A GUIDE TO THE ECONOMIES IN TRANSITION

The collapse of communism in 1989 was a landmark in the history of the twentieth century. This volume provides a unique review by one author of developments in economies in various stages of transition to democracy and the market. The speed of change presents formidable problems, but in *A Guide to the Economies in Transition* Ian Jeffries takes up that challenge.

The book is divided into four parts: Part I examines theoretical issues in the transition from command to market economies; Part II covers events in the fifteen, now independent, countries of the former Soviet Union; Part III looks at the countries of Eastern Europe; and finally, Part IV covers non-European states (China, Cuba, Mongolia, North Korea and Vietnam). It is now increasingly recognized that economic developments need to be analysed in their political context. This accessible book attempts to do just that and information is presented chronologically when appropriate. It is best seen as a companion volume to *Socialist Economies and the Transition to the Market: A Guide*, carrying on where the one left off. Both volumes provide a unique level of reference, and are valuable sources for anyone working in this area.

Ian Jeffries is Lecturer in the Centre of Russian and East European Studies in the University of Wales.

A GUIDE TO THE ECONOMIES IN TRANSITION

Ian Jeffries

London and New York

First published 1996
by Routledge
11 New Fetter Lane, London EC4P 4EE

Simultaneously published in the USA and Canada
by Routledge
29 West 35th Street, New York, NY 10001

Routledge is an International Thomson Publishing company

Typeset in Garamond by
Pure Tech India Ltd., Pondicherry
Printed and bound in Great Britain by
Mackays of Chatham PLC, Chatham, Kent

British Library Cataloguing in Publication Data

A catalogue record for this book is available from the British Library

Library of Congress Cataloguing in Publication Data

Jeffries, Ian.
A guide to economies in transition / Ian Jeffries. p. cm.
Includes bibliographical references and index.
ISBN 0–415–13684–9
1. Former Soviet republics–Economic conditions. 2. Europe, Eastern–Economic conditions–1989- 3. Communist countries–Economic conditions. I. Title.
HC336.27.J44 1996
330.947–dc20 95–40969
CIP

ISBN 0–415–13684–9

CONTENTS

TABLES

ACKNOWLEDGEMENTS

Many people in Swansea have helped me in my gargantuan task of keeping up with events in thirty-five countries. I rely totally on rapid and assured access to a vast range of material and the library staff go well beyond the call of duty in this regard: Gwen Bailey, Merlyn Brown, Dianne Evans, David Painting, Hazel Pember, Ann Preece, Jane Richards, Clive Towse and Carole Williams. Jeremy Collins, Paul McGrath, Nigel O'Leary, Taufiq Choudhry and David Brooksbank sorted out all my computer problems. The earliest possible access to the quality newspapers and magazines has, as always, been ensured by the college newsagent Russell Davies. The porters in the library, the Abbey and Fulton House have continued to assist in many much appreciated ways.

My sources of information have been greatly expanded by the kind mailing (free of charge) of invaluable reports by the Deutsche Bank, the Hongkong and Shanghai Bank, the World Bank and the Commission of the European Communities.

The staff of Routledge have transformed the frenetic activities of a workaholic academic into another splendidly produced book: Alan Jarvis, Alison Kirk, Sally Close, John Dust, Ruth Jeavons and Natalie Brightbard. Ray Offord has once again ensured that copy-editing of the highest standard has been undertaken.

Ian Jeffries
Centre of Russian and East European Studies, University of Wales

INTRODUCTION

This book is best described as a 'companion' or 'complementary' volume to *Socialist Economies and the Transition to the Market.* The latter was published in 1993 and so it is time to update both the theoretical debate and, more particularly, the actual events in all the individual countries. With the disintegration of the Soviet Union, Yugoslavia and Czechoslovakia the country count is now a staggering thirty-five (and may conceivably rise). I do not attempt to duplicate the material in the previous volume, so the reader is recommended to consider the two in tandem.

I have always included the basic political background in all my so-called 'economics' textbooks, since I believe that the separation of the two disciplines is artificial. In this book I go a stage further. There is a welcome, growing realization in the study of the transition from 'communism' to 'capitalism' of the importance of linking the two disciplines together in order to maximize our understanding of an exciting, immensely important and essentially new area of study. The method chosen in Russia's first phase of large privatization, by way of example, was largely politically inspired. I hope that this volume will provide an overview of the main ideas involved in and the events occurring during the transition. But a generous amount of descriptive economic and political information (often presented chronologically) is also put at the disposal of the reader, the intention here being to provide a 'quarry' from which to dig out any desired facts and figures relating to the period up to the autumn of 1995. The sources of the data are many and varied and I make no apology for making full use of quality newspapers and magazines. Their correspondents do a fine job of reporting fast-changing events and their contributions are often underestimated or not sufficiently acknowledged. The number of languages involved typically rules out access to source material and I am exceedingly grateful for reports in English when trying to cope with a large number of countries. It is obviously not possible to mention every single correspondent or researcher, but I have done what I can. Those not named will, I am sure, understand. I have had to make full acknowledgements of items in newspapers, bank reports, magazines and newsletters in the text itself. The vast number of such items rule out conventional referencing.

I am not an econometrician and so in none of my books have I ever pretended to analyse economic data in any sort of sophisticated manner. Indeed, I am mostly interested in how economic and political systems actually change. But I think the reader should be aware of the broad economic magnitudes and these I present in tables that are meant to be as simple as possible. There are often many differing estimates and not infrequently the same source changes the figures from one issue to the next! Rather than drawing up immensely complicated tables showing a multitude of estimates, I have tried to look for the most representative figures. These usually speak for themselves and thus I avoid tediously stating the obvious. The one set of figures that presented most problems was for the budget deficit or surplus as a percentage of GDP. The reasons for this are admirably discussed in EBRD (1995: 21–2), e.g. 'the tradition in many East European countries of handling many activities of the state and municipalities off-budget' and 'the fact that chronically loss-making enterprises in some countries are kept alive through their access to credits from the banking system. Such credits may conceptually constitute government subsidies.' I decided, therefore, to rely largely on the European Bank for Reconstruction and Development's figures for the 'general government balance' for the countries of Eastern Europe and the former Soviet Union (the 'general government balance' includes the state, municipalities and extra-budgetary funds). Figures for 'net foreign debt' are generally taken from the United Nations Economic Commission for Europe, defined as 'gross debt less foreign exchange reserves of the central bank' (1995: 138). Frequent use is also made of the term 'net foreign direct investment', defined as 'net of inward investment and investment made abroad' (p. 151). (The commission draws attention to the negative aspects of foreign direct investment, such as 'rent-seeking' in situations where markets are not competitive or the state lacks regulatory powers. Foreign companies aiming to dominate markets in transitional economies are inclined to pressurize the government to protect the domestic market from foreign competition: p. 7.) (Note that throughout this book any reference to dollars means US dollars.)

For ease of reading I have tried to standardize the country chapter subheadings as far as possible, dealing in turn with political events, macroeconomic stabilization, prices, privatization, foreign trade, foreign aid, direct foreign investment, agriculture and economic performance. Thus the index omits (unhelpful) masses of page numbers referring to these broad topics. Chapter 1, of course, deals with general issues such as privatization.

Part I deals with the general issues involved in the transition from command to market economies. I am not a theorist, but I hope that I may give readers some insights into the issues involved. I do not like to thrust my own views down anyone's throat, but, for what they are worth, they are to be found in Chapter 1. My feeling is that the often emotional rhetoric conceals much more agreement than might be supposed at first reading. My plea is for modesty and pragmatism in approaching the subject and in offering advice.

Part II covers the events in the fifteen now independent countries of the former Soviet Union. Because of its dominance Russia is placed first, the other fourteen countries follow in alphabetical order and Chapter 18 looks at economic relations between Russia and what it calls its 'near abroad'. The collapse of trade was a profound shock to all the countries, but those dependent on (increasingly expensive) energy imports were doubly hit.

Russia obviously requires a generous amount of space. The need to ensure the lumbering giant's successful transition to democracy and the market is of paramount importance. That the Soviet Union disintegrated without massive conflict is still a remarkable fact, especially since 25 million ethnic Russians were stranded in the 'near abroad'. This can be stated despite the vicious wars in the Caucasus and Tajikistan. Russia itself, of course, has not been free of strife. Yeltsin dissolved parliament on 21 September 1993 and blasted the White House into submission on 4 October, while the invasion of Chechenia, colossally destructive in human and material terms, began on 11 December 1994. Apart from this resort to force, a number of other factors have taken their toll on the (elected) president's popularity. They include Yeltsin's erratic (at times even bizarre) behaviour and, above all, the distress of the economic transition (aggravated by rapidly widening inequalities in the distribution of income and by the power of organized crime; corruption and crime are, to varying degrees, a cancer in all transitional societies). The reformers did badly in the general election of 12 December 1993, but parliament's authority is relatively weak compared with the powers granted to the president under the new constitution. Although the 'honeymoon' period with the West is now over, relations remain essentially sound. This is not, of course, to underestimate the pain caused by Russia's diminished international status (which partly explains the anger shown at Nato's military action against the Bosnian Serbs) and by the prospect of Nato expanding in an easterly direction. The support that the West should give Yeltsin personally has long been a bone of contention, especially in the light of his occasional resort to force (as in Chechenia) to solve problems. Even his supporters vary considerably in their enthusiasm, the less partisan seeing Yeltsin merely as the only alternative to a president of the extreme left or right. But it is a sign of Russia's political progress that anxieties about Yeltsin's health and judgement have subsided considerably with the appearance of realistic and reassuring alternatives, not least Viktor Chernomyrdin.

The way Russia has handled the transition to the market has aroused passionate debates, including the following:

1. The extent of the fall in GDP, although there seems to be a consensus that the turning point for industrial production was around the summer of 1994 (the reasons for the relatively low rate of unemployment, even using standard international definitions, are arousing considerable interest).

2. 'Big bang' price liberalization at the beginning of 1992.

3. While the speed of large privatization in industry has been remarkable, the emphasis placed in the first phase (which ended on 1 July 1994) on 'insiders' (existing workers and managers) has brought forth the most damning of criticisms from some quarters. In contrast, private (family) farms have made very little progress.

4. The extent to which the West has provided and should provide aid, and on what conditions. Jeffrey Sachs's attacks on the IMF make particularly entertaining reading. I have always been at one with Sachs in his view that the West is very shortsighted when it comes to providing aid. There is much greater agreement on what should be done to raise the relatively small amounts of direct foreign investment for a country of Russia's size (the contrast with China is staggering).

Yeltsin admitted on 16 February 1995 that 'Two serious attempts were made to curb inflation in the years of reform . . . The third attempt must be a success'. The two earlier attempts led to tortuous negotiations with the IMF and a huge decline in the nominal exchange rate of the rouble against the US dollar.

The Baltic States of Estonia, Latvia and Lithuania have made a decisive break with their Soviet past and are generally streets ahead of their former fellow republics in the transition to democracy and the market. But it has not been all plain sailing. The passage of a new citizenship law was particularly stressful in Latvia (a country which has also had to struggle with banking crises). Although great progress has been made on the inflation front, the loss of output has been considerable (left-of-centre parties have done well in recent elections in Lithuania and Estonia). Nevetheless, the economic circumstances in the other former republics of the Soviet Union are generally much bleaker. The term 'Ukrainianization' came to mean having the worst of both worlds, massive falls in output and hyperinflation at the same time, due to the old system collapsing and next to nothing being done to help construct a new one. But the election of President Kuchma in July 1994 seems to have been a turning point for Ukraine.

Initially the Commonwealth of Independent States (CIS) seemed to be more a means of achieving a 'peaceful divorce', but from 1993 onwards Russia's military and economic dominance (especially its supplies of energy and raw materials) gave it a new lease of life. The CIS now entwines all the countries of the former Soviet Union except the three Baltic States and in ways that are firmer than seemed likely at one stage. Nevertheless, the exact future form and importance of the CIS remain uncertain. Each of the twelve countries now has its own currency (even Tajikistan as of 10 May 1995). The proposed monetary union between Russia and Belarus did not come off. But the 14 May 1995 referendum in the latter country produced a decisive vote in favour of economic union with Russia and it is not out of the question that political reunification may come about eventually. The degree of enthusiasm for further economic integration varies considerably between other CIS members, e.g. Kazakhstan is much more eager than Azerbaijan.

Part III covers the countries of 'Eastern Europe'. I retain this general term even though it is becoming increasingly common practice to hive off the countries of 'Central Europe', namely Hungary, Poland, the Czech Republic and Slovakia (East Germany is, of course, a special case and appears in Part III because of its socialist past). The reasons for the popular distinction, it seems, are not only historical and geographical but also related to perceived differences in progress towards the market and Western-type democracy. It would probably be more diplomatic of me, from the point of view of the countries concerned, to sail with the prevailing wind. But I retain the term 'Eastern Europe' and not only for convenience. I would argue that to differentiate 'Central Europe' creates new and rather artificial dividing lines and that such a division is nowhere near as clear-cut as is often made out. Thus parties with roots in the communist past have won recent elections in Hungary, Poland and Slovakia, while Slovenia looks very ill at ease in a 'Balkan' setting and Bosnia has historically represented the best traditions of a tolerant society. Albania achieved outstanding growth rates in 1993 and 1994 (albeit after substantial output falls in the previous three years). GDP growth in Romania was also positive in both years.

Albania's surprising bounce back in 1993 was helped by a rapid return to private farming, rapid small privatization and generous Western aid. Political problems include deep concern about the authoritarian traits and actions of President Sali Berisha and complaints from the Greek minority. Economically, large privatization has been slow and there is a high rate of unemployment.

In the December 1994 general election the Bulgarian Socialist Party did even better than expected, winning an absolute majority of seats in the National Assembly. Bulgaria has taken more strides towards economic liberalization and stabilization than it has sometimes been given credit for, but large privatization has been at a snail's pace, the increasing economic power of the *nomenklatura* (using business and political connections) is little short of sinister, and private agriculture has not been adequately supported.

Czechoslovakia split into two at the beginning of 1993 (despite the lack of popular support for such a move), with Slovakia having by far the worst of the bargain. It lost its subsidies from the Czech Republic, inherited a disproportionate amount of obsolete heavy and defence industry, and was forced to build parts of its own administrative system from scratch because of the former dominance of Prague. The return to power of Vladimir Meciar in the general election of 30 September–1 October 1994 was not greeted with enthusiasm in the West because of his generally lukewarm attitude towards economic reform, his authoritarian inclinations and his appeal to nationalism (there is a large Hungarian minority). The hope is that political and economic realities and the inducement of possible future membership of the EU and Nato will keep the country broadly on course. In mid-1995 the government announced that the voucher privatization programme was to be scrapped. Although unemployment was still in double figures, economic performance in 1994 was generally very encouraging. Moreover, the 19 March 1995 agreement with Hungary about borders and minority rights is an encouraging start, despite some apprehension about its exact significance in reality. In contrast, the Czech Republic is now generally seen as the most successful transitional country in an all-round sense, the odds-on favourite for first in the race to join the EU. Prime Minister Vaclav Klaus would probably not win any 'Mr Charm' contest, but he has found a successful blend of no-nonsense 'selling' of market reform and pragmatism (such as using subsidies to avoid sudden, large-scale bankruptcies and lay-offs). Unemployment is low and the voucher-based privatization programme has stormed ahead. (Regardless of its drawbacks, my own personal preference is for a voucher scheme to be at the heart of a large privatization programme on the grounds of social equity, the gaining of mass support and getting the privatization show on the road; I would favour a small proportion of shares going to existing workers and managers for incentive purposes.) But problems in the Czech Republic include financial scandals and a lot of enterprise restructuring still to be done. President Vaclav Havel remains the conscience of the nation.

The early optimism of Chancellor Kohl proved to be unwarranted. Despite massive public financial flows from West to East Germany and many positive achievements, the economic and social strains of reunification remain considerable. Chancellor Kohl only narrowly retained power in 1994 and the Party of Democratic Socialism did well in East Germany in the local and national elections. The Treuhandanstalt was wound up at the end of 1994 amid controversy over many aspects of the privatization programme, e.g. the speed of the process, the (associated) disappointing amount of revenue raised and the early stress on physical restitution. Unemployment remains high (e.g. money wages sprinted ahead of productivity increases, thus reducing competitiveness). Growth in East Germany is still far from being entirely self-sustaining, but there are encouraging signs of progress in that direction and GDP has rebounded after a massive fall. Deindustrialization came to a halt in 1994. Many people in East Germany feel belittled by the process of reunification and constant vigilance is needed to hold in check the forces of the extreme right in the whole of the country.

After being considered the number one in the transitional race early on, Hungary has proved something of an economic disappointment of late (although it has attracted the largest volume of direct foreign investment in Eastern Europe, excluding East Germany of course; the Czech Republic is in second place in that regard). In the May 1994 general election economic platforms did not play a big role in the campaigning. The Hungarian Socialist Party won an overall majority of seats, but it still formed a coalition government with the Alliance of Free Democrats. The electorate seems to have wanted a more competent and experienced team of economic managers and one more aware of the plight of those most adversely affected by change. But Prime Minister Gyula Horn has been criticized for his aloof prevarication over privatization and foreign investment. A stiff austerity package was not announced until March 1995.

The merits and effects of Poland's pioneering 'big bang' and 'shock therapy' policy of January 1990, under the stewardship of Leszek Balcerowicz, remain the subject of much debate. But it is clear that Poland was the first transitional country to achieve positive growth (in 1992) and inflation has been much reduced (although it is still at an uncomfortable level). It is also true, however, that in the September 1993 general election there was a decisive shift to left-of-centre parties with roots in the communist past. Promises of a somewhat slower pace of market reform and better protection for those members of society most disadvantaged by events since 1989 proved to be appealing (there are a relatively large number of pensioners of various sorts). The Alliance of the Democratic Left formed a coalition government with the Polish Peasant Party. But politically Poland seems dogged by squabbling, among the coalition partners, within parliament, and between parliament and President Walesa. The president seems rather desperate to avoid being more or less sidelined and to improve his poor popularity rating (and thus stand a realistic chance of winning the next presidential election). This political wrangling has not dramatically worsened Poland's economic progress overall, so far at least. The large privatization programme has been adversely affected (aggravated by the power of workers' councils) and the record on direct foreign investment could be improved. But the private sector has expanded rapidly thanks to the growth of new firms, rapid small privatization and asset sales in larger enterprises.

Romania has never shaken off the dominance of personalities and parties with roots in the communist past. President Ion Iliescu and the Social Democracy Party of Romania (formerly the Democratic National Salvation Front) show little sign of losing that pre-eminence. The technocratic government of Nicolae Vacaroiu has survived any number of votes of no confidence. Although large privatization has been slow (hopefully really beginning to get going in the second half of 1995) and (predominant) private agriculture lacks adequate support in terms of infrastructure and legal entitlement, Romania's progress as regards economic liberalization and IMF-approved stabilization programmes has often been underplayed. GDP growth turned positive in 1993. It would be wise not to underestimate the capacity of extreme nationalists to turn the problem of the large Hungarian minority into a hornets' nest.

Eastern Europe is a veritable hotchpotch of nationalities. Nowhere has the evil of intolerant nationalism raised its ugly head more than in the former Yugoslavia. Until mid-September 1995 some 70 per cent of Bosnia-Hercegovina lay in the hands of the Bosnian Serbs, who had 'ethnically cleansed' whole areas and committed even worse crimes in the name of Serb nationalism. My own sympathies are very much with the tradition of ethnic tolerance practised in Bosnia. William Pfaff rightly argues that 'The Serbs themselves have made it impossible to respond to their legitimate concerns and demands. Rather than propose their case rationally, and argue it before the international community, they chose the course of demagogy, grotesque demands for an inflated Greater Serbia, the deliberate fostering of ethnic hatred and military aggression, terrorism and ethnic cleansing' (*IHT*, 2 September 1995, p. 4). There are, of course, few angels in such a situation. The Bosnian Croats have a lot to answer for and there are Bosnian government supporters who have tarnished their side's image. But the burden of guilt rests massively on the shoulders of the Bosnian Serbs. Until the late summer of 1995 the West's role bore comparison in some respects with the appeasement of 1938. Nato's commencement of massive military action (justified, in my opinion) against the Bosnian Serbs on 30 August 1995, following Croatia's routing of the ethnic Serbs in the Krajina, shifted the military balance. On 8 September 1995, while Nato air strikes continued, the foreign ministers of Bosnia, Croatia and Serbia (negotiating on behalf of the Bosnian Serbs) agreed to the 'basic principles' of a political settlement.

The book ends with the September 1995 agreement on Bosnia, described by US special envoy Richard Holbrooke as 'an important milestone in the search for peace'. (The USA took over the reins of negotiations in August 1995 at a time when the credibility of the UN, Nato and the EU was at a dangerously low ebb.) There is a long and dangerous haul ahead, but the agreement provides a glimmer of hope. I would not even rule out the possibility that the various ethnic groups in Bosnia may eventually begin to live together again in greater harmony. This seemingly ludicrous degree of optimism derives from three considerations:

1. Of the 1.75 million Yugoslavs who died in the Second World War, around a million were killed by other Yugoslavs (the Croats and Serbs were the principal protagonists). Atrocities were committed by all sides, but the Croat fascist (Ustasha) regime is generally held responsible for the deaths of over 500,000 Serbs and 70,000 Jews. Even allowing for Tito's heavy hand, it is still remarkable how Yugoslavia progressed in the post-war period.

2. The hope that the majority of ethnic Serbs in Bosnia, Croatia and the Federal Republic of Yugoslavia will begin to realize the extent to which their hate-filled, power-mad leaders have deceived them.

3. A tolerant, multi-ethnic society is not simply a worthwhile end in itself. I would argue that economic development is enhanced when human resources are fully utilized, and the international community is undoubtedly more willing to provide aid on a large scale to such a society. The September 1995 agreement seems like *de facto* partition along largely ethnic lines, but a flourishing economic centre (with an incentive to maintain its tradition of ethnic tolerance) could well prove attractive to suspicious ethnic Croats and Serbs.

Slovenia, markedly homogeneous in ethnic composition, stands out like a beacon in the morass of the former Yugoslavia, having had the lightest of brushes with the Yugoslav army. It has surged towards stabilization and the market (although large privatization was slow up to mid-1995, a much speedier process was envisaged thereafter). Slovenia is a good bet for relatively early entry into the EU.

The rest of the area has been damned in varying degrees by war and/or sanctions. It is ironic (and sad) that the international community came to be heavily dependent on the goodwill of the arch-villain Slobodan Milosevic to bring the Bosnian Serbs to heel. The sanctions Milosevic imposed on the Bosnian Serbs have in reality been very leaky and the international community dangled the offer of a partial lifting of its sanctions on Serbia in the hope of inducing Milosevic to recognize Bosnia (and Croatia) diplomatically. The overriding goal of communist-turned-nationalist Milosevic has always been to retain personal power (as opposed to creating a Greater Serbia) and he certainly sees Radovan Karadzic as a rival. It is worth noting that Milosevic did not lift a finger to help the Serbs of Krajina when Croatia took back western Slavonia in the lightning attack of 1–2 May 1995 and when Croatia routed the Croatian Serbs in Sectors North and South Krajina on 4–7 August 1995. As noted above, the September 1995 agreement on Bosnia was negotiated by Serbia's foreign minister on behalf of the Bosnian Serbs. Within Serbia (which dominates its increasingly dissatisfied partner, Montenegro, in the rump Federal Republic of Yugoslavia) the Albanians in Kosovo continue to be repressed and the Serbian economy is generally in poor shape. The hyperinflation in late 1993 reached all-time, world-record proportions. It was only brought under control (at least temporarily) with an anti-inflation package at the beginning of 1994 which included a 'super-dinar' backed by gold and hard currency reserves and convertible into the Deutschmark at par.

President Franjo Tudjman (seriously at fault for his stridently nationalistic tone when independence was declared) would have been very happy to carve Bosnia up between Croatia and Serbia, but was forced to at least shelve the idea. A significant part of Croatia was under the control of the Croatian Serbs until the devastating Croatian successes in the military campaigns of 1–2 May and 4–7 August 1995. There have been some encouraging signs of economic recovery of late, but defence expenditure remains a heavy drain on the budget and the problem of eastern Slavonia hangs like the sword of Damocles over the country.

Macedonia under President Kiro Gligorov struggles to maintain its unity under pressure from a large (and in many ways discontented) Albanian minority and the legacy of a bitter quarrel with Greece, which imposed economic sanctions until October 1995. The economy has not been helped by Macedonia having to support (in reality in a very leaky fashion) sanctions against the Federal Republic of Yugoslavia. Large privatization was very limited as of mid-1995, but the programme has attracted a great deal of attention and rapid progress was expected thereafter.

Part IV covers China, Cuba, Mongolia, North Korea and Vietnam. China's gradual and partial approach to economic reform has paid off handsomely in terms of world-beating growth rates, although inflation and corruption have caused increasing concern. The relevance of the Chinese model to the countries of Eastern Europe and the former Soviet Union has become a subject of intense interest in itself. The 'post-Deng' era seems to be going reasonably smoothly in advance of the ailing Deng Xiaoping's actual death (although the eagerness of rivals to demonstrate their nationalist credentials has resulted in some friction in international affairs, especially in relations with the USA and with those countries claiming all or part of the Spratly Islands). Although President Jiang Zemin has begun to attack certain high-ranking officials associated with Deng for corruption, Deng Xiaoping's argument that economic success is essential to preserve the power of the Communist Party and to increase China's standing in the world seems to have won the day. It is difficult to see any of the major planks of policy being overturned:

1. The Household Responsibility System in agriculture. This is not to underestimate the problems in this sector, such as the relatively slow rate of growth of agricultural output, the small size of plots and the increasing disparity between urban and rural incomes (which, together with the lack of jobs, encourages massive migration of people to the towns).

2. The 'open door' policy. China is now the eleventh largest exporter in the world and is second only to the USA as a recipient of direct foreign investment. While the yuan is far from being fully convertible, progress is being made. The foreign debt is manageable. But China's growing weight in the world (some argue that in purchasing-power parity terms it is the third largest economy in the world after the USA and Japan) has led to friction with trading partners. China did not succeed in becoming a founder member of the World Trade Organization (the successor to Gatt) in January 1995 and only a last-minute deal the following month saved a trade war with the USA over intellectual property rights (though the USA had caved in the previous year over the linkage between trade and human rights).

3. A flourishing non-state sector. The 'township–village enterprises' have attracted considerable theoretical and empirical interest.

Politically China still stresses the 'stability and unity' of the country and is quite willing to disregard Western contempt for China's record on human rights. The fear of social unrest stemming from large-scale bankruptcies and unemployment helps explain the continuing willingness to fork out large subsidies (feeding inflation through increases in the money supply) and the lack of progress with the new pilot scheme for radically reforming the operation of state enterprises. Other nagging problems include widespread corruption, slow price reform (there has even been some retrogression owing to unease over inflation) and increasing regional power (which raises concern over the political unity of the country, widens regional income inequalities, hinders control over investment and adds to the difficulty of collecting tax revenue).

The collapse of communism, especially the demise of the Soviet Union, left Cuba in dire straits (although some sectors have fared better than others and the government claims modest growth for the economy as a whole in 1994 and an even better performance in the first half of 1995). Aid and much of foreign trade disappeared. Fidel Castro has thus been forced to make ideologically painful concessions to the market and to introduce severe austerity measures. The illegal flood of refugees to the USA in 1994 forced the USA to reach a deal with Cuba. Ever responsive to domestic political pressures, the USA actually tightened an already short-sighted and irrational sanctions regime against Cuba (the Clinton administration is under pressure from Republicans to tighten it even more). The economic reforms introduced by Cuba have been considerable, e.g. in 1993 the possession and (conditional) use of foreign currencies like the dollar was made legal, there was further relaxation of controls on the private sector and state farm workers were allowed to form semi-autonomous co-operatives. In 1994 all (licensed) producers of agricultural products were permitted to sell output on the market once state delivery quotas had been met. In addition, there has been decentralization in foreign trade and every effort has been made to earn hard currency through tourism and direct foreign investment. Foreign companies have been showing greater interest of late and Cuba clearly hopes that the new foreign investment law, passed by the National Assembly on 5 September 1995, will provide an added incentive.

The Mongolian People's Revolutionary Party dominates the parliamentary scene, but it has been pragmatic as regards economic policy, its candidate in the presidential election of June 1993 fared badly against the incumbent Pulsalmaagiyn Ochirbat (an independent-minded democrat and economic reformer) and there are other encouraging signs of checks and balances emerging in Mongolian society. Mongolia has always been a very poor country and the loss of large-scale aid from the Soviet Union was a real blow. The West provides only partial recompense and relations with the IMF have not always been smooth. The 1990s have been very difficult years economically, with a sharp decline in foreign trade and shrinking GDP up to 1993. But 1994 saw growth and progress was made on the inflation front. Economic reforms have not always been consistently applied, but there has neverthless been substantial progress in liberalizing prices and foreign trade (the tugrik was allowed to float in May 1993). Privatization, employing a voucher scheme, has been rapid, although the extent of 'insider' control by existing workers and managers has caused concern. Most livestock is now privately owned. Direct foreign investment has not exactly flooded into Mongolia.

North Korea remains in essence an old-fashioned 'communist' state built around the cult of personality. Speculation is still rife because so little is really known about what goes on within the country. In 1994 world attention was focused on two major events. On 8 July Kim Il Sung died of a heart attack at the age of eighty-two. His (in all senses) colourless son, Kim Jong Il, seems to have been grudgingly accepted as successor but has yet to be formally named president and/or general secretary of the Korean Workers' Party. Nevertheless, the world breathed a sigh of relief when a deal was negotiated (on 21 October 1994) with the USA on North Korea's nuclear programme amid uncertainty as to whether any nuclear weapons had actually been produced. In return for ending its programme North Korea was to be given replacement light-water reactors and supplies of oil in the meantime (but the North's objection to South Korea being the source of the new reactors led to further tortuous negotiations and the US claims that some of the fuel meant for heating and electricity production has been diverted to industrial use). The economic situation remains desperate, with the 1990s seeing aggregate output falling every year to date according to Western figures. In June 1995 South Korea and Japan agreed to deliver emergency supplies of rice and in the late summer of 1995 North Korea appealed to the international community for emergency relief to counter the effects of severe flooding. There have been no major economic reforms, although Kim Jong Il is generally considered to be interested in change and foreign investment continues to be sought in the (what are in effect) special economic zones. Progress in the front-ranking Tumen project, however, has been very limited so far.

Vietnam is a poor country by any standard. It has a high unemployment rate and a very large proportion of its population lives below the poverty line. But Vietnam has achieved considerable success in the 1990s in terms of growth rates and bringing down the rate of inflation. Market-orientated reforms have continued and the non-state sector is flourishing. Although land still belongs to the state, land use regulations have been relaxed. Vietnam is the world's third largest exporter of rice. The number of state enterprises has been considerably reduced through mergers and closures, but the pilot 'equitization' programme announced in 1992 to privatize partially a small number of them has not got very far to date. Vietnam continues to integrate itself into the world economy. Aid pledges have been generous, although the low disbursement rate is the cause of some concern. Vietnam is attracting a lot of attention from foreign investors, helped by speedier authorization, more relaxed regulations and the approval of export processing zones. A major stimulus was President Clinton's announcement on 3 February 1994 that the USA was to lift its economic embargo, full diplomatic relations with the USA being formally established on 5 August 1995. On 28 July 1995 Vietnam became the seventh member of Asean.

Part I
GENERAL ISSUES

1

GENERAL ISSUES IN THE TRANSITION FROM COMMAND TO MARKET ECONOMIES

'BIG BANG' AND GRADUALISM

Two hundred years after the French Revolution of 1789 the world witnessed the stunning collapse of communism. Not surprisingly, the question of how to handle the transition from 'communism' to 'capitalism' has led to immense controversy. There is even controversy about how unique the process is. Sachs, for example, argues that the conversion of a socialist into a capitalist economy is 'in many ways . . . a well-trodden path . . . Although parts of the transformation represent uncharted territory (such as massive privatization of industry), many other aspects of Eastern Europe's reform tasks are quite familiar. Many other countries that were once cut off from the rest of the world by inward-looking, authoritarian regimes have successfully opened up and become integrated into the global mainstream economy' (Sachs 1994: 2–3). Sachs surely understates, to a marked degree, the differences in jettisoning a command economy. But it was clear pretty early on that the rhetoric about how to handle the economic transition concealed considerable (and increasing) agreement.

Part of the problem is the attempt by theorists to impose neat categories on a messy world, an essentially new area of economics where even clear definitions are hard to come by. The term 'shock therapy' is more often than not still used in a broad sense to cover both severe austerity measures and a rapid and comprehensive change in the economic system. But it can still (and, in my opinion, should) just imply the former (while 'big bang' should refer to the latter). Otherwise there can be confusion. The claim in 1993 that Russia had not undergone 'shock therapy', for example, makes sense only if the narrower definition is used. Clearly, chronic inflation has to be tackled as a matter of urgency. But in general any adverse effects on output and employment must be taken into account and care should be taken to ensure that the magnitude of stabilization measures is proportionate to the scale of the inflationary problem. Richard Portes (*Transition*, 1994, vol. 5, no. 8, p. 13) also has a point when he says that 'If immediate stabilization is not feasible, there may still be very useful things that can be done, which by constructing parts of the microfoundations may also make stabilization that much easier when it does become feasible.'

No one has ever suggested that 'everything' can be done 'at once', so the question essentially revolves around how much can or should be attempted at the 'same' time. Personally I have always been sceptical about the wisdom and feasibility of a 'big bang' solution, but equally aware that doing next to nothing brings about economic catastrophe (the term 'Ukrainianization' is frequently used in this context, referring to the early years of Ukrainian independence). Consequently, I see merit in the idea of (1) a 'critical mass' of co-ordinated measures on a sufficient scale to provide an irreversible and on-going momentum to the reform process and (2) a credible programme for which a democratically elected government must seek and maintain popular approval (as rightly stressed by the United Nations Economic Commission for Europe 1993: 9). Choosing the appropriate blend and scale of measures best suited to individual countries is a political art. (The initial circumstances vary between countries, such as the size of the private sector, the extent of the previous reforms, the burden of foreign debt and the availability of aid.)

The debate seems to me to boil down to what is politically and economically feasible. It is also worth bearing in mind that 'the range of sensible strategies is limited and there may be little margin for choice' (Portes 1994: 1180). Many of the alleged protagonists would probably agree that as much as possible should be done as quickly as possible, but the snag is that this begs all sorts of questions. There is no room for arrogance and dogmatism here. Pragmatism should be the order of the day and the policies of Vaclav Klaus, the prime minister of the Czech Republic, are well worth studying in this regard. This free-marketeering but pragmatic politician has engineered a remarkably successful transition while using subsidies to avoid sudden, large-scale bankruptcies and lay-offs (the interested reader will find an extended quotation below).

Arguments in favour of the 'big bang' approach

Sachs (1994) provides an excellent summary of the arguments in favour of a 'big bang' approach, with specific reference to Poland from the start of 1990 (Sachs tends to use the terms 'big bang' and 'shock therapy' interchangeably). The main pillars of Poland's reform programme were:

1. Macroeconomic stabilization.
2. Liberalization, including the end of central planning, the end of bureaucratic controls over prices, international trade and the use of raw materials, and the establishment of a legal environment to support decentralized

actions of private property owners (such as a commercial code, company law and a system of judicial enforcement of contracts).

3. Privatization (Sachs notes the delays in large privatization in Poland).

4. A 'social safety net' (especially an unemployment compensation scheme).

5. The need for international aid (and a generous trade policy by Western countries) (pp. 45–6).

The need for liberalization of foreign trade, including rapid current account convertibility, is emphasized: 'International competition would provide the competition in the internal market that Polish firms themselves would not provide at the start. If free trade could be introduced, prices could be liberalized' (p. 50).

Sachs stresses the urgency of taking advantage of the political 'honeymoon' period to pursue rapid and comprehensive economic reforms. Moreover, the lack of experienced personnel led the new administration in Poland to rely on market forces as much as possible (p. 43). Pinto *et al.* (1993: 255) argue that 'Poland's experience shows that shock therapy can have valuable effects by giving an unambiguous signal, changing relative prices, and indicating the government's commitment to hard budgets.'

Clague (1992) supports 'big bang' ideas (although the terms he uses are the 'incentives approach' and the 'minimum bang'). He argues that the difference between the 'big bang' and the evolutionary approach 'lies primarily in judgments about what is politically feasible' (p. 15). Åslund (1994a: 37) thinks that 'the interesting limitation is what is practically and politically possible, and nothing else'. Rausser and Johnson (1993: 675) argue that orthodox reform prescriptions cannot be implemented effectively without (1) a constitution that clearly defines and secures basic political, civil and economic freedoms and (2) a legal and regulatory infrastructure that creates a fertile environment for a vibrant market economy.

'A common error is to evaluate a defined economic policy by comparing . . . phenomena which can be ascribed to the period since the policy began to be implemented with the situation which preceded it.' To a large extent, however, the fall in output in 1991 in all the countries connected with the former Soviet Union was caused by the collapse in trade. Thus 'a particular policy should always be evaluated by comparing the phenomena which can be ascribed to it with the phenomena which would have arisen as an effect of a realistic alternative policy, conducted under similar initial conditions and in similar circumstances' (Balcerowicz 1994: 19–20). Balcerowicz also argues that it is a fallacy to believe that a gradualist approach is milder in terms of its social consequences when one is dealing with hyperinflation. 'What is crucial in such circumstances is to change the basic monetary conditions and to eliminate or at least reduce inflationary expectations. In such a situation a consistent and credible radical stabilization is much more likely to succeed and could be far less costly than a gradualist approach' (pp. 38–9). 'A preoccupation with structural factors and the corresponding neglect of macroeconomic ones freezes the poor economic structure . . . there are no incentives for people and [other resources] to move to other sectors . . . tough stabilization and comprehensive liberalization seem to be the necessary conditions for any meaningful structural change.' Such an environment 'encourages many state enterprises to restructure, transferring their resources to the private sector, and/or to change their sphere of operations' (p. 40).

Roland (1994a) delineates the political economy of the choice between 'big bang' and 'gradualism':

1. 'Advocates of "big bang" are less concerned with *ex ante* than with *ex post* political constraints. With respect to *ex ante* political constraints, the basic idea is that there is a *window of opportunity*, a grace period . . . How does the "big bang" approach deal with *ex post* political constraints? . . . it is best understood as a strategy of *fait accompli* to constrain a successor government by increasing the costs of reversal of policies adopted today' (p. 29). For example, 'by lifting price controls and disbanding administration, one makes it more costly to reinstate price controls. By distributing freely state assets to the population and to workers, one runs down government wealth and makes it more costly to re-nationalize or to expand government expenditures' (p. 30).

2. 'Gradualism is directly concerned with *ex ante* feasibility constraints . . . A gradual resolution of uncertainty gives an option for early policy reversal at a low cost if the outcome turns out to be bad. Policy reversals do not necessarily mean a return to a communist regime . . . The *ex ante* existence of this reversal option increases the willingness of the population to engage in the reform process. Gradualism also allows, in case of a successful outcome, the building of constituencies for further reform' (p. 32).

Criticisms of the 'big bang' approach

The problem of defining terms is increasingly recognized. Roland points out that it is very difficult to know what is meant by the term 'big bang' (comment in *Economic Policy*, no. 18, p. 139). Reforming everything at once is a physical impossibility, so all programmes are a mixture of rapid and slow elements. Few people disagree that it is desirable to be radical and decisive where possible, but political constraints sometimes make it impossible. Sometimes gradualism may help to overcome them. China is a good example of the way in which early successes can create a constituency for further reform. Van Brabant (1993: 94–5) thinks that 'outside advisers' 'have obfuscated the tasks of the transformation by focusing too much on pitting the potential virtues of shock therapy against the potential drawbacks of gradualism. All too often many of the participants in these debates have ignored that any substantial transformation programme must embody elements of both. Not only that, these elements can only be tailored relative to the specific conditions of time and place to any given PET [European planned economy in transition], rather than in terms of a preset technocratic blueprint.'

Critics attack the feasibility and wisdom of attempting a rapid and comprehensive approach. Two major criticisms of the 'big bang' school are that:

1. There is undue optimism about the time needed to accomplish and the costs incurred in the transition (e.g. the time needed for behaviour patterns, including informal codes of behaviour such as 'gentlemen's agreements', attitudes and institutions to change). There is also the related point that the cost of making a mistake is likely to be large. The general lack of personnel qualified to deal with the changed political, administrative and economic conditions also hinders the transition substantially. (It is ironic that this very deficiency is one factor that has added to the appeal of former communists, offering their administrative experience to manage the transition.)

2. Its adherents advocate policies of rapid market adjustment that even their own governments would not follow (the problems and time dimension of West European integration are often quoted as a comparison).

In an interview in *The Guardian* (Supplement, 26 January 1994, p. 7), Jacques Attali (the former president of the EBRD) stated, 'I have always said that they will need at least twenty years to get out of the mire and sufficient resources from Western institutions. Otherwise, the desperate populations of these countries will start to think a return to military dictatorship is a small price to pay for a return to employment, social protection and accessible consumer goods. Western Europe has no global vision of a continental union. Everybody is fixated with their own national problems. We really need a new generation of visionary statesmen . . . there is the dream of a continental union, which I favour, which would include all Europeans "from the Atlantic to the Urals", including the Turks. That is probably the most desirable, but also the least likely.'

The United Nations Economic Commission for Europe (1994: 1–2) emphasizes that 'for many people in Eastern Europe and the former Soviet Union, the transition process appears as a social crisis'. A November 1993 United Nations Children's Fund (Unicef) report is cited, which says that 'in seven of the nine transition economies monitored by Unicef, the crisis "appears most pronounced and general in the fields of poverty, mortality (particularly for males in the 40–59 age group), marriage and birth rates, pre-school education and youth, and overall crime", the data showing "clear and sizeable deteriorations in each of these areas". The situation appears to have stopped deteriorating in Hungary, Slovakia and the Czech Republic, but only in the last country are there any signs of a return to normal conditions.'

The United Nations Children's Fund published a report on 26 January 1994 detailing the unexpectedly high social costs of the transition since 1989 in nine countries (Albania, Bulgaria, the Czech Republic, Hungary, Poland, Romania, Russia, Slovakia and Ukraine) (Frances Williams, *FT*, 27 January 1994, p. 2; Adrian Bridge, *The Independent*, 28 January 1994, p. 10). The increase in poverty and widespread social disintegration have been reflected in rising death rates, falling birth rates, fewer marriages, an increasing number of suicides, the spread of infectious diseases (such as diphtheria and tuberculosis), falling school enrolment (coupled with increasing truancy) and a crime wave of 'truly alarming proportions'. 'These costs are not only the cause of unnecessary suffering and waste of human lives, but they also represent a source of considerable instability and social conflict that could threaten the entire reform process.'

Another Unicef report, published on 6 October 1994, covered Russia, Albania, Bulgaria, the Czech Republic, Slovakia, Hungary, Poland, Romania and Ukraine in the period 1989–93. There was 'a deterioration of unparalleled proportions in human welfare throughout most of the region.' There were 800,000 excess deaths (more than would have occurred if 1989 death rates had prevailed): 'Such a death toll, mainly among males aged 30–55 and across so many countries, is without precedent in peacetime.' Russia, Ukraine and south-eastern Europe were worst affected. The Czech Republic and Slovakia were largely untouched (extreme poverty was contained to less than 4 per cent), while by 1993 Poland showed signs of returning to pre-transition mortality rates. 'In parts of eastern Europe this health, nutrition and mortality crisis represents a clear threat to the political viability of the entire reform process. The whole transition could grind to a halt as mortality rises, health services worsen and consensus-building skills are slowly and painfully learned.' (Frances Williams, *FT*, 7 October 1994, p. 2; *The Guardian*, 7 October 1994, p. 12; *IHT*, 8 October 1994, p. 5.) The United Nations Economic Commission for Europe (1994) makes two other points:

1. The recession has been relatively less prolonged in the Czech Republic, Hungary, Poland and Slovenia, where, on current indications, a gradual recovery may now be emerging. But it should be emphasized that 'many of the achievements so far are more likely to impress professional economists and international officials than the long suffering electorates of the countries concerned. Even in this group, with the possible exception of the Czech Republic, there is still widespread disillusionment with the transition process and dissatisfaction with the fall in living standards: the essentially political task of organizing and maintaining popular support for the ultimate objectives of market-based economies and democratic institutions remains as urgent as ever' (p. 1). (This is an interesting observation in the light of the swing to the left in the general elections in Poland in September 1993 and in Hungary in May 1994.)

2. 'The persistence over many years of a harsh macroeconomic environment runs the risk of tipping the balance of the economy from a situation in which the majority of enterprise managers perceive a reasonable likelihood of viability in the market economy to a situation in which viability appears improbable. If the enterprise is thought to have "no chance" under market conditions, management and employees will be prone to seek survival strategies for the "enterprise community" which may not be market-conforming . . . If loss-making becomes prevalent there is a danger that the incentive for managers to push forward with restructuring is dulled' (p. 160). (See Nove in the section on industrial policy below.)

A 'big bang' approach may be accused of largely avoiding the issue of choosing the proper sequence of reforms in each particular case (it has always been recognized, of course, that restructuring and large privatization take a long time to accomplish). Jackman (1994) points out that the 'orthodox' approach has been to argue for restructuring to be as rapid as possible and to rely primarily on unemployment benefit (the 'social safety net') to protect the unemployed. But governments in Eastern Europe and, even more so, in the former Soviet Union have tended to support most of their enterprises. Bankruptcies and closures have been rare, and implicit and explicit subsidies continue. Even so, unemployment has risen and is placing heavy burdens on budgets. 'In these circumstances, arguments for a "gradualist" approach, not to the restructuring programme as a whole but to the rate of run-down of production and employment in state firms, are gaining ground. It will often be less costly in both social and fiscal terms to maintain employment than close down an enterprise, and there is no reason to think the growth of new private firms will be impeded as a result. In particular . . . private firms are generally not recruiting unemployed people' (p. 344). (Growing private firms recruit their workers primarily from those employed in the state sector rather than from the unemployed: p. 334.)

Ellman (1993) draws a distinction between 'constructivists' (who wish to build 'capitalism' quickly) and 'Popperians' (who anticipate a long and difficult process of socio-political–economic transformation, which may take decades, with no guarantee of success) (pp. 7–8). Ellman sees the three main issues in the transition as stabilization, institutional change (likely to be a long process: p. 18) and the difficult process of structural change (although they can be related) (p. 28).

Murrell (1993: 113) is critical of 'big bang' advocates such as Lipton and Sachs: 'Their discussion does not examine existing institutional structures and how to change them to reach the goal [the creation of a Western-type economic system], but rather focuses on ways, the methods, and the strategies to replace these structures entirely. There is complete disdain for all that exists . . . History, society, and the economics of present institutions are all minor issues in choosing a reform programme . . . Given that existing structures are the problem, society must be sidestepped in the reform process.' Murrell (1992b) favours an evolutionary approach. He argues that an understanding of the success of capitalism requires primary emphasis to be placed on mechanisms that produce growth and change as opposed to equilibrium processes. In Schumpeterian fashion he thus focuses on the role played by innovation rather than on allocative efficiency. The evolutionary approach stresses 'the existence of rigidities in organizational behaviour and the importance of entry and exit processes to the dynamism of capitalism' (p. 52). For example, during the transition privatization should be given a lower priority than policies encouraging the growth of new private firms (pp. 36, 46). Murrell also argues that some of the existing structures could be used. Thus 'during the transition there might be a case for direct controls on state enterprises to promote macroeconomic stability, rather than relying upon solely market-based measures' (p. 47); 'monetary policy might need to be more stringent and foreign currency less available for the private sector, if the state eschews all non-market means of controlling its own enterprises' (p. 51).

Alexander Solzhenitsyn recommends an evolutionary approach for Russia: 'The major mistake of reformers is that they followed the habitual revolutionary road – "to destroy the foundations and then . . ." – But even a fool can see that what is required in this case is an evolutionary approach, a smooth and slow transition. The old economic mechanism has to be preserved, but reanimated from below' (*Moscow News*, 29 July–4 August 1994, p. 13).

Neuber (1993: 511–30) develops an interdisciplinary approach, highlighting the interdependence of economic, political, institutional and cultural factors. 'Although the creation of market-enhancing institutions figures in the transition blueprints, their lagged creation is not seen as an indispensable condition for the initial stages. Underlying that faithful leap into a market setting characterized by a hybrid institutional environment is the neoclassical assumption that markets operate in a frictionless world, the institutions of which do not play any instrumental role' (p. 514). 'A principal objective of this paper has been the identification of shortcomings of the neoclassical paradigmatic approach adopted by advisers and practitioners alike in Eastern Europe. The erroneous belief in the automaticity of market-based incentives and signals, especially when coupled with the advocacy of wholesale import of institutions that neglects the existence of surviving institutions, however much disliked, has led to a vast underestimation of the difficulties and subtleties involved' (p. 527).

'Big bang' price liberalization: the pros and cons

It is worth reading the section on price reform in Russia in Jeffries (1993: 99–103) and in this volume (pp. 172–5).

Brada (1993: 90–1) points out that the liberalization of prices (assuming a relatively stable level of aggregate prices such as would exist if there were no repressed or open inflation) should lead to a more rational allocation of resources, and both queues and forced substitution of goods would disappear. He argues that the equilibrium of the consumer market, the reassertion of consumer sovereignty and the better assortment of goods available to consumers are gains that are largely dismissed by critics of the 'big bang'.

Woo (1994: 278–9) argues in favour of a 'big bang' approach. The common consequence of partial price reform is that the state is obliged to accede to requests for subsidies from loss-making firms that have their output prices controlled. There is little incentive for such firms to increase their efficiency because it is hard for the government to determine whether the losses are due to price controls or to mismanagement and misappropriation. Furthermore, the common knowledge that prices are being phased out means that intertemporal speculation of storable goods is promoted, resulting in inventories being too large and shortages more severe.

Balcerowicz puts forward a number of arguments in favour of a comprehensive liberalization of most prices: (1) to make use of the political 'honeymoon' period; (2) it is a necessary (and largely sufficient) means of removing widespread shortages quickly, which is in turn necessary for consumers' well-being and for the more efficient operation of enterprises; and (3) slow price liberalization would prolong the existence of distorted prices: the performance of enterprises cannot be judged reliably and the soft budget constraint is likely to persist as loss-makers are able to blame distorted prices (Balcerowicz 1994: 42). The actual choice in Eastern Europe 'was between maintaining widespread price controls with the corresponding shortages and distortions, or liberalizing prices within initially very imperfect market structures . . . a comprehensive price liberalization should be complemented by comprehensive liberalization of foreign trade' (p. 28).

In contrast, McKinnon (1994: 462) believes that 'the big bang argument for total price decontrol is flawed if the important actors bidding for scarce resources have soft budget constraints . . . until budget constraints are hardened, uncontrolled bidding by state enterprises will cause the producer price level to increase indefinitely'.

China shows that gradual reform is possible, although it does lead to corruption. In Russia price controls on energy have led to illegal exports of oil and gas. For a strong defence of the Chinese approach see Wang Xiaoqing (1993). He argues that successful price reform needs enterprise reform and adjustment of the industrial structure. China's growth has encouraged competition and technological advance. Hussain and Stern (1994: 7) argue that one lesson of the Chinese experience is that 'market transactions can flourish even under a heavily distorted price structure and in particular economic sectors, whilst others remain closed. Once established they themselves can become a powerful force for a rationalization of prices.

Experience with market transactions enhances the capacity of economic agents to adapt to changes in relative prices.'

It may be unwise to release prices in 'big bang' fashion when the authorities do not possess effective instruments of monetary control. Rapid price and trade liberalization may be destabilizing, with inelastic supply responses and inadequate instruments and institutions for creating and maintaining macroeconomic stability (United Nations Economic Commission for Europe 1993: 9–10). (Note also the point that underdeveloped financial markets may make bond sales difficult and thus force governments to rely excessively on the printing press.)

Qian (1994) develops a theory of shortage in socialist economies based on the soft budget constraint. He takes the case where the same good is demanded both by firms (subject to a soft budget constraint) as an input and by households (hard budget constraint) as a consumer good (the many examples of these goods in short supply include electricity and cars). Qian argues that 'if the seller cannot perfectly separate firms from households, a high market-clearing price will exclude many households from receiving consumer goods but will not deter inefficient projects from starting because of the soft budget constraint. This clearly leads to social welfare losses. However, at a lower price, social welfare may be higher. The idea is that, although a bad project [one that requires more time and capital for completion than its lender expected] may be able to secure the funds it needs under the soft budget constraint, it may not be able to obtain all the inputs it requires if they are in short supply . . . Therefore, shortage may discourage a manager who knows his project is bad from applying for finance in the first place. This would improve the average quality of the projects. Of course, setting the price below the market-clearing level has inefficient consequences in terms of misallocation, project completion delays, and supply distortions . . . the incentive effect may outweigh these adverse outcomes, however, in certain situations. In such a case, increasing the price to the market-clearing level is welfare-reducing' (p. 146). In terms of the transition, Qian suggests that 'financial discipline together with the corresponding institutional changes is needed at the time of price liberalization. To the extent that the two reforms are complementary, price liberalization without hardening the budget constraint of the firms may induce adverse welfare consequences' (p. 147).

There is the argument that price liberalization preceding demonopolization of the state sector is more effective when there is an already flourishing private sector which can respond (thus Poland was in a better position to free prices than Russia).

A plea for pragmatism

Portes (1994: 1180) argues that 'the range of sensible strategies is limited and there may be little margin for choice. Some elements of stabilization and liberalization make sense only when done simultaneously. The range observed across countries is in fact surprisingly limited and mainly a function of initial conditions.'

The prime minister of the Czech Republic, Vaclav Klaus, reiterates his welcome plea for pragmatism. The creation of a normally functioning society and economy requires a comprehensive and painful transformation. 'Such a change takes years to complete; it cannot be accomplished merely with some sort of overnight shock therapy.' Nevertheless, the transition is proving a successful one. 'For the countries of Central and Eastern Europe, the important thing now is to push ahead with the process of self-transformation, and to resist any temptation to settle for half-measures or to make useless political and social concessions.' The reforming politician must beware of 'reform fatigue'. He must be able to formulate a clear vision of a future which is both attractive and achievable. He must explain this vision to his citizens and defend it against populists. He must implement a consistent reform strategy and introduce unpopular and painful measures as and when they are needed. He must not defer to 'rent-seekers' and lobbyists who pursue their own short-term advantage to the detriment of society as a whole. 'The reforming politician must take into account the fact that radical transformation of any society is a complex and dynamic process, not merely an exercise in applied economics or political science.' The people that such changes affect are not passive objects, but are human beings who must be offered a fair deal politically as well as economically. A system of political parties has to be created as the means for achieving a basic political and social consensus. 'To privatize, deregulate and liberalize, and yet to retain an appropriate degree of macroeconomic stability; such is the essential aim.' Although most of Europe's post-communist countries have already introduced a first set of reform measures, 'some have done so hesistantly or inconsistently, falling short of the critical mass of reforms needed to change the basic system and so deliver some tangible results'. Where that is so, initial euphoria has evaporated and with it the early mood of national unity. In some cases there is a high degree of political instability. It is not easy to find 'an optimal equilibrium point in the real world between the freedom of individuals and the need for regulation by the state – not to mention by supranational institutions' (Vaclav Klaus, *The Economist*, 10 September 1994, pp. 45–6).

Empirical evidence

As the transition proceeds in various countries there is increasing debate about how far the empirical evidence supports the various 'schools' of thought. But there is even disagreement about how to categorize actual programmes. Åslund and Layard (1993), while praising the progress made in Russia in freeing prices and in privatization, claim that 'shock therapy' (in the sense of strict fiscal and monetary policies) has not been carried out. Murrell (1993: 125–31) argues that Poland's 'big bang' of January 1990 was a departure from a progression of reforms, but that gradually policy returned to its natural path in the ensuing months. But even in the early part of 1990 the radical policy was held up by existing institutions, the Church and Solidarity in particular (as opposed to a top-down policy simply being implemented by technocrats). He argues that the important new private sector was actually temporarily slowed by the abortive attempt to produce quick results in the state sector (such as by means of trade liberalization). In mid-1990 monetary and credit policy was eased and trade protectionism was enhanced in August 1991. Large privatization was delayed. Thus the aim of the programme was 'to change irrevocably the course of policy and to wrest policy from the influence of the dominant elements of existing society. In fact, Polish society took back the reforms; the continuous progression of policy before and after the big bang is much more remarkable than any discontinuity . . . Judged on its own terms, as an instrument to side-step society and create a new configuration of political and economic forces, shock therapy was a failure in Poland. But the Polish economy is now showing its first signs of success, after policy was rescued from the shock therapists' (pp. 130–1). Murrell thinks that a similar thing happened in Russia, but the destruction of the old administrative institutions was 'hardly matched by the creation of market-oriented institutions of economic control' (p. 137).

In total contrast, Sachs and Woo (1994: 103) argue that Vietnam's 'gradual reform during 1985–88 failed to address serious macroeconomic imbalances . . . In 1989 Vietnam adopted a "big bang", liberalizing prices, devaluing 450 per cent to unify the exchange market, sharply tightening credit, and returning collective farms to families with long leases.'

(Note that transitional economies were not helped by economic recession in the West in the early 1990s.)

TRADE LIBERALIZATION AND PROTECTION

The United Nations Economic Commission for Europe (1993: 189) criticizes the idea that exchange rate policy can be used instead of transitional protection such as tariffs (i.e. the idea that a sufficiently low exchange rate can make most loss-making industries efficient). Not only would this lead to an excessive reduction in real wages throughout the economy, but, because of large disparities in the profitability of individual enterprises, the exchange rate would have to depreciate to absurdly low levels. But the most important reason is the presence of 'value-added subtractors'. Under new relative prices some activities may yield negative value added, especially energy-intensive sectors. In these circumstances devaluation cannot help and such activities would have to be discontinued.

Whether the exchange rate should be fixed or flexible 'is one of those either–or choices that many economists and inexperienced policy makers are fond of. In practice, the question is more what kind of crawling peg should be established and at what intervals the exchange rate should be adjusted to avoid damaging the currency's credibility and, by extension, the credibility of transition policies as a whole' (Van Brabant 1994: 173). Van Brabant argues that 'a managed nominal exchange rate would be preferable to a heavily undervalued fixed rate, such as has been introduced in several PETS [planned economies in transition] since 1989' (p. 174).

Williamson (1993: 32–4) makes a case for transitional tariff protection of 'senile' industries. 'An important cause of demand-shift in an economy integrating itself into the world economy is from the production of import substitutes to that of exports . . . it is inefficient to have large pools of resources that are made idle years before they can be reabsorbed elsewhere . . . it is better that, until they can be reabsorbed elsewhere, resources should produce goods of low value-added than that they should not add any value at all.' But Williamson is very sceptical of McKinnon's argument that industries producing negative value added (at world prices) should be granted temporary protection in order to see whether they can adjust to the new input prices.

Demekas and Khan (1991: 21) stress the need to switch (1) from quotas to tariffs and (2) to a more uniform tariff structure (in order to minimize production distortions and reduce the vulnerability of governments to lobbying from vested interest groups). Portes (1994: 1189) believes that a moderate tariff can yield useful revenue while temporarily protecting 'senile' industries. Non-selective export promotion services are an example of a useful industrial policy.

CORPORATE FINANCE

Market-based versus bank-based systems

Begg (1993: 1–5) provides a useful summary of the relative merits of (1) a market-based system relying on stock markets (as in the USA and UK) and (2) a bank-based system in which banks become long-term suppliers of finance to companies (as in Germany and Japan). The important distinction is the way the two systems award control rights to those providing the finance.

1. The market-based system allows the prime role to be played by stock and bond markets. Bond holders can force companies into bankruptcy, while the existence of publicly quoted shares raises the possibility of a take-over. The arguments in favour of take-overs include managers being deterred from departing too far from the interests of shareholders. The main argument against is the charge of 'short-termism'; managers are

deterred from taking decisions bringing long-term benefits since an initial dip in profits will depress share prices and encourage hostile take-over bids. (The growth of institutional investors such as pension and insurance funds is said to aggravate the problem of 'short-termism': Mullineux and Belka 1993: 3.) (It is commonly pointed out that it is especially important to take a long-run view in transitional economies.)

2. The bank-based system extends the role of banks to ownership and control of companies (via 'supervisory boards'). There is little second-hand trading of shares on secondary markets. In countries such as Poland state banks have been the most important financial institutions in the early stages of the transition and are likely to continue to be so in the medium term (Mullineux and Belka 1993: 3). The counter-argument is the lack of suitable banks in the transitional economies.

(See also Portes 1994 in the section on enterprise debt and restructuring below.)

Taxation

Ickes and Slemrod (1992) and Holzman (1992) deal with the problems of tax policy during the transition. Cnossen (1992: 250–1) discusses an appropriate value-added tax (VAT) for the countries of Eastern Europe, proceeding from the point of view that the tax should be used almost exclusively to generate revenue in as neutral and administratively feasible a manner as possible. While income tax can be employed to achieve distributional objectives and excise and import duties to attain allocative goals, the focus of VAT should be on revenue. If VAT is not to resemble the kind of bookkeeping exercise of the old turnover tax in socialist countries, the introduction of VAT should be preceded by a substantial degree of price liberalization and enterprise autonomy.

Hussain and Stern (1993) point out that the usual model is the West European tax structure (p. 67). The following are typical: personal income tax (including social security contributions); a substantial shift from taxes on enterprises to taxes on persons and the introduction of corporation tax integrated with personal income tax; VAT and excise taxes on selected commodities; and property taxes (p. 76). They recommend that reform of the public finances and the institution of a new social security system should be contemporaneous with rather than follow enterprise reforms. (Note the extra incentive to use the West European system as a way of easing the path to membership of the EU.)

Heady *et al.* (1994) argue that 'simply transplanting West European [tax] practice is unlikely to be optimal, due to severe limitations in administrative capacity, reflecting both the lack of trained personnel, and administrative traditions which are incompatible with tax enforcement in a market economy. These limitations imply that tax reform should be gradual and that, initially, maximum use should be made of simple, albeit perhaps inelegant, systems' (p. 79). Apart from administrative limitations, there is also the 'clean sheet' argument for not simply copying Western tax systems, i.e. a unique opportunity to start from scratch (p. 71). Heady *et al.* also argue that 'the key priority in tax reform has been to make a transition from the arbitrary and negotiable tax structures characteristic of centrally-planned economies to a more uniform and rule-based taxation system' (p. 79).

McKinnon (1992b) explains why 'price inflation and a general loss of macroeconomic control are almost endemic in a liberalizing socialist economy . . . The ability of the reform government to collect taxes and control the supply of money and credit is unwittingly undermined by the process of liberalization itself' (p. 109). 'Rather than a "big bang" where all centralized socialist controls are simultaneously dismantled . . . [McKinnon] . . . holds that there is a natural or optimum order of economic liberalization. Moves to dismantle the apparatus of central planning, decontrol prices, privatize property, free foreign trade, and so on need to be supported by a proper sequence of fiscal, monetary, and foreign exchange measures' (pp. 109–10).

'Raising adequate revenue is essential if inflation is to be contained in economies whose capital markets do not yet allow adequately for non-monetary financing of government deficits' (EBRD 1994: iv).

Enterprise debt and restructuring

(See Ickes and Ryterman above.)

Begg and Portes (1993a: 116–17) propose immediate recapitalization; the government should take over all the non-performing loans from banks and replace them at par with Treasury bills. If the aim is to support unprofitable state enterprises, the government should do so by means of explicit, cash-limited fiscal subsidies. This policy is advocated despite credibility and moral hazard problems (creating expectations of future write-offs). (To guard against any moral hazard it is necessary to introduce an effective system of bank regulation and supervision: Mullineux and Belka 1993: 5.)

Portes (1994: 1187) argues that the single most important error in actual sequencing was not to have implemented a financial clean-out: recapitalizing the banks, cancelling the debts of state enterprises at the time of privatization and instituting cash-limited fiscal subsidies to the state enterprises meanwhile, so that the banks would not have to extend them new loans or capitalize their arrears. Stock markets were and are clearly not going to be a major mechanism for financial intermediation or corporate control for many years to come. The banks had to take on the task and they were too weak to do so. Investment and the growth of new private firms have thereby suffered. Both monetary tightness and the need to maintain high intermediation margins to build up a capital base, in the absence of recapitalization, have contributed to high real interest rates and thus to low real investment.

Hexter (1993: 111–12) points out the temptation for governments in the short run to support insolvent enterprises by means of credit creation rather than the budget (the tax base is inadequate, while explicit budgetary subsidies may violate IMF targets). Hexter argues that loans should be written down to realizable values in the books of banks. Then banks should be recapitalized either by transferring the below-market-value loans to a government-sponsored 'hospital' bank, and substituting the guarantees/bonds of the government, or by a cash infusion. The worst of the loss-making enterprises will have to retrench or be closed (an adequate social security safety net is needed to make this course of action politically acceptable). Some banks will have to retrench or even be closed, while the 'survivor' banks must be privatized as rapidly as possible.

Levine and Scott (1993: 319) argue that in transitional economies the large stocks of loans issued by state banks to state enterprises in the socialist era are impeding the transition to a market economy by slowing the privatization of enterprises and banks, hindering the efficient operation of firms and banks, encouraging *ad hoc* government intervention and reducing government credibility. Replacing bank claims on enterprises with claims on the government at the time of privatization will yield important efficiency gains and may not add much to the fiscal burden.

Van Wijnbergen (1993) links the questions of restructuring, privatization, bankruptcy and debt. A substantial acceleration of privatization is the only safeguard against the reappearance of the debt problem (p. 23). Outsiders cannot know whether the poor circumstances of an enterprise are due to inefficient management, to efficient management responding to distorted incentives, or to the fact that it has no prospects with the current capital structure. Thus enterprise restructuring is unavoidable, advice which goes against the widespread view that it is best left to new private owners (p. 22). In Eastern Europe current profits are a very poor guide to future profitability and the application of Western bankruptcy procedures leads to a bias towards liquidation and delay (p. 35). Van Wijnbergen argues that reorganization and debt–equity swaps offer a more promising way of making efficient use of assets (p. 118). While foreign participation is to be welcomed, the main resort should be to rely on management buy-outs or bank-inspired restructuring. Thus the programme should rely on the government as little as possible, passing the initiative for enterprise reform to the next-in-line class of creditors (the banks and the enterprise's management, possibly joined by its workers) (p. 118). Thus Van Wijnbergen argues that a much more effective way of debt restructuring is to introduce effective ownership into the process. Some of the debt should be converted into equity and this should be the main focus of the restructuring exercise rather than debt write-down schemes and full collection of what remains (p. 23).

Debt should be written off just enough to restore solvency and no more (p. 26).

(For a detailed analysis of banks and capital markets during the transition, see the special issue entitled 'Banks and capital markets in former centrally planned countries: their role in establishing a market economy' of *Journal of Banking and Finance*, 1993, vol. 17, no. 5.)

THE ROLE OF THE STATE IN THE TRANSITION

It is ironic that, given the much reduced role of the state in non-planned economies, there is increasing recognition that the transition to the market is too important to be left to the market, e.g. state control is needed to ensure that the privatization process is not abused by the *nomenklatura* (the importance of high ethical standards in government is crucial, of course) and to protect the most vulnerable sections of society. Bruno, for example, has contributed to the debate. 'Experience shows that even the most *laissez-faire* economies are susceptible to market failures (e.g. in financial markets) and that governments may have to intervene in the micro-economy. All the more reason to believe that in the transition a hands-off approach cannot be optimal. The obvious example is that of financial restructuring. The danger of repeating old central planning mistakes is obviously always there, but this cannot justify ducking the issue of how best to intervene in the transition' (1993b: 245).

Industrial policy deals essentially with structural changes in the economy. Hughes and Hare (1991) argue the case for an industrial policy based on calculations of long-term competitiveness rather than the government being influenced by the lobbying of various pressure groups (see main text). Hare (1993: 43–64) produces measures of the 'social profitability' of different industries, using world prices. He considers them to be a more reliable guide to long-term profitability than current domestic prices ('the distortions in domestic prices are large enough to rule out reliance upon domestic measures of profitability or value added': p. 54). 'It would be a serious mistake for all apparently loss-making firms to be allowed to fail. Since current financial performance is so misleading, even after the initial stages of economic reforms, governments should not leave decisions about closures and other forms of restructuring assets solely in the hands of banks and other financial institutions. Aside from the remaining distortions in markets for goods and services . . . financial institutions themselves are not well enough developed to undertake such an important task' (p. 47).

Hughes and Hare (1994) again argue that what is needed is 'a methodology which makes it possible to rank enterprises and branches in terms of their viability and competitiveness, that is after removing the effects of the present distortions. We do this by using world market prices as a basis for revaluing the outputs and inputs into different branches of the economy, and calculating various measures of social profitability' (p. 201). 'The use of world market prices and alternative assumptions about the shadow pricing of capital and labour enabled us to calculate three measures of the shadow rate of profit, corresponding to short-run, medium-run and long-run analysis . . . The advantage of having three measures . . . is that it enabled us to differentiate between branches where adjustment was really very urgent . . . those where it was efficient to employ existing workers in the medium run but not to undertake further investment with current technology . . . and those where returns are already sufficiently high to make additional investment socially profitable, even with existing ("old") technology' (p. 218). In his comment on the paper Andrew Glyn argues that the most appropriate basis for ranking industries is value added at world prices per person employed (p. 225).

Landesmann (1993) favours an active state industrial policy in the transition, such as on training and infrastructure, in order to improve the response to market signals. Nove (1994) argues in favour of a government-co-ordinated investment programme because of the decline of investment. 'The danger is not of "creative destruction" envisaged by Schumpeter, but just of destruction, de-industrialization, with nothing creative taking its place. Here, in my view is *the* Achilles heel of the transition models. The necessary adjustments on the supply side . . . require investment' (p. 865). The chances of success would be higher if 'the government, instead of giving sole emphasis to macroeconomic stabilization, launched and publicized a recovery programme, and mobilized opinion and private (and foreign) capital to that end' (p. 869).

OTHER MODELS FOR THE TRANSITION

There is considerable debate about the relevance of other models.

Asian models

Frances Williams (*FT*, 16 September 1993, p. 6) summarizes a report by Unctad (the United Nations Conference on Trade and Development) which is critical of the East European experience. The report not only notes the fall in output in Eastern Europe (average annual growth rates of −14.9 per cent in 1991 and −15.9 per cent in 1992) but also says that many of the countries find themselves in 'a twilight world where there is neither plan nor market'. In contrast the report praises the East and South East Asian economies for the positive role played by government in supporting private business and exports. The Asian experience (characterized by high average rates of growth) shows that export success requires not only 'getting prices right' but also 'active government support and . . . well-targeted protection of domestic producers.' (China is praised in the report.) Criticisms include the following:

1. The relevance of the (four) 'Pacific Tigers' (Hong Kong, Singapore, South Korea and Taiwan) is limited by the fact that they simply experienced a change from one form of market system to another.

2. Riedel (1993: 412) argues that 'Unfortunately, in dwelling on the role of trade and industrial policy, many students of the East Asian "Tigers" have overlooked their relative performance in the more fundamental duties of government in a market economy, which are first and foremost supplying public goods and maintaining macroeconomic stability.'

3. The World Bank's *The East Asia Miracle: Economic Growth and Public Policy* is summarized in *The Economist* (2 October 1993, pp. 73–4), *FT* (27 September 1993, pp. 3, 18, 34), *IHT* (5 October 1993, p. 15) and Tony Killick (*Development Policy Review*, 1994, vol. 12, no. 1, pp. 69–79). Numbered among its conclusions are the following: (1) the eight countries studied (Hong Kong, Indonesia, Japan, Malaysia, Singapore, South Korea, Taiwan and Thailand) did not follow a single economic model, e.g. Hong Kong is basically *laissez-faire*, while Japan and South Korea have been the most interventionist; (2) industrial policies to 'pick winners' have usually failed (market forces would have brought about the desired changes in industrial structure), but there have been more favourable aspects, e.g. export promotion, which has helped keep domestic prices in line with world prices and encouraged competition and the use of foreign technology; in Japan and South Korea there have been government-sponsored and strictly monitored competitions to choose selected firms (note also the general commitment to successful agriculture); (3) the region's success mainly reflects getting 'economic fundamentals' right, such as sound macroeconomic policies (leading to relatively low inflation), a proper legal framework, a high rate of saving and high rates of investment in physical and human capital (especially in primary, secondary and technical education); (4) development has lessened poverty and income inequalities and this has enhanced the legitimacy of government policies; (5) the East Asian experience is not easy to export, e.g. the work ethic is relatively strong and the bureaucracy is of an unusually high calibre, while intervention is less feasible today (because of factors such as Gatt rules and a more integrated global capital market).

China as a model

Hussain and Stern (1993) argue that when China embarked on the reform process in 1978 the economy was relatively stable, the reforms were introduced from the top and there was no political democratization. In contrast, in some economies in Eastern Europe and the former Soviet Union law and order have broken down and the government is unable to take or implement decisions (pp. 63–4). The combination of old-style planning and markets creates problems of co-ordination which worsen over time (e.g. above-plan output sold at negotiated prices), but it can help to reduce uncertainty and maintain stability in the initial stages of transition. If economic reforms bring tangible benefits to a majority of the population while losers are protected, a constituency in favour of reform can emerge. Hussain and Stern do not argue that a slow rate of transition is always superior, only that the idea that there is no alternative to the fast route cannot be accepted without the most careful scrutiny. The evidence from theory and from history in favour of the fast route cannot be regarded as overwhelming (p. 83).

Brus (1993: 428–9) sees value in what he calls a '"dual track" system whereby target planning and state allocation of resources were preserved for a given limit of productive capacity, while "above quota" output was freed with regard to the direction of sales, sources of supply and – most importantly – pricing . . . The "dual track" policy has not eliminated the usual weakness of the state sector in terms of competitiveness and financial discipline (the need for large-scale subsidization remains one of the main problems for China's budget), and has inevitably created new problems by opening the door to corrupt exploitation . . . Nevertheless, on balance it has to be judged positively: from the short-term point of view – because it injected a measure of business behaviour into the management of state enterprises without waiting for change in the ownership structure and without threatening to produce major social tensions by abrupt cessation of the familiar type of employee-entitlements, leading *inter alia* to a massive surge in joblessness; from the longer-term point of view – because it paved the way, both ideologically and practically, towards full subordination of the present state sector to market co-ordination.' (See also the section on the linkage between political and economic reform.)

Jefferson and Rawski (1994: 66) argue that China's recent history proves that a gradual reform of state industry is a feasible alternative, one that is capable of generating very substantial results. China's industrial success is partly attributable to favourable initial conditions, but the contrast between China's performance in terms of industrial output, real wages, employment and exports and the performance of industry in states that have attempted to accelerate the pace of institutional change is too large to be explained solely by differences in initial conditions. 'We cannot avoid speculating that China is not the only venue in which the optimal path from plan to market might involve a lengthy interlude of gradual reform and a succession of transitional structures that deviate widely from standard market institutions.'

Elsewhere, Rawski (1994: 274) comments that economists who advocate sweeping reform have expressed the fear that gradualism may permit conservatives to mobilize against reform. In China events have moved in the opposite direction. 'The reform experience of China and other transitional economies shows that a penchant for excessive abstraction often leads economists to overlook essential features of actual market systems . . . One obvious lesson is that partial, gradual reform of public-sector industry can produce substantial results. Early privatization of industry may be useful in some circumstances, but it is not essential in every country . . . Chinese industry will still have achieved fifteen years of substantial growth, export success and technical advance under institutional arrangements that many economists see as unworkable.' But 'China's success with gradualism does not mean that other ex-socialist nations should rush to embrace Chinese policies . . . initial conditions strongly affect policy outcomes . . . Take the example of administrative capacity, which is widely neglected in the discussion of reform issues. China's stable and relatively effective bureaucracy finds it difficult to cope with multiple reforms'.

'The 1978–84 [agricultural] spurt gave enormous credibility to market-oriented reforms and to the individuals who designed those reforms. The political lesson for future reformers from China's experience is obvious but forgotten – try to begin the reform process with a clear winner' (Perkins 1994: 27).

Bolton argues that the main sources of inefficiency in production are the lack of competition in product markets combined with the separation of ownership and control. 'Because of this separation it is not clear *a priori* that private ownership is a more efficient arrangement than public ownership. Moreover, competition in product markets . . . can be introduced whether firms are private or state-owned' (1995: 2). Two important factors explaining the success of township–village enterprises (TVEs) in China 'are the introduction of a vastly improved governance structure and the high levels of competition in product markets (both inside China and in world markets)'. Local governments may be better monitors than a board of directors or a bank. They represent the interests of the whole community, they may have stronger incentives to induce TVEs to internalize some of the negative externalities and they may be able to foster greater co-operation between workers, managers and themselves. 'Whether TVEs actually do control managerial performance better than private firms cannot be established definitely, but the huge success of TVEs is sufficient to take this alternative form of governance structure seriously' (p. 7). There is the argument that there are factors specific to China, but the Chinese experience suggests that 'alternative policy options to full scale privatization ought to be considered more carefully'. These options could include the introduction of greater competition prior to privatization (such as by breaking up existing conglomerates) and greater involvement by local government in the supervision of firms (p. 7). 'The Chinese experience also demonstrates that substantial efficiency improvements can be obtained through partial reforms and through decentralized reform . . . The additional advantage of the Chinese reform is that it is much easier to correct policy errors and to push good reforms; also it is easier for economic agents to adapt to the gradual transformation of the economy' (p. 8).

Brada (1993: 96–7) argues that applying the Chinese lesson to Eastern Europe or Russia may be neither as desirable nor as feasible as it seems (apart from the unacceptable level of control exercised by the communist party). The starting conditions in China were in many respects favourable, e.g. as regards macroeconomic disequilibrium (the sharp increase in the savings rate also helped to keep inflation under control) and the large proportion of the work force employed in agriculture (which was relatively independent of machinery and intermediate inputs from industry).

Weitzman (1993: 550–5) descibes the township–village enterprise as the driving force of the Chinese model. The TVE is a 'vaguely defined co-operative . . . a communal organization about as far removed from having a well-defined ownership structure as can be imagined . . . Legally, the TVE is collectively owned by all the people in the community where it is located. There is no stipulation of any individual owners nor does anyone have rights to appropriate assets of the firm. There are no shares at all, formally speaking . . . Reward structures are extremely vague and informal.' But Weitzman argues that there is a need for a certain cultural inheritance if this form of organization is to work, a culture which enables the group to solve conflicts informally. Thus it may not be a realistic option for Eastern Europe to be thinking in terms of the Chinese model. Weitzman and Xu (1993) point out that in property rights theory 'the existence of well-defined private property rights is viewed as a basic precondition to the proper functioning of a capitalist market economy' (p. 5). But 'it seems fair to say that the property rights literature is often presented as if it were culture-free, of universal applicability' (p. 23). In the case of TVEs, conventional property rights theory misses a crucial dimension: 'The key missing element is the ability of a group to solve potential conflicts internally, without explicit rules, laws, rights, procedures and so forth' (p. 19). But 'the costs of changing culture are presumably very high, if culture is changeable at all. So it simply may not be a realistic option for Eastern Europe to be thinking in terms of the Chinese model' (p. 27). Nevertheless, not all the Eastern European countries are the same and it may be argued that Russia is a more relevant case (p. 28). (See also Weitzman and Xu 1994.) (See the analysis of TVEs by Naughton in Chapter 27 on China.)

Cyril Lin (as reported by Alexander Nicholl, *FT*, 24 May 1993, p. 17) argues that China is unique among the (former) socialist economies in that it has excess aggregate supply: 'An overstocked supply of consumer goods is chasing recalcitrant buyers.' In contrast the countries of the former Soviet bloc are experiencing declining output and instability, making it impossible for them to be gradualist.

Qian and Xu (1993) stress the important role that regional decentralization has played in China (e.g. in expanding the non-state sector) compared with the socialist countries of Eastern Europe and the Soviet Union.

The relevance of China's economic system to Russia in particular has also been tackled. John Gittings (*The Guardian*, 19 April 1993, p. 6) points out that Russian diaspora has nothing like the same entrepreneurial talent or capital as the overseas Chinese, who have invested massively in China). Russia lacks the proximity of the dynamic economies of East and South East Asia, in search of cheap labour, and Russia inherited huge and highly mechanized farms. (Note that the commonly cited figure of 50 million to 55 million overseas Chinese includes the populations of Taiwan and Hong Kong. Gungwu points out that the figure, excluding these, is generally in the 25 million to 30 million range, 80 per cent of whom live in South East Asia: 1993: 927.)

Sachs (Lipton and Sachs 1992: see comment, p. 277) argues that the lessons of Chinese gradualism have little relevance to Russia. Three-quarters of the Chinese population live in the countryside, so that the agrarian reforms after 1978 liberalized a huge proportion of the economy. Rapid growth has taken place outside the planned sector, while state industries have continued to suffer enormous financial losses. In contrast Russia is heavily industrialized and urbanized. Almost all economic activity in Soviet Russia was state-controlled. Sachs (*The Independent*, 11 October 1993, p. 18) also argues that 'In China there is very little social protection. Its growth is fuelled by tens of millions of peasant farmers who are willing to work for subsistence wages in new private factories to escape even more dismal conditions in the countryside. China's state enterprises lose money at an extraordinary rate, but fortunately account for less than 20 per cent of the work force. In Russia more than 80 per cent of workers were in the state sector at the start of the reforms in 1992.'

Sachs and Woo (1994: 103–43) argue that China's experience does not show that gradual reform is superior. Differing performance primarily reflects different economic structures prior to reform. China was a peasant agricultural society (in 1978 71 per cent of the labour force was in agriculture and only 15 per cent in industry, 2 per cent in construction and 2 per cent in transport), while Eastern Europe and the former Soviet Union were urban and overindustrialized (in Russia in 1985 the respective figures were 14 per cent, 32 per cent, 10 per cent and 10 per cent: p. 106). In China the state sector as a whole accounted for only 18.6 per cent of total employment in 1978, compared with 93.1 per cent in Russia in 1985 (p. 108). Jobs in state enterprises in all the countries were so heavily subsidized that workers refused to move to new industries elsewhere. But rapid growth in China was possible because the large agricultural sector contained vast surplus labour and did not enjoy subsidies or soft budget constraints. This labour fuelled the rapidly growing new industries in the non-state sector, while the reallocation of labour allowed all groups to gain. In Eastern Europe and the former Soviet Union, however, the much more important state sector impeded the necessary structural adjustment. Gradualism would not work because curtailing subsidies would produce losers who would use their power to resist this adjustment. Gradualism would not result in sufficient productivity gains to overcome the losses. (Woo goes so far as to argue that 'gradual reform in China was not the optimal reform for China': 1994: 306.)

Layard (*Economics of Transition*, 1993, vol. 1, no. 3, p. 358) argues that Russia has a huge industrial sector which must be improved. It is no good simply relying on entry by new firms. In China this was possible because the industrial sector was small and there was a large rural labour supply on which new enterprises could draw. In Russia only 11 per cent of the work force is employed in agriculture, compared with 60 per cent in China. Riedel (1993: 411–12) argues that 'What differentiates the socialist economies in Asia from those in Europe is their large labour force which is ready and willing . . . to go to work in export-oriented industries at wages only slightly above the subsistence level. It is the abundance of their human resources that has allowed the East Asian countries to build dynamic, export-oriented industries side-by-side with the inefficient, often state-owned, capital-intensive industries built up during the previous stage of autarkic industrialization. Eastern Europe and Russia, lacking human resources on the same scale as in Asia, do not have the same luxury; instead they must dismantle the old industry before they can build the new.'

'In Russia, as elsewhere in Eastern Europe (though not in Central Asia), political reform preceded effective economic reform, ruling out the Chinese way' (Flemming and Matthews 1994: 79).

Anatole Kaletsky (*The Times*, 23 September 1993, p. 29) argues that Boris Yeltsin made a mistake 'by accelerating economic liberalization instead of trying to rebuild the political foundations of the Russian state. Experience suggests that a properly functioning market economy can only be created by a strong government, working in a stable, or at least controlled, political framework. This does not mean that China is right to maintain repression, while liberalizing the economy. Political freedom and human rights may well be more important – even to many Russians – than economic growth. Instead the right conclusion is perhaps that economic liberalization must proceed gradually, and radical reform must be avoided, until the political framework is rebuilt.'

Even those who most vociferously deny the relevance of the Chinese experience to Eastern Europe and Russia do admit that China has had its economic successes. It is thus well worth noting Peter Nolan's point that what 'most economists of China have put forward is that its industrial performance in the 1980s would have been much better if it had followed the path of a rapid transition to a market economy. A large body of informed opinion both inside and outside the country considered that in the early 1980s China's policy makers should have liberalized industrial prices, eliminated the industrial material balance planning system, opened the industrial economy to the forces of international competition . . . and rapidly privatized state industry' (quoted by Wang Xiao-qing 1993: 3). Dic Lo (*The CEA (UK) Newsletter*, 1993, vol. 5, no. 3, p. 17) asks, 'if "big bang" is more rational, why is it that the actual performance of Eastern Europe has been far worse than that of China? Moreover, if a "second best" reform model can be accompanied by more than a decade of rapid economic growth, isn't it implying that the model is at least no less successful than that of the "first best"?' (Dic Lo argues that there is a substantial literature which tends to support the view that China's rapid growth has in the main been based on productivity improvement rather than resource mobilization. Moreover, there has been stagnation in many Third World countries, which are generally endowed with vast rural economies. This seems to support the argument that the existence of a large agricultural sector is not an adequate explanation of China's experience: p. 18.)

Nolan (1993) offers a strong defence of the Chinese model.

THE CAUSES AND EXTENT OF THE FALL IN OUTPUT

The causes of the fall in output

Williamson (1993: 25–39) provides a very useful taxonomy of the possible causes of the fall in output in transitional economies and distinguishes between 'avoidable' and 'unavoidable' losses:

1. Demand factors can be subdivided into (1) external demand: exogenous decline (a world recession, for example); overvalued currency (an avoidable loss when excessive); (2) internal demand: Keynesian demand deficiency, including the special case of a shortage of foreign currency, i.e. the government is forced to deflate because of a balance of payments constraint (Williamson argues that Czechoslovakia provided an even clearer case than Poland, where recession was primarily due to an excessively contractionary macroeconomic policy); 'demand shift' (resources have to be shifted to the production of the goods now in demand), including the special case where goods that were formerly produced are no longer wanted.

2. Supply factors can be subdivided into: (1) exogenous shocks (typically bad weather or natural disasters, but the example cited here is a fall in the output of oil in the former Soviet Union); (2) price changes that make some part of the former output uneconomic; (3) dislocation of input supplies; (4) a credit squeeze; (5) monoply pricing (exploitation of monopoly power after privatization).

Flemming and Matthews (1994: 66–7) also use the traditional division of factors:

1. On the demand side are the effects of fiscal and monetary tightening, destocking and reduced effective export demand.

2. On the supply side are the effects of destroying the planning mechanism before less formal market communication networks linking producers and the users of their products are in place. 'While many enterprises see this as a demand shock – potential users are slow to make themselves known after the state orders cease – looked at as a whole the productive system has lost a co-ordination mechanism and is less able, in the short run, to produce – an adverse supply shock. Until new market institutions and contractual arrangements emerge, old contracts and networks of exchange persist, if only on a barter basis.'

Bruno (1993a) argues that macroeconomic stabilization policies need to take account of the particular institutional features of the East European countries (p. 5). The size of the actual fall in output came as a great surprise (p. 10). Bruno gives a number of policy examples. Banks have an incentive to lend to insolvent enterprises in order to protect their portfolios, and so potentially profitable enterprises are crowded out by high interest rates and/or credit ceilings. The result is either an excessive fall in output as the money supply is reduced or a distorted composition of output decline (p. 15). In the early stages of transition the demand for foreign currency is strong because of the lack of alternative hedges against inflation (e.g. when there are negative interest rates on bank accounts). A free float of the domestic currency could be disastrous if far-reaching price liberalization is carried out, especially when appropriate fiscal and monetary policies are not in place (e.g. the Russian rouble). It is a mistake to let the exchange rate be determined by market forces unless alternative domestic financial assets with positive real interest rates are introduced at the same time (p. 16). Bruno believes that the conventional wisdom remains substantially correct, i.e. that an economy in fundamental macroeconomic disequilibrium cannot successfully transform its microeconomic structure. But the more recent experience teaches us that macroeconomic adjustment can often not be achieved without at least some simultaneous structural reform, such as reform of the tax and financial systems. 'The general lesson to be learned here is that the policy reform package has to place even greater emphasis on setting up institutions and rules of behaviour for the micro-units. Otherwise the stabilization part of the reform might also fail' (Bruno 1993b: 245).

It could be argued that a considerable part of what has been produced in the past was of relatively poor quality and that the output collapse has therefore been exaggerated. But Bruno argues that the size of the output fall 'transcends such explanations' (1993a: 10). It seems that about half the fall in output in each of the East European countries was due to the collapse of Comecon trade, the rest by various internal supply and demand factors associated with the overshooting of the price shock and the sharp initial stabilization and liberalization move (p. 10).

Borensztein *et al.* (1993: 2, 4, 16) offer some tentative explanation for the output decline in Bulgaria, Czechoslovakia and Romania in 1990–91, countries chosen because they were previously perhaps the most rigidly centralized economies in the region. The authors pose two questions:

1. To what extent can 'structural change' (a reallocation of resources from less to more profitable sectors, i.e. industry-specific factors) account for the output decline as opposed to a macroeconomic recession (i.e. aggregate or national factors)? Empirical analysis, they suggest, indicates that very little of the output decline during this early period of the transition was attributable to structural change. Because not much structural change had taken place the shock of it was still to come.

2. To what extent have demand-side (the collapse of domestic and foreign markets) rather than supply-side forces (e.g. disruption in the supply of domestic or foreign inputs) been dominant in generating the output decline? The authors conclude that supply disturbances predominated in Bulgaria and Czechoslovakia, while in Romania the results were less conclusive in that the relative importance of supply and demand shocks seems to have varied over time.

Calvo and Coricelli (1993: 32–3) note that the fall in output in Eastern Europe during the transition has been greater than expected. They argue that a large proportion of the fall in output can be explained by 'trade implosion' or 'trade destruction', i.e. trade is destroyed for lack of market institutions, not simply as a result of changes in relative prices or movements along transformation frontiers. Trade implosion helps explain the collapse of both domestic and international trade (especially Comecon trade) and ultimately some part of the collapse in output. They single out the credit market as one of the key underdeveloped institutions in Eastern European countries and advance the hypothesis that the fall in output associated with monetary contraction may be significant when credit markets are underdeveloped. For example, they suggest that at least 20 per cent of the decline in output in Poland in the first quarter of the stabilization programme can be attributed to the initial credit contraction.

The United Nations Economic Commission for Europe (1993: 75–6) thinks that many factors contributed to the large falls in output in the European transitional economies. The leading role was played by the distorted structures inherited from the past, the implementation of radical economic reforms and the collapse of intra-Comecon trade in 1991. Weak supply responses to the new economic environment and changed demand also played a role. In the former Yugoslavia and Soviet Union the collapse of inter-republic trade was an important additional factor. The simultaneous impact of several adverse developments caused a deeper recession than expected. Country-specific features also played an important part. Judging from the fact that the largest losses coincided with the introduction of radical economic reforms (1990 in Poland, 1991 in other East European countries and 1992 in the countries of the former Soviet Union), it seems likely that tight stabilization policies which strongly compressed domestic demand were responsible for a large part of the output contraction. The rapid collapse of Comecon trade in 1991 exacerbated the impact of radical economic reforms both on the demand side (loss of traditional export markets) and on the supply side (constraints arising from reduced imports of fuels and raw materials). Some estimates suggest that about half the 1991 fall in output was due to the collapse of Comecon. But the economic downturn was also due to radical transformation and a rapidly changing economic environment. In consequence a part of the capital stock was made obsolete.

Schmiedling (1993: 216–53) argues that 'the institutional void which the collapse of socialism left in its wake is an important cause of the transformation crisis' (p. 216). 'An institutional near-vacuum is a major cause of the crisis' (p. 253). Schmiedling defines institutions broadly, comprising 'not only bureaucracies and administrations but also, and more importantly, the entire body of formal laws, rules and regulations as well as the informal conventions and patterns of behaviour' (p. 233). 'In Central and Eastern Europe, the socialist bureaucracies and firm managers have steered a highly complex division of labour. After the collapse of socialism, these economies are now lacking – for the time being – the fundamental institutional devices for the reliable co-ordination of such an extended division of labour. Until the ultimately far superior institutional devices of capitalism have evolved and until economic agents place sufficient trust in them and have accumulated the necessary institution-specific human capital, the additional transaction costs can overcompensate the positive incentive effects of the switch from socialism to a more market-based economic order' (pp. 247–8).

Portes (*Transition*, 1994, vol. 5, no. 8, p. 13) argues that 'It is difficult to distinguish in the data between demand and supply shocks. The fall in CMEA trade is big enough to account for a lot, but exports to the West from most countries rose immediately and by almost as much. The military–industrial complex is not big enough, even in Russia, to account for a substantial share of the lost production. My own preferred story is a combination of excessive monetary contraction . . . and the inadequacy of supply response (itself due to inadequate microfoundations) in the face of shifts in demand that would have required reallocation.'

Rosati (1994) concludes that the popular argument on the irrelevance of the observed output fall because of deficient and biased statistics, the reporting malpractices of enterprises and the discontinuation of 'socialist' production carries less weight than is commonly believed. The recession could have been less severe had some other policies been adopted. A closer scrutiny of demand-side and supply-side factors indicates that, while both categories played a role, the impact of the former on the output decline has been much more pronounced. Macroeconomic stabilization policies in Poland in 1990 were too restrictive because of erroneous assumptions about the size of the inflationary 'overhang' and about the dynamics of expectation in the first stage of transition (pp. 434–5). The Soviet trade shock accounted for between one-third (Poland and Czechoslovakia) and two-thirds (Hungary and Bulgaria) of the GDP fall registered in 1991 (p. 429).

The extent of the fall in output and sectoral differences

The United Nations Economic Commission for Europe (1994) says that it is possible that the present official figures overstate the depth of the fall in output, but it seems unlikely that subsequent revisions will transform the slump in output into a mild recession (p. 1). The fall of GDP by 3 per cent in 1993 in Eastern Europe as a whole can be regarded as an improvement compared with the falls in 1990 (7.9 per cent), 1991 (12.3 per cent) and 1992 (7.4 per cent). But 1993 was another year of recession, bringing the total fall between 1989 and 1993 to nearly 29 per cent below its transition level (pp. 52, 58). 'Even though the overall reliability and accuracy of macroeconomic statistics may legitimately be questioned because of difficulties connected with measuring changes in real output and demand levels under conditions of high inflation and rapidly growing unregistered private sector activities, it is very unlikely that even more elaborate and accurate estimates would yield a fundamentally different picture of the macroeconomic performance of transition countries' (p. 58). The most apparent change in Eastern Europe in sectoral terms is the expansion of services, not only the growth of small-scale enterprise in retail trade, restaurants, etc., but also the creation of new financial, legal and business services (p. 2).

Dobozi and Pohl (1995: 17–18) argue that 'electric power consumption is a far better indicator of true economic activity in Eastern Europe and the former Soviet Union than any of the officially reported economic statistics that are widely used by the IMF, the World Bank and the international community at large . . . Until better national income data become available, a much simpler method would be to rely on power consumption data, a more reliable indicator of short-run activity.' In Central and Eastern Europe the 22 per cent average accumulated decline in electric power consumption between 1989 and 1993 is in harmony with the reported 24 per cent average accumulated decline in economic activity. A fairly large discrepancy is found in the Czech Republic, where electric power consumption fell only half as much (11 per cent) as GDP (22 per cent). This may indicate a large shift into new activities, such as services. The discrepancy is much more dramatic in the countries of the former Soviet Union. Electric power consumption declined cumulatively by 15 per cent during 1989–93, while official statistics report a GDP decline of 54 per cent. In Georgia official GDP declined by 80 per cent, while power use was down by 40 per cent.

Official economic statistics for Russia and Ukraine appear to suffer from a gross downward bias. The countries that have been hit particularly hard include the Baltic States, Bulgaria and Romania, all of which have suffered external trade disruption (and, in some cases, slow reforms), and Armenia and Georgia, which have faced severe civil disturbances. (Åslund also supports the use of electricity consumption in the case of Russia. See the section on Russian economic performance in Chapter 3 for this and a critique of the argument.)

Ellman (1993) stresses that the distribution of the falls in output in Poland in 1990 was perverse, with the biggest falls in the consumer goods sector (such as textiles) (hit by the decline in demand) rather than in the capital and intermediate goods sectors (where most of the wasteful production is probably concentrated). Zukowski (1993: 1173) notes that the most adversely affected sectors in Poland in 1990 were light industry, food processing and transport equipment, while in 1991 they were capital and intermediate goods (e.g. electrical goods and metallurgy).

The light and food industries were severely depressed by the acute contraction of domestic demand in the initial stage of the reform process, although in some East European countries output in those branches began to recover as policy was eased (e.g. Poland in 1991 and Czechoslovakia the following year) (United Nations Economic Commission for Europe 1993: 79). The fall in output in transition economies in 1990–92 was essentially across-the-board and affected all major sectors, which suggests that the changes in relative prices were not the main factor behind the output declines (Rosati 1994: 425).

The then economics minister, Andrei Nechayev, said that the slump in output in Russia had taken place evenly in all sectors, rather than through the driving out of the inefficient. This was due to the lack of a mechanism for reorganizing enterprises, such as a bankruptcy law (*CDSP*, 10 March 1993, vol. XLV, no. 6, p. 11). In a February 1994 article Andrei Illarionov (the former economic adviser to the Russian prime minister) argued that 'the total depth of the decline, which began back in 1990, amounts to approximately 40 per cent of the gross domestic product. But to a significant extent this is not simply a quantitative decline but the result of deliberate changes in the structure of production involving the partial elimination of "production for production's sake" . . . roughly 10 per cent of the decline in production was useful, while the other 30 per cent was undoubtedly harmful and damaged both the economy and consumption' (*CDSP*, 1994, vol. XLVI, no. 6, p. 20).

The Deutsche Bank (*Focus: Eastern Europe*, 1994, no. 104, p. 5) thinks that in Russia 'the slump in industrial output has not been confined to those sectors which are in any case due for restructuring, such as the production of arms and goods that no one wants to buy. The full force of collapsing production has also been felt in the civilian goods sectors that are vital to the nation's supplies.' Flemming and Matthews (1994: 77) note that in Russia 'the data suggest that at the low point in mid-1992 production of consumer goods was half that of 1991.' Nolan (1992: 15) takes a dim view of some of the services *currently* being provided in transitional economies, such as petty retailing and prostitution. He considers that some of the switch to service employment can be humiliating for people who previously had jobs in the state sector.

(Throughout Eastern Europe unemployment has affected certain groups in particular, especially the young, the unskilled and women. An increasing proportion have been unemployed for a long time. Regional unemployment is also an acute problem. The highest rates are to be found in areas where, for example, agriculture accounts for a high share of activity and where heavy industries are in decline. The lowest rates are to be found in the capital cities and their surrounding regions, where services are relatively important: Commission of the European Communities, *Employment in Europe*, 1992, pp. 117–18; 1993, pp. 78–9.)

Kolodko (1993c: 345–54) discusses what he calls the 'perverse effect of fiscal adjustment in transition economies': 'Although fiscal adjustment policies were designed to balance budgets in the short run, it turned out that they, in conjunction with additional unique and specific factors, also brought about the resurgence of even more serious fiscal disequilibria in the medium and long run.' For example, excessive public expenditure cuts can lead to infrastructural bottlenecks which slow down activity later on. Enterprises and banks enjoy temporary high profits at first even when output is declining. In the case of the former this is due to factors such as products produced with existing cheap inputs sold at higher prices due to liberalization (real wages were then falling). In the case of banks there is usually a wide spread between short-term lending and borrowing rates at first (due to such factors as the high proportion of bad loans on bank balance sheets: Bruno 1993b: 235).

Ickes and Ryterman (1993: 250–1), in an article on Russia, argue that 'the attempt to impose a tight credit policy in a financially underdeveloped economy is the fundamental cause of the explosion in inter-enterprise arrears . . . in an economy in transition with an underdeveloped financial system, monetary policy must be sufficiently restrictive to encourage enterprises to adjust, but not so restrictive that enterprises choose to react in a way that undermines the process of economic reform. If the government chooses to tighten credit too quickly or too severely, then the credibility of the policy, once again, will be brought into question. Moreover, as long as financial markets are underdeveloped, tight credit policies have deleterious unintended consequences, such as gridlock in the payments system and arrears in the payment of taxes. This suggests that efforts to impose financial discipline on enterprises must be associated with progress in the development of the financial system in Russia.'

PRIVATIZATION

Restructuring versus privatization

The United Nations Economic Commission for Europe (1994: 10) argues that a clear distinction needs to be drawn between the minimum degree of financial and organizational restructuring required to find buyers for the enterprise and *strategic* restructuring (such as decisions about net investments and new products), which should be the responsibility of the new owners. Usually, restructuring means both efficiency- and competition-orientated measures to enhance productive and allocative efficiency, e.g. the breaking up of large enterprises and the separation out of the core businesses, the hiving-off of social assets, employment shedding, the closure of unviable activities and the restructuring of balance sheets to deal with the problem of enterprise debts (p. 159).

An empirical study (see Chapter 24 on Poland) in favour of restructuring before privatization is to be found in Pinto *et al.* (1993): But it is stressed that privatization is the known ultimate goal. Somogyi (1993: 6) cites Newbery's argument that monopolies should be broken up before privatization, since 'splitting up enterprises before they are privatized keeps open options for subsequent merger where there are genuine synergies. It will, on the other hand, be much harder to break up monopolies after they have been privatized.' See Roland (1994b) on the speed of privatization (below).

Corporatization (commercialization)

Frydman *et al.* (1993: 35, 140) define corporatization as the process by which state enterprises are converted into commercial companies with structures familiar in the West (such as joint stock or limited liability companies; the shares of the former, which may also enjoy limited liability, are publicly traded, whereas the shares of the latter are not publicly traded). Prior to privatization the state or appropriate municipality remains the owner. Simoneti (1993: 99) points out that this may be achieved relatively quickly. Corporatization provides a clear organizational structure in companies and clearly defined property rights (e.g. workers' councils are a problem otherwise). Clague (1992: 15) advocates rapid commercialization, in which state enterprises 'are put in the charge of boards of directors and allowed to act independently'. (Note that 'independently' means separating management from the state, so that it is no longer under ministerial control.)

Van Wijnbergen (1993: 21–2) argues that while it may be possible to operate a clear-cut state enterprise efficiently, and it is certainly possible for a private enterprise to function efficiently, it is clearly not possible to run an enterprise efficiently whose current and future ownership status is in limbo. Thus it is essential to clarify the medium-term ownership structure, the first decision being whether to privatize an enterprise or to keep it in state hands even in the long run (one of a 'small sub-set' of enterprises: p. 118). Enterprises not permanently under state ownership should be immediately transformed into joint stock companies, with the intention of rapidly privatizing them.

Voucher (mass) privatization

Boycko *et al.* (1994) usefully remind us that 'the decision to pursue mass privatization and even the specific design of the programmes are largely dictated by politics. Nonetheless, politically feasible programmes can also be made attractive from an economic standpoint in terms of maximizing value, fostering free and efficient markets, and promoting corporate governance' (p. 249). For example:

1. The most important factor determining the choice of decentralized auctions in Russia was the political reality: 'the managerial lobby in Czechoslovakia was considerably weaker, and the central government considerably stronger, than in Russia . . . In Russia . . . privatization had to start on the voluntary basis, with managers of companies who wanted to privatize leading the process . . . In order for the managers to consent to voucher auctions, then, the process had to be decentralized and pushed to localities' (p. 263).

2. Vouchers in Russia are denominated in currency, while those in (the former) Czechoslovakia are denominated in points. 'A currency denomination makes vouchers appear like securities and gives a much clearer impression of a government give a way to the public. In Russia, where the public acceptance and support of privatization was *much* more tenuous than in Czechoslovakia, the popularity of a giveaway became the engine of privatization' (p. 260).

The importance of political factors in determining the shape of privatization programmes needs stressing. For example, the director of the Slovenian privatization agency has said that 'the political conditions here would make it impossible to do it all through the state like in Germany, because all managers here believe they already own the companies' (reported by Patrick Blum, *FT*, Survey, 12 April 1994, p. 32).

Restitution

There is also an important political aspect to restitution, namely reviving the middle class. Fischer (1992b: 230) argues that restitution (which, however, should not take the form of physical restitution) 'not only strengthens the credibility of a country's commitment to the rights of private property, but also prevents the legal confusion over ownership that could arise if the issue were left to be settled later in the courts.' The longer the time span, of course, the more difficult restitution becomes.

Auctions and competitive tenders

Closed auctions involve sealed bids, while at open auctions bidders have to gather physically at a specified time and place and openly compete with other bidders (Ash and Hare 1994: 623). With auctions price alone decides who can purchase, whereas with competitive tenders the purchaser must satisfy a number of other conditions (Frydman and Rapaczynski 1993: 55).

Demougin and Sinn (1994) highlight the virtues of the 'participation contract', where, instead of cash, the government receives a certain percentage of future profit. The participation model may help overcome the risk aversion of potential investors, because the government shares the risk of failure by reducing or giving up its claim to receive the sales price. A risk-theoretic competitive auction model is developed, where, instead of making cash bids, bidders are allowed to offer participation contracts which specify the percentage 'sleeping' ownership ceded to the government and the volume of reorganizational investment. The bid that promises the highest expected present value of the cash flow accruing to the government is selected (pp. 204–5). 'The participation contract mitigates the problem of missing capital markets because it allows the investor to pay later and it mitigates the problem of missing risk markets because it allows the investor to pay only if, and to the extent that, distributable profits become available.' It is shown that 'with a competitive bidding process, the participation contract will generate more revenue for the government than cash sales and, what is more, that it will also induce more private investment' (p. 226).

Spontaneous privatization

Frydman *et al.* (1993: 34) distinguish between 'illegal' and 'quiet' forms of spontaneous privatization. The latter involves no formal illegality but relies on acts which do not involve the open, public and competitive sale of state property.

(Note the argument in favour of involving the *nomenklatura* in the sale of state assets. The idea is not only to channel their perhaps ill-gotten gains into productive activities, but also to channel their energies away from political subversion of the new regime.)

('Many of Central Europe's budding conglomerates are former foreign trade organizations . . . One reason is that, of all command economy sectors, foreign trade was the closest thing to real-world business': *Business Central Europe*, June 1994, p. 7.)

When the sale of enterprise or investment fund shares should be allowed

There is the argument that for a limited time the sale of initial allocations of enterprise or investment fund shares should not be allowed. The purpose is to prevent wealthy traders from acquiring large blocks of shares cheap at a time when real incomes have fallen and many individuals are anxious to sell (e.g. Russia). The counter-argument is that even temporary restrictions would hinder the process whereby firms and individuals can accumulate sufficient shares to exercise effective control over management (Demekas and Khan 1991: 25).

Investment funds

Investment funds can use vouchers deposited with or sold to them by individuals (Flemming and Matthews 1994: 74).

Fischer (1993b: 239–40) states that the difference between holding companies and mutual funds is that the latter are expected to take a more passive role in enterprise management (exercising discipline over enterprise management by sales and purchases of shares). Holding companies take an active role in management, being represented on corporate boards. He suggests that shares should be distributed so that each enterprise is allocated predominantly, but certainly not exclusively, to one holding company.

Investment funds may resist any attempt to end their lives. Frydman and Rapaczynski (1993: 50), for example, point out the danger of creating powerful bureaucracies with a permanent hold on the enterprises in their portfolios. There is the possibility of collusion with other funds, leading to such abuses as the division of markets by common consent, the fixing of prices and the entrenchment of a complex system of state subsidies. The United Nations Economic Commission for Europe (1993: 216) sees the danger that investment funds could become vehicles of state intervention.

Jenkins (1992) suggests that some portion of the assets of state enterprises to be privatized should be used partially to offset the state's pension liabilities in order to relieve budgetary pressures on strained social security systems. Professionally managed private pension plans, initially funded by newly privatized assets, could assist in the transition to market economies by contributing to the development of capital markets. Furthermore, linking the process of privatization with the creation and funding of private pension funds would disperse private ownership and substantially alleviate the problem of selling or distributing hard-to-value state assets.

Worker share ownership and management or employee buy-outs

Acks and FitzRoy (1993) argue in favour of a majority equity shareholding for employees in order to avoid excessive wage claims and to maximize co-operation. But banks should have the remaining equity and majority board membership for control purposes.

Bogetic (1993) argues in favour of a flexible approach to privatization, reflecting the differing circumstances of different countries. But he sees merit in minority employee ownership on the grounds of speed, the incentive to take a long-term view of the welfare of the enterprise and the existence of a group of shareholders able to exercise some control over management. Disadvantaged groups such as retired employees, workers in unprofitable enterprises and the unemployed could have some proportion of shares reserved for them.

Note that a proportion of the shares allocated to workers could be non-voting in order to mitigate the less favourable aspects of worker ownership while maintaining positive interest in the success of the enterprise (e.g. the Russian programme).

Frydman and Rapaczynski (1993: 54) say that management and employee buy-outs are surprisingly few in number. One reason is the problem of credit. Sources of genuine investment credit are, for all practical purposes, non-existent. Even if they are available the enterprises involved cannot easily be evaluated by the potential creditors.

The ability to appoint the management of state enterprises about to be privatized has the potential drawback of introducing political patronage into the procedures.

The speed of privatization

The possible adverse effect of rapid large privatization on asset prices is dealt with in Chapter 22 on East Germany.

Metcalf and Ambrus-Lakatos (1992) do not deal with natural monopolies or contracting out, only with enterprises free of market failure. They suggest a moderately gradual approach for the following reasons: (1) to enable assets to be valued properly; (2) to reduce the transitional unemployment effects and the associated demands on the fiscal system; and (3) the need to develop the supporting service sector (such as banking, capital markets and accounting).

Rausser (1992: 326) argues that privatization by itself cannot be expected to achieve efficiency. There is also need for an anti-monopolization (anti-trust) policy, an open trade policy and an open foreign investment policy. These measures, coupled with appropriate management incentives for state enterprises, 'may result in a set of conditions where the speed of implementing privatization is no longer crucial' (p. 328).

Laban and Wolf (1993: 1199–209) attempt to throw light on the slow progress of mass privatization programmes in Eastern Europe. They present a model based on a positive spill-over between aggregate privatization and the individual expected return to privatization, derived from a potential populist backlash if costly reforms do not bring forth sufficient aggregate privatization. 'The value of an individual industrial enterprise offered for sale in the post-socialist economies depends positively on the overall success of the privatization programme. A sufficiently large *aggregate* expected volume of privatization may then be required to render the acquisition of enterprises attractive to the *individual* investor. The implied critical mass effect distinguishes the task facing the East European economies from the privatization programmes recently implemented in the OECD and brings about the possibility of a self-fulfilling low-expectation trap . . . the individually expected return to buying a state-owned enterprise increases with the likelihood of policy continuation, which in turn increases with the aggregate amount of privatization . . . if the effect is sufficiently pronounced *critical-mass* effects can arise: the acquisition of a state-owned enterprise becomes profitable for an individual if a critical number of other agents are also expected to commit . . . The possibility of a co-ordination failure leading to a sub-optimal outcome provides a possible rationale for government intervention during the transition to markets' (p. 1201). 'While rapid front-end reform steps may rule out a return to old-style socialism, they do not prevent a backsliding into semi-state managed capitalism. Indeed . . . a socially unbuffered "big bang" increases the probability of such a shift. The challenge, then, rests in determining the optimal degree of gradualism as a trade-off between the efficiency losses from slower reform and the gain in political stability accompanying a more gradual approach' (p. 1209).

Roland and Verdier argue that a 'big bang' policy announcement may fail to deliver the desired policy outcome because of failures in co-ordination. 'If there are economies of scale to the size of the private sector, a policy of full and fast privatization may generate enough growth so as to absorb the labour force made redundant by privatization. However, as decisions by private investors on the acquisition of firms are made independently, the investor response may not be strong enough to avoid large-scale unemployment, leading to partial renationalization, the prospect of which may even further deter private investors. A low-level privatization equilibrium may then arise if a critical mass of privatization is not achieved, despite the government's preference for fast and complete privatization' (Roland 1994a: 31). Political uncertainty plays a role in slowing privatization down. Roland and Verdier model a situation where there is a policy of free and equal distribution of shares to the population. 'There are conditions where under which such policies may eliminate a potential policy reversal. However, to the extent that the sunk costs of restructuring are incurred by the acquirer, the free distribution of part of the shares of the enterprise deprives the acquirer of some future dividends from this investment. Under costly restructuring, policies of free distribution may therefore deter potential private investors and even reduce welfare' (1994: 162).

(Externalities relating to the growing size of the private sector include improved input supply, the diffusion of management techniques, the build-up of a climate of trust with repeated contracting and the desire to emulate successful rivals: p. 163.)

Roland (1994b) argues that political constraints necessitate a gradual approach to restructuring and that gradualism has implications for the speed and sequencing of privatization. He especially warns of the danger of too rapid privatization of firms where restructuring should be delayed for political reasons. This may not only lead to partial renationalization but may also prevent a gradual hardening of budget constraints (p. 1158). A condition for successful gradual privatization is a screening mechanism to separate firms of different qualities. It is crucial that a process of separating good from bad firms takes place and that channels of finance for good and bad firms remain separate. Basically, good firms would become independent of the government through privatization and face hard budget constraints, while bad firms would remain under government control with strengthened controls. If all firms get financed through the banking system, bad firms are likely to spoil the whole financial system (p. 1167).

The sequencing of privatization

Husain and Sahay (1992) analyse the problem of sequencing an input-producing upstream sector and a final goods-producing downstream sector. Efficiency gains under perfect competition are maximized when the sector facing less uncertainty is privatized first. Thus, if shocks to final goods demand are more critical than shocks to raw material supply, it is optimal to privatize the upstream sector first. But if supply shocks are relatively large the downstream sector should be privatized first. When the privatization of a sector leads to the creation of an oligopoly, the associated distortion is minimized by privatizing the sector that is less concentrated and less capable of extracting oligopoly rents. When all factors are taken into consideration, optimal sequencing of privatization under imperfect competition involves maximizing the gains from increased flexibility and minimizing the distortion arising under oligopoly.

Maciaszek-Roberts (1993a) restricts the sequence of privatization to the choice between whether to privatize an intermediate goods sector first or a consumer goods sector first. A simulation exercise is undertaken, using data from Poland before the transition. The results show that in many respects the privatization of an intermediate goods sector is better for the economy; output and GDP fall less and the price level is lower than in the experiments with a consumer goods sector. When a consumer goods industry is privatized, however, households gain more because of higher incomes. Elsewhere (Maciaszek-Roberts 1993b: 97–106), consideration is given to privatization in Poland, where whole industries are to be privatized. The main finding is that there is a very strong positive correlation between the overall performance of the economy as a result of privatizing a given sector and the index of forward linkage. (A high degree of forward linkage means that the output of a given sector is widely used by other sectors.) 'The simulation analysis shows that the macroeconomic performance as a result of privatizing a sector does not depend as much as one might have thought on the high profitability of the sector in question. The impact on other sectors, measured by the index of forward linkage, is the main determinant' (pp. 105–6).

AGRICULTURE

Brada and King (1993) examine the technical efficiency of state and private farms in Poland in the period 1960–74. They find that the average technical efficiency of the two types of farm does not differ, although the dispersion of efficiency levels is greater among state farms than among private ones (p. 41). They conclude that the internal organization of state farms does not make them inherently less technically efficient than private farms. But the effects of agricultural policies and the administrative distribution of inputs do lead to the sub-optimal allocation of resources in Polish agriculture. (There is clear evidence of allocative inefficiency, with state farms oversupplied with fertilizer and machinery: p. 41.) Thus it is the environment of socialized agriculture rather than the socialized nature of farms that leads to the poor performance of the agricultural sector. This implies that the privatization of agriculture alone will not lead to any great upsurge in agricultural productivity resulting from improved incentives and improvements in the internal organization of farms. But large gains might be achieved by reallocating inputs between the two sectors of agriculture, largely by creating efficient, and unbiased, input markets (p. 54).

Pryor (1992: 294–5) reflects on the privatization of agriculture. He points out the difficulties of dividing up large-scale, high-technology equipment and large buildings and also of creating a new service sector. 'Decollectivization' is easier where farming is not highly input-intensive or mechanized, where agricultural workers are not highly specialized, where the rural work force is relatively young, where collectivization has not lasted a long time, where collective (as opposed to state) farms predominate, and where the government is strong enough to overcome political resistance. There are problems in creating a reliable and accessible source of inputs, providing for the profitable sale of products and establishing outlets for credit and consumer goods. The costs of decollectivization are high, especially in the short run. It is difficult where the system has been in existence for several decades and where the level of agricultural technology has become relatively high.

Ash (1993: 497) notes that 'apart from the legal problems associated with restitution, the rural population, in general, remains unwilling to take on the risk of private farming due to the recession, preferring instead the security of state and collective farm employment.'

Cochrane (1993) argues that one of the most fundamental lessons that the countries of Central Europe can learn from their past is that the radical restructuring of agriculture now under way will not succeed unless governments follow the transition through completely. The emerging private sector in Central European agriculture will not thrive without the creation of new institutions to support it. There is an urgent need for co-operatives, credit institutions, new marketing structures, and extension services (p. 855). 'Land markets, which would facilitate the consolidation of so many small farms as less efficient farmers sell out to the more efficient, have been hampered by delays in granting title, lack of credit, and lack of an information system. The marketing system inherited from the communist period does not serve private farmers very well; the word "co-operative" has taken on negative connotations; credit is difficult to come by; and extension services targeting small, private farms are almost completely lacking. The new private farmers, while free for the first time in forty-five years to make their own production and marketing decisions, lack the information and management expertise to make the appropriate decisions' (p. 853).

THE LINKAGE BETWEEN POLITICAL AND ECONOMIC REFORM

The Economist (Survey, 30 October 1993, p. 23) argues that 'The political secret of Asia's success stories is to have their governments fairly impervious to the kind of plea for favours – which economists call "rent-seeking" – that modern democratic governments find impossible to resist.' *The Economist* (29 January 1994, pp. 27–8) also argues that 'reform can thrive on crisis, when crisis provides opportunities for decisive action by small, determined groups . . . in principle all reformers' freedom of action is greatest at their moment of taking office, because harsh decisions can be blamed on their predecessors . . . One of the few features common to successfully reforming countries has been a leader with a clear sense of where he wants his country to go and a willingness to stick by his purpose when the going gets rough.'

Havrylyshyn *et al.* (1994) argue that serious economic reform can be thwarted by the ability of powerful interest groups to block changes which threaten the 'rents' they receive from the partially reformed economy (e.g. from control over export licences, subsidized energy imports and state credits to enterprises) (p. 371). 'The semi-reformed economy is full of rent-seekers with strong motives to resist change . . . price distortions and their associated rents attract powerful lobbies which fight to preserve or even increase the distortions and prevent further reform' (pp. 373–4).

There is the argument that democracy is more likely to ensure the maintenance of property rights than dependence on the whims of a dictator or his successor. 'It is plausible to believe that, over time, democracy entrenches economic freedoms, making them more stable and more credible' (*The Economist*, 27 August 1994, p. 19). Woo (1994: 290) argues that 'sustained economic reforms do not require Stalinist-style political repression; what is definitely required is a commitment by the political leadership to economic prosperity and not to ideological purity.'

Nolan (1992: 18) argues that political stability is needed for economic progress. In China there is the danger of political instability if the Communist Party falls, but Nolan is optimistic that democracy will take root in the long run with successful economic development.

'Authoritarian rule is no guarantee of economic success for the simple reason that there are various kinds of autocracy . . . A populist autocracy is no better for the economy than a weak democracy, and if a weak democracy were to be replaced by authoritarian rule it would most likely be of the populist type' (Balcerowicz 1994: 36).

Robert Scalapino (*IHT*, 8 February 1993, p. 2) argues that economic development will lead to greater political openness in China: (1) economic development promotes diversity of regional development, professions and class structure, a diversity which means that it becomes increasingly impossible to maintain highly centralized political controls; (2) economic development builds a middle class, a highly educated urban group that demands more genuine political participation; (3) economic development breaks down isolation, making society more porous and susceptible to external influences.

The 'opening up' qualities of foreign investment and tourism are often stressed.

Brus (1993: 439–40) concludes an interesting discussion related to the economic progress of China by saying 'that, at least up to a point, another scenario – of a reformist, evolutionary nature – is *feasible*, and that – contrary to the conventional wisdom, shared in the past by this author as well – mono-archy [a monopolistic Communist Party-state] may play a positive role in this process. The supposition that in the longer run the feedback effect would enhance the likelihood of political pluralization ("democratization") sweetens somewhat the bitter taste of this conclusion for those who value freedom as good in itself.'

In reply to the rhetorical question whether China 'should emulate the disastrous example of the former Soviet Union and implement glasnost before economic reform is well established', John Gray answers that 'to flirt with similar policies in China today would be irresponsibility of the highest order' (*The Guardian*, 4 April 1994, p. 22).

AID

The conditions of aid

Where conditions are necessary there is increasing recognition of the need to consider not just narrow macroeconomic criteria but also democratic developments and economic reform in a broad sense. The IMF is criticized by some for what are seen as its often inappropriate conditions. But supporters argue as follows: (1) IMF pressure helps governments overcome internal resistance to essential but painful economic reforms by providing an outside 'scapegoat'; (2) IMF approval of an economic programme is the gateway to other sources of finance. (Note that the IMF's new instrument called the 'systemic transformation facility' involves less demanding conditions.)

Jeffrey Sachs argues that 'Rather than concentrating nearly all its efforts on budget-cutting, as it does now, the IMF should aim to combine fiscal constraint with ample foreign loans, exchange rate stabilization, increasing central bank independence and debt relief, all designed to restore confidence in the currency and in the government's ability to honour its (restructured) debts'. The package should mobilize sufficient support in the short term to enable the government to continue providing essential services. Once stability is achieved, the reforming government can proceed to more fundamental institutional reform in areas such as taxation. 'A key step in restoring confidence lies in stabilizing the exchange rate quickly . . . An injection of foreign exchange is often required to set up a stabilization fund; yet the IMF has preferred to play only a small role at the start of such reforms, albeit helping several countries to stay the course later on . . . The IMF continues to neglect currency stabilization: it has held back money needed for stabilization funds in Russia and Ukraine.' Sachs also maintains that the IMF should help governments mobilize international financing of budget deficits early in the reform process and so minimize the risk that a 'fragile' government might be brought down by hostile reaction to heavy spending cuts and tax increases (*The Economist*, 1 October 1994, p. 28).

Three issues of the *Journal of Comparative Economics* (1995, vol. 20, nos 1, 2 and 3) carry a series of papers dealing with the varying assessments of the role of international financial institutions, such as the IMF, the World Bank and the EBRD. There is a very useful summary in no. 1 (pp. 49–56) by Josef Brada, Roland Schönfeld and Ben Slay. Yearly World Bank lending to Eastern Europe and the former Soviet Union averaged $3 billion to $4 billion during the period 1991–93, a sum representing about one-sixth of total bank lending (p. 52). Cumulative World Bank commitments in the period from 1990 to the end of February 1994 came to $13.81 billion (Christine Wallich; p. 66). Cumulative IMF commitments and disbursements during the period 1990–93 came to $13.1 billion and $9.2 billion respectively (Salvatore Zecchini; p. 120). Jan Winiecki's paper is said to be the strongest critique of the financial institutions, e.g. high real interest rates mean that large state enterprises crowd smaller but more efficient firms out of credit windows, while limits upon wage growth in state enterprises (which reinforce managers' resistance to wage demands to only a limited extent) generally serve to politicize labour relations (p. 54).

The volume of aid

Summers (1992: 31) states that Marshall Plan aid (over a four-year period) represented 2 per cent a year of the GDP of the recipient countries. In terms of Eastern Europe's GDP, 2 per cent amounts to only $5 billion a year (or $20 billion over four years).

The United Nations Economic Commission for Europe (1993: 19, 239–40), while stressing the uncertainty surrounding the figures, has calculated the cumulative commitments of international assistance to the countries of Eastern Europe (including the Baltic States; from the beginning of 1990 to the end of June 1992) and for the countries of the former Soviet Union (excluding the Baltic States; up to November 1992). The total of commitments amounted to Ecu 118.785 billion ($145 billion):

1. *The recipients.* Eastern Europe, Ecu 46.965 billion ($60 billion); the former Soviet Union, Ecu 71.821 billion ($84 billion). The individual East European countries: Albania, Ecu 0.727 billion; Bulgaria, Ecu 2.128 billion; Czechoslovakia, Ecu 5.082 billion; Hungary, Ecu 7.888 billion; Poland, Ecu 18.175 billion; Romania, Ecu 4.175 billion; the former Yugoslavia, Ecu 3.212 billion; Estonia, Ecu 0.137 billion; Latvia, Ecu 0.132 billion; Lithuania, Ecu 0.125 billion.

2. *The donors.* Multilateral aid, Ecu 14.327 billion: IMF, Ecu 7.626 billion; World Bank, Ecu 5.38 billion; EBRD, Ecu 0.81 billion. Bilateral aid, Ecu 104.457 billion: the EU, Ecu 73.459 billion (Germany, Ecu 46.713 billion); the USA, Ecu 11.185 billion; Japan, Ecu 4.509 billion.

In 1992 some $40 billion of financing was made available to all the transition countries (compared with net government transfers from West to East Germany of $75 billion in 1991 and $96 billion in 1992). But only a small proportion consisted of grant aid or concessionary finance as defined by the OECD's Development Assistance Committee and there was actually a net outflow of resources from most of the East European countries when debt servicing and other income payments are taken into account.

In contrast to the net outflow from Eastern Europe in 1992, there was a net inflow of resources in 1993. Russia, however, experienced a net outflow in 1993 (United Nations Economic Commission for Europe 1994: 142).

The OECD has calculated that the net flow of all public and private money from all OECD countries to all the ex-communist countries was only $20 billion; developing countries received $60 billion, by way of contrast (Flora Lewis, *IHT*, 26 January 1994, p. 4).

At the Clinton–Yeltsin summit held in Vancouver on 3–4 April 1993 Yeltsin said of aid that 'Too little is not very good, because it is not enough to enable you to solve problems. Too much could also be bad, because it could be used by communists to target us. The opposition will say we are shackled by the West. We need an optimal amount, enough to keep us on course and not allow the revanchists to return.'

The type of aid

The United Nations Economic Commission for Europe (1993: 17–19) argues that the relative proportions of technical assistance (to create the institutional structures of a market economy and to train people to operate it effectively) and financial aid should be the reverse of those in the Marshall Plan, which was largely composed of grants and was short on technical assistance. (The Marshall Plan also insisted on the recipient countries drawing up their own assessment of their needs within a five-to-ten-year programme.)

Silberman *et al.* (1994: 21–6) advocate a 'bottom up' form of technical aid (pioneered in the Marshall Plan) in the shape of rigorous work-study tours of private businesses in advanced market economies. Large numbers of people from transitional societies would be exposed to market-based practices, experiences which could be shared with their compatriots on returning home. The advantages include rapid, cost-effective, tangible improvements in productivity. The productivity study tours would allow participants to identify for themselves those aspects of management and production techniques deemed most useful.

The peace dividend

Increasing UN commitment to places like the former Yugoslavia reduces the peace dividend somewhat, but the potential savings are still large. The Stockholm International Peace Research Institute reported a 15 per cent fall in world military spending in 1992. But the industrialized countries still spent $540 billion, roughly 65 per cent of the world total (*FT*, 16 June 1993, p. 3).

The European Bank for Reconstruction and Development

A very critical article appeared in *The Financial Times* (13 April 1993, pp. 1, 6). It alleged that from April 1991 to the end of 1992 the EBRD had disbursed only Ecu 126 million (£101 million) in loans and investments to Eastern Europe and the countries of the former Soviet Union, while it had spent £201.5 million on furnishing and equipping its offices, paying staff, travel and administrative overheads. (By way of comparison with this seemingly slow rate of disbursement, there had been $7 billion, or £4.6 billion, of equity investment in the Czech Republic, Hungary and Poland by multinational companies and private investors over the preceding three years.) But by the end of 1992 the EBRD had *approved* projects with an EBRD contribution of Ecu 1.8 billion. The 1993 targets are Ecu 700 million to Ecu 820 million in disbursements and Ecu 2.0 billion to Ecu 2.6 billion in new projects. One of the investment tenets is that equity injections should be only a small proportion of the amount the bank lends. (Other criticisms included the relatively narrow range of countries favoured, namely Czechoslovakia, Hungary, Poland and Russia, and the relatively narrow range of sectors favoured, such as telecommunications. Note that the USA has been sceptical of the value of the EBRD from the beginning and Congress has repeatedly delayed approving the USA's annual contribution.)

Jacques Attali, then president of the EBRD, provided additional information (*The Times*, 14 April 1993, p. 16). To date the EBRD had committed more than Ecu 2 billion (£1.6 billion or $2.41 billion) to eighty-eight projects, of which about Ecu 200 million had been disbursed by the end of March 1993. In working with corporations, banks, governmental organizations and other institutions the bank had mobilized approximately an additional Ecu 6 billion. A further Ecu 66 million in technical co-operation grant funds had been committed by the bank.

The 1992 Annual Report of the EBRD says that in 1992 fifty-four investment projects were approved, with a total EBRD contribution of Ecu 1.2 billion. But only Ecu 126 million was disbursed, consisting of Ecu 75.8 million of loans and Ecu 50 million of equity investments.

Jacques Attali resigned on 25 June 1993, although there was general acknowledgement of his visionary defence of causes East European. Although he had been expected to stay on until a successor had been appointed, the publication of a highly critical audit committee report led to him leaving his desk on 16 July 1993. Although the committee found no evidence of fraud, a string of criticisms were made. They included the unjustified use of private aircraft instead of ordinary flights, the lack of competitive tendering in some instances and slow reimbursement of personal expenses charged to the corporate credit card. (Some reimbursement took place after the inquiry was announced, while supporting invoices were not always provided.) His contractual termination 'golden handshake' was forfeited in return for the EBRD making no claims against Attali for acts and omissions made in 'good faith'.

Jacques de Larosière was appointed president of the EBRD on 19 August 1993. A former managing director of the IMF for eight years, he became governor of the Bank of France in 1987. On 8 November 1993 a radical reorganization of the EBRD was approved. The division into the development banking department (responsible for infrastructure projects) and the merchant banking department (responsible for encouraging the private sector) was scrapped. Two new departments were established, covering the more northerly and the more southerly of the twenty-five countries catered for (most of the countries in the latter group are less developed and therefore need more attention to infrastructure). Sectoral specialists were to be attached either to each of the departments or to a separate support group. There was to be greater concentration on increasing operations and personnel in the receiving countries themselves.

The EBRD's record for 1991 (nine months' operations), 1992, 1993 and 1994 respectively is as follows: approvals, Ecu 350 million, Ecu 951 million, Ecu 2.062 billion and Ecu 2.409 billion; signed loans and equity commitments, Ecu 53 million, Ecu 826 million, Ecu 1.642 billion and Ecu 1.878 billion; net disbursements, zero, Ecu 127 million, Ecu 409 million and Ecu 591 million. In 1993 the EBRD made a net profit for the first time (Ecu 4.1 million), compared with losses of Ecu 6 million in 1992 and Ecu 7 million in 1991. (*FT*, 8 April 1995, p. 2; *Business Central Europe*, April 1995, pp. 38–40; *The Guardian*, 8 April 1995, p. 37.)

In 1994 73 per cent of all investment went to private companies – up from less than half in 1991. The EBRD has invested less than Ecu 1 billion in equity, compared with almost Ecu 4 billion in loans (*The Economist*, Survey, 1995, p. 20). Private-sector lending accounted for 73 per cent of total commitments in 1994, compared with 56 per cent of total lending in 1993 (*Transition*, 1995, vol. 6, no. 4, p. 6).

For an analysis of the origins of the EBRD in terms of organizational theory, see Weber (1994).

Phare and Tacis

The Economist (10 April 1993, p. 21) reports that Phare and Tacis, managed by the European Commission, supply about 70 per cent of the West's technical aid. By the end of 1992 Ecu 2.3 billion ($2.6 billion) had been committed by Phare, but only Ecu 888.8 million had actually been paid out, while the respective figures for Tacis were Ecu 815.4 million and Ecu 32.6 million (*Business Central Europe*, December 1993/January 1994, p. 18).

The EU's Phare and Tacis programmes provide grants (not loans) for technical assistance to Eastern European countries (plus the Baltic States) and to the countries of the former Soviet Union (excluding the Baltic States) respectively. By the end of 1994 Ecu 3.784 billion had been committed by Phare and Ecu 1.747 billion by Tacis. The programmes have been criticized for being over-centralized, unwieldy, constrained by short-term budgets, possessing weak monitoring systems and duplicating the work of other organizations. As a result of these criticisms changes have been made, e.g. a shift away from technical assistance into investment support and the direct financing of projects. Multi-annual budgeting has been approved, there is co-financing with other multilaterals and Phare's SME (small and medium-size enterprise) programme is considered a success (*Business Central Europe*, April 1995, pp. 37, 44–8).

PARTNERSHIP FOR PEACE

On 21 October 1993 Nato decided to adopt a US proposal that non-aligned and former communist countries should be offered a Partnership for Peace rather than immediate membership. The idea was formally accepted at the Nato summit held in Brussels on 10–11 January 1994 as a way of reconciling conflicting pressures: (1) the eagerness of the East European and Baltic States in particular to join in order to benefit from Nato's security guarantees (especially after the 12 December general election in Russia and the failure of the West to deal with the crisis in Bosnia); (2) the desire to avoid a security vacuum in Eastern Europe; (3) the danger of stirring nationalist passions in a Russia perceiving potential isolation (the Russian government favours a fortified OSCE to replace Nato; on 10 January 1994 Vladimir Zhirinovsky warned that the incorporation of Eastern Europe 'would mean Nato took the path of preparing for World War Three'); (4) the fear of involving Nato in a still unstable region and drawing new lines of division in Europe; (5) the fear of weakening Nato if countries unready to join were admitted.

A communiqué issued on 11 January 1994 stated, 'We expect and would welcome Nato expansion that would reach to democratic states to our east, as part of an evolutionary process, taking into account political and security developments in the whole of Europe.' No former communist country (a member of the North Atlantic Co-operation Council) would be excluded from consideration as a future member, but there was no guarantee of membership, no timetable was laid out and no detailed and specific eligibility criteria were listed (as opposed to the general requirement to be, for example, a democracy accepting existing national borders and ensuring democratic civilian control of the military). What was promised was closer co-operation with Nato on a bilateral, individually tailored basis, which might lead to future membership. (The idea was to sign a standard framework and individual deals could be worked out in detail later.) The forms of co-operation include information exchange, transparency in defence planning and budgeting, joint planning, exercises and training (including training for peacekeeping duties), and consultation during a crisis for any country ('a direct threat to its territorial integrity, political independence or security').

Membership has gradually expanded:

1. As of 3 March 1994: Estonia, Latvia, Lithuania, Poland, Hungary, Slovakia, Ukraine, Albania, Bulgaria and Romania. (The Czech Republic joined soon afterwards.)
2. Moldova (the twelfth member, 16 March 1994).

3. Georgia (the thirteenth member, 23 March 1994).
4. Slovenia (the fourteenth member, 30 March 1994).
5. Azerbaijan (4 May 1994).
6. Russia (22 June 1994; this would have made Russia the twenty-first member, but on 1 December 1994 Russia refused to finalize plans for military co-operation; Russia finally joined on 31 May 1995).
7. Uzbekistan (the twenty-second member, 13 July 1994).
8. Austria (the twenty-fifth member, 10 February 1995).
9. Russia (31 May 1995). The number of members is now twenty-six.

Some of the countries not mentioned, because the dates of entry are unknown to the author, are Kazakhstan, Kyrgyzstan, Turkmenistan, Finland and Sweden. A Nato report on the expansion of full membership was expected by late summer 1995, in time for consideration at the Nato meeting in December that year. On 9 May 1994 the Western European Union offered 'associate partner' status to Bulgaria, the Czech Republic, Hungary, Poland, Romania, Slovakia, Estonia, Latvia and Lithuania.

THE STABILITY PACT

A conference on Stability in Europe was held in Paris on 26–27 May 1994 (it was French-inspired). It represented a sort of 'preventative diplomacy' in the sense of heading off border and ethnic minority problems of the sort that have devastated much of the former Yugoslavia. A necessary (but not sufficient) condition for entry to the EU and Nato was to be the signing of 'good neighbour' accords, with guarantees of borders and minority rights. Two regional round tables were set up, one for the Baltic region and one for Central and Eastern Europe. Bilateral agreements were to be signed within one year. Together with existing friendship agreements, these were to form part of the Stability Pact. The countries taking part were Bulgaria, the Czech Republic, Hungary, Poland, Romania, Slovakia, Estonia, Latvia and Lithuania. Slovenia was prevented from participating as a full member by Italy (owing to demands for compensation for property allegedly seized by Slovenia after the Second World War).

A non-binding set of principles to 'render irreversible the advance of democracy and institute durable good-neighbourliness in Europe' was agreed at the meeting held in Paris on 20–21 March 1995. All the individual deals were to be monitored by OSCE, e.g. the one signed by Hungary and Slovakia on 19 March 1995. All fifty-two countries present were OSCE members, but some members were not represented, e.g. Croatia, Slovenia and the Federal Republic of Yugoslavia.

2

FOREIGN TRADE

The transitional countries were unfortunate in that the early 1990s were years of economic recession in the West. But the United Nations Economic Commission for Europe (1993: 6, 129) is encouraged by the growth of East European exports to Western markets. Exports of manufactures have risen faster than total exports, with consumer goods and engineering leading the way. Exports from Eastern Europe have indeed been growing fast, but only from a small base; while the former market is small, its share of Western European exports rose from 3 per cent to 5 per cent in 1992 (United Nations, *World Economic Survey 1993*, pp. 5, 62). The Commission of the European Communities (*Employment in Europe 1993*, p. 76), however, sees 'evidence of a shift in the composition of exports away from more sophisticated, high value-added manufactures, such as machine tools, towards basic products, fuel and raw materials'.

The share of world trade accounted for by the countries of Eastern Europe and the former Soviet Union fell from 3.5 per cent in 1990 to 2.4 per cent in 1993 (Deutsche Bank, *Focus: Eastern Europe*, 1994, no. 121, p. 3).

TRADE WITH THE EUROPEAN UNION

In 1991 the East European countries increased their exports to the EU by 20.6 per cent and in 1992 by about 17 per cent (in 1992 imports from the EU increased by 22 per cent) (Deutsche Bank, *Focus: Eastern Europe*, 30 July 1993, no. 85, pp. 3–4).

Kramer (1993: 236) stresses how important it is to adopt a generous stance on imports from Eastern Europe in order to ensure political stability. A successful process of political transformation in Eastern Europe is very much in the EU's interest.

Messerlin (1993: 91–3) argues that the 1991 association agreements ('Europe Agreements') between the EU and Czechoslovakia, Hungary and Poland were less generous than they seemed. The general provision was that EU tariffs were to be eliminated in 1992. But there was a lot of double counting, i.e. some concessions had been granted before. In addition the concessions were more selective than they looked at first glance. Seven groups of products (comprising major East European exports) were to have their EU tariffs eliminated more slowly, e.g. those on coal by 1996, those on steel by 1997 and those on textiles by 1998. The EU concessions on agricultural products consisted of two broad commitments over a five-year period, namely reductions in tariffs or levies of up to 60 per cent and increases in quotas or ceilings by 36 per cent. But Messerlin says that in reality the concessions were small and uncertain. Messerlin also examines the relatively small impact that the elimination of EU trade barriers to East European exports would have on EU production. For a detailed discussion of the relatively small impact on EU economies even in the case of 'sensitive' sectors like agriculture and food processing, steel, chemicals, textiles, clothing and footwear see Rollo and Smith (1993). Rollo (*FT*, 18 June 1993, p. 15) also points out that 'sensitive products' account for 25–40 per cent of East European exports to the EU, whereas significant liberalization of trade in these goods should not cause notable harm to EU producers (their losses are more or less balanced by savings to EU consumers and taxpayers).

Other figures also put some perspective on the situation. In 1992 Bulgaria, Czechoslovakia, Hungary, Poland and Romania accounted for just 1.6 per cent of total EU imports (compared with Austria's 1.9 per cent and Sweden's 2.1 per cent), while the EU accounted for more than half their total trade (*FT*, 6 May 1993, p. 3; 16 June 1993, p. 19); Eastern Europe has less than 5 per cent of the European steel market (*IHT*, 17 February 1993, p. 21); Czech steel exports were less than 1 per cent of total EU consumption (*The Guardian*, 20 February 1993, p. 35); Hungary accounts for less than 1 per cent of EU imports (*IHT*, 30 April 1993, p. 15). According to *The Economist* (Survey, 3 July 1993, p. 17), Eastern Europe accounts for about 3 per cent of the EU's trade. David Marsh and Lionel Barber (*FT*, 7 June 1993, p. 13) add the following points about the EU's trade relations with Czechoslovakia, Hungary, Poland, Bulgaria and Romania:

1. The EU's trade surplus increased from Ecu 1.4 billion in 1991 to Ecu 2.5 billion in 1992 ($3.2 billion: *The Economist*, 19 June 1993, p. 45). (Up to 1990 the EU ran a deficit. In 1990 trade was roughly in balance: *The Economist*, Survey, 3 July 1993, p. 17.)

2. Encouraging East European exports now will stimulate growth in the region and thus expand markets for future EU exports.

3. Trade liberalization has a much larger effect proportionately on Eastern Europe than on the EU. In 1992 the former accounted for only 1.7 per cent of the latter's foreign trade (less than Austria or Sweden), while the reverse figure was about 50 per cent (compared with 25 per cent in 1989). Even in the case of 'sensitive' goods Eastern Europe's share of the EU's imports in 1991 was just 1.7 per cent in the case of chemicals, 2.3 per cent for agricultural products, 2.7 per cent for iron and steel and 2.8 per cent for textiles.

As Leszek Balcerowicz puts it, 'Western governments do not seem to realize their own potential to damage or increase the chance for successful economic reform in the former socialist countries through actions that appear to be quite marginal to them . . . What for Western countries is a marginal restriction of access to their markets may cause great harm to countries undergoing radical economic reform, reducing their chances of success' (cited by Reginald Dale, *IHT*, 7 December 1993, p. 9).

The United Nations Economic Commission for Europe (*Economic Bulletin for Europe*, November 1993; as quoted by Frances Williams, *FT*, 10 December 1993, p. 6) described the protectionist measures adopted by Western Europe as 'especially petty and ungenerous', given that Western exporters have gained most from the liberalization of East–West trade. Between 1989 and 1992 East European exports to OECD countries rose in value by 43 per cent, whereas the reverse figure was 67 per cent. As a result the OECD trade balance swung from a small deficit to a sizeable surplus. In the first half of 1993 East European exports to the West fell by some 14 per cent, while the reverse flow featured a rise of 11 per cent. US Senator Sam Nunn (*IHT*, 28 December 1993, p. 4) argues that 'today's Iron Curtain of West European trade barriers is a greater threat to Eastern Europe's long-term prospects for democratic and free market reform than a distant, weakened and demoralized Russian army.'

Edward Balls (*FT*, 13 September 1993, p. 6) summarizes a study commissioned by the Commission of the European Communities (*Trade and Foreign Investment in the Community's Regions: the Impact of Reform in Central and Eastern Europe*, Regional Development Studies, no. 7). The study contradicts the view that the EU's 'lagging' regions (Greece, Portugal, the Irish Republic, Northern Ireland, southern Italy and most of Spain) stand to be hurt more if trade with Eastern Europe is liberalized. In the short term the EU as a whole would be a net loser from open trade if reforms succeeded in Eastern Europe, although the fall in output would be a mere 0.2 per cent. As East European imports of manufactures and agricultural goods grew, so the net impact of open manufacturing trade would turn positive and outweigh agricultural losses. By the year 2010 total EU output would have risen by an estimated 0.8 per cent. But the 'lagging' regions would be net beneficiaries even in the short run, with Greece, southern Italy and Spain reaping most of the benefit. Output would rise for all the main categories of manufactures in the 'lagging' regions except iron and steel. And the projected gains in manufacturing output are substantial (0.4 per cent by 1995 and 2.2 per cent by 2010). For Spain and Portugal such relative success is almost entirely due to a mix of industries and products which are better suited to the import needs of Eastern Europe. For Greece this industry effect is enhanced by its geographical position.

'The main threat to Eastern European exports comes from actual, threatened and "latent" trade remedy action employed for purposes of managing trade to support industrial policy objectives in the EU.' At the end of May 1994 nineteen anti-dumping measures imposed by the EU were in force, along with twelve other trade restrictive measures. Over the past four years trade among the former Comecon members has shrunk by 50 per cent and has been refocused on the West (EBRD report of October 1994: *FT*, 20 October 1994, p. 3; *The Guardian*, 20 October 1994, p. 20).

Since the association agreements were signed some trade restrictions have been implemented (the economic recession in the main Western countries exacerbated the situation, especially the need for output reductions in products like steel in Western Europe). For example, on 25 February 1993 the EU imposed special tariffs for up to three years on steel from Eastern Europe, supposedly under the anti-dumping clauses of the association agreements. Jacques Attali (*The Guardian*, 19 March 1993, p. 22) argues that this was a short-sighted move because of the danger that East European steel will be diverted into armaments for export. On 6 April 1993 the EU imposed a one-month ban on imports of live animals, meat, milk and dairy products from Eastern Europe on the grounds of preventing the spread of foot and mouth disease. (Actually suspect cattle had been transported to Italy from Croatia.) The East European countries, suspecting that this was merely a protectionist ploy, retaliated. Most of the bans were lifted later that month, following agreement on a tightening up of both quarantine rules and export certification procedures. (Poland's ban was not lifted until mid-July.)

On 22 June 1993, however, the European Council summit agreed a package of measures to hasten the political and economic integration of associated countries with the EU. Duties would be abolished on industrial (mainly chemical) products after two rather than four years and on products such as footwear, glassware, cars and electrical goods after three rather than five years. Tariffs on textiles (originally scheduled to end in 1998) and on steel (1997) would end a year earlier than planned. Quotas and ceilings would be raised and at a faster rate than envisaged previously. Levies and duties on agricultural products would be reduced by 60 per cent six months ahead of time and a 10 per cent increase in quotas would also be introduced six months in advance. But EU membership would be conditional on a number of stiff criteria: 'stability of institutions guaranteeing democracy, the rule of law, human rights, respect for and protection of minorities, the existence of a functioning market economy as well as the capacity to cope with competitive pressure and market forces.'

Portes (1994: 1188–9) argues that the 'hub-and-spoke pattern of trade relations marginalizes the individual Eastern countries, artificially discourages economic relations among them and favours investment in Germany or Austria to supply the East rather than in the East itself . . . All this argues for mapping out a clearer path to accession that would multilateralize the Europe agreements so as to create a comprehensive free trade area, then deepen integration in an approach to something like the EU–EFTA "European Economic Area".'

ENTRY TO THE EUROPEAN UNION

The prospects of entry to the EU in the foreseeable future vary substantially. Normally the Czech Republic, Hungary and Poland are put well in the lead (with Slovakia not far behind), with the year 2000 seen as the earliest conceivable date even for those countries. But a study by the European Commission suggested that the Czech Republic and Slovenia may be the only countries economically strong enough to be admitted by the end of the decade. Slovenia already has a higher *per capita* income than Greece or Portugal (John Palmer, *The Guardian*, 24 September 1994, p. 14).

Entry for any East European country is made much more difficult by (1) the prospect of the free movement of labour in conditions of high unemployment in Western Europe and (2) the massive additional demands placed on the regional/social funds and the Common Agricultural Policy (CAP) by generally poorer and more agrarian countries. (There is the argument, of course, that such widening would be an effective way of finally destroying the grotesquely protectionist CAP! In 1993 the respective shares of agriculture in GDP and employment were as follows: Bulgaria, 10.4 per cent and 17.4 per cent; Poland, 6.5 per cent and 26.9 per cent; Romania, 21 per cent and 32.2 per cent; Slovakia, 4.5 per cent and 10.3 per cent; the Czech Republic, 5.5 per cent and 6.5 per cent; Hungary, 8.9 per cent and 8.1 per cent; the EU of twelve countries, 2.8 per cent and 5.8 per cent: Deutsche Bank, *Focus: Eastern Europe*, 1995, no. 128, p. 7.)

'Most Central European countries began their agricultural reform with widespread liberalization . . . But these improvements have been overshadowed by the reinvention of government intervention. Credit subsidies have been doled out to protect farmers against high real interest rates; trade barriers have been raised against imports; various forms of market regulation have been introduced to stabilize domestic prices' (*The Economist*, 20 August 1994, p. 32). For example:

1. All the countries subsidize some agricultural credit, e.g. Bulgaria has passed laws forcing commercial banks to provide cheap loans and in 1994 the Czech Republic set up a special fund to guarantee loans and subsidize interest rates.

2. Most countries have raised tariffs on agricultural imports. Some, like Hungary, have reintroduced import licences. Others, such as the Czech Republic, Poland and Slovakia, have introduced variable import levies (which fluctuate to keep domestic prices stable when import prices change).

3. There are floor prices for many products and government agencies have been created to buy them at these prices and then either sell them

when prices rise or export them with a subsidy. Hungary and Poland have also introduced some production quotas.

'If all these policies sound depressingly familiar, it is because most of them are copies of those practised by the EU. The real reason for introducing them is domestic political pressure. But talk to any official in a Central European agriculture ministry and you will be told that the ministry is simply introducing habits common in Western Europe in preparation for EU membership' (p. 32).

Van Brabant (1994) considers the arguments that the future of transitional economies lies 'in fostering close, and nearly exclusive, ties with the West . . . are simply not very credible in the short to medium run . . . The goodwill built up through long-established trade and business contacts has recently been wasted in the haste of destroying the old without putting anything viable in its stead' (p. 190). 'Much existing capacity lies idle' and 'only some of the group's comparative advantages have been extensively exploited' (pp. 190–1). A multilateral clearing mechanism offering some external finance and constructive surveillance might, he suggests, provide one useful channel. But a European guarantee that such an interim solution would indeed be only temporary would be helpful (pp. 190–1).

Inotai (1994) is a stern critic of the idea of any kind of Central (and/or Eastern) European payments union. The European Payments Union (EPU) set up after the Second World War 'rested on altogether different conditions. The participating countries had a strong interest in mutual trade, and had historically developed complementary trade patterns . . . Intra-regional trade amounted to 60–70 per cent of total trade, or ten times the current proportion of trade among the Visegrad countries' (p. 38). The situation is different today. 'Regional trade has practically collapsed and there is little interest in reviving any Comecon-like co-operation' (p. 38). During the Comecon era 'a radial political and economic pattern was developed, in keeping with the Soviet priority of maintaining bilateral contacts with the small Central and East European countries'. Today 'intra-regional trade is a very modest fraction of total trade – less than 5 per cent for Hungary and Poland, and less than 10 per cent for the Czech Republic and Slovakia' (p. 37).

DEVELOPMENTS

21 December 1992. The Visegrad countries (the Czech Republic, Slovakia, Hungary and Poland) sign up to the Central European Free Trade Association (effective 1 March 1993). (For details of this and subsequent developments, see *Business Central Europe*, July–August 1995, p. 9. For example, members hope to sign an agreement to reduce duties on agricultural products by 50 per cent from 1 January 1996.)

4 October 1994. EU foreign ministers agree to invite Poland, Hungary, the Czech Republic, Slovakia, Bulgaria and Romania to take part in EU ministerial and summit meetings on a regular basis from 1995 onwards. The foreign ministers also agree to call on the European Commission to produce papers detailing how the East European countries can prepare for entry.

29 October 1994. Leon Brittan (UK commissioner) loses that part of his portfolio dealing with Central and Eastern Europe and the former Soviet Union to Hans Van den Broek (Netherlands).

10 December 1994. The six countries attend the final session of the EU meeting in Essen (Germany).

1 February 1995. EU association agreements come fully into effect for Bulgaria, the Czech Republic, Romania and Slovakia. (Agreements with Hungary and Poland entered into full force on 1 February 1994.)

(See the Stability Pact discussed in Chapter 1.)

Part II

THE COUNTRIES OF THE FORMER SOVIET UNION

3

RUSSIA

THE DEMISE OF THE SOVIET UNION

As I see it, the Soviet Union did not collapse because of its economic weaknesses. The economic system could have trundled on despite falling further and further behind in relative terms. It was the collapse of the political system that was the key. Command economies can survive only if commands are generally obeyed. Gorbachev was not a tyrant who was willing to use the security forces to enforce compliance at home or in Eastern Europe. The Soviet political system was, ironically, also undermined by the very success of foreign policy. The end of the Cold War deprived the Communist Party of an important source of legitimacy.

Berkowitz *et al.* (1993: 50, 56) conclude that: 'The CIA failed to foresee . . . the sharp decline of the economy and the break-up of the Soviet Union at the end of the 1980s . . . [But] the CIA was not significantly better or worse than academic specialists . . . neither anticipated the intensity of potential ethnic separation nor even considered the possibility that the Communist Party would lose legitimacy completely and that the Soviet political and economic system would disintegrate. It perhaps should be said that neither did Gorbachev and his advisers . . . The CIA's assessment in the early 1980s, which was shared by the scholarly community generally, was that there was a very "low probability" that the system would collapse from popular unrest or from internal strains. Subsequent events have not proven that assessment to have been wrong, contrary to what many critics now assert. The system in fact did not collapse from internal strains and there was no public unrest. It collapsed for another reason that no one foresaw; namely, the cumulative sequence of events that culminated in the dissolution of the Party by the very man who had been elected five years earlier to lead the Party and had no intention at that time of contributing to its dissolution. The profession . . . did not foresee the possibility of one particular outcome, that the Party would be destroyed by the hand of the Party leader himself . . . Had that scenario been put forward for consideration, it would no doubt have been generally considered as of extremely low probability, and properly so. Low probability events do occur, however, and the occurrence of such an event does not signify that those who had judged that event to be improbable were wrong.'

THE SEARCH FOR A NEW CONSTITUTION

It is not uninteresting to note that the Western word 'parliament' comes from the verb to speak, while the Russian 'duma' comes from the more compliant verb to think. Formally the Congress of People's Deputies was the only body that had the authority (with a two-thirds majority) to amend the 1970s constitution (already subjected to hundreds of amendments) or to adopt a new one. In order to bypass the Congress (and its standing representative, the Supreme Soviet) Yeltsin appointed a constituent assembly which initially sat on 5–16 June 1993. The assembly comprised a wide range of interests, including the president, parliament, political parties, the Constitutional Commission, the various regional authorities in the Russian Federation (including Moscow and St Petersburg), trade unions, the Church and the business community. The aim was to draw up a new constitution laying out the division of power between the president and parliament and between the federal and regional authorities.

On 30 April 1993 Yeltsin put forward the draft of a new constitution with a strong presidency and considerable regional devolution of authority (although no unilateral secession would be permitted). Some of the controversial proposals included the following: (1) no vice-president; (2) if the Federal Assembly failed to confirm the president's candidate for prime minister (or the president's call for his dismissal) the president could dissolve parliament and set the date for a fresh election (this procedure could be followed when any 'crisis of state power' could not be resolved on the basis of constitutional procedures); (3) acting on representations from the prime minister and after consulting the Council of the Federation, the president was to appoint and dismiss federal ministers; (4) the president could still dismiss the government even if parliament rejected his call for a vote of no confidence; (5) the president 'conducts negotiations and signs international treaties of the Russian Federation and acts on behalf of the state in international relations'.

The Federal Assembly was to consist of two chambers. The following proposals were originally put forward:

1. *Council of the Federation.* There were to be two representatives appointed from each subject (member) of the federation, namely the chairman of the council and the governor (most governors were appointed by Yeltsin). (Note that Chechenia boycotted the negotiations.) The president could be removed from office if more than two-thirds of the deputies were in favour.

2. *State Duma*. This was to consist of 300 deputies elected from territorial constituencies on the basis of proportional representation.

But the summer of 1993 saw much wrangling over many of the president's proposals. On 5 June Khasbulatov and many representatives of parliament walked out of the assembly. There was much debate about the degree of regional devolution. On 14 May 1993 Vologda Province proclaimed itself a 'state-territorial member of the Russian Federation' (but with the same constitutional rights as a republic). On 1 July Sverdlovsk Province more openly declared itself 'the Urals Republic' and on 8 July the Primorski (Maritime) territory (centred on Vladivostok) threatened to proclaim itself a 'republic within the federation' if it did not get increased autonomy. As a way to satisfy the thirst of such lower-level authorities for republic status the president suggested that they should be given equal 'economic rights'. The president made many concessions (e.g. about his right to dissolve parliament) and a draft constitution was approved on 12 July for consideration by the lower-level authorities. But the disputes did not end. On 13 August the regional representatives informed Yeltsin that the Council of the Federation should be only a 'consultative' body and not the 'legitimate body of power' that he wanted (in order to bypass the existing parliament when it came to adopting a new constitution). The president also consented to work with the existing parliament's drafting committee. On 19 September 1993 the regional representatives failed to agree on the setting up of the Council of the Federation and two days later Yeltsin announced the dissolution of parliament and elections on 12 December for the State Duma (see below). The draft constitution was published on 9 November 1993 (see, for example, *CDSP*, 1993, vol. XLV, no. 45, pp. 4–16). It was to be subject to a referendum (formally a 'national vote': 'Do you agree with the constitution of the Russian Federation?') on 12 December, a simple majority being required for acceptance with a turnout of at least 50 per cent. The draft reflected Yeltsin's strengthened position following the dissolution of parliament. A powerful presidency was the key feature, i.e. the executive gained at the expense of the legislature.

The procedures for changes in the constitution are as follows. 'A federal law is considered to have been adopted if it is approved by a majority of at least three-quarters of the total number of members of the Council of the Federation and at least two-thirds of the number of deputies to the State Duma. The President of the Russian Federation has fourteen days to sign and promulgate an adopted federal constitutional law' (see below for procedures where there is disagreement). 'If a proposal to revise chapters 1, 2 or 9 of the constitution of the Russian Federation is supported by a three-fifths vote of the total number of members of the Council of the Federation and of deputies to the State Duma, a Constitutional Assembly is convened in accordance with federal constitutional law. The Constitutional Assembly either confirms the immutability of the constitution of the Russian

Federation or works out the draft of a new Russian Federation constitution, which may be adopted by the Constitutional Assembly by a two-thirds vote of the total number of its members or may be submitted to a nationwide vote. When a nationwide vote is conducted, the constitution of the Russian Federation is considered to have been adopted if more than half the voters who took part in the balloting voted in favour of it, provided that more than half of all eligible voters took part.'

The main clauses of the constitution are as follows:

1. 'The Russian Federation/Russia is a democratic and federal state based on the rule of law, with a republican form of government.' 'Basic human rights and liberties are inalienable and belong to everyone from birth.' 'A citizen of the Russian Federation may hold citizenship in a foreign state (thus dual citizenship).' 'Private, state, municipal and other forms of ownership enjoy equal recognition and protection under the Russian Federation . . . The right of private property is protected by law.' An ombudsman is to be appointed by the State Duma.

'The Russian Federation consists of republics, territories, provinces, federal cities, an autonomous province and autonomous regions, all of which are equal members of the Russian Federation.' There are eighty-nine 'members' or 'subjects' of the federation, twenty-one republics, six territories, forty-nine provinces, two federal cities (Moscow and St Petersburg), one autonomous province (the Jewish Autonomous Province) and ten autonomous regions.

Many of the concessions granted to 'members' or 'subjects' during the negotiations prior to the dissolution of parliament were withdrawn. All subjects have equality of rights and responsibilities. An earlier draft referred to the republics as 'sovereign states within the Russian Federation', but the term 'sovereignty' was omitted in the final draft. Subjects do not have the right to secede. Relevant clauses include the following. 'If there is a contradiction between a federal law and another Act issued under the Russian Federation, the federal law prevails.' 'The status of a member of the Russian Federation may be changed on the basis of mutual consent by the Russian Federation and the member of the Russian Federation, in accordance with federal constitutional law.' 'The borders between members of the Russian Federation may be changed with their mutual consent.' 'The following matters fall within the jurisdiction of the Russian Federation . . . the federal structure and territory of the Russian Federation . . . determining the status and protecting the border . . . of the Russian Federation.'

(On 9 November 1993 Yeltsin cancelled Sverdlovsk Province's declaration of itself as 'the Urals Republic'. The fifteen Soviet republics, based on the most populous nationalities, were supposed to give a semblance of statehood, a reflection domestically of 'internationalism'. Although it was constitutionally feasible, in reality there was no possibility of secession. The sixteen autonomous republics of Russia became full republics when the Soviet Union disintegrated. Four new republics were created in the early 1990s and Chechenia split away from Ingushetia in 1992. Thus there are now twenty-one republics.)

2. *The president.* 'The President of the Russian Federation is head of state.' (Note that there is no vice-president.) 'In accordance with the constitution of the Russian Federation and federal laws, the President of the Russian Federation determines the basic guidelines of the state's domestic and foreign policy . . . exercises leadership in Russian Federation foreign policy . . . conducts negotiations and signs international treaties of the Russian Federation.' 'The same person may not hold the position of President of the Russian Federation for more than two consecutive terms.' (Each term lasts for four years.) The President of the Russian Federation:

'Appoints the chairman of the government of the Russian Federation [the prime minister], with the consent of the State Duma . . . makes decisions on dismissing the government . . . acting on a proposal by the chairman of the government of the Russian Federation, appoints vice-chairmen [deputy prime ministers] of the Russian Federation and federal ministers to their posts and relieves them of their duties' (see below when there is disagreement).

'Presents to the Council of the Federation for appointment to positions as judges of the Constitutional Court of the Russian Federation, the Supreme Court of the Russian Federation and the Higher Court of Arbitration of the Russian Federation [economic disputes are dealt with by this court], and also a candidate for the post of Prosecutor-General of the Russian Federation . . . submits a proposal to the Council of the Federation on relieving the Russian Federation prosecutor-general of his duties . . . appoints judges of other federal courts.' 'Judges are not subject to removal from office.' ('The powers of a judge may be terminated or suspended only on grounds and according to procedures established by federal law.')

'Appoints the Supreme Commander of the Russian Federation Armed Forces and relieves members of their duties . . . The President of the Russian Federation is the Supreme Commander in Chief of the Russian Federation Armed Forces . . . in the event of aggression against the Russian Federation, or a direct threat of aggression, the President of the Russian Federation may introduce martial law throughout the Russian Federation or in specific localities, giving immediate notification of his action to the Council of the Federation and the State Duma . . . Under circumstances and in accordance with procedures stipulated by federal constitutional law, the president may introduce a state of emergency throughout the Russian Federation or in specific localities, giving immediate notification to the Council of the Federation and the State Duma.'

'The President of the Russian Federation issues decrees and directives . . . [which] . . . are binding throughout the Russian Federation . . . [but which] . . . may not be at variance with the constitution of the Russian Federation or with federal laws.'

'In all cases in which the President of the Russian Federation is unable to perform his duties, those duties are temporarily performed by the chairman of the government of the Russian Federation. The acting president of the Russian Federation has no power to dissolve the State Duma, to schedule referendums, or to propose amendments of the constitution of the Russian Federation or the revision of its provisions.'

'The President of the Russian Federation may be removed from office by the Council of the Federation only on the basis of an accusation that charges the president with high treason or the commission of another grave crime, an accusation brought by the State Duma and confirmed by a finding of the Russian Federation Supreme Court on the presence of the elements of the crime in the actions of the President of the Russian Federation and by a finding of the Russian Federation Constitutional Court on compliance with the established procedure for bringing the accusation . . . A decision by the State Duma on bringing an accusation and a decision by the Council of the Federation on removing the president from office must be adopted by a two-thirds vote of the total number of members of each chamber and on the initiative of at least one-third of the deputies of the State Duma, and there must be a finding by a special commission formed by the State Duma . . . A decision by the Council of the Federation on removing the President of the Russian Federation from office must be adopted no later than three months after the State Duma has brought an accusation against the President.'

3. *The Federal Assembly.* This consists of two chambers, the Council of the Federation (the upper house) and the State Duma (the lower house):

The members of the Council of the Federation (CF) consist of two representatives of each member of the Russian Federation, one from the representative body of state power and one from the executive body of state power (CF representatives were, in reality, to be elected for the first term of office: see 12 December general election). The following matters fall under the jurisdiction of the Council of the Federation: confirming border changes between members of the Russian Federation; confirming presidential decrees on the introduction of martial law or on the declaration of a state of emergency; deciding the question of using Russian armed forces outside the territory of the Russian Federation; scheduling presidential elections; removing the president from office; approving nominations for judges of the Constitutional Court, the Supreme Court and the Higher Court of Arbitration; approving the nomination for prosecutor-general or relieving him of his duties.

The following matters fall under the jurisdiction of the State Duma: approving the nomination for prime minister; deciding on the question of confidence in the government; approving the presidential nomination for the chairman of the central bank of Russia and relieving him of his duties; bringing accusations against the president with the aim of removing him from office.

Legislation can be initiated by the president, the Council of the Federation, the State Duma, the government and the legislative (representative) bodies of the members (subjects) of the federation. Draft laws are submitted to the State Duma. Draft laws relating to fiscal matters may be submitted only 'if there is a finding by the government of the Russian Federation . . . The government of the Russian Federation works out the federal budget, presents it to the State Duma and ensures its fulfilment.' Federal laws are adopted by the State Duma (by simple majority unless otherwise stipulated by the constitution). Federal laws adopted by the State Duma are forwarded to the CF for its consideration (simple majority voting applies). If the CF rejects a federal law there is a conciliation process. If it fails the State Duma can vote again, albeit requiring a two-thirds majority this time. Federal laws adopted by the State Duma are subject to mandatory consideration by the CF if they concern the federal budget, taxes, monetary policy, customs regulations, international treaties, the state border, or war and peace. A federal law must be submitted to the president. If he rejects the law the State Duma and the CF must reconsider. But the two chambers can overrule the president: 'If, when the federal law is reconsidered, it is approved, in the words previously adopted, by a majority of at least two-thirds of the total number of members of the Council of the Federation and deputies to the State Duma, it must be signed by the President of the Russian Federation within seven days and promulgated.'

'Where nominations for chairman of the government of the Russian Federation have been rejected three times by the State Duma, the President of the Russian Federation appoints a chairman of the government of the Russian Federation, dissolves the State Duma and schedules new elections.' 'The State Duma may express lack of confidence in the government of the Russian Federation. A resolution of no confidence in the government of the Russian Federation is adopted by a majority vote of the total number of deputies to the State Duma . . . [if this takes place] . . . the president has the right to announce the dismissal of the government of the Russian Federation or to disagree with the decision of the State Duma. If the State Duma, within three months' time, again expresses no confidence in the government of the Russian Federation, the President of the Russian Federation announces the dismissal of the government or dissolves the State Duma.' (Note that the president cannot dissolve the State Duma within a year of a general election.)

Comments. 'The Russian constitution is based on the French system, and it contains the latter's major inherent flaw: the premier and his government are responsible to both the president and the legislature' (Hough 1994: 21).

THE FEDERAL STATE

Demographic features of the federal state

The population of Russia was 148.3 million at the start of 1993 (*IHT*, 12 February 1993, p. 11). There are more than 100 nationalities, the main ones being Russians (81.3 per cent), Tatars (3.6 per cent), Ukrainians (2.7 per cent), Chuvash (1.2 per cent), Dagestanis (1.0 per cent) and Baskirs (0.9 per cent) (*The Independent*, 24 April 1993, p. 11).

The percentage of ethnic Russians in the population of each of the twenty-one republics (in 1989 in descending order) was as follows: Khakassia, 79.5; Karelia, 73.6; Buryatia, 70.0; Adygeya, 68.0; Mordovia, 60.8; Altai, 60.4; Udmurtia, 58.9; Komi, 57.7; Yakutia (Sakha), 50.3; Mari-El, 47.5; Tatarstan, 43.3; Karachevo-Balkaria, 42.4; Bashkortostan, 39.3; Kalmykia, 37.7; Kalbardino-Balkaria, 32.0; Tuva, 32.0; North Ossetia, 29.9; Chuvashia, 26.7; Ingushetia, 23.0; Chechenia, 22.0; Dagestan, 9.2 (*The Economist*, 14 January 1995, p. 33).

The economics of the federal state

Åslund argues that 'Since most economic powers have devolved from Moscow to regional governments, there is little incentive to claim independence' (1994b: 61–2).

Twenty-three of the eighty-nine 'members' of the federation collect sufficient taxes to meet their own needs; the others need federal subsidies (*Moscow News*, 14–20 October 1994, p. 8). A presidential decree of 22 December 1993 allowed the members of the federation to vary the tax rate on profits in the range from 13 per cent to 25 per cent (of which 13 percentage points were to go to the federal budget and the remainder was to go to the local budget) (*CDSP*, 1994, vol. XLVI, no. 19, p. 10).

Tyumen accounts for roughly two-thirds of oil output and is now permitted to sell up to 10 per cent of its production on its own account. Other regions are also allowed to sell some oil on their own account (Deutsche Bank, *Focus: Eastern Europe*, 1995, no. 126, pp. 4–5).

Bilateral agreements

The shelling of parliament on 4 October 1993 was a turning point for the nature of the federal state in Russia. The danger of Russia disintegrating through 'members' ('subjects') of the federation breaking away seemed to be over (note that Yeltsin had previously tried to curry favour with regional leaders in his dispute with parliament by offering greater autonomy). Before the Chechen crisis erupted a number of bilateral, power-sharing agreements ('treaties') had been drawn up between the centre and the 'members':

1. *Tatarstan.* A bilateral power-sharing treaty with the autonomous republic of Tatarstan was signed on 15 February 1994 by President Yeltsin and President Mintimir Shamiyev. Tatartstan agreed to drop the terms 'sovereign state' and 'subject of international law' from its constitution and to pay federal taxes (*CDSP*, 1994, vol. XLVI, no. 7, p. 11). Tatarstan would retain its own constitution, have its own police force and have substantial freedom in economic affairs. It would not be allowed to decide for itself the share of tax revenue to remit to the centre, but it actually transfers to Moscow only 10 per cent of the taxes it collects (ordinary provinces transfer up to 80 per cent) (*Business Central Europe*, October 1994, p. 24). Tatars who do not wish to serve in the federal army may opt to perform some other service specified by the Tatar authorities.

Tatarstan has introduced a three-year tax holiday for foreign companies and joint ventures. In addition local property and profit tax exemptions are available for all manufacturing and service companies with at least 30 per cent foreign ownership and assets worth at least $1 million (*IHT*, Survey, 2 December 1994, p. 12).

2. *Bashkortostan.* The power-sharing agreement with this oil-producing (6 per cent of total output) autonomous republic was signed on 3 August 1994. The republic had already adopted its own constitution, but there would be a federal constitutional and macroeconomic policy framework and the federal government would be responsible for foreign affairs and defence. The republic would have significant powers, e.g. its own judiciary, certain tax-raising authority and the right to conclude foreign economic agreements.

All the republic's natural resources, including oil, were put under its exclusive 'ownership'. As regards industrial facilities the republic retained, among other things, all oil refineries and petrochemical enterprises. The federal government was allocated the defence and coal industries. The republic renounced the system whereby taxes are paid only to the republic government, which then decides how much to give the federal government. The division of taxes going to the federal government was as follows: VAT, 75 per cent; revenue from foreign-economic activity (i.e. duties), 100 per cent; the 38 per cent tax on profits, 13 percentage points (*CDSP*, 1995, vol. XLVII, no. 6, p. 8).

John Lloyd (*FT*, 25 February 1995, p. 7) argues that these sorts of arrangements are 'likely to be available only to relatively wealthy regions and republics that pay more into the federal budget than they receive. Moscow is unlikely to be so generous with parts of the federation that rely on the centre for finance.'

3. *Yakutia.* The bilateral agreement was signed on 29 June 1995. Under the 1991 agreement the sovereignty of the Republic of Sakha-Yakutia was recognized and Moscow undertook to finance Yakutia's social sphere in exchange for 100 per cent ownership of the republic's minerals. But Moscow's failure to meet its commitments led to the 1995 agreement. Under this the republic (1) has the right to diplomatic representation in the world and (2) finances its own social sphere (such as education and health) in return for ownership of 26 per cent of diamond output, 30 per cent of gold output and a slightly smaller percentage of oil and gas output (*Moscow News*, 30 June–6 July 1995, p. 1; *CDSP*, 1995, vol. XLVII, no. 26, pp. 14–15).

The Chechen crisis

The background

Chechenia had a population of about 1.2 million, about three-quarters of whom were Chechens. The 900,000 Chechens were Sunni Moslems; there were a further 400,000 scattered throughout the world (Deutsche Bank, *Focus: Eastern Europe*, 1994, no. 117, p. 3). Before 1991 about one-third of the population of 1.2 million were ethnic Russians. By autumn 1994 around 150,000 remained (Anatol Lieven, *The Times*, 30 December 1994, p. 12). As of January 1995 the population was 1,006,000, of which 22 per cent were Russians (*The Economist*, 14 January 1995, p. 33). Some 380,000 Russians lived in Chechenia, but by December 1994 only 100,000–110,000 remained (*CDSP*, 1995, vol. XLVI, no. 51, p. 4). 'Along with Chuvashia and Tuva, it is the only one of the three dozen republics where the titular group forms a majority' (Jonathan Steele, *The Guardian*, 18 March 1995, p. 24). 'In only . . . the neighbouring smaller Caucasian one of North Ossetia, even tinier Tuva (on the Siberian border with Mongolia) and the Chuvash republic (. . . in central Russia), does the local ethnic group hold an outright majority' (*The Economist*, 10 June 1995, p. 16).

It has always had a fearsome reputation as a warrior nation. It took years of fighting before Russia finally conquered the Chechens (Chechenia formally became part of Russia in 1859, but the Caucasian wars lasted from 1817 to 1864). In 1922–24 the Chechens and Ingushes formed two autonomous regions and in December 1936 the two united as an autonomous republic. Stalin banished the Chechens to the Central Asian republics in February 1944, because of the alleged danger of collaboration with the Nazi invaders. The move led to massive loss of life. According to *The Economist* (10 June 1995, p. 43), perhaps 240,000 out of a population of 800,000 died in the process. But some estimates go up to half the population. Khrushchev allowed them to return in 1957, when the republic was reconstituted as Chechenia-Ingushetia.

In 1973 the northern Caucasus region produced over 23 million tonnes of oil (about 5.7 per cent of the Russian total), a little over half of which came from Chechenia. But the region produced only 5.5 million tonnes in 1992 (1.4 per cent of the Russian total), with Chechenia's contribution slightly over 3 million tonnes. Russia has imposed economic sanctions since 1991. Unemployment is supposed to have topped 50 per cent. Average incomes were 30 per cent of those in Moscow in 1991 and only 3.6 per cent in March 1994 (Deutsche Bank, *Focus: Eastern Europe*, 1994, no. 117, p. 4).

In 1992 oil production was 3 million tonnes and in 1993 2.5 million tonnes (*CDSP*, 1995, vol. XLVI, no. 51, p. 7). Oil production was 4.5 million tonnes in 1992, 2.6 million tonnes in 1993 and 1.2 million tonnes in 1994 (*Moscow News*, 20–26 January 1995, p. 8). According to the Russian government, oil production in 1994 was 2 million tonnes (*IHT*, 30 January 1995, p. 13).

The toll

Parliament's human rights commissioner Sergei Kovalyov issued a report on 21 February 1995. His team's estimate was that between 25 November 1994 and 25 January 1995 24,400 civilians were killed in Chechenia, including 3,700 children under the age of fifteen, 4,650 women over fifteen, 2,650 men over fifty and 13,350 unarmed men between fifteen and fifty. The number of armed Chechen men killed was put at 650. No figure was given for Russian military losses, but Russian military officials had put the number of Russian troops dead and missing at more than 1,000. Most of the civilian casualties were believed to have been ethnic Russians who were unable to leave Grozny because, unlike Chechens, they could not go to the countryside to join relatives. The number of refugees was put at 400,000. (Reports in *IHT*, *The Independent*, *The Times* and *The Guardian* of 22 February 1995. See also *CDSP*, 1995, vol. XLVII, no. 8, p. 10.)

On 9 February 1995 the Russian army put the number of Chechen militants killed in the period 11 December 1994 to 8 February 1995 at 6,690. Russian army losses (excluding Interior Ministry troops) were put at over 1,100. There were also several hundred missing and unidentified corpses (*CDSP*, 1995, vol. XLVII, no. 6, p. 4).

Russian officials put the number of Russian servicemen killed as of 24 February 1995 at 1,146, those missing at 374, the number wounded or ill at 5,000 and the number of unidentified bodies in morgues at about 100 (reports in *IHT* and *The Guardian* of 25 February 1995; see also *CDSP*, 1995, vol. XLVII, no. 8, p. 11). The Russian Ministry of Defence reported that Russian troops had killed about 7,000 Chechen fighters (*The Times* and *IHT* of 1 March 1995).

On 23 March 1995 Anatoli Kulikov, the commander of Russian forces in Chechenia, said that Russian forces had included as many as 58,000 men; 1,385 troops had been killed and 4,439 wounded. Russian forces initially faced 15,000 'well prepared, well trained and excellently armed men' and an additional 30,000 'semi-trained' local militia. 'They are considerably less now' (Steven Erlanger, *IHT*, 24 March 1995, p. 5). General Kulikov talked of 1,426 Russian soldiers killed, 4,630 wounded and ninety-six taken prisoner (*The Daily Telegraph*, 31 March 1995, p. 18), while on 19 April 1995 he estimated that some 9,500 Chechen militia had been killed (*CDSP*, 1995, vol. XLVII, no. 16, p. 5). Official Russian figures show that between 11 December 1994 and 10 April 1995 1,721 Russian servicemen were killed, 6,301 wounded and 336 declared missing (*CDSP*, 1995, vol. XLVII, no. 15, p. 10). On 30 July 1995 Anatoli Kulikov (now interior minister) revealed that 1,800 Russian troops had been killed, 6,500 wounded and 250 classified as missing (*The Times*, 31 July 1995, p. 11).

By mid-February 1995 Grozny had no more than 60,000 residents left, compared with over 300,000 two months before (*CDSP*, 1995, vol. XLVII, no. 7, p. 7). Grozny was devastated by the heavy bombardment, which turned it into a wasteland. Steven Erlanger (*IHT*, 30 March 1995, p. 5) described 'a city of 400,000 only four months ago, but now a blasted landscape in which 120,000 dazed people try to live . . . Even those Chechens who hate Mr Dudayev, and there are many, are outraged by the seemingly wanton destruction of Grozny and the civilian deaths there, which number at least 10,000, aid agencies estimate.' Some 250,000 Chechens have been displaced (Steven Erlanger, *IHT*, 10 April 1995, p. 5). There are an estimated 250,000 people now living in Grozny, well below the prewar total of 400,000. Across Chechenia about 400,000 have been displaced (*The Economist*, 10 June 1995, p. 43).

Public opinion in Russia

There have been a number of public opinion polls:

1. January 1995: 66 per cent against sending Russian troops into Chechenia and only 21 per cent in favour (*CDSP*, 1995, vol. XLVII, no. 3, p. 17).
2. January 1995: 71 per cent against sending Russian troops (*CDSP*, 1995, vol. XLVII, no. 4, p. 12).
3. January 1995: 46 per cent want a cessation of the Russian army's military action in Chechenia, while 31 per cent wanted more decisive use of force to eliminate the rule of Dudayev (*CDSP*, 1995, vol. XLVII, no. 6, p. 19).
4. Polls suggest that two-thirds of Russians oppose the war (*The Economist*, 25 February 1995, p. 43).

5. 'Three months into the war, opposition has slackened' (Jonathan Steele, *The Guardian*, 18 March 1995, p. 24).

A chronology of developments

27 October 1991. Dzhokhar Dudayev is elected president (he was previously a Soviet air force general).

2 November 1991. 'Independence' is declared. (Russian forces soon beat a hasty retreat after some resistance and the refusal of the Russian parliament to ratify the move.)

June 1992. Russia declares Ingushetia a semi-autonomous republic.

2 April 1993. Dudayev dissolves parliament after an attempt at impeachment and rule by presidential decree begins. (Fighting with opposition forces begins in mid-1993.)

27 May 1994. There is an attempted assassination (the third) of President Dudayev.

13 June 1994. There is open fighting in Grozny with a rival clan led by Ruslan Labazanov.

29 July 1994. The Russian government (which supports the opposition) issues a statement attacking the Dudayev regime as 'illegitimate' and promises Russian 'intervention' (Yeltsin ruled out the use of troops) to ensure the rule of law and protection of Russian citizens. (Chechenia was considered a hive of criminality in general, but a series of hijackings in southern Russia particularly angered the Russian government.)

2 August 1994. The opposition Provisional Council of Chechenia (led by Umar Avturkhanov) claims to have assumed power, but this is denied by the Dudayev regime and proves not to be the case. (Ruslan Khasbulatov returned to Chechenia in early August 1994 on an allegedly peacekeeping operation to prevent civil war, but mediation soon turned into an attempt to encourage co-operation between the opposition forces. He went back to Moscow on 3 December.)

10 August 1994. Russia imposes an air blockade.

11 August 1994. Dudayev orders a mobilization (of men) to counter a suspected Russian invasion.

2 September 1994. Heavy fighting breaks out.

5 September 1994. Labazanov's stronghold of Argun is taken by Dudayev's forces.

15 September 1994. Dudayev imposes martial law and a 10 p.m. to 6 a.m. curfew.

30 September 1994. Grozny airport comes under helicopter attack by opposition forces. Khasbulatov issues an ultimatum to Dudayev to resign or face an all-out attack on the capital, Grozny.

15 October 1994. Opposition forces attack Grozny.

25 November 1994. Opposition forces attack Grozny once again (and fail once again). Some of the Russians aiding the opposition are captured (the Russian government says they are mercenaries).

29 November 1994. Yeltsin issues an ultimatum. If there is no cease-fire within forty-eight hours Russia will intervene militarily and impose a state of emergency.

Unidentified planes (generally presumed to be Russian) bomb Grozny airport and a military airport in the capital.

30 November 1994. The military airport is again bombed.

1 December 1994. There is more bombing, but the deadline passes.

Yeltsin offers an amnesty to Chechens who put down their weapons.

2 December 1994. A visiting delegation from the Russian parliament requests an end to Russian bombing.

5 December 1994. Defence Minister Grachev admits that Russian planes did the bombing.

6 December 1994. Grachev and Dudayev meet. They agree that there will be no military solution to the problem and that the captured Russian troops will be released.

7 December 1994. Yeltsin's 'security council' says that 'all constitutional measures must be taken to disarm and liquidate illegal armed groupings.' Yeltsin tells the council that Russia's constitution and laws must be observed 'unwaveringly'.

There is a report of bombs falling.

9 December 1994. Yeltsin issues a decree entitled 'On measures to bring an end to the activities of illegal armed formations on the territory of the Chechen republic and in the zone of the Ossetian–Ingush conflict'. 'Activity aimed at violating the integrity of the Russian Federation, undermining the security of the state, creating armed formations or stirring up national or religious discord is prohibited and unlawful . . . The Russian Federation government . . . is instructed to use all means at the state's disposal to . . . disarm all illegal armed formations.'

11 December 1994. Russian forces invade Chechenia, but stop short of Grozny (negotiations were to take place the following day). They meet resistance in both Ingushetia and Dagestan.

Yeltsin says that 'the government's actions were prompted by the threat to the integrity of Russia and to the safety of its citizens both in Chechenia and elsewhere, and by the destabilization of the political and economic situation. Our goal is to find a political solution to the problems of a member of the Russian Federation, the Chechen republic, and to protect its citizens from armed extremism . . . I order all officials responsible for conducting measures to restore constitutional order in the Chechen republic not to use violence against the civilian population.'

The initial political reaction in Russia itself was split in ways which made strange bedfellows. Yegor Gaidar, Grigori Yavlinsky and Gennadi Zyuganov (the leader of the Communist Party) opposed the move. Sergei Kovalyov, member of the State Duma and human rights commissioner, was an especially vocal critic from the start. Supporters of the move included Vladimir Zhirinovsky, Foreign Minister Andrei Kozyrev (who resigned from his party, Russia's Choice, over the issue) and Boris Fyodorov (who later called for the dismissal of the government for incompetence; he opposed the use of violence against civilians and the use of conscripted servicemen). Alexander Solzhenitsyn thinks that only a third of Chechenia, the northern part, should remain within Russia.

McFaul argues that 'Yeltsin did not order his troops into Chechenia to save the Russian Federation. He moved against Chechenia to save his presidency' (McFaul 1995: 151). The December 1993 election, for example, convinced Yeltsin of the need to tap the nationalist and law-and-order vote (p. 151). Another factor was the personal interest of members of the 'party of war' exercising increasing influence over the president, e.g. Defence Minister Pavel Grachev (to deflect attention from corruption in the army) and Alexander Korzhakov (a nationalist and 'law and order' man in charge of Yeltsin's personal security and totally dependent on Yeltsin for his political power) (pp. 153–6).

12 December 1994. Russian forces inch forward to try to surround Grozny, meeting pockets of resistance.

13 December 1994. Advancing Russian forces meet stiff resistance.

A resolution of the State Duma declares 'the work of federal bodies of power with regard to a political settlement' of the Chechen crisis to be 'unsatisfactory', expressing 'serious concern . . . that the developing situation is beginning to threaten the vital interests and territorial integrity of the Russian Federation'. Chechenia is 'an inalienable part of the territory of the Russian Federation.' The deputies decide to 'advise the president and the government to use all political and legal means to end the armed confrontation in the Chechen republic'. The resolution was passed by 289 votes to four, with one abstention.

14 December 1994. The Chechen delegation walks out of the negotiations and Russia reminds Chechenia of the 15 December deadline for laying down their arms.

15 December 1994. Yeltsin announces a forty-eight-hour extension of the deadline (midnight Saturday).

16 December 1994. One of the commanders of the three Russian divisions (Major-General Ivan Babichev) refuses to continue fighting. He says that firing on civilians is unconstitutional.

18 December 1994. The deadline passes and Russia resumes bombing.

19 December 1994. The centre of Grozny is bombed, targets including the television tower.

20 December 1994. There is heavy fighting and Russia closes the borders with Georgia and Azerbaijan.

21 December 1994. There is heavy bombing of Grozny, targets including an oil refinery.

22 December 1994. Continued heavy bombing results in increasing civilian casualties. There are rumours of sackings and resignations in the army and of Grachev taking personal command of the conflict.

23 December 1994. Moscow claims that Grozny has been surrounded. (This proves to be untrue. Moscow has engaged in disinformation, e.g. the claim that the Chechens themselves, for propaganda purposes, have engaged in self-inflicted bombing.)

The State Duma passes a resolution (by 228 votes to thirty-eight with three abstentions) calling for an end to hostilities and a resumption of peace talks. Efforts to call for a vote of no confidence in the president fail. (Note that critics among military personnel include General Boris Gromov, a deputy defence minister and former commander of Soviet forces in Afghanistan, and General Alexander Lebed, commander of the Fourteenth Army in the Dniestre region. They both oppose a military solution.)

Yeltsin says that 'The first stage is coming to an end. We are going to look at when we can wind up the participation of the military and proceed to the second stage, forming administrative organs in the Chechen republic.' (Yeltsin spent much of the time in hospital owing to a minor nose operation.)

27 December 1994. In a television address Yeltsin says that: 'Russian soldiers are defending the unity of Russia . . . The Chechen republic is a part of the Russian Federation . . . Not a single territory has the right to secede from Russia . . . The regime in Grozny is illegal . . . there are neither authorities nor law there today . . . The regime set up in the republic has become a source of great criminal danger, above all for Russia . . . the longer the situation in the Chechen republic goes on the greater the destructive impact on Russia's stability. It has become one of the main internal threats to our state's security . . . the explosion of banditry on Chechen soil threatens our entire country . . . The first stage of solving the crisis has been fulfilled. The ring has tightened around Grozny. Legality and order will be restored on the territory of Chechenia . . . For the sake of preserving lives I have given an order to halt the bombing raids which can lead to casualties among the civilian population of Grozny.'

(The international community has generally seen the crisis as an internal Russian one, but there has been increasing criticism of the effects on civilians. Concern has also been expressed about unannounced Russian troop movements in the light of treaties on conventional forces.)

28 December 1994. There is bombing of the outskirts of Grozny and Russian forces escalate their assault on the city.

29 December 1994. Dudayev declares his 'readiness personally to head talks with the Russian side, at the level of Chernomyrdin.' He is willing to do so without preconditions (such as a withdrawal of Russian forces).

31 December 1994. There is an all-out assault on Grozny.

1 January 1995. Russian forces reach the centre of Grozny.

2 January 1995. Russian forces incur heavy losses on men and equipment as they are forced to withdraw from the centre of Grozny. (Prior to the invasion Defence Minister Grachev thought that a regiment of Soviet paratroops could take Grozny in 'two hours'. Military observers severely criticized the sending in of tanks unaccompanied by ground troops. The tanks were easily surrounded and destroyed. Moreover, the Russian troops were mainly inexperienced conscripts.)

3 January 1995. There is a renewed Russian assault on Grozny.

Forces led by Ruslan Labazanov attack Russian troops (*The Economist*, 7 January 1995, p. 30).

4 January 1995. Yeltsin orders Russian planes to stop bombing Grozny.

5 January 1995. Air raids continue, but it is not clear whether they are on Grozny itself or outside the city.

The EU delays signing an interim trade agreement with Russia (until 17 July 1995) as a form of protest.

6 January 1995. The 'security council' (currently comprising twelve members, excluding Yeltsin) resolves to carry on with the assault on Grozny. (There has been increasing concern about how Yeltsin, the security chiefs and a small number of presidential advisers have dominated policy-making. Among the main individuals were Defence Minister Pavel Grachev, Interior Minister Viktor Yerin, head of counter-intelligence Sergei Stepashin, Nationalities Minister Nikolai Yegorov and the head of the 'security council', Oleg Lobov. The influence of the chief of presidential security and Yeltsin's bodyguard since 1985, General Alexander Korzhakov, has caused particular disquiet in a more general sense, e.g. his attempts to prevent the liberalization of oil exports. The term 'party of war' was coined by the critics of the attack on the Chechen republic.)

Yeltsin demands 'absolutely clear information' about whether bombing raids have continued against his orders, since he says 'there is information' that they have.

Yeltsin is reported to have sacked the head of the Russian Television and Radio Company because of its open coverage of the crisis. (The latter actually remained at his post and it seems the order was revoked because of the adverse publicity.) The attempts to distort information and manipulate the media have caused increasing concern. But the resistance of much of the media, especially newspapers, to such pressure has been encouraging.)

President Clinton sends a letter to Yeltsin calling for a halt to the assault because of the number of civilian casualties.

7 January 1995. The bombing of Grozny from the air continues. Russian forces gradually move towards the centre with greater success owing to a change in tactics (intense shelling combined with the use of more experienced troops advancing from building to building and street to street). The presidential palace burns fiercely.

The first senior Russian casualty occurs when General Viktor Vorobyov is killed in a mortar attack (he was commander of the Interior Ministry special task force).

8 January 1995. Russian forces advance ever closer to the centre of Grozny.

9 January 1995. Chernomyrdin calls for a forty-eight-hour truce.

10 January 1995. There is only a brief lull in the fighting. The Chechens do not respond to an ultimatum to lay down their arms even with the inducement of an amnesty.

Yeltsin creates a five-strong inner circle (permanent members) of the 'security council', only these having voting rights (note, however, that the council is only a consultative body): existing 'security council' members Yeltsin (chairman), Chernomyrdin and Oleg Lobov (secretary) are joined by two new ones, Ivan Rybkin (speaker of the State Duma) and Vladimir Shumeiko (speaker of the Council of the Federation).

The other members of the 'security council' are Sergei Shakhrai (deputy prime minister), Pavel Grachev (defence minister), Viktor Yerin (minister of internal affairs), Andrei Kozyrev (foreign minister), Sergei Stepashin (director of the counter-intelligence service), Yevgeni Primakov (director of the Foreign Intelligence Service), Sergei Shoigu (minister of civil defence affairs, emergency situations and the elimination of the consequences of natural disasters) and Andrei Nikolayev (director of the Federal Border Service).

Grigori Yavlinsky, on a visit to the UK, calls for Yeltsin's resignation.

The Council of Europe suspends Russia's application for entry.

11 January 1995. There is an emergency meeting of the State Duma. Liberal factions fail in their attempt to introduce legislation preventing the president from using the military to resolve internal disputes. For example, Russia's Choice wanted to try to alter the constitution and give parliament greater powers.

Dudayev is interviewed in a location on the southern outskirts of Grozny: 'Only a peaceful solution is possible . . . Full or partial independence; it is a relative matter. Russia has interests in the Caucasus. But Russia cannot ignore our interests . . . All these issues, everything, can be settled in a day or an hour, with a stroke of a pen at the negotiating table . . . But winning militarily is impossible.'

Yeltsin assumes direct control of the General Staff (i.e. direct control of the army).

The inner circle of the 'security council' decides to disarm illegal armed groups belonging to commercial structures throughout Russia (i.e. private security forces).

12 January 1995. A fact-finding mission by OSCE is agreed.

Nikolai Fyodorov, the president of the Chuvash republic (Chuvashia), issues a decree allowing servicemen from the republic to refuse to fight in internal conflicts within Russia.

13 January 1995. The State Duma (sitting in emergency session) passes a non-binding resolution by 236 votes to one, urging the president and the government to 'take all measures to stop the combat action in the Chechen republic and create the conditions for a political settlement'.

15 January 1995. Despite a fierce onslaught Chechen defenders still control some buildings in the centre of Grozny, including the presidential palace.

16 January 1995. Chernomyrdin calls for an immediate cease-fire and for negotiations to start simultaneously.

Finance Minister Panskov is made a member of the 'security council'.

17 January 1995. After talks with Chernomyrdin Chechen representatives claim that a cease-fire has been agreed in principle for the following day.

Oleg Soskovets remains head of the task force co-ordinating the activity of federal bodies of power in restoring the economy and the social sphere in Chechenia (*CDSP*, 1995, vol. XLVII, no. 3, p. 23).

18 January 1995. Yeltsin rules out direct talks with Dudayev: 'We are ready for talks, but not for talks with Dudayev, who simply organized genocide against his own people.'

The fierce Russian assault on Grozny continues.

19 January 1995. The presidential palace falls to Russian troops.

Yeltsin declares that 'The military stage of restoring the Russian constitution in the Chechen republic is effectively complete.'

It is rumoured that three generals (deputy defence ministers) critical of the Chechen policy have been sacked, namely Boris Gromov, Georgi Kondratiev and Viktor Minorov (see the entry for 9 February 1995). General Eduard Vorobyev, first deputy commander of land forces, is transferred to the army reserves. (Grachev ordered him to tender his resignation on 17 December 1994 after declaring his troops unprepared for the assault on the Chechen republic. 'I have one ready' he is said to have replied.) (It was announced on 13 February 1995 that Gromov had been demoted to chief military adviser to the Foreign Ministry.)

20 January 1995. The fighting continues in other parts of Grozny.

UN relief supplies reach Chechen refugees after three weeks' delay due to Russian bureaucracy.

21 January 1995. Fighting continues in other parts of Grozny and increasingly affects smaller surrounding towns.

23 January 1995. A meeting of EU foreign ministers 'deplores the serious violations of human rights and international humanitarian law which are still occurring there'.

25 January 1995. The 'security council' congratulates Defence Minister Grachev 'for the completion of military operations in the conflict zone.'

It is announced that Interior Ministry troops will begin to play the primary role in Chechenia.

27 January 1995. Nikolai Yegorov is replaced as co-ordinator of the Chechen campaign ('for health reasons') by Nikolai Semyanov.

An OSCE fact-finding mission leaves Moscow for the war zone.

30 January 1995. The mission reports on its visit to Grozny: 'disproportionate and indiscriminate force' used by Russian forces; 'unbelievable devastation'; violations of human rights on both sides; a cease-fire recommended, to enable aid to get through, civilians to be evacuated and corpses to be cleared from the streets.

1 February 1995. An arrest warrant is issued for Dudayav, the charges including treason.

4 February 1995. The Moscow-backed Provisional Council (led by Umar Avturkhanov) issues a critical statement. It accuses Russian forces of 'Barbaric, senseless and cruel bombardments and shellings of the living quarters of Grozny . . . It is stated that there are cases of looting, robbery, unmotivated killings of civilian population. These practices provoked dozens of Chechens who were hitherto loyal to federal bodies of power to take up arms.'

The Chechens shoot down a Russian fighter bomber, the first.

7 February 1995. The Chechens prepare to retreat from Grozny.

8 February 1995. The Chechens are to move their headquarters from Grozny.

9 February 1995. Yeltsin sacks two deputy defence ministers, General Georgi Kondratiev (a critic of the Chechen policy) and General Matvei Burlakov (the target of a corruption investigation).

12 February 1995. The Chechens claim to have blown up a former Soviet missile launching site, killing 250 Russian soldiers.

13 February 1995. A (two-day) partial cease-fire is agreed (involving heavy weapons) in talks brokered by Ingushetia. (The cease-fire was being repeatedly broken within hours.)

15 February 1995. A two-day (complete) cease-fire is agreed. (There were frequent violations.)

16 February 1995. Yeltsin commented on the Chechen crisis in his 'state of the nation' speech to a joint session of parliament: 'Abcesses like the Medellin cartel in Colombia, the "golden triangle" of South East Asia and the criminal dictatorship of Chechenia do not heal themselves . . . The state can and must use the force of its authority to preserve sovereignty, independence and integrity. But our state turned out to be unprepared for effective military action. This is the cause of casualties, here lie the roots of the violations of the rights of citizens in the course of the military operations . . . failures, setbacks and mistakes in command are a painful blow to patriotic and civic feelings . . . in 1995 decisive measures must be taken to reorganize the armed forces.'

17 February 1995. A day-to-day extension to the cease-fire is agreed.

19 February 1995. The cease-fire ends and the Russian commander says that it will not be extended.

21 February 1995. Russian forces cut off the last road into Grozny.

23 February 1995. On Defenders of the Fatherland Day (national army day) Yeltsin says that 'The army is starting to disintegrate a bit . . . We have to be tough and firm, so military people believe that there will be reforms.' He promises to help fund the reforms.

25 February 1995. An accidental blast kills twenty-five Russian servicemen.

6 March 1995. The Russian military say they have full control of Grozny.

9 March 1995. Yeltsin accepts in principle a permanent OSCE mission in Chechenia, but the exact terms have not been decided.

The Dudayav regime places Chechenia on a war footing and introduces *shariah* law.

10 March 1995. The State Duma sacks the parliamentary human rights commissioner Sergei Kovalyov. (He has been criticized in particular for advocating foreign observers in Chechenia; he still retains the presidential position.)

14 March 1995. Dzhokhar Dudayev, in a published article, calls for (1) a real and unconditional cease-fire monitored by international observers, (2) direct negotiations at any mutually agreed level under the auspices of international mediators and (3) the holding of presidential and parliamentary elections in 1995 under international supervision. 'We are not secessionists. We are not demanding complete independence. We are not criminals. Nor did we start this war' (*IHT*, 14 March 1995, p. 8).

23 March 1995. Russian forces claim that the town of Argun (east of Grozny) has fallen and that the Chechens have moved their military headquarters from Shali (south-east of Grozny); some Chechen fighters remain in Shali, their self-declared capital.

29 March 1995. It is announced that Russian troops have surrounded Shali and Gudermes (east of Grozny and second in size only to the capital).

US Secretary of State Warren Christopher describes the assault on Chechenia as 'tragically wrong.' He warns that 'the evaluation of Russia's participation in Western institutions will be affected by the world's judgement' of the military campaign.

30 March 1995. Gudermes falls to the Russian forces.

31 March 1995. Shali falls.

9 April 1995. Samashki falls. (Russian troops are accused of massacring civilians.)

10 April 1995. Two more villages to the west of Grozny fall.

14 April 1995. A Russian attack on Bamut (south-west of Grozny) is repulsed.

Anatoli Kulikov, the commander of Russian forces since early February, is replaced by Mikhail Yegorov.

18 April 1995. Bamut falls.

19 April 1995. Russian forces withdraw from Bamut after being shelled by Chechen forces in surrounding hills.

27 April 1995. Yeltsin announces a cease-fire until 12 May because of the fiftieth anniversary of the defeat of Nazi Germany (celebrated on 9 May). (The clashes continued.)

29 April 1995. Dudayev rejects the cease-fire.

1 May 1995. Chechens launch an attack on Russian forces in Grozny.

Russia imposes a two-month dusk-to-dawn curfew on the region.

22 May 1995. It is announced that direct talks between Dudayav and the Russian government will be held under the auspices of OSCE, starting on 25 May in Grozny.

23 May 1995. It is revealed that twenty-five Russian soldiers captured by the Chechens have been surgically castrated.

25 May 1995. Talks (without Dudayev in person) begin and end without agreement, but further talks are agreed in principle.

4 June 1995. Russian forces capture the Chechen headquarters town of Vedeno in the south-east.

13 June 1995. Russian forces capture Shatoi (south of Grozny and the last major Chechen stronghold).

14 June 1995. Chechen forces led by Shamil Basayev attack the town of Budyonnovsk, north of the Chechen border in the Stavropol region of Russia. There is significant loss of life and many hostages are held in a hospital. The Chechens demand the withdrawal of Russian forces from Chechenia.

17 June 1995. Attempts by Russian forces to storm the hospital fail. (Yeltsin was in Canada attending the G7 summit; apparently he ordered the attack before he left on 16 June.)

18 June 1995. Prime Minister Chernomyrdin offers a cease-fire in Chechenia, fresh talks with the Dudayev administration and safe passage for the Chechens in exchange for the release of the hostages.

19 June 1995. The Chechens are allowed to leave accompanied by Russian 'volunteers' to ensure their safe passage to Chechenia.

Fresh talks begin in Grozny.

20 June 1995. The 'volunteers' are released when the Chechens return home.

The talks result in a three-day cease-fire. According to OSCE, the framework agreement also 'foresees an end to military activity, the mutual release of detained people, an end to terrorist acts and diversions, disarmament and the gradual withdrawal of troops.'

21 June 1995. The State Duma passes a vote of no confidence in the government by 241 to seventy-two, with twenty abstentions.

30 June 1995. Yeltsin accepts the offers to resign of Viktor Yerin (interior), Sergei Stepashin (security), Nikolai Yegorov (nationalities) and Yevgeni Kuznetsov (governor of the Stavropol region), but not those of Pavel Grachev (defence), Oleg Lobov (secretary of the 'security council') and Alexei Ilyushenko (acting procurator-general).

1 July 1995. The State Duma fails to pass a vote of no confidence in the government. Only 193 voted for (at least 226 were needed), while 117 voted against and there were forty-eight abstentions.

4 July 1995. Yeltsin issues a decree allowing a permanent Russian armed presence in Chechenia.

5 July 1995. The new nationalities minister is Vyacheslav Mikhailov and Viktor Yerin is appointed deputy director of the Foreign Intelligence Service.

6 July 1995. Anatoli Kulikov, commander of Russian forces in Chechenia, becomes interior minister.

12 July 1995. A move to set up a committee to consider the impeachment of Yeltsin receives only 168 votes (226 were needed).

24 July 1995. The new head of the Federal Security Directorate is Mikhail Barsukov, promoted from being head of the Kremlin's security organization (the Main Security Directorate). (Alexander Korzhakov was subsequently promoted to lieutenant-general and became head of the Kremlin's security organization.)

30 July 1995. A cease-fire agreement is signed. Forces are to be disengaged, prisoners are to be exchanged, Chechen help is to be given in the search for those responsible for the Budyonnovsk crisis, and gradual disarmament is to be achieved. (The Chechen fighters are to be gradually disarmed, except for twenty-five-member 'self-defence' units, and only two Russian brigades are to remain ultimately, one provided by the regular army and one by the Interior Ministry.) (At first Dudayev denounced the agreement, but then accepted it.)

31 July 1995. The Constitutional Court rules that the 9 December 1994 presidential decree authorizing the use of force against 'illegal armed units' was constitutional (despite the fact that no state of emergency had been declared).

3 August 1995. A pre-recorded speech by Yeltsin is shown on television.

7 August 1995. Yeltsin returns to work.

25 August 1995. Oleg Lobov is made Yeltsin's personal representative in Chechenia.

MILITARY AFFAIRS, DISARMAMENT AGREEMENTS AND PARTNERSHIP FOR PEACE

Lambeth (1995: 90) states that more than 75 per cent of eligible Russian youths now routinely evade conscription. He argues that the Russian military have largely remained above politics and helped to stabilize the nation amid reforms. Other sources say that less than 20 per cent of draft-age youths are joining up (Bruce Clark, *FT*, Survey, 10 April 1995, p. xiii) and that 84 per cent of eligible conscripts evaded military service in 1994 compared with 48 per cent in 1989 (including legal exemptions) (John Thornhill, *FT*, 2 May 1995, p. 3).

The Nuclear Non-proliferation Treaty (NNPT) was signed in 1968 and came into effect in 1970.

28 February 1993. Yeltsin suggests that 'the moment has come for the UN to accord Russia special powers to guarantee peace and stability in the former Soviet Union.' (On 4 March 1993 Yeltsin stressed that security coverage should be extended only to those countries requesting it.)

22 April 1993. The office of the prosecutor-general says that Defence Minister Grachev and others are possibly implicated in 'illegal deals' involving the sale of military property in East Germany. Gennadi Burbulis is to be questioned about a different corruption case.

4 July 1993. President Clinton announces an extension (until the end of September 1994) of the ban on the testing of nuclear weapons, provided other countries do the same.

27 July 1993. Yeltsin dismisses Viktor Barannikov (security minister) for 'personal violations of ethical norms [allegedly helping relatives to take trips abroad] as well as serious flaws in his work, including the leadership of the border guard troops attached to the ministry.' (He had been reprimanded the previous day over the loss of Russian soldiers guarding Tajikistan's border with Afghanistan. Note the entry for 21 March 1993.) Barannikov's successor was Nikolai Golushko.

28 July 1993. The praesidium of the Supreme Soviet declares the dismissal of Barannikov to have 'no legal force'; it is claimed that under a constitutional amendment adopted in December 1992 only parliament may dismiss the ministers of security, defence and foreign affairs.

8 September 1993. Russia and the USA agree to increase military co-operation, including joint military exercises (probably in both countries and in Germany) for UN peacekeeping purposes.

2 November 1993. Russia announces a new military doctrine: (1) a defensive posture is adopted, with no country considered to be an adversary; (2) the 'no first use' of nuclear weapons pledge is abandoned (first made in 1982 by Brezhnev for generally perceived propaganda purposes rather than as a credible policy); (3) no reference is made to the final desired size of the armed forces (previously set at 1.5 million); (4) regional conflicts are considered the main danger and so the priority will be rapid deployment forces; (5) the use of the armed forces is permitted when Russia's security is threatened from within by nationalist or separatist forces, when the constitutional order is in danger of being undermined by force, when, for example, nuclear or chemical installations are attacked, or against illegal armed groups; (6) in the interests of Russia and of other CIS members (and by mutual consent) there may be cases where Russian forces and equipment are based outside Russia; (7) the armed forces may undertake peacekeeping operations for the UN or as a result of bilateral or multilateral deals.

29 December 1993. Defence Minister Grachev thinks that the target size of the armed forces should be 2.1 million instead of 1.5 million: 'We plan to have 2.1 million by the end of 1994 [no more than 150,000 men would go during 1994]. We'll keep the army at about that size, not at 1.5 million.' (The Soviet armed forces reached a peak of nearly 5 million in 1988.)

10–11 January 1994. The Partnership for Peace policy is formally agreed at the Nato summit.

18 January 1994. Foreign Minister Kozyrev, referring to the former Soviet Union, says that 'We should not withdraw from those regions which have been a sphere of Russian influence for centuries . . . Although military domination is not in Moscow's interests, it would be dangerous to create a vacuum, because it might be filled by unfriendly forces.' (The significance of the statement was played down, with Kozyrev allegedly talking in the broadest possible terms, in the light of great concern expressed in the West and the Baltic States in particular.) (An estimated 200,000 Russian troops are stationed abroad: Celestine Bohlen, *IHT*, 26 January 1994, p. 1.)

25 January 1994. The UN Conference on Disarmament begins to discuss a nuclear test ban treaty.

15–16 February 1994. On the first day of a two-day visit to Russia by the British prime minister, John Major, the two countries agree to stop targeting each other with nuclear missiles from May 1994. On the second day a future state visit to Russia by Queen Elizabeth II is announced (the first by a reigning British monarch since 1908).

22 February 1994. A senior CIA officer (Aldrich Ames) is arrested in the USA on a charge of spying since 1985 for the former Soviet Union and Russia.

24 February 1994. Yeltsin delivers his state-of-the-nation speech to a joint session of parliament. The theme is the need to strengthen Russian statehood both (1) at home, e.g. to tackle crime and to regulate the market: 'without a strong, effective state we cannot overcome the economic crisis or set up a true market system'; and (2) in foreign affairs, e.g. to defend the interests of ethnic Russians in the 'near abroad', 'The main task of our foreign policy is the consistent advancement of Russia's national interests.' 'Russia is against widening Nato by admitting various countries on the European continent and not Russia'.

2 March 1994. Russia announces its intention of signing a Partnership for Peace agreement with Nato.

15 March 1994. President Clinton extends the US moratorium on nuclear weapon testing for a further year (to September 1995).

6 April 1994. Yeltsin approves the military's plans to negotiate for the establishment of about thirty permanent bases (some new) in the 'near abroad'. (There was great confusion. For example, Russia had to make clear that the Skrunda radar base in Latvia was not one of them, while Foreign Minister Andrei Kozyrev was not even consulted about the decree.)

18 May 1994. Nato offers Russia a 'special' ('enhanced') partnership or relationship. (There is much concern about the use of terminology.)

25 May 1994. The FBI (USA) is to set up its first permanent office in Moscow. (It is concerned about the international links between criminal gangs and especially the danger of illegal sales of nuclear material.) (The office, in the US embassy, was opened on 4 July by FBI chief Louis Freeh. The following day he signed a co-operation agreement.)

30 May 1994. It is announced that Russia and the USA are no longer targeting each other with long-range nuclear missiles.

9 June 1994. Nato offers Russia an 'extensive and far-reaching individual partnership programme, corresponding to its size, importance, capabilities and willingness to contribute.' Nato also calls for relations to be developed 'in appropriate areas' outside the Partnership for Peace programme, e.g. nuclear safety and non-proliferation (this is what is known as 'sixteen plus one'). (Note that there was no mention of a 'special' partnership/relationship and any veto over Nato decisions was ruled out. On 24 May Defence Minister Grachev said that Russia would join the programme, although he did not say when. He hinted at a veto and proposed subordination of Nato, Russia and the CIS to the CSCE.)

22 June 1994. Russia becomes the twenty-first signatory of the Partnership for Peace with Nato. Russia and Nato also agree to (but do not actually sign) a separate document ('summary of conclusions'), involving 'enhanced dialogue' on broader political and security matters (such as nuclear disarmament and non-proliferation). The document establishes the following: (1) 'the development of a far-reaching co-operative Nato–Russia relationship, both inside and outside Partnership for Peace'; (2) recognition of Russia as 'a major European, international and nuclear power'; (3) information-sharing, political consultations and security co-operation. (Other countries have simply signed the Partnership for Peace and only later begun to refine their links with Nato.)

Foreign Minister Kozyrev says that 'we do not preclude the possibility that we or other countries should join Nato, but there should be no haste.'

21 August 1994. Theo Waigel, the German finance minister, says that 'Our financial aid to Russia will depend on Moscow's willingness to co-operate with us in the fight against the international smuggling of nuclear materials. I hope other industrialized countries will align themselves with us.'

Since May 1994 Germany had been the scene of four such incidents, the most serious on 10 August (although there was later to be an inquiry into allegations that the German security services themselves had set it up; three smugglers were given prison sentences on 17 July 1995, but the German judge expressed concern at the role of a paid agent of German intelligence in luring the smugglers). The sources and significance of these nuclear materials were the subject of considerable debate, but on 22 August German and Russian negotiators came to a preliminary agreement to co-operate. On 24 February 1995 the Russian Interior Ministry reported that 80 per cent of storage sites lacked basic equipment at their gates for detecting radioactive materials.

2 September 1994. Russian and US troops begin (nine-day) joint exercises in Russia for UN peacekeeping purposes.

President Jiang Jemin of China begins a four-day visit (the first by a head of state since Mao in 1957). Presidents Yeltsin and Jiang Jemin agree on the following: Russia and China to cease targeting each other with strategic nuclear weapons; not to use force against each other; to reduce the number of troops stationed along the border; the disputed western part of the border is finally settled; to enhance trade and economic co-operation in general.

16 September 1994. A presidential decree lays down stricter controls on nuclear materials.

26 September 1994. In an address to the UN General Assembly President Yeltsin proposes that the five major nuclear powers should sign a new treaty on: (1) stopping the production of enriched materials for nuclear weapons (and banning the reuse of such materials); (2) reducing the number of nuclear warheads and carriers; and (3) a permanent test ban. He also supports an extension of the Nuclear Non-proliferation Treaty. (Note that the Russian parliament has yet to ratify the Start 2 treaty.)

27–28 September 1994. Presidents Clinton and Yeltsin hold a summit meeting in the USA. They agree to speed up the timetable of the Start 2 treaty, specifically to start dismantling the warheads as soon as the agreement has been ratified by both countries 'instead of taking the nine years allowed.' (Note that Russia's ratification of Start 1 depends on Ukraine signing the NNPT.)

20 October 1994. The funeral takes place of the *Moskovsky Komsomolets* journalist Dmitri Kholodov. He was killed (on 17 October) by a bomb in a briefcase he thought contained information on corruption (such as the illegal sale of equipment) in the Western Group of Forces (that part of the army formerly in East Germany). He was due to appear at a parliamentary hearing.

25 October 1994. Defence Minister Grachev announces plans to reduce the army from 2.3 million (at the start of 1994) to 1.9 million by January 1995 and 1.7 million by the end of 1995.

1 November 1994. Yeltsin dismisses First Deputy Defence Minister Matvei Burlakov 'in connection with the current investigations' into corruption in the armed forces. (Burlakov had been commander of the Western Group of Forces and was appointed first deputy on 23 August 1994.)

14 November 1994. Yeltsin declares that the army should be reduced in size to 1,917,400 by 1 January 1995, 1.7 million by 1 January 1996 and, ultimately, 1.5 million.

1 December 1994. Kozyrev objects to the Partnership for Peace proposals and refuses to finalize plans for military co-operation. (He was annoyed by Nato's proposals for enlargement, specifically US pressure to speed up the process of including East European countries. Nato set up a commission to define the conditions of entry and to report within a year.)

4 December 1994. Yeltsin speaks against Nato's encroachment on Eastern Europe.

5–6 December 1994. At the CSCE conference in Budapest Yeltsin again criticized Nato: 'Europe is in danger of plunging into a cold peace.'

16 February 1995. In his state-of-the-nation speech Yeltsin talked of: 'Upholding Russia's position within the framework of OSCE and increasing the role of this organization in the interests of all its members . . . Russia does not claim a right to "veto" the entry of new members into Nato, but it will not agree to the hasty expansion of that alliance either . . . The creation of a stable security mechanism for the twenty-first century is at the centre of political interaction with the European states. That mechanism could rely on existing organizations and institutions, above all OSCE's potential and possibilities' (*CDSP*, 1995, vol. XLVII, no. 8, p. 14).

16 March 1995. Yeltsin says 'We are against a sudden, accelerated, large-scale expansion of Nato.'

20 March 1995. Kozyrev, on Nato, asks, 'Why rush things if we run the risk of creating new lines of division?' Nato 'should be replaced by a new model based on comprehensive security . . . The gap between Nato's very active moves to study potential enlargement and its passive attitude in developing this new model of comprehensive security is a very wide one and it could be dangerous.'

3 April 1995. The USA fails to change Russia's plans to sell light-water nuclear reactors to Iran. (The USA fears that this will help Iran develop nuclear weapons.)

Defence Minister Grachev warns that if Nato continues its 'rush to expand to the east' Russia may take 'counter-measures', such as refusing to abide by the 1990 Conventional Forces in Europe (CFE) Treaty and seeking closer co-operation with other CIS countries.

16 April 1995. Grachev, referring to Chechenia, says that 'only when conditions are stable can Russia fulfil all the conditions of the CFE treaty'.

30 April 1995. Yeltsin signs a decree extending military service from eighteen months to two years. (The shorter period was introduced in

1993.) In addition, only those students doing postgraduate scientific work or graduates immediately starting work in state organizations will be allowed to defer military service.

10 May 1995. At the summit meeting between Yeltsin and Clinton Russia agrees to subject the proposed sale of nuclear reactors to Iran to a joint Russia–USA commission (in order to ensure that 'only the peaceful part remains') and to cancel a separate agreement involving a gas centrifuge plant (used for enriching uranium). Yeltsin also promises to activate membership of the Partnership for Peace scheme by the end of May.

11 May 1995. The Nuclear Non-proliferation Treaty is extended indefinitely.

31 May 1995. Russia agrees (1) to join the Partnership for Peace and (2) to a second document involving a 'special relationship' with Nato (arrangements for an 'enhanced dialogue' over matters such as nuclear proliferation and peacekeeping). But Andrei Kozyrev still objects to Nato's ideas on expansion in Eastern Europe.

General Lebed offers his resignation as commander of the Fourteenth Army (in the Dniestre region of Moldova). (Yeltsin rejected his resignation on 6 June, even though Grachev had accepted it. But on 14 June Yeltsin too accepted Lebed's resignation.)

11 August 1995. President Clinton endorses a permanent end to the testing by the USA of all nuclear weapons.

8 September 1995. Yeltsin says that the bombing of the Bosnian Serbs 'is the first sign of what might happen when Nato comes right up to the borders of the Russian Federation'. When this happens 'you can say that there will be two military blocs and there will be a return to what we had before'. 'Those who insist on the expansion of Nato are making a major political mistake. The flames of war could ignite across the whole of Europe.' If Nato were to expand, Russia would 'immediately establish constructive ties with all ex-Soviet republics and form a bloc'.

A CHRONOLOGY OF EVENTS PRIOR TO THE DISSOLUTION OF PARLIAMENT ON 21 SEPTEMBER 1993

9 February 1993. Yeltsin appears to be willing to call off the April referendum. He calls for early elections (spring 1994 for parliament and spring 1995 for the presidency) and a one-year moratorium on political conflict. (He is concerned that a referendum could prove to be politically destabilizing. There may be less than the minimum required 50 per cent turnout, he may not get the minimum 50 per cent number of 'yes' votes and many regions may refuse to participate at all.)

11 February 1993. Yeltsin threatens to hold the referendum unless agreement is reached with parliament.

12 February 1993. The Constitutional Court rules that the 28 October 1992 presidential decree outlawing the National Salvation Front was unconstitutional. (On 14 February a congress was held in Moscow to reconstitute the Communist Party, with some of the coup leaders in attendance.)

16 February 1993. Yeltsin and Khasbulatov (speaker of parliament) agree to call a special session of the Congress of People's Deputies to ratify a 'constitutional agreement' (defining the powers of the executive and the legislature) that teams appointed by the government and parliament will attempt to draw up within ten days. The joint commission of experts will be headed by First Deputy Prime Minister Vladimir Shumeiko and First Deputy Speaker of Parliament Nikolai Ryabov. The government lets it be known that the referendum will go ahead if no agreement is reached.

19 February 1993. Yeltsin, through a spokesman, calls on parliament to dismiss Khasbulatov.

25 February 1993. The first Clinton–Yeltsin summit is set for 3-4 April 1993 in Vancouver. (Note the timing, shortly before the 11 April referendum.)

2 March 1993. Yeltsin talks of a 'final option' if the compromise negotiations fail.

3 March 1993. Senior army commanders urge Yeltsin to take 'resolute measures' to end the political crisis.

5 March 1993. The Supreme Soviet votes against Yeltsin's power-sharing proposals and convenes an emergency session of the Congress of People's Deputies starting on 10 March.

6 March 1993. Yeltsin offers to compromise.

7 March 1993. Yeltsin vows to go ahead with the referendum if the Congress of People's Deputies rejects his proposals.

10–13 March 1993. The eighth (and special) session of the Congress of People's Deputies takes place. It proved to be a very acrimonious session and ended with no agreement. Yeltsin attended but did not speak on the first day, walked out on the second day, led the government walk-out on the third day, and did not even attend the fourth and final day. He failed to persuade the Congress to compromise on political power sharing.

The Congress cancelled the 11 April referendum and reinstated its power to suspend any presidential decree deemed unconstitutional (pending a decision by the Constitutional Court) and to dismiss the president should he act unconstitutionally. The only concessions were made to the government. Although Prime Minister Chernomyrdin spoke in favour of a strong presidency and of continuing the economic reform process, he thanked the Congress for the following concessions: the government was empowered directly to initiate legislation and the heads of the central bank, the Federal Property Fund, the State Pension Fund and the statistical service could sit in on cabinet meetings (though still remaining responsible to parliament).

The vagueness of the (much amended) 1978 constitution and the general lack of clarity about decision-making powers left the status of presidential decrees and the previously called-for referendum in the air. (The Congress argued that even a million signatures could not override its power over a referendum.) Yeltsin vowed to refer question of the referendum to the Constitutional Court and to hold at least a (non-binding) plebiscite. He would lay two questions before the people on 25 April 1993, namely whether they would support a strong presidency and the private ownership of land.

15 March 1993. Yeltsin issues the following statement via his spokesman: 'Attempts are being made to concentrate all power in the hands of the soviets [councils], to restore the levers of power to the communist *nomenklatura* and to undo the achievements of August 1991.'

16 March 1993. During a visit by President Mitterrand of France, Yeltsin warns that the resurgence of communist forces poses an 'imminent danger'. Yeltsin stresses the need for Western aid: 'We cannot wait for Tokyo [the G7 meeting] in June or July. It may prove too late.'

20 March 1993. In a television address to the nation Yeltsin announces that he has that day signed a Decree on Special Rule pending the Resolution of the Crisis of Power. On 25 April 1993 there will a popular 'vote of confidence' in the president and vice-president. (The published version confined the vote to the president, Rutskoi having refused to sign the decree.) The nation will also vote on the draft of a new constitution and a draft law on elections to a new federal parliament (followed by fresh parliamentary elections if it is passed). The Congress and the Supreme Soviet may still operate but may not overturn presidential decrees. Yeltsin later issues a decree renaming the Kremlin guard as the presidential guard and puts it under presidential control.

21 March 1993. The Supreme Soviet votes to ask the Constitutional Court for a ruling on the president's actions. Vice-President Alexander Rutskoi and Security Council Secretary Yuri Skokov refuse to sign the decree and the chairman of the Constitutional Court, Valery Zorkin, blunders by speaking of an 'attempted coup' before even consulting the other twelve members of the court. But Yeltsin is supported by the government, whose statement speaks of 'the efforts of the democratically elected president to prevent anarchy, chaos, political confrontation, separatism, nationalism and crime'. The government's statement is signed by the ministers of defence (Pavel Grachev, who constantly stresses the neutrality of the army), security (Viktor Barannikov) and the interior (Viktor Yerin), who pledge loyalty to the 'principles of the constitution'. The Western governments back Yeltsin.

22 March 1993. Yeltsin says that he is placing television, radio and the newspapers under presidential protection in order to ensure their freedom, thwarting any attempt by parliament to subject the mass media to its control. Yeltsin asks the Interior Ministry to guarantee the security of the premises. Justice Minister Nikolai Fyodorov resigns, but Prime Minister Chernomyrdin says that 'no reforms, not even the normal functioning of the economy, is possible unless the political crisis is halted'.

23 March 1993. Yeltsin signs another decree threatening to dismiss local officials who do not carry out decrees.

The Constitutional Court (established by parliament in November 1991), although it had not actually seen the presidential decrees, decided by nine votes to three that Yeltsin had violated a number of provisions of the constitution and the federal treaty. But there was no ruling on impeachment. (It was reported that a phrase explicitly calling Yeltsin's actions impeachable had been removed before the findings were published.) The court also conceded that the president could ask for a popular vote, but only on the question of trust in himself (and not, for example, on the question of where power should lie). The preamble to the findings also accepted the need to end the crisis over the division of power, to continue political and economic reform and to safeguard the unity and integrity of the country.

Khasbulatov said that 'there is every ground for impeachment . . . We face a direct attempt at a *coup d'état*.' (Yeltsin had already indicated that he would ignore an impeachment vote; a successful one requires a two-thirds majority vote of the 1,033 deputies of the Congress of People's Deputies; the vice-president would take over for three months, after which a fresh election would be held.)

24 March 1993. Yeltsin causes a stir when he actually publishes the final version of his decree. It contains no reference to 'special rule' and accepts the Constitutional Court as arbiter of the constitutionality of presidential decrees. The decree refers to 'urgent measures . . . aimed at stabilizing the situation and providing conditions for economic reform'. There are brief talks between the two sides, but no agreement is reached (Khasbulatov suggested things like early elections and cabinet changes, but rejected a national vote). The Supreme Soviet approves another extraordinary session of the Congress of People's Deputies.

25 March 1993. Khasbulatov says, 'I am not a supporter of impeachment.' (By then it was clear that the required 689 votes were not attainable.) He suggests a coalition government and simultaneous presidential and parliamentary elections.

26–29 March 1993. The ninth (and special) session of the Congress of People's Deputies takes place.

Yeltsin attended and in his speech on the opening day insisted on a popular vote of confidence in himself and on a new constitution. He challenged the Congress to submit itself to a popular vote. Yeltsin promised that henceforth reforms would have 'a strong social orientation'. Economics Minister Andrei Nechayev was dismissed (Andrei Shapovaliants was later named acting minister) and Deputy Prime Minister Boris Saltykov was demoted to minister of science and technology. Vasily Barchuk lost his

Ministry of Finance to the strengthened Boris Fyodorov. Yeltsin invited names of candidates for government posts. Valery Zorkin, chairman of the Constitutional Court, warned that any attempt to impeach the president could have catastrophic consequences and called for fresh presidential and parliamentary elections (based on a new bicameral parliament). Rutskoi supported a plebiscite. Yeltsin gained general support from republic and regional leaders.

On 27 March, the second day of the Congress, not enough votes were cast even to get impeachment on the agenda. But the compromise proposals presented to the Congress by Yeltsin and Khasbulatov the following day provoked a violent reaction from a Congress generally unwilling to bring about its own dissolution. The proposals were as follows: there would be no popular vote in April and early elections would be held in November 1993 for both the presidency and a new two-chamber parliament (although deputies would receive their salaries and privileges until their mandate expired in 1995). In angry response the Congress agreed to vote not only on the impeachment of the president but also on the dismissal of the speaker. But the impeachment motion was defeated, with 617 votes for (689 were needed) and 268 against. The vote of no confidence in Khasbulatov was also defeated; only a simple majority was needed (517), but there were just 339 votes in favour and 558 against. The Congress did vote (537 to 263) to place the state radio and television stations under parliamentary control and to disband the Federal Information Centre (which oversees state media and is headed by a Yeltsin appointee, Mikhail Poltoranin). Yeltsin's response was to carry on with plans for a popular vote of confidence in April. He also signed decrees introducing measures designed to protect the weakest segments of society, such as doubling the minimum monthly wage to 4,500 roubles, raising student grants and setting up special, subsidized shops for poor people. The military also benefited (e.g. better housing), as did health workers, and regional governments were given the right to freeze the prices of basic goods and services, although at their own expense. (Yeltsin also reimposed a state of emergency in parts of North Ossetia and Ingushetia.) (The following day a decree promised to guarantee people's savings.)

The final day of the Congress saw bitter denunciations of Yeltsin (who did not attend) and no resolution of the crisis. An approved resolution accused the president of 'serious violations' of the constitution and said that he 'bore personal responsibility for the increasing confrontation between the branches of authority and different sections of society'. The Congress called for a coalition government and the dismissal of the president's representatives in the regions. The Constitutional Court was asked to judge the legality of the president's recent decrees and declared them null and void pending a decision. Congress also asked the court to investigate whether a speech made by Yeltsin at a public rally constituted grounds for impeachment (he said, for example, that he would ignore the decisions of Congress). The Congress did accept a referendum on 25 April, but four questions were to be put to the people: 'Do you have confidence in the President of the Russian Federation, B. N. Yeltsin?'; 'Do you approve of the socio-economic policy carried out by the President of the Russian Federation and the government of the Russian Federation since 1992?'; 'Do you consider it necessary to hold an early election for the presidency of the Russian Federation?'; 'Do you consider it necessary to hold early elections for the People's Deputies of the Russian Federation?' No specific date was set for either election, but it was laid down that to be accepted each of the four questions had to gain 50 per cent of the votes of all eligible voters (i.e. not just 50 per cent of those who actually cast ballots).

1 April 1993. Yeltsin accepts the Congress's referendum but challenges the '50 per cent of eligible voters' rule in the Constitutional Court.

5 April 1993. Yeltsin asks the Russian people to say 'yes' to all four questions in the referendum.

6 April 1993. Vice-President Alexander Rutskoi says that 'If the situation is not changed in the next two or three months, we shall get something between civil war and dictatorship.' He advocates a government reshuffle and says that there is a need to revive the centrally planned economy in the next six months in order to avert total collapse.

9 April 1993. Yeltsin repeals the decree doubling petrol prices and the rents of state apartments in the big cities.

14 April 1993. The trial of twelve of the leaders of the August 1991 coup attempt begins. They are all charged with 'treason against the motherland' ('betraying the native land in the form of a conspiracy to seize power') and five are also charged with exceeding their legal authority. Alexei Tizyakov falls ill and two days later the trial is suspended. On 19 May 1993 the three presiding (military) judges of the Supreme Court rule that the prosecuting team should be dismissed and the matter referred to the Supreme Soviet. The prosecutor-general and his deputy (although not actually part of the prosecuting team) had earlier written and published a book (*The Kremlin Conspiracy*) in which they described the defendants as 'criminal'. On 7 September 1993 the Constitutional Court ruled that Tizyakov could be tried separately and the prosecuting team should remain in place.

15 April 1993. Yeltsin appoints Oleg Lobov as first deputy prime minister in charge of the economy. Lobov has close links with industry and believes in increased state intervention (such as more price controls and increased centralized investment). He is, in theory at least, senior to Fyodorov, who is responsible for economic reform.

Yeltsin reduces Rutskoi's perquisites, such as depriving him of his personal doctor and most of his bodyguards and replacing his Mercedes with a Volga. Yeltsin also intends to deprive Rutskoi of his agriculture portfolio. (Rutskoi is against an overhasty dismemberment of collective farms.)

16 April 1993. The CIS meeting in Minsk supports Yeltsin in his campaign.

20 April 1993. Yeltsin announces a decree increasing subsidies for children's programmes. Rutskoi says that he will stand for the presidency if Yeltsin resigns.

21 April 1993. The Constitutional Court rules that the first two questions in the referendum need gain only 50 per cent of votes actually cast in order to win acceptance, but the minimum 50 per cent turnout condition still applies.

22 April 1993. The office of the prosecutor-general says that Defence Minister Grachev and others may be implicated in 'illegal deals' involving the sale of military property in East Germany. Gennadi Burbulis is to be questioned about a different corruption case.

23 April 1993. Yeltsin reveals the outlines of a draft constitution with strong presidential powers, which is to be implemented if he is supported in the referendum.

Yeltsin strips Rutskoi of his agriculture portfolio.

24 April 1993. In a television speech Yeltsin indicates that questions 1 and 4 are the most important. (Many of his supporters were recommending a 'no' to question 3, although Yeltsin himself had earlier urged a straight 'yes' to all four questions.) Yeltsin promises army officers a plot of land on retirement, which they can own or sell.

25 April 1993. There is a surprisingly high turnout of 64.6 per cent of the 107.3 million registered voters and an unexpectedly strong show of support for Yeltsin and, to a lesser extent, for his economic policy. (Note that the number of registered voters was given as 106.2 million for the 12 December 1993 general election.) Question 1 receives a 'yes' vote of 58.7 per cent of those who voted and question 2 a 'yes' vote of 53.0 per cent. Question 3 receives 31.7 per cent of eligible voters and question 4 43.1 per cent, indicating a much stronger desire for early parliamentary elections than for an early presidential election.

Support was stronger in the towns than in the countryside, although the gap was not as wide as anticipated. There were considerable regional variations. For example, Yeltsin scored especially well in cities like Moscow (75.2 per cent) and St Petersburg (a 72.8 per cent 'yes' vote). Chechenia did not take part at all and in Tatarstan the turnout was so low (22 per cent) that the result was declared invalid. In Ingushetia question 1 received a 'yes' vote of only 2.4 per cent and in Dagestan it was 14.28 per cent.

During the election campaign Yeltsin made some costly promises, some of which were honoured. For example, on 1 April 1993 the minimum monthly wage was doubled to 4,500 roubles and on 1 May 1993 the minimum monthly pension was raised from 4,275 roubles to 8,122 roubles.

Yeltsin did promise to postpone an increase in petrol prices, but changed his mind on 24 May.

28 April 1993. Yeltsin dismisses Rutskoi from his position as head of the Interdepartmental Committee on Crime and Corruption and takes over the role himself.

29 April 1993. Yeltsin unveils his draft constitution to heads of the eighty-nine republics, regions and districts. The Federation Council is to give its judgement by 20 May.

30 April 1993. Yeltsin appoints Oleg Soskovets as a first deputy prime minister (making three in total, Oleg Lobov and Vladimir Shumeiko being the other two). A former steel industry director and minister, his portfolio is the industrial sector as a whole.

1 May 1993. The National Salvation Front defies a ban on holding a procession to Red Square in Moscow and a large number on both sides are hurt in serious fighting with the police. (One policeman subsequently died.)

11 May 1993. Yeltsin dismisses Yuri Skokov (secretary of the 'security council') and Georgi Khizha (industry minister and deputy prime minister). Both are lukewarm about reform and Skokov openly criticizes the president prior to the referendum.

Yeltsin suggests that regional leaders should form a constituent assembly to draw up a constitution. In addition 'this gathering should be transformed into a Council of the Federation which will subsequently become one of the chambers of the future parliament'.

12 May 1993. Yeltsin issues a decree calling for a special assembly of the Council of the Federation to be held on 5–10 June to 'consider and finalize preparations' for a new constitution. The consenting eighty-eight republics, regions and districts (eighty-nine with Chechenia, which opted out) will each have two representatives and these will be joined by representatives of the president and parliament (e.g. Nikolai Ryabov, the deputy speaker of parliament, is to receive an invitation; in a speech to parliament on 14 May Ryabov endorses the assembly). Parliament aims to have its alternative constitution drafted by 6 July 1993.

14 May 1993. Despite Ryabov's endorsement of Yeltsin's assembly, parliament votes to refer Yeltsin's constitutional programme to the Constitutional Court for a judgement on its legality.

19 May 1993. The Constitutional Court rules that *Izvestia* should remain independent and not be taken over by parliament.

10 June 1993. Marshal Yevgeni Shaposhnikov is appointed head of the 'security council' (as a replacement for Yuri Skokov). (Shaposhnikov's office as commander-in-chief of the CIS was abolished as unnecessary: *CDSP*, 1993, vol. XLV, no. 24, p. 17. The joint command of the CIS was abolished on 15 June: *The Economist*, 28 August 1993, p. 20.)

27 July 1993. Yeltsin dismisses Viktor Barannikov (security minister) for 'personal violations of ethical norms [allegedly helping relatives to take trips abroad] as well as serious flaws in his work, including the leadership of the border guard troops attached to the ministry'. (He had been reprimanded the previous day over the loss of Russian soldiers guarding Tajikistan's border with Afghanistan. Note the entry for 21 March 1993. Barannikov died of a heart attack on 21 July 1995.) Barannikov's successor is Nikolai Golushko.

28 July 1993. The praesidium of the Supreme Soviet declares the dismissal of Barannikov to have 'no legal force'; it is claimed that under a constitutional amendment adopted in December 1992 only parliament may dismiss the ministers of security, defence and foreign affairs.

1 August 1993. Yeltsin's representative (the military governor) is assassinated in North Ossetia (he was also governor of Ingushetia).

10 August 1993. Yevgeni Shaposhnikov resigns as secretary of the 'security council'.

12 August 1993. Yeltsin insists on an autumn 1993 parliamentary election even if the Congress of People's Deputies refuses to set a date.

18 August 1993. The commission set up by Yeltsin to combat corruption (and whose chairman is the minister of justice, Yuri Kalmykov, appointed on 5 August) proposes that the chief prosecutor, Valentin Stepankov, should be dismissed and that the Constitutional Court should 'review the conduct' of Vice-President Rutskoi (allegedly diverting state funds into a Swiss bank account). (Note that mutual accusations of corruption have been rife.)

20 August 1993. Mikhail Fedotov, the minister for the press and information, offers to resign because of parliament's attempts to increase its control over the media by establishing special supervisory councils. But he favours free media in general, free of any presidential control as well.

21 August 1993. The minister of foreign economic relations, Sergei Glazyev, offers his resignation. He claims that he has made enemies in his attempts to reduce corruption in the trade department by reducing (on 18 August) the number of companies allowed to export oil and metals. He not only accuses the mafia, but also says that Kalmykov (who named the department as a major culprit in illegal exports) and Shumeiko have been trying to hound him out of office. (His offer to resign was not accepted.)

1 September 1993. Yeltsin issues a decree suspending Vice-President Alexander Rutskoi and First Deputy Prime Minister Vladimir Shumeiko. 'The situation that has come about as a result of reciprocal accusations of corruption and legal claims against one another by officials in the system of executive power is seriously undermining the state authority of the Russian Federation . . . Rutskoi . . . and . . . Shumeiko . . . are temporarily suspended from the performance of their duties.' (The period will depend on the results of an official investigation.) (Rutskoi considers that Yeltsin is acting unconstitutionally, while Shumeiko claims that he asked to be relieved of his duties in order to concentrate on clearing his name. Both have been accused of misuse of state funds earmarked for essential imports, Shumeiko allegedly authorizing the transfer of state funds to a company in Switzerland which failed to deliver the whole consignment.)

3 September 1993. The Supreme Soviet refers Yeltsin's suspension of Rutskoi to the Constitutional Court.

16 September 1993. It is announced that Yegor Gaidar is to return to the government on 18 September as a first deputy prime minister in charge of the economy (there are three first deputy premiers altogether). (Gaidar had been elected president of the All-Russia Association of Private Enterprises and Enterprises undergoing Privatization at its founding congress held on 2–3 April 1993.) Oleg Lobov is to be moved to another post.

18 September 1993. A decree issued by Yeltsin formally appoints Gaidar and also appoints Oleg Lobov as secretary of the 'security council' and Nikolai Golushko as security minister. Rutskoi is deprived of his last role, namely as stand-in for the president when he is abroad.

Yeltsin offers to call an early presidential election not less than six months after early parliamentary elections.

THE DISSOLUTION OF PARLIAMENT

On 21 September 1993, in a television and radio address, Yeltsin announced the dissolution of parliament and elections on 11–12 December for the lower house (the State Duma) of a new bicameral Federal Assembly (with a presidential election to follow; on 23 September the date was set for 12 June 1994 and Yeltsin said that he would stand). (Deputies were to receive a year's pay and to go on enjoying other benefits, such as apartments. But later it was announced that only those who left the building before 3 October and who did not participate in the disturbances were still eligible.) The president was to rule by decree until the new parliament began its work.

'Parliament has been seized by a group of people who have turned it into the headquarters of irreconcilable opposition. Hiding behind deputies, this group is pushing Russia towards the abyss. My duty as president is to state that the current corps of deputies has lost its right to be in control of crucial levers of state power. The security of Russia and its peoples is more precious than formal obedience to contradictory norms created by the legislature, which has finally discredited itself. The measures that I have to take as president are the only way to protect democracy and freedom in Russia, to defend reform and the still weak Russian market. There will not be fresh elections to the Congress or the Supreme Soviet. There will be no more sessions of the Congress. According to a presidential decree signed today, the Congress of People's Deputies and the Supreme Soviet cease to perform their legislative functions. The authority and powers of the people's deputies of the Russian Federation are regarded as void . . . every one of them has the right to be nominated a candidate to stand in the elections to the Federal Assembly. Russia needs deputies who do not play political games at the expense of the people. We need people who are more professional, more civilized and more democratic, and I believe there are such people in Russia. The already weak legal foundation of the already weak Russian state is being deliberately eroded. Laws are being approved for the sake of momentary political goals. The only way to overcome the paralysis of state power is to renovate it fundamentally on the basis of the rule of the people and constitutionality. The current situation does not allow that; neither does it allow of the passage of a new constitution. Being the guarantor of the security of the state, I must offer a way out of the stalemate and to break this disastrous, vicious circle. These measures are necessary in order to protect Russia and the whole world against the catastrophic effects of the disintegration of Russian statehood, against the triumph of anarchy in a country with a huge nuclear arsenal. This is my only aim.'

Rutskoi denounced the move as an 'overt *coup d'état*' and announced that he had assumed the presidency. Khasbulatov talked of a 'state coup', called for a general strike and called upon the army not to obey Yeltsin. In a defiant emergency session the Supreme Soviet approved Rutskoi's presidency (and appointed an alternative government, including ministers of security, defence and the interior) and denounced Yeltsin's actions as unconstitutional. The Constitutional Court ruled (by nine votes to four) that Yeltsin had violated the constitution and so this provided grounds for impeachment. (The court was advised not to convene again until a new parliament had been elected.) The Congress of People's Deputies could muster only 638 deputies (689 were needed for a quorum; deputies' travel allowance and foreign passports had been taken away). But this was deemed enough for the Congress to be quorate when Yeltsin supporters were dismissed and Yeltsin was impeached on 23 September. The next day Congress voted in favour of simultaneous elections for a new parliament and the presidency in March 1994. But the parliament was more or less ignored. Yeltsin had its finances terminated, telephones disconnected, electricity and heating cut off, water flow reduced, assets seized and its newspaper (*Rossiskaya Gazeta*) closed down; the special radio and television programmes devoted to parliament were taken off the air. The country remained quiet and the number of people actively participating in the events was tiny, much smaller than in August 1991, when the participation rate was already low. (One source puts the number taking part in the revolt on 3–4 October, according to 'modest calculations', at some 4,000: *Moscow News*, 8 October 1993, p. 4). Many people were, however, fed up with the political squabbling, with what *The Times* aptly called the 'Moscow Punch and Judy show' (*The Times*, 2 October 1993, p. 15).

Prime Minister Chernomyrdin (and the rest of the government, with the exception of the minister of foreign economic relations, Sergei Glazyev, who resigned) backed Yeltsin (as did the central bank and the prosecutor-general, Valentin Stepankov) and said that the heads of the ministries of the interior, security and defence had also expressed support. Yeltsin received generally strong support internationally (including the republics of the former Soviet Union; a supportive CIS meeting was held in Moscow on 24 September). The picture among the regions of Russia itself was more mixed; most of the administrators (governors or chiefs of administration) appointed by Yeltsin supported the president (the Bryansk governor was dismissed for his opposition), but Yeltsin himself estimated that the (elected) regional councils were split more or less evenly. (Yeltsin's actions were not supported by twenty-nine of the fifty-eight provincial and territorial soviets: *CDSP*, 1993, vol. XLV, no. 38, p. 11.) A gathering in St Petersburg of thirty-nine regional representatives on 26 September suggested simultaneous elections for parliament and president and the cancellation of the decrees issued by both sides since the crisis began. (Jonathan Steele reported the following: the Interfax news agency said that only 52.6 per cent of the elected regional councils and 80 per cent of the regional governors, most of whom had been appointed by Yeltsin, backed the president's declaration of a state of emergency: *The Guardian*, 6 October 1993, p. 10.) (The idea of regional representatives being 'for' or 'against' Yeltsin was an oversimplification. There was also a desire to remain above the fray.)

On 27 September Yeltsin rejected the idea of simultaneous elections: 'Dual power is very dangerous today. A power vacuum is even more dangerous, when both powers are engaged in elections and have no time to work.' Parliament's deputy speaker, Nikolai Ryabov, was appointed head of the commission to oversee the new election. Yevgeny Ambartsumov (head of parliament's foreign affairs committee) also went over to the Yeltsin side. The radio and television were biased in favour of Yeltsin and most newspapers were supportive too.

(Yeltsin used the occasion to issue a number of economic decrees. See the section below on economic policy after the dissolution of parliament.)

23 September 1993. A policeman and an elderly onlooker are killed in an attack by opponents of Yeltsin on the headquarters of the CIS military command.

24 September 1993. Yeltsin orders Interior Ministry troops and riot police to surround parliament (the 'White House') and orders those defending the building to disarm.

28 September 1993. The White House is sealed off with razor wire and defenders are given until 11 a.m. the next day to hand over their weapons. People are allowed to leave the White House, but not to enter or return.

29 September 1993. Another ultimatum is issued: weapons to be handed in and the building cleared by 4 October.

A traffic policeman is crushed by a vehicle in scuffles with demonstrators.

30 September 1993. Patriarch Alexei II, the head of the Russian Orthodox Church, persuades the two sides to enter into negotiations with him as mediator.

Representatives of sixty-two regional bodies warn Yeltsin to reverse the decree dissolving parliament and to lift the siege of the White House. They say that they themselves should handle the new elections.

1 October 1993. The negotiators agree to the restoration of services in exchange for the handing in of weapons (except those legally held by parliamentary guards). But parliament rejects the deal and makes further demands (such as the removal of the troops surrounding the parliament). Journalists are allowed back into the White House.

Trade unions are deprived of their role in administering the social security system. (The Federation of Independent Trade Unions united the old official union movement. In late October 1993 the leadership changed, with Mikhail Shmakov replacing Igor Klochkov, who had earlier been forced to resign after criticizing Yeltsin's dissolution of parliament. The FITU claims that total membership of all trade unions is around 57 million, between 85 per cent and 90 per cent of the old number: Jonathan Steele, *The Guardian*, 30 October 1993, p. 13.)

2 October 1993. Police and demonstrators clash and some people are hurt.

3 October 1993. Armed demonstrators (some put the number at around 10,000) break through the cordon around parliament to join those inside and then move on to attack other buildings, including that of the mayor, the Ostankino television station and Itar-Tass. There is loss of life in heavy fighting. Yeltsin dismisses Rutskoi (who, together with Khasbulatov, called on the crowd to attack the mayor's office and the television centre) as vice-president (and names Prime Minister Chernomyrdin as his replacement), declares a seven-day state of emergency in Moscow and calls in the army. (The state of emergency meant that rallies and demonstrations were banned and news censorship was imposed. People without residence permits could be expelled. Thousands were subsequently affected, especially criminals and market traders from the Caucasus and Central Asia. Human rights groups protested that many were maltreated and expelled simply because they belonged to ethnic minorities. The figure for deportations during the state of emergency given by Helsinki Watch was around 9,000: *The Independent*, 17 November 1993, p. 12.)

4 October 1993. The 'second October revolution' comes to a rapid end when the army (around 1,300 troops) blasts the White House into submission with the aid of tanks (it subsequently became known as the 'Black House'). (It was subsequently revealed that Defence Minister Grachev was reluctant to use force.) There is heavy loss of life (the exact number of dead and wounded was not subsequently given). (On 5 October the provisional toll for Sunday 3 and Monday 4 October was put at 127 dead and around 600 injured. The number initially detained was put at 1,452. On 6 October the number of dead was lowered to 118 and 467 were in hospital. The next day the figures were put at 187 dead, including seventy-six civilians, and 437 wounded. Subsequently the number of dead was generally put in the range 140–50. *Izvestia*, for example, put the figure at 145 for the period 3–4 October: 25 December 1993, p. 1. The prosecutor-general's report, published on 6 September 1995, put the figure at 123; 'both sides were found responsible' for the conflict.)

In a speech to the nation Yeltsin says that 'All that was and still is going on in Moscow was an armed revolt planned in advance. It was organized by communists seeking revenge, by fascist leaders and some of the former deputies. The armed fascist–communist revolt in Moscow will be suppressed in the shortest possible time.' Both Rutskoi and Khasbulatov are arrested (they sought international mediation to ensure their safety on surrendering). Also placed in custody are (previously cashiered) General Albert Makashov (who organized parliament's armed resistance and led the attack on the Ostankino television station) and the three parliamentary appointees for security (Viktor Barannikov), defence (Vladislav Achalov) and the interior (Vladimir Dunayev). Some publications are suspended, including *Pravda* (Communist Party), *Den* (neo-fascist), *Sovietskaya Rossiya* (nationalist) and (surprisingly) the more moderate *Rabochaya Tribuna* ('Workers' Tribune'). Also suspended are a range of opposition parties and organizations, including the Russian Communist Workers' Party (founded in November 1991, one of whose leaders, Viktor Antipov, was arrested on 7 October for helping to organize armed resistance at the White House), Working Russia (founded in October 1992), the National Salvation Front (an umbrella communist–extreme nationalist organization, i.e. a 'far left–far right' or 'red–brown' organization; it was set up in October 1993), Pamyat ('Remembrance', founded in 1986; neo-fascist, virulently anti-semitic) and the Officers' Union (founded in 1992 by servicemen, led by Stanislav Terekhov and openly opposed to Yeltsin's reforms). A curfew is imposed in Moscow from 11 p.m. to 5 a.m. (The curfew was later renewed.)

5 October 1993. There are further dismissals, namely the prosecutor-general, Valentin Stepankov (replaced by Alexei Kazannik), and the governors (chief administrators) of the provinces of Novosibirsk (in Siberia) and Amur (in the Far East). Moscow City Council and Moscow's district councils ('soviets') are dissolved.

6 October 1993. In an address to the nation Yeltsin says that 'What happened in Moscow last Sunday was not spontaneous action of some sort. All of it has another name – an armed rebellion, planned and prepared by the leaders of the former Supreme Soviet, the former vice-president and the leaders of a number of parties and public organizations . . . Fascists and communists, the swastika and the hammer and sickle, came together in this dark deed.' He confirms the December election for the Duma and encourages local councils to hold fresh elections at the same time (he calls on those councils which took an 'intransigent stand' to dissolve themselves).

Opposition publications remain suspended, but general press censorship is lifted.

The chairman of the Constitutional Court, Valery Zorkin, resigns (the court was created by a 12 July 1991 decree and parliamentary approval was obtained in October). He remains a member of the court, since the appointment is supposed to be for life, but the deputy chairman Nikolai Vitruk assumes the top position. (In fact, following a newspaper interview given on 1 December 1993 in which Zorkin criticized the constitution, six of his fellow judges dismissed him.)

The guards attending Lenin's mausoleum in Red Square are removed for the first time since August 1924 (the present mausoleum was opened in 1929).

7 October 1993. The Constitutional Court is suspended until a new constitution is adopted. On the day the dead are buried Yeltsin promises to banish the spectre of 'communist fascism'.

8 October 1993. The Communist Party is suspended (leader Gennadi Zyuganov; a membership of 600,000 is claimed, very large in Russian terms, but critics say that only 10 per cent are paid-up members). Also suspended is the People's Party of Free Russia.

9 October 1993. Yeltsin issues a decree suspending all councils in cities, towns and villages (their functions will be taken over by mayors). The republic and regional councils are to be subordinate to local governors. Local council elections are to be held in December and the republics are advised to do the same. A special commission will look into local government reform.

The state of emergency in Moscow is extended for a week, although the curfew is to last from midnight to five in the morning.

10 October 1993. Yeltsin announces that there will also be elections to the Council of the Federation in December.

11 October 1993. Yeltsin begins a three-day (long delayed) official visit to Japan. (Yeltsin promised to withdraw the remaining 5,000 troops from the Kuril Islands.)

13 October 1993. According to Yeltsin, the newly elected parliament will have the final say on the date of the presidential election.

Makashov is charged with organizing mass disturbances (this carries a maximum jail sentence of fifteen years).

14 October 1993. Fifteen newspapers are closed down permanently, such as *Den*, *Pravda* and *Sovietskaya Rossiya* are allowed to reregister under different titles and with new editors. (The editor of *Pravda* resigned on 28 October, but the paper reappeared under its own name on 2 November.)

15 October 1993. It is announced that a referendum on the constitution will be held on 12 December.

Rutskoi and Khasbulatov are charged with 'organizing mass disorder'.

Ilya Konstantinov, leader of the National Salvation Front, is arrested.

18 October 1993. The state of emergency in Moscow is not renewed.

19 October 1993. The following six organizations are suspended and barred from participating in the election: National Salvation Front; Russian Communist Workers' Party; Union of Officers; Russian Communist Youth League; Russian National Unity; Union for the Defence of the Social Rights of Servicemen. But the Communist Party of Russia and the People's Party of Free Russia (formerly led by Rutskoi) are allowed to participate in the election. (Note that individual members of banned organizations are still permitted to take part in the election unless they are in prison.)

22 October 1993. Yeltsin orders elections to new-style local parliaments in Moscow, St Petersburg and more than sixty regions, to be held between December 1993 and March 1994. But Yeltsin does not order elections in the twenty republics; he merely 'recommends' that the republics should reorganize their elected bodies, 'taking the decree into consideration'. (References to the sovereignty of the constituent republics are removed from a new draft constitution.) Future regional parliaments will have the right to pass laws (which the old 'soviets' did not). But the new parliaments (elected for two years and comprising no more than fifty deputies) will not be able to contradict federal laws, presidential decrees or government orders. In addition local laws, passed by parliament, have to be signed by the chief of regional administration (most chiefs are appointed by Yeltsin). The decree comes into force immediately, but it will be submitted for approval to the new Russian parliament once elected.

29 October 1993. A Special Information Court is to be set up 'to protect the mass media against unlawful interference into their activities during the electoral campaign'. Thus the aim is to ensure the independence of the press and equal access to the mass media for all candidates.

1 November 1993. Moscow City Council bans all demonstrations on 7 November.

2 November 1993. Yeltsin is to establish a commission to study abuses of human rights. The chairman is Sergei Kovalev and the members include Andrei Kozyrev and Yelena Bonner (wife of the late Andrei Sakharov).

6 November 1993. After much speculation Yeltsin says that 'I am against holding the next presidential election in June 1994. I believe the present presidential mandate should be fully used and exercised until [June] 1996' (earlier Yeltsin had indicated that the new parliament would decide).

7 November 1993. The seventy-sixth anniversary of the Bolshevik revolution passes off without incident, with a massive security presence in Moscow confronting a tiny number of would-be demonstrators.

9 November 1993. The draft constitution is published (see above).

10 November 1993. Prime Minister Chernomyrdin, by a personal order, transfers the allocation of export quotas to Oleg Soskovets, reserving for himself the dealing out of centralized credits (*CDSP*, 1994, vol. XLVI, no. 3, p. 6).

15 November 1993. All visitors from the other countries of the former Soviet Union who stay in Moscow for more than twenty-four hours have to register with the police and pay a daily residence fee of 750 roubles. The penalty for non-compliance is deportation or a fine of up to 430,000 roubles. Some exemptions were granted the following day, namely refugees, the handicapped, visitors seeking medical treatment, scientists, performing artists and others with official invitations. (St Petersburg subsequently required foreigners to obtain residence permits for a stay longer than three days.)

4 December 1993. There are reports that Russia's Choice, the Party of Russian Unity and Accord, Yabloko and the Russian Democratic Reform Movement have agreed at the local level to withdraw other candidates where one is clearly in the lead. (But this co-operation largely failed to materialize.)

6 December 1993. Yeltsin decrees a 90 per cent increase in the minimum wage (to 14,620 roubles a month), student grants and benefit and other social payments. Budget-financed organizations are to pay the minimum wage from 1 December 1993 and other organizations by 1 March 1994.

Some coal miners go on strike over grievances such as delays in wage payments and planned pit closures.

8 December 1993. The salaries of government workers are approximately doubled.

9 December 1993. On the second day of a three-day visit to Brussels Yeltsin signs a declaration with the EU promising greater economic and political co-operation.

11 December 1993. Pensions are increased by 80 per cent.

THE GENERAL ELECTION OF 12 DECEMBER 1993

Of the twenty-one parties and blocs that had registered by the deadline of midnight 6 November 1993 (thirty-five were in the running), eight were subsequently disqualified for not meeting one or more of the conditions (e.g. the Russian National Union, the National Republican Party of Russia, the Constitutional Democratic Party and the New Russia Bloc). Each party or bloc had to collect at least 100,000 signatures from eligible voters in order to be registered. In addition, since no more than 15,000 signatures could come from any one of the eighty-nine 'federation subjects', the support of at least seven subjects was required. Polls were considered valid in any constituency if 25 per cent or more of the electorate voted (compared with 50 per cent previously). There was a 5 per cent threshold for any party or bloc to be allocated those seats in parliament to be decided on a proportional representation basis.

(There had been earlier efforts to form an overtly pro-Yeltsin party, but Yeltsin was reluctant to attach his name to any particular one. Prime Minister Chernomyrdin, too, did not overtly support any particular party or bloc, although apparently he favoured the Party of Russian Unity and Accord.)

The two representatives from each of the eighty-nine federation 'members' or 'subjects' were to be elected under a first-past-the-post system (rather than appointed, as originally conceived), although for one term of office only (thereafter the representatives were to be nominated by the members). There were to be 450 deputies in the State Duma, half elected by proportional representation from national party lists (to encourage the growth of parties) and half by single-member constituencies under a first-past-the-post system (no party affiliation was to accompany any candidate's name on the ballot paper). (Originally 400 deputies were mooted, elected on a 130 and 270 split respectively.) The first term of office for both houses was reduced to two years (as opposed to the four years proposed earlier). (Note that Chechenia boycotted the election.)

The parties, leading personalities and platforms

Russia's Choice. Yegor Gaidar, Anatoly Chubais, Andrei Kozyrev, Boris Fyodorov, Sergei Filatov, Mikhail Poltoranin, Gennadi Burbulis, Sergei Kovalev and Ella Pamfilova (i.e. many members of the pre-election cabinet and presidential advisers). Founded 16–17 October 1993 in Moscow, the bloc comprises several parties and movements, such as Democratic Russia, the Peasants' Party of Russia, the Association of Privatized and the Private Entrepreneurs and the Party of Democratic Initiative. Its motto is 'Freedom, property and legality' and its symbol is Peter the Great. The draft constitution is supported. The bloc advocates radical economic reform, although promising protection for the poorest members of society. The inflation target is set at 4–5 per cent a month by the end of 1994. (During the election campaign more populist measures were promised, such as greater protection for industry from foreign competition and greater stress on reorganizing enterprises than on closing them down.)

Party of Russian Unity and Accord. Sergei Shakhrai, Alexander Shokhin, Oleg Soskovets and Konstantin Zatulin (head of Entrepreneurs for a New Russia). Founded 16 October 1993 in Novgorod (genuine regional devolution is advocated), the bloc comprises important members of the pre-election administration. Its motto is 'Stability, family, property and motherland'. The draft constitution is supported on the whole. The party is concerned about 'shock therapy' and thus advocates a more gradual process of market reform, with greater protection offered to industry and the poorest members of society. Shakhrai recommends 'an active industrial policy, directed to the support of branches and enterprises able to become the locomotives of economic growth' (cited by John Lloyd, *FT*, 17 November 1993, p. 25). Strong links with the CIS are advocated.

The Yavlinsky–Boldyrev–Lukin bloc. (Subsequently nicknamed Yabloko, or 'Apple', an acronym loosely derived from the surnames of the three leaders.) Grigori Yavlinsky, Yuri Boldyrev and Vladimir Lukin. Formed in October 1993. The bloc is supported by parties such as the Republican Party of the Russian Federation, the Social Democratic Party and the Russian Christian Democratic Party. Generally seen as 'centrist' in terms of policy, a more gradual process of market reform is espoused along with a strong federal state. (There seem to be differences of attitude within the bloc towards the draft constitution.) The bloc is critical of the government's policy of stressing financial stabilization before the creation of a competitive market economy. Financial stabilization cannot be achieved overnight. As Yavlinsky puts it, 'Gaidar . . . simply made state monopolists into private monopolists. My programme is to demonopolize, to privatize much further, and only then can you stabilize the currency' (quoted by John Lloyd, *FT*, 11 December 1993, p. 10). Yavlinsky also stresses the need for economic and monetary co-ordination between CIS members. (In a later article he spelt out his idea of an economic union in order to encourage trade, economic growth and social stability. There should be a customs union, a payments union and co-ordinated economic policies and legislation: *IHT*, 12 October 1994, p. 4.)

Civic Union for Stability, Justice and Progress. Arkady Volsky (head of the Russian Union of Industrialists and Entrepreneurs), Nikolai Bekh, Alexander Vladislavlev. Founded 26 October 1993, it has the support of the Social Democratic Centre (headed by Oleg Rumyantsev) and the Russian Union of Youth. The draft constitution is not supported. A centrist party of 'reasonable realists', it rejects 'shock therapy' and advocates more gradual market reform, greater state regulation of the economy, increased state investment in industry and greater protection of industry. Economic reform, it argues, should not mean the destruction of the country's scientific and technological potential. The government should control the export of raw materials and privatization is not an end in itself. Specific policies include higher taxes on the wealthy, subsidies aimed at consumers rather than producers and an incentive system to ensure the effective use of land. Active participation in the CIS is recommended.

Alexander Tsipko is a Civic Union intellectual who clearly belongs to the 'evolutionary' school in the theory of the transition. The reformers 'act like Bolsheviks. They treat the country like an empty field, ready for their experiments – only now it is the imposition of capitalism and not of communism . . . This was a country created by the Soviet period. You cannot make that disappear suddenly. You must recognize and work with it' (cited by John Lloyd, *FT*, 9 December 1993, p. 2).

Democratic Party of Russia. Nikolai Travkin, Oleg Bogomolov and Stanislav Govorukhin. Policies include moderate, evolutionary reform, restrictions on land sales, protection for domestic industry, strengthened Russian statehood and a strong political centre. The draft constitution is not supported.

Russian Democratic Reform Movement. Anatoly Sobchak, Gavriil Popov, Alexander Yakovlev, Yevgeni Shaposhnikov and Sviatoslav Fyodorov. Founded in October 1993. Advocates a genuine federation with meaningful decentralization (the draft constitution is supported on the whole). There is support for 'realistic' economic reform (with greater support for production and entrepreneurship) but stress on the party's independence from Yeltsin. Policies include wider access to higher education, greater protection for pensioners and the low-paid, and wider ownership of private land.

The Communist Party of the Russian Federation. Gennadi Zyuganov. (The party list includes Vladimir Khryuchkov and Anatoly Lukyanov.) A membership of 600,000 is claimed, but disputed. The party advocates a 'planned market economy', with a powerful role for the state, e.g. generous social protection, wages indexed to inflation and protection of industry. 'Shock' therapy would be abandoned. The party does not oppose a wider spread of ownership; 'destatization' cannot be achieved overnight. Neither is it opposed to private farming, but it does reject the buying and selling of land. Zyuganov talks in terms of reforms with 'a human face' and being more 'socially orientated' (Jonathan Steele, *The Guardian*, 25 November 1993, p. 12). Yeltsin's draft constitution is opposed.

Agrarian Party of Russia. Mikhail Lapshin, Valentin Rasputin, Viktor Shcherbak and Alexander Zaveryukha. (Vasily Starodubtsev is on the list of candidates.) Founded in February 1993. The draft constitution can be adopted 'as a basis'. There should be a state-regulated change-over to a socially orientated market economy. The state should manage the economy, provide easy credits for domestic producers and offer social protection. The programme acknowledges diversity of ownership and accepts 'sensible destatization'. Domestic producers should be protected, especially farmers. It opposes the 'reckless' buying and selling of land (although not private farming as such) and offers strong protection for collective and state farms in particular.

Liberal Democratic Party of Russia. Vladimir Zhirinovsky. (Zhirinovsky never joined the Communist Party. He came third out of five behind Yeltsin and Nikolai Ryzhkov in the Russian presidential election of June 1991 with 6.2 million votes, or 7.8 per cent of those cast.) He was born in Kazakhstan and his father was apparently from a Jewish family, referred to by Zhirinovsky simply as 'a lawyer'. It is alleged that he changed his name from Eidelshtein to Zhirinovsky in June 1964, the latter being the name of his mother's first husband. Founded in June 1989 and reregistered in December 1992. Extreme right-wing, ultra-nationalistic and antisemitic. There was a promise to 'raise Russia off its knees'. The draft constitution is supported. (But greater centralization is advocated. Russia should be divided into territorial units 'without any nationality-based overtones', according to Zhirinovsky.) Populist economic and anti-crime measures are advocated. Economic promises include the following: restoration of 'lost' savings; increased pensions; a halt to the run-down of the military and of the defence industry (including conversion to civilian output) as well as more housing for military personnel; arms exports to be encouraged; no aid to be given to other countries, including the countries of the former Soviet Union; cheap vodka; lower business taxes; and a ban on trading within Russia by non-Russians. There should be state ownership of land, but renting and inheritance should be allowed. (After the election Zhirinovsky talked of a 'mixed economy' with equal rights for the state and private sectors. There should be reform, but it should not mean the destruction of the state sector and collective farms.) (The Liberal Democratic Party has in mind a form of state capitalism, with the state remaining in control of strategic sectors such as defence and the railways. The state would control the privatization process, with only Russian citizens allowed to hold certificates paying an annual dividend. The state would ensure that Russia does not become simply a supplier of raw materials to the West: Kipp 1994: 79–81.)

Zhirinovsky has been associated with some very wild ideas, although during and especially after the campaign a more moderate style was adopted. The following are taken from *The Financial Times* (14 December 1993, p. 2), *The Guardian* (14 December 1993, p. 12) and *The Daily Telegraph* (14 December 1993, p. 1):

1. *Antisemitism.* 'Although we are not antisemitic we won't tolerate an increase in the strength of the Jews.' 'It is certain that representatives of Zionism have also made their contribution to the decay of the Russian media.' 'Zionists who control international banks.'

2. *Crime.* 'We'll set up courts on the spot and shoot the leaders of criminal bands.'

3. *Foreign policy.* Against the 'Westernization' of Russia. The protection of Russians in the 'near abroad' would include dumping nuclear waste along the borders of the Baltic States if they mistreated their ethnic Russian citizens (after the election Zhirinovsky said that economic sanctions could be employed). (Within Russia itself ethnically based autonomous republics would be abolished.)

Strong support is given to Serbia and Iraq (volunteers have been sent to fight on the side of Iraq).

The Kuril Islands dispute. 'I would bomb the Japanese. I would sail our large navy around their small island and if they so much as cheeped I would nuke them.' 'Not a single foreign ship will enter the sea between the Russian mainland and the Kurils, so that all the seafood will get on to the tables of the Russian people.'

Germany and Japan. 'When I am sitting in the Kremlin if a German so much as challenges Russia you will pay for everything . . . the third time will be the last time if you meddle again . . . [I will not hesitate] . . . to create new Hiroshimas and Nagasakis . . . You will get your own Chernobyl in Germany' (*The Times*, 15 December 1993, pp. 1, 13).

4. *Territorial ambitions.* Advocates a return to Russia's 'natural historic borders', i.e. a return to the old Tsarist empire, including parts of Poland and Finland (although during the campaign it was stressed that force would not be used and economic forces in particular would be instrumental in inducing countries to rejoin the empire). 'Russia should not permit its borders to shrink. The only possible version is to move the border farther, to Russia's former borders.' 'How I dream of our Russian soldiers washing their boots in the warm waters of the Indian ocean.' (Zhirinovsky's solution to the North–South problem is for the former to take over the latter: Russia – Central Asia and the Middle East; Europe – Africa; USA/Canada – Latin America; China/Japan – East and South East Asia). 'It is difficult to establish borders today. We need to provoke wars between native tribes. To do this we do not even need to wage war actively, we simply need to avoid interfering. They will simply slaughter each other (Armenians against Azerbaijanis . . . Tajiks against Uzbeks and so on) . . . They . . . will come rushing to ask Russia to accept them as districts or provinces' (*The Times*, 17 December 1993, p. 13). (After the election Zhirinovsky talked of the need to withdraw Russian troops from all foreign countries. He also said that the former Soviet republics would soon 'beg with tears in their eyes to be taken back into the Russian state.')

Constructive Ecological Movement ('Cedar'). Anatoli Panfilov. Established in March 1993 and registered in August 1993. Mainly stresses solving Russia's severe environmental problems. The platform says that 'our goal is to make Russians' physical and moral health a priority of government policy'. The draft constitution is favoured on the whole. Favours more socially orientated market reforms.

Women of Russia Bloc. Alevtina Fedulova, Yekaterina Lakhova and Natalya Gundareva. Formed in October 1993. Main platform is a strengthening of the role of women in society by providing the conditions enabling women to have a choice of whether to work or not, e.g. a generous child benefit scheme. Improved health care is stressed. Slogan 'There is no real democracy without women'. There should be less social tension on the way to the market; social policy is a priority and there should be less spending on defence. There is support for (inherited) land leasing but not sales. No stand is taken on the constitution.

Dignity and Compassion Alliance. Mikhail Trunov and Vyacheslav Grishin. Founded in 1992. Represents vulnerable groups, such as invalids, pensioners, war veterans, Chernobyl victims and cultural figures. Broadly in favour of reform, but concerned to protect those most in need, i.e. reforms should be for people and not at their expense.

The Future of Russia – New Names. Vyacheslav Lashchevsky. Established in October 1993. Most leaders in this youth movement come from the Russian Union of Youth (successor to the Komsomol). Policies include a gradual adoption of the market system ('a market economy in the interests of broad strata of society'), a reasonable and equitable tax system, a reduction in the government apparatus (there is recognition of the supremacy of the 'rights, liberties and vitally important values of the individual and society over the state'), a truly federal state and higher domestic and foreign investment. The referendum on the draft constitution should be postponed since it is too early to vote.

The result of the elections

The turnout was 54.8 per cent (58.2 million of the 106.2 million registered voters took part; note that the 25 April 1993 referendum gave a figure of 107.3 million registered voters). (Note that on 5 May 1994 a commission, set up by the president and headed by Alexander Sobyanin, reported massive fraud during the election; the commission's figures were 49 million or 46.1 per cent. The findings were not accepted by the president's office and the electoral commission.) The constitution was approved by 58.4 per cent of those who cast their votes.

Eight of the thirteen participating parties or blocs passed the 5 per cent threshold. Table 3.1 shows the distribution of seats in the State Duma. The election was declared illegal in six constituencies. The picture of the total distribution of seats became muddled later on as factions developed and changed.

Overall the election produced no decisive result. Although Russia's Choice gained most seats in the State Duma, Zhirinovsky's (misleadingly named) Liberal Democratic Party (LDP) did surprisingly well in the party list section. This came as a bombshell at home and abroad. The initial panic subsequently turned into a generally held opinion that the LDP's success was largely a protest vote against the dire economic circumstances of a large section of the population (associated in people's minds with radical economic reform), the very high level of crime, national humiliation at the decline of a great power and foreign 'meddling'. Zhirinovsky did well among the armed forces (Yeltsin thinks Zhirinovsky gained about one-third of the votes). On a more positive note, Zhirinovsky (previously treated by many as something of a clown) ran a very effective (and well financed) campaign. His simple messages took full advantage of people's misery and

Table 3.1 Russia: the general election of 12 December 1993: the State Duma

Party or bloc	*Party list*		*Constituency seats*	*Total seats*
	% vote	*Seats*		
Russia's Choice	15.38	40	30	70
Liberal Democratic Party	22.79	59	5	64
Communist Party	12.35	32	16	48
Agrarian Party	7.90	21	12	33
Yabloko	7.83	20	3	23
Women of Russia	8.10	21	2	23
Russian Unity and Accord	6.76	18	1	19
Democratic Party	5.50	14	1	15
Russian Democratic Reform Movement	4.06	0	4	4
Dignity and Compassion	0.70	0	2	2
Civic Union	1.92	0	1	1
The Future of Russia – New Names	1.25	0	1	1
Independents	–	–	141	141
Total				444*

* Election declared illegal in six constituencies.

prejudices. The reformist parties were deeply divided, unable to unite through policy differences and personal rivalries.

Comments on the 12 December 1993 election and public opinion polls

Hough (1994) describes the results of a major public opinion poll undertaken during the three weeks preceding the 12 December 1993 election. 'One fact is abundantly clear from our survey data: the Russian population does not see the choice as one between radical economic reform and a return to the past . . . The great bulk of the population takes a centrist position on economic change' (pp. 5–6). 'The support either for very radical reform or for a return to the past . . . has become quite small . . . the centre is still strong in the Duma' (p. 34). 'Perhaps the most consistent political fact about Russia is the much stronger support for the radicals in the large cities than in the countryside and small towns' (p. 24).

Sakwa (1995: 220–1) concludes that: 'If the elections had been held only on a proportional system, the LDPR would have been the single largest group in the Duma; but if the old two-stage first-past-the-post system had been retained, the LDPR would hardly have figured. The confused results reflect genuine confusion in the Russian political scene. A large number were seduced by the promises of easy solutions and the restoration of Russia's great power status; but a solid bloc at the same time voted for the continuation of reforms. The population had sent two mutually exclusive signals: in apparently accepting the constitution they were voting for stability; but in voting for the opposition they were rejecting the existing basis for order. In the constituency elections the personal factor was generally more important than programmes, and conjunctural factors (like the non-payment of wages in many sectors since September) amplified the protest vote. The elections revealed not so much "support" for nationalist or neo-communist parties as disenchantment with the democrats . . . the protest vote was less against a centre that barely existed than a mark of dissatisfaction with the venality of post-communist politics and the persistence of elite structures across the August divide . . . The strong showing for Zhirinovsky reflected the insurgency of outsider groups against the embryonic post-communist "new class". The results suggest a highly discerning and sophisticated pattern of voter behaviour . . . the party list vote was used as a classic instance of the "protest" vote . . . whereas in the single-member constituencies the electorate voted *for* rather than *against* particular candidates and programmes.'

DEVELOPMENTS AFTER THE DECEMBER 1993 GENERAL ELECTION

15 December 1993. Presidential adviser Sergei Stankevich says he has resigned. (There followed a series of staff dismissals by Yeltsin.)

17 December 1993. Tougher immigration rules are decreed, including more thorough scrutiny of identification papers and asylum requests. Tougher controls are also decreed for the employment of foreigners. Work permits are needed (costing the equivalent of the minimum monthly wage) and citizens of Russia should have priority access to vacant positions.

18 December 1993. Prime Minister Chernomyrdin speaks out against 'shock' therapy: 'We should face the truth and admit that many people voted against the hardships and mistakes of the current reforms, rather than for a particular programme . . . As many as 35 million Russians live below the poverty line, which means that some 30 per cent of the electorate were potentially "against". Naturally, any "shock" methods must be precluded in the future . . . I said it a year and a half ago and I am ready to repeat it now; it is wrong to jump in the river without testing the water first . . . The election defeat is a personal evaluation of Gaidar's work, not as a representative of the whole government but as the person responsible for the Economics Ministry. The same goes for Chubais. It is their personal defeat. They should think it over hard. They have a lot to think about now.' The focus, the prime minister says, should be less on monetary and spending controls and more on social protection and on investment in efficient state and private enterprises in order to create jobs.

19 December 1993. Gaidar and others call for an 'anti-fascist front'.

21 December 1993. Yeltsin describes the election success of Zhirinovsky as 'a protest against poverty'. 'Do not forget the poor. There are many of them. It was they who voted for the Liberal Democratic Party. They were not voting for its leader or its programme, but against poverty.'

Yeltsin abolishes the Security Ministry (successor to the KGB, although it had been made progressively much weaker than its predecessor). It is to be replaced by the Federal Counter-intelligence Service (the Foreign Intelligence Service deals with security matters abroad).

22 December 1993. Yeltsin says that 'no matter whom the voters cast their ballots for, they were agreed on one point: Russia needs strong rule, Russia needs order . . . and they are exasperated by the rise in crime . . . to a considerable extent people's patience has been exhausted. For two years they have tightened their belts and put up with difficulties. Now they want results.' But 'Gaidar remains, which means the course he is pursuing with the president and the government also remains . . . basic foreign policy remains in place.' The rate of inflation has started to slow down, however, and 'if the trend continues we shall seriously change our social policy'. Yeltsin also says that he intends to stay in office until the end of his term in June 1996, to form his own party, to work with the new parliament, and to make the state mass media accountable to the president rather than the government. (As an indication of the greater attention paid to social protection, the IMF is to send a team in January 1994 to help design a social security system.)

Alexander Yakovlev is appointed chairman of the Russian Federal Television and Radio Service.

28 December 1993. Zhirinovsky is ordered to leave Bulgaria after insulting the Bulgarian president (he said the president should be 'pensioned off' and introduced a Bulgarian colleague and adviser as the future president).

29 December 1993. Zhirinovsky is refused entry to Germany. The Romanian parliament condemns his portrayal of Romania as an 'artificial state' (made up of territory seized from Russia, Bulgaria and Hungary) peopled by 'Italian Gypsies'.

1 January 1994. In his New Year's address Yeltsin pays particular attention to the need to defend the interests of ethnic Russians living in other countries of the former Soviet Union (the 'near abroad').

10 January 1994. A decree issued by Yeltsin makes the Defence, Interior and Foreign Ministries accountable to the president as well as the committees responsible for espionage, frontier troops, information, television and radio.

11 January 1994. The Federal Assembly convenes. Yeltsin personally addresses the Council of the Federation, calling for co-operation and on deputies not to 'stop half-way' on the path to economic reform: 'Now is the time we need our second wind.' In contrast, Prime Minister Chernomyrdin informs the State Duma that 'the government will not allow ill-considered leaps forward and unreasonable shock actions . . . The limit of the people's patience is nearly exhausted.' He calls for 'a new stage of economic reforms, a stage of stabilization during which we should provide the right conditions for producers.' (On 13 January Vladimir Shumeiko was elected speaker of the Council of the Federation; the following day Ivan Rybkin of the Agrarian Party was elected speaker of the State Duma.)

13–14 January 1994. US President Clinton visits Moscow and urges 'more reform, more support' (i.e. carry on with the reform programme and switch expenditure, with the help of the USA, to social programmes in order to mitigate the adverse effects of reform). Russia and the USA agree that by 30 May 1994 'no country will be targeted by the strategic forces of either side.' (Russia, Ukraine and the USA also signed an agreement to dismantle the remainder of Ukraine's nuclear weapons: see the chapter on Ukraine.)

16 January 1994. Gaidar resigns from the government: 'I cannot work without having the necessary levers at my command . . . where decisions I have taken are not approved and at the same time decisions I regard as dangerous are adopted by the government . . . I cannot serve in the government and at the same time be in opposition to it . . . I would stay in the government if I had the least hope of improving things, but I have not.' Gaidar cited his opposition to the decisions to form a monetary union with Belarus (which he considers inflationary) and to spend $500 million on a new building for parliament: 'those things were examples of contributing factors, of which a great many had accumulated'. There was 'a much more serious problem . . . stay . . . but at the same time serve more and more as a cover for a policy I do not agree with' (*CDSP*, 1994, vol. XLVI, no. 3, p. 7). The social security minister, Ella Pamfilova, also announced her intention to resign, saying, 'this is not an ultimatum – it is an act of despair': 'when your advice is ignored it is simply pointless'. (She complained about the amount of money spent on refurbishing the White House when social services urgently needed resources. Her final and irrevocable intention to resign was not actually announced until 16 February: 'my departure is a protest against the discrediting of the idea of the current reforms . . . I consider it dishonest to participate in conducting a policy that I do not agree with and cannot bear responsibility for': *CDSP*, 1994, vol. XLVI, no. 7, p. 18.)

17 January 1994. Yeltsin issues a statement on Gaidar: 'Accepting his resignation, I would particularly like to stress the unchangeability of the president's course towards deep and democratic reform of Russian society, its economy and political institutions. The policy of reforms will be continued.' Russia's Choice's parliamentary faction also issues a statement: 'The economic and political situation in Russia has changed considerably. The leadership of the Russian government regularly departs from the course of stabilization and reform while declaring it is true to it. In this situation the departure of Russia's Choice representatives responsible for economic and social policy is the only possible decision.'

18 January 1994. Boris Fyodorov refuses the post of finance minister (without the rank of deputy prime minister). The conditions he laid down were not accepted, e.g. that Viktor Gerashchenko (chairman of the central bank) and Alexander Zaveryukha (deputy prime minister in charge of agriculture) should be dismissed and that he should be in charge of monetary policy. Fyodorov also leaves Russia's Choice and joins the 'Union of 12 December', an alliance of liberal independents formed after the election and led by Irina Khakamada (Andrei Makarov also joins).

20 January 1994. Prime Minister Chernomyrdin announces the new government: first deputy prime minister, Oleg Soskovets; deputy prime ministers, Anatoli Chubais (privatization), Alexander Zaveryukha (agriculture) and Yuri Yarov (social issues); economics, Alexander Shokhin (the government would try to 'cling to a narrow corridor between hyperinflation and a stop in industrial production'; he became deputy prime minister in charge of the economy on 24 March 1994); foreign affairs, Andrei Kozyrev; nationalities and regional policy, Sergei Shakhrai.

Chernomyrdin (whose position has strengthened) declares that 'The government will not retreat from the course of continuing and deepening reform . . . The course adopted by the government in 1993 remains unchanged . . . [but the new government must] . . . correct the course of reforms . . . The period of market romanticism is now over. But we will not permit its replacement by a fetishism of production . . . The current government considers the fight against inflation its utmost aim. But in fighting inflation we will switch from mainly monetarist methods to mostly non-monetarist methods widely tested abroad' (he seems to have in mind such measures as demonopolization and price and wage controls). Chernomydin forecast that the monthly inflation rate would be 15–18 per cent in the first half of 1994, 12–14 per cent in the second half and 8–9 per cent by the end of the year (the previous target was 5 per cent). (Note that on 30 January the prime minister talked of 15–18 per cent monthly inflation by December 1994.) ('It is vitally important that every member of the Russian government fully understands that a strong rouble is the indispensable condition for the revival of the Russian economy, and the Russian state as a whole': Chernomyrdin, *FT*, 16 May 1994, p. 15.)

The new more 'centrist' government (more in tune with parliament) was generally expected to pay greater attention to production, adopt a more selective approach to the allocation of credit (e.g. to encourage exports) and lay greater emphasis on demonopolization. Fyodorov is of the opinion that inflation will increase and that 'the government will evidently be one that is incapable of advancing reform'.

21 January 1994. Prime Minister Chernomyrdin says that 'The mechanical transfer of Western economic methods to Russian soil has caused more harm than good.' A government spokesman talks in terms of using only 'elements of Western market economics'.

Izvestiya: 'The government of reformers has ceased to exist in Russia. It is replaced by directors and apparatchiks who know only how to administer and issue credits' (cited in *The Independent*, 22 January 1994, p. 10).

Western advisers Jeffrey Sachs and Anders Åslund resign, saying that 'the aims and policies announced by the prime minister are strongly contrary to our views.' Sachs says that 'This is a massive failure of Western efforts. There was nothing inevitable about this result. We had a lot of ability to affect things and failed to do it. But the IMF, which held back $15 billion in Western aid this year, always claimed that everything was going fine and fails to see the consequences of its failure to deliver aid.' (For further comments by Sachs, see the section on 'aid'.)

23 January 1994. Leonid Abalkin, Nikolai Petrakov and Stanislav Shatalin (former advisers to Gorbachev), among others, are asked to prepare a report on fighting inflation by 'non-monetary means' and preventing a further decline in industrial and agricultural production.

25 January 1994. A presidential decree grants a 90 per cent increase in the salaries of government employees, backdated to 1 January.

26 January 1994. Fyodorov's resignation is formally accepted after a further period of negotiations (Sergei Dubinin, a deputy finance minister in charge of legal and insurance issues, becomes acting finance minister). Fyodorov warns of an 'economic coup' and a 'social explosion': 'the presence in the cabinet of the lifeless and illiterate ideology of Gosplan red industrialists, in the conditions of a market economy, would inevitably bring the country to ruin and the peoples of this country to a dreadful decline in their living standards. Ukrainianization has crossed over the border into Russia . . . It is inadmissible that people who have inflicted colossal economic and political damage on the state, who are resolute and open opponents of the course of reforms, should keep their posts in government.'

The public prosecutor's office instigates criminal proceedings against Zhirinovsky, charging him with spreading war propaganda.

8 February 1994. Andrei Illarionov resigns as chief economic adviser to the prime minister: 'I entered the government to conduct economic reforms, not to bury them.'

15–16 February 1994. On the first day of a two-day visit to Russia by the British prime minister, John Major, the two countries agree to stop targeting each other with nuclear missiles from May 1994. On the second day a future state visit to Russia by Queen Elizabeth II is announced (the first by a reigning British monarch since 1908).

16 February 1994. Two prominent Liberal Democrats leave the parliamentary faction in protest at Zhirinovsky (Vladimir Borzyuk and Vladimir Novikov). (Viktor Kobelev, Alexander Pronin and Vyacheslav Marychev have already left: *CDSP*, 1994, vol. XLVI, no. 14, p. 8.)

23 February 1994. The State Duma passes by 253 votes to sixty-seven (with twenty-eight abstentions; note that Russia's Choice voted against) the following resolution: there will be an amnesty for those involved in 'crimes in the sphere of political and economic activity'. Those concerned include (1) those involved in the events of 19–21 August 1991 and 3–4 October 1993; (2) elderly and ill criminals; (3) first-time petty offenders; (4) people convicted of economic crimes in the Soviet era. (Note that the president cannot veto this amnesty.) The State Duma also cancels a previous decision to investigate the events of 3–4 October 1993.

24 February 1994. Yeltsin delivers his state-of-the-nation speech to a joint session of parliament. The theme was the need to strengthen Russian statehood (1) at home, e.g. to tackle crime and to regulate the market: 'without a strong, effective state we cannot overcome the economic crisis or set up a true market system'; and (2) in foreign affairs, e.g. to defend the interests of ethnic Russians in the 'near abroad', 'The main task of our foreign policy is the consistent advancement of Russia's national interests.' 'Russia is against widening Nato by admitting various countries on the European continent and not Russia'. 'I shall defend and uphold the course of economic transformation . . . As long as inflation is not curbed, the crisis will be insurmountable . . . [but] . . . The task is to find a reasonable balance between the pace of reform and its social cost . . . [but] . . . The past two years have shown that reform is not the only thing that exacts social costs. Even greater harm is being caused by delaying urgently needed changes in the economic mechanism. It is time to establish effective state regulation that is compatible with market mechanisms . . . The year 1994 must be the year in which the effective structural reorganization of the Russian economy begins.'

The only reference to the State Duma's amnesty was Yeltsin's view that 'societal reconciliation is not all-forgiveness. Mercy is only mercy when it is not at variance with the law or the norms of morality.'

(Zhirinovsky's comment: 'I would have said that 10,000 criminal gangs must be eliminated within three months or the interior minister will be dismissed.')

26 February 1994. Among those released from prison are Rutskoi and Khasbulatov. (The latter vows to retire from politics and concentrate on academic studies of economic policy. The prosecutor-general, Alexei Kazannik, resigns, saying that he cannot carry out Yeltsin's request to suspend the amnesty (Yeltsin's argument is that parliament has in effect pardoned men not actually convicted). (Kazannik later said that 'my resignation is connected with the fact that demands were being made on me to break the law, but I am unable to break the law': *CDSP*, 1994, vol. XLVI, no. 9, p. 1. On 7 April 1994 the Council of the Federation refused to accept his resignation.)

The G7 countries hear that Russia aims to reduce the monthly inflation rate to 7–9 per cent by the end of 1994 and to reduce the budget deficit to 5 per cent of GDP. But they insist that Russia must reach agreement with the IMF before IMF help is forthcoming and negotiations about official debt rescheduling resume (the current Paris Club agreement expires at the end of April). However, the World Bank is encouraged to help set up a social security net in Russia (specifically to use $500 million of its restructuring fund for the purpose).

28 February 1994. Nikolai Golushko, head of the Federal Counter-intelligence Service, is dismissed (he was replaced by Sergei Stepashin on 3 March).

4 March 1994. Yeltsin calls for co-operation with parliament in the form of a Memorandum on Civic Peace and Accord: 'today in Russia democracy means above all stability, order and co-operation'. On the economy: 'Making inflation moderate, controllable and predictable is a paramount task. The target remains the same – about 5 per cent a month by the end of the year. The government set this figure in the programme adopted on 6 August 1993 and so far there is no convincing evidence that it needs to be reconsidered.'

Prime Minister Chernomyrdin says: 'The basic constraint is lowering the inflation rate to the 7–9 per cent [per month] range by the end of the year. And to have the federal budget no larger than 9–10 per cent of the gross domestic product . . . these parameters should be regarded as maximum allowable figures, especially those for the inflation level . . . we shall actively seek reserves that will make it possible to draw steadily closer to the target of 3–5 per cent by the end of the year that was mentioned in the president's message. These are certainly rather rigorous limits.' (The government's draft budget mentions an average monthly inflation rate of 11–12 per cent in 1994. The budget deficit is planned to be 10.2 per cent of GNP, compared with 10.5 per cent in 1993.)

Prime Minister Chernomyrdin: 'Our choice is fairly limited. If we let inflation rip we shall end up in a spiral fall from which we will not be able to extract ourselves. But if we stop production we shall end up with a seething country, collapse and chaos. Today's most important task is to walk along the edge of a razor blade without falling to one side or the other.' In reply to central bank chairman Geraschenko's view that inflation was a lesser evil than mass unemployment he says: 'if you want to have a weak state then go and give out money. If not, do not. Future Russian generations will never forgive us if we leave them a weak country.' (Later in the month he told the upper house of parliament that 'many, perhaps everybody, wants to be kind. But either we come to grips with the problem of financial discipline or we shall never extricate ourselves from this crisis.')

Gaidar's comment on the razor's edge analogy: 'There is no such dilemma. Economic decline is by and large caused by our failure to adhere to tough monetary policies.'

9 March 1994. Yeltsin refuses to meet former US president Richard Nixon on the grounds that the latter had earlier met Rutskoi and Zyuganov.

11 March 1994. The Supreme Court rules that the August 1991 coup leaders must stand trial, albeit with new judges.

15 March 1994. Nixon meets Zhirinovsky.

16 March 1994. The 'Accord for Russia' is formed by communists, agrarians and nationalists (although not by the Liberal Democrats) in order 'to prevent the final collapse of historic Russia'.

18 March 1994. The newspaper *Obshchaya Gazeta* publishes what it says is the outline of a planned coup by senior government officials (the document became known as 'Version Number One'). (On 25 March it was reported that the article was a fabrication by one of the newpaper's own editorial staff, who said it was meant to be a work of fiction.)

22 March 1994. Michel Camdessus, managing director of the IMF, at the end of a visit to Russia agrees in principle to the second tranche ($1.5 billion) of the 'systemic transformation facility' (see the section on aid for the conditions laid down). (The IMF formally agreed to the second tranche on 20 April.)

Boris Fyodorov spoke out very strongly for ensuring strict conditionality (*FT*, 28 March 1994, p. 12): 'Is it not clear that, for three months, not a single economic policy measure has been enacted? . . . The sooner this money is handed over the sooner we shall see a change in policy – in the wrong direction . . . The $1.5 billion is immaterial to Russia . . . Its importance is that it would be taken as a seal of approval on "corrections" to the policy. This is now a purely political matter. The stakes are high. The idea is to abandon Western-type economic policies, with Western approval.' Fyodorov suggests that 'a budget should first be approved by parliament and the new government's track record examined. The government's performance on inflation . . . starts only in May, because of the three- or four-month time lag between credit policies and the inflation resulting from them. There is no valid reason to hurry before being reasonably sure that this government's new virtue is real . . . I think it is important for creditors to be sure that fiscal discipline is in place, and that obligations really will be honoured . . . I am sure that a weakening of the Western position on stabilization will be detrimental to my country.'

Jeffrey Sachs (*FT*, 31 March 1994, p. 21) calls the IMF action 'understandable': 'After withholding a $1.5 billion loan from the Russian reformers in the second half of 1993 on the grounds that the budget deficit was too high, it finally agreed the loan, in spite of a vastly larger deficit today. IMF action in the past contributed to Russia's gathering storm. Its action last week was a desperate move to help head off Russia's descent into chaos. Russian reformers are understandably nonplussed. Last year, with reformers in the cabinet, the IMF withheld financing when the budget deficit was about 10 per cent of gross domestic product; now it lends money to a 'cabinet of lobbies' with a deficit about 15 per cent of GDP and rising . . . The draft budget on which the IMF agreement is based is dubious. And yet the IMF's move was understandable . . . If the IMF had continued to withhold the funds, it would have amounted to the West's abandonment of Russia's reform hopes. Prime Minister Viktor Chernomyrdin's new-found prudence, whether feigned or real, would have been buried immediately by a political avalanche . . . The $1.5 billion means little, since it covers less than two weeks of Russia's budget deficit. Only a much larger aid programme, with a wiser stabilization strategy, could do the job.' (See the section on aid.)

31 March 1994. COCOM is disbanded.

2 April 1994. At the Liberal Democratic Party's congress, Zhirinovsky is given the power to control all party affairs until 2 April 2004 (including finances and the appointment or dismissal of any party office-holder). The congress will not meet again until 1997.

Several thousand nationalists and communists march through Moscow to commemorate those who lost their lives in the events of early October 1993. Rutskoi takes part in the commemoration (on 5 April he ruled out any co-operation with Yeltsin).

6 April 1994. Yeltsin publishes his 'Memorandum on Civic Peace and Accord'. Violence should be avoided in the pursuit of political goals. Among other things the memorandum specifically proposes that signatories should refrain from trying to change the constitution in any major way, from pushing for pre-term presidential and parliamentary elections, from stirring up passions related to the events of August 1991 and October 1993 and from calling for politically motivated strikes. Hoped-for signatories include the president, party leaders, regional leaders, union leaders, company managers and ministers. (There was a signing ceremony on 28 April, but among the absent signatures were those of the Communist Party, the Agarian Party and Yabloko. Yabloko refused because Zhirinovsky signed.)

26 April 1994. An elected member of the State Duma (and banker), Andrei Aizderdzis, is assassinated by the mafia. (He belonged to the New Regional Policy faction.)

1 May 1994. May Day is quiet, with only a few peaceful marches taking place.

11–13 May 1994. Yeltsin visits Germany.

16 May 1994. Sergei Shakhrai remains a deputy prime minister, but loses his position as minister for nationality affairs and regional policy to Nikolai Yegorov.

17 May 1994. Shakhrai submits his resignation as deputy prime minister (but it was not accepted).

26 May 1994. Prime Minister Chernomyrdin begins a four-day visit to China.

27 May 1994. Alexander Solzhenitsyn returns to Russia. (He was deported on 14 February 1974. He undertook a staged train journey from Vladivostok to Moscow in order to acquaint himself with the new Russia and ordinary people; he arrived in Moscow on 21 July.) (Anne McElvoy maintains that 'while Solzhenitsyn remains broadly supportive of the president, backing him against the challenge to his power by parliament last October, he has strongly criticized Yeltsin's economic reforms as hasty and incongruent with Orthodox traditions of social organization, and berated him for failing to attend sufficiently to the needs of ethnic Russians stranded in the other former Soviet republics': *The Times Magazine*, 21 May 1994, p. 19. Solzhenitsyn thinks that Yeltsin's economic policy has led to 'theft and chaos': *The Economist*, 28 May 1994, p. 41. John Lloyd says that Solzhenitsyn 'sees the liberal reformers as dangerous, guilty of reckless experiments with the country on a par with those of the Bolsheviks eight decades ago, of having reduced Russia to poverty, dependence and criminality . . . Russia . . . should define itself as the Slav area – the Russian Federation itself, Ukraine, Belarus and northern Kazakhstan . . . even though he has made it clear he has no time for the more rabid expressions of the idea, such as those of Vladimir Zhirinovsky: *Weekend FT*, 28 May 1994, p. i. Solzhenitsyn has called Zhirinovsky a 'clown': *IHT*, 28 May 1994, p. 4. The efforts to liberalize the economy are 'brainless': Richard Beeston, *The Times*, 30 May 1994, p. 9. Solzhenitsyn has criticized price liberalization, where monopolies raise prices rather than output, and uncontrolled privatization, which has turned into robbery: Jonathan Steele, *The Guardian*, 30 May 1994, p. 8. Privatization has meant the 'plunder of national wealth': Andrew Higgins, *The Independent*, 30 May 1994, p. 7.) 'What we have is oligarchy and not democracy.' There should be local elections of 'honourable, selfless people who understand that power is not a privilege but a tough job . . . Gorbachev destroyed the system that existed. But it should not have been destroyed, only revitalized slowly, slowly from the bottom up, starting with the distribution of plots of land, the organization of small workshops, stalls . . . The freeing of prices is rob-bing the people, privatization is privateering, it should be dealt with by the public prosecutors and the courts' (*The Guardian*, 16 June 1994, p. 12).

8 June 1994. Russia and the OECD sign an accord on co-operation in developing a market economy in Russia, thus giving Russia observer status (note that some help has already been given).

12 June 1994. Yegor Gaidar forms a new party called Democratic Choice of Russia. (He was elected leader the following day.)

14 June 1994. The state prosecutor asks the Duma to withdraw Zhirinovsky's immunity from prosecution in order to face charges of 'incitement to war' and stirring up national hatred.

24 June 1994. Russia and the EU sign a partnership and co-operation agreement, which involves a strengthening of political and economic ties (for details, see foreign trade, below).

10 July 1994. Yeltsin joins the G7 meeting (8–10 July) as a full and formal participant in the political (but not economic) talks. (Informally the new grouping became known as the 'political G8'.)

11 August 1994. The verdict on the trial of General Varennikov is delivered. (The trial began on 7 July. Varennikov was the former commander of Soviet ground forces; his troops suppressed the democracy demonstrations in Vilnius in January 1991, when fourteen people lost their lives. Varennikov turned down the pardon granted by parliament to those involved in the August 1991 coup attempt and insisted on a trial – although a jail sentence was automatically ruled out whatever the verdict.)

The Military Collegium of the Russian Supreme Court found that Varennikov was not guilty of treason for his participation in the abortive coup of August 1991: 'In Varennikov's actions there was no plan to impair the defence capacity and security of the Soviet Union. He was guided exclusively by the state interests of the USSR.'

Gorbachev, who testified, did not come very well out of the court's verdict: 'If Gorbachev did not approve, he made no effort to prevent them from trying to save the country by introducing a state of emergency.'

19 August 1994. Gorbachev plans to help create a 'democratic movement alternative to the present regime'.

15 September 1994. Zhirinovsky wins a libel action against Yegor Gaidar and *Izvestia* for calling him a fascist (both have to pay 500,000 roubles).

('The situation is made confusing for outsiders by the lack of an assumed link in Russia between fascism and antisemitism. The word "fascist" is an insult to men like Zhirinovsky – who has won libel cases after being called that – because it is linked specifically with Nazi Germany': James Leek, *The Guardian*, 14 March 1995, p. 11.)

21 September 1994. President Clinton ends the need for an annual waiver of the Jackson–Vanik amendment (which links 'most favoured nation' status with emigration policy), but every six months a report must be submitted to Congress on the state of Russia's emigration policy.

4 October 1994. A presidential decree makes regional administrators ('governors') subject to presidential appointment instead of being elected (*IHT*, 5 October 1994, p. 2). The decree bans all elections for governors (*FT*, 6 October 1994, p. 2).

5 October 1994. The new session of parliament begins.

Viktor Ilyukhin, the chairman of the State Duma's security committee, says that Yeltsin 'has been suffering from alcoholism for a long time and cannot run the country'.

7 October 1994. The Council of Europe turns down Russia's application for membership on two grounds:

1. Constitutional guarantees of human rights 'seem to be more theory than practice. In many important fields the essential legal codifications have not yet been reformed as planned . . . traditional authoritarian thinking still seems to be dominant . . . the concept that it should . . . be for the judiciary to protect the individual has not yet become a reality in Russia'. The concerns of the Council of Europe included the difficulty of ensuring fair trials and the poor pre-trial conditions for remand prisoners.

2. The difficulty of actually implementing laws, e.g. enforcing property rights.

11 October 1994. 'Black Tuesday', so named because of the dramatic fall (21.5 per cent) in the exchange value of the rouble against the US dollar (see Table 3.3).

12 October 1994. Yeltsin talks of 'sabotage or the manifestation of a policy of extreme irresponsibility and slovenliness by the special groups of people who organized the rouble's disastrous fall'. He sacks acting Finance Minister Sergei Dubinin, demands that the State Duma should dismiss Viktor Gerashchenko (the chairman of the central bank) and orders an inquiry into the rouble's fall.

The State Duma decides to debate a motion of no confidence in the government on 21 October.

The rouble strengthens.

13 October 1994. The rouble rebounds strongly (ending the day stronger than before the 11 October collapse).

Andrei Vavilov takes over as temporary acting finance minister.

Presidential spokesman Vyacheslav Kostikov talks of a plot by commercial banks linked with the communist and nationalist opposition.

14 October 1994. Gerashchenko offers his resignation in a letter to Yeltsin and the president issues a decree formally endorsing it.

17–20 October 1994. Queen Elizabeth II visits Russia (the first reigning British monarch to do so).

19 October 1994. Rumours that Chernomyrdin has offered to resign on health grounds are denied.

Tatyana Paramonova is appointed temporary head of the central bank (the State Duma rejected her permanent appointment on 23 November, but she stayed on).

20 October 1994. The funeral takes place of the *Moskovsky Komsomolets* journalist Dmitri Kholodov. He was killed (on 17 October) by a bomb in a briefcase he thought contained information on corruption (such as the illegal sale of equipment) in the Western Group of Forces (that part of the army formerly in East Germany). He was due to appear at a parliamentary hearing.

27 October 1994. The prime minister gives his budget speech.

It is announced that the agriculture minister, Viktor Khlystun, is to be replaced by Alexander Nazarchuk (of the Agrarian Party).

The motion of 'no confidence' in the government fails to attain the requisite minimum 226 votes. The votes were 194 for the motion, fifty-four against and fifty-five abstentions.

Protest rallies take place across the country in response to an appeal by the Federation of Independent Trade Unions. Among the issues were the non-payment of wages, worsening economic conditions and widening income differentials. According to the union, more than 8 million people participated (*CDSP*, 1994, vol. XLVI, no. 43, p. 10).

4 November 1994. Alexander Shokhin, economics minister and deputy prime minister, tenders his resignation after the appointment of Vladimir Panskov as finance minister.

5 November 1994. Anatoli Chubais is appointed joint deputy prime minister in charge of economic policy.

8 November 1994. Yevgeni Yasin is appointed finance minister.

9 November 1994. Two new deputy prime ministers are appointed, Oleg Davydov (the foreign trade minister) and Alexei Bolshakov (formerly in charge of a high-speed rail link, who is given responsibility for CIS relations).

11 November 1994. The State Duma passes a bill involving compulsory Aids testing for foreigners unable to furnish proof of freedom from the disease. (An amendment was passed by the State Duma on 24 February 1995. The measure would apply only to those visitors staying for more than three months. Yeltsin gave his approval on 3 April 1995. The measure was supposed to come into force on 1 August 1995, but it was postponed. According to official figures, there are around 1,000 HIV-positive cases registered: *IHT*, 12 August 1995, p. 5.)

15 November 1994. Vladimir Polevanov, the governor of the Amur region, is appointed deputy prime minister and chairman of the State Committee on Property (the privatization headship formerly held by Chubais).

Polevanov was dismissed on 24 January 1995 after (1) advocating renationalization in such sectors as energy, defence and aluminium (those enterprises 'improperly privatized'); (2) objecting to the influence of foreign investment and (3) barring Western advisers and their Russian employees from the agency (except with his written permission), allegedly in order to protect national secrets. Polevanov became deputy director of the control commission (oversight administration) in the presidential apparatus. Chubais assumed overall responsibility for privatization on 12 January 1995 and on 26 January 1995 his ally Pyotr Mostovoi became acting head of privatization.

1 December 1994. The New Regional Politics faction is formed in the State Duma by over sixty deputies.

2 December 1994. Yeltsin's personal guard, which is commanded by Alexander Korzhakov, raids the headquarters of the Most group. This business group is headed by Vladimir Gusinsky, a close associate of Yuri Luzhkov (the mayor of Moscow).

(The Chechen crisis has already been dealt with in the section on the federal state. The assault began on 11 December 1994.)

5 January 1995. The new justice minister is Valentin Kovalyov (he was elected to the State Duma on the Communist Party list, but he is not a formal member of the party; he has supported Yeltsin on the Chechen issue).

28 January 1995. The Regions of Russia association is formed, headed by Vladimir Medvedev (president of the Union of Petroleum Industrialists). The association supports the retention of state regulation of the economy 'for the transitional period', state protectionism, 'domestic goods producers', 'the satisfaction of defence requirements' and the idea that 'every region must be given the right to choose the direction of its economic and social development on its own' (*CDSP*, 1995, vol. XLVII, no. 5, p. 16).

8 February 1995. Coal miners stage a one-day strike over back pay and subsidies to the industry. The miners claim that as many as 500,000 took part (this represents 80 per cent of the work force in the industry; 189 out of Russia's 228 underground mines and twenty-one open-cast mines were affected: *CDSP*, 1995, vol. XLVII, no. 5, p. 5).

13 February 1995. The Constitutional Court resumes work under the chairmanship of Vladimir Tumanov.

18 February 1995. Boris Fyodorov organizes the first meeting of a new political movement called Forward Russia (Forza Rossiya).

Alexander Yakovlev forms the Russian Party of Social Democracy (it is pro-Yeltsin).

19 February 1995. Yeltsin bans media advertising of tobacco, alcohol and unofficial medical practices. (This is officially aimed at improving the death rate, but critics see the danger of a weakening of the media through a reduction in revenue.)

1 March 1995. The prominent television journalist Vladislav Listyev is murdered, perhaps by the mafia. (He was executive director of the main television station, Ostankino. In April it was to be transformed into a public company called Public Russian Television, with the state's stake reduced to 51 per cent. Listyev was so concerned about the way the highly lucrative advertising was arranged via middlemen that he had ordered a temporary halt as of 1 April in order to devise a new system.)

1–2 March 1995. Foreign Minister Kozyrev visits China.

2 March 1995. Yeltsin vows to take tough action against the mafia and sacks the chief of police and the prosecutor-general of Moscow. (Apart from journalists and businessmen, three MPs have been murdered: Andrei Aizderdzis on 26 April 1994, Valentin Martemyanov in November 1994 and Sergei Skorochkin in early February 1995.)

4 March 1995. The funeral has mass public support.

6 March 1995. The EU delays signing an interim trade accord with Russia until progress is made on settling the Chechen crisis, e.g. moves towards political dialogue with Chechen leaders, access for humanitarian aid for refugees and continuing co-operation with OSCE.

7 March 1995. The mayor of Moscow, Yuri Luzhkov, threatens to resign if the police chief and prosecutor-general of the city are not reinstated (Yeltsin confirmed the sackings the day before).

10 March 1995. The State Duma passes (non-binding) votes of no confidence on Interior Minister Viktor Yerin and Prosecutor-General Alexei Ilyushenko.

12 March 1995. Russia's Choice announces that it will not support Yeltsin if he decides to stand in the next presidential election.

16 March 1995. Alexander Yakovlev resigns as chairman of Ostankino, talking of the lack of professionalism of the (money-orientated) staff (but he remains head of the successor Russian Public Television).

19 March 1995. The Party of People's Conscience is formed, with Alexei Kazannik (the former public prosecutor) as chairman. It claims to be a centrist party, whose charter denounces 'the adventurist policy of Russia's executive branch in all spheres of public life' (e.g. in Chechenia and the attack on the White House in October 1993).

2 April 1995. Alexander Rutskoi's political movement Derzhava (Power) nominates him as its presidential candidate.

7 April 1995. The Federal Counter-intelligence Service (limited to domestic operations) becomes the Federal Security Service, with expanded powers: (1) at home, for example, it is able to search homes and businesses without a warrant as well as to run its own prisons and (2) it is once again able, in conjunction with the Foreign Intelligence Service, to operate abroad.

18 April 1995. Referring to the 'near abroad', Kozyrev says that 'There may be cases when the use of direct military force will be needed to protect our compatriots abroad.'

25 April 1995. Chernomyrdin announces that he will form a new party.

This was generally seen as a 'centre–right' party, stressing 'stability'. Ivan Rybkin, speaker of the State Duma, was envisaged as setting up a 'centre–left' party (later called Harmony).

8 May 1995. V-E (Victory in Europe) Day, the fiftieth anniversary of the German surrender, is celebrated in Moscow with the unveiling of a bronze statue of Marshal Georgi Zhukov (his role was deliberately minimized by a jealous Stalin).

The 'Great Patriotic War' was won at the cost of almost 27 million Soviet citizens. In the period prior to the fiftieth anniversary war veterans were awarded privileges such as prison amnesties and pension bonuses.

9 May 1995. President Clinton and other heads attending the fiftieth anniversary watch a parade by Second World War veterans in Red Square (fifty heads were invited, but not all attended the parade, including those of France and Germany). President Clinton and most other heads avoid a large military parade of current forces because of the situation in Chechenia.

10 May 1995. At the summit meeting between Yeltsin and Clinton Russia agrees to subject the proposed sale of nuclear reactors to Iran to a joint Russia–USA commission (in order to ensure that 'only the peaceful part remains') and to cancel a separate agreement involving a gas centrifuge plant (used for enriching uranium). Yeltsin also promises to activate membership of the 'Partnership for Peace' scheme by the end of May.

12 May 1995. Chernomyrdin launches Our Home is Russia, a party with the stress on 'stability'.

23 May 1995. Yeltsin vetoes two State Duma decisions: (1) to maintain equal division of the 450 seats into party list and constituency candidates (Yeltsin wants a 150/300 split) and (2) to require candidates to step down from government office fifty days before the general election.

15 June 1995. The Council of the Federation votes in favour of the first State Duma decision (Yeltsin was expected to agree with this in return for the State Duma abandoning its second decision).

29 June 1995. A US shuttle links up with the Mir space station.

11 July 1995. Yeltsin is taken into hospital with heart trouble (he was expected to leave on 17 July, but his stay was extended until 24 July; he then spent some time in a sanatorium).

14 July 1995. Yeltsin signs a decree fixing 17 December 1995 as the date for parliamentary elections.

20 August 1995. There is an election in Yekaterinburg (formerly Sverdlovsk), the first in Russia for a regional governor for two years. The candidate of Our Home is Russia is defeated by a former governor, dismissed by Yeltsin in 1994 (*IHT*, 24 August 1995, p. 2).

6 September 1995. It is announced that the presidential election will be held on 5 November 1995.

THE ECONOMY

From plan to market

'The country runs on a mixture of inertia and anarchy' (Leyla Boulton, *FT*, 19 April 1993, p. 17). Whereas by the end of 1991 enterprises were extensively using barter for inter-enterprise transactions, by March 1992 they were seeking sales for roubles and credit from banks. Prices were beginning to play their role as an allocation instrument (United Nations, *World Economic Survey 1993*, p. 34).

Sachs (*The Independent*, 11 October 1993, p. 18) argues that 'Much progress has been made in the area of privatization, where the government's voucher programme has been popular and effective. Great advances have been made in dismantling price controls and abolishing the planning system. Yet the reformers have been completely stymied on macroeconomic stabilization and have been unable to abolish highly corrupted and inefficient controls on international and internal trade . . . these controls, such as export licences, are not only economically unjustified, but are also the seedbed of Russia's extraordinary corruption' (see the remainder of the quotation in the section on Western aid).

'The Russia emerging today is very different from what pessimists have prophesied. It is not falling apart but coming together. The new political institutions function. Strikes are rare and no serious social unrest is on the horizon. Incredibly, most of the Russian economy, measured by employment or output, has been privatized in just two years. Russia has already become a market economy, but one in the midst of long-overdue and massive restructuring. In short, Russia has undergone fundamental changes and appears to be on the right track' (Åslund 1994b: 58). Åslund accepts that 'major problems such as crime and inflation remain,' but 'even monthly inflation fell to 5 per cent in June [1994]' (p. 58). 'More daunting is the task of building a system of law,' but 'the situation . . . is far from hopeless' (p. 59). 'After an astounding 50 per cent surge in the number of registered crimes from 1990 to 1992, the rate levelled off in 1993 and dropped by 6 per cent in 1994 . . . Russia already has a functioning market economy characterized by real economic interests that defend themselves' (Anders Åslund, *IHT*, 25 April 1995, p. 8).

'Commercial relations between enterprises, based on freely agreed contracts, have supplanted administrative allocation in most parts of the economy. The market economy is rapidly taking over' (*RET*, 1993, vol. 2, no. 1, p. 5). 'The results of the widespread deregulation of 1992 continued to be felt. Queues virtually disappeared, and increasingly goods became allocated by market mechanisms rather than bureaucratic methods. There remains, however, a good deal of managed trade between enterprises, and much of the trade between Russia and the states of the CIS is conducted on an intergovernmental basis' (*RET*, 1993, vol. 2, no. 4, p. 5).

'Several important elements of market relations have appeared recently: economic freedom, the right of ownership and functioning markets for goods and services. But it is too early to say that the Russian economy is living according to the laws of the market. What we have now is a combination of new but still weak market mechanisms and old command levers. The administrative–distributive system has not vanished without trace; it has assumed new forms' (part of Boris Yeltsin's speech to a joint session of parliament delivered on 24 February 1994: *CDSP*, 1994, vol. XLVI, no. 8, p. 7).

As the economy disintegrated in the late Soviet and early post-Soviet period the regions of Russia came to play a more important economic role. Indeed, in a more general sense it can be argued that local government assumes greater importance in conditions of economic and political instability. Not only is central authority weakened, but the local population finds it easier to identify with and has more confidence in local administration.

'If the Soviet experience is any guide, it seems that to make an economy work coherently in Russia you have to choose what to control: the money supply, through fiscal and monetary discipline and a normal central bank, or human minds, through fear, propaganda and the secret police. But if you do neither, you end up with chaos' (Andrei Ostalsky, *FT*, 2 February 1994, p. 19).

'State procurement still covers a large part of transactions in most former Soviet republics' (Kasper Bartholdy and Ivan Szegvari, *Economics of Transition*, 1993, vol. 1, no. 4, p. 511).

'Although isolated market elements have appeared in the economy, the bulk of it still has not been transformed, and therefore we are unable to do anything substantive at this time about either the budget deficit or inflation' (Grigori Yavlinsky, *CDSP*, 1994, vol. XLVI, no. 11, p. 14).

'With regard to the state sector, control of firms' production via state orders has been relaxed. They are no longer mandatory in several states [of the former Soviet Union] and cover decreasing shares in most states. They are now used mainly to cover essential needs of the public sector, to effect inter-republic trade agreements and to ensure control over strategic exports for hard currency' (Gertrude Schroeder, *Post-Soviet Affairs*, 1993, vol. 9, no. 4, p. 298).

By 1992 almost no branch ministries were left in Russia. Most of them had transformed themselves into trade associations, performing such functions as lobbying for state subsidies, co-ordinating input supplies and production, investment and financial assistance, marketing and R & D. The associations appear to have played a very important support role in 1990–91. But by the summer of 1992 it was clear that the need for many of their functions would decline as their member enterprises learned how to operate independently (especially functions such as input supply and distribution) and other supporting institutional arrangements emerged (Joskow *et al.* 1994: 327–30). The Russian anti-trust law was adopted by parliament in March 1991 and became effective on 1 May 1991 (p. 331). Not much conventional anti-trust enforcement has been done; the anti-monopoly law has not been used to break up any enterprises (p. 359).

Criticisms of the way Russia's transition is being handled

'Russia, which managed to discredit the idea of socialism, is going to do the same with capitalism' (a Russian joke, quoted by Shlapentokh 1993: 19).

'Under the leadership of Lenin, Brezhnev, Gorbachev and others we were brought to the edge of a great abyss. But under the leadership of Boris Yeltsin we have taken a great step forward' (a popular joke circulating in 1993).

John Gray (*The Guardian*, 11 March 1994, p. 22) is very critical of the advice given by former advisers such as Sachs and Åslund: 'In Russia . . . market institutions exist outside any framework of law or civil society, in a kind of anarcho-capitalism of *nomenklaturist* privatization and of competing mafias. To suppose that such wild or anarchic capitalism will converge on any Western model, in a process of slow evolution, is a dangerous delusion. It is far more likely to issue in precipitate economic collapse . . . or in an authoritarian political backlash, as has already occurred in Russia. To imagine that policies of shock therapy which may have had some success in countries . . . where the legal infrastructure of a market economy was already in place, could work in countries such as Russia where it is almost entirely lacking betrays a staggeringly cavalier attitude to the realities of life in Russia. The truth is that we cannot know what mix of economic policies and institutions will be best for the Russian peoples. Their problems will be solved, in so far as they are soluble, by skilful improvisation, encompassing the development of policies offering a safety net for those dislocated by unemployment, not by the importation of bankrupt Western models.'

'Russia's transition to the market, largely on the advice of Western governments, has been handled so abruptly and hastily that it has given capitalism an almost irretrievably bad name, at least among a majority of the current generations of Russians' (Jonathan Steele, *The Guardian*, 19 May 1994, p. 26).

'The major mistake of reformers is that they followed the habitual revolutionary road – "to destroy the foundations and then . . ." But even a fool can see that what is required in this case is an evolutionary approach, a smooth and slow transition. The old economic mechanism has to be preserved, but reanimated from below' (Alexander Solzhenitsyn, *Moscow News*, 29 July–4 August 1994, p. 13).

Solzhenitsyn continued his criticisms in his address to the State Duma on 28 October 1994. 'We lost our chance in August 1991. We put back in power the very same communist officials we painted in democratic colours.' After travelling through many Russian provinces and holding hundreds of meetings, and later by reading thousands of letters that followed, I get the impression that 'the great mass of our people are disheartened, are stunned and in shock from humiliation and shame over their powerlessness, that they are not convinced that the reforms taking place and the policies of the government truly serve their interests. The people at the bottom have been virtually excluded from life. Everything that is being done in the country is taking place without them. They are left with a poor choice: either drag out an impoverished and submissive existence, or look for other ways: take up illegal activity, or deceive the state or one another.' Today it must be acknowleged that we are emerging from communism in the most distorted, painful and absurd manner. 'We all know that prices were freed to suit the monopolists. We know that not one citizen used a voucher to obtain (not even remotely) his share of the national property. We know from the press, here and there, about scandalous instances of privatization for a song. Somebody got some piece of property almost free, while the state received nothing. And we know that the state robbed 70 million depositors. . . . It taught them a cruel lesson: never trust the state and never do any honest work . . . We have often heard it said and still hear: "Why are you worried? The market will put everything in its place!" The market will not put the state system in place. The market will not create the moral foundations of society . . . What kind of society do we have today? It is hardly a democracy. What we have, let us admit it honestly, is an oligarchy. That is, rule by a limited, exclusive group of persons . . . I have found the key: do not fail to vote in local elections.' Solzhenitsyn believes that there is a simultaneous need both for a strong central authority with a vertical chain of command and for wide-ranging activeness on the part of the people. He believes that a much more apt term than local self-government would be *zemstvo* (the elective body of local self-government in rural Russia during Tsarist times). 'There should be a strong presidency . . . Who seriously believes in the CIS? Or that it will continue to exist? . . . The time has come for us to get completely out of Central Asia and the Transcaucasus . . . We must strive to establish a single state alliance of the three Slavic republics [Russia, Belarus and Ukraine] and Kazakhstan . . . To sell land at auction to the fast-ripening *nouveau riche* is tantamount to selling Russia itself.'

Oleg Bogomolov (*Moscow News*, 15–21 April 1994, p. 4) argues that: 'Having forgotten about our large domestic market . . . we followed the IMF recommendations and liberalized our foreign trade after the Polish model. One result was an immense outflow of capital and raw materials . . . We failed to consider that Russia has no private sector in agriculture and trade . . . As a result, we are experiencing runaway inflation and a production plunge incomparable to anything registered in Poland. Worse, we still place ideology above reality, and try to make ourselves believe in monetarist conceptions that have patently failed. We try to prove that the central bank causes inflation, that the economy is being ruined by an oversupply of money and not by the fact that the population lacks money, which means that effective consumer demand is extremely low . . . I believe that the main cause of instability and polarization in Russian society is the failure of 'shock therapy' and inadequacies in reform planning . . . 'shock therapy' was not properly prepared, it lacked social support, its proponents did not care about securing the people's approval, or the price it would be ready to pay.'

Grigori Yavlinsky (*CDSP*, 1994, vol. XLVI, no. 11, p. 14) argues that: 'It is impossible to attain macroeconomic stabilization before a sizeable sector that is really private has emerged in the country's economy and before structural and institutional reorganization has taken place . . . Although isolated markets have appeared in the economy, the bulk of it still has not been transformed, and therefore we are unable to do anything substantive at this time about either the budget deficit or inflation . . . The destruction of production monopolies is a task of enormous importance. However, in most cases it is being held back by the fact that gigantic state (or post-state) enterprises . . . support the entire vital systems of large cities: housing, medical care, children's institutions, recreation facilities and even education depend to a large extent on state enterprises . . . Therefore, the first step on the road to structural reorganization, conversion of the military–industrial complex and the break-up of monopolies must be the separation of social infrastructures from state and post-state enterprises.' He later added that 'bringing down inflation in the Russian economy within a short period is impossible; its roots are deeply institutional and structural in nature . . . the main objective of economic policy is not to combat inflation, but to bring about institutional and structural transformations in the economy against the backdrop of a relatively stable and predictable budget and monetary policy' (*CDSP*, 1994, vol. XLVI, no. 16, p. 10).

Note that, in contrast, Åslund argues that: 'One of the greatest myths is that Soviet production was enormously monopolized. The truth is the opposite. In the USSR, there were surprisingly many producers of various goods and the big enterprises were not dominant and not even particularly big by any international comparison. The problem was instead the regulation of the market that created trade monopolies . . . since the Russian belief was that the economy was dominated by gigantic producer monopolies, the anti-monopoly policy was characterized by price regulation, which further entrenched the trade monopolies. In reality, however, more liberalization and stabilization were needed, so that enterprises could compete and would feel forced to compete, as they would run out of money otherwise' (1996: forthcoming).

McKinnon (1994) believes that 'it was a major mistake for the Russian Federation, in January 1992, to suddenly decontrol virtually all prices within the state sector and to stop trying to enforce normal patterns of delivery within that sector' (p. 459). 'The big bang argument for total price decontrol is flawed if the important actors bidding for scarce resources have soft budget constraints . . . until budget constraints are hardened, uncontrolled bidding by state enterprises will cause the producer price level to increase indefinitely' (p. 462).

The title of Yuri Afanasyev's (1994) article reveals his extremely gloomy view of events, especially in the aftermath of the 12 December 1993 election: 'Russian reform is dead: back to central planning'. He believes that 'the political rearrangement in Russia that began with the attrition of reform forces in mid-1992 has come to an end . . . now it is clear that there will be no reforms, not even bad ones . . . Under the guise of social welfare policies, a planned economy will be re-established' (p. 21). 'The looming prospect of a return to the so-called planned economy is . . . disastrous. Russia's age-old penchant for subordinating economic considerations to demands for control by political leaders is again at work. Despite reforms since the time of Peter the Great, the economy remains a pre-modern, artificial construct completely dependent on the state life-support system and incapable of surviving by market-driven decisions' (p. 24). 'Today the gigantic super-monopoly of the state determines the gross national product. Central planning and distribution agencies have changed names but not functions. Ministries and institutions now call themselves "holding companies" and "concerns", but they still suppress all market-oriented competition.' Afanasyev maintains that the central bank has taken on many distribution functions, distributing finances at the federal level (which, he says, is essentially the same as distributing resources and planning the volume of production). At the regional level, he believes, distribution is controlled by the local *nomenklatura*. 'In fact, such distribution is the main work of all government administrations – in oblasts, republics and Moscow . . . The 400 or so monopolistic government agencies in various branches of industry all require subsidies. At their initiative new duties are being imposed on agricultural and industrial goods, thus eliminating competition, expanding opportunities for price increases and creating hothouse conditions for incompetent administrators. Pseudo-commercial banks that merely redistribute state finances and do not depend on deposits from people or enterprises now prevail. Among them are banks covering various branches of industry that add to the monopolies' strength. Fear of competition has led to a ban on foreign banks.' Afanasyev thinks that agriculture remains in a terrible state. 'A gigantic monopoly, Agroprom [Agro-Industrial Committee], is the main social brake on the development of agricultural production, the introduction of private land ownership and the formation of private farms or voluntary co-operatives. To this day peasants of the collective farms turn in produce and receive goods in return. A product–money relationship is lacking. In an astonishing and unexpected form, the archaic communal system of the Russian village, combined with Agroprom's socialist practices, has become an insurmountable obstacle to reform . . . Unlike Western subsidies . . . Russian subsidies go not to farmers but to Agroprom, a system without analogy in any developed country' (p. 25). 'Now is not the first time that reforms have been halted not only by the evil intentions of those in power but by three social forces that predominate in Russia. In production, the main driving force is the military–industrial complex. Its primary interest is receiving additional payments from the state budget. The second force is the collective peasantry, debased, used to a parasitic life style, thievery and shoddy work, supported by the agrarian *nomenklatura*. Their only hope is also the state. The third force is the bureaucracy, 20 million almost totally corrupt clerks who seek additional opportunities for bribes and form the black market. All three forces are aligned against the market economy and democracy' (p. 26). (See also his article in *CDSP*, 1994, vol. XLVI, no. 6, pp. 10–12.)

In a later article he states that: 'Russia has by no means been advancing towards the market and democracy . . . but in a directly opposite direction . . . It has not only not been reformed, but for the time being is not even being reformed . . . it is an over-centralized state-distribution system . . . if some stumps of this vast structure still function today it is . . . on account of the inertia of the old Soviet system; for example, operation with the help of barter or mutual exchange along the lines of directors' personal contacts. The centralization of the Russian economy is primarily explained by the fact that it has always been extremely militarized . . . Half of it [the economy] is a shadow economy . . . that is, half of the country's material wealth is owned by the mafia' (Yuri Afanasyev, *Moscow News*, 30 December 1994–5 January 1995, p. 3).

Peter Reddaway is of the opinion that: 'The bonds holding the state, political system and society together have slackened – the result of trying to carry out simultaneous political and economic revolutions in a society unready for them. Economic reform has been too ambitious and doctrinaire. This has caused the old state-run system to be replaced not by a true market economy, but by an unstable semi-market system, preyed on by a growing army of *mafiosi* and bribe-taking officials (Peter Reddaway, *IHT*, 14 January 1995, p. 6).

Crime

The scale of the problem

Stephen Handelman (1994) describes a deeply disturbing degree of criminality (though, of course, there is a history of crime throughout the Tsarist and Soviet eras). 'Organized crime is the most explosive force to emerge from the wreckage of Soviet communism. The so-called Russian "mafiya" has undermined reform, spawned extraordinary levels of violence in major cities, and helped fuel a growing ultra-nationalist backlash . . . Russia's crime syndicate constitutes a serious threat to post-Soviet democracy . . . The mafiya, Russian-style, is a hydra-headed phenomenon that feeds on the emerging market economy' (p. 83). Between 3,000 and 4,000 gangs operate in Russia. Although total gang membership is estimated at less than 100,000, 'the hazy boundary between criminal and legal business activity has allowed mafiya groups to penetrate most areas of the Russian economy, giving them disproportionate influence' (p. 83). According to the

Russian Ministry of Internal Affairs (MVD), organized crime controlled as much as 40 per cent of the turnover in goods and services by 1993. No criminal enterprise of this complexity could have succeeded without the support and encouragement of officials at every level. According to government investigators, more than half the criminal gangs in 1992 had ties with government. A number of cartels are fronts for the former Soviet elites, the '*nomenklatura* capitalists' (p. 84). The mixture of unbridled capitalism, organized crime and official chicanery has produced a crisis of government (p. 88). 'Russian policy-makers committed a fundamental mistake: they tried to develop a free market before constructing a civil society in which such a market could safely operate' (p. 89). 'The Russian mafiya's connection with government, born of its symbiotic relationship with the former communist establishment, makes organized crime a dagger pointed at the heart of Russian democracy. The danger is especially apparent outside the urban centres of Moscow and St Petersburg, where local crime lords and their government allies have filled the vacuum created by the departure of communist authority. These alliances are joined for political as well as economic reasons. As regional leaders seek more power over resources, they share a common interest with black-marketeers and underworld figures in resisting central control' (p. 90). 'The strong support for the neo-fascist Vladimir Zhirinovsky in the 12 December 1993 parliamentary elections owed at least as much to the backlash against crime as to economic populism' (p. 92). 'Organized crime has reinforced the old structures in their battle to retain control over key sectors of the economy and strengthened popular hostility towards the free-market democratic policies pursued by pro-Western reformers' (p. 94). The central problem is 'the legal vacuum at the heart of the Russian economy. Western advice and assistance in creating a commercial infrastructure, including a viable banking system and regulatory agencies, and in developing a legal framework for business activities would go far toward meeting the security concerns of Russian and foreign investors . . . International assistance in bringing Russia's justice and law enforcement system into the modern era is therefore crucial' (pp. 94–5). The MVD estimates that in 1993 $25 billion was transferred from CIS states to Western banks by organized crime (p. 95). 'As Russians increasingly identify free-market democracy with organized crime and corruption, they will turn toward much less congenial forms of governing. Unchecked economic chaos and gang violence could well foster the rise of a hostile, authoritarian power on the Eurasian continent, instead of the prosperous partner the West requires for a stable twenty-first-century world' (p. 96).

The danger of crime undermining democracy is well illustrated by a comment from a Russian citizen: 'We pretend to vote and the government pretends to govern. It is the mafia which runs everything' (cited by Anatol Lieven, *The Times*, 9 May 1994, p. 10).

The official figures record there are 5,700 criminal groups in Russia, with 100,000 members and operations in twenty-nine countries (*The Independent*, 26 May 1994, p. 1). There are an estimated 5,800 organized criminal gangs in Russia with more than twenty members; 200 were large syndicates with international operations (Tim Kelsey, *The Independent*, 12 July 1994, p. 17). *The Economist* (9 July 1994, p. 20) also mentioned the figure of 5,800 gangs. New estimates suggest that there are over 8,000 gangs, with 35,000 members (*The Economist*, 12 August 1995, p. 4).

The Analytical Centre for Social and Economic Policy (a presidential think-tank) estimates that 70–80 per cent of all private firms (local and foreign) and virtually all cafés, restaurants and retail shops pay 10–20 per cent of their earnings to mafia groups (*Business Central Europe*, July–August 1994, p. 27).

'The reformers . . . have been unable to abolish highly corrupted and inefficient controls on international and internal trade . . . these controls, such as export licences, are not only economically unjustified, but are also the seedbed of Russia's extraordinary corruption' (Jeffrey Sachs, *The Independent*, 11 October 1993, p. 18).

'The links between Russian criminal gangs and organized crime in the West are developing rapidly and ominously . . . These ties are becoming a serious menace to business.' (Marshall Goldman estimates that there are about 4,000 racketeering gangs, called 'mafias' in Russia. He says that they have gained great sway over 70–80 per cent of domestic businesses and are now demanding tribute from and even partnership with foreign businesses.) The going rate for 'protection' seems to be 20 per cent of income. 'The government appears helpless. But the imminent, much greater threat is the new international connections' (Flora Lewis, *IHT*, 13 October 1994, p. 9).

Thomas Friedman (*IHT*, 4 May 1995, p. 8) considers that: 'It is not the street crime that threatens Russia. It is the official corruption, the cheating of the state and businesses by their own employees and the mafia, which, if unchecked, is going to undermine Russian reform from within. It is already eroding the credibility of the government and courts, diverting resources, lowering tax revenues and driving away investors . . . rampant corruption could leave all those left out of the game looking for a man-on-horseback, maybe a fascist, to crack down.'

Åslund is optimistic about the prospects of controlling organized crime. 'The stage is now set for a long and intense struggle between law and crime, but there is little reason to believe that society will lose' (1994b: 69). After an astounding 50 per cent surge in the number of registered crimes from 1990 to 1992, the rate levelled off in 1993 and dropped by 6 per cent in 1994 (Åslund, *IHT*, 25 April 1995, p. 8).

Edward Luttwak (*The Guardian*, 31 July 1995, p. 11) also sees a brighter side to organized crime: 'it is the only counterweight to the greater number of firms backed by corrupt officials which now engage in ruthless monopolistic practices . . . Only the local criminal mafia may be able to resist the ex-Party mafia, if the two are not one and the same.'

There is also the common argument that today's criminals will eventually turn into advocates of law and order in order to protect their gains from future criminals.

Events relating to corruption and crime

27 July 1993. Yeltsin dismisses Viktor Barannikov (security minister) for 'personal violations of ethical norms [allegedly helping relatives to make trips abroad] as well as serious flaws in his work, including the leadership of the border guard troops attached to the ministry'. (He had been reprimanded the previous day over the loss of Russian soldiers guarding Tajikistan's border with Afghanistan. Note the entry for 21 March 1993.) Barannikov's successor was Nikolai Golushko.

28 July 1993. The praesidium of the Supreme Soviet declares the dismissal of Barannikov to have 'no legal force'; it is claimed that under a constitutional amendment adopted in December 1992 only parliament may dismiss the ministers of security, defence and foreign affairs.

18 August 1993. The commission set up by Yeltsin to combat corruption (and whose chairman is the minister of justice, Yuri Kalmykov, appointed on 5 August) proposes that the chief prosecutor, Valentin Stepankov, should be dismissed and that the Constitutional Court should 'review the conduct' of Vice-President Rutskoi (allegedly diverting state funds into a Swiss bank account). (Note that mutual accusations of corruption have been rife.)

1 September 1993. Yeltsin issues a decree suspending Vice-President Alexander Rutskoi and First Deputy Prime Minister Vladimir Shumeiko. 'The situation that has come about as a result of reciprocal accusations of corruption and legal claims against one another by officials in the system of executive power is seriously undermining the state authority of the Russian Federation . . . Rutskoi . . . and . . . Shumeiko . . . are temporarily suspended from the performance of their duties.' (The period will depend on the results of an official investigation.) (Rutskoi considers that Yeltsin is acting unconstitutionally, while Shumeiko claims that he had requested to be relieved of his duties in order to concentrate on clearing his name. Both have been accused of misuse of state funds earmarked for essential imports, Shumeiko allegedly authorizing the transfer of state funds to a company in Switzerland which failed to deliver the whole consignment.)

12 September 1993. Russia and Italy agree to co-operate in the fight against organized crime.

15 November 1993. All visitors from the other countries of the former Soviet Union who stay in Moscow for more than twenty-four hours have to register with the police and pay a daily residence fee of 750 roubles. The penalty for non-compliance is deportation or a fine of up to 430,000 roubles. Some exemptions were granted the following day, namely refugees, the handicapped, visitors seeking medical treatment, scientists, performing artists and others with official invitations. (St Petersburg subsequently required foreigners to obtain residence permits for a stay longer than three days.)

17 December 1993. Tougher immigration rules are decreed, including more thorough scrutiny of identity papers and requests for asylum. Tougher controls are also decreed for the employment of foreigners. Work permits are needed (costing the equivalent of the minimum monthly wage) and citizens of Russia should have priority access to vacant positions.

21 December 1993. Yeltsin abolishes the Security Ministry (successor to the KGB, although it had been made progressively much weaker than its predecessor). It is to be replaced by the Federal Counter-intelligence Service (the Foreign Intelligence Service deals with security matters abroad).

27 January 1994. Yeltsin is advised to create a special security force, answerable to him, in order to fight organized crime.

24 February 1994. Zhirinovsky states that 'I would have said that 10,000 criminal gangs must be eliminated within three months or the Interior Minister will be dismissed.'

26 April 1994. An elected member of the State Duma (and banker), Andrei Aizderdzis, is assassinated by the mafia. (He belonged to the New Regional Policy faction.)

14 June 1994. A presidential decree outlines a tough anti-crime programme. This enables the police to hold suspects for up to thirty days without charge (instead of two days), to scrutinize the financial affairs (including bank accounts) of suspects and their relatives without a court order, to search premises and cars without a warrant, and to use in court evidence gathered during these searches and by undercover methods such as phone-tapping and infiltration of criminal groups. (The reaction was very mixed. Opponents said that the decree was unconstitutional and/or a danger to human rights.)

1 March 1995. The prominent television journalist Vladislav Listyev is murdered, perhaps by the mafia. (He was the executive director of the main television station, Ostankino. In April it was to be transformed into a public company called Public Russian Television, with the state's stake reduced to 51 per cent. Listyev was so concerned about the way the highly lucrative advertising was arranged via middlemen that he had ordered a temporary halt as of 1 April in order to devise a new system.)

2 March 1995. Yeltsin vows to take tough action against the mafia and sacks the chief of police and the prosecutor-general of Moscow.

(Apart from journalists and businessmen, three MPs have been murdered: Andrei Aizderdzis on 26 April 1994, Valentin Martemyanov in November 1994 and Sergei Skorochkin in early February 1995.)

4 March 1995. The funeral has mass public support.

7 March 1995. The mayor of Moscow, Yuri Luzhkov, threatens to resign if the police chief and prosecutor-general of the city are not reinstated (Yeltsin confirmed the sackings the day before).

7 April 1995. The Federal Counter-intelligence Service (limited to domestic operations) becomes the Federal Security Service, with expanded powers: (1) at home, for example, it is able to search homes and businesses without a warrant as well as to run its own prisons and (2) it is once again able, in conjunction with the Foreign Intelligence Service, to operate abroad.

25 August 1995. Yeltsin states that 'Crime has become a real threat to the national security of Russia'.

Macroeconomic stabilization

'Shock therapy'

It has been argued that Russia has not actually implemented 'shock therapy', e.g. Åslund and Layard (1993). Here it is important to bear in mind that a narrow definition is being used, namely macroeconomic stabilization (austerity) measures. 'The reformers have been completely stymied in macroeconomic stabilization' (Jeffrey Sachs, *The Independent*, 11 October 1993, p. 18).

A January 1994 report entitled 'Russia's finances in 1993' and prepared under the direction of Boris Fyodorov concluded that 'a policy under which a budget deficit amounting to 10 per cent of the gross national product was financed by monetary emissions, inflation for the year came to 900 per cent, the population's cash income and average wages in all branches of the economy rose faster than prices, unemployment remained at a level of 1 per cent, and there were no enterprise bankruptcies or shutdowns cannot be called shock therapy by any criteria . . . in 1993 Russian courts of arbitration actually did register eight instances of bankruptcy. However, there are 220,000 enterprises in Russia, about one-third of which are operating at a loss . . . 70–75 per cent of Russian inflation can in fact be accounted for by the monetary factor' (*CDSP*, 1994, vol. XLVI, no. 6, pp. 14–15). Fyodorov himself has said that 'many people in the West, it seems, prefer to close their eyes to the simple fact that there never was any shock therapy, ever, in Russia' (*FT*, 28 March 1994, p. 12).

Illarionov (*CDSP*, 1994, vol. XLVI, no. 6, p. 14) says that the increase in the money supply in Russia was 130 per cent in 1991, 640 per cent in 1992 and 380 per cent in 1993. And, as a logical result, prices increased by 150 per cent, 2,500 per cent and 800 per cent respectively. 'When, during what period, has shock therapy (tough monetary and financial policy) ever been conducted in Russia? Even in the first five months of 1992 . . . the average monthly rate of increase in the money supply exceeded 11.4 per cent. To say nothing of the second half of 1992, when . . . it soared to 28 per cent, or 1993, when . . . it dropped to 14 per cent.'

Gaidar (*CDSP*, 1994, vol. XLVI, no. 6, p. 9) admits that although 'in those first months of 1992 a serious step was taken . . . within just a few months our policy began to spin its wheels. Under pressure from lobbying groups, particularly in the former Supreme Soviet, our firm line in budget and monetary policy was broken.'

It is reported that Mikhail Berger of *Izvestiya* thinks that 'shock therapy' in Russia lasted just sixteen days. It ended on 18 January 1992, when the decision to provide state subsidies to the coal mining industry was taken (*CDSP*, 1994, vol. XLVI, no. 3, p. 3).

The budget deficit was reduced from 31 per cent of GDP in 1991 to 1.5 per cent in the first quarter of 1992 (with all budget deficits expressed in annualized terms). But the budget deficit increased to 11 per cent of GDP in the second quarter and to 15 per cent in the third quarter (Woo 1994: 277–8).

In his state-of-the-nation speech on 16 February 1995 Yeltsin says that 'Two serious attempts were made to curb inflation in the years of reform . . . For various reasons the job was not implemented in full. The third attempt must be a success.'

The budget deficit and its financing

The consolidated budget on a rouble cash flow basis was 20 per cent in 1991 (*RET*, 1993, vol. 2, no. 3, pp. 6, 9). In 1992 the budget deficit on a 'rouble cash flow' basis was 4.7 per cent of GDP, but the 'overall government deficit on an accrual basis' was of the order of 20 per cent of GDP. The former excludes (1) extra-budgetary funds such as the Pension Fund, (2) off-budget interest rate subsidies and import subsidies and (3) unpaid obligations to the domestic economy and to foreign creditors. The budget deficit must be financed either by increasing base money or by borrowing at home or abroad (*RET*, 1993, vol. 2, no. 4, p. 10). The projected budget deficit for 1995 was 5.5 per cent of GDP, compared with roughly 10 per cent in 1994 and 15 per cent in 1993 (after allowing for quasi-budgetary credits) (*RET*, Monthly Update, 14 April 1995, p. 2). The consolidated budget deficit in 1994 was 9.9 per cent of GDP. The federal deficit on a cash flow basis was 10.4 per cent of GDP (close to the 9.6 per cent planned), of which more than 70 per cent was financed with credits from the central bank (*RET*, 1995, vol. 3, no. 4, pp. 4, 9).

The 'cash deficit' was 8.8 per cent of GDP in 1992 and 9.5 per cent of GDP in 1993, but the 'overall deficit' was 31.2 per cent in 1992 and 14.1 per cent in 1993. The former excluded (1) extra budgetary funds (revenue), such as pension funds (2.5 per cent and 0.6 per cent of GDP respectively), (2) import subsidies (11.9 per cent and 2.3 per cent of GDP respectively),

(3) central bank subsidies to banks for lending to enterprises (9.3 per cent and 2.1 per cent of GDP respectively) and (4) central bank subsidies to former Soviet republics (3.7 per cent and 0.8 per cent of GDP respectively) (*The Economist*, 16 July 1994, p. 41). Transfers to other ex-Soviet states and import subsidies have now stopped (*The Economist*, 11 March 1995, p. 36).

The budget deficit on a 'cash basis' excludes arrears in foreign debt payments (United Nations Economic Commission for Europe 1994: 126).

It is now the federal budget, rather than the consolidated state budget (including the regions), which is the central focus of debate. The federal budget has now been adjusted to include all interest rate subsidies, all foreign currency income and outlays and the formerly extra-budgetary production funds (the social funds, which are larger, remain outside the budget). (Note that import subsidies were abolished in late 1993.) (*RET*, 1994, vol. 3, no. 2, p. 9.) Unlike local budgets the federal budget can be financed by money creation. The federal budget deficit (on a cash flow basis) in 1993 was 10.4 per cent of GDP (*RET*, 1994, vol. 3, no. 3, p. 10).

The Economist (27 March 1993, p. 25; 3 July 1993, p. 72) reports the following, based on Sachs. In 1992 the budget deficit was 8 per cent of GDP, virtually all of which was financed by central bank credit, i.e. by creating money. In total in 1992 the central bank issued credits to the value of 40 per cent of GDP, of which about 8 percentage points were used to finance the budget deficit, 22 percentage points went to state enterprises (more than two-thirds of which was channelled through commercial banks and the rest through the Ministry of Finance; enterprises used nearly all their central bank credit not for investment or financing output but to replenish working capital, 10 per cent going into rouble bank accounts and 6–8 per cent into legal dollar accounts plus an unknown amount into illegal capital flight) and 10 percentage points went to the other republics of the former Soviet Union. The share of central bank credit in 1992 was as follows: the budget 21 per cent, state enterprises 54 per cent and other republics 25 per cent (*FT*, 3 April 1993, p. 2). According to *RET* (1993, vol. 2, no. 1, pp. 6–7), the extra central bank credit during 1992 amounted to 43 per cent of national income. The credits, as a percentage of GDP, were divided as follows: Ministry of Finance, 15 per cent (including 8 per cent for enterprise loans); commercial loans, 18 per cent (for lending to enterprises); other CIS states, 11 per cent.

On 10 April 1993 the Russian government and central bank agreed to limit the growth of new centralized credit for the second quarter of 1993 over the first to 30 per cent. Fyodorov's intention was progressively to limit the increase to 20 per cent in the third quarter and 15 per cent in the fourth quarter (but on 6 August the government raised both targets to 30 per cent). In the fourth quarter of 1992 the increase was 105 per cent and in the first quarter of 1993 it was 54 per cent (*CDSP*, 1993, vol. XLV, no. 15, p. 10).

Fyodorov reduced the credit issued from 42 per cent of GDP in the fourth quarter of 1992 to 25 per cent in the third quarter of 1993 (*The Economist*, 29 January 1994, p. 29).

The money supply was swollen by a factor of 7.4 in 1992 and 4.8 in 1993 (Gaidar, *CDSP*, 1994, vol. XLVI, no. 6, p. 9). According to Andrei Illarionov (*CDSP*, 1994, vol. XLVI, no. 6, p. 14), the money supply increased by 130 per cent in 1991, 640 per cent in 1992 and 380 per cent in 1993 (Illarionov resigned as chief economic adviser to the prime minister on 8 February 1994).

In the past two years the government has financed four-fifths of its budget deficit by, in effect, printing money (*The Economist*, 29 October 1994, p. 20).

In the first quarter of 1994 credit from the central bank accounted for 82 per cent of the total budget shortfall (*RET*, 1994, vol. 3, no. 1, p. 12). The budget deficit is financed mainly from the central bank. In the first half of 1994 this type of financing amounted to 80 per cent of the federal budget shortfall. But in order to reduce this inflationary method of finance the government now also sells government bonds and gold certificates. Net borrowing through these operations yielded a sum equivalent to nearly 14 per cent of the federal budget deficit. The remaining 6 per cent was covered by the partial sale of the IMF loan received in April 1994 (*RET*, 1994, vol. 3, no. 2, p. 13). 'In 1994 72 per cent of the state budget deficit was covered by credits from the central bank, that is, by printing money that had nothing behind it' (Anatoli Chubais, *CDSP*, 1995, vol. XLVII, no. 22, p. 7).

On 28 January 1995 the State Duma passed a law (which needed to be ratified by the Council of the Federation) banning the central bank from financing the budget by credits not approved in the budget. The budget adopted for 1995 included no central bank credits (the 5,000 billion credits voted for the first quarter did not break the rule, since the government planned to repay them later in the year). But it was still possible for the central bank to buy a limited amount of Treasury bills on the secondary market, thereby expanding the money base. The deficit was to be financed by issues of Treasury bills and private saving certificates and by foreign borrowing (*RET*, Monthly Update, 21 February 1995, p. 2).

The government's economic programme announced on 25 January 1993

The details are to be found in *CDSP* (1993, vol. XLV, no. 4, pp. 7–8; vol. XLV, no. 5, pp. 11–15). Inspired by Boris Fyodorov, the priority was financial stabilization (only thirty-five years of age when appointed, Fyodorov oversaw both the Ministry of Finance and the Ministry of Economics and was one of the authors of the '500-day confidence mandate': see Jeffries 1993: 71). The basic aims for 1993 were:

1. To reduce the monthly inflation rate to 5 per cent by the end of the year by, for example, tightening control over the supply of money and credit (Fyodorov says that 'There has not been one [a tough credit policy] since the first quarter of 1992').

2. To reduce the budget deficit in 1993 to no more than 5 per cent of GDP by, for example, cutting defence spending and subsidies to loss-making enterprises, although increasing social security spending to protect those most adversely affected by reform (in 1992 total state subsidies equalled 29 per cent of GNP: Deutsche Bank, *Focus: Eastern Europe*, 21 May 1993, no. 79, p. 4). There should also be government control over credits issued to other states of the former Soviet Union. Government securities were to be sold to help finance the deficit.

The first (three-month) Treasury bills were sold on 18 May 1993. The target was 15 per cent of the deficit (*The Economist*, 20 March 1993, p. 122). Currently about 10 per cent of debt is covered by issuing government bonds (Deutsche Bank, *Focus: Eastern Europe*, 31 July 1994, no. 112, p. 4). There was a gold-backed bond issue on 27 September 1993. On 15 February 1994 foreigners were allowed to buy up to 10 per cent of the Treasury bill issue.

In the first half of 1994 the budget deficit came to 10.9 per cent of GDP and the central bank's share in covering this was 67.3 per cent (*CDSP*, 1994, vol. XLVI, no. 36, p. 16).

3. To stabilize the rouble exchange rate in the second half of the year.

4. To slow the rate of decline in production, gradually stabilize output and contain the growth in unemployment.

Prime Minister Chernomyrdin also saw the need to toughen financial and credit policy, although he pointed out that 'We are on a "narrow path" between the abyss of hyperinflation, the sheer cliff of economic collapse and the blind alley of insoluble social problems. Therefore, at this point the government does not have a wide choice of options.'

On 24 May 1993 the government and the central bank signed a statement of intent promising the IMF that they would restrict credit expansion and try to bring inflation down to 10 per cent a month at most by the end of 1993 and the budget deficit to 8.3 per cent of GDP in 1993 (on a 'cash' basis). There was a commitment to switch, on 15 July, to a central bank interest rate 'at a level no more than seven points lower than the basic market-based interbank interest rate'.

The interest rate the central bank charged commercial banks for credit was as follows: 8 per cent (1991); 20 per cent (1 January 1992); 50 per cent (7 April 1992); 80 per cent (23 May 1992); 100 per cent (30 March 1993); 110 per cent (2 June 1993); 120 per cent (22 June 1993); 140 per cent (29 June 1993); 170 per cent (15 July 1993); 200 per cent (1 October 1993); 210 per cent (15 October 1993); 205 per cent (29 April 1994); 185 per cent (2 June 1994); 170 per cent (later in the month); 155 per cent (30 June 1994); 150 per cent (1 August 1994); 130 per cent (22 August 1994); 200 per cent (6 January 1995; up from 180 per cent); 195 per cent (mid-May 1995); 180 per cent (20 June 1995). (Note Aslund's point that 17.5 per cent a month amounts to 592 per cent a year and not the 210 per cent cited by the Russian authorities: *FT*, 12 April 1994, p. 18). The interest rate on three-month interbank credit turned positive in real terms in November 1993 (*RET*, Monthly Update, 30 April 1994, p. 3).

A massive fall in the exchange rate of the rouble on 11 October 1994 ('Black Tuesday') led to a large rise in the rate of interest, from 130 per cent to 170 per cent (see the entry for that date in the chronology).

In September 1993 it was decided to do away with subsidized credits for enterprises. Credits would henceforth to be issued at a uniform central bank interest rate (United Nations, *World Economic and Social Survey*, 1994, p. 37). There was a pledge to refuse to continue 'to provide credits for the mutual offsetting of enterprises' non-payments' (*CDSP*, 1993, vol. XLV, no. 20, p. 8).

Bankruptcy

A bankruptcy law came into effect on 1 March 1993 (*CDSP*, 1993, vol. XLV, no. 5, p. 21; no. 12, p. 29). A decision on the bankruptcy of an enterprise can be made only by a court of arbitration in response to an appeal by the insolvent enterprise itself, its creditors or a prosecutor. The court has the right to either liquidate or (the preferred option) to reorganize and clear up the finances of the enterprise. After proceedings have been initiated through the courts, approximately two to two and a half years must pass before an enterprise can finally be declared bankrupt and be closed. During that time measures have to be taken to reorganize its finances and operations or other means used to try to save it. On 22 December 1993 Yeltsin signed a decree entitled 'On measures to implement the Acts on the bankruptcy (insolvency) of enterprises', which needed the approval of the Federal Assembly. One of the procedures was as follows: 'as the property owner, the State Committee for the Management of State Property, as represented by the Federal Administration on Bankruptcy, decides that a debtor must submit a statement of bankruptcy to a court of arbitration; it goes to the court itself if the debtor is reluctant to do so on its own.'

Leyla Boulton (*FT*, 17 September 1993, p. 3) reports the first enterprise to be bankrupted under the new law (a cellulose plant in Archangel). According to Jill Barshay (*FT*, 29 December 1993, p. 2), only one small kitchen knife factory has filed successfully. Boris Fyodorov is quoted as saying, 'What kind of shock therapy is it if inflation runs at 20 per cent a month? If the whole nation had just five bankruptcies during a year?' (*IHT*, 2 February 1994, p. 4). *The Economist* (19 March 1994, p. 83) reported that bankruptcy proceedings had begun against fewer than fifty industrial firms;

all were small and not one had been forced into liquidation, according to the Federal Bankruptcy Agency. The agency later reported that it had liquidated or sold 400 state enterprises (*The Economist*, 18 February 1995, p. 82). In the first two years after price liberalization in January 1992 not a single enterprise was allowed to go under. But the Federal Bankruptcy Agency was established in late 1993 and by January 1995 the agency had taken action against 400 state enterprises that had defaulted on their debts. Courts had placed over 500 privatized firms in receivership (*The Economist*, Survey, 8 April 1995, p. 13). Only one coal mine has been closed since the launch of radical reform (p. 19).

Prime Minister Chernomyrdin has talked in terms of three categories of basic industries (*FT*, 16 May 1994, p. 15): (1) enterprises that have successfully completed a period of adaptation to new market conditions and are already increasing turnover; (2) enterprises which have yet to undergo such a period of adaptation, but which display the necessary potential to do so and have some hope of succeeding; this group is by far the most numerous and its enterprises should get state help; (3) enterprises which are beyond salvation and should be closed down in accordance with the law on bankruptcy; a list of such enterprises has already been prepared.

A new bankruptcy decree was signed by the president on 2 June 1994 in which specific criteria were drawn up for declaring enterprises insolvent. Control of insolvent enterprises would be handed to officials of the Federal Bankruptcy Agency, which liquidates the enterprises to cover debts or auctions them off at investment tenders. While investors who purchase insolvent enterprises would be responsible for paying the enterprises' debts, there would be an opportunity to gain full control (in the first phase of privatization it was unusual for any single investor to gain a stake greater than 25 per cent). In mid-July 1994 the agency declared the first three insolvencies (*RET*, 1994, vol. 3, no. 2, p. 34). By the end of September 1994 516 enterprises had been officially declared insolvent, fifty-six of which were auctioned off (*RET*, 1994, vol. 3, no. 3, p. 9). As of 23 January 1995 1,358 enterprises had been declared bankrupt out of 6,448 examined by the Federal Bankruptcy Agency. Sixty-one had been auctioned off during liquidation or privatization procedures (*RET*, 1995, vol. 3, no. 4, pp. 7, 99).

In a late November 1994 speech Chernomydin referred to about fifty enterprises having been declared bankrupt (*CDSP*, 1994, vol. XLVI, no. 47, p. 2).

The presidential decrees issued on 23 May 1994

These included the following:

1. Measures to combat tax evasion. For example, banks were only allowed to open accounts for enterprises that are registered with the tax

authorities. Moreover, an enterprise could only have one bank account. Banks were to notify the tax authorities of all transactions by physical persons involving sums in excess of $10,000.

2. The government was ordered to submit a draft law by 15 September 1994, which would reduce both the number of taxes and the tax rates (e.g. VAT and profit tax by 10–20 per cent) in order to stimulate output.

3. The introduction of the concept of the 'state-owned and state-operated enterprise'. Here the management (which can be changed) has only the power of day-to-day management and not full managerial authority, because of factors such as the illegal use of state funds, misuse of state property and the absence of profit for two consecutive years.

4. Highly indebted enterprises can be sold off; the buyer must then discharge the enterprise's debt within one month (foreigners are allowed to be buyers). Alternatively bankruptcy proceedings can be brought against the enterprise.

5. Enterprises which have foreign exchange at their disposal would be required to convert it in order to finance rouble expenditures.

6. An increase in the wage fund that exceeded the level of price increases by more than 70 per cent would be subject to a fine. (*RET*, 1994, Monthly Update, 30 June 1994, p. 3; *CDSP*, 1994, vol. XLVI, no. 21, pp. 9–10; *IHT*, 24 May 1994, p. 11, and 27 May 1994, p. 13; *FT*, 24 May 1994, p. 2; *The Independent*, 24 May 1994, p. 10.)

(On 28 October 1993 a decree demanded that all regional bodies which failed to pay their financial contributions to the central budget should be penalized in the period from 1 November 1993 to 31 January 1994, e.g. by the ending of subsidies, credits, export quotas and delivery of products, including imports, dealt with by the federal authorities.

The share of the 'territories' in total tax revenue was 44.1 per cent in 1992 and 58.8 per cent in 1993, while the respective shares of budgetary expenditure were 38.6 per cent and 50.1 per cent: Tesche 1994: 116–17.)

The July 1993 currency reform

The gradual replacement of old notes had been decided upon before, but on Saturday 24 July 1993 the chairman of the Russian central bank, Viktor Geraschenko, made a surprise and dramatic announcement about the currency. All rouble notes printed before 1993 (specifically 1961–92 notes) were to be invalid as of 12.01 a.m. on Monday 26 July. Russian citizens were to have until 7 August to change up to 35,000 old roubles; additional sums were to be placed in the state savings bank, where they would not be able to be withdrawn for six months and would earn interest at the 'established rate' (generally thought to be significantly below inflation). (The central bank estimated that 88 per cent of roubles in circulation were already in new notes, so only 12 per cent would have to be swapped: *The*

Guardian, 26 July 1993, p. 6; according to the central bank, the withdrawn banknotes would account for no more than 10 per cent of the total money supply in circulation in Russia: *CDSP*, 1993, vol. XLV, no. 30, p. 1; according to Western experts working in Moscow, the average Russian citizen had little more than 5,000 roubles in old paper money: p. 1; the central bank claimed that each Russian held only 8,000 roubles in pre-1993 notes, but this was shown to be hopelessly wrong: *The Economist*, 31 July 1993, p. 35.)

The alleged reasons for the move were as follows: (1) to reduce inflation; (2) to counter illegal activities (only legally earned roubles would be exchangeable); (3) to make counterfeiting more difficult; (4) to force other republics still using the rouble to synchronize monetary and fiscal policy with Russia (the bank claimed that rouble notes from other republics were undermining Russia's monetary policy and that it would be ready to supply them with new roubles if they would synchronize their monetary and fiscal policies with Russia's: *CDSP*, 1993, vol. XLV, no. 30, p. 5), otherwise they would not be issued with 1993 rouble banknotes and would thus have to introduce their own currency (the Finance Ministry estimated that 20 per cent of all roubles were held outside Russia: *The Guardian*, 26 July 1993, p. 6). It has also been suggested that the recent strengthening of the rouble against the US dollar was also a factor in the sense that roubles accumulated through dollar sales made a tempting target (*Moscow News*, 30 July 1993, p. 2). (Note that 'citizens of other states who are temporarily in the Russian Federation' would only be able to exchange up to 15,000 roubles and even then only on 26 July. The rest would have to go into the state savings bank.)

Yeltsin did not cancel the ruling, but a decree issued on 26 July substantially diluted it. The maximum amount of old rouble notes Russian citizens could exchange was raised to 100,000 and the period of time was extended to 31 August. In addition there was to be no quantity limit on the exchange of 10,000 rouble notes dated 1992 and all pre-1993 notes of ten roubles or less could still be used up to the end of August. (The official aim of forcing individuals to place sums exceeding 100,000 old roubles in bank accounts earning interest at a rate well below inflation was to make entrepreneurs declare untaxed revenues: Leyla Boulton, *FT*, 16 August 1993, p. 2.)

The currency ruling of the central bank was ill prepared, e.g. there was a wholly inadequate supply of new notes. There was much confusion, distress, panic buying of goods and panic selling of old notes. The prime minister had been involved in the decision and called a surprise cabinet meeting the day before the announcement (at which Chubais and Sergei Shakhrai had apparently spoken against the decision), but the Finance Ministry was not invited (Fyodorov was in the USA at the time and was not informed) and Yeltsin was on holiday (it is not clear whether he knew in advance of the announcement). This led to the allegation that the unpopular currency reform was a move inspired by parliament (parliament, to which the central bank is accountable, had gone into recess the day before the announcement) and the central bank in order to undermine Yeltsin.

(Note that, shortly before, parliament had passed measures to counter various Yeltsin policies and the to-and-fro battle continued until the president dissolved parliament on 21 September 1993:

1. On 19 July spending increases were approved which, if implemented, would have doubled the budget deficit to around 25 per cent of GDP (Yeltsin could veto the budget, but the president's veto could be overruled by a two-thirds majority in parliament: *The Economist*, 31 July 1993, p. 36). Veto and counter-veto followed until the dissolution of parliament.

2. On 20 July parliament cancelled the presidential decree of 8 May on voucher privatization. Parliament voted to transfer control of the privatization programme from the State Property Committee to the government, which, in turn, could delegate authority to ministries and departments (the aim was to encourage employee ownership and ministerial control). Parliament also voted to impose tighter controls on foreign banks. (Another battle between president and parliament commenced, as discussed below.)

3. The procurator (prosecutor)-general was given permission to investigate allegations of corruption against First Deputy Prime Minister Vladimir Shumeiko and Deputy Prime Minister Mikhail Poltoranin.

4. Parliament had also voted to restrict the activities of foreign religious organizations via a registration process.

But Khasbulatov (who seemed to know in advance) became very critical of the central bank's ruling. He called it 'a confiscatory measure and a direct violation of human rights.' On 28 July the praesidium of the Supreme Soviet declared that the central bank's limits on the exchange of notes were to be lifted; all pre-1993 notes were to remain valid until they could be replaced. But on 6 August parliament did not call for the ('understandable') ruling to be overturned and merely criticized the way the move had been managed (a resolution was also passed to remove Geraschenko from the cabinet).

Boris Fydorov said that his ministry 'did not take part in the preparation of this decision and considers it to be economically and politically harmful'. He described it as 'useless and unjustified' and 'a deliberate political provocation aimed at causing dissatisfaction among the population with the president, his government and the course he is pursuing . . . a direct deception of the people . . . [and] . . . a blow against economic reforms'. He called for the resignation of the chairman of the central bank, Viktor Gerashchenko. 'The action undertaken by the central bank of Russia to exchange old paper money is illegal from a juridical standpoint; it is senseless from an economic standpoint; from a political standpoint it is certainly harmful to Russia's interests, since it is a flagrant provocation aimed at undermining the people's confidence in the president, the government and the social and economic policy that is being pursued; and, finally, from a moral standpoint it insults and mocks the people of Russia . . . Moreover, the action that has been undertaken flagrantly tramples on the rights of citizens and enterprises in the rouble zone that have the misfortune to be using Soviet and Russian paper money . . . If the main objective of the exchange . . . was supposed to be protection against rouble intervention by the CIS countries, then this action was senseless from the very start . . . Even if only adult citizens of Russia exchange their money . . . [the theoretical figure that could be presented for exchange] . . . exceeds all possible estimates of the total amount of old-issue money . . . After the ceiling on the amount that can be exchanged was raised to 100,000 roubles per person . . . the total sum that theoretically can be offered for exchange grew to . . . two and a half times the total amount of both old- and new-issue cash roubles and five times the total amount of old-issue cash (Fyodorov, *CDSP*, 1993, vol. XLV, no. 31, p. 5).

General criticisms of the central bank ruling by reformers and government advisers included the following: (1) old roubles would actually be encouraged to flood into Russia from the other republics to be exchanged on the black market, while old unexchanged rouble notes would flow from Russia into the other countries still using them; (2) it would undermine confidence in the rouble (just at the time, moreover, when the exchange rate against the US dollar was beginning to stabilize); (3) there was no consultation with other countries and international organizations; loss of confidence in Russia could lead to the loss of aid; (4) trade links between the republics of the former Soviet Union would be further impaired; (5) it was possibly a way to cover up corruption and mismanagement, while the real criminals would either hold their wealth in forms such as hard currency or find a way round the regulations. Åslund discerned criminal motives in the central bank's action. He argues that it was no coincidence that it was taken 'immediately after the central bank's audit by the firm Coopers & Lybrand, according to whose report the passing of questionable sums through the bank cannot be ruled out . . . It seems to me that there is only one explanation . . . The central bank sold money to other republics and the central bank's officers got something for it.'

More radical proposals for monetary reform include that for a currency board, which would hold 100 per cent foreign reserves against roubles in circulation (i.e. there would be zero domestic credit creation). A fixed exchange rate would be maintained between the rouble and a suitable foreign currency such as the dollar (Steve Hanke and Kurt Schuler, *FT*, 12 August 1993, p. 13). In an article in *Transition* (1994, vol. 5, no. 4, p. 4) Hank and Schuler think that, rather than converting the central bank into a currency board, it might be more feasible to establish a currency board in order to issue a parallel currency (the resistance from vested interests dependent on subsidized loans would be less and the required foreign reserves smaller). The parallel rouble would be fully convertible, with an exchange rate fixed in terms of the reserve currency but floating in terms of the central bank rouble. Under this arrangement the central bank could, for a time, continue to be used to finance soft budget constraints. The central bank should be abolished when the real value of its roubles falls to less than 10 per cent of all domestic currency.

Jude Wanniski (*IHT*, 2 October 1993, p. 4) argues that if the government wishes to halt the rampant inflation, it has to start by reducing the oil price, signalling that it intends to increase the purchasing power of the rouble. 'A gold-backed bond issue, collateralizing the state's vast wealth, would then have credibility. The public finance problem would be resolved.'

Policy after the dissolution of parliament on 21 September 1993

On 4 October 1993 the central bank announced that as of 1 January 1994 all transactions in foreign cash were to be banned and that all enterprises had to return foreign banknotes to banks by 31 December 1993. But Russian citizens and enterprises would still have the right to maintain foreign currency accounts. Transactions by hard currency credit and charge cards would still be permitted. Permission to trade in foreign cash was to cease on 1 November. (After the dissolution of parliament Fyodorov put the central bank under the guidance of the government's credit commission, a committee to set macroeconomic targets: Jeffrey Sachs and Charles Wyplosz, *FT*, 11 January 1994, p. 17. In October 1993 Yeltsin placed the central bank under presidential authority: Ickes and Ryterman 1993: 252.)

The government's economic programmes

A three-stage programme was announced by the prime minister on 6 August 1993: (1) the 'crisis development' stage until mid-1994: the aim was to bring down the budget deficit to 8–10 per cent of GDP and monthly inflation to 5–7 per cent (the target for the growth of centralized credit was 30 per cent for both the third and the fourth quarters of 1993; there would be more selective support for enterprises); (2) the 'stage of stabilization' until the end of 1995: the priority was to stimulate investment through large privatization; by the end of the period the state sector was to account for only 35 per cent of GDP; (3) the prime minister forecast that the economy would begin to grow again in 1996 after beginning to stabilize in the second half of 1994. (The 'war of decrees' continued until Yeltsin dissolved parliament on 21 September 1993.) The targets revealed on 5 November 1993 were a monthly inflation rate of 3–5 per cent by the end of 1994 and a budget deficit of 5 per cent in 1994 (*CDSP*, 1993, vol. XLV, no. 52, p. 22).

The 1994 budget was finally approved by both houses of parliament on 24 June 1994. Although the budget deficit was supposed to be kept within 10 per cent of GDP (a figure of 9.6 per cent was agreed), there was general scepticism as to whether this was attainable (on the expenditure side there was heavy pressure from such powerful lobbies as defence and agriculture, while tax revenues were running well behind forecast levels). In an article in the *FT* (16 May 1994, p. 15) Prime Minister Chernomyrdin said that a budget deficit of 9 per cent of GDP would allow the monthly inflation rate to be lowered to 7–8 per cent by the end of 1994. (Some 5 per cent of the budget deficit was to be financed by the sale of state bonds: *Moscow News*, 22–28 April 1994, p. 7). There followed a debate about the extent to which the government had adhered to the macroeconomic stabilization programme.

Åslund (1994b: 63–4) describes Chernomyrdin's efforts to keep the lobbies at bay. In January 1994 Chernomyrdin seemed to promise considerable subsidies to agriculture, but he actually put up some resistance. Agriculture did end up receiving subsidies amounting to about 4 per cent of GDP. 'This measure was unfortunate but commensurate with the agrarian representation in the Duma' (p. 64). Throughout the spring of 1994 the military–industrial complex demanded up to 87,000 billion roubles (including arms procurement), while the draft budget offered 37,100 billion roubles (equivalent to 5.1 per cent of expected GDP in 1994). When the State Duma finally adopted the 1994 budget the figure was raised to only 40,000 billion roubles. 'The Russian military–industrial complex has proven to be a far weaker lobby than the agrarians' (p. 64). A positive interest rate was achieved in November 1993 and since February 1994 Russia has had 'a real interest rate of about 100 per cent a year – the highest rate in the world' (p. 63).

For the past year Russia has had some of the highest real interest rates in the world (*The Economist*, 8 October 1994, p. 24). In July and August 1994 the central bank issued credits worth 18,000 billion roubles (equivalent to 4 per cent of GDP) to the government at an interest rate of 10 per cent a year (*The Economist*, 22 October 1994, p. 119).

Jochen Wermuth, an adviser to the Russian Ministry of Finance, argued that an unprecedented austerity programme had been implemented in 1994. Shortfalls in revenue were met with severe expenditure cuts and real interest rates remained high. Critics of the government pointed to the fall in budgetary revenue from 29.5 per cent of GDP in the fourth quarter of 1993 to 26.3 per cent in the first half of 1994. But government expenditure was cut from 35.3 per cent of GDP to 32.8 per cent. Central bank lending to the government at 10 per cent a year was well below market rates, but credit ceilings meant that such lending fell over the first half of 1994 from 8.8 per cent of GDP to 7.9 per cent. The IMF's monetary base target was met despite the spring's soft credits and additional borrowing from the central bank in July and August. On 9 October 1994 the government set a budget deficit target for 1995 of 4–5 per cent of GDP, with the aim of financing a large part of the deficit by issuing Treasury bills and with what could well be the last significant injection of foreign credits (*FT*, 19 October 1994, p. 20).

In the first nine months of 1994 the federal government collected only 37.3 per cent of expected tax and other revenues (*FT*, 22 October 1994, p. 2). By the end of September 1994 only around 10 per cent of the budget had been financed by Treasury bills sales. Tax revenues fell in 1994 to a mere 11 per cent of GDP (*FT*, 24 December 1994, p. 2). The high growth of money in the third quarter of 1994 was due to a large credit injection at the end of the summer for agriculture, the northern regions and the defence industry (*RET*, Monthly Update, 17 November 1994, p. 7).

In late summer 1994 4,200 billion roubles' worth of soft credits went to defence and investments (John Lloyd, *FT*, 12 October 1994, p. 25).

In early October 1994 the Ministry of Defence was awarded extensive credit to cover its energy debt (*IHT*, 11 October 1994, p. 11).

Sachs argues that 'the general cause of the rouble's downward trend is easy to pinpoint. After pursuing a tight monetary policy for half a year, the government and the central bank flooded the market with new credits in the last three months to cover the government's budget deficit and relieve favoured enterprises of bulging debts' (*IHT*, 17 October 1994, p. 8). Sachs then asserts that 'Russian monetary policy has been in the hands of a few powerful people who understand little and care little about normal monetary policy and instead view central bank credits as a resource to be manipulated at will for short-run advantage' (p. 8). On a more positive note, Sachs suggests that the central bank should be given political independence and a clear mandate to protect the currency. 'The bank should stabilize the market value of the currency relative to the dollar or some other international currency. It should limit central bank credits to maintain the exchange rate target' (p. 8). Such a clear rule, he says, would speed economic recovery by bolstering confidence in the currency, thus allowing interest rates to fall. 'Under the Russian–IMF approach, because confidence in the rouble was so low, interest rates had to be held at 15 per cent a month to encourage roubles rather than black market dollars. After a few months of such punishing rates, it was not surprising that the Russians abandoned the IMF programme last summer . . . It is not too late to make the rouble a stable currency, backed by an IMF stabilization fund' (p. 8).

The 1995 budget was outlined by Prime Minister Chernomyrdin on 27 October 1994 in a speech to the State Duma, which approved it on 23 December. The budget deficit was to be kept to 7.8 per cent of GDP and the monthly inflation rate was to be reduced to 1 per cent by the end of 1995. Just under half was to be financed by borrowing from abroad, especially from the IMF. (Although the budget for 1995 included no central bank credits, it was still possible for the central bank to buy a limited number of Treasury bills on the secondary market, thereby expanding the money base: *RET*, Monthly Update, 21 February 1995, p. 2.)

On 7 February 1995, after three weeks of negotiations, the IMF suspended negotiations about a $6.25 billion stand-by loan and a $6 billion stabilization fund. The IMF was concerned about unfavourable fiscal and monetary trends, exacerbated by the cost of the war in Chechenia. Negotiations were resumed on 23 February and the following day the State Duma passed the budget for 1995 on its third reading. The budget deficit was to be a satisfactory 7.8 per cent of GDP and the aim was to bring the monthly inflation rate down to under 2 per cent by the end of 1995. The State Duma failed to override Yeltsin's veto of the proposed massive increase in the minimum monthly wage from 20,500 roubles to 54,500 roubles. On 10 March 1995 Michel Camdessus announced that he was recommending the IMF board to permit the stand-by loan, but that it should be paid out in monthly rather than quarterly tranches in order to ensure compliance with the terms. When the State Duma passed the budget on its fourth reading on 15 March 1995 (the Council of the Federation gave its approval on 22 March) it was announced that the budget deficit would be 5.6 per cent of GDP, owing to GDP being greater than first calculated. The deficit of 73.2 trillion roubles was to be financed by the issuing of domestic bonds (30.6 trillion roubles) and by foreign loans (42.6 trillion roubles), primarily from the IMF (*IHT*, 23 March 1995, p. 7). The IMF's decision to lend Russia $6.4 billion, announced on 10 March 1995, would help the government to finance two-fifths of the deficit (*The Economist*, Survey, 8 April 1995, p. 19). Subsidies to state industries accounted for half of the planned expenditure, especially agriculture and coal (*The Economist*, 11 March 1995, p. 36). The IMF approved a $6.8 billion stand-by loan on 11 April 1995.

Yeltsin issued three decrees on 1 March 1995. The main features were:

1. Only the president would henceforth be able to permit spending greater than or revenue less than that envisaged in the budget.
2. The cancellation of the tax and import duty exemptions enjoyed by certain companies and organizations engaged in foreign trade.
3. Further trade liberalization, although controls would remain for natural monopolies in sectors such as oil and gas, communications and some forms of transport.
4. The granting of ministry status to the State Anti-monopoly Commission and the Federal Commission on Securities and Capital Markets.

RET (Monthly Update, 21 March 1995, p. 2) argued that the Russian economy was set for a period of sustained disinflation: 'For the next few months the main factor will be the tighter economic policy of the last six months. Between October and December [1994] monetary growth averaged 6 per cent per month and in the first two months of this year there has been no growth at all in the monetary base.'

Inter-enterprise debt

The so-called 725 accounts system netted out the debts between enterprises and extended credits to net creditor enterprises. According to a declaration of the central bank on 15 October 1992, credits within the 725 system could be used freely to repay debts to enterprises in other republics, to pay back loans from banks, or to pay taxes; with permission they could also be converted into roubles or conventional non-cash accounts. All centralized credits granted to pay off their debts should be paid back by 30 December 1992. The fate of enterprises unable to repay debts owed to the banks by the end of 1992 was left to be determined (*RET*, 1992, vol. 1, no. 3, pp. 13, 40).

A significant element of corruption has been detected, e.g. when directors are bribed to supply goods on credit (Chrystia Freeland, *FT*, 12 August 1994, p. 2).

The size of the debt

Inter-enterprise debt grew from 48 billion roubles at the beginning of 1992 to over 3,000 billion roubles (70 per cent of GDP) by mid-1992 (IMF, *World Economic Outlook*, May 1993, p. 61).

Inter-enterprise debt was essentially eliminated during the payments crisis in summer 1992 by a massive credit injection, but by summer 1993 the debt had reportedly reached 60 per cent (in real terms) of the pre-crisis level (OECD, *Economic Outlook*, December 1993, p. 116). A figure of 112,000 billion roubles is mentioned by *Transition* (July–August 1994, vol. 5, no. 5, p. 19). But a mid-September 1994 source breaks the figure down into sub-categories; 55,000 billion roubles of non-payments between enterprises; 12,000 billion roubles of settlements beween banks; 12,000 billion roubles owed to the federal budget in back taxes (*CDSP*, 1994, vol. XLV, no. 37, p. 17). Inter-enterprise debt is the largest category of total enterprise arrears, amounting to 63.8 per cent as of 1 June 1994. The second largest category is tax arrears, followed by bank loan arrears and then wage arrears (*Transition*, 1994, vol. 5, no. 9, p. 5). By December 1994 inter-enterprise debt amounted to 196,000 billion roubles (*RET*, 1995, vol. 3, no. 4, p. 112).

Richard Layard (*FT*, 14 March 1995, p. 20) rejects the claim that Russia's factory managers have accumulated massive inter-factory debt while counting on the government to bail them out. The average delay in paying suppliers is rather less than in Western Europe. Most bail-outs go to agriculture, coal or defence and not to privatized industry.

An analysis of the debt

Ickes and Ryterman (1993) analyse the problem in depth. 'The attempt to impose a tight credit policy in a financially underdeveloped economy is the fundamental cause of the explosion of inter-enterprise arrears' (p. 250). 'An outcome of the debt accumulation has been a breakdown in economic stabilization. And, more ominously, arrears have proven to be a safety valve that enables enterprises to postpone adjustment . . . Arrears arise because enterprises find the adjustment to markets costly. When enterprises provide credit to trading partners of unknown viability, they discover that they can obscure their own viability. This loss of information undermines the commitment of government to policies such as bankruptcy and liquidation . . . To prevent the creation of new arrears, their primary underlying cause – the absence of financial discipline due to the underdevelopment of the financial system – must be addressed' (pp. 232–4). The Russian government's strategy comprised three main components: (1) to freeze all arrears incurred prior to 1 July 1992; these would be eliminated through the cancellation of mutual debt; (2) to set up a new agency to deal with the net debtor enterprises that remained after mutual cancellation (enterprise assets to be sold off); (3) to introduce measures to prevent the recurrence of debt, such as the threat of bankruptcy or liquidation and financial penalties (p. 234). The central bank imposed a regime of pre-payment on enterprises, i.e. enterprises were required to pay for purchases prior to their delivery. The central bank instructed commercial banks to create special off-balance sheet accounts for arrears, one for arrears to Russian enterprises (no. 725) and another to enterprises in other parts of the former Soviet Union (no. 721). Once all arrears had been identified and registered, the process of clearing mutual claims could begin (p. 236). When the offsetting of claims had been completed, the sum of the remaining credit (or debit) balances was 402 billion roubles (the gross debt had been 3.2 trillion roubles) (p. 237). The clearing of payables and receivables in the 725 accounts had been completed by the end of November 1992 and the clearing of interstate accounts by the end of December. (By the end of November 1992 the liabilities of net debtor enterprises within the 725 system amounted to 350 billion roubles: *RET*, 1993, vol. 2, no. 1, p. 21.) Enterprises were permitted to use net balances in their 725 accounts to settle debits in their 721 accounts and to settle overdue payments to the state budget. The remaining balances were to be frozen pending further instructions from the central bank. By the end of November these funds were so insignificant that permission was given to transfer them to enterprise bank accounts. But the system of pre-payment did not deal with the underlying financial problems of enterprises: 'the problem of financing production has been transferred from enterprises to the central bank. Central bank credit in the second half of 1992 increased dramatically, with devastating implications for the government's stabilization programme . . . Between June and October central bank credit to commercial banks trebled . . . These credits were then lent on to enterprises, often at interest rates that were highly subsidized' (pp. 238–9). 'Soon after the clearing process was completed estimates of the level of inter-enterprise arrears appeared which suggested that, by January 1993, the 5 trillion rouble level had been reached, approximately 20 per cent of GNP. This explosion in the level of inter-enterprise arrears clearly indicates that the combination of mutual clearing and pre-payment failed to stem the flow of new arrears. In particular, it failed because the Russian government and the central bank failed to signal their commitment to impose financial discipline on enterprises' (p. 240).

A number of measures have subsequently been taken to deal with the problem:

1. A decree of 20 October 1993 stated that all inter-enterprise debt had to be converted into three-month promissory notes. Non-payment of these bills on maturity would lead to automatic bankruptcy, although privatization could take place by swapping debt for equity. An insolvent enterprise could also be leased by an outside investor, who would be able to purchase (at a discount) 20–30 per cent of the shares of the enterprise if it was still operating after a year (*RET*, 1993, vol. 2, no. 4, p. 65). The promissory notes would enable creditors to sell debt to others, who could then try to recover the amount owing through the bankruptcy procedures.

2. On 4 February 1994 the government proposed a two-stage scheme. In the first stage the government would repay some of its own debt to enterprises on condition that the funds were used to repay their creditors. In the second stage enterprises would be forced to allocate part of their revenue to meet the debts owed to the tax authorities, the workers and suppliers in prescribed proportions.

3. A decree of 23 May 1994 allowed the government to start bankruptcy proceedings against enterprises that were more than three months late in paying their taxes. It also attempted to speed up the introduction of a system of promissory notes (*FT*, 24 May 1994, p. 2). The decree set a firm timetable for paying overdue debts and required enterprises to withdraw funds from hard currency accounts if they were unable to pay with roubles (*IHT*, 24 May 1994, p. 2).

4. A decree 'On the sale of state debtor-enterprises' was signed on 2 June 1994. Insolvent enterprises ineligible for state assistance would be subject to sale under competitive conditions. The manager would be automatically replaced prior to the sale. The buyer would be responsible for the enterprise's debts and for undertaking a certain minimum investment (*CDSP*, 1994, vol. XLVI, no. 22, p. 11).

5. A presidential decree of 20 December 1994, effective 1 January 1995, concerned non-payment. The bill for an item delivered under contract must be paid within three months of receipt of the item. If the bill is not paid the money owed to the enterprise is written off as a loss; bankruptcy agencies acquire the right to recover the money as state revenue (*CDSP*, 1995, vol. XLVI, no. 51, p. 23).

In February 1995 Yeltsin complained that the work of the government commission on the non-payment problem had been unsatisfactory (*CDSP*, 1995 vol. XLVII, no. 7, p. 4).

Prices

In early 1992 about 80 per cent of wholesale prices and 90 per cent of retail prices were freed of administrative controls. In 1993 the prices of petrol, coal, grain and bread were also decontrolled. There are, however, widespread direct and indirect price controls set by local authorities (on about 30 per cent of consumer prices). In addition price and profitability ceilings apply to monopolies (EBRD 1994: 35).

Prices were liberalized for most goods on 2 January 1992. During 1992 price liberalization proceeded in three phases. On 2 January most federal controls were lifted, except on utilities, transport, telecommunications, energy and certain foods. In March all federal controls on consumer goods were abolished and local authorities increasingly reduced their own controls (which had to be financed out of local budgetary funds). Local authorities directly control municipal transport prices and public housing rents. Indirect price controls through profitability limits also affect for many industries, e.g. the 600 enterprises officially designated as monopolies face a profitability limit of 25 per cent (*RET*, 1993, vol. 2, no. 1, pp. 7, 23; no. 4, p. 28).

The majority of goods and services are now sold at free-market prices. Since the beginning of 1994 there have been no price controls on goods and services officially designated as monopolies (other than those considered natural monopolies, e.g. gas and some transport and communications). Previously monopoly prices were controlled either by setting an upper limit, a maximum coefficient of price increase or a marginal profitability level (there was frequently evasion of these controls). Average commodity prices on the commodity exchanges are gradually approaching world price levels. By the start of 1994 domestic prices merged with world prices for sugar and petrol, but the crude-oil price is still 50 per cent of the world price (*RET*, 1994, vol. 3, no. 1).

During the second quarter of 1994 there were no significant changes in price policy. The majority of goods and services are sold at free-market prices, but the prices of products and services of natural monopolies continue to be regulated at the federal and local levels (e.g. electricity and heating supply, railway tariffs, basic communication services, housing and communal services). Since the beginning of 1994 other monopolies have not been subject to price regulation, but the authorities interfere if monopoly power is abused. At the regional and local levels there is price regulation of basic foods, some non-food goods and some services (e.g. direct price-fixing and limits on trade mark-ups and profitability). But there were fewer of these by mid-1994 (*RET*, 1994, vol. 3, no. 2). During the second quarter of 1994 the ratio of domestic to world fuel prices declined. In May–June the domestic price of crude oil was one-third the world level, while the relative price of oil products was much higher, owing to high excise taxes. Diesel and petrol prices were still very close to their world price. The price of wheat remained at 50 per cent of the world price (p. 40). Energy prices have been kept low by quota restrictions on exports (p. 6). *RET* now takes user prices reported by Goskomstat rather than prices listed on the Russian commodity exchanges. In March 1995 the domestic crude oil price was 38 per cent of the world level, while the price of petrol and diesel oil exceeded that on the world market, as did sugar. The relative price of wheat was nearly 70 per cent of the world price (*RET*, 1995, vol. 4, no. 1, pp. 44–5).

As of the beginning of March 1995 state-regulated prices accounted for 22–24 per cent of GDP. The aim is to reduce this to 15–16 per cent (*CDSP*, 1995, vol. XLVII, no. 9, pp. 4–5).

Oil and gas prices

Note that export quotas and inadequate pipeline capacity increase domestic supply and help keep prices below world market levels (see foreign trade, below).

In September 1992 the price of oil was effectively liberalized (it was subject to a progressive tax on prices above 4,000 roubles a tonne. Retail prices, however, were still controlled and subsidized. In February 1993 gas prices were still controlled at 3,600 roubles per thousand cubic metres (wholesale price; the residential price was 600 roubles) (*RET*, 1993, vol. 2, no. 1, p. 23).

In the summer of 1992 the price of a tonne of oil was about 2,000 roubles or 10–20 per cent of the world price (Lipton and Sachs 1992: 231).

In early 1993 the price of natural gas was only 5–10 per cent of the world price and in the case of oil around one-quarter in February 1993 (IMF, *World Economic Outlook*, May 1993, p. 61).

Another source put the domestic price of oil at less than one-third of the world price and other energy prices even lower (Edward Balls, *FT Survey*, 27 May 1993, p. ii).

Oil prices are currently about 30 per cent of world prices (*Izvestiya*, 1 June 1993, p. 4). At the end of 1993 the price of crude oil was only one-third of the world level (Flemming and Matthews 1994: 67). Another source put it at 25 per cent (*IHT*, 27 November 1993).

On 1 February 1993 the base price of crude oil was increased to 9,000 roubles per tonne from the old base introduced in September 1992 of 4,000 roubles a tonne (prices charged by producers above the base incur a penalty or tax, an amount set for each hundred roubles on an escalating scale; the price cap introduced in the 17 September 1992 decree remains, i.e. no more than 1.5 times extraction costs (Sagers 1993: 350). On 1 February 1993 industrial users of gas saw the 'base' price rise from 1,100 (established in May 1992) to 3,600 roubles per thousand cubic metres (4,000 roubles including VAT and transport charges). This new 'base' price is the maximum price, whereas previously the government had set a range of prices and imposed a penalty or tax. At the existing exchange rate the new price was only about 10 per cent of the world market price, but possibly as high as 25 per cent on a purchasing power parity basis. Households faced an increase from 260 to 600 roubles (Sagers 1993: 279–80). (To be precise, on 1 February the wholesale price of gas was raised from the previous level of between 1,100 and 1,600 roubles, while the price of gas for households was raised from 216 roubles: *RET*, 1993, vol. 2, no. 1, p. 55.)

At the current exchange rate the world price of gas is 50,000 roubles per thousand cubic metres (*Moscow News*, 11 February 1993, p. 6).

Layard (*Economics of Transition*, 1993, vol. 1, no. 3, p. 359) claims that in June 1993 the domestic price of oil was only 13 per cent of the world price and the price of natural gas was only 4 per cent of the West European price.

On 1 July 1993 a series of taxes on any oil sales made at more than 550 roubles a barrel were abolished; despite the tax the average price of oil was over 2,000 roubles a barrel, still only a ninth of the world market price (*The Economist*, 7 August 1993, p. 67). The price of gas was raised more than fourfold on 20 July 1993.

Crude-oil prices are a third of world prices (*Business Central Europe*, July–August 1994, p. 33).

In September 1994 the price of crude oil was about 30 per cent of the world level, the price of petrolem being higher because of a higher share of taxes (*RET*, 1994, vol. 3, no. 3, p. 46). In December 1993 the domestic price of crude oil was 58 per cent of the world price, but by December 1994 it was only 25 per cent (*RET*, 1995, vol. 3, no. 4, p. 44).

As for other energy prices, the price of coal was allegedly freed on 1 July 1993, but controls remained in reality (*FT*, 22 July 1993, p. 30).

Railway enterprises were allowed to fix their own tariffs on 1 August 1993 (*The Economist*, 4 December 1993, p. 97).

Price changes following the dissolution of parliament on 21 September 1993

Bread prices were to have been freed on 1 October 1993, but this step was delayed until 15 October. (According to one source, although Yeltsin decontrolled the price of bread by decree in October 1993, a law passed by the old Supreme Soviet that banned reaping more than 15 per cent profit from baking and selling bread expired only on 1 January 1994. Bread factories, worried about a political backlash, still do not allow the retail shops they supply to add more than a 15 per cent mark-up on their bread. Some local authorities have also imposed profit restrictions: *IHT*, 8 April

1994, p. 13.) There were also substantial rises in housing rents and interest rates were also increased. By way of compensation social security benefits were raised by 81 per cent as of 1 October and the pay of 'people working in bodies of representative power of members of the Russian Federation and in bodies of local self-government, judicial bodies and the Russian Prosecutor's Office' by 80 per cent as of 1 September. Funding was to be found in savings on subsidies to agriculture and industry.

PRIVATIZATION

The speed of privatization has been very rapid, but the nature of the programme has been highly controversial. Moreover, there has not always been consistency or unanimity about the desired speed of the process even within the government itself. Some members have blown hot and cold, e.g. on 1 April 1993 Prime Minister Chernomyrdin compared the process with forced collectivization.

Small privatization

A small-scale enterprise is one with less than 200 employees and assets of less than 1 million roubles as of 1 January 1992. Small enterprises are typically the property of municipal governments. The small-scale privatization programme is largely decentralized, with local governments having substantial independence in establishing many of the procedures and logistics involved. Small enterprises are sold either through unconditional auctions or tender offers (the latter are open or closed bid auctions in which the purchaser accepts some stipulations regarding the operation of the firm after privatization, e.g. with regard to employment; during 1992 70 per cent of small-scale sales were tender offers). Preference is given to workers by granting a 30 per cent discount on the auction price to successful bids from workers' collectives. The collectives are also allowed to spread 75 per cent of their payments over three years at zero interest. It is, therefore, not surprising that at the end of 1992 worker collectives owned 60 per cent of the shares in privatized small-scale enterprises, other firms owned 27 per cent and individuals owned 13 per cent. (See *RET*, 1993, vol. 2, no. 1, pp. 5, 8, 50–2, for the details of both small-scale and large-scale privatization.)

Large privatization

A large-scale enterprise is defined as one which had assets larger than 50 million roubles or employed more than 1,000 people on 1 January 1992, while a medium-size enterprise had assets between 1 million roubles or employed between 200 and 1,000 people. More than 5,000 of these medium and large enterprises (accounting for about half the industrial capital) were scheduled to be privatized before the end of 1993 (about half the shares were to go to managers and workers and 80 per cent of the rest were to be sold for vouchers). The privatization process involves deciding upon one of the three options (see Jeffries 1993: 477; if the collective cannot agree on any option, Option 1 is selected by default), transforming the enterprise into a joint stock company, and then distributing the shares in accordance with the chosen option. (Sutela says that under Option 1 the controlling stake was to be sold in a single block to an investor or a consortium through a tender or auction; 10 per cent was to be auctioned to the public at large, who could pay with vouchers. The government seemingly believed that Option 1 would be the most popular of the three, but by summer 1993 some 70–80 per cent of enterprises to be privatized had opted for Option 2: 1994: 420.)

When an option is chosen a local branch of the State Committee for the Management of State Property must approve the plan and then the enterprise is registered as a joint stock company. (As of the end of 1992, 64 per cent of workers' collectives in medium and large enterprises had chosen Option 2, 34 per cent had chosen Option 1, and only 2 per cent had chosen Option 3.) After incorporation the shares that are not taken by workers or managers under the chosen option are auctioned to the public (according to a March 1993 decree these sales must occur within two months of incorporation). (Preliminary surveys indicate that management teams end up with an average of about 13 per cent of the shares, which they either get at subsidized prices from the government, or acquire from workers, or buy in voucher auctions: Boycko *et al.* 1994: 257.)

In 1993 39 per cent of all Russian industry was privatized by voucher auction. More than 8,000 large and medium-sized enterprises were involved. The share of charter capital sold at voucher auctions average 21 per cent. Allowing for investment tenders (whoever commits themselves to the highest investment over some minimum requirement wins), outside investors have accounted for 30–35 per cent of the shares of privatized firms. Enterprise managers and employees are generally majority stockholders. The role of investment funds is highlighted by the fact that individual investors accounted for no more than 15–20 per cent of the total number of vouchers used in auctions. Foreign and private investors are now allowed to purchase privatization vouchers and participate in auctions without explicit permission from the Ministry of Finance (the draft state programme was published on 17 December 1993, although restrictions were not lifted on foreigners interested in buying shares in sectors such as defence, mining, fuel and energy) (*RET*, 1993, vol. 2, no. 4, pp. 65–7, 102).

By July 1994 more than 70 per cent of all enterprises had been privatized under Option 2, which allowed workers and managers to buy 51 per cent of the voting shares at a discount and with deferred payments. Another 21 per cent of enterprises chose Option 1, which directly gave workers 25 per cent of the shares (non-voting) and also gave them the opportunity to buy another 10 per cent of shares at a 30 per cent discount to book value (*RET*, 1994, vol. 3, no. 2, pp. 79–80). During the first stage of privatization, which ended on 1 July 1994, in 64 per cent of cases managers and workers acquired at least 51 per cent of the voting shares (the second option). Another 25 per cent chose the first option. Cash auctions were limited to 3 per cent of shares (*RET*, 1994, vol. 3, no. 3, pp. 93–4). On average shares in 18 per cent of the chartered capital were sold in open auctions for vouchers (p. 94).

Managers and workers own more than 50 per cent of most privatized firms (Maxim Boycko and Andrei Schleifer, *Transition*, November–December 1994, vol. 5, no. 9, p. 8).

Workers and managers often end up with more than 70 per cent of the shares in privatized companies; 'concessions to the management do not appear large on the surface, but in truth they are simply enormous' (Maxim Boycko, Andrei Shleifer and Robert Vishny, cited in *The Economist*, 12 March 1994, p. 46).

On average, insiders own some 70 per cent of the privatized enterprises (Yevgeny Yasin, cited by John Lloyd, *FT*, 30 June 1994, p. 27).

Vouchers with a face value of 10,000 roubles (corresponding to the historical book value) began to be distributed to the population on 1 October 1992 (by the end of January 1993 96 per cent of the population had received their vouchers). The vouchers were originally to remain valid (exchangeable for shares) until the end of 1993, but this deadline was subsequently shifted to 1 July 1994 (in some cases the deadline was extended further; the 28 June 1994 presidential decree gave workers the right to buy shares in their enterprises until the end of July; the city of Moscow was given permission to use vouchers for sales of city assets until the end of 1994; a presidential decree also authorized people to use vouchers in regional, as opposed to federal, privatization programmes until 30 November 1994: *RET*, 1994, vol. 3, no. 2, p. 82).

The market price of vouchers has fluctuated considerably. Compared with a nominal value of 10,000 roubles, for example, the value was 4,500 roubles in April 1993 and 27,760 roubles on 5 November 1993.

A 1 October 1992 decree increased the proportion of those shares auctioned to the public which must be purchased with vouchers rather than cash. The proportion was raised from 35 per cent to 80 per cent in the case of federal enterprises and from 45 per cent to 90 per cent for municipal government enterprises (*RET*, 1992, vol. 1, no. 3, p. 37). According to Anatoli Chubais (*FT*, 2 April 1993, p. 15), the inflation-adjusted book value is probably twenty to thirty times higher, so, on average, early investors were able to exchange each voucher for shares representing 74,000–110,000 roubles' worth of property. Most enterprises are offering 30 per cent of their shares for sale at auction. (Sutela cites an August 1993 source, which said that on average only 22.5 per cent of the shares of a given enterprise were sold in voucher auctions: 1994: 421; note that 'in auctions vouchers have actually the role of points', i.e. how many shares vouchers buy depends on the demand for shares in a particular enterprise.) In order to emphasize the unity of the country, 'cross-over' ownership is used, which means that residents of various regions can own property in other regions (*CDSP*, 1993, vol. XLV, no. 4, p. 33). The decree of 8 May 1993 laid down that at least 29 per cent of the stock of all enterprises changing their ownership status was to be sold for vouchers at voucher-based auctions beginning no later than three months after enterprises had become joint stock companies (*CDSP*, 1993, vol. XLV, no. 19, p. 24; no. 20, p. 27). Sutela (1994: 422) says that a presidential decree of July 1993 not only repeated this minimum proportion (and shortened the period allowed to two months), but also demanded that vouchers must be used as payment for not less than 80 per cent of the total number of shares for sale in each enterprise. But the presidential decrees, Sutela claims, fell victim to the political struggle.

Boycko *et al.* (1994: 249) usefully remind us that 'the decision to pursue mass privatization and even the specific design of the programme are largely dictated by politics'. Factors include the initially relatively sceptical public view of the value of privatization, a weak central government and a powerful managerial lobby (see the chapter on general issues for details). Sutela (1994: 418–19) also argues along these lines: 'The authors of the privatization programme evidently believed that breaking the ownership position of the branch ministries was the overwhelming priority if the irreversibility of the transformation was to be ensured . . . as the political situation remained unsettled, such bastions of the *ancien régime* had to be abolished as fast as possible . . . Russian privatizers judged the speed deemed necessary could not be attained without "bribing" the insiders.'

A 'war of decrees' followed until Yeltsin dissolved parliament on 21 September 1993. On 20 July 1993 parliament cancelled the presidential decree of 8 May and voted to transfer control of the privatization programme from Chubais to the cabinet. On 26 July Yeltsin issued another decree, which reinforced the earlier one, e.g. the three-month gap before the beginning of the auction was reduced to two months and it was more clearly established that voucher investment funds could only use the vouchers collected from the public for purchasing shares (*CDSP*, 1993, vol. XLV, no. 30, pp. 30–1). On 6 August parliament blocked the decree (by referring it to the Constitutional Court for a ruling) and on 10 August Yeltsin retaliated by issuing a counter-decree. A late October 1993 presidential decree strengthened the rights of shareholders by obliging the directors of public companies to pass on financial data and to keep accessible share registers: *The Economist*, 13 November 1993, p. 120.) A presidential decree that came into force on 1 January 1994 restricted directors' ability to rig shareholders' meetings and otherwise to ignore shareholders' wishes. For example, it banned all limitations on the sale of shares (a common tactic to prevent outsiders from gaining influence had been to forbid workers to sell their shares). The decree also stipulated that employee shareholders could not make up more than one-third of the board, which must have at least nine members for companies with over 10,000 shareholders (*The Economist*, 12 March 1994, p. 46). (Note also that the decree reduced restrictions on the direct use of vouchers by foreigners. Foreigners are now able to buy shares in companies via investment funds or to go direct to management and workers to negotiate an acquisition: *Business Central Europe*, April 1994, p. 45.)

No property restitution to former owners has taken place (EBRD 1994: 34).

The effects of privatization

There is considerable debate on the effects of privatization.

Generally negative comments

According to *The Economist*, few formerly state-owned enterprises have changed their behaviour or their management since privatization. In many companies a pact has been struck whereby workers are not dismissed provided they use their shares to support management. This has been encouraged by loose monetary policy (*The Economist*, 20 November 1993, p. 48). *The Economist* (12 March 1994, p. 46) quotes Grigori Yavlinsky: 'What has happened so far is not privatization, it is collectivization, which puts the workers and managers in charge of enterprises. Their interest is in increasing wages, not investment.'

Brzezinski (1994: 69) also argues that although 'much has been made by administrative spokesmen of Russia's allegedly large-scale privatization . . . most of the major industrial privatizations have involved essentially paper transfers of ownership to enterprise management, and sometimes to its work force, with the central government's purchases and subsidies unaltered'.

'The much-touted privatization often consists of management buy-outs by the same factory directors who were responsible for the communist disaster' (*Newsbrief*, August 1994, vol. 14, no. 8, p. 57).

'According to authoritative accounts disseminated at the spring meetings of the IMF and World Bank . . . the privatization effort has been a farce. The vouchers given to workers, managers and the general public passed through their hands so quickly that no one is certain what happened to them . . . workers were often blackmailed over the future of their jobs, and managers over the future of their control, and persuaded, with hard cash, to part with their patrimony . . . As a result the vouchers have been passed on to forces (including organized crime) which appear to have little interest in the establishment of free markets, private property and the service of shareholders . . . David Roche, of investment bankers Morgan Stanley, has estimated that 70–80 per cent of the privatized enterprises and commercial banks are paying a commission to organized crime, gobbling up 50 per cent of profits . . . The economics of privatization in Russia has become that of madness' (Alex Brummer, *The Guardian*, 29 April 1994, p. 22).

Sutela argues that: 'There has been little change in enterprise personnel . . . as is shown, for instance, by the arrears crisis, many enterprise directors have continued to behave as if the regime had not changed. Indeed, expectations of continued soft budget constraints have been self-fulfilling . . . enterprise managers deliberately suspend payments even when enterprises have sufficient funds, trusting that a general bailing out will be forthcoming. The expectations were proved correct in summer 1992 . . . the privatizers have vested much of their political credibility in the process of property transfer. It may simply be infeasible to impose hard budget constraints on enterprises that have been privatized in an environment characterized by so much political fighting' (Sutela 1994: 424–6).

Fyodorov is also critical: 'The problem is that privatization so far has not led to real improvements in efficiency or productivity. If you have a state enterprise and you take the state away but the management stays the same, the bureaucracy stays the same and the productivity stays the same, you have not achieved much. These companies pay no dividends. They do not allow outsiders as shareholders. They do not show the share register to anyone. It is not privatization. It is only part of the process. The second part is you kick out the bad management and you cut the work force and that has not happened' (Boris Fyodorov, *IHT*, 17 October 1994, p. 2).

(See Alexander Solzhenitsyn's address to the State Duma on 28 October 1994 in the chronology of political events.)

In a survey of enterprises undergoing privatization Ash and Hare (1994: 633) conclude that 'most firms reported extremely defensive reasons for privatization, seeking to change as little as possible while retaining substantial insider control'. The method of privatization opted for by most enterprises, which allows the *status quo* to be maintained, 'appears to be slowing down, at least in the short term, the adoption of market behaviour and hence progress towards a properly functioning market economy' (p. 632).

Alexander Bekker summarizes a lecture given by Yelena Belyanova in February 1995 (*CDSP*, 1995, vol. XLVII, no. 10, pp. 7–8). When voucher-based privatization ended, half the enterprises had no outside shareholders at all and two-thirds of them had no outside shareholders on their boards of directors. Supplier or customer enterprises were represented on boards of directors in a quarter of enterprises, investment funds in only 9 per cent and banks in 7 per cent. Only an insignificant number of the enterprises that have been converted to joint stock companies have shares traded on the stock market and most of these shares have low liquidity. A study showed that directors strove to achieve financial stability as first priority, with output not far behind. The significance of profit was only slightly over half the significance attached to output and was comparable with the ratings given to wages and number of employees. Paying off debt on schedule is not a priority because the threat of bankruptcy has not yet become real for Russian enterprises. The survival of enterprises has depended not so much on their competitiveness, profitability and financial situation as on the effectiveness of their lobbying (which depends on what and how much an enterprise produces and how many employees it has). A quarter of all industrial enterprises are money-losers and the same proportion break even. Although the incentive to increase the economic effectiveness of production is diminished by these circumstances, a pro-market model of enterprise behaviour is making headway.

Generally positive comments

Åslund (1994b: 67–8) states that 'managers are supreme to an extent unknown in the West.' Between 1989 and mid-1993 hardly any state enterprise managers were fired, 'allowing them to be criminally negligent of their workers'. A common complaint is that managers give themselves extraordinary salaries and fringe benefits, while 'much of Russia's capital flight appears to have gone from state enterprises to their managers'. But the powers of managers have been reduced:

1. A democratically elected parliament, consisting of political parties, has diminished their political influence.
2. The monetary squeeze has transformed managers into competitors.
3. Mass privatization has shifted power relations both in society and in business. Some 70 per cent of industrial enterprises have been privatized. Two-thirds of shares ended up in the hands of employees of those enterprises (altogether 40 million Russians have become shareholders). Consequently, managers' jobs are no longer safe. About 10 per cent of them are replaced at the initial shareholder meetings. In such cases small groups of insiders band together with outside owners against incumbent directors.

Joseph Blasi (*IHT*, 1 July 1994, p. 4) believes that 'Privatization has made huge strides in Russia. I am sure of that after eighteen months of studying 200 large state-owned enterprises that have been privatized. The average enterprise in this study has about 3,000 employees, and the enquiry has involved on-site interviews lasting up to six hours with company managers and local officials in nearly half the Russian Federation's eighty-eight regions, or states. The results are heartening. Employees are now majority shareholders at most companies, but managers exercise firm control, while outside investors have growing influence over many enterprises. The public also has a stake. And many companies are becoming more efficient than they ever were under the old Soviet system.' The specific findings were as follows:

1. Employees bought an average of 66 per cent of each enterprise (senior management got 8 per cent) and 21 per cent went to outsiders. The Russian government retained 13 per cent, and its shares were to be sold later to outsiders (particularly Russian or foreign investors who agree to put in money).

2. The outside owners of the 200 enterprises were mainly well known Russian investment funds, individual citizens, other Russian companies or foreign investors. There were only a few cases of shadowy, unidentified owners.

3. The formal privatization process was nearly complete and there was considerable evidence that the enterprises were becoming more efficient. More than 60 per cent of sales at the 200 enterprises were to private businesses.

4. The companies had cut employee rolls by 20 per cent since 1991 and the managers say they would have cut 20 per cent more if a social safety net had been in place.

5. More than half the 200 enterprises had already changed their product lines to reflect the products that consumers really wanted to buy.

6. Major outside shareholders (Russian companies and investment funds, and some foreign investors) had begun to demand fundamental change, even seizing control (this happened at the Vladimir tractor factory near Moscow).

7. Russian enterprises never had worker control. Fewer than 5 per cent of the 200 enterprises had any rank-and-file employee representation on company boards. Trade union power had largely vanished. If anyone had too much power it was the managers.

8. On the negative side, companies were starved of capital and were operating at significantly reduced levels, unable to find buyers for their products. Some senior managers still needed to learn how to negotiate with investors. There was a need for better accounting systems so that managers could figure out the profitability of different products. The boards at most of the 200 enterprises were made up entirely of senior managers, so outside shareholders had little chance to advise or discipline top management.

Fan and Schaffer conclude that they: 'See signs that Russian enterprises have made substantial progress in adjusting to the new market conditions . . . enterprises are changing their product mixes to meet changes in the composition of demand. They are looking for new customers, though progress in terms of exports is still limited. They are shedding labour and containing wage costs, with the hardest-hit sectors decreasing employment and cutting wages the most. Finally, enterprises are making efforts to control the levels of their receivables . . . However, there are also signs that adjustment in the enterprise sector is uneven and that the overall pace of adjustment is slow by CEE [Central and Eastern European] standards . . . A major reason for the unevenness and slower pace of adjustment by Russian enterprises is the continued, large government financial transfers to the enterprises, especially the larger ones' (1994: 183–4).

Despite problems 'many privatized enterprises have indeed begun to change their product lines, reduce employment and involve foreign companies in joint ventures. Major investors, who accumulated blocks in voucher auctions and post-auction trading, have actively challenged and even displaced old-school managers.' Perhaps most important, 'privatization has created a political constituency of entrepreneurs who, rather than concentrate their lobbying efforts on extracting further state subsidies, expect the government to go ahead with further reform in such areas as corporate governance, securities markets and law enforcement' (Maxim Boycko and Andrei Shleifer, *Transition*, 1994, vol. 5, no. 9, p. 8).

Buck *et al.* (1994) see an unexpected benefit in employee buy-outs (EBOs). 'Employee shareholders are . . . unlikely to want to hold shares in the long term, given their relatively undiversified status. As they sell their shares, the EBO is likely to degenerate . . . Yet, paradoxically, the likely degeneration of the EBO in large firms is its major strength.' They acknowledge the shortcomings of the EBO in decision-making and governance, but argue that its benefits have been underestimated. It is 'a flexible and versatile structure that can be expected to evolve gradually to produce the more conventional governance structures (with external, core investors) capable of achieving the real transformation of large manufacturing firms, as opposed to mere shifts in ownership' (p. 4). This versatility 'offers real prospects of gradual transformation in the long term: incompetent managers will find it difficult to hold on to power when individual employees exercise their right to sell stock to would-be core investors from outside' (p. 13). 'The choice of the EBO as the dominant vehicle of privatization has, perhaps accidentally, produced a flexible structure capable of evolution without interference from the state' (p. 14).

David Hearst (*The Guardian*, 25 June 1994, p. 12) reported a World Bank study which detected signs of change in newly privatized enterprises: 47 per cent of them had changed their product mix, while 57 per cent had introduced incentive-orientated work schemes. About 10 per cent of the privatized enterprises had changed management by mid-1994 (EBRD 1994: 34). At one in every ten shareholders' meetings held in 1994, shareholders voted to sack the management (*The Economist*, Survey, 8 April 1995, p. 10). Richard Layard (*FT*, 14 March 1995, p. 20) states that 'Managers now own around a third of shares in the typical firm, which gives them a powerful incentive to maximize shareholder value, and restructuring is going ahead fast.' 'What the privatization system has done, whatever its much criticized flaws, is to create 40 million shareholders where there were none before, people who have a stake in the new system. The intent was to make the shift from communism irreversible, and it may well have succeeded.' Although it should be noted that 'property rights are still insecure and poorly defined, as the new money and the old industrial managers fight it out for control of Russia's assets' (Thane Gustavson and Daniel Yergin, *IHT*, 8 May 1995, p. 10).

Privatization of oil, natural gas and public utilities

Oil and gas

Russia is the third largest producer of oil in the world, behind Saudi Arabia and the USA (*IHT*, 6 July 1994, p. 6). Although the oil enterprises are formally independent, the government still has the right to determine how 80 per cent of their output is distributed. The government principally uses quotas, which dictate how much oil each Russian oil company has to deliver to the central government, how much to the regions and, most important, how much can be exported (see foreign trade) (*The Economist*, 16 July 1994, p. 70). The industry has been split up into a number of corporations, with the state holding company Rosneft acting as overseer. The state will have a controlling stake in each corporation for at least three years, while up to 15 per cent of shares could go to foreigners. According to Joskow *et al.* (1994: 365), there are a number of competing integrated oil production and refining enterprises, separated from pipeline transport and product distribution enterprises. The details vary:

1. *Yuganskneftgaz.* The auction of vouchers for 12 per cent of the shares was to close on 19 November 1993. Workers and managers were to receive 50 per cent of shares and the other 38 per cent was to be held by Yukos, a state-owned holding company (part of which was, in turn, to be privatized) (*The Economist*, 13 November 1993, p. 120).

2. *Lukoil.* Lukoil accounts for about 15 per cent of Russia's output of oil and gas (*IHT*, 24 October 1994, p. 9). Lukoil is the largest of the oil companies (*FT*, 4 July 1994, p. 2). In April 1994 Lukoil swapped 7.4 per cent of its shares for privatization vouchers. It intends to sell, for cash, 20.4 per cent of its shares to Russian investors and another 15 per cent to foreigners. The government will keep 45 per cent of the company for at least three years (*The Economist*, 16 July 1994, p. 70). Some Lukoil shares are already owned by foreigners, including a 3.5 per cent stake by Crédit Suisse First Boston, while a 5 per cent stake has been distributed free among the company's managers (*FT*, 6 January 1995, p. 2).

Natural gas

On 25 April 1994 28.7 per cent of Gazprom's shares were publicly auctioned for vouchers reserved for Russian citizens. Gazprom was to buy 10 per cent of its own shares (all or some of which could, later on, be sold to foreigners). The staff of Gazprom already owned 15 per cent of the shares (since February), 5.2 per cent were to be reserved for inhabitants of the Yamal-Nenetsk autonomous region in the far north and the state would hold the remaining 42 per cent for at least three years (Leyla Boulton, *FT*, 23 February 1994, p. 3, and 27 April 1994, p. 3).

3. *Surgutneftgaz*. Produces about 11 per cent of oil output (*FT*, 21 February 1995, p. 23).

4. *Rosneft*. Produces over a third of oil output. On 3 April 1995 it was announced that it was to be transformed into a joint stock company. The government was to retain 51 per cent of shares for three years (John Thornhill, *FT*, 5 April 1995, p. 3).

5. *Gazprom*. Gazprom has a monopoly of gas exports (*The Economist*, 16 July 1994, p. 70). Fifteen per cent of shares were distributed to Gazprom personnel, a third went to the personnel of related industries in the gas-producing regions and about 40 per cent were turned over to public auction (*Moscow News*, 25 November–1 December 1994, p. 8).

Gazprom controls 24 per cent of the world's known natural gas reserves, supplies nearly a fifth of total West European gas demand and is Russia's largest single source of hard currency. Unlike the oil industry there has been no attempt to split Gazprom into smaller units. In 1994 34 per cent of its shares were sold for privatization vouchers in a closed auction held mainly in gas-producing regions. Employees hold an additional 15 per cent share, while the state retains a 40 per cent stake. Later in 1995 it was planned to sell to foreign investors 9 percentage points of the 10 per cent of the shares held by the company (*FT*, 10 January 1995, p. 17, and 27 March 1995, p. 19). The sale of 9 per cent of its shares to foreigners was postponed on 26 March 1995 (*FT*, 27 March 1995, p. 19).

Gazprom is the largest gas company in the world, accounting for 22 per cent of world production. In 1993 Russian gas output totalled 618 billion cubic metres, of which Gazprom accounted for 578 billion cubic metres (*Business Central Europe*, March 1995, p. 41).

Gazprom supplies up to 40 per cent of the world demand for natural gas. The privatization programme meant that 40 per cent of shares became federal property, 15 per cent of shares were distributed by closed subscription among the workers' collective, 10 per cent were sold for vouchers to the joint stock company itself, 1.1 per cent were distributed to the authorized capital of the joint stock society Rosgazifikatsia and 33.9 per cent of shares were sold at regional voucher auctions. Workers' collectives were not allowed to sell shares for three years and persons who bought shares at voucher auctions have to send in a written proposal in order to sell them (*Moscow News*, 17–23 February 1995, p. 8).

Electricity

The United Energy System runs the electricity grid and owns part or all of the various power plants. It was to offer 20 per cent of its shares to the public as part of the mass privatization programme. The government was to retain 51 per cent of shares and continue to control electricity prices (Leyla Boulton, *FT*, 27 January 1994, p. 2). Joskow *et al.* (1994: 365–6) describe the interim structure as follows: a holding company with the fifty largest generating plants maintained as separate subsidiaries; a national high-voltage grid and despatch centres; regional control of distribution, smaller generating facilities and combined power and heat facilities.

Telecommunications

Rostelkom controls some 80 per cent of telephone lines (practically all long-distance domestic traffic and much of the international traffic). The state owns 51 per cent of shares and 22 per cent of shares were to be offered to the public on 14 March–12 April 1994 (*FT*, 18 February 1994, p. 2).

Investment funds

Investment funds are permitted to own no more than 10 per cent of the voting shares of any one joint stock company. Moreover, an investment fund cannot hold shares in a joint stock company when the value of those shares amounts to more than 5 per cent of the assets of the investment fund. Enterprises of which the state owns more than 25 per cent of the authorized capital cannot purchase shares in privatized state enterprises (Ash and Hare 1994: 622). (Organizations 25 per cent or more owned by the state cannot bid in share auctions.)

Each investment fund was initially allowed a maximum of 10 per cent of the shares of any one enterprise (*CDSP*, 1993, vol. XLV, no. 4, p. 33). Then a presidential decree, signed by Yeltsin on 24 December 1993, raised the percentage to 25 per cent (*CDSP*, 1994, vol. XLVI, no. 2, p. 22). A decree of 8 May 1993 ordered that funds could use vouchers only to invest in equity and could not trade in vouchers themselves (*Business Central Europe*, July–August 1993, p. 57). More than 300 funds had been registered by the end of 1992 (*CDSP*, 1993, vol. XLV, no. 4, p. 33). There are now 657 registered investment funds (Celestine Bohlen, *IHT*, 19 March 1994, p. 2).

Following a number of scandals involving investment funds, a 12 June 1994 presidential decree banned dishonest advertising ('On the protection of consumers from unfair advertisements'). Another decree was entitled 'On the protection of the interests of investors'. The decree included the following clauses: 'the issuer of ordinary shares and/or their seller shall not be able to promise or grant guarantees of a definite size of dividend or a definite growth rate for the shares'; 'joint stock companies in cases envisaged by the given decree must be carried out in a mass communication organ'; 'in the event of patently false information being published by the issuer . . . the organ which registered the corresponding prospectus of the issue shall have the right to cancel in the prescribed manner the registration of the securities' issuance' (*Moscow News*, 1–7 July 1994, p. 8).

The MMM affair of 1994 exposed the lack of adequate financial legislation and even of enforcement of the existing laws (MMM claimed that the investment fund had 10 million 'shareholders', but other estimates ranged from 2 million to 5 million). The MMM company ran (among other things) a so-called investment fund, essentially a pyramid scheme. It relied on a boastful but hugely successful advertising campaign to ensure enough revenue from the sale of new 'shares' for a while to buy back shares at a huge profit for early investors. There was then no legislation specifically outlawing pyramid schemes. The Finance Ministry, the Anti-monopoly Ministry and the tax inspectorate criticized MMM on 22 July 1994 and this triggered a panic (inevitable at some stage given the nature of the scheme) and a plummeting of the 'share' price. On 31 July the prime minister announced that the government would not bail investors out despite criticism that the government should have acted very much earlier. The chairman of MMM, Sergei Mavrodi, refused to co-operate in the investigation and on 4 August the tax police used force to raid his home for documents. Mavrodi was arrested on tax charges and he retaliated by closing all offices (most had already been closed). On 15 August he was formally charged with tax evasion as general director of one of his other companies (Invest Consulting) and with obstructing the investigation. Further developments:

22 August 1994. The Moscow offices of MMM reopen for the sale of 'tickets'. Each ticket is sold for 1,515 roubles on the strength of a promise to exchange (at an unspecified time in the future) 100 tickets for an MMM share. (People were gambling that the share price would rise to at least 151,500 roubles. This was not illegal, but the government issued warnings.)

4 September 1994. The government bans MMM from advertising on those parts of the media that are state-run. The ban also extends to any similar organizations violating existing laws.

13 October 1994. Mavrodi is released on bail (he was due to contest a by-election on 30 October).

30 October 1994. Mavrodi wins a seat in the State Duma and is thus able to claim immunity from prosecution.

1 November 1994. Mavrodi announces that existing shares are to be 'temporarily suspended' until 1 January 1995. (New shares began to be issued.)

7 November 1994. A presidential decree deals with the securities market. A special licence is needed to deal in securities and in financial markets. The government ('in concert with the central bank') has until the end of 1994 to stop unlicensed activity and illegal issuing of securities (temporary authorization was later allowed until 1 March 1995). The decree also sets up a Federal Commission on Securities and the Capital Market (Anatoli Chubais as chairman) to ensure implementation of the rules and regulations governing activity.

Regional aspects

The process of privatization is taking on a decidedly regional character. Nizhny Novgorod has attracted considerable attention, but other towns have also started, e.g. Volgograd (8 February 1993), Tomsk (25 February 1993) and Yekaterinburg (formerly Sverdlovsk) (2 April 1993). A report in *Izvestiya* of 6 March 1994 said that 'four months from now check-based privatization will come to an end . . . More than thirty regions, led by Moscow, are stubbornly resisting this process, are boycotting check-based public auctions, and have not sold even 20 per cent of the property subject to mandatory privatization' (*CDSP*, 1994, vol. XLVI, no. 11, p. 12). (The mayor of Moscow, Yuri Luzhkov, argues that the government's voucher privatization programme benefits speculators. He prefers sales or leasing, the revenue from which would benefit Moscow.)

The best progress has been made in Moscow, Rostov, Krasnodar and Stavropol, while the least progress has been made in the central region, the southern regions, Siberia and the far east. The supply of enterprises for sale through voucher auctions often does not match the regional distribution of vouchers and a national voucher auction system is still in the process of being developed (Ash and Hare 1994: 626). Because the implementation of the privatization programme is so decentralized, a great deal of progress can be achieved without reference to Moscow-based ministries or the central government. 'Hence once the initial legislation has been passed, political disunity at the centre has not stopped privatization' (p. 633).

As of 1 November 1994 the extent of small privatization varied greatly, e.g. 98 per cent in Moscow and Krasnodar and 19 per cent in Tatarstan (and, interestingly, only 21 per cent in Nizhny Novgorod) (*RET*, 1995, vol. 3, no. 4, p. 97).

The extent of privatization

Table 3.2 gives an overall view.

In January–October 1992 the private sector accounted for 6.7 per cent of industrial output (United Nations Economic Commission for Europe 1993: 215).

Table 3.2 Russia: privatization

Date		*Total no. of enterprises privatized*	*Percentage of industrial workers in private enterprises (workers in medium-sized and large industrial enterprises)*
1992	March	1,352	
	April	2,995	
	May	5,855	
	June	8,933	
	July	12,015	
	August	17,230	
	September	22,572	
	October	29,235	
	November	34,932	
	December	46,815	0.2
1993	January	54,243	1.1
	February	57,989	2.0
	March	59,495	4.6
	April	66,000	8.6
	May	68,000	11.3
	June	72,000	15.5
	July	78,000	19.1
	August	81,000	22.9
	September	82,000	26.8
	October	83,000	30.9
	November	86,000	35.1
	December	89,000	40.0
1994	January	91,000	43.1
	February	93,000	49.1
	March	95,000	54.0
	April	98,000	59.8
	May	99,000	65.0
	June	102,000	81.8
	July	104,000	
	August	106,000	
	September	108,000	
	October	109,000	
	November	110,000	
	December	112,000	
1995	January	113,000	
	February	114,000	
	March	115,000	
	April	116,000	

Source: *Russian Economic Trends* (various issues)

The end of August 1993 marked the first nine months of voucher privatization, during which period Russia had over 4,000 voucher auctions and over 25 per cent of industrial workers ended up working for private companies (Boycko *et al.* 1994: 264). Boycko is reported as saying that 'forty million Russians have become shareholders. That is more than half the adult population of Russia.' Some 70 per cent of small businesses and 15,000 medium and large enterprises have been privatized. Privatized enterprises now employ more than 70 per cent of the industrial work force (Elif Kaban, *The Times*, 2 July 1994, p. 12). Mass privatization officially ended on 1 July 1994. Some 14,000 medium-sized and large enterprises have been privatized. Two-thirds of the industrial labour force is now employed by privatized firms. More than 40 million Russians became shareholders in either privatized enterprises or investment funds (Maxim Boycko and Andrei Shleifer, *Transition*, 1994, vol. 5, no. 9, p. 8).

By the end of August 1993 an estimated 20 per cent of industrial workers were employed by enterprises already privatized (*The Economist*, 2 October 1993, p. 24). By the end of 1993 just over 40 per cent of the work force in manufacturing was employed by private companies (*The Economist*, 12 March 1994, p. 46). CIA analysts estimate that the private sector (including co-operatives, leased enterprises and joint ventures) employed 15 per cent of the work force in 1991, while today it employs 42 per cent of the work force and produces 35–40 per cent of GDP (*The Economist*, 11 December 1993, p. 28). By 1 July 1994 more than 14,000 large and medium-sized enterprises had been put into private hands; over 70 per cent of industrial workers were employed by private firms (*The Economist*, 9 July 1994, p. 13). The private sector now produces 58 per cent of official GDP (*The Economist*, 8 October 1994, p. 24). The privatization of 15,779 medium-sized and large enterprises in a period of just eighteen months has helped to form a private sector which in 1994 produced 62 per cent of officially recorded GDP (*The Economist*, Survey, 8 April 1995, p. 3). By the end of June 1994 86 per cent of the industrial labour force was working in the private sector (p. 6). Over 95 per cent of shops are now privately owned (p. 13).

'By now two-thirds of Russian industry, big and small, is in private hands' (Richard Layard, *FT*, 3 June 1994, p. 17). Around 86 per cent of Russia's industry is in mainly private hands (Richard Layard, *FT*, 14 March 1995, p. 20).

On 28 December 1993 Anatoli Chubais announced that the private sector accounted for 40–50 per cent of the economy as a whole and employed more than 40 per cent of the total work force (compared with 15 per cent in 1991) (*IHT*, 29 December 1993, p. 1; *The Independent*, 29 December 1993, p. 8). On 23 March 1994 Chubais said that 'more than half of gross national product is being produced outside the state sector'. To date 15,000 major industrial enterprises and about 80,000 small and medium-sized ones have been privatized (*CDSP*, 1994, vol. XLVI, no. 12, p. 20). Chubais has estimated that by December 1993 65.5 per cent of all small enterprises had been privatized and by March 1994 the figure had risen to nearly 80 per cent (*CDSP*, 1993, vol. XLV, no. 51, p. 19; *FT*, 21 March 1994, p. 19).

Some 70 per cent of large and medium-sized enterprises were involved by 1 July 1994 (*CDSP*, 1994, vol. XLVI, no. 26, p. 6). By that date, according to official statistics, more than 50 per cent of workers were employed in the private sector and 70 per cent of state industry had been turned over to private owners (*FT*, 10 August 1994, p. 2). By mid-1994 the non-state sector of the economy accounted for more than half of all employed people (*CDSP*, 1994, vol. XLVI, no. 32, p. 13).

In mid-1994 the private sector accounted for roughly 50 per cent of GDP (EBRD 1994: 10).

Over three-quarters of all industrial workers are now employed in the non-state sector, while more than half GNP is produced there (*Moscow News*, 13–19 January 1995, p. 8).

The small privatization of 1992–93, which involved firms of less than 200 employees, placed almost 70 per cent of the firms in retail trade and other services (including restaurants and food catering) into full private ownership. By the end of September 1993 over 40 per cent of industrial output was produced by divested enterprises (United Nations, *World Economic and Social Survey*, 1994, p. 36).

Up to 40 per cent of the labour force now works in the private sector (Anders Åslund, *The Independent*, 11 December 1993, p. 19). Some 70 per cent of industrial enterprises have been privatized, while 40 million Russians have become shareholders (Åslund 1994b: 67–8).

By 6 June 1994 126 million out of 148 million vouchers had been used (*CDSP*, 1994, vol. XLVI, no. 23, p. 15). (The figure rose to 136 million by the end of June 1994: *RET*, 1994, vol. 3, no. 2, p. 82.)

The number of medium-sized and large enterprises (out of roughly 14,500) privatized were as follows: December 1992, eighteen; January 1993, 105; February 1993, 201; March 1993, 378; April 1993, 558; mid-1993, more than 2,300; September 1993, about 4,500; October 1993, over 5,000 (various issues of *RET*, *CDSP*, *The Economist*, *FT* and *IHT*).

In 1993 39 per cent of all Russian industry was privatized by voucher auction. More than 8,000 large and medium-sized enterprises were involved. By December 1993 only 44 million vouchers of the 144 million vouchers had actually been invested in privatized enterprises. More than 69 per cent of small-scale activity is now in private hands (*RET*, 1993, vol. 2, no. 4, pp. 65–7). By the end of March 1994 more than 70 per cent of all small-scale retail, catering and personal service enterprises were under private ownership (*RET*, Monthly Update, 30 April 1994, p. 14). By April 1994 nearly 11,000 medium-sized and large enterprises had been privatized. Their employees represented nearly 70 per cent of the total industrial labour force (*RET*, 1994, vol. 3, no. 1, p. 74). The voucher-based first stage of privatization ended on 1 July 1994. More than 13,000 large and medium-sized industrial enterprises had been sold through voucher auctions since the mass sell-off began in December 1992. More than 40 million Russians had become share owners in enterprises or in investment funds. More than 75 per cent of the industrial labour force had moved into the private sector. The government has retained a controlling share in some 358 enterprises and a 'golden share' (with veto power over strategic enterprise decisions) in 211 enterprises (*RET*, 1994, vol. 3, no. 2, pp. 79–80). More than 75 per cent of small-scale activity was in private ownership by mid-1994 (p. 82). Thus over half of all workers in Russia now work in private enterprise (p. 8). By 1 July 1994 15,052 medium-sized and large industrial enterprises had been sold through voucher auctions (*RET*, 1994, vol. 3, no. 3, pp. 93–4). The workers accounted for 84 per cent of total industrial employment (p. 94; a figure of 81 per cent was later given: 1995, vol. 3, no. 4, p. 94) ('privatized' enterprises meaning those over half private: p. 6). At the end of June 1994 the market share of private enterprises was 75 per cent in retail trade, 66 per cent in catering and 77 per cent in personal services (p. 96).

Yeltsin said that by the end of 1994 over 110,000 state and municipal enterprises had changed their form of ownership. The non-state sector accounted for 62 per cent of GDP (*CDSP*, 1995, vol. XLVII, no. 7, p. 2).

Post-voucher privatization

Prime Minister Chernomyrdin said that 'in the second half of the year a new stage of privatization policy will begin. The basic form of privatization at this stage will be commercial and, principally, investment competitions with rather rigorous conditions ensuring the reorganization and modernization of enterprises and the influx of investments needed for this purpose, including foreign investments . . . We must bring the reforms to the enterprise level and reinforce them with real changes in the economic behaviour of our country's goods producers. To this end it is necessary, first of all, to get a mechanism into operation for the financial reorganization of bankrupt enterprises . . . The focus of all our efforts in privatization is now shifting from the distribution and redistribution of property to the creation of conditions for increasing the economic effectiveness and competitiveness of production, improving management and providing incentives for investment' (*CDSP*, 1994, vol. XLVI, no. 9, p. 11). 'From 1 July the remaining shares in state hands will be sold not for vouchers but for money' (Prime Minister Chernomyrdin, *FT*, 16 May 1994, p. 15).

According to Privatization Minister Chubais (*CDSP*, 1994, vol. XLVI, no. 11, p. 12), in a 6 March 1994 interview, 'the concept of what is to follow check-based privatization has not yet been confirmed; it is still in the developmental stage'. On 23 March 1994 he said that a concept for the post-voucher privatization of industry, in which the main emphasis would be on the 'investment component', was being worked out and would be submitted for the broadest discussion (*CDSP*, 1993, vol. XLVI, no. 12, p. 20).

The plan for post-voucher privatization was revealed on 12 April 1994. One key element was the sale of primarily large blocks of shares (more than 51 per cent of authorized capital) to 'major strategic investors' (*CDSP*, 1994, vol. XLVI, no. 15, p. 22). The post-voucher privatization bill ran into trouble in parliament, the State Duma rejecting it on 13 July and referring it to a commission for further consideration the following day.

Yeltsin signed a presidential decree on 22 July 1994 incorporating various concessions. The plan called for remaining state enterprises to be sold voluntarily through investment tenders. The main features of the new programme were as follows:

1. A switch from vouchers to cash sales at auctions or stock markets. The shares to be sold were those still held by the state in privatized enterprises or those in enterprises still fully owned by the state. The starting price was to be 140 per cent of the value of enterprises' assets as of 1 January 1994, rather than being based on the 1992 asset valuation used in the first phase. In 'strategic sectors', including energy, metals and armaments, the state would retain the right to hold a 51 per cent stake for a further three years (*RET*, 1994, vol. 3, no. 3, p. 93).

2. The formation of 'strategic private investors'. The scheme would allow investors to acquire 'substantial stakes' in enterprises (*RET*, 1994, vol. 3, no. 3, p. 93). The programme is designed to attract 'strategic investors' through direct sales of shares representing 20 per cent of state assets (*Transition*, 1994, vol. 5, no. 6, p. 19).

3. Reduced privileges for 'insiders'. Workers would either be able to buy up to 20 per cent of the enterprise that employs them at a 30 per cent discount or 51 per cent at the market price. One of the options would allow the enterprise to give 25 per cent of the non-voting stock away and to sell a further 10 per cent of voting stocks to employees at a discount (*RET*, 1994, vol. 3, no. 3, p. 94).

4. The enterprise could retain 51 per cent of the revenue raised from its privatization and these funds were to be used for investment. The other 49 per cent would be split between the federal and local governments.

5. Any company with state ownership less than 25 per cent would have the automatic right to issue secondary shares.

6. The freehold of commercial land could now be bought and sold for the first time, with enterprises able to sell or mortgage any land they owned (*RET*, 1994, vol. 3, no. 3, p. 94).

7. Regions would be given greater authority. For example, local authorities would have the right to set the price, above a government-established minimum threshold, at which shares in privatized enterprises could be sold to the public. The final decision on the sale of the largest enterprises (employing more than 50,000 workers or with assets of over 200 billion roubles) would be switched from the Privatization Ministry to the presidential office.

8. Foreigners would be involved to a greater extent (although special permission would still be needed in areas such as defence and oil).

9. The shifting of social provision from enterprises to local authorities.

10. A July 1994 presidential decree stipulated that enterprises with assets worth more than 200 billion roubles in 1992 or those employing more than 50,000 people could be privatized only with the consent of the State Duma.

The Red October confectionery enterprise launched its public share offer for cash (55 per cent of stock) in December 1994. The plan was to sell most of the shares to individuals.

The second stage of privatization has been slow, in part owing to depressed share prices (*RET*, Monthly Update, 21 March 1995, p. 10). But a list has now been published of more than 7,000 enterprises of which the state intends to sell some shares over the course of 1995 (*RET*, Monthly Update, 14 April 1995, p. 10).

The city of Moscow was given permission to control its own privatization programme: (1) the initial price for investment tenders and auctions could be determined by the city; (2) some of the privatization revenues previously granted to privatized firms could be spent on the reorganization of other Moscow enterprises; (3) land would be available to enterprises only on a forty-nine-year lease; (4) the city would have the right to supervise closely the projects financed through investment tenders (*RET*, Monthly Update, 21 February 1995, p. 9).

It was announced on 13 April 1995 that 7,186 enterprises that had not been sold in the first stage were to be sold by the end of the year. The enterprises were 'not strategically important' and not part of the 'defence or oil complexes'. The government was then drafting a decree on the sale of shares in timber and oil holdings and a state commission would review whether the government should retain ownership of some large industrial enterprises (*IHT*, 14 April 1995, p. 13).

A presidential decree of 11 May 1995 established new rules for distributing the proceeds from sales of shares in federally owned enterprises: 55 per cent of the funds was to go to the federal budget (up from 10 per cent), 10 per cent to republican budgets, 4 per cent to local budgets, and 14 per cent to the enterprise itself (down from 51 per cent) (*CDSP*, 1995, vol. XLVII, no. 19, p. 15; *RET*, 1995, vol. 4, no. 1, p. 95).

RET (Monthly Update, 11 July 1995, p. 11) argued that it was unlikely that the government would offer company shares as collateral with preferential rights to a consortium of banks lending to the government. But it was possible that separate arrangements could be made with individual banks in which shares would be provided as collateral or in which the role of trust management on behalf of the government would be put out to tender.

On 5 September 1995 the government confirmed that it would allow a group of Russian banks to assume management control of the state's shareholdings in several enterprises for use as collateral in return for loans to the government (John Thornhill, *FT*, 6 September 1995, p. 13).

The state property agency was by 11 September 1995 to draw up a list of large enterprises in which the government was to sell its remaining shares (Gazprom managed to exclude itself from the list). A decree signed by Yeltsin on 31 August 1995 outlined a scheme less favourable to the interested banks than they had hoped for: (1) anyone would be able to take part, with assets going to those offering the largest loans, (2) the winning bidders would not have voting rights on 'major' issues affecting enterprises whose shares they hold and (3) holders would have to sell the shares within three years and do so 'publicly and competitively' in open auctions regulated by a government agency (*The Economist*, 9 September 1995, pp. 97–8).

In August 1995 the government announced that as from the following month it intended to begin speeding up the second stage of privatization. Some 140 important enterprises were listed, including the sale of shares in oil companies such as Lukoil (15 per cent), Sidanko (15 per cent) and Yukos (7 per cent) and in Unified Energy Systems (the national grid; 10 per cent) (*IHT*, 10 August 1995, p. 13; *FT*, 17 August 1995, p. 2).

FOREIGN TRADE

The importance of foreign trade

The USSR was a largely closed economy. Its share of world trade turnover in 1990 was about 4.5 per cent (compared with the USA, 16.3 per cent; West Germany, 12 per cent; and Japan, 9.5 per cent) (*RET*, 1993, vol. 2, no. 4, p. 85).

The Gatt's annual world trade report noted that in 1991 the former Soviet Union had been among the world's top twenty traders, but that its successor is now not even among the top twenty-five (*IHT*, 29 March 1993, p. 7).

Geographical distribution of trade

Nearly two-thirds of exports now go to the West and two-thirds of imports come from the West (*RET*, 1994, vol. 3, no. 2, p. 7). In 1994 some 70 per cent of exports went to industrialized countries, particularly the EU

(*Transition*, January–February 1995, p. 20). In a February 1995 speech Yeltsin stated that the CIS countries accounted for only 20 per cent of foreign trade, compared with 56 per cent in 1991 (*CDSP*, 1995, vol. XLVII, no. 8, p. 13).

In 1992 the volume of foreign trade fell by 23 per cent (*CDSP*, 1993, vol. XLV, no. 6, p. 10). In 1992 exports fell by 25 per cent and imports fell by 21 per cent (*Moscow News*, 18 February 1993, p. 4).

Russia and the EU

5 April 1993. EU foreign ministers agree to widen the terms of the European Commission's mandate for negotiating a partnership agreement with Russia to include the attainment of a free-trade agreement 'when economic and political circumstances in Russia are suitable'. But eventual membership of the EU is not an issue.

24 June 1994. Russia and the EU sign a partnership and co-operation agreement, which involves a strengthening of political and economic ties. Russia is recognized as an economy in transition rather than a state trading country. The main specific economic elements are as follows:

1. A relaxation of trade restrictions. Tariffs will be gradually lowered, with the possibility of a free-trade agreement after 1998 if Russia makes sufficient progress along the path of a market economy. In the meantime EU quotas on imports from Russia will be removed (with the exception of certain textile and steel products; agricultural products are unaffected by the agreement), while Russia can introduce limited import restrictions in sectors facing severe job losses or market shares. Safeguard clauses can be activated by either side to counter sudden surges of imports proved to be substantially harmful to domestic producers (e.g. uranium from Russia).

2. Measures to improve the business environment in Russia for foreign investors, e.g. removing obstacles to the free flow of capital and profit repatriation. (Once established in Russia, EU companies cannot be subjected to restrictive legislation for three years following the passage of any new law: *FT*, 25 June 1994, p. 2).

3. The 1993 presidential decree restricting the activities of foreign banks in Russia will be scrapped by 1996. The five banks which have already been given licences prior to the decree will be immediately freed of the restrictions (see the section below for details on foreign investment).

In 1993 the EU took about 50 per cent of Russian exports, minerals accounting for 44 per cent and wood products 14 per cent. The value of these exports was $17.4 billion, while EU exports to Russia came to $13.5 billion. One-third of EU exports were electrical machines and parts, while processed foodstuffs made up 16 per cent (Lionel Barber, *FT*, 25 June 1994, p. 2).

17 July 1995. The EU and Russia sign a trade agreement (delayed by the EU as a protest against the handling of the Chechen crisis).

The regulation of foreign trade

The key feature of trade in 1992 was the existence of export quotas for raw materials. These were allocated by administrative methods. In addition, on 1 July 1992 the export tax on raw materials was raised to 40 per cent. Up to 1 July 1992 exporters had to sell 10 per cent of their hard currency earnings to the central bank at the market exchange rate. As of 1 July 1992 this was increased to 20 per cent and at the same time exporters became obliged to sell 30 per cent of their earnings to commercial banks. The raw material quotas were regularly violated (illegal exports of raw materials may have amounted to more than $5 billion). For this reason, in early 1993 a programme of centralized exports for raw materials was introduced: Russian producers sell goods to the government at rouble prices and the government then sells the goods on the world market at a mark-up averaging 30 per cent of the rouble purchasing price. As regards imports there were no tariffs until the government introduced a 5 per cent tariff on 1 July 1992 (increased to an average rate of 15 per cent on 1 September). The coverage of both VAT and excise taxes was expanded to include imports as of February 1993. The 20 per cent VAT was applied to all imported goods except some types of food, medicine, clothing and furniture. The government subsidizes imports of critical materials like grain and medicines. Trade with the former Comecon countries fell by more than 56 per cent in 1992. Trade with other socialist countries also fell sharply, but that with industrial economies was similar to 1991 (*RET*, 1993, vol. 2, no. 4, pp. 41–2).

In 1992 barter accounted for 8.5 per cent of exports and in 1993 for 11.5 per cent; the respective figures for imports were 8.3 per cent and 13.8 per cent (*Moscow News*, 15–21 April 1994, p. 10).

1 November 1993. The number of commodities subject to export taxes is reduced from fifty-three to twenty-nine and the average level of export tax is reduced. All import subsidies are to be abolished at the beginning of 1994 (*RET*, 1993, vol. 2, no. 4, pp. 54–6). On 10 November 1993 duties are raised on a range of imported goods, chiefly alcohol, tobacco and cars (p. 101).

15 March 1994. A package of higher or new tariffs is imposed, e.g. on aircraft and foodstuffs respectively (although some imported spares have their rates reduced). The average tariff rate rises from 8 per cent to 14 per cent (*Business Central Europe*, May 1994, p. 13). (But on 15 April 1994 it was announced that the measures would be halted until 1 July. In addition most tariffs would be lower than originally planned.)

11 June 1993. Russia formally applies to join Gatt.

1 November 1993. A resolution cuts export tariffs by half on average (as of 1 November import subsidies have been halted, with the exception of centralized purchases of medicines). There will be a sharp reduction in the list of products subject to licensing and quotas. Import tariffs will be set at 5 per cent to 15 per cent (*CDSP*, 1993, vol. XLV, no. 44, pp. 21–2).

On 23 May 1994 a presidential decree scrapped quotas and licences as of 1 July 1994, including oil and gas but excluding certain materials subject to international agreements (such as uranium, aluminium and diamonds). All tax concessions for exporters (mainly for energy supplies) were also to be removed. Import tariffs were raised on 1 July, including, for the first time, tariffs on food. But on 1 July two new decrees appeared:

1. The first one prolonged, until the end of 1994, the existing procedure for exporting oil and petroleum products on the basis of previously distributed quotas. All tax exemptions for exporters of oil for state needs were to be retained and only specifically authorized organizations have the right to export oil.

2. The second decree, issued by the government, was concerned mainly with those highly exportable 'strategic commodities' (such as natural gas, electricity and timber) which ceased to be regulated by export quotas. These were to become subject to a special registration procedure. The decree also retained export quotas for a number of specific commodities agreed with the EU (e.g. aluminium and textile articles). The existing special export regime for goods like weapons and nuclear materials was left untouched (*RET*, 1994, vol. 3, no. 2, pp. 7, 65–6).

In December 1994 it was proposed that, as of 1 January 1995, oil export quotas were to be scrapped and domestic producers obliged to supply up to 65 per cent of output to the domestic market. Exports would continue to be regulated by tariffs and other methods, while the system of fourteen approved 'special exporters' would be maintained.

On 31 December 1994 Chernomyrdin signed a resolution (which needed to be approved) lifting the export quotas but ruling out domestic quotas. The fourteen approved 'special exporters' would remain, as would export taxes. The existing pipeline capacity was to be allocated by a government committee, largely on the basis of each oil producer's total output (*RET*, Monthly Update, 17 January 1995, p. 3).

Andrei Illarianov described as a 'myth' the idea that the new scheme meant the liberalization of oil exports. The real object was to create an impenetrable barrier to the gradual equalization of domestic and world prices for energy resources and to preserve a source of corruption (*CDSP*, 1995, vol. XLVII, no. 4, p. 22). (On 15 February 1995 the top fourteen oil producers formed the Union of Oil Exporters in order to co-ordinate their exports.)

Chernomyrdin signed yet another decree on 30 January 1995, which seemed effectively to neutralize that of the 31 December 1994. The powers of a newly created commission which grants access to the pipelines were set out. The commission was instructed to take into consideration the supply of the domestic market and state contracts for oil exports (Chrystia Freeland, *FT*, 4 February 1995, p. 2).

Yeltsin signed two more decrees on 6 March 1995 (effective 15 May 1995). These revoked the special trading privileges enjoyed by certain enterprises (including the fourteen 'special exporters' of oil) in the form of exemptions from quotas and import and export duties (Chrystia Freeland, *FT*, 7 March 1995, p. 1).

The system of special exporters has been abolished (as of 25 March 1995) and quotas for domestic supplies have been banned except in special circumstances (*RET*, Monthly Update, 21 March 1995, p. 2). Quantitative restrictions on exports and imports can be introduced by the government only if they are necessary for the implementation of international agreements. Exports cannot be limited by insisting upon a compulsory level of supply for the domestic market (*RET*, 1995, vol. 4, no. 1, p. 76). Any oil-producing company can now gain access to the pipelines; capacity is initially allocated in proportion to output, but can then be traded (p. 4).

Yeltsin signed two decrees on 6 March 1995 liberalizing foreign trade:

1. Abolition of the special dispensations granted for export and import operations granted to certain groups (e.g. athletes and disabled people), enterprises (e.g. Gazprom) and regions.

2. 'Restricting exports of goods and services by establishing mandatory amounts of deliveries to the domestic market is not permitted' (exceptions to this rule include defence). The system of special exporters was abolished (*CDSP*, 1995, vol. XLVII, no. 10, p. 5).

The exchange rate

The exchange rate was unified in mid-1992 and the rouble has been floating since then. The rouble is convertible for most current account purposes, including profit repatriation for foreign investors. There are restrictions on the capital account. There is a 50 per cent export surrender requirement for foreign exchange (EBRD 1994: 35, 111).

On 1 July 1993 the rules governing the mandatory sale of 50 per cent of hard currency earnings were changed. Henceforth all 50 per cent had to be sold on currency exchanges rather than 20 per cent (30 per cent had previously been bought by the central bank) (*CDSP*, 1993, vol. XLV, no. 26, p. 25).

In December 1994 the central bank ordered the exchange to impose a maximum daily fluctuation of 10 per cent in the rouble exchange rate with effect from 1 January 1995. On 5 July 1995 it was announced that for the period 6 July–1 October 1995 the central bank would keep the exchange rate within a band of 4,300–4,900 roubles to the US dollar (*IHT*, 6 July 1995, p. 13). On 24 August 1995 the duration of the band was extended to the end of 1995 (*The Economist*, 2 September 1995, p. 103). (On 24 August

Table 3.3 Russia: the value of the rouble on the Moscow Interbank Currency Exchange (no. of roubles to $1)

1992		*1993*		*1994*		*1995*	
Date	*Roubles*	*Date*	*Roubles*	*Date*	*Roubles*	*Date*	*Roubles*
14 January	180	14 January	442	14 January	1,356	13 January	3,776
18 February	170	18 February	559	18 February	1,567	18 January	3,883
17 March	161	18 March	667	18 March	1,722	25 January	3,988
14 April	155	15 April	779	15 April	1,793	26 January	4,004
14 May	128	18 May	934	18 May	1,880	16 February	4,293
16 June	119	16 June	1,104	16 June	1,959	15 March	4,744
16 July	136	16 July	1,020	15 July	2,024	11 April	4,991
18 August	163	18 August	985	18 August	2,141	12 April	5,008
15 September	204	15 September	1,010	15 September	2,301	29 April	5,130[3]
15 October	338	15 October	1,116	10 October	3,081	2 June	4,943
17 November	448	17 November	1,201	11 October[1]	3,926	8 June	4,911
17 December	416	17 December	1,247	12 October	3,736	9 June	4,943
				13 October	2,994	20 June	4,546
				14 October	2,988	27 June	4,516
				17 October	2,996	7 July	4,581
				17 November	3,157	11 July	4,550
				29 November	3,232	24 August	4,428
				9 December	3,261	7 September	4,479
				12 December[2]	3,323	15 September	4,465
				14 December	3,368	16 October	4,506
				15 December	3,383	8 November	4,523
				16 December	3,395		
				29 December	3,550		

1 'Black Tuesday'.
2 The attack on the Chechen Republic began on 11 December 1994.
3 All-time low for the rouble against the dollar.
Source: *Russian Economic Trends* (various issues)

a banking crisis began, with banks ceasing to lend to each other. In order to ease the liquidity crisis the central bank stepped in with short-term loans to a number of large banks and with purchases of government bonds.)

The (nominal) value of the rouble on the Moscow Interbank Currency Exchange is given in Table 3.3.

AID

The 1 April 1992 $24 billion aid package

There is still dispute about how much of the 1 April 1992 $24 billion aid package was actually spent.

1. Only about $16 billion was actually disbursed (James Sterngold, *IHT*, 16 April 1993, p. 7).

2. On 31 January 1993, at the Davos World Economic Forum, Russian officials and their Western advisers said that less than half had actually been

paid out and that almost $10 billion of that was in the form of short-term credits (*IHT*, 1 February 1993, p. 7).

3. Stanley Fischer (*IHT*, 7 April 1993, p. 8) calls the $24 billion package a 'fiasco'; less than half was delivered.

4. The managing director of the IMF, Michel Camdessus, said that in 1992 Russia had received all the $24 billion except for the $6 billion stabilization fund, i.e. debt relief worth $7.2 billion (note that there is controversy about how to take account of Russia's non-payment of debt), $12.6 billion in fresh credit (note that this is disputed) and $1 billion from the IMF (Leyla Boulton, *FT*, 4 February 1993, p. 3).

5. The Institute of International Finance estimates that Western official support totalled $17.55 billion in 1992. While the $1 billion from the IMF was $9 billion less than projected, largely because of the non-activation of the stabilization fund, official debt rescheduling was higher than expected and made up most of the shortfall (Peter Norman, *FT*, 24 April 1993, p. 2).

The size of Russia's debt and debt repayment

At the end of 1993 Russia's foreign debt was $83 billion, with about $26 billion of it being owed to commercial creditors and over $40 billion owed to creditor governments in the Paris Club (*RET*, 1994, vol. 3, no. 1, p. 58).

Russia's foreign debt consists of two parts: (1) the debts of the former Soviet Union, which were inherited by Russia in exchange for sole Russian entitlement to all assets abroad formerly owned by the republics of the USSR (around $80 billion by the end of 1993, of which about $40 billion was owed to Paris Club governments, nearly $26 billion to the London Club banks and the rest to 'non-organized' creditors, mainly Western exporters to the former Soviet Union); and (2) the purely 'Russian' debts, accumulated over 1992–93 and totalling approximately $18 billion. In 1993 the total amount due was almost $40 billion, which was comparable to total annual exports. But only $3 billion was actually repaid. In 1994 total debt service due was $32.5 billion. Russia is actually a net international creditor and is owed $150 billion by debtors to the Soviet Union. But the largest debtors (such as Cuba, Vietnam and Mongolia, which account for 38 per cent of total debt) are insolvent (*RET*, 1994, vol. 3, no. 2, pp. 70–1).

Russia's foreign debt at the end of 1994 was estimated at $91 billion (later put at $93.6 billion), but the figure rose to $120 billion (later put at $121.6 billion) if debts to former Comecon countries were included (these will probably never be settled in cash). Purely Russian debt, accumulated after 1992, was estimated at $11.2 billion (later put at $11.3 billion). In 1993 only $3.6 billion was actually paid out of the $31 billion due in debt servicing. In 1994 total debt service due was $32.5 billion, but only $3.7 billion had been paid by the end of September (*RET*, 1995, vol. 3, no. 4, pp. 79–80; vol. 4, no. 1, p. 84). (Russia repaid less than $2 billion in 1992, stopped repaying principal a year before and stopped paying interest at the end of 1992: *The Economist*, 3 April 1993, pp. 104–5. In 1994 Russia repaid $4.5 billion: *Moscow News*, 26 May–1 June 1995, p. 2.)

Of the $90 billion debt some $45 billion is owed to Paris Club governments, $35 billion is owed to London Club banks and the remaining $10 billion comprises liabilities that sprang from foreign trade credits (*Transition*, September 1994, vol. 5, no. 7, p. 18).

Of the $80 billion debt, $10 billion was contracted by the Russian Federation during 1993–94 (United Nations Economic Commission for Europe 1994: 114).

Russia has virtually given up hope of getting back the $150 billion owed by countries in the Third World and the former Soviet bloc (*IHT*, 26 March 1993, p. 11).

Volsky estimates that Third World countries owe Russia around $100 billion (*IHT*, 31 January 1994, p. 12).

A later estimate by the Russian government put developing countries' debt at $140 billion (*FT*, 4 July 1994, p. 3).

According to Bruce Clark (*FT*, 9 July 1994, p. 2), Russia is owed up to $140 billion by 'former client states' of the Soviet Union.

Konstantin Kagalovsky, the IMF's executive director for Russia, says that Russia is owed $147 billion (John Lloyd, *FT*, 17 September 1994, p. 24).

Capital flight

There are various estimates:

1. It has been estimated that illicit capital flights in 1992 more than matched the total foreign assistance of some $13 billion. Capital outflow in 1992 was at least $8.1 billion, including $1.4 billion (a sum which excludes debt servicing) officially recorded (*The Economist*, 1 May 1993, p. 110). According to official figures, Russian enterprises and individuals hold $24 billion in offshore accounts. But at least as much again is held illegally offshore (*The Economist*, Survey, 8 April 1995, p. 15).

2. John Lloyd (*FT*, 16 April 1993, p. 4) quotes an estimated $15 billion to $25 billion illegally deposited by Russian companies and individuals in Western bank accounts. The Russian Ministry of Finance has estimated that the illegal annual outflow amounted to $15 billion to $20 billion in both 1992 and 1993 (Anthony Robinson, *FT*, 4 July 1994, p. 3).

3. Marshall Goldman (*IHT*, 24 April 1993, p. 4) also quotes a capital flight figure of $15 billion to $25 billion a year.

4. The Institute of International Finance estimated capital flight from Russia at $8 billion in 1992 (Peter Norman, *FT*, 24 April 1993, p. 2).

5. *Business Central Europe* (October 1993, p. 53) cites the OECD's estimate of $10 billion to $20 billion in 1992.

6. Russian enterprises have $20 billion illegally deposited abroad (Deutsche Bank, *Focus: Eastern Europe*, 1993, no. 90, p. 7).

7. Åslund is quoted as saying that 'To judge from conversations with well informed businessmen and government officials, 10 to 20 per cent of the oil and at least one-third of the metals exported from Russia in 1992 were smuggled out of the country. Naturally the revenues from these sales stayed in bank accounts abroad (Ian Davidson, *FT*, 1 June 1993, p. 38). In 1994 capital flight fell to $5 billion (Anders Åslund, *IHT*, 25 April 1995, p. 8).

8. The central bank estimates that by June 1993 all Russian banks together were holding $15.5 billion abroad (*FT*, 1 November 1993, p. 16).

9. In February 1994 Gaidar said that foreign deposits by Russian citizens and companies over the previous years were already in the tens of billions of dollars and were growing rapidly.

10. Some $15 billion a year leaks out (*CDSP*, 1993, vol. XLV, no. 48, p. 11).

11. Russian customs officials estimate that in 1993 a third of Russia's $48 billion of export revenues (i.e. $15.5 billion) never came back from the West (Ann Imse, *IHT*, 15 February 1994, p. 11).

12. The Institute of International Finance estimates that during the period from the start of 1991 to the end of 1993 exports of oil, gas and other products were worth some $90 billion; capital flight came to $40 billion (Anthony Robinson, *FT*, 19 April 1994, p. 2). The institute says that half the $40 billion capital flight consisted of unrepatriated revenue from exports (Peter Passell, *IHT*, 30 April 1994, p. 13).

13. The IMF estimates that capital flight declined from $13 billion in 1992 to $8 billion in 1993 (Richard Stevenson, *IHT*, 11 May 1994, p. 11). *The Economist* (28 May 1994, p. 115) cites estimates in the range of $12 billion to $15 billion for 1993.

14. Capital flight rose from a cumulative total of $10.6 billion in 1991 to $43.1 billion in 1994. The legally held portion rose from $7.6 billion to $24.9 billion (it consists of enterprises' hard currency deposits in Russian banks plus cash dollars, held mostly by individuals, including those operating in the grey economy). The illegal portion increased from $3 billion to $18.2 billion (assets mainly held abroad, as cash, securities or real property; in 1994 most of the increase was in interest earned and there was little new export of illegal capital) (*RET*, Monthly Update, 14 April 1995, p. 4).

On 15 October 1993 a scheme to tackle the problem of illegal capital flight was announced. The banks would be involved in monitoring foreign exchange earnings, as of January 1994 in the case of the exporters of strategic commodities (such as oil and precious metals) and March 1994 for the others.

Views on aid to Russia

Jacques Attali (the former chairman of the EBRD) thinks it 'folly' to ask Russia to repay any of the Soviet debt and proposes that Western governments should compensate Western banks for debts incurred by the former Soviet Union (*FT*, 31 March 1993, p. 22). But he believes that Russia must repay its own debts, albeit restructured (*Moscow News*, 23 April 1993, p. 9).

Stanley Fischer (*IHT*, 7 April 1993, p. 8) offers the following advice. To stabilize the economy Russia will need direct financial assistance of $12 billion a year for the next two years, plus even further debt relief, from the West. The large sums, mainly export credits, that flowed into Russia in the previous year were not tied to economic reform and were totally ineffective. Fischer recommends looser conditions than the IMF normally imposes for macroeconomic stabilization in order to escape from a Catch-22 situation ('The West rightly fears that economic assistance would simply be wasted. But without Western financial assistance the Russians will not be able to balance the budget and bring inflation down to a level that will allow other reforms to succeed': reported in *FT*, 5 April 1993, p. 4). The key is to start the aid programme with direct assistance from Western governments, but with looser conditions than the IMF normally applies. After the initial $12 billion a year for two years, Western aid can decline. The West should relieve Russia of the need to repay the remainder of its $85 billion debt for five years. When the time is right to stabilize the exchange rate of the rouble, Russia should also have access to the $6 billion stabilization fund. The essential requirement is to rein in the growth of credit, and Russia also needs to agree on a budget deficit target and on the need to adhere to a single rate of exchange. (*The Economist*, 27 March 1993, p. 14, notes that the Russian government can use dollar aid to buy roubles on the Moscow market. This would increase the value of the rouble and help finance the budget deficit without printing money.)

The Financial Times thinks that the West 'should decide that $24 billion a year in long-term assistance (a mere 0.2 per cent of its aggregate gross domestic product) is a price well worth paying for the chances of successful Russian reform . . . all assistance must be conditional, but the conditions should be neither over-detailed nor excessively unrealistic' (4 March 1993, p. 19). 'What is needed . . . is true stabilization. That could be achieved through a programme to peg the exchange rate, combined with elimination of inflationary financing of the budget deficit. More funding would be needed than is now available. Much of it could be raised domestically, some in higher domestic revenue and some in domestic borrowing, but a precondition would be more Western finance. Some 4–5 per cent of Russian gross domestic product in external assistance, for two or three years, might do the trick. The bill for the West would be perhaps $14 billion a year' (20 June 1994, p. 17).

Sachs (*The Independent*, 11 October 1993, p. 18) says that although Russia started its reforms in January 1992 in 'dire financial conditions'. 'It took the West nearly eighteen months to grant Russia a debt standstill in the Paris Club and to grant it its first $600 million from the World Bank . . . The long delay of the G7 was nearly fatal. By failing to move early on, the West left the Russian reformers confused and anxious to find political allies among the old guard. In the middle of 1992 they vainly tried to compromise with so-called centrist forces representing parts of the old *nomenklatura* . . . To date, the Western world in its entirety has provided less grant aid to Russia in two years than the US alone provides to Egypt each year.'

Aid agreements

14 November 1992. An agreement is signed with the World Bank for a $600 million credit (*CDSP*, 1992, vol. XLIV, no. 46, p. 22).

28 January 1993. The G7 countries complete plans for a $700 million Nuclear Safety Fund to improve safety at nuclear reactors in Eastern Europe. The fund is to be administered by the EBRD and other countries are expected to join the fund.

23 March 1993. Western commercial banks agree the sixth roll-over of debt repayment for another three months to the end of June 1993 (*IHT*, 26 March 1993, p. 11). (A third roll-over was subsequently agreed to the end of September and others followed.)

2 April 1993. The Paris Club of creditor countries formally reschedules over ten years $15 billion due to be paid by Russia in 1993 ('formally' because most of it would not have been paid anyway). There will be a six-month grace period and $3.5 billion will be repaid over the following twelve months ($1.95 billion in 1993). The governments hope that Western banks will grant relief on 'comparable terms'.

3 August 1993. The London Club of Western bank creditors agrees to accept $0.5 billion of the $3.5 billion in interest owed in 1993, with the repayment of the remaining $3 billion postponed for five years. (It was estimated that in 1993 Russia would have to make only about 8 per cent of payments due in 1992 and 1993 to the London Club and to the Paris Club: *IHT*, 4 August 1993, p. 11.) Towards the end of December 1993 a new roll-over replaced the old one, expiring on 31 March 1994 (Leyla Boulton, *FT*, 31 December 1993, p. 2).

4 June 1994. Western creditor governments agree to reschedule $7 billion of the debt due in 1994 (Russia allocated $4.1 billion for debt servicing in that year) (Leyla Boulton, *FT*, 6 June 1994, p. 3).

23 June 1994. The World Bank announces a loan of $820 million for uses such as agricultural reform, banking and roads.

5 October 1994. Preliminary agreement is reached with the London Club of creditors to reschedule Russia's commercial bank debt (there is a five-year grace period and the following ten years will be allowed to pay off the debt). Russia agrees to pay $500 million in interest before the end of the year.

The Clinton–Yeltsin summit in Vancouver, 3–4 April 1993

The Clinton–Yeltsin summit was held in Vancouver. It was the first between the USA and Russia (and the former Soviet Union) to concentrate on economic rather than military matters. Prior to the summit President Clinton had stressed the urgency of aid to Russia and the need for an emergency meeting of the G7 countries. On 1 April 1993 he said that: 'Nothing could contribute more to global freedom, security and prosperity than the peaceful progression of Russia's rebirth. It is not an act of charity. It is an investment in our own future. While our efforts will entail new costs, we can reap even larger dividends for our safety and prosperity. The danger is clear if Russia's reforms turn sour, if it reverts to authoritarianism or disintegrates into chaos. The world cannot afford the strife of the former Yugoslavia replicated in a nation spanning eleven time zones and armed with a vast arsenal of nuclear weapons.'

The main element was a bilateral US aid package, aimed at furthering democracy and the market in Russia, and was seen as the starting point of both an international aid programme and a second bilateral US package to be taken to Congress. The package itself comprised the following features: (1) there were almost no new funds, what there were consisting largely of aid already approved by Congress but not yet spent; the aid could, therefore, be spent quickly; (2) though modest, the aid was meant to have a visible impact by being targeted, 'people to people', microeconomic in nature; three-quarters was to be 'targeted on partners outside Moscow' (e.g. local governments, businesses and individuals). The $1.6 billion package was broken down into $690 million in grants and $932 million in credits and guarantees. It included the following elements: (1) $700 million in grain credits on concessionary terms; (2) $215 million for the dismantling of nuclear weapons; (3) a $95 million 'privatization fund'; humanitarian aid, such as $194 million for food and $30 million for medicines; (4) $48 million for a 'democracy corps' to further democracy and market skills: $6 million to rehouse returning army personnel; $38 million to improve oil pipelines (it was hoped in the future to arrange a barter deal in which US companies would be persuaded by US Export–Import Bank credits to aid the Russian energy industry; repayment would be in the form of future oil deliveries).

At the Vancouver summit the USA also promised to support Russia in other ways, e.g. in the application to join Gatt, exports of Russian military equipment and a review of the restrictions on US exports to Russia of sensitive technology. Canada pledged aid worth $200 million.

The G7 meeting in Tokyo, 15–16 April 1993

The first emergency meeting of the G7 countries was held in Tokyo. The communiqué said that 'Our assistance will be pragmatic, visible, tangible and effective, tailored to Russian absorptive capacity and phased with the progress of the reform.' The $43.4 billion aid package was larger than expected. There was more old than new, but the exact proportion was not clear. For example, *Business Central Europe* (May 1993, p. 53) estimates that previous commitments account for $21 billion. Deutsche Bank (*Focus: Eastern Europe*, 21 April 1993, no. 74, p. 2), however, thinks that the 'bulk' of the aid package is not new. Georges Skorov (*IHT*, 25 June 1993, p. 6) argues that only about $5 billion is new.

1. The $15 billion of debt rescheduling announced by the Paris Club of creditor countries on 2 April 1993.
2. The $6 billion currency stabilization fund created on 1 April 1992 but never used.
3. The $4.1 billion IMF stand-by loan agreed in 1992, dependent on reducing inflation and the budget deficit.
4. The World Bank would provide $3.4 billion in loan commitments (e.g. for restructuring industry), a $1.1 billion 'import rehabilitation' loan (for vital imports) and a $0.5 billion oil sector loan.
5. A total of $10 billion in export credits and guarantees by Western governments.
6. A $3 billion 'systemic transformation facility' from the IMF. Not only was this new, but some of the conditions laid down were also new. The first instalment of $1.5 billion was to be disbursed simply when a commitment to economic change was made (the IMF actually approved the first tranche on 30 June 1993), although the second depended on the curbing of inflation and the budget deficit. The second tranche, due in September, was delayed because of the IMF's concern that its conditions were not being met (*IHT*, 21 September 1993, p. 13). It was not until 22 March 1994 that Michel Camdessus, the managing director of the IMF, agreed in principle to the second tranche; formal IMF approval had to wait until 20 April 1994. The agreed conditions included cutting planned expenditure programmes in the event of tax deficiencies and/or spending overruns and a target monthly inflation rate of 7 per cent by the end of 1994 (see the chronological entry for 22 March 1994 in the politics section above).
7. A total of $300 million for a small business development fund financed mainly by the EBRD; the creation of a Russian bank for small and medium-sized enterprises is envisaged.

The US proposal for the setting up of a $4 billion fund to promote the privatization of large enterprises is merely to be studied before the July 1993 full G7 meeting in Tokyo. The USA promised $500 million if the other G7 countries provided $1.5 billion, with the remainder coming from international institutions. The 7–9 July 1993 G7 meeting in Tokyo, which

Yeltsin joined on the second day, actually recommended a $3 billion fund. This sum, most of which was not new and which was to be spent over an eighteen-month period, was smaller than originally intended by the USA but larger than forecast at one stage. The $3 billion consisted of the following: $1 billion in credits for Russian enterprises to import equipment; $0.5 billion in technical assistance; $0.5 billion from the World Bank to help divest enterprises of the burden of providing social services; $1 billion from the World Bank ($0.475 billion), the International Finance Corporation ($0.1 billion) and the EBRD ($0.425 billion) for privatization and restructuring. About $0.5 billion of the $3 billion represented grant aid and the rest consisted of loans.)

Bilateral commitments are also made, although the exact amount of additional aid is uncertain:

1. *Japan*. $1.82 billion, $1.1 billion in trade insurance, a $400 million loan facility and $320 million in grants for food, medical equipment and technical assistance. Japan has already pledged $2.4 billion (mainly trade insurance), about a third of which has been disbursed (*FT*, 13 April 1993, p. 3). Japan itself claims to have pledged aid worth $5 billion to Russia and other CIS countries (Jonathan Steele, *The Guardian*, 8 July 1993, p. 12).

2. *The USA*. $1.8 billion, including $300 million for the other countries of the former Soviet Union; $1.3 billion in grants and $500 million for a privatization fund.

3. *The UK*. At the Tokyo meeting the UK pledged $686 million, $500 million in export credits and $186 million in technical aid. (On 2 April 1993 it was announced that the 'know-how fund' was to be increased from £60 million to £120 million.)

4. *Germany*. Germany did not announce additional bilateral aid because of the large commitments already made. On 25 March 1993 Chancellor Kohl said that 'We Germans have provided more than 50 per cent of all Western aid so far, with more than DM 80 billion . . . with that we have reached the limit of what we can afford.' Robert Thomson (*FT*, 15 April 1993, p. 3) reports German officials' estimates that Germany had contributed 67 per cent of the bilateral aid promised by the G7 countries over the past two years and 75 per cent of that already disbursed. The Deutsche Bank (*Focus: Eastern Europe*, 21 April 1993, no. 74, p. 5) estimates that prior to the Tokyo conference Germany had contributed 56 per cent of Western aid, the USA just over 9 per cent and France just below 3 per cent. Japan had contributed less than 3 per cent of Western aid to the countries of the former Soviet Union (p. 4). According to its government, Germany has committed $50 billion to the Soviet Union or its successor states since 1989 (more than half the Western total) compared with the USA's $9 billion and Japan's $3 billion (*The Economist*, 3 July 1993, p. 37). (Between 1990 and 1993 the EC contributed almost 75 per cent of world aid to the countries of the former Soviet Union: Lionel Barber, *FT*, 20 January 1994, p. 2.)

The Institute of International Finance considered that only $32 billion of the $43.2 billion would be actually provided in 1993, mainly because IMF disbursements would probably be around $4 billion rather than $13.1 billion (specifically Russia would be unlikely to qualify for the $6 billion stabilization fund and only around half the stand-by loan and 'systemic transformation facility' would be disbursed) (Peter Norman, *FT*, 24 April 1993, p. 2).

Criticisms of the Western aid effort

Jeffrey Sachs and Charles Wyplosz (*FT*, 11 January 1994, p. 17) are very critical of the Western aid effort and of the IMF in particular. 'The Western aid effort for Russia has been a debacle. Over the past two years much aid has been promised but very little has been delivered. Technical assistance and food aid aside, almost no programmes have taken off.' Reformers consequently suffered at the polls. As early as 1991 Western governments sought to avoid budgetary responsibility for Russia's reforms by assigning the lead role to the IMF, 'a cautious, narrowly focused bureaucracy ill-suited for a task needing breadth of vision and risk-taking'. Sachs and Wyplosz argue that foreign aid can be crucial for stabilization. It helps the government pay the bills (such as for social programmes) in a non-inflationary way, while it also fosters government unity, increases public confidence in the reforms and signals that the government has staying power. The reformers did badly in the election of 12 December 1993. 'They were undone by government inconsistencies and inaction – not by too much reform.' The West had failed to help push through basic improvements in the economy and to help finance an adequate social safety net. The West promised a $28 billion package for 1993, of which about $5 billion was actually delivered. Some $13 billion was to come from the IMF, of which $1.5 billion arrived; $3 billion was to come from the World Bank, of which $600 million arrived. Most of what actually came was in the form of export credits, which were of very limited use for the reforms. Sachs and Wyplosz suggest that Western governments should provide about 4 per cent of Russian GNP ($14 billion) in quick-disbursing funds for socially orientated projects such as housing for the military, support for targeted social relief and funds to close coal mines and compensate miners and their families. The programmes should be monitored by G7 governments rather than the IMF. Another $8 billion – from the World Bank, the EBRD and the export credit agencies – could support long-term industrial restructuring, with investment funds and programmes for promoting small businesses. The IMF would make available $6 billion in loans subject to normal conditions, but it would not have the overall lead or be able to block disbursement of other funds. 'Payment of less than one-tenth of 1 per cent of Western GNP, or $14 billion, is surely the most important investment in Russia's democratic future and, thus, in Western security.'

In an article in the *IHT* (24 January 1994, p. 4) Sachs continued his attack on the IMF and the World Bank. 'The financial crisis left behind by the communist regime was too deep. The reformers could not win without outside help, but help never arrived, and the reformers paid the price, losing badly in the December elections.' Sachs estimates that of the roughly $18 billion that the IMF and the World Bank were to lend to Russia in 1993, only $2 billion was handed over. The main goals of financial policy, he maintains, should have been to reduce the budget deficit, to float new government debt on the domestic market in order to cover the budget deficit without printing new money, to staunch the flow of cheap government loans to weak industries and to establish a separate Russian currency so that Russia could pursue a monetary policy independent of its neighbours. At the same time international grants and loans should have been provided to help the government pay its bills. 'The IMF failed miserably in advising the Group of Seven countries and the Yeltsin administration on Russia's financial reconstruction. It discouraged Russia from rapidly introducing a separate national currency. For two years it downplayed Russia's need and ability to issue domestic treasury bonds, focusing nearly all its efforts on pressuring the Russians to make politically impossible cuts in the budget deficit. It advised Russia against the stabilization of the rouble exchange rate and held back a rouble stabilization fund designed to support such a policy. Most remarkably, it never acknowledged the urgency of mobilizing international assistance to help Russia finance its deficit. The IMF's relentless advice was to cut the deficit, not to find acceptable and non-inflationary ways to finance part of it.' Sachs believes that the World Bank also failed in its most important task, namely to help finance a viable social support system.

In an article in the *FT* (31 March 1994, p. 21) Sachs continued in the same vein. 'IMF incantations of budget cutting and tight monetary policy are insufficient. Almost no stabilization programme in history has worked the way the IMF recommends in Russia. Real stabilization programmes . . . start from the proposition that a country needs a stable convertible currency as the *first* step towards ending high inflation, not the last. After currency stability is achieved, and inflation is lowered as a direct result, then cuts in the budget become politically and economically more likely.' To achieve such a stable currency typically requires large-scale help from the outside world to back the currency and to help finance the budget deficit, as well as immediate relief on debt servicing. 'The foreign help should surely come together with significant deficit cutting, but well before the fundamental budgetary problems are fully resolved.' Sachs considers that the IMF blundered badly on these points. It delayed the introduction of a separate Russian currency in 1992, with the result that Russia was bombarded with inflation from the other states. 'The IMF has argued constantly against pegging the exchange rate until several months *after* inflation is ended, so guaranteeing a vicious circle of currency depreciation and rising deficits, not a virtuous circle of currency stability and falling budget deficits.' The IMF has failed to mobilize international assistance to help Russia fund its budget deficit. Russia went into default in January 1992, but the Russian government did not receive its first working capital loan, from the World Bank (for $600 million), until nearly eighteen months later. Even debt service relief is not fully in place.' (See also Sachs's attack on floating exchange rates in the section on the rouble zone.)

Sachs (1995: 60) returned to the attack later on, claiming that 'Not only the Russian economy, but also Russian democracy has been put recklessly at risk by Western neglect.' The Western effort has failed at three levels:

1. 'The Marshall Plan architects had one brilliant insight that is missing today: the purpose of economic assistance is *political*, to support fragile democratic regimes attempting to implement more basic reforms' (p. 60). 'Fragile regimes are likely to collapse before they can implement needed market reforms if aid is not present as a *temporary* support' (p. 61). One of the basic principles of aid-giving in general is that it should be limited in time to no more than five consecutive years, since the goal is to bolster fragile governments and not to finance economic development. Some cases where serious reversals occur may merit throwing out another aid lifeline, however, if a new reformist government takes power at a later date (p. 61).

2. The sums have been derisory. In the fiscal year 1995 Russia would receive roughly $380 million in US aid. This was about one-sixth of US aid to Egypt or roughly 0.005 per cent of US GDP (compared with Marshall Plan commitments to Europe in fiscal year 1949 of 2 per cent of GDP).

3. The USA has failed almost entirely in leading a co-ordinated Western effort to aid Russia. Virtually all Western 'aid' has come in the form of export credits to Russian enterprises, with short periods for repayment, rather than in the form of grants and long-term loans to the Russian budget (almost all the Marshall Plan support was in the form of grants). Repayments of these loans have been straining the Russian budget. Overall support from Western governments for the budget, vitally needed for stabilization, has been essentially nil. Very little co-ordination of the G7 aid packages ($24 billion announced in 1992 and $28 billion in 1993) was ever undertaken to bring those packages to fruition. In 1994 there was essentially a complete collapse in US attempts to mobilize international assistance, and the IMF and World Bank have proved to be hugely inefficient (pp. 60–1).

In 1992 Russia received $14.1 billion in loans and grants disbursed by the West. All but $1.6 billion were in loans, mostly trade credits. Russia paid the West $1.6 billion in debt service, nearly all of it interest (*RET*, 1993, vol. 2, no. 1, p. 43).

In 1992 the USA announced $24 billion in aid; some $15 billion arrived. In 1993 the G7 countries offered $43 billion, including $15 billion of debt relief; the debt relief came, but only $5 billion with it (*The Economist*, 15 January 1994, p. 18).

Michel Camdessus, the managing director of the IMF, has acknowledged that the IMF has lent a total of only $2.5 billion to Russia so far, rather than the $14 billion announced in separate packages by the G7 countries. He has also pointed out that Western donors have delivered $20 billion of the $21 billion promised by the G7 countries and that official and commercial debt rescheduling, as well as money provided by Germany to rehouse Russian military personnel, has brought the total of external financial assistance to $58 billion (George Graham, *FT*, 2 February 1994, p. 2). Camdessus has said that of $55 billion in aid packages over the last two years by the G7 countries, $38 billion has been delivered, primarily in bilateral assistance (*IHT*, 2 February 1994, p. 1).

Former (late) US president Richard Nixon, shortly after a visit to Russia in March 1994, commented as follows: 'I found no one who had a good word to say for the US aid programme. The issue is not the amount but how it is administered. Rip-offs, shakedowns and corruption among recipients, along with incompetence among administrators, have created enormous disillusionment.'

FOREIGN INVESTMENT

An investment is considered to constitute direct foreign investment when a lasting relationship is established between a legal person or entity resident in one country (the foreign investor) and an entity resident in another country (the foreign investment enterprise) in which the foreign investor obtains a controlling interest. This type of investment can be contrasted with (foreign) portfolio investment, in which the investor is not interested in exerting significant influence over management decisions. Portfolio investment from abroad was considerable during most of 1994 (e.g. that into Russian equities and government securities was nearly $800 million in the first half of 1994), but fell sharply after the invasion of Chechenia on 11 December 1994. All foreign investment must be registered. Direct foreign investment in some sectors (such as banking, insurance and heavy industry when damage to the environment could result) also requires authorization. The defence sector is closed to foreign investment, as is gambling (Barbara Peitsch, *The OECD Observer*, April–May 1995, no. 193, pp. 32–4).

The laws on joint ventures have been repeatedly changed over the past year and foreigners have lost any shred of preferential treatment (*The Economist*, 27 February 1993, p. 100).

A presidential decree of 23 May 1994 awarded a three-year profit tax holiday for joint ventures registered after 1 January 1994 with at least 30 per cent foreign ownership and worth at least $10 million, provided that they are not liquidated within six years. In the fourth year enterprises would pay a quarter of the usual tax rate and half in the fifth year (*CDSP*, 1994, vol. XLVI, no. 21, p. 9).

At present foreigners can only lease land (for up to ninety-nine years) (*The Daily Telegraph*, 2 February 1993, p. 10).

Considerable confusion and anguish stemmed from a presidential decree of 22 December 1993. The decree was meant to close a tax loophole (loans were previously exempt from taxation and so enterprises made fake loans to one another to avoid paying VAT). A 23 per cent tax was thus imposed on all loans, even genuine ones. As a result of the outcry the government promised to amend the decree.

On 27 September 1993 a decree was issued to ensure that federal rules applied to foreign investment (to be submitted for consideration to the Federal Assembly of the Russian Federation).

There are heavy VAT and profit taxes imposed on direct investments by foreigners. Alternative forms of investment have arisen in response, such as placing money in special tax-free investment funds or making capital contributions to existing Russian companies. The newness of the relevant investment laws, the unknown status of numerous proposed laws and the volatile political situation are hindrances (Rodney Burton and Diane Juzaitis, *IHT*, 25 March 1995, p. 21).

Investment is so risky in Russia that investors require an extremely high expected return. A survey was carried out in February 1995 of twenty Western investment banks, brokerages and accounting firms, along with several major companies engaged in direct foreign investment. The disincentives, in order of ranking, were as follows:

1. Legal disincentives were the most serious (average rank 1.7), especially fears about shareholder rights, weak contract enforcement and securities regulation.

2. Economic disincentives (2.9), especially high inflation, the incoherence of the tax system and exchange rate fluctuations.

3. Political disincentives (3.0), especially scepticism about commitment to reform, fears about renationalization and doubts about parliamentary elections.

4. Financial disincentives (3.7), especially lack of information about potential business partners, repatriation of profits and lack of a credit rating in Russia.

5. General disincentives (4.1), especially the worldwide retreat from emerging markets, fear of crime/the mafia and discrimination against foreigners.

6. Logistic disincentives (5.6), especially the communications infrastructure, the transport infrastructure and technological constraints (*RET*, Monthly Update, 21 March 1995, pp. 3–4).

Banks

Crédit Lyonnais Russie (St Petersburg) was the first to obtain a licence in December 1991. New regulations were published on 15 April 1993. Foreign banks could open only one branch office besides their head office, while the total capital of all foreign banks operating in Russia could not exceed 12 per cent of the aggregate capital of the Russian commercial banks in 1993 (the annual limit will vary). The aggregate capital of foreign banks represents 6 per cent of the Russian total (John Lloyd, *FT*, 16 April 1993, p. 4). As of 1 April 1994 the seventeen banks with more than 50 per cent foreign capital accounted for a little over 7 per cent of the total authorized capital of banks (*Moscow News*, 19–25 August 1994, p. 10).

Parliament was due to consider finalizing a bill excluding, until January 1996, banks with more than 50 per cent foreign participation from dealing with Russian customers, including joint ventures, i.e. confining them to transactions with foreign nationals and non-resident legal entities. But parliament was dissolved by Yeltsin on 21 September 1993. The ban finally came into force on 19 November 1993, although those banks already dealing with residents as of 15 November were allowed to continue. Of the twelve foreign banks that had by then received licences, only two (Crédit Lyonnais Russie and BNP-Dresdner) already had resident clients (*Moscow News*, 19–25 August 1994, p. 10). Finance Minister Fyodorov justified the move in terms of protecting Russian banks from losing their best clients and staff during the transitional stage. A presidential decree of 10 June 1994 lifted the restrictions on banks from those countries with which Russia had signed investment protection agreements. The partnership and co-operation agreement with the EU of 24 June 1994 immediately lifted the restrictions on the five EU banks which had already been given licences prior to the November 1993 decree, namely Crédit Lyonnais Russie and Société Générale of France, Ing and ABN-Amro of the Netherlands, and Dresdner of Germany. The restrictions would be scrapped for other banks by 1996.

The volume of foreign investment

Western concerns say that their capital investment totals nearly $3 billion. But the amount of foreign capital that has actually been put into Russian joint ventures is estimated by Russian economists at about $1 billion (*CDSP*, 27 January 1993, 1992, vol. XLIV, no. 52).

The Deutsche Bank (*Focus: Eastern Europe*, 1993, no. 94, p. 8) estimated a figure of $1.5 billion by mid-1993 (by then Russia may have accounted for only 10 per cent of the total direct foreign investment going into the East European and CIS countries: 1993, no. 94, p. 4).

The government has set up the Russian International Co-operation and

Development Agency under the direction of Deputy Prime Minister Alexander Shokhin. Prime Minister Chernomyrdin said on 31 January 1993, at the Davos World Economic Forum, that foreign investment in Russia in 1992 did not even exceed $200 million.

The Guardian (31 January 1993, p. 10) reports $200 million of direct foreign investment committed in 1992, with total foreign capital inflows of only $1 billion.

Net direct foreign investment was $100 million in 1991, $800 million in 1992, $682 million in 1993 and $577 million in January–September 1994 (United Nations Economic Commission for Europe 1995: 151).

In 1993 Russia attracted around $700 million of direct investment from foreign companies (*The Economist*, 19 March 1994, p. 101); another estimate put the figure at around $400 million (Deutsche Bank, *Focus: Eastern Europe*, 1994, no. 104, p. 6).

The actual stock of paid-in capital at the start of 1994 did not exceed an estimated $2.5 billion, with commitments of about $5 billion (*Business Central Europe*, April 1994, p. 43).

Accumulated investment at the end of 1993 amounted to $2.7 billion (*CDSP*, 1994, vol. XLVI, no. 26, p. 17).

At an international conference held in Moscow on 27 June 1994 it was revealed that the cumulative total of foreign investment was $2.7 billion; around $1 billion was expected in 1994, compared with $1.5 billion in 1993 (Lee Hockstader, *IHT*, 28 June 1994, p. 2).

The Deutsche Bank (*Focus: Eastern Europe*, 1994, no. 107, pp. 1–6) provides the following information: (1) by the end of 1993 direct foreign investment totalled around $2 billion (in 1992 $290 million flowed in, and in 1993 $400 million); (2) by the end of 1993 there were 11,700 foreign-invested enterprises, of which 40 per cent were wholly-owned subsidiaries; (3) foreign-invested enterprises accounted for 2.5 per cent of economic output, 4 per cent of exports and 0.5 per cent of the work force.

At the end of 1993 total foreign investment amounted to $2.7 billion, an increase of $1.4 billion for the year (*Transition*, 1994, vol. 5, no. 6, p. 19).

Foreign direct investment amounted to $2 billion in the period 1990–93: $100 million in 1991, $800 million in 1992 and $1.1 billion in 1993 (EBRD 1994: 123).

In 1994 official figures put the year's inflow at $2 billion, but unofficial sources say that another $1 billion entered unrecorded (Stephanie Flanders, *FT*, Survey, 10 April 1995, p. iv).

In 1994 the inflow of portfolio investment amounted to $1.6 billion and that of direct foreign investment to about $1 billion (*IHT*, Survey, 8 June 1995, p. 18).

At the end of 1994 direct foreign investment (commitments) had reached nearly $4 billion. The bulk had gone into energy and mining. In

1994 enterprises with foreign investment were responsible for 17 per cent of exports (Barbara Peitsch, *The OECD Observer*, April–May 1995, no. 193, p. 32).

In 1993 foreign investment accounted for 2.6 per cent of total investment; it rose to 3.8 per cent in 1994 (*Moscow News*, 13–19 January 1995, p. 8).

A report of early October 1993 talked in terms of 11,000 foreign-invested enterprises in Russia, some 2,000 of which were wholly foreign-owned. Foreigners were still very reluctant to invest in 'production', preferring 'middleman operations' (70 per cent of enterprises were involved in this kind of activity). Enterprises with foreign capital accounted for only 1 per cent of the 'total production of goods and services' (*CDSP*, 1993, vol. XLV, no. 40, p. 33). In 1992 joint ventures accounted for 11 per cent of total exports (*Moscow News*, 29 October 1993, p. 7).

AGRICULTURE

Reforms and problems

In 1992 26 per cent of the population were rural and agriculture accounted for 20 per cent of employment in the period 1990–92 (industry 46 per cent and services 34 per cent) (*The Economist*, Survey, 8 April 1995, p. 4).

The December 1992 decrees ordered state and collective farms to decide their own future forms of organization by 1 March 1992 and to re-register by 1 January 1993 (more than three-quarters of state and collective farms had actually been re-registered by the beginning of 1993: *CDSP*, 1993, vol. XLV, no. 5, p. 22). Unprofitable farms were to be declared bankrupt by 1 February 1992 (to be taken over by profitable enterprises or, as a last resort, have their assets sold at auction). The options were (1) to form a joint stock company (where farmers hold shares); (2) to form an agricultural co-operative; (3) to divide the farm into individual private farms (land was to be divided up equally, but, in the case of property, factors such as past wages, age and qualifications were to be taken into account); in the case of a peasant association, services such as input supply could be performed by a specialized organization; (4) to retain the previous state or collective farm form of organization (Wegren 1992b: 657–61).

Pallot (1993: 212) points out that during the December 1992 Congress it was agreed that the waiting period for sales should be reduced from ten to five years for certain categories of rural land, such as that under dachas, orchards and 'private plots'.

According to Siszov (1993: 500), land could be sold only for the purposes of running personal plots and dacha or house building. If a farmer received land free of charge it could not be sold for ten years. Purchased land could not be sold for five years.

Wegren (1994) makes some further points:

1. 'Yeltsin has been largely successful in creating a new set of rural institutions in the Russian countryside. But the underlying culture has changed very little . . . a collectivist and egalitarian culture still exists in the countryside' (p. 216). 'One of the most striking features of land reform in Russia is the lack of spontaneous decollectivization by collective and state farm workers themselves . . . by 1 July 1993 over 90 per cent of all state and collective farms had reorganized. Of those farms which had reorganized . . . *collective* forms of organization retained much more popularity than expected . . . the most popular forms of reorganization were: joint stock companies, which retain collective ownership; the retention of a farm's previous status, chosen by more than one-third of reorganized farms; and the creation of "comrade societies with limited responsibility", a form chosen by more than half of the farms undergoing reorganization . . . of the farms that remained intact after reorganization . . . an overwhelming 92 per cent chose a form of collective labour organization' (p. 219).

2. The Law on Peasant Farms adopted on 27 December 1990 stipulated the right of 'every able-bodied citizen' who possessed 'specialized agricultural knowledge or past specialized training' to organize a peasant farm. The Russian Land Code of 1991 added that any citizen at least eighteen years old who had experience in agriculture and the corresponding skills, or who had past specialized training, could receive land. The aim of a new decree issued by Yeltsin in mid-1993 was the situation where 'every citizen may acquire land' (p. 222).

3. During the first two years of the land reform most new private farmers were in fact former urban residents who had migrated back to the countryside (p. 222).

4. There are two main ways for an individual to receive land free from the state in order to begin peasant farming operations: (1) from a Special Land Fund; initially this consisted of land that state or collective farms did not want, were not using, or which had been used unproductively in the recent past; only this sort of land was available under Gorbachev, but in early 1991 Yeltsin signed a decree that allowed up to 10 per cent of a farm's land to be withdrawn and placed in this fund; and (2) from a state or collective farm.

5. 'Although in reality the state continues to require obligatory deliveries to it, state prices are much more influenced by market prices' (p. 217). 'Early in 1993 the government created a federal grain fund to which farms of all types were required to deliver grain. The Law on Grain, signed by Yeltsin in May 1993, states that the government will select, on a competitive basis, purchasers who will buy grain at negotiated, market prices . . . In reality, state purchasers are simply the state grain elevators . . . and there is no competitive selection process. Grain elevators are issued state credits to buy grain. The prices offered by these grain elevators are state-set firm

prices . . . The federal grain fund requires a farm to deliver about one-third of its grain to state elevators, while the local grain fund requires another 10–12 per cent . . . in October 1993 obligatory deliveries were abolished, although food funds will remain during 1994' (p. 237). (According to *RET*, the practice of grain procurement at officially set prices was abolished in mid-September 1993: 1993, vol. 2, no. 4, p. 28. The central reforms in 1993 were the freeing of grain prices, the decision to procure grain, meat and milk at market prices, and the lifting of the time limit on the sale of land: p. 52.)

Van Atta (1994) argues that 'At present the new individual farmers are finding their interests increasingly aligned with the old large farms, rather than with the macroeconomic reformers who advocate tight state credit. Without any alternative source of capital, private owners can only demand state subsidies and protectionist policies just as their bitter enemies, the farm chairmen, have been doing' (p. 162). 'Until a market-orientated credit system is put in place, few farms are likely to be broken up successfully, since it is impossible for the new owners to purchase the items they need to run their farms' (p. 186). 'The ultimate success of agrarian reform will require policies that prevent the destruction of the independent farmers' movement or its absorption by the old agarian interests' (p. 187).

By the end of 1992, of the 32,000 collective farms, state farms and other agricultural enterprises, 16,183 (or 50.4 per cent) had been converted to other forms of operation. Those converted comprised joint stock companies (5,644), co-operatives (1,625), associations of peasant farms (944) and other forms (5,072) (*CDSP*, 1993, vol. XLV, no. 3, p. 28). By March 1993 22,000 collective and state farms (87 per cent of the total) had been re-registered. Of these the collectives of 7,500 farms (one-third of those re-registered) decided to retain their former status, while the rest preferred other forms of organization (*CDSP*, 1993, vol. XLV, no. 21, p. 20). (Note that the deadline for re-registering had been formally extended from the end of 1992 to March 1993.)

By 1 July 1993 23,400 collective and state farms (91 per cent of their total number) had been re-registered; 7,900 (34 per cent) of re-registered farms reaffirmed their former status (the respective figures for 1 July 1992 were 8,400, or 33 per cent, and 3,700, or 44 per cent). By 1 July 1993 11,000 farms (47 per cent of all re-registered farms) had re-established themselves as various forms of partnership. In addition there were 300 public stock companies (Siszov 1993: 499).

Today 90 per cent of farmland is in the hands of co-operatives, limited liability partnerships and private farmers (*CDSP*, 27 April 1994, vol. XLVI, no. 13, p. 19).

Table 3.4 shows data on private farms. Some 39 per cent of the land allotted to private farming had become the farmers' own property

Table 3.4 Russia: private farms

End of year	*No. of private farms*	*Average size (ha)*	*Agricultural land (%)*	*Agricultural output (%)*	*Average number employed*
1990	4,432	46.3			
1991	49,013	42.0			
1992	182,787	42.5	3.65	1.0	3
1993	270,000	43.0	5.0	2.0	
1994	279,200	43.0	5.2		

Sources: *Russian Economic Trends* (various issues), United Nations Economic Commission for Europe (1993: 206), Wegren (1992b: 646, 665), Siszov (1993: 501), Shaw (1992: 554), Nikonov (1992: 1159–60), *CDSP* (various issues), Pallot (1993: 112)

(compared with 25 per cent six months earlier), 32 per cent was held in lifelong heritable possession and 29 per cent was leased (*CDSP*, 1993, vol. XLV, no. 5, p. 22). In a survey 80 per cent of farmers named high prices for equipment and building materials as the chief hindrance to the development of their farms; more than 5,000 private farms ceased operating in 1992 (p. 23).

There are now nearly 250,000 private farmers in Russia, but they control only a tiny proportion of farming land and produce only 3 per cent of the 'overall commercial agricultural output' (Gillian Tett, *FT*, 3 June 1993, p. 36).

A lack of machinery suitable for small farms (as well as difficulties in obtaining other inputs) hinders the development of the 260,000 private farms (*The Economist*, 7 August 1993, p. 64).

In 1991 private plots (i.e. excluding newly created independent private farms) accounted for 35 per cent of agricultural output (United Nations Economic Commission for Europe 1993: 81).

The 277,000 private farms work 5 per cent of agricultural land and have less than 2 per cent of livestock. Even so, goods provided by private agricultural producers (traditional small plots tended by city dwellers plus the new private farmers) grew from 24 per cent of the total in 1990 to 38 per cent in 1993 (United Nations, *World Economic and Social Survey*, 1994, p. 36).

In 1993 50 million private plots and 270,000 private farms accounted for 36 per cent of official agricultural production (Åslund 1994b: 68).

It is sometimes said that the agrarian sector is now 94 per cent private, but this includes the collective and state farms that have been converted to joint stock companies (*CDSP*, 5 October 1994, vol. XLVI, no. 36, p. 6).

The percentage contribution to gross agricultural output for 1990, 1991, 1992 and 1993 respectively by type of enterprise was as follows: agricultural enterprises (such as collective farms, state farms, joint stock companies, partnerships and co-operatives, which together had 90 per cent of cultivated land at the beginning of 1994), 76, 72, 66 and 62; household plots (5 per cent of cultivated land), 24, 28, 33 and 36; new private farms (5 per cent of cultivated land), 0, 0, 1 and 2 (*RET*, 1994, vol. 3, no. 2, pp. 62–3). By the end of September 1994 new private farms accounted for 5.2 per cent of cultivated land. Their main output is grain, where their share of output in 1993 was 5 per cent, whilst for all other agricultural goods their share is only 1 per cent (*RET*, 1994, vol. 3, no. 3, pp. 70–1).

Policy after the dissolution of parliament on 21 September 1993

On 27 October 1993 Yeltsin issued a decree liberalizing the sale of land in agricultural areas entitled 'On the regulation of land relations and the development of agrarian reform in Russia'. 'Citizens and juristic persons who own land have the right to sell, bequeath, give away, mortgage, lease or exchange land, or pass it wholly or in part as a contribution to the authorized capital of joint stock companies, associations and co-operatives, including those with foreign investments.' Regions would decide the maximum amount of land an individual could own. The use of hired farm labour would not be allowed, i.e. owners must work the land themselves or form co-operatives. Potential owners would have to have an agricultural education and some farming experience. Local authorities would have the right to take back land left uncultivated or used 'irrationally' (the decree was primarily aimed at agricultural land, but local authorities would be allowed to change the use to commercial). The aim was to promote viable private farms. Foreigners would be allowed to rent land ('under certain conditions'), but not to buy land themselves (although joint ventures would be able to buy land).

The right to buy land would be given to all existing members of collective and state farms, including pensioners and children. Certificates (vouchers in effect) would be distributed according to job and length of service. According to *The Economist* (18 June 1994, p. 55), the first certificate entitles each holder to a certain number of hectares (calculated by dividing the area of the farm by the number of claimants) and the second certificate entitles the holder to a share of farm assets such as buildings and machinery (the value of each individual certificate depends on how many years the holder has worked on the farm). These certificates would be used in auctions to bid for farm land and property or could be sold to their fellow farmers (the first certificates were issued on 23 October 1993). 'The owners of land have the right . . . to sell shares in land to other members of the collective, as well as to other citizens and juristic persons, for the production of agricultural products. At the same time, members of the collective are to take preference over other purchasers in acquiring shares of land.' Farmers would have a choice of becoming individual proprietors, joining together in new co-operatives or selling their land to others in the village. A pilot scheme involving six collective and state farms in the Nizhny Novgorod area was announced on 26 October 1993. Help was given by the International Finance Corporation. Encouragement was given to form co-operatives (in order to create viable units) and most in fact did this (John Lloyd, *FT*, 2 April 1994, p. 26). The resulting farms were large-group farms (Van Atta 1994: 185).

On 10 March 1994 Prime Minister Chernomyrdin paid a visit and said that 'I am convinced this programme should become the national programme for all Russia. I have supported it and will support it'; he also said, however, that the scheme would be used 'as the basis' for the national programme. Agriculture Minister Alexander Zaveryukha also expressed support.

As of early February 1995 seven agricultural enterprises in Nizhny Novgorod province had gone through a reform process based on this model. Heavy pressure from the agrarian lobby had postponed the plan to make the programme a national one (*CDSP*, 1995, vol. XLVII, no. 7, p. 12).

But 'efforts to repeat it [the Nizhny Novgorod scheme] across the country have got nowhere' (*The Economist*, 11 March 1995, p. 36). 'Nizhny Novgorod is the only region in Russia to have tried systematically breaking up its collective farms – ninety of them so far' (*The Economist*, 25 March 1995, p. 52).

The 27 October 1993 decree also said that 'as of [1 January] 1994, compulsory deliveries and other forms of forced taking of agricultural products for state resources are to be abolished.' Yeltsin signed a decree entitled 'liberalizing the grain market in Russia' on 27 December 1993 (*CDSP*, 1993, vol. XLV, no. 52, p. 24).

On 1 February 1995 Chernomyrdin signed a government decree which stated that in order to withdraw land from a collective, would-be private farmers would have to obtain the unanimous consent of other members (Chrystia Freeland, *FT*, 21 February 1995, p. 2).

ECONOMIC PERFORMANCE

Inflation

By way of comparison with Russia's record on inflation, during the German inflation of 1922–23 the average inflation rate was 322 per cent a month or 40 per cent a week (*RET*, 1992, vol. 1, no. 3, p. 16). (The monthly peak was 45,213 per cent in October 1923.)

The annual rate of inflation peaked in 1992, but it remains at a level

Table 3.5 Russia: selected economic indicators

Economic indicator	*1990*	*1991*	*1992*	*1993*	*1994*
Rate of growth of GDP (%)	−4.0	−13.0	−19.0	−12.0	−15.0
Rate of growth of industrial output (%)	−0.1	−8.0	−18.0	−16.2	−21.7
Oil output (million tonnes)	516	462	399	354	316
Natural gas output (billion cubic metres)	641	643	641	619	607
Rate of growth of agricultural output (%)	−3.6	−4.5	−9.0	−4.0	−9.0
Grain output (million tonnes)	116.7	89.1	106.9	99.1	81.3
Grain imports (million tonnes)			26	11	
Inflation rate (%)	5.6	92.7	1,353.0	896.0	302.0

Sources: Various issues of *Russian Economic Trends*; United Nations Economic Commission for Europe, *Economic Survey of Europe*; United Nations, *World Economic and Social Survey*; IMF, *World Economic Outlook*; Deutsche Bank, *Focus: Eastern Europe*; *Economics of Transition* and *Business Central Europe*; EBRD (1995: 44)

Table 3.6 Russia: monthly rate of inflation (%)

Month	*1991*	*1992*	*1993*	*1994*	*1995*
January	6.2	245.3	25.8	17.9	17.8
February	4.9	38.0	24.7	10.8	11.0
March	6.3	29.9	20.1	7.4	8.9
April	63.5	21.7	18.8	8.5	8.5
May	3.0	12.0	18.1	6.9	7.9
June	1.2	18.6	19.9	6.0	6.7
July	0.6	10.6	22.4	5.3	5.4
August	0.5	8.6	25.8	4.6	4.6
September	1.1	11.5	23.1	7.7	4.5
October	3.5	22.9	19.5	15.0	4.7
November	8.9	26.1	16.4	15.0	
December	12.1	25.4	12.5	16.4	

Source: *Russian Economic Trends* (various issues)

high enough for attention to be focused on the monthly figures (see Tables 3.5 and 3.6).

Output

There is considerable debate about the output figures, but Table 3.5 indicates that GDP growth was negative through 1994. There seems to be general agreement that industrial production stopped falling in mid-1994.

Over the past three years Russia's output has declined by 38 per cent. The USA's fell by a mere 30 per cent in the Great Depression between 1930 and 1933 (*The Economist*, 15 January 1994, p. 71).

The output of machinery, forging/pressing and rolling stock has fallen to the levels of the 1950s, of coal and tractors to those of the 1960s, and of crude oil and pipe/rolled steel to those of the 1970s (Deutsche Bank, *Focus: Eastern Europe*, 21 May 1993, no. 79, p. 4).

A flourishing private economy in services and trade is under-reported and virtually untaxed. As a result, up to 40 per cent of the economy may not be taxed at all and GDP may be underestimated by as much as 15 per cent (Leyla Boulton, *FT*, Survey, 27 June 1994, p. ii). According to the Washington-based Bureau of National Affairs, the 'black' economy accounts for 20 per cent of GDP (*Business Europa*, February–March 1995, p. 45). Managers today have a strong incentive to under-report production to avoid paying taxes, while official GDP figures do not reflect what is happening in the new private sector. Guesses at how big the unrecorded economy may be begin at 25 per cent of official GDP and rise from there. The service sector now accounts for half of officially recorded GDP (*The Economist*, Survey, 8 April 1995, p. 14). Various estimates put the shadow economy in the range 20 per cent to 40 per cent of GDP (*Moscow News*, 26 May–1 June 1995, p. 9).

Åslund (1994b: 66) says that electricity consumption is universally closely correlated with real GDP. In 1992 official GDP in Russia fell by 19 per cent, but electricity consumption declined by only 6 per cent. In 1993 the respective decreases were 12 per cent and 5 per cent. 'The latter figures probably reflect the development of the economy more accurately, indicating that the depression of the Russian economy is wildly exaggerated' (p. 66). This becomes all the more evident when consumption is considered. 'Private consumption has started rising as a share of GDP from a paltry 40 per cent . . . real income rose by no less than 9 per cent [in 1993]' (p. 66). ('After four years of sharp fall in GDP, the decline in output appears to have bottomed out': Anders Åslund, *IHT*, 24 April 1995, p. 8.)

A criticism levelled at Åslund is that 'no mention is made of the possibility that high electricity consumption may merely reflect waste. Estonia . . . has managed to reduce electricity consumption by considerably more than the corresponding decline in GDP, an indication of the results that a true success story would have to generate.' Moreover, 'at least some of the output decline is real, most importantly the decline in oil production . . . Aggregate investment in 1994 may be a full 70 per cent below the 1990 level. It is hard not to call that a collapse' (DIW, *Economic Bulletin*, December 1994, vol. 31, no. 12, p. 1). (Real investment is low and in 1994 it was a quarter down on the previous year. It would not appear to be due to an absolute shortage of funds. The problem is that investment is so risky that investors require an extremely high expected return: *RET*, Monthly Update, 21 March 1995, p. 3. Capital investment fell by 26 per cent in 1994: *RET*, 1995, vol. 3, no. 4, p. 67. In 1994 Russians saved an amount equal to 33 per cent of GDP, but in Russia an amount equal to only 16 per cent of GDP was invested: *The Economist*, Survey, 8 April 1995, p. 15.)

Valeri Markov and Alexander Bulatov dismiss electricity statistics as indicators of aggregate industrial production because most electricity is used for household and municipal consumption and prices remain controlled (cited in *Comparative Economic Studies*, 1994, vol. XXXVI, no. 4, p. 42).

The weaker the statistical system the more useful electricity consumption as a measure of economic activity becomes. But it assumes constant ratios between electricity use and value added, and these may have changed a lot, in either direction, during the transition. In Eastern Europe the efficiency of electricity use may have risen, but this is perhaps less intuitively clear in the case of the CIS countries, where the payment discipline for electricity is weak (Kasper Bartholdy, *Transition*, 1995, vol. 6, no. 4, p. 3).

Noren (1993: 447) argues that 'As the influence of demand-side factors in the economy began to increase, the supply-side influences linked to trade disruptions and payments problems lost some of their significance. Either their constraints on production were not binding because of the overriding constraint imposed by the lack of demand, or they began to weaken as enterprises and governments adjusted to the new situation in economic life . . . By the end of 1992 Russia had passed an important milestone on the transition to a market economy – the rise to prominence of demand factors in determining the level and composition of output.'

Industrial production ceased to fall during the summer of 1994. In October 1994 a substantial rise was recorded (*RET*, Monthly Update, 17 November 1994, p. 3). Real industrial production has been fairly steady since October 1994 (on a seasonally adjusted basis) (*RET*, Monthly Update, 14 April 1995, p. 9).

The decrease in industrial production stopped in June 1994 (Deutsche Bank, *Focus: Eastern Europe*, 1994, no. 112, p. 3).

The decline in industrial output may have bottomed out; output has been steady for the past three months. Estimates of the size of the grey economy are inexact, but conservative guesses range from 25 per cent to 40 per cent of the officially recorded economy (*The Economist*, 8 October 1994, p. 23).

Industrial production did not fall in June, July or August 1994 (compared with the previous month). The importance of services has sharply increased (53.3 per cent of GDP in the second quarter of 1994). In the first eight months of 1994 real personal income rose by 12 per cent compared with the same period of 1993. The proportion of people with incomes below the minimum living standard was 24.4 per cent in the fourth quarter of 1993 and 13.9 per cent in the second quarter of 1994 (*CDSP*, 1994, vol. XLVI, no. 36, p. 16).

Industrial production troughed in May 1994 and has grown by around 1 per cent a month since (Jochen Wermuth, *FT*, 18 October 1994, p. 20).

'The Russian recession apparently levelled off in the first quarter of 1995' (OECD, *Economic Outlook*, June 1995, p. 111).

'The great Russian depression . . . appears to be bottoming out. The output of Russian industry has been drastically reshaped by market forces . . . The private sector is growing rapidly and the overall economy may be as much as 50 per cent larger than official statistics indicate' (Thane Gustavson and Daniel Yergin, *IHT*, 8 May 1995, p. 10).

In 1994 services accounted for half of GDP, compared with one-third in 1990 (*Transition*, January–February 1995, p. 20).

Conversion

In 1993 civilian goods accounted for 80 per cent of the military–industrial complex's total output (compared with 62 per cent in 1991). It produces 90 per cent of refrigerators and 100 per cent of television sets. About a quarter of the complex's enterprises have been privatized (*CDSP*, 1993, vol. XLV, no. 4, p. 8, and no. 52, p. 23).

Defence procurement fell by 32 per cent in 1991 and by 68 per cent in 1992 (*The Economist*, 28 August 1993, p. 20). In 1992 expenditure on arms and military equipment fell by about 68 per cent (*CDSP*, 1993, vol. XLV, no. 4, p. 13). In 1992 defence spending fell by around two-thirds (United Nations Economic Commission for Europe 1993: 230).

'Today only 3 million Russians actually produce arms. The conversion of the military industry has, to a large extent, already succeeded' (Åslund 1994b: 66).

Unemployment and wage policy

The figures for unemployment in Table 3.7 are generally considered to be underestimates. But even the adjusted figures are relatively low by Western standards and attempts have been made to find the reasons. Unemployment is a mainly urban phenomenon and women fare much worse than men.

Unemployment benefit for redundant workers is a percentage of their former money wage: for three months they get 100 per cent (from their employers); then (from the Employment Service) 75 per cent for the next three months, 60 per cent for the next four months and 45 per cent for the next five months. After that they can get 'material assistance' of not more than the minimum wage. With high inflation the real value of benefit falls rapidly. Consequently, most unemployed people receive the minimum wage, which is the minimum guaranteed level of unemployment benefit. All unemployed people not made redundant by a former employer are entitled to the minimum wage, which has fluctuated around 10 per cent of the average wage (*RET*, 1994, vol. 3, no. 2, pp. 48–9).

RET (1993, vol. 2, no. 1, pp. 45, 48; no. 4, pp. 60–1) provides the following information. At the end of February 1993 only 0.6 per cent of the labour force who were 'out of employment' (workers so defined must

Table 3.7 Russia: unemployment

		'Out of employment'		'Registered'	
Date		*No.*	%	*No.*	%
1991	July	351,000		16,000	
	December	469,000	0.6	62,000	0.1
1992	January	485,000		69,000	
	July	843,000		248,000	0.4
	December	982,000	1.4	578,000	0.8
1993	January	1,029,000	1.5	628,000	0.9
	July	989,000		717,000	1.0
	December	1,085,000	1.5	836,000	1.1
1994	January	1,165,000	1.6	894,000	
	July	1,581,000		1,324,000	
	December	1,878,000	2.5	1,637,000	2.2
1995	January	1,963,000	2.6	1,710,000	
	July	2,394,000	3.0	2,048,000	

Source: *Russian Economic Trends* (various issues)

be registered with a local office of the Federal Employment Service) were receiving benefit. From September 1992 onwards redundant workers were automatically included in the more restrictive 'registered unemployment' category as long as they registered with the FES, but they do not receive benefit during the first three months of unemployment because they are still being paid by their former employers. The unemployment numbers may be biased downward: (1) those who do not register with the FES are not counted; the advantages of registration are generally quite low, since the average level of benefit for those eligible is poor (on the other hand, workers may be reluctant to dissociate themselves from their enterprises because of non-cash benefits such as housing, subsidized meals and health services); (2) an estimated 9 per cent of the industrial work force at the end of 1992 were working (often involuntarily) reduced hours. At the end of 1992 72 per cent of the unemployed were female. The level of employment has been falling: 73.8 million in 1991, 72.3 million in 1992 and 71 million in 1993.

According to the methodology used by the International Labour Organization (those out of work and actively seeking employment), 3.8 million were unemployed (5 per cent of the active population). If the 'partially' ('potentially') unemployed had been included (i.e. people who would have been laid off in other countries), the figure would have gone up to 7.8 million or 10.4 per cent (*Izvestiya*, 21 December 1993, p. 1). In 1993 almost 4 million people or 5 per cent of the labour force would have been classified as unemployed under the methodology developed by the ILO (United Nations, *World Economic and Social Survey*, 1994, p. 36). These two estimates have been officially published in Russia since November 1993 (United Nations Economic Commission for Europe 1994: 7). The ILO estimated that the real level of unemployment was six or seven times the official rate of about 1.5 per cent (Frances Williams, *FT*, 8 February 1994, p. 2). The head of the federal employment service estimated that if hidden unemployment had been included (e.g. part-time work and unpaid 'holidays') the figure would have risen from 5 million to 7 million or 7–10 per cent of the working population (reported by John Lloyd, *FT*, 7 October 1993, p. 5). In the first quarter of 1994 5.9 per cent of the work force were unemployed by the standard international definition, compared with 4.8 per cent in 1992 and 5.5 per cent in 1993 (*RET*, 1994, vol. 3, no. 1, p. 69). As of June 1994 4.5 million people or 6 per cent of the labour force were unemployed using ILO methodology. Another 6 per cent were employed part-time or 'on leave' without pay or with partial pay. Thus the 'total potential unemployment' was 12 per cent of the economically active population (*CDSP*, 1994, vol. XLVI, no. 32, p. 13).

An ILO report of late October 1994 is summarized by Frances Williams (*FT*, 1 November 1994, p. 2). Based on standard international definitions, open unemployment is at least five times as high as the official Russian figures. Around 35 per cent of those still 'in work' had no job to do. They included those on involuntary short-time working and those (a fifth of all industrial workers) on long-term 'administrative leave' receiving little or no wages. The creation of hidden unemployment was a rational response by managers who would otherwise have had to pay wages or severance pay. Nearly half the enterprises surveyed were in wage arrears and more than 60 per cent had not paid wages in full. Official figures showing a rise in average real wages referred to contractual wages and not those actually paid.

According to the labour force survey, 7.1 per cent of the work force were unemployed at the end of 1994 (compared with 5.5 per cent at the end of 1993); a further 6.4 per cent were either on short-time work or on administrative leave. During 1994 workers were on strike for an average of eleven days per thousand workers. This is more than double the figure for 1993, but only one-thirtieth of the average for OECD countries over the previous decade (*RET*, Monthly Update, 21 February 1995, p. 8). Long-term unemployment is a growing problem. In March 1993 2 per cent of the unemployed had been out of work for more than a year and 42 per cent for more than four months. As of December 1994 the respective figures had reached 17 per cent and 50 per cent (*RET*, 1995, vol. 3, no. 4, p. 87).

The unemployment rate is 7.1 per cent, but if the partially unemployed are taken into account the rate rises to 13.5 per cent. Women and young people accounted for two-thirds of the unemployed in 1994 (*Transition*, January–February 1995, p. 21).

According to official calculations, 25 million Russians would be thrown out of work if subsidies to loss-making enterprises were eliminated (*Newsbrief*, January 1994, vol. 14, no. 1, p. 2). If all the unprofitable enterprises were to shut down at once, at least 50 per cent of the adult population would be thrown out of work (Deutsche Bank, *Focus: Eastern Europe*, 1994, no. 104, p. 6).

Since January 1992 enterprises have been free to set the wages of their employees. There is, however, an 'excess wage' tax built into the profits tax, generally limiting the tax deductibility of wage payments to four times the minimum wage.

'Excessive' wage increases are subject to punitive taxation (EBRD 1994: 35).

In March 1994 accumulated wage arrears amounted to some 40 per cent of the monthly wage bill in industry, construction and agriculture (*RET*, Monthly Update, 30 April 1994, p. 3). In the first quarter of 1994 wage arrears roughly equalled two weeks' wages (*RET*, 1994, vol. 3, no. 1, p. 37). At the end of the third quarter of 1994 arrears as a percentage of the wage bill were 44 per cent in industry, 85 per cent in agriculture and 26 per cent in construction (*RET*, 1994, vol. 3, no. 3, p. 50).

At the beginning of 1994 the total amount of overdue pay was almost 800 billion roubles; employees of 24,000 enterprises had not received their pay by the established dates (*CDSP*, 1994, vol. XLVI, no. 29, p. 7). As of 1 August 1994 the sum had risen to 3,800 billion roubles: more than 20 million people at 34,000 enterprises were involved (*CDSP*, 1994, vol. XLVI, no. 33, p. 22).

Åslund says that in August 1993 only 56 per cent of workers polled had received their latest monthly wage in full and on time. Nevertheless, apart from coal miners, Russian workers rarely strike, even when they have not been paid for months. Nor are workers likely to strike, because they lack both organization and leaders. Real wages seem perfectly flexible. Workers are kept on the payroll for these reasons and because they are a useful pawn in negotiations with the authorities over subsidies. Thus unemployment stays low, with the most plausible estimate at around 6 per cent (1994b: 67). 'Unemployment has stayed at a moderate 7.5 per cent of the labour force and the labour market remains highly flexible, with one-quarter of workers changing jobs each year' (Anders Åslund, *IHT*, 24 April 1995, p. 8).

Labour market surveys are a much better indicator of real joblessness, but unemployment is still only 6.5 per cent according to these. Only a few industries, such as agriculture or coal, continue to receive big state subsidies. Overall employment has fallen by only 2 million (or 2.4 per cent of the work force) since 1992. Richard Layard argues that the labour market is both very buoyant and remarkably flexible. Its buoyancy is reflected in the large number of new jobs being created, while its flexibility stems from the fact that employees are willing to accept much lower real wages rather than lose their jobs. Even in declining sectors enterprises are paying their workers less and sending them on unpaid leave rather than sacking them. Because unemployment benefit is so low and social services (such as schools and clinics) are often attached to enterprises, it makes sense for the worker to stay. The enterprise gains by not having to pay redundancy money and by the fact that cheap labour helps mitigate the effects of the excess wage tax. But Guy Standing of the ILO has recalculated the figures, recording all those on short working hours and unpaid leave as unemployed, and comes up with a rate (excluding agriculture) of 35 per cent (*The Economist*, 18 February 1995, p. 90).

Living standards

There is considerable controversy about what has happened to living standards. Lipton and Sachs (1992: 220–2) dispute the common assertion that real living standards fell by around 50 per cent. They argue that price liberalization basically restored wage–price relations that had prevailed before the 1987 changes in enterprise autonomy, without representing an actual fall in living standards. Over the period 1985 to December 1991 average industrial real wages increased by 79 per cent. But because the supply of consumer goods grew little if at all, and certainly not commensurately with the increase in rouble wages, excess demand developed. There were price controls and, therefore, intensifying shortages and lengthening queues in official markets and inflation in black markets. The statistical real wage was thereby disconnected from actual living standards. If anything an inverse relationship occurred; higher real wages resulted in longer queues and thereby a loss of work and leisure time. The costs in terms of lower living standards are exaggerated (p. 246). Even if the reforms *per se* do not reduce living standards sharply, the backdrop is still one of a falling trend in such key sectors as energy. An income squeeze resulting from trends that preceded the reforms might be widely blamed on the reforms themselves. Also it is likely to be the case that income inequality has risen as a result of the reforms, with pensioners probably being squeezed relative to younger workers (pp. 247–8). The United Nations (*World Economic Survey 1993*, p. 33) adds that surveys indicate that nearly half the working population now hold more than one job, often in the growing non-state and informal sectors which are not reported in the official data. Thus the officially measured 50 per cent fall in average real wages in the year to December 1992 is an overstatement.

The Economist (6 February 1993, p. 36) notes that the average wage buys only 60 per cent of what it could buy before the January 1992 price liberalization and is lower in real terms than the average wage in 1985. But this ignores the previous shortages. The average standard of living may not have fallen by as much as is claimed, but fallen it has, especially for the old and unemployed. Each month the Russian government calculates a 'minimum subsistence level'. In November 1992 the minimum was 3,285 roubles a month; 29 per cent of the population had incomes below that level, while less than 1 per cent had incomes over 10,000 roubles a month.

The minimum for January 1993 was 5,073 roubles, which was more than the pension (increased to 4,275 roubles a month on 1 February 1993) and over twice the minimum wage (increased from 900 to 2,250 roubles on 1 January 1993). Minimum pensions and wages were to be indexed to inflation quarterly, starting on 1 February and 1 April 1993 respectively (p. 35).

RET (1992, vol. 1, no. 3, p. 21) refers to a 'physiological minimum' of 1,939 roubles a month in August 1992; about 30 per cent of the population received less.

The number of people living below the minimum subsistence level increased from 12 per cent to 29 per cent in the twelve months to the end of 1992 (United Nations Economic Commission for Europe 1993: 4–5).

There has been a halving of living standards over the past year (*The Economist*, 1 May 1993, p. 13).

Measured living standards per head fell by half in 1992 (real average 55.6: January 1991 = 100), with pensioners and others dependent on state incomes especially adversely affected (Edward Balls, *FT Survey*, 27 May 1993, pp. II–III).

According to official statistics, average real income fell by 56 per cent in 1992 (Deutsche Bank, *Focus: Eastern Europe*, 22 March 1993, no. 71, p. 3).

In 1992 37 per cent of the population were below the poverty line, defined as an income which would allow a level of food consumption adequate to maintain a normal body weight at an average level of activity (Ellman 1994: 341).

A Unicef report claimed that the number of people living in extreme poverty soared from 2.5 per cent in 1991 to 23.2 per cent in 1992 (*The Guardian*, 7 October 1994, p. 12).

The 'real living standard' of the population in January 1993 was around 63 per cent of the December 1992 level and about 30 per cent of the December 1991 level (*Moscow News*, 12 March 1993, no. 11, p. 5). Comparing consumer prices and money income the standard of living in 1992 was below 44 per cent of that of 1991, while the proportion of the population below the poverty line was about 40 per cent (*Moscow News*, 18 February 1993, p. 4).

Since the reform began there has been a severe fall in living standards. The measured after-tax real wage is now roughly three-quarters of its level in 1985 and about half its unsustainably high level in 1991. Compared with 1985 the average pension has fallen by a quarter relative to the average wage. In November 1992 about 30 per cent of the population had incomes below the 'physiological minimum' level of living (*RET*, 1993, vol. 2, no. 1, pp. 5, 32). Taking all factors into account living standards fell by roughly 20 per cent in 1991–93 (although living standards actually rose slightly in 1993) (*RET*, 1993, vol. 2, no. 4, p. 32).

'After a decline in the standard of living of about one-fifth in 1991 and 1992, life improved considerably in 1993 and 1994. Real incomes increased by 10 per cent in 1993 and even more in 1994' (Anders Åslund, *IHT*, 24 April 1995, p. 8).

In a 9 February 1994 article, Illarionov said that 40 million Russians (27 per cent of the population) were below the minimum living standard (*CDSP*, 1994, vol. XLVI, no. 6, p. 21).

It is estimated that some 30 per cent of the population received less than the minimum subsistence income in the last quarter of 1993, compared with 26 per cent at end-1992 and 12 per cent at end-1991. Pensions averaged 30 per cent of monthly wages in 1993 (United Nations Economic Commission for Europe 1994: 70).

In July 1994 24.5 million citizens (or every sixth resident of Russia) had an income lower than the minimum living standard (*CDSP*, 1994, vol. XLVI, no. 33, p. 21).

The proportion of the population with an income below the subsistence level was 29.4 per cent in the fourth quarter of 1993, 30.7 per cent in the first quarter of 1994 and 38.5 per cent in the second quarter of 1994 (*Transition*, 1994, vol. 5, no. 6, p. 18).

According to Goskomstat, real household incomes rose by 18 per cent in the year to July 1994 and real household consumption by 10 per cent. The number of people officially recorded as living below the poverty line has halved from just over 40 million in June 1993 to 20 million in June 1994 (*The Economist*, 8 October 1994, pp. 23–4).

The proportion of people with incomes below the minimum living standard was 24.4 per cent in the fourth quarter of 1994 and 13.9 per cent in the second quarter of 1994 (*CDSP*, 1994, vol. XLVI, no. 36, p. 16).

The real income of the population during the first half of 1994 was 10 per cent higher than one year earlier. A new class of 'super rich' is emerging in Russia, but the share of the population below the minimum subsistence level has been falling (from an average of 31 per cent in the first half of 1993 to 17 per cent in the first half of 1994) (*RET*, 1994, vol. 3, no. 2, p. 41). Real incomes grew by 16 per cent during 1994 (compared with 10 per cent in 1993), although real incomes were still some 30 per cent below pre-reform levels. Over the year 24 per cent of the population received incomes below an official subsistence level of income, compared with 31 per cent in 1993 (*RET*, 1995, vol. 3, no. 4, p. 46).

In 1994 about 23 per cent of the population had money incomes below the minimum subsistence level. Russians with the highest incomes had fifteen times as much as the lowest. In 1993 the ratio was 11 : 1 and in 1991 it was 4.5 : 1 (*Transition*, January–February 1995, p. 21).

The top 10 per cent of the population now earn fourteen times the income of the poorest 10 per cent, compared with 5.4 times three years ago (*FT*, 31 December 1995, p. 2).

Health and the environment

The population was 148.3 million at the start of 1993 (*IHT*, 12 February 1993, p. 11).

The population of Russia actually fell in 1992, by 1.4 per cent (United Nations, *World Economic Survey 1993*, p. 33).

The death rate per thousand was 14.6 in 1993, a rise compared with the 1992 figure of 12.2. The birth rate, on the other hand, fell from 10.7 per thousand in 1992 to 9.2 in 1993 (*RET*, 1993, vol. 2, no. 4, p. 41).

The infant mortality rate increased from 17.4 per thousand in 1990 to 19.1 per thousand in 1993 (John Lloyd, *FT*, 14 February 1994, p. 1).

By the end of 1993 male life expectancy had fallen to just fifty-nine years, putting Russia on a par with India and Egypt (*The Economist*, 9 July 1994, p. 40).

The figure of fifty-nine years in 1993 compares with the 1980s peak of sixty-five in 1987 (61.45 in 1979–80): 'This steep and rapid decline is a remarkable demographic phenomenon. By 1993 male life expectancy at birth in Russia had fallen below the level of the medium income countries and had probably fallen to a level about that of Indonesia in the second half of the 1980s' (Ellman 1994: 334, 351–2).

The suicide rate in 1993 reached 38 per 100,000, up from 26.5 in 1991 (the rate in the USA is 12 per 100,000). Overall 2.2 million Russians died in 1993, 360,000 more than in June 1995 the previous year. Deaths exceeded births by nearly 800,000 in 1993. Life expectancy during the final years of the Soviet period was 64.5 years for men and 74 for women. Today's figures are 58.5 and 68.5 respectively in Russia, compared with 72.7 (for white males) and 79.4 (for white females) in the USA (Gennadi Gerasimov, *IHT*, 29 December 1994, p. 4).

In 1994 male life expectancy was 58.3 years (Alexei Yablokov, *The Economist*, 29 April 1995, p. 10).

In August 1993 there were many reports of an increasing incidence in some countries of the former Soviet Union of diseases such as diphtheria, typhoid, cholera, malaria, anthrax and even bubonic plague (a case reported in Kazakhstan). Explanatory factors include the worsening economic situation, the increased mobility of people and the fear of inoculation with unsterilized needles.

The Russian environment minister revealed that about 15 per cent of Russia could be considered an environmental disaster zone. Some 100,000 people lived on land where radiation levels were too high. Half of Russia's 222 million hectares of arable land was unsuitable for farming and only 20 per cent of industrial waste was adequately treated (*The Independent*, 28 December 1993, p. 7).

The chief environmental adviser to the president has said that between 14 per cent and 16 per cent of the Russian land mass can be considered environmental disaster zones, an area inhabited by roughly 40 million people. Some 40 per cent of the ground water supply is now heavily polluted. The official data show that 1.2 per cent to 1.3 per cent of oil going through pipelines is lost every year, but unoffical data suggest that the figure may be 2 per cent or even 3 per cent (Erik Ipsen, *IHT*, 24 April 1995, p. 6).

There have been disturbing reports about oil spills. For example, major environmental damage was caused by a leaking pipeline in the Komi republic, near Usinsk (300 km from the Arctic Ocean). It came to world attention in September 1994, but it looked as though the pipeline had been leaking badly since February 1994 (*CDSP*, 1994, vol. XLVI, no. 43, pp. 18–19).

Losses due to broken pipes and defective plant are high. The Russian environment ministry cites an annual loss of 20 million tonnes of crude oil. In 1985 Russia was the number one oil producer, accounting for almost 20 per cent of world output. Since 1992 it has slipped into third place behind Saudi Arabia and the USA. In 1994 Russia's oil output was 311 million tonnes, with its share of world production falling to roughly 10 per cent (Deutsche Bank, *Focus: Eastern Europe*, 1995, no. 126, p. 3).

4

ARMENIA

POLITICS

The political background

Around 95 per cent of the population in Soviet Armenia was Armenian. In 1992 only 2 per cent of the population were ethnic Russians (*The Economist*, 10 July 1993, p. 33). Ethnic Armenians account for 93 per cent of the population, Russians 2 per cent, Kurds 2 per cent and others 3 per cent (*FT*, Survey, 7 June 1995, p. 35). Unofficial estimates indicate that more than 500,000 Armenians have fled in the last three years, reducing the population to 3 million (Raymond Bonner, *IHT*, 28 April 1994, p. 12). Another source cites estimates of those leaving in the previous year in the range 300,000 to 800,000 (*CDSP*, 1994, vol. XLVI, no. 16, p. 21).

There are thought to be some 3.5 million Armenians in the diaspora, the trigger for which was the massacres of 1915 perpetrated by the Ottoman Turks (Haig Simonian, *FT*, Survey, 7 June 1995, p. 38).

Political developments

2 February 1993. Prime Minister Khozrov Arutyunyan and his government are dismissed (he thought the economic programme did not sufficiently protect the interests of the neediest segments of society). Grant Bagratian was made premier. Strongly pro-reform, he was a deputy prime minister who had pioneered land privatization.

7 September 1993. Armenia agrees (subject to ratification) to take part in the rouble zone (see rouble zone).

28 December 1994. President Levon Ter-Petrossian suspends the opposition Armenian Revolutionary Federation (Dashnak) for six months and the party's members will be allowed to stand only as individuals in the 5 July 1995 general election.

The president talked of terrorism and drugs, calling Dashnak a 'terrorist, fascist organization' (the mayor of Yerevan had been murdered a couple of weeks earlier). Eleven opposition publications were closed.

12 January 1995. The suspension of Dashnak is upheld by the Supreme Court, but on the grounds that its ruling Athens-based 'bureau' has foreign citizens as members (James Meek, *The Guardian*, 19 April 1995, p. 10).

5 July 1995. The general election takes place and also a referendum on whether to adopt a powerful presidency. The ruling party is the All-Armenian National Movement. 'Most analysts expect the new parliament to have a close resemblance to the current legislative body, which is dominated by state factory directors, local politicians and other allies of Mr Ter-Petrossian' (Chrystia Freeland, *FT*, Survey, 7 June 1995, p. 35).

Candidates competed for seats in the 190-member National Assembly. Forty seats were allotted to party lists and 150 seats to single-member constituencies. The Dashnak suspension has already been mentioned, but nine other parties were excluded from the election (on technical grounds such as allegedly forged signatures). Thirteen parties and around 2,000 candidates (including some thirty 'independents' from Dashnak) took part.

OSCE observers thought the election 'generally free but not fair.' Apart from the banning of certain parties from participating, mention was made, for example, of the manipulative use of the media by the government and inadequate explanation of the new constitution.

According to preliminary figures, the Republic bloc (headed by the All-Armenian National Movement) won twenty out of the forty seats allotted to party lists. There were reports that the bloc also won a convincing victory in the election for the 150 seats allotted to single-member constituencies. 'All told, the ruling party is assured of at least two-thirds of the seats in parliament' (*CDSP*, 1995, vol. XLVII, no. 28, p. 19).

The referendum on the constitution needed at least one-third support from eligible voters for the constitution to be approved. The draft constitution envisaged a powerful presidency, e.g. with the ability to dissolve parliament and appoint senior members of the judiciary. 'In all, 68 per cent of the voters cast their ballots in favour of it' (*CDSP*, 1995, vol. XLVII, no. 28, p. 19).[1]

THE ECONOMY

'As Armenian officials explain, the economic blockade has acted as an unlikely catalyst for reforms, forcing Yerevan to adopt radical economic measures that more prosperous former Soviet republics could afford to delay' (Chrystia Freeland, *FT*, Survey, 7 June 1995, p. 35).

Financial policy

Armenia's own currency (the dram) was introduced on 22 November 1993. Armenians were entitled to exchange up to 50,000 roubles for drams, with higher sums frozen in special accounts.

Old (pre-1993) roubles were finally declared invalid in March 1994 (Deutsche Bank, *Focus: Eastern Europe*, 1994, no. 113, p. 5). The dram became the sole legal tender on 1 March 1994 (EBRD 1994: 17).

Monetary policy was tightened sharply in the spring of 1994 (EBRD 1995: 11). Interest rates became highly positive in real terms from June 1994 onwards (p. 52).

In mid-December 1994 the IMF approved a $25 million systemic transformation facility. The government aims to bring monthly inflation down from 26.3 per cent in 1994 to 5 per cent in 1995 (*Transition*, January–February 1995, p. 23). Since May 1994 the nominal exchange rate has been stable and the dram has sharply appreciated in real terms. The monthly inflation rate averaged 46 per cent in the first quarter of 1994, but fell to 1.2 per cent in March 1995 (Chrystia Freeland, *FT*, Survey, 7 June 1995, p. 35).

Prices

Comprehensive price liberalization was introduced in January 1992. Controlled prices and subsidies still exist for bread, medical care, energy and certain public utilities (EBRD 1994: 17). Further price liberalization took place in the fourth quarter of 1994 (EBRD 1995: 52).

Privatization

A draft privatization programme envisages the partial sale of state enterprises (perhaps up to 30 per cent of total state assets) through the use of vouchers. But details have not been issued (*Business Central Europe*, November 1993, p. 60). The declared intent was to privatize all small-scale enterprises and a quarter of large manufacturing enterprises by 1995 (*Business Central Europe*, December 1993/January 1994, p. 74).

In mid-1994 the private sector accounted for roughly 40 per cent of GDP (EBRD 1994: 10). The law of 27 August 1992 was amended in November 1993. At least five large-scale enterprises have been privatized. The government intends to distribute freely to the population 20 per cent of the shares in 70 per cent of large and medium-sized industrial enterprises. No property restitution had taken place by summer 1994 (p. 16). The distribution of mass privatization vouchers began on 10 October 1994. Six hundred small enterprises were privatized in the fourth quarter of 1994 and another 40 per cent of the housing stock and agricultural land was privatized in the second half of 1994 (EBRD 1995: 52).

Legislation passed in July 1992 provided for the privatization of small and large enterprises. By September 1992 300 small enterprises and forty-five large enterprises had been privatized. Vouchers need to be issued (Havrylyshyn *et al.* 1994: 383).

Armenia has launched a campaign to sell 64 per cent of shares in ten of its largest enterprises for vouchers and cash. The enterprises would be transformed into joint stock companies and also open to foreign investors. Shares would be on sale for two months (*FT*, 17 March 1995, p. 2). The government pledged to implement a mass privatization programme in 1995. A textile enterprise was one of the first ten enterprises privatized in May 1995 under the voucher sell-off scheme, workers receiving a 20 per cent stake for free and then buying another 16 per cent with their vouchers. Vouchers are freely transferable and there are no limits on foreign participation. There were plans to sell another fifty enterprises in the following two months and to offer 900 medium-sized and large enterprises by the end of 1995 (Matthew Kaminski, *FT*, Survey, 7 June 1995, p. 36).

Foreign trade

A system of state-negotiated barter arrangements with other countries of the former Soviet Union still dominates trade. Otherwise there are few explicit tariff or non-tariff barriers to trade (EBRD 1994: 17).

The government adopted a floating exchange rate regime in the second half of December 1993, after a short period with a fixed peg to the dollar. The exchange rate is determined in an auction in which currency surrendered by enterprises is offered for sale to financial institutions. Full convertibility for current account purposes has not yet been achieved (EBRD 1994: 17). There are restrictions on current and capital account convertibility. There is a 50 per cent export surrender requirement of foreign exchange at the official rate (p. 111).

Agriculture

By the end of 1992 there were 243,000 private farms, with an average size of 2 ha (*CDSP*, 1993, vol. XLV, no. 5, p. 22); they accounted for 37.4 per cent of total agricultural land (United Nations Economic Commission for Europe 1993: 206).

As of 1 April 1993 there were 246,000 private farms, with an average size of less than 2 ha; a large proportion of the publicly owned farms have been transformed into peasant farms (*CDSP*, 1993, vol. XLV, no. 21, p. 20).

Privatization covers more than 90 per cent of arable land (*Business Central Europe*, December 1993/January 1994, p. 74).

Privatized agricultural units account for more than 60 per cent of arable land (EBRD 1994: 16). Another 40 per cent of the housing stock and agricultural land was privatized in the second half of 1994 (EBRD 1995: 52).

In the land privatization programme of spring 1991 each collective farm was divided into as many parcels as there were households. The head of each household drew a lot, each lot corresponding to one of the parcels of land. Another important development, which was to be fully implemented in 1995, was a new system of taxation. Taxes were to be based on the *potential* production of land, thus helping to compensate for differences in land quality and providing an incentive to sell land that cannot be farmed properly (the three-year moratorium on the sale of land has now expired). More than 80 per cent of agricultural land is now in the hands of private farmers (Chrystia Freeland, *FT*, Survey, 7 June 1995, pp. 35–6).

Economic performance

Table 4.1 paints a generally pretty grim picture, especially on the inflation front. But GDP rose in 1994.

Table 4.1 Armenia: selected economic indicators

Economic indicator	*1990*	*1991*	*1992*	*1993*	*1994*
Rate of growth of GDP (%)	−7.4	−10.8	−52.4	−14.8	5.4
Rate of growth of industrial output (%)	−7.5	−7.7	−48.2	−10.3	6.9
Rate of growth of agricultural output (%)	−11.4	11.0	−13.0	24.0	3.0
Inflation rate (%)	10.3	100.3	824.5	3,731.8	5,267.8
Budget surplus or deficit (% GDP)		−1.9	−37.6	−48.2	−16.1
Current account ($ billion)			−0.04	0.0315	
Unemployment (end of year, %)		3.5	3.5	6.2	6.0

Sources: Various issues of United Nations Economic Commission for Europe, *Economic Survey of Europe*; United Nations, *World Economic and Social Survey*; IMF, *World Economic Outlook*; Deutsche Bank, *Focus: Eastern Europe*; *Economics of Transition* and *Business Central Europe*; EBRD (1994: 150; 1995: 27)

Industry is operating at 30 per cent capacity owing to a fuel shortage that results in electricity being available for only two hours a day (Raymond Bonner, *IHT*, 28 April 1994, p. 12). In late May 1995 Armenia announced that the nuclear plant at Medzamor was to be restarted. (It was mothballed in February 1989 three months after a massive earthquake. The reactor was restarted on 25 October 1995.)

NOTE

1. 'Mr Ter-Petrossian emerged from the elections with effective control of all three branches of government, including 160 of 190 parliamentary seats and the right to appoint all judges' (Steve LeVine, *IHT*, 28 November 1995, p. 7).

5

AZERBAIJAN

POLITICS

The political background

In 1989 the ethnic composition of the population was as follows: Azeri 78.1 per cent; Russian 7.9 per cent; Armenian 7.9 per cent; other 6.1 per cent (*Economic Bulletin for Asia and the Pacific*, 1991, vol. XLII, nos 1 and 2, p. 2).

The population comprises 82 per cent Azeris, 6 per cent Armenians, 6 per cent Russians and 2 per cent Kurds (Deutsche Bank, *Focus: Eastern Europe*, 31 August 1993, no. 86, p. 3).

Business Central Europe (July–August 1993, p. 64) estimated the population split as 83 per cent Azeri, 6 per cent Armenian, 6 per cent Russian and 5 per cent 'other'. In the Soviet era Nagorno-Karabakh's 174,000 population was split 76 per cent Armenian to 23 per cent Azeri (most Azeris have now been displaced). In 1991 the proportion of Russians was 4.1 per cent (*The Economist*, 10 December 1994, p. 52).

The ancient name for Nagorno-Karabakh was 'Artsak'. Azerbaijan is currently the only country of the former Soviet Union without Soviet troops or military bases (with the exception of Lithuania since the end of August 1993).

Political developments

9 March 1993. An agreement is reached with Turkey about an oil pipeline.

2 April 1993. A two-month state of emergency is declared after strong Armenian gains in the fighting over Nagorno-Karabakh (opening up another corridor to Armenia). There are many refugees.

5 April 1993. The UN Security Council calls on Armenian forces to withdraw from Azerbaijani territory.

8 April 1993. Russia announces a cease-fire, but the two opposing camps deny that such an agreement has been reached.

30 April 1993. Under international pressure Armenian forces begin to withdraw from Azerbaijani territory.

7 June 1993. Rebel Azerbaijani troops under recently dismissed Colonel Surat Huseinov capture Gyanja, the second largest town in the country, in protest at the military defeats over Nagorno-Karabakh. They later make strong territorial gains.

14 June 1993. The Armenians in Nagorno-Karabakh announce their acceptance of a cease-fire which had been earlier brokered by Russia, the USA and Turkey (it had been set to start on 29 May). But fighting appears to have gone on as the political situation in Azerbaijan continued to deteriorate.

15 June 1993. Gaidar Aliev (who was removed from the Soviet politburo in October 1987 and is now head of the Azerbaijani enclave and autonomous republic of Nakhichevan in Armenia) accepts the post of chairman of parliament as the authority of the president continues to fall.

18 June 1993. President Albufez Elchibey (who was democratically elected, supported by Turkey but not Russia and was a former dissident jailed when Aliev was in charge of Soviet Azerbaijan) flees Baku for his home territory of Nakhichevan (it seems as though army commanders refused to offer protection from the rebels). But he does not resign as president. Aliev takes over as acting head of state.

24 June 1993. Parliament votes to hand over power to Aliev.

27 June 1993. The rebel forces pledge allegiance to Aliev.

The last large Azeri town in Nagorno-Karabakh falls to the Armenians.

The signing of an oil contract with Western multinational companies planned for 2 July, is postponed.

30 June 1993. Surat Huseinov is appointed prime minister and 'supreme commander' of all the security forces.

24 July 1993. A three-day cease-fire is supposed to come into effect with Armenian forces in Nagorno-Karabakh as of midnight (subsequently extended to 2 August).

23 August 1993. The Azerbaijani towns of Cebrayil (21–22 August) and Fizuli (23 August) fall to the Armenians, who now occupy large swathes of Azerbaijan around Nagorno-Karabakh, in effect substantially closing the land gap with Armenia (despite condemnation by the UN Security Council). Jebrail fell the following day.

29 August 1993. A national vote of confidence in Elchibey's presidency is held via a referendum, which goes decisively against the former president (97 per cent in a 92 per cent turnout).

4–5 September 1993. The town of Goradiz falls to the Armenians.

6 September 1993. Aliev hints that Azerbaijan may join the CIS. (Presidential elections are set for 3 October 1993.)

20 September 1993. Parliament votes to join the CIS.

24 September 1993. Azerbaijan joins the CIS.

3 October 1993. Aliev wins the presidential election with 98.8 per cent of the vote (the turnout was more than 95 per cent).

21 October 1993. The cease-fire, which had been extended to 5 November, breaks down. (A counter-offensive by Azerbaijan began in mid-December 1993. There was some success at first, but the Armenians had regained the upper hand by early 1994.)

20 February 1994. Russia brokers a cease-fire over Nagorno-Karabakh (to begin on 1 March).

28 July 1994. An indefinite extension of the 17 May cease-fire agreement is announced (those of 9 and 11 May had broken down).

3 October 1994. Aliev proclaims a state of emergency and talks of an attempted coup. (On 29 September two senior officials were murdered and several members of the Interior Ministry's special police force were arrested. Some of their colleagues seized the general prosecutor for a short while. Rebel forces were then besieged.)

5 October 1994. Aliev declares the coup attempt to have failed.

6 October 1994. Parliament supports Aliev's call for the dismissal of Prime Minister Surat Huseinov for alleged involvement in the coup attempt.

5–6 December 1994. The CSCE meeting in Budapest decides in principle to send a multinational peacekeeping force to Nagorno-Karabakh. But conditions are laid down, such as the declaration of a formal truce, negotiations starting between the warring factions and prior approval being given by the UN Security Council.

16 March 1995. Aliev talks of an attempted coup and the country being 'on the brink of civil war'. Baku is put on a war footing. (On 13 March an attempt was made to disband an elite police force commanded by Deputy Interior Minister Rovshan Javadov and his brother Makhir; the former also lost his deputy premiership. They were supporters of Surat Huseinov and of former president Ayaz Mutalibov. They accused the government of corruption and demanded the resignation of Aliev and the formation of a coalition government. There were reports of fighting in the north and the headquarters of the elite police force was put under siege in Baku.)

17 March 1995. The rebellion is crushed and Rovshan Javadov is killed.

31 March 1995. The Grey Wolves opposition party is banned (*The Economist*, 22 April 1995, p. 48).

The war toll

The war has so far claimed 15,000 lives and produced a million refugees (*IHT*, 30 July 1993, p. 2).

UN estimates put the number displaced from their homes at 800,000–1,000,000 (Hugh Pope, *The Independent*, 22 September 1993, p. 13).

About 10,000 people have been killed in the five years of fighting over Nagorno-Karabakh and about 20 per cent of Azerbaijan is now occupied (Jonathan Rugman, *The Guardian*, 7 September 1993, p. 8).

The sixth year of the war may have claimed more than 15,000 lives on both sides; about 1 million have become refugees (Steve LeVine, *FT*, Survey, 7 March 1994, p. 13).

Over 20,000 have been killed and over 1 million have become refugees (*IHT*, 13 May 1994, p. 2).

There are over 40,000 dead and more than 1 million homeless (Caroline Cox and John Eibner, *IHT*, 21 November 1994, p. 7).

On 3 November 1993 Aliev talked of 16,000 Azeris dead and 22,000 wounded. In December 1994 Aliev talked of more than 20,000 having been killed in and around Nagorno-Karabakh since 1988 (*The Guardian*, 28 December 1994, p. 11).

THE ECONOMY

The economic system

The pre-independence management structure and the relationship between enterprises and ministries remain largely intact (EBRD 1994: 19).

Financial policy

The manat was introduced in August 1992 alongside the rouble (for cash transactions only). It was to replace the latter entirely on 15 June 1993, but the deadline was postponed first until 1 July and then until 1 September 1993. After the Russian currency reform of late July 1993 Azerbaijan vowed to end dependence on the rouble as soon as possible.

Since May 1994 wage ceilings have been imposed on enterprises (EBRD 1994: 19).

A bankruptcy law, published in December 1994, was to come into force in 1995 (EBRD 1995: 53).

Prices

In January 1992 70–80 per cent of producer and consumer prices were liberalized, with further rounds later in 1992 and 1993. This has left bread and energy as the main goods subject to continued price controls. Energy prices are still about a quarter of world market prices (EBRD 1994: 19).

Bread prices were raised by 850 per cent on 23 November 1993.

Subsidies on bread were eliminated on 1 February 1995 (EBRD 1995: 53).

Privatization

Political instability has badly affected the economic reform programme. For example, the privatization Act was only passed in January 1993 (Deutsche Bank, *Focus: Eastern Europe*, 31 August 1993, no. 86, p. 6).

Business Central Europe (November 1993, p. 60) reported that the voucher system had been thrown out by parliament earlier in the year.

In mid-1994 the private sector accounted for roughly 20 per cent of GDP (EBRD 1994: 10). The size of the private sector, including informal activity, is likely to be within the range 15–25 per cent. The government programme put forward in April 1994 envisaged the privatization of medium-sized enterprises in 1996–98 and of large ones from 1998. Around 30 per cent of small enterprises were earmarked for privatization in 1994–95. There is no individual property restitution law (p. 18). A privatization programme, due to come into force in 1995, has yet to be approved by the National Assembly (EBRD 1995: 53).

Foreign trade

Foreign trade is largely centrally controlled. Extensive export quotas are backed by a licensing system and export taxes. Most imports are arranged by bilateral agreement. Since May 1994 the official manat exchange rate has been set weekly, based on a weighted average of exchange rates quoted by authorized commercial banks. Both current and capital account convertibility is heavily restricted. There is mandatory surrender of proceeds from non-strategic exports at the official rate (EBRD 1994: 19). Strategic exports, mostly raw materials, are sold through bilateral trading agreements at fixed prices (p. 111). Trade with Russia dropped sharply when Russia halted rail traffic to Azerbaijan through Chechenia in September 1994 (EBRD 1995: 53).

In 1991 Azerbaijan accounted for only just over 2 per cent of Soviet oil production, but supplied 70 per cent of Soviet oil equipment (Deutsche Bank, *Focus: Eastern Europe*, 31 August 1993, no. 86, pp. 3–4).

Exporters have to sell 60 per cent of their export revenues to the state (Deutsche Bank, *Focus: Eastern Europe*, 1994, no. 113, p. 6). The government requires 85 per cent of hard currency earned from the sale of 'strategic' goods (almost 75 per cent of all traded goods) to be surrendered to the state in exchange for domestic currency (Steve LeVine, *FT Survey*, 7 March 1994, p. 12).

Foreign investment

A progressive law was passed in 1992, e.g. joint ventures with a foreign stake of more than 30 per cent pay a corporate tax rate of 25 per cent instead of 35 per cent (*Business Central Europe*, July–August 1993, p. 64).

The January 1992 law says that foreigners can hold up to 100 per cent of capital (though only 49 per cent in the case of banks), but for the time being it is not possible to purchase real estate (Deutsche Bank, *Focus: Eastern Europe*, 1993, no. 86, p. 6).

An agreement in principle with a BP-led consortium of Western oil companies to develop oilfields in the Caspian Sea was signed on 1 November 1993. The deal was finally signed on 20 September 1994, with the nine Western companies taking a 70 per cent stake, the Azerbaijani State Oil Company 20 per cent and Russia's Lukoil 10 per cent (derived from the State Oil Company's original 30 per cent stake). The agreement specifies that 80 per cent of the profit goes to Azerbaijan. (Note that Russia's Foreign Ministry refused to recognize the deal, even though a representative of the Russian Ministry of Fuel and Power attended the signing ceremony.) It was announced on 13 November 1994 that Iran was to be offered a 5 percentage point share (coming out of Azerbaijan's 20 per cent), but the offer was withdrawn when the USA raised objections. On 13 March 1995 President Aliev announced that he had agreed to increase Turkey's share from 1.75 per cent to 6.75 per cent, with the extra 5 percentage points coming from the State Oil Company's stake (the deal was signed on 13 April 1995). (October 1995: pipelines via Russia and Georgia.)

Agriculture

Azerbaijan prohibits private land ownership by its nationals and legal entities, although leasing is allowed (EBRD 1994: 74).

Economic performance

A pretty dismal scene on the GDP and inflation fronts is depicted in Table 5.1.

Table 5.1 Azerbaijan: selected economic indicators

Economic indicator	*1990*	*1991*	*1992*	*1993*	*1994*
Rate of growth of GDP (%)	−11.7	−0.7	−22.6	−23.1	−21.9
Rate of growth of industrial output (%)	−6.3	4.8	−23.7	−7.0	−24.8
Rate of growth of agricultural output (%)	−0.1		−25.0	−15.0	−13.0
Inflation rate (%)	7.8	105.6	912.6	1,129.7	1,664.4
Budget surplus or deficit (% GDP)		−5.0	2.8	−13.0	−18.0
Current account ($ billion)		0.153	0.488	0.002	−0.179
Unemployment (end of year, %)	0.0	0.1	0.2	0.7	0.9

Sources: Various issues of United Nations Economic Commission for Europe, *Economic Survey of Europe*; United Nations, *World Economic and Social Survey*; IMF, *World Economic Outlook*; Deutsche Bank, *Focus: Eastern Europe*; *Economics of Transition* and *Business Central Europe*; EBRD (1994: 151; 1995: 28)

6

BELARUS

POLITICS

Almost 80 per cent of the population are Belorussians and only 13 per cent are Russians (*The Banker*, March 1993, p. 47). In 1992 13 per cent of the population were ethnic Russians (*The Economist*, 10 July 1993, p. 33), while about 96 per cent of Belarussians speak Russian as their main tongue (*The Economist*, 20 May 1995, p. 37). There are 600,000 Poles (*The Economist*, Survey, 13 March 1993, p. 18).

4 February 1993. Start 1 is ratified by parliament.

15 January 1994. President Clinton visits Belarus.

26 January 1994. Stanislav Shushkevich, chairman of parliament, loses a vote of no confidence. The alleged reason was corruption (using government workers to help relatives build dachas), but his dismissal was probably on account of his strongly pro-reform and pro-independence stance (there had been a clash between him and Prime Minister Vyacheslav Kebich over these issues).

28 January 1994. Mechislav Grib becomes chairman of parliament (he is strongly pro-Russia).

3 March 1994. Russian gas supplies are reduced because of delays in payment.

23 June 1994. A second round of the presidential election will be needed, but there is a surprising result in the first round (turnout 79 per cent). The populist Alexander Lukashenko wins 44.82 per cent of the vote on an anti-corruption platform (during the campaign he vowed to 'defeat the mafia, which like an all-devouring octopus has ensnared all government organs with its tentacles'). (Lukashenko also made the following promises: suppress inflation; restrict price rises through state regulation; stop privatization in its present form and confiscate the 'ill-gotten gains' of the private sector; provide generous credits for agriculture and industry; 'a job and a home for every Belorussian'; restore severed economic contacts with the republics of the former Soviet Union and especially Russia; compensate people for the losses caused by the devaluation of their bank deposits. (The

FT notes the inconsistency of his policies, e.g. he has said that an economic union with Russia should be complemented by a political one, but he has also advocated substantially increasing the independence of the central bank of Belarus and initiating 'a regime of direct economic management of state enterprises': 13 July 1994, p. 23. Formally, Lukashenko supports monetary union on the terms agreed in September 1993. Post-election, Lukashenko said that he is 'the guarantor of the unshakability of our statehood': *CDSP*, 1994, vol. XLVI, no. 28, p. 15. In April 1994 Lukashenko began his campaign with talk of taking Belarus into the Russian Federation. But in mid-May he did a U-turn and by the time the election came he was stressing that reforging broken economic links with Russia did not mean surrendering independence: Rich 1995: 48.)

Lukashenko was formerly vice-chairman of a collective farm, deputy director of a construction association and director of a state farm. In parliament he voted against the creation of the CIS in 1991 because it meant the end of the Soviet Union and supported the August 1991 coup attempt in the Soviet Union.)

Vyacheslav Kebich won only 17.33 per cent of the vote (he is an advocate of close links with Russia, including a merging of the two economies; during the campaign he promised full indexation of pensions and savings by 1995 and to avoid bankrupting ailing industrial enterprises). (Stanislav Shushkevich came fourth with only 9.9 per cent of the vote.)

10 July 1994. Lukashenko wins a massive 80.1 per cent of the vote, compared with Kebich's 14.2 per cent.

12 July 1994. Prime Minister Kebich and the rest of the government resign.

20 July 1994. Lukashenko appoints as the new prime minister the banker and market reformer Mikhail Chigir. The pro-market governor of the central bank, Stanislav Bogdankevich, is retained (he is against monetary union with Russia).

29 July 1994. Michel Camdessus, the managing director of the IMF, meets Lukashenko. The latter adopts a pro-economic reform tone in his inaugural speech.

3 August 1994. President Lukashenko meets President Yeltsin.

30 September 1994. Parliament supports President Lukashenko's 'anti-crisis' (radical economic reform) programme, but rejects his request for additional powers to implement the measures. The aim is to bring down the monthly rate of inflation to 7–8 per cent by June 1995.

30 October 1994. The Pope announces Belarus's first ever cardinal.

December 1994–January 1995. In mid-December 1994 an opposition member of parliament presented a report alleging corruption in the president's own team. Lukashenko immediately imposed a media clampdown – broadcasting from parliament was stopped, some newspapers appeared with blank spaces, others failed to appear at all and one editor was dismissed on government orders and accused of corrupt dealings in foreign currency. Lukashenko later denied the media clamp-down and dismissed the official allegedly responsible. Back in August 1994 parliament had endorsed Lukashenko's proposed reform package, but then consistently refused to vote him the sweeping executive powers to implement it by decree. The president was accused, among other things, of incompetence and inaction. Despite opposition from parliament Lukashenko, at the end of November 1994, enacted a decree setting up 'vertical' local authority chains of command reporting directly to him and bypassing the elected local councils. Already the IMF has backtracked on a planned $398 million credit because of insufficient progress in rebuilding and liberalizing the economy. The chances of pulling Belarus out of economic disaster seem increasingly remote. The relatively young advisers and supporters have quietly melted away (Rich 1995: 49). For example, the young economic adviser Viktar Hanar resigned in December 1994 (*EEN*, 1995, vol. 9, no. 3, p. 8).

Lukashenko is accused of press censorship in his attempt to prevent the publication of a report on corruption in the president's team (*CDSP*, 1995, vol. XLVII, no. 2, p. 27).

6 March 1995. Belarus and the EU sign a trade and co-operation agreement.

20 March 1995. The EU agrees to lend Belarus Ecu 75 million.

12 April 1995. Armed soldiers expel nineteen nationalist deputies from parliament, on hunger strike over the president's plan to hold a referendum at the same time as the 14 May general election (the hunger strikers objected to the president's threat to dissolve parliament if he did not get his way).

Parliament rejected three of the four proposed questions in the referendum, namely on extending the president's powers (including the right to dissolve parliament if it 'systematically or seriously violates the constitution'), on re-establishing Russian as a 'state language' (with equal status) and on what should be the national flag and coat of arms (specifically restoring the Soviet-era flag, albeit minus the hammer and sickle and the inscription 'Workers of the World Unite'). The one approved was whether to forge economic links with Russia. (Parliament later approved all four questions and also made 7 November, the anniversary of the Bolshevik Revolution, a national holiday.)

14 May 1995. The referendums and the general election take place. All four questions were strongly approved. Lukashenko responded by saying that 'Slav unity is the most important issue in our lives. If the people call for it we shall also have a political union that is even closer than the Soviet Union was. For the moment I am talking about economic union.'

The election was held on a first-past-the-post basis, so that a candidate obtaining 50 per cent plus one vote in the first round would win (the second round was fixed for 28 May). The new parliament had 260 seats (down from 315 elected seats owing to boundary changes).

Broadly there was a 'democratic' bloc, a socialist bloc and a large number of independents (many of whom were protégés of Lukashenko) (*EEN*, 28 April 1995, vol. 9, no. 9, p. 4). Agrarians, communists and a non-party *nomenklatura* ('party of power') were likely to win most of the votes. Of the 2,348 candidates only about two-thirds listed themselves as belonging to any of the twenty-two fledgling official parties (Matthew Kaminski, *FT*, 15 May 1995, p. 3). The competing parties or blocs were as follows:

Belorussian Popular (National) Front. Led by Zenon Poznyak. Pro-democracy and economic reform. In favour of developing a national consciousness and against union with Russia.

Bloc of Democratic Forces. This coalition of the five leading non-socialist parties (set up at the end of January 1995) comprises the Belarussian Social Democratic Hramada, the Belarussian Peasant Party, the Belarussian Christian Democratic Party, the Party of the Belarussian Popular Front and the National Democratic Party of Belarus. The agreed platform stresses democracy (including guaranteed minority rights), the strengthening of state sovereignty, market reforms, privatization, a reduction in inflation and a social security system.

United Democratic Party and Civic Accord. They set up a centrist coalition in February–March 1995.

Despite a turnout of 65 per cent, very few deputies were elected in the first round (the most commonly cited figure was eighteen). This poor response pleased Lukashenko, who indicated his contempt for the election by declaring in advance that he would not be voting for any candidate and actually crossed out all names on the ballot paper on the day. OSCE observers were concerned about certain 'irregularities'.

After the second round, held on 28 May, the number of elected deputies went up to only 119 (the most commonly cited figure), leaving parliament well short of the quorum mandated in the constitution.

'Virtually all the 120 deputies are Communists, Agrarians or non-party candidates opposed to market reforms. The Belarussian National Front, the biggest progressive grouping, did not gain a single seat' (Matthew Kaminski, *FT*, 30 May 1995, p. 2).

The average turnout was 56 per cent, but good turnouts in the countryside contrasted with a poor one in Minsk. Communists, the Agrarian Party and local chief administrators (the 'party of power') did well (*CDSP*, 1995, vol. XLVII, no. 22, p. 21).

Of the 119 elected deputies, thirty were from the Agrarian Party and twenty-seven were communists. 'Fifteen seats house the "party of power", i.e. those who work in the president's immediate entourage and their subordinates in the hierarchy of executive structures.' The remaining deputies belonged to no particular party, but included representatives of the so-called New Left. The Belarussian Popular Front suffered total defeat (*Moscow News*, 4–10 August 1995, p. 4).

On 14 June 1995 the old parliament refused to reduce the quorum requirement. Thus Lukashenko was to govern by means of presidential decrees until the November elections (*CDSP*, 1995, vol. XLVII, no. 24, p. 22).

On 17 August 1995 workers on the Minsk underground began a strike. This led to the detention of several trade union leaders, MPs and other opposition figures (*EEN*, 1995, vol. 9, no. 17, p. 3). The state prosecutor started criminal proceedings against the organizers of the strike. The strike (and the previous one by tram drivers elsewhere) 'was symptomatic of worker unrest throughout the country. The late payment of wages, which are anyhow barely enough for subsistence, appears to have reached crisis point'. On 1 September the Free Trade Union was formally banned by the administration. Any party or organization which supports the strike is also to be banned (*EEN*, 1995, vol. 9, no. 18, pp. 1–2).

THE ECONOMY

The economic system

The Economist (20 February 1993, p. 45) saw delays in the reform process. The State Planning Committee still set some plan targets for enterprises and there was rationing. The budget deficit in 1992 was 4.6 per cent of GDP, according to official figures. Nearly a third of Russian oil was bought at market rates.

According to Deutsche Bank (*Focus: Eastern Europe*, 28 February 1994, no. 102, p. 3), only fragments of an initial programme planned for 1992–93 have been put into practice.

Financial policy

The Banker (March 1993, p. 47) reported Belarus's desire to remain in the rouble zone. While negotiations with Russia were continuing Belarus froze those with the IMF on a programme of macroeconomic and structural reform.

Coupons (rubels) have been introduced alongside the rouble for cash transactions (the coupon fell against the rouble). Belarus has thought about introducing its own currency (the taler), but after the Russian currency reform of late July 1993 it was announced that the country would remain in the rouble zone (see below for further details and the 7 September 1993 agreement discussed in Chapter 18).

On 11 October it was announced that the use of foreign currencies in all cash and domestic transactions was to be banned. Coupons (rubels) would be the sole means of payment in retail trade by the end of 1994 and enterprises would have to comply within a week.

The currency was redenominated in September 1994 and the rubel was made the sole legal currency in October 1994 (EBRD 1995: 53).

The negotiations about the formation of an economic and monetary union with Russia

7 January 1994. Belarus and Russia signed a declaration of intent to form an economic and monetary union, but the subsequent negotiations failed. This was largely because of the extent of loss of Belarussian sovereignty and the adverse effects on output and employment because of uncompetitiveness, but also partly because of the inflationary effects within Russia (Belarus's expectation of relatively cheap energy was also a factor).

12 April 1994. The prime ministers of Belarus (Kebich) and Russia (Chernomyrdin) sign a treaty on (staged) monetary union, but it has to be ratified by both parliaments. The zaichik ('hare' or 'bunny') would be exchanged at par with the rouble up to a certain limit for individuals and to a higher limit for corporate entities (the black market rate was roughly 10 : 1 in mid-April 1994: *RET*, 1994, vol. 3, no. 1, p. 16). The Russian central bank would control monetary policy, foreign trade regulations would be co-ordinated and budgetary systems gradually unified. As regards the free-trade zone, customs duties would be abolished as of 1 May 1994 (although a number of customs restrictions would remain, as would the import quota system: *CDSP*, 1994, vol. XLVI, no. 15, p. 3). Russia would not be charged transit fees or for military facilities.

16 June 1994. Russia decides to charge the world price for oil as a way of encouraging Belarus to accept monetary union.

3 July 1994. Prime Ministers Kebich and Chernomyrdin sign a protocol on monetary union (*EEN*, 1994, vol. 8, no. 14, p. 8).

4 July 1994. Belarus and Russia sign a free trade agreement.

3 August 1994. President Lukashenko meets Yeltsin and Chernomyrdin. Talks about monetary union are postponed until September.

9 September 1994. Russian Prime Minister Chernomyrdin says that monetary union is ruled out for the time being because Russia is so far ahead. The issue will be reconsidered 'if the levels of development of the Russian and Belarussian economies become more nearly equal.'

15 September 1994. Chernomyrdin says that 'Right now unification would mean Russia taking on the additional burden of a neighbouring state's problems. We cannot afford that.' Unification can be discussed seriously only if 'the level of Belorussia's economic development becomes equal to that of Russia' (*CDSP*, 1994, vol. XLVI, no. 37, p. 24).

26 May 1995. At the CIS meeting in Minsk Yeltsin calls for deeper integration with Belarus, including a currency union (Chrystia Freeland, *FT*, 27 May 1995, p. 2).

Prices

Producer prices were liberalized in early 1992, but ceilings on profit margins for traders were subsequently introduced to check the increase in retail prices. Prices of products produced by monopolistic enterprises are also controlled by ceilings on profit margins (EBRD 1994: 19). The prices of food products were liberalized in late 1994 by presidential decree, but food rationing for some basic products was introduced in early 1995, indicating that some controls remain. Rents and public utilities' prices were raised in early 1995, but remained well below costs (EBRD 1995: 17–18, 53).

On 1 September 1994 fuel prices rose by an average of 50 per cent; petrol prices jumped by 30–40 per cent (*Transition*, 1994, vol. 5, no. 8, p. 16).

Economic policy in the Lukashenko era

Subsidies were to be lifted on bread and milk on 9 August 1994.

Lukashenko has begun to implement a somewhat *ad hoc* emergency economic programme; subsidies have been reduced and part of the energy debt is to be repaid by giving Russia shares in oil refineries (*EEN*, 1 September 1994, vol. 8, no. 18, p. 7).

In mid-August there were substantial price increases, e.g. a twentyfold increase in the price of milk and a tenfold increase in the price of bread. Housing and energy costs have also risen. Enterprises are being given new rights to trade and hold hard currency (*Business Central Europe*, September 1994, p. 22).

On 29 September 1994 Lukashenko presented his reform package to parliament. The intention was to reduce the monthly rate of inflation to 7–8 per cent and to halt the production slump and the decline in the standard of living by mid-1995. Near-term plans included cutting off the flow of easy-term credits to loss-making enterprises, drastically limiting social benefits to numerous categories of citizens and charging world prices for energy (*CDSP*, 1994, vol. XLVI, no. 39, p. 23). The programme called for the monthly rate of inflation to be reduced from about 30 per cent to 11 per cent by the end of the year and to 7 per cent by July 1995 (*Transition*, 1994, vol. 5, no. 8, p. 16). The following day parliament supported the president's 'anti-crisis' programme, but rejected his request for additional powers to implement the measures.

The IMF has withheld $250 million, although $206 has already been loaned (*FT*, 25 March 1995, p. 3). An IMF mission withheld a $250 million stand-by credit in March 1995, owing to unsatisfactory progress with the economic reforms (Belarus had received a $100 million systemic transformation facility loan the previous month) (*CDSP*, 1995, vol. XLVII, no. 13, p. 20).

Privatization

By November 1992 200 state enterprises, employing 1.4 per cent of the work force, had been privatized (United Nations Economic Commission for Europe 1993: 206).

In July 1992 a law on the privatization of housing came into effect. On 19 January 1993 a law was passed on the privatization of commercial and industrial enterprises providing for the issue of vouchers to the population (*The Banker*, March 1993, p. 46).

According to *Business Central Europe* (September 1993, p. 20), the voucher privatization law was enacted in August 1993 but would not take effect until July 1994. The original plan was to privatize 500 large enterprises by the end of 1993 and to transfer 50 per cent of the economy to the private sector by 1997. According to the latest draft programme, up to 50 per cent of state property would be sold using vouchers, workers would be offered shares in their own enterprises at a discount of 20 per cent, and the number of vouchers citizens would be entitled to depends on age and type of work (*Business Central Europe*, November 1993, p. 60). The mass privatization voucher programme scheduled for July 1994 was delayed owing to lack of popular interest and organizational difficulties. Some fifty large enterprises (representing around 20 per cent of total production) were scheduled for privatization by the end of 1994, but the government hinted at a freeze (*Business Central Europe*, October 1994, p. 82).

The privatization law was adopted in January 1993. This envisaged granting 50 per cent of state property to the population and selling the remainder. The programme involved the planned voucher privatization of two-thirds of the economy, with the remaining third including defence industries and natural monopolies. Workers were to be given a 20 per cent discount off the final selling price (Havrylyshyn *et al.* 1994: 384). The distribution of vouchers began on 1 April 1994 and the sale of assets was set to begin on 1 July (*Transition*, 1994, vol. 5, no. 4, p. 15).

So far only 50 per cent of enterprises in the trade and catering sector have been privatized (Deutsche Bank, *Focus: Eastern Europe*, 22 March 1994, no. 100, p. 44).

Only 3 per cent of state-owned industry and agriculture is in private hands (Leyla Boulton, *FT*, 17 February 1994, p. 2).

In mid-1994 the private sector accounted for roughly 15 per cent of GDP (EBRD 1994: 10). Large-scale privatization under the 1993 law began in June that year and about 300 enterprises were privatized by the end of the year. Two-thirds of state assets were to be privatized by 1997, with half involving the distribution of vouchers to the general population. A voucher-based programme was launched in July 1994 (for small-scale privatization as well). No property restitution has taken place to date. The 1992 bankruptcy law has been inoperative (p. 18). By late 1994 only 3 per cent of state enterprises had been privatized (EBRD 1995: 53).

All privatization is now on hold following the 14 May 1995 referendum and general election (*EEN*, 25 May 1995, vol. 9, no. 11, p. 5).

Foreign trade

Foreign trade has been liberalized and a unified exchange rate introduced (*Business Central Europe*, March 1994, p. 19).

Import subsidies were abolished in August 1993. There are few quantitative or licensing restrictions on imports. Quantitative restrictions and taxes on exports were substantially reduced in early 1994. There are restrictions on current and capital account convertibility. There is a floating exchange rate regime with heavy central bank intervention (EBRD 1994: 19, 111).

The reform package outlined in late September 1994 envisaged the scrapping of most export licences and quotas, except for textiles and defence products, by the end of 1994. Import licences would be retained only for goods that could endanger domestic industry (*Transition*, 1994, vol. 5, no. 8, p. 16).

A customs union agreement with Russia was reached in early 1995 (EBRD 1995: 53). Parliament ratified the February agreement, which was to come into effect on 6 May 1995 (*EEN*, 1995, vol. 9, no. 9, p. 3). At the CIS meeting in Minsk on 26 May 1995 Russia and Belarus signed a customs union agreement, border posts being removed.

Foreign investment

Legislation on foreign investment is relatively generous (Deutsche Bank, *Focus: Eastern Europe*, 1994, no. 100, p. 44).

By mid-1993 foreign capital commitments amounted to over $420 million (*Business Central Europe*, April 1994, p. 46). By the end of 1993 there were 1,097 joint ventures registered, with a mere $450 million invested (*Business Central Europe*, October 1994, p. 82).

Agriculture

A law on the privatization of farms has been deferred (*The Banker*, March 1993, p. 46). By the end of 1992 there were 2,000 private farms, with an average size of 19 ha (*CDSP*, 1993, vol. XLV, no. 5, p. 22); they accounted for only 0.41 per cent of total agricultural land (United Nations Economic Commission for Europe 1993: 206). At the end of 1992 there were 2,100 private leaseholders, with an average of 20 ha apiece (Kaser 1995: 37). As of 1 April 1993 there were 9,400 private farms, with an average size of 20 ha (*CDSP*, 1993, vol. XLV, no. 21, p. 20).

Economic performance

Table 6.1 paints a grim picture on the GDP and inflation fronts.

Table 6.1 Belarus: selected economic indicators

Economic indicator	*1990*	*1991*	*1992*	*1993*	*1994*
Rate of growth of GDP (%)	−3.0	−1.2	−9.6	−9.5	−21.5
Rate of growth of industrial output (%)	2.1	−0.2	−9.4	−7.4	−19.3
Rate of growth of agricultural output (%)	−8.7	−4.9	−9.0	4.0	−14.0
Inflation rate (%)	4.5	83.5	969.0	1,188	2,200
Budget surplus or deficit (% GDP)		3.6	−1.6	−8.3	−1.5
Current account ($ billion)			0.372	0.781	
Unemployment (end of year, %)			0.5	1.3	2.1

Sources: Various issues of United Nations Economic Commission for Europe, *Economic Survey of Europe*; United Nations, *World Economic and Social Survey*; IMF, *World Economic Outlook*; Deutsche Bank, *Focus: Eastern Europe*; *Economics of Transition* and *Business Central Europe*; EBRD (1994: 152; 1995: 29)

7

ESTONIA

POLITICS

The political background

Citizenship

In the 1934 population census 88 per cent were Estonians, 8.2 per cent Russians, 1.7 per cent Germans, 0.7 per cent Swedes and 0.4 per cent Jews (Henn-Juri Uibopuu, *The World Today*, June 1992, p. 109). The 1989 census revealed that 61.5 per cent of the population of 1.6 million were Estonians, 30.3 per cent were Russians and 3.1 per cent were Ukrainians (Gwiazda 1994: 77). Only 14 per cent of Russians have mastered the Estonian language (p. 79). 'Many Russians, Ukrainians and Belorussians living in the Baltic States regard the countries as their home. They (about 30–35 per cent) too voted in the referenda for the independence of the Baltic republics and they now feel betrayed by their Estonian, Latvian and Lithuanian fellow citizens. The native people of the Baltic countries, however, remain distrustful of the Russian minority' (p. 78).

There are around 500,000 Russian-speakers. So far 40,000 have applied to leave the country and 60,000 have applied for citizenship (John Lloyd, *FT*, 25 July 1994, p. 2). As of 1 October 1994 there were 52,411 Russian citizens of Estonia (*The Baltic Observer*, 13–19 October 1994, p. 6). There are about 451,000 non-citizens; some 53,000 residents have chosen Russian citizenship (*The Baltic Observer*, 10–16 November 1994, p. 2).

On 21 June 1993 a new nationality and citizenship law was introduced according to which non-citizens (citizens being those with that status on 16 June 1940 or their descendants) had to register and apply for citizenship (which required two years' residence from 30 March 1990, a language test and the taking of an oath of loyalty) or residence permits within two years. (Less than 3 per cent of ethnic Russians had attained Estonian citizenship by July 1993: *Business Central Europe*, November 1993, p. 74.)

On 27 June 1993 the new nationality and citizenship law was suspended until the Council of Europe and the CSCE had been consulted. The president signed the amended law on 12 July 1993. There were a number of clarifications about residence, e.g. pensioners and those lawfully employed in the civilian sector were protected, while soldiers and criminals were not (*The Economist*, 31 July 1993, p. 41). Now residence permits would be denied only to people who posed a threat to security, people who had been sentenced to lengthy terms but amnestied before completing them, and active-duty officers of foreign armies and members of their families (*CDSP*, 1993, vol. XLV, no. 28, p. 24).

On 19 January 1995 a new citizenship law was adopted, establishing six years as the period of residence required prior to naturalization instead of three years. The previous law stated that applicants for citizenship had to have lived in Estonia for two years and could become naturalized citizens one year after submitting the application. The new law replaced the two-plus-one-year scheme with a five-plus-one-year scheme. As of December 1994 the number of people who had been granted citizenship was 48,000. As of October 1994 52,000 people had received Russian citizenship. Out of a population of some 1.5 million 962,000 are Estonians and 436,000 are Russians (*The Baltic Observer*, 26 January–1 February 1995, p. 4). Since 1992 about 100,000 of Estonia's 500,000 Russian-speakers have obtained citizenship and are able to vote. Half of them lived in Estonia before the Second World War and qualified for automatic citizenship, while the rest passed a language exam and a minimum residence requirement (*The Baltic Observer*, 9–15 March 1995, p. 7).

A survey has shown that only 2 per cent of ethnic Russians planned to leave Estonia (Andrew Higgins, *The Independent*, 19 April 1995, p. 8).

A poll has shown that almost 75 per cent of ethnic Russians in the Baltic States do not want to emigrate to Russia (Michael Binyon, *The Times*, 19 April 1995, p. 10).

Non-citizens who had failed to apply for work and residence permits by 12 July 1995 would be given a chance to apply late (*The Baltic Observer*, 29 June–5 July 1995, p. 1). There are 400,000 non-citizens. Over 73,000 have chosen Russian citizenship since the collapse of the Soviet Union (p. 3).

Russian troops in Estonia

William Schmidt (*IHT*, 13 November 1993, p. 2) reported that fewer than 17,000 Russian troops (out of a total of 145,000 in 1991) remained in the Baltic States (none in Lithuania and most of the remainder in Latvia). Anatol Lieven (*The Times*, 18 March 1994, p. 13) put the numbers at around 12,000 in Latvia and less than 2,000 in Estonia (2,300 according to *IHT*: 7 April 1994, p. 5).

10 July 1994. At the G7 ('political G8') meeting, Yeltsin rules out the removal of all remaining Russian troops by 31 August because of the dispute over the citizenship and housing of retiring Russian military officers. But he agrees to meet the Estonian president.

26 July 1994. Presidents Yeltsin and Meri sign an agreement. A statement says that 'the presidents of Russia and Estonia signed an agreement today that the rights of the Russian military pensioners would be respected equally to the rights of Estonian citizens. They also signed an agreement in accordance with which Russian troops are withdrawn from Estonia before 31 August.' Retired military servicemen will be denied a residence permit only if they are a threat to national security. (The most generally given figure for the number of troops remaining was about 2,000 and that for retired/retiring Russian officers was about 10,000. The equality of treatment was not exactly clear in some respects. Pensions would be awarded, but it seemed that citizenship would not be offered to those below the usual retiring age.)

31 August 1994. The last Russian troops pull out (although 210 'military specialists' will remain for about a year to decommission two nuclear reactors, used for training purposes, at the Paldiski nuclear submarine base).

Political developments prior to the 5 March 1995 general election

The 20 September 1992 general election produced a five-party coalition ('Fatherland Coalition') of conservatives and Christian Democrats led by Prime Minister Mart Laar. Parliament elected Lennart Meri as president.

25 June 1993. Russia cuts off gas supplies (for several days, allegedly because of non-payment).

17 July 1993. Two heavily Russian-dominated towns in north-eastern Estonia held a referendum on local autonomy ('a territorial autonomous entity within the Estonian Republic'). The turnout was relatively low, but a large 'yes' was given by those who did vote. The respective turnouts for Narva and Sillamae were as follows: 57.4 per cent and 61.5 per cent; the respective 'yes' votes were 97 per cent and 98.6 per cent. (Note that foreign non-citizens can vote in local elections. Candidates did well in the elections held in September 1993. Candidates have to be citizens, but the Estonian government granted that status to about thirty-five Russians to allow them to stand: William Schmidt, *IHT*, 13 November 1993, p. 2.)

13 August 1993. The National Court annuls the referendums.

10 September 1993. The Pope visits Estonia.

14 June 1994. The finance and education ministers resign.

18 September 1994. The Estonian Social Democrats decide to leave the coalition government.

26 September 1994. Prime Minister Mart Laar loses a vote of no confidence in parliament on the grounds of 'improper conduct of affairs of state' (i.e. there were allegations that old rouble notes had been sold improperly, perhaps to Chechenia; note that this was in violation of the agreement with Russia). (One report talked of political in-fighting, charges of financial impropriety and discontent with the high cost of reform: *The Baltic Observer*, 13–19 October 1994, p. 1.)

28 September 1994. The ferry Estonia sinks with massive loss of life (the ferry belongs to a joint venture between a Swedish company and the state-owned Estonian Shipping Company).

13 October 1994. Parliament rejects President Meri's candidate for prime minister (central bank governor Siim Kallas).

27 October 1994. Environment Minister Andres Tarand is appointed prime minister. He belongs to no party, but does support the Green movement.

23 November 1994. President Yeltsin visits the disputed border area and vows never to give it up (the area was considered to be part of Estonia in the 1920 Tartu Peace Treaty, but it was annexed by the Soviet Union in 1945).

The 5 March 1995 general election

There were 1,256 candidates for the 101 seats. Sixteen parties/coalitions contested the election and nine failed to reach the 5 per cent threshold. There was a decisive swing to centre–left parties. Reasons included the economic pain of transition (felt especially by groups such as the elderly and farmers) and the desire for greater political stability. The government had been accused of financial impropriety (see above). The young, inexperienced, fractious, free-market radicals were swept aside. There was general agreement among the parties broadly to go ahead with economic reform, but the more left-leaning parties stressed a gentler transition to capitalism (with stronger social guarantees), slower progress towards the EU and closer ties with Russia.

The turnout of the nearly 800,000 eligible voters was 67 per cent. Below is the resulting distribution of votes and seats in the 101-member parliament:

1. *Coalition Party/Rural Union* (32.3 per cent of the vote; forty-one seats). This centre–left grouping was formed in January 1995. The leader of the Coalition Party is Tiit Vahi, who was a state enterprise director in the Soviet era, caretaker prime minister in 1992 and currently chairman of the Tallinn City Council. He supports a market economy, but one with a stronger social safety net (increased pensions were promised).

The leader of Rural Union is Arnold Ruutel, who was Estonian president from 1983 to 1992. The party favours increased support for the rural sector.

2. *Reform Party* (16.3 per cent of the vote; nineteen seats). The leader of this right-wing party is Siim Kallas, the governor of the central bank. The party favours fast reform and believes that the country cannot afford higher social spending.

3. *Centre Party* (14.2 per cent of the vote; sixteen seats). The leader of this broad-based coalition is Edgar Savisaar, who headed the last government of the Soviet era.

4. *Fatherland Party/Estonian Independence Party* (7.1 per cent of the vote; eight seats).

5. *Moderates* (6 per cent of the vote; six seats). The leader is the current prime minister, Andras Tarand, who is pro-reform but sees the necessity of social guarantees.

6. *Our Home is Estonia* (5.9 per cent of the vote; six seats). This is the party of ethnic Russians, Russian-Estonian citizens being allowed to vote for the first time in a parliamentary election. The platform is mildly left, advocating slower privatization, greater social guarantees. Support for Estonian independence is tempered by support for closer ties with Russia.

7. *Right Wingers* (5.1 per cent of the vote; five seats). Led by former speaker of parliament Ulo Nugis.

Political developments after the 5 March 1995 general election

31 March 1995. Coalition Party/Rural Union and the Centre Party agree to form a coalition government.

12 April 1995. Estonia and the EU initial an associate membership agreement (it was signed on 12 June 1995).

16 April 1995. The government takes office, with Coalition/Rural Union having ten ministers and the Centre Party five (including Edgar Savisaar as interior minister; the other ministries are economics, transport and communications, social affairs, and culture and education). Prime Minister Tiit Vahi promises to continue with the policies of the previous government, but has made commitments to help farmers (with low-interest loans and tax concessions) and old-age pensioners.

24 May 1995. Estonia and Ukraine sign a free-trade agreement.

THE ECONOMY

The economic background

Oil shale is by far the most important source of energy. Between 1990 and 1993 it increased as a proportion of primary energy consumption by 8 percentage points to 63 per cent, owing to the sharp decline in imports of crude oil and natural gas from Russia. Environmental damage is largely caused by the use of shale for electricity generation (DIW, *Economic Bulletin*, 1995, vol. 32, no. 2, p. 21).

Financial policy

The fight against inflation has been a key feature of government policy. Hence the stress on budgetary control (e.g. in late December 1994 a balanced budget for 1995 was passed by parliament: *Business Europa*, February–March 1995, p. 35). According to Deutsche Bank (*Focus: Eastern Europe*, 1995, no. 131, p. 7), there is a legal obligation to balance the budget.

Estonia's own national currency, the kroon ('crown'), was introduced on 20 June 1992 as the sole legal tender (it was agreed that roubles were to be returned to the Russian central bank within a month).

A currency board rule operates under which new issues of kroons are tied to the growth of foreign reserves (these were boosted by the return of gold reserves held in trust by Western governments from before the Soviet occupation) (Hansson 1993: 177–8).

Banknotes and deposits in kroons placed with the Bank of Estonia qualify for a guarantee of exchange at the established rate of exchange (Bennett 1993: 454).

The kroon has been successfully pegged to the Deutschmark at a rate of eight to one; the kroon can be devalued only by an Act of parliament (Deutsche Bank, *Focus: Eastern Europe*, 19 April 1993, no. 73, p. 3; 1994, no. 113, p. 12).

In deciding to peg the kroon to the Deutschmark Estonia was backed by initial foreign currency reserves of $120 million, a $40 million stabilization loan from the IMF and 11.3 tonnes of gold retrieved from Western governments; the rate of the kroon against the Deutschmark has held, the annual inflation rate has come down from over 500 per cent to 30 per cent and foreign currency reserves have more than doubled (Adrian Bridge, *The Independent*, 26 July 1993, p. 21). It is often claimed that a currency board system means that the money supply is completely backed by foreign assets. But this cannot be correct, as countries with a currency board are certain to have a commercial banking system, which will create credit on the basis of this monetary base, which is 100 per cent backed (Gavin Peebles, review, *Europe-Asia Studies*, 1994, vol. 46, no. 6, p. 1061). Lithuania now has a currency board-like system similar to that of Estonia rather than an orthodox currency board system. The central banks of both countries retain considerable discretion in monetary policy, retaining powers such as setting reserve requirements for commercial banks (Steve Hanke and Kurt Schuler, *Transition*, 1994, vol. 5, no. 6, p. 13). The emission of kroon currency is tied by law to the authorities' holdings of gold and foreign currency. The danger that irresponsible or incompetent commercial banking practices could detach the broader money supply has been avoided by tough bank regulation (*Transition*, 1994, vol. 5, no. 6, p. 9).

The kroon is convertible on current account, but only partially convertible on capital account (IMF, *World Economic Outlook*, May 1993, p. 67). There is full current account convertibility and virtual capital account convertibility (EBRD 1994: 109). The few remaining subsidies (e.g. on housing) are currently being cut (p. 23).

Large capital inflows, fuelled by foreign aid and investment and balance of payments financing, have caused a rapid rise in the money supply and thus boosted inflation (Philippe Legrain, *FT*, 21 June 1994, p. 3).

The governor of the central bank cannot be fired and future governors will nominate their own successors (John Lloyd, *FT*, 3 May 1994, p. 19). Two large banks have failed (IMF, *World Economic Outlook*, June 1995, p. 55).

Prices

Prices for household energy, municipal transport and housing are gradually being raised to cost recovery levels (EBRD 1995: 55).

Privatization

Although about 30 per cent of services and small enterprises have been auctioned, progress in privatizing large enterprises has been slow so far. A new privatization law was adopted in June 1993. A basic feature is the restitution of property lost in and after 1940. An elaborate system of vouchers has been instigated. About 15 per cent of claims have been resolved to date. Where physical restitution is impracticable, compensation vouchers are issued. In addition 'work contribution' vouchers are distributed, based on years of work in Estonia between 1945 and 1991. These are interchangeable and can be used in the privatization of housing, land, collective farm implements and state enterprises or redeemed for shares in the compensation fund. There have also been pilot commercial sales of property, with thirty large state enterprises having already been sold. A small percentage of shares, determined individually for each enterprise, will be reserved for sale in exchange for citizen vouchers. But the majority of shares will be sold for cash to strategic investors in the tender for sale of fifty-two state enterprises announced in May (Lucja Swiatkowski Cannon, *FT*, 13 July 1993, p. 15). The asset transfer per adult averaged $1,000 (Lucja Swiatkowski Cannon, *FT*, 9 September 1994, p. 17). In a pilot programme planned for the autumn of 1994 four large enterprises were to sell about 30 per cent of their shares for vouchers in the initial public offerings on the stock exchange. And the government is diversifying privatization methods, beyond the tender offers (Lucja Swiatkowski Cannon, *Transition*, 1994, vol. 5, no. 7, p. 16).

By the end of May 1994 an estimated 50 per cent of state-owned enterprises and business units had been transferred to private ownership or control. Privatization does not emphasize pay-offs to insiders (except for a discount to insiders at small-scale auctions). Instead a range of divestiture methods has been adopted: (1) restitution of homes, farms and businesses expropriated during the communist periods; (2) auctions of small-scale business units; (3) a tender process for medium-size and large enterprises thought to be of interest to foreign or domestic investors; (4) lease arrangements for parts or all of certain enterprises; (5) joint ventures between state enterprises and foreign companies; (6) an active bankruptcy process which turns over the assets of liquidated enterprises to private entrepreneurs; (7) a voucher programme which would allow holders to exchange vouchers for shares in enterprises, investment funds, (residential) housing or land. (Each resident over the age of eighteen was to receive 'national vouchers', the number depending on years of schooling or work between 1 January 1945 and 1 January 1992; 'compensation vouchers' were to be issued either to persons whose property was illegally expropriated but cannot be returned or to people who were deported during the Soviet era; tradability of vouchers was made complete at the end of May 1994.) By the end of May 1994 over 1,000 small business units had been auctioned off, representing about 85 per cent of the small businesses originally designated for sale. A sixth tender, comprising about forty to fifty enterprises thought to be of interest to foreign investors was scheduled for the autumn of 1994. Twenty large enterprises were to be privatized through a public offering (John Nellis, *Transition*, July–August 1994, vol. 5, no. 6, pp. 7–9).

Around 20 per cent of state-owned stock was to be sold to voucher holders (*Business Central Europe*, November 1993, p. 61). Tenders for ninety large enterprises have drawn offers for most of them; thirteen had been sold by August 1993 (p. 74).

A law on large privatization was passed in August 1992. The first thirty-eight enterprises were registered for international tender and by March 1993 more than 100 domestic and non-resident bids had been submitted (Deutsche Bank, *Focus: Eastern Europe*, 1993, no. 73, p. 3).

Initially, vouchers could not be sold but could be passed on to relatives. But a law was passed at the end of June 1994 allowing voucher holders to sell them to other people who have lived in the country for more than fifteen years; as of August 1994 vouchers could be exchanged for shares in enterprises to be privatized (*IHT*, 2 August 1994, p. 11).

Vouchers were to be distributed from July 1994 onwards and fifty medium-sized enterprises were to be sold off by the end of the year (*Business Central Europe*, March 1994, p. 51). Beginning in 1992, with Germany's Treuhandanstalt as a model, Estonia sold enterprises to investors outright through tenders for large enterprises (thus having regard for investment and employment and not just going for the highest sale price) and auctions for small enterprises. By the end of 1994 small privatization was virtually complete and nine tenders had been run listing 300 large enterprises. The 290th contract is currently being negotiated. In November 1994, bowing to popular demand for free shares, Estonia introduced a new method, which combines tenders with a public share offering. A majority owner is found by tender (for investment and corporate guidance), while the remaining shares are sold to the public for vouchers (*Business Central Europe*, March 1995, p. 18).

About half of all companies slated for privatization have been offered to the international and national markets by means of four tenders, with the fifth being launched. Foreign investment is actively being sought. Price is only one consideration in the tenders, others including viability of plan, job guarantees and investment pledges (*IHT*, 24 March 1994, p. 9).

Estonia has opted for an agency modelled on the East German Treuhand-anstalt. Of more than 500 enterprises slated for sale, fifty-two had been sold by the start of 1994. A new wave of auctions is under way (Philippe Legrain, *FT*, 21 June 1994, p. 3).

Small privatization began in 1991 and 50 per cent of the target projects (shops, restaurants, handicrafts) have been sold (Deutsche Bank, *Focus: Eastern Europe*, 19 April 1993, no. 73, p. 3). Small privatization is nearly complete and of the approximately 300 larger industrial enterprises that are capable of surviving more than 250 had been sold off in nine international bids by the end of 1994 (22 June 1995, no. 121, p. 6).

The main aim of the Land Reform Act is to return land to its former owners (compensation, solely in the form of vouchers, is meant to be the exception). Non-residents were previously not allowed to buy land, although leasing for ninety-nine years was available (Deutsche Bank, *Focus: Eastern Europe*, 19 April 1993, p. 3).

On 15 April 1993, however, Estonia became the first republic of the former Soviet Union to allow foreigners to buy land (subject to purchases being part of a major enterprise) (*Business Europa*, August–September 1993, p. 35). Only seven out of 300 large state enterprises have been sold to date (p. 35).

Anthony Robinson (*FT*, Survey, 19 April 1994, p. 30) comments as follows:

1. Small privatization is virtually complete (with the exception of rural land and property, where restitution and other legal problems are still obstacles).

2. Large privatization started to take off only in August 1993 with the creation of the Privatization Agency. The agency is modelled closely on East Germany's Treuhandanstalt (tenders, open to foreign firms, take account not only of price but also of factors such as investment and employment programmes).

3. Since April 1993 foreigners have been allowed to buy land, but only in the sense of a particular land use connected with their investment, not of land as such.

4. There is a list of more than twenty sectors which are currently restricted for foreigners (e.g. electricity, harbours, gas, liquor and tobacco).

5. In 1993 the Privatization Agency signed fifty contracts for the sale of assets.

6. In 1994 the aim was to prepare some 155 out of the remaining 500 industrial enterprises for sale by tender.

The Privatization Agency expects to conclude the bulk of its large-scale privatizations by 1995. A final international tender round, covering about fifty enterprises, is soon to be announced, concurrently with a local tender round. A final local tender round will be held in spring 1995 (*The Baltic Observer*, 13–19 October 1994, p. 7). Roughly 60 per cent of state industry and 90 per cent of small businesses have been privatized. Large privatization was expected to be finished by the end of 1995 (*The Baltic Observer*, 23 February–1 March 1995, p. 15). The majority of state enterprises have been privatized, leaving only a few dozen large organizations with extensive infrastructures to be dealt with. The Privatization Agency sold 339 enterprises in 1994 (*The Baltic Observer*, 6–12 April 1995, p. 9).

In December 1994 forty-two large enterprises were up for sale under the fifth and last international tender. Estonia had sold 192 enterprises, putting about 80 per cent of state property in private hands (excluding transport and public utilities). Foreigners accounted for about 40 per cent of investment. The Privatization Agency planned to finish its work by 1995. Public utilities, railway lines, harbours and oil shale industries were then to be put up for sale (Matthew Kaminski, *FT*, 13 December 1994, p. 2).

The private sector now accounts for 40 per cent of the economy (Matthew Kaminski, *FT*, 27 September 1993, p. 4).

In mid-1994 the private sector accounted for roughly 55 per cent of GDP (EBRD 1994: 10). The government's ambition is to complete large privatization by the end of 1995. By May 1994 more than 85 per cent of small enterprises had been privatized through employee buy-outs and auctions (p. 22). In 1993 fifty-four large enterprises were privatized out of a total of 155. The 1993 law allows for the use of vouchers as well as cash and instalment purchases for domestic buyers (p. 63). Privatization of large enterprises accelerated in the second half of 1994 in a 'multi-track' approach which includes national and international tenders and public share offerings. Privatization through evaluated bids, modelled after the Treuhandanstalt, is near completion. This approach is supplemented by public share offerings, the first of which took place in November 1994 and the second of which was initiated in early March 1995 (EBRD 1995: 55).

The IMF believes that in the Baltic States the informal sector or grey economy may be responsible for as much as 20 per cent of the region's GDP (*The Baltic Observer*, 9–15 March 1995, p. 14). 'In 1993 the share of the illegal economy [in Estonia] was 13.1 per cent, while at present it is difficult to find the precise percentage' (*The Baltic Observer*, 20–26 April 1995, p. 8).

Foreign trade

Virtually no restrictions on foreign trade remain (EBRD 1994: 23). A free-trade agreement with the EU came into effect in January 1995. Trade in 'sensitive' products (including agriculture and textiles) was to be governed by specific provisions. Unusually there was no transition period and reciprocity was granted upon entry into force (EBRD 1995: 55).

In 1991 more than 56 per cent of exports went to Russia alone and 95 per cent to the Soviet Union as a whole. Russia accounted for 46 per cent of imports (the Soviet Union for 85 per cent). In 1993 Russia's share went down to 20 per cent of exports and 19 per cent of imports (the respective figures for the former Soviet Union were 38 per cent and 30 per cent). Finland is now the main trading partner (22 per cent of exports and 25 per cent of imports) (Anthony Robinson, *FT*, Survey, 19 April 1994, pp. 29, 31). (Note that, owing to factors such as oil shale deposits, Estonia is self-sufficient in electricity production and meets 65 per cent of its total energy requirements: p. 32.)

In 1992 the CIS accounted for only 50 per cent of merchandise trade, compared with 90 per cent in 1991 (Deutsche Bank, *Focus: Eastern Europe*, 19 April 1993, no. 73, p. 5). No Baltic State conducts more than 12 per cent of its trade with another. In 1993 the CIS accounted for 29 per cent of exports (Russia alone 23 per cent) and 22 per cent of imports (Russia 17 per cent) (United Nations Economic Commission for Europe 1994: 106).

On 13 September 1993 Estonia, Latvia and Lithuania signed a free-trade agreement (*Business Central Europe*, November 1993, p. 18). The agreement came into force on 1 April 1994. Agricultural products are excluded and tariffs or quotas are allowed for the time being on some industrial goods. Extraordinary measures are permitted in the case of a 'serious threat' to a domestic market and temporary restrictions are allowed when 'moral values' or national security are adversely affected (*The Baltic Observer*, 24 February–2 March 1994, p. 12; 7–13 April 1994, p. 9). At least for an initial period some restrictions on the export of raw materials would be maintained by all three countries; in Latvia and Lithuania export tariffs would be employed and in Estonia quotas would be used (EBRD 1994: 113).

In 1993 the main trading partners were Finland (23.9 per cent), Russia (19.2 per cent), Germany (9.7 per cent) and Sweden (9.4 per cent) (*IHT*, 14 June 1994, p. 11).

Foreign investment

Foreigners are allowed to own land (Matthew Kaminski, *FT*, 13 December 1994, p. 2).

Net foreign direct investment was $58 million in 1992, $160 million in 1993 and $251 million in January–September 1994 (United Nations Economic Commission for Europe 1995: 151). Nearly $200 million had been attracted by the beginning of 1994, $66.2 million in 1993 alone (*Business Central Europe*, April 1994, p. 46).

Foreign direct investment amounted to $180 million in the period 1990–93 (EBRD 1994: 123). By the end of 1994 foreign direct investment amounted to $440 million (Deutsche Bank, *Focus: Eastern Europe*, 1995, no. 126, p. 18).

Foreign direct investment, the total stock of which was about $471 million by the end of 1994, has contributed significantly to a vigorous recovery in output. No restrictions on capital flows or repatriation of profits exist, but tax incentives have been eliminated (IMF, *World Economic Outlook*, June 1995, p. 63).

Agriculture

A separate law deals with the privatization of collective farms, three-quarters of which have been dismantled on the basis of resolved restitution claims or leases based on anticipated restitution (Lucja Swiatkowski Cannon, *FT*, 13 July 1993, p. 15).

Land has been sold to the highest bidder and the former owners have been compensated with shares in industrial enterprises (Matthew Kaminski, *FT*, 18 August 1993, p. 26).

Bruce Clark (*FT*, Survey, 19 April 1994, p. 32) comments that the privatization process has been slow. In Soviet times there were about 350 large farms. The proportion of land farmed privately is still only 14 per cent, while the 'socialist sector' has undergone a very limited break-up, with about 1,000 co-operatives and public companies.

On 31 July 1995 the government agreed to introduce agricultural subsidies in order to placate farmers angry that it had failed to fulfil an election pledge to introduce protective tariffs (*The Baltic Observer*, 27 July–9 August 1995, p. 3).

Economic performance

GDP grew in 1994. Agriculture has taken a pounding. The annual inflation rate reached a peak of over 1,000 per cent in 1992, but considerable progress has been made since then (see Table 7.1).

If job-seekers who do not qualify for benefit are included, the unemployment rate rises from 1.8 per cent to 4.3 per cent (*The Baltic Observer*, 9–15 March 1995, p. 14).

Table 7.1 Estonia: selected economic indicators

Economic indicator	*1990*	*1991*	*1992*	*1993*	*1994*
Rate of growth of GDP (%)	−8.1	−11.0	−14.2	−6.7	6.0
Rate of growth of industrial output (%)	−5.6	−7.2	−38.9	−19.0	−5.0
Rate of growth of agricultural output (%)	−13.1	−20.7	−21.1	−16.8	−9.0
Inflation rate (%)	23.1	210.6	1,076	89.8	47.8
Net foreign debt ($ billion)			−0.2	−0.3	−0.1
Budget surplus or deficit (% GDP)	2.9	4.6	0.5	−1.4	0.9
Current account ($ billion)		0.570	0.083	0.012	−0.171
Unemployment (end of year, %)	0.0	0.1	1.9	2.6	2.2

Sources: Various issues of United Nations Economic Commission for Europe, *Economic Survey of Europe*; United Nations, *World Economic and Social Survey*; IMF, *World Economic Outlook*; Deutsche Bank, *Focus: Eastern Europe*; *Economics of Transition*, *Business Central Europe* and *The Baltic Observer*; EBRD (1994: 156; 1995: 33)

8

GEORGIA

POLITICS

The political background

In 1992–93 800,000 people left Georgia, one-third of them Georgians (*CDSP*, 1994, vol. XLVI, no. 20, p. 12). The civil wars have resulted in 4,000 dead and more than 250,000 refugees (*Business Central Europe*, March 1994, p. 18). There is a small OSCE mission in South Ossetia.

Political developments

16 March 1993. Shevardnadze accuses Russian forces of backing the 'separatists' in Abkhazia, including the bombing of Sukhumi (the regional capital of Abkhazia and a port).

In 1986 the (Moslem) Abkhazians accounted for only 17 per cent of the (0.53 million) population of the province (Georgians 44 per cent and Russians 16 per cent). In Georgia as a whole the 5.2 million population was split as follows: Georgians, 68.8 per cent; Armenians, 9 per cent; Russians, 7.4 per cent (5.9 per cent in 1991, according to *The Economist*, 10 December 1994, p. 52); Azeris, 5.1 per cent; Ossetians, 3.2 per cent; Abkhazians, 1.7 per cent.

Abkhazia (the name means 'country of the soul') came under Tsarist rule in 1810. It was a separate Soviet republic until 1930, when Stalin (a Georgian) attached it to Georgia (Hugh Pope, *The Independent*, 29 September 1993, p. 13). According to Raymond Bonner (*IHT*, 9 June 1994, p. 6), in August 1992 Defence Minister Tengiz Kitovani invaded Abkhazia without the approval of Shevardnadze. Georgian troops engaged in wholesale looting, raping and killing.

19 March 1993. A Russian warplane is brought down by Georgian forces.

7 April 1993. An agreement is reached with Russia to allow Russian troops to stay until 1995.

13 April 1993. A Treaty of Friendship and Mutual Assistance is signed with Ukraine.

7 May 1993. The defence minister, Tengis Kitovani, is dismissed by parliament.

14 May 1993. Yeltsin and Shevardnadze agree a cease-fire between Georgian and Abkhazian forces starting 20 May.

2 July 1993. Parliament endows Shevardnadze with special powers, e.g. to appoint and dismiss all cabinet ministers (except the prime minister) and to issue decrees.

Heavy fighting is reported in Abkhazia.

6 July 1993. Martial law is declared in Abkhazia for a period of two months.

25 July 1993. After an acrimonious debate parliament grants Shevardnadze authority to approve a peace agreement in Abkhazia. Georgian troops will be removed and replaced by Russian military personnel. Monitoring will be performed by UN observers (approved by the UN Security Council earlier in the month provided there was a cease-fire). Abkhaz guerrillas will withdraw from the 'zone of conflict' and those from outside will leave Abkhazia. Local autonomy would be restored.

27 July 1993. A cease-fire is signed, effective as of noon 28 July.

6 August 1993. Prime Minister Tengiz Sigua and his government resign when parliament rejects the proposed budget (the background is the state of the economy and the military situation). Shevardnadze is appointed caretaker premier (Otar Patsatsia was approved as prime minister by parliament at the end of the month).

28–29 August 1993. Armed supporters of ousted president Zviad Gamsakhurdia take over three towns in western Georgia (the Mingrelia region) and another one on 7 September.

12 September 1993. Shevardnadze assumes the post of interior minister.

14 September 1993. Shevardnadze is granted emergency powers (for two months starting 20 September, during which parliament will be suspended) only after he has said he will resign. (The state of emergency was later extended to 20 January 1994. In November 1993 Shevardnadze formed his own political party, the Citizens' Union.)

16 September 1993. Abkhazian separatists (led by parliamentary speaker Vladislav Ardzindba) break the cease-fire and attack Sukhumi (the Georgians are caught off guard, having withdrawn many of their forces and much of their heavy weaponry). Russia demands a halt to the fighting (Russia later cuts off fuel supplies).

19 September 1993. A truce is signed, but Abkhazian separatists continue to attack Sukhumi. The Mingrelian 'rebels' (who are nationalists opposed to the Abkhazians; the nationalists claim that rogue Russian military units are helping the Abkhazians) say that they will come to the aid of the Georgian defenders.

24 September 1993. Zviad Gamsakhurdia returns to the Mingrelia region. His priority is to defeat the Abkhazians, but he also calls for Shevardnadze's resignation and the restoration of power to what he calls the 'legitimate authorities'.

27 September 1993. Sukhumi falls. Shevardnadze, who had joined his forces there, escapes.

28 September 1993. Shevardnadze returns to the Georgian capital Tbilisi. He claims that Sukhumi will be recaptured (although perhaps by the next generation) and that 'The plan to occupy Sukhumi was masterminded at Russian [military] headquarters.'

30 September 1993. The loss of Abkhazia is almost complete. The conflict to date has resulted in more than 30,000 dead and 100,000 made homeless (*The Daily Telegraph*, 1 October 1993, p. 15; *IHT*, 1 October 1993, p. 2).

1 October 1993. The Abkhazians claim that their territory is now 'completely liberated'. Georgian government troops clash with supporters of Gamsakhurdia.

2–3 October 1993. Supporters of Gamsakhurdia take control of the port of Poti and the small town of Khoni.

4 October 1993. Government forces retake Khoni.

8 October 1993. Shevardnadze announces that Georgia will seek to join the CIS (a majority in parliament agreed on 20 October and Shevardnadze signed the decree on 24 October). (Parliament ratified a bill on 1 March 1994.)

17 October 1993. Supporters of Gamsakhurdia take Samtredia and Khoni.

18 October 1993. Shevardnadze appeals to Russia for military support after admitting that 'the Georgian army has practically disintegrated'.

20 October 1993. Russian troops begin deploying along the rail link with the Black Sea (there were subsequently many reports of Russian equipment and even some personnel helping Georgian forces). (Note that agreement was reached to allow some 20,000 Russian troops to stay. The troops were to have been withdrawn in 1995.) Government forces claim that they have retaken Poti, Lanchkhuti and Khoni.

22 October 1993. Government forces claim that they have retaken Samtredia.

25 October 1993. Government forces claim they have retaken Poti. (But the situation was fluid. Russian troops took over key transport points on 4 November.)

26 October 1993. Senaki falls to government forces (there followed a counter-attack by Gamsakhurdia's supporters, taking Khobi and Senaki, only to lose them again.)

29 October 1993. Shevardnadze claims there is an alliance between Gamsakhurdia's supporters and the Abkhazians.

6 November 1993. Zugdidi, Gamsakhurdia's stronghold, falls to Georgian government forces.

9 November 1993. Russia warns Georgian government forces and Abkhaz separatists not to attack each other.

30 November–1 December 1993. UN-sponsored talks in Geneva produce agreement. The elements include the cessation of hostilities, the exchange of prisoners of war, the return of refugees, the creation of a commission of inquiry into the status of Abkhazia, an appeal for a UN peacekeeping force and a pledge to begin political negotiations in January 1994.

5 January 1994. There is debate about whether Zviad Gamsakhurdia committed suicide on 31 December 1993 when surrounded by enemy forces.

3 February 1994. Presidents Yeltsin and Shevardnadze sign a ten-year treaty of friendship and military co-operation. Russia is to retain three military bases in Georgia and station troops on Georgia's border with Turkey. Russia will also provide help with training and equipping the Georgian army.

4 April 1994. The Georgian government and the Abkhaz separatists agree to allow refugees to return and also make an appeal for a UN peacekeeping force. The conflict has left 3,000 dead (James Meek, *The Guardian*, 5 April 1994, p. 9). (The problem of resettling refugees continued.)

9 June 1994. Yeltsin issues a decree for the sending of peacekeeping troops to Abkhazia (the Council of the Federation approved this on 21 June).

22 July 1994. The United Nations Security Council approves the use of Russian peacekeeping troops on condition that UN military officers monitor the operation.

10 February 1995. Abkhaz 'rebels' say they will give up demands for independence. The invasion of Chechenia is cited as the reason, the West being unwilling to help independence-seekers (*The Economist*, 18 February 1995, p. 46).

2 May 1995. Shevardnadze issues a decree on the disarming of unrestrained gunmen. The decree was mainly aimed at the Mkhedrioni (Horsemen) led by Dzhaba Ioseliani. Set up six years ago, they actively participated in the overthrow of Zviad Gamsakhurdia's regime during the Azkhazian and civil wars and were granted official status in 1993 as the Corps of Rescuers. But their criminal activities forced Shevardnadze to act and Ioseliani decided to comply (*Moscow News*, 12–18 May 1995, p. 5).

24 August 1995. Parliament approves a new constitution, a strong presidency being a key feature.

29 August 1995. Shevardnadze survives, with only minor injuries, an assassination attempt when a car bomb explodes outside parliament. (He was on his way to a signing ceremony for the new constitution.)

30 August 1995. Shevardnadze, who was elected speaker of parliament on 11 October 1992, announces that he is to stand in the presidential election of 5 November 1995.[1]

2 September 1995. The security minister is dismissed.

THE ECONOMY

The economic system

Most of the formal economy remains subject to a system of state orders (EBRD 1994: 24).[2] Peter Nasmyth (*FT*, Weekend, 4 March 1995, p. ii) portrays the situation thus: 'Georgia was once the Soviet Union's wealthiest *per capita* republic with flourishing wine, mineral and film industries. Geographically, it is in the centre of the Caucasus; economically, it lies between the free market and a free mafia. Georgia lacks a solid legal structure for commerce, although moves are being made . . . Georgians continue to base much of their trade system on the old Caucasian tradition of "friendship". Insurance, personal investment, even policing remain heavily dependent on personal or family contact . . . Three years of an unregulated free market have spawned a chaos of new enterprises. Inevitably there have been casualties . . . Most big businesses pay for the "friendship" of the mafia. The system has grown from the huge black economy built in the Soviet period.'

Financial policy

On 5 April 1993 coupons were introduced as a supplement to the rouble. The Russian currency reform of late July 1993 speeded up Georgia's plans. On 2 August 1993 coupons officially became the only legal tender. But, while coupons are accepted in state shops and to pay rent and bills for fuel and services, roubles and dollars are used to buy other goods (the coupon has dramatically plummeted in value against the dollar and even the rouble) (*IHT*, 11 August 1994, p. 9). The coupon is used only to buy rationed staple goods and for rent, water and electricity (Deutsche Bank, *Focus: Eastern Europe*, 1994, no. 113, p. 6). In April 1993 there was talk of eventually introducing a new currency (the lari). The lari was to be introduced in the first half of 1995 (*Transition*, 3 March 1995, vol. 6, no. 3, p. 17).[3]

Restrictions on the convertibility of coupon deposits into cash were removed in September 1994. In November 1994 the general rate of VAT was raised from 14 per cent to 20 per cent and certain VAT exemptions were eliminated (EBRD 1995: 56).

Mohammad Shadman-Valavi of the IMF, in a letter to the *Financial Times* (8 March 1995, p. 24), depicted a much improved outlook. He said that decisive steps had been taken in late 1994 to stabilize and restructure the economy in the form of a comprehensive programme developed in close consultation with the IMF and the World Bank. These measures halted hyperinflation and led to a sharp nominal appreciation of the exchange rate of the coupon against the US dollar. The IMF had disbursed about $40 million under the systemic transformation facility.

In mid-December 1994 the IMF approved a $40 million systemic transformation facility loan. The aim of the government's programme was to reduce the monthly rate of inflation to 1 per cent by the end of 1995 (*Transition*, January–February 1995, p. 23).

Prices

Price controls were lifted from most goods and services in 1991 and 1992. Price controls continue to apply to goods such as bread and milk (EBRD 1994: 25). In the second half of 1994 further steps were taken to raise the remaining controlled prices towards full cost-recovery levels (EBRD 1995: 56).

On 17 September 1994 there were massive increases in the prices of goods and services such as bread (nearly 300 times!), transport and electricity. The minimum monthly wage was increased.

With prices recently liberalized, massive price increases have occurred, e.g. 1,000 per cent for electricity, 4,900 per cent for a metro ticket and 19,000 per cent a loaf of bread (*Business Central Europe*, March 1995, p. 66).

Privatization

Some work has been done on a privatization programme, but the details remain sketchy (*Business Central Europe*, November 1993, p. 60).

Around 100 large industrial enterprises were to be privatized in the first batch of mass privatization. The scheme involves 20 per cent of shares being given to workers, who would be able to buy an additional 10 per cent at a discount. The remaining 70 per cent would be sold for cash or vouchers (Havrylyshyn *et al.* 1994: 385).

In mid-1994 the private sector accounted for roughly 20 per cent of GDP (EBRD 1994: 10). The proportion is probably 20–30 per cent of GDP. The government plans to use a voucher programme to privatize most medium-sized or large enterprises.[4] So far three of the over 900 enterprises have been privatized. By April 1994 about 22 per cent of the almost 5,000 small enterprises had been privatized. No property restitution has taken place (p. 24).

The port of Batumi is to become a free economic zone (*Moscow News*, 3–9 March 1995, p. 7).

Foreign trade

Import licences are generally not required and there are no significant import quotas. But there is an 8 per cent tax on non-FSU (former Soviet Union) exports and there are significant export licensing requirements (EBRD 1994: 111). There is a floating unified exchange rate regime (p. 25).

Convertibility is heavily restricted. The rate floats within these parameters. A 32 per cent export surrender requirement was implemented in June 1993 (p. 111).

Foreign aid

EU aid accounts for about half the state budget (Bruce Clark, *FT*, 28 February 1995, p. 18).

Foreign investment

Despite thousands of registered joint ventures, few if any are in operation (*Business Central Europe*, March 1995, p. 66).

Agriculture

Nikonov (1992: 1161) maintains that peasants are granted land free of charge in the mountainous zone (up to 5.5 ha) and in the valleys (1.25 ha). The right to buy and sell is exercised through the Land Bank following a two-year moratorium. All inefficient and unprofitable collective farms have been reorganized as associations, co-operatives, partnerships or small-scale enterprises. More than 20,000 peasant (farmer) holdings are operating.

Georgia has rapidly disbanded state and collective farms and transferred land to private farmers (Ash 1993: 497).

More than half of agricultural land has been privatized in small plots via leasing (private land ownership rights have not yet been granted). The government intends to keep approximately 25 per cent of agriculture in state hands (EBRD 1994: 24).

Georgia has achieved virtual privatization under leasehold, but continues to forbid private ownership of land. But by mid-1994 over half of agricultural land was under private lease (Kaser 1995: 38).

Economic performance

Table 8.1 shows Georgia's dreadful economic performance through 1994.

Around 90 per cent of the population now live below the poverty level (*The Guardian*, 7 August 1993, p. 11). Fear of widespread hunger resulted in promises of emergency relief from the UN World Food Programme and the EU. Georgia is one of the few countries in the world which has seen agriculture's share of GDP increase at the expense of services and manufacturing. Georgia imports 90 per cent of its energy, for which it cannot pay. There are regular power cuts (*Business Central Europe*, March 1995, p. 66).

Table 8.1 Georgia: selected economic indicators

Economic indicator	*1990*	*1991*	*1992*	*1993*	*1994*
Rate of growth of GDP (%)	−12.4	−13.8	−40.3	−39.2	−35.0
Rate of growth of industrial output (%)	−29.9	−24.4	−43.3	−21.0	−39.7
Rate of growth of agricultural output (%)	6.9	−10.6	−34.2	−41.6	−15.0
Inflation rate (%)	3.3	78.5	913.1	3,126	7,400
Budget surplus or deficit (% of GDP)		−3.0	−28.0	−34.0	−17.0
Current account ($ billion)			−0.248	−0.191	−0.500
Unemployment (end of year, %)			1.0	2.0	2.8

Sources: Various issues of United Nations Economic Commission for Europe, *Economic Survey of Europe*; United Nations, *World Economic and Social Survey*; IMF, *World Economic Outlook*; Deutsche Bank, *Focus: Eastern Europe; Economics of Transition* and *Business Central Europe*; EBRD (1994: 158; 1995: 35)

The Itar-Tass news agency said that a special UN report released on 17 September warned of the possibility of famine. Of late inflation had been averaging 2,000 per cent per month (*The Baltic Observer*, 22–28 September 1994, p. 22). But there has been progress in the battle against inflation. Since January 1995 inflation has been below 3 per cent a month (*The Economist*, 27 May 1995, p. 51).

NOTES

1. Shevardnadze easily won the 5 November 1995 election, with 74.3 per cent of the vote. Parties supportive of Shevardnadze won the general election.
2. The state order system was completely phased out on 1 June 1995 (EBRD, *Transition Report*, 1995, p. 43).
3. The exchange of old for new money began on 25 September 1995 and the lari became the sole legal tender on 2 October 1995.
4. A voucher-based programme for large privatization was adopted in March 1995 (EBRD, *Transition Report*, 1995, p. 43).

9

KAZAKHSTAN

POLITICS

The political background

Kazakhstan is well endowed with natural resources (Deutsche Bank, *Focus: Eastern Europe*, 1993, no. 70, pp. 1–9, and 1995, no. 126, p. 8; *FT*, 8 April 1993, p. 6). There is, for example, oil, natural gas, coal (25 per cent of Soviet production in 1991), gold, nickel, copper, lead and zinc. It inherited about 20 per cent of the Soviet Union's arable land, and grain, meat and wool are important (in 1991 agriculture accounted for 37 per cent of national income). There is a relatively diversified industrial base compared with the other Asiatic republics. There are large oil reserves, but the country is dependent on Russian pipelines for oil exports.

In 1989 the ethnic composition of the population was as follows: Kazakhs, 42 per cent; Russians, 38 per cent; Ukrainians, 5.4 per cent; other, 14.6 per cent (*Economic Bulletin for Asia and the Pacific*, 1991, vol. XLII, nos 1 and 2, p. 2). Kazakhs are of mixed Turkish and Mongol descent. In 1992 Kazakhs accounted for 41 per cent of the population and ethnic Russians 38 per cent (FEER, *Asia 1994 Yearbook*, 1994, p. 108). In 1990–93 the share of Russian residents decreased from 40.8 per cent to 36.4 per cent (*CDSP*, 1994, vol. XLVI, no. 13). *The Economist* (12 March 1994, p. 77) put the current figures at 43 per cent and 36 per cent respectively.

Some 350,000 ethnic Russians have left the Central Asian republics over the past three years (John Lloyd, *FT*, 9 April 1994, p. 3). In 1993 365,000 Russian-speaking people left Kazakhstan and moved to Russia (*Moscow News*, 20–26 May 1994, p. 3). In 1993 222,100 emigrated (*CDSP*, vol. XLVI, no. 24, p. 13). *The Economist* (21 May 1994, p. 53) cites one estimate of 300,000 going to Russia in 1993. In 1994 254,500 Russian-speakers moved to Russia, mostly from the Central Asian states. (Steven Erlanger reported that altogether nearly 3 million Russians had emigrated to Russia from the other countries of the former Soviet Union during the previous three years: *IHT*, 8 February 1995, p. 11. As many as 3 million ethnic Russians have fled the former Soviet republics since 1991. A survey has shown that economic concern is far more important than human rights, the latter rating only 9 per cent: Andrew Higgins, *The Independent*, 19 April 1995, p. 8. In 1993 over 920,000 people moved to Russia from other successor states of the Soviet Union: United Nations Economic Commission for Europe 1995: 228.)

The name of the capital city, Alma Ata, is now written Almaty.

'It is clear that the evolving political system of Kazakhstan is characterized by the absolute dominance of the executive branch of power, vested in the president and in the cabinet, which is appointed by him and responsible solely to him . . . titular nationality accounts for only 40 per cent of the population . . . Preservation of ethnic tranquillity has been one of the greatest achievements of his [Nazarbayev's] presidency so far' (Nourzhanov and Saikal 1994: 226–7). 'Having endorsed a transition to a market economy, the government of Kazakhstan has in reality been reluctant to decentralize the national economy, fearing the political decentralization that would inevitably follow' (p. 227).

Political developments

8 December 1993. Parliament votes to dissolve itself and calls for early elections.

10 December 1993. Parliament votes to allow President Nazarbayev to rule by decree until the new parliament is elected on 7 March 1994.

13 December 1993. Parliament ratifies the Nuclear Non-proliferation Treaty.

7 March 1994. The general election takes place for the 177 parliamentary seats. The turnout is 73.8 per cent. President Nazarbayev (controversially) fills forty-two seats by appointment. While the Nazarbayev-sponsored Union of People's Unity of Kazakhstan wins only twenty-five seats, the majority of the sixty 'independent' candidates are believed to be pro-president because they hold state or government positions. Eleven seats are won by the official federation of trade unions. Parties opposed to Nazarbayev on at least some issues may have won less than thirty seats. The Lad (Harmony Slavic) Party (backed by ethnic Russians) wins four seats.

Observers from the CSCE declared that the election did not meet internationally acceptable standards. The allegations included, for example, 'arbitrary and capricious' disqualification of some candidates, incidents of ballot stuffing, the casting of perhaps more than one-third of votes by proxy (an individual was allowed to cast multiple ballots provided the relevant passports were brought along) and distortion in the media. Ahmed Rashid (*FEER*, 16 March 1995, p. 24) said that Nazarbayev had vetted all the candidates.

29 March 1994. Nazarbayev supports the idea of transforming the CIS into a 'Euro-Asian Union', with a single parliament and currency.

6 July 1994. It is announced that before the year 2000 the capital will move from Almaty (Alma Ata) to Akmola (farther north, nearer the border with Russia).

11 October 1994. The government resigns when President Nazarbayev criticizes it for the slow pace of reform: 'the government is not capable of fulfilling the obligations placed upon it'.

12 October 1994. A new government is confirmed. The new prime minister, Akezhan Kazhegeldin, is reportedly pro-market.

23 November 1994. The USA discloses that it has purchased and transported to the USA highly enriched (weapons grade) uranium. (Russia approved the deal.)

20 January 1995. Presidents Yeltsin and Nazabayev agree to unite the armies of Russia and Kazakhstan: 'Beginning in 1995, the two sides will start work on forming joint armed forces.'

11 March 1995. President Nazarbayev dissolves parliament and announces plans to rule by decree pending new parliamentary elections. This action is the result of the Constitutional Court ruling that the 1994 general election was illegal: the authorities had violated the principle of 'one citizen, one vote' in counting ballots and had set up a voting system that favoured the winning party (e.g. constituency boundaries had been tampered with).

Parliament had earlier voted against measures (supported by the president) to allow the privatization of land and to give the Russian language equal status (*The Economist*, 18 March 1995, p. 80).

14 March 1995. The Constitutional Court's ruling is contested by 130 members of parliament, who claim that the irregularities were confined to only one electoral district.

15 March 1995. Some of the deputies begin a hunger strike and about 100 of them form an alternative 'people's parliament'.

25 March 1995. Nazarbayev announces that a referendum is to be held on 29 April on the question of postponing for four years the presidential election scheduled for 1 December 1996.

29 April 1995. The turnout for the referendum is 91.3 per cent and the 'yes' vote is 95.4 per cent.

30 August 1995. There is a 90 per cent turnout for the referendum on the constitution. The 'yes' vote is 89.14 per cent. Under the constitution the president is able to dissolve parliament if it holds a vote of no confidence or twice rejects his nominee for prime minister. The constitution also allows the president to rule by decree and to call a state of emergency. Parliament is able to oust the president only if he is incapacitated by illness or is found to have committed treason (*FT*, 31 August 1995, p. 3).

THE ECONOMY

Financial policy

Steve LeVine (*FT*, 8 April 1993, p. 6) reports that inflationary pressures are aggravated by a generous social policy and heavy subsidization of state enterprises. Problems with the IMF include the fund's advice that Kazakhstan should leave the rouble zone and establish its own currency because of Russia's poor record of combating inflation. (Wages are officially adjusted to compensate for 70 per cent of the inflation rate: Deutsche Bank, *Focus: Eastern Europe*, 27 September 1994, no. 115, p. 4. There is no insolvency law: p. 5.)

Kazakhstan had debated whether to introduce its own currency, but after the Russian currency reform of late July 1993 agreement was reached with Russia (on 7 August 1993) that the country would remain in the rouble zone (see the 7 September 1993 agreement discussed in Chapter 18). But the tougher conditions imposed by Russia in late September for the supply of new rouble notes led to the introduction of the tenge on 15 November 1993. Roubles could be exchanged for the tenge at the rate of 500 to one and each Kazakh citizen could exchange up to 100,000 roubles. Cash amounts exceeding the limit could be put into special bank accounts and special commissions would establish whether the sums had been legally earned. According to *The Financial Times* (11 January 1995, p. 3), a presidential decree made the tenge the only means of commercial payment.

Following the introduction of the tenge, the aim became the reduction of the monthly rate of inflation to 3 per cent by the end of 1994 and the restriction of the budget deficit to 4 per cent of GDP in 1994. In late January 1994 the IMF agreed to lend SDR 185 million, the first SDR 62 million being made available immediately (as the second drawing on the 'systemic transformation facility') and the rest subsequently on the usual terms. In addition Japan agreed to provide $145 million in aid. The agreements followed a meeting of donor countries two weeks earlier at which aid pledges totalled $1 billion (George Graham, *FT*, 28 January 1994, p. 6). The IMF has granted $1.3 billion to support the tenge (Steve LeVine, *FT*, 15 February 1994, p. 6). The IMF-inspired target for the budget deficit is 4.6 per cent of GDP (Deutsche Bank, *Focus: Eastern Europe*, 27 September 1994, no. 115, p. 4). There has been extremely cautious and often uncoordinated gradualism as well as neglect of monetary and budgetary policy requirements (p. 2). One positive feature is the creation of a so-called 'rehabilitation fund' with whose help thirty to thirty-five enterprises are to be restructured and made competitive (p. 6).

In June 1994 a fifteen-month stabilization programme was announced, much in line with IMF recommendations. The programme included measures to reduce inflation to 10 per cent a month by the end of the year (Nourzhanov and Saikal 1994: 227).

A new bankruptcy law was submitted to parliament in late 1994 (EBRD 1995: 58).

Prices

In January 1992 most prices were freed. By mid-1994 only the prices of transport and communication services, bread and bakery products, baby food, some energy products and imported medicine remained subject to control (EBRD 1994: 27). Substantial progress was made in late 1994 in liberalizing the prices of a number of sensitive products, including bread (EBRD 1995: 58).

Steve LeVine (*FT*, 8 February 1994, p. 4) reported on the new reform programme: the prices of consumer goods were freed on 1 January 1994; the budget deficit for 1994 was set at 4 per cent of GDP; state salaries were frozen.

A proposal to free the price of bread and flour has been rejected by parliament on fifteen occasions (*The Economist*, 15 October 1994, p. 88). The government resigned on 11 October 1994 and the prime minister immediately pushed through the liberalization of bread prices (*Business Central Europe*, November 1994, p. 11).

Privatization

About 5,000 small enterprises were privatized in 1992. The programme envisaged the privatization of more smaller enterprises (with up to 200 employees and fixed assets of up to 5 million roubles) by the end of March 1993 and the conversion of medium-sized and large enterprises into joint stock companies in readiness for their sale to their employees and private companies (*Central Asia Newsfile*, February 1993, no. 4, p. 4).

Privatization was suspended for six months from May to September 1993. Under current legislation half the value of sales must be made up of privatization housing vouchers; these were issued to all citizens, on the basis of length of service, to pay towards privatized housing, but in many cases they remained unused (*Moscow News*, 24 September 1993, p. 8).

According to *Business Central Europe* (September 1993, p. 51), a slow approach is favoured, with the emphasis on pre-privatization restructuring. Details of the March 1993 programme are to be found in the November 1993 issue (p. 61): (1) 51 per cent of the shares of enterprises were to be given to forty investment funds, 10 per cent were to go to employees and the balance was to stay in state hands; (2) all citizens would receive vouchers (those in very poor regions would get 20 per cent more), but the vouchers would have no set value and would not be tradable; the public would have indirect access to shares by placing their vouchers with the funds (managed by state-approved professionals), in which they would have voting rights; (3) foreigners would not be allowed to participate (note that this ban was lifted later on: *Moscow News*, 12 November 1993, p. 8); (4) sectors omitted from the scheme (and sold, if at all, on a case-by-case basis) include defence, construction enterprises of 'national importance', energy production and distribution, mining, metallurgy, commercial banking and foreign trade. Most of Kazakhstan's 1,500 largest enterprises (those employing at least 5,000 people) would be restructured before being sold and foreigners would be encouraged to bid for them.

In 1993 the US tobacco company Philip Morris became the first private owner of a large Kazakh enterprise. The government has now issued a list of thirty-eight more state enterprises to be auctioned to foreigners. The government also promised that, at a later date, about 7,500 state enterprises would be auctioned to Kazakh citizens under a voucher scheme (Steve LeVine, *FT*, 8 February 1994, p. 4).

A mass privatization programme was to begin on 29 April 1994. Over the following fifteen months about 3,500 medium-sized enterprises (accounting for around 70 per cent of businesses and 30 per cent of the entire economy) were to be auctioned off to investment funds. Citizens were to be allowed to buy into these funds with their (free) vouchers. Foreigners would be excluded from the auctions, but would be able to buy shares in and assets of privatized enterprises at a later stage once trading began. State enterprises employing fewer than 500 people were already being sold off. In 1994 thirty-eight large industrial enterprises of more than 2,000 employees were due to be sold. (*The Economist*, 30 April 1994, p. 81; *The Daily Telegraph*, Survey, 21 March 1994, p. 28.)

The first auction sale of enterprises in the mass privatization programme was held in May 1994. Fifty enterprises were offered to the 140 licensed investment funds (*Business Central Europe*, June 1994, p. 49). A figure of thirty-nine was mentioned later (*Business Central Europe*, July–August 1994, p. 15). Almost 4,000 small and medium-sized enterprises have already been privatized. But the government generally retains a 39 per cent share, to be sold off for cash in the future (*Business Central Europe*, September 1995, p. 70).

In mid-1994 the private sector accounted for roughly 20 per cent of GDP (EBRD 1994: 10). The large privatization programme for 1993–95 involved the auction sale of shares to private investment funds. The first funds were created in July 1993 and vouchers were distributed to citizens during the second half of the year. The privatization of the largest enterprises started in July 1993 and proceeds on a case-by-case basis. By mid-1994 about one-fifth of small service entities had been privatized. The aim is to privatize all enterprises in the wholesale trade, in retail trade, in storage and in distribution in the near future. There has been no property restitution to date (p. 26). By the end of 1994 at least 55 per cent of small enterprises had been privatized. In late 1994 the government announced its intention to increase the number of large state enterprises to be sold on a case-by-case basis from ten to 170. Medium-sized enterprises have been privatized by selling shares for vouchers in auctions. It remains unclear whether the target of privatizing 20 per cent of all medium-sized enterprises in the mass privatization programme by the end of 1994 was achieved (EBRD 1995: 58).

Foreign trade

Though the foreign trade system was streamlined in 1994, state-owned trading continues to be prominent and the taxation of imports and exports (mostly at low rates) remains somewhat discretionary (EBRD 1994: 27). There are few quantitative restrictions on imports. There are no export subsidies. There are export taxes on many products, but such taxes were cut substantially in 1994. Exporters outside the state-order system have to be licensed. There are restrictions on the export of certain (mainly strategic) products. The tenge floats, but there is intervention. There is current account convertibility for enterprises, but there are restrictions on capital account. There is a 50 per cent surrender requirement for export proceeds to the interbank market (p. 111). Some progress has been made in reducing the number of commodities covered by export quotas (now seven) and there are plans to reduce the number of products requiring export licences (EBRD 1995: 58).

Foreign investment

Kazakhstan is now second only to Russia among the countries of the former Soviet Union in attracting foreign invesment; favoured sectors include oil and tobacco (Steve LeVine, *FT*, 15 February 1994, p. 6). Foreign investment is estimated to be about $500 million (*The Daily Telegraph*, Survey, 21 March 1994, p. 28). By the end of 1993 commitments amounted to about $9 billion, of which only $500 million had been disbursed (*Business Central Europe*, April 1994, p. 46). Foreign direct investment amounted to $400 million in the period 1990–93 (EBRD 1994: 123).

According to a United Nations survey released in late March 1995, Kazakhstan has attracted more long-term foreign investment than any other country in the former Soviet Union or Eastern Europe. More than $46 billion in foreign investment commitments had been attracted over the previous five years (39 per cent of the region's total) (*Transition*, 1995, vol. 6, no. 3, p. 17).

Agriculture

Nikonov (1992: 1161) said that private land ownership was then not legally recognized in Kazakhstan, Kyrgyzstan, Tajikistan, Turkmenistan and Uzbekistan (see the country profiles for more recent developments). These states never had private ownership of land. The land was allotted to extended families and they were nomads within the boundaries of the area owned by their tribe. The transition to settled life was completed in the 1920s. Life-long possession of land with the right to inherit is recognized in law.

Note that the previous nomadic way of life makes privatization more difficult than usual.

An Itar-Tass report of mid-December 1994 said that the prime minister was to propose legislation allowing individuals to own land (*Business Europa*, February–March 1995, p. 32). (See the entry for 11 March 1995.)

By the end of 1992 there were 8,500 private farms, with an average size of 400 ha (*CDSP*, 1993, vol. XLV, no. 5, p. 22); they accounted for only 1.72 per cent of total agricultural land (United Nations Economic Commission for Europe 1993: 206). As of 1 April 1993 there were 11,100 private farms, with an average size of 531 ha. More than 20 per cent of the collective and state farms and inter-farm and other agricultural production enterprises have been privatized. Almost 800 collective enterprises (including thirty-seven joint stock companies), about 100 agricultural co-operatives, 400 small enterprises and 800 private farms have been formed in their place (*CDSP*, 1993, vol. XLV, no. 21, p. 20).

Private farms and plots account for 35–70 per cent of the major agricultural outputs (EBRD 1994: 26). The privatization scheme has been extended to the agricultural sector on a (non-tradable) lease basis, since private land ownership is prohibited (EBRD 1995: 17).

The Kazakh leadership supports private land ownership. The draft constitution containing the clause was to be circulated for discussion (*CDSP*, 1995, vol. XLVII, no. 27, p. 21).

Economic performance

Table 9.1 paints a pretty grim picture on the GDP and inflation fronts. But agriculture has not done too badly.

Table 9.1 Kazakhstan: selected economic indicators

Economic indicator	*1990*	*1991*	*1992*	*1993*	*1994*
Rate of growth of GDP (%)	−0.4	−13.0	−13.0	−12.0	−25.0
Rate of growth of industrial output (%)	−0.8	−0.9	−13.8	−14.8	−28.5
Rate of growth of agricultural output (%)	6.8	−10.0	1.0	−5.0	−17.0
Inflation rate (%)	4.2	90.9	1,381	1,663	1,880
Budget surplus or deficit (% GDP)	1.4	−7.9	−7.3	−1.2	−6.5
Current account ($ billion)			−0.6	−0.6	
Unemployment (end of year, %)	0.0	0.0	0.5	0.6	1.0

Sources: Various issues of United Nations Economic Commission for Europe, *Economic Survey of Europe*; United Nations, *World Economic and Social Survey*; IMF, *World Economic Outlook*; Deutsche Bank, *Focus: Eastern Europe*; *Economics of Transition* and *Business Central Europe*; EBRD (1994: 160; 1995: 37)

10

KYRGYZSTAN

POLITICS

The political background

In 1989 the ethnic composition of the population was as follows: Kyrgyz, 52.4 per cent; Russian, 21.5 per cent; Uzbek, 12.9 per cent; Ukrainian, 2.5 per cent; Tatar, 1.6 per cent; other, 9.1 per cent (*Economic Bulletin for Asia and the Pacific*, 1991, vol. XLII, nos 1 and 2, p. 2). Ian Pryde (*The World Today*, November 1992, pp. 208–11) points out that the president, Askar Akayev, has a policy of national harmony (the 4.5 million population comprised 52 per cent Kyrgyz, 21 per cent Russians, 13 per cent Uzbeks and the rest numerous other nationalities). Kyrgyzstan has decided not to form its own army. A June 1994 report stated that over the previous four years the number of Russians had decreased by almost 200,000 and so the proportion of ethnic Russians in the population had fallen to 17 per cent (*CDSP*, 1994, vol. XLVI, no. 24, p. 13). Kyrgyz now comprise 56 per cent of the population (*The Economist*, 10 September 1994, p. 76).

Political developments

13 December 1993. The government resigns when Prime Minister Tursun Chyngyshev is accused of corruption (involving gold mining).

30 January 1994. President Akayev wins a national vote of confidence in his economic reform programme (the referendum turnout was 95.3 per cent and the 'yes' vote was 96.3 per cent).

President Akayev is reported as saying that the country is doomed by its backwardness to return to Russia's economic orbit. Kyrgyzstan could not attract 'serious' foreign investment and would remain 'on the sidelines of economic progress' for at least ten to fifteen years (*FT*, 13 June 1994, p. 4).

5 September 1994. The government resigns and the president calls an early general election (on 24 December 1994; it will be preceded by a referendum on a constitutional amendment specifying a bicameral government).

22 October 1994. Two questions were asked in the referendum, which attracted a turnout of at least 87 per cent:

1. Whether changes in the constitution could be decided by referendum. Approved by nearly 75 per cent.

2. Whether the present single-chamber parliament of 350 members should be changed to a bicameral parliament of 105 members. One chamber would consist of thirty-five full-time deputies, while the other would comprise seventy deputies elected on a regional basis and sitting less frequently. Approved by nearly 73 per cent.

5 February 1995. The first round of the general election takes place, for seats in the thirty-five-member Legislative Assembly and the seventy-member People's Assembly (which will meet only twice a year).

The turnout was variously estimated at 43 per cent and 62 per cent. Some 1,400 candidates took part, mostly independents or ones nominated by various social and workers' organizations. One estimate was that only about 160 candidates represented viable political parties, while another was that something over 20 per cent of the candidates were members of the twelve registered political parties. Only sixteen candidates gained the required 50 per cent or more of the vote in the first round, leaving eighty-nine seats to be decided in the second round on 19 February (only the top two candidates from the first round competing). After the 19 February round a total of seventy-eight candidates were successful (twenty-eight in the Legislative Assembly and fifty in the People's Assembly), so at least one more round would be needed.

Some concern has been expressed. Anthony Daniels (*The Daily Telegraph*, 14 February 1995, p. 21) said that some adults had more than one vote; though illegal this was allowed in order to ensure a 50 per cent turnout. Ahmed Rashid (*FEER*, 16 March 1995, p. 24) argues that President Akayev has allowed a political opposition, but that he has enhanced the power of the presidency in order, it is alleged, to control the economy better and stamp out corruption. The government has genuinely tried to encourage democratic participation, but the political process itself is in chaos, with frequent cabinet changes and intense power struggles within the ruling elite.

Ian Pryde (*The World Today*, June 1995, pp. 115–16) states that in the previous parliament there emerged two factions 'divided less by political orientation than by their attitude to the endemic corruption among official and public figures who had taken advantage of their position and privileges to line their own pockets'. At the time of their election nearly 30 per cent of the new deputies were being investigated for illegal financial dealings. 'Parliamentary privileges, notably immunity from further investigation and criminal prosecution, gave corrupt businessmen a strong incentive to seek election to parliament . . . large sums of black money [were spent] in often bitter campaigns, and numerous cases of vote-rigging and outright physical intimidation were reported.' The election brought about a crucial change in the balance of power in the country:

1. The Islamic south managed to get many of its own candidates elected, showing that it was no longer prepared to accept traditional northern dominance.

2. The twelve largest parties were able to win only a few seats.

3. The new parliament consists almost entirely of ethnic Krygyz, leaving other nationalities with virtually no representation.

Pryde is critical of the OSCE observers, who concluded that, despite the massive number of irregularities and violations, the voting had on the whole been free and fair. Pryde also presents in detail the arguments of those who disagree with the generally favourable impression given in the West of the Akayev regime.

Huskey (1995: 828–9) states that 'Akayev began to employ methods of rule in mid-1994 that had more in common with authoritarian than liberal regimes . . . the reasons for the turn to the right in Kyrgyz politics remain a subject for debate.' As for the election, Huskey argues that political parties 'have not yet succeeded in making the transition from groups of notables to mass-based organizations capable of generating electoral support'. He believes that 'The most formidable blocs in the new parliament will include central and local executive officials, as well as directors of factories and business organizations . . . They are drawn largely from the ranks of the old *nomenklatura*.'

9 February 1995. Kyrgyzstan and the EU sign a ten-year partnership and co-operation deal, to come into force within two months of ratification. Elements include the mutual granting of 'most favoured nation' status and the abolition of quantitative trade restrictions.

THE ECONOMY

The economic background

Natural resources are not so much limited as needing time to develop, e.g. mercury, gold, coal, uranium, marble, oil and gas. Only 7 per cent of Kyrgyzstan is arable, of which 72 per cent is irrigated. The emphasis in agriculture is on livestock. The country accounted for only 0.6 per cent of Soviet industrial production in 1990. The country has made most progress among the Asiatic republics in price liberalization (Deutsche Bank, *Focus: Eastern Europe*, 1993, no. 70, pp. 1–9).

On 18 February 1993 Kyrgyzstan became a member of the International Finance Corporation, the first of the Central Asian republics to do so.

Financial policy

On 10 May 1993 the som ('catfish') replaced the rouble and was allowed to float. The new currency is supported by $400 million from the IMF, the World Bank and Japan (John Lloyd, *FT*, 22 May 1993, p. 2).

The som was allowed to float, although there is some state intervention. The som is in principle convertible for transactions related to foreign trade of the enterprise sector. But there are restrictions on the capital account (EBRD 1994: 29, 111).

The value of the som has been relatively stable, helped by the independence of the central bank (*CDSP*, 22 June 1994, vol. XLVI, no. 21, pp. 21–2).

With IMF and World Bank support the som has remained at about eleven to the US dollar for a year (Steve LeVine, *FT*, 10 May 1995, p. 3).

Moldova and Krygyzstan have implemented successful stabilization programmes, reducing monthly inflation to 2–5 per cent in May–June 1994 in the wake of tough fiscal and credit policy adjustments over the previous six months (Kasper Bartholdy, *Economics of Transition*, 1994, vol. 2, no. 3, p. 405). The monthly inflation rate fell from 3 per cent in July 1994 to 0.2 per cent in September (*Transition*, 1994, vol. 5, no. 8, p. 16).

The World Bank has reported that 'The liberalization programme has been largely completed.' But Kyrgyzstan is still struggling to control the budget deficit (John Thornhill, *FT*, 1 June 1995, p. 4).

Prices

There are few direct controls on prices. Significant adjustments were made to administered prices for bread, rents and other items during 1993. The maximum retail margins imposed on all goods after the introduction of the som were lifted on imported goods in August 1993 and on most domestically produced goods in November 1993. In March 1994 all retail margins were eliminated except for that on bread (EBRD 1994: 29).

Privatization

Since relatively few ethnic Kyrgyz live in towns they are given interest-free loans to allow them to participate in purchases. The 9 August 1991 decree laid down that every adult citizen would be given a voucher. Large privatization involves 50 per cent of the shares being retained by the state, 30 per cent being sold to employees of the affected enterprises at a 30 per cent discount and the remaining 20 per cent being sold to the public (who may use their vouchers), to foreigners (with special permission) or to other related enterprises (e.g. a long-standing supplier). The privatization process was initiated by the 10 January 1992 decree (Kaser and Mehrotra 1992: 41–2).

Interest-free loans are available to encourage private purchases of small and medium-sized enterprises (Deutsche Bank, *Focus: Eastern Europe*, 1993, no. 70, p. 5).

Sheila Jones (*FT*, 16 February 1993, p. 4) reported that 11 per cent of state property, mainly in retailing and services, had been privatized. The aim was to privatize over a third of industry, agriculture and services by the end of 1993 and two-thirds by the end of 1994. The voucher scheme involves distribution according to salary and years of work (*The Economist*, 20 February 1993, p. 75).

An article published on 9 July 1994 reported that the first stage of privatization had been concluded. But although some 230,000 people had participated, only a few thousand people had become owners of major enterprises, property, land and other state-owned facilities. Deputies, government members and the heads of provinces and districts became major landowners and businessmen; the lion's share of capital is now concentrated in their hands. A parliamentary commission was set up to investigate the issue (*CDSP*, 1994, vol. XLVI, no. 27, p. 20).

Most small businesses are private (John Lloyd, *FT*, 16 September 1994, p. 4).

In mid-1994 the private sector accounted for roughly 30 per cent of GDP (EBRD 1994: 10). The predominant method of large privatization has been the transfer of shares to work collectives, with the state usually retaining a significant proportion of the shares. No voucher auctions have taken place and competitive bidding has been used for only 1.4 per cent of total privatized assets. At the end of 1993 the government significantly accelerated the pace of privatization. By January 1994 about 4,450 enterprises (accounting for 33 per cent of total fixed enterprise assets) were privatized. New provisions in January 1994 involved the privatization of all small enterprises through auctions and/or competitive bidding with the use of cash and vouchers. The main methods for the privatization of medium-sized and large enterprises were to be competitive cash bidding (by individual investors for up to 70 per cent of the equity) and voucher auctions (open to individuals and investment funds for 25 per cent of the equity), while 5 per cent of the equity would be preserved for the labour collectives. The privatization of small trade outlets, retail and service establishments is largely complete, comprising 80 per cent of fixed assets in these units. There is no property restitution programme (p. 28).

By the end of 1994 some 45 per cent of all enterprises had been privatized under the new privatization programme, up from a third in mid-1994. The distribution of vouchers had started in February 1994 and by November 75 per cent had been distributed. By November 1994 cash auctions involving eighty-four enterprises and voucher auctions involving 185 enterprises had taken place and 1,000 enterprises were to be privatized by the end of 1996. Twenty-three licensed specialized investment funds were created in the second half of 1994, taking 50 per cent of the shares in the voucher auctions. Some trading in privatization vouchers began in September 1994 and a full stock market was set to start trading in early 1995 (EBRD 1995: 59).

The World Bank has said that 'The privatization programme is progressing well', while the prime minister has reported that 'More than 64 per cent of our firms have been privatized and there is no such thing as a state-owned farm' (John Thornhill, *FT*, 1 June 1995, p. 4).

Foreign trade

After a first wave of reforms, when restrictions on imports, quotas for exports and foreign exchange surrender requirements were abolished, some momentum was lost in 1993. The government moved to reintroduce compulsory state orders, export licences and prohibitive export taxes. These measures, together with the continued dominance of trade and distribution by the Ministry of Industry, Trade and Material Resources and the Ministry of Agriculture created a system whereby about 70 per cent of output became subject to direct or indirect state control. In external trade the state's direct involvement has been mainly through clearing agreements which allow goods to be exchanged between republics on a barter basis. In early 1994 the trade system was substantially liberalized. Remaining import and export licensing agreements were lifted and export taxes reduced. The state order system for exports has been replaced by voluntary supply contracts (EBRD 1994: 29, 111). Since mid-1994 the central bank has been *de facto* pursuing a policy of a fixed exchange rate (at ten to eleven som to the US dollar) (EBRD 1995: 59).[1]

Foreign aid

In May 1993 Kyrgyzstan agreed a programme with the IMF and received $23 million as the first slice of an $85 million aid package (John Lloyd, *FT*, 21 May 1993, p. 5). On 14 May 1993 the World Bank approved a credit of $60 million, the first of its kind to any Central Asian state (Ahmed Rashid, *FEER*, 17 June 1993, p. 30).

Kyrgyzstan has been promised more than $680 million in foreign aid (including some previously committed funds) by the end of 1995 after winning the approval of international financial institutions for its reform programme (John Thornhill, *FT*, 1 June 1995, p. 4).

The foreign debt is $365 million (*IHT*, 15 April 1995, p. 10).

Foreign investment

In early September 1994 the president signed a decree allowing foreign investors to take all their profits out of the country in hard currency or goods they have produced. The decree also cancelled a 5 per cent tax on profits taken abroad (*Transition*, 1994, vol. 5, no. 7, p. 19).

Agriculture

The 19 April 1991 decree forbids the buying and selling of land, although every citizen has the right to enjoy the use of and to bequeath a plot (albeit not to be divided); equal rights are granted to different forms of land management; inefficient state and collective farms should be disbanded (Kaser and Mehrotra 1992: 41). The transfer of land for fifty years has been confirmed. But a law has recently been adopted on the possibility of selling the right to the use of land (*CDSP*, 22 June 1994, vol. XLVI, no. 21, pp. 21–2).

Ian Pryde (*The World Today*, November 1992, p. 208) reports how the traditionally nomadic Kyrgyz lost much of the best land in the north to Russian and Ukrainian settlers in the nineteenth century. In the south the Uzbeks have been working the land for generations. (A similar situation prevails in industry, which is dominated by Russians and Ukrainians.) In consequence, many Kyrgyz have been demanding a halt to the privatization programme. But although the privatization of land has been postponed the president is intent on pushing ahead with privatization in the not-too-distant future.

See the comments by Nikonov in Chapter 9 on Kazakhstan.

By the end of 1992 there were 8,600 private farms, with an average size of 43 ha (*CDSP*, 1993, vol. XLV, no. 5, p. 22); they accounted for 3.7 per cent of total agricultural land (United Nations Economic Commission for Europe 1993: 206). As of 1 April 1993 there were 16,700 private farms, with an average size of 23 ha (*CDSP*, 1993 vol. XLV, no. 21, p. 20).

Land leases of up to forty-nine years have been introduced, which can be used as collateral and are inheritable (thus mitigating the constitutional prohibition of private land ownership). Obligatory state purchase of agricultural produce was largely phased out in 1994 (EBRD 1995: 59).

All collective farms were supposed to be dissolved by the end of 1994 and all state farms by the end of 1995. It was stated that by mid-November 1994 17,000 of the 21,700 farms were privately owned (Kaser 1995: 38–9).

The prime minister has said that 'there is no such thing as a state-owned farm' (John Thornhill, *FT*, 1 June 1995, p. 4).

Economic performance

Table 10.1 paints a generally pretty grim picture on the GDP and inflation fronts, although the inflation rate dipped noticeably in 1994.

According to the government, most enterprises are working at 25 per cent capacity or less (*The Economist*, 29 October 1994, p. 98).

Table 10.1 Kyrgyzstan: selected economic indicators

Economic indicator	*1990*	*1991*	*1992*	*1993*	*1994*
Rate of growth of GDP (%)	3.0	−5.0	−19.1	−16.0	−26.5
Rate of growth of industrial output (%)	−0.6	−0.3	−26.8	−25.3	−30.0
Rate of growth of agricultural output (%)	1.3	−10.0	−6.0	−9.0	−15.0
Inflation rate (%)	3.0	85.0	854.6	1,209	278.2
Budget surplus or deficit (% GDP)	0.3	4.6	−17.4	−13.5	−8.4
Current account ($ billion)		−0.136	−0.061	−0.256	−0.194
Unemployment (end of year, %)	0.0	0.0	0.1	0.2	0.8

Sources: Various issues of United Nations Economic Commission for Europe, *Economic Survey of Europe*; United Nations, *World Economic and Social Survey*; IMF, *World Economic Outlook*; Deutsche Bank, *Focus: Eastern Europe; Economics of Transition* and *Business Central Europe*; EBRD (1994: 161; 1995: 38)

NOTE

1. In March 1995 the authorities introduced full current account convertibility (EBRD, *Transition Report*, 1995, p. 47).

11

LATVIA

POLITICS

Citizenship

Henn-Juri Uibopuu (*The World Today*, June 1992, pp. 109–11) provides the following information. The census of 1935 split the population into 73 per cent Latvians (compared with about 52 per cent today), 12.5 per cent Russians (33 per cent in 1989), 5.2 per cent Jews, 3.9 per cent Germans, 2.8 per cent Poles, 1.3 per cent Livs and 0.4 per cent Estonians.

In 1989 52 per cent of the 2.7 million population were Latvians, 34 per cent were Russians, 4.5 per cent were Belorussians, 3.5 per cent were Ukrainians and 2.5 per cent were Poles (Gwiazda 1994: 77). About 20 per cent of Russians have mastered the Latvian language (p. 79). In 1993 the respective proportions were 54.2 per cent, 33.1 per cent, 4.1 per cent, 3.1 per cent and 2.2 per cent (*FT*, Survey, 18 November 1994, p. 32).

The 15 October 1991 (guidelines for the) citizenship law stipulated, for example, at least sixteen years' lawful residence and a language test (see below for changes). A letter in *The Economist* (29 January 1994, p. 8) said that less than 40 per cent of Russians had taken Latvian citizenship.

26 November 1993. Parliament approves the first reading of the new, controversial citizenship law. The requirements include a minimum ten-year residence, a conversational knowledge of Latvian and a loyalty oath. Former KGB or army officers are permanently barred and 'naturalization quotas' are proposed. (Currently only 66 per cent of the population are citizens: *FT*, 27 November 1993, p. 2.)

21 June 1994. Parliament approves a highly controversial law on citizenship (there are currently 700,000 non-citizens: *Moscow News*, 1–7 July 1994, p. 4; currently there are about 740,000 non-citizens, 30 per cent of the population, and 1,744,507 Latvian citizens: *The Baltic Observer*, 16–22 June 1994, p. 4). Non-citizens born in Latvia (around 200,000) are able to apply for citizenship after 1996. But about 500,000 (mainly ethnic Russians) born outside Latvia will be subject to a strict annual quota after the year

2000 (the quota will be 0.1 per cent of the number of Latvian citizens in the previous year, i.e. around 2,000 people: *CDSP*, 1994, vol. XLVI, no. 23, p. 16). President Guntis Ulmanis needs to approve the law. Non-citizens cannot vote or own land.

There was considerable international criticism. At home the Union of Non-citizens estimated that there were 800,000 'forced non-citizens' residing in Latvia. In March 1991, when a referendum was held, many of them supported independence and democracy. Around 637,000 subsequently declared their desire to be citizens (*The Baltic Observer*, 21–27 April 1994, p. 13). There are 690,000 non-citizens (*The Baltic Observer*, 17–23 March 1994, p. 4).

28 June 1994. The president orders parliament to reconsider the law.

22 July 1994. A revised law on citizenship is passed. Instead of quotas, residents previously involved with specific organizations hostile to Latvia's independence will not be granted citizenship (such organizations include the Union of Veterans of the Armed Forces of the USSR and the KGB). A one-year deadline is introduced for Latvian officials to process naturalization applications. (Under the previous draft the naturalization of some 400,000 non-citizens would have proceeded with tight quotas. The new law allows for naturalization of persons born in Latvia to begin in 1996 and for all non-citizens born outside Latvia to begin in the year 2003: *The Baltic Observer*, 28 July–3 August 1994, p. 3.)

27 October 1994. Parliament approves the first reading of the draft aliens law (there have to be three readings in parliament and the president has to consent). The draft law grants automatic permanent resident status to citizens of the former Soviet Union and their descendants who were inhabitants of Latvia before 1 July 1992. Some 22,000 Russian military pensioners and their families will receive permanent resident status under the law, although they will be barred from applying for citizenship. Under Latvia's citizenship law non-citizens who have lived for five years as permanent residents in Latvia since 4 May 1990 will be eligible to apply for naturalization. The first applicants will be considered on 1 January 1996. For those who emigrated to Latvia after 1 July 1992 the five-year term will be counted from the date of the issue of their permanent residence permit. Nearly half of Latvia's 2.6 million population are Russian-speakers, most of whom emigrated during the half-century of Soviet control. Of these over 500,000 lack citizenship (*The Baltic Observer*, 3–9 November 1994, p. 2).

31 January 1995. Latvia becomes the Council of Europe's thirty-fourth member (the last of the Baltic States; note also that there is an OSCE mission in Latvia).

16 March 1995. Parliament amends the citizenship law. Two groups would be granted citizenship without having to take language tests: (1) ethnic Latvians who did not return to Latvia until after the Second World

War and (2) residents who have completed a course of general education taught in Latvian (this would affect mainly Russian-speaking young people who were born in Latvia and graduated from Latvian schools). Approximately 70,000 people would be affected, including 25,000 to 28,000 repatriated from Russia (*The Baltic Observer*, 23–29 March 1995, p. 1).

The general election of 5–6 June 1993

A large proportion of the population were not eligible to vote because of the strict law on citizenship. The right to vote was confined to pre-1940 citizens and their descendants, which meant that about 40 per cent of 'non-citizens' were eligible (i.e. only about 20 per cent of the electorate were non-Latvian). According to Jonathan Steele (*The Guardian*, 10 June 1993, p. 12), of the 2.34 million registered as residents in March 1993, 667,000 or 28.5 per cent were 'non-citizens'.

There was a 5 per cent threshold for each of the twenty-three participating parties. The turnout was about 90 per cent. Below is the resulting distribution of votes and seats in the new 100-member Saeima or parliament (it replaced the Supreme Council):

1. *Latvian Way* (32.38 per cent of the vote; thirty-six seats). The party is a centre–right coalition of moderate nationalists, former communists and emigrés, stemming from the Latvian Popular Front and the pre-election government. The leader is Anatolijs Gorbunovs, the chairman of parliament and former ideology secretary of the Latvian Communist Party. The party advocates a 'gradual' citizenship process and is a firm supporter of the market economy.

2. *Latvian National Independence Movement* (13.35 per cent of the vote; fifteen seats). The party is right-wing and nationalist, adopting a hard line on citizenship. It is led by Joachim Siegerist, a German-speaking emigré.

3. *Harmony for Latvia* (11.99 per cent of the vote; thirteen seats). The leader is Janis Jurkans (a former foreign minister) and the party has a generous attitude towards naturalization.

4. *Latvian Peasants' Union* (10.64 per cent of the vote; twelve seats). The leader is Ivars Berkis. The party advocates a 'gradual' approach to citizenship and priority support for agriculture.

5. *Fatherland and Freedom* (six seats). The party wishes to 'decolonize' Latvia by forcibly repatriating Russians.

6. *Christian Democrat Union* (six seats).

7. *Democratic Centre Party* (5 per cent of the vote; five seats). The party is liberal on the citizenship issue.

8. *Equal Rights Movement* (seven seats). Defends the rights of Russians and advocates immediate citizenship for 'non-citizens'. It is led by Sergejs Dimanis.

Political developments after the June 1993 general election

8–10 September 1993. The Pope visits Latvia.

15 March 1994. An agreement is announced with Russia: Russian troops will be withdrawn by 31 August 1994, although Russia will retain the use of the Skrunda radar station for four years after that (a formal agreement was signed by the presidents on 30 April 1994). (The non-operational part of the station was demolished on 4 May 1995 despite Russia's objections.)

Under the agreement the 22,000 Russian military pensioners (and their families) are, for example, able to buy and sell property. But they are ineligible to receive Latvian citizenship and so unable to vote (*The Baltic Observer*, 1–7 September 1994, p. 1).

6 July 1994. President Clinton visits Latvia, the first US president to visit any of the Baltic States. He promises support for the removal of Russian troops, but encourages a tolerant attitude towards the Russian minority. A USA–Latvia trade and investment accord is signed and more US aid is promised. (The USA never recognized the Soviet Union's claim to the Baltic States.)

14 July 1994. The government resigns after rejecting demands for increased tariff protection for imported foodstuffs from the Latvian Peasants' Union (one of Latvian Way's two junior partners in the coalition government).

18 August 1994. The Latvian National Independence Movement's proposed government is rejected by parliament. (President Guntis Ulmanis then invited Latvian Way to try to form the next government.)

31 August 1994. The last Russian troops pull out (except for the 600 or so military specialists operating the Skrunda radar station until August 1998).

15 September 1994. Maris Gailis of Latvian Way becomes prime minister.

Latvian Way formed a coalition government with the eight-member, centre–left Political Union of Economists (which had split away from Harmony for Latvia). Two former members of the Latvian Peasants' Union also joined the government.

Ironically, parliament later approved increased tariffs on food imports, effective 1 December 1994 (*The Baltic Observer*, 6–12 October 1994, p. 2).

12 April 1995. Latvia and the EU initial an associate membership agreement (it was signed on 12 June 1995).

23 May 1995. Latvia and Ukraine sign a friendship and co-operation agreement.

27 July 1995. Alfred Rubiks, the former leader of the Latvian Communist Party, is given an eight-year prison sentence for conspiring to overthrow the Latvian government in support of the coup attempt against Gorbachev in August 1991.

THE ECONOMY

Financial policy

The fight against inflation has been a key feature of government policy. Hence the concern with budgetary control (e.g. on 8 December 1994 parliament decided that the budget deficit for 1995 should not exceed 1.7 per cent of GDP: *The Baltic Observer*, 15–21 December 1994, p. 2).

The Latvian rouble (rublis) was introduced as a parallel currency on 7 May 1992 and was allowed to float against other currencies in October. But on 20 July the Russian rouble was entirely withdrawn from circulation, to be exchanged at a rate of ten to one rublis (United Nations Economic Commission for Europe 1993: 170, 233).

The first lats went into circulation on 5 March 1993, alongside the rublis. The phased introduction of the lat was to have been completed by the end of June 1993. Exporters are free to move their foreign exchange earnings wherever they please and there are no restrictions on the purchase of foreign currency by importers, tourists and foreign investors. The result is *de facto* convertibility of the lat (Deutsche Bank, *Focus: Eastern Europe*, 23 April 1993, no. 75, p. 3).

The IMF talks of current account convertibility and partial capital account convertibility (*World Economic Outlook*, May 1993, p. 67).

Steve Hanke (*FT*, 5 May 1994, p. 24) argues that 'although Latvia has a central bank that can engage in discretionary monetary policy, it has been operating as if it was a currency board. Moreover, the Latvian central bankers have kept the politicians at bay by threatening to introduce currency board legislation, if the politicians should meddle in monetary affairs.'

According to the United Nations Commission for Europe (1994: 121), in addition to current account operations capital account transactions have also been largely decontrolled.

The lat is totally convertible, with both local and foreign companies enjoying free access to international capital markets (*IHT*, Survey, 4 November 1994, p. 12).

The exchange rate was freely determined on the market until February 1994. It is still not officially pegged to a currency or currency basket. The central bank (the banks' direct trading partner, since the currency exchange is still not fully functional as yet) exerts considerable influence on the exchange rate. According to the central bank, the lats has been informally pegged to Special Drawing Rights (SDRs) since February 1994 (Deutsche Bank, *Focus: Eastern Europe*, 28 August 1994, no. 113, pp. 12–13).

The lat is informally pegged to the SDR via central bank intervention in foreign exchange markets. Base money is fully backed by net international reserves. There is complete and effective current and capital account convertibility, with no repatriation or surrender requirements (EBRD 1994: 29, 109).

The monthly rate of inflation was reduced from 50 per cent in January 1992 to 0.3 per cent in April 1993, while the exchange rate against the dollar has stabilized since the lat became the sole currency at the end of June 1993 (Adrian Bridge, *The Independent*, 26 July 1993, p. 21).

Einars Repse (*Finance and Development*, December 1993, pp. 28–9) says that Latvian roubles were no longer legal tender after 18 October 1993; there is an independent central bank.

The central bank is independent. Its chairman (Einars Repse) and council are appointed by parliament, but are not dismissible for a six-year term. Most restrictions on foreign exchange were lifted in 1992 (*FT*, Survey, 18 November 1994, p. 30).

A series of financial scandals has badly dented the image of the Latvian banking system (*The Baltic Observer*, 18–24 May 1995, p. 1). On 22 May 1995, for example, the central bank suspended the operations of the Banka Baltija, the largest commercial bank. The following day the government and the central bank announced that they had agreed on a 100 per cent takeover of the bank, as opposed to the 51 per cent mentioned earlier. On 19 May the finance minister had announced his intention to resign over the growing budget deficit and the problems of financing it (*The Baltic Observer*, 25–31 May 1995, pp. 1, 7, 15). On 25 May the Bank of Latvia made a six-month loan to the government in return for a commitment to draft a non-deficit budget for 1996. The state budget crisis started in April 1995 when a dramatic decrease in state revenues and problems in the commercial banking system increased the budget deficit substantially (*The Baltic Observer*, 1–7 June 1995, p. 7). On 13 June 1995 the first demonstration by depositors took place. On 20 June the government asked the central bank to bring bankruptcy proceedings against Banka Baltija, which was declared insolvent by the Latvian Economic Court on 27 June 1995. On 27 June it was announced that the former president and chairman of the Banka Baltija were to be arrested on criminal charges. New banking laws were passed by parliament on 27 July 1995 to increase regulatory control and to provide guidelines for a compensation scheme. Depositors in Bank Baltija were to be partially compensated and the government was working on a plan to provide cheap credits to businesses who lost money in the bank. Nine commercial banks have been declared bankrupt since February 1994 (*The Baltic Observer*, 27 July–9 August 1995, p. 2).

Prices

Price liberalization began in early 1991 and was virtually complete by late 1992. No formal price controls remain. Rents and public transport and heating prices are set by municipalities (EBRD 1994: 29).

Privatization

The legal framework of privatization has almost been completed, including restitution, land privatization and a voucher scheme (the November 1992 legislation allows the free distribution of vouchers partly on the basis of length of residence in Latvia). But implementation has been slow (Deutsche Bank, *Focus: Eastern Europe*, 23 April 1993, no. 75, p. 4).

A mere 7 per cent of the 'total volume' of state property was privatized in 1992 (*Moscow News*, 18 February 1993, p. 7).

Most progress has been made in the small privatization of shops, restaurants and handicrafts. Large enterprises have to determine their own privatization strategies. An enterprise may be purchased by its employees, by domestic and/or foreign investors or by the state. An auction is also possible (Deutsche Bank, *Focus: Eastern Europe*, 23 April 1993, p. 4).

According to *Business Central Europe* (November 1993, p. 61), voucher distribution began (slowly) in the summer of 1993, allocation depending on length of residence with extra amounts going to 'real Latvians', restitution claimants and political victims. Vouchers can be used to buy enterprises, land and housing. State enterprises have to set aside 25 per cent of their shares for vouchers.

Latvia has sold only forty-two enterprises to date, but the plan is to push 75 per cent of state enterprises into the private sector by 1996 (*Business Central Europe*, June 1994, p. 20). Plans to privatize as many as 300 enterprises by the end of 1994 have proved to be unrealistic, with only six large enterprises sold so far (*Business Central Europe*, December 1994–January 1995, p. 74). The privatization agency's first tender in December 1994 attracted a good deal of foreign interest. A second is under way. Tendering is designed to speed up privatization and attract investors. The agency planned to privatize 250 enterprises in 1995, with a minimum of fifty by public offering. Core investors were to be found in each case, with a minimum of 25 per cent of the shares sold through the Riga stock exchange for vouchers (*Business Central Europe*, March 1995, p. 18).

The delay has been caused by a quarrel between the newly set up privatization agency and government ministries over where responsibility lies and whether to opt for hard currency or voucher sales. Although the aim is to privatize about 200 enterprises a year, only about eighty-five out of a list of 703 have actually changed hands so far (Philippe Legrain, *FT*, 21 June 1994, p. 3).

Initially ministries were permitted to privatize at their own speed the enterprises for which they were responsible. Privatizations were achieved, but went largely to existing management, which brought in financial partners without effective oversight. The law provided that managers could lease their plant and buy it over a set period of years. In 1993 the government decided to restructure a process clearly seen to be failing and set itself the target of privatizing 75 per cent of all state property by 1996. Instead of a decentralized approach based on the ministries two new institutions were established, namely the Privatization Agency (to put into effect the privatizations themselves) and the State Property Fund (to manage the existing state portfolio). Forty-four enterprises were to be put up for tender in November 1994 (*FT*, Survey, 18 November 1994, pp. 29, 31).

According to Adrian Bridge (*The Independent*, 8 June 1993, p. 12), only citizens are allowed to own land.

On 14 January 1994 a British-led consortium took a 49 per cent stake in Lattelekom. This was the first internationally tendered privatization of a state telecommunications company in any country of the former Soviet Union.

The State Property Fund, in business since 1 September 1994, was at that time the residual 'owner' of 1,500 industrial enterprises. Enterprises are handed over to the Privatization Agency (founded on 22 April 1994), which handles the sale. The privatization law of early March 1994 includes an element of employee ownership and tenders involving not only price but also job and investment guarantees. The plan was to put 121 large industrial enterprises up for auction in December 1994. The main phase of the privatization programme was to be completed by 1996, with the state retaining important stakes in certain key industries and enterprises. The small privatization was to be virtually complete by the end of 1994. About 70 per cent of industry is still in state hands, but the agency has started its programme of transferring 75 per cent of state enterprises into private hands over the next three years (*IHT*, Survey, 4 November 1994, p. 12). On 22 December 1994 the Privatization Agency successfully concluded its first international tender involving forty-five enterprises, while the second one (forty-six enterprises) was completed on 27 April 1995. The third, scheduled for September 1995, was to feature forty to fifty enterprises (*IHT*, Survey, 9 June 1995, p. 20). The head of the privatization programme stated that 'By the end of 1996 all of our industrial enterprises, with a few key exceptions, will have been sold to the private sector or put into liquidation' (p. 19).

In mid-1994 the private sector accounted for roughly 55 per cent of the GDP (EBRD 1994: 10). In 1993 state sector employment fell to 50 per cent of total employment and the non-state sector's share of industrial output was 30 per cent. Large privatization is lagging behind other areas of reform; only eighty-five enterprises were privatized by April 1994 out of a total of 698 to be privatized. The law of February 1994 streamlined the process of privatization by creating an independent Privatization Agency and State Property Fund. Methods were to include tenders, auctions and liquidation. Vouchers were to be used for up to 25 per cent of capital and investment funds were to be set up. The government is committed to privatize 75 per cent of state property by the end of 1996. Small privatization is, by contrast, advanced, with two-thirds of enterprises transferred by April 1994 (trade and services) (EBRD 1994: 28). Voucher privatization began in January 1995. Plans were put forward to sell off fifty enterprises during 1995 using vouchers (EBRD 1995: 60).

The deadline for applying for vouchers was extended from the end of 1994 to the end of April 1995. Latvia is now seeking to attract investors both from within and without the country, using auction and international tender, and employing a system requiring investments to be half in vouchers and half in cash. The first international tender was arranged in December 1994 and bids were received for forty-five enterprises. A second offering, of fifteen to thirty enterprises, was to take place in March 1995. The Privatization Agency aimed to sell seventy enterprises through the new stock market by the end of 1995 (*The Baltic Observer*, 23 February–1 March 1995, p. 15). The Riga stock exchange was formally opened on 25 July 1995.

Foreign trade

Trade has been largely freed of quantitative restrictions. There are export taxes on raw materials, precious metals and antiques, but there are few quantitative restrictions (EBRD 1994: 29, 109). A free-trade agreement with the EU came into effect in January 1995. Latvia benefited from a transitional period of four years for industrial products, while the EU was to open its market immediately. Trade in 'sensitive' products (including agricultural goods and textiles) was to be ruled by specific provisions (EBRD 1995: 60).

In 1993 the CIS accounted for 46 per cent of exports (Russia alone 28 per cent) and 38 per cent of imports (Russia 28 per cent) (United Nations Economic Commission for Europe 1994: 107).

The EU now accounts for over 31 per cent of exports (virtually zero in 1991) and 40 per cent of imports. The free-trade agreement signed by Latvia and the EU on 18 July 1994 was to take effect at the beginning of 1995. All EU tariffs and quotas on Latvian goods were to be removed, with the exception of those on such 'sensitive' items as steel and textiles. Latvia was to be allowed to maintain various tariffs for a four-year transitional period (*IHT*, Survey, 4 November 1994, p. 13).

Free-trade agreements have been signed with the EFTA countries (Deutsche Bank, *Focus: Eastern Europe*, 23 April 1993, no. 75, p. 6).

Foreign investment

Foreigners were only able to lease land for up to ninety-nine years (*IHT*, Survey, 4 November 1994, p. 12). But on 24 November 1994 new legislation was passed by parliament allowing foreign enterprises from countries that have bilateral agreements with Latvia on investment protection and promotion to purchase the land on which the enterprises are situated (*The Baltic Observer*, 1–7 December 1994, p. 2).

Foreign investment to date has been negligible (Deutsche Bank, *Focus: Eastern Europe*, 23 April 1993, no. 75, p. 4). Foreign direct investment totalled $112 million by June 1994 (1995, no. 126, p. 19).

By mid-1993 Latvia had attracted a little over $120 million (*Business Central Europe*, April 1994, p. 46).

Only $60 million was invested in 1993 (Philippe Legrain, *FT*, 21 June 1994, p. 3).

Foreign direct investment amounted to $103 million in the period 1990–93 (EBRD 1994: 123). Foreigners may not own land, but are able to lease land for up to ninety-nine years (p. 126).

At the end of March 1995 total direct foreign investment had reached $371 million (*Business Europa*, July–August 1995, p. 37).

Net foreign direct investment was $43 million in 1992, $39 million in 1993 and $187 million in 1994 (United Nations Economic Commission for Europe 1995: 151).

Agriculture

In line with the 24 November 1994 changes in the law on land reform in cities, the law on rural land reform was amended on 8 December 1994. Land can be sold to Latvian citizens, state and municipal institutions, and legal persons and enterprises that are registered in Latvia and in which more than half the registered capital is owned by Latvian citizens. Land may also be sold to Latvian-registered foreign businesses from countries with which Latvia has concluded agreements on the promotion and protection of foreign investments (*The Baltic Observer*, 15–21 December 1994, p. 2).

Economic performance

GDP growth was positive in 1994. The annual inflation rate reached a peak not far short of 1,000 per cent in 1992, but considerable progress has been made since then (see Table 11.1).

The economy made a return to growth in mid-1994 (*IHT*, Survey, 4 November 1994, p. 11).

Many firms have drastically reduced work hours or laid employees off under the euphemism 'unpaid vacation' (which enables employers to avoid paying severance benefits). According to one report, if this hidden unemployment is included the real unemployment rate is closer to 20 per cent. But that may be an exaggeration, because many of the people who have joined the 'hidden unemployed' have managed to find 'hidden employment' (*The Baltic Observer*, 9–15 March 1995, p. 14).

Table 11.1 Latvia: selected economic indicators

Economic indicator	*1990*	*1991*	*1992*	*1993*	*1994*
Rate of growth of GDP (%)	2.9	−8.3	−34.9	−14.9	2.0
Rate of growth of industrial output (%)	−0.2	−0.7	−34.8	−38.1	−4.1
Rate of growth of agricultural output (%)	−10.2	−3.9	−15.7	−22.4	−20.0
Inflation rate (%)	10.5	124.4	951.2	109.1	35.7
Net foreign debt ($ billion)			−0.1	−0.1	−0.1
Budget surplus or deficit (% GDP)	2.0	6.0	0.0	1.0	−1.7
Current account ($ billion)			0.021	0.220	−0.119
Unemployment (end of year, %)	0.0	0.1	2.1	5.8	6.5

Sources: Various issues of United Nations Economic Commission for Europe, *Economic Survey of Europe*; United Nations, *World Economic and Social Survey*; IMF, *World Economic Outlook*; Deutsche Bank, *Focus: Eastern Europe; Economics of Transition, Business Central Europe* and *The Baltic Observer*; EBRD (1994: 162; 1995: 39)

12

LITHUANIA

POLITICS

Citizenship

Henn-Juri Uibopuu (*The World Today*, June 1992, pp. 109–11) provides the following information. The 1923 census split the population into 84 per cent Lithuanians (still almost 80 per cent today), 7.6 per cent Jews, 3.2 per cent Poles, 2.5 per cent Russians (8 per cent in 1989), 1.4 per cent Germans and 0.7 per cent Latvians.

In 1989 79.6 per cent of the 3.7 million population were Lithuanians, 9.4 per cent were Russians and 7.0 per cent were Poles (Gwiazda 1994: 77). Around 34 per cent of Russians have mastered the Lithuanian language (p. 79).

In 1993 the split was 80.3 per cent Lithuanians, 9.1 per cent Russians, 7.4 per cent Poles and 3.2 per cent 'other' (*Business Central Europe*, April 1994, p. 82).

The 10 December 1991 citizenship law stipulated that applicants have to prove ten years' lawful residence and take an oral and written language test. But all residents of the former Soviet republic were given citizenship (*Newsbrief*, 1993, vol. 13, no. 9, p. 65).

Citizenship also requires the signing of an oath of loyalty (Gwiazda 1994: 79).

Political developments

14 February 1993. Algirdas Brazauskas wins the presidential election with 60 per cent of the vote. His campaign platform included the acceleration of privatization and a warm welcome to private investment. During the campaign Brazauskas was critical of the previous government's agrarian policy, which stressed the return of land to the previous owners or their heirs (see below). He argued that the return of land should not be automatic and stressed compensation instead. The tax system should be used to penalize those who leave land idle or use it poorly. There should be a ceiling on the profits of monopolistic food producers such as dairies and meat packers.

22 August 1993. Russia breaks off talks over troop withdrawals and says that the remaining 2,500 (out of the original 22,000) will not now leave by the 31 August 1993 deadline. Lithuania has submitted a claim for compensation for the military occupation. (In fact the troops did leave on schedule.)

4–8 September 1993. The Pope visits Lithuania, the first visit to any of the republics of the former Soviet Union.

4 January 1994. Lithuania applies to join Nato.

27 January 1994. Lithuania becomes the first country of the former Soviet Union to sign a Partnership for Peace agreement with Nato.

26 March 1995. In local elections 1,488 seats were contested. The turnout was only 42.4 per cent. There was a swing to the right. The results were as follows: Conservative Party (Homeland Union), 29.1 per cent of the vote and 426 seats; Christian Democratic Party (partner of the Conservative Party) 16.9 per cent of the vote and 247 seats; Lithuanian Democratic Labour Party, 19.9 per cent of the vote and 291 seats.

12 April 1995. Lithuania and the EU initial an associate membership agreement (it was signed on 12 June 1995; as part of the agreement Lithuania promised to lift the ban on the sale of land to foreigners).

5 July 1995. Economics Minister Aleksandras Vasiliauskas is dismissed. The prime minister was unhappy at the slow pace of development of a law on the second stage of privatization, which was not passed until 4 July (*The Baltic Observer*, 13–19 July 1995, p. 3).

THE ECONOMY

The economic background

The Ignalina nuclear plant supplies 85 per cent of Lithuania's electricity (*FT*, 10 November 1993, p. 12).

Financial policy

The fight against inflation has been a key feature of government policy. Hence the concern for budgetary control. The 1995 budget was passed by parliament on 14 December 1994. The budget deficit was to be 1.9 per cent of GDP (*Business Europa*, February–March 1995, p. 39).

The coupon (talonas) was introduced alongside the rouble in April 1992, but it became the only legal tender on 1 October 1992 (United Nations Economic Commission for Europe 1993: 170). It was then allowed to float. The litas was introduced on 25 June 1993; the talonas was to be withdrawn entirely by 20 July.

In April 1994 Lithuania switched from a managed float to a currency board, with the litas pegged by law to the US dollar (EBRD 1995: 7).

A currency board-like system was installed on 1 April 1994; the litas must be fully backed by foreign reserve currencies and gold and is freely convertible at a fixed rate of four litai per US dollar (Steve Hanke, *FT*, 5 May 1994, p. 24; see also *Business Central Europe*, May 1994, p. 19). The amount of lits in circulation is tied to the amount of foreign currency and gold reserves in the Bank of Lithuania. Only three other countries in the world have currency board arrangements, namely Argentina, Estonia and Hong Kong (*The Baltic Observer*, 19–25 May 1994, p. 11).

In addition to current account operations, capital account transactions have also been largely decontrolled (United Nations Economic Commission for Europe 1994: 121). There is full current account and (virtually) capital account convertibility (EBRD 1994: 109).

Prices

The prices of food, consumer and industrial goods were fully liberalized during 1991–92. Restrictions remain on energy and housing (EBRD 1994: 31).

Privatization

The Vilnius stock exchange opened on 14 September 1993.

The mass privatization programme has resulted in the sale of 1,586 state enterprises since 1991. A bankruptcy law had been introduced a year earlier, but no actual bankruptcies have yet been reported (Matthew Kaminski, *FT*, 15 September 1993, p. 34).

According to *Business Central Europe* (November 1993, p. 61), of the 5,582 enterprises included in the first wave begun in February 1991, 3,672 had been privatized by July 1993. Most were sold via bidding rounds using vouchers. Voucher holders have to pay the state 5 per cent of the vouchers' nominal value. Vouchers can be used to pay off outstanding housing loans or sold back to the state. By December 1993 Lithuania had denationalized 69 per cent of designated state enterprises, 86 per cent of farm properties and 97 per cent of all apartments (*Business Central Europe*, April 1994, p. 82). (According to Andrew Baldwin, by the end of March 1994 89 per cent of the 2,300 enterprises had been sold off by share subscription plus 87 per cent of the 2,700 enterprises in the programme designated for sale by auction. Moreover, 99 per cent of farm enterprises had been privatized: letter to *Business Central Europe*, May 1994, p. 4.) Since early 1991 Lithuania has sold an astounding 90 per cent of the assets registered in its initial programme, about 5,303 enterprises and over 5,000 flats (*Business Central Europe*, March 1995, p. 18).

Employees are offered first rights to stock, up to 30 per cent of the total; up to 70 per cent is then sold at auction, with the remaining percentages being auctioned at a later date; vouchers are used instead of money. The voucher privatization programme was scheduled for completion by the end of 1994 (*Business Europa*, February–March 1994, p. 28).

Almost 97 per cent of apartments and houses have been privatized. Of the 2,300 commercial and industrial enterprises to be sold by subscriptions for shares, 88 per cent have been privatized. Of the 2,700 to be privatized by auction, 88 per cent have been sold, representing 77 per cent of the state capital invested in them (*The Baltic Observer*, 24 February–2 March 1994, p. 9).

On 10 February 1994 President Brazauskas complained that 'almost half of all vouchers have yet to be used' (*The Baltic Observer*, 3–9 March 1994, p. 9). About 30 per cent of all the vouchers received by citizens have not been used so far. The 1 July 1994 deadline for the use of vouchers has been extended to the end of the year. Despite the relatively rapid progress, only 40 per cent of all state assets have been privatized to date (*The Baltic Observer*, 21–27 April 1994, p. 12). Over 80 per cent of large industry has been privatized and close to 60 per cent of workers are now in the private sector (*The Baltic Observer*, 23 February–1 March 1995, p. 15). By the end of 1994 Lithuania had privatized over 95 per cent of all domestic apartments, 85 per cent of all agricultural land and assets, and around 83 per cent of all state enterprises that were put under the privatization programme. Despite the slower rate at which larger enterprises have been privatized and the relative lack of large new businesses, over half GDP is now attributable to the private sector. Most privatization has been done under the 1991 law, which involved the distribution of free vouchers to the whole population (exchangeable for housing, land or shares). Certain groups, such as employees and managers, were given privileges in buying shares (workers have the right to buy up to 51 per cent of an enterprise), but these are slowly being eliminated. By the end of 1994, of the 114 enterprises originally advertised on the privatization list, only three had attracted foreign investors and thirty-nine had been sold by tender to Lithuanian investors. There has been criticism that the process of privatization has not been transparent enough and that some shady deals have been done (power resides in the ministries). In January 1995 the government announced that the voucher scheme was officially to end in July 1995. The draft law drawn up in the summer of 1994 originally recommended that two new organizations should be established, a state property fund (to look after state enterprises until they came to be sold) and a privatization agency (which would sell them). The split between ownership and sale was recommended mainly because ministries and municipalities are often reluctant to relinquish control. But as the draft law progressed the two new organizations were replaced by a co-ordinating body controlled by the ministries. The exact shape of future privatization was not certain at the time of writing, but there was likely to be greater encouragement of foreign investment, the introduction of a number of new methods of privatization and flexible rules for tenders (e.g. stress on investment plans) (*The Baltic Observer*, 2–8 March 1995, p. 8). A law on the second stage of privatization was not passed until 4 July 1995, months behind schedule. Many large enterprises have yet to pass into private hands (*The Baltic Observer*, 13–19 July 1995, p. 3). The second stage was to start in September 1995, involving the sale of the remaining shares for cash. A new Privatization Agency was to be set up. By August 1995 83 per cent of all 'objects' destined for privatization had been denationalized. In 1991 10.5 billion vouchers were distributed for the privatization of 9,418 enterprises; by August 1995 6,670 enterprises had been privatized. But some 1 billion vouchers remained unused by the 1 July 1995 deadline. With some exceptions (e.g. their continued use for the purchase of flats and garden plots) the vouchers were annulled, even though the government had originally pledged to exchange them for government bonds. As of August 1995 20 per cent of all privatized property belonged to investment funds, while 30 per cent of former state property had gone to employees of the privatized enterprises on privileged terms. Another 36 per cent was acquired by 'separate natural and juridical persons'. Ten enterprises have been subjected to bids for hard currency, but only four of them have been bought by foreign bidders (*The Baltic Observer*, 17–23 August 1995, p. 5). The actual sale of state property was to begin at the start of 1996 (*The Baltic Observer*, 14–20 September 1995, p. 6).

By January 1995 about 78 per cent of all state enterprises by number and 44 per cent in terms of capital assets had been privatized (United Nations Economic Commission for Europe 1995: 215). As of 30 June 1995 about 5,620 of the country's 6,700 state enterprises marked for privatization had been sold (*Transition*, 1995, vol. 6, nos 7–8, p. 19). Over half the work force is now employed in the private sector (*Business Central Europe*, June 1994, p. 19). More than two-thirds of enterprises slated for sale have been privatized and more than half the work force is now in the private sector (Philippe Legrain, *FT*, 21 June 1994, p. 3).

In mid-1994 the private sector accounted for roughly 50 per cent of GDP (EBRD 1994: 10). Originally only voucher (large) privatization had been envisaged, but some cash auction sales have also taken place. Previous preferences for employees and management (up to 50 per cent of shares reserved) are being eliminated. By the end of 1993 1,915 enterprises had been privatized out of 2,203 in the privatization programme and a total of some 5,500 state enterprises. There has been substantial progress in the sale of small enterprises. The deadline for applications from former landowners was March 1994 (p. 10). Privatization of the largest state enterprises was to accelerate in 1995 and the privatization of utilities was to begin (EBRD 1995: 60).

Foreign trade

Foreign trade has been largely freed of non-tariff restrictions (EBRD 1994: 31). There have been no import quotas since October 1993 except for health and safety reasons. The export licensing system was abolished in July 1993, but there are some export taxes on raw materials and foodstuffs and some quantitative restrictions (p. 109). A free-trade agreement with the EU came into effect in January 1995. Lithuania was to benefit from a transition period of four years for industrial products, while the EU was to open its market immediately to most Lithuanian products. Trade in 'sensitive' products (including agricultural goods and textiles) was to be ruled by specific provisions (EBRD 1995: 60).

In 1993 the CIS accounted for 63 per cent of exports and 84 per cent of imports (especially energy and raw materials) (United Nations Economic Commission for Europe 1994: 108).

In 1994 26.4 per cent of imports came from the EU, of which 13.8 percentage points came from Germany (*The Baltic Observer*, 9–15 March 1995, p. 15).

On 13 February 1993 the government announced that Russia had agreed to take roubles as payment for a backlog of energy debts, but that from 1 March 1993 hard currency would be used in settlements (Leyla Boulton and Chrystia Freeland, *FT*, 20 February 1993, p. 2).

Parliament now requires state enterprises to sell 25 per cent of their export earnings to the state (Leyla Boulton, *FT*, 16 February 1993, p. 3).

Foreign investment

By the beginning of 1994 some $200 million had been attracted, $76.5 million in 1993 alone; there are generous tax holidays (*Business Central Europe*, April 1994, pp. 46, 82).

Official figures put the total amount of committed foreign investment at $200 million. The corporate profit tax is reduced for the first five years and there is no tax on money taken out of the country (*The Baltic Observer*, 13–19 October 1994, p. 6). Foreign countries invested $112 million between 1 January 1987 and 27 July 1995. Some $25 million was invested in 1993 and $31.75 million was invested during the first seven months of 1995 (*The Baltic Observer*, 4–10 August 1994, p. 9). More than $120 million has been invested in Lithuania since 1987 (*The Baltic Observer*, 10–16 November 1994, p. 12). The World Bank estimates that foreign investment amounts to a mere $16 million (*The Baltic Observer*, 2–8 March 1995, p. 8).

Foreign direct investment amounted to $310 million at the end of 1994 (Deutsche Bank, *Focus: Eastern Europe*, 1995, no. 140, p. 6).

Net foreign direct investment was $10 million in 1992, $31 million in 1993 and $33 million in January–September 1994 (United Nations Economic Commission for Europe 1995: 151).

Foreign direct investment amounted to $45 million in the period 1990–93 (EBRD 1994: 123). Joint ventures and firms with foreign capital may only lease land and buildings (for up to ninety-nine years) necessary to carry out business (p. 30). On 22 February 1995 parliament began consideration of a constitutional amendment that would allow foreign citizens to buy land (*The Baltic Observer*, 2–8 March 1995, p. 16). Lithuania is the only post-communist state in Central and Eastern Europe which prevents foreign companies or individuals from owning land. There are mixed feelings within the country over whether to allow foreigners to acquire property, but there is pressure from the EU to permit foreign firms to acquire immovable property together with the land on which it stands (*The Baltic Observer*, 16–22 March 1995, p. 16).

A new law on land went into effect in July 1994. It permits the transfer of land among Lithuanian citizens, but foreign ownership of land is not allowed (EBRD 1995: 60).

On 28 June 1995 parliament passed a law allowing the creation of Free Economic Zones, where companies will be subject to tax and customs concessions (*The Baltic Observer*, 6–12 July 1995, p. 10).

Agriculture

Reform started in 1989 when the process of re-establishing individual farms began. Between the summer of 1989 and the autumn of 1990 around 6,000 private farms acquired land use rights. The main laws on restructuring the agricultural sector were adopted during the period 1990–92. Citizens of Lithuania who owned property, including land, before 1940 (or their heirs) were able to claim physical or monetary restitution. The maximum size of land holding was set at 80 ha. In 1991 94,000 ha of land were given to 5,900 farmers, an average area per farmer of 16 ha. The privatization of agricultural assets was carried out by issuing vouchers. The following forms of agricultural enterprises resulted: individual (private) farms; partnerships (general and limited) based on joining privately owned land; joint stock companies (open and closed); state enterprises in which property belongs to the state (local municipality); state stock companies, joining state and private property. The share of agricultural output produced by individual properties has increased significantly, but even so in 1991 large-scale farms accounted for 79 per cent of grain, 95 per cent of sugar beet, 96 per cent of flax, 67 per cent of meat and 54 per cent of milk (Kazlauskiene 1992: 1174–5).

Agriculture was disrupted by the chosen methods of privatization and this featured strongly in the presidential campaign (see above). The collectives began to be dismantled by 'outside' officials and there were many claims to property (mostly from people now living in the towns).

Matthew Kaminski (*FT*, 18 August 1993, p. 26) puts part of the blame for falling output on the small size of many plots. The 1,058 collectives were quickly split up into 413,000 plots of no more than 3 ha each. The average size of farm fell to 9 ha in the summer of 1993. Parliament then prohibited the division of farmland below 20 ha.

Collective farming has passed into the history books, with over 80 per cent of the unindexed (initial) value of enterprises in agriculture privatized to date (*The Baltic Observer*, 24 February–2 March 1994, p. 9). By the end of 1994 Lithuania had privatized 85 per cent of all agricutural land and assets (*The Baltic Observer*, 2–8 March 1995, p. 8).

At the end of 1993 individual private farmers, partnerships and households held 80 per cent of agricultural land (EBRD 1994: 30).

The government aims to maintain control of 80 per cent of the country's (valuable) forests. Pre-war owners can claim only up to 25 ha of forest land (*Business Europa*, February–March 1994, p. 28).

Farm subsidies were cancelled in November 1992, but were reintroduced on 10 February 1995 for cattle and milk purchases (*The Baltic Observer*, 23 February–1 March 1995, p. 10).

Economic performance

GDP growth was positive in 1994. The annual inflation rate reached a peak of over 1,000 per cent in 1992, but considerable progress has been made since then (see Table 12.1).

If job seekers who do not qualify for benefit are included, the unemployment rate rises from 1.9 per cent to 4.8 per cent. There is also hidden unemployment. Many firms have drastically reduced work hours or laid employees off under the euphemism 'unpaid vacation' (which enables employers to avoid paying severance benefits) (*The Baltic Observer*, 9–15 March 1995, p. 14).

Table 12.1 Lithuania: selected economic indicators

Economic indicator	*1990*	*1991*	*1992*	*1993*	*1994*
Rate of growth of GDP (%)	−5.0	−13.1	−39.3	−23.7	1.7
Rate of growth of industrial output (%)	−2.8	−3.5	−30.0	−34.2	2.0
Rate of growth of agricultural output (%)	−9.0	−4.6	−23.6	−8.0	22.0
Inflation rate (%)	8.4	224.7	1,020.5	410.4	72.2
Net foreign debt ($ billion)				−0.2	
Budget surplus or deficit (% GDP)	−4.5	5.0	0.5	2.4	1.5
Current account ($ billion)			0.322	−0.083	−0.107
Unemployment (end of year, %)	0.0	0.3	1.0	2.5	4.2

Sources: Various issues of United Nations Economic Commission for Europe, *Economic Survey of Europe*; United Nations, *World Economic and Social Survey*; IMF, *World Economic Outlook*; Deutsche Bank, *Focus: Eastern Europe*; *Economics of Transition*, *Business Central Europe* and *The Baltic Observer*; EBRD (1994: 163; 1995: 40)

13

MOLDOVA

POLITICS

The political background

In 1992 ethnic Russians constituted 13 per cent of the population (*The Economist*, 10 July 1993, p. 33).

Hella Pick (*The Guardian*, 21 September 1993, p. 22) says that, although the Communist Party was banned, the Government of National Accord that emerged after the 1990 election was dominated by former members of the Communist Party.

There is now an OSCE mission in the Dniestre region. The self-proclaimed Republic of Transdniestria covers about 12 per cent of Moldova. The 600,000 population of the former is divided between Moldovans (40 per cent), Ukrainians (28 per cent), Russians (26 per cent) and miscellaneous (6 per cent) (*EEN*, 1995, vol. 9, no. 12, p. 5).

Political developments

11 May 1993. Peace talks begin with leaders of the Dniestre region.

EEN (2 February 1993, vol. 7, no. 3, pp. 7–8) argued that President Mircea Snegur had accumulated almost absolute power.

27 February 1994. In the general election parties favouring union with Romania are decisively rejected (the Christian Democratic Popular Front, with 7.53 per cent of the vote, and the Bloc of Peasants and Intellectuals, with 9.21 per cent; these parties, with only twenty of the 104 seats in parliament, also claimed that the IMF-approved economic reform programme would now be under threat). The largest percentage of the vote (43.13 per cent of the vote and fifty-seven seats) went to the Agrarian Democratic Party, led by Andrei Sangheli (who subsequently became prime minister) and Petru Luchinsky. (The party advocates improved relations with Russia and making concessions to the Dniestre region.) The Socialist Bloc (which favours close links with Russia and the CIS) came second, with

22 per cent of the vote and twenty-eight seats. The Dniestre region largely boycotted the election (and the subsequent plebiscite), but the turnout was still about 75 per cent.

6 March 1994. The question asked in the plebiscite was whether the people supported 'an independent Moldova within its 1990 borders, which maintains neutrality, established ties with other nations and provides equal rights for all citizens'. The turnout was 65 per cent and the 'yes' vote was over 90 per cent.

1 April 1994. Parliament suspends the 1989 language law, which made Romanian the official language (a compulsory test would have been necessary for state employment). Romanians make up 65 per cent of the population (*IHT*, 2 April 1994, p. 2).

8 April 1994. Parliament ratifies the agreements on participation in the CIS and CIS economic union.

10 August 1994. Russian and Moldovan negotiators come to a preliminary agreement on the withdrawal, over a three-year period, of the 15,000 Russian troops from the Dniestre region (whose representatives walked out of the talks). (There was formal approval on 21 October.) (Dniestre plans a currency reform to be introduced on 1 September 1994, in which coupons will replace stamped Soviet rouble notes: *IHT*, 11 August 1994, p. 9.)

27 August 1994. The new constitution goes into effect. The official language is Moldovan and autonomy is granted to the Dniestre and Gagauz regions.

5 March 1995. A local referendum to determine the borders of the Gagauz region is held in the areas where the Gagauz population is concentrated.

In December 1994 the Moldovan parliament adopted a law granting the Gagauz region a special status that allows for its secession from Moldova in the event of a change in the republic's legal status, such as reunification with Romania. The Gagauz region was to have three official langauages (Gagauz, Moldovan and Russian) and its own anthem, emblem and flag (*CDSP*, 1995, vol. XLVII, no. 16).

The law adopted by the Moldovan parliament on 23 December 1994 granted the Gagauzians wide authority for local self-administration. The Gagauzians, Orthodox Christians of Turkic origin, 'created a republic in August 1990, defending its notional borders with pitchforks. They elected a parliament in October 1990 and a president in December 1991.' Moldova is home to over 153,000, of whom 135,000 are settled in the southern districts (*EEN*, 1995, vol. 9, no. 10, p. 7).

26 March 1995. The Dniestre region holds an unauthorized referendum on preventing the withdrawal of Russia's Fourteenth Army (under General Lebed). There is an overwhelming 91.3 per cent vote to retain the army. Local elections are also held.

16 April 1995. Ethnic Russians and Ukrainians in the Dniestre region boycott official local elections.

5 July 1995. An agreement is reached to use the Moldovan currency (the leu) in the Dniestre region. The Dniestrian coupon is to remain in circulation until macroeconomic reform has been carried out in the region and financial legislation conforms to Moldovan law (*EEN*, 1995, vol. 9, no. 15, p. 6).

15 July 1995. The Party of Revival and Reconciliation in Moldova is established, to be led by President Mircea Snegur. In June he resigned from the ruling Agrarian Democratic Party of Moldova. The split was sparked by the president's proposal to amend the July 1994 constitution (which refers to the language as Moldovan and the people as Moldovans) in order to make Romanian the official state language (*EEN*, 1995, vol. 9, no. 15, p. 5). (Thirteen MPs have defected to the Party of Revival and Reconciliation in Moldova from the Agrarian Democratic Party: *EEN*, 1995, vol. 9, no. 18, p. 8.)

THE ECONOMY

The economic system

EEN (2 February 1993, vol. 7, no. 3, pp. 7–8) argued that economic reforms were minimal. But *The Banker* (March 1993, p. 47) saw some progress. Moldova had gone some way towards creating the legal and institutional infrastructure of a market economy. Privatization laws had been passed and privatization was being extended to agriculture. A free-trade zone had been established with Romania (a committee also liaises between the two parliaments).

Financial reform

The IMF (*World Economic Outlook*, May 1993, p. 67) reported that coupons (used for cash payments) circulated alongside the rouble after June 1992. The coupon became the sole domestically accepted currency in July 1993. Moldova's own currency, the leu, was introduced on 29 November 1993.

The leu is traded on the currency exchange and has been made convertible for residents (Deutsche Bank, *Focus: Eastern Europe*, 1994, no. 113, p. 7).

The exchange rate is now largely market-determined, with thrice-weekly currency auctions. The Dniestre region introduced a separate currency in late August 1994. Most payments and transfers for current transactions and some capital transfers are now free of controls. There has been a reduction in the surrender requirement; repatriation of export earnings is required, but only 35 per cent is compulsorily sold on the domestic interbank market (EBRD 1994: 31).

Moldova has agreed with the IMF to a stabilization programme (e.g. a budget deficit of no more than 3.5 per cent of GDP in 1994), the complete liberalization of consumer goods prices by July 1994, trade liberalization and accelerated privatization (*CDSP*, 1993, vol. XLV, no. 46, p. 30).

Moldova and Kyrgyzstan have implemented successful stabilization programmes, reducing monthly inflation to 2–5 per cent in May–June 1994 in the wake of tough fiscal and credit adjustments over the previous six months (Kasper Bartholdy, *Economics of Transition*, 1994, vol. 2, no. 3, p. 405).

Moldova 'has surprisingly emerged as one of the economic success stories of the former Soviet Union'. On 14 March 1995 a memorandum of intent was signed by the central bank and the IMF, with Moldova pledging to keep the budget deficit below 3.5 per cent of GDP and annual inflation down to 10 per cent in 1995. As a result of the austerity programme launched in 1994 the monthly inflation rate was 2.3 per cent in February 1995 (Chrystia Freeland, *FT*, 15 March 1995, p. 3).

A bankruptcy law was adopted in 1992, but was hardly used in 1993 (EBRD 1994: 30).

Prices

In January 1992 most consumer goods prices were liberalized. The exceptions were the prices of bread and dairy products, some transport prices and utility charges. Initially indirect price control remained through heavy producer regulation and strict retail margin controls, but 1993 saw some liberalization and an increase in milk prices to 75 per cent of production costs (EBRD 1994: 31).

Moscow News (12 November 1993, p. 81) talked of the first steps having been taken towards free prices, e.g. most jewellery and some goods made of natural fur and leather. The mark-up on the prices of twenty-five types of socially important goods (such as meat, dairy products, bread, fruit and vegetables and children's clothing and shoes) is limited to 20 per cent of the wholesale price.

Privatization

Only housing and agriculture have been partly privatized to date. But a privatization law has been passed recently by parliament. A third of state property is to be privatized by issuing vouchers to citizens (allocation depending on years of work), who have two years to exchange them for shares in the 1,600 enterprises (*Business Central Europe*, September 1993, p. 74; November 1993, p. 60). Jill Barshay (*FT*, 1 March 1993, p. 3) said that the aim was to privatize one-third of state property by the end of 1994.

Vouchers are to be used in the privatization of 1,200 enterprises, accounting for 45 per cent of the total value of state property (*Moscow News*, 24 September 1993, p. 7).

Three unfinished construction projects were auctioned off on 11 September 1993, launching the privatization drive (*IHT*, 13 September 1993, p. 11). The privatization of small enterprises was to be completed by July 1994 (*CDSP*, 1993, vol. XLV, no. 46, p. 30). *Business Europa* (February–March 1994, p. 44) adds the following: (1) most shops and small businesses were to be sold for vouchers at auction, with very few enterprises sold for cash; (2) voucher holders would be allowed to combine their vouchers in investment funds; (3) foreigners would be allowed to invest post-privatization; (4) the first auctions were held in October 1993.

In mid-1994 the private sector accounted for roughly 20 per cent of GDP (EBRD 1994: 10). The private sector is thought to account for 10–25 per cent of GDP, including an allowance for informal sector activity. The March 1993 large privatization plan envisaged the privatization within two years of about 1,600 enterprises (accounting for 40–45 per cent of state assets), mostly through the distribution of ownership vouchers to the whole population. The programme also includes 124 medium-sized and large enterprises under the control of the Ministry of Privatization and State Property. Some state corporations are to remain in state ownership, including some utilities, scientific institutes and large food-processing companies. The sale to private entities of small units began in September 1993 with the first, relatively modest auctions. No property restitution for pre-communism owners has taken place (p. 30). The target of privatizing 35 per cent of the total value of state-owned assets by the end of 1994 was not achieved. But by then four public auctions had been organized to privatize around 700 medium-sized to large state enterprises, 408 of which passed into private hands. Further small-scale privatization had been undertaken (EBRD 1995: 61).

The privatization plan, involving the auctioning of 1,600 enterprises, got under way in the summer of 1994 (*Business Europa*, November–December 1994, p. 43).

Foreign trade

The state monopoly on foreign trade was abolished in 1992. There are few import licences, but there are licensing requirements for seventy-seven export categories and some export quotas (EBRD 1994: 31, 111). In August 1994 Moldova signed a partnership and co-operation agreement with the EU.

Foreign aid

IMF credits have been arranged, e.g. in September and October 1993 (see 'Financial reform' above).

Agriculture

Agricultural privatization is under way (but not subject to the voucher scheme), with the transfer of shares in some state and collective farms to present and former farm employees. At least 10 per cent of state holdings in agriculture were transferred to private owners in 1992 and further sales took place in 1993. The intention is to privatize nearly two-thirds of farm assets. The privatization of agro-processing enterprises is to involve 50 per cent share distribution to suppliers, 20 per cent to employees and 30 per cent to the Ministry of Privatization (EBRD 1994: 30). Since December 1994 it has been possible to sell land to domestic investors and to use land as collateral (EBRD 1995: 61).

At the end of 1992 there were 500,000 private farms, with an average size of 3 ha; they accounted for 60 per cent of total agricultural land (United Nations Economic Commission for Europe 1993: 206).

As of 1 April 1993 there were about 500,000 private farms, with an average size of 3 ha. Almost 40 per cent of the collective and state farms and inter-farm and other enterprises and organizations had been re-registered by the start of 1993. The collectives of 94 per cent of the enterprises decided to retain their current status, while the rest were transformed into lease-based enterprises, joint stock companies, co-operatives or other arrangements (*CDSP*, 1993, vol. XLV, no. 21, p. 20).

Economic performance

Table 13.1 shows a pretty dismal scene, although some progress has been made on the inflation front. Agricultural output grew by 3 per cent in 1993.

Table 13.1 Moldova: selected economic indicators

Economic indicator	*1990*	*1991*	*1992*	*1993*	*1994*
Rate of growth of GDP (%)	−1.5	−11.9	−29.0	−8.7	−22.1
Rate of growth of industrial output (%)	3.2	−11.1	−27.1	−10.0	−29.9
Rate of growth of agricultural output (%)	−12.8	−10.0	−16.0	7.0	−28.0
Inflation rate (%)	4.2	114.0	1,276	837.0	327.0
Net foreign debt ($ billion)				0.2	0.3
Budget surplus or deficit (% GDP)	3.0	0.0	−23.4	−8.8	−8.0
Current account ($ billion)		−0.476	−0.039	−0.182	−0.180
Unemployment (end of year, %)	0.0	0.0	0.7	0.7	1.0

Sources: Various issues of United Nations Economic Commission for Europe, *Economic Survey of Europe*; United Nations, *World Economic and Social Survey*; IMF, *World Economic Outlook*; Deutsche Bank, *Focus: Eastern Europe*; *Economics of Transition* and *Business Central Europe*; EBRD (1994: 164; 1995: 41)

14

TAJIKISTAN

POLITICS

The political background

In 1989 the ethnic composition of the population was as follows: Tajiks 58.8 per cent; Uzbeks 22.9 per cent; Russians and Ukrainians 10.4 per cent; and others 7.9 per cent (*Economic Bulletin for Asia and the Pacific*, 1991, vol. XLII, nos 1 and 2, p. 2). In 1992 Tajiks accounted for 58.8 per cent of the population, Uzbeks 23 per cent and Russians 11 per cent (FEER, *Asia 1994 Yearbook*, 1994, p. 110). According to incomplete data, 778,500 people have left Tajikistan (*CDSP*, 15 June 1994, vol. XLVI, no. 20, p. 12). The Russian community is now down to about 180,000, from 350,000 in 1991 (Anthony Hyman, *The World Today*, November 1993, p. 207). In 1991 ethnic Russians accounted for 7 per cent of the population, but most Russian civilians have now cleared out (*The Economist*, 21 May 1994, p. 53).

Around 70 per cent of the state budget comes from Russia, there are 25,000 Russian troops protecting the border with Afghanistan and the defence minister is a Russian general. Forty observers authorized by the UN Security Council in December 1994 were due to arrive in Tajikistan in early 1995 to monitor the cease-fire (Andrew Meier, *IHT*, 3 January 1995, p. 4).

There is now an OSCE mission in Tajikistan.

Political developments

29 July 1993. The government offers the 'rebels' an amnesty to hand in weapons up to 9 September 1993.

7 August 1993. Russia, Kazakhstan, Kyrgyzstan, Tajikistan and Uzbekistan meet in Moscow (the others have helped Tajikistan militarily). (Note that Turkmenistan did not attend the meeting.) They appeal to the UN to mediate with Afghanistan and to send UN observers to the border. Yeltsin appeals for talks between the government of Tajikistan and the opposition.

17 August 1994. Russia, Tajikistan, Turkmenistan and Uzbekistan sign a border security treaty, formalizing the presence of Russian troops in all three Asiatic states. Tajikistan is forced to give shares in its industry in return for Russian loans (Ahmed Rashid, *FEER*, 15 September 1994, p. 17).

7 September 1994. The presidential election (and a referendum on the new constitution), set for 25 September, is postponed until 6 November to allow opposition candidates to take part.

17 September 1994. A temporary cease-fire is arranged (until the election), to come into force when UN observers arrive.

20 October 1994. The first day of the cease-fire (extended for three months on 6 November). Prime Minister Munavarsho Nazriev is killed when his car runs over a landmine.

6 November 1994. Imamali Rakhmonov wins the presidential election. According to official figures, the turnout was 95 per cent and Rakhmonov won 60 per cent of the vote compared with Abdumalik Abulajanov's 35 per cent (Abulajanov is the ambassador to Moscow: Andrew Meier, *IHT*, 3 January 1995, p. 4). There were claims of irregularities in the election, e.g. ballot stuffing and intimidation.

3 January 1995. Six Russian troops are killed in a border clash with guerrillas.

24 February 1995. The People's Unity Party headed by Abdulmalik Abulajanov withdraws from the general election.

26 February 1995. The general election takes place. There are 181 seats in parliament. Ahmed Rashid (*FEER*, 16 March 1995, p. 24) was scathing in his criticism: 'Tajikistan . . . held a farce of an election for a new 181-member parliament. The only candidates allowed to stand were those who supported President Imamali Rakhmonov. The turnout was reported to be 85 per cent, even though Rakhmonov's writ only runs in about half the country. Western countries refused to send observers to the Tajikistan elections, saying they could not be fair. The Islamic opposition . . . refused to take part. The only opposition party allowed to stand – and that too just five seats – was the People's Unity Party led by former prime minister Abdumalik Abulajanov. But it too pulled out of the polls, because of what it called "anti-democratic practices by the Rakhmonov regime".'

7 April 1995. At the start of a major offensive, more than twenty CIS soldiers are killed in a border clash. (By 13 April thirty-five CIS troops had been killed, although opposition forces suffered far greater casualties.)

13 April 1995. Yeltsin promises more military aid to Tajikistan.

14 April 1995. Six more CIS troops are killed.

The war toll

There are a number of estimates of the effects of the civil war by the time it had begun to quieten down around about February 1993: as many as 15,000 people had been killed since May 1992 (*IHT*, 1 April 1993, p. 5); official sources said that at least 20,000 had been killed and 600,000 made homeless since spring 1992 (*The Guardian*, 1 April 1993, p. 9); about 7 per cent of the population, or 350,000 people, had been displaced, about a quarter of them fleeing to Afghanistan (*FT*, 19 February 1993, p. 3). Another source puts the number who died in 1992 at 20,000–50,000 (*The Economist*, 7 August 1993, p. 58).

The conflict has resulted in 50,000 dead and 500,000 homeless people (Ahmed Rashid, *FEER*, 16 September 1993, p. 24). Rashid later talked of more than 30,000 dead (*FEER*, 3 February 1993, p. 16); the civil war since 1992 has claimed 30,000 dead (*FEER*, 16 March 1995, p. 24). Gillian Tett (*FT*, 16 November 1993, p. 3) talked of up to 100,000 dead, as did *The Times* (plus 350,000 homeless) (7 March 1994, p. 17).

A report of early November 1993 talked in terms of 778,500 refugees outside Tajikistan, e.g. 339,000 in Turkmenistan, 144,750 in Russia and 100,000 in Afghanistan (*CDSP*, 1993, vol. XLV, no. 44, p. 44). Around 600,000 live as refugees in Tajikistan while another 95,000 have fled to Afghanistan. There was heavy fighting around the capital Dushanbe in February and March; the Islamic forces say they are in no position to launch a major offensive, but will continue to keep the regime under pressure (Ahmed Rashid, *FEER*, 3 June 1993, p. 24). There are frequent opposition raids across the border with Afghanistan and Russian involvement in support of the government has increased.

Nearly 150,000 Russian-speakers (including ethnic Ukrainians, Germans and Koreans) have left Tajikistan; this is well over a quarter of the pre-independence total and the exodus has led to skill shortages (*Central Asia Newsfile*, February 1993, no. 4, p. 1). Of the 380,000 Russian-speakers who lived in Tajikistan before the troubles began about 300,000 have left, the bulk going to Russia (*CDSP*, June 1993, vol. XLV, no. 22, p. 1). The war has taken perhaps 50,000 lives and forced more than 650,000 to flee. Clan and regional loyalties have played an important role in the fighting (Andrew Meier, *IHT*, 3 January 1995, p. 4).

THE ECONOMY

The economic background

The civil war has caused much economic damage and held back economic reform.

Since only 6 per cent of the land is arable (of which 74 per cent is irrigated), grazing predominates. Tajikistan is dependent on food imports. There are deposits of lead, zinc, wolfram, uranium and gold, but they have yet to be developed. In 1991 industry accounted for 19.6 per cent of national income. There has been some reversal of price liberalization (Deutsche Bank, *Focus: Eastern Europe*, 1993, no. 69, pp. 1–9).

Tajikistan has substantial gold reserves, one of the world's biggest silver deposits, hydro-electric power and commercially exploitable amounts of oil (Jonathan Rugman, *The Guardian*, 6 March 1995, p. 10).

On 4 June 1993 Tajikistan became the last of the republics of the former Soviet Union to join the World Bank (*Business Central Europe*, July–August 1993, p. 45).

The economic system

Movement towards a market system has remained largely on paper; more retail prices remain controlled and subsidized than elsewhere in the CIS (Kaser and Mehrotra 1992: 48–9).

Enterprises still operate under the system of state orders and state instructions to enterprise management (EBRD 1994: 38).

'Tajikistan has reverted to a barter economy, with huge flea markets stretching along the roadsides . . . Corruption is pandemic . . . financial aid from abroad seems likely to be limited, given the slow pace of market reform, as well as qualms about the lack of democracy' (Jonathan Rugman, *The Guardian*, 6 March 1995, p. 10).

Financial policy

On 7 September 1993 Tajikistan agreed (subject to ratification) to remain in the rouble zone (see Chapter 18). The conversion from old to new roubles was completed on 6–8 January 1994, with the aid of a credit from Russia. If Tajikistan meets all the conditions laid down within six months (such as subordination to the Russian central bank, the co-ordination of tax, customs and budget policies and the implementation of economic reforms) the credit need not be repaid (*CDSP*, 1994, vol. XLVI, no. 2, p. 28).

According to *Business Central Europe* (July–August 1994, p. 74), in May 1994 a transitional currency (coupon) replaced the new rouble. But the goal is still monetary union with Russia.

In January 1994 monetary reform was implemented which aimed to introduce the new rouble as the main means of payment. But the supply of new roubles was inadequate to support full conversion along these lines and all deposits remained inconvertible into new roubles. The monetary reform effectively cut the currency in circulation by two-thirds. In response the price level halved in January 1994 and rose only slowly thereafter as new credits became available from Russia (EBRD 1995: 11–12). After the failure to introduce the new Russian rouble as legal tender in 1994 it was planned to introduce an interim Tajik rouble in 1995. But monetary union with Russia remains the ultimate policy goal (p. 65).

Tajikistan introduced its own currency (the Tajik rouble) on 10 May 1995.

'The currency shortage has forced Tajikistan to use barter and IOUs. The introduction of the [new] currency is part of a new economic recovery programme that includes a 250 per cent increase in state-subsidized bread prices next week and is aimed at ensuring the rescheduling of $731 million of foreign debt' (Steve LeVine, *FT*, 10 May 1995, p. 3).

About 40 per cent of the budget is spent on defence (Jonathan Rugman, *The Guardian*, 6 March 1995, p. 10).

Prices

In January 1992 the government lifted price controls on 80 per cent of goods. Further liberalization of prices has reduced the number of goods under price controls to about 2 per cent of the total. Price controls apply mostly to staple consumer goods such as flour and milk (EBRD 1994: 39).

Bread prices were freed on 20 August 1995, with the poor to be compensated for the price rise (*FT*, 23 August 1995, p. 4).[1]

Privatization

Although a law on divestment and privatization became effective on 21 February 1991 and a State Property Committee was created in August that year, virtually all transfers were a leasing to or buy-out by employees. In principle equity not so taken up can be sold to foreigners or offered to the public at auction, but the IMF mission in February 1992 found no actual purchases under these provisions (Kaser and Mehrotra 1992: 50). In mid-1994 the private sector accounted for roughly 15 per cent of GDP (EBRD 1994: 10). At least 10–20 per cent of GDP is generated in the private sector, including informal sector activity. By mid-1994 152 out of a total of 1,304 medium-sized and large enterprises had been privatized in the agriculture, trade, transport and construction sectors. The 1993–95 programme proposes to add seventy-nine such enterprises to the list. There has been no property restitution to pre-communism owners (p. 38). Privatization has stalled since 1993 (EBRD 1995: 65). Only 5 per cent of state enterprises have been privatized (Jonathan Rugman, *The Guardian*, 6 March 1995, p. 10). On 25 August 1995 Tajik radio reported that state property was to be 100 per cent privatized in 1996 (*Transition*, September 1995, p. 23).

Foreign trade

A command system, based on state orders, quotas, export licences and centralized trading, still dominates production and trade (EBRD 1994: 39). There is a 30 per cent export revenue surrender requirement (p. 111).

A December 1994 decree introduced further liberalization of currency restrictions, lifting all capital control restrictions on individuals and allowing foreign exchange accounts to be opened locally (EBRD 1995: 65).

Agriculture

The 15 December 1990 Land Code says that the state retains ownership of land, but usufruct on up to a ten-year lease is allocated by local authorities (Kaser and Mehrotra 1992: 49). (See the comments by Nikonov in Chapter 9 on Kazakhstan.)

By the end of 1992 there were about 100 private farms, with an average size of 10 ha (*CDSP*, 1993, vol. XLV, no. 5, p. 22); they accounted for only 1 per cent of total agricultural land (United Nations Economic Commission for Europe 1993: 206). As of 1 April 1993 there were only eight private farms, with an average size of 45 ha (*CDSP*, 1993, vol. XLV, no. 21, p. 20).

In 1994 ninety-nine-year leases were introduced, thus mitigating the effects of the prohibition of private land ownership (EBRD 1995: 65).

Economic performance

Table 14.1 paints a pretty awful picture on the GDP and inflation fronts.

Table 14.1 Tajikistan: selected economic indicators

Economic indicator	*1990*	*1991*	*1992*	*1993*	*1994*
Rate of growth of GDP (%)	−0.6	−7.1	−28.9	−11.1	−21.4
Rate of growth of industrial output (%)	1.9	−7.4	−35.7	−19.5	−30.0
Rate of growth of agricultural output (%)	−9.2	−9.9	−27.7	−4.0	−3.0
Inflation rate (%)	4.0	111.6	1,156.7	2,194.9	341.0
Budget surplus or deficit (% GDP)	3.5	−16.4	−29.9	−24.7	−6.4
Current account ($ billion)			−0.053	−0.207	−0.116
Unemployment (end of year, %)	0.0	0.0	0.3	1.1	1.8

Sources: Various issues of United Nations Economic Commission for Europe, *Economic Survey of Europe*; United Nations, *World Economic and Social Survey*; IMF, *World Economic Outlook*; Deutsche Bank, *Focus: Eastern Europe*; *Economics of Transition* and *Business Central Europe*; EBRD (1994: 170; 1995: 47)

NOTE

1. Cotton prices are still controlled. In 1995 cotton producers had the right to dispose of 30 per cent of the crop, but in 1996 the entire crop was to be at their disposal (*Transition*, 1995, vol. 6, nos 9–10, p. 23).

15

TURKMENISTAN

POLITICS

The political background

In 1989 the ethnic composition of the population was as follows: Turkmens, 68.4 per cent; Russians, 12.6 per cent; Uzbeks, 8.5 per cent; Kazakhs, 2.9 per cent; other, 7.6 per cent (*Economic Bulletin for Asia and the Pacific*, 1991, vol. XLII, nos 1 and 2, p. 2). In 1992 Turkmens accounted for 72 per cent of the population, Uzbeks 13 per cent and Russians 12.6 per cent (FEER, *Asia 1994 Yearbook*, 1994, p. 111). A more recent figure for Russians is 9 per cent (Anthony Hyman, *The World Today*, November 1993, p. 206).

In November 1993 Russia cut Turkmenistan's access to the European natural gas market (Steve LeVine, *FT*, 3 January 1995, p. 4). In August 1994 Turkmenistan, Iran and Turkey agreed to build a gas pipeline from Turkmenistan through the other two countries to connect with the European network (*The Economist*, 29 October 1994, p. 98).

Political developments

23 December 1993. Turkmenistan and Russia agree that ethnic Russians in Turkmenistan should have dual citizenship and that Russian troops should guard Turkmenistan's borders with Iran and Afghanistan. Russian military personnel will help train the army. (The agreement stipulates that Russia will be allowed to intervene militarily if its interests are threatened, including 'protection of Russian minorities': Ahmed Rashid, *The Daily Telegraph*, 25 January 1994, p. 13.) Yeltsin is awarded the title of 'Honorary Citizen of Turkmenistan'.

16 January 1994. President Saparmuryad Niyazov claims to have won a 99.99 'yes' vote (turnout 99.9 per cent) in a referendum to extend his term of office to 2002 (Ahmed Rashid puts the official 'yes' vote at 98 per cent:

FEER, 17 February 1994, p. 30). In celebration of the referendum result the president decreed that gas and electricity would henceforth be free for all Turkmen (Ahmed Rashid, *FEER*, 17 February 1994, p. 30). (Since the beginning of 1993 only consumption of domestic gas, electricity and water in excess of 'need' has been charged for: *International Labour Review*, 1993, vol. 132, no. 4, p. 427.)

11 December 1994. There was a 99.8 per cent turnout in the general election (according to official figures). Candidates for parliament (the Majlis) were all unopposed and nearly all were members of the one permitted political party, the Democratic Party of Turkmenistan. All of them won. The parliament will be a fifty-member version of the 175-member assembly inherited from Soviet days (*The Economist*, 17 December 1994, p. 68). 'There were only fifty candidates from the ruling Democratic Party for the fifty seats. Predictably, all won' (Ahmed Rashid, *FEER*, 16 March 1995, p. 24).

12 July 1995. There is a protest march in the capital, demonstrators calling for fresh parliamentary and presidential elections.

THE ECONOMY

Economic reform

The Economist (22 January 1994, p. 59) saw not much reform having taken place.

Financial policy

Turkmenistan's own currency, the manat, was introduced on 1 November 1993.

The manat was made the sole legal tender on 20 December 1994. In mid-February 1995 banks were required to surrender 75 per cent of their 1994 profits to the state and to cut lending rates to 15 per cent per annum (EBRD 1995: 65).

A bankruptcy law was passed in June 1992, but few enterprises have been forced into bankruptcy (EBRD 1994: 38).

Prices

The prices of nineteen consumer goods remain controlled and subsidized by the state, including bread, butter and vodka. Certain other items, including electricity and gas, are free (EBRD 1994: 39). The government provides free gas, electricity and water to its citizens and basic foodstuffs are available at very low prices for ration coupons (*The Baltic Observer*, 19–25 January 1995, p. 12).

Before November 1993 only the prices of imports and products using a high proportion of imported feedstuffs were liberalized (Deutsche Bank, *Focus: Eastern Europe*, 1994, no. 100, p. 45).

A fresh round of reforms was announced on 1 November 1993, including the freeing of prices on all but forty staple products and a tightening of monetary and fiscal policy (*IHT*, 2 November 1993, p. 11).

According to the *FT* (2 November 1993, p. 4), the prices of the largely state-controlled staples were to be raised and a privatization programme (excluding the oil and gas sectors) was also due to be launched.

But both attempts at price liberalization (most recently in November 1993) were scrapped after only a few days, according to *Business Central Europe* (March 1994, p. 74).

Privatization

The 19 February 1992 privatization law set out the following principles (Kaser and Mehrotra 1992: 47–8): land, water and energy deposits would remain state property; staff can determine by majority vote the form of divestment of the enterprise in which they work; employee buy-outs are facilitated by the distribution of part of the profits and of the depreciation fund; foreigners could buy shares in privatized enterprises within a quota but priority would be given to Turkmen citizens; a voucher scheme for citizens would be formulated by presidential decree.

Privatization has been slow (Deutsche Bank, *Focus: Eastern Europe*, 28 February 1993, no. 70, p. 5).

An 11 March 1993 source (*CDSP*, 1993, vol. XLV, no. 10, pp. 25–6) said that President Niyazov had signed a resolution on state support for 'entrepreneurial activity', including the establishment of a joint stock bank and the creation of seven economic zones for free enterprise. But the president said that 'We will not take the path of large-scale, uncontrolled privatization or of handing enterprises over to their collectives.'

Only 15 per cent of the economy is privatized (EBRD report of October 1994: *IHT*, 20 October 1994, p. 9).

Deutsche Bank (*Focus: Eastern Europe*, 22 March 1994, no. 100, p. 45) says that the emphasis is now on rapid and comprehensive privatization (although the state will maintain control in the oil and gas sectors, for the time being, through a majority stake in the major companies).

In mid-1994 the private sector accounted for roughly 15 per cent of GDP (EBRD 1994: 10). Large privatization remains largely at the planning stage. Little has been achieved to date in small privatization, but there has been substantial growth in the number of small private enterprises. There is no programme of property restitution (p. 38). By late 1994 about 850 small entities in the service sector had been sold. A presidential decree of 13 May 1994 (formalized further in October 1994) foresaw a voucher-type privatization process with preference granted to members of workers' collectives. But preparations for implementation are at an early stage (EBRD 1995: 65).

Foreign trade

Centralized state trading remains a prevalent influence on both foreign trade and production. Outside this system licences can be obtained for most imports and exports, but duties and tariffs can be very high (EBRD 1994: 39).

At the beginning of November 1993 full currency convertibility and a unified exchange rate for the purpose of trade transactions were introduced in principle (EBRD 1994: 39). There are various restrictions on current account convertibility and there are capital controls. There is a 50 per cent surrender requirement at the official rate and there are multiple exchange rates for different transactions (p. 111).

The manat was launched at a rate of two to the US dollar, but galloping inflation has undermined the currency. The commercial exchange rate has been brought more closely into line with black market rates. The manat has been pegged at 230 to the US dollar, down from the old official rate of ten and commercial rate of seventy-five. At the same time the commercial rate offered by state banks and the largely disused official rate have been unified. Individuals are allowed to buy up to $500 at the new rate (*The Baltic Observer*, 19–25 January 1995, p. 12).

Agriculture

The Land Code of 12 October 1990 termed land 'the property of the whole people'. Each citizen has the right to the use of a plot of land and leases (including to foreigners) can be granted for up to twenty-five years. The 23 April 1992 law allows collective and state farms to be divided up into leaseholds for the lifetime of a citizen, with the right of inheritance, to be used not only for farming but also for handicrafts and buildings (Kaser and Mehrotra 1992: 47).

About 90 per cent of Turkmenistan is desert and only 2 per cent is arable land (98 per cent of which is irrigated). (Ahmed Rashid puts the desert area at two-thirds and the arable area at 2.5 per cent: *FEER*, 17 February 1994, p. 30.) The acquisition of agricultural land is allowed only in the form of a long-term lease (see the comments by Nikonov in the section on Kazakhstan). In 1991 agriculture accounted for 46 per cent of national income (Deutsche Bank, *Focus: Eastern Europe*, 28 February 1993, no. 70, pp. 1–9). Another (11 March 1993) source, however, reports that a law on the introduction of private land ownership has been adopted. Every citizen has the right to own up to 50 ha of land or to lease up to 500 ha on a long-term lease (*CDSP*, 1993, vol. XLV, no. 10, p. 26).

A small share of land has been leased to private individuals. Land ownership has been legalized (EBRD 1994: 38).

By the end of 1992 there were 100,000 private farms, with an average size of 10 ha; they accounted for 2.8 per cent of total agricultural land (United Nations Economic Commission for Europe 1993: 206).

Some 60 per cent of food is still imported (Ahmed Rashid, *FEER*, 17 February 1994, p. 30).

Economic performance

The inflation record is pretty awful, but the output picture is somewhat better and the budgetary situation is quite encouraging (see Table 15.1).

Table 15.1 Turkmenistan: selected economic indicators

Economic indicator	*1990*	*1991*	*1992*	*1993*	*1994*
Rate of growth of GDP (%)	1.8	−4.7	−5.3	−10.0	−19.5
Rate of growth of industrial output (%)	3.2	4.8	−14.9	4.0	−25.0
Rate of growth of agricultural output (%)	7.0	−4.0	−9.0	16.0	2.0
Inflation rate (%)	4.6	102.5	492.9	3,102.4	2,397.0
Budget surplus or deficit (% GDP)	1.2	2.5	13.2	−0.5	−1.1
Current account ($ billion)				0.677	0.500
Unemployment (end of year, %)			0.0	0.0	

Sources: Various issues of United Nations Economic Commission for Europe, *Economic Survey of Europe*; United Nations, *World Economic and Social Survey*; IMF, *World Economic Outlook*; Deutsche Bank, *Focus: Eastern Europe*; *Economics of Transition* and *Business Central Europe*; EBRD (1994: 171; 1995: 48)

16

UKRAINE

POLITICS

The political background

Ukrainians constitute 72.7 per cent of the population and Russians 22.1 per cent (Andrew Higgins, *The Independent*, 26 March 1994, p. 8). There are 300,000 Poles, 180,000 Hungarians and 25,000 Slovaks (*The Economist*, Survey, 13 March 1993, p. 18).

Jewish leaders claim that there are 500,000–600,000 Jews in Ukraine, the fifth largest Jewish population in the world. There is a revival of Jewish culture and Jewish leaders praise official attitudes since independence, e.g. handing back the properties of Jewish institutions seized by the Soviet Union and the condemnation of antisemitism (James Rupert, *IHT*, 31 March 1995, p. 2).

Ukraine has not yet adopted a (new) constitution (*EEN*, 5 October 1994, vol. 8, no. 20, p. 3).

Crimea

17 June 1993. Yeltsin and Kravchuk agree in principle to divide the Black Sea Fleet evenly (after joint management till 1995) and for the Russian navy to stay in the port of Sevastopol on the Crimea (problems had arisen on 29 May when ships flew different flags).

3 September 1993. The Massandra agreement: Kravchuk and Yeltsin seemingly agree in principle to the following (parliamentary ratification is needed): (1) Ukraine will sell its half of the Black Sea Fleet to Russia in exchange for debt relief (if a joint commission's estimate of the ships' value exceeds the debt, estimated at around $2.5 billion mainly for oil and gas deliveries, Russia will pay the difference); the port of Sevastopol will be available for lease; (2) Ukraine will send the (approximately 1,800 originally) nuclear warheads on Ukrainian soil to Russia for dismantling and, in return, will receive enriched uranium (a by-product of the dismantling) for the civilian nuclear power stations. (There was, however, some ambiguity about what was said concerning the fleet. Kravchuk later talked about agreeing simply to study the idea and about 'some' ships being sold. The communiqué published on 4 September said that officials were 'to prepare within a month proposals for solving the problem of the Black Sea Fleet'. Note that Ukraine has not yet ratified either Start 1 or the Nuclear Non-proliferation Treaty.)

30 January 1994. The second round (the first was on 16 January) of the election of a 'president' of the Ukrainian Autonomous Republic of Crimea (a position not recognized by the Ukrainian government) results in a victory for Yuri Meshkov (72.92 per cent of the vote in a 75.1 per cent turnout; he won 38.5 per cent in the first round). He campaigned on a separatist/independence within Russia platform (up to 70 per cent of the 2.65 million population of the Crimea are ethnic Russians), although he fudged this message when it became clear that he would win and suggested a referendum on 27 March ('Are you in favour of an independent Crimea in union with other CIS states?'). Mykola Bagrov, the only other run-off candidate, won 23.35 per cent of the vote (he was the only one of the original six candidates to stand on an unambiguous 'stay within Ukraine' ticket; he won 17.55 per cent of the vote in the first round).

(Tatars currently number 250,000: *EEN*, 27 April 1994, vol. 8, no. 9, p. 2. The Tatars are descendants of Genghis Khan's 'Golden Horde' of Mongols in the thirteenth century. They ruled the 'Crimean Khanate', under Ottoman protection, until 1783, when the strategically situated peninsula was annexed by Russia under Catherine the Great. In May 1944 Stalin deported the Tatars to the Central Asian republics for allegedly collaborating with Nazi Germany; there was great loss of life on the way. Khrushchev presented Crimea to the Ukrainian Soviet Socialist Republic in 1954 on the 300th anniversary of the unification of Russia and Ukraine. The Tatars started to return to the Crimea in large numbers in the Gorbachev era.)

15 March 1994. Kravchuk pronounces unconstitutional an 'opinion poll' in the Crimea arranged for 27 March by Yuri Meshkov (a non-binding test of whether there is support for increased regional autonomy, enhanced decree-making powers for the Crimean president and dual nationality). Kravchuk issues a decree outlawing the plebiscite. Plebiscites (on regional autonomy, making Russian an official language and close links with Russia and the other CIS states) were also to be held in Donetsk and Lugansk in the Russified eastern and southern parts of Ukraine.

15 April 1994. After the worrying clashes of 8–10 April involving Ukrainian and Russian sailors, Presidents Kravchuk and Yeltsin come to another agreement on the Black Sea Fleet. Ukraine will receive 15–20 per cent of the fleet and there will be separate bases.

22 April 1994. Talks on the Black Sea Fleet end in failure. Although it appears that Ukraine may be prepared to accept something like a 20 per cent share, the talks founder on the question of bases (e.g. Russia wants the sole use of Sevastopol).

18 May 1994. A presidential decree subordinates the Crimean Justice, Security and Interior Ministries to the central Ukrainian authorities.

20 May 1994. Crimea's regional parliament (in the absence of Yuri Meshkov) votes by sixty-eight to two to restore Crimea's separate constitution, originally passed on 5 May 1992 (on that date parliament announced 'the creation of a sovereign state, the Republic of Crimea', i.e. one in which Ukrainian rights would be only those voluntarily delegated by the Republic of Crimea, but backed off under pressure from Ukraine: see Jeffries 1993: 107). The Crimean constitution calls for the following: (1) relations between Crimea and Ukraine to be governed by treaty; (2) the right to confer Crimean citizenship (hence dual citizenship); (3) the right to a separate foreign policy (including the ability to sign treaties with foreign partners) and to separate military forces. Crimea's parliament also votes to halt the conscription of Crimean men into the Ukrainian army.

The Ukrainian parliament responds by suspending Crimea's constitution and giving the Crimean assembly a 30 May deadline to bring their legislation into line with Ukrainian law. President Yeltsin of Russia says that he has warned President Kravchuk of Ukraine by telephone that 'force must not be used against Crimea under any circumstances. Crimea is a sovereign republic within Ukraine and has the right to its own political positions, the right to make its own decisions.' (On 24 May 1994 Kravchuk said that 'A president can only issue warnings to his own government bodies and ministers and not to the presidents of other countries. This is at variance with accepted norms, undemocratic and to no one's benefit.')

1 June 1994. The deadline having passed (negotiations did not resolve the problem), parliament rejects Kravchuk's proposal that a constitutional court should be set up to resolve the status of Crimea. Instead, parliament passes a resolution which suspends the Crimean constitution and calls upon the president to draw up a list of 'concrete measures' by 6 June to ensure compliance.

2 June 1994. The Crimean parliament rejects Yuri Meshkov's proposal to rule by decree in order to push through economic reform.

3 June 1994. Crimea's negotiators sign a communiqué in which they recognize 'the territorial integrity of Ukraine, of which Crimea is a part' and 'the supremacy of the Ukrainian constitution over all Ukrainian territory.'

23 August 1994. The city council of Sevastopol (Crimea) declares it a Russian city.

29 September 1994. The Crimean parliament strips Meshkov of nearly all his powers. (A deadline of 1 November was set by the Kiev parliament for Crimea to bring its laws and constitution into line with those of Ukraine.

An extension did not change the situation and so on 17 November 1994 Crimea's amendments were declared null and void.)

8 February 1995. Ukraine and Russia initial a friendship treaty. There is agreement in principle to divide the Black Sea Fleet. Russia will lease the main fleet base at Sevastopol.

17 March 1995. The Ukrainian parliament abolishes both the (1992) constitution and the presidency of the Crimean autonomous republic. Parliament also instructs the prosecutor-general to consider whether criminal charges should be brought against Crimean President Yuri Meshkov 'in view of gross violations of Ukraine's constitution and laws . . . for exceeding his authority and powers'. The Crimean parliament is given until 15 May 1995 to draw up a more acceptable constitution.

18 March 1995. The Crimean authorities call on Russia to help. (The Russian government thinks that the Crimean issue is an internal Ukrainian affair. The general view is that after the assault on Chechenia, which began on 11 December 1994, Russia could hardly encourage separatism in the Ukraine.)

22 March 1995. The Crimean parliament dismisses the Crimean prime minister, Anthony Franchuk.

31 March 1995. Kuchma decrees that his consent is necessary for the appointment of the prime minister and the rest of the cabinet in Crimea until a new constitution is adopted. He reinstates Franchuk (whose son is married to Kuchma's daughter).

15 April 1995. Yeltsin says that he will not sign a friendship treaty with Ukraine until the dispute over Crimea has been solved, until the 'interests and human rights' of ethnic Russians have been heeded.

25 April 1995. The Crimean parliament votes to hold a referendum on 25 June on the reinstatement of the Crimean constitution and president.

31 May 1995. The Crimean parliament votes to cancel the referendum.

9 June 1995. Yeltsin and Kuchma sign an agreement on sharing the Black Sea Fleet. Although the fleet is to be equally shared, Ukraine will eventually end up with only 18.3 per cent of the fleet after 'selling' most of its vessels to Russia (including the possibility of partial debt cancellation or rescheduling). The port of Sevastopol will be shared and Russia will pay rent in the form of energy supplies or debt forgiveness. The details of the agreement will be sorted out in future negotiations.

25 June 1995. There is a riot by Tatars after the funeral of two Tatars killed by racketeers two days earlier. Five more Tatars were killed on 25 June (*CDSP*, 1995, vol. XLVII, no. 26, p. 10).

6 July 1995. The Crimean parliament elects a new chairman. Yevgeni Supriunyuk promises that 'All the actions of the Crimean parliament will be in accordance with Ukrainian law.'

29 August 1995. President Kuchma lifts direct presidential rule, allowing the Crimean parliament to name a new government (*IHT*, 30 August 1995, p. 6).

Chernobyl

Chernobyl provides 7 per cent of the country's energy (Georges de Menil, *IHT*, 15 March 1995, p. 80). Chernobyl generates 7 per cent of electricity (*The Independent*, 28 March 1995, p. 8). The working reactors of the Chernobyl plant generate 5 per cent of electric energy (*Moscow News*, 21–27 April 1995, p. 1).

Current generation is dominated by thermal plants (66 per cent), nuclear accounting for 27 per cent (John Leslie, *FT*, 17 November 1993, p. 20). Nuclear power accounts for a third of electricity and the share has been rising (*The Economist*, 2 July 1994, p. 14). Up to 40 per cent of energy is obtained from five nuclear power stations (*Transition*, January–February 1995, p. 20).

An EU report attributes forty-two definite deaths to the Chernobyl accident; the Ukrainian government's estimate is 8,000 (*FT*, 15 November 1993, p. 21). A report by an association of victims of the disaster estimated that about 7,000 had died or committed suicide (*CDSP*, 1995, vol. XLVII, no. 17, p. 23).

21 October 1993. The Chernobyl nuclear power station, due to close by the end of the year, is to stay open 'for a period determined by its technological condition' ('until its resources are exhausted'). The moratorium on the construction of new nuclear plants is also lifted, with work resuming on plants at three sites.

8 April 1994. After talks with the USA, Ukraine agrees 'in principle' to shut down the remaining nuclear power reactors at Chernobyl ('at the earliest possible time', according to the Americans: the text of the US–Ukraine agreement says that 'The Ukrainian side agreed to cease operation of the Chernobyl plant once it had reached a balance in the energy system and found the resources to take the plant out of operation').

10 July 1994. The G7 countries agree to offer initially up to $200 million in grants as an inducement to close down the Chernobyl plant, this being in addition to the EU's offer of Ecu 500 million ($600 million) in loans and grants for nuclear safety in general. The G7 countries also held out the prospect of aid worth up to $4 billion over the next two years if Ukraine embarks on a genuine economic reform programme.

26 March 1995. A group of Western experts for the European Commission produce a highly critical report. There is need, for example, to replace the concrete container (or 'sarcophagus'), the new (airtight) one covering not only Unit 4 (which exploded in 1986), but also the adjoining Unit 3 (which should be closed down).

13 April 1995. Kuchma announces that Chernobyl will be closed down before the year 2000 (more specifically the two out of four reactors still operating; one was closed in 1991 after a fire). A gas-fired power station will compensate (he implied that the West would pay the lion's share of the

$4 billion estimated by Ukraine to be needed to close and replace).

26 April 1995. The Ukrainian minister of health claims that 125,000 people in Ukraine died as a result of Chernobyl and 2 million people were suffering ill health (Anne McElvoy, *The Times*, 27 April 1995, p. 10).

16 May 1995. The government announces that one of the remaining reactors will be closed in 1997 and the other in 1999.

Political developments before the 1994 general election

20 May 1993. Prime Minister Leonid Kuchma offers to resign when parliament refuses to extend his powers to rule by decree for one year (due to end the following day). Kuchma also requests further powers, e.g. control over the national bank, the state property fund (which is in charge of privatization) and the anti-monopoly committee. President Leonid Kravchuk asks parliament to make the president head of government, with power to rule by decree.

21 May 1993. Kuchma's offer to resign is not accepted by parliament. President Kravchuk is granted the power to issue decrees on economic measures not governed by existing legislation.

2 June 1993. Parliament rejects Kravchuk's request for extra powers (Kuchma supported the president and thought he should have the right to choose the prime minister).

9 June 1993. A strike by coal miners in the Donbas region begins, which later spreads. The strikers make not only pay demands but also political demands, such as greater regional autonomy for the eastern (mainly Russian-speaking) part of Ukraine, Kravchuk's resignation and a national referendum on whether to hold fresh presidential and parliamentary elections.

16 June 1993. Kravchuk issues a decree making himself head of the government and the security services. An emergency committee is to be created to deal with the day-to-day management of the economy, headed by Kuchma (who would control the central bank and the state property fund).

17 June 1993. Parliament approves a referendum on the question of confidence in the president and parliament for 26 September 1993 (it did not take place).

19 June 1993. Kuchma attacks Kravchuk's proposals on the grounds that the prime minister's role is diminished.

20 June 1993. The coal miners' strike ends with an offer of large wage increases (pay is to be indexed to inflation) and price subsidies.

21 June 1993. Kravchuk suspends his decree.

2 July 1993. Parliament declares that Ukraine 'owns' the nuclear weapons on its soil, but is still committed 'to becoming a non-nuclear state some time in the future' (Kravchuk supported this sentiment a short while later).

8 July 1993. Kuchma suggests the need for a state of emergency, but Kravchuk disagrees.

3 September 1993. Kuchma offers to resign, saying that 'I am convinced that Ukraine needs urgent political reforms, without which no economic reforms can occur' (parliament would need to give its approval).

21 September 1993. Parliament accepts Kuchma's resignation. It also passes a vote of no confidence in the government and asks Kravchuk to name a new one.

22 September 1993. The conservative Yefim Zvyagilsky is appointed acting prime minister. (He was appointed first deputy prime minister in June to help deal with the strike by coal miners, having previously been a high-ranking official in that industry.)

24 September 1993. The election dates are fixed, for parliament on 27 March 1994 (second round on 10 April) and for the presidency on 26 June 1994.

27 September 1993. Kravchuk gains full executive control of the government, including direct control of the economy. (Note that in August Deputy Prime Minister Viktor Pinzenyk, charged with economic reform, left the cabinet. Shortly afterwards Economics Minister Bannikov resigned.)

28 September 1993. A ten-member committee is established to co-ordinate the reform efforts.

4 October 1993. Defence Minister Konstantin Morozov (an ethnic Russian) submits his resignation.

19 October 1993. Kravchuk says that, since the West has failed to help Ukraine to disarm, there is no alternative but to reserve the right to keep the forty-six SS-24 nuclear missiles (though they have been taken off active military alert and are no longer aimed at the USA).

18 November 1993. Parliament ratifies the Start 1 treaty, but only partially and conditionally (eliminating 42 per cent of its 1,656 nuclear warheads and 130 of its 176 long-range nuclear missiles). Ukraine refuses to approve the giving up of all nuclear weapons and to sign the NNPT. Conditions are laid down, such as security guarantees and aid for disarmament.

17 December 1993. It is announced that non-resident citizens of the former Soviet Union visiting or living in Kiev have to register with the police and pay a daily fee (since the previous month Lviv has required non-Ukrainians to register with the police).

20 December 1993. Ukraine says it has deactivated seventeen of the forty-six SS-24 nuclear missiles by moving their warheads away from the launchers.

14 January 1994. Presidents Yeltsin, Clinton and Kravchuk sign an agreement in Moscow to send Ukraine's remaining nuclear weapons to Russia for dismantling. The details are not given, but Ukraine receives, for example, security and territorial guarantees, financial help and fuel rods for the civilian nuclear power industry (made by converting uranium from the weapons). (It was by no means certain that the Ukrainian parliament would ratify the agreement. Ukraine inherited 1,240 nuclear warheads on 176 intercontinental missiles, 130 SS-19s and forty-six SS-24s, and 564 cruise missiles.)

25 January 1994. A US intelligence report concludes that the worsening economic situation could spark an ethnic conflict capable of splitting the country and creating a new dispute over nuclear weapons (*IHT*, 26 January 1994, p. 1).

3 February 1994. Parliament removes the conditions (of 18 November 1993) it imposed on ratifying the Start 1 treaty.

22 February 1994. President Kravchuk announces that he will not stand for a second term of office in June.

3 March 1994. Russian gas supplies begin to be reduced because of payment problems (Turkmenistan had cut off supplies on 20 February). (Ukraine was subsequently given until 10 April to pay off its debt to Gazprom. A deal was agreed in principle on 12 April involving the $900 million debt for oil and gas supplies; aspects included sending gas equipment to Russia and allowing Russia to receive assets from the privatization of the gas industry in Ukraine. On 17 August Russia's Gazprom agreed to receive 25 per cent of the gas debt in payments spread over three months and the remainder in equity shares in Ukrainian gas enterprises. Ukraine is $5 billion in debt to Russia; 20 per cent of it is for Russian deliveries of gas for 1994: *Transition*, 1994, vol. 5, no. 7, p. 3.)

4 March 1994. Kravchuk visits the USA and is told that aid is to double to $700 million (half in the form of economic aid and half to help dismantle nuclear weapons). (Another $100 million was announced by the USA on 21 March, both for dismantling nuclear warheads and for conversion purposes.)

23 March 1994. A partnership and co-operation agreement is signed with the EU (the first for a republic of the former Soviet Union). The agreement includes increased trade and economic co-operation (free trade by 1998 if Ukraine achieves the transition to a market economy).

The 1994 general election

The turnout was much higher than anticipated, 75.6 per cent in the first round and 66 per cent in the second round (Kravchuk had, in fact, anticipated a situation where he could impose direct presidential rule). International observers from the United Nations and the CSCE were not altogether happy, raising doubts about the fairness of the electoral process (e.g. incidents of bribery, dubious invalidation of ballot papers and observers being denied access to polling stations).

There was no element of proportional representation. All 450 (single-member) constituencies could be won only by a 50 per cent turnout of the electorate and a 50 per cent 'yes' vote. In consequence there were a number of rounds of voting (e.g. on 27 March, 3 April, 10 April, 24 July and

7 August). There were 5,833 candidates. Although thirty-two parties competed, the vast majority of candidates (around three-quarters, according to Bojcun 1995: 233) were 'independents' with no or at least undeclared party allegiances (in Table 16.1 Bojcun's figures are given; the official returns identified elected deputies as independents if they were so registered as candidates, but in fact a number of so-called 'independents' campaigned as members of political parties: Bojcun 1995: 241–2). Represented among the independents were managers of state enterprises and collective farms, private businessmen, academics and reformist economists (e.g. Viktor Pinzenik and Volodymyr Lanovoi; the latter has remarked that 'it is not the president who rules the country, but an economic *nomenklatura*, which acts like a mafia': *The Economist*, 7 May 1994, pp. 9–10). (The managers and other members of the former *nomenklatura* were known as the 'party of power', which broadly supported Kravchuk.)

The results are given in Table 16.1. Only 338 seats were decided in the March–April rounds. The election produced a broad 'east' (pro-independence and pro-reform) and 'west' (left-wing, pro-Russia and anti-radical reform) split, with a large 'swamp' of independents in the middle. The prospects for economic reform did not look good at the time.

The plebiscites in the Crimea, Donetsk and Lugansk (see entry for 15 March 1994) produced overwhelming 'yes' votes. The Crimean president,

Table 16.1 Ukraine: the general election of March–April 1994

Party	*Seats in the Supreme Council*	
	Author's own estimates	*Bojcun (1995: 239)*
Ukrainian Communist Party	86	86
Rukh	20	25
Peasant Party	18	18
Ukrainian Socialist Party	14	14
Ukrainian Republican Party	8	11
Congress of Ukrainian Nationalists	5	7
Inter-regional Reform Bloc	4	15
Labour Party	4	4
Ukrainian Democratic Renaissance Party	4	4
Ukrainian National Assembly	3	3
Civic Congress of Ukraine	2	2
Democratic Party of Ukraine	2	3
Social Democratic Party of Ukraine	2	2
Ukrainian Conservative Republican Party	2	2
Christian Democratic Party of Ukraine	1	1
Independents	163	136
Total	338	338[1]

1 The Communist Party of Crimea won five seats.

Yuri Meshkov, recommended a boycott of the national vote, but his Russia Bloc triumphed in the regional election (with communists doing well also).

Only nineteen of the remaining 112 seats were decided on 24 July 1994, four won by candidates not affiliated to any party and the rest by candidates from small centrist groups. The turnout was very low.

Currently there are 392 MPs in parliament, leaving fifty-eight seats vacant (*EEN*, 21 September 1994, vol. 8, no. 19, p. 3).

In December 1994 it was decided to curtail parliamentary elections for a year after several rounds of voting had failed to produce clear winners in a number of districts. There are nearly fifty vacancies in parliament (*Business Europa*, February–March 1995, p. 48).

Comments on the election

Anders Åslund describes the election as one in which 'voters turned against Mr Kravchuk's corrupt supporters and elected liberals and old-line communists who oppose him . . . Mr Kravchuk, an opportunistic old-line communist ideologue who changed his stripes, has refused serious economic reform. His sympathy for the *nomenklatura* was shown by his ousters of officials who favour reform. Enterprising members of the former elite have been given excellent opportunities to enrich themselves . . . 74 per cent of the electorate voted, mostly for politicians perceived to be honest' (*IHT*, 11 June 1994, p. 8). Åslund maintains that the by-elections have 'gradually moderated parliament's original communist orientation. Slightly more than one-third of the deputies are pro-communist, that is, Communists, Socialists or Agrarians. About one-third belong to an amorphous centre and one-third are reformers or nationalists' (1995: 131).

Bojcun concludes that 'parties of the left have emerged as the strongest single bloc, reversing their decline, indeed ostracism, before and immediately after independence. Their success on this occasion is undoubtedly due to the electorate's reaction to the deepening economic crisis . . . The crisis is attributed in the public's mind to the loss of an ordered economy, regulated by the state, and to the emergence of the new "robber barons" undertaking the primitive accumulation of their wealth through appropriation of state assets . . . and profits from trade' (Bojcun 1995: 246). 'The national democrats proved unable to broaden their base because they did not convince the electorate that they had a serious strategy to combat the economic crisis' (p. 246). 'On the whole, the centrist parties performed poorly' (p. 243). 'The geographical split of the vote for the left and national-democratic blocs between the eastern and western *oblasti* brings to the fore again a division of Ukraine that has deep historical roots . . . None of the parties, blocs nor even the independents can claim to have a national presence' (p. 247).

The main parties, leading personalities and platforms

1. Left-wing parties:

Ukrainian Communist Party. Led by Pyotr Simonenko. Banned after the August 1991 coup attempt, but reinstated in June 1993. The party opposes radical economic reform and advocates close economic and political links with Russia.

Peasant Party. Established in December 1991.

Ukrainian Socialist Party. Established in October 1991.

2. Centrist parties:

Inter-regional Reform Bloc. Co-chaired by former prime minister Leonid Kuchma, who has said that 'our aim is rapid market reform and strategic partnership with Russia' (*The Independent*, 26 March 1994, p. 8).

Ukrainian Democratic Renaissance Party.

Civic Congress of Ukraine.

Social Democratic Party of Ukraine.

Labour Party.

Christian Democratic Party of Ukraine.

Civic Congress. In favour of close links with Russia.

3. Nationalist parties:

Ukrainian National Assembly. Neo-fascist party espousing extreme nationalism, anti-Russian sentiments and populist economic measures. Its motto is 'Force, order, prosperity'. Its paramilitary organization is called 'Ukrainian People's Self-defence'.

Ukrainian Conservative Republican Party. Extreme nationalist.

Social Nationalist Party. Extreme nationalist.

Congress of Ukrainian Nationalists.

Rukh. Rukh (Popular Movement of Ukraine) is led by Vyacheslav Chornovil. Moderate nationalist. Initially the dominant political force, which rallied the nation in support of independence. But then split into factions and thereby lost influence. Broadly in favour of economic reform.

Ukrainian Republican Party. Moderate nationalist.

Democratic Party of Ukraine. Moderate nationalist.

Political developments after the 1994 general election

19 May 1994. Alexander Moroz (Socialist Party) is elected speaker of parliament.

2 June 1994. Parliament rejects Kravchuk's call for the June presidential election to be postponed (Kravchuk registered as a candidate on 4 May).

14 June 1994. Kravchuk signs a partnership and co-operation agreement with the EU (the first involving a former Soviet republic). Greater political and economic co-operation involves, for example, mutual trade concessions (including the prospect of a free-trade agreement after 1998 if Ukraine makes sufficient progress towards a market economy). (The nuclear issue overshadowed the agreement, both the NNPT and Chernobyl and other civilian power stations.)

16 June 1994. Vitaly Masol is made prime minister. (He was prime minister 1987–90 and believes in greatly strengthening economic links with Russia.)

26 June 1994. The first round of the presidential election (seven candidates) produces no outright winner, but the 'west–east' divide deepens. Kravchuk (who steadily gained ground during the campaign as the compromise nationalist candidate) won 37.72 per cent of the vote (largely in the 'west'). Leonid Kuchma won 31.27 per cent of the vote, largely in the 'east' (his platform stressed close economic links with Russia and other CIS countries, greater autonomy for Russian-speaking areas within Ukraine – a treaty-based relationship with Crimea – and more rapid economic reform – a 'controlled transformation' to a market economy; but during the campaign he rejected the idea of abandoning a separate currency and joining the rouble zone, 'because that would mean the end of our independence': *FT*, 13 July 1994, p. 23). Alexander Moroz (who is against the private ownership of land) won 13 per cent of the vote and Volodymyr Lanovoi (the economic reformer) only 9.3 per cent. The second round of voting is due on 10 July. (The turnout was high, around 70 per cent.)

6 July 1994. The reformist Petro Hermanchuk becomes minister of finance.

10 July 1994. The second round of the presidential election produces a somewhat surprising win for Kuchma, who seems to have picked up votes in central regions, in particular from people dissatisfied with economic conditions (the population of the central area is largely ethnic Ukrainian, but many people speak Russian as their first language). He won 52 per cent of the vote, compared with 45 per cent for Kravchuk. (The average turnout in both rounds was 68 per cent.)

The G7 countries agree to offer initially up to $200 million in grants as an inducement to close down the Chernobyl plant, this being in addition to the EU's recent offer of Ecu 500 million ($600 million) in loans and grants for nuclear safety in general. The G7 countries also hold out the prospect of aid worth up to $4 billion over the next two years if Ukraine embarks on a genuine economic reform programme.

13 July 1994. Kuchma says, 'I have never suggested that Ukraine should return to the Russian empire.'

19 July 1994. Kuchma is sworn in as president. In his address he warns that 'harsh and unpopular measures will have to be taken' to halt the country's economic decline. 'The country faces a hard winter ahead', but that will be 'its final, most difficult period of trial'. He indicates his support for joining the economic union of CIS states and proposes to make Russian a second official language. (Kuchma has been reported as saying that 'we can be truly independent only if we are powerful economically': Jim Hoagland, *IHT*, 26 July 1994, p. 6. In a post-election interview Kuchma stated the following: 'I am an advocate of economic changes that are evolutionary, not revolutionary. To conduct reforms political will is necessary. I have it'. 'I want us to have equally good relations with Russia, with Germany, with Taiwan etc. . . . Ukraine should become a bridge between Russia and the technologically developed West.' 'I do not consider it [the federalization of Ukraine] possible today, and above all I want to urge everyone to unite.' Note that Crimea voted 89.7 per cent in favour of Kuchma: *CDSP*, 1994, vol. XLVI, no. 27, p. 4.)

21 July 1994. Kuchma signs a tough anti-crime decree. The provisions include the following: (1) the police are allowed to hold suspected criminals for up to thirty days; (2) premises where criminals may gather (such as hotels and dormitories) may be raided without a search warrant; (3) commercial documents from private companies may be seized; (4) half the proceeds of raids on illegally obtained property will go to law enforcement budgets.

27 July 1994. Kuchma meets the managing director of the IMF, Michel Camdessus. (An economic programme is to be drawn up in collaboration with the IMF by October 1994.)

8 August 1994. Kuchma issues a decree asserting the right of the president to appoint officials, including deputy ministers and committee heads. Local council and executive heads are also required to obey presidential directives. (Just before Kuchma took office parliament abolished the seats in local government reserved for presidential representatives. Note that the president has no right to replace the prime minister without the consent of parliament.)

28 August 1994. Kuchma issues a decree joining the forces of the general prosecutor, the Interior Ministry and the security service in the fight against 'the most difficult cases of crime in financial and banking services, trade and those committed by public servants'.

11 September 1994. President Meshkov of Crimea dissolves parliament and assumes 'full powers'. He orders a referendum on a new constitution and fresh parliamentary elections. (On 7 September the Crimean parliament voted to reduce the powers of the president. On 13 September parliament was reopened. On 15 September the prime minister, Yevgeny Saburov, offered his resignation.)

26 September 1994. Leonid Kravchuk wins a seat in parliament.

11 October 1994. President Kuchma presents his economic reform proposals to parliament ('On the way to radical economic reform'). They include reductions in subsidies and privatization in agriculture and other sectors (small privatization to be completed by the end of 1995 and medium and large privatization by 1998).

18 October 1994. Parliament lifts the ban on the Communist Party. (On 10 November it was decided that a new vote would have to be taken because of irregularities in the first one.)

19 October 1994. Parliament endorses Kuchma's economic programme by 231 votes to fifty-four.

26 October 1994. The IMF agrees to provide a $371 million credit.

31 October 1994. Kuchma names the reformist Viktor Pinzenyk as first deputy prime minister for economic reform. (Note that Roman Shpek is the economics minister, Igor Mityukov is the new deputy prime minister for financial affairs, Viktor Yushchenko is head of the central bank and Yuri Yekhanurov is in charge of privatization.)

15 November 1994. Ukraine is promised an additional $234 million in disarmament aid (*FT*, 17 November 1994, p. 2).

16 November 1994. Parliament ratifies the NNPT, subject to certain conditions (e.g. the signing of security guarantees at the 5–6 December 1994 meeting of the CSCE). (The Start 1 and 2 treaties were made conditional on Ukraine's ratification of the NNPT.)

22 November 1994. The USA offers an extra $100 million in aid.

5 December 1994. Ukraine formally signs the NNPT at the CSCE meeting in Budapest, thus allowing Start 1 to take effect.

22 December 1994. The World Bank approves a $500 million loan.

17 February 1995. Agreement is reached on Ukraine's debt for natural gas supplies from Russia. Elements include debt restructuring, barter deals and debt–equity swaps.

1 March 1995. Vitaly Masol resigns as prime minister. Yevgeny Marchuk, first deputy prime minister, pragmatist and firm ally of Kuchma, becomes acting premier.

20 March 1995. Ukraine signs an agreement to restructure $2.5 billion of its debt to Russia (owed partly to the Russian government and partly to Gazprom).

4 April 1995. Parliament passes by 292 to fifteen a vote of no confidence in the government (ministers will stay on until Kuchma nominates a new cabinet).

18 April 1995. Parliament rejects Kuchma's proposals to enable the president to dissolve parliament, appoint a prime minister and form a government (*EEN*, 1995, vol. 9, no. 9, p. 1).

11–12 May 1995. President Clinton visits Ukraine and praises the progress made on nuclear disarmament and economic reform.

18 May 1995. Parliament passes Kuchma's 'law on power' by one vote, giving decisive political advantage to the president (*EEN*, 1995, vol. 9, no. 11, p. 1). The president now has full control over ministerial appointments (*The Economist*, 27 May 1995, p. 6).

1 June 1995. Parliament vetoes Kuchma's decree of 31 May to hold a plebiscite to push forward economic and constitutional changes (the question asked citizens whether they 'trust president or parliament'). (Kuchma's decree came after parliament had again failed to ratify constitutional amendments passed on 18 May giving the president broad powers to form a cabinet without parliamentary approval and to control local government: Chrystia Freeland and Matthew Kaminski, *FT*, 2 June 1995, p. 3.)

5 June 1995. Kuchma issues a decree invalidating parliament's veto.

7 June 1995. The president and parliament agree to sign a 'constitutional accord'. Parliament votes to cede the president (temporary) extra powers (e.g. the right to appoint ministers without having to refer them to parliament, greater powers to issue decrees and the right to appoint local administrators), while Kuchma agrees to a one-year deadline for a new constitution, to yield the power to dissolve parliament and to cancel the plebiscite.

8 June 1995. Kuchma appoints Yevgeny Marchuk as prime minister.

3 July 1995. Roman Shpek becomes deputy prime minister in charge of the economy. President Kuchma says that he intends to offer Viktor Pinzenyk a position with responsibility for overall economic strategy. (In the middle of talks with the IMF Pinzenyk was reappointed deputy prime minister for economic reform: *The Economist*, 12 August 1995, p. 4.)

THE ECONOMY

The economic background

As much as 40 per cent of Ukraine's industrial capacity in the Soviet era was devoted to making armaments (Chrystia Freeland, *FT*, 26 August 1993, p. 14). Roughly 40 per cent of total Soviet military production was located in Ukraine (Deutsche Bank, *Focus: Eastern Europe*, 1993, no. 87, p. 4).

Havrylyshyn *et al.* (1994) put the early reluctance to engage in serious economic reform down to factors such as the ability of powerful interest groups to block changes which threatened the 'rents' they received from the partially reformed system (e.g. from control over export licences, subsidized energy imports and state credits to enterprises) (p. 371). 'The semi-reformed economy is full of rent seekers with strong motives to resist change, while the ill-defined nature of political groupings and allegiances makes it difficult to arrange the kind of social compromise necessary to achieve much-needed reform . . . price distortions and their associated rents attract powerful lobbies which fight to preserve or even increase the distortions and prevent further reform' (pp. 373–4).

The economic system

The advent of a new government in October 1992 brought about a degree of liberalization (some relaxation of controls over prices and exports and the introduction of a foreign exchange auction), but in the summer of 1993

Ukraine's new government began to reintroduce administrative controls. By mid-1994 the degree of administrative control over the economy was virtually the same as it had been immediately following independence (*Transition*, 1994, vol. 5, no. 7, p. 2).

State orders in 1992 accounted for about 75 per cent of turnover in industrial inputs. Sectoral ministries played a major role intermediating between enterprises, both to ensure that the basic inputs needed to meet the state order were made available and to allocate goods delivered under state orders to enterprises that required them for further processing (Sundakov *et al.* 1994: 420).

'At present the Ukrainian economy is more liberalized than the Russian economy' (Åslund 1995: 142). 'The government was too weak to maintain the centralized system of allocation; by 1994 it had effectively broken down. Therefore, enterprises increasingly became dependent on actual demand, and much of the necessary downscaling of obsolete and uneconomic production took place. Many enterprises closed down because of insufficient demand, while others adjusted' (p. 129).

Financial policy

The value of the Ukrainian coupon (karbovanets or *zaichik*, meaning 'little hare' or 'bunny', from the design) has plummeted even against the Russian rouble. As of 18 February 1995 the use of foreign currency as legal tender is to be forbidden (*Moscow News*, 20–26 January 1995, p. 9). As of 18 February 1995 all financial transactions are to be concluded in karbovanets (*Business Central Europe*, February 1995, p. 50).

The stabilization effort in 1992 relied more on administrative methods, e.g. the imposition of limits on both wage increases and profit margins on goods (ceilings on some food prices) at the end of January. The economic programme adopted in February 1993 aimed to reduce the budget deficit in 1993 to 6 per cent of GDP and monthly inflation to 3–4 per cent by the end of the year. Strict wage restraint is also a feature (United Nations Economic Commission for Europe 1993: 231).

The government criticized a very large increase in credit by the central bank in March 1993, which was used to wipe out the debts of enterprises (including those owed to Ukrainian by Russian enterprises).

The *EEN* (11 May 1993, vol. 7, no. 10, p. 4) reported a 'lack of direction' in the government, one of the main aims of which was to reduce inflation to 5 per cent a month by the end of 1993. The budget was passed on 9 April 1993, but the reformist Deputy Prime Minister Viktor Pinzenyk resigned his economic reform portfolio four days later (although he remained deputy premier).

Anne McElvoy (*The Times*, 13 November 1993, p. 12) reported the order to close the currency exchange 'temporarily' in an attempt to regulate the exchange rate. Kravchuk then presented a three-stage programme envisaging the introduction in 1994 of currency and price liberalization.

In early December 1993 a joint statement by the government and the central bank said that 'Issuing loans in Ukraine is banned until the end of the year because of the country's very difficult financial situation' (*FT*, 7 December 1993, p. 2). (The governor of the national bank, Victor Yushchenko, has said that 'parliament has the right to order me to emit credits, and it is controlled by lobbies': *The Economist*, Survey, 7 May 1994, p. 7.)

A new stabilization plan (the eighth in two years) has already been discredited by the granting in January of substantial extra subsidies to agriculture. The forecasts for 1994 of 5–8 per cent monthly inflation and a balanced budget look hopelessly unrealistic (*The Economist*, 22 January 1994, p. 35). Near the end of February 1994 the brief three-month clampdown on the money supply was abandoned when credits totalling 10 per cent of GNP were issued (Jill Barshay, *FT*, 3 March 1994, p. 3). A tight credit squeeze was introduced in December 1993, but the policy was reversed at the end of February 1994. The government agreed an emission equal to half the 1993 GNP in the first quarter of 1994 (John Lloyd, *FT*, 13 April 1994, p. 25).

In January 1994 the governor of the central bank, Viktor Yushchenko, launched a very severe monetary squeeze (although there was a wave of new credits in July, mainly for agriculture) (Chrystia Freeland, *FT*, 8 August 1994, p. 2). The counter-inflationary effects of the tight monetary policy have been undermined by the large budget deficit (*FT*, 14 October 1994, p. 16). The monthly inflation rate was brought down from 90 per cent in December 1993 to 5.2 per cent in May 1994 (Jill Barshay, *FT*, 23 June 1994, p. 3).

On 29 September 1994 a preliminary agreement was signed with the IMF. In exchange for $360 million (part of the 'systemic transformation facility') Ukraine would undertake a stabilization and liberalization programme (e.g. a budget deficit of 10 per cent of GDP, price and foreign trade liberalization, and speedier privatization).

The karbovanets has been stabilized, trading at 150,000 to the US dollar since February 1995 (Matthew Kaminski, *FT*, 6 June 1995, p. 3). Since January 1995 the street and official exchange rates have converged and stabilized. On 1 August the exchange rate was 152,300 to the dollar. In late July Kuchma announced that the karbovanets would be replaced by the grivna in October 1995 (Matthew Kaminski, *FT*, 2 August 1995, p. 2).

As of 1 August 1995 there was a ban on the use of foreign currency for cash payments in the retail and service sectors. Deposits from businesses must be converted into karbovanets within a day (*IHT*, 2 August 1995, p. 2).

There has been little enforcement of the May 1992 law on bankruptcy (EBRD 1994: 40).

'So far not a single enterprise has been formally declared bankrupt' (*The Economist*, 22 July 1995, p. 20).

Kuchma's economic reform package

'On the way to radical economic reform' was presented on 11 October 1994 and approved by parliament on 19 October. The programme comprised:

1. A macroeconomic stabilization package, with the budget deficit being reduced to 10 per cent of GDP by the end of 1994 and 5 per cent in 1995. Price liberalization (e.g. a sevenfold increase in bread prices) would mean a saving on subsidies, although there would be extra expenditure on the indexing of pensions and wages and improvements in social welfare. (Local authorities can subsidize certain staple commodities such as bread out of their own budgets: *Moscow News*, 11–17 November 1994, p. 4.)

By the end 1994 the volume of state-regulated retail prices was to be reduced from 80 per cent to 65 per cent of all prices. Most prices would be freed from 1995, excluding those set by monopoly producers (*IHT*, 28 October 1994, p. 13). The aim was to increase domestic energy prices to world levels by mid-1995 (*FT*, 28 October 1994, p. 19).

2. Trade liberalization and the unification of exchange rates (see below).

On 3 March 1995 Ukraine signed a stand-by agreement with the IMF. In return for a $1.5 billion stand-by loan and a $373 million systemic transformation facility Ukraine agreed to keep its budget deficit to 6.4 per cent of GDP, to reduce the monthly inflation rate to 1 per cent by the end of the year and to undertake reforms such as further price liberalization and the limitation of export quotas to grain.

Parliament approved the budget on 6 April 1995. The budget deficit in 1995 was to be 7.3 per cent of GDP, including external debt servicing. More than half the deficit was to be financed by printing money (Matthew Kaminski, *FT*, 7 April 1995, p. 3). (According to IMF methods of calculations, the budget deficit would amount to 3.5 per cent of GDP: Matthew Kaminski, *FT*, 13 March 1995, p. 3. Including an allowance for expected aid, the budget deficit would come to 3.2 per cent of GDP: *The Economist*, 18 March 1995, p. 43.)

On 9 April 1995 the IMF approved a total of $1.96 billion, including a $1.57 billion stand-by loan and a $392 million systemic transformation facility.

In January 1995 a new enterprise profits tax was introduced, which changed from gross to net income (EBRD 1995: 67).

Åslund believes that Kuchma has 'transformed Ukraine's international agenda by putting economic reform first. Saying that he did so for the sake of Ukraine's sovereignty, he succeeded in bringing eastern and western Ukraine together' (1995: 141). 'Thanks to IMF and World Bank agreements Ukraine is effectively bound to its present course of reforms, rendering success likely . . . Yet pressure for credits may still defeat the reformers.

The most obvious threat comes from agriculture, but that danger is widely anticipated . . . Like Yeltsin in the spring of 1992 he [Kuchma] may be convinced that industrial lobbies are justified in making certain demands' (p. 142).

Prices

After the price liberalization in 1991 and 1992 price regulation intensified at the beginning of 1993. Prices are set administratively for housing and transport, goods of 'social significance' and goods produced in monopolistic sectors. In addition profit margins are subject to regulatory limits (EBRD 1994: 41). In October 1994 most energy and agricultural prices, communal tariffs and rents were increased in real terms. Further liberalization steps followed in December 1994 and in February 1995. Energy prices have been moving significantly towards cost recovery levels for domestic production and world price levels for imports. Public utility prices increased from 2–3 per cent of cost in September 1994 to 40 per cent by February 1995 and were expected to rise to 60 per cent of cost by July 1995 (EBRD 1995: 66).

By early 1992 the Ministry of the Economy estimated that the percentages of retail and wholesale turnover accounted for by various categories of prices were as follows: free, 21 and 26; administered, 12 and 17; regulated (limits on profit margins principally), 67 and 57. But in many cases it is unlikely that profit margin regulation provided more than symbolic constraint. In July 1992 the majority of profit margin limits were abolished. But the relative price freedom came to an end in December 1992 when the category of regulated prices was substantially expanded and the effectiveness of regulation strengthened (Sundakov *et al.* 1994: 414–16).

In December 1992 subsidies were abolished on almost all agricultural products, resulting in food price increases in state shops of 300–500 per cent (United Nations Economic Commission for Europe 1993: 231).

On 10 September 1993 the prices of food, electric power and some other goods and services were increased 300–500 per cent (there were some cash awards and wage rises to compensate). On 28 October 1993 price increases and state purchasing in key industries were enforced (*EEN*, 1993, vol. 7, no. 22, p. 1).

Wholesale and retail price controls were imposed; prices were to rise with energy cost increases only and profits were to be strictly limited. The state order system was re-instituted, requiring most enterprises to sell a portion of their production to the state at fixed prices (Jill Barshay, *FT*, 9 November 1993, p. 3). Wholesalers were allowed to raise their prices only in line with input costs and manufacturers of 'strategic products' (such as food and fuel) had to deliver an average of 40 per cent of their output to the central ministries (*The Economist*, 20 November 1993, p. 48).

According to Kasper Bartholdy and Ivan Szegvari (*Economics of Transition*, 1993, vol. 1, no. 4, p. 511), 'the Ukrainian authorities reactivated the old central planning mechanism, reintroducing pervasive price controls and a comprehensive state-order system as the basis for the distribution of production.'

The June 1993 agreement between Kravchuk and Yeltsin foresaw world prices for energy supplies from Russia from the start of 1994.

Domestic industry and agriculture are charged a fraction of world prices (ranging from between 25 per cent for electricity and gas to 33 per cent for coal) and households are charged only a fraction of what the industries pay (Daniel Kaufmann, *Transition*, September 1994, vol. 5, no. 7, p. 5).

At the start of November 1994 the price of bread quadrupled and public transport fares increased tenfold (*EEN*, 1994, vol. 8, no. 23, p. 1).

On 1 June 1995 utility prices for individual consumers were increased, e.g. doubled in the case of heating and by 40 per cent for water (*Transition*, 1995, vol. 6, nos 5–6, p. 19).

Even energy prices have reached world market levels. The subsidies that remain (for rents and natural gas for households and for collective transport) have been sharply reduced (Åslund 1995: 138).

Privatization

The first auctions in the small privatization programme took place in Lvov on 20 February 1993 with the help of the International Finance Corporation (Chrystia Freeland, *FT*, 22 February 1993, p. 16). Workers employed in shops, restaurants and small businesses were able to obtain a 30 per cent discount off the bid price and to make a 30 per cent down-payment with a year to pay the remainder. Leasing was the main form.

Only around 100 out of 68,000 state enterprises have been privatized (*IHT*, 21 May 1993, p. 2).

In 1992 only sixty-eight out of 200,000 state enterprises were privatized (*Business Europa*, August–September 1993, p. 20).

By October 1992 enterprises accounting for 21 per cent of retail sales had been leased to private management. Also operating under leasing arrangements were 1,431 medium-sized manufacturing enterprises, with ownership divided between lessees and the state (Havrylyshyn *et al.* 1994: 391).

Less than 2 per cent of industry has been privatized (*The Economist*, 27 November 1993, p. 17).

Less than 10 per cent of total assets have been officially privatized (Daniel Kaufmann, *Transition*, 1994, vol. 5, no. 7, p. 1).

Less than 10 per cent of enterprises have been privatized (Jill Barshay, *FT*, 2 August 1994, p. 14).

Little progress has been made with large privatization. By early 1994 only about 4 per cent of the 60,000 small units to be privatized had been sold, but the informal economy is growing rapidly. There has been no property restitution for former owners (EBRD 1994: 40).

Only 1 per cent of state housing has been sold to the private sector (*The Times*, 21 May 1993, p. 9).

A decree issued in January 1993 to allow the sale of medium-sized and large enterprises from July was rejected by parliament (United Nations Economic Commission for Europe 1993: 232).

Business Central Europe (September 1993, p. 51) reports the first two large-enterprise pilot privatizations (vouchers were involved).

Citizens were to receive 'property certificates' in October 1993. Unlike vouchers they cannot be bought and sold; they are registered in the name of their holders as deposit bank accounts (*Moscow News*, 8 October 1993, p. 9). As a way of trying to prevent the use of 'illegal capital' buyers have to produce income declarations (p. 9).

Parliament's latest programme calls for the privatization of 8,000 state enterprises (28 per cent of the total) by the end of 1994 (Jill Barshay, *IHT*, 15 March 1994, p. 15).

The privatization 'trial of 150 enterprises' has begun (John Lloyd, *FT*, 13 April 1994, p. 25).

Over the summer of 1994 150 large and medium-sized enterprises were privatized using vouchers. Another 300 enterprises were to be put out to tender in the autumn (Chrystia Freeland and Matthew Kaminski, *FT*, 28 November 1994, p. 3).

On 29 July 1994 parliament (ostensibly because of corruption) voted 180 to sixty-two to order the state property fund to 'halt the conclusion of agreements involving buying and selling . . . until parliament approves the industries and objects which are not to be privatized'. The government was ordered to draw up a list of enterprises in the transport, energy and communications sectors which are of 'national significance' and should therefore remain in state hands. The list was to be drawn up by 15 August and presented to parliament for approval in September (later extended). The resolution also ordered a review of the mechanism by which foreign investors participate in privatization.

'I intend to activate small-scale privatization and initiate mass privatization before the end of this year' (President Leonid Kuchma, *FT*, 30 September 1994, p. 18).

President Kuchma issued a decree aimed at privatizing more than 8,000 state enterprises in 1995. The decree sought to guarantee the right of Ukrainian citizens to use privatization certificates and create a market for shares. Shares were to be sold to insiders (employees and enterprise managers) and at auction. Managers would have the right to buy up to 5 per cent of the shares in a given enterprise (*Transition*, November–December 1994, vol. 5, no. 9, p. 17).

In December 1994 parliament lifted its suspension of mass privatization. Hitherto less than 5 per cent of small-scale units had been privatized and there had been virtually no mass privatization (EBRD 1995: 16). The aim of the draft legislation was to privatize 8,000 medium-sized and large enterprises (and another 12,700 small enterprises) in 1995. Up to 5 per cent of shares would go to management, with the rest to be sold in auctions (about 70 per cent of general vouchers issued to the population at large and 30 per cent to savings account holders). The first auctions were scheduled for the first quarter of 1995 in five pilot regions. A December 1994 decree provided incentives to accelerate small privatization (p. 66). Over 200 investment trusts and funds are operational (p. 67).

Ninety per cent of all assets are still owned by the state. Ukraine launched its mass privatization in late January 1995. Vouchers, which were distributed to citizens at that time, are not tradable. Bids could be made by individuals or pooled investment funds. Up to 70 per cent of an enterprise could be sold by voucher and the rest by means such as hard currency tenders. Kuchma's November 1994 decree envisaged the privatization of up to 8,000 medium-sized and large enterprises in 1995. His December 1994 decree charged the regions with completing small-scale privatization in 1995. The head of large privatization said 150 enterprises could be ready by February 1994. But about half the enterprises were leased by workers and ineligible for privatization. Parliament was drawing up a list of about 5,400 enterprises in the coal, steel and chemical sectors to remain in state hands. Pilot schemes for fifty-seven enterprises were planned in five regions, to be followed by nationwide auctions in April 1994. In the long run foreign investors would gain access to assets through the secondary market (Matthew Kaminski, *FT*, 28 January 1995, p. 2).

In late January 1995 Ukraine began the process of offering shares in what officials said would be about 8,000 state enterprises, which were to be auctioned off over two years. Officials said that the auction would sell to Ukraine's citizens about 75 per cent of state industry, permit significant foreign investment and lead to the activation of the stock market. The government was at first offering shares in about sixty enterprises and using adverts to encourage citizens to pick up privatization certificates. The new, reformist head of the state property fund is Yuri Yekhanurov (James Rupert, *IHT*, 3 February 1995, p. 11).

Kuchma aims to auction 8,000 large enterprises in 1995. But fewer than half of them are likely to be sold off, since many of the best enterprises have already been either bought by their own workers or put on a list of 'strategic' enterprises that parliament has decided should not be sold (*The Economist*, 11 February 1995, p. 86). Fewer than 200 large enterprises have been auctioned off so far. Parliament has drawn up a list of 6,100 'strategic' enterprises that cannot be privatized at all (including some bakeries as well as defence plants and telecom firms) (*The Economist*, 22 July 1995, p. 20).

Nationwide auctions were due to begin in April 1995, preceded by pilot auctions in five regional centres (*Business Central Europe*, March 1995, p. 20).

President Kuchma has signed a decree proclaiming that 90 per cent of all small municipal enterprises should be privatized by the end of 1995 (Åslund 1995: 138).

The size of the private sector

The Centre for Market Reforms estimates that the black economy is providing between 25 per cent and 30 per cent of GNP. Everybody is substantially underreporting their turnover (David Hearst, *The Guardian*, 26 March 1994, p. 12).

According to official data (which do not fully reflect the growing black economy), the private sector accounted for 30 per cent of GNP in the first quarter of 1994 (*FT*, 29 June 1994, p. 23).

Misha Glenny (*IHT*, 15 July 1994, p. 5) cites one estimate that half of all economic activity is illegal.

Perhaps more than half of economic activity is accounted for by the unofficial private economy (Chrystia Freeland and Matthew Kaminski, *FT*, 14 October 1994, p. 16).

Some 10 per cent of the economy is in private hands (*Newsbrief*, February 1994, vol. 14, no. 2, p. 12).

In mid-1994 the private sector accounted for roughly 30 per cent of GDP (EBRD 1994: 10). This figure takes into account the contribution of the large informal sector (p. 40). According to official estimates, the private sector has grown to at least 40 per cent of GDP of which three-quarters is likely to be in the informal sector (EBRD 1995: 66).

Foreign trade

Foreign trade was recentralized in late 1993, leaving most transactions subject to bilateral agreements and state orders. There have been few import tariff rates since the beginning of 1993 and there are no significant quotas. As far as exports are concerned, since March 1994 there have been explicit export quotas and licences for virtually all products. There are heavy restrictions on convertibility. There is a floating rate with intervention (EBRD 1994: 111). In October 1994 most export quotas and licensing requirements were abolished. Export licences remained for only four important commodities (grain, coal, cast iron and scrap metal). In December 1994 these were lifted on all but grain, which was to be liberalized by mid-1995. Unification of multiple exchange rates had almost been achieved by October 1994. The official exchange rate is now determined on the interbank currency exchange. Access to the interbank market has since been broadened. In late January 1995 additional US dollar auctions were introduced and banks were allowed to sell foreign exchange direct to their customers (with a margin no greater than 10 per cent of the auction price) (EBRD 1995: 66).

Export licences have been reduced to four items, namely grain, coal, precious, ferrous and non-ferrous scrap metal and pig iron (*Moscow News*, 4–10 November 1994, p. 4).

After 16 August 1993 exporters were obliged to exchange 50 per cent of hard currency earnings for karbovanets at a fixed rate of 5,970 to the US dollar, instead of 15 per cent at the floating rate determined in the hard currency auctions; Ukrainian citizens were allowed to buy or sell foreign currency in unrestricted quantities at the floating rate (*IHT*, 12 August 1993, p. 11; Leyla Boulton, *FT*, 16 August 1993, p. 2). There were, however, exemptions from this general rule (*Moscow News*, 27 August 1993, p. 1).

On 3 November 1993 the buying and selling of foreign currency were suspended and all auction centres and exchange points were to be closed down. Hard currency transactions were to be confined to government-authorized exports and imports at the fixed central bank exchange rate.

In January 1994 new rules laid down that exporters had to surrender 40 per cent of their hard currency receipts to the central bank for 12,610 karbovanets to the US dollar; another 10 per cent had to be sold at 25,000, the same rate at which the traders could sell the remaining half (*Business Central Europe*, February 1994, pp. 48–9).

A decree signed by President Kuchma on 23 August 1994 included the following: (1) a call for the reopening of the interbank currency exchange on 1 October 1994; (2) the central bank would gradually bring the official exchange rate into line with the market rate (possibly by the end of 1994); factors taken into account were to include the inflation rate, the money supply and the balance of payments (a unified, market-determined exchange rate would finally come about when the IMF provided a stabilization fund); (3) in the meantime enterprises would still have to surrender 50 per cent of their hard currency earnings, but 20 per cent would be sold at the market rate and only 30 per cent at the official rate.

In an article in the *FT* (30 September 1994, p. 18), Kuchma said that 'I want to peg the exchange rate of our currency from the beginning of 1995 and exchange our provisional coupon for our national currency [the grivna].'

The exchange rate was unified on 1 November 1994. A single hard currency rate has been restored. The interbank hard currency exchange operates once a week and only a 2.5 per cent deviation from the rate is allowed in hard currency transactions (*Moscow News*, 4–10 November 1994, p. 4).

Ukraine now pays around 70 per cent of the world market price for Russian oil (Chrystia Freeland, *FT*, 18 May 1993, p. 4; Jill Barshay, *FT*, 23 November 1993, p. 2). Lee Hockstader (*IHT*, 9 November 1993, p. 8) reports a figure of 80 per cent for oil and gas.

Ukraine relied on Russia for 90 per cent of its oil and gas (Jill Barshay, *FT*, 23 November 1993, p. 2). Ukraine imports almost two-thirds of its energy needs, buying oil, natural gas and coal from Russia, Turkmenistan and Poland (*The Guardian*, 30 December 1994, p. 11). Ukraine imports 87 per cent of its oil and 83 per cent of its natural gas, mostly from Russia and Turkmenistan. A new oil terminal in Odessa has been approved, with the aim of diversifying energy sources. In 1994 Ukraine produced 4 million tonnes of oil and 17 billion cubic metres of natural gas (Matthew Kaminski, *FT*, 24 January 1995, p. 5). Gas accounts for 40 per cent of energy consumption (Matthew Kaminski, *FT*, 1 May 1995, p. 2).

On 14 June 1994 President Kravchuk signed a partnership and co-operation agreement with the EU (for details, see the entry for that date above). On 1 June 1995 President Kuchma signed an interim trade agreement with the EU.

Foreign aid

Jeffrey Sachs (*FT*, 17 February 1995, p. 17) described the EU's response as 'extremely feeble'. The EU had found about Ecu 85 million in loans for balance of payments purposes, but Ecu 65 million of this was to be used to repay debts to the EU that were falling due. The IMF was to put up another $1.5 billion. The overall sums were 'minuscule' and fell short even of the 'inadequate' pledges given at the G7 summit in the summer of 1994, when $4 billion was promised. 'Without significant external assistance most financially strapped governments cannot win the time needed for basic reforms.' The IMF should provide $3 billion, half to help the budget and half to help back a new Ukrainian currency. The World Bank should put up another $1.5 billion for urgent balance of payments support (as opposed to the $0.5 billion on offer), while European countries should together mobilize $1 billion in urgent additional support.

The EU has not released the $100 million it conditionally agreed to lend Ukraine in (December) 1994 and said it would not consider a 1995 loan until the conditions had been met. The main condition was to close Chernobyl (Georges de Menil, *IHT*, 15 March 1995, p. 8). On 22 May 1995 the EU agreed to a package worth up to Ecu 220 million, linked with the government's decision to close Chernobyl (see the entries for 13 April and 16 May 1995). The first tranche was worth Ecu 100 million, but the exact size of the second would depend on the contributions of other donors.

Foreign investment

The total sum of Western investments is $900 million. In 1992 joint ventures accounted for only 0.2 per cent of industrial output and 5.7 per cent of exports (*Moscow News*, 7 May 1993, p. 4).

Foreign capital levels approached $700 million at the beginning of 1993 (*Business Central Europe*, April 1994, p. 46).

Ukraine is the only former Soviet republic (apart from Russia) that has been able to secure more than $1 billion in direct foreign investment (Barbara Peitsch, *The OECD Observer*, April–May 1995, p. 32).

Net direct foreign investment was $200 million in 1992, $200 million in 1993 and an estimated $225 million in 1994 (United Nations Economic Commission for Europe 1995: 151).

Total foreign investment since independence reached $500 million by August 1995 (*The Economist*, 2 September 1995, p. 41).

A November 1994 decree introduced private land ownership, subject to constraints on use. But foreign land ownership is not permitted (EBRD 1995: 66).

Agriculture

President Kuchma issued a decree authorizing the private ownership of agricultural land for the first time. The decree allowed landowners to sell, lease or bequeath their land to Ukrainian citizens provided it continued to be used for agricultural purposes (*Transition*, November–December 1994, vol. 5, no. 9, p. 17). (See 'Foreign investment' above.)

A decree of late 1992 allowed property title to tenants of rural household plots and gave them the right to sell. Kuchma's decree of November 1994 allowed each farm member to receive a certificate of ownership of a parcel of land or of a share in group property. Such certificates could be traded, bartered, inherited or mortgaged. Members of existing state and collective farms were to be invited to take voluntary decisions on their mode of ownership, but size limits were to be fixed on any one individual's property. But parliament has challenged the legality of the right to transact land, thereby delaying implementation (Kaser 1995: 37).

The 13 million private smallholders satisfy 25 per cent of food consumption (Edward Balls and Chrystia Freeland, *FT*, 23 February 1993, p. 18).

By the end of 1992 there were 14,400 private farms, with an average of 20 ha (*CDSP*, 1993, vol. XLV, no. 5, p. 22); they accounted for 0.7 per cent of total agricultural land (United Nations Economic Commission for Europe 1993: 206). As of 1 April 1993 there were 20,700 private farms, with an average size of 20 ha (*CDSP*, 1993, vol. XLV, no. 21, p. 20).

In 1993 individuals held only 11 per cent of all agricultural land, yet they produced 43 per cent of all livestock and 37 per cent of crops (Daniel Kaufmann, *Transition*, 1994, vol. 5, no. 7, p. 5).

Roughly 60 per cent of the population have a piece of land on which they grow most of their own food (*The Economist*, Survey, 7 May 1994, p. 6). 'A quarter of the harvest is still bought by the state, often at below world-market prices. The distribution system is in the hands of government monopolies.

Land privatization, promised by Mr Kuchma, has got nowhere because parliament has refused to approve it' (*The Economist*, 2 September 1995, p. 41).

Reformers see the need to improve incentives for farmers who are currently forced to sell at low state-determined prices and to restructure the inefficient collectives still dominant in Ukraine. A government spokesman has outlined a plan to put 60 per cent of land in public hands (the state currently owns 93 per cent). Subsidies to agriculture eat up half the state's budget (Matthew Kaminski, *FT*, 18 October 1994, p. 32). In January 1995 Kuchma signed an edict permitting farmers to sell their produce on commodity exchanges or to trading houses after the state quotas for certain goods (such as grain and sugar) had been met. The Ministry of Agriculture sets price floors on the commodity exchanges. State contracts were supposed to be phased out over the following two years (Matthew Kaminski, *FT*, 28 June 1995, p. 35). Of 4.5 million farmers only about 35,000 are private. By acreage collectives make up 70 per cent of the total, state farms around 15 per cent, private farms 2.5 per cent, and small subsidiaries and household plots 12 per cent. President Kuchma puts the contribution of the private sector as a whole to total agricultural output at 44 per cent. State orders for grain in 1995 cover some 25 per cent of the total harvest, compared with 50 per cent in 1994. The World Bank has urged Ukraine to remove ceilings on profit margins and mark-ups and generally to free prices. Parliament has so far failed to pass a law backed by President Kuchma that would allow land to be bought or sold (Matthew Kaminski, *FT*, 14 July 1995, p. 25). On 17 August 1995 the quotas and licences applying to grain exports were 'temporarily' reimposed owing to the disappointing grain harvest (they had been removed only at the beginning of that month) (Matthew Kaminski, *FT*, 18 August 1995, p. 21).

Economic performance

'Ukrainianization' is a term the country would sooner forget. But Kuchma seems determined to pull the country round and there was progress on the inflation front in 1994 (see Table 16.2).

Table 16.2 Ukraine: selected economic indicators

Economic indicator	*1990*	*1991*	*1992*	*1993*	*1994*
Rate of growth of GDP (%)	−3.0	−11.9	−17.0	−17.1	−23.0
Rate of growth of industrial output (%)	−0.1	−4.8	−6.4	−22.4	−27.7
Rate of growth of agricultural output (%)	−3.7	−19.0	−9.0	−2.0	−16.0
Inflation rate (%)	4.2	91.2	1,209.7	4,734.9	891.2
Budget surplus or deficit (% GDP)	2.6	−13.7	−29.3	−9.7	−9.1
Unemployment (end of year, %)	0.0	0.0	0.3	0.4	0.4

Sources: Various issues of United Nations Economic Commission for Europe, *Economic Survey of Europe*; United Nations, *World Economic and Social Survey*; IMF, *World Economic Outlook*; Deutsche Bank, *Focus: Eastern Europe*; *Economics of Transition* and *Business Central Europe*; EBRD (1994: 172; 1995: 49)

17

UZBEKISTAN

POLITICS

The political background

In 1989 the ethnic composition of the population was as follows: Uzbeks, 68.7 per cent; Russians, 10.8 per cent; Tatars, 4.2 per cent; Kazakhs, 4.0 per cent; Tajiks, 3.9 per cent; other, 8.4 per cent (*Economic Bulletin for Asia and the Pacific*, 1991, vol. XLII, nos 1 and 2, p. 2). In 1992 Uzbeks accounted for 71 per cent of the population, Russians 10.8 per cent, Tajiks 4 per cent and Tatars 4.2 per cent (FEER, *Asia 1994 Yearbook*, 1994, p. 112). A more recent figure for Russians is 8 per cent (Anthony Hyman, *The World Today*, November 1993, p. 206).

According to official statistics, 98,000 emigrated in 1991 (partially offset by 58,000 immigrants). Although the numbers emigrating fell in 1992, around 100,000 left the country in 1993 through Russian embassy channels alone (*CDSP*, 1994, vol. XLVI, no. 24, p. 12).

Political developments

The opposition parties in Uzbekistan have been clamped down on and the US State Department has revealed significant abuses of human rights. President Karimov argues that restrictions on opposition parties are necessary to prevent the spread of Islamic fundamentalism. On 21 January 1993 the Supreme Court suspended the activities of Birlik (the main Uzbek nationalist opposition party) for three months (FEER, *Asia 1994 Yearbook*, 1994, p. 112). The Birlik (Unity) Popular Movement (formerly the Democratic Party of Uzbekistan) has still not been allowed to register as a political party (*The Economist*, 15 May 1993, p. 88). The Erq (Will) opposition party is legal, but has been harassed (Anne McElvoy, *The Times*, 26 May 1993, p. 12).

25 December 1994. The general election takes place. There are 250 members of the new parliament (the former Supreme Soviet had 500 deputies). Thirty-nine seats need further rounds of voting, but the People's Democratic Party (successor to the Communist Party) and its supporters win handsomely: People's Democratic Party, fifty-four seats; Party of National Progress, six seats; local government candidates, 145 (most, perhaps 93 per cent, belong to the PDP). The Party of National Progress was created by the government as a party of business. The Birlik and Erq parties did not take part in the election.

Ahmed Rashid (*FEER*, 16 March 1995, p. 24) assessed the results thus: 'His [Karimov's] People's Democratic Party won 231 seats, with the remainder going to close allies in the Party of National Progress, which Karimov set up two years ago. Opposition parties, most of whose members have been jailed or forced into exile, have been barred since 1992 and were barred from standing in the elections . . . the turnout was high. Some 93 per cent of Uzbekistan's people voted, many because government officials forced them to.'

26 March 1995. There is a referendum on the question of postponing the presidential election scheduled for December 1996 until December 2000.'

There was a turnout of 99.3 per cent and 99.6 per cent of voters said 'yes', according to official figures. Only those voting against had to enter cubicles to make their mark, while those voting 'yes' simply placed the voting paper unmarked in the ballot box (*The Economist*, 8 April 1995, p. 81).

THE ECONOMY

The economic background

Nearly 80 per cent of Uzbekistan is desert and only 9 per cent is arable land (it is a net importer of food). It has major gas deposits and some oil. There has been some reversal of price liberalization (Deutsche Bank, *Focus: Eastern Europe*, 1993, no. 70, pp. 1–9).

Financial policy

The government has pursued a cautious policy on reform and restructuring, arguing against shock therapy (Kaser and Mehrotra 1992: 43). The coupon system differs from that introduced during 1991 in a number of other Soviet republics. Coupons did not replace Soviet roubles, but accompanied 70 per cent of all wages and collective farm dividends and were necessary to purchase most goods and services in state shops. In late July 1992 it was announced that coupons were to replace the rouble and that coupons, in turn, were to be replaced by a new currency (p. 46).

Uzbekistan had debated whether to introduce its own currency, but after the Russian currency reform of late July 1993 agreement was reached with

Russia (on 7 August 1993) that the country would remain in the rouble zone (see the 7 September 1993 agreement discussed above in the section on the rouble zone and the tougher conditions imposed by Russia in late September). But the *sum* was introduced on 15 November 1993 in the form of coupons (one coupon = one rouble). These were to circulate together with new rouble notes and lower-denomination old rouble notes. At the beginning of 1994 the coupon became the sole legal tender. The sum itself was introduced on 1 July 1994 (coupons were to be deposited in state banks and exchanged after a month in order to restrict the initial circulation to current salaries; the coupon remained legal tender during the first month).

Originally the sum coupon was pegged at par with the rouble, but since mid-April 1994 the exchange rate has been determined via a managed floating system. Nevertheless, there is still a wedge between the official rate and the street rate. This reflects less than full convertibility, including for current account transactions. A fully fledged national currency was introduced in July 1994 (EBRD 1994: 41). There is a 30 per cent surrender requirement at a rate set by the central bank (p. 111).

The government planned to ban the use of foreign currencies in commercial transactions as of 15 October 1994. All payments and settlements between individuals and legal entities were to be conducted only in the sum (*IHT*, 11 October 1994, p. 11).

All restrictions on the purchase of foreign currency from commercial banks were lifted on 1 July 1995 (*Transition*, 1995, vol. 6, nos 7–8, p. 20).

A law on bankruptcy was adopted in May 1994, but no bankruptcy proceedings have yet been initiated (EBRD 1994: 40).

On 1 March 1995 the IMF approved a loan under the systemic transformation facility. The first instalment of $74 million was to be used to support the government's programme of macroeconomic stabilization and systemic reform. The chief objective of the government was to reduce the monthly rate of inflation to 2 per cent by the end of 1995. The second tranche of the loan was to depend on implementation of the stabilization programme. Negotiations were also taking place with the World Bank for a loan of $160 million (*CDSP*, 1995, vol. XLVII, no. 5, pp. 23–4).

Prices

The bulk of consumer prices were liberalized in January 1992. After a partial reversal liberalization was resumed in mid-1993. By early 1994 only the prices of basic necessities remained fixed. On other goods, however, there are indirect price controls through ceilings on mark-ups for trade organizations and profitability ceilings for a range of producers in monopolistic positions (EBRD 1994: 41). In the second half of 1994 the scope of the state order system was greatly reduced (see 'Agriculture' below) and there were also fewer administered prices. In early 1995 the remaining rationing of staple food was abolished and limits on profit margins were removed for all goods except natural monopolies and certain medicines. Domestic prices were to continue to be adjusted to cover fully the cost of supply. Producer prices for oil were supposed to be raised to world market levels by the fourth quarter of 1995 (EBRD 1995: 68).

Full price liberalization was once again postponed in January 1994 (*Business Central Europe*, May 1994, p. 74).

Bread and flour prices have tripled, with virtually all adults receiving income compensation (Steve LeVine, *FT*, 6 September 1994, p. 5).

Subsidies on basic foodstuffs and public transport were axed in 1994, while those on utilities are being reduced (*The Economist*, 7 January 1995, p. 56).

Privatization

The law of 19 November 1991 foresaw leasing, transformation into co-operatives, sale by auction, sale by tender and, for some housing, gratis hand-over to tenants. There is no offer of vouchers, but the possibility is envisaged of a buy-out by staff, who can be given a share of the enterprise's profit and depreciation fund to assist purchase. State cotton plantations, energy, metallurgy, mining, railway and air transport, pharmaceuticals and high-technology industries are not to be privatized (Kaser and Mehrotra 1992: 45).

An ultra-cautious approach is taken towards privatization (*Business Central Europe*, November 1993, p. 60).

To date privatization has been minimal; in February 1994 the first auction of state property (such as hotels and shops) was held (Ahmed Rashid, *FEER*, 31 March 1994, p. 61). Around 53,000 state enterprises were partially or fully privatized in 1993, but most of them were very small. The government is now starting to sell off larger enterprises, using management or employee buy-outs and auctions. In March 1994 locals (and to a limited extent foreigners) were allowed to bid for fifteen state enterprises. Industries such as mining, cotton and energy will remain under majority state ownership for some time to come (*Business Central Europe*, May 1994, p. 74) (metallurgy and transport too: Havrylyshyn *et al.* 1994: 392).

Steve LeVine (*FT*, 8 February 1994, p. 4) reports the announcement of a reform programme by presidential decree on 23 January 1994. There were promises for the first time to auction off state enterprises publicly, foreigners being allowed to bid. The decree enacted a five-year tax holiday for manufacturers established under more than 50 per cent foreign ownership (those with a lower percentage are exempt from tax on their first two years' profits: Ahmed Rashid, *FEER*, 31 March 1994, p. 60) and also promised a phasing out of import duties in July 1995. Since becoming independent

Uzbekistan has taken the route of 'collectivization', i.e. the transfer of enterprises to their employees in fixed-price shares.

The programme includes a speeding-up of privatization, encouragement of the private sector and the cancellation of many import duties until July 1995 (*The Economist*, 19 March 1994, p. 80).

Uzbekistan has drafted an ambitious privatization programme. The plan calls for selling off leading enterprises in the mining, fuel and cotton industries (*IHT*, 18 February 1995, p. 11).

The private sector contributes around 10 per cent of GDP (Deutsche Bank, *Focus: Eastern Europe*, 22 March 1994, p. 42).

In mid-1994 the private sector accounted for roughly 20 per cent of GDP (EBRD 1994: 10). A presidential decree was issued in March 1994. About 4,000 medium-sized or large enterprises were marked for privatization in 1994 and the first auctions took place in March. By mid-1994 more than 50,000 small enterprises had been privatized or leased. There has been no property restitution (EBRD 1994: 40). Privatization moved forward after March 1994 with the extension to medium-sized and large enterprises. By the end of 1994, according to official figures, 67 per cent of the number of enterprises (50 per cent of GDP) had been privatized or corporatized. Housing privatization was almost complete, and small privatization and the sale of many consumer services were also advanced (EBRD 1995: 16). The official estimate of the size of the non-state sector had risen to 50 per cent of GDP by the end of 1994, including joint stock companies irrespective of the size of the state's stake. This share was planned to increase to 60 per cent by the end of the 1995. With encouragement from the IMF and the World Bank the government committed itself to pushing ahead with the privatization of medium-sized to large enterprises and with agricultural reforms. A new cash-based comprehensive privatization scheme was to be adopted by the end of March 1995. The methods of privatization were to be diversified and a total of 1,796 enterprises were earmarked for privatization during 1995 (p. 68).

Foreign trade

Trade with CIS countries is largely determined by bilateral intergovernmental agreements. In early 1994 it was made legal for individuals to engage in foreign trade. At the same time the customs duties on all imports were suspended until mid-1995 and the number of product categories subject to export quotas and export licensing systems was reduced from seventy to twenty-six (EBRD 1994: 41). There are few quantitative restrictions on imports. The state foreign trade monopoly was lifted in March 1994 (p. 111). As of December 1994 the number of products subject to export licences was reduced from twenty-six to eleven. Customs duties on all imports were to be suspended until mid-1995, when the government was to consider putting in place a homogeneous and low import tariff structure. The exchange rate was unified in October 1994. The gap between the official market rate and the black market rate narrowed and the exchange rate stabilized at twenty-five sum to the US dollar after mid-November 1994 (EBRD 1995: 68).

Foreign aid

On 2 March 1995 the World Bank reported that donor countries and international institutions had pledged more than $900 million in loans and grants (*FT*, 3 March 1995, p. 7).

Foreign investment

Uzbekistan has attracted more than $2 billion in commitments (*Business Central Europe*, April 1994, p. 82).

Foreign direct investment amounted to $145 million in the period 1990–93 (EBRD 1994: 123).

Agriculture

See the comments by Nikonov in Chapter 9 on Kazakhstan. Nikonov (1992: 1161) says that Uzbekistan has chosen its own way. Efforts are directed towards expanding individual peasants' private plots. Irrigated lands are added to previously allotted individual subsidiary plots. In 1991 individual subsidiary farming accounted for 60.6 per cent of total agricultural output. In addition 8,000 farmer holdings have been established. Unprofitable state farms have been transformed into co-operative and leased enterprises.

Another source informs us that by the end of 1992 nearly 6,000 private farms had been established, with an average size of 8 ha (*CDSP*, 1993, vol. XLV, no. 5, p. 22); they accounted for only 0.18 per cent of total agricultural land (United Nations Economic Commission for Europe 1993: 206). As of 1 April 1993 there were 5,800 private farms, with an average size of 9 ha (*CDSP*, 1993, vol. XLV, no. 21, p. 20).

The private sector is well advanced. In the autumn of 1991 loss-making state farms were sold off to staff or transformed into co-operatives; together with other collective farms the latter were to be distributed among members by the end of 1993 (Kaser and Mehrotra 1992: 45).

Van Atta (1993: 598–604) takes a detailed look at the agrarian scene in Uzbekistan:

1. He argues that only very limited agrarian reform has been undertaken to date. The regime clearly intends to maintain the old Soviet-style system of state orders and subsidies. President Karimov's strategy has been to

stabilize agricultural production before attempting any reform. The supply of inputs and the processing and sale of agricultural products remain in the hands of the state. The government provides the all-important water free.

2. State orders for cotton are being reduced (in 1994 70 per cent of the crop will have to be delivered and then orders are supposed to decline by 5 per cent a year for several more years), but the state still controls all the cotton gins and the distribution network. At present only 10 per cent of cotton production is processed as finished goods within Uzbekistan and the aim is to increase the proportion.

3. The way the government intends to increase incentives for individual farm workers is to lease land and assets to individuals and families within the framework of the existing collective and state farms.

4. Because the collective and state farms concentrated so intensively on cotton, much food comes from the private plots. In 1991 the president claimed that private plots produced 40 per cent of foodstuffs on 4.5 per cent of the land. By mid-1993, as a result of extra land being made available, the plots accounted for between 11 per cent and 12.5 per cent of agricultural land. The plots now account for 70 per cent of milk, 50 per cent of meat and 50 per cent of potatoes, vegetables and fruit.

5. The July 1990 law allowed individuals to lease but not to buy land. Even after January 1992 Uzbekistan retained retail price controls on basic foodstuffs and the system of state orders for agricultural production. The law on peasant farms was adopted on 3 July 1992. Individual peasant families were allowed to obtain a share of land and assets from the farm in order to establish their own private farms. But the right to leave with a land share was absent. So peasant farms can be established only as share-cropping operations within the large farms, when an entire state or collective farm is reorganized into peasant farms by its membership or on (the very little) unused yet suitable land. Peasant farmers were to be given a state order for 50 per cent of their crops and freed from all taxes for two years.

6. A decree issued on 10 January 1993 concerned the denationalization of around 700 state farms. The farms were to be reorganized into collective farms or 'associations of peasant farms'. It is not exactly clear what these terms mean. Perhaps the new collective farms may grant peasant farmers the nominal right to leave the farm with a share of land and capital assets, while the associations theoretically make the peasant households legally independent proprietors. 'In general, however, the peasant farms created when entire farms are reorganized are not legally independent, and the change more resembles "internal khozraschyot" than it does the creation of truly independent farms' (p. 603).

7. The government reported that by mid-1992 4,378 peasant farms existed, compared with 1,358 at the start of 1991 and 1,868 at the start of 1992 (over this period of time the average size increased from 6.7 ha to 7.3 ha and then to 8.1 ha). The statistics are supposed to reflect the number of farmers

who have received title to their land. But Van Atta was told unofficially that 'there are only about 250 genuinely private, or peasant, farms in Uzbekistan. These peasant farms are not "family" farms in the Western sense. Instead . . . they are "clan" or group farms, with the oldest competent male officially regarded as the "farmer" ' (pp. 603–4).

About a quarter of state farms were to be privatized before the end of 1994. Over 10 per cent of the cultivated land has been leased to private farmers (EBRD 1994: 40). Uzbekistan still prohibits private ownership of land by its nationals and legal entities, although leasing is permitted (p. 74). Some 25 per cent of all irrigated land was planned to be leased to private farmers by mid-1995, rising to about 40 per cent by the end of the year. The scope of the state order system was greatly reduced in the second half of 1994. State orders (involving obligatory production targets and administrative price setting) are now in place only for cotton and grain, and their coverage has been reduced to 60 per cent and 50 per cent of production (from 67 per cent) respectively. These state orders were scheduled to be eliminated within three years (EBRD 1995: 17, 68).

According to *Business Central Europe* (March 1995, p. 11), the first private land auction has been held.

Economic performance

Economic performance in terms of output is not so bad, but inflation is still a problem (see Table 17.1).

Table 17.1 Uzbekistan: selected economic indicators

Economic indicator	*1990*	*1991*	*1992*	*1993*	*1994*
Rate of growth of GDP (%)	1.6	−0.5	−11.1	−2.4	−2.6
Rate of growth of industrial output (%)	1.8	1.8	−12.3	−8.3	1.0
Rate of growth of agricultural output (%)	6.3	−1.0	−7.3	−0.7	−1.0
Inflation rate (%)	3.1	97.0	645.0	534.0	723.0
Budget surplus or deficit (% GDP)	−1.1	−3.6	−12.0	−20.0	−2.0
Current account ($ billion)			−0.239	−0.429	−0.432
Unemployment (end of year, %)	0.0	0.0	0.1	0.2	0.3

Sources: Various issues of United Nations Economic Commission for Europe, *Economic Survey of Europe*; United Nations, *World Economic and Social Survey*; IMF, *World Economic Outlook*; Deutsche Bank, *Focus: Eastern Europe*; *Economics of Transition* and *Business Central Europe*; EBRD (1994: 173; 1995: 50)

18

ECONOMIC RELATIONS BETWEEN RUSSIA AND THE OTHER COUNTRIES OF THE FORMER SOVIET UNION (THE 'NEAR ABROAD')

THE PAYMENTS MECHANISM

The pre-July 1992 payments mechanism is discussed by *RET* (1993, vol. 2, no. 4, pp. 18, 96–7), Lipton and Sachs (1992: 226, 237–8), Michalopoulos and Tarr (1993: 22–5) and the United Nations (*World Economic Survey 1993*, p. 119). Although Russia alone controlled the printing of rouble notes (widespread shortages of cash roubles developed), before 1 July 1992 the central bank of each country in the rouble zone had the ability to create rouble credits acceptable as a means of payment throughout. Since Russia had a large trade surplus, the enterprises of the other republics receiving credits from their own central banks made net payments to Russia (especially for fuels and energy). These swelled bank deposits and thus the money supply in Russia. The lack of monetary control and co-ordination was exacerbated by the introduction of currency in the form of coupons in some countries. In the words of the IMF (*World Economic Outlook*, May 1993, p. 65), the Russian central bank had the sole power to issue rouble currency, but the other banks could extend credit themselves by creating new commercial bank reserves, borrowing from the Russian central bank and, in many cases, issuing coupons.

In order to staunch the outflow of goods (Russia's trade surplus was expanding) and control the provision of credit to other states, in July 1992 Russia established a network of bilateral correspondent accounts for the other central banks (more strictly, according to Eichengreen, correspondent banks existed from the beginning of 1992, but the credit ceilings were not enforced in the first half of the year: 1993: 315). A halt was called to the automatic crediting of other countries running trade deficits with Russia and it was laid down that Russian goods could be purchased only with rouble deposits in Russian banks (gained through exports to Russia or permitted credit limits). The Russian central bank thus constrained the movement of non-cash roubles in settlements between enterprises. It forbade direct settlements, shifting them to a state-to-state basis through these correspondent accounts held by the various national banks (Noren 1993: 437). The system did not work smoothly because of Russia's large trade surplus. The correspondent accounts began to serve as mechanisms for bilateral barter in which energy-exporting states, including Kazakhstan, tended to run substantial trade surpluses without there being any obvious mechanism to encourage them to increase their imports from 'weak rouble' states. The idea of an inter-state bank, discussed below, is meant to facilitate mutual account settlement so that surpluses earned with one trading partner can be used to offset deficits with another (United Nations, *World Economic Survey 1993*, p. 119).

The United Nations Economic Commission for Europe (1993: 171) points out the emergence not only of national cash surrogates but also of 'national roubles' used in non-cash settlements. This was due chiefly to large imbalances in trade between the republics. The central banks of Russia and the Baltic States were increasingly reluctant to accept non-cash roubles in payment for exports to deficit countries such as Ukraine. Towards the end of 1992 Latvia introduced differentiated exchange rates for non-cash roubles originating in various states and the practice was quickly adopted by the central banks of some other countries (Russia and Belarus).

The Russian authorities even tried to limit monetary growth in the rouble area by restricting deliveries of cash roubles. But several republics responded by introducing parallel currencies or coupons (Havrylyshyn *et al.* 1994: 357).

A distinctive feature of 1993 and 1994 was that the majority of payments between Russia and the other countries of the former Soviet Union now go directly through commercial banks rather than via the central banks (*RET*, 1994, vol. 3, no. 1, p. 28).

Sachs is reported as saying that Russia continues to subsidize the other countries through cheap resources and credits, to the tune of 10 per cent of national output (Peter Passell, *IHT*, 20 March 1993, p. 11). The Deutsche Bank (*Focus: Eastern Europe*, 1993, no. 67, p. 4) quotes the World Bank's estimate that Russian subsidies (the supply of commodities at bargain prices) to the other countries of the former Soviet Union amounted to $20 billion in the first half of 1992. According to Fyodorov, in 1992 Russia provided $17 billion in aid (21.4 per cent of GDP) to CIS countries in the form of cash transfers, credits and low prices (*CDSP*, 1993, vol. XLV, no. 28, p. 30). The $17 billion constituted, for example, soft credits and goods sold at below market prices. In 1992 Russian subsidies in cash and kind accounted for 69 per cent of Uzbekistan's GDP and 67 per cent of Turkmenistan's GDP (*The Economist*, 20 November 1993, p. 115). The IMF/World Bank calculate that the loss of cheap credits and subsidized energy would cost Ukraine, Armenia, Azerbaijan, Georgia, Moldova, Kazakhstan,

Kyrgyzstan, Tajikistan and Uzbekistan together $15.5 billion or almost 15 per cent of Russia's GNP (John Lloyd and Steve LeVine, *FT*, 12 November 1993, p. 2).

Orlowski (1993: 1005–6) has calculated the value of 'indirect transfers' between the Soviet republics in 1990 through underpriced oil and natural gas and overpriced other goods (compared with world market prices). Two republics made net transfers (as a percentage of their own GDP) to the other republics, namely Turkmenistan (10.8 per cent) and Russia (3.7 per cent). The others were net recipients (in descending order as a percentage of their GDP): Moldova, 24.05 per cent; Lithuania, 17.09 per cent; Georgia, 16.02 per cent; Estonia, 12.08 per cent; Latvia, 10.43 per cent; Azerbaijan, 10.09 per cent; Armenia, 9.16 per cent; Belorussia, 8.91 per cent; Tajikistan, 6.08 per cent; Ukraine, 3.61 per cent; Kirghizia, 2.72 per cent; Uzbekistan, 1.26 per cent; Kazakhstan, 0.50 per cent.

The rouble zone

There was considerable controversy about whether to retain or abandon the rouble zone. For example, the EBRD advised the former Soviet republics to abandon it. Separate national currencies or smaller currency zones could improve the prospects for production and trade. The rouble zone was undermined by unco-ordinated credit policy. The argument was that outside the rouble zone countries would adopt more prudent fiscal and monetary policies (*FT*, 12 February 1993, p. 3).

At first the IMF advised the countries of the former Soviet Union to remain in the rouble zone, but now favours independent currencies. But Jeffrey Sachs is still very critical of the IMF for advising each of the countries of the former Soviet Union to adopt a floating exchange rate regime (*FT*, 29 July 1994, p. 13). 'The most urgent question facing the IMF – whether in Ukraine, Russia, Kazakhstan or elsewhere – is how to help a bankrupt government trying to end high inflation. The IMF's approach is straightforward – sharp cuts in the budget deficit, a low target growth of the money supply, high real interest rates, and a floating exchange rate. But while these policies will end high inflation in the long run, they almost invariably lead to an unnecessarily deep recession; indeed, often to a reversal of the policies themselves, as recent history in Ukraine and other former Soviet Union countries confirms. The IMF has always blamed the governments for not following through, not recognizing that its advice has played a significant role in these failures.' Sachs argues that there is a better way. Stabilization policies in Israel in 1985, Bolivia in 1986, Mexico in 1987, Poland in 1990, Argentina in 1991 and Estonia in 1992 were based on a different principle. The governments of these countries recognized that low money growth was insufficient. It was also necessary to bolster expectations of low inflation and to increase confidence in the money in order to build up money holdings and to reverse capital flight. This was accomplished by a strong government commitment to a stable exchange rate, at least for several months, together with other fiscal, monetary and privatization measures along normal IMF lines. Sachs argues that exchange rate stabilization serves several key functions in ending high inflation. It directly limits price increases in tradable goods (thereby providing a 'nominal anchor' to the price level), it ties the government to a highly visible target, it co-ordinates future price expectations around a common standard and it raises confidence in the currency (especially when the pegged exchange rate is backed by international resources or gold, as in the case of the most highly successful programmes). 'The situation [in Kyrgyzstan] cries out for a defence of the currency, backed by an international stabilization fund. Instead, the IMF plan calls for more budget cuts and a further decline in the ratio of money to GDP.' (See also Sachs's attack on the IMF in the section on aid to Russia in Chapter 3.)

The Economist (30 July 1994, p. 77) also recommends a fixed exchange rate regime. 'Following the advice of the IMF, most ex-Soviet republics allowed their new currencies to float freely . . . If the governments concerned had instead pegged their exchange rates to a stable currency, they would have had a more visible anchor against inflation . . . If the exchange rate is pegged, prices of traded goods stabilize quickly, because they are subject to competition from abroad at the fixed exchange rate. With a pegged rate, the goal of monetary policy becomes that of defending the exchange rate . . . Pegging the exchage rate is not a substitute for cutting budget deficits and keeping monetary policy tight, but – if these things are done – it can make it easier to bring down inflation.' The exchange rate stabilization school thinks it 'far more efficient . . . to give a clear signal of confidence through a pegged exchange rate early on'.

On 7 September 1993 Russia, Belarus, Armenia, Kazakhstan, Tajikistan and Uzbekistan agreed (subject to ratification) to form a rouble zone. The others would synchronize their fiscal and monetary policies with Russia, whose central bank would be the only authority allowed to issue roubles. In the meantime the others would use their own currencies or receive new rouble notes with special markings to invalidate their use within Russia.

But Russia began to impose more stringent conditions soon after the dissolution of its parliament on 21 September 1993: (1) the supply of new rouble notes to other countries would be in the form of a credit for a term of half a year at the central bank's interest rate (then 210 per cent); the credit would not be repayable by those countries which, at the end of the period, showed 'readiness for joint functioning' and promised not to introduce national currencies for five years (to prevent new roubles flooding back into Russia); (2) security (collateral) in the form of the gold and hard currency reserves of the other countries (*Moscow News*, 12 November 1993, p. 5; 19 November 1993, p. 4). President Nazarbayev of Kazakhstan replied that 'We have made all possible concessions, but now Moscow has asked us to do the impossible, to hand over to them billions of dollars.' Kazakhstan then introduced its own currency (see the response of the individual countries below).

Prices

Tarr (1994: 1–24) estimates the impact on the fifteen countries of the former Soviet Union of shifting to world prices in their trade had that been accomplished in 1990 or 1989. He concludes that energy and raw material exporters, especially Russia, Turkmenistan and Kazakhstan, are the gainers, while countries that concentrate on food and machinery exports (notably Belarus, Estonia, Latvia, Lithuania and, in particular, Moldova) are the biggest losers.

In the first quarter of 1993 Russian supplies under bilateral intergovernmental agreements to other rouble zone countries were priced at about half the world market price for oil and one-third for gas. But other deliveries were priced close to world market levels (Bartholdy and Szegvari 1993: 285). By mid-1993 Russia's energy export prices stood at about half the world market level, up from one-third in the first quarter of the year. Price subsidies to other CIS countries were to be almost entirely phased out by the start of 1994 (Bartholdy and Flemming, *Economics of Transition*, 1993, vol. 1, no. 3, p. 369).

CIS countries continued to benefit from low Russian domestic oil prices immediately after the collapse of the Soviet Union, but the price they paid rose to much higher world market levels calculated in US dollars when they left the rouble zone and created their own currencies. Their oil purchases were still in fact heavily subsidized, although no longer to the previous extent, as the price was calculated at an exchange rate considerably lower than in official trading. Some portions were guaranteed at even lower prices under bilateral agreements (Deutsche Bank, *Focus: Eastern Europe*, 28 February 1995, no. 126, p. 7).

Trade

The average share of intra-regional trade in the total trade of the republics of the former Soviet Union (71.8 per cent in 1988) was higher than that of the EU (59.2 per cent) (Kaser and Mehrotra 1992: 5).

Trade between the states of the former Soviet Union fell by over 30 per cent in 1991 (Michalopoulos and Tarr 1993: 22). In 1993 total trade among the fifteen countries of the former Soviet Union declined to a third of its 1990 level, while trade with the rest of the world fell to 46 per cent compared with 1990. By late 1993 all countries except Tajikistan had introduced their own currencies. The new currencies, with the exception of the Baltic currencies (and possibly the Russian rouble) were not convertible and could not be used in trade. Denominating trade in roubles, however, was risky because of the rouble's instability. Barter continued to be the favoured instrument of trade among most of the new states. For countries other than the Baltic States, annually renegotiated intergovernmental barter agreements provide the framework for allocating goods through state ministries or agencies. This mandatory trade leads to widespread distortions, even though prices fixed in the agreements are getting closer to world market levels and the goods included in the agreements have narrowed to a few commodities (Constantine Michalopoulos and David Tarr, *Transition*, 1994, vol. 5, no. 9, pp. 1–4).

The United Nations Economic Commission for Europe (1993: 76, 139) puts the falls at 5 per cent in 1990, more than 25–35 per cent in 1991 and 25 per cent in 1992. According to official Russian statistics, Russia's trade with the 'near abroad' in 1993 was 50 per cent in volume terms below the level of 1991 (United Nations Economic Commission for Europe 1994: 105).

According to Russian reports, trade with the 'near abroad' fell by 21 per cent in 1993. From 1991 to 1993 Russian exports to the CIS fell as follows: oil, 60 per cent; natural gas, 8 per cent; coal, 68 per cent; petrol, 60 per cent (Deutsche Bank, *Focus: Eastern Europe*, 1994, no. 118, p. 4).

Trade among the former Comecon partners and among the republics of the former Soviet Union shrank by half or more between 1989 and 1993. Over 70 per cent of intra-CIS trade in 1992–93 was conducted on the basis of bilateral agreements on strategic supplies at regulated prices, which often diverged widely from world prices (EBRD 1994: 104).

In a February 1995 speech Yeltsin stated that the CIS countries accounted for only 20 per cent of Russia's foreign trade, compared with 56 per cent in 1991 (*CDSP*, 1995, vol. XLVII, no. 8, p. 13).

In 1994 Russia established a free-trade regime with nearly all CIS states. Some Russian exports to the CIS (fuels, metals, timber and chemicals) still remain subject to export taxes. Export quotas now apply only to the fourteen most important raw materials (*RET*, 1994, vol. 3, no. 2, p. 71).

THE COMMONWEALTH OF INDEPENDENT STATES (CIS)

At first the CIS seemed to be merely a way of allowing a 'peaceful divorce', but from 1993 onwards Russia's military and economic dominance (especially its supplies of energy and raw materials) gave it new life. Political and economic desperation drove reluctant countries to become members and today only the Baltic States have refused to join (Azerbaijan joined on 24 September 1993; on 8 October 1993 Shevardnadze announced that Georgia would seek to join the CIS, he signed a decree on 24 October and parliament ratified a bill on 1 March 1994: see the chapters on the countries concerned for details).

The 22 January 1993 meeting of the CIS was held in Minsk. Azerbaijan was then only an observer and Estonia, Latvia, Lithuania and Georgia were not members of the CIS, either. Seven members signed a charter on closer political and economic integration. Ukraine, Moldova and Turkmenistan signed only the memorandum, allowing them more time to reflect. The idea was that the other seven would ratify the charter during the course of the year, which would also allow time for suggested changes to and amplification of the charter.

All ten members of the CIS accepted the idea of an inter-state bank. This would act as a multilateral clearing house for inter-state trade, but not as a central bank in charge of the money supply. The rouble would be the clearing bank's unit of account and the intention is that monetary policy should be co-ordinated. Russia would have 50 per cent of the shares and votes, while the allocation of the remaining percentages would depend on the share of each country in inter-state trade in 1990. But decisions would require a two-thirds majority.

On 17 March 1993 Yeltsin pessimistically concluded that the CIS to date had been 'unable to fulfil the hopes vested in it'. But he proposed closer integration.

At the CIS meeting in Moscow on 14 May 1993 nine of the ten members signed the following declaration of intent: 'Heads of state of the Commonwealth announce their determination to proceed along the path of in-depth integration, the creation of a common market for the free movement of goods, services, capital and labour within the common "economic space" of the states, and to move by phases towards an economic union.' Yeltsin (optimistically) said that an inter-state bank would be set up by 1 October 1993. Turkmenistan did not sign and asked for further time to consider. (Turkmenistan is concerned to protect the price of its natural gas, but it signed during the 23–24 December 1993 meeting: *CDSP*, 1993, vol. XLV, no. 52, p. 16.) Ukraine stressed that it was only a declaration of intent.

On 15 June 1993 defence ministers announced that they would recommend to their governments the disbandment of the Supreme Command of the Commonwealth Joint Armed Forces and its replacement by a 'united headquarters for co-ordinating military co-operation' (i.e. the end of joint forces). Marshal Yevgeni Shaposhnikov would be replaced by a lower ranking individual.

The declaration on economic integration of 10 July 1993

On 10 July 1993 in Moscow Russia, Belarus and Ukraine signed a surprise 'declaration on economic integration', which envisaged the drawing up of a full treaty by 1 September 1993. The declaration called for the following:

1. The creation of a customs union and a single market in goods and services, labour and capital: 'the interests of our states dictate the need to maintain a single economic space'.

2. The unification of monetary, fiscal, price and tax policies.

3. Respect for territorial integrity. 'The governments proceed from the fact that economic integration cannot be effective without wider, multilateral joint action in the political, defence and legislative spheres'.

4. The economic union is open to all the countries of the former Soviet Union, but only on condition that they do not belong to another economic grouping that would prevent them carrying out the foreign economic policies of the new union.

The CIS Treaty of Economic Union of 24 September 1993

Of the republics of the former Soviet Union only the Baltic States were totally absent from the Moscow meeting, Azerbaijan joining the CIS and (non-member) Georgia sending an observer. Not all members of the CIS signed the framework agreement (individual countries need to agree on the details), Turkmenistan and Ukraine remaining associate members pending discussion and possible ratification by their parliaments (the former affiliated as a full member at the 23–24 December 1994 CIS meeting). The treaty aimed 'gradually to build a common economic space on the basis of market relations' by means of the following:

1. The gradual reduction and eventual abolition of trade barriers. The aim was the free movement of goods, capital and manpower. Unified customs regimes were eventually to be established.

2. Equal legal status for all enterprises in the economic union to encourage joint ventures (partly to enable Russia to exchange energy supplies for shares in partners' enterprises).

3. A payments union or multi-currency clearing system operated via an inter-state bank (ten CIS states formed the bank on 16 December 1993: *RET*, 1993, vol. 2, no. 4, p. 102). It would eventually be transformed into a currency union under which members' currencies would float against the rouble within agreed limits. Those countries retaining the rouble would allow their fiscal and monetary policy to be synchronized with that of Russia.

The CIS meeting in Moscow on 15 April 1994

There was agreement on the setting up of an Inter-state Economic Commission, aimed at integrating the economies and eventually creating a customs union. Ukraine joined the economic union as an associate member. There was also agreement in principle to co-ordinate border policing and peacekeeping duties.

The CIS meeting in Moscow on 9 September 1994

There was agreement on the formation of a payments union and an Inter-state Economic Commission. But Azerbaijan and Turkmenistan did not sign and requested more time to consider. The commission is sited in Moscow, its purpose being to implement decisions. It undertakes administrative functions of common concern delegated by members (e.g. the co-ordination of power, oil and gas pipelines, transport and communications; analysis of the economies and the progress of economic reforms; the drawing up of joint economic programmes). Russia has 50 per cent of the votes (Ukraine 14 per cent; Belarus, Kazakhstan and Uzbekistan 5 per cent each; and the other members 3 per cent each). Some major decisions need a 75 per cent vote, e.g. quotas, currency reserves and new funds. (Ukraine was still only an associate member of the CIS economic union and, therefore, could not sign up for the payments union and could be only an associate member of the commission.)

The CIS meeting on 21 October 1994

Although the Inter-state Economic Commission, a payments union and a customs union were again on the agenda, it seems that countries would be able to opt out.

The CIS meeting in Almaty on 10 February 1995

This was the seventeenth meeting of the CIS, one at which very little was achieved. Yeltsin complained about the 'unsatisfactory work during the past year . . . there have been lots of agreements, but no sign of their implementation'. He called on heads of state to 'make a breakthrough, first and foremost, in the area of economics' (*CDSP*, 1995, vol. XLVII, no. 6, p. 23). Russia's proposal for the joint defence of external borders was rejected. Ukraine and Azerbaijan were categorically opposed, while Russia, Kazakhstan, Tajikistan and Kyrgyzstan were strongly in favour. A non-binding (fully supported) 'Memorandum on Peace and Accord' urged members to refrain from putting military, political and economic pressure on each other. Members pledged to oppose any actions that undermined the stability of existing borders. The meeting confirmed the appointment of Alexei Bolshakov as chairman of the Inter-state Economic Commission.

The CIS meeting in Minsk on 26 May 1995

One of the few concrete results was the signing by Russia and Belarus of a customs union agreement, border posts being removed.

The summit almost unanimously (Turkmenistan abstained from the voting) agreed to create the inter-state currency committee to promote the mutual conversion of national currencies and to ease mutual payments (*Moscow News*, 2–8 June 1995, p. 2).

OTHER DEVELOPMENTS

In January 1994 Kazakhstan and Uzbekistan agreed to form an economic union. The aim was free trade and capital movements and to co-ordinate monetary, fiscal and labour policies. Kyrgyzstan agreed to join on 1 February 1994. (For details, see *The Economist*, 15 January 1994, p. 66; Steve LeVine, *FT*, 27 January 1994, p. 4.) These three countries have been accepted as members of the Asian Development Bank, while Azerbaijan, Tajikistan and Turkmenistan wish to join (*Business Central Europe*, September 1993, p. 511).

On 8 July 1994 Kazakhstan, Kyrgyzstan and Uzbekistan agreed to form a defence and economic union (*Transition*, 1994, vol. 5, no. 6, p. 21). As of July 1994 customs duties had already been eliminated and a payments clearing system was being established (EBRD 1994: 113). On 12 February 1995 they agreed to set up a development bank.

On 28 January 1995 Russia, Belarus and Kazakhstan agreed to form a customs union, although membership would be open to others. The three countries agreed to unify their economic, monetary and foreign trade policies. The customs union would be set up in two stages: (1) unification of trade regimes and customs regulations and the lifting of all restrictions on mutual trade and (2) formal unification into a single customs zone. All restrictions on mutual trade in strategic raw materials were to be lifted in the first quarter of 1995 and unified foreign trade regulations and customs duties were to be introduced in the second quarter of the year (*IHT*, 30 January 1995, p. 11).

In mid-March 1995 there was a meeting of the Economic Co-operation Organization (ECO). Iran, Pakistan and Turkey had set up a body called Regional Co-operation for Development in 1964 to promote trade and development. It was rechristened the ECO in 1985 and in February 1992 Azerbaijan, Kazakhstan, Kyrgyzstan, Tajikistan, Turkmenistan and Uzbekistan joined (as well as Afghanistan). At the March 1995 meeting the three founder members agreed to contribute $714 million to establish a trade and development bank, due to open in July 1995 in Istanbul. Delegates also agreed to set up a shipping company, an airline and an insurance company (Ahmed Rashid, *FEER*, 30 March 1995, pp. 66, 68).

THE RELEVANCE OF THE EUROPEAN PAYMENTS UNION

The main features of and arguments surrounding the relevance of the European Payments Union (EPU) are discussed in Jeffries (1993: 351).

But the issue continues to be debated. Eichengreen (1993: 310–53) argues against applying the idea to the former Soviet Union. Instead he advocates the relatively rapid introduction of (current account) convertibility of independent currencies coupled with macroeconomic stabilization. The circumstances of the early post-war period were very different. For example, the rest of the world is not as prepared to accept terms-of-trade losses as was the USA in 1950; the structural creditor problem would be especially severe, given Russia's dominance; the problem of trade diversion within the former Soviet Union would be much more severe (i.e. a payments union would reinforce the previously already excessive level of intra-regional trade as compared with trade with the rest of the world; in addition the problem of monopolistic enterprises would not be solved). Eichengreen argues that the EPU played a historically specific role, namely helping to reach what he sees as a solution to the struggle over income distribution within individual countries (specifically a social compact whereby labour would moderate wage claims in return for increased investment; this is controversial, e.g. Fischer comments that it was mistrust of the market system that ruled out a rapid return to convertibility as an alternative: p. 349).

Part III

THE COUNTRIES OF EASTERN EUROPE

19

ALBANIA

POLITICS

The political background

The Democratic Party won ninety-two out of the 140 seats in the March 1992 general election, the Socialist Party thirty-eight, the Social Democratic Party seven, the Union for Human Rights two and the Albanian Republican Party one seat (Deutsche Bank, *Focus: Eastern Europe*, 1995, no. 125, p. 7).

The Berisha regime has shown worrying signs of authoritarianism (see below for details and, for example, *EEN*, 1993, vol. 7, nos 9, 16 and 17; *The Economist*, 9 April 1994, p. 39).

The Greek minority

In 1937 the Kingdom of Albania had a population of 1,003,097, of which 92 per cent were Albanians, 4.7 per cent were Greeks and 3.3 per cent were 'others'. Around 71 per cent of the population were Moslems, 19 per cent were Orthodox Christians (mainly in the south) and 10 per cent were Roman Catholics (chiefly in the north). No geological survey had yet taken place. Only about 23 per cent of the land was arable and just 11 per cent was actually cultivated, mostly in the north. (*Albanian Life*, 1994, issue 56, no. 1, p. 7.)

Today about 98 per cent of the population are Albanians, 1.7 per cent are Greeks and the rest are mainly Macedonians, Vlachs and Gypsies (Tony Barber, *The Independent*, 30 June 1993, p. 8).

25 June 1993. Albania expels a Greek Orthodox priest, accusing him of stirring up secessionist feeling among the minority Greeks in southern Albania (he allegedly distributed literature claiming the area was Greek territory, specifically as northern Epirus).

The next day, in retaliation, Greece started to expel large numbers (possibly up to 30,000 up to July) of (mostly) illegal Albanian immigrants (*EEN* puts the total number deported at over 120,000: 15 March 1995, vol. 9, no. 6, p. 4; in 1994 Greece deported 70,000 Albanians: *The Economist*, 1 April 1995, p. 46). There were originally perhaps around 300,000 Albanian immigrants in total in Greece. A figure of around 200,000 was later mentioned by Kerin Hope (*FT*, 15 April 1994, p. 3) and *IHT* (23 April 1994, p. 15). There are now 150,000 Albanians working illegally in Greece (Kerin Hope, *FT*, 6 April 1995, p. 2).

There were also incidents along the border and among the Greek minority in Albania. *EEN* paints a dismal picture of corruption, thuggery and exploitation in the cross-border movements of Albanians (1993, vol. 7, no. 22, pp. 4–7). In total probably some 500,000 Albanians work abroad (*The Economist*, 1 April 1995, p. 46).

It is difficult to know how many ethnic Greeks there are in Albania. The Greek government, it is typically claimed, says that there are around 300,000 ethnic Greeks in Albania, but most Western estimates are around the 200,000 mark (although *EEN* puts the number at a probable 100,000: 15 March 1995, vol. 9, no. 6, p. 4). The Albanian government puts the number at only 60,000. Nicholas Gage (*IHT*, 7 October 1994, p. 4) says that the Greek government's estimate is 400,000, that of Albania 60,000 and that of the CIA 280,000. (The last population census in the early 1980s put the number at 54,000 and 49,000 voted for the Greek minority party in the March 1992 election: Pavli Qesku, Albania's ambassador to Great Britain, *The Independent*, 25 August 1993, p. 35.)

10 April 1994. Two Albanian border guards are killed in a raid on a training camp near the border with Greece. Reciprocal expulsions of diplomats follow. (The attack was led by members of the Greek nationalist 'North Epirus Liberation Front', which are demanding the annexation of the area by Greece: Deutsche Bank, *Focus: Eastern Europe*, 1995, no. 125, p. 8. North Epirus is the name given by Greek nationalists to southern Albania.)

30 May 1994. Greece lodges a formal complaint about the arrest of members of the Greek minority in Albania.

7 July 1994. In another border incident a Greek soldier is wounded.

15 August 1994. The trial begins of five ethnic Greeks (members of Omonia: 'Concord' or 'Harmony'). They are charged with (1) treason and spying (military espionage on behalf of the Greek secret service) in an attempt to 'change Albania's frontiers' and (2) illegal possession of weapons. Although the charge of treason is dropped (because it derived from the penal code operating in the communist period), they are still accused of attempting to 'annex southern Albania'. On 7 September they were given prison sentences of six to eight years. They were convicted, among other things, of 'collaborating with Greek secret services to arm the Greek minority in Albania' and informing Greek intelligence of Albanian troop movements. (The appeal produced only a slight reduction in the sentences. But one was pardoned in December 1994 and the other four had their sentences suspended by the Supreme Court on 8 February 1995.)

Greek retaliation took a number of forms: (1) the expulsion of Albanians – perhaps 70,000 by early October; (2) the blocking of EU financial aid worth Ecu 35 million to Albania (the veto was lifted in November 1994); (3) the closing of one of the main crossing points to Albanians and a slowing of commercial traffic.

23 August 1994. A Greek plane (stolen, according to the Greek government) flies into Albanian air space and drops leaflets calling for the removal of the Albanian government.

16 September 1994. Greece accuses Albania of closing its borders to Greek traffic.

13–14 March 1995. The Greek Foreign Minister Carolos Papoulias visits Albania. The visit is considered a success, e.g. work is to begin on a treaty of peace and friendship. Key issues agreed on were the establishment of private Greek language schools, economic co-operation (such as protection of foreign investment and the creation of a joint Greek–Albanian bank) and the settlement by negotiation of the legal status of Albanian migrant workers in Greece (*EEN*, 1995, vol. 9, no. 6, p. 4).

20 March 1995. Greek security forces arrest several members of the North Epirus Liberation Front as they are preparing to mount a raid across the Albanian border.

Political developments

1 July 1992. Around 6,000 people try to commandeer ships in two ports to flee the country.

19 January 1993. Thousands again try to flee to Italy.

26 January 1993. Nexhmije Hoxha, the widow of Enver Hoxha, is jailed for nine years for misappropriation of state funds (increased to eleven years on 17 May).

12 February 1993. A friendship and co-operation treaty is signed with Bulgaria.

25 April 1993. The Pope visits Albania.

12 July 1993. The leader of a small opposition party is sentenced to six months in prison for denouncing President Berisha in the party newspaper.

27 July 1993. Parliament votes to deprive former prime minister Fatos Nano of his immunity from arrest. Criminal proceedings are started against him for alleged 'abuse of duty and the falsification of official documents in connection with Italian aid' (the single agency he was alleged to have insisted on using overcharged and delivered some foodstuffs which were unfit for human consumption). (He was arrested on 30 July, while other members of the socialist party have also been arrested. On 3 April 1994 he was sentenced to twelve years in prison. 'Since Mr Nano's arrest, public political rallies have been banned, except those of the Democratic Party. Indoor meetings organized by the opposition parties are routinely disrupted or banned': *The Economist*, 9 April 1994, p. 39.)

19 August 1993. Seven senior communists are placed under arrest, including Ramiz Alia (already under house arrest for abuse of power) and Foto Cami (also already under house arrest). (The trial of Alia and nine others, including former prime minister Adil Carcani, began on 21 May 1994. Alia was charged with misappropriation of state funds and abuse of power, including the policy of shooting Albanians trying to flee the country. On 2 July 1994 he was given a jail sentence of nine years, but he was released from jail on 7 July 1995.)

31 August 1993. Former prime minister Vilson Ahmeti is sentenced to two years in prison for alleged abuse of power (for squandering funds in a failed attempt at debt rescheduling; specifically for authorizing a French businessman to negotiate Albania's foreign debt without checking his credentials).

20 September 1993. Momir Bulatovic, the president of Montenegro, visits Albania.

8 and 14 October 1993. The USA and Albania respectively sign an accord on military co-operation. It affirms 'the readiness to broaden and expand defence and military relations between the two countries' with training programmes for Albanian officers and high-level meetings on 'the international security environment'.

Early November 1993. There are protests about a new press law, which gives state institutions the power to withhold information they consider secret or harmful to public or private interests. Newspapers can be confiscated if an article is judged harmful to the public interest (*Albanian Life*, 1994, issue 56, no. 1, p. 33).

9 November 1993. Finance Minister Genc Ruli resigns (amid allegations of corruption) and Trade Minister Artan Hoxha is dismissed. (The governor of the central bank was also dismissed.)

20 November 1993. Leka I (proclaimed king by Albanian exiles after the death of King Zog in 1961) visits Albania for the first time since his family fled after the Italian invasion in April 1939. The authorities order him to leave after just a day because his passport is stamped 'Kingdom of Albania'.

3 March 1994. A new right-wing political alliance is formed (the Democratic Party of the Right). One of its main aims is the return of former landowners' property (*EEN*, 13 April 1994, vol. 8, no. 8, p. 8). (It had difficulty getting registered.)

30 October 1994. The Pope announces Albania's first ever cardinal.

6 November 1994. President Berisha holds a referendum on the new constitution after failing to achieve a two-thirds majority in parliament.

Berisha is unsuccessful in the referendum, with only just over 40 per cent voting 'yes' (*Albanian Life*, 1995, issue 57, no. 1, p. 31). According to

Deutsche Bank (*Focus: Eastern Europe*, 1995, no. 125, p. 7), the turnout was 84 per cent.

The proposed new constitution separated judicial, executive and legislative powers and granted freedom of religion. But opposition was strong because it granted substantial powers to the president, including the following rights: to nominate the prime minister; appoint or dismiss ministers at the suggestion of the prime minister; preside over the cabinet on special occasions and set the agenda; dismiss or arrest the chairman and members of the Supreme Court and Constitutional Court with the approval of parliament.

At the end of December 1994 both coalition partners of the Democratic Party, the Republican Party (one representative) and the Social Democratic Party (seven representatives), announced the end of their co-operation (Deutsche Bank, *Focus: Eastern Europe*, 1995, no. 125, p. 7).

After the failure of the referendum nine out of nineteen cabinet ministers were replaced. Berisha's administration then lost the last of its support as the Republican Party pulled out of the coalition on the grounds that the government was incapable of fighting corruption and inefficiency (*Albanian Life*, 1995, issue 57, no. 1, p. 31).

5 March 1995. Eduard Selami is ousted as chairman of the Democratic Party.

26 March 1995. Around 1,000 young Albanians storm the US embassy in Tirana on rumours that visas and work permits were about to be issued. Police open fire and two demonstrators are reportedly injured.

THE ECONOMY

Financial policy

The *EEN* (20 July 1993, vol. 7, no. 15, p. 8) reports improvements in line with IMF-agreed targets, e.g. the banking system has been rationalized, both the money supply and inflation have been brought under control and the lek has become both semi-convertible and stable against the dollar.

According to Ian Traynor (*The Guardian*, 24 July 1993, p. 35), the central bank has been radically restructured to concentrate on credits to small businesses, while the bulk of state industry has effectively closed down; the president estimates that the budget deficit has been reduced from 50 per cent to 20 per cent of GDP.

The monthly inflation rate was zero in June 1993 (David Ottaway, *IHT*, 24 July 1993, p. 5). The National Bank of Albania enjoys formal independence modelled on the German Bundesbank.

The banking law, which separated the functions of the central bank and the commercial banks, was not implemented until June 1992 (Pashko forthcoming).

A bankruptcy law was adopted in 1992, but no bankruptcies have yet taken place. A rapid accumulation of inter-enterprise arrears in 1991–92 was halted in early 1993 by a settlement system relying on payment before delivery. Arrears were netted out and a strictly limited number of financially viable enterprises were granted the means to write off their claims on non-viable enterprises (EBRD 1994: 16).

The law on social assistance became fully operational only in July 1992. Unemployment benefit is limited to one year, with 70 per cent of the previous year's average wage being paid for the first six months and 60 per cent for the next six months (Pashko 1993: 912–13). A wage inflation tax is in operation (p. 915).

A nominal wage ceiling was introduced in September 1992, which may be exceeded only by certain relatively successful enterprises (Deutsche Bank, *Focus: Eastern Europe*, 1995, no. 125, p. 3).

Prices

In August 1992 almost all prices were freed and the few controlled prices of basic food products were raised by 300–400 per cent (United Nations Economic Commission for Europe 1993: 221).

Price liberalization has been comprehensive, although twenty-five items remain subject to administrative price-setting (EBRD 1994: 17).

Privatization

The urban private sector had been abolished by the late 1960s (Sjöberg forthcoming).

Under legislation passed and decisions taken in August 1991 state enterprises were to be auctioned, sold through shares, distributed free through vouchers or shares (up to 30 per cent of the enterprise value), or disposed of by a combination thereof. The sale of state assets would typically proceed by giving the employees of the enterprise the first option to buy, then by auctioning the property to all Albanian citizens, and finally, in the case of unsold properties, by opening the auction to foreign individuals and companies. As of early 1992 only the privatization of small retail shops and other commercial services had progressed substantially, while only around 20 per cent of state enterprises in the food industry had been privatized (Blejer *et al.* 1992: 56–7).

By January 1992 almost 75 per cent of retail trade and small services was in private hands (Pashko forthcoming).

Nearly all retail shops are now privately owned (Deutsche Bank, *Focus: Eastern Europe*, 15 February 1995, no. 125, p. 4).

On 7 January 1993 a presidential decree was issued on the privatization of all state-owned housing and apartments, a process to be completed by the end of the year (*Albanian Life*, 1993, no. 1, p. 43).

A restitution law passed in May 1993 allows former owners to claim back their land even if it has been built over. It offers compensation to people who have already bought shops or apartments (*The Economist*, 5 June 1993, p. 45).

The law provides only for compensation of up to 10 per cent for country owners (mostly land) and even then only in the form of bank guarantees (*EEN*, 22 June 1993, vol. 7, no. 13, p. 5). The purchase of land is currently forbidden in order to prevent 'tenants' from selling the pre-1946 landowners' land (*EEN*, 21 September 1993, vol. 7, no. 19, p. 8). In the towns former owners can 'share' their old shops with current owners. Until 1995 retailers, traders and other small entrepreneurs who have established businesses will have to pay rent to the former owners, as will tenants who live in expropriated housing; in 1995 the property expropriated in 1948 will revert to the original owners or their descendants (*EEN*, 20 July 1993, vol. 7, no. 15, p. 8; vol. 7, no. 16, p. 3).

The private sector now employs 100,000 people out of a work force of around 1 million (Ian Traynor, *The Guardian*, 24 July 1993, p. 35; David Ottaway, *IHT*, 24 July 1993, p. 5).

Large and medium privatization has not been proceeded with. Instead, the state has concentrated on trying to regain control over the state sector by re-establishing the state's ownership rights, which were assumed by enterprises after liberalization (Pashko forthcoming).

At the end of 1992 300 enterprises were categorized as 'large'. But so many jobs have been cut that they now fall into the 'small' category. It now appears that the aim is to sell them as quickly as possible through the programme for the privatization of smaller enterprises (Deutsche Bank, *Focus: Eastern Europe*, 15 February 1995, no. 125, p. 4).

The aim is for privatization to be largely complete by the end of 1996 (Sjöberg forthcoming).

In mid-1994 the private sector accounted for roughly 50 per cent of GDP (EBRD 1994: 10). According to laws passed in 1993 former owners or their heirs can claim compensation for or restitution of non-agricultural land. In the case of property that has already been privatized there is co-ownership between the new and former owners. The privatization of large enterprises has been insignificant. The privatization of small enterprises progressed rapidly in 1991–92 as many were taken over by employees. The privatization of retail shops is virtually complete (p. 16). In November 1994 the Enterprise Restructuring Agency completed its plan of action for the forthcoming six months. It sought to initiate the liquidation or privatization of twenty large 'problem' enterprises (workers laid off would receive one year's wages in compensation). As of December 1994 about 2,500 small and medium-sized enterprises had been sold. At the end of 1994 the government decided to proceed with the privatization of utilities, including water, electricity and telecommunications (EBRD 1995: 52).

Foreign trade

Limited currency convertibility and a floating exchange rate were introduced for the lek in July 1992 (United Nations Economic Commission for Europe 1993: 221).

There are no quantitative restrictions on imports and only eight product groups are subject to export licences. The exchange rate is freely determined in the interbank market. Current account transactions are largely free of restrictions. Heavy controls are maintained on capital transactions, but there are no controls on the repatriation of capital placements by foreign investors (EBRD 1994: 17, 109).

A free-trade agreement with EFTA was signed in December 1992 (*Business Europa*, May–June 1993, p. 25).

Albania became a net importer of total energy in 1988 (Blejer *et al.* 1992: 20). Domestic oil production was 2.25 million tonnes in 1974 (the peak), 2.0 million tonnes in 1990 and 1.0 million tonnes in 1991 (Blejer *et al.* 1992: 20; *Business Europa*, May–June 1993, p. 28).

The more than 300,000 Albanians who work abroad (most of them in Greece) send back an estimated $400 million a year (Henry Kamm, *IHT*, 4 August 1993, p. 5). Deutsche Bank (*Focus: Eastern Europe*, 22 March 1994, no. 100, p. 35) put the figure at $500 million, but later talked of a conservative estimate of $200 million to $250 million transferred annually (15 February 1995, no. 125, p. 5). In 1993 remittances amounted to $500 million, supplemented by goods to the value of $6 million (*Business Central Europe*, May 1994, p. 80). Anthony Robinson (*FT*, 29 June 1994, p. 3) says that remittances from the more than 300,000 Albanians abroad rose from virtually zero in 1991 to $150 million in 1992 and $334 million in 1993. By way of comparison, the value of exports of goods was $70 million in 1992 and $112 million in 1993; the respective figures for official aid were $374 million and $303 million. The estimated $400 million annually accounts for half the state budget (Helena Smith, *The Guardian*, 13 March 1995, p. 9). About $400 million, over half of national income, comes from remittances (*EEN*, 15 March 1995, vol. 9, no. 6, p. 4).

Foreign aid

As shown in Jeffries (1993), Albania has become highly dependent on foreign aid. The EU has provided some $200 million in food aid (Ian Traynor, *The Guardian*, 24 July 1993, p. 35).

On 26 August 1992 the IMF approved a $29 million loan.

Albania would have been in dire straits without the nearly $1.5 billion of food aid, grants and low interest loans provided by governments and international institutions over the previous three years; they pledged to continue this aid at an annual rate of around $300 million until 1996 (Anthony Robinson, *FT*, Survey, 21 July 1994, p. 31).

Food aid amounted to more than $600 million in the period 1991–92, a sum equivalent to 63 per cent of GDP (Pashko forthcoming).

Gross foreign debt was around $900 million at the end of 1994. Albania, whose payments problems started in 1990, barely services its outstanding foreign debt. It is seeking to negotiate a debt agreement with foreign commercial banks, to which it owes around $400 million. In July 1993 the IMF approved a loan of $60 million, while by mid-1994 the World Bank had approved project financing of over $120 million (Deutsche Bank, *Focus: Eastern Europe*, 1995, no. 125, pp. 5–6).

Gramoz Pashko is cited as saying that 'Foreign aid, remittances from Albanians working abroad and embargo-breaking now account for three-quarters of national income' (James Hansen, *IHT*, 1 April 1995, p. 11). (Albania is the biggest breaker of the embargo on fuel supplies to the Federal Republic of Yugoslavia: Raymond Bonner, *IHT*, 3 April 1995, p. 1.)

Foreign investment

In the first half of 1993 alone ninety-seven joint ventures invested nearly $60 million (*Business Central Europe*, February 1994, p. 66).

Only $20 million in foreign investment has been attracted to date (*The Economist*, 5 June 1993, p. 45). One of the president's staff says that the stock of direct foreign investment at the end of 1993 was $130 million; others have claimed that some $260 million had been attracted between September 1990 and November 1993. Yet no significant foreign investor has yet completed a project that involves building new premises (*The Economist*, 5 March 1994, p. 91).

Total foreign investment commitments exceed $300 million (*Business Central Europe*, July–August 1994, p. 23).

Net direct foreign investment was $20 million in 1992, $48 million in 1993 and an estimated $48 million in 1994 (United Nations Economic Commission for Europe 1995: 151).

Some $80 million of foreign equity capital has flowed in to date; over $200 million of foreign capital is committed to projects, Italian companies accounting for 53 per cent and Greek investors for 20 per cent (Laura Silber, *FT*, Survey, 21 July 1994, p. 33).

Foreign direct investment amounted to $39 million in the period 1990–93 (EBRD 1994: 123). Foreign individuals or companies cannot own land, but they are permitted to lease for up to ninety-nine years (p. 16).

Direct foreign investment rose from $60 million at the end of 1992 to $290 million at the end of 1993, when a new law was approved by parliament permitting unlimited foreign investment throughout the country (Deutsche Bank, *Focus: Eastern Europe*, 1995, no. 125, p. 6).

President Berisha is cited as saying that the government would introduce legislation within two months allowing foreign ownership of real estate (James Hansen, *IHT*, 1 April 1995, p. 11).

Agriculture

Most collective farms were abandoned spontaneously in 1991 and their assets (including the land) were taken over by their members. Legal division of land was not supposed to start before June 1992, but by then 77 per cent of the cultivated land was already in private hands. By the end of 1992 90 per cent of land had been disposed of and 80 per cent of peasant families had become land owners (United Nations Economic Commission for Europe 1993: 203).

Antonia Young and Agim Prodani (*Albanian Life*, 1993, no. 1, p. 33) painted a dismal portrait of the situation in agriculture. The hesitancy over the question of land ownership resulted in the destruction of crops, machines and cattle farms. In autumn 1991 only 50 per cent of the arable area was planted. A year after the promulgation of the land privatization law, nearly all land (about 520,000 ha) that once belonged to the agricultural co-operatives had been privatized. In the mountainous areas especially land was not distributed among members of the ex-co-operatives in line with the law but taken over by the former owners (mostly for their own consumption). The situation on state farms was even worse. Some were almost paralysed, either through vandalism or the collapse of the irrigation system. On a brighter note four joint ventures for state farms and eight for food processors were to be established with Italian, Greek and French companies. Nearly 12 per cent of the small food-processing industry has been privatized. The government has decided that all state farms established on the land of former co-operatives will be privatized and distributed to individual farmers. The rest of the state farms will be developed in the form of joint ventures or share companies.

Former landowners are only allowed to reclaim a maximum of 15 ha from their pre-communist holdings. Alternatively they may seek compensation for up to 30 ha. Compensation is in the form of bonds (*EEN*, 21 September 1994, vol. 8, no. 19, p. 6). Most state farms are now partially or wholly farmed by former employees, who hope to receive title to their allotted land in three years or so (*EEN*, 21 September 1993, vol. 7, no. 19, p. 8). Though in the case of state farms the law does allow for the transfer of ownership to individuals, in practice this category of private farmer is a tenant. Most of the state farms remain intact, although in several cases individuals have been allowed to use state farm land for their own benefit (*EEN*, 21 September 1994, vol. 8, no. 19, p. 6).

The average holding is just under 2 ha. More than 90 per cent of agricultural land and livestock has been shared out among workers on collective farms. Cereal production fell by about 60 per cent in 1991–92, but milk and meat production increased by 30 per cent (Kerin Hope, *FT*, 15 June 1993, p. 34).

By the end of 1993 92 per cent of agricultural land had been privatized, mostly as a result of spontaneous take-overs in the period 1991–92 (EBRD 1994: 16).

By the end of 1993 more than 90 per cent of former co-operative land and nearly two-thirds of land previously owned by state farms had been privatized (*Business Central Europe*, February 1994, p. 66).

Sjöberg (forthcoming) warns that these estimates of the extent of privatization need to be treated with caution.

The land has been split up into small units averaging 1.4 ha (3.5 acres) (Henry Kamm, *IHT*, 4 August 1993, p. 5).

The average holding is around 1.4 ha. The future lies in a consolidation of strips into larger units once peasants are permitted to buy and sell their land; this was forbidden for the first two years (Anthony Robinson, *FT*, Survey, 21 July 1994, p. 33).

Whereas in 1990 50 per cent of agricultural production came from co-operatives, today 95 per cent is contributed by private farmers (Deutsche Bank, *Focus: Eastern Europe*, 15 February 1995, no. 125, p. 4).

Economic performance

Albania's economic performance up to 1989 is summarized in Table 19.1 and after 1990 in Table 19.2.

The United Nations classified Albania as a 'least-developed country', the only one ever in Europe (Henry Kamm, *IHT*, 4 August 1993, p. 5). James Hansen cites a World Bank estimate of *per capita* income at just below $300 a year (*IHT*, 1 April 1995, p. 9). But there have been some very encouraging signs of recovery in the economy, especially in agriculture. Strong growth of GDP was recorded in 1993 and 1994. Substantial progress has also been made on the inflation front, the annual rate peaking in 1992.

There are widely varying estimates of unemployment:

1. Industrial unemployment was 50 per cent at the end of 1991 and did not improve during the first half of 1992 (Pashko 1993: 913). Unemployment in the state sector was 39 per cent at the end of 1992 (Pashko forthcoming).

2. About half the working population is theoretically unemployed, but many are already abroad (Ian Traynor, *The Guardian*, 24 July 1993, p. 35).

3. The unemployment rate is about 40 per cent of the remaining work force, after around 10 per cent of the population has fled abroad to find work. More than 300,000 work abroad, mostly in Greece (Henry Kamm, *IHT*, 4 August 1993, p. 5).

4. In June 1993 the recorded unemployment rate was 33 per cent, but the Ministry of Labour put it at just over 18 per cent. The difference was not explained (*Employment Observatory*, December 1993, no. 5, p. 12).

5. Unemployment in the towns is probably around 60 per cent (*The Economist*, 2 April 1994, p. 43).

Table 19.1 Albania: selected economic indicators 1961–89

Economic indicator	*1961–70*	*1971–75*	*1976–80*	*1981*	*1982*	*1983*	*1984*	*1985*	*1986*	*1987*	*1988*	*1989*
Average annual rate of growth of NMP (%)	7.4	6.7	2.7	6.0	2.7	0.5	–2.9	1.8	6.2	–2.2	–0.5	11.7
Average annual rate of growth of GDP (%)								1.8	3.1	–0.8	–1.4	9.8
Average annual rate of growth of industrial output (%)									5.0	1.5	2.1	5.0
Average annual rate of growth of agricultural output (%)									4.0	0.5	–6.2	10.7
Unemployment rate (%)									5.4	5.2	6.0	6.7
Gross foreign debt ($ million)												74.4

Sources: Blejer *et al.* (1992: 4, 26); Pashko (1993: 907–19); *Economics of Transition*, 1993, vol. 1, no. 1, p. 128; Sandström and Sjöberg (1991: 937–43); Åslund and Sjöberg (1991: 6–20); United Nations Economic Commission for Europe (1992: 86)

Table 19.2 Albania: selected economic indicators 1990–94

Economic indicator	*1990*	*1991*	*1992*	*1993*	*1994*
Rate of growth of GDP (%)	−10.0	−27.7	−9.7	11.0	7.4
Rate of growth of industrial output (%)	−7.6	−36.9	−44.0	−10.0	−2.0
Rate of growth of agricultural output (%)	−6.9	−24.0	18.0	14.0	6.8
Inflation rate (%)	0.0	36.0	225.2	85.0	22.6
Net foreign debt ($ billion)	0.1	0.5	0.6	0.6	0.7
Budget surplus or deficit (% GDP)	−3.7	−44.0	−22.0	−16.0	−14.0
Current account ($ billion)	−0.122	−0.293	−0.442	−0.369	−0.238

Sources: Various issues of United Nations Economic Commission for Europe, *Economic Survey of Europe*; IMF, *World Economic Outlook*; Deutsche Bank, *Focus: Eastern Europe*; Commission of the European Communities, *Employment Observatory*; *Economics of Transition* and *Business Central Europe*; EBRD (1994: 149; 1995: 26); Blejer *et al.* (1992: 2, 4); Pashko (1993: 907–19; forthcoming)

6. More than 300,000 Albanians work abroad, mainly in Greece, Italy and Germany. In 1993 unemployment still hovered around 30 per cent of the remaining non-agricultural work force (Anthony Robinson, *FT*, Survey, 21 July 1994, p. 32).

7. Unemployment as a percentage of the non-agricultural labour force was 37 per cent at the end of 1992 and 44 per cent by mid-1993. Some 200,000 to 300,000 have left the country to work elsewhere (Sjöberg forthcoming).

8. The (end of year) unemployment rate was 9.8 per cent in 1990, 9.4 per cent in 1991, 24.2 per cent in 1992, 22.0 per cent in 1993 and 19.0 per cent in 1994 (United Nations Economic Commission for Europe 1994: 86, and 1995: 111).

9. The unemployment rate was 17.5 per cent at the end of 1993 (EBRD 1994: 149).

10. Unemployment fell to 18 per cent at the end of September 1994 (*Business Europa*, February–March 1995, p. 28).

11. Unemployment, according to official data, reached a peak of 26.3 per cent at the end of 1992 and fell to 19.6 per cent at the end of 1993 and to 17.5 per cent at the end of 1994. But real unemployment (i.e. including those seeking work but excluded from the statistics) was at least 30 per cent at the end of 1993 (Deutsche Bank, *Focus: Eastern Europe*, 1995, no. 125, p. 3).

12. The rate of open unemployment was 30 per cent at the end of 1993 and 21 per cent at the end of 1994 (IMF, *World Economic Survey*, June 1995, p. 53).

13. Registered unemployment was 9.8 per cent at the end of 1990, 9.4 per cent at the end of 1991, 26.7 per cent at the end of 1992, 23.3 per cent at the end of 1993 and 18.4 per cent at the end of 1994 (*Employment Observatory*, 1995, no. 7, p. 38).

20

BULGARIA

POLITICS

Political developments before the 18 December 1994 general election

14 July 1992. Grisha Filipov (prime minister 1981–86) is arrested on charges of corruption.

22 January 1993. Todor Zhivkov and others are to be charged with treason (he is alleged, for example, to have proposed that Bulgaria should become the sixteenth republic of the Soviet Union).

14 February 1993. Bulgaria and Albania sign a treaty of friendship and co-operation.

Late May 1993. A new informal pro-presidential party, Civic Alliance for the Republic, is formed (mainly by Bulgarian Socialist Party reformists and social democrats led by former BSP liberal Alexander Tomov) (*EEN*, 1993, vol. 7, no. 13, p. 7).

5 August 1993. Andrei Lukanov is charged with 'grave misappropriation of large funds' (diverting state funds to leftist governments and overseas communist parties in the late 1980s).

9 August 1993. Zhivkov is charged with diverting funds to left-wing governments and overseas communist parties.

2 September 1993. Former prime minister Georgiu Atanassov begins a ten-year prison sentence.

December 1993. A new party, the Centre for New Politics, is launched. It is led by Dimitur Ludzhev and other UDF breakaways (*EEN*, 1994, vol. 8, no. 1, p. 4).

18 January 1994. Zhivkov's appeal against a seven-year jail sentence for embezzlement of public funds is rejected.

9 February 1994. The Berov government survives its fifth no-confidence vote (there was also one at the end of May 1993, for example).

April 1994. In April President Zhelev demanded that the government should resign, accusing it of failing to push economic reforms (John Pomfret, *IHT*, 14 May 1994, p. 11).

19 May 1994. The Berov government survives its sixth no-confidence vote (all tabled by the Union of Democratic Forces).

6 June 1994. The Bulgarian Socialist Party re-elects Zhan Videnov as party chairman (he took over in December 1991).

2 September 1994. The Berov government resigns (its resignation approved by parliament on 8 September) and calls for an early general election. (The Movement for Rights and Freedoms withdrew its support for the government.)

17 October 1994. Reneta Indzhova is named interim prime minister until the 18 December 1994 general election. (She is the first woman to be prime minister. She helped the UDF draw up its economic programme and was a former privatization director.)

The general election of 18 December 1994

The turnout was over 75 per cent. There was a 4 per cent threshold for parliamentary representation. The Bulgarian Socialist Party did even better than expected, winning an absolute majority of seats in the National Assembly (see Table 20.1). Only five parties won seats in the National Assembly. Smaller ones failed to do so, e.g. the Democratic Alternative for the Republic (a centre–left coalition). The parties with seats in the National Assembly were as follows:

Bulgarian Socialist Party. Leader Zhan Videnov. (The Bulgarian Socialist Party was joined in an election pact by the Bulgarian Agrarian Party 'Alexander Stamboliski' and the Political Club 'Ecoglasnost': Deutsche Bank, *Focus: Eastern Europe*, 1995, no. 130, p. 3.)

Union of Democratic Forces. Leader Filip Dimitrov (he resigned after the election and was replaced by Ivan Kostov).

People's Union. A coalition of the Democratic Party (which split from the UDF) and the Agrarian Party.

Movement for Rights and Freedoms. Leader Ahmed Dogan.

Bulgarian Business Bloc. Leader Georgi Ganchev (a former emigré). (The bloc became part of the coalition government, but Ganchev was later

Table 20.1 Bulgaria: the general election of 18 December 1994

Party	*Seats in the National Assembly*	*Vote (%)*
Bulgarian Socialist Party	125	43.5
Union of Democratic Forces	69	24.23
People's Union	18	6.15
Movement for Rights and Freedoms	15	5.44
Bulgarian Business Bloc	13	4.72
Total	240	

disqualified as an MP because he held a US passport at the time of the election: *EEN*, 14 April 1995, vol. 9, no. 8, p. 1, and 28 April 1995, vol. 9, no. 9, p. 8.)

Political developments after the 18 December 1994 general election

24 January 1995. The new government is announced. Membership includes Roumen Getchev (vice-premier in charge of the economy and privatization; he favours growth to a lower rate of inflation), Dimitar Kostov (finance), Kyril Tsochev (trade), Georgi Pirinski (foreign affairs) and Dimitar Pavlov (defence).

1 February 1995. The EU association agreement comes fully into effect.

THE ECONOMY

The Berov government's financial programme

The IMF-approved target was to keep the budget deficit in 1993 to within 7.9 per cent of GDP (passed by parliament in June). The *EEN* (19 January 1993, vol. 7, no. 2, pp. 7–8; 2 March 1993, vol. 7, no. 5, p. 7) reports the attempt to reinvigorate the National Council for Social Co-operation. This was designed to co-opt union support over privatization and redundancies (it is composed so far of the two major trade union groups, Podkrepa and the Confederation of Independent Trade Unions, the smaller union Edinstvo, the Bulgarian Chamber of Commerce and the Union of Private Enterprise).

The 1994 budget was passed on 28 February 1994, with the IMF setting tough targets (a budget deficit of 6.2 per cent of GDP and an inflation rate of 30 per cent). The IMF approved funding on 18 March (*EEN*, 1994, vol. 8, no. 6, p. 7). *Business Central Europe* (March 1994, p. 20) put the planned budget deficit at 6.5 per cent of GDP and the *FT* (29 March 1994, p. 3) put it at 6.7 per cent.

VAT was introduced on 1 April 1994, having been postponed by around six months (the standard rate is 18 per cent, but staple foods, school books, medicines and domestic utilities are zero-rated).

Parliament approved the 1995 budget on 5 May 1995, the budget deficit being targeted at 5.6 per cent of GDP.

Prices

In February 1991 90 per cent of prices were liberalized. The government frequently adjusts administered prices (EBRD 1994: 21).[1]

After the February 1991 stabilization programme only the prices of goods accounting for about 10 per cent of trade turnover (in 1991) were subject to state intervention, either indirectly via margins in the case of basic food products, medicines and oil products, or directly in the case of energy (Wyzan forthcoming).

In April 1992 new price limits were set for some of the fourteen important food items under government control, while the prices of the remainder were liberalized. New minimum procurement prices for a number of agricultural products were also fixed. Price increases of 35 per cent for electricity and 60 per cent for coal were announced. A package of compensation measures for the population was also approved (Frydman *et al.* 1993: 6).

In February 1993 petrol prices rose by 50 per cent. In May electricity prices were to rise by 50 per cent for households and 10 per cent for industry. Coal and central heating prices were also to be increased (Anthony Robinson, *FT Survey*, 5 May 1993, p. 32).

Price controls have been maintained on a number of products and services, e.g. energy, telecommunications, water supply and transport (*Transition*, April 1994, vol. 5, no. 4, p. 9).

On 1 February 1995 there were price increases for fuel, energy and other goods such as flour (*Transition*, January–February 1995, p. 21).

Banks

The National Bank of Bulgaria is an independent institution accountable only to parliament. Progress has been made in 'bank consolidation', i.e. the merging of some eighty state commercial banks into eight to ten banking groups (Virginia Marsh, *FT Survey*, 5 May 1993, p. 30). Smaller commercial banks with bad loan portfolios are being merged into stronger banks (United Nations Economic Commission for Europe 1993: 222). By mid-1994 fifty-nine banks had been reduced to six; all except the State Savings Bank had been transformed into joint stock companies (Wyzan forthcoming).

On 1 October 1993 the government issued twenty-five-year bonds to cover the worst of its state enterprises' bad debt (*Business Central Europe*, November 1993, p. 49). In March 1994 the government took steps to refinance some of the bad loans arranged in the socialist era by banks to enterprises, issuing bonds to convert enterprise debt into government debt (Virginia Marsh and Anthony Robinson, *FT*, 29 March 1994, p. 3).

A programme implemented during 1994 to recapitalize banks provided 'bad loan bonds' to cover non-performing bank assets (which remain on the balance sheets of banks). The bonds have a twenty-five-year maturity and a five-year grace period, and pay a fraction of market interest rates for seven years. The low interest rates have created severe liquidity problems for the banks, which the past government addressed by repeated cash recapitalizations during 1994 (partial repurchasing of the 'bad loan bonds') (EBRD 1995: 54).

There is still no bankruptcy law and only a few (mainly small) enterprises have been closed down (Virginia Marsh and Anthony Robinson, *FT*, 29 March 1994, p. 3).

There is no separate bankruptcy law. Provisions for bankruptcy are included in a 1989 law, but the environment is very protective of debtor enterprises and allows indefinite deferral of creditor claims (EBRD 1994: 20). A bankruptcy law was passed by parliament in July 1994, but banks are not covered (EBRD 1995: 54).

Of the 3,500 state enterprises scheduled for privatization two-thirds are operating at a loss. But there have been no closures, a bankruptcy Act passed in July 1994 existing only on paper (Deutsche Bank, *Focus: Eastern Europe*, 31 May 1995, no. 130, p. 5).

Manpower

There have been some strikes, e.g. in the ore and coal-mining industries in December 1993. Issues included overdue wages and government-guaranteed jobs for those laid off by mine closures. According to *EEN* (1993, vol. 8, no. 1, p. 4), there is a strong pro-reform lobby among workers, who are desperate to see foreign investment.

The government imposes a ceiling on wage increases in enterprises (EBRD 1994: 21).

Privatization

Small privatization was launched and aborted in March–June 1991. Although some sales of petrol stations took place, the programme was considered to be a failure on the whole. New legislation was then introduced. The only significant privatization was in housing (even in 1985 85 per cent of the housing stock was in private hands). With large privatization, preferential sales to employees up to 20 per cent of shares are allowed. Each employee or retired person is entitled to a 50 per cent discount up to an amount equal to between eight and twelve months' salary, depending on length of service. Employee shares have no voting rights for the first three years. If more than 30 per cent of employees vote to enter an auction or tender for their company and are successful, the price will be reduced by 30 per cent (Frydman *et al.* 1993: 29–32).

According to Anthony Robinson (*FT Survey*, 5 May 1993, p. 31), 20 per cent of shares have to be set aside for purchase by investment funds.

The 1992 restitution law states that owners or their heirs have the right to reclaim houses, shops and other property confiscated between 1947 and 1952. To date 23,500 out of 51,300 claims have been settled (*The Independent*, 29 January 1993, p. 11).

By the end of June 1993 56.5 per cent of small-scale urban properties (83 per cent of shops and restaurants) had been restored to their former owners (Wyzan forthcoming).

The pace of large privatization has been very slow. According to Anthony Robinson (*FT Survey*, 5 May 1993, p. 31), not a single medium or large state enterprise has been privatized. Twelve enterprises are in the process of being privatized, while eighty-four have been selected for the first round. The sale of Balkan Bulgarian Airlines was planned to be completed by the autumn of 1993 (up to 49 per cent of the shares would be on offer to foreign investors; 40 per cent would probably remain with the state, the remainder going to employees and other domestic investors) (p. 31). The share of the private sector has risen from 5 per cent to 20–25 per cent of GDP (p. 29).

The private sector now accounts for between 25 per cent and 30 per cent of economic activity, although 90 per cent of industry is still formally in state hands and privatization remains slow (Anthony Robinson, *FT*, Survey, 13 October 1994, p. 13). Legislation to set up the mass privatization programme was approved just before the Berov government resigned on 2 September 1994. Direct sales to investors have resulted in the privatization of thirty medium-to-large enterprises. Although formal privatization has been slow, state and municipal enterprises have been subjected to 'hidden' privatization. This usually involves the formation of private companies to supply state enterprises with inputs at high prices and of other companies to take their subsidized output for resale at market prices. In this way enterprises accumulate inter-enterprise debts and losses while allowing a new class of millionaires to develop. The process of nationalizing losses and privatizing profits is widespread throughout the former Soviet bloc but has been most blatant in countries such as Bulgaria and Romania (p. 14).

According to official estimates, the private sector as a whole accounted for 5 per cent of GDP in 1991, 10 per cent of GDP in 1992 and 12–13 per cent in 1993 (United Nations Economic Commission for Europe 1993: 215; 1994: 57).

In mid-1993 the private sector accounted for 20 per cent of GDP and 22 per cent of employment (compared with 4 per cent of employment in 1990 and 14 per cent in 1992) (*Employment Observatory*, 1993, no. 5, pp. 1, 4, 26). In 1994 the private sector accounted for 27.5 per cent of GDP, 20 per cent of industrial production and 80 per cent of agricultural production (*Employment Observatory*, 1995, no. 7, p. 3).

Up to a third of the economy is now thought to be in private hands (Julian Borger, *The Guardian*, 8 March 1994, p. 13).

According to *Transition* (April 1994, vol. 5, no. 4, pp. 9–10), the private sector's contribution to GDP increased from around 5 per cent of GDP before 1989 to 37 per cent in 1993 (although some official estimates put it at

18 per cent). The sector now accounts for more than 50 per cent of all retail and wholesale trade.

The private sector accounted for 9.1 per cent of GDP in 1990, 11.8 per cent in 1991, 15.3 per cent in 1992 and 19.4 per cent in 1993 (Wyzan forthcoming).

The private sector's share of GDP is about 40 per cent (*The Economist*, 29 October 1994, p. 56). Only thirty-four large and medium-sized enterprises have been privatized (*The Economist*, 7 January 1995, p. 33).

In mid-1994 the private sector accounted for roughly 40 per cent of GDP (EBRD 1994: 10). Between 30 per cent and 50 per cent of GDP is generated in the private sector, mostly in the trade/retail and service sectors. Large privatization has been slow. By mid-1994 one in sixteen large enterprises had been privatized, while seventeen out of 870 medium-sized enterprises had been privatized. The mass privatization programme involves 340 enterprises. Small privatization has been slow. By March 1994 only sixty-nine out of the 5,000 enterprises had been sold by ministries and ninety-three had been sold by municipalities. But some 25,000 small and medium-sized enterprises were created in 1992 alone through the restitution of urban business properties (p. 20). During the third and especially the fourth quarter of 1994 thirty medium-sized state enterprises were privatized, bringing the total to forty-seven (compared with a target set in 1993 of eighty enterprises). A programme for the mass privatization of medium-sized enterprises was submitted to parliament on 22 March 1995. This was to involve the privatization of 100–150 enterprises between November 1995 and October 1996 and a further 100 enterprises between February 1996 and January 1998. Payment would be in the form of vouchers (15–20 per cent), cash (50 per cent) and 'bad loan bonds' issued by the government as part of the bank recapitalization scheme (30–35 per cent). Vouchers would be tradable on the stock market. The first list of enterprises was to be made public in November 1995 (EBRD 1995: 54).

Under the plan approved by the cabinet on 27 March 1995 the first stage of mass privatization was to run from November 1995 to October 1996. By the end of 1995, it was hoped, 20 per cent of state-owned enterprises (600) would be in private hands. Some 50 per cent of the value of the enterprises was to be offered for cash, while the rest would be sold for bonds and privatization coupons (*Transition*, 1995, vol. 6, no. 3, pp. 5, 17). In May 1995 the government talked of privatization being carried out in two stages, starting in January 1996 and ending in late 1997. Some 150 enterprises were to be selected for privatization (those not to be privatized included the Kozloduy nuclear power station, the military–industrial complex, the Bulgarian Telecommunications Company, the Post Office and one or two major banks). The private sector's share of GDP (30 per cent in 1994) was projected to reach 55–60 per cent by the end of 1996 and 70–75 per cent in late 1997 (*Transition*, 1995, vol. 6, nos 5–6, p. 19).

It was estimated that the list of enterprises was to be ready by 20 September 1995 so that it could be presented to parliament by the end of that month. It was thought that the first wave of the programme should begin in March 1996. Bulgarians were to have the option of either investing vouchers in investment funds or participating directly in auctions. Immediate direct sales on the stock exchange were rejected, but shares in enterprises acquired through vouchers could be offered on the exchange six months after an auction (Theodor Troev, *FT*, 9 August 1995, p. 2).

The first two large state enterprises have been privatized, the first in May 1993 when a Belgian company bought a starch and sweetener manufacturer. But the sale of Balkan Bulgarian Airlines was not proceeded with. The private sector, mostly small businesses, accounts for 20–30 per cent of economic activity, according to a World Bank representative (*IHT*, 1 December 1993, p. 14).

Business Central Europe (February 1994, p. 51) reveals that only seven deals were concluded by the Privatization Agency in 1993. The delay in 'open' privatization has allowed 'hidden' or '*nomenklatura*' privatization to thrive; 60 per cent of trade and 20 per cent of industry are now in private hands. The draft 1994 privatization programme includes 315 companies (about 10 per cent of the total).

Pomfret also makes the point that the *nomenklatura* have exploited business and political connections: 'Many of these people have become fabulously rich running private trading companies that buy from and sell to Bulgaria's state-run factories, creating a bizarre economic subsystem in which production is state-run but profits are private . . . Essentially, private trading companies control everything sold to the factories and market their production too. Such enterprises can be lucrative through kickbacks or manipulation of antiquated accounting methods. The private trading companies can make windfall profits selling raw materials at market prices, buying finished products at low prices and then selling them at a profit. As the state-run enterprises slip deeply into debt, the private trading companies reap huge profits' (John Pomfret, *IHT*, 14 May 1994, p. 11). 'Diplomats and political observers agree that Bulgaria's state enterprises are being comprehensively asset-stripped by managers and private businessmen with close ties to the former communists' (Julian Borger, *The Guardian*, 17 December 1994, p. 9).

The economic power of the *nomenklatura* is particularly strong in Bulgaria. 'By supplying raw materials at market prices to state firms run by friends, and then buying back the finished products cheaply, companies can make money twice, first on the raw materials and then by selling the finished goods. The state firm then makes a thumping loss – but that is passed on to the government . . . What Bulgarians call the "mafiaization" of the economy' (*The Economist*, 7 January 1995, p. 33).

According to official figures, the private sector contributed 22 per cent of GDP in 1994. But a World Bank estimate, which encompasses illegal and quasi-legal activities as well as legal activities outside the government tax base, puts the figure at 50 per cent. The World Bank also suggests that at least 90 per cent of profits in the economy may accrue to the informal private sector. Since the private sector accounts for only 5 per cent of long-term assets, less than 10 per cent of total credits, 22-26 per cent of employment and 10–12 per cent of labour income, this suggests that private-sector profits are somehow channelled from the state enterprise sector. After 1991, as a general rule, private firms took over distribution, marketing and foreign trade functions. Private wealth has been created through siphoning profits from state enterprises (Zeljko Bogetic and Arye Hillman, *Transition*, 1995, vol. 6, no. 3, pp. 4, 6).

(The 'Group of 13' is the name given to the business lobby founded by the largest private companies. The group controls a large part of the private sector: Virginia Marsh, *FT*, 10 May 1994, p. 3. The 'Group of 13' is 'said to be owned and operated by former communists who are now exerting mafia-like influence in the country's private sector': *Business Europa*, November–December, 1994, p. 35. Until mid-1994 the most important of the groups were united in the so-called 'Group of 13'; seven now remain in the group: *Transition*, 1995, vol. 6, no. 3, p. 5.)

On 2 August 1993 the government announced its privatization scheme to be presented to parliament; the scheme rules out a mass programme via *free* vouchers (*EEN*, 10 August 1993, vol. 7, no. 16, p. 4).

The privatization law was passed in early June 1994 (*Business Central Europe*, July–August 1994, pp. 17–18). (The mass privatization programme came into force on 28 June: *FT*, 29 June 1994, p. 3.) Between 1 September and 14 October 1994 Bulgarians aged twenty or more would be eligible to buy vouchers worth 30,000 lev (they would have to pay 1,500 lev, two weeks' average wages, and the rest between 1999 and 2005); some 150,000 vouchers worth 100,000 lev each would be issued to cover restitution claims; vouchers would be placeable in special investment funds; the first wave would include some 500 medium-sized and large (but non-strategic) enterprises valued at 180 billion lev, to be followed, if successful, by a second wave of up to 700 enterprises (*Business Central Europe*, October 1993, p. 62). (Wyzan (forthcoming) puts the number of enterprises on the list at 340. The target was to sell 320 enterprises – including seventy large ones – in 1994, or around 10 per cent of the state sector. 'Strategic' sectors were to be excluded, e.g. armaments, transport, oil refining and energy generation: *Transition*, 1994, vol. 5, no. 4, p. 9.)

Two years after the passing of a privatization law which envisaged the sale of more than 3,000 enterprises, the agency responsible for selling medium-sized and large enterprises has completed fewer than twenty transactions. Ministries have sold only 200 small enterprises (Virginia Marsh and Anthony Robinson, *FT*, 29 March 1994, p. 3).

Thirty-four medium-sized and large enterprises have been privatized (Jane Perez, *IHT*, 19 December 1994, p. 5).

Mark Milner (*The Guardian*, 3 September 1994, p. 35) puts the total number of state enterprises at over 5,000 (to date 146 enterprises have been sold, sixty-three of them by the end of 1993).

The private sector's share of GDP in 1994 was a third. So far only around 275 enterprises have been privatized out of a scheduled total of some 3,500 enterprises (Deutsche Bank, *Focus: Eastern Europe*, 31 May 1995, no. 130, pp. 4–5).

Foreign trade

The foreign trade regime is liberal, although tariff rates have tended to increase. Quantitative restrictions apply to only a limited number of imports and exports (EBRD 1994: 21). There is a floating exchange rate regime. There are few restrictions on current account transactions, but heavy controls on the capital account (p. 109).

The central bank sets the (unified) exchange rate against the dollar on the basis of events the previous day.

On 26 February 1993 it was announced that a trade agreement with EFTA was to come into effect, after ratification, on 1 July 1993. The EFTA countries would dismantle trade barriers more quickly (there would be restrictions mainly on steel and textiles during the interim period), Bulgaria having until the end of 2002 to phase out tariffs and other restrictions.

On 8 March 1993 an association agreement with the EU was announced (*EEN*, 1993, vol. 7, no. 6, p. 5). There would be a ten-year transition to free trade (although EU restrictions on Bulgarian agricultural exports would remain indefinitely). Bulgarian pig iron and tobacco, for example, would be subject to stringent quotas until the sixth year, when, in theory, there will be completely free access to the EU for all Bulgarian industrial goods.

The current temporary 2 per cent import surcharge is to be gradually reduced to 1 per cent in 1995 and is expected to be phased out altogether by the end of 1995 (*Transition*, April 1994, vol. 5, no. 4, p. 9).

According to official figures, the countries of the former Soviet Union accounted for only 28 per cent of foreign trade in 1992 (compared with 75 per cent in 1989). In contrast the EU's share had risen to 31 per cent (Virginia Marsh, *FT Survey*, 5 May 1993, p. 31). Exports to the former Comecon countries may have fallen by about 66 per cent in 1991 and by a further 15–25 per cent in 1992 (Borensztein *et al.* 1993: 6). In 1992 the OECD countries accounted for 42.2 per cent of exports, compared with 26.3 per cent in 1991, while the respective figures for imports were 43.8 per cent and 32.8 per cent (Wyzan forthcoming).

Foreign aid

On 3 March 1993 a moratorium on interest payments on foreign commercial bank debt was announced (*EEN*, 16 March 1993, vol. 7, no. 6, p. 5; 14 April 1993, vol. 7, no. 8, p. 5). But in late March the government decided to resume partial payment of interest. According to *Business Central Europe* (November 1993, p. 14), Bulgaria halted interest payments on commercial debt in June and again in September 1993. Bulgaria had a foreign debt of $12.95 billion, of which $9.25 billion was owed to the London Club of bank creditors (*EEN*, 4 June 1994, vol. 8, no. 1, p. 4).

On 21 March 1994 the EU agreed to an Ecu 110 million balance of payments loan (*FT*, 22 March 1994, p. 2).

On 25 November 1993 Bulgaria reached a debt reduction and rescheduling agreement in principle with creditor commercial banks. Further negotiations were meant to be completed by the 30 June 1994 deadline. On 15 April 1994 the Paris Club agreed to reschedule $200 million of debt repayments due in the year to March 1995. On 29 June 1994 Bulgaria signed an agreement with the London Club which provided for a 47.1 per cent reduction in the $8.16 billion debt to commercial banks. Parliament ratified the deal on 27 July 1994.

Foreign investment

Foreign citizens and legal entities may not buy land. Foreign persons and firms with over 50 per cent foreign participation may not buy agricultural land. Foreign persons can own buildings and usufructural rights over non-agricultural land, but cannot acquire title to the underlying real estate. Foreign persons or firms with a foreign majority participation must have special permission to engage in the following: the production of or trade in weapons or ammunition; the exploration for or the extraction of natural resources from the territorial sea, the continental shelf, or the exclusive economic zone. Such persons or firms must also apply for permission from the Bulgarian National Bank if they wish to operate in banking or insurance (Frydman *et al.* 1993: 20).

Parliament has ruled that foreign companies have to start paying the same profit tax (40 per cent) as local ones (*Business Central Europe*, November 1993, p. 49).

Net direct foreign investment in 1991 was only $56 million and in 1992 was only $42 million (Deutsche Bank, *Focus: Eastern Europe*, 1993, no. 91, p. 10). The United Nations Economic Commission for Europe (1994: 136, and 1995: 151) puts net direct foreign investment at $4 million in 1990, $56 million in 1991, $42 million in 1992, $55 million in 1993 and $48 million in January–September 1994.

According to *Business Central Europe* (February–March 1994, p. 33), the two years to the end of August 1993 saw only $216 million of direct foreign investment.

By the end of 1993 foreign investment totalled only $220 million (Virginia Marsh and Anthony Robinson, *FT*, 29 March 1994, p. 3). The Deutsche Bank (*Focus: Eastern Europe*, 1995, no. 127, p. 10) put the figure at $300 million by July 1994.

The figure for foreign investment was $230 million at the end of April 1994 (Wyzan forthcoming).

Foreign direct investment amounted to $164 million in the period 1990–93 (EBRD 1994: 123).

Agriculture

In 1990 all farm debts were written off (Pryor 1992: 279).

The process of land restitution began in February 1991. The law provided for restitution to former owners or their heirs of the land forcibly collectivized in the 1950s. The aim was to re-establish the land ownership structure as of 1946 (note that before 1946 63.1 per cent of farms were 5 ha or less in size). Provision has also been made for auctioning off about 400,000 ha of state land to peasants who have never owned land. As of August 1992 around 10 per cent of land had been returned to its former owners and an additional 20 per cent was expected to have been returned by the autumn of the following year (Frydman *et al.* 1993: 32–3).

According to Franz-Lothar Altmann (*The World Today*, June 1993, p. 113), the spring 1991 law was amended a year later and restrictions on the number of hectares to be available for restitution were lifted. By the end of 1992 about 27 per cent of agricultural land had been returned to private owners.

The Bulgarian Socialist Party was trying to get the government to share its views regarding farming co-operatives inheriting the land and other assets of the former collective farms. Some 800 of these co-operatives had been set up in BSP-controlled districts, even though they were technically illegal. Three weeks earlier the government came close to approving legislation giving land to peasants who promised to farm their allocated land. But on 3 March 1993 President Zhelev insisted that land must first be restored to its original owners and only afterwards could co-operatives be established. Private farmers who do not belong to co-operatives are now being discriminated against by, for example, being given poor land (*EEN*, 16 March 1993, vol. 7, no. 6, p. 5; 21 September 1993, vol. 7, no. 19, p. 4). By the end of 1992 only 6 per cent of farmland had been returned to private ownership, but this figure rose to 23 per cent (*EEN*, 20 July 1993, vol. 7, no. 15, p. 3) and then 35 per cent at most (*EEN*, 10 August 1993, vol. 7, no. 16, p. 4).

According to the United Nations Economic Commission for Europe (1993: 203), by the end of 1992 only 10 per cent of arable land had been restored to the original owners.

Around 30 per cent of the land is now worked by farmers who own it (*Employment Observatory*, December 1993, no. 5, p. 4).

Virginia Marsh and Anthony Robinson (*FT*, Survey, 5 May 1993, p. 32) reported that many animals had been slaughtered for such reasons as livestock being given to peasants who had no land and the selling-off of co-operatives' fodder before animals were returned to individual farmers. Government policy included the following: a desire to avoid breaking up all the large farms (especially those with long-maturity crops such as vineyards and orchards); restitution is a priority, but private co-operatives ought to be encouraged (the opposition UDF opposes these co-operatives). By mid-April 1993 only 13.3 per cent of arable land had been returned to owners within its final borders.

There are more than 1.7 million conflicting restitution claims. More than 90 per cent of the land that has passed into private hands is in tiny plots of less than 1 ha. Because much of the land has been transferred on a temporary basis pending final decisions on claims, the land cannot yet be used as collateral or sold (*The Economist*, 7 August 1993, p. 63).

The average plot size is 0.16 ha (Mark Milner, *The Guardian*, 4 September 1993, p. 35).

Some 50 per cent of farmland is now in private hands, most of it outside the highly productive regions. About 25 per cent of land has been returned to the former owners (42 per cent of agricultural land reserved for restitution has been distributed so far). To help farmers obtain bank credit, land protocols or temporary land titles can be used as collateral under the amended law. Government controls include price floors and minimum import prices for some agricultural products. Prohibitions on grain exports were expected to be phased out by September 1994 and replaced by export taxes (*Transition*, April 1994, vol. 5, no. 4, pp. 9–10).

EEN (18 August 1994, vol. 8, no. 17, p. 5) refers to 'the parlous state of agriculture generally – endless derelict collective farms and acres of fertile but abandoned land. The vaunted privatization of land is a fiction: about half the land may have been privatized, but the poor security of ownership and the extreme difficulty of getting credit or vital agricultural inputs makes farming a nightmare.'

Theodor Troev is not so pessimistic (*FT*, Survey, 13 October 1994, p. 14). But he notes that about 60 per cent of the new landowners now live in cities or towns and many are unable or unwilling to return to farming. Some work their newly returned plots of land only at weekends and with simple implements. The average size of newly returned plots is 1.6 ha. Some new co-operatives have been formed. It may take another year before land restitution is complete. Only 50 per cent of farmland had been returned with full title by the end of September 1994, while 60 per cent should be returned by the end of 1994. The privatization of state agricultural enterprises is now slowly moving ahead (e.g. pig farms, poultry farms, mills, machine repair works and fisheries) (p. 14).

By the end of 1994 57.3 per cent of farmland had been restituted (EBRD 1995: 54).

Laws to return property to pre-communist owners have left many ethnic Turks landless (in total Turks account for 10 per cent of the population) (Tim Judah, *The Times*, 29 December 1994, p. 11).

Around 59 per cent of all arable land has been restored to previous owners or their heirs. The Bulgarian Socialist Party has criticized the land reform for interfering with the cultivation of large land blocks. The party has therefore asked parliament to amend the law so as to restrict owners of small plots of land which are part of larger land blocks from trading with them or planting crops different from those in the rest of the block (*The Guardian*, 25 March 1995, p. 39).

On 27 April 1995 President Zhelev vetoed the changes in the Land Act which had been passed by parliament on 14 April (*EEN*, 1995, vol. 9, no. 9, p. 6). The amendments specified the following:

1. Only the amount of land declared on entering the collective farm would be returned to the claimant. Opponents argued that peasants had routinely declared less land in order to avoid the heavy taxes on private farmers.

2. The owner's original land would remain part of the co-operative. Opponents argued that this could mean a claimant receiving inferior land as compensation.

3. A seller of land could resort to the free market only if the offer were to be successively rejected by owners of neighbouring plots, by relatives and by the municipal authorities. Moreover, the sale price would be fixed by the state.

4. People who received land from the communist regime would receive full title and pay prices set by the state, while former owners would receive compensation.

The amended Land Act has now passed into law (*EEN*, 25 May 1995, vol. 9, no. 11, p. 7).

Parliament passed the controversial amendment on 14 April 1995. Owners wishing to sell their land have to offer it in the first place to the state, which has two months to decide whether to buy it. The amendment also restricts the right to sell small plots that are part of larger land blocks or to plant crops different from those in the rest of the block. The opposition vowed to refer the matter to the Constitutional Court (*Transition*, 1995, vol. 6, no. 4, p. 19). The court rejected some of the provisions of the amended Land Act.

Economic performance

Bulgaria has had a rough transition, but it seems as though GDP growth was slightly positive in 1994. The annual inflation rate peaked in 1991, but inflation is still troublesome (it was higher in 1994 than in 1993) and the unemployment rate is still in double figures (see Tables 20.2 and 20.3).

Table 20.2 Bulgaria: selected economic indicators

Economic indicator	*1990*	*1991*	*1992*	*1993*	*1994*
Rate of growth of GDP (%)	−9.1	−11.7	−7.3	−2.4	1.4
Rate of growth of industrial output (%)	−16.5	−27.3	−15.9	−6.9	4.1
Rate of growth of agricultural output (%)	−6.0	−0.3	−12.0	−18.2	−1.1
Inflation rate (%)	23.9	333.5	82.0	72.8	96.3
Net foreign debt ($ billion)	10.4	11.5	12.1	12.5	10.0
Budget surplus or deficit (% GDP)	−12.8	−14.7	−15.0	−15.7	−7.0
Current account ($ billion)	−1.200	−0.800	−1.100	−1.500	−0.100

Sources: Various issues of United Nations Economic Commission for Europe, *Economic Survey of Europe*; OECD, *Economic Outlook*; IMF, *World Economic Outlook*; United Nations, *World Economic and Social Survey*; Deutsche Bank, *Focus: Eastern Europe*; *Economics of Transition* and *Business Central Europe*; EBRD (1994: 153; 1995: 30); *Transition*, 1994, vol. 5, no. 4, pp. 9–10; Wyzan (forthcoming)

Table 20.3 Bulgaria: unemployment

Date		*Number unemployed*	*Unemployment rate (%)*
1990	June	22,400	0.5
	December	72,200	1.8
1991	January	74,000	1.9
	February		2.6
	March	124,100	3.4
	April		4.4
	May		5.1
	June	223,000	5.8
	July		7.0
	August	302,000	7.9
	September	342,000	8.6
	October		9.1
	November		10.0
	December	425,000	10.5
1992	January		10.7
	February		10.9
	March		11.2
	April		11.5
	May		
	June		13.1
	July		
	August	506,000	14.0
	September		14.8

Table 20.3 Continued

Date		*Number unemployed*	*Unemployment rate (%)*
	October		
	November		
	December	576,900	15.6
1993	January		
	February		
	March	604,500	16.0
	April		
	May		
	June	586,500	15.5
	July		16.2
	August		
	September	598,700	15.7
	October		15.9
	November		16.1
	December	626,100	16.4
1994	January		
	February		
	March		16.1
	April		16.1
	May		14.5
	June	509,000	13.3
	July	514,000	13.5
	August		
	September		12.7
	October		
	November		
	December		12.8

Sources: Various issues of United Nations Economic Commission for Europe, *Economic Survey of Europe*; OECD, *Economic Outlook*; Commission of the European Communities, *Employment Observatory*; Deutsche Bank, *Focus: Eastern Europe*; *Economics of Transition* and *Business Central Europe*; *Transition*, 1994, vol. 5, no. 4, p. 10; EBRD (1994: 153; 1995: 30); Frydman *et al.* (1993: 8)

NOTE

1. The share of unrestricted prices was reduced from 90 per cent of the basket of goods in the consumer price index in 1991 to 69 per cent in mid-1994. At present the figure is 54 per cent (EBRD, *Transition Report*, 1995, p. 18).

21

THE FORMER CZECHOSLOVAKIA

Czechoslovakia

SEPARATION

Basic data on the Czech Republic and Slovakia on separation

The respective percentage shares for the Czech Republic and Slovakia in 1992 were as follows (*FT Survey*, 24 March 1993, p. i): population, 66 and 34; NMP, 70.2 and 29.8; industrial output, 71.8 and 28.2. According to official statistics, the respective percentage shares for 1992 were as follows (DIW, *Economic Bulletin*, 1994, vol. 31, no. 3, p. 13): population, 66.2 and 33.8; GDP, 72 and 28; exports, 74 and 26; direct foreign investment, 92 and 8.

In 1992 the population of the Czech Republic was 10.4 million and GDP per person was $2,550, while the respective figures for Slovakia were 5.26 million and $1,820 (*The Economist*, Survey, 13 March 1993, p. 18).

More than 100,000 Slovaks have been attracted to the Czech Republic, but only 200 Czechs have opted to become Slovak citizens (*The Economist*, 31 July 1993, p. 42). According to Tony Barber (*The Independent*, 12 November 1993, p. 12), perhaps as many as 300,000 Slovaks opted to stay in the Czech Republic, many of them professional people.

Note that Slovakia has had to do much more than the Czech Republic in building up its administrative system, owing to the dominance of Prague. For example, it had to build up a central bank and a central statistical office from scratch (United Nations, *World Economic and Social Survey*, 1994, p. 31).

Arms production

Arms production reached a peak in Czechoslovakia in 1987, when it accounted for around 3 per cent of total industrial output and employed 1.3 per cent of the total labour force. Slovakia's share of arms production was at least 60 per cent. This implies that arms production was less than 2 per cent of industrial output in the Czech Republic but 5–6 per cent in Slovakia. This amounts to a regional problem in both Slovakia and the Czech Republic (in southern Moravia and Prague) (Capek and Sazama 1993: 225). Almost two-thirds of the Czechoslovak armaments industry was previously concentrated in Slovakia (DIW, *Economic Bulletin*, 1994, vol. 31, no. 3, p. 14). Czechoslovakia was the world's seventh largest arms exporter, selling about 80 per cent of its output of military hardware abroad (the former Warsaw Pact took two-thirds of exports) (*The Economist*, 10 April 1993, p. 76). In 1990 arms exports to many countries (e.g. Iran) were banned. Arms production in Slovakia has now fallen to just over 10 per cent of the 1988 level in that region, while Czech arms production has fallen by around 30 per cent since 1988 (on 11 June 1993 the Czech arms regulations were amended to incorporate a 'case by case' approach) (*The Economist*, 6 November 1993, p. 106).

According to Kiss (1993: 1046–7), in 1987 military production represented about 3 per cent of GDP and 10.5 per cent of total industrial production in Czechoslovakia. The proportion of military production exported was 77.6 per cent (50–60 per cent of total production went to the other Warsaw Pact countries). By 1990 military output had already fallen by nearly 50 per cent and the proportion of output exported was 52.3 per cent.

Williamson (1993: 30) is not the only one to argue that Czechoslovakia provided an even clearer case than Poland of a country 'where recession was primarily due to an excessively contractionary macroeconomic policy'.

The trade and payments arrangements between the two countries

The common currency ended much sooner than expected because of the lack of synchronization of monetary and fiscal policy. The two currencies (the Czech and Slovak crowns; stamped old notes at first) were actually introduced on 8 February 1993 at par. Avoiding the mistakes made when Comecon collapsed, the Czech Republic and Slovakia established an Ecu-denominated payments clearing system. This is backed by an Ecu credit facility (net trade deficits were to be settled in convertible currency at the end of each month: United Nations, *World Economic and Social Survey*, 1994, p. 31). Balances over Ecu 130 million must be repaid within a month; the first equalization payment, in convertible currencies, was made by Slovakia in December 1993 (DIW, *Economic Bulletin*, 1994, vol. 31, no. 3, p. 18). According to *Business Central Europe* (June 1993, p. 18), the Ecu trade clearing system is very slow. Payment for a sale from one republic has to be converted into Ecus before being transferred to the other republic, where it is converted back into crowns. Consequently enterprises do not record all their transactions.

The Slovak crown quickly began to be devalued against the Czech crown to try to tackle the Slovak trade deficit and stem the fall in trade between the two countries. Anthony Robinson (*FT Survey*, 24 March 1993, p. ii) reported a possible 30–40 per cent decline in such trade in 1993 unless special measures were taken to finance trade over and above the Ecu 130 million credit facility. It has been estimated that a 10 per cent fall in trade with Slovakia leads to a 1 per cent fall in Czech GDP and the reverse figure for Slovakia is twice that. Foreign trade (including that with Slovakia) now accounts for nearly 50 per cent of Czech GNP. In 1992 Slovakia took 23 per cent of the Czech Republic's exports and over 40 per cent of Slovakia's trade is with the Czech Republic (p. ii).

Capek and Sazama (1993: 230) estimate that 11.5 per cent of Czech sales are in Slovakia, while the reverse figure is 26.9 per cent. In 1992 Slovakia exported one-third of its industrial output to the Czech Republic, while the reverse figure was only 15 per cent (OECD, *Economic Outlook*, June 1993, p. 122).

The IMF granted the Czech Republic a special credit of $240 million after the introduction of the Czech crown (Deutsche Bank, *Focus: Eastern Europe*, 26 February 1993, no. 69, p. 5).

The initial attempt to establish co-ordinating institutions to govern economic relations, including a monetary union and customs, quickly disintegrated. The Czech Republic in particular has moved speedily to introduce border controls and to place trade relations with Slovakia on a similar footing to its trade with other partners (Heady *et al.* 1994).

In the first half of 1993, compared with the same period of 1992, Czech exports to and imports from Slovakia fell by 24 per cent and over 26 per cent respectively (United Nations Economic Commission for Europe 1994: 96). In 1993 Czech exports to Slovakia declined by over 30 per cent and Czech imports from Slovakia dropped by some 15 per cent (United Nations, *World Economic and Social Survey*, 1994, p. 32).

On 7 June 1995 the Czech government announced that it had decided to cancel the Ecu-denominated payments system. A 10 per cent devaluation of the Slovak crown in July 1993, partially offset by a 4 per cent revaluation in May 1995, coupled with the imposition of a 10 per cent Slovak import surcharge, led to a $750 million bilateral trade surplus for Slovakia over the last year (Anthony Robinson and Vincent Boland, *FT*, 8 June 1995, p. 3).

The value of the former Czech subsidy to Slovakia

The amount transferred from the Czech Republic to Slovakia has been estimated at about 15 per cent of Slovakia's income in the 1950s and 5–7 per cent in the 1980s. The transfer was the equivalent of roughly 4.5 per cent and 3 per cent respectively of the Czech Republic's income (Capek and

Sazama 1993: 216). Between 1981 and 1988 transfer payments represented an average of 3.1 per cent of Czech 'produced national income' and 6.8 per cent of Slovakian 'appropriated national income' (DIW, *Economic Bulletin*, 1994, vol. 31, no. 3, p. 13). In 1992 the Czech Republic transferred 25 billion crowns or the equivalent of 7 per cent of Slovak GDP (United Nations, *World Economic and Social Survey*, 1994, p. 32). There are varying estimates of the value of the Czech subsidy: (1) $700 million annually (Anthony Robinson, *FT*, Survey, 24 March 1993, p. ii); (2) $700 million to $1 billion annually (Tom Redburn, *IHT*, 24 March 1993, p. 11).

THE ECONOMY

Privatization

Monopoly

In 1990 the largest 100 enterprises accounted for 26 per cent of industrial employment and 51 per cent of the total assets of state industrial enterprises (Frydman *et al.* 1993: 41).

The private sector

According to official figures, the entire private sector's contribution as a percentage of GDP was 4.1 per cent in 1989, 5.2 per cent in 1990, 9.3 per cent in 1991 and 20 per cent in 1992 (United Nations Economic Commission for Europe 1993: 215).

The private sector accounted for about 10 per cent of GDP in 1991 and 16–20 per cent of GDP in 1992 (Schwartz and Lopes 1993: 17).

The first wave of privatization

Corporatization was launched in 1990 (Frydman *et al.* 1993: 91). The management of each enterprise was given a deadline of 31 October 1991 to submit a 'basic project'. Others, including foreigners, could submit an unlimited number of 'competing projects'; the deadline of 30 November was extended to 20 January 1992 (p. 80). The projects were evaluated by the founder (e.g. branch ministry or local authority) and then sent to the appropriate Czech or Slovak privatization ministry or to the federal ministry for the final decision. By the end of February (the deadline) 8.57 million people had registered for coupons (79 per cent of the eligible number) (p. 85). In the first round 437 investment funds operated (p. 87). If an investment company (group) administered several funds there could be no more than 40 per cent of any enterprise in the entire portfolio (p. 88). The funds controlled 72 per cent of all points (p. 86). Some 53 per cent of the total book value of enterprises in the first round was to go to vouchers and 65 per cent of the total equity (the book value of all shares) (p. 84).

Nearly 50 per cent of the investment points were held by only nine of the investment funds (e.g. Harvard Capital and Consulting Company), while a mere 28 per cent were retained by individuals (Anthony Robinson, *FT*, 17 February 1993, p. 13). After the first wave almost 70 per cent of shares were controlled by the top fourteen funds (*Business Central Europe*, July–August 1993, p. 49). According to Mladek and Hashi (1993: 83), the ten largest funds controlled over 40 per cent of all voucher points and 60 per cent of those voucher points transferred to all the funds. Nine of the ten funds are controlled by large domestic and foreign banks (the exception is Harvard Capital and Consulting).

According to *Business Central Europe* (June 1993, p. 53), the legislation prohibited banks from establishing investment funds with the intention of purchasing shares in other banks. But some banks have circumvented the law by establishing independent subsidiaries to set up funds.

The shares were to have been transferred to investors on 29 March 1993, but the distribution was held up by the Czech government (not the Slovak government) because of the dispute with Slovakia over asset sharing in general (Slovak citizens hold about 18 per cent of the shares in Czech companies: *IHT*, 23 March 1993, p. 15). Not until 12 May 1993 was it announced that shares in Czech enterprises would be transferred to Slovak investors. The distribution of shares began in the Czech Republic on 24 May 1993, with shares tradable on 22 June. According to Mladek and Hashi (1993: 86), Czech citizens spent only 3.5 per cent of their voucher points on enterprises in Slovakia, while Slovak citizens spent 23.2 per cent of their voucher points on enterprises in the Czech Republic.

In the first wave the asset transfer was about $1,000 per voucher holder (Lucja Swiatkowski Cannon, *FT*, 9 September 1994, p. 17).

Small privatization

In 1991 some 20,000 small production units and shops were sold at auction. In most cases property was let on a long-term lease; only in a quarter of cases was the property actually sold (Simoneti 1993: 92). No privileges were granted to management or employees during small-scale privatization (United Nations Economic Commission for Europe 1994: 165).

Agriculture

The aim was to return land to the original owners, with a limit of 250 ha of agricultural land and 150 ha of arable land (the maximum established during the 1921 land reform). The law also contained provision for a grant of 'equivalent' land if the original land could not be returned (Cochrane 1993: 852).

In agricultural co-operatives over 50 per cent of members had no title to the land going back to the time before collectivization (land had remained formally private even in communist times). Roughly half the land used by the co-operatives was formally owned by absentee landowners who were not members, since they had chosen to leave the land (Frydman *et al.* 1993: 54). The privatization of state farms was to begin in 1993 (p. 90).

There was no write-off of farm debts (Pryor 1992: 279).

Original owners were given until 31 December 1992 to make their claims. The public response was very poor (Frydman *et al.* 1993: 55). Only 180,000 out of 3.5 million people eligible had by then applied for land; private farms account for barely 5 per cent of agricultural output in both the Czech Republic and Slovakia (*The Economist*, 7 August 1993, p. 63).

Table 21.1 Czechoslovakia: unemployment

Date		*No. unemployed*	*Rate of unemployment (%)*
1990	June	12,600	0.2
	December	77,000	1.0
1991	January	119,478	1.5
	February	152,323	1.9
	March	184,720	2.3
	April	223,208	2.8
	May	255,635	3.2
	June	300,767	3.8
	July	363,000	4.6
	August	400,000	5.1
	September		5.6
	October		6.0
	November	500,000	6.3
	December	524,000	6.6
1992	January	550,000	7.1
	February		6.9
	March		6.5
	April		6.0
	May		5.6
	June		5.5
	July		5.4
	August		5.3
	September		5.2
	October		5.1
	November		5.1
	December		5.1

Sources: Various issues of *Czechoslovak Economic Digest*; United Nations Economic Commission for Europe, *Economic Survey of Europe*; OECD, *Economic Outlook*; Commission of the European Communities; *Employment Observatory*; *Economics of Transition*; Deutsche Bank, *Focus: Eastern Europe*

Foreign trade

In 1992 OECD countries accounted for 63 per cent of exports (*Employment Observatory*, 1993, no. 4, p. 2).

Foreign investment

A foreign investor domiciled abroad could not acquire land in Czechoslovakia, except by descent and special legal provisions (mainly the restitution laws). A Czechoslovak entity, however, even if wholly owned by the above, or a foreign person with a registered domicile in Czechoslovakia, could purchase land without any limitations (Frydman *et al.* 1993: 61).

The net flow of direct foreign investment was $188 million in 1990, $592 million in 1991 and $1.054 billion in 1992 ($983 million for the Czech Republic and only $71 million for Slovakia) (United Nations Economic Commission for Europe 1993: 239).

Economic performance

The main indicators are shown in Tables 21.1 and 21.2.

Table 21.2 Czechoslovakia: selected economic indicators

Economic indicator	*1990*	*1991*	*1992*
Rate of growth of GDP (%)	−0.4	−14.7	−7.1
Rate of growth of industrial output (%)	−3.5	−24.7	−11.5
Rate of growth of agricultural output (%)	−3.9	−8.4	−11.8
Inflation rate (%)	10.8	58.9	10.8
Net foreign debt ($ billion)	7.0	6.3	5.3
Budget surplus or deficit (% GDP)	0.1	−2.0	−3.3
Current account ($ billion)	−1.1	0.4	0.2

Sources: Various issues of United Nations Economic Commission for Europe, *Economic Survey of Europe*; OECD, *Economic Outlook*; IMF, *World Economic Outlook*; Deutsche Bank, *Focus: Eastern Europe*; *Economics of Transition* and *Business Central Europe*.

The Czech Republic

POLITICS

The political background

Under the go-ahead but pragmatic leadership of Prime Minister Vaclav Klaus the Czech Republic has become the number one economic and political success story in Eastern Europe. He has engineered a remarkably successful and rapid transition, while using subsidies to avoid sudden, large-scale bankruptcies and lay-offs. Klaus has also done a good job of 'selling' a consistent policy line to the Czech public.

Communist or socialist parties appear to have little chance of making a comeback. David Ottaway (*IHT*, 28 May 1994, p. 5) suggests two possible reasons: (1) the 'velvet revolution' was so rapid that little real reform took place within the Communist Party; (2) in reality Prime Minister Klaus has followed a highly statist approach to economic reform, carefully incorporating trade unions as partners and allowing heavy state spending on social welfare measures and subsidies to hold down unemployment (see the section on bankruptcy below).

The Economist (22 October 1994, p. 26) talks of a tacit social contract in which workers accept low wages in exchange for high employment and a low cost of living (note that housing rents and most utility prices are controlled).

'From now on the main thrust of government and business policy will shift increasingly from the macro to the micro level, concentrating above all on the restructuring of the industrial sector. Here, Premier Klaus appears to have been right. His view has been that the process of restructuring, which will take a very heavy toll, can be more easily weathered, at a more bearable social cost, in a period of economic growth than during the adjustment recession' (Deutsche Bank, *Focus: Eastern Europe*, 22 December 1994, no. 123, p. 3).

Political developments

26 January 1993. Vaclav Havel is elected president by parliament.

30 June 1993. The Czech Republic is admitted to the Council of Europe.

26 August 1993. During a visit by Yeltsin a friendship and co-operation treaty with Russia is signed.

24 October 1993. Jiri Hajek, one of the founders of Charter 77, dies.

11–12 January 1994. President Clinton vists Prague. (On the second day he met the leaders of the Czech Republic, Slovakia, Hungary and Poland mainly to discuss the Partnership for Peace policy.)

1 July 1994. Over 1,000 Gypsies become non-citizens when the deadline passes for Slovak citizens wishing to claim Czech citizenship. Citizenship requires proof of two years' fixed residence and a five-year trouble-free police record (*EEN*, 1994, vol. 8, no. 25, p. 4). Almost all the 250,000 Gypsies were classified as Slovaks even though two-thirds were born on Czech territory and the rest were (usually forcibly) moved from Slovakia by the communists (to replace the Sudeten Germans, for example) (Tom Goss, *FT*, Survey, 19 December 1994, p. vi). The law, which came into effect on 1 January 1993, states that anyone under forty whose parents were registered as Slovaks in Czechoslovakia is classified as Slovak and has to apply for Czech citizenship.

6 July 1994. It is announced that Radio Free Europe/Radio Liberty will move to Prague.

29 October 1994. The Pope announces that a Czech has been made a cardinal.

2 November 1994. Jaroslav Lizner, director of the Centre for Coupon Privatization (which processes applications from would-be investors), is arrested on charges of taking bribes.

18–19 November 1994. In local elections the Civic Democratic Party wins over 32 per cent of the vote.

1 February 1995. The EU association agreement comes fully into effect.

22–23 April 1995. A new communist party is established. The Party of Czechoslovak Communists is led by Miroslav Stepan.

20–22 May 1995. The Pope visits the Czech Republic. The Pope canonizes the seventeenth-century priest Jan Sarkander, amid considerable controversy over his role in the Counter-reformation.

THE ECONOMY

Financial policy

The new West European-type taxation system is designed to widen the tax base and shift the burden from enterprises to individuals and consumption. The introduction of VAT on 1 January 1993 caused initial confusion. The aim is to bring the general VAT rates into line with those of Western Europe (Deutsche Bank, *Focus: Eastern Europe*, 31 August 1993, no. 86, p. 8).

'The Czech Republic is one of the most heavily taxed countries in Europe, with the top rate of income tax running at 42 per cent and the [top] rate of VAT at 23 per cent. As a result, large-scale tax evasion and tax avoidance are the order of the day. At the same time the heavy tax burden discourages investment, especially as the government is adamant in its refusal to grant any tax privileges to domestic or foreign investors' (Otto Pick, *The World Today*, November 1994, p. 208).

Wages are regulated through a tax on 'excessive increases'. It was initially imposed during 1991, reintroduced in the second half of 1992 for enterprises with majority state or municipal ownership and reintroduced on 1 July 1993 for all enterprises with more than twenty-five employees (EBRD 1994: 23). The tax on 'excessive wages' has been reduced (EBRD 1995: 55). On 12 July 1995 the wage regulations introduced in July 1993 were abolished on the grounds that they had proved unsuccessful, e.g. the regulation specifying that wage increases could not exceed inflation by more than 5 per cent was taken as a binding commitment rather than an option (Deutsche Bank, *Focus: Eastern Europe*, 1995, no. 135, p. 7).

The Czech National Bank was to repay all $471 million in outstanding debt to the IMF by the end of September 1994, two years ahead of schedule. Earlier in the year the bank had repaid a $430 million IMF loan not due until 1995 (*Transition*, 1994, vol. 5, no. 6, p. 21).

The aim was to achieve a balanced budget in 1995 (*Business Europa*, February–March 1995, p. 33).

There has been a series of financial scandals (*The Economist*, 11 February 1995, p. 47).

Prices

The only remaining significant price controls pertain to utility charges, rents and public services. In addition mark-ups are closely regulated in the energy sector (EBRD 1994: 23).

The government planned to liberalize the rents of non-residential property fully by 1 June 1995 (*Business Europa*, February–March 1995, p. 35).

The bankruptcy law

Bankruptcy legislation was approved by parliament in 1991. But the enactment of the law was postponed twice and it has been in effect only since April 1993. Debtor companies whose shares will be at least 50 per cent voucher-privatized are protected from bankruptcy during privatization, specifically until two months after the shares are transferred to new owners. The law also provides a three-month protection period (which may be extended to six months with court approval) to allow firms to come to an agreement with creditors (Brom and Orenstein 1994: 899). Only a handful of firms have been declared bankrupt since 1990 (p. 898).

The bankruptcy law took effect on 22 April 1993 (Patrick Blum, *FT*, 22 April 1993, p. 2). There is a period of three to six months during which debtors and creditors are able to try to reach agreement. Failing that the enterprise is declared bankrupt and its assets are seized. Debtors have only fifteen days to apply for three months' protection and creditors have only thirty days to file claims.

Private farmers were to be protected from bankruptcy until December 1994. Enterprises in the voucher scheme are protected until two months after the transfer of at least 34 per cent of the shares to the new owners (EBRD 1994: 22).

Only thirty bankruptcies have been declared; creditors are not keen to sue because they are unlikely to recoup much of their debt (Susan Greenberg, *The Guardian*, 30 October 1993, p. 39). The number of petitions filed is 1,448; sixty-six cases have been wound up. For example, tax bills are being deferred to avoid bankruptcies (Deutsche Bank, *Focus: Eastern Europe*, 16 February 1994, no. 10, p. 4). In its first year of operation only 133 (mainly small) enterprises went bust (*The Economist*, 22 October 1994, p. 26). As of November 1994 only 319 companies had gone bankrupt, a mere thirty-seven of which were state-owned enterprises (*Business Central Europe*, March 1995, p. 64).

Privatization

Up to the end of 1992 the former large state industrial enterprises were broken up on average into three independent enterprises either prior to or during the privatization process (United Nations Economic Commission for Europe 1994: 167). The average number of employees per industrial enterprise has fallen from 1,665 in 1990 to 360 (*Transition*, July–August 1994, vol. 5, no. 6, p. 21).

The Prague stock exchange opened on 6 April 1993.

A draft law would return properties expropriated from Jews during the period of Nazi rule. The Jewish community, which now numbers only 3,000, compared with 120,000 before the Second World War, will be handed back synagogues, cemeteries, libraries and other community buildings that were confiscated by the Nazis and are still in state hands. The law was passed on 2 May 1994 (Adrian Bridge, *The Independent*, 20 January 1994, p. 12).

In July 1994 the Constitutional Court ruled as follows: (1) the residence clause (claims could be made only by permanent residents) had to be removed; (2) the six-month deadline set in 1991 for claims to the property by those living in exile was too short and November 1994 should be the new deadline (Deutsche Bank, *Focus: Eastern Europe*, 1994, no. 112, p. 7).

On 8 March 1995 the Constitutional Court upheld a 1945 decree issued by President Eduard Beneš stripping ethnic Germans of their property (*IHT*, 9 March 1995, p. 2).

The second and final wave of large (voucher) privatization was to involve 861 enterprises. (The original deadline for submitting 'basic privatization projects' to branch ministries was 16 August 1992 and other interested parties were allowed two more months to submit 'competing projects'. The final choice was to be made jointly by the branch ministries and the republican Ministries of Privatization: Mladek and Hashi 1993: 88.) The process was to take place in the second half of 1993 (voucher sales starting at the end of July, later postponed to 30 September; the deadline of 30 November 1993 for the registration of voucher booklets by individuals and registration for privatization by enterprises was later postponed to 8 December and 31 December respectively). The first of the auction rounds was later fixed for 11 April–12 May 1994. The second wave of voucher privatization was completed on 25 November 1994 (EBRD 1995: 55).

Greater use was to be made of methods such as direct sales, auctions and tenders; only 30 per cent of the book value of enterprises was to be accounted for by vouchers, as opposed to 60 per cent in the first round (Deutsche Bank, *Focus: Eastern Europe*, 31 March 1993, no. 72, p. 7). Only 65 per cent of people entrusted their vouchers to investment funds, compared with 72 per cent in the first round (*Business Central Europe*, April 1994, p. 58). According to *Prague News* (7–21 April 1994, p. 1), the 353 investment funds will have some 60 per cent of registered vouchers at their disposal, 10 percentage points less than in the first wave. The law sets a legal limit of 20 per cent on the participation of any one fund in the assets of any particular company (p. 3).

Most investment funds are owned by the large banks, of which the state still owns (on average) 40 per cent and to which former state enterprises are heavily indebted. The banks are naturally reluctant to call in their loans (Portes 1994: 1186–7).

In mass privatization the large banks have become, through their investment funds, the most significant owners of the privatized sector (Brom and Orenstein 1994: 893). The government still owns approximately 40 per cent of each of the largest banks (p. 895). In the first round more than 50 per cent of all vouchers were invested with the thirteen largest investment funds (p. 895). The National Property Fund appears to hold about 20 per cent of the property privatized to date through vouchers and other methods (p. 897). Despite a variety of concerns expressed during the implementation of mass privatization, the investment funds 'have maintained liquidity, have taken a long-term and active role in enterprise management and are acting like "real" owners' (p. 917).

After the second round of privatization the state retained a significant stake in only a few large utilities such as the national power utility CEZ and the petrochemical conglomerate Chemapol. Chemapol was the subject of much indecision about whether to involve foreign companies and only at the 13 July 1994 cabinet meeting was it decided to allow an international oil consortium to take a large minority stake (*EEN*, 1994, vol. 8, no. 15, p. 4; *EEN*, Czech Republic Country Briefing, 21 July 1994, p. 3).

The National Property Fund still has a stake of more than 20 per cent in 400 enterprises (*The Economist*, 20 May 1995, p. 93).

Investment funds control about 29 per cent of all outstanding shares, while the National Property Fund holds 40 per cent and industrial and portfolio investors own 25 per cent. The top twenty or so investment funds obtained 90 per cent of those vouchers entrusted (Vincent Boland, *FT*, Survey, 2 June 1995, p. vi).

On 28 June 1995 a Dutch–Swiss consortium was declared the successful competitor to buy a 27 per cent stake in SPT Telecom, while on 11 July 1995 it was announced that a Western consortium was to take a 49 per cent stake in the two main oil refineries.

The size of the private sector

The private sector's share of GDP rose from close to zero in 1989 to about 18 per cent in 1992 and some 50 per cent in 1993 (United Nations Economic Commission for Europe 1994: 168).

The private sector still accounts for only around 15 per cent of GDP, but it is growing fast (*The Economist*, Survey, 13 March 1993, p. 10).

The rapidly growing private sector provides work for 10 per cent of all employed persons, compared with 5 per cent in Slovakia (Deutsche Bank, *Focus: Eastern Europe*, 29 December 1992, no. 65, p. 6). Virtually non-existent before the revolution, the private sector accounted for a good 10 per cent of GDP in 1991 and close to 20 per cent of GDP in 1992 (Deutsche Bank, *Focus: Eastern Europe*, 1993, no. 82, p. 4).

The private sector has expanded from virtually zero in 1989 to around 20 per cent of the economy (Anthony Robinson, *FT Survey*, 24 March 1993, p. ii).

The private sector's share of GDP has increased from 4.2 per cent in 1989 to nearly 30 per cent today; the government expects the figure to rise to 85–90 per cent by the end of the second wave of privatization in 1994 (*The Guardian*, 9 October 1993, p. 39).

By mid-1993 the private sector accounted for 40 per cent of GDP; it accounted for 1 per cent of employment in 1989 and over 30 per cent in 1992 (*Employment Observatory*, 1993, no. 5, pp. 1, 26).

At the end of the third quarter of 1993 the private sector contributed 44.7 per cent to industrial output and 75 per cent to construction (*Business Europa*, February–March 1994, p. 19).

Estimates of the private sector's share of the economy vary from 40 per cent to 60 per cent, but its share of industrial production remains below 20 per cent; almost two-thirds of the work force is still employed in the public sector (Patrick Blum, *FT*, 16 November 1993, p. 2).

The private sector's share of GDP rose from 17.3 per cent in 1991 to 52.1 per cent in the final quarter of 1993 (*Business Central Europe*, June 1994, p. 11).

The private sector's share of GDP rose from 21.9 per cent in 1992 to 39.4 per cent in 1993 (*Transition*, 1994, vol. 5, no. 4, p. 13).

Three sources say that the private sector now accounts for around 60 per cent of GNP (Deutsche Bank, *Focus: Eastern Europe*, 22 March 1994, no. 100, p. 16; *EEN*, 4 January 1994, vol. 8, no. 1, p. 3; Susan Greenberg, *The Guardian*, 26 February 1994, p. 33).

In mid-1994 the private sector accounted for roughly 65 per cent of GDP (EBRD 1994: 10).

Anthony Robinson (*FT*, 13 September 1994, p. 2) cites an official estimate that around 80 per cent of the economy will be privatized by the beginning of 1995.

Some 80 per cent of GDP is now in the hands of the private sector, but the government still owns an average of 40 per cent of privatized companies through the National Property Fund (*The Times*, Survey, 2 May 1995, p. 11).

The grey economy is probably the equivalent of some 12 per cent of GDP (*The Economist*, 22 October 1994, p. 29).

Foreign trade

Capital account transactions remain subject to some control (EBRD 1994: 23). On 1 January 1995 the yearly amount that Czech citizens were allowed to exchange for hard currency went up from 12,000 to 100,000 koruny. There is the possibility that the central bank may allow the koruna to fluctuate in a wider band against the US dollar and the Deutschmark (perhaps as much as 2 per cent) than the current 0.5 per cent limit (*IHT*, 3 January 1995, p. 10). On 1 October 1995 a new foreign exchange law came into operation which conforms to Article 8 of the IMF's guidelines on convertibility, i.e. full convertibility for current account transactions and partial liberalization for capital account transactions. In an interview given early in 1993 Prime Minister Vaclav Klaus thought that the Czech Republic would be ready to join the EU in two or three years. Not as regards living standards, but ready in political, economic and social terms; by then the Czech Republic would, in all important respects, be a standard, normal European country (*IHT*, 1 February 1993, p. 2).

The Czech Republic officially became a member of Gatt in mid-April 1993. On 23 June 1993 the EU and the Czech Republic initialled a bilateral association agreement to succeed the one with Czechoslovakia. On 4 October 1993 a trade and co-operation agreement was signed (which needed to be ratified by the Czech parliament). It involves more rapid liberalization of trade in industrial goods than previously (Deutsche Bank, *Focus: Eastern Europe*, 1993, no. 91, p. 9). In 1994 46 per cent of Czech trade was with the EU (*The Times*, Survey, 2 May 1995, p. 11).

Foreign investment

There is now no special treatment of foreign investors, with the exception of small tax advantages (Patrick Blum, *FT*, Survey, 24 March 1993, p. iii). There are now no discriminatory tax or subsidy benefits for inward foreign investments (Frances Williams, *FT*, 28 September 1994, p. 6). The government remains adamant in its refusal to grant tax privileges to domestic or foreign investors (*Transition*, July–August 1994, vol. 5, no. 6, p. 21). The Czech Republic eliminated nearly all special incentives in 1993 (EBRD 1994: 125). There are free economic zones. Enterprises which are more than 30 per cent foreign-owned are exempt from customs duty for one year (p. 127).

Germany accounted for 32.2 per cent of foreign investment and the USA for 29.5 per cent by the end of 1992 (*Business Central Europe*, September 1993, p. 47).

Between 1989 and early 1993 foreign investment amounted to $2.18 billion, with Germany accounting for 40 per cent, the USA 21 per cent and France 15 per cent (*Business Europa*, May–June 1993, p. 31).

The Deutsche Bank (*Focus: Eastern Europe*, 1993, no. 94, p. 9) estimates that, as of mid-1993, Germany accounted for one-third of direct foreign investment, the USA 28 per cent and France 13 per cent. Direct foreign investment totalled roughly $2.1 billion by the end of 1993 and $3.1 billion by the end of 1994 (*Focus: Eastern Europe*, 1995, no. 129, p. 12).

Direct foreign investment in 1993 was only $561 million; the total was $1.9 billion by September 1993 (the USA 55 per cent, Germany 11 per cent and Austria 8 per cent) (*Business Central Europe*, April 1994, p. 38). The total was $2.7 billion by September 1994 (*Business Central Europe*, December 1994 to January 1995, p. 72).

By the end of 1994 direct foreign investment amounted to $3.1 billion, of which Germany accounted for 36.2 per cent and the USA 21.2 per cent (*FT*, Survey, 2 June 1995, p. i).

Direct foreign investment plunged from $1 billion in 1992 to $568 million in 1993 (*Transition*, 1994, vol. 5, no. 6, p. 21).

Net direct foreign investment was $180 million in 1990, $511 million in 1991, $983 million in 1992, $517 million in 1993 and $779 million in 1994 (United Nations Economic Commission for Europe 1995: 151).

Foreign direct investment was $983 million in 1992 and $606 million in 1993 (EBRD 1994: 123).

Agriculture

The land bill (restitution of land to former members) has not yet been implemented, nor has there been a ruling on Church property (Deutsche Bank, *Focus: Eastern Europe*, 26 February 1993, p. 3).

A survey in *The Financial Times* (11 January 1993, p. 8) talked of private individuals becoming owners and part-owners of state farms, while co-operatives were being transformed into owners' co-operatives. Shares were being determined by the amount of capital employed and by the length of employment of the individual owners.

The majority of restitution claims are for less than 2 ha and less than a third of farmland is in private hands. The former collectives are now co-operatives and associations, which dominate the scene (they are to be included in the second wave of privatization) (*Business Central Europe*, September 1993, p. 25).

Karel Dyba, the Czech minister in charge of the economy, said that agricultural employment had fallen by half to 300,000 since 1990, compared with a decline in industrial employment of 15–20 per cent (*The Economist*,

13 November 1993, p. 107).

'Gone are the former agricultural co-operatives. In their place stand more than 600 share-owning co-operatives and some 1,500 commercial co-operatives' (*The Times*, Survey, 10 July 1995, p. 10).

Table 21.3 The Czech Republic: unemployment

Date		*Per cent*
1990	December	0.7
1991	December	4.1
1992	January	4.4
	February	4.1
	March	3.7
	April	3.2
	May	2.9
	June	2.7
	July	2.7
	August	2.7
	September	2.6
	October	2.5
	November	2.5
	December	2.6
1993	January	3.0
	February	3.0
	March	2.9
	April	2.7
	May	2.6
	June	2.6
	July	2.8
	August	3.0
	September	3.2
	October	3.2
	November	3.3
	December	3.5
1994	January	3.8
	February	3.7
	March	3.5
	April	3.3
	May	3.1
	June	3.1
	July	3.2
	August	3.2
	September	3.2
	October	3.1
	November	3.1
	December	3.2

Sources: Various issues of United Nations Economic Commission for Europe, *Economic Survey of Europe*; OECD, *Economic Outlook*; IMF, *World Economic Outlook*; Deutsche Bank, *Focus: Eastern Europe*; *Economics of Transition* and *Business Central Europe*; EBRD (1994: 155; 1995: 32)

Table 21.4 The Czech Republic: selected economic indicators

Economic indicator	*1990*	*1991*	*1992*	*1993*	*1994*
Rate of growth of GDP (%)	−0.4	−14.2	−6.4	−0.9	2.6
Rate of growth of industrial output (%)	−3.5	−22.3	−7.9	−5.3	2.3
Rate of growth of agricultural output (%)	−2.3	−8.9	−12.1	−2.3	−7.4
Inflation rate (%)	10.8	56.7	11.1	20.8	10.0
Net foreign debt ($ billion)	4.0	7.0	6.8	4.7	3.1
Budget surplus or deficit (% GDP)	0.1	−2.0	−3.3	1.4	1.0
Current account, including trade with Slovakia 1992 and onwards ($ billion)	−1.1	0.4	0.6	0.4	0.3

Sources: Various issues of United Nations Economic Commission for Europe, *Economic Survey of Europe*; OECD, *Economic Outlook*; IMF, *World Economic Outlook*; Deutsche Bank, *Focus: Eastern Europe*; *Economics of Transition* and *Business Central Europe*; EBRD (1994: 155; 1995: 32)

Economic performance

The unemployment rate is amazingly low (see Table 21.3) and inflation has been kept under control (the annual rate in the peak year of 1991 was only 56.7 per cent and the figure for 1994 was around 10 per cent). But the generally considered front runner in the transition race has not been without its economic pain, e.g. GDP did grow until 1994 (see Table 21.4).

Prime Minister Klaus thought that the 'bottom of the valley' had been reached in the second quarter of 1992; GNP started to improve in the third quarter and again in the fourth quarter of 1992 (*IHT*, 1 February 1993, p. 2).

According to *The Economist* (18 February 1995, p. 90), there are a number of factors explaining the low rate of unemployment. For example, an incomes policy ensuring low real wages, special public works programmes, the separation from Slovakia (where a lot of moribund industry was situated) and a tourist boom centred on Prague.

The low overall unemployment masks a massive sectoral reallocation of labour. Employment in manufacturing fell by almost 30 per cent between 1989 and 1994, compared with an aggregate employment decline of about 16 per cent. Employment also fell precipitously in agriculture, but picked up sharply in trade, financial services and tourism (EBRD 1995: 4–5).

Slovakia

POLITICS

The Hungarian minority

30 June 1993. Slovakia is admitted to the Council of Europe (despite Hungary's concern about Slovakia's Hungarian minority).

8 January 1994. Leaders of the Hungarian minority met at Komarno. Before the meeting there had been speculation that there might have been calls for a self-governing province, but the actual declaration was very moderate. The government's proposed revamping of regional boundaries was strongly opposed, since the Hungarians would be a minority in every case. Instead the Komarno declaration suggested maintaining a Hungarian majority in areas where there had historically been one. The eight-point programme included a call for broad autonomy at local government level and in cultural affairs. (In August 1993 a ban had been imposed on the use of Hungarian on road signs. A ban had also been imposed on the use of non-Slovak Christian names on official documents.)

3 June 1994. A draft law allowing bilingual road signs for villages with over 20 per cent Hungarian population was defeated in parliament by one vote. (Those voting against were not only Slovak nationalists but also ethnic Hungarian MPs objecting to the exclusion of villages bearing the names of Slovak heroes.) (Note that in mid-May a law was passed allowing Hungarian women to use their names on official documents without adding the Slovak '-ova' ending.)

8 July 1994. The road sign bill is passed in parliament. The votes were seventy-six for, forty-nine against and six abstentions.

19 March 1995. Slovakia and Hungary sign, as part of the European Stability Pact, an agreement guaranteeing borders and minority rights.

22 April 1995. Around 6,000 ethnic Hungarians hold a rally in Komarno. The protest is led by teachers protesting against the Slovak government's plan to introduce bilingual education at schools in ethnic Hungarian areas, i.e. Slovak-language education in ethnic Hungarian schools would become compulsory (*EEN*, 1995, vol. 9, no. 9, p. 4).

Political developments prior to the 1994 general election

Two-thirds of Slovaks still say they are against the split (Ian Traynor, *The Guardian*, 19 March 1994, p. 11).

26 January 1993. Roman Kovac fails to be elected and fails again on the following day.

15 February 1993. Michal Kovac is elected president.

20 February 1993. The IMF breaks off discussions, saying that the government is in disarray and that the fund is unable to gather even the most basic economic data (Tom Redburn, *IHT*, 24 March 1993, p. 13). Slovak officials protest that Slovakia is 'not a banana republic' (*EEN*, 2 March 1993, vol. 7, no. 5, p. 4). The IMF returns in May after the government has passed laws on bankruptcy, privatization and income taxation (*Business Central Europe*, June 1993, p. 18). In mid-June the IMF agrees to a loan of $90 million under the 'systemic transformation facility' (and the option of a further $90 million in six months) in return for commitments such as keeping the budget deficit to 5 per cent of GDP at most and holding inflation at 1 per cent per month (*Business Central Europe*, July–August 1993, p. 45; *IHT*, 10 July 1993, p. 11; *EEN*, 20 July 1993, vol. 7, no. 15, p. 6; Deutsche Bank, *Focus: Eastern Europe*, 1993, no. 82, p. 7).

18 March 1993. Ludovit Cernak, the economics minister, resigns. He is the chairman of the Slovak National Party and, until his resignation, the only cabinet minister not a member of the Movement for a Democratic Slovakia (MDS). He is unhappy about the appointment of a former communist as defence minister and about what he considers to be Meciar's undemocratic style and lukewarm attitude towards economic reform. (His replacement is Jan Ducky.)

19 March 1993. Foreign Minister Milan Knazko is dismissed and is replaced by Jozef Moravcik. Knazko accuses Meciar of having a dictatorial manner, of lying 'as a general method of working', of being too populist and of adopting an unpredictable foreign policy stance. (These two events were followed by the resignation of the chairman of the council of the MDS, Rudolf Filkus: *EEN*, 30 March 1993, vol. 7, no. 7, p. 2; and by the splitting away of the MDS's liberal faction called the Alliance of Democrats, led by Knazko: *EEN*, 22 June 1993, vol. 7, no. 13, p. 8; Knazko took seven others with him to form the Independent Club of Deputies: *The Economist*, 7 August 1993, p. 40.)

7 April 1993. Hungary agrees to the Gabcikovo dam dispute being referred to the International Court of Justice.

26 August 1993. During a visit by Yeltsin a friendship and co-operation treaty with Russia is signed.

4 September 1993. Meciar calls for cuts in family allowances in order 'to achieve a reduction in the extended reproduction of the socially unadaptable and mentally backward population.' (This was generally taken to be a reference to Gypsies: according to the *World Directory of Minorities*, in 1989 Czechoslovakia had 410,000 Gypsies, 2.66 per cent of the population; unofficial estimates put the figure at around 500,000 Gypsies in Slovakia alone, or not far short of 10 per cent of the population: Tony Barber, *The Independent*, 7 September 1993, p. 9; *IHT*, 7 September 1993, p. 2.) (Meciar claims he was misquoted. The government released an official translation, which said that Gypsies 'should be perceived as a problem group that is growing in size . . . This means that if we do not deal with them now, they will deal with us later . . . Another thing we have to consider is extended reproduction of socially unadaptable populations': *The Economist*, 18 September 1993, p. 52.)

20 October 1993. A coalition government is formed with the Slovak National Party.

10 February 1994. Ten members of the MDS form a faction called Alternative for Political Realism. They advocate a transitional 'government of experts', excluding all party leaders, until a new election is held in early November 1994.

24 February 1994. Foreign Minister Jozef Moravcik resigns.

25 February 1994. Deputy Prime Minister Roman Kovac resigns.

9 March 1994. President Kovac attacks Meciar (e.g. he charges the prime minister and his government with seeking to finance the MDS out of privatization revenue).

11 March 1994. Meciar loses a vote of no confidence in parliament (the vote was seventy-eight in favour of the motion and two against, with seventy abstentions).

14 March 1994. The government resigns, Meciar refusing to stay on until an interim administration can be set up. Jozef Moravcik becomes interim prime minister and forms a five-party coalition government on 16 March: Moravcik's new Democratic Union of Slovakia (originally called the Alternative for Political Realism); the Party of the Democratic Left (led by Peter Weiss); the Christian Democratic Party (led by Jan Carnogursky); the Alliance of Democrats (led by Milan Knazko); and New Alternative (led by Ludovit Cernak). (Moravcik said that the government's priorities were 'to speed up economic transformation, depoliticize the privatization process and take more effective steps to attract foreign investors': Anthony Robinson, *FT*, 5 April 1994, p. 2.) (There have been allegations of unethical practices in some of the privatization procedures, e.g. preferential share prices in return for contributions to MDS party funds. There were allegations that Meciar pushed through around forty privatization deals favouring his political supporters just before he resigned. Twenty-five were later revoked.)

17 March 1994. A general election is called for 30 September–1 October 1994.

13 April 1994. The new economic programme is announced.

23 May 1994. The Party of the Democratic Left forms an alliance with the Green Party, the Social Democratic Party and the Slovak Farmers' Party.

24 July 1994. Meciar signs an accord with the leaders of five Gypsy parties. The leaders will instruct members to vote for Meciar in the forthcoming election in return for a 1 million crown loan and a car (*The Guardian*, 26 July 1994, p. 10).

The general election of 30 September–1 October 1994

Eighteen parties competed for the 150 seats on a proportional representation basis via party lists (with a 5 per cent threshold). The turnout was 74.6 per cent. Seven parties made it to parliament.

The Movement for a Democratic Slovakia won a surprisingly high percentage of the vote (see Table 21.5). Meciar's campaign platform, however,

Table 21.5 Slovakia: the general election of 30 September–1 October 1994

Party	*Vote (%)*	*Seats*
Movement for a Democratic Slovakia	34.96	61
Common Choice	10.41	18
Hungarian Coalition	10.18	17
Christian Democratic Movement	10.08	17
Democratic Union of Slovakia	8.57	15
Association of Slovak Workers	7.34	13
Slovak National Party	5.40	9
Total		150

was entirely predictable, stressing nationalism and promising a slower transition and improved economic conditions (such as more jobs, lower prices and increased pensions). Meciar spoke against the current voucher privatization programme, alleging that control of state assets would go to 'anonymous persons' and that foreign capital might 'buy out' the country. Instead he favoured existing management and workers and giving Slovaks first refusal on sales. (He also wished to prevent the privatization of utilities and the defence sector: Deutsche Bank, *Focus: Eastern Europe*, 1994, no. 120, p. 5.)

Common Choice won a surprisingly small percentage of the vote.

The main parties were as follows:

Movement for a Democratic Slovakia. Led by Vladimir Meciar.

Common Choice. A coalition of four left-wing parties, the foremost being Peter Weiss's Party of the Democratic Left (the others were the Social Democratic Party of Slovakia, the Green Party and the Slovak Farmers' Party).

Christian Democratic Movement. Led by Jan Carnogursky.

Democratic Union of Slovakia (Deus). Led by Jozef Moravcik.

National Democratic Party. Led by Ludovit Cernak.

Association of Slovak Workers. Led by Jan Luptak. Communist.

Slovak National Party. Led by Jan Slota. Extreme nationalist.

Alliance of Democrats. Led by Milan Knazko.

Hungarian Coalition. A coalition of three ethnic Hungarian parties (the Hungarian Christian Democrats, the Hungarian Civic Party and Co-existence; Co-existence is led by Miklos Duray).

Political developments after the 1994 general election

4 November 1994. Meciar supporters become chairmen of parliamentary committees and win key positions in the areas of privatization (chairman of the National Property Fund), state radio and television (heads of councils), and the intelligence service.

Prime Minister Jozef Moravcik tenders his resignation, but agrees to head a caretaker government until a new one is formed.

18–19 November 1994. In local elections the Movement for a Democratic Slovakia wins 22.8 per cent of the vote.

11 December 1994. A coalition government is formed, with the Movement for a Democratic Slovakia contributing twelve ministers, the Association of Slovak Workers four and the Slovak National Party two.

13 December 1994. Meciar becomes prime minister for the third time. The ministers include the following: economics, Jan Ducky; finance, Sergei Kozlik; privatization, Peter Bisak (Association of Slovak Workers, a party generally anti-privatization); defence, Jan Sitek (Slovak National Party); education, Eva Slavkovska (Slovak National Party).

1 February 1995. The EU association agreement comes fully into effect.

19 March 1995. Slovakia and Hungary sign, as part of the European Stability Pact, an agreement guaranteeing borders and minority rights.

THE ECONOMY

Financial policy

In mid-1993 measures were taken to curb the fast expanding budget deficit, both measures to raise revenue and measures to reduce spending (DIW, *Economic Bulletin*, 1994, vol. 31, no. 3, p. 19). On 22 December 1993 parliament approved the draft budget for 1994, albeit by a narrow majority. The budget deficit was forecast by the government at 4–5 per cent of GDP. The IMF has stipulated that the deficit should not exceed 5 per cent of GDP (Deutsche Bank, *Focus: Eastern Europe*, 1993, no. 97, pp. 4, 9). The IMF target for the budget deficit in 1994 was 4 per cent of GDP, while the official government target for 1995 was 3 per cent of GDP (Deutsche Bank, *Focus: Eastern Europe*, 7 November 1994, no. 129, p. 6). The government target for the budget deficit in 1995 was 4 per cent of GDP (*Business Europa*, February–March 1995, p. 13).

The IMF approved $263 million in credits on 22 July 1994.

There is a tax on 'excessive' wage increases (EBRD 1994: 37).

Wage ceilings have been set in the public sector and may be exceeded only if sufficient profits are achieved. There are no controls on private-sector wages (Deutsche Bank, *Focus: Eastern Europe*, 7 November 1994, no. 120, p. 4).

On 24 February 1995 the Meciar government resolved the budget proposals for 1995. The budget deficit was to be a maximum 3 per cent of GDP, with a target inflation rate for the year of 10 per cent (Deutsche Bank, *Focus: Eastern Europe*, 28 February 1995, no. 126, p. 13). Parliament endorsed the budget in early March 1995. The central government budget (i.e. excluding social insurance, local budgets and extra-budgetary funds) was to be a maximum 3 per cent of GDP (Deutsche Bank, *Focus: Eastern Europe*, 1995, no. 127, p. 6).

The current bankruptcy law became effective in June 1993 and allows creditors to bring cases to court after a three-month protective period (EBRD 1994: 36).

Prices

The only remaining significant price controls pertain to utility charges, rents and public services. In addition mark-ups are closely regulated in the energy sector (EBRD 1994: 37).

Privatization

Share trading on the Bratislava stock exchange began on 1 July 1993.

The Slovak government intended to embark on the second wave of large privatization in the summer of 1993 (involving 514 enterprises), but the start was rescheduled for early 1994 and then September 1994 (with the transfer of shares scheduled for spring 1995).

The Deutsche Bank (*Focus: Eastern Europe*, 1993, no. 97, p. 4) puts the number at 365 smaller enterprises and 154 larger ones. Preference would be given to potential buyers able to guarantee certain investments and the creation of new jobs. Vouchers were to play only a 'supplementary' or 'residual' role. A maximum of 30 per cent of the capital of state enterprises was to be set aside for vouchers, while up to 100 per cent of capital could be acquired by means of auctions and tenders (*Focus: Eastern Europe*, 23 April 1993, no. 76, p. 5). A later report cites a figure of 420 enterprises in the second wave. It was originally planned that vouchers would be involved mainly in large enterprises, while smaller and medium-sized enterprises were to be privatized by standard methods (direct sale and auction) (7 November 1994, no. 120, p. 5).

Roughly one-third of the shares were to be distributed through vouchers (EBRD 1994: 36). The plan has come under fire for allocating only 25 per cent of the shares to voucher privatization (Vincent Boland, *FT*, 25 August 1994, p. 2).

On 17 February 1994 an opposition version of the privatization law was passed by parliament, favouring a variety of proposals. So far management-led projects (often involving buy-outs) have been favoured (*Business Central Europe*, March 1994, p. 15). Participants over sixty years of age have been allowed a 30 per cent discount (*Business Central Europe*, September 1994, p. 53). The programme involves up to 310 enterprises and 166 investment funds (*Business Central Europe*, February 1995, p. 18).

The programme involves 380 enterprises (*IHT*, 3 September 1994, p. 11).

On 5 September 1994 voucher booklets went on sale for 1,000 crowns each. There are 300–600 enterprises to choose from. The government also plans to sell shares direct to Slovaks or foreigners through public auctions or on the stock exchange.

Parliament approved a list of about 180 firms, but that represented only a quarter of state assets up for sale. The rest would go through trade sales and public offerings, in which small investors could participate (*Business Central Europe*, October 1994, p. 15).

On 7 September the government decided not to add any more enterprises to the (already vague) list of those due to be privatized until after the election (*The Economist*, 10 September 1994, p. 89).

On 20 September 1994 a decision on direct sales of state assets was postponed until after the election. The National Property Fund opened on 1 August for bids for stakes in state enterprises not included in the voucher privatization programme, which is not affected by the suspension (Vincent Boland, *FT*, 21 September 1994, p. 2).

On 11 August 1994 President Kovac called a referendum for 22 October 1994 to decide whether Slovak citizens buying state property under the privatization programme should have to disclose the source of their funds (in early August the government had passed a law requiring buyers to give documentary evidence of the origins of their funds). But the referendum attracted only a 20 per cent turnout instead of the minimum necessary 51 per cent.

On 4 November 1994 parliament voted to cancel all privatization contracts involving (around fifty) direct sales to Slovak investors signed since 6 September. But on 25 May 1995 the Constitutional Court pronounced that 'Parliament has six months to redraft the law to make it conform with the Slovak constitution. Otherwise it will be annulled' (*FT*, 26 May 1995, p. 3).

The second round of coupon privatization was set to begin on 15 December 1994, but the planned start was later postponed to 1 July 1995.

The government plans to curb the influence of the 166 investment funds, making them more like portfolio managers and less like strategic investors. The proposals are designed to reduce the maximum stake an investment fund can take in enterprises to be sold in the next privatization round from 20 per cent to 10 per cent. It is also possible that the voting rights an investment fund is able to exercise in a privatized enterprise may be reduced to 5 per cent regardless of the size of its stake. Reflecting the government's desire to retain control of enterprises which may be privatized, the maximum stake in any one entity to be included in the next round will be 46 per cent, compared with 97 per cent in the first round. The government estimates that the average stake to be sold will be 33–35 per cent (Vincent Boland, *FT*, 5 April 1995, p. 32).

The sell-off theoretically included 549 enterprises. In July 1995 a voucher sale was to put up equity in some 200 enterprises. No more than 46 per cent in any one of these enterprises was to be sold via vouchers, with the average size of the stake being 25 per cent. The remaining assets earmarked for sale were to be divested gradually by way of direct sale or tender, most being sold on easy terms to enterprise managers, trade unions and employees. The government intended to keep 'strategic' enterprises such as energy utilities, arms manufacturers and big financial institutions under its firm control. Foreigners were to get a chance to invest primarily through joint ventures (*The Economist*, 6 May 1995, p. 99).

In June 1995 the government unexpectedly revealed a new programme, scheduled to begin on 1 July. Vouchers were to be replaced by five-year state bonds, these being eventually convertible into shares or housing. 'The bond scheme effectively disenfranchises the investment funds from the privatization process.' The remaining equity was to be gradually divested by way of direct sales and auctions, with preference given to management buy-outs on easy terms (*Business Central Europe*, July–August 1995, p. 15). There has been 'a major crackdown on the investment funds . . . a new law bars them from exercising corporate governance in companies they control' (*Business Central Europe*, September 1995, p. 58).

On 12 July 1995 parliament approved legislation ending coupon privatization (replacing the coupons with bonds) and the following day approved legislation restricting the powers of investment funds (*EEN*, 1995, vol. 9, no. 15, p. 8).

(Note that there is some uncertainty about what the bonds can be used for.)

The size of the private sector

According to official figures, the private sector as a whole accounted for around 20 per cent of national income in 1992 (United Nations Economic Commission for Europe 1993: 215).

Another source puts the figure at around only 10 per cent of GDP, although rapidly growing (Patrick Blum and Anthony Robinson, *FT Survey*, 2 November 1993, p. 14).

In 1993 it seemed that more than one-third of GDP was produced in the private sector (United Nations, *World Economic and Social Survey*, 1994, p. 35).

The private sector now generates 35–40 per cent of GDP (*Business Central Europe*, February 1994, p. 19).

In the first half of 1993 the private sector accounted for 36.9 per cent of GDP, 18.1 per cent of industrial output, 51.2 per cent of construction and 83.8 per cent of trade receipts (*Business Europa*, February–March 1994, p. 20). The non-state sector now has a 58 per cent share of industrial output (*Business Europa*, April–May 1995, p. 40).

According to the Statistical Office, the private sector accounted for about 40 per cent of GDP in mid-1994 (*Transition*, 1994, vol. 5, no. 6, p. 22).

The private sector accounts for about 40 per cent of GDP (Deutsche Bank, *Focus: Eastern Europe*, 7 November 1994, no. 120, p. 4).

The private sector's share of GDP is about 55 per cent (*The Economist*, 29 October 1994, p. 56).

In mid-1994 the private sector accounted for roughly 55 per cent of GDP (EBRD 1994: 10). Official sources estimate that the proportion of output produced by the private sector had risen to 58 per cent by the end of 1994 (EBRD 1995: 64).

Foreign trade

There are some quantitative restrictions on imports, e.g. on some agricultural products, textiles, clothing, steel and coal. Import licences are required for oil, gas and weapons. Export licensing affects for some products, e.g. livestock, textiles and steel (EBRD 1994: 109).

Slovakia officially became a member of Gatt in mid-April 1993.

On 23 June 1993 the EU and Slovakia initialled a bilateral association agreement to supersede the one with Czechoslovakia. On 4 October 1993 a trade and co-operation agreement was signed (which needed to be ratified by the Slovak government). It involves a more rapid liberalization of trade in industrial goods than previously (Deutsche Bank, *Focus: Eastern Europe*, 1993, no. 91, p. 9). In 1993 the EU accounted for 34.2 per cent of foreign trade (*FT*, Survey, 16 December 1994, p. i).

Some restrictions on the capital account remain (EBRD 1994: 37). On 10 July 1993 the Slovak crown was devalued by 10 per cent against the basket of five hard currencies to which the crown is linked and against the 'clearing Ecu' used in trade with the Czech Republic (Deutsche Bank, *Focus: Eastern Europe*, 1993, no. 83, p. 5). (In February 1993 the IMF had called for a devaluation of up to 30 per cent: Anthony Robinson, *FT*, 6 August 1993, p. 13.) As of 15 July 1994 the currency basket comprised only the Deutschmark (60 per cent) and the US dollar (40 per cent) (Deutsche Bank, *Focus: Eastern Europe*, 1994, no. 112, p. 10).

In July 1993 a 20 per cent surcharge was imposed on imported consumer goods (United Nations Economic Commission for Europe 1994: 120). On 3 March 1994 a 10 per cent import surcharge was introduced on numerous consumer goods. The Czechs responded by devaluing the Czech crown by 3 per cent against the clearing currency (the Ecu) used in bilateral trade (Deutsche Bank, *Focus: Eastern Europe*, 1994, no. 103, p. 10). A 10 per cent surcharge on imports was imposed between March and August 1994 (EBRD 1994: 109).

Foreign investment

Tax allowances are designed to attract foreign investment. While domestic and foreign investors are generally to be treated equally, the aim is to make tax incentives more favourable to foreigners in particular cases (Deutsche Bank, *Focus: Eastern Europe*, 23 April 1993, no. 76, p. 4). For example, joint ventures with a foreign stake of at least 30 per cent (or involving an investment of at least DM 1 million) pay a maximum profit tax of 30 per cent for the two years (sometimes longer) after the general tax-free first (profitable) year for enterprises registered after the start of 1993 (Deutsche Bank, *Focus: Eastern Europe*, 28 May 1993, no. 80, p. 9). Domestic companies registered after 31 December 1992 also benefit from tax allowances (Deutsche Bank, *Focus: Eastern Europe*, 1993, no. 83, p. 4).

There are free economic zones. If foreign ownership is greater than 30 per cent or 10 million crowns duty-free importation of investment goods is available until the end of 1995 (EBRD 1994: 127).

Net direct foreign investment was $18 million in 1990, $82 million in 1991, $100 million in 1992, $144 million in 1993 and $79 million in January–September 1994 (United Nations Economic Commission for Europe 1995: 151).

Direct foreign investment totalled $231 million by the end of 1992, $340 million by the end of 1993 and $450 million by the end of 1994 (Deutsche Bank, *Focus: Eastern Europe*, 1995, no. 131 p. 17).

By the end of September 1993 direct foreign investment totalled $346.3 million (*EEN*, 4 January 1994, vol. 8, no. 1, p. 1).

Direct foreign investment was $151 million in 1992 and $135 million in 1993 (*Business Europa*, July–August 1994, p. 49).

In 1993 Slovakia attracted $135 million, the total by December 1993 being $366 million (Austria 23.8 per cent, Germany 21.1 per cent, the USA 12.8 per cent and the Czech Republic 10.9 per cent) (*Business Central Europe*, April 1994, p. 42).

Direct foreign investment was $71 million in 1992 and $160 million in 1993 (EBRD 1994: 123).

Agriculture

Private farms still play a negligible role, with an average size of less than 1 ha (*Business Central Europe*, September 1993, p. 25).

Economic performance

Slovakia has not fared as well as its former twin. Unemployment is still in double figures (see Table 21.6). But the annual inflation rate reached a peak

Table 21.6 Slovakia: unemployment

Date		*Per cent*
1990	December	1.6
1991	December	11.8
1992	January	12.7
	February	12.7
	March	12.3
	April	11.8
	May	11.3
	June	11.3
	July	11.1
	August	10.9
	September	10.6
	October	10.4
	November	10.3
	December	10.4
1993	January	11.2
	February	11.8
	March	12.0
	April	12.0
	May	12.0
	June	12.5
	July	13.3
	August	13.5
	September	13.7
	October	13.8
	November	14.0
	December	14.4
1994	January	15.2
	February	
	March	14.5
	April	14.2
	May	13.9
	June	14.1
	July	
	August	14.4
	September	14.3
	October	14.4
	November	14.5
	December	14.8

Sources: Various issues of United Nations Economic Commission for Europe, *Economic Survey of Europe*; OECD, *Economic Outlook*; IMF, *World Economic Outlook*; Deutsche Bank, *Focus: Eastern Europe*; *Economics of Transition* and *Business Central Europe*; EBRD (1994: 168; 1995: 45)

of only 61.2 per cent in 1991 and the record in this regard is relatively good (though still not in single figures in 1994). As with the Czech Republic, GDP grew in 1994 (see Table 21.7).

Table 21.7 Slovakia: selected economic indicators

Economic indicators	*1990*	*1991*	*1992*	*1993*	*1994*
Rate of growth of GDP (%)	−0.4	−14.5	−7.0	−4.1	4.8
Rate of growth of industrial output (%)	−4.0	−25.4	−14.1	−13.5	6.4
Rate of growth of agricultural output (%)	−7.2	−7.4	−13.9	5.5	9.1
Inflation rate (%)	10.8	61.2	10.1	23.1	13.4
Net foreign debt ($ billion)	1.9	2.1	2.5	3.2	2.6
Budget surplus or deficit (% GDP)	0.1	−2.0	−13.1	−6.7	−3.7
Current account ($ billion)	−1.1	0.4	0.2	−0.4	0.7

Sources: Various issues of United Nations Economic Commission for Europe, *Economic Survey of Europe*; OECD, *Economic Outlook*; IMF, *World Economic Outlook*; Deutsche Bank, *Focus: Eastern Europe*; *Economics of Transition* and *Business Central Europe*; EBRD (1994: 168; 1995: 45)

22

EAST GERMANY

POLITICS

What happened to Honecker and other GDR leaders

A new estimate (by the 'Thirteenth of August Association') of the number of people who died in one way or another trying to escape the GDR was published on 10 August 1993. The official German estimate had recently been raised from 290 to 372. In contrast the latest estimate put the number at 588: 172 at the Berlin Wall; 290 at the land border between the GDR and the Federal Republic; eighty-one on the Baltic Sea; twenty-five GDR border guards; four Soviet soldiers; and thirty West Germans.

27 January 1993. The Berlin Court wishes Honecker to stand trial for manslaughter.

20 April 1993. Hans Modrow goes on trial accused of vote-rigging in Dresden in the local elections of May 1989 (i.e. in the socialist era). Although he is found guilty on 27 May, the judge decides that he carries 'the least possible guilt' and so is given the lightest possible sentence (a warning and a fine).

4 May 1993. The trial begins of 'spymaster' Markus Wolf, accused of treason, espionage and bribery (for paying agents' fees). Wolf was director of the external intelligence agency 1953–86. He fled to the Soviet Union in 1990, but returned in September 1991. (He was sentenced to six years' imprisonment on 6 December 1993.)

16 September 1993. Heinz Kessler (GDR defence minister), Fritz Streletz (his deputy) and Hans Albrecht (a GDR district party leader) were given jail sentences of seven and a half, five and a half and four and a half years respectively (the sentences would, however, be served at home). As members of the GDR National Defence Council they were charged with complicity in the 'shoot to kill' policy and specifically with incitement to manslaughter in seven separate cases. In his summing-up the presiding judge said that although they were not directly involved they were important links in the chain of command: 'They recognized that the killing of their own citizens may not have been correct. But they accepted it as necessary for the state.'

20 October 1993. A former East German border guard is convicted of murder and sent to prison for ten years for shooting a would-be escapee from the GDR. It is the first case of murder. The guard was originally sentenced to six years' imprisonment for manslaughter in December 1992.

26 October 1993. Erich Mielke is sentenced to six years in jail for the alleged murder of two policemen in August 1931 (he was released on 1 August 1995, having been in prison for four years).

29 May 1994. Erich Honecker dies in Chile aged eighty-one (of cancer of the liver).

5 September 1994. The trial begins of Erich Mielke, on the charge of responsibility for the shooting of six people trying to flee the GDR. (The trial was adjourned and then abandoned altogether on 3 November 1994 on the grounds of Mielke's ill health.) (Note that the trial of Willi Stoph was abandoned in mid-August 1993.)

2 November 1994. The trial begins of Wolfgang Vogel, the lawyer who negotiated the 'sale' of dissidents or the exchange of spies. He is charged with extortion, perjury and blackmail (e.g. those leaving the GDR were paid nothing or very little for their property).

9 January 1995. Seven members of the GDR politburo are charged with manslaughter in connection with the death of people trying to leave the GDR. Those accused are Egon Krenz, Kurt Hager, Harry Tisch, Günter Schabowski, Günter Kleiber, Erich Mückenberger and Horst Dohlus.

14 March 1995. It is announced that seven members of the GDR politburo are to be charged with forty-seven cases of manslaughter and twenty-four cases of attempted manslaughter in connection with those trying to flee the GDR in the period 1962–89. Erich Mückenburger and Kurt Hager are accused of 'actively contributing' to politburo decisions, while the others (including Egon Krenz) are accused of failing to use the opportunity to change the decisions.

23 May 1995. The Constitutional Court announces the following: 'Citizens of the former East Germany, who before restoration of German unity spied for the secret services of their state, exclusively from the territory of East Germany against West Germany, may no longer be prosecuted after reunification because of their espionage . . . Special mitigating circumstances, including the possible cessation of proceedings against them, should be considered when determining the legal consequences for those East German citizens who did this on West German territory.' The court noted that all still remained culpable for other crimes, such as murder and extortion, committed in the course of their espionage.

The far right

In 1992 the extreme right committed 2,584 acts of violence (90 per cent of them against foreigners) and killed seventeen people (*IHT*, 30 August 1993, p. 4). (Note that there is also deep concern about the desecration of Jewish cemeteries and memorials and attacks on groups such the disabled.) Rita Süssmuth, speaker of the German parliament, said that 'As a result of right-wing violence since 1991 more than 4,500 acts of violence have occurred, twenty-six people murdered and 1,800 injured' (*The Daily Telegraph*, 10 November 1993, p. 14).

In 1993 the extreme right committed 1,814 acts of violence and killed eight people. The number of attacks on foreigners was 1,322, compared with 2,283 in 1992. The number of attacks on Jews was also lower (forty-six instead of sixty-three). But the number of attacks on the homeless and handicapped increased from 145 in 1992 to 324 in 1993 (*IHT*, 14 January 1994, p. 5). In 1994 the extreme right committed 1,489 acts of violence and there were no deaths (*IHT*, 7 July 1995, p. 7).

7 March 1993. The far right makes gains in the Hesse (West Germany) local elections, winning 8.3 per cent of the vote.

29 May 1993. Two Turkish women and three Turkish girls are killed in an arson attack. There follow the first large-scale demonstrations by the Turkish community. From the start of 1993 until this time three other people have died in assaults by the extreme right (*IHT*, 31 May 1993, p. 5). There are 6.4 million foreigners in Germany, of whom 1,854,945 are Turks (*The Times*, 2 June 1993, p. 10). Very few foreigners become German citizens because of the very strict requirements.

11 June 1993. The National Bloc becomes the fifth neo-Nazi party to be banned.

14 July 1993. The Home Faithful Organization of Germany becomes the sixth neo-Nazi party to be banned.

15 September 1993. The government asks the Constitutional Court to ban the Free German Workers' Party (a ruling is needed because it is a registered party).

12 May 1994. Neo-fascists run riot in Magdeburg, attacking foreigners in broad daylight.

24 February 1995. Two neo-Nazi organizations, the Free German Workers' Party and the National List, are banned (making ten in all).

The new asylum law

1 July 1993. The new asylum law (passed by the Bundestag on 26 May) takes effect. In essence it is now possible to turn back at the border those asylum seekers 'with manifestly unfounded claims' if they come from a 'safe country of origin' (a country which has signed the Geneva convention on refugees). Those who have travelled through a third country considered to be 'safe' (i.e. politically non-repressive) can also be sent back to that country. The authorities now have to decide on individual cases within nineteen days instead of taking an average of twelve months (*FT*, 6 August 1993, p. 2). Before the changes about 4 per cent of asylum seekers were being granted permission to stay (*IHT*, 26 May 1993, p. 2). (Chancellor Kohl claims that in 1992 Germany had to deal with 79 per cent of those seeking asylum in the EC: *IHT*, 17 June 1993, p. 1. As of January 1991 the 10 million immigrants in the EC constituted 2.8 per cent of the EC's 344 million population. Germany accounted for 23 per cent of the EC's population, but 43 per cent of immigrants: *IHT*, 22 June 1993, p. 6.) (There were 438,191 asylum seekers in 1992, 322,599 in 1993 and 127,210 in 1994: *IHT*, 7 January 1995, p. 2.)

Political developments

19 January 1993. Gunter Rexrodt becomes economics minister.

7 May 1993. Germany and Poland sign a treaty on the return of asylum seekers, to take effect later in the year (note the earlier treaties with Bulgaria and Romania).

1 October 1993. Hans Tietmeyer becomes president of the Bundesbank.

12 October 1993. It is announced that the target date for transferring the seat of government from Bonn to Berlin is the end of the year 2000.

25 November 1993. Steffan Heitmann (justice minister of Saxony in East Germany), Chancellor Kohl's candidate for the 23 May 1994 election, withdraws from the presidential race.

5 December 1993. The Party of Democratic Socialism does well in the Brandenburg state election, winning 21.2 per cent of the vote (compared with 16.5 per cent in 1990).

23 May 1994. Roman Herzog is elected president to replace Richard von Weizsacker. (The new president was sworn in on 1 July 1994.)

12 July 1994. The Federal Constitutional Court rules that German troops may take part in UN peacekeeping and peacemaking operations (including those outside the Nato area) provided a simple majority in the Bundestag approves each operation: 'The constitution requires the federal government as a rule to seek enabling agreement by the Bundestag in advance before committing the armed forces in action . . . Peace forces and their task of securing peace are part of the United Nations' system of collective security.' The vote should be taken 'on tasks that are bound up with membership of a system of mutual collective security. For that reason, German soldiers may also be employed within the framework of UN peacekeeping troops even when they have a mandate to use force.'

31 August 1994. The last Russian troops leave (East) Germany (the last in the former Eastern Europe). The ceremony was attended by Chancellor

Kohl and President Yeltsin. (Russian troops also leave Estonia and Latvia, having already left Lithuania.)

8 September 1994. The last allied troops (US, French and British) leave Berlin.

11 September 1994. The Party of Democratic Socialism (PDS) does well in state elections in Saxony (16.5 per cent of the vote, compared with 10.2 per cent in 1990) and Brandenburg (18.7 per cent of the vote, compared with 13.4 per cent in 1990). (The party did well in local elections in June and July 1994.) (Note that Berlin and Brandenburg are to merge in 1999.)

16 October 1994. The general election is narrowly won by Chancellor Kohl's ruling CDU/CSU–FDP coalition. Its majority is only ten.

The distribution of seats in the 672-seat Bundestag is as follows (number of seats and percentage of the vote):

1. CDU/CSU: 294 (CDU 244 and CSU 50) and 41.5 per cent (43.8 per cent in 1990).
2. FDP: forty-nine and 6.9 per cent (11 per cent in 1990).
3. SPD: 252 and 36.4 per cent (33.5 per cent in 1990).
4. Greens: forty-nine and 7.3 per cent (3.8 per cent in 1990; Alliance 90, 1.3 per cent in 1990).
5. PDS: Thirty and 4.4 per cent (2.4 per cent in 1990). Although the PDS did not attain the threshold 5 per cent, it won four seats in East Berlin. Three constituency seats need to be won to entitle a party to gain a proportionate share of votes when its share of the total vote falls below 5 per cent. The PDS won 17.7 per cent of the vote in East Germany, compared with 0.9 per cent in West Germany (mostly in West Berlin). The four seats in East Berlin (out of five) were won by Gregor Gysi, Christa Luft, Manfred Müller and Stefan Heym. Stefan Heym is not a party member, but stood as a PDS-backed independent. A writer who chose to return to the GDR from the USA, he was a critic of the communist regime. He favoured a socialist and democratic East Germany and opposed rapid reunification.

The far right Republican Party won only 1.9 per cent of the vote.

The names of the parties in full are the Christian Democratic Union, the Christian Social Union, the Free Democratic Party, the Social Democratic Party, the Greens and the Party of Democratic Socialism. The results of the December 1990 election are discussed in Jeffries (1993: 394).

29 January 1995. At the end of its congress the PDS defined itself as a left-wing democratic party, e.g. anti-communists were no longer barred from membership.

27 April 1995. Berlin and Brandenburg announce that they are to merge (but the approval of parliament and the people of Berlin and Brandenburg via a referendum is needed).

Demography

There have been marked demographic changes in East Germany (DIW, *Economic Bulletin*, October 1993, vol. 30, no. 8, pp. 12–20). The population has declined by around 1 million since the beginning of 1989, while that of West Germany has increased by around 3.6 million. Although the birth rate in East Germany had already begun to fall in 1989, the decline since then has been extraordinary (causal factors include rising unemployment and the uncertainty surrounding individual and family futures). The figures here are for the number of children that 1,000 women have on average in the course of their lives: 1987, 1,740; 1988, 1,670; 1989, 1,560; 1991, 977; 1992, 770 (estimated).

Between 1989 and 1992 the crude birth rate per thousand population fell from 12 to 5.6, while the marriage rate per thousand population fell from 7.9 to 3.1 (Eberstadt 1994a: 138, 144). 'Such an abrupt and precipitous drop in fertility is unprecedented for an industrialized society during peacetime . . . Eastern Germany's adults appear to have come as close to a temporary suspension of childbearing as any such population in human experience' (pp. 138–9). 'The worsening of Eastern Germany's mortality patterns since 1989 represents a sharp departure from the past' (p. 147). 'This conjuncture of extreme and anomalous tendencies – the upswing in mortality and the collapse of births and new marriages – portrays a society convulsed by its stresses' (p. 149). (See also Eberstadt 1994b.)

There is also a more positive explanation for the fall in the birth rate, namely the initial optimism that younger people will have the ability to travel and improve their employment prospects (Steve Crawshaw, *The Independent*, 9 February 1995, p. 12).

Since reunification 1.4 million East Germans have settled in West Germany, while only 350,000 West Germans have made the move in the opposite direction (Jochen Thies, *The World Today*, December 1994, vol. 50, no. 12, p. 223).

In 1993 about 180,000 moved from East Germany to West Germany, while around 135,000 moved in the opposite direction (*IHT*, 3 March 1994, p. 2).

In 1993 218,888 ethnic Germans came to Germany from the former Soviet Union and Eastern Europe (compared with 230,565 in 1992).

Germany has a population of 80 million, including some 6.5 million 'non-Germans', i.e. 8.1 per cent of the population (*The Economist*, Survey, 21 May 1994, p. 16).

There are 6.9 million foreigners in Germany, 8.5 per cent of the population compared, with less than 3 per cent in Western Europe as a whole (the figure was 1.2 per cent for the Germany of 1960) (Rick Atkinson, *IHT*, 16 November 1994, p. 6).

THE ECONOMY

The terms of reunification

Jonathan Steinberg (*FT*, 13 October 1994, p. 25) reports a conversation with one of the economists who advised the Bundesbank on the exchange rate between the Deutschmark and the East mark on reunification. Experts at the time decided that it should 1:2.5, but Chancellor Kohl ignored them.

Monetary policy

On 4 February 1993 the Bundesbank lowered the Lombard rate from 9.5 per cent to 9.0 per cent and the discount rate from 8.25 per cent to 8.0 per cent. On 18 March 1993 the discount rate was further reduced to 7.5 per cent. On 22 April 1993 the Lombard rate was reduced to 8.5 per cent and the discount rate to 7.25 per cent, followed on 1 July by further reductions to 8.25 per cent and 6.75 per cent respectively. On 29 July 1993 the Lombard rate (only) was reduced, to 7.75 per cent. Both rates were reduced on 9 September 1993 (the Lombard to 7.25 per cent and the discount to 6.25 per cent) and on 21 October 1993 (to 6.75 per cent and 5.75 per cent respectively). The discount rate only was reduced on 17 February 1994, to 5.25 per cent. Both rates were reduced on 14 April 1994 (the Lombard rate to 6.5 per cent and the discount rate to 5 per cent) and on 11 May 1994 (to 6 per cent and 4.5 per cent respectively). The discount rate only was reduced (to 4.5 per cent) on 30 March 1995, while both rates were reduced on 24 August 1995 (to 5.5 per cent and 3.5 per cent respectively).

Fiscal policy

The total net borrowing requirement of the general government in Germany rose from DM 89.1 billion in 1991 to DM 93.1 billion in 1992, although the ratio of net borrowing to GDP fell slightly from 3.2 per cent to 3.1 per cent. But these figures exclude off-budget borrowing by the Treuhandanstalt, the railways and the postal services, which in total accounted for another 2 per cent of GDP in 1992 (United Nations Economic Commission for Europe 1993: 56–7).

The extended public-sector budget deficit (including territorial authorities, social security, the Treuhandanstalt and public enterprises) was 2.9 per cent in 1990, 4.5 per cent in 1991, 4.7 per cent in 1992, 5.2 per cent in 1993 and an estimated 4.2 per cent in 1994 (OECD, *Economic Outlook*, December 1994, p. 65).

The total public-sector budget deficit (including regional and local governments, the Treuhandanstalt, the railways and social insurance, but excluding the Federal Post Office) as a percentage of GDP was 3.8 per cent in 1990,

4.4 per cent in 1991, 5.3 per cent in 1992, 5.8 per cent in 1993 and an estimated 4.3 per cent in 1994 (Deutsche Bank, *Focus: Germany*, 1994, no. 144, p. 3).

In 1992 the budget deficit in Germany was 4 per cent of GDP, but it rose to 7 per cent when the off-budget liabilities were included (*FT*, 26 April 1993, p. 14).

Investment in East Germany

West German companies allocated DM 80 billion to East Germany in 1992, a 60 per cent increase over the previous year. Non-German companies put in nearly DM 30 billion and local companies invested several billion. With DM 110 billion, East Germany's share of national capital investment amounted to nearly 26 per cent (almost twice the 1991 figure) (Survey of East Germany, *IHT*, 16 December 1992, p. 11).

The Treuhandanstalt survey (*IHT*, 23 April 1993, p. 9) informs us that in 1992 DM 115 billion was invested in East Germany in 'capital goods, production facilities and structures', a 35 per cent increase over 1991. The percentage sources of the investment were as follows: West German companies, 31.3; East German and non-German companies, 20.9; federal, state and local governments, 15.7; the federal rail system, 11.3; apartment and house owners, 11.3; telecommunications authorities, 9.5.

In 1992 60 per cent of total fixed capital formation in the industrial and extractive industries was due to West German firms. The forecast is that investment by West German firms in East Germany in 1993 will total just short of DM 55 billion, a 17 per cent increase on 1992 (DIW, *Economic Bulletin*, July 1993, vol. 30, no. 5, pp. 11–12).

Some DM 140 billion of private investment has been used to modernize the capital stock of East Germany's enterprises and to improve the quality of distribution. In 1993, for the first time, investment *per capita* in East Germany exceeded that in West Germany (Judy Dempsey, *FT*, 30 December 1994, p. 12).

East Germany accounted for 15 per cent of the total inflow of foreign investment into Germany in the period from 1990 to mid-1993 (DM 2.531 billion out of a total of DM 16.388 billion; note that investment financed out of retained profits by subsidiaries of foreign companies located in West Germany is not included here) (Deutsche Bank, *Focus: Germany*, 1994, no. 129, p. 4).

Investment grants and tax incentives are to be extended from 1995 to 1998 (Judy Dempsey, *FT*, 19 July 1994, p. 3).

Public transfers from West to East Germany

West Germany's share of Marshall Plan aid amounted to approximately 2 per cent of GNP (Rothschild 1993: 262).

In 1990 the government optimistically forecast that fiscal expenditures in East Germany would be in the range DM 25 billion to DM 50 billion a year (Hughes Hallet and Ma 1993: 416).

Total financial transfers (to state and local governments and to social insurance institutions) amounted to DM 151.0 billion in 1992, DM 162.4 billion in 1993 and DM 165.6 billion in 1994 (in addition, the Treuhandanstalt borrowed DM 29.6 billion, DM 38.1 billion and DM 37.1 billion respectively) (DIW, *Economic Bulletin*, May 1995, vol. 32, no. 5, p. 16).

Total financial transfers amounted to DM 128.4 billion in 1991, DM 155.6 billion in 1992 and DM 163.5 billion in 1993 (DIW, *Economic Bulletin*, May 1994, vol. 31, no. 5, p. 16).

Net government transfers from West to East Germany amounted to $75 billion in 1991 and $96 billion in 1992 (United Nations Economic Commission for Europe 1993: 19).

Total financial transfers to East Germany rose from DM 132.1 billion in 1991 to DM 156.2 billion in 1992 and to DM 170 billion in 1993 (*FT*, Survey, 4 May 1994, p. ii). Net transfers in 1993 amounted to DM 130 billion, the equivalent of 4.6 per cent of West German GDP and 47 per cent of East German GDP (*FT*, 1 September 1994, p. 23).

Gross public-sector transfers in 1993 were predicted to be DM 182 billion (i.e. without deducting additional revenues generated by unification). This is the equivalent of just over 6 per cent of West German GDP and some two-thirds of East German GDP. The net sum will probably be about DM 140 billion (Deutsche Bank, *Focus: Eastern Europe*, 16 June 1993, no. 109, p. 3). Total net transfers were DM 130 billion in 1991 (of which the Treuhandanstalt accounted for DM 24 billion), DM 145 billion in 1992 (DM 30 billion), DM 167 billion in 1993 (DM 38 billion) and DM 176 billion in 1994 (DM 37 billion) (Deutsche Bank, *Focus: Germany*, 1995, no. 159, p. 4).

In an election campaign speech delivered on 15 September 1994 Chancellor Kohl stated that between October 1990 and the end of 1994 nearly DM 500 billion would have been pumped into East Germany (*IHT*, 16 September 1994, p. 2).

Der Spiegel reports that around DM 65 billion of public funds has gone astray (cited in *FT*, 15 February 1995, p. 2). (The government vehemently denies large-scale fraud.)

The 'solidarity pact'

The 'solidarity pact' was proposed by Chancellor Kohl on 7 September 1992. The participants were the government, the opposition, industry and the trade unions and the aim was to tackle the economic cost of reunification (an estimated DM 110 billion in public transfers in 1995) and the distribution of the burden. It was hoped that trade unions would moderate wage demands, industry would invest more in East Germany and the Bundesbank would feel able to respond to a successful pact by lowering interest rates.

Agreement at the level of government and opposition was reached on 13 March 1993. The government, the Social Democrats and the sixteen *Länder* (eight of the eleven West German *Länder* were controlled by the Social Democrats) agreed the following in the hope of reducing the budget deficit in the medium term:

1. As regards taxation, there was to be a 7.5 per cent 'solidarity surcharge' on income tax for 1 January 1995 (except for the lowest-paid) and an increase in wealth tax. The *Länder*'s share of VAT was to increase from 37 per cent to 44 per cent.

2. Federal government spending was to be cut by DM 9.2 billion overall, but there was to be no reduction in welfare expenditure (e.g. unemployment benefit). The actual spending cuts were left vague, although there was to be a campaign against false welfare claims. The borrowing limits of the Treuhandanstalt were to be raised (perhaps by DM 30 billion; in order to finance the restructuring of 'core' industries and the cleaning up of the environment), as were those of the Bank for Reconstruction (from DM 30 billion to DM 60 billion in order to finance housing modernization in East Germany).

Manpower

Wages and productivity

In the second half of 1991 average hourly wages in East Germany were 43 per cent of those in West Germany (DIW, *Economic Bulletin*, 1993, vol. 29, no. 12, p. 7).

In 1990 East German productivity was only 26 per cent of the West German level, according to an estimate quoted by Hughes Hallet and Ma (1993: 417).

In the second half of 1991 labour productivity in East Germany stood at 32 per cent of the West German level, according to the Federal Statistics Office (Quentin Peel, *FT*, 9 September 1992, p. 4).

At the end of 1991 the average income of a West German industrial worker was just under 50 per cent of the West German level (Deutsche Bank, *Focus: Germany*, 5 October 1992, no. 93, p. 3). In 1991 GDP per member of the labour force was just under 32 per cent of the West German level, while disposable *per capita* income was just over half the West German level (p. 2).

In 1992 average monthly *per capita* earnings were DM 2,450 in East Germany, compared with DM 3,910 in West Germany, i.e. the ratio of East German to West German wages increased from 49 per cent to about

63 per cent in one year. In 1992 there was a 17.5 per cent increase in East German unit wage costs (Deutsche Bank, *Focus: Germany*, 20 January 1993, no. 100, p. 4). In 1992 wages and salaries increased by 25 per cent (Deutsche Bank, *Focus: Germany*, 1992, no. 94, p. 11).

On 19 January 1994 Chancellor Kohl said that the incomes of private households in East Germany had almost doubled since mid-1990 and had reached more than 70 per cent of western levels (David Gow, *The Guardian*, 21 January 1994, p. 12).

Public service workers in East Germany receive 80 per cent of the West German wage levels; the proportion was to be raised to 82 per cent on 1 October 1994 and 84 per cent in 1995 (*IHT*, 12 March 1994, p. 13).

The Financial Times refers to the following figures:

1. East German unit labour costs are 80 per cent above the West German level, while East German wage tariffs are 73 per cent of the West German level (19 February 1993, p. 15).

2. Productivity in East German manufacturing industry is 30 per cent, while wages are 70 per cent, of the West German level (16 March 1993, p. 21).

3. East German wage costs were 31 per cent of companies' sales in 1991, compared with 20 per cent in West Germany (16 April 1993, p. 3).

4. In 1992 hourly wages in East Germany were 65 per cent of the West German level, while output per worker was only 40 per cent (20 August 1993, p. 13).

5. Immediately after currency union unit wage costs were around 20 per cent higher than those in West Germany; gross wages per employee as a percentage of the West German level were 47.6 per cent in 1991, 62.1 per cent in 1992 and 68.5 per cent in 1993; as a percentage of the West German level unit wage costs in East Germany were 165.7 per cent in 1991, 155.2 per cent in 1992 and 144.3 per cent in 1993 (Survey, 4 May 1994, p. ii).

6. Since productivity levels are on average between 30 per cent and 40 per cent of West German levels while wages are about 80 per cent, the result is that labour unit costs are 70 per cent higher (Survey, 4 May 1994, p. i).

7. An estimate by a securities house says that productivity in East German industry is about 65 per cent below West German levels, while wages in East Germany are 70–80 per cent of West German levels; that puts unit labour costs about 70 per cent higher (14 October 1993, p. 15).

8. The Halle Institute says that productivity is still only 40 per cent of the West German level (3 November 1994, p. 2).

9. Unit labour costs are 50 per cent higher than in West Germany (Survey, 21 November 1994, p. vi); unit labour costs are 44 per cent higher than those in West Germany (p. ix). East Germany still contributes only 2 per cent to Germany's total GDP (p. ix).

10. In 1993 GDP per employee was 46 per cent of the West German level, while *per capita* wages and salaries were 70 per cent of West German levels (30 December 1994, p. 12).

11. In the second half of 1994 wages reached 70 per cent of the West German level, while productivity was only 54 per cent (21 July 1995, p. 2).

Unit wage costs in East Germany are 60 per cent higher than those in West Germany (*The Economist*, 15 May 1993, p. 92).

The DIW (*Economic Bulletin*, July 1993, vol. 30, no. 5, p. 10) reports that unit wage costs in East German industry are still about twice as high as in West Germany. Unit wage costs are still around 50 per cent higher than in West Germany (May 1994, vol. 31, no. 5, p. 15). If West Germany is indexed as 100, the figures were 175.8 in 1991, 162.0 in 1992 and 149.4 in 1993 (p. 14). Average unit wage costs are still a third higher than in West Germany (DIW, *Economic Bulletin*, December 1994, vol. 31, no. 12, p. 22).[1]

Note that unit wage costs vary greatly between sectors and between companies (Deutsche Bank, *Focus: Eastern Europe*, 1994, no. 107, p. 4).

Unit wage costs in industry are 70 per cent above the West German level (*Transition*, July–August 1994, vol. 5, no. 6, p. 20).

East German productivity is 39 per cent and pay 63 per cent of the West German level (David Gow, *The Guardian*, 2 April 1993, p. 11).

As of December 1994 eastern hourly wage rates were 84 per cent of the western level (*Transition*, 1995, vol. 6, no. 4, p. 14).

Labour unrest

The March 1991 agreement between the trade union I G Metall and employers in the steel, engineering and metal goods sectors laid down that on 1 April 1993 wages for steelworkers were to rise by 21 per cent and those for the other workers by 26 per cent. These would bring East German wages in those sectors up to about 80 per cent of the West German levels. But in March 1993 the employers invoked a 'revision clause' in the agreement to justify only a 9 per cent wage offer (the clause allowed either side to challenge the agreement on the grounds of changed economic circumstances). Ballots among the workers in various East German states on 26–28 April and 12 May 1993 produced overwhelming support for strike action (around 85 per cent and 82 per cent respectively). The strikes brought about one tentative agreement on 14 May 1993: 1 June 1993, 75 per cent of West German pay; 1 September 1993, 77 per cent; 1 December 1993, 80 per cent (instead of 1 April); three further increases after mid-1994; 1 July 1996, full parity (instead of April 1994), although it could be delayed for six months under certain adverse circumstances. An opt-out 'hardship clause' allowed companies in financial difficulties to engage in local negotiations with the union to offer lower wage increases. Ballots on the deal among workers did not produce clear-cut results. There was resistance from engineers and metalworkers in Berlin–Brandenburg. (One estimate put the 1993 wage increase at around 15 per cent: *FT*, 19 May 1993, p. 17.) Even more resistance from steelworkers led to an improved offer for them on 23 May: 80 per cent of the West German level on 1 June 1993, 90 per cent on 1 October 1994 and parity on 1 April 1996. The offer was accepted in a ballot held on 25 May 1993.

Employment

Employment is down to around 6 million, of whom almost 500,000 are working under government job-creation schemes (DIW, *Economic Bulletin*, November 1992, vol. 29, no. 9, p. 2). The figure for the number employed was down to 6,170,000 in 1992 (*FT*, 28 October 1992, p. 2).

In West Germany over 30 per cent of all employed persons are engaged in manufacturing, while in East Germany the proportion is now around 20 per cent and still tending downwards in 1993 (Deutsche Bank, *Focus: Germany*, February 1993, no. 102, p. 3).

Overall the number of jobs available fell from 9.3 million in 1989 to 6.2 million in 1993. The 3.17 million employed in manufacturing are now down to 1.29 million (Judy Dempsey, *FT*, Survey, 4 May 1994, p. iv).

Unemployment

The unemployment rate was much the same at the end of both 1992 (13.9 per cent) and 1994 (13.5 per cent), although it had reached 17.1 per cent in February 1994. But the 'short time' working number has fallen substantially (see Table 22.1). Long-term unemployment is now a serious problem.

The underemployment rate in 1992 was 32.8 per cent. This figure takes account not only of the jobless rate but also of factors such as job creation schemes, early retirement, short-time working and retraining (Deutsche Bank, *Focus: Eastern Europe*, 1993, no. 113, p. 2).

The Federal Statistical Office has calculated that the East German unemployment rate, taking into account schemes such as early retirement, short-time working and retraining, amounts to 35 per cent (John Eisenhammer, *The Independent*, 2 April 1993, p. 23).

Judy Dempsey (*FT*, Survey, 4 May 1994, p. iv) cites a figure of 37 per cent, although she later mentions the Halle Institute's lower estimate of 28 per cent (*FT*, 2 August 1994, p. 3). A figure of 35 per cent is mentioned in a later survey (*FT*, 21 November 1994, p. ix).

Judy Dempsey (*FT*, 28 January 1994, p. 17) provides the following figures for 1993: jobless, 1,146,000; on job creation schemes, 240,714; on 'short time' working, 135,000; retraining, 392,000; taken early retirement, 849,000; commuters, 360,000.

Table 22.1 East Germany: unemployment and 'short time' working

Month		*Unemployment*		*'Short time' working*
		No. unemployed	*Unemployment rate (%)*	*No.*
1992	December	1,100,400	13.9	241,000
1993	January	1,194,400	14.7	237,000
	February	1,190,700	14.5	
	March		15.0	246,000
	April	1,120,000	14.7	
	May	1,100,000	14.4	
	June	1,100,000	14.4	
	July	1,170,000	15.3	155,331
	August	1,174,000	15.4	
	September	1,159,166	15.2	143,000
	October	1,165,736	15.3	135,000
	November	1,150,000	15.1	
	December	1,189,000	15.4	125,449
1994	January	1,293,423	17.0	115,900
	February	1,300,000	17.1	
	March	1,260,000	16.8	135,000
	April	1,220,000	16.2	
	May	1,160,000	15.4	118,000
	June	1,120,000	14.8	
	July	1,140,000	15.1	90,000
	August	1,110,000	14.7	
	September	1,040,000	13.8	
	October	1,000,000	13.3	
	November		13.0	
	December	1,015,000	13.5	

Sources: Various issues of Deutsche Bank, *Focus: Germany*; DIW, *Economic Bulletin*; *The Financial Times* and *The International Herald Tribune*

By the start of 1993 more than 2 million of the 3.3 million jobs which still existed in East German manufacturing industry at the start of 1990 had been lost (DIW, *Economic Bulletin*, 1993, vol. 29, no. 12, p. 7).

By the end of 1991 only 300,000 out of the former agricultural work force of 850,000 still had a job and 158,000 of those were on short time (*FT*, 6 February 1992, p. 30). Agriculture now employs only around one-third of the number of people it did in 1990 (DIW, *Economic Bulletin*, February 1993, vol. 29, no. 12, p. 4).

The problem of wage subsidization

Snower (1992: 1–6) argues that the social and budgetary costs associated with revenue- or profit-sharing subsidies are likely to be lower than those associated with wage subsidies. Given the structure of wage bargaining in East Germany, wage subsidies may be expected to lead to excessive real wage increases. Revenue- or profit-sharing subsidies do not suffer this disadvantage; revenue- or profit-sharing may be expected to bring the labour market close to full employment even when the associated subsidies are negligibly small.

Snower criticizes the argument that labour migration tends to be more sensitive to the unemployment differential (between the two Germanies) than the wage differential. That argument does not take account of the German unemployment benefit system, which makes the size of the unemployment benefit dependent on the previously earned wage. This militates against wage constraint. The narrowing of wage differentials may well have had a stronger effect in keeping East German workers where they are than a narrowing of unemployment differentials would have had.

Begg and Portes (1993b) strongly defend wage subsidies: 'Since the major distortion arises in the labour market, it is tackled most efficiently in the labour market. We propose a simple, uniform, universal wage subsidy declining over time according to a pre-specified schedule. The subsidy would be 75 per cent of the wage bill in the first year, 50 per cent in the second year, 25 per cent in the third year, and would disappear thereafter . . . our temporary wage subsidy would be accompanied by the scrapping of the plethora of *ad hoc* subsidies which have largely been introduced to cushion inappropriate labour costs . . . in fact, there is only one other measure that it is necessary to adopt: bad debts must not be allowed to infect the present and the future' (pp. 395–6). Begg and Portes reject the counter-arguments to wage subsidies, such as the budgetary cost, the fear that trade unions will appropriate the subsidies in the form of higher wages without any change in employment and the danger of freezing the existing industrial structure (pp. 398–9).

(See Hughes Hallet and Ma 1993, 1994, below, in the section on the economic outlook.)

Privatization

On 19 January 1993 the government proposed a one-year extension of the Treuhandanstalt (THA), i.e. to the end of 1994. According to draft legislation, the THA was then to be largely decentralized and as many of its duties as possible transferred to the private sector (Deutsche Bank, *Focus: Germany*, 1993, no. 123, pp. 6–7). But the plans to relieve the government of responsibility for major portions of future privatization and control mandates and to create private-sector successor organizations failed because of political reservations. Since the beginning of 1995 the work of the THA has been divided among several public-sector institutions (Deutsche Bank, *Focus: Germany*, 1995, no. 149, pp. 5–7).

1. *Bundesanstalt für Vereinigungsbedingte Sonderaufgaben*. Its functions include the monitoring of investment and job commitments.

2. *Beteiligungs-Management-Gesellschaft Berlin*. Its main task is to privatize the remaining saveable enterprises which have not yet been privatized or not yet privatized in full. It is responsible for the four 'management KGs'.

3. *Liegenschaftsgesellschaft der Treuhandanstalt*. It deals with real estate (excluding agricultural and forestry assets).

4. *Bodenverwertungs und -verwaltungs GmbH* (BVVG). This is an independent company (whose shares were taken over in full by banks as of 1 January 1995) which acts on behalf of the federal government. It manages and sells agricultural and forestry assets.

Some 20 per cent of contracts relating to investment and job commitments are not upheld (*IHT*, 23 June 1993, p. 9).

Table 22.2 shows the privatization details. At the end of 1994 a long-term solution was still needed for sixty-six (mainly industrial) enterprises with up to 500 employees (Deutsche Bank, *Focus: Germany*, 1995, no. 149, p. 3). Agreed privatization revenues added up to more than DM 65 billion, although less than half had actually flowed into the THA by then. THA debt rose from DM 14.1 billion in December 1990 to DM 194 billion by the end of November 1994 (pp. 3–4).

Privatization proceeds have fallen well short of target; it was originally believed that more than DM 600 billion would be raised through the sale of some 13,000 enterprises (Judy Dempsey, *FT*, 26 July 1994, p. 2). In fact the THA has run up debts of DM 270 billion, of which DM 100 billion has been spent on restructuring enterprises and subsidizing jobs (Judy Dempsey, *FT*, 30 December 1994, p. 12).

The original THA forecast of privatization proceeds was DM 600 billion, but even the most optimistic forecasts do not place the final total at more than DM 60 billion (Demougin and Sinn 1994: 228).

The German government 'vastly overestimated the market value of East Germany . . . the Treuhandanstalt initially assessed East Germany's industrial properties at a value of about DM 600 billion, but that . . . shrank . . . to ultimately show a net deficit of around DM 250 billion' (Richard Smith, *IHT*, 3 April 1995, pp. 17–18).

Of the enterprises unsold at the end of 1992, around 1,800 employed fewer than 100 people and forty employed more than 1,500 (Deutsche Bank, *Focus: Germany*, 1993, no. 103, p. 5). Foreigners purchased the following number and made the following investment pledges by the end of 1992: Switzerland, 100; UK seventy-three and DM 1.5 billion; France, sixty and DM 4.8 billion; USA, fifty-six and DM 2.8 billion; Canada, DM 1.8 billion (pp. 2–3). About 10 per cent of former GDR state property has been sold to foreigners (Birgit Breuel, *Moscow News*, 10–16 June 1994, p. 9). By the end of September 1994 the respective figures were: Switzerland 139 and DM 1.191 billion; UK, 124 and DM 2.825 billion; Austria, 100 and

Table 22.2 East Germany: the Treuhandanstalt

Measure	*31 December 1991*	*31 December 1992*	*31 December 1993*	*31 December 1994*
Number of enterprises privatized	5,200	11,000	13,118	13,800
Number of enterprises remaining		2,575	266	
Number of employees remaining		458,100	100,000	
Management buy-outs		1,950		2,679[1]
Enterprises under foreign ownership:		548	818	855[2]
Pledged investment (DM billion)		17	25.6	21.8[2]
Job commitments		121,500	146,000	150,187[2]
Liquidations:				
Embarked on		2,220	3,130	3,527[1]
Completed		32		157
Privatization proceeds (DM billion)	19.5	40.1	45.0	64.9[1]
Contractual investment pledges (DM billion)	114	170	183	206[1]
Contractual job pledges (million)		1.4	1.5	1.5[1]
Employees remaining in THA-owned enterprises[3]			203,000[4]	
Agricultural properties privatized		13,100	18,500[4]	
Hectares of agricultural land		28,000	32,000[4]	

1 September.
2 End of September.
3 Nearly 3 million at the beginning of 1991.
4 31 October.
Sources: Various issues of Deutsche Bank, *Focus: Germany*; *The Financial Times* and *The International Herald Tribune*

DM 1.016 billion; Netherlands, ninety-six and DM 1.191 billion; France, eighty-eight and DM 5.454 billion; USA, seventy-seven and DM 3.685 billion; Italy, thirty-eight and DM 0.702 billion; Denmark, twenty-six and DM 0.545 billion; Luxembourg, twelve and DM 0.406 billion; Canada, ten and DM 1.849 billion; others 145 and DM 2.935 billion. In total the figures were 855 and DM 21.798 billion (Deutsche Bank, *Focus: Germany*, 1995, no. 149, p. 4).

The 'management KG'

Further comments are as follows:

1. The THA survey (*IHT*, 23 April 1993, p. 9) defines 'management KGs' as limited partnerships or holding companies with private-sector management and capital funding from the THA. The five management KGs supervise between seven and twenty-one enterprises, with a total of sixty-nine enterprises and 32,000 people.

2. The Commerzbank report in *The Economist* (22 May 1993, p. 78) describes the 'management KG' as a sort of holding company for restructuring purposes, operating largely independently of the THA and comprising potentially viable enterprises still awaiting buyers. These enterprises would be reorganized and made competitive.

3. Priewe (1993: 343) adds that non-saleable but viable enterprises are grouped together into 'management limited partnerships'. These are legally private companies in which the THA has a majority share and which are managed by ex-THA managers now acting as private entrepreneurs and minority owners. These firms are supposed to be privatized after a few years of intensive economic rehabilitation financially supported by the THA. Only a limited number of such projects have been started.

4. At the end of 1994 the THA was still sponsoring four 'management KGs', with sixty-six enterprises in their fold. The fifth one (with eight enterprises) was sold *en bloc* to an investment group in late autumn 1995 (Deutsche Bank, *Focus: Germany*, 1995, no. 149, p. 4).

Restitution claims

Judy Dempsey (*FT*, 26 February 1993, p. 2; 1 April 1993, p. 2; 2 April 1993, p. 2; 25 August 1993, p. 2) provides the following information on total restitution claims:

1. By the time of the deadline for submission (31 December 1992) 1.21 million individuals had submitted claims on 2.63 million property titles. But fewer than 15 per cent of claims had been settled by then. By August 1993 nearly 25 per cent of claims on property confiscated by the Nazis (1933–45) and the socialist regime (after 1949) had been resolved (the unification treaty says that 'expropriations on the basis of Occupation law are irrevers-

ible', but there is still debate on the issue). (In a later article Judy Dempsey refers to 1.248 million claims being originally registered to 2.8 million property titles: *FT*, 26 August 1994, p. 2.)

2. A proposed tax on returned property (to help pay for monetary compensation) caused considerable controversy. So much so that on 23 November 1993 the German government agreed to issue bonds to cover the compensation payments.

3. In a later article (*FT*, Survey, 4 May 1994, p. iv), Judy Dempsey notes that 'recently' those who had property expropriated between 1945 and 1949, while not entitled to restitution, had won the right to a more limited form of compensation. All told, 30 per cent of claims have been resolved. (Note that in August 1994 Gorbachev and Shevardnadze denied that the exclusion of restitution claims for the period 1945–49 was part of the unification treaty.)

4. The federal government originally chose restitution of property rather than compensation partly for financial reasons. A compensation package for those unwilling or unable to claim the property itself was finally agreed by the Bundestag on 20 May 1994 (*FT*, 21 May 1994, p. 2; 27 May 1994, p. 16). At the same time a limited compensation fund has been granted to former landowners whose property was expropriated by the Soviet authorities between 1945 and 1949. The new measures involve the setting up of a DM 18 billion compensation fund, issued in bonds. Some DM 12 billion was to be allocated to former owners whose property was confiscated in 1933–45 and 1949–90. The amount of compensation for each individual was to be based on the 1935 value of property and multiplied by several times, depending on the type of property (land, housing or business). The bonds would not be fully redeemable until 2004. In addition DM 3.4 billion compensation was put aside and would allow former landowners to buy back a percentage of their property at below market prices. A further DM 2 billion was granted to East Germans who had suffered under the Nazis but received no compensation under the communists.

Until recently landowners whose land was confiscated by the Soviet administration between 1945 and 1949 had no right to any form of compensation or restitution. An exception was made for those with holdings smaller than 100 ha. In late 1994 the federal government finally agreed to a system whereby the former 1945–49 landowners would have some limited right to compensation and the right to buy and rent land in East Germany. In most cases these former owners can claim, through buying, only 10 per cent of land (though not the original land). They also have the right to buy, at a small reduction, land from the BVVG. East Germans can buy land at about a third of the market price (*FT*, 26 January 1995, p. 35).

5. By June 1994 38 per cent of claims had been settled, excluding enterprises; more than 43 per cent of claims for businesses had been settled (Judy Dempsey, *FT*, 26 August 1994, p. 2).

Some 80 per cent of those who got their property back promptly sold it again, usually to westerners (*The Economist*, Survey, 21 May 1994, p. 28).

Agriculture

By March 1992 two-thirds of all enterprises in agriculture and forestry were still awaiting privatization (DIW, *Economic Bulletin*, 1993, vol. 29, no. 12, p. 9).

Pryor (1993: 250–1) notes the formation of a new type of co-operative farm, where land is rented from those receiving title to it and farmed collectively. In some cases limited liability corporations have been formed. 'At this point it is difficult to judge whether these new small co-operatives are merely a transitional form to private farming, or whether they will last' (p. 252). In 1990 there was a partial write-off of farm debts (p. 279).

The LPGs (Agricultural Producer Co-operatives) had accumulated debts of about DM 8 billion, which the federal government has since picked up (Judy Dempsey, *FT*, 26 January 1995, p. 35).

After unification the right to restitution and compensation was granted to former owners of land under 100 ha. But this right did not extend to the owners of the large estates which had been expropriated by the Soviet authorities in 1945–49. The THA began to privatize or lease 1.3 million ha of land, a third of the total arable land in East Germany. By mid-1994 the THA will have leased out 700,000 ha, many on twelve-year contracts (Judy Dempsey, *FT*, Survey, 4 May 1994, p. iv). (EU regulations entailed setting aside 15 per cent of arable land, but East Germany's exceeded the planting area. Around 850,000 used to work on the land, but that number has fallen to about 200,000.) (The Bodenverwertungs und -verwaltungs Gesellschaft is charged with administering the THA's portfolio of 3.7 million ha of agricultural land and 2 million ha of forest land: p. vii.)

In the early days of unification the THA started selling agricultural land. But because most of the buyers were coming from West Germany a system of leasing land to easterners at preferential rates was introduced. Under the terms of the unification treaty former Nazi victims and those whose land was confiscated by the Nazis have full rights of restitution and compensation. These rights also apply to former landowners whose land was confiscated by the communists between 1949 and 1990. As regards the former landowners, usually belonging to the Prussian aristocracy, whose land was expropriated by the Soviet administration between 1945 and 1949, the situation has changed somewhat. Such owners have no right to restitution, but they do have a right to buy land back, rent it or, following a law passed in September 1994, receive limited compensation, or to buy a certain amount of property in East Germany at preferential rates. In general those wishing to buy land in East Germany can circumvent outstanding property claims held by easterners if they can prove that they will invest and create jobs. In such cases the former landowners can repossess land only if the investment plans are matched (Judy Dempsey, *FT*, 5 October 1994, p. 34).

A 1993 report is cited by Lueschen (1994). The average size of farm in East Germany was as follows: private farms, 114 ha; partnerships, 328 ha; 'juridical persons' (e.g. co-operatives and corporations), 1,754 ha. By way of contrast, in 1991 the average full-time farm in West Germany was only 31.4 ha (p. 39). By the end of 1992 the number of agricultural workers had plummeted from 850,000 to 160,000. By December 1992 around 516,000 agricultural workers had taken early retirement, 25,000 were working part-time, 105,000 had moved to other jobs and 160,000 were unemployed (p. 41).[2]

Criticisms and alternative models of privatization

The DIW (*Economic Bulletin*, March 1993, vol. 30, no. 1, p. 13) offers the following comments. Forced privatization, attempting to maintain the pace in depressed conditions, means that enterprises are sold 'at any price'. In fact this often means a 'negative price', whereby the THA is not able to ensure that the new owners hold to their investment and job commitments. Many of the enterprises sold are already in difficulties. On a more positive note, the DIW recommends that all THA enterprises (with the exception of those being liquidated) should receive adequate equity capital plus a supplement to compensate them for their difficult initial situation. This would effectively guarantee their survival for a limited period (they would be financially autonomous, e.g. make their own investment decisions). There should be no resort to arbitrary subsidization. The firms that fail to seize the opportunity offered them will have to be liquidated. Privatization could continue but without undue haste. ('Although the Treuhandanstalt attempted in the course of privatization to retain industrial research capacities by setting up the Forschungs-GmbH, it made little effort to maintain research jobs when selling firms to Western investors. This must be seen as a serious failure of privatization policy': DIW, *Economic Bulletin*, 1995, vol. 32, no. 3, p. 10.)

Priewe (1993: 341–6) sums up the THA's strategy for privatization as one in which preference is given to rapid privatization with limited prior restructuring (concentrated on the legal and financial aspects). Economic restructuring is delegated to the new owners. Privatization is achieved predominantly by way of sales or donations to western investors, following individual negotiations concerning investment and employment promises. Where this option is not available other means, such as management buy-outs or sales to intermediaries, are employed. As a result Priewe offers a number of criticisms. They include the following: (1) the combination of a buyers' market and insistence on rapid privatization sometimes forces the THA into hasty sales at less than the 'true' value; (2) in numerous cases enterprises have been sold to West German investors, often to market-dominating companies, although they would have been independently viable either immediately or after restructuring; thus many opportunities for revitalizing competition in a united Germany have been missed; (3) enterprises regarded as viable, but only slowly being privatized, are forced into inactivity in the interim so as not to conflict with any plans future investors may have in mind.

Roesler (1994: 514) argues that the THA 'has privatized to a concept that has worked overwhelmingly badly, creating large financial, economic and social costs, and threatening political stability in the East, if not the whole of Germany'.

Sinn (1992: 166–7) recommends a 'participation model' (social compact) in which the THA keeps a stake in the enterprise (preferably a minority one) without voting rights. The THA should distribute its shares to the population, at least a third to the employees of the privatized firms. In return the employees would accept a union wage 'freeze' (in the sense of keeping the gap between wages in east and west constant for a certain number of years). Sinn also adds some useful material omitted in Jeffries (1993):

1. The period 1945–49 witnessed Soviet expropriations which covered practically all big firms, including the joint stock companies, all banks, the entire insurance industry, many medium-sized firms, all mines and all Nazi property. Moreover, they included agricultural property of 100 ha and above, amounting to about 40 per cent of all private and agricultural and forestry areas (p. 154).

2. Of the original 8,000 enterprises, 6,100 were to be privatized and 1,900 were public utility companies that were to be given to local municipalities. The total number of factories behind the legal entities was around 40,000 (p. 157).

3. The Obstacle Removal Law of March 1991 (p. 156). The government can rule out restitution by itself investing in the property. Current owners who bought property under the rules of the Modrow government are able to retain their ownership. Investors and restituted owners who do not keep to their commitments can be forced to return the property to the government. The legislation does not entirely resolve the problem of investment deterrence since it still takes time to negotiate with the former owners to see whether they are willing to match the investor's offer.

4. As regards indebtedness, the aim is to equalize a firm's starting chances. A firm rich in equity has to accept an interest-bearing liability from the THA, while an equity-poor firm receives an interest-bearing claim against the THA.

The THA maintains that West German companies have not in fact closed East German enterprises down in order to prevent competition (Judy Dempsey, *FT*, 25 May 1993, p. 21). But Dempsey maintains that in the early days West German companies bought the cream of East German enterprises to keep out foreign competition. They also bought enterprises for the real estate and then closed them down (*FT Survey*, 25 October 1993, p. x). Dempsey also reports Birgit Breuel's belief that the THA was a cleverly conceived scapegoat to deflect criticism of adverse effects, such as job losses, away from politicians (p. x).

Only two public offerings of purely East German companies have been floated on the stock exchange and one of them was a flop (Sachsenmilch AG, which almost went out of business) (Richard Smith, *IHT*, 20 April 1994, p. 21).

Output and exports

The output figures have been adjusted quite frequently, but GDP growth has been robust since 1992 (see Table 22.3).

A broad-based process of self-supporting economic growth is still not in sight. Growth in East Germany is still largely based on investment by West German firms and investment in the construction sector, both of which are heavily dependent, directly or indirectly, on government support (DIW, *Economic Bulletin*, September 1993, vol. 30, no. 7, p. 7). It seems that the process of economic restructuring has made considerable progress, and, in certain areas at least, a self-sustaining growth has been initiated (DIW, *Economic Bulletin*, May 1994, vol. 31, no. 5, p. 9). In 1993, for the first time, manufacturing industry made a contribution to output growth after a long period in which economic growth had been the result solely of expansion in the construction industry and the service sector (p. 14). 'Almost five years after economic reunification the question must be addressed as to whether the process of recovery in East Germany has acquired its own momentum. There is some initial evidence for this claim' (*Economic Bulletin*, May 1995, vol. 32, no. 5, p. 8). But 'the current expansion is still not

Table 22.3 Germany: rates of growth of GDP and prices (%)

Territory	*1991*	*1992*	*1993*	*1994*
GDP				
Germany	2.8	2.2	−1.1	2.9
West Germany	5.0	1.8	−1.7	2.3
East Germany	−19.2	7.8	5.8	9.2
Inflation				
Germany	4.8	4.7	3.9	2.7
West Germany	3.8	4.1	3.2	2.6
East Germany	12.8	9.9	8.4	3.0

Sources: Estimates by the German Research Institutes (now six with the inclusion of the Halle Institute for Economic Research) in DIW, *Economic Bulletin* (various issues)

self-sustaining; the volume of government financial support is still considerable. The progress achieved in economic terms does suggest, however, that government support can steadily be wound down' (pp. 17–18).

There have been sectoral variations. While the capital goods industries (such as steel, chemicals and mechanical engineering) continued to decline in 1992, the other main sectors of manufacturing grew (Deutsche Bank, *Focus: Germany*, 22 February 1993, no. 102, p. 1). Manufacturing industry has probably fallen to about a third of the GDR level (p. 2). In the first half of 1992 the manufacturing sector contributed only 15.6 per cent of total East German output compared with 30.3 per cent in West Germany (p. 3).

The prospects for various industries are analysed by the DIW (*Economic Bulletin*, 1992, vol. 29, no. 9, pp. 6, 13). Those struggling most are foundries and firms in mechanical and electrical engineering, the sheet metal and chemical industries, wood processing and clothing and textiles. Those suffering to a less than average extent are quarrying and stone processing, iron, steel and light metal construction, printing, and artisanal firms in the food and vehicle branches. Firms in shipbuilding or chemicals and the iron industry expect turnover to fall. Prospects are not much rosier in paper processing or mechanical and electrical engineering. But future turnover trends are viewed much more positively in plastics and wood processing, quarrying, vehicles and sheet metal production. Printers are optimistic.

One estimate of the growth of industrial output in 1993 was about 5 per cent. The main growth sectors were those geared to the domestic market, such as construction, printing, plastics and food. But output would probably fall in sectors focusing on foreign trade, such as engineering, chemicals, steel and textiles (Deutsche Bank, *Focus: Germany*, 23 April 1993, no. 107, p. 2).

The Deutsche Bank (*Focus: Eastern Europe*, 9 June 1994, no. 107, pp. 1–7) said that the upswing in 1993 was still not self-sustaining. At the end of 1991 industrial production was just over 60 per cent of the level of the second half of 1990. Manufacturing remained at this low level in 1992. It was only in 1993 that production rose: by March 1994 it was around 84 per cent of the level of the second half of 1990. In March 1994 637,000 were employed in manufacturing, compared with an average of 2.8 million in 1990. Consequently, only 10 per cent of the work force is now employed in industry (in West Germany the figure is roughly twice as high).

The process of deindustrialization in East German manufacturing came to a halt in 1994. In 1993 the overall growth of industrial production was 9 per cent, but major sectors such as chemicals and mechanical engineering were still contracting. In 1994 most sectors registered growth (overall industrial growth an estimated 18 per cent), the exceptions being fine ceramics, leather goods and mechanical engineering (Deutsche Bank, *Focus: Germany*, 1994, no. 143, p. 6).

It will be at least a decade before the economic basis of self-sustaining growth is secure (*Transition*, July–August 1994, vol. 5, no. 6, p. 20).

East German exports fell by around 20 per cent in 1992, reaching close to a quarter of the 1989 level. East Germany's share of pan-German exports fell to about 2 per cent (Deutsche Bank, *Focus: Germany*, 1993, no. 101, p. 3). In 1993 the East German share of total German exports was 2 per cent, compared with 30 per cent in 1989 (Judy Dempsey, *FT*, 22 June 1994, p. 4). For Germany as a whole, the current account of the balance of payments was in deficit to the tune of DM 33 billion in 1991 and DM 38 billion in 1992 (p. 5). In 1992 East German exports were only around a third of the 1989 level and imports were about a quarter (DIW, *Economic Bulletin*, 1993, vol. 30, no. 5, p. 12).

The economic outlook

Hughes Hallet and Ma (1993: 427) conclude their simulation exercise with the verdict that the full convergence of the two Germanies without a *mezzogiorno* problem will take thirty to forty years. On the basis of current policies the catch-up after fifteen years will be in the range 50–60 per cent, although 70 per cent is also possible with some policy changes. The unification process would be accelerated if East German wages were to be constrained relative to those in West Germany or if taxes were to be increased. But the same effects could be obtained more effectively with a self-eliminating employment subsidy in East Germany.

Hughes Hallet and Ma (1994) argue that if a *mezzogiorno* problem, in which investment and/or labour have to be supported by continuing transfers, and possible migration flows to West Germany, are to be avoided, there has to be convergence in productivity levels. Full convergence, without a *mezzogiorno* problem, is likely to take thirty to forty years (the official predictions are in the range of five to ten years: p. 1745). On the basis of current policies the catch-up after fifteen years will be around 50 per cent to 60 per cent, although 75 per cent is also possible with some policy changes. Policies which promote price and wage flexibility in East Germany are recommended (pp. 1731, 1758). A capital subsidy scheme would reduce the relative price of new capital but do nothing to preserve employment at the same time. Wage subsidies encourage employment, but do nothing to expand investment (p. 1756). The unification process would be speeded up if East German wage growth were restrained, or taxes increased, or if capital was subsidized. But the same effects can be obtained more effectively with self-eliminating employment subsidies or, better still, self-eliminating revenue subsidies in East Germany. Subsidizing production units (rather than production factors) is the superior strategy because it does not distort the optimal factor input ratios. But both schemes have the advantages of inducing price flexibility and of complete credibility in not overloading the budget deficit for too long (p. 1758).

Jürgens *et al.* (1993: 229–43) argue that the future could hold either vigour and growth or stagnation and permanent second-class status for the economy and the labour movement in East Germany, depending largely on actor strategy and choice. The rapid spread of privatization and open markets on the one hand is tending to undermine the influence of trade unions. On the other hand, institutional transfers from West Germany (especially of co-determination law and centralized, regional-level collective bargaining) are giving unions and works councils increased leverage. Jürgens *et al.* are cautiously optimistic about the future prospects of trade unions and industrial relations. But it all depends. If unions and works councils are flexible and innovative they will improve the chances of a future of modernization and the exercise of substantial influence in East Germany.

NOTES

1. Until mid-1992 the wages of East German industrial workers rose far faster than productivity. Since then unit labour costs have been falling, but in the second half of 1994 average unit labour costs in manufacturing industry were still a quarter above those in West Germany (DIW, *Economic Bulletin*, 1995, vol. 32, no. 9, p. 4).
2. There are now about 25,000 farms in East Germany compared with the 5,000 mostly state-owned collectives which existed in 1989. The larger units have been split up into smaller holdings, many of which are now family run. The average West German farm covers around 33 ha, while the average East German farm covers 157 ha. Animal breeding has been adversely affected, e.g. the size of the cattle, dairy and pig herds in East Germany has slumped by 65 per cent since 1989 (Michael Lindemann, *FT*, Survey, 23 October 1995, p. 11).

23

HUNGARY

POLITICS

The political background

The population of Hungary is markedly homogeneous. Hungarians constitute 92 per cent of the population, Gypsies 5 per cent, Germans 2 per cent and South Slavs 1 per cent (*The Independent*, 7 May 1994, p. 11).

Political developments prior to the 1994 general election

16–18 April 1993. At its fifth congress the Federation of Young Democrats permits those over thirty-five years of age to join the party. Viktor Orban is re-elected president. The party is pro-market and pro-democracy.

30 April 1993. A treaty is signed by Hungary and Ukraine which states that 'neither country has, nor will have, any territorial claims on the other'. Ukraine gives guarantees about the treatment of its Hungarian minority (*EEN*, 1993, vol. 7, no. 10, p. 2).

1 June 1993. Istvan Csurka and three other members on the extreme right wing of the Hungarian Democratic Forum are expelled from the parliamentary party. A nationwide party meeting on 5 June confirmed the decision, saying that Csurka's movement Hungarian Way was incompatible with membership of the party. He then formed the Hungarian Justice Party on 22 June 1993 (later called Hungarian Justice and Life after its 1930s namesake).

22 August 1993. The electoral deal agreed in July between the Alliance of Free Democrats and the Federation of Young Democrats is widened to include the Entrepreneurs' Party (led by Peter Zwack) and the Agrarian Alliance. For example, joint candidates may be put up in the second round of voting (*EEN*, 25 August 1993, vol. 7, no. 17, p. 3, and 29 March 1994, vol. 8, no. 7, p. 4).

4 September 1993. Admiral Miklos Horthy (the 'Regent' of Hungary, pending a Habsburg 'restoration', from March 1920 to October 1944, who died in Portugal in 1957) is reburied in Hungary amid controversy.

12 December 1993. Prime Minister Jozsef Antall dies at the age of sixty-one (of heart trouble after battling against cancer for a number of years). Peter Boross, the interior minister, is asked to carry on as acting prime minister (parliament elected him prime minister on 21 December).

February 1994. The dismissal or forced retirement of 129 journalists from the state-owned radio is seen by opposition parties as another example of government interference in the media.

1 April 1994. Hungary formally applies to join the EU (the first ex-socialist country to do so).

Agreement in principle is reached that Russia will pay off its remaining debt to Hungary of $900 million by the deadline in 1996 through means such as debt–equity swaps and arms deliveries. In 1993 Hungary acquired armaments worth $800 million in part payment of the total debt of $1.7 billion (Nicholas Denton, *FT*, 2 April 1994, p. 2).

The 1994 general election

There were two rounds, on 8 and 29 May 1994. The 386 seats were contested on (1) a proportional basis (5 per cent threshold), in which 152 candidates were elected via regional party lists (Budapest was counted as one of the twenty 'counties' for the purpose) and fifty-eight were allocated to the highest-scoring runners-up; (2) a first-past-the-post basis, involving 176 individual constituencies. A second round of voting was held when no candidate won 50 per cent of the vote and/or the turnout was less than 50 per cent.

Before the election result was known Nicholas Denton and Edward Mortimer (*FT*, 5 May 1994, p. 25) observed that 'economic policy as such has been almost absent from the Hungarian election campaign . . . economic policy is not what divides the parties. Voters' feelings about the economy may be the decisive factor in the election, but the political class reserves its passion for the "national question". This is, in essence, a question about what makes a Hungarian: ethnicity or citizenship? . . . Hungarians are being asked to choose between left and right, not in the sense of socialism versus capitalism, but in the much older sense of "cosmopolitan" freethinkers versus Christian nationalists.'

The main parties

Hungarian Democratic Forum. Led by Peter Boross. Conservative.

Christian Democratic People's Party. Led by Laszlo Surjan. Conservative. Opposes the sale of land to foreigners.

Independent Smallholders' Party. Led by Jozsef Torgyan. Pro-farming.

Hungarian Justice and Life Party. Led by Istvan Csurka. Neo-fascist.

Alliance of Free Democrats. The parliamentary group is led by Gabor Kuncze. The party president is Ivan Peto. Liberal, but seen as perhaps having moved somewhat to the left. Still to the right on economic policy.

Federation of Young Democrats (Fidesz). Led by Viktor Orban. Liberal, strongly pro-market (e.g. advocates a more investment-friendly corporate tax regime). Economic growth should have a higher priority than reducing inflation. Weakened by criticism about some dubious business deals and the defection to the Alliance of Free Democrats of Gabor Fodor.

Hungarian Socialist Party. Led by Gyula Horn. Generally pro-market and offers no dramatic change in economic policy. But the party does contain diverse elements as regards economic policy. Finance supremo Laszlo Bekesi is very much to the right, while Sandor Nagy (head of the National Association of Trade Unions, which claims around 1 million members) was second only to Gyula Horn on the party list. The party advocates a 'social pact' between government, employers and trade unions. Greater social protection for the most disadvantaged would be one element of the pact. Although privatization was supported, the process would be brought under parliamentary control in order to stop abuses (Bekesi was reported not to be keen on the small shareholder programme).

Workers' Party. Led by Gyula Thurmer. Communist.

The result (see Table 23.1)

The first round. There was a 68.9 per cent turnout in the first round, although only 127 parliamentary seats were decided (only two of the 176 constituency seats, both won by the Hungarian Socialist Party). Overall the vote was for the centre (especially the centre left) and against extremism. Headlines included one which said, 'Socialists first, liberals second'.

1. The Hungarian Socialist Party, as predicted, came out well in front with 32.5 per cent of the vote (fifty-five seats). Although it had promised no radical shift in policy, it benefited from the support of those who most felt

Table 23.1 Hungary: the general election of May 1994

Party	*Seats*	*Vote (%)*
Hungarian Socialist Party	209	53.9
Alliance of Free Democrats	70	18.1
Hungarian Democratic Forum	37	9.6
Independent Smallholders' Party	26	6.8
Christian Democratic People's Party	22	5.8
Federation of Young Democrats	20	5.3
Others	2	0.5
Total	386	100

the pain and uncertainty of economic transition (aggravated by the increasing disparities in income and wealth) and of those who perceived a seemingly relatively united, competent, experienced and tolerant team. Thus the support was widespread, from pensioners and the unemployed to managers and university graduates in general.

2. The Alliance of Free Democrats did even better than expected, winning 19.8 per cent of the vote (twenty seats).

3. The Hungarian Democratic Forum won 11.8 per cent of the vote (eighteen seats).

4. The Christian Democratic People's Party won 7 per cent of the vote.

5. The Independent Smallholders' Party won 8.5 per cent of the vote.

6. Fidesz won 7 per cent. (At a post-election conference the party changed its name to the Federation of Young Democrats–Hungarian Civic Party and confirmed the move to the right: *EEN*, 12 May 1995, vol. 9, no. 10, p. 10.)

7. Hungarian Justice and Life won 1.43 per cent.

The second round. The Hungarian Socialist Party did even better in the second round than had been generally forecast. Despite winning a surprising overall majority of seats, a coalition government with the Alliance of Free Democrats was still sought by the party leaders in order to ensure that there would be no slide into inflationary spending increases arising from pressure from the more social welfare-orientated elements within the party.

The coalition government

An agreement was signed on 24 June 1994. The Alliance of Free Democrats were awarded three of the twelve ministerial posts, namely interior and deputy prime minister (Gabor Kuncze), culture and education (Gabor Fodor) and 'infrastructure', combining transport, telecommunications and water (Karoly Lotz). But there would be joint decision-making at the cabinet level between the two coalition partners over policy and personnel, the so-called 'guarantee of joint government'. Among the posts occupied by members of the Hungarian Socialist Party were those of prime minister (Gyula Horn), finance and the economy (Laszlo Bekesi), foreign affairs (Laszlo Kovacs), defence (Gyorgy Keleti) and industry and trade (Laszlo Pal).

Political developments after the 1994 general election

14 July 1994. The prime minister says he is ready to sign new bilateral agreements with Romania and Slovakia on the inviolability of borders, provided the rights of the Hungarian minorities are guaranteed.

15 July 1994. The new session of parliament begins.

28 July 1994. Expo '96, the world fair planned to take place in 1996, is cancelled by parliament on the grounds of cost. (The project was conceived in the late 1980s as a joint project with Austria, but Austria pulled out because of the expense. It was meant to celebrate the 1,100th anniversary of the founding of the state. Seven Magyar – nomadic – tribes from east of the Urals arrived in the Carpathian basin in 896.)

5 September 1994. The Romanian foreign minister, Teodor Melescanu, visits Hungary.

11 December 1994. In the local elections the ruling coalition parties do well, although not quite as well as in the general election.

28 January 1995. Finance Minister Laszlo Bekesi resigns (effective 1 March). The main reason is the prime minister's decision to take responsibility for privatization away from the Finance Ministry and put it in the hands of a new privatization minister. (The previous privatization commissioner, Ferenc Bartha, was effectively dismissed on 12 January; the government said he had agreed to leave 'by mutual consent'. The governor of the central bank, Peter Akos Bod, was forced to resign in December 1994.)

31 January 1995. The prime minister says that 'It is of strategic importance that the country should not be dependent either on foreigners or on domestic private businesses in terms of its power supply.' He also says that the central bank should co-ordinate its policies more with the government.

Two former militiamen are sentenced to five years in prison for crimes against humanity, specifically for taking part in the firing on unarmed civilians demonstrating on 8 December 1956 (forty-six died, but there was no proof that the two militiamen were directly responsible).

1 March 1995. The West approves of the new appointments to the presidency of the central bank (Georgyi Suranyi, a banker and former president of the central bank 1990–91) and to the Finance Ministry (Lajos Bokros, a banker and former chairman of the Budapest stock exchange). (They were recommended by the prime minister on 7 February, but formally took up their duties on 1 March. Tamas Suchman was nominated as privatization minister on 21 February.)

13 March 1995. The ministers of welfare and national security offer to resign when the government's package of austerity measures is announced (see below).

15 March 1995. The education minister offers his resignation.

19 March 1995. Hungary and Slovakia sign, as part of the European Stability Pact, an agreement guaranteeing borders and minority rights.

19 June 1995. Parliament re-elects Arpad Goncz as president.

22 June 1995. Industry and Trade Minister Laszlo Pal is dismissed (effective 15 July) for his resistance to gas and electricity privatization. He is replaced by Imre Dunai.

THE ECONOMY

Financial policy

On 11 February 1993 the finance minister, Mihaly Kupa, resigned and was replaced the following day by the industry minister, Ivan Szabo.

The budget deficit in 1992, planned to be 70 billion forints, turned out to be 190 billion forints or 7 per cent of GDP (*The Economist*, Survey, 13 March 1993, pp. 15–16). The Deutsche Bank (*Focus: Eastern Europe*, 26 February 1993, no. 68, p. 2) reported that the IMF accepted the 1993 draft budget deficit of 185 billion forints or 6.2 per cent of GNP. Frydman *et al.* (1993: 101) note that the aim was to reduce subsidies as a percentage of GDP to less than 4 per cent in 1993 (compared with 13 per cent in 1989 and 7.3 per cent in 1991). A tough budget was presented by the finance minister, Ivan Szabo, on 17 May 1993 in order to bring the budget deficit down to 6.8 per cent of GDP in 1993 and to 5.5 per cent of GDP in 1994. This was in line with the new IMF agreement of that month (replacing the February 1991 to February 1994 one which had been suspended in July 1992; the new agreement involved an eighteen-month structural adjustment programme and a $600 million stand-by credit). On 15 September 1993 a new IMF stand-by loan of $480 million was arranged, with Hungary agreeing to keep the budget deficit to 6.5 per cent of GDP in 1993 and to 5.5 per cent of GDP in 1994.

On 1 January 1993 the VAT system was reformed. The old rates of 0 per cent, 18 per cent and 25 per cent were amended to 0 per cent (medicines and household electricity), 6 per cent (most goods for daily consumption, formerly zero rated) and 25 per cent respectively. On 7 July 1993 the government succeeded in getting these rates amended as part of an austerity package. On 2 August 1993 VAT on household energy was raised from zero to 10 per cent (medicines would remain exempt until the end of 1994) and that on food and other staples was increased from 6 per cent to 10 per cent.

The taxing of wage increases above a set limit was abolished in 1993 (EBRD 1994: 27). Hungary abandoned wage controls in 1993 (*Business Central Europe*, July–August 1994, p. 24). (An excess wage tax was introduced in 1991, exceptions including joint ventures where the foreign stake was over 20 per cent; the scheme was modified in 1992: Frydman *et al.* 1993: 100.)

The Horn government's financial policy

21 September 1994. A supplementary budget for 1994 is presented. Austerity measures are to reduce the budget deficit to 6.6 per cent of GDP (Deutsche Bank, *Focus: Eastern Europe*, 1994, no. 116, p. 9).

But the government retroactively raised pensions by 8 per cent across the board from January and deferred an increase in VAT and energy prices from October 1994 to 1995 (*FT*, 21 October 1994, p. 2).

27 December 1994. The budget for 1994 is passed, with a planned deficit of 5.5 per cent of GDP.

13 March 1995. An unexpectedly tough package of austerity measures is announced. Apart from expenditure cuts, including social welfare spending, increases in wages in the public sector are to be limited to 3 per cent, the forint is devalued by 9 per cent against the US dollar (with subsequent small weekly devaluations for the rest of the year) and an 8 per cent increase in import duties is announced, with the exception of machinery/equipment, energy and components of exportables (the surcharge was to be phased out during the first half of 1997). But on 30 June the Constitutional Court declared some of the cuts in social spending to be unconstitutional because inadequate notice was given. The government compensated with alternative spending cuts.

Banking

There was a partial write-off of bad debt in 1991, and in late 1992 some more bad debt was converted into state bonds (*The Banker*, February 1993, p. 38, and July 1993, p. 27).

The state guaranteed half of inherited bad debt, while in March 1993 the state agreed to swap low-interest twenty-year bonds for bad debt. Under the voluntary scheme participating banks must write off 20–50 per cent of loans swapped (*Business Central Europe*, June 1993, p. 37).

In January 1993 the government set up the Hungarian Investment Bank, which took over some 100 billion forints' worth of bad debt in return for the banks buying special twenty-year Treasury bonds (*Banking World*, September 1993, p. 28).

But both the World Bank and the OECD stress the need for further reform of the financial system as a whole. Problems include bad debt, wide spreads between deposit and lending rates and the level of government taxation; in 1992 bank lending to the enterprise sector was curtailed (Nicholas Denton, *FT*, 1 November 1993, p. 17).

In late 1992 fourteen state banks received some 70 billion forints in twenty-year government bonds in exchange for 105 billion forints' worth of bad debts, which were placed in the Hungarian Development Organization; in December 1993 the government unveiled a $1.4 billion rescue plan for ten banks, including three of the largest (*Business Europa*, February–March 1994, p. 11).

In autumn 1992 the government launched a 'consolidation scheme'. In the first round (effected in March 1993) the chosen banks exchanged non-performing loans for twenty-year state bonds. In the second round

(December 1993) a state-financed capital injection of twenty-year bonds was combined with the purchase by the state of bank claims for state bonds. There was another injection of bonds in May 1994. The Foreign Trade Bank was privatized in 1994. The law on commercial banks requires a reduction in state ownership of all banks, except the National Savings Bank, to less than 25 per cent by the end of 1997 (EBRD 1994: 27).

Prices

In January 1991 the share of decontrolled consumer prices was raised to about 90 per cent (including the retail prices of petrol and fuel oil; other energy prices were raised substantially, while producer prices for coal, firewood, electricity and natural gas remained controlled). Central control remained for textbooks, for one type of milk, for white bread and for public utilities; local governments set local transport fares and rents for government-owned apartments (Boote and Somogyi 1991: 13).

More than 90 per cent of prices, weighted by their share of the consumer price index, are free of administrative controls (EBRD 1994: 27).

On 1 January 1995 the price of household electricity went up by 65 per cent and that of household gas by 53 per cent (wholesale 26 per cent). The government agreed to raise domestic gas prices to market levels by 1997 as part of its commitment to the World Bank (*Business Central Europe*, March 1995, p. 26).

Below-cost prices for gas and electricity were to be phased out before January 1997 (EBRD 1995: 57).

Bankruptcies

Hare (1993: 48) describes the bankruptcy law as very tough on paper (firms with payments overdue by more than three months have to register at the bankruptcy court). But in practice most cases are resolved by negotiation between creditors and firms, relatively few going into liquidation.

In 1992 almost 15,000 enterprises filed for bankruptcy protection or liquidation, but only around thirty had actually been closed down by the start of 1993 (*Business Central Europe*, June 1993, p. 7).

Up to August 1993 some 5,000 bankruptcy and over 15,000 liquidation requests had been lodged (United Nations Economic Commission for Europe 1994: 193). As well as the scale of applications, abuses of the liquidation process are likely to lead to formal amendment of the bankruptcy law. Many enterprises apply in order to obtain legal cancellation of all their debts so that they can re-establish their business activities with a clean balance sheet (United Nations Economic Commission for Europe 1993: 175).

According to the OECD, one in six registered companies (producing about 14 per cent of GDP) have been affected by the bankruptcy legislation (Nicholas Denton, *FT*, 1 November 1993, p. 17).

The law was substantially amended in September 1993. Enterprises with overdue liabilities were no longer forced to declare themselves bankrupt and a qualified majority of creditors could decide on an out-of-court restructuring against the will of a minority of shareholders. The earlier version had been criticized for forcing potentially profitable enterprises into liquidation (EBRD 1994: 26).

Privatization

The employment limit on private businesses was abolished in 1990 (Boote and Somogyi 1991: 9).

In 1990 the 100 largest industrial enterprises accounted for 13 per cent of the work force and 48 per cent of the total assets of state industrial enterprises (Frydman *et al.* 1993: 97). In March 1991 the government's aim was to reduce the share of state-owned assets in the 'competitive' economy – which excludes those large enterprises expected to remain under direct state control – to about 50 per cent by 1994 (p. 125). Corporatization by the end of 1992 became mandatory for all enterprises (p. 131). As regards small privatization, 80 per cent of sales are by open auction; real estate is often not sold; more than 30 per cent of shops had been privatized by the end of April 1992 (p. 136).

Frydman *et al.* (1993: 135) and Frydman and Rapaczynski (1993: 55) provide the following information on 'self-privatization'. The invitation for consulting firms to participate was issued at the beginning of June 1991; in the first stage 400 small enterprises were eligible (p. 135). The (voluntarily) participating enterprise has to employ an independent consulting company from a list drawn up by the State Property Agency. The enterprise may propose a plan, but the consulting company is ultimately responsible for the actual sale (for which it receives a percentage of the price plus a bonus dependent on the speed at which the transaction is completed).

By the end of 1992 some 15–18 per cent of state property had been privatized (the government's strategy was to reduce the public sector's share of GDP from 90 per cent in 1990 to about 40 per cent by the end of 1994) (*Business Europa*, August–September 1993, p. 23).

According to the OECD, around 18 per cent of state enterprise assets had been privatized by the end of 1992. This was well short of the government's target of privatizing half the state sector by the end of its term in 1994 (Nicholas Denton, *FT*, 1 November 1993, p. 17; *FT*, Survey, 17 November 1993, p. 47). In 1989 Hungary had about 2,000 state enterprises. By September 1993 the State Property Agency had sold 273 enterprises outright, disposed of majority shareholdings in 144 others and minority shareholdings in seventy-one. A further 370 enterprises were liquidated (p. 47). The Hungarian State Property Agency says that in 1993 404 companies passed from state ownership to the private sector and some portion of a further 185 companies was sold (*FT*, 2 March 1994, p. 22).

Large privatization has been gradual but steady. Out of almost 2,000 enterprises owned by the State Property Agency when it started operations in 1990, 569 had been fully privatized by mid-1994, while state ownership in 167 had been reduced to a minority share. In addition more than 400 of the 4,000 enterprises had been liquidated (EBRD 1994: 26). When it started operations in 1990 the State Property Agency had 1,848 large enterprises. By the end of 1994 653 were fully privately owned and state ownership of a further 204 had been reduced to less than 50 per cent. Of the original 1,848 enterprises 437 were in liquidation by December 1994. The state retained on average 53 per cent of the shares in the remaining 1,411 enterprises (EBRD 1995: 57).

Up to July 1994 the State Property Agency and the State Holding Company had sold 47 per cent of the former state-owned stock. The remaining 720 enterprises that comprise the former's portfolio are still to be sold, while most of the 166 enterprises in the latter's portfolio are to be privatized completely and the remaining forty-five or so only partially (Helgard Wienert, *The OECD Observer*, April–May 1995, no. 193, p. 38).

The State Property Agency estimates that 47 per cent of state property has been privatized (*FT*, Survey, 11 November 1994, p. 29).

By the end of 1994 Hungary has sold off about 40 per cent of state enterprises by book value (*The Economist*, 20 May 1995, p. 93).

On 2 March 1993 the government set in motion its Small Investor Shareholder Programme, to involve the population in the privatization process through inducements such as favourable credit terms (Nicholas Denton, *FT*, 3 March 1993, p. 3, and 16 October 1993, p. 2; *Business Central Europe*, May 1993, p. 11, October 1993, p. 61, and April 1994, p. 22; Deutsche Bank, *Focus: Eastern Europe*, 31 August 1993, no. 86, p. 8; Nicholas Clegg, *FT*, 19 October 1993, p. 4). Citizens (on payment of a 2,000-forint registration fee) would receive interest-free loans of up to 100,000 forints (repayable over five years). The loans do not require collateral and the scheme as a whole does not require the support of parliament. Shares can only be traded once the loans have been paid off. The first enterprises (out of around seventy in total) selected for the programme were due to be sold in January 1994, but the start was delayed somewhat (it began with one enterprise on 18 April 1994).

On 28 February 1994 it was announced that four public offerings were to be made in April (a hotel group, a plastics manufacturer, a brewer and a food retailer).

Nicholas Denton (*FT*, 4 February 1993, p. 3) reports that on 3 February 1993 the government announced that it intended to privatize the main national utilities (e.g. telecommunications, gas distribution and electricity; state commercial banks were also mentioned). No precise timetable was mentioned, but some privatizations could be completed before the end of the year. To date consumer goods and food companies have provided the privatization momentum. On 19 December 1993 it was announced that a German–US consortium had taken a 30 per cent stake in Matav (the national telecommunications company), the first privatization in that sector in the whole of Eastern Europe (some of the state shares were to be sold off in autumn 1994). On 6 April 1994 parliament voted through an Act dealing with the restructuring and privatization of electricity generation and distribution: the monopoly was to be broken; foreign companies were to be involved; the state was to retain a stake of 25 per cent plus one share in three larger conventional power stations and to keep full control of the Paks nuclear power station; the state would also retain variable percentages of shares in the five regional distribution networks (Nicholas Denton, *FT*, 7 April 1994, p. 2; Lucy Hooker, *The Guardian*, 2 April 1994, p. 35). In September the date of privatization was fixed for 1995. Further details were announced on 29 November 1994. MVM is the state electricity company. The state was to retain full control of the nuclear plant and the national grid but would sell off 50 per cent (minus one vote) of the national distribution centre. The government also planned to sell 100 per cent, less one golden share, of the regional electricity companies and the non-nuclear power stations (both of which are under MVM), with 50 per cent plus one share going to strategic investors. The intention was to sell off 100 per cent (minus one golden share) of the five regional gas suppliers. Thirty to 35 per cent of MOL (the oil and gas monopoly) was to be sold off to strategic investors and the aim was to reduce state ownership to 25 per cent plus one vote. The gas companies were expected to be sold first. The plan was to sell 50 per cent (plus one vote) to strategic investors via an international tender early in 1995. The remainder would be sold later to institutional and local investors on local and international stock exchanges (Virginia Marsh, *FT*, 30 November 1994, p. 53; *Transition*, 1995, vol. 6, nos 5–6, p. 14).

In June 1995 the government revised its utility privatization plans. The November 1994 strategy envisaged a one- to two-year timetable. But the government now intends to sell a majority stake in MOL as soon as possible, although the privatization of MVM was to be spread over two phases (ending in 1997). In the first phase a strategic partner would be offered a 24 per cent stake in the core company, which will retain the national grid and the Paks nuclear plant. It was to hive off MVM's power generators and distribution companies and offer minority stakes in most of them also to strategic partners. With regard to the gas supply companies it has kept to its original plan to sell off a majority stake, but has reduced the stake to be offered from 100 per cent minus one to 60 per cent (Virginia Marsh, *FT*, 24 July 1995, p. 18).

Total proceeds from privatization collected by the State Privatization Agency in 1991 amounted to 39.2 billion forints ($500 million), representing about 2 per cent of the consolidated state budget (Frydman and Rapaczynski 1993: 55). Foreigners have accounted for a large proportion of privatization sales since 1990. In 1991 80 per cent of state assets were bought by foreigners and in 1992 the figure was still around 60 per cent (*The Banker*, July 1993, p. 35).

Committees of inquiry have been set up to look into the activities of the State Property Agency, which manages the privatization process. Allegations include secrecy, political interference, corruption and lack of supervision (*EEN*, 11 May 1993, vol. 7, no. 10, pp. 1–2). (See also *Business Central Europe*, June 1993, pp. 19–20.)

On 4 October 1994 the government sacked eight of the ten board members of the State Holding Company (AV Rt) and ordered an investigation into allegations of corruption against the general manager, Lajos Csepi. The holding company was set up in 1992 to manage the 160 enterprises in which the state wished to sell a strategic stake but retain majority ownership. In future greater emphasis would be placed on privatization via cash sales, flotation on the stock market and sales to institutional investors. Until now trade sales to strategic investors, often by tender, have been the preferred method (Virginia Marsh, *FT*, 5 October 1994, p. 2).

The Horn government's privatization programme

The government approved its privatization programme on 3 November 1994, but it was not until 9 May 1995 that parliament gave its approval (sources include Virginia Marsh, *FT*, 20 September 1994, p. 3; 4 November 1994, p. 2; Survey, 11 November 1994, pp. 29–31):

1. The aim was to complete the sale of most state enterprises by the end of the government's term of office in 1998. (Horn expects the share of private property in the economy to reach two-thirds by then: *Transition*, January–February 1995, p. 19.)

2. The State Property Agency (AVU; the trustee for enterprises to be privatized) and the State Holding Company (AV Rt; charged with managing enterprises remaining in the public sector) were to be merged (into the Hungarian Privatization and Holding Company; this was established on 19 June 1995).

3. Cash sales of large enterprises (with transparent procedures) were to take pride of place as a means of raising revenue and rapid sale was to be preferred to restructuring. Strategic investors would be sought.

4. As regards medium-sized enterprises, the priority is finding good partners and providing for long-term survival.

5. Small enterprises will be sold for cash if possible. But if an enterprise cannot be sold in any other way a new scheme is available. If the employees

and management buy 10 per cent of the shares, 40 per cent may be paid for in ten years and then they receive the remaining 50 per cent of shares free of charge.

6. The number of enterprises under majority state ownership would be reduced to 161 (from 252 under current law). Forty-six enterprises would be kept in full state ownership, including postal services and the railways. The state would maintain a majority stake in the electrical grid and in the only nuclear power plant, while it would maintain 25 per cent ownership in large banks (EBRD 1995: 57). (Details of the privatization of the electricity and gas sectors are given above.)

The size of the private sector

The 66,000 small private firms and 180,000 one-man firms account for 40 per cent of output (*The Economist*, Survey, 13 March 1993, p. 9). The private sector's share of GDP is 55 per cent (*The Economist*, 29 October 1994, p. 56).

Assessment is fraught with difficulties, but official government estimates indicate that in 1992 about one-third of GDP originated in the private sector (Bartholdy 1993: 124).

The Deutsche Bank (*Focus: Eastern Europe*, 1 July 1993, no. 82, p. 4) merely gave a range of 33–45 per cent of GDP, but later gave a more definite figure of around 50 per cent (22 March 1994, no. 100, p. 16).

The United Nations Economic Commission for Europe (1993: 215) also gives (officially estimated) ranges for the private sector as a whole: 1990, 10.0–15.8 per cent of GDP; 1991, 18.2–41.0 per cent of GDP; 1992, 25–45 per cent of GDP.

A figure of 30 per cent of GDP has been mentioned (Nicholas Denton, *FT*, 1 November 1993, p. 17).

According to the OECD, wholly and partly privately owned firms now employ 36 per cent of the work force (*Economic Outlook*, December 1993, p. 115).

In March 1994 it was announced that the government had reached its target of 50 per cent of GDP contributed by the private sector eight months ahead of schedule (*IHT*, Survey, 19 April 1994, p. 17).

Some estimates put the black economy at 25 per cent of GDP (Nicholas Denton, *FT*, 14 September 1993, p. 3). According to *The Economist* (7 May 1994, p. 45), if the black economy is included the private sector accounts for 60 per cent of GDP. Up to two-fifths of the 500,000 officially unemployed people probably live off a black economy whose value may amount to nearly a third of GDP (*The Economist*, 11 March 1995, p. 50). Estimates put the grey economy as large as one-third of official GDP (*Business Central Europe*, May 1995, p. 59).

In mid-1994 the private sector accounted for roughly 55 per cent of GDP (EBRD 1994: 10).

Foreign trade

Trade liberalization has been gradually phased in. There are now very few remaining licensing/quota restrictions on imports and exports. The forint is generally convertible for current account transactions (there are restrictions as regards tourism by Hungarian citizens), while capital account transactions are gradually being liberalized (EBRD 1994: 27).

The forint operates on an 'adjustable peg to basket' system (IMF, *World Economic Outlook*, May 1993, p. 66).

Changes in the official exchange rate in excess of plus or minus 4 per cent are decided by the government (United Nations Economic Commission for Europe 1994: 122).

The central bank can devalue or revalue the currency by as much as 5 per cent on its own initiative. Moves of more than 5 per cent require government approval (*IHT*, 11 October 1994, p. 11).

In December 1991 the weighting was fixed at 50 per cent US dollar and 50 per cent Ecu, but on 2 August 1993 the Deutschmark replaced the Ecu. On 23 April 1994 the weighting became 70 per cent Ecu and 30 per cent US dollar.

The president of the National Bank of Hungary is reported as saying that full convertibility would gradually be achieved over the course of 'several years' (*The Banker*, July 1993, p. 38).

On 1 June 1994 it became legal for foreigners to convert forints earned from exporting to Hungary into foreign currency (*Business Central Europe*, July–August 1994, p. 51).

At the end of February 1993 Hungary and EFTA signed a free-trade agreement, to come into force on 1 July (the actual date turned out to be 1 October). An association agreement with the EU came into force on 1 February 1994. Under the agreement 80 per cent of industrial exports to the EU are free of tariffs and quota limits. Over the next three years the remaining goods (including textiles, steel and most agricultural products) will also be freed of restrictions. Hungary is given an extra seven years to remove all similar barriers to imports from the EU (*IHT*, Survey, 19 April 1994, p. 19).

In 1992 75 per cent of exports went to OECD countries (*Employment Observatory*, 1993, no. 4, p. 2).

In 1992 70.5 per cent of exports went to OECD countries, 49.8 per centage points of which went to the EU (Deutsche Bank, *Focus: Eastern Europe*, 1993, no. 85, p. 6).

Foreign investment

Direct foreign investment in Eastern Europe and the former Soviet Union amounted to $12.417 billion in the period 1990–93. Hungary, the Czech

Republic and Slovakia alone accounted for two-thirds of the total. 'Annual measured FDI inflows into Eastern Europe and the former Soviet Union rose tenfold between 1990 and 1993. Even so, however, they represented only approximately 10 per cent of total FDI flows into developing countries in 1993' (EBRD 1994: 122).

Nicholas Denton (6 October 1993, p. 8) reported more than $5.5 billion in accumulated direct foreign investment since 1988, more than half the total for Eastern Europe the government claims. On 5 October 1993 Eastern Europe's first independent investment and trade development agency (ITD Hungary) was set up, with the focus on attracting investment into motor components, food processing and tourism. In 1992 foreign investment was an estimated $1.7 billion.

Direct foreign investment in 1992 matched the $1.5 billion figure of the previous year (Deutsche Bank, *Focus: Eastern Europe*, 26 February 1993, no. 68, p. 3). The cumulative totals by the end of the period were as follows: 1989, $0.22 billion; 1990, $0.57 billion; 1991, $2.1 billion; 1992, $3.4 billion; 1993, $5.6 billion; 1994, $7.1 billion (Deutsche Bank, *Focus: Eastern Europe*, 1993, no. 84, p. 8; 1995, no. 134, p. 14).

Net direct foreign investment in Hungary was $311 million in 1990, $1.46 billion in 1991 and $1.47 billion in 1992; the respective total figures for Bulgaria, the former Czechoslovakia, Hungary, Poland and Romania combined were $573 million, $2.261 billion and $2.825 billion; Hungary and Czechoslovakia together accounted for some 90 per cent of the total (United Nations Economic Commission for Europe 1993: 19, 239). In 1993 the net flow into Hungary was $2.328 billion and in 1994 it was $1.097 billion (United Nations Economic Commission for Europe 1995: 151).

In 1993 Hungary attracted $2.5 billion, bringing the total up to $7.1 billion by the end of the year (*IHT*, Survey, 19 April 1994, p. 18).

Hungary has attracted a total of $7.1 billion of foreign investment (Nicholas Denton, *FT*, 1 March 1994, p. 3).

Total direct foreign investment reached $5.5 billion at the end of 1993 and $6 billion at the end of April 1994 (*Transition*, 1994, vol. 5, no. 6, p. 22).

By September 1994 the total was $6.5 billion (*Business Central Europe*, December 1994–January 1995, p. 72).

Direct foreign investment amounted to $5.441 billion in the period 1990–93 (EBRD 1994: 123).

Some $7.2 billion has entered the country during the last four years in the framework of privatization and direct investment (State Property Agency, *FT*, Survey, 11 November 1994, p. 29).

By the start of 1994 Eastern Europe had attracted $18.3 billion (actually paid up), of which Hungary accounted for a third; more than $10 billion (over 55 per cent) of the total went to Hungary, the Czech Republic and Poland (Frances Williams, *FT*, 10 May 1994, p. 6).

In 1993 only $5 billion flowed into the former Soviet bloc countries (excluding East Germany), representing just 3 per cent of all foreign direct investment. Within Central and Eastern Europe Hungary accounted for 35.9 per cent, the former Czechoslovakia for 26.4 per cent, Poland for 15.7 per cent, Romania 1.4 per cent and Bulgaria 1.2 per cent (Mark Milner, *The Guardian*, 3 September 1994, p. 35).

In the seventeen years following the 1972 legislation a total of $600 million in direct foreign investment flowed into Hungary. Today foreign investors have a 7–8 per cent share of the economy, while 2,000 of the 14,000 foreign-invested companies are fully foreign-owned (*Business Europa*, January–February 1993, p. 2).

Foreign-owned companies have contributed the equivalent of 6 per cent of GDP (*Business Central Europe*, October 1993, p. 11).

Foreigners are estimated to hold 7 per cent of the total capital of Hungarian companies; their share of joint ventures amounts to 66 per cent (Deutsche Bank, *Focus: Eastern Europe*, 10 February 1994, no. 99, p. 2).

Some 20 per cent of industrial output is now produced by companies with Western capital (*Business Central Europe*, December 1994–January 1995, p. 10).

Frydman *et al.* (1993: 123) draw attention to what they call a remarkable feature of foreign investment in Hungary, namely the relatively high incidence of minority stakes held by foreigners.

Nicholas Denton (*FT*, 6 October 1993, p. 8) reported that the old law on foreign investment was to be replaced by the end of 1993. The latest draft proposed tax relief for reinvested profits and for companies in high-technology sectors, but on a largely discretionary basis.

Foreign companies enjoy the same rights and follow the same procedures as their local counterparts, except in the purchase of agricultural land and certain residential property (*IHT*, Survey, 7 October 1993, p. 9).

A new land law was passed by parliament on 6 April 1994. Although existing holdings were not affected, new purchases of land by foreign individuals and companies would be banned. Non-Hungarian investors would be allowed to lease no more than 500 ha and then only for ten years as a rule. The measures would apply only in the interim period leading up to EU accession and until land prices reached 'realistic' levels (Nicholas Denton, *FT*, 7 April 1994, p. 28).

Since the beginning of 1994 Hungary has ceased to offer incentives to new foreign investors (Frances Williams, *FT*, 28 September 1994, p. 6). Hungary has abandoned its general incentive scheme (*Business Central Europe*, April 1994, p. 37). Hungary has abolished tax holidays for enterprises with foreign participation, but the Horn government has promised to reinstate broader incentives (EBRD 1994: 125).

On 12 January 1995 the sale of Hungar Hotels was postponed (an agreement was cancelled when a US company refused to pay the higher price demanded by the new Hungarian government for a 51 per cent stake). On the same day the privatization commissioner, Ferenc Bartha, was dismissed.

Agriculture

In 1992 34 per cent of the population was rural and agriculture accounted for 15 per cent of employment in the period 1990–92 (industry 31 per cent and services 54 per cent) (*The Economist*, Survey, 8 April 1995, p. 4).

The basic aim of legislation reforming the collective farms was to force them to transform themselves into new business organizations (such as private or public companies) or, if they so wished, into new, free co-operatives. Although the deadline has technically gone by (the end of 1992) many issues remain unresolved. Few members of the former collectives who had re-established as new co-operatives opted to take their land and other assets out in order to farm independently. The privatization of state farms has also been slow (Matthew Harley, *OECD Observer*, 10 February 1994, p. 33).

Only 119 co-operatives have been liquidated so far and only 10 per cent of the membership has opted for individual farming (United Nations Economic Commission for Europe 1993: 204).

Restitution has produced 2 million owners of small plots, most of whom lease their land to private farmers. The average size of private farms is only 6 ha (*Business Central Europe*, September 1993, p. 25).

Pryor (1993: 279) notes that Hungary has not written off farm debts.

In February 1993 an Agricultural Marketing Regime was established. This allows EU-like guaranteed prices, production quotas and trade restrictions (*The Economist*, 7 August 1993, p. 64). Despite this an OECD report found that the level of agricultural subsidy in Hungary was lower than in any of the twenty-four OECD countries except New Zealand. The report also coincided with an announcement that Hungary was to require licences for imports of dairy, sugar and pasta products in 1994, thus reversing a long process of liberalization that had freed all but 10 per cent of imports. In 1994 12 per cent of imports would require official permission (Nicholas Denton, *FT*, 15 December 1993, p. 28).

All the collective farms have been privatized, but many cannot be broken up because of legal conflicts about land ownership (*The Economist*, 7 August 1993, p. 63).

According to *Business Central Europe* (December 1993 to January 1994, pp. 14–15), co-operatives have been broken up, but new owners often lack the knowledge (or willingness) to work the land.

Economic performance

Hungary is no longer the 'golden boy' of the transition (see Tables 23.2 and 23.3). GDP growth did not resume until 1994 and unemployment was still

Table 23.2 Hungary: selected economic indicators

Economic indicator	*1990*	*1991*	*1992*	*1993*	*1994*
Rate of growth of GDP (%)	−3.5	−11.9	−3.0	−0.9	2.0
Rate of growth of industrial output (%)	−9.6	−18.2	−9.8	4.0	9.5
Rate of growth of agricultural output (%)	−4.7	−6.2	−20.0	−6.9	2.4
Inflation rate (%)	28.9	35.0	23.0	22.5	18.8
Net foreign debt ($ billion)	20.2	18.7	17.1	17.9	21.8
Budget surplus or deficit (% GDP)	0.5	−2.2	−5.6	−6.4	−8.2
Current account ($ billion)	0.127	0.267	0.324	−3.455	−3.911

Sources: Various issues of United Nations Economic Commission for Europe, *Economic Survey of Europe*; OECD, *Economic Outlook*; IMF, *World Economic Outlook*; Deutsche Bank, *Focus: Eastern Europe*; *Economics of Transition* and *Business Central Europe*; EBRD (1994: 159; 1995: 36); Lorinc (1992: 1002)

Table 23.3 Hungary: unemployment

Date		*No. unemployed*	*Unemployment rate (%)*
1989	December		0.3
1990	January	23,426	0.4
	June	41,800	0.8
	December	81,400	1.7
1991	January	103,000	2.0
	February	128,386	2.5
	March	144,800	3.0
	April	164,000	3.5
	May	165,022	3.6
	June	185,600	3.9
	July	218,000	4.6
	August	251,000	5.2
	September	294,100	6.1
	October	317,700	6.5
	November	351,300	7.3
	December	406,100	7.5
1992	January[1]	442,532	8.2
	February		
	March		8.9
	April		9.3
	May	522,000	10.0
	June		10.1
	July		10.9
	August		11.1
	September		11.4
	October		11.6
	November		
	December	663,027	12.3
1993	January		13.3
	February	705,000	13.6
	March	697,585	13.4
	April	685,078	13.2

Table 23.3 Continued

Date		*No. unemployed*	*Unemployment rate (%)*
	May	677,997	13.0
	June	657,331	12.6
	July	677,097	13.0
	August	675,016	13.0
	September	669,761	12.9
	October	655,044	12.6
	November		
	December	632,100	12.6
1994	January		
	February		12.6
	March		12.2
	April		
	May		11.4
	June	549,882	11.0
	July		11.1
	August		11.0
	September		
	October		
	November		10.4
	December		10.4

1 A new basis of calculation was introduced in January 1992.
Sources: Various issues of United Nations Economic Commission for Europe, *Economic Survey of Europe*; OECD, *Economic Outlook*; IMF, *World Economic Outlook*; Deutsche Bank, *Focus: Eastern Europe*; Commission of the European Community, *Employment Observatory*; *Economics of Transition* and *Business Central Europe*; EBRD (1994: 159)

over 10 per cent at the end of 1994. Inflation has never been out of control, but the inflation rate was still not in single figures in 1994. The deterioration of the current account of the balance of payments in 1993 and 1994 caused considerable concern. Debt servicing amounts to 40 per cent of export earnings (*Business Central Europe*, April 1995, p. 13).

24

POLAND

POLITICS

Political developments prior to the September 1993 general election

10 March 1993. The trial starts of the former interior minister General Czeslaw Kiszczak and a number of policemen. They are charged with the shooting of nine coal miners in 1981.

At the end of March 1993 President Walesa approved of the new 'non-party forum for reform' (based on Solidarity organizations in the large enterprises). It believes, for example, that Polish citizens should be given low-interest, twenty-year loans (investment vouchers) to buy state property. The president is thought to see the new movement as a political platform for himself. (Solidarity now has around 2 million members, compared with 8 million in 1981, according to *EEN*, 16 February 1993, vol. 7, no. 4, p. 5. The *EIU Country Profile*, 1992–93, p. 6, estimated a membership of 2.4 million in 1989.) The OPZZ trade union has 4.5 million members, compared with only 2 million or so for Solidarity (*The Economist*, Survey, 16 April 1994, p. 10).

15 April 1993. A new electoral law is proposed (passed by the Sejm on 28 May and approved by the president on 30 May). Parties have to obtain at least 5 per cent of the votes before being allotted parliamentary seats; the threshold for alliances is to be 8 per cent.

29 April 1993. The small Peasant Alliance leaves the coalition government over agricultural policy.

28 May 1993. The Suchocka government fails by one vote in the Sejm to survive a vote of no confidence. The origins of the vote lie in an industrial dispute over a pay claim by Solidarity on behalf of teachers, nurses and other public-sector workers.

30 May 1993. President Walesa dissolves parliament and calls a general election for 19 September (the election must follow within four months of the dissolution). Walesa did not accept the resignation of Suchocka, who stays on as caretaker prime minister. The president declares his support for economic reform and vetoes the pension increase approved earlier by parliament (it would have added 21,000 billion zlotys to the 81,000 billion zlotys agreed with the IMF).

25 August 1993. On an official visit to Poland Yeltsin pledges to withdraw the last Russian troops by 1 October instead of 31 December 1993 (they actually left on 18 September), says that he does not oppose Poland's aspiration to join Nato, lays a wreath at the Katyn monument (in memory of the massacre of Polish officers by Soviet security forces in 1940) and signs a trade and energy pact (including a gas pipeline). A joint declaration says that 'in the long term, such a decision [to join Nato] taken by a sovereign Poland in the interests of overall European integration does not go against the interests of other states, including the interests of Russia'. However, in a letter dated 30 September 1993 to the USA, Germany, France and the UK, Yeltsin warned against expanding Nato into Eastern Europe (he argued that the 1990 German reunification treaty ruled this out). Instead Russia and Nato should jointly secure Eastern Europe's security until such time as Russia became a member of Nato. On 21 October 1993 Nato decided to adopt a US proposal to offer non-aligned and former communist countries a Partnership for Peace, i.e. bilateral, individually tailored arrangements. There would be no security guarantees, but co-operation could include things like joint exercises, joint training for peacekeeping missions and crisis consultation.

17 September 1993. The remains of General Wladislaw Sikorski are reburied in Krakow, having lain in Newark (England). (He is a Polish hero, having been prime minister in the early 1920s and Polish leader in exile during the Second World War until he died in a mysterious air crash on 4 July 1943.)

The general election of 19 September 1993

The turnout, although higher than in the October 1991 election, was still only 51.5 per cent. The new rule was in operation whereby a party had to cross a threshold 5 per cent of the vote in order to be allotted parliamentary seats and an alliance had to obtain at least 8 per cent of the vote. As a result the number of parties represented in the Sejm went down from twenty-nine to six, excluding the German minority, which had four guaranteed seats (see Table 24.1; the opinion polls predicted the result fairly accurately). Even so, a coalition government was still needed. (The 100 seats in the Senate were distributed as follows: ADL, thirty-seven; PPP, thirty-six; Solidarity, nine; DU, four; LU, two; BBWR, two; no other party had more than one of the remaining ten seats.)

The election campaigns produced a broad consensus in favour of continuing the economic reforms and rash promises were generally absent. But the election saw a decisive shift towards those left-of-centre parties with

Table 24.1 Poland: the general election of 19 September 1993

Party	*Vote (%)*	*Seats in Sejm*	*Seats (%)*
Alliance of the Democratic Left	20.41	171	37.17
Polish Peasant Party	15.40	132	28.69
Democratic Union	10.59	74	16.08
Labour Union	7.28	41	8.91
Confederation for an Independent Poland (KPN)	5.77	22	4.78
Non-party Bloc in Support of Reform (BBWR)	5.41	16	3.48
		4[1]	0.9
Total		460	

1 Special allotment of seats to German minority under special arrangements (0.71 per cent of the vote).

roots in the old system promising a somewhat slower pace of market reform, better protection for those members of society most disadvantaged by events since 1989 and greater political stability. The victims of the economic transition included the unemployed, state-sector workers and farmers. The importance of pensioners needs emphasizing. There are 9 million pensioners (including 2.5 million receiving disability pensions) out of a voting population of 27 million. 'Fear of alienating pensioners' votes has blocked all attempts at needed reforms of the welfare payments system' (such as indexing pensions to the consumer price index rather than to wages). As a result 'transfers to households' rose from 17.4 per cent of total government expenditure in 1991 to 21.3 per cent in 1994. The World Bank says that total spending on benefits to pensioners increased from 9.4 per cent of GDP in 1988 to 21 per cent in 1994 (Christopher Bobinski, *FT*, Survey, 28 March 1995, p. viii). The portion of the budget spent on pensions rose from 15 per cent in 1991 to 23 per cent in 1994 (*Business Central Europe*, April 1995, p. 14). Roughly 32 per cent of the entire Polish adult population is covered by pensions, with an astounding 9 per cent of the adult population on disability pensions. In the USA pensioners account for about 21 per cent of the adult population. From 1989 to 1993 the number of Polish pensioners increased by 28 per cent (Jeffrey Sachs, *Transition*, 1995, vol. 6, no. 3, p. 3).

Wlodzimierz Cimoszewicz, chairman of the victorious Alliance of the Democratic Left, argued that 'People are very critical of social and economic policy and they want a change. Thirty-nine per cent of families are living below the poverty line, according to official statistics. They do not accept the idea of very fast, ideologically motivated privatization [a "get-rich-quick" scheme]. They do not oppose reforms, but they are very critical of their practical effects' (quoted in *The Times*, 21 September 1993, p. 12, and *The Daily Telegraph*, 21 September 1993, p. 12). Alexander Kwasniewski, the leader of the ADL, said that 'We are not communists; we are not post-communists; we are social democrats. It is wrong to refer continually to historic emotions. The old system collapsed. We understand the change, the change in the world. We are a new party. People voted for reform, but reform with some human sense' (quoted in *The Daily Telegraph*, 21 September 1993, p. 12). The Alliance's support came from a wide range of groups within Polish society (*Business Central Europe*, October 1993, p. 13), e.g. it got 17 per cent of the business vote, more than any other single party (*Business Central Europe*, November 1993, p. 9). (It is said that a third of Poles have done better since the fall of communism, a third hope to do better and a third have done worse; class distinctions have sharpened: *IHT*, 22 September 1993, p. 8.)

The right wing suffered both from the swing to the left and from its own internal divisions. Church-backed parties suffered from the backlash against policies such as the strict abortion law of March 1993 and (to a lesser extent) the reintroduction of religious teaching into the school curriculum. Solidarity had already atomized.

The Western countries and international organizations like the IMF saw some dangers in the election result. For example, the reform process as a whole could be slowed to an unwelcome extent and increased spending on unemployment benefit, housing, education and health (coupled with higher wages in the state sector) could fuel inflation. In addition the right wing could resort to extra-parliamentary (possibly even violent) activity. But it is worth pointing out that the West itself is partly responsible for the result, not least the EU's shortsighted protectionist attitude towards imports such as steel and agricultural products from Poland.

The parties and their platforms

Alliance of the Democratic Left (ADL). Leader, Alexander Kwasniewski (aged thirty-nine and minister for youth and sport in the last communist government). The alliance includes Social Democracy of the Polish Republic, the Polish Socialist Party (led by Piotr Ikonowicz) and the OPZZ trade union. The alliance is not without internal tensions, primarily between the veterans and the newer breed of politician, but it was well organized and motivated. The election platform offered a general continuance of the economic reform programme, but with greater protection for the groups in society most disadvantaged by the transition to the market (such as the unemployed, pensioners and state-sector workers). (In a post-election interview Kwasniewski talked of four-year implementation of the electoral platform promise of 100 per cent indexation for pensions: *Business Central Europe*, November 1993, p. 14.) There would be increased spending on welfare benefits, health and education, but there need be no large increase in the programmed budget deficit (e.g. a more effective tax system would raise revenue). (After the election Kwasniewski talked of 'introducing better collection and getting more from VAT . . . increasing personal taxes to 50 per cent . . . in the long run we want to decrease taxes, especially for economic activity – the 40 per cent corporate tax is much too much'; the budget deficit should be 5.5 per cent of GDP at most: *Business Central Europe*, November 1993, p. 14.) There should be a greater stress on employee buy-outs in the privatization programme. Foreign investment would be welcome (described on another occasion as 'essential') provided it promoted jobs and did not pollute the environment. The alliance disapproved of the idea of a strong presidency and of the growing power of the Catholic Church. Future membership of Nato (especially if Russia and Ukraine were allowed to join as well) and the EU would be sought.

Polish Peasant Party (PPP). Leader, Waldemar Pawlak. The main plank of the election platform of this well organized party was greatly increased state support for and trade protection of agriculture (farmers have in many respects been adversely affected by the transition to the market). The party was very critical of the existing programme to privatize industry and was prepared to see both the budget deficit and inflation rise.

Democratic Union (DU). Leading figures included Hanna Suchocka (the pre-election prime minister), Tadeusz Mazowiecki and Bronislaw Geremek. The DU has its roots in Solidarity's intellectual and white-collar supporters and naturally wanted to continue the last government's reform programme.

Labour Union (LU). Leader, Ryszard Bugaj. Formed in 1992, the party comprises former Solidarity activists and is critical of the privatization programme.

Confederation for an Independent Poland (KPN). Leader, Leszek Moczulski. A nationalistic, right-wing party.

Non-party Bloc in Support of Reform (BBWR). Leader, Andrzej Olechowski (a former finance minister and currently an economic adviser to the president). The Polish initials BBWR are the same as Marshal Pilsudski's parliamentary bloc. The BBWR was founded in late June 1993 to support Walesa and his idea of a new constitution with a powerful president (Walesa's interest cooled as the high hopes for the bloc faded).

The parties and alliances which did not attain sufficient votes to be awarded seats in the Sejm were as follows (in alphabetical order):

Centre Agreement. Leader, Jaroslaw Kalczynski. A single party, but supported by the *Third Republic Movement* (led by Jan Pary) and several smaller Christian democratic groups. It won 4.42 per cent of the vote for the Sejm.

The Fatherland. An electoral alliance comprising four parties: *Christian National Union* (leader, Wieslaw Chrzanowski), which formed part of the outgoing government; *Conservative Party* (leader, Alexander Hall); *Christian Democratic Party* (leader, Pawel Laczkowski, a deputy prime minister in the outgoing government); *Christian People's Party* (leader, Jozef Slisz).

The alliance is right-wing and backed by the Church (e.g. it would ban abortion). The alliance won 6.4 per cent of the votes for the Sejm.

Liberal Democratic Congress. Leaders, Jan Krzysztof Bielecki (a former prime minister) and Donald Tusk. (The privatization minister in the outgoing government, Janusz Lewandowski, is a member of the party.) Strongly favours continuing the economic reform programme. It won 3.99 per cent of the vote for the Sejm.

Movement for the Republic. Leader, Jan Olszewski (a former prime minister). A single party, but includes a number of small, right-wing groups.

Olczyzna-Lista Polska. An alliance of extreme right-wing parties (including several dissenters from the *Christian National Union*).

Party X. Led by the populist Stanislaw Tyminski.

People's Agreement. Leader, Gabriel Janowski (a former minister of agriculture). A rurally based party born of Solidarity.

Samobrona. A rural 'self-defence' party, xenophobic and antisemitic.

Solidarity. Leader Marian Krzaklewski. It won 4.9 per cent of the votes for the Sejm.

The new government

The ADL would have preferred a coalition with the DU and LU, but the DU declined an invitation to talks and the LU soon withdrew from them. The PPP, in turn, was not keen on a coalition with the ADL but eventually agreed to form a government under Prime Minister Waldemar Pawlak. (Kwasniewski did not even take a cabinet post; he was to be consulted about key government appointments and was to head the parliamentary constitutional committee drafting the new constitution.) Pawlak was sworn in on 26 October 1993. The other cabinet posts were: interior, Andrzej Mielczanowski (the sole survivor from the previous government); foreign affairs, Andrzej Olechowski; defence, Piotr Kolodziejczyk (note that these three posts are presidential appointments); finance, Marek Borowski (also deputy prime minister); privatization, Wieslaw Kaczmarek; labour, Leszek Miller; agriculture, Andrzej Smietanko; trade and industry, Marek Pol; foreign trade, Leszek Podkanski; transport, Boguslaw Liberadzki; communications, Andrzej Zielinski; construction, Barbara Blida; justice (and deputy prime minister), Wlodzimierz Cimoszewicz; education (and deputy prime minister), Alexander Luczak.

An early casualty was Marek Borowski, who resigned as finance minister on 8 February 1994. The immediate issue was Premier Pawlak's earlier dismissal of Deputy Finance Minister Stefan Kawalec (blamed for undervaluing shares in a bank privatization). Borowski claimed that the authority for any such action lay with him, while he also demanded greater control over financial policy. On 25 March 1994 President Walesa rejected Dariusz

Rosati as finance minister and deputy prime minister and it was not until 28 April that Grzegorz Kolodko was appointed.

Despite all this, on 5 March 1994 the Sejm approved a surprisingly low budget deficit of 4.1 per cent of GDP for 1994. Walesa approved it on 12 April.

Political developments after the September 1993 general election

6 October 1993. The coal miners' strike ends (generous redundancy payments are awarded).

7 March 1994. The Solidarity trade union begins a series of strikes in protest at the austerity measures.

8 April 1994. Poland formally applies to join the EU (second only to Hungary).

21 April 1994. Strikes begin in four open-cast lignite mines in protest at government restructuring plans.

24 April 1994. The Democratic Union and the Liberal Democratic Congress merge to form the Freedom Union.

27 April 1994. Some (hard coal) miners go on strike.

28 April 1994. Solidarity calls a national strike in protest at government wage controls in state enterprises (it proposes a tripartite commission of government, trade unions and employees to deal with wage policy). (More than 10 per cent of industries took part in the eight-hour strike: *IHT*, 29 April 1994, p. 2.)

1 July 1994. The Senate approves the bill already passed by the Sejm to liberalize the abortion law (allowing abortion within the first three months of pregnancy 'in difficult personal and economic circumstances'). (The strict law of March 1993 allowed abortion only in cases where the mother's life or health was in danger, pregnancy was the result of rape or incest or the foetus was irreparably damaged. Doctors performing illegal abortions faced up to two years in prison.)

(Note that the Sejm has also voted to postpone the ratification of the concordat with the Vatican until there is a new constitution. The concordat includes the right of the Church to teach religion in school.)

4 July 1994. Walesa says that he will veto the abortion bill (a two-thirds majority in parliament is needed to overturn a presidential veto).

7 July 1994. President Clinton, during a visit to Poland, promises eventual Nato membership. But no date is given. A modest amount of extra aid is also promised.

2 September 1994. The Sejm fails to overturn the president's veto of the abortion bill by the necessary two-thirds majority (there were 232 votes for, 157 against and twenty-two abstained, i.e. forty-two votes short).

16 September 1994. The Sejm passes a controversial official secrets bill. This introduces prison sentences of up to ten years for journalists who reveal confidential information held by the government to be vital to the strategic, diplomatic and economic interests of the state.

12 October 1994. The Sejm votes through a motion of censure on President Walesa, accusing him of trying to destabilize the constitutional order by putting the armed forces under his direct control via the general staff (on 10 October he demanded the resignation of the defence minister).

27 October 1994. Foreign Minister Andrzej Olechowski tenders his resignation as of December 1994 after being accused of being paid (illegally for ministers) a second salary (in this case from a bank). (He had suspended his resignation on 31 October 1994 while the courts clarified the legal situation. The constitutional tribunal concluded that Olechowski had not broken the law by serving on the bank's board, but that he should not draw the bank salary if he remained in government service. Nevertheless he resigned on 13 January 1995 after accusing the government of being more interested in furthering relations with Russia than in pressing for Poland's rapid entry into Nato and the EU: the government wanted 'our region, from the Baltic to the Adriatic, to be a neutral sphere linked by economic and political institutions and preferably demilitarized': quoted by Ian Traynor, *The Guardian,* 26 January 1995, p. 11.)

10 November 1994. At the request of the prime minister, President Walesa dismisses the foreign minister (Piotr Kolodziejczyk) and replaces him with Jerzy Milewski. The reason given by the prime minister was failure 'to normalize the situation in the defence ministry'. (Kolodziejczyk complained that the military were slipping out of civilian control: *The Guardian*, 26 January 1995, p. 11.)

27 January 1995. The fiftieth anniversary of the liberation of Auschwitz by Soviet forces is marred by a dispute over the ceremony between Poland and Jewish groups, the latter claiming that the extent of Jewish suffering has been understated by the former.

30 January 1995. Poland and Russia agree to write off debts owed to each other.

2 February 1995. Walesa takes the first formal step towards dissolving parliament by asking the chairmen of the two chambers for their views on dissolution and taking the contested 1995 budget (which the president has refused to sign) to the Constitutional Court. Walesa also accuses parliament of failing to replace corrupt ministers.

4 February 1995. The Sejm resolves that the president has no legal right to dissolve parliament and any further steps will lead to his impeachment.

6 February 1995. Walesa calls for Pawlak's resignation, citing incompetence and lack of progress with economic reforms.

7 February 1995. Pawlak resigns as prime minister. The speaker of the Sejm and member of the ADL, Jozef Oleksy, is nominated to replace him (he was given the Sejm's approval on 1 March).

18 February 1995. Poland and Russia sign a $2.5 billion deal to construct a natural gas pipeline to Western Europe.

4 March 1995. The Sejm approves the new cabinet. Walesa's nominees are given defence (Zbigniew Okonski), foreign affairs (Wladyslaw Bartoszewski) and the interior (Andrzej Milczanowski). Other members of the government include Grzegorz Kolodko (finance), Wieslaw Kaczmarek (privatization) and Leszek Miller (labour).

7 March 1995. The new prime minister promises tough action against organized crime.

2 April 1995. Freedom Union elects Leszak Balcerowicz as leader and nominates Jacek Kuron as presidential candidate.

28 April 1995. Foreign Minister Bartoszewski addresses the German parliament (President Walesa was not invited to the 8 May commemoration in Germany of the end of the Second World War).

19 November 1995. Kwasniewski wins the presidency with 51.7 per cent of the vote. Walesa receives 48.3 per cent. The turnout was 68 per cent.

THE ECONOMY

'In 1989 we had but one asset. That was the enthusiasm born of the newly-won freedom. And we invested that asset in economic reform. We succeeded in securing such an emotional upswing that the fall of 30 per cent in living standards in the first two years of reform caused neither strikes nor uprisings' (Bronislaw Geremek of Democratic Union, *Moscow News*, 15–21 April 1994, p. 4).

Financial policy and institutions

Subsidies to state enterprises decreased from 4.5 per cent of GDP in 1989 to 1.1 per cent in 1993 (Blanchard 1994: 1169). Inter-enterprise debt rose rapidly in 1990 and 1991, but by the end of the latter year the debt was decreasing and it is no longer a financing option for loss-making enterprises. Tax arrears have also declined since the end of 1991 (p. 1170).

Table 24.2 provides information on the budget surplus or deficit as a proportion of GDP (see p. 502).

12 February 1993. The Sejm approves the 1993 budget, including a budget deficit of 5.1 per cent of GDP.

5 July 1993. VAT is introduced (standard rate 22 per cent).

5 March 1994. The Sejm approves a budget deficit of 4.1 per cent of GDP for 1994.

End of June 1994. Finance Minister Kolodko's 'Strategy for Poland 1994–97' is approved by the Sejm. The reform process is to continue, but with a fairer sharing of the burden. Targets include an average growth rate of 5 per cent and end-of-1997 figures of less than 10 per cent for inflation, 14 per cent for unemployment and 2–3 per cent of GDP for the budget deficit.

30 December 1994. The Sejm approves a budget deficit of 3.3 per cent of GDP for 1995 (Walesa did not approve until March 1995, owing to the political situation described above).

1 January 1995. In a revalorization of the currency four zeros are removed, e.g. 10,000 old zlotys = 1 new zloty. The two currencies will circulate side by side for two years. The grosz is reintroduced (100 groszy = 1 zloty).

Prices

Since 1992 all prices have been market-determined except those of electricity, gas, central heating, hot water, basic medicines, rents in housing belonging to local authorities, television fees and spirits (EBRD 1994: 33). Prices in the energy sector were raised further in the January 1995 budget and were to reach recovery levels in 1996 (EBRD 1995: 61).

Banks

Private banks were allowed in 1989 and by the end of 1991 they appear to have accounted for about 13 per cent of all deposits. Some 10 per cent of the private banks are foreign-owned. Commercial banks in general are allowed to take equity stakes in enterprises, but central bank approval is needed if an individual stake exceeds 25 per cent. Likewise, lending to any one enterprise needs approval if the figure is greater than 15 per cent of the bank's capital. Commercial banks were converted into joint stock companies in October 1991 as a prelude to privatization (Eastwood and Durski 1993: 3–7).

The National Bank has said that it will stop issuing licences to foreign banks. But foreigners will still be able to buy a majority stake in existing banks (*Business Central Europe*, September 1993, p. 51).

A law to deal with bad debt came into effect in March 1993 as an incentive to restructure insolvent enterprises. A bank holding 30 per cent of the debt can apply for a debt–equity swap (*Business Central Europe*, June 1993, p. 9).

Enterprise adjustment

There have been a number of studies:

1. *The World Bank study.* Pinto *et al.* (1993) survey seventy-five state enterprises drawn widely from five manufacturing sectors, specifically metallurgy, electro-machinery, chemicals, light manufacturing (such as textiles and leather) and food processing. (See also Hume and Pinto 1993: 18–20.) The analysis covers the period June 1989 to June 1992. They conclude that

state enterprises have generally been much more responsive and adaptable than expected in terms, for example, of increasing profitable sales, improving distribution, shedding labour and reducing other costs (the differing performance of enterprises within each sector is taken as an additional favourable sign of adaptation to market forces). Managers stressed the need for restructuring before privatization (which is still the known ultimate aim, it should be stressed); 'Poland's experience shows that shock therapy can have valuable effects by giving an unambiguous signal, changing relative prices, and indicating the government's commitment to hard budgets. But Poland's experience also shows that rapid changes in ownership may be unnecessary, and that restructuring before privatization may be desirable' (p. 255).

Three main reasons are given for these encouraging signs of adaptation: (1) a hardening of budget constraints (after mid-1991 managers were finally convinced that no bail-outs would occur, there was tighter control over commercial bank lending in late 1991 and stronger enterprises became increasingly reluctant to help weaker ones through inter-enterprise credit); (2) competition from imports and the resulting improvement in relative price determination; (3) managers' expectation that improved performance will be rewarded when privatization takes place and that their reputation (and hence compensation and ability to borrow to purchase shares in their enterprises) will depend upon their perfomance today.

2. In contrast, Estrin and Richet (1993) paint a more gloomy picture. They look at adjustment in the period 1989–92 in a detailed analysis of three state enterprises, each from a different sector (iron and steel, electronics and white goods). Enterprises were studied to see whether they were adjusting variously according to differences in their market power, financial status, exposure to world and domestic competition and the collapse of Comecon, and comparative advantage. No evidence was found of this. In all three cases adjustment was relatively modest and the governance of enterprises had hardly changed (pp. 1–2). Managers had to concentrate above all on declining demand, both at home and in (former) Comecon markets: 'while managers may have been in principle more autonomous, the rapidly declining financial situation in all three companies has severely restricted their ability to manoeuvre' (p. 12). 'The cases provide little evidence of a profit orientation. The primary concern seems to have been to keep the firm going and to maintain employment, with little apparent thought for either optimal responses or personal enrichment' (p. 14). The responses in more detail were as follows: (1) regarding financial autonomy, 'responses have been surprisingly modest, with only the simplest changes introduced as yet; for example, in accounting procedures'; (2) regarding product market liberalization, 'it is in this area that enterprise adjustments have been greatest. All three firms have developed marketing departments, and sought new markets at home (often attempting to develop their own distribution net-

work) and in the West' (pp. 14–15); (3) regarding factor markets, 'labour market adjustments could include a shift from benefit to cash compensation, new wage payments, widening wage differentials and tighter labour discipline . . . [but] . . . there is no mention in the three cases of such adjustment' (p. 15); (4) 'there is almost no evidence of clarification of ownership rights or of an emerging system of corporate governance' (p. 15). 'In summary, responses have been much more rapid in product than factor markets, or with regard to ownership. All firms have focused on new marketing devices, product differentiation, export promotion and to a lesser extent improved financial planning. Few have made significant progress in altering personnel priorities or in diversifying their dealings with the capital market' (p. 16). Enterprises have been 'overwhelmed by huge changes in their market environment, particularly in their ability to sell their output, and are making as yet only minimal adjustments in their behaviour' (p. 16). The magnitude of the fall in demand 'has left all three firms with excess capacity, large wage bills and rising debt. The demand shock was clearly associated with the Polish "big bang" transition policy, and appears to have weakened the ability of firms to respond, even in those sectors which in principle stand to gain from the changes in relative prices and costs. In addition, the shortage of capital has severely restricted the ability of firms to embark on restructuring, or to invest in order to exploit the new opportunities opened up by the reforms' (p. 17).

3. Blanchard (1994: 1171) sees little evidence of restructuring beyond labour shedding.

The 'enterprise pact'

The 'enterprise pact' was signed on 22 February 1993 by representatives of the government, state employers and trade unions (the only significant trade union not to sign was the militant Solidarity 80). Ratification by the Sejm was needed. The major aims of the pact were to stave off labour unrest, to combat inflation and to accelerate restructuring and privatization. The main aspects of the pact were as follows:

1. Employees in state enterprises not included in the mass privatization programme (and excluding certain 'strategic' enterprises) were to have six months to decide on the form of privatization, otherwise the Privatization Ministry would take the decision for them. Employees would be given 10 per cent of the shares regardless of the form of privatization. The financial conditions would be eased where employees decide to take over their enterprise and lease its assets from the state.

2. Workers' councils were to be abolished, but workers were to have 30 per cent representation on non-executive boards of directors. Both private and state enterprises employing more than 2,500 people were to have at least one worker in top management.

3. The tax burden and wage controls on state enterprises were to be eased. For example, the 'dividend' (an asset tax on the share of an enterprise's equity that is centrally financed) was to be eliminated and replaced by an arrangement whereby one-third of profits could be used for wage payments provided one-third was spent on investment and the remaining third was paid in corporate tax. The *popiwek* was to be replaced by a tripartite national negotiating commission.

The *popiwek* was a tax on wage increases above a statistically determined norm. The excess wage tax was considered a necessary concomitant of macroeconomic policy under conditions of almost universal state ownership in industry. Initially it was applied, for political reasons, to both state and private firms. After a year, however, it was removed from the latter (Sachs 1994: 55–6). The *popiwek* ceased to apply at the end of March 1994. After much delay and resistance President Walesa signed a modified version of the law at the end of June 1994; the law, effective 1 August 1994, puts a cap on wage increases in state enterprises. According to one source, the *popiwek* system was to have been replaced by a mechanism of centralized wage bargaining at the beginning of 1995. But implementation of the new scheme awaits presidential approval (United Nations Economic Commission for Europe 1995: 178).

4. Broad economic strategy would be discussed at a national tripartite commission representing government, employers and trade unions (set up in February 1994).

5. Loss-making state enterprises were to have until 31 March 1994 to agree a programme with their bank creditors on debt relief (rescheduling or partial write-offs) and enterprise restructuring. If the reconciliation process did not succeed liquidation proceedings would be started. Government bonds would be available to banks to replace bad debt. On 19 March 1993 the Law on the Financial Restructuring of Enterprises and Banks was passed by the Sejm (*Business Central Europe*, May 1993, pp. 60–1; *The Economist*, 27 March 1993, pp. 49–50, and Survey, 13 March 1993, p. 17; *Finance and Development*, 1994, vol. 31, no. 2, p. 46). Both banks and enterprises would be able to deal with their debt problem by means of devices such as debt–equity swaps. The government was to strengthen banks with World Bank credit and the unused stabilization fund. The banks would be able to sell shares acquired or even their claims for debt repayment. Each bank would keep special accounts for its problem loans, swapping them for interest-earning government bonds. The hope was that banks would use their influence to help restructure enterprises. Enterprises too large or politically sensitive to close down rapidly would be helped by a special government fund.

(Note that bankruptcy law has been based on the 1934 and 1981 legislation: United Nations Economic Commission for Europe 1993: 175.)

Privatization

Demonopolization was initiated in the period 1989–90 with the break-up of large state enterprises (United Nations Economic Commission for Europe 1994: 205).

Large privatization has been delayed by political wrangling and powerful workers' councils. But Balcerowicz (1994: 29) argues that overall privatization has been quite rapid by comparison with other countries, thanks mostly to the rapid growth of the private sector and the related privatization of the assets of state enterprises. Bankruptcies of large enterprises have been rare, but many of them have undertaken radical divestiture by selling off or leasing out substantial parts of their assets.

The sectoral approach to privatization is merely a preparatory programme in which an overall privatization policy can be developed as regards a number of state enterprises (Frydman *et al.* 1993: 181). This is not really privatization. It is a method of grouping together a number of enterprises (not necessarily all the enterprises in an industry) for the purpose of systematic analysis, which may ultimately result in privatization (pp. 197–8). The reasons include lowering the cost of foreign consultants, dealing with specific problems and offering several enterprises for sale at the same time (Simoneti 1993: 90).

It must be stressed that liquidation does not necessarily involve only failing enterprises (Frydman *et al.* 1993: 181).

On 18 March 1993 the Sejm rejected the privatization programme involving 600 medium-sized and large enterprises. The government then decided to submit a revised programme in which only 200 enterprises would be involved in the first stage. These would be transferred to five investment funds (still managed by Western agents, but the agents' rights and duties would be strictly defined), whose shares would be distributed free to pensioners and public-sector workers as compensation for a failure (subsequently deemed illegal) to index pensions and state employees' pay in 1991. The privatization of the remaining 400 enterprises would take place more slowly via another fifteen investment funds. Each of the roughly twenty funds would have a lead 'shareholding' of 33 per cent in twenty to thirty enterprises, with 27 per cent of the shares being split evenly between the other funds, 30 per cent going to the Treasury and 10 per cent to employees (*Business Central Europe*, October 1993, p. 60). The proportion going to the state has been put at 25 per cent and that to employees free of charge at 15 per cent (EBRD 1994: 64; Lucja Swiatkowski Cannon, *FT*, 9 September 1994, p. 17). After ten years the shareholders would decide what to do with the funds. Another concession was that enterprises on the list would be able to opt out. The Sejm passed the amended programme on 30 April 1993 (it still needed the approval of Senate and president).

The start of 1994 was set for the launch of the twenty National Management Wealth Funds and the issue of shares would begin in the first quarter.

People would then have six months to register and claim their certificates. Enterprises have to set aside up to 20 per cent of shares for their workers (including management), with 10 per cent being given away and up to 10 per cent being available for sale at a 50 per cent discount (Anthony Robinson, *FT*, 17 June 1993, p. vi).

Equity in 444 state enterprises was to be handed over to fifteen investment funds run by local and foreign fund managers for a period of ten years (paid an annual fee and a bonus at the end of the period linked to the value of the fund) (Christopher Bobinski, *FT*, Survey, 28 March 1995, p. vi).

'Capital privatization (transformation)' refers to public offerings, trade sales, management and employee buy-outs or a combination of these methods. As of July 1992 only thirty-two enterprises had been more than 51 per cent privatized by such methods (Frydman *et al.* 1993: 181).

By the end of September 1992 only forty-three of the large enterprises had been privatized through capital privatization (public tender or direct offer to a potential investor) and some 250 cases were being processed. In addition 349 enterprises had been taken over by the employees or management (leasing of property) and around 300 were being processed. Another 100 enterprises had been liquidated and sold and a further 700 were being processed (Mullineux and Belka 1993: 11).

According to Lucja Swiatkowski Cannon (*FT*, 9 September 1994, p. 17), by July 1994 there had been only twenty-four public offerings on the Warsaw stock exchange and about sixty sales to foreign investors. There had been, however, about 1,000 privatizations via the 'liquidation' of medium-sized enterprises through employee ownership and leases.

Shops and wholesalers are now more than 90 per cent private. Some 900 larger companies have been privatized through 'liquidation' (which usually entails the sale or lease of a company's assets to its employees). By early February 1994 100 companies had been sold to investors or privatized through the stock market (*The Economist*, Survey, 16 April 1994, p. 15). By early 1995 200 had been sold to strategic investors or through the stock market (*The Economist*, 20 January 1995, p. 75).

By the end of 1993: (1) 'capital privatization' (the sale of enterprises to outsiders through sales or auctions) accounted for only about 100 out of 8,000 state enterprises (under this arrangement workers get 20 per cent of the shares at a discount but lose control of the enterprise); (2) 'liquidation' accounted for 850 enterprises (this allows workers and managers to buy their enterprise by paying 20 per cent of the estimated value of the enterprise and making lease payments, at attractive terms, for the remainder over a period of five to ten years; they have typically been small to medium-sized enterprises with under 200 employees); (3) even if sales of the assets of insolvent enterprises ('asset sales') are added, amounting to an additional 1,010, the total number came to about 2,000 enterprises, or 25 per cent of state enterprises. The private sector accounted for 84 per cent of employment in trade (Blanchard 1994: 1172; Aghion and Blanchard 1994: 6–7).

Privatization is giving foreign trade companies a new lease of life, several of them beginning to buy industrial enterprises and turn themselves into holding companies (Christopher Bobinski, *FT*, 1 December 1993, p. 52).

According to the Deutsche Bank (*Focus: Eastern Europe*, 31 October 1993, no. 91, p. 8), 2,385 of the 8,440 medium-sized and large state enterprises existing at the start of 1990 are now fully or partly in private hands; the number has gone up to around 3,200 (19 July 1994, no. 111, p. 5). As of 28 November 1994 5,096 of the 8,441 medium-sized and large enterprises were still owned by the state (no. 123, p. 10).

The 1990 large privatization programme envisaged a multi-track approach. At the end of 1993 12 per cent of the 8,772 enterprises owned by central government agencies at the outset of the reforms had been privatized (EBRD 1994: 32). By the end of 1994 32 per cent of the 8,772 larger state enterprises owned by the central government and about 20 per cent of the 4,500 enterprises owned by regional governments had been privatized (EBRD 1995: 61).

Policy after the September 1993 general election

Prime Minister Pawlak displayed considerable reluctance to approve the remaining enterprises in the programme (ninety-eight or 100 or so enterprises, according to various sources) involving the National Wealth Management Funds. In fact he only signed on 19 October 1994 after he had excluded from the list twenty enterprises of interest to the rural sector. His reluctance stemmed from (1) suspicion both of the role of foreign managers and of big business in general, (2) a feeling that the enterprises were being undervalued and (3) an inclination to think that restructuring ought to precede privatization (Christopher Bobinski, *FT*, 20 October 1994, p. 3). The mass privatization list was initially planned to comprise 444 enterprises, but the actual number has fluctuated and is still not definitive (*IHT*, 19 June 1995, p. 13). The prime minister approved board members for the fifteen funds on 7 December 1994.

The draft law on restitution was to be submitted to the Sejm in May 1995. Only property confiscated between 1944 and 1962 in violation of the law at the time would be covered. Compensation would be in the form of 'privatization coupons', with no restitution in kind (*Transition*, 1995, vol. 6, no. 3, p. 18). The law was approved by the Sejm on 30 June 1995 and the presidential veto was overridden on 21 July. On 31 July Walesa sent the bill to the Constitutional Court.

The mass privatization list finally comprised 413 enterprises (with additional enterprises to be added later in 1995). The managements of the fifteen

National Wealth Management Funds (National Investment Funds) were to receive fees, an annual claim to 1 per cent of the assets of their funds and longer-term bonuses. Starting in November 1995 the privatization units purchased (for a nominal fee) by Poles were to be converted into fifteen shares (one for each NWMF) and these were to be tradable on the Warsaw stock exchange (possibly starting in early 1997). The shares of the enterprises were to be allocated in a complex system of lottery rounds beginning on 17 July 1995. This was to be followed by a trading process. Initially the government was to transfer 60 per cent of its holdings in the 413 enterprises to the NWMFs. Each of the NWMFs was to take a 33 per cent 'lead shareholding' in twenty-eight of the 413 enterprises and the NWMFs were also to take 'minority shareholdings' of 27 per cent in other enterprises. At a later stage the government was to allocate, free of charge, 15 per cent of the shares to employees of the participating enterprises. A further 15 per cent were to be allocated to social funds and other recipients. By then 90 per cent of the shares of the 413 enterprises would be in the hands of funds, workers or institutions, leaving a balance of 10 per cent with the Treasury (Anthony Robinson, *FT*, 14 July 1995, p. 2; *IHT*, 18 July 1995, p. 13). The new privatization law was designed to speed privatization by cutting back the power of employees and management to delay sales. Individual sales of state-sector enterprises would henceforth have to be approved by the entire cabinet (rather than by the privatization minister) and the government would have to win parliamentary approval for decisions to sell off key sectors such as telecommunications, ports, railways and the remaining banks (Christopher Bobinski, *FT*, 22 July 1995, p. 2). At the end of September 1995 the government added another 101 enterprises to the list, making 514 enterprises in total. The distribution of vouchers started on 22 November 1995.

The size of the private sector

Blaszczyk and Dabrowski (1993) point out that the way the private sector is defined has changed. For example, the official figures for the private sector given by the communist regime for 1989 and earlier excluded co-operatives, since 'most co-operatives were really controlled by the communist party and state administration' (p. 81).

1. The old official figures for the private sector as a whole for 1989 were as follows (pp. 9, 32–3, 65): 19.2 per cent of NMP (plus roughly another 10 per cent if the modern definition is used), of which the former non-agricultural sector accounted for 9.2 percentage points; 33.3 per cent of (end-of-year) employment (47.2 per cent if the modern definition is used), of which the former non-agricultural sector accounted for 10.1 percentage points; 7.4 per cent of industrial output (16.2 per cent by the modern definition); 21.9 per cent of construction output (25.5 per cent); 5.9

per cent of transport output (11.5 per cent); 4.8 per cent of domestic trade (59.5 per cent).

2. Figures for the private sector using modern definitions are for 1991 and 1992 respectively (end of the year in the case of employment): industrial output, 24.6 per cent and 31.0 per cent; industrial employment 35.8 per cent and 41.4 per cent; construction output, 62.2 per cent and 77.7 per cent; construction employment, 59.5 per cent and 71.8 per cent; transport output, 25.2 per cent and 39.3 per cent; transport employment, 26.0 per cent and 23.1 per cent; domestic trade employment (no figures for output are given), 88.3 per cent and 90.5 per cent; total non-agricultural employment, 40.3 per cent and 44.4 per cent (including agriculture the total employment figure at the end of 1992 amounted to 58.4 per cent).

The private sector as a percentage of GDP was 28.6 per cent in 1989 (the non-agricultural sector 19.0 per cent and agriculture 9.6 per cent), 30.9 per cent in 1990 (25.0 per cent and 5.9 per cent), 42.1 per cent in 1991 (36.9 per cent and 5.2 per cent), 47.2 per cent in 1992 (41.7 per cent and 5.5 per cent) and probably over 50 per cent in 1993. In terms of employment the respective figures were 44.3 per cent, 21.7 per cent and 22.6 per cent in 1989, 45.8 per cent, 22.6 per cent and 23.2 per cent in 1990, 51.1 per cent, 26.7 per cent and 24.4 per cent in 1991, 54.6 per cent, 29.8 per cent and 24.8 per cent in 1992 and 59.9 per cent in September 1993 (United Nations Economic Commission for Europe 1994: 205, 207).

The private sector as a percentage of GDP was 28.6 per cent in 1989, 30.9 per cent in 1990, 30 per cent in 1991, 40 per cent in 1992 and 45 per cent in 1993 (*Economics of Transition*, 1994, vol. 2, no. 1, p. 121).

The Economist (23 January 1993, p. 24) provides the following figures for the percentage share of the private sector in sectoral output in 1989 and 1991 respectively: industrial production, 16 and 24; construction, 33 and 55; commerce, 60 and 83; transport, 12 and 24. In terms of employment, the respective percentage figures were 44 and 51 (including private agriculture) and 22 and 27 (excluding private agriculture). The private sector as a whole accounted for 29 per cent and 42 per cent of GDP respectively. By the end of 1992 a quarter of manufacturing was in private hands, along with 70–80 per cent of construction, 35 per cent of exports, 55 per cent of imports, and almost all publishing, restaurants and shops. Overall, 55–60 per cent of the work force was employed in the private sector and nearly half of GDP originated there. (Private companies produce two-thirds of output if activity hidden from official statisticians is counted: 27 November 1993, p. 113.) The 1.8 million or so private non-agricultural firms now employ 30 per cent of the work force and produce about 40 per cent of GDP (their output rose by more than 40 per cent in 1993; most employ five or fewer people) (*The Economist*, Survey, 16 April 1994, p. 16). Agriculture produces 8 per cent of GDP and accounts for about 30 per cent of employment (p. 5). The private sector accounts for 37 per cent of industrial output (p. 19). The private sector's share of GDP is about 55 per cent (29 October 1994, p. 56).

The United Nations Economic Commission for Europe (1993: 215, 220) cites the official estimates of the percentage of GDP contributed by the private sector: 1990, 30.9 per cent; 1991, 42.1 per cent; 1992, 45–50 per cent (the sector employed more than 60 per cent of the work force).

John Pomfret (*IHT*, 18 June 1993, p. 9) reports the official figures for the share of the private sector as a proportion of GDP as 47 per cent in 1992 (*The Economist* puts the figure at 45 per cent: 28 August 1993, p. 36), compared with 10 per cent in 1989. Pomfret's figures are confirmed by George Blazyca (*Business Europa*, November–December 1993, p. 10).

The half of total employment in the private sector at the end of 1990 was divided 26 per cent for agriculture and 24 per cent for the non-agricultural sector (Eastwood and Durski 1993: 5).

The private sector accounts for 50 per cent of GDP and 55 per cent of jobs (Deutsche Bank, *Focus: Eastern Europe*, 1 July 1993, no. 82, p. 4). The private sector now generates about 60 per cent of GDP. In 1994 it accounted for 38 per cent of industrial sales (23.4 per cent in 1992) and 38.4 per cent of industrial employment (4 July 1995, no. 133, pp. 2–3).

The private sector now accounts for more than 60 per cent of the economy and around 60 per cent of total employment (Anthony Robinson, *FT Survey*, 18 March 1994, p. ii).

In mid-1994 the private sector accounted for roughly 55 per cent of GDP (EBRD 1994: 10). Around 93 per cent of trading activity is now in private hands (p. 13). In 1993 the private sector accounted for 46 per cent of total employment (p. 32).

The number of registered individual proprietorships rose from 813,500 at the end of 1989 to 1,523,400 at the end of June 1992, the increase in the number of small business owners representing almost 5 per cent of the working population. Total employment in these enterprises increased from 1,475,500 to 2,800,400, an increase of almost 9 per cent of the total labour force. As regards larger enterprises, the number of private commercial law partnerships (partnerships, limited liability companies and joint stock companies) rose from 11,693 to 51,174 (Lipton and Sachs 1992: 250–1).

At the end of 1992 there were still 7,342 state enterprises in total, but around 40 per cent of industrial output is now produced by the private sector (Christopher Bobinski, *FT*, 1 May 1993, p. 2).

The private sector's share of industrial output rose from 24 per cent in 1991 to 31 per cent in 1992 (OECD, *Economic Outlook*, June 1993, p. 121) and 33 per cent in the first half of 1993 (OECD, *Economic Outlook*, December 1993, p. 113).

Kolodko (1993a: 59) maintains that while state industrial output declined by 25 per cent in 1990, that of the private sector actually increased by 8.5 per cent; the fall in total industrial output was 23 per cent.

Foreign trade

Most quantitative trade restrictions and export subsidies were eliminated in 1990. But in sectors such as automobiles import barriers can be substantial. There have been several upward revisions of import tariffs after the sharp reductions in 1990 (EBRD 1994: 33). Largely current account convertibility exists, with limits on residents' capital account transactions. There is a pre-announced crawling peg regime (p. 109). The regime was adjusted in September 1994 and in February 1995, the combined effect of which was to slow the monthly rate of currency depreciation from 1.5 per cent to 1.2 per cent (EBRD 1995: 61).

The zloty is pegged to a basket of five currencies (the US dollar, the Deutschmark, the pound sterling, the French franc and the Swiss franc) under a crawling peg mechanism. The central bank pre-announces the exchange rate and commercial banks can buy and sell currency within two percentage points above and below the central rate (*The Economist*, 15 April 1995, p. 99).

As of 16 May 1995 the central bank was able to set daily rates within a band 7 per cent either side of a fixed mid-rate and to intervene in the interbank foreign exchange market (previously the zloty's underlying rate was fixed in agreement between the central bank, the Finance Ministry and the Foreign Trade Ministry). The policy under which the zloty is devalued by 1.2 per cent a month to match domestic inflation was maintained (Christopher Bobinski, *FT*, 12 May 1995, p. 2).

The free-trade agreement with EFTA, signed in December 1992, was not ratified in time to take effect on 1 May 1993 as planned. The association agreement with the EU came into force on 1 February 1994.

In 1992 72.2 per cent of exports went to OECD countries, 57.9 percentage points of which went to the EU (Deutsche Bank, *Focus: Eastern Europe*, 1993, no. 85, p. 6).

The EU took 44 per cent of exports in 1990 and 63 per cent in 1993 (the respective figures for Eastern Europe and the countries of the former Soviet Union were 21.5 per cent and 12.9 per cent). Average tariffs were cut to 5.5 per cent in the early days of reform, but have crept back to over 18 per cent. Products like food, textiles and clothing are the most heavily protected (*The Economist*, Survey, 16 April 1994, pp. 15, 21).

The EU and other developed markets account for more than 70 per cent of foreign trade (Anthony Robinson, *FT*, Survey, 28 March 1995, p. ii). Some 63 per cent of exports go to the EU, from which Poland takes 57 per cent of imports (p. ix). A surplus of $557 million in 1989 in agricultural trade with the EU turned into a deficit of $333 million by 1993 (p. v).

Foreign aid

Contributing governments have recently allowed the $1 billion stabilization fund to be directed to aiding the financial restructuring of enterprises (*The Economist*, 20 February 1993, p. 48).

3 March 1993. During the visit of Prime Minister Suchocka the UK agrees that its $100 million part of the stabilization fund can be used to recapitalize the banking system.

9 March 1993. The IMF approves a one-year $655 million stand-by credit.

April 1993. The World Bank agrees loans totalling $750 million for bank restructuring and agriculture.

11 May 1993. It is announced that limited interest payments to Western commercial banks (10 per cent of that due) will be resumed on 20 May. Poland owes the banks $12.1 billion, which has gone unserviced since autumn 1989 (Anthony Robinson and Christopher Bobinski, *FT*, 29 May 1993, p. 9; *FT Survey*, 17 June 1993, p. iv). Negotiations with creditor banks had got under way in February 1993 after a break of almost two years (Deutsche Bank, *Focus: Eastern Europe*, 17 May 1993, no. 78, p. 5).

11 March 1994. Poland and the London Club of commercial banks sign an agreement in principle to reduce (by 42.5 per cent) and reschedule the $13.2 billion debt over a thirty-year period. (The formal signing took place on 14 September 1994. The value of the reduction will rise to more than 49 per cent: *Transition*, 1994, vol. 5, no. 7, p. 19.)

Foreign investment

Blaszczyk and Dabrowski (1993: 54) point out that the first foreign investments started with the Polonia companies owned by ex-Polish citizens (1976 legislation) and that in 1982 the opportunity was extended to all foreigners in the form of so-called foreign small-scale enterprises. The 1985 law allowed the creation of joint venture companies.

The volume of foreign investment has been relatively disappointing, especially at first.

Poland has phased out almost all tax advantages for foreign investments (Nicholas Denton, *FT*, 6 October 1993, p. 8).[1]

Net direct foreign investment was $88 million in 1990, $117 million in 1991, $284 million in 1992, $580 million in 1993 and $527 million in January–October 1994 (United Nations Economic Commission for Europe 1995: 151).

Around $4 billion in foreign equity investment has been committed (as opposed to actually used) to date (Anthony Robinson, *FT Survey*, 17 June 1993, p. vi).

Direct foreign investment amounted to $3 billion at the end of 1993 and $4.4 billion at the end of 1994 (Deutsche Bank, *Focus: Eastern Europe*, 1995, no. 126, p. 20).

Direct foreign investment was around $600 million in 1993 (*The Economist*, 19 March 1994, p. 101).

Foreign investment amounted to $1.59 billion in 1993, bringing the total up to $3 billion by the end of the year (*Business Central Europe*, April 1994, p. 42).

Direct foreign investment amounted to $839 million in the period 1990–93 (EBRD 1994: 123).

Agriculture

Around 40 per cent of Poles still live in rural areas and 17 per cent continue to depend exclusively on agriculture for their livelihood. Farm incomes have fallen by more than 50 per cent (Anthony Robinson, *FT*, Survey, 28 March 1995, p. v).

In 1992 37 per cent of the population was rural and agriculture accounted for 27 per cent of employment in the period 1990–92 (industry 37 per cent and services 36 per cent) (*The Economist*, Survey, 8 April 1995, p. 4).

On 9 April 1993 the agriculture minister, Gabriel Janowski, resigned because the government refused to introduce minimum grain prices.

Olko-Bagienska (1992: 1178) makes the point that the ownership transformation of state farms has been slower than that of agribusiness and food processing (where farmers tied by contract to specific plants are able to purchase shares at a discount when they are privatized through the capital method: p. 1177). Problems include the duality of ownership, whereby state farms own the movable assets while the Treasury owns the land and improvements. The privatization of state farms was expected to speed up with the establishment of the Agricultural Property Agency (modelled on the German Treuhandanstalt).

Christopher Bobinski (*FT Survey*, 17 June 1993, p. x) and *Business Central Europe* (September 1993, p. 25) report that the agency was actually set up in 1992 to take over and sell the 1,495 state farms (covering 3.1 million ha of arable land). But by the end of March 1993 only 24,000 ha (less than 1 per cent of state arable land) had found new owners and another 204,000 ha had been leased (7 per cent of state arable land). Farm incomes have fallen by half since 1988.

Economic performance

There was positive GDP growth as early as 1992, Poland's being the first transitional economy to achieve this (despite the political wrangling). But unemployment was 16 per cent at the end of 1994 and the inflation rate in 1994 was still around 30 per cent (see Tables 24.2 and 24.3).

Output stabilized in mid-1992, while unemployment steadily increased until mid-1993 (Blanchard 1994: 1169).

Table 24.2 Poland: selected economic indicators

Economic indicator	*1990*	*1991*	*1992*	*1993*	*1994*
Rate of growth of GDP (%)	−11.6	−7.6	2.6	3.8	5.0
Rate of growth of industrial output (%)	−26.1	−11.9	3.9	5.6	13.0
Rate of growth of agricultural output (%)	−2.2	−1.6	−12.8	1.5	−4.0
Inflation rate (%)	585.8	70.3	43.0	35.3	32.2
Net foreign debt ($ billion)	43.7	44.8	43.1	43.3	35.9
Budget surplus or deficit (% GDP)	3.1	−6.5	−6.7	−2.9	−2.5
Current account ($ billion)	0.700	−2.200	−0.269	−2.300	−0.944

Sources: Various issues of United Nations Economic Commission for Europe, *Economic Survey of Europe*; OECD, *Economic Outlook*; IMF, *World Economic Outlook*; Deutsche Bank, *Focus: Eastern Europe*; *Economics of Transition* and *Business Central Europe*; EBRD (1994: 165; 1995: 42); Kolodko (1993b: 126)

Table 24.3 Poland: unemployment

Date		*No. unemployed*	*Unemployment rate (%)*
1989	December		0.1
1990	January		0.3
	February		0.8
	March		1.5
	April		1.9
	May		2.4
	June		3.1
	July		3.8
	August		4.5
	September		5.0
	October		5.5
	November		5.9
	December	1,126,100	6.1
1991	January		6.8
	February		7.0
	March	1,322,100	7.3
	April	1,370,000	7.5
	May	1,435,500	7.9
	June	1,574,100	8.6
	July	1,749,900	9.6
	August		10.1
	September	1,970,900	10.7
	October		11.1
	November		11.4
	December	2,155,600	11.8
1992	January	2,230,100	12.2
	February		12.5
	March		12.2
	April	2,238,400	12.2
	May		12.3
	June		12.6
	July	2,400,000	13.1
	August		13.4

Table 24.3 Continued

Date		*No. unemployed*	*Unemployment rate (%)*
	September		13.6
	October		13.6
	November		13.6
	December	2,509,300	13.6
1993	January		14.0
	February		14.4
	March	2,648,700	14.4
	April		14.4
	May		14.6
	June	2,701,800	14.8
	July	2,800,000	15.4
	August		15.4
	September	2,830,000	15.4
	October	2,809,000	15.3
	November		15.5
	December	2,889,600	15.7
1994	January		16.0
	February		16.1
	March		16.0
	April		15.7
	May	2,800,000	15.5
	June		16.6
	July		16.6
	August		16.9
	September		16.5
	October		
	November		16.1
	December		16.0

Sources: Various issues of United Nations Economic Commission for Europe, *Economic Survey of Europe*; OECD, *Economic Outlook*; IMF, *World Economic Outlook*; Deutsche Bank, *Focus: Eastern Europe*; Commission of the European Community, *Employment Observatory*; *Economics of Transition* and *Business Central Europe*; EBRD (1994: 165); Frydman *et al.* (1993: 154); Ash (1992: 14); Gora (1991: 157)

There has been considerable debate about how to interpret the figures for output, living standards and unemployment. Sachs argues that 'There has been no significant fall in living standards. Real incomes did not plummet. Unemployment, while high, is not soaring to the levels that were feared.' Moreover, 'the lost production reflects the cut-backs in production of enterprises that lack customers, mainly the cut-back of Poland's excessively large heavy industry' (1994: 67). Unemployment is highest in the rural areas and 'Polish analysts have concluded that a significant number of those reporting unemployment are in fact working in the second economy, or on the farms, and are collecting unemployment compensation as a form of income supplement for their other jobs. It is widely estimated, within the Polish government and by independent experts, that around one-third of the unemployed fall within this category. The actual unemployment is probably closer to two-thirds of the measured rate' (pp. 72–3). There was an export boom: 'After two decades of failed export promotion, most Polish analysts ascribed the failure to generate growing exports as a reflection of the low quality of Polish goods rather than of the profound export bias of the old system (due to an overvalued exchange rate, excess domestic demand and explicit trade barriers)' (p. 64). 'Ricardo taught us that trade depends on comparative advantage . . . any country can engage in free trade' (p. 51). The inflation rate had reached 34 per cent in the month of August 1989 (an annual rate of more than 3,000 per cent) and in October 1989 it had reached 54 per cent (an annual rate of more than 17,000 per cent) (p. 40).

The Economist (Survey, 13 March 1993, p. 9) refers to what Balcerowicz calls 'pure socialist production' (goods that no one wanted; output that existed only under central planning, between 10 per cent and 20 per cent of most countries' GDP). The Polish Research Institute calculated that when this is taken into account a fall in output of 18–20 per cent in 1990–92 turns into a decline of 5–10 per cent (and much of that was due to the collapse of Comecon).

If the output of unregistered private-sector operations and of the informal economy is included, the decline in GDP from 1990 to 1993 would probably come to barely 5 per cent rather than 14 per cent (Deutsche Bank, *Focus: Eastern Europe*, 1994, no. 100, p. 7). Official data show that between 1989 and 1991 GDP fell by 18 per cent. But the actual decline is now thought to have been between 5 per cent and 10 per cent (*The Economist*, Survey, 8 April 1995, p. 13). Ellman (1993: 30) makes the point, however, that the distribution of the falls in industrial output in 1990 was perverse, with the biggest falls in the consumer goods sector (such as textiles), hit by the decline in demand, rather than in the capital and intermediate goods sectors (where most of the wasteful production is probably concentrated). In 1990 the most adversely affected sectors were light industry, food processing and transport equipment, while in 1991 they became capital and intermediate goods (e.g. electrical goods and metallurgy) (Zukowski 1993: 1173). The growth of industrial output started in the second quarter of 1992 (United Nations Economic Commission for Europe 1993: 220). Balcerowicz (1993: 40) cites estimates that about 50 per cent of those officially registered as unemployed are in fact active in the secondary economy. The black economy, which includes much of the private sector, may add up to 20 per cent or more to GDP (*The Economist*, Survey, 16 April 1994, p. 6). The World Bank has calculated that 14–15 per cent of the population live in poverty (*Transition*, 1994, vol. 5, no. 6, p. 18; Deutsche Bank, *Focus: Eastern Europe*, 31 July 1994, no. 112, p. 8).

NOTE

1. Poland has opened its first free enterprise zone. The zone enjoys corporate tax relief (Christopher Bobinski, *FT*, 11 October 1995, p. 3).

25

ROMANIA

POLITICS

The political background

There is still disagreement as to how spontaneous the 1989 revolution was. The general view is that the uprising was a popular one, but soon taken over by the National Salvation Front (apparently formed some six months earlier).

Caritas ('Charity') was a pyramid scheme started by Ion Stoica in June 1992 (the claim was that profits were to go to 'good works', hence the name). Cluj became the main centre (Stoica enjoyed the support of the extreme right-wing nationalist leader Gheorghe Funar, the mayor of Cluj). Pyramid schemes promise large returns, but are bound to fail in the long run because out-payments rely on ever-increasing new donations. Regular payments began to be missed in autumn 1993, but it was not until February 1994 that the local authorities closed down a recently opened branch in Snagov. Action was then taken against other schemes. On 19 May Stoica announced that he was to close the scheme down. He was arrested on 24 August 1994 and in mid-June 1995 he was sentenced to six years in jail.

The government survived a series of no-confidence votes in 1993, e.g. one in December. In February 1994 negotiations about a possible coalition government began between the Social Democracy Party of Romania (see below) and the extreme right-wing nationalist parties.

The Hungarian minority

There are 1.7 million ethnic Hungarians and 2 million Gypsies (*FT*, 13 May 1994, p. 2). Another source puts the figure in the range 1.6 million to 2 million Hungarians (*IHT*, 6 July 1994, pp. 1, 4).

20 July 1993. An accord is signed aimed at improving the rights of the ethnic minorities, e.g. more elementary school lessons in history and geography taught in minority languages, multilingual street signs in areas where a minority represents at least 30 per cent of the population and more university places for Hungarian teachers.

4 October 1993. The Council of Europe votes to admit Romania as the thirty-second member (Hungary abstained in the vote). The formal admission ceremony was held on 7 October.

10 August 1994. The government rejects calls for 'special status' from the Hungarian minority (e.g. greater control over education and cultural matters) and for this special status to be included in the treaty currently under discussion between Romania and Hungary (Tony Barber, *The Independent*, 11 August 1994, p. 10).

On 10 December 1994 the Democratic Union of Hungarians in Romania (DUHR) declared that it wanted the right to autonomous self-determination (*Business Europa*, February–March 1995, p. 44). In mid-January 1995 the DUHR resolved to form special 'councils of local government' in anticipation of an ethnic Hungarian autonomous region. Both it and the Romanian Social Democratic Party have now left the Democratic Convention (*EEN*, 2 March 1995, vol. 9, no. 5, p. 6).

The education law passed by parliament at the end of June 1995 established Romanian as the national language and main language of education. The new law met resistance from ethnic Hungarians.

Political developments

8 May 1993. The Romanian Communist Party has been resurrected (*EEN*, 1993, vol. 7, no. 10, p. 8).

30 May 1993. Petre Roman announces that the National Salvation Front is to merge with the former Democratic Party to form the Democratic Party-National Salvation Front (DP-NSF).

28 August 1993. Four ministers leave the cabinet, including Misu Negritoiu (the reform-minded independent deputy prime minister in charge of economic policy, who resigns). Emilian Ijdelea, the president of the Romanian Development Agency responsible for foreign investment and the development of small and medium-sized enterprises, was dismissed (there have been allegations about corruption in government; Ijdelea accused certain government ministers of personally intervening in state contracts: *EEN*, 7 September 1993, vol. 7, no. 18, p. 4). Aurelian Dochia, the head of the privatization agency, resigned later on; he was in favour of bringing the State Ownership Fund under government control to prevent its board, dominated by members of the Social Democracy Party of Romania (leader Adrian Nastase; formed in late summer 1993; formerly the Democratic National Salvation Front), from stressing management or employee buy-outs (Virginia Marsh, *FT*, 9 September 1993, p. 3).

29 December 1993. Parliament agrees (with many members choosing not to vote) that the government should be able to rule by decree during the recess in January 1994.

26 January 1994. Romania becomes the first country to sign a Partnership for Peace agreement with Nato.

30 January 1994. A military agreement is signed with Russia.

21 June 1994. The Democratic Agrarian Party says it will withdraw its support from the ruling Social Democracy Party of Romania.

1 July 1994. The government survives its fifth vote of no confidence.

19 August 1994. Two members of the right-wing Romanian National Unity Party (though from the more moderate wing of it) are made ministers (of agriculture and of communications).

7 October 1994. Former King Michael is denied entry to the country.

14 October 1994. A British couple, who bought a baby and then attempted to smuggle it out of the country, are given jail sentences of twenty-eight months each. The three men convicted of arranging the sale are given thirty-two months and the teenage parents will serve a year in jail when they are eighteen.

2–4 November 1994. President Iliescu visits the UK. He is to pardon the British couple if their appeal fails.

9 November 1994. The Chamber of Deputies approves legislation which specifies that the punishment for flying foreign flags or singing foreign anthems may be up to three years in jail.

16 November 1994. The court of appeal reduces the prison sentence on the British couple to two years, suspends the sentence and orders the couple to leave the country.

23 December 1994. The Vacaroiu government survives another vote of no confidence.

1 February 1995. The EU association agreement comes fully into effect.

THE ECONOMY

Financial policy

On 23 July 1993 Romania failed to reach a new agreement with the IMF (to replace the stand-by agreement that expired in March) owing to the lack of success against inflation. Generous pay rises had been granted and the issue of enterprise closures had not been tackled. Inter-enterprise debt, which had been written off in January 1992, has risen again and now amounts to the equivalent of 20 per cent of GDP (Virginia Marsh and Robert Corzine, *FT*, 27 July 1993, p. 3). Inter-enterprise arrears now exceed the 1993 level of budgetary expenditure (Chrystia Freeland and Virginia Marsh, *FT*, Survey, 3 May 1994, p. 29).

'Excessive' wage increases are taxed (EBRD 1994: 33). In March 1995 the government issued an emergency decree under which enterprises under majority state ownership were only allowed to grant wage increases in line with productivity growth (DIW, *Economic Bulletin*, 1995, vol. 32, no. 7, p. 16).

Parliamentary approval was given to a bankruptcy law and to the privatization of large enterprises in July 1991, but no bankruptcies have yet been reported (United Nations Economic Commission for Europe 1993: 223). A draft bankruptcy law has long been under debate in parliamentary committees (EBRD 1994: 32). A bankruptcy law was passed by parliament on 21 March 1995, but this does not apply to the largest state enterprises.

The Vacaroiu government's financial programme

The programme was outlined in March 1993. The government survived a vote of no confidence on 19 March by 260 to 192, a motion brought by opposition parties dubious of the degree of commitment of the government to economic reform.

The aim was to reduce inflation to around 80 per cent in 1993 and to 15 per cent by 1996 (*EEN*, 30 March 1993, vol. 7, no. 7, pp. 3–4). The budget deficit for 1993 was set at 4 per cent of GDP. The government planned to increase its investment by raising corporate taxation. Profit tax would rise from 30–40 per cent to 40–60 per cent, although exporters would be eligible for discounts of up to 50 per cent (Virginia Marsh, *FT*, 22 February 1993, p. 4).

An austerity package was agreed with the IMF on 9 December 1993. Parliament passed the IMF memorandum of understanding in January 1994 and the IMF formally approved the package on 11 May 1994 (the loan was worth $720 million). The aim was to reduce the inflation rate from the then level of 300 per cent to 75 per cent in 1994 and 35 per cent in 1995; the conditional reward was to be an IMF loan of $696 million, $130 million from the World Bank and $50 million of co-financing (*EEN*, 1994, vol. 8, no. 4, p. 7). Agreement was reached to float the leu, adjust interest rates to market requirements, speed up privatization and restructuring, reduce the budget deficit to 3.5 per cent of GDP, improve the insolvency law and reduce the trade deficit (Deutsche Bank, *Focus: Eastern Europe*, 1994, no. 113, p. 3).

On 5 April 1994 the World Bank approved a $175 million loan for a petroleum project and subsequently disbursed the $180 million second tranche of a structural adjustment loan (Anthony Robinson and Virginia Marsh, *FT*, Survey, 3 May 1994, p. 29).

On 6 April 1994 parliament endorsed the budget deficit target of 3.5 per cent of GDP.

Parliament approved the budget for 1995 on 1 March 1995. In line with IMF guidelines, the target budget deficit was 2.7 per cent and the target inflation rate was 29 per cent.

'The Romanian leu has been stable against the dollar for the past year, thanks to a tough stabilization programme backed by the International Monetary Fund' (Alfred Moses, *IHT*, 17 March 1995, p. 8).

The labour market

The main unions, Fratia, or Brotherhood, Alfa, the National Confederation and the Ceres Agricultural Union, together represent the 'vast majority' of the 10 million-plus work force (*EEN*, 11 May 1993, vol. 7, no. 10, pp. 2–3).

On 14 June 1993 CNSLR and Fratia merged to form a new union representing 3.7 million workers or about a third of the work force (Virginia Marsh, *FT*, 15 June 1993, p. 2).

The National Confederation of Free Trade Unions in Romania (CNSLR) and Fratia merged in June 1993 to form CNSLR-Fratia, claiming 3.7 million members. Together with the second largest trade union, Alfa Cartel, they represent 4.8 million workers or 40 per cent of the work force (*Business Central Europe*, March 1994, p. 14).

Chrystia Freeland (*FT*, Survey, 3 May 1994, p. 30) puts the combined membership figure at 5.5 million or more than half the work force (the two unions are strong advocates of market reform).

According to Julian Borger (*The Guardian*, 28 February 1994, p. 7), Alfa Cartel claims 1.2 million members. The third largest trade union is National Union Bloc.

The 1 May 1993 price rises led to trade union pressure for wage increases. The 6 May accord, signed the day before a threatened general strike, involved wage increases and a mechanism partly indexing wages to the cost of a basket of basic goods and to productivity in individual enterprises (*EEN*, 1993, vol. 7, no. 10, p. 2). The *Financial Times* (19 May 1993, p. 2) reported that the government had agreed to raise the public-sector minimum monthly wage from 17,600 lei to 30,000 lei (the big trade unions comprise more than 6 million workers). Bread prices had already risen by 450 per cent since 1 May. Steel workers began a strike on 17 May and rail workers on 14 June 1993. There were serious strikes in August 1993 by coal miners in the Jiu valley and by train drivers, but a tough approach by the government resulted in these ending with moderate pay awards.

18 November 1993. Workers demonstrate in considerable numbers against the government and its economic policy (trade unions generally want improved pay and social security benfits, but also faster economic reform).

29 November 1993. A further demonstration takes place and a general strike is threatened.

16 December 1993. The third demonstration takes place. It was followed by a one-hour strike by an estimated million workers in late January 1994, a one-day strike on 4 February 1994, a one-day strike by an estimated 2 million workers on 28 February 1994 and another by over 700,000 the following day (1 March).

14–16 June 1994. There are demonstrations by workers in Bucharest.

Mid-December 1994. There are strikes by steel workers in Resita over back-pay and subsidies.

15 December 1994. There is a warning strike by coal miners and oil workers in several regions. Rail workers demonstrate in Bucharest.

21 March 1995. Around 40,000 workers protest in Bucharest over a government decision to freeze public-sector wages at the November 1994 level (*FT*, 22 March 1995, p. 3).

3–5 June 1995. Energy workers go on strike.

The five largest unions are threatening large-scale strikes (starting 4 June) unless the government agrees to higher wages and amends a government decree which penalizes state enterprises offering salaries over a certain level without corresponding increases in productivity (*EEN*, 25 May 1995, vol. 9, no. 11, p. 5).

Banks

In 1991 the government bought from the banks 90 per cent of their non-performing claims and then cancelled the loans. There was another injection of capital in 1992 (EBRD 1994: 33).

The state used its deposits with banks to write off some of the inherited bad loans. Since then banks have been ordered to arrange a one-off, short-term loan to customers to repay overdue debts (to be followed by bankruptcy proceedings if debts fall overdue again, although there is still no bankruptcy law as such) (*Business Central Europe*, June 1993, p. 37).

The government has continuously, in effect, written off enterprise debts by means of credit infusions (Ronnas forthcoming).

On 21 March 1995 the Chamber of Deputies passed a bankruptcy law. It had already been passed by the Senate on 6 December 1994, but it still needed to be promulgated by the president (*Business Europa*, February–March 1995, p. 44; Virginia Marsh, *FT*, 22 March 1995, p. 3).

Prices

In November 1990 about 50 per cent of prices were liberalized (although this probably represented a far lower proportion in terms of transactions). While maintaining controls, other prices were raised substantially (especially those of many basic consumer goods). The second round of price liberalization occurred on 1 April 1991. By mid-1991 about 80 per cent of prices were free. The final stage of price liberalization took place in July 1991, with controls applied only to fourteen categories of products (five basic food items and others such as domestic fuel, local transport and rents) (Demekas and Khan 1991: 17–21).

Half the prices in the consumer goods basket were freed in November 1990. Price liberalization picked up again in 1993 as consumer subsidies were phased out, mark-up limits were eliminated (in June) and the number of consumer goods under direct price control fell to five (EBRD 1994: 33).

Most of the remaining consumer subsidies were removed on 1 May 1993, the third and final stage of the process. As a consequence the price of bread and other staple commodities quadrupled and that of electricity quintupled (*EEN*, 11 May 1993, vol. 7, no. 10, p. 3). On 1 July 1993 VAT at 18 per cent replaced the 1–30 per cent turnover tax (*EEN*, 6 July 1993, vol. 7, no. 14, p. 7). The government has announced large price increases for petrol, natural gas, electricity (42 per cent) and thermic energy beginning 7 April 1994 (*Transition*, 1994, vol. 5, no. 4, p. 13).

Privatization

Note that the March 1990 law governing the private sector was subsequently abrogated and the employment ceilings removed.

Between August and the end of December 1992 fifteen enterprises were privatized (United Nations Economic Commission for Europe 1993: 223).

The 1991 privatization law envisaged selling off 70 per cent of the equity of the state's 6,300 commercial enterprises over a seven-year period. But by the end of May 1993 only ten enterprises (out of the 1,100 designated for the whole year) had been privatized and all these were either management or employee buy-outs (*Business Central Europe*, June 1993, p. 21). (A later figure of seventeen is cited by another source: *Business Europa*, August–September 1993, p. 11.) By mid-June 1993 only fifty small enterprises had been sold, all to their managers or workers (*Business Central Europe*, October 1993, p. 62). Most of the thirty-two enterprises in the pilot programme have been sold off, mostly through management and worker buy-outs. Only 10 per cent of the enterprises targeted for privatization in 1993 have been privatized to date (*Business Central Europe*, December 1993 to January 1994, p. 54). Under a 1991 law the State Ownership Funds were to sell off one-seventh of their 70 per cent stake in 6,000 enterprises each year. But they have actually managed something closer to 3 per cent (*Business Central Europe*, December 1994–January 1995, p. 15). The private sector now accounts for 70 per cent of retail trade and 30 per cent of exports (*Business Central Europe*, April 1995, p. 74). The private sector accounts for 35 per cent of GDP, compared with 32 per cent in 1993. Only 900 of the 6,000 enterprises slated for privatization under the existing law have been sold, mainly through management–employee buy-outs; only about a dozen of them have been large enterprises employing over 2,000 workers (*Business Central Europe*, May 1995, p. 18). Romania successfully offered sixty state enterprises for public sale at the beginning of May 1995 (*Business Central Europe*, June 1995, p. 45).

By the end of 1993 some 430 small enterprises had been privatized, but very few larger ones (Ronnas forthcoming).

Virginia Marsh provides the following information:

1. Only 1 per cent of the equity of the 6,280 state enterprises earmarked for privatization has been sold. In 1993 only 220 small enterprises were sold off, compared with a target of 800–1,000 (*FT*, 31 December 1993, p. 2).

2. In 1993 management or employee buy-outs were the main methods of privatization. Just 250 mainly small enterprises were privatized, well short of the initial target of 800–1,000. A public offering of up to ten state enterprises was planned for summer 1994, while the government promised the IMF to privatize 2,000 enterprises by the end of the year. Although only 1 per cent of the state economy has been sold off under privatization, there are now 500,000 private enterprises (*FT*, Survey, 3 May 1994, p. 30).

3. Some 500 small enterprises have been privatized via management and/or employee buy-outs (*FT*, 27 June 1994, p. 29).

4. On 7 November 1994 the government opened public offerings for three medium-sized enterprises, the first such offerings for eighteen months. Only two enterprises have been sold so far under the privatization scheme (*FT*, 8 November 1994, p. 2).

The 6,200 enterprises represented 55 per cent of the stock value of state enterprises. The remaining 45 per cent (around 330 large, 'strategic' enterprises) were to be self-administered state enterprises (*régimes autonomes*) (Franz-Lothar Altmann, *The World Today*, June 1993, p. 114).

5. Romania has sold off about 900 mainly small state enterprises under the 1991 scheme, with most purchased by management and employee groups. The Chamber of Deputies passed a delayed mass privatization programme on 21 March 1995. It had already been approved by the Senate, but needed to be promulgated by the president. The programme aimed to sell off about 3,000 state enterprises (around half of those earmarked for privatization under a 1991 law) within the next year (*FT*, 22 March 1995, p. 3).

6. The programme aimed to sell off shares in some 2,500 mainly small and medium-sized enterprises. The prospects for cash sales were not good, owing to factors such as the intention to offer enterprises at highly inflated book values. The vast majority of the 1,000 mainly small enterprises sold off by the State Ownership Fund to date have been privatized through management or employee buy-outs (*FT*, Survey, 25 May 1995, p. 34).

Another five public offerings were planned for the second half of September 1994 (the new mass privatization programme covers about 3,000 commercial enterprises) (*Business Journal Romania*, 25 August 1994, p. 5).

The list of 3,000 state firms was published at the end of August 1994 (*EEN*, 1994, vol. 8, no. 19, p. 5); the proposed new privatization bill involves 30 per cent of all state assets (p. 8).

A new privatization law was passed by parliament on 21 March 1995. Romanians would be able to purchase state assets using 'certificates of ownership' distributed to individuals in 1992 and higher-value coupons which were to be distributed. The new law envisaged the eventual sale through various means of 3,000 enterprises (down from 6,000 in the preceding law). A total of 1,500 enterprises were to be sold in 1995. The prices of assets sold for certificates and coupons were not to be determined through mechanisms such as auctions, but each enterprise was to be offered at a price based on the 1992 book value, adjusted for inflation (EBRD 1995: 62). Use of the original (1992) vouchers was to be limited and their value fixed, because the government was concerned about 'speculation' (Virginia Marsh, *FT*, 20 April 1995, p. 2). A privatization law covering 3,000 small and medium-sized state enterprises has been tied up in legislative wrangling since September 1994. The state sector accounts for 96 per cent of industrial production, but the private sector as a whole accounts for almost half the total work force (Alfred Moses, *IHT*, 17 March 1995, p. 8). The state sector still accounts for 90 per cent of industrial production. Under the mass privatization programme vouchers with a face value of 875,000 lei (equivalent to four times the average monthly take-home wage) were to be allocated to citizens over the age of eighteen (the new vouchers were non-transferable and, therefore, could not be obtained by investment funds). But the 1992 vouchers were valued at only 25,000 lei. Both sets of vouchers could be exchanged for shares in the 2,500 enterprises to be sold off. The vouchers represented only the population's 30 per cent share in the total equity of the roughly 5,000 enterprises the state still owned. They could be used to buy 60 per cent of the 2,500 enterprises earmarked in the scheme. In addition, the State Ownership Fund was to sell equity for cash (*The Economist,* 10 June 1995, p. 99). Over 1,200 enterprises have been privatized. The new privatization law was passed at the end of June 1995. Both types of voucher had to be used to acquire shares before the end of 1995 in about 3,000 enterprises. The mass privatization programme was officially started on 1 August 1995. The exchange of vouchers for shares was to take place between October and the end of December 1995. The new stock exchange was opened on 23 June 1995 (*EEN*, 1995, vol. 9, no. 16, pp. 5–6). In mid-August 1995 a list of 3,907 enterprises to be privatized was published (*Transition*, September 1995, p. 20).

Frydman *et al.* (1993: 230) provide figures showing the share of the various sectors in terms of employment at the end of 1991: state, 65.1 per cent; private, 34.9 per cent (private companies, 6.9 per cent; individual and co-operative farmers, 23.1 per cent; non-agricultural co-operatives, 4.9 per cent).

In 1992 the private sector as a whole accounted for around 26 per cent of GDP and employed over 35 per cent of the total work force of nearly 11 million (United Nations Economic Commission for Europe 1993: 215, 223).

According to *Business Europa* (August–September 1993, p. 9), the shares of the private sector were 25 per cent of GDP (3.6 million people employed), 45.7 per cent of total services, 45.8 per cent of retail trade, 26.4 per cent of the export trade and 27.5 per cent of the import trade.

By mid-1993 the private sector accounted for 30 per cent of GDP (*Employment Observatory*, 1993, no. 5, p. 1).

The private sector now accounts for roughly 30 per cent of GDP, compared with less than 5 per cent in 1989 (Deutsche Bank, *Focus: Eastern Europe*, 22 March 1994, no. 100, p. 30). In 1993 and 1994 the figure was 32 per cent and 35 per cent respectively (22 May 1995, no. 129, p. 3). Altogether about 1,000 enterprises have been transformed into private property. Many of them have been privatized through management and employee buy-outs and only about 100 have changed hands through public tenders. Privatization started in the early 1990s with the transformation of about 6,000 state enterprises into commercial companies. Seventy per cent of the capital of these companies was committed to the State Ownership Fund and 30 per cent to five Public Ownership Funds. The new law aimed to accelerate the process, the first phase of which obliged 3,000 enterprises to go ahead with privatization. Up to 60 per cent of the capital (30 per cent from the Public Ownership Funds and up to 30 per cent from the State Ownership Fund) was to be handed over to citizens in exchange for new and old vouchers. The idea was for the remaining 40 per cent either to go to foreign strategic investors or to be sold via auctions and public tenders (p. 7).

The preliminary findings of the national statistics commission for 1992 are reported by Virginia Marsh (*FT*, 4 February 1993, p. 3). The private sector, concentrated in trade and services, contributed more than 25 per cent to GDP (compared with less than 5 per cent in 1989: Deutsche Bank, *Focus: Eastern Europe*, 17 June 1993, p. 1). The 400,000 private companies and businessmen registered since 1989 handled 32 per cent of imports and 26 per cent of services, doubling their share of retail sales to 45 per cent. Industrial production was still more than 90 per cent state-controlled. In 1993 the private sector accounted for 30 per cent of GDP (Virginia Marsh, *FT*, 2 February 1994, p. 2); the private sector now employs more than a quarter of the 10.5 million work force (mainly in agriculture) and accounts for 55 per cent of retail trade and 30 per cent of foreign trade (*FT*, Survey, 3 May 1994, p. 30). By mid-1993 the private sector accounted for 30 per cent of GDP (*Employment Observatory*, 1993, no. 5, p. 1).

In 1993 25 per cent of GDP was produced in the private sector (United Nations, *World Economic and Social Survey*, 1994, p. 5).

In mid-1994 the private sector accounted for roughly 35 per cent of GDP (EBRD 1994: 10). At the end of 1993 the figure was over 31 per cent (42 per cent of employment), compared with 16 per cent in 1990. About 270 small enterprises were privatized under the privatization programme in 1993 and another 250 during the first four months of 1994, mostly by management–employee buy-outs (EBRD 1994: 32). The State Ownership Fund is obliged to reduce its shareholdings by at least 10 per cent a year (p. 61). By the end of 1994 891 enterprises had been privatized, primarily through management–employee buy-outs (EBRD 1995: 62).

In 1994 the private sector accounted for 35 per cent of GDP (32 per cent in 1993), 9 per cent of industrial output (7 per cent in 1993) and 69 per cent of retail trade (55 per cent in 1993) (DIW, *Economic Bulletin*, 1995, vol. 32, no. 7, p. 22).

'We now have more than 500,000 new economic agents . . . accounting for one-third of GDP and one-third of the work force.' But only some 700 enterprises, out of a total of 6,700, have been privatized so far (President Iliescu, *The Guardian*, 5 November 1994, p. 39).

As of July 1992 there were 327,967 privately owned companies registered, of which 13,431 were foreign-owned or joint ventures with foreign capital participation (*Business Europa*, January–February 1993, p. 43).

About 50 per cent of state housing had been sold to the public by mid-1991 (Demekas and Khan 1991: 26).

Foreign trade

Most licensing requirements for exports and imports were eliminated in May 1992, leaving quantitative import restrictions on only a few products related to public health or security (e.g. arms and drugs). There are no duties on exports, although there are some export quotas (such as for certain raw materials and drugs and, on occasion, agricultural products). Export licensing requirements have been reduced since June 1993. The tariff treatment of imports is fairly liberal. The leu is virtually fully convertible for the purpose of foreign trade transactions and for the capital and profits of foreign investors. There are exchange restrictions on residents wishing to holiday abroad and there are controls on the capital account. There is a floating exchange rate (EBRD 1994: 33, 109).

The foreign exchange market was liberalized on 8 April 1994. Enterprises and banks sell lei for dollars in daily auctions, with the exchange rate determined by the market (*Business Central Europe*, June 1994, p. 53). There are still controls on capital account transactions.

An association agreement was signed with the EU on 1 February 1993.

A free-trade agreement with EFTA was signed in December 1992, effective as of 1 May 1993.

The USA granted 'most favoured nation' status on 13 October 1993.

In 1994 more than half of exports went to countries in the EU and EFTA (Deutsche Bank, *Focus: Eastern Europe*, 1995, no. 129, p. 5).

In 1994 the EU accounted for 47.1 per cent of exports (39.3 per cent in 1993) and 50.3 per cent of imports (42.1 per cent in 1993) (DIW, *Economic Bulletin*, 1995, vol. 32, no. 7, p. 18).

Foreign investment

Foreign investors are able to acquire ownership rights over enterprise buildings and other real estate, but cannot directly hold title to land or own residential buildings other than those 'auxiliary to an investment'. But Romanian companies with a majority foreign participation may own land if the Romanian partners contribute it as their share for the duration of the joint venture (Frydman *et al.* 1993: 228).

According to one report, on 28 June 1993 parliament rejected an amendment to the law which would have clarified the question of foreign ownership of land; it did, however, allow full repatriation of profits by eliminating the annual limits of 8–15 per cent (*FT*, 29 June 1993, p. 2).

The constitution forbids land ownership by foreign individuals. The rejected amendment would have allowed foreign companies participating in joint ventures with local firms or with Romanian subsidiaries to own real estate (*Business Europa*, August–September 1993, p. 10).

The reluctance to allow foreign ownership of land may be partly due to the fear of Hungarians buying up land in Transylvania, home of most of Romania's Hungarian minority (Mark Milner, *The Guardian*, 24 July 1993, p. 35).

At the end of March 1992 there were 10,394 commercial companies with foreign capital (1,589 in 1990); the total registered foreign capital was $323.1 million (Frydman *et al.* 1993: 235).

The gross inflow of direct foreign investment was $108 million in 1990, $156 million in 1991, $269 million in 1992 and $227 million in 1993 (Deutsche Bank, *Focus: Eastern Europe*, 1994, no. 106, p. 9). Direct foreign investment totalled $1.3 billion by the end of 1994 (1995, no. 135, p. 17).

Foreign investment was $269 million in 1991 and $466 million in 1992 (*Business Central Europe*, May 1993, p. 25).

By the end of May 1993 only $672 million in direct foreign investment had been committed (Virginia Marsh, *FT*, 30 June 1993, p. 3). The figure for 1992 alone was $270 million (Virginia Marsh, *FT*, 31 December 1993, p. 2). A further $227.4 billion was committed during 1993, bringing the total to $760.5 million since 1990 (Virginia Marsh, *FT*, Survey, 3 May 1994, p. 32).

The total by mid-1994 was $888.2 million (*Business Journal Romania*, 25 August 1994, p. 9).

Total foreign investment is a little more than $1 billion (Alfred Moses, *IHT*, 17 March 1995, p. 8).

Direct foreign investment amounted to $415 million in 1994 and by the end of that year reached a cumulative total of almost $1.3 billion (DIW, *Economic Bulletin*, 1995, vol. 32, no. 7, p. 20).

Net direct foreign investment was $37 million in 1991, $73 million in 1992, $95 million in 1993 and $294 million in 1994 (United Nations Economic Commission for Europe 1995: 151).

Direct foreign investment amounted to $140 million in the period 1990–93 (EBRD 1994: 123).

Nathaniel Nash (*IHT*, 1 March 1995, p. 2) cites a study analysing the multiplier effects of investment by the Coca-Cola Company in Romania. 'Overall, at least eleven jobs were created elsewhere in the economy for each job that Coke created directly . . . more than double the rate for the soft-drink industry in the United States.' This is because Coke sells its soft drinks in Romania primarily through small retailers and kiosk owners.

Agriculture

Julian Borger (*The Guardian*, 2 March 1994, p. 12) cites a recent Romanian estimate that during the 'systematization' programme twenty-nine towns were destroyed and thirty-seven were 'crippled' (losing between a quarter and half of their pre-communist buildings). According to Borger, Ceausescu's inspiration for the 'agro-industrial centres' were the towns he had seen in China and North Korea.

In 1990 out of a total of 14.8 million ha of agricultural land, about 9.4 million ha was arable land (of which co-operatives owned 51.3 per cent and state farms 20.4 per cent; the remaining 28.3 per cent of arable land, mostly hilly and mountainous areas, belonged to individual farmers). The following are eligible for land: co-operative members who contributed land, or their heirs; co-operative members who have not contributed land but have worked in the co-operative for at least three years; Romanian citizens whose land has been abusively expropriated, or their heirs; and, to the extent that land is available, any other Romanian citizens willing to work the land, and civil servants who work in the countryside (Frydman *et al.* 1993: 253). Agricultural co-operatives were dissolved in 1991. Nearly 80 per cent of arable land is now privately operated, while state farms have been transformed into state-owned commercial companies (p. 231).

Chrystia Freeland (*FT*, Survey, 3 May 1994, p. 32) describes the initial situation in agriculture after 1989 as an anarchic free-for-all, formalized by the 1991 land reform. The sale of newly privatized rural properties is banned for ten years, but larger farms are being created through leasing. Peasants account for 45 per cent of the population.

Over 80 per cent of the area farmed had been privatized by the end of 1992 (United Nations Economic Commission for Europe 1993: 223).

Roughly 80 per cent of arable land has been split into too small parcels and as deeds of ownership were not handed out in time the farmers were virtually unable to raise credit for the purchase of inputs (Deutsche Bank, *Focus: Eastern Europe*, 17 June 1993, no. 81, p. 4).

Definitive (as opposed to provisional) title deeds have been issued for only 3.8 per cent of the land (*Business Europa*, August–September 1993, p. 12). A recent survey shows that a quarter of all land holders have 1 ha or less of land, 38 per cent have 1–3 ha and 20 per cent have 3–5 ha (p. 13). The difficulty of using land as collateral has led to the 'association movement', whereby holders group together to form larger holdings and to try to benefit from government or internationally backed cheap loans (p. 13).

Ronnas (forthcoming) cites a 1992 survey which put the average holding at 2.5 ha.

Only around 5 per cent of new landholders have received full title to their land (*Business Central Europe*, November 1993, p. 15).

Fewer than a fifth of farmers have received full title to the land returned to them (although the private sector now accounts for 80 per cent of agricultural output) (Virginia Marsh, *FT*, 2 February 1993, p. 2). Although most agricultural land is now worked by private farmers, only 15 per cent of the 5.1 million private landowners have received full title (*FT*, 30 March 1994, p. 3). On 29 March 1994 parliament approved a law introducing a tax on individual land ownership, specifically a tax on estimates of production from the land (implemented on 1 July 1994); agricultural companies such as state farms would continue to pay tax on profits (p. 3).

The Ministry of Agriculture says that over 90 per cent of land due to be given back is in private hands and that 99 per cent of landowners have been given documents stating how much land is theirs. But farmers' groups claim that by mid-June 1994 only 24 per cent of landowners had received full legal title to their property (*Business Central Europe*, July–August 1994, p. 15).

Although 80 per cent of agricultural land is now classified as being in private ownership, many farmers have merely acquired provisional property titles. Around 60 per cent of farmers are still in possession of only provisional property deeds (DIW, *Economic Bulletin*, July 1995, vol. 32, no. 7, p. 22).

About 80 per cent of agricultural land has been restored to its former owners and their heirs, but at least 65 per cent of the so-called 'owners' have not yet received definitive title deeds (*EEN*, 10 August 1995, vol. 9, no. 16, p. 5).

Cochrane (1993) argues that Romania has found itself with a large number of small farms but without the infrastructure necessary to support them (p. 851). Of the countries of Eastern Europe only Romania has seen the widespread formation of new co-operative arrangements. New private farmers have been encouraged to join associations. These are of two types: loosely organized 'family associations' and more formally structured associations that are legally registered (p. 853).

Associations tend to be newly organized joint production units, with most resembling voluntary production co-operatives (Brooks and Meurs

1994: 25). In 1992 many households continued to choose associations over private farming. A 1992 publication found that 23 per cent of arable land was farmed by registered associations, 20 per cent by informal associations, 49 per cent by households and (presumably) 8 per cent by state farms. The size of the average private (household) farm was 2.5 ha split into three parcels. An August 1991 survey found that the average association farmed 1,400 ha and had 300 members (p. 26). An important advantage of associations was input supply, especially machinery services for mechanized grain farming (pp. 28–30).

In 1990 all farm debts were written off (Pryor 1992: 279).

Economic performance

Positive GDP growth was achieved as early as 1993. Agriculture has performed relatively well throughout, but inflation is still a worry and unemployment was still over 10 per cent at the end of 1994 (see Tables 25.1 and 25.2).

Crude-oil production, which peaked at about 15 million tonnes a year in the mid-1970s, totalled only 6.7 million tonnes in 1994. The respective figures for natural gas production were 36 billion cubic metres and 19.6 billion cubic metres (*FT*, Survey, 25 May 1995, p. 34).

Table 25.1 Romania: selected economic indicators

Economic indicator	*1990*	*1991*	*1992*	*1993*	*1994*
Rate of growth of GDP (%)	−5.6	−12.9	−10.0	1.3	3.4
Rate of growth of industrial output (%)	−23.7	−22.8	−21.9	1.3	3.3
Rate of growth of agricultural output (%)	−2.9	0.8	−13.3	12.8	0.2
Inflation rate (%)	5.1	174.5	210.9	256.1	136.8
Net foreign debt ($ billion)	0.8	1.5	2.7	3.2	2.8
Budget surplus or deficit (% GDP)	1.2	0.6	−4.6	−0.1	−3.0
Current account ($ billion)	−1.65	−1.37	−1.46	−1.235	−0.271

Sources: Various issues of United Nations Economic Commission for Europe, *Economic Survey of Europe*; OECD, *Economic Outlook*; IMF, *World Economic Outlook*; Deutsche Bank, *Focus: Eastern Europe*; *Economics of Transition* and *Business Central Europe*; EBRD (1994: 166; 1995: 43)

Table 25.2 Romania: unemployment

Date		*No. unemployed*	*Unemployment rate (%)*
1991	January		0.0
	February		0.1
	March	79,200	0.2
	April		0.6
	May	138,900	0.9
	June	169,900	1.2

Table 25.2 Continued

Date		*No. unemployed*	*Unemployment rate (%)*
	July	217,100	1.4
	August	237,800	1.6
	September	260,500	1.7
	October		1.7
	November		1.8
	December	337,500	3.1
1992	January		2.9
	February		3.4
	March		4.6
	April		4.8
	May		
	June		5.9
	July	700,000	6.0
	August		6.9
	September		7.6
	October		
	November		
	December	929,000	8.2
1993	January		8.5
	February		8.8
	March	1,060,400	9.5
	April		9.5
	May		9.3
	June	1,035,400	9.3
	July		9.4
	August		
	September	1,046,400	9.2
	October		9.3
	November		9.6
	December	1,170,000	10.2
1994	January		
	February		11.1
	March		11.3
	April		11.2
	May		11.0
	June		10.8
	July		
	August		10.5
	September		
	October		
	November		10.8
	December		10.9

Sources: Various issues of United Nations Economic Commission for Europe, *Economic Survey of Europe*; OECD, *Economic Outlook*; Commission of the European Communities, *Employment Observatory*, Deutsche Bank, *Focus: Eastern Europe*; *Economics of Transition* and *Business Central Europe*; Frydman *et al.* (1993: 215); EBRD (1994: 166)

26

THE FORMER YUGOSLAVIA

Bosnia-Hercegovina

THE VARIOUS PLANS FOR BOSNIA-HERCEGOVINA

The Vance–Owen plan

There were three main parts to the Vance–Owen plan:

1. *The 'map'*. Bosnia was to be divided into ten largely autonomous provinces, with the three main ethnic groups (Moslem, Serb and Croat) to varying degrees in the majority in three provinces each (although all main groups had to be represented in provincial governments). In the provincial government of Sarajevo the three groups would be represented equally. The capital itself was to be a demilitarized 'open city'. There could be negotiations only on marginal boundary changes. There was a change on 25 March 1993. President Izetbegovic signed a somewhat modified map (the Croats agreed). Sarajevo province was to be expanded and placed under the dominance of the Moslem majority. The city of Sarajevo itself was to be a separate capital district administered by the coalition government. Croatian provincial majorities would be reduced from three to two, with Travnik coming under dual Croat/Moslem control. (The Bosnian government and the Croats also agreed to the arrangements for the interim government prior to elections. The Serbs rejected both this and the map.)

In terms of total land area the three Serb provinces would amount to 43 per cent of the total area of Bosnia (instead of the 70 per cent then occupied). The Serbs complained about the extent of the loss of territory and the separation of their provinces (on 23 April 1993 Lord Owen raised the possibility of a UN-patrolled, demilitarized northern corridor linking Serb areas, but this was rejected). The Serbs also complained about the paucity of resources within their provinces. Steve Cole (*IHT*, 8 March 1993, p. 4) reports a Belgrade estimate that under the plan Moslem provinces would control about one-third of all businesses that existed before the war, just over half Bosnia's electricity, 70 per cent of coal, 65 per cent of bauxite and 72 per cent of alumina. The Serbs would have the majority of iron ore and timber and a quarter of electricity, some of it in regions Serbs had taken by force. According to Western estimates, as much as two-thirds of former Yugoslavia's military production was in Bosnia. Under the Vance–Owen plan most military factories would come under Moslem or Croatian control, according to UN and US analysts.

Although the Bosnian government ultimately signed the revised map under international pressure, it has always maintained that it still meant accepting the results of 'ethnic cleansing' to a considerable extent and, indeed, 'ethnic cleansing' would be encouraged (on 19 May 1993 even the UN human rights investigator, Tadeusz Mazowiecki, said that owing to the lack of an effective international response the Vance–Owen plan had actually accelerated 'ethnic cleansing').

2. *The constitutional aspects.* Bosnia's sovereignty was to be preserved within existing borders. But the plan envisaged a highly decentralized state in which the functions of the central government were to be very restricted. One of them would be foreign affairs and it was made clear that the provinces would not have the right to forge international relations of their own: 'the provinces shall not have any legal personality and may not enter into agreements with foreign states or international organizations'. The Serbs wanted an independent 'state within a state', including the right to self-determination (i.e. to join a 'Greater Serbia' if they so wished). The Bosnian government feared that the high level of ethnically based provincial autonomy, coupled with a weak central government, would lead to the break-up of the country. Instead Bosnia should be a decentralized country in which eight to ten regions (not based on ethnic dominance) would have a high degree of autonomy.

The central government would reflect the ethnic mix (a lower house elected by proportional representation and an upper house appointed by the provincial governments). The post of president was to rotate among the ethnic groups.

There was to be strong international involvement to ensure respect for human rights (e.g. attempts would be made to reverse 'ethnic cleansing' and agreements to release property under duress would be made null and void).

3. *The military agreement.* This provided for a comprehensive ceasefire and the withdrawal of forces to the respective provinces. Heavy weapons would be placed under UN supervision. UN peacekeeping forces would oversee the whole agreement and ensure freedom of movement. The military part of the Vance–Owen plan was not signed by the Bosnian government until 3 March 1993 (i.e. later than the Croats and Serbs).

The Serb–Croat plan for Bosnia

The essential elements of the Serb–Croat plan of 16 June 1993 for the future of Bosnia were as follows:

1. *The map.* The territorial division between the three constituent *republics* was to be the subject of negotiations.

At the time the Serbs claimed to control 72 per cent of the territory of Bosnia and the Croats claimed 19 per cent; if true this left the Bosnian government with 9 per cent (10 per cent was the most frequently mentioned figure, but the percentage varied because of the fighting, e.g. Moslem successes in central Bosnia against the Croats). The Serbs also claimed that the (socialist) Yugoslav land register had given them 64 per cent of the land, the Serbs being mainly rural (it has been argued, in the light of the significant support given to the Bosnian government by urban Serbs and Croats in particular, that the Bosnian war could in some respects be seen as a rural–urban conflict). The Serbs mostly proposed up to 30 per cent of the land for the Moslems (although it was claimed that this would represent more than 50 per cent of the 'wealth'/'economic value'/'resources'). But other figures were mentioned, e.g. on 28 July 1993 a division of 60 per cent for the Serbs, 26 per cent for the Moslems and 14 per cent for the Croats was proposed. The Serbs also wanted either to divide Sarajevo or to create a new city in the western part of the capital.

The Croats had at one time suggested 45 per cent for the Serbs, 35 per cent for the Moslems and 20 per cent for themselves. The Croats felt as though they might lose out in the territorial division and so no definite joint set of figures appeared in the Serb–Croat plan (although Lord Owen said on 6 August 1993 that the Serbs and Croats had agreed on 30 per cent for the Moslems). On 13 August 1993 President Izetbegovic said that the Bosnian government would be satisfied with 40 per cent of the land.

A frontier commission would deal with any subsequent changes to the finally agreed republican borders. The commission would comprise a member from each republic and a member each from the UN and the EU.

2. *The constitutional aspects.* A *confederation* of three constituent peoples.

The three constituent *republics* would carry out most functions of government. 'The republics shall not enter into agreements with foreign states or international organizations which harm the interests of other republics.' 'All matters of vital concern to any of the constituent peoples and their republics shall be regulated in the constitutions of the republics' (i.e. union decisions would be taken by consensus). (Note that there is intentionally nothing in reality in these proposals stopping the Serbs or the Croats joining a 'Greater Serbia' or a 'Greater Croatia'.)

Before democratic elections took place in the republics a provisional union government ('co-ordinating committee') would be set up, consisting of nine members (three from each of the three republics). The post of president would rotate every month and that of the foreign minister would rotate every four months.

After elections in the republics the union structures would be set up. 'The presidency of the confederation shall be composed of the three presidents of the republics. There shall be a confederal council of ministers composed of nine members, three from each of the republics. The posts of the prime minister and foreign minister shall rotate at agreed intervals. The confederal parliament shall be indirectly elected by the legislatures of the three republics.'

'A constitutional court, with a member from each republic, shall resolve disputes between the republics and the confederation.' In the event of disagreement the International Court of Justice in the Hague would arbitrate.

3. *The military agreement*. There should be progressive demilitarization under UN–EU supervision: a cease-fire, a withdrawal of heavy weapons and UN monitoring.

The Bosnian presidency's plan for Bosnia

The Bosnian collective presidency was subject to increasing internal division during July 1993, but a draft set of counter-proposals was nevertheless put forward on 20 July. It was largely based on the Vance–Owen plan:

1. *The map*. No percentage figures were presented for territorial division. Indeed, even the number of *provinces* was left vague (four to eighteen).

2. *The constitutional aspects*. There would be a pluralistic, democratic and secular *federation*, but with 'substantial provincial, cultural and social autonomy'. Each ethnic group would have parity at the federal level, but the *provinces* 'cannot be constituted solely on ethnic principles'. Instead the provinces would be established on the basis of economic, geographical, communications, historical and cultural criteria. A temporary UN protectorate would be asked for in the event of no agreement between the warring factions.

The Owen–Stoltenberg plan for Bosnia

This 'compromise' plan (the first draft of which was released for general publication on 6 August 1993 and the second on 20 August) was, in fact, largely based on the Serb–Croat set of proposals:

1. *The map*. The *republics* are essentially ethnic-based. The two negotiators had been bargaining for a minimum of 30 per cent of the area for the Bosnian government. The actual proposed territorial division just met this aspiration, with the Serbs attaining 52.5 per cent (in one contiguous republic and borders with the Federal Republic of Yugoslavia and with Croatia, including the Serb-held parts; thus the Serbs would relinquish around a fifth

of the land they captured by force or through 'ethnic cleansing': *The Times*, 1 September 1993, p. 8) and the Croats 17.5 per cent (in two pieces, bordering on Croatia). (The Bosnian government aspired to 40 per cent and objected to the fact that the Serbs would hold on to land in eastern and northern Bosnia in particular ethnically cleansed by force.) But the land-locked Bosnian republic would be in four pieces. The Bosnian government enclaves of Gorazde and Zepa/Srebrenica in eastern Bosnia would be linked with one another by road and Gorazde would be linked with the main central region by corridor. There would also be linkage by road to Bihac in the north-west. There would be access to the river Sava in the north (and control of the town centre and the river port area of Brcko) and access to the port of Ploce on the Adriatic in Croatia proper. (The co-chairmen estimated that around 40,000 additional UN troops would be needed to carry out the plan. Nato's estimate is that about 50,000 would be needed in total, compared with 77,000 for the Vance–Owen plan.)

On 16 August 1993 an interim plan for Sarajevo was announced, to be implemented once an overall peace accord had been reached. Sarajevo would be placed under UN administration for up to two years. The UN administrator, appointed by the UN secretary-general, would have the support of a ten-strong advisory body comprising four Moslems, three Serbs, two Croats and a person representing the city's minorities (a Jew, for example). Sarajevo would be demilitarized except for UN forces. There would be nine municipalities, the tenth, Pale (the Serbs' headquarters during the war), being excluded. (Pessimists see the likelihood of a permanent division of a city renowned for its tolerance and harmony.)

On 20 August 1993 the co-chairmen proposed that the same sort of formula should be used for Mostar, except that the EU ought to be asked instead of the UN (on 12 September the EU agreed to provide a German-led civilian administration in the event of an overall settlement).

2. *The constitutional aspects.* The 'Union of the Republics of Bosnia-Hercegovina' would be a *confederation*. The union government would have residual powers only, specifically confined to foreign policy and foreign trade. The union government would be charged with safeguarding human rights, supposedly including efforts to reverse 'ethnic cleansing' or at least to award compensation for property which cannot be restored. (But implementation would be another matter; indeed, further 'voluntary' movements by frightened people would be likely to enhance ethnic separation. The union would have a supreme court, a constitutional court and a human rights court. There would also be a group of ombudsmen 'to protect human dignity, rights and liberties'.) There would be no union army or police, central bank or single currency. None of the three *republics* was to be able to secede from the union without the agreement of the UN Security Council. (But a major criticism of the scheme is that there is nothing in reality to prevent them seceding. A not unduly cynical interpretation is that

Owen and Stoltenberg were well aware that a 'Greater Serbia' and 'Greater Croatia' would be formed eventually.) Dual nationality would be allowed of the union and the republics. But only the union would be recognized internationally and be allowed membership of the UN and other international organizations.

The three republic presidents would form the union presidency, whose chairmanship would rotate every four months. The posts of prime minister and foreign minister would rotate annually between the three republics (although not from the same republic at the same time). There would be no direct election of the union parliament, which would be composed of 120 representatives elected in equal percentages from the legislatures of the three republics. The republics would be allowed to draw up their own constitutions, although they would have to provide for 'democratic forms'.

Internal border controls would not be permitted and there would be free movement of people, goods and services throughout the union. (Croatia also agreed to guarantee the union and the constituent republics access to the sea.)

3. *The military agreement.* There would be a comprehensive cease-fire once a general peace agreement had been reached. Demilitarization was called for, the republics being called upon 'to disarm and disband existing forces progressively'. The union would not be allowed to have any military forces.

The Bosnian government–Croat plan for Bosnia

Note that before the latest war 750,000 Croats lived in Bosnia-Hercegovina. Some 500,000 lived in Sarajevo and central Bosnia, while the rest lived in the almost ethnically pure area of western Hercegovina: *The Economist*, 15 January 1994, p. 41. It was the former who really suffered when fighting broke out between Croats and Bosnian government forces. Hercegovina is one of the poorest parts of the country.

The preliminary plan was outlined on 1 March 1994 in Washington (the USA was the broker; Charles Redman was the US special envoy to the former Yugoslavia). The document was signed by Bosnia's prime minister (Haris Silajdzic), the representative of the Bosnian Croats (Kresimir Zubak) and Croatia's foreign minister (Mate Granic). (The first two signed the document relating to the federal constitution at the formal ceremony in Washington on 18 March 1994, while Presidents Izetbegovic and Tudjman signed the document spelling out the principles of confederation with Croatia.) The details were to be thrashed out in further negotiations, but the basic ideas were as follows:

1. A federation split up into cantons based not only on ethnic make-up but also on economic, geographical and other factors. The central government is responsible for defence (there is one army), foreign affairs and economic policy (including foreign trade), while the cantons have authority

over the police, education, housing and public services. The two levels of government are jointly responsible for human rights. The exact boundaries of the federation have yet to be decided.

2. The federal parliament consists of the House of Representatives (democratically elected on a proportional basis) and the House of Peoples (with equal numbers of Bosnian Moslems and Croats). The House of Peoples elects the (rotating) president and vice-president, each from separate communities and each serving for alternate one-year terms over a four-year period. The president chooses the prime minister, who has to come from the other ethnic group. In fact any minister and deputy minister must belong to a different ethnic group. (On 31 May 1994 it was announced that the Croat Kresimir Zubak was to be president for the first six months, the Moslem Ejup Ganic vice-president and the Moslem Haris Silajdzic prime minister.)

3. The status of Sarajevo is to be decided. Mostar will be placed under EU administration for two years (the administrator was to be Hans Koschnick, the former mayor of Bremen; the agreement was not actually signed until 5 July 1994 and EU administration did not start until 23 July 1994).

4. A loose confederation with Croatia. Bosnia and Croatia would remain independent states, but there would be a common market for the free movement of goods, a customs union and a monetary union. There would also be defence arrangements. All these matters would be decided by a confederative council comprising an equal number of Bosnian Moslems, Bosnian Croats and Croats.

5. All refugees have the right to return freely and to receive compensation for damaged property. An exchange of prisoners is to take place.

6. It is open to the Bosnian Serbs to join the federation.

Additional information

1. On 11 May 1994 the Bosnian government and the Bosnian Croats agreed that the federation should comprise 58 per cent of the territory of Bosnia-Hercegovina. There would be eight cantons, four of them with a Moslem majority, two with a Croat majority and two composed of more or less equal members of both communities (Travnik in central Bosnia and Mostar in the south).

2. The Sarajevo-based Serb Citizens' Council reported in May 1994 that only 41 per cent of Bosnian Serbs lived in territory controlled by Radovan Karadzic. Out of the 1.3 million Serbs in pre-war Bosnia-Hercegovina 600,000 had fled the country since the war began, 100,000 had died and 200,000 were still living 'under the legitimate Bosnian government' (70,000 in Sarajevo) (*FT*, 26 May 1994, p. 3). (The Bosnian Serbs dispute these figures. Their spokesman, Srdja Trifkovic, says that the implication is that the '73 per cent of the former Yugoslav republic of Bosnia-Hercegovina

under Serb control is inhabited by merely 400,000 Serbs. In fact there are 1.1 million . . . that there are 200,000 Serbs under Muslim rule . . . is also untrue . . . there are some 80,000 of these unfortunates and there would not be more than a handful left if they were free to leave . . . we learn that 600,000 Serbs have "left" . . . a callous misnomer for over half a million Serbs . . . are victims of "ethnic cleansing" . . . the figure of 100,000 dead Serbs is wishful thinking . . . slogans of multi-ethnicity have never been anything but a smokescreen for Muslim domination': letter to *The Guardian*, 1 June 1994, p. 19.)

Later developments

Formally the federal government already exists, its ministers doubling up as ministers of the Bosnian or Herceg-Bosna ('Croatian Republic of Herceg-Bosna') governments. The federal parliament has held several meetings, but few of its laws have been implemented. There are still two legal, fiscal and monetary systems. Only one of the eight new cantons actually exists. One difficulty is the absence of a finalized territory and another is that the Bosnian government wants a single, integrated army, while the Croats want two armies under a joint headquarters (which has been set up) (*The Economist*, 11 February 1995, p. 52).

The Bosnian government and the Bosnian Serbs, unable to resolve many issues, agreed on 5 February 1995 to submit all disputes to an international arbitrator, whose decisions were to be binding on both parties.

The 'contact group's' plan for Bosnia-Hercegovina

The foreign ministers of the 'contact group' in this instance were from the USA, Russia, Germany, France, the UK and Greece (they were backed up at the 'political G8' meeting on 10 July 1994). They presented the map to the factions on 6 July 1994 and gave them until 19 July to make up their minds. If the Serbs did not accept the map they would face tightened sanctions, the expansion of weapon exclusion zones in Bosnia and even the prospect of a lifting of the arms embargo against the Bosnian government. If the Serbs accepted and the Bosnian government did not the former would be rewarded by an easing of sanctions. The key features of the map were as follows:

1. The Bosnian Serbs would receive 49 per cent of the land area.

2. The Bosnian government would receive 51 per cent of the land area. Land removed from Serb control would include land around Bihac and Brcko (the Serbs would retain a narrow land corridor through the Posavina corridor).

3. The Bosnian government would retain the eastern enclaves of Srebrenica, Zepa and Gorazde and these would be corridor-linked with each other

and with Sarajevo. Sarajevo itself would be placed under UN administration for two years pending a settlement.

4. There would be no 'grey zones'. This idea originated with the Bosnian government to accommodate the 7 percentage point difference between the preferred 58 per cent and the 51 per cent on offer. (The 'grey zones' were Serb-held areas which formerly had a Moslem majority and which suffered the worst 'ethnic cleansing'. The suggestion was that they should come under international administration and thus refugees would be allowed to return home.)

The Bosnian Serbs objected that there was a need for: (1) self-determination; (2) an equal share of resources as well as land; (3) a contiguous area; (4) access to the Adriatic Sea; (5) a split Sarajevo.

Later developments

2 December 1994. The 'contact group' proposes amendments: (1) the territorial division 'can be adjusted by mutual agreement between the parties'; (2) 'constitutional arrangements agreeable to the parties need to be drawn up which preserve the integrity of Bosnia and allow equitable and balanced arrangements for the Bosnian–Croat and Bosnian–Serb entities' (thought to imply the Bosnian Serbs being allowed to confederate with the Federal Republic of Yugoslavia). The Bosnian Serbs will not have to withdraw physically from any land until negotiations are concluded.

14 February 1995. The 'contact group' countries put forward tentative proposals further to ease sanctions on the Federal Republic of Yugoslavia in return for recognition of Bosnia and Croatia, acceptance of the 'contact group's' plan for Bosnia and the Z-4 plan for Croatia, and ending all military support for the Bosnian and Croatian Serbs. But there were disagreements, e.g. France preferred the complete suspension of sanctions, while the USA favoured progressive relief.

'The "contact group" should give the Serbs three months to sign its peace plan. If they fail to sign, the arms embargo against the Bosnian government should be lifted . . . The deadline should be no later than 1 May, however, because the Serbs will launch new offensives during the spring . . . We are asking for the right to receive weapons, not ground troops . . . Defenders of the embargo also claim that ending it would lead to a collapse of the UN mission in Bosnia. Yet the majority of humanitarian organizations have already pledged to remain even if the UN troops leave. In addition, many countries have pledged to replace departing European units . . . Defenders of the embargo also say that lifting it would provoke pre-emptive attacks by the Serbs. What is stopping them now? It is our army and the will of the people that have prevented our country from being totally overrun' (Haris Silajdzic, the prime minister of the Republic of Bosnia-Hercegovina, *IHT*, 23 February 1995, p. 8).

8 September 1995. The foreign ministers of Bosnia, Croatia and Serbia agree on the 'basic principles' of a political settlement in Bosnia. The details are to be found in the chronology.

A CHRONOLOGY OF EVENTS

20 January 1993. Croatia and Slovenia join the IMF and World Bank.

22 January 1993. The Croats launch an offensive in parts of the Serb-occupied Krajina region of Croatia across the UN cease-fire lines. The Serbs seize their heavy weapons held in UN depots. The Serbs had not relinquished control to Croat authorities as agreed in the so-called 'pink zones' (the proposed demilitarized buffer zones along the borders of Krajina). The Croats also alleged that the UN terms in general had not been fulfilled, such as disarmament, the return of Croatian refugees and the repair of the Maslenica bridge linking the northern and southern Adriatic coastlines of Croatia (the bridge was successfully retaken by the Croats). The UN mandate was due to end on 21 February 1993.

25 January 1993. The UN Security Council condemns the Croatian offensive and demands the withdrawal of troops. But the Security Council also demands that the Serbs should return their heavy weapons for supervision by the UN.

26 January 1993. President Tudjman offers to withdraw if Croatian police are allowed to install civilian authority and the Serbs are disarmed (including the handing over of their heavy weapons to the UN).

28 January 1993. The Croats retake the Peruca dam, which the Serbs almost succeeded in blowing up with mines.

30 January 1993. The Geneva session of the Vance–Owen discussions ends with only the Croats signing all three parts of the proposals. The negotiations continue in New York. Cyrus Vance and Lord Owen intend to go to the UN Security Council for endorsement and subsequent enforcement of their plan.

4 February 1993. UN Secretary-General Boutros Boutros-Ghali supports the Vance–Owen plan. The new Clinton administration in the USA also accepts the plan provided all parties agree to it (the US government stressed that it would not force the Bosnian government to accept).

The new Clinton administration took some time to finalize its attitude towards the Vance–Owen plan (the delay was criticized for building up the hopes of the Bosnian government and thereby hindering negotiations). During the US presidential election campaign Bill Clinton had advocated a much more supportive stance towards the Bosnian government, considering such actions as recommending to the UN Security Council the use of air strikes against the Serbs and the lifting of the arms embargo on the Bosnian government. He was critical of important aspects of the Vance–Owen plan, e.g. it rewarded aggression by conceding the results of 'ethnic cleansing' and its proposed division of Bosnia was impractical and unenforceable. In the end, however, the USA broadly backed the Vance–Owen plan. The USA disclosed its detailed plan on 10 February 1993 and included the possibility of US ground troops becoming involved. The new secretary of state, Warren Christopher, said that the administration would be 'prepared to do its share to help implement and enforce' a viable settlement, 'including possible US military action'. The USA would contribute to a UN multinational *peacekeeping* (but not peacemaking) force to implement a settlement, i.e. provided it had already been agreed to by the warring parties. The plan also tightens economic sanctions against Serbia, calls on all parties to halt the violence, seeks enforcement of the 'no fly' zone, and insists that the only solution lies in negotiations between Bosnia, Serbia and Croatia. A special US envoy to the talks, Reginald Bartholomew, was announced. A war crimes tribunal was to be sought to punish those responsible for atrocities. Protection was to be afforded to Kosovo and Macedonia to stop the conflict spreading. An important aspect of policy was to involve Russia in the negotiations (not only to enhance the prestige of Boris Yeltsin, but also because of Russia's historical friendship with Serbia).

7 February 1993. In the election for the (less important) Croatian upper house of parliament Tudjman's Croatian Democratic Community Party won most of the county seats.

11 February 1993. The Bosnian government refuses to accept further international aid for Sarajevo until aid reaches the Moslem areas of eastern Bosnia (aid was resumed on 22 February).

12 February 1993. Boutros Boutros-Ghali proposes a limited extension of the UN mandate in Croatia from 21 February to 31 March 1993.

14 February 1993. Russia appoints Vitali Churkin as its special envoy to the negotiations.

17–21 February 1993. The UN High Commission for Refugees took a controversial decision to suspend relief operations in Bosnia, but after much criticism (including that from Boutros Boutros-Ghali) aid was formally resumed (some had continued anyway).

19 February 1993. The UN Security Council renews the mandate of the UN peacekeeping force in the former Yugoslavia from 21 February to 31 March 1993. It is specifically mentioned for the first time that all Unprofor forces will work under Charter 7 of the UN charter, i.e. military means are allowed for self-protection purposes to ensure the implementation of UN resolutions (previously this applied only to the forces escorting aid convoys). The UN force in Croatia is also allowed to carry heavier weapons.

22 February 1993. The UN Security Council unanimously approves the setting up of an international court for war crimes (the first since Nuremberg and Tokyo after the Second World War, although the death penalty is not available this time). The Security Council 'decides that an international tribunal shall be established for the prosecution of persons responsible for serious violations of international humanitarian law committed in the territory of the former Yugoslavia since 1991'. (The South African judge Richard Goldstone was named as prosecutor on 8 July 1994.)

23 February 1993. President Clinton and UN Secretary-General Boutros Boutros-Ghali agree to US aid air drops (parachuted relief supplies) to Moslems in Bosnia under UN supervision (extended to Serbs and Croats in Bosnia the following day). They began on 28 February.

The UN Human Rights Committee condemns Serb atrocities (such as rape) in Bosnia, but mention is also made of 'violations by all sides to the conflict'. In addition backing was given to the findings of Mazowiecki (the UN's special investigator on human rights).

2 March 1993. Russia and Germany offer to help with the air drops.

Cerska falls to the Serbs (part of a 'land grab' in eastern Bosnia by the Serbs to create 'facts on the ground' in case a peace treaty is eventually signed; the Serbs also wish to establish land corridors between the provinces allocated to them in the Vance–Owen plan).

3 March 1993. The Bosnian government signs the military agreement, the Croats and the Serbs having already signed. The agreement provides for a comprehensive cease-fire, the demilitarization of Sarajevo and the 'control' of heavy weapons by the UN (originally the term 'monitoring' was used and Karadzic objected to the change). The armed forces and weapons will be withdrawn when a final settlement is reached.

The UN Security Council condemns the continued Serbian aggression in Bosnia.

8 March 1993. Boutros Boutros-Ghali suggests that outside force may be needed to ensure Serbian compliance (e.g. to eject Serbs from non-Serb territories). Lord Owen, however, confines possible use of force to recalcitrant warlords. He also says that if the Bosnian government signs the Vance–Owen plan the proposals should be taken to the UN for approval. Non-compliance by the Serbs should be met with tightened sanctions.

The Bosnian government orders a counter-offensive in eastern Bosnia.

13 March 1993. The first confirmed bombing raids by Serbian planes take place. Three planes bomb villages in eastern Bosnia. One report talks of 465 violations of the flight ban in total since October 1992 (*IHT*, 18 March 1993, p. 2).

President Izetbegovic of Bosnia consults his colleagues in Sarajevo and is given conditional power to sign the Vance–Owen plan. Izetbegovich talks of his desire for the following: a strict timetable for implementation with the UN having enforcement powers (including physical control of heavy weapons); Sarajevo open to free passage immediately; no ethnic areas; three additional provinces, under UN control.

Philippe Morillon, the (French) commander of UN forces in Bosnia, vows to stay in Srebrenica in eastern Bosnia until aid gets through.

19 March 1993. The first land convoy since 10 December 1993 gets through to Srebrenica, returning with wounded, women and children. (Note that the Serbs continue to impede many aid convoys.)

21 March 1993. Morillon negotiates for the evacuation of Serbs from Tuzla and for air and land corridors from Srebrenica, although he descibes the negotiations as separate and not part of a reciprocal deal.

22 March 1993. The Bosnian government brings charges against the Federal Republic of Yugoslavia before the International Court of Justice in The Hague, including genocide and other war crimes. Public hearings are to begin on 1 April. (The court is the main judicial arm of the UN. It cannot force countries to implement its decisions, but it influences international opinion and its recommendations can be enforced by the UN Security Council.)

23 March 1993. In a pessimistic assessment, Lord Owen criticizes the Bosnian government's boycott of the most recent negotiations (due to the fighting in eastern Bosnia). He thinks that the Serbs will not sign the Vance–Owen plan. Of Karadzic, Lord Owen says that 'It is very clear that he still wants his Republic of Srpska' (the self-proclaimed Serbian state in Bosnia). But Karadzic says he will continue to negotiate.

24 March 1993. The evacuation of wounded by helicopter from Srebrenica begins, but shelling by Serbs quickly leads to its suspension.

25 March 1993. The first session involving all three parties leads to a major breakthrough. President Izetbegovic of Bosnia-Hercegovina (in that capacity) signs a somewhat modified map after coming under international pressure. The change is agreed to by the Croats (who continue to do well out of the plan; in any case there is little doubt that the ultimate aim is still a 'Greater Croatia'). The change involves expanding Sarajevo province and placing it under the dominance of the ethnic (here Moslem) majority (as in the other provinces). The city of Sarajevo itself is to be a separate capital district administered by the coalition government. Croatian provincial majorities are reduced from three to two, with Travnik coming under dual Croat/Moslem control. The Moslems and Croats also agree to set up a federal border police. They also sign what has become part of the Vance–Owen plan, namely an agreement on the interim government prior to elections.

The Serbs signed neither the map nor the interim government and thus became isolated. Karadzic reserved his position. President Clinton indicated that he would again consider such actions as lifting the arms embargo on the Bosnian government if the Serbs refused to sign up to all aspects of the Vance–Owen plan.

26 March 1993. The three military factions agree to a cease-fire starting at noon on 28 March.

27 March 1993. France joins the air drops.

28 March 1993. The cease-fire begins at noon. Germany joins the air drop.

29 March 1993. The evacuation of Srebrenica continues, by road. Lives are lost along the way to Tuzla owing to overcrowding of the lorries.

30 March 1993. Two Bosnian Serbs are sentenced to death in Sarajevo for murder, rape and robbery in the first war crimes trial. Morillon says that the cases should be turned over to an international war crimes tribunal.

31 March 1993. Another evacuation of Srebrenica by lorry is chaotic and lives are lost in the pandemonium. A temporary halt is called to further evacuations until control is established. (Note that the UN was criticized by local Moslem forces for abetting ethnic cleansing, but the UN argued, apart from the humanitarian case, that most of those evacuated had already been ethnically cleansed from areas outside Srebrenica.)

The UN Security Council votes to enforce the 'no fly' zone, although, at Russia's behest, aircraft on the ground are excluded (provided there is no danger to the enforcing planes, such as radar locking on to them). There is a seven-day period of grace before it comes into effect and a further seven days before enforcement commences.

1 April 1993. The Serbs say that they will allow only empty lorries into Srebrenica, thus preventing aid deliveries but furthering the evacuation. The Bosnian Serb 'parliament' begins its discussions on whether to accept the Vance–Owen proposals.

2 April 1993. Thorwald Stoltenberg, the foreign minister of Norway, accepts the invitation to replace Cyrus Vance, who wishes to retire at the end of the month on the grounds of ill health. The cease-fire begins to break down, with fighting around Srebrenica.

3 April 1993. The Bosnian Serb 'parliament' rejects the Vance–Owen map, but suggests direct talks between the three warring parties. There is heavier fighting, especially in eastern Bosnia. The Security Council asks the UN to send more peacekeeping troops to Srebrenica.

4 April 1993. Local Moslem forces prevent the continued evacuation of Srebrenica on the grounds that it furthers 'ethnic cleansing'.

5 April 1993. The UN aims to evacuate up to 15,000 refugees from Srebrenica (in addition to the 5,000 or so already moved out). The population of the town had been swollen to 20,000 and that of the enclave as a whole to 40,000–60,000.

The Western European Union (WEU) is to tighten the economic blockade of Yugoslavia on the Danube by means of patrol boats (crews would also be provided).

6 April 1993. Local Moslem authorities again refuse to allow further evacuation from Srebrenica (they demanded a UN battalion of peacekeepers and the flying out of wounded soldiers).

The Croats and Serbs reach agreement on a cease-fire in the Krajina region of Croatia (although it needs ratification by Serb deputies meeting on 10 April). Croatian forces are to withdraw behind the 1992 cease-fire line, the Serbs are to return their heavy weapons to UN custody and the 'pink zones' are to be placed under the control of the UN protection force (instead of being under the authority of the Serbian police). (It seems that most of the terms of the agreement were not carried out and periodic shelling continued.)

The first anniversary of the siege of Sarajevo. The Bosnian Medical Crisis Committee provided the following figures for the end of March 1993 (*IHT*, 7 April 1993, pp. 1, 4). Nearly 140,000 civilians had been killed or classified as missing throughout Bosnia, including 8,565 in Sarajevo. An additional 2,500 Bosnian soldiers had died in the siege of Sarajevo, while 50,000 residents of the city had been wounded (nearly 16,000 seriously).

8 April 1993. The evacuation of Srebrenica continues.

The Serbs discover arms on a UN aid convoy from Sarajevo to one of its districts.

The German Constitutional Court gives provisional permission for Germans to take part in the enforcement of the 'no fly' zone as radar operators in Awacs surveillance flights. This is the first combat role for German armed service personnel since the Second World War (the court was called in to determine whether the constitution allowed them any role outside the Nato area).

The International Court of Justice (which pronounces on inter-state disputes in the light of international law) gives its verdict on the charges brought by the Bosnian government. 'The government of the Federal Republic of Yugoslavia should immediately, in pursuance of its undertaking in the [1948 Genocide] Convention, take all measures within its powers to prevent commission of the crime of genocide . . . ensure that any military, paramilitary or irregular armed units which may be directed or supported by it . . . do not commit any acts of genocide.' (On 13 September 1993 the International Court said that its 8 April ruling had to be 'immediately and effectively implemented' by Yugoslavia because of the 'commission of heinous acts' in Bosnia which had 'shocked the conscience of the world'. But the court was not satisfied that both sides had done all they could to prevent genocide and refused to give any ruling that would have led to a lifting of the arms embargo against the Bosnian government.)

Macedonia is admitted to the UN (member no. 181) under the temporary name of 'The former Yugoslav republic of Macedonia', pending international arbitration over a final name. (On 13 October 1993 China recognized the country as 'The Republic of Macedonia'. On 21 October 1993 Belgium became the eleventh EU member state to recognize Macedonia, although under its temporary name.)

9 April 1993. The Serbs agree to enforce the cease-fire around Srebrenica, but not to allow the stationing of UN troops there. Morillon is prevented from returning to the town.

10 April 1993. The cease-fire is not enforced and the evacuation of Srebrenica is again halted.

12 April 1993. Enforcement of the 'no fly' zone begins, the first ever combat role for Nato (although, of course, under the authority of the UN). There had been over 500 violations of the flight ban prior to this (*IHT*, 13 April 1993, p. 1). (In fact, the violations continued.)

Srebrenica comes under heavy shelling and there are a large number killed (fifty-six, including fifteen children) and even more injured. Sarajevo is also shelled.

The discussion in the UN Security Council about tighter sanctions on Yugoslavia, already delayed, is postponed to 26 April at the request of Russia (the problem of the traditional sympathy in Russia for the Serbs is aggravated by the forthcoming referendum in Russia on 25 April).

There are many reports of a potential problem as regards the quantities of food aid supplied by donor countries.

13 April 1993. The evacuation of Srebrenica continues.

France announces that Morillon is to be replaced (retracted on 18 April).

The former British prime minister Margaret Thatcher (now Baroness Thatcher) launches a savage attack on Western policy towards Bosnia. 'We cannot go on with this policy, namely feeding people but leaving the innocent to be massacred. That seems to me to leave two possibilities. The first is to see the Bosnian Muslims are armed; after all, everyone has a right to self-defence . . . and also to give full air cover, if need be with ground attack. The other alternative is an ultimatum to the Serbs about the Owen–Vance plan . . . I am ashamed of the EC . . . the West, by not doing more, has been a little like an accomplice to massacre . . . I have never suggested that we put in ground forces, except to implement the Owen–Vance plan.'

16 April 1993. The imminent fall of Srebrenica to the Serbs produces a very strong international reaction. The UN Security Council declares the town and its environs a 'safe area' (an area safe from 'armed attack or any other hostile act'; the idea stemmed from the 'safe havens' for the Kurds in Iraq), calls for an end to the fighting and threatens stronger measures if UN troops are not allowed through. President Clinton rules out only ground troops (peacemaking as opposed to peacekeeping) and Lord Owen raises the possibility of severing Serb military supply lines in Bosnia (e.g. by bombing roads and bridges).

17 April 1993. The UN Security Council, with Russia and China abstaining, votes to tighten sanctions on Yugoslavia unless the Vance–Owen plan is accepted. Implementation is delayed until 26 April (the day after the Russian referendum). The sanctions are as follows: (1) a ban on the transport of goods to or through Yugoslavia except for permitted humanitarian supplies; (2) a ban on Yugoslav traffic on the Danube outside the Federal Republic of Yugoslavia's own borders, while other vessels passing through Yugoslavia must be approved and carry a monitor; (3) a maritime exclusion zone barring all unauthorized vessels (Yugoslav vessels are prohibited from passing through the territorial waters of UN member countries); (4) the freezing of financial assets held overseas; (5) the impounding of Yugoslav means of transport found abroad, which can be confiscated if found violating sanctions (those from other countries can be detained if suspected of violating sanctions and confiscated if found guilty); a ban on services to Yugoslavia except for postal, telecommunication and legal services and those specifically permitted.

A cease-fire is agreed, to start the following day. Srebrenica is declared a demilitarized area, but only Moslem forces have to hand in their weapons (to UN troops by 21 April).

18 April 1993. About 150 (Canadian) UN troops arrive. An airlift by helicopter starts to evacuate the seriously sick and wounded. Karadzic talks of 'the twilight of the international community'. 'They can do whatever they want. We have to follow our own needs and our own survival.'

There is fierce fighting in parts of central Bosnia, such as Vitez, between Croats and Moslems. The main cause is the wish to have full control over areas allotted under the Vance–Owen plan (including a struggle for control of transport routes, especially those needed for the supply of arms). The Croats (guilty of most of the 'ethnic cleansing') demand that Moslem soldiers should withdraw or take orders from them. The critics of the Vance–Owen plan argue that such fighting is to be expected, since the plan actually encourages ethnic cleansing.

19 April 1993. The helicopter airlift is completed.

20 April 1993. Local Moslem forces prevent further evacuation of Srebrenica.

There are reports of atrocities, especially of atrocities committed by Croats.

The Serb 'parliaments' in Croatia and Bosnia declare a 'Union of Parliaments' and fix the first session for 24 April.

21 April 1993. The UN troops declare Srebrenica to be demilitarized, with Moslems' weapons handed in and being destroyed (although it seems that many Moslem fighters took to the hills, probably with their weapons). The UN troops declare themselves ready to defend the remaining inhabitants.

22 April 1993. The defence of Srebrenica is more clearly spelt out. The UN forces will protect the demilitarized zone as peacekeepers; if somebody tries to enter by force then force will be used in self-defence.

23 April 1993. Lord Owen raises the possibility of a UN-patrolled, demilitarized zone 5 km either side of the road in northern Bosnia (the 'corridor') linking Serbian areas to help ensure free access. Local police will be entitled to be armed (handguns only). Otherwise there will be a ban on the transport of arms or military personnel belonging to the warring parties. The Serbs reject the proposal.

The Bosnian Serbs' self-styled 'parliament' reconvenes.

24 April 1993. The Moslems and Croats agree a cease-fire (the response was patchy).

Lord Owen suggests that there may be some limited room for altering provincial boundaries in negotiations when the three sides sign all sections of the Vance–Owen plan.

26 April 1993. Full sanctions come into force when the Bosnian Serb assembly ('parliament') rejects the remaining elements of the Vance–Owen plan (the map and the arrangements for the interim administration). This was despite a letter from Slobodan Milosevic (president of Serbia), Momir Bulatovic (president of Montenegro) and Dobrica Cosic (president of Yugoslavia) which said that 'This is a question of war and peace and we choose peace. You have no right to jeopardize and expose ten million Yugoslav citizens to international sanctions . . . This is not a time to compete in patriotism. It is a time for a careful, farsighted and courageous decision. An unnecessary war can bring nothing but evil and suffering.'

27 April 1993. A Serbian unit from the Krajina region of Croatia attacks Bihac in north-west Bosnia (Karadzic disowns the move). The UN force commander in Bosnia orders UN troops in the enclave to protect citizens if they are attacked. Bosnian Serbs attack towns in eastern Bosnia such as Gorazde.

Fresh from his referendum win, Yeltsin warns that 'The Russian Federation will not protect those who resist the will of the world community. Serbian nationalists and other parties in the conflict who rely on force will bear the brunt of UN retaliation. The time has come for decisive measures to quell the conflict.'

28 April 1993. A UN Security Council fact-finding mission to Bosnia recommends that Sarajevo, Gorazde, Tuzla and Zepa should be designated 'safe areas'. (Gorazde's population has increased from 37,000 to 60,000.)

29 April 1993. The Bosnian Serb 'parliament' is to reconvene on 5 May to reconsider the Vance–Owen plan.

Unprofor reveals that thirty-nine of its (24,915) members have been killed in the whole of the former Yugoslavia since March 1992 and 414 wounded. On 2 June 1993 it was announced that the numbers had reached forty-two and 500 respectively. A later source reveals that of Unprofor's 27,088 troops fifty-five had died and 613 had become casualties (*The Guardian*, 27 August 1993, p. 6). (The UN has 10,300 troops in Bosnia, 2,900 in Sarajevo; Russia has no troops in Bosnia but 860 in Croatia: *The Independent*, 1 September 1993, p. 7.)

1 May 1993. After intensive deliberations the Clinton administration comes to the conclusion that 'military steps' are to be recommended (these are not publicly revealed but apparently include air strikes and an end to the arms embargo on the Bosnian government). A series of consultations begins.

2 May 1993. The possibility of Western military action, the tightened embargo and Yeltsin's success in the 25 April referendum result in sufficient

Yugoslav pressure being put upon Karadzic to sign the remaining parts of the Vance–Owen plan (including the map). (It was agreed that the withdrawing Serbian forces would be replaced by UN and not Bosnian government or Croat forces.) Karadzic threatens to resign if the Bosnian Serb 'parliament' ('the assembly of the Republic of Srpska') does not back him when it reconvenes on 5 May. But Karadzic also emphasizes that the idea of a separate Serbian state is 'neither dead nor buried, only postponed.' (There was considerable support for the argument that the long-term aims of the Serbs remained the same.)

There is a cautious international response to these developments. President Clinton, for example, says that 'We will judge intentions by actions.' Sanctions would be lifted only gradually, in line with the implementation of the Vance–Owen plan. Lord Owen estimates that 50,000 UN troops will be needed to implement the Vance–Owen plan.

3 May 1993. The USA continues its attempts to reach consensus on military action against the Bosnian Serbs in case the Vance–Owen plan is not implemented.

4 May 1993. The Serbs attack Zepa.

5 May 1993. Russia agrees to send peacekeeping troops to Bosnia if the Vance–Owen plan is accepted by all sides (specifically to guard the land corridor between Serbia and Bosnian Serb territory). If there is no agreement the USA and Russia 'will immediately resume discussion of new, tougher measures. No measures are prejudged or excluded from consideration.'

Lord Owen makes the controversial statement that UN forces should be prepared to fight if necessary to enforce the plan; they should be employed even if the Bosnian Serb 'parliament' rejects the Vance–Owen plan.

6 May 1993. The Bosnian Serb 'parliament' does not accept the Vance–Owen plan and instead votes fifty-one to two (with twelve abstentions) to hold a referendum on 15–16 May 1993 in the Serb-held areas of Bosnia (remaining non-Serbs would be eligible to vote). This was despite the personal appearances of and appeals to accept the plan by the three Yugoslav presidents (the Greek Prime Minister Constantine Mitsotakis was also present). In response the Serbian government vows to cut off all but humanitarian supplies (food and medicines) to the Bosnian Serbs; its statement says that 'Reasons no longer exist for further assistance in money, fuel, raw materials, etc.'. The Yugoslav federal government backs the statement. (The blockade was formally to begin on 8 May, but no UN monitors were allowed and the sanctions were not implemented.)

The UN Security Council grants 'safe area' status to Sarajevo, Bihac, Gorazde, Tuzla and Zepa.

9 May 1993. A cease-fire between the forces of the Bosnian government and Bosnian Serbs comes into effect. It is agreed that Srebrenica and Zepa should be designated 'demilitarized zones'. In the case of Zepa this involves

UN troops collecting all weapons inside the zone, with Moslem fighters refusing to comply being asked to leave. Once the Serbs are satisfied that the zone is demilitarized, they will begin to pull back.

Heavy fighting breaks out in Mostar between Croats and Moslems. There is further evidence of 'ethnic cleansing' by the Croats.

10 May 1993. The UN Security Council condemns the Croat attack and demands the withdrawal of their forces from Mostar. A cease-fire is declared between the Croats and Moslems, but fighting continues.

11 May 1993. Presidents Milosevic, Cosic and Bulatovic and the Croatian Serb leader Goran Hadzic issue an invitation to the Bosnian Serbs to attend a joint parliamentary session in Belgrade on 14 May rather than hold a referendum on the Vance–Owen plan. (The invitation was not taken up.)

The USA has failed to date to persuade the Europeans to support its proposal that the embargo on arms sales to the Bosnian government should be lifted. (The Clinton administration had suggested a 'lift and strike' strategy, lifting the embargo and bombing the Serbs until Bosnian government forces were sufficiently armed to prevent a predicted pre-emptive Serbian offensive; the Europeans, while not ruling out air strikes in principle, suggested that US troops should join in defending the 'safe areas'.)

The strongest evidence of a growing rift between the USA and Europe over Bosnia comes in comments made by Joseph Biden (Democrat, Delaware), a member of the Senate Foreign Relations Committee. He sees in European policy 'a discouraging mosaic of indifference, timidity, self-delusion and hypocrisy. Let's not mince words. European policy is based on cultural and religious indifference if not bigotry, and I think it's fair to say this would be an entirely different situation if the Muslims were doing what the Serbs have done. The truth of this is not lost on the Islamic world. Let me speak as plainly as I can. I can't even begin to express my anger for a European policy that's now asking us to participate in what amounts to a codification of a Serbian victory.' What is happening in Bosnia is not a civil war 'but a blatant act of Serbian expansion'; the Serbs are guilty of 'fascist thuggery'. The European troops in Bosnia should be removed if they are going to be used as an excuse to avoid taking military action.

12 May 1993. Another cease-fire in Mostar fails to hold. The Croats are proved to be holding Moslems in detention camps.

13 May 1993. Another cease-fire in Mostar fails to stop the fighting.

The EU sends a letter to President Tudjman of Croatia. It warns of the possibility of sanctions if Croat attacks on Moslems do not stop.

14 May 1993. A Serb attack on the northern Bosnian town of Brcko (on the important supply corridor linking Serb areas) is a serious violation of the cease-fire.

The pan-Serb assembly meets in Belgrade, with the Bosnian Serbs and the Croatian Serbs sending only observer delegations. A large number of ultranationalists walked out before the vote was taken to accept the Vance–Owen plan.

15–16 May 1993. Two questions are asked in the Bosnian Serb referendum: 'Are you for or against the Vance–Owen plan?' 'Are you for or against an independent Republic of Srpska which has the right to unite with other nations and states?' It was announced that 96 per cent of voters had rejected the plan and a similar percentage had voted in favour in response to the second question. On 19 May, when the result was announced, the so-called 'parliament' declared that it would abide by the cease-fire agreements with the Moslems and Croats. Karadzic declared that the Vance–Owen plan was 'dead', but that the Bosnian Serbs were ready to accept a confederation of separate ethnic states. The international community considered the referendum to be irrelevant and meaningless (given the 'ethnic cleansing' that had gone on).

16 May 1993. Bosnian Serbs and Croats sign a cease-fire, to come into effect throughout Bosnia on 18 May.

Russia's foreign minister, Andrei Kozyrev, calls for the 'progressive implementation' of the Vance–Owen plan even in the event of a 'no' vote in the referendum. He indicates that Russia is prepared to contribute troops to monitor the borders of Bosnia. On 18 May Kozyrev publicly outlined a four-point programme: (1) the complete implementation of UN sanctions; (2) the sealing of the border between Serbia and Bosnia; (3) the immediate creation of safe 'havens' in Sarajevo and six enclaves; (4) the setting up of an international war crimes tribunal.

18 May 1993. A 21 May meeting of the foreign ministers of the UN Security Council (called by Russia in its capacity as rotating president) is called off when the USA refuses to attend. (This was generally considered to be another indication of friction.)

Another cease-fire between Moslems and Croats is announced, to come into effect the following day (but some fighting still went on).

19 May 1993. Tadeusz Mazowiecki, the UN human rights investigator, says that owing to the lack of an effective international response the Vance–Owen plan has actually accelerated 'ethnic cleansing'.

20 May 1993. It appears that the Croats have released most of the 1,800 or so Moslem detainees.

21 May 1993. President Cosic of Yugoslavia rejects the proposal to place UN monitors on the border between Serbia and Bosnia to ensure the implementation of Yugoslav sanctions on the Bosnian Serbs.

22 May 1993. The foreign ministers of the USA, France, Russia, the UK and Spain, meeting in Washington, reveal a joint programme to contain the Bosnian crisis:

1. 'The economic sanctions imposed by the UN Security Council against Serbia and Montenegro must be rigorously enforced by all members of the UN until the necessary conditions set out in Security Council resolution

820, including the withdrawal of Bosnian Serb troops from territories occupied by force, are met for lifting the sanctions.'

2. 'We note the pledge of the Belgrade authorities to close the border with Bosnia-Hercegovina, in order to accept the peace plan. We are watching to see whether the border closure is effective. Although the primary responsibility for enforcing this step belongs to Belgrade, we can assist, for instance, by placing monitors on the borders or providing technical expertise or conducting aerial surveillance. We also note the willingness expressed by the Zagreb authorities for monitoring to take place along the border between Croatia and Bosnia-Hercegovina.'

3. 'The concept of "safe areas" in Bosnia could make a valuable contribution . . . The USA is prepared to help protect Unprofor forces.' (Note that the USA refused to contribute troops; the six areas already designated were Sarajevo, Bihac, Gorazde, Srebrenica, Tuzla and Zepa.)

4. 'We support the rapid establishment of the war crimes tribunal, so that those guilty of atrocities may be brought to justice.'

5. 'Negotiated settlement in Bosnia, building on the Vance–Owen process [note the word "process" rather than "plan"] and international co-operation, is the way a durable peace can be established . . . To the extent that the parties decide to implement promptly mutually agreed provisions of the Vance–Owen plan, this is to be encouraged.'

6. 'We are deeply concerned about the fighting between Bosnian Croat and Bosnian government forces and the related "ethnic cleansing", and we agree that Croatia should be put on notice that assistance to Bosnian Croat forces engaged in these activities could result in the international community imposing sanctions.'

7. 'We will co-operate closely to enhance efforts to contain the conflict and prevent the possibility that it will spill over into neighbouring countries . . . It is essential that everyone in the region understands that aggression against the former Yugoslav republic of Macedonia would have grave consequences. We will support an increase in the international presence there. The USA is considering a contribution to this . . . We favour an increase in the international monitoring presence in Kosovo. Human rights should be respected in this formerly autonomous region, although we do not support declarations of independence there.'

8. 'We will keep open options for new and tougher measures, none of which is prejudged or excluded from consideration.'

(Note that Lord Owen and Thorwald Stoltenberg were not consulted, and Germany and Italy complained that they too were not asked to attend the meeting.)

The supporters of the new plan stressed the importance of the Western powers and Russia taking a united stance, given the history of Germany siding with Croatia and France and Russia siding with Serbia. On 23 May Karadzic praised the 'more realistic approach . . . The reality is that Bosnia-

Hercegovina is already divided.' Karadzic promised to co-operate 'provided that our sovereignty is respected'. He called for talks with Croats and Moslems to create separate ethnic states in Bosnia.

President Izetbegovic of Bosnia, on the other hand, described the plan as 'totally unacceptable'. It rewards 'Serbian aggression and genocide'. 'The aggressor is not going to withdraw from the occupied territories and our people who have been evicted will not be allowed to return to their homes.' The idea of 'safe areas' was an attempt to put the Bosnian people in 'reservations'. Other critics of the programme made the following points, among others: (1) the refusal to use force means that Serbian gains would undoubtedly remain; the Vance–Owen plan was effectively dead and the new programme merely an exercise in diplomatic face-saving; (2) monitoring (not control) of the Bosnian–Serb border depended on Serbian permission (ruled out by the Yugoslav president); (3) the 'safe areas' would become no more than refugee camps, with no chance of becoming self-reliant (the Moslems would become the Palestinians of Europe; there were already reports of a breakdown of law and order in Srebrenica); shortly before, President Clinton himself had raised the spectre of another Lebanon or Northern Ireland, while the US secretary of state, Warren Christopher, had only two weeks earlier described such areas as ethnic ghettos that would mean acceptance of 'ethnic cleansing' (the USA was clearly reluctant to go along with the programme, but did so in order to preserve a united front); (4) the US protection (if asked for and only via air strikes) applied only to Unprofor forces and not to Bosnian civilians.

25 May 1993. Milosevic rules out UN monitors on the border between Serbia and Bosnia.

The UN Security Council approves the setting up of a war crimes tribunal for the former Yugoslavia, the first since the Nuremberg trials (although the death penalty is not available this time).

27 May 1993. The Serbs continue to attack Maglaj as part of the aim of securing a northern corridor (the attack had begun almost two weeks before). Serious fighting between Croats and Moslems in Mostar is reported.

28 May 1993. The Serbs launch a large-scale attack on Gorazde, the last large town in eastern Bosnia not to have been captured or neutralized by the Serbs. The Bosnian government claims that the neutralization of a 'safe area' simply allows the Serbs to redirect their units elsewhere.

29 May 1993. Three Italian aid convoy drivers (not under UN escort) are murdered (probably by Moslems).

30 May 1993. Heavy fighting breaks out in Sarajevo.

1 June 1993. Two Danish aid convoy drivers and a local interpreter (with a UN escort) are killed outside Maglaj (by deliberate Serb shelling).

President Dobrica Cosic of Yugoslavia loses his position after a no-confidence vote in the federal parliament. He was accused of encouraging the army to stage a coup, holding secret negotiations with the Croats over Krajina and being willing to divide Kosovo. The ousting is seen as a victory for Milosevic and Vojislav Seselj (leader of the extreme nationalist Serbian Radical Party). But it is also seen as a further widening of the rift with Montenegro, whose parliamentarians supported Cosic. Montenegro also favours allowing UN monitors along the Serb–Bosnia border to enforce Serbia's sanctions against the Bosnian Serbs.

A demonstration in Belgrade by supporters of opposition parties (the immediate cause of which was the assault in parliament on a Party of Serbian Renewal MP by a Serbian Radical Party MP) is violently crushed by the large, well paid and heavily armed police force (one policeman dies; the police are a powerful, 70,000–80,000 strong force (up from 40,000) deliberately built up by Milosevic as a counter to the army, where Cosic has support).

2 June 1993. Following the demonstration, Vuk Draskovic (leader of the Party of Serbian Renewal) is arrested and badly beaten by the police (there was no international outcry, mainly because at the time Milosevic was being courted to help bring over the Bosnian Serbs). (On 1 July Draskovic went on hunger strike; he had been charged with obstructing the police and incitement to riot. On 9 July Milosevic granted a pardon and ordered his release after belated international pressure and the threat of internal demonstrations. On 6 October the last charge of assaulting a policeman was dropped.)

Cosic declares that 'What happened in the federal parliament was a classic Stalinist act, hounding the president out of office through slander.' Milosevic 'could not bear my opposing of his self-will in his own passionate love of power.' Milosevic 'had misinterpreted my normal working meeting with the Yugoslav army . . . he panicked and imagined a military coup was being prepared to throw him out of power. The ideological pupil of Stalin and Tito invented the minutes.'

3 June 1993. Karadzic announces that he has ordered a cease-fire in Gorazde, but fighting continues.

4 June 1993. The UN Security Council approves the sending of troops to the six 'safe areas', with the ability to use force (including calling air strikes) to protect themselves. The troops are authorized 'to take the necessary measures, including the use of force' if the aid convoys are obstructed or there are 'bombardments against the safe areas by any of the parties or armed incursions into them' (it is not clear whether the protection applies only to Unprofor troops). The secretary-general is asked to report on how many of the existing 9,000 UN troops in Bosnia can be redeployed to the areas and member countries are appealed to for additional troops.

The Bosnian ambassador to the UN, Mohammed Sacirbey, is highly critical of the concept of 'safe areas'. He argues that 'new non-safe areas' are thereby created. 'What motivates at least some of the co-sponsors is a diplomatic cover to mitigate the need and responsibility for more resolute and comprehensive measures.' Srebrenica is an 'open concentration camp' where disease, hunger and despair 'have replaced shells and bullets as the tools of genocide'.

6 June 1993. The Serb assembly in the Krajina region of Croatia announces that a referendum is to be held on 19–20 June on the question of whether to link up with the Bosnian Serbs (with the option of joining Serbia later on).

7 June 1993. The Bosnian government accepts the 'safe areas' subject to the following conditions: they are expanded to include economic hinterlands; they are linked by UN-protected corridors; the UN posts monitors along the borders of Bosnia; Serb artillery is withdrawn out of range; there is international endorsement of the Vance–Owen plan as a final settlement.

Moslem forces drive Croat militia and civilians from Travnik with heavy loss of life (Travnik was originally designated a Croat area, but, as was seen above, the 25 March 1993 amendment placed it under dual Croat–Moslem control). Around 1,000 of the Croat militia volunteer to surrender to the Serbs. This retaliatory large-scale 'ethnic cleansing' by Moslems (many of whom had themselves been victims elsewhere) is seen by critics as the direct result of a Western policy that has failed to deter Serbian and Croat aggression.

9 June 1993. The Bosnian military commander orders a cease-fire.

10 June 1993. Nato agrees to provide aircraft to defend Unprofor troops if requested 'in performance of the overall mandate' (there was disagreement as to whether the protection applied to the troops throughout Bosnia or just to those in the 'safe areas').

The USA offers to send 300 troops to Macedonia as observers (there are already over 700 (Nordic) UN peacekeeping troops monitoring the borders).

A cease-fire between Moslem and Croat forces is supposed to come into effect in central Bosnia.

An 'unofficial' Moslem aid convoy (organized by the mayor of Tuzla; it went ahead against UN advice) is stopped near Novi Travnik by the Croats and some drivers are killed.

11 June 1993. Croat militia fire on part of the convoy near Vitez and on UN troops who decided to escort the convoy. The (British) troops return fire and shoot at three Croats, definitely killing one, probably killing another and wounding the third. (It is worth a reminder at this stage that the rules of engagement for UN troops, broadly self-defence, are less than clear and that the troops have to negotiate convoys through often hostile roadblocks.)

13 June 1993. The Bosnian collective presidency orders a cease-fire between Moslems and Croats. (The Bosnian army chief and the Bosnian Croat military leader were responsible for carrying out the cease-fire, but it did not seem to be very effective.)

14 June 1993. Boutros Boutros-Ghali recommends at least 7,500 additional UN troops to guard the safe areas.

15 June 1993. The military commanders of the three warring factions in Bosnia agree to a cease-fire as of noon on 18 June.

A local deal between Serbs and Croats in Celibici (south-west Bosnia) involves a formal exchange of people and property.

16 June 1993. Presidents Izetbegovic, Milosevic and Tudjman meet in Geneva under the auspices of the UN and the EU. Milosevic and Tudjman agree to a confederation of three ethnic states in Bosnia, but Izetbegovic walks out because of the continuing Serb attack on Gorazde (where UN monitors are finally allowed through by the Serbs). The Moslem state would be divided into two (central Bosnia around Sarajevo, Zenica and Tuzla and Bihac in the north-west); there would also be access to the (Croatian) port of Ploce on the Adriatic. The Croat state would also be divided in two. The Serb state would be in one contiguous area.

The new Yugoslavia is expelled from the seat at Gatt held by the former Yugoslavia.

17 June 1993. Lord Owen admits that the Vance–Owen plan is essentially dead and recommends negotiations on the Serb–Croat plan as the only realistic alternative. Izetbegovic says that the new plan would only encourage further 'ethnic cleansing'. General criticisms include the following: in the absence of a Western threat to use force Bosnia will shrink to a rump Moslem state as 'Greater Serbia' and 'Greater Croatia' are formed; ethnic cleansing is rewarded and indeed further encouraged; borders are changed by force, setting a dangerous precedent; Serbian aggression will be directed to other areas such as Kosovo.

18 June 1993. Germany rejects an accusation by US Secretary of State Warren Christopher. Christopher maintains that Germany bears 'particular responsibility' for events in the former Yugoslavia by having pressed allies into early recognition of Croatia, Slovenia and Bosnia.

The UN Security Council agrees to send 7,600 troops to defend the safe areas and welcomes the US offer of 300 troops for Macedonia.

The cease-fire is ignored to a considerable extent.

19–20 June 1993. A referendum is held by the Serbs in Croatia. The question asked is 'Are you for a sovereign Republic of Krajina and its unification with other Serbian countries?'

20 June 1993. President Izetbegovic says that the use of chemical weapons cannot be ruled out if the arms embargo remains.

Lord Owen, addressing EU foreign ministers, suggests negotiating for a 'viable mini-state' for the Moslems.

21–22 June 1993. At the EU summit Chancellor Kohl of Germany argues unsuccessfully in favour of a partial lifting of the arms embargo on the Bosnian government (he had received a letter from President Clinton which said, 'I would urge that you support lifting the embargo when you meet with your colleagues tomorrow'). The summit pledged more money and troops for the 'safe areas'.

President Izetbegovic also requested a limited amount of arms for defensive purposes, arguing that nothing else would make the 'aggressors' negotiate seriously. (Note that there are rumours of a split in the Bosnian collective presidency, with some in favour of a more positive attitude towards negotiations on the Serb–Croat plan. The leader of the isolated and relatively unscathed north-western enclave of Bihac, Fikret Abdic, is considered to be a possible alternative president; he actually received more votes than Izetbegovic in the 1990 election; Abdic is a wealthy businessman who has gone on trading (via Agrokomerc) with the Croats and the Serbs. In 1987 Abdic was jailed for issuing unbacked promissory notes in the Agrokomerc scandal, an enterprise that he had built up.)

21 June 1993. Cyrus Vance adopts an attitude different from that of Lord Owen. Vance says, 'I'm very saddened by what I think is a tragic mistake in moving to a new plan. It will end up rewarding those involved in ethnic cleansing.'

22 June 1993. An aid convoy reaches Gorazde.

23 June 1993. The Geneva talks resume. Seven of the nine-member (three from each of the main ethnic groups) Bosnian collective presidency attend. President Izetbegovic and Vice-President Ejup Ganic refuse to join the other members (who include the Croatian and Serbian members of the presidency; there were increasing signs of tension within the presidency). (The presidency was supposed to rotate, but a special clause in the constitution was invoked in December 1992 to enable Izetbegovic's term to be extended for the duration of the war.)

25 June 1993. Zoran Lilic (a supporter of Milosevic) becomes the new president of the Federal Republic of Yugoslavia.

27 June 1993. Serbs and Croats join forces to fight the Moslems in northern and central Bosnia and agree to a truce in south-west Bosnia.

29 June 1993. The (fifteen-member) UN Security Council rejects a proposal to lift the arms embargo on the Bosnian government. Nine abstained and six voted for the proposal (of the five permanent members, namely the USA, France, the UK, Russia and China, only the USA voted for the proposal; the UK, France and Russia would have used their veto if necessary).

The collective Bosnian presidency meet and appoint a three-member committee to draw up a joint response to the Serb–Croat plan.

A joint Serb–Croat offensive in central Bosnia causes a setback for Bosnian government forces.

30 June 1993. The UN mandate in Croatia is further extended, for three months.

1 July 1993. Gorazde comes under heavy artillery attack by the Serbs.

The Serbs try to exact money tolls per vehicle (allegedly for road repairs) from aid convoys (they already typically receive part of the aid in kind), but the UN refuses.

2 July 1993. Maglaj is encircled.

The Federal Republic of Yugoslavia refuses to allow the mandate of CSCE observers within the republic to be extended.

The US State Department repeats the threat originally made by ex-president Bush in December 1992: the USA 'remains prepared to respond against the Serbs in the event of conflict in Kosovo caused by Serbian action' (US officials say it would mean bombing Serbia: *The Economist*, 24 July 1993, p. 41).

4 July 1993. Philippe Morillon is replaced by another Frenchman as commander of UN forces in Bosnia.

7 July 1993. Amnesty International reports that in 1992 in Bosnia 'the majority of the victims were Muslims and the main perpetrators were local Serbian armed forces' (*The Times*, 8 July 1993, p. 12).

Croatian police raid the offices of the Croatian Party of Rights. (Its leader, Dobroslav Paraga, and others are to be tried for allegedly attempting to overthrow Tudjman's government. The CPR's policy is to restore the Second World War Ustasha state, and it has a military wing called the Croatian Armed Forces.)

8 July 1993. Izetbegovic accepts that Bosnia could become a confederation of ethnic states if the Serbs and Croats presented no alternative. In a radio interview he says that 'Bosnia is not going to commit suicide. Illusions cannot keep people alive. We have to say clearly: if it is going to be division it is going to be ethnic division, unfortunately. It is acceptable to us only if we are forced. The other option is war without end. It is a very ugly option.'

The communiqué of the G7 meeting (held in Tokyo on 7–9 July) says that 'We cannot agree to a solution dictated by the Serbs and the Croats at the expense of the Bosnian Muslims. We will not accept any territorial solution unless it has the agreement of the three parties. If the Serbs and Croats persist in dismembering Bosnia through changes of border by force or ethnic cleansing, they will place themselves beyond the pale of the international community and cannot expect any economic or commercial assistance, especially reconstruction aid . . . Stronger measures are not excluded.' ('Stronger measures' apparently referred to the lifting of the arms embargo on the Bosnian government.)

9 July 1993. Izetbegovic, in contradiction of his statement the day before, says that 'The [collective] presidency has accepted [by seven to three] the proposal according to which Bosnia-Hercegovina would be constituted along the lines of a federal state. The number of units has not been defined, but there is no question of Sarajevo being divided along ethnic lines. In other words, the ethnic division of Bosnia-Hercegovina has been refused.'

10 July 1993. Trnovo falls to the Serbs.

11 July 1993. The Bosnian presidency puts forward its official response for the future of the country: 'the constitutional make-up of Bosnia-Hercegovina should be along the lines of a federal state in which all citizens of three nationalities will have equal rights'.

13 July 1993. The Organization of Islamic Conference offers more than 17,000 troops to boost the UN protection force in Bosnia, the countries involved being Iran (up to 10,000), Pakistan (3,000), Bangladesh (1,220), Malaysia (1,500), Tunisia (1,000), the Palestinian delegation (1,000) and Turkey (a brigade). The UN is once again called upon to lift the arms embargo on the Bosnian government (it will be recalled that the UN Security Council imposed an arms embargo on the whole of the former Yugoslavia on 25 September 1991).

A US State Department report calculates that a Milosevic map dividing Bosnia into three ethnic areas (Serbs 60 per cent, Moslems 25 per cent and Croats 15 per cent) could require the resettlement of between 1.5 million and 2 million people. There are currently 3.8 million people displaced by the war, compared with 2.4 million in December 1992 (*IHT*, 14 July 1993, p. 2).

The UN appeals for $1 billion to $1.5 billion in additional aid from donor countries. Between September 1991 and the end of June 1993 the total aid of $1.285 billion for the former Yugoslavia was donated as follows: the EU, $872 million (68 per cent of the total); the USA, $164 million (13 per cent); Japan, $32 million (2 per cent); others, $217 million (17 per cent) (*FT*, 14 July 1993, p. 2).

14 July 1993. Nato declares itself ready to defend Unprofor troops as of 22 July.

16 July 1993. Fears of another clash between Croats and Serbs over the Krajina are allayed somewhat by an agreement to replace the Maslenica bridge (destroyed in November 1991) with a pontoon bridge on 18 July. But the bridge and Zemunik airport (Zadar) are to be placed under UN protection and closed to the troops of both sides. Croat forces are supposed to withdraw from the territory captured in January. (On 27 July, however, Croatia said that it would withdraw its troops by the 31 July deadline only if the Serbs placed their heavy weapons in UN depots.)

18 July 1993. Some Serb shelling in the area delays proceedings somewhat, but both the bridge and the airport are formally opened by President Tudjman.

19 July 1993. The EU decides to send a mission to warn Croatia of possible loss of trade privileges if 'ethnic cleansing' and attacks on Moslems in Bosnia persist.

25 July 1993. A cease-fire is supposed to come into effect in Sarajevo, but fighting continues and a UN base in the capital is shelled by Serb forces.

26 July 1993. The UN threatens retaliation if its forces are attacked again.

The Geneva talks resume.

29 July 1993. The leaders of the warring factions agree to order an immediate cease-fire in Bosnia; their army commanders are instructed to meet under UN auspices in Sarajevo for as long as discussions in Geneva go on in order to discuss violations. (The fighting continued although the commanders did meet.)

President Clinton threatens retaliatory air strikes against the Serbs if UN troops are attacked again (he even hints at air strikes in defence of Sarajevo).

30 July 1993. President Izetbegovic and the other leaders of the warring factions agree to the constitutional aspects of the Owen–Stoltenberg 'compromise' plan. (But the talks soon stall.)

31 July 1993. Izetbegovic is criticized by some members of the Bosnian collective presidency. In a letter to Lord Owen Izetbegovic says that 'Yesterday I gave my preliminary approval of the draft . . . my approval was given upon your statement that the agreement does not question the status of the state for a future union and . . . its membership of the United Nations . . . I have to inform you . . . that I still have reservations regarding the wording.'

The Clinton administration announces its intention of proposing to a Nato meeting on 2 August that air strikes should be used not only to protect aid convoys but also to attack Serb positions shelling Sarajevo and other towns.

1 August 1993. The Serbs start shelling Croatian areas near the Maslenica bridge and Zemunik airport.

2 August 1993. The Maslenica bridge is partially disabled by Serb shelling and the airport is also shelled.

3 August 1993. After pressure from the USA, Nato issues the following statement: 'The alliance has now decided to make immediate preparations for undertaking, in the event that the strangulation of Sarajevo and other areas continues, including wide-scale interference with humanitarian assistance, stronger measures including air strikes against those responsible, Bosnian Serbs and others, in Bosnia-Hercegovina . . . Full co-ordination will be carried out with the United Nations.' (But there was considerable friction at first between Nato and the UN about the precise control over and extent of the air strikes.)

The three Croat members of the Bosnian presidency at the Geneva talks walk out and join the delegation from Croatia in protest at the Moslem military offensive in central Bosnia.

4 August 1993. The Serbs claim to have captured Mount Igman, the last of the high ground surrounding Sarajevo, which controls the most important Bosnian government military supply route into the city. (But it seems that the supply route was not actually cut off by the Serbs at any stage.)

5 August 1993. The talks are formally postponed until 9 August (Izetbegovic walked out on 2 August, offering to return if Serbian troops withdrew from the newly captured strategic heights). Karadzic offers to withdraw Serbian troops from Mount Igman and Mount Bjelasnica (UN forces should replace them to prevent the return of government troops) and to open two routes into the city (for UN military, relief and commercial traffic).

The desk officer on Bosnia in the US State Department, Marshall Freeman Harris, resigns: 'I can no longer serve in a Department of State that accepts the forceful dismemberment of a European state and that will not act against genocide and the Serbian officials who perpetuate it . . . The administration is driving the Bosnian government to surrender its territory and its sovereignty to the victors in a war of aggression.' (The next day witnessed the resignation of Jon Western, an analyst dealing with issues such as war crimes in the Bureau of Intelligence and Research. On 23 August 1993 Stephen Walker, a State Department official in the Office of East European Affairs, resigned: 'I can no longer countenance US support for a diplomatic process that legitimizes genocide and aggression.' These resignations followed that of George Kenney on 25 August 1992, the Yugoslav desk officer in the Bush administration.)

6 August 1993. The threat to use air strikes results in open criticism. The UN commander of UN forces in Bosnia, the Belgian Francis Briquemont, says that air strikes would complicate the situation on the ground and UN troops could suffer retaliatory attacks. Lord Owen says that the threat is a factor contributing to the Bosnian government's absence from the talks. (The US government tells the Bosnian government that there will be no air strikes unless it rejoins the talks.)

8 August 1993. Ratko Mladic, the military commander of the Bosnian Serbs, says that he has come to an agreement with General Briquemont on withdrawal from the two mountains.

9 August 1993. Nato's 'Operational options for air strikes in Bosnia-Hercegovina' says that 'It is essential that the Bosnian Serbs lift without delay the siege of Sarajevo and the heights around the city, and the means of access are placed under the control of Unprofor . . . the air strikes are limited to the support of humanitarian relief, and must not be interpreted as a decision to intervene militarily in the conflict.' Events that could trigger ('phased and proportionate') air strikes include interference with humanitarian road convoys and airlifts, failure to restore public services such as water and energy, and continuation of the shelling of Sarajevo and other 'safe areas'. The threat of air strikes is further weakened by the other conditions laid down, apart from the fact that the Nato council must agree unanimously. The UN secretary-general, Boutros Boutros-Ghali, has a veto: 'The first use of our air power in the theatre shall be authorized by him.' Normally he would have to approve requests from the commander of UN forces in the former Yugoslavia (the Frenchman General Jean Cot) via the commander of UN forces in Bosnia (the Belgian General Francis

Briquemont). Such requests are unlikely, given the concern of the UN commanders about Unprofor forces suffering retaliatory attacks.

The Serbs claim to have withdrawn from Mount Bjelasnica, but Mount Igman (the more important) remains occupied. President Izetbegovic refuses to join the talks scheduled to start today because of this.

10 August 1993. There are rumours that the Serbs may even have reoccupied Mount Bjelasnica.

11 August 1993. Owen and Stoltenberg give the Serbs until noon the following day to complete the withdrawal, while Izetbegovic gives them two days or he will abandon the talks.

The Bosnian government delegation (and others, such as Jim Hoagland, *IHT*, 11 August 1993, p. 6) accuses Owen and Stoltenberg of pressing it to accept the partition of Sarajevo. The co-chairmen deny applying pressure, saying that they had only suggested that the UN should come up with some sort of temporary arrangement for a year or so to let passions cool (but the co-chairmen do seem to think that the Serbs have legitimate territorial claims).

The three military commanders agree a comprehensive cease-fire, to take effect once the other matters are settled.

12 August 1993. There is confusion about whether Serbian troops have left the two mountains. The UN is to fix a definite line for the troops to withdraw behind.

Karadzic denies that he threatened to acquire nuclear weapons if Nato took military action.

13 August 1993. The Geneva talks are formally postponed until 16 August to give the UN a chance to verify that the Serbs have withdrawn from the two mountains (the UN said there were some 'stragglers').

14 August 1993. The UN confirms that the Serbs have more or less withdrawn. They are replaced by UN forces to prevent the retaking of the mountains by Bosnian government forces.

'Operation Irma' begins. This is an airlift of some sick and wounded people from Bosnia for treatment in British, Swedish and Irish hospitals (the Irish airlift did not start on 14 August; other countries joined in, such as Norway, Finland, Italy, France, Poland and the Czech Republic). ('Operation Irma' was so named after five-year-old Irma Hadzimuratovic, who was airlifted from Sarajevo to London on 9 August after being critically injured in a mortar attack during which her mother died. Heavy publicity in the Western media led to public reaction and government action. The little girl symbolized the suffering of her people. There was considerable friction initially, with, for example, the UN being accused of bureaucracy and the British government being accused of cheap publicity-seeking. Irma died on 1 April 1995.)

16 August 1993. The Geneva talks resume. There is agreement that UN military observers should be free to go anywhere in Bosnia. The three sides agree in principle that Sarajevo should be placed under temporary UN administration and demilitarized (except for UN forces) once a general agreement has been reached (all except the tenth municipality, Pale, the Bosnian Serbs' present headquarters, which will remain under Serb control). A committee of three will be set up to make detailed recommendations regarding the future status of the city. (A more detailed scheme was unveiled on 18 August: see the section on the Owen–Stoltenberg plan, above.)

Unprofor's chief spokesman, the Canadian lieutenant-colonel Barry Frewer, makes the highly controversial statement that the situation of Sarajevo can no longer really be described as a siege, only as 'encirclement'; the Serbs are only in 'tactically advantageous situations around the city'. (He and other Unprofor commanders also consider that it was not the threat of air strikes that caused the withdrawal of Serbian troops from the two mountains.)

The International Committee of the Red Cross confirms that the Croats are forcing Moslem captives to dig trenches and build military installations in the front lines of their siege of eastern Mostar.

18 August 1993. A row breaks out between the USA and Unprofor personnel in Bosnia. The British brigadier Vere Hayes, chief of staff of Unprofor in Bosnia, says, 'What does President Clinton think he is up to? . . . Air power won't defeat the Serbs.' General Francis Briquemont says of air strikes: 'It was a Nato warning, so it's a problem for Nato, but Nato is not the UN.'

19 August 1993. The first aid convoy (on this occasion just carrying medical aid) since 15 June 1993 reaches Croat-held western Mostar. (The UN stopped aid convoys then because of the Croat refusal to allow the convoys into Moslem-held eastern Mostar, which had not received aid since 2 June 1993. The Croats reneged on their promise to allow an aid convoy into eastern Mostar on 20 August, but allowed a medical one in the following day. Fighting between Croat and Bosnian government forces started in Mostar on 9 May 1993.)

20 August 1993. Owen and Stoltenberg present a 'compromise' peace plan to the three delegations for consideration by their respective parliaments or assemblies until 30 August 1993 (see above, on the Owen–Stoltenberg plan). The Serb and Croat representatives in Geneva give a generally positive response (Milosevic is particularly enthusiastic), but the response of the Bosnian government side is generally negative (e.g. the Serbs would hold on to land ethnically cleansed by force; the Bosnian foreign minister, Haris Siladjic, is particularly opposed).

The UN High Commission for Refugees says that 'credible reports from people fleeing the [Mostar] region point to a new campaign of so-called "ethnic cleansing" that is as brutal as any so far witnessed in the Bosnian conflict . . . There are numerous reports of brutal "ethnic cleansing", murder, looting, rape and other abuses by Bosnian Croat forces throughout the region.' About 1,500 mostly draft-age Moslem men are thought to be held in extremely poor conditions in Bosnian Croatian detention centres in the Mostar region of south-western Bosnia. The commission also reports 'various abuses' (including looting and vandalism) by Bosnian government forces against Croat families.

21 August 1993. A group of elderly Jews leaves Sarajevo. (The city has a history of tolerance here as well. For example, in 1492 around 14,000 Sephardic Jews thrown out of Spain found refuge in Sarajevo: *The Economist*, 21 August 1993, p. 33.)

A Ukrainian member of Unprofor is sent home in disgrace for black-marketeering, bringing the total to thirteen. Three French soldiers have also been sent home for war profiteering. (This was considered to be the tip of the iceberg. On 25 August a UN investigation started into allegations of widespread black-marketeering, possibly also involving aid provisions and drugs. Prostitution was also a feature of life for some Unprofor troops.)

22 August 1993. The UN warns that many people in eastern Mostar are on the verge of starvation.

There are reports of fighting in some parts of Bosnia between Serbs/Croats and Bosnian government forces in a grab for disputed territory (e.g. around Brcko and Mostar).

The Maslenica bridge in Croatia reopens amid Serb shelling in the area.

23 August 1993. The Croats continue to prevent the UN running further aid convoys into eastern Mostar.

24 August 1993. The failure of another attempt to send an aid convoy into eastern Mostar leads to the USA carrying out a food air drop.

The Bosnian Croats declare Mostar the capital of their republic and reject the idea of temporary EU administration.

25 August 1993. The first food convoy reaches western Mostar (and eastern Mostar in the early hours of the following day).

26 August 1993. There is, in effect, another purge of the Yugoslav army. Forty-two generals and admirals, including the chief of staff, are 'retired'.

28 August 1993. The civilian part of the UN aid convoy is allowed to leave eastern Mostar (having been held up by residents hoping to help prevent Croatian shelling). (But over fifty Spanish Unprofor troops escorting the convoy were forced to stay behind until 31 August.)

30 August 1993. The fiftieth anniversary of the founding of the famous liberal and secular newspaper *Oslobodenje* ('Liberation'), which has, in support of religious tolerance and ethnic harmony, gone on publishing in Sarajevo throughout the siege.

The start of a three-day conference in Geneva on the protection of war victims (it was decided to take stronger action to enforce rules protecting civilians in wartime).

31 August 1993. The Geneva talks resume after the consultation period (a day late, owing to transport problems experienced by the Bosnian government delegation).

1. The Serbs report a large majority in favour of accepting the Owen–Stoltenberg plan. They also suggest that some limited exchange of land can take place after the signing of the plan.

2. The Croats (who on 28 August formally proclaimed their own republic of Herceg-Bosna) have brought with them a demand for some territorial adjustments but offer to forgo them if the other two parties agree to the map as it is.

3. The Bosnian government reports that the plan is acceptable only as 'a basis for further negotiations'. A claim is made for an extra 4 per cent of land (part of the land taken by force and 'ethnic cleansing'), Izetbegovic describing this as the 'minimum of minimums' in order to produce a viable state. Specifically there should be (1) corridors (rather than roads) connecting the central portion to the Moslem enclaves (as is already the case with Gorazde) and the enclaves in eastern Bosnia with each other (plus Moslem control of towns in the west and north, e.g. the northern town of Prijedor with its corridor to Bihac) and (2) access to the Adriatic via a corridor (from Stolac in the south-west) to Neum. These corridors would be under the control of the Moslem-led government (Neum and the adjacent 20 km or twelve-mile stretch of coastline is the only part of Bosnia-Hercegovina fronting the sea and in the Owen–Stoltenberg plan it was to be under 'union' control). The Bosnian government also requests firm international guarantees to implement the final settlement.

In a letter to *The Independent* (31 August 1993, p. 25), David Alton (a British MP) and others write that total support for the Bosnian government is well over 60 per cent, since at least 18 per cent of the population are non-Moslems supporting the central government (many of them in mixed marriages). (David Ottaway says that multi-ethnic families make up almost 30 per cent of Bosnia's 4.4 million population: *IHT*, 4 September 1993, p. 2.)

The Bosnian government and Serbian delegations agree a five-point plan involving a cease-fire, the exchange of prisoners, the setting up of a telephone 'hot line' between Sarajevo and the Serbs' headquarters at Pale, the establishment of a joint commission to restore communications and utilities such as water, gas and electricity, and an appeal to local media to avoid 'provocative' language.

1 September 1993. The peace talks collapse over the map. The Croats walk out, refusing to cede Moslem control over Neum (they stress that it would cut off Dubrovnik from the rest of Croatia proper; the only offer was the opportunity for the Moslems to buy land in Neum to build their own port). The Serbs concede only a two-mile (3 km) corridor linking the Moslem enclaves of Gorazde and Zepa/Srebrenica.

Baroness (Margaret) Thatcher and George Shultz (former US secretary of state) and many others sign an open letter to President Clinton advocating Nato air strikes against the Serbs and lifting the arms embargo on the Bosnian government. The letter criticizes the Geneva talks, describing them as leading to the destruction of Bosnia and 'more killing, broken families and the expulsion of millions'. The Owen–Stoltenberg plan is unworkable.

2 September 1993. The USA blames Serb and Croat intransigence for the failure of the Geneva talks and supports the Bosnian government's claims. President Clinton says that 'If, while talks are in abeyance, there is abuse by those who would seek to interfere with humanitarian aid (attacking protected areas, resuming the sustained shelling of Sarajevo, for example) then first I would remind you that the Nato military option is very much alive.'

6 September 1993. Macedonia agrees to tighten sanctions controls on its border with the Federal Republic of Yugoslavia after pressure from the UN and from the USA in particular. (There are reports that other countries such as Bulgaria and Romania have also tightened up sanctions.)

7 September 1993. Representatives of the UN High Commissioner for Refugees release reports of interviews with former Moslem internees in Croat detention camps in Bosnia. A picture of deplorable treatment and conditions emerges. (Further reports indicate that continued fighting in central Bosnia has resulted in large population movements.)

9 September 1993. President Clinton says that any US troops used in Bosnia to implement an agreed plan would be under Nato and not UN control.

The Croats capture three Serbian villages on the Krajina front line (the Serbs retaliated with extensive shelling and on 12 September a surface-to-surface missile hit a suburb of Zagreb). (A cease-fire was agreed on 15 September, with the Croats promising to withdraw from the villages and the UN taking control. The Croats did withdraw, but left behind mass destruction and dead civilians. It was later described as a 'scorched earth' policy. The UN human rights investigator Mazowiecki classified it as an atrocity, with sixty-seven dead and forty-eight still unaccounted for.) (The war in Croatia has to date resulted in at least 10,000 dead: Robert Block, *The Independent*, 15 September 1993, p. 12.)

10 September 1993. A rebel Serbian unit takes control of the Serb-held town of Banja Luka (perhaps the future capital of the Bosnian Serb republic), allegedly in order to stamp out corruption and war profiteering (other factors included poor living standards and conditions for soldiers and their families). (On 14 September the resignation of the Bosnian Serb government was demanded, alleging that many in the assembly had enriched themselves. The rebellion was ended on 17 September after a promise to address the unit's grievances over living conditions and war profiteering; there is a rumour that one rebel leader was arrested.)

12 September 1993. The EU agrees to provide a German-led civilian administration for Mostar in the event of an overall settlement in Bosnia.

14 September 1993. Izetbegovic and Tudjman meet in Geneva and agree a cease-fire between Bosnian government and Croat forces by 10 a.m. on 18

September at the latest (fighting continued even beyond the deadline). New negotiating committees would deal with remaining disputes after the signing of a peace agreement, including territory and access to the sea.

15 September 1993. Bosnian government forces are blamed for a village massacre of Croats (twenty-seven civilians and eleven members of the armed forces).

16 September 1993. A dramatic accord is signed by President Izetbegovic and Momcilo Krajisnik (chairman of the Bosnian Serb assembly):

1. After reaching an agreement on territorial division (this would be deferred, working groups considering the problem after the signing of a peace agreement) and 'during the initial two-year period of the union's existence, there shall be provision for a referendum to be held on a mutually agreed date within the republics of the union on the question of whether citizens of any particular republic agree to remain in the union or to leave the union.'

2. 'In the case of the dissolution all rights of the Union of the Republics of Bosnia and Herzegovina, including membership of the United Nations, shall be automatically vested in the republic with a predominantly Moslem majority.'

3. Both the Bosnian Moslem and the Serb republics would have access to the sea.

4. A cease-fire by noon on 18 September, the release of detainees (detention camps to close) and unhindered access for relief convoys.

Lord Owen and Thorwald Stoltenberg invited the three parties 'to consider signing the peace package as a whole' in Sarajevo on 21 September.

20 September 1993. The co-chairmen sponsor talks between the three warring factions aboard the British aircraft carrier HMS *Invincible* in the Adriatic. The talks scheduled for the following day in Sarajevo are called off, but President Izetbegovic agrees to put various proposals to the Bosnian parliament on 27 September (later postponed by a day).

The Serbs seem to be willing to grant only a wider corridor between Sarajevo and the eastern Bosnian enclaves. But the problem of access to the sea is solved when a Franco-German scientific delegation confirms that Neum would be unsuitable as a deep-water port. Instead the Bosnian state would be allowed a ninety-nine-year lease on a facility in the port of Ploce in Croatia proper and would be given a port (near the village of Celjevo) 12 km upstream on the river Neretva, which runs through Ploce. A 1 km-wide corridor will connect the river port (in the Croatian republic of Bosnia) to the Bosnian republic. The Bosnians and the Croats would develop a stretch of land near Neum for tourism.

21 September 1993. Ten people are reported to have died of starvation in the central Bosnian (Moslem) town of Zenica.

24 September 1993. Croats helping to defend Sarajevo are ordered to withdraw to barracks by Bosnian government forces (the ultimatum was then postponed for seven days). There are reports of Serb–Moslem co-operation against the Croats, e.g. Bosnian government troops being allowed to leave the capital to fight around Mostar and even rumours of arms provision. (On 6 November the Croat force was ordered to disband and integrate into the Bosnian government forces.)

27 September 1993. The Bosnian Moslem Assembly (Sabor) meets to discuss the proposals. The 352 members are drawn from Moslem political, military, religious and intellectual circles (Serbian and Croatian members of the government are only observers). (There is concern that this represents a move away from a multi-ethnic state.)

Of the 349 who voted the following day, 218 voted for conditional acceptance only (namely that territories seized by force where there was formerly a Moslem majority should be returned), fifty-three said yes unconditionally and seventy-eight voted against. (The eighteen members of the cabinet were in favour of acceptance, only asking that Nato and the UN should ensure implementation of the plan.)

The 'Autonomous Province of Western Bosnia' is declared by the Bihac assembly. The next day Izetbegovic ordered the military authorities to take control amid popular anti-central-government demonstrations. Their control turned out to be patchy and far from secure. On 29 September parliament voted sixty-one to one to remove Fikret Abdic from the collective leadership (see the entry for 21–22 June 1993). On 3 October government forces stormed a radio station and shot a policeman dead. The fighting then escalated. On 21 and 22 October 1993 respectively the Croats and the Serbs recognized the break-away province and signed separate peace agreements with Abdic.

29 September 1993. The sixty-nine deputies in the Bosnian parliament voted as follows: fifty-eight in favour of acceptance only on the conditions specified by the Moslem assembly; four opted for unconditional acceptance; and seven voted against.

30 September 1993. General Rasim Delic, commander of the Bosnian army, orders his men to cease military action against the Croats.

1 October 1993. Croatia agrees to a twenty-four-hour extension of the UN mandate in the four designated areas of the Krajina (there has been continual Croat unhappiness at the inadequate implementation of the original agreement).

2 October 1993. The Bosnian Serb assembly withdraws its offer of land concessions and access to the river Sava at Brcko. (The Croats then followed by withdrawing their concessions.)

5 October 1993. The UN Security Council authorizes six more months of peacekeeping by UN troops in Croatia (and in other parts of the former Yugoslavia), but warns the Federal Republic of Yugoslavia that the lifting of sanctions will now also depend on its behaviour towards Croatia: 'full normalization of the international community's position towards those concerned will take into account their actions in implementing all relevant resolutions of the Security Council, including those relating to the UN peacekeeping plan for Croatia'.

6 October 1993. Attention is focused on the long-running siege of Maglaj and Tesanj by the Serbs and the difficulties of delivering aid. (The first land convoy for nearly six months reached Maglaj on 25 October.)

11 October 1993. General Philippe Morillon suggests temporary UN protectorate status for the disputed areas of Bosnia.

16 October 1993. There is a very heavy bombardment of Sarajevo.

17 October 1993. President Clinton says that 'I felt very strongly that the United Nations made a grave error by applying the arms embargo on Yugoslavia to Bosnia after they recognized Bosnia. I had the feeling that the British and the French felt it was far more important to avoid lifting the arms embargo than to save the country . . . John Major told me he wasn't sure he could sustain his government.' (Major denied that he said this.)

20 October 1993. The UN war crimes commission finds evidence that the Serbs have used rape as a weapon of terror in the war in Bosnia (the largest number of victims were Moslems and the largest number of perpetrators were Serbs). But the number of provable cases may be substantially lower than the 20,000 mentioned in the EU report of late 1992. Reports have been collected on about 3,000 cases and about 800 victims are identifiable by name (*IHT*, 21 October 1993, p. 2).

21 October 1993. Milosevic dissolves parliament and calls a Serbian general election for 19 December 1993 (though not for the presidency) in order to thwart Vojislav Seselj's motion of no confidence (which was due to be voted on on 25 October). (Seselj is leader of the Serbian Radical Party, which advocates the annexation of Macedonia and mass expulsions of non-Serbs from Kosovo and other areas in Serbia. He rejects any compromise over Serb-held areas in Croatia and Bosnia. Arrests of some of his supporters began on 5 November. Seselj is reported to have said publicly that Serbs should deal with their opponents by 'gouging their eyes out with rusty spoons': John Kifner, *IHT*, 24 November 1993, p. 4.)

23 October 1993. Bosnian government forces launch a major attack on Croat-held Vares (virtually free of fighting until taken over by radical Croat nationalists). They claim that the Croats massacred some of the inhabitants of the village of Stupni Do (UN forces found evidence for this). On 3 November Croat forces withdrew from Vares, followed by Croat civilians, and Bosnian government forces moved in the next day.

25 October 1993. Bosnian Foreign Minister Haris Silajdzic is made prime minister and a member of the collective presidency.

26 October 1993. The Bosnian army and police use force to regain control of Sarajevo from powerful criminal gangs that dominate the black market. (Ramiz Delalic, known as 'Celo' surrendered, while Musan Topalovic, known as 'Caco', was shot dead.)

UN relief operations to many parts of central Bosnia are suspended when a convoy is fired on and a Danish lorry driver killed (Moslem forces were blamed).

31 October 1993. The Autocephalous Montenegrin Orthodox Church is re-established despite resistance from the Serbian Orthodox Church (the two were merged in 1920). The new patriarch is Antonije Abramovic, who lived in Canada for more than forty years.

1 November 1993. 'Secret' talks begin in Norway between Croatia and the Serbs of Krajina (but they broke up two days later without success).

3 November 1993. The Serbian Unity Party is founded by Zeljko Raznjatovic (popularly known as 'Arkan', leader of the 'Serbian Tiger Brigade' and accused of war crimes; he represents the Serbs of Kosovo in the Serbian parliament). The major aim is a 'Greater Serbia'. (He is a supporter of Milosevic.)

9 November 1993. Although the Serbs began the shelling, it is the Croats who finally destroy the famous Mostar bridge (*Stari Most* or 'Old Bridge'). (It was built over the river Neretva in 1557–66 on the orders of the Ottoman emperor Suleiman the Magnificent.)

15 November 1993. The Bosnian government threatens to take the UK to the International Court of Justice for failure to prevent genocide. The UK is alleged to be at the forefront of resistance to lifting the arms embargo. (The threat was removed on 20 December.)

18 November 1993. The three warring factions sign an accord in Geneva guaranteeing the safe passage of humanitarian aid. The UNHCR will recommend to the UN secretary-general that aid deliveries should recommence.

22 November 1993. At the instigation of France and Germany, EU foreign ministers agree to support the idea of a 'gradual suspension of sanctions' (the term 'lifting' was avoided, owing to US coolness towards the idea), i.e. some UN sanctions on the Federal Republic of Yugoslavia to be lifted in exchange for more land for the Bosnian state in order to end the deadlock. (The lifting of all sanctions would depend on the solution of broader problems, such as the Krajina and Kosovo.) The EU also threatens to use force against renegade groups ('uncontrolled elements') continuing to block aid deliveries in spite of higher-level agreements.

24 November 1993. Aid finally gets through to a number of towns in central and eastern Bosnia (e.g. Travnik and Srebrenica).

The International Helsinki Federation for Human Rights (IHF) publishes a report entitled *From Autonomy to Colonization: Human Rights Violations in Kosovo, 1989–1993*. 'The methods of harassment range from verbal insults and meaningless identity checks in the street to arbitrary detention and torture or ill-treatment – not infrequently with fatal consequences, including death – and summary shootings of demonstrators or killing of unarmed individuals . . . The region has been placed under virtual colonial control which has resulted in a total marginalization of the Albanian majority in Kosovo. The entire province has been gradually Serbianized . . . The IHF is deeply concerned that the Serbian oppressive policies carried out in Kosovo aim at a permanent change in the demographic structure of the region.' The Serbian parliament has adopted legislation providing cash incentives for Serbs to settle in Kosovo, while restrictions have been imposed on the freedom of movement of ethnic Albanians, on the use of the Albanian language and on the holding of private property.

25 November 1993. In a public speech in London Lord Owen forecasts that Bosnia will disintegrate. The Serb and Croat areas will eventually join Serbia and Croatia respectively and an independent Moslem state will be set up (this new state is not to be feared he says). He blames the USA for the failure of the Vance–Owen plan.

29 November 1993. EU-sponsored talks begin in Geneva, involving representatives of the warring factions, the USA and Russia. There is agreement that the peace negotiations should resume.

2 December 1993. The first round of the new negotiations ends without agreement.

12 December 1993. It is predicted that the Serbs of Krajina will elect Milan Babic as 'president', thus defeating Milan Martic (backed by Milosevic). But Martic wins the re-run on 23 January 1994.

16 December 1993. Germany, the UK, France, the Netherlands, Denmark and Italy establish formal diplomatic links with the Former Yugoslav Republic of Macedonia. (Finland followed the next day and Japan on 21 December.)

17 December 1993. Bosnian government and Bosnian Croat forces agree a cease-fire from midnight 23 December 1993 to midnight 3 January 1994. Serbian forces will take part provided they are not attacked.

19 December 1993. The Serbian general election takes place (see under 'Serbia' below).

20 December 1993. The UN General Assembly resolves to lift the arms embargo on the Bosnian government.

21 December 1993. Talks resume in Geneva, and the Serbs and Croats suggest the following split of Bosnia: 'Moslems', 33.33 per cent; Croats, 17.5 per cent; Serbs, 49.17 per cent (the most commonly cited figures for the current occupation of Bosnia are 15 per cent, 15 per cent and 70 per cent respectively). But the Bosnian government rejects the proposal, specifying the extra land needed for a viable state: (1) corridors connecting the eastern enclaves with the main central area; (2) a corridor connecting Prijedor with Bihac; (3) the ethnically cleansed districts in western, northern and eastern Bosnia that formally had a 'Moslem' majority. Access to the sea (via 'Croatian' Bosnia) at Neum was also demanded rather than the Prevlaca peninsula (on the border between Croatia and Montenegro). Other issues included access to the river Sava in the north and the Serb demand for the division of Sarajevo (the Serbs reintroduced the idea of exchanging 'Serb' land in Sarajevo for 'Moslem' land in eastern Bosnia such as Srebrenica).

22 December 1993. The talks shift to Brussels, where a Christmas truce is declared (until mid-January 1994, when the talks are due to resume). (The fighting did not stop.)

23 December 1993. The current round of talks ends without agreement.

28 December 1993. The long-delayed departure from Sarajevo begins of the people on an evacuation list (1,265 were registered originally, but not all turned up).

29 December 1993. The Montenegrin parliament reinstates Cetinje as the capital of Montenegro, but the seat of government is to stay in Podgorica.

4–5 January 1994. The foreign ministers of Croatia and Bosnia meet in Vienna. A plan to halt hostilities is to be put to the two presidents at their meeting in Bonn on 8 January (the meeting actually started a day late).

5 January 1994. Lord Owen says that 'We all know that there is a very substantial element of the Croatian army in Bosnia-Hercegovina' (this comment followed an earlier threat by President Tudjman to intervene directly in Bosnia if the 'Moslem' offensive continued). (On 7 January UN officers confirmed that regular Yugoslav troops were being deployed in Bosnia: Laura Silber, *FT*, 8 January 1994, p. 2.)

It is announced that the British lieutenant-general Sir Michael Rose will replace the Belgian lieutenant-general Francis Briquemont at the end of January as commander of UN forces in Bosnia (the change-over actually occurred on 24 January). (Lieutenant-general Briquemont was to have ended his duties in July, but he became very critical of the lack of UN forces: 'There is a fantastic gap between all those Security Council resolutions and the resources available to execute them.' Note that he still thinks that air strikes will not work. On 23 January he said that 'there is a fantastic crisis because the politicians are writing and voting I do not know how many resolutions, but we have no means to execute them.' He believes that Unprofor field commanders should be empowered to call in 'close air support' when UN forces are attacked or threatened, but he is not in favour of air strikes in a wider sense: 'air strikes involve war and intervention, and we cannot solve the problem like that': *The Daily Telegraph*, 24 January 1994, p. 11.)

6 January 1994. Warren Zimmerman (the last US ambassador to Yugoslavia) resigns from the foreign service section of the US State Department dealing with refugee affairs in protest at the administration's policy towards Bosnia. (He recalled that Nato had threatened air strikes if the siege of Sarajevo was not lifted and humanitarian aid convoys were impeded: see 9 August 1993 entry.)

7 January 1994. It is reported that General Jean Cot, commander of UN forces in the former Yugoslavia, has asked the UN secretary-general to delegate the authority to call up air strikes in defence of UN forces (the request was refused).

9–10 January 1994. Presidents Izetbegovic and Tudjman meet in Bonn.

10–11 January 1994. On the first day of the Nato summit President Clinton, in a comment relating to the Nato threat to use air strikes, said that Nato's credibility was at risk. 'I welcome the reassertion by the Alliance . . . of our warning against the strangulation of Sarajevo and the safe areas. But if we are going to reassert this warning, it cannot be seen as mere rhetoric. Those who attack Sarajevo must understand that we are serious. If we leave the sentence in the declaration we have to mean it.'

The communiqué issued on 11 January said that: 'We reaffirm our readiness, under the authority of the United Nations Security Council and in accordance with the Alliance decisions of 2 and 9 August 1993, to carry out air strikes in order to prevent the strangulation of Sarajevo, the safe areas and other threatened areas in Bosnia-Hercegovina. We urge Unprofor authorities to draw up urgently plans to ensure that the blocked rotation of the Unprofor contingent in Srebrenica can take place [Dutch troops to replace the Canadians there] and to examine how the airport at Tuzla can be opened for humanitarian relief purposes.'

18 January 1994. The Geneva talks resume.

It is announced that General Jean Cot is to be replaced at the end of March 1994 (i.e. ahead of schedule).

19 January 1994. The Geneva talks end without agreement, although fresh talks are fixed for 10 February.

Croatia and the Federal Republic of Yugoslavia agree to set up 'official representation' offices in Belgrade and Zagreb respectively by 15 February in order to 'facilitate relations and contacts between the two states'.

20 January 1994. By a fairly narrow majority the European parliament recommends that the Council of Ministers should replace Lord Owen as EU mediator. Both he and Thorwald Stoltenberg (the UN negotiator) 'have achieved no results and consistently attempt to divide Bosnia-Hercegovina along ethnic lines even though it is a member of the United Nations'. Parliament calls for 'the nomination of a new European Union negotiator with a proper mandate and a new strategy for exercising it'.

21 January 1994. EU governments issue a statement of support for Lord Owen.

The UN secretary-general, Boutros Boutros-Ghali, says that he will approve air strikes if his special adviser (Yasushi Akashi) so recommends: 'If it [the UN troop rotation in Srebrenica] does not happen, then we will have to make the decision to use air power.'

The State Duma in Russia votes in favour of a motion recommending that the Russian government should lift sanctions against Serbia and oppose Nato air strikes against the Bosnian Serbs.

23 January 1994. A UN report alleges that some Unprofor troops and some of their civilian personnel in former Yugoslavia have been conducting a black-market trade in fuel, coffee, cigarettes and alcohol. Troops were associated with prostitution in Sarajevo and other areas, although there was no evidence that they ran brothels. There was abuse of UN identification cards and press passes. There was no widespread or organized corruption and serious violations declined in mid-1993. Twenty-three UN soldiers, from Ukraine and Kenya, have been sent home to face disciplinary action and seven locally recruited civilian employees have been dismissed.

24 January 1994. General Cot says that 'in the case of a massive attack against the safe areas or anywhere else, the only means we have of reacting immediately is close air support. Immediately means three minutes. That would be perfect. Half an hour, that would be nice. But it is certainly not three hours.'

25 January 1994. Russia's special envoy on former Yugoslavia, Vitali Churkin, calls for an urgent meeting of the UN Security Council. He will press for a resolution providing for strict observance of a cease-fire, security of aid convoys and the strengthening of the 'safe areas'. He does not exclude the use of force to protect Unprofor personnel, but he believes that the Security Council should have the final say over air strikes.

28 January 1994. The UN secretary-general delegates the authority to his special representative in the former Yugoslavia, Yasushi Akashi, to approve any request from the Unprofor commander in Bosnia for 'close air support' in Srebrenica and Tuzla.

31 January 1994. The Bosnian Serbs order full military mobilization and put the economy on a war footing (earlier in the month UN officials reported cases of Bosnian refugees in Serbia being ordered to report for duty in the Bosnian Serb army; the UN has also warned Croatia about doing the same thing).

1 February 1994. Dutch troops begin relieving the Canadians in Srebrenica.

2 February 1994. The prime ministers of Pakistan (Benazir Bhutto) and Turkey (Tansu Cilla) visit Sarajevo. The two lady prime ministers call for a lifting of the arms embargo on the Bosnian government.

3 February 1994. The UN Security Council warns Croatia that economic sanctions may be imposed if its (3,000–5,000) troops are not withdrawn from Bosnia. (The Bosnian government puts the number of Croatian troops at 20,000.)

The new commander of Unprofor troops in Bosnia, Lieutenant-General Rose, begins a tougher approach to aid convoys; force is to be used when necessary.

5 February 1994. A mortar bomb kills sixty-eight people in a Sarajevo market and injures more than 200 others.

6 February 1994. The UN secretary-general, in a letter to Nato's secretary-general, Manfred Wörner, says: 'The mortar attacks last week against civilian targets in Sarajevo, at least one of which has been established by the UN Protection Force to be the work of Bosnian Serb forces, make it necessary to prepare urgently for the use of air strikes to deter further such attacks . . . I should be grateful if you could take action to obtain, at the earliest possible date, a decision by the North Atlantic Council to authorize the commander-in-chief of Nato's southern command to launch air strikes, at the request of the United Nations, against artillery or mortar positions in or around Sarajevo.'

7 February 1994. EU foreign ministers call for an early meeting of the Nato council: 'the aim should be to bring about the immediate lifting of the siege of Sarajevo, using all the means necessary, including the use of air power'.

8 February 1994. Mate Boban is forced to resign as leader of the Bosnian Croats.

9 February 1994. Just prior to the Nato declaration Lieutenant-General Rose announces that Bosnian Serb and Bosnian government commanders have agreed an 'immediate' cease-fire in and around Sarajevo (noon the following day was mentioned as the start of the truce). Heavy weapons were to be placed under UN control and then gradually withdrawn to sites chosen by UN forces. (The following day UN troops began to move into six front-line zones.)

10 February 1994. Nato's communiqué reads that the council: 'condemns the continuing siege of Sarajevo and, with a view to ending it, calls for the withdrawal, or regrouping and placing under Unprofor control, within ten days, of heavy weapons (including tanks, artillery pieces, mortars, multiple rocket launchers, missiles and anti-aircraft weapons) of the Bosnian Serb forces located in an area within 20 km of the centre of Sarajevo, and excluding an area within 2 km of the centre of Pale [the Bosnian Serbs' headquarters] . . . calls upon the government of Bosnia-Hercegovina, within the same period, to place the heavy weapons in its possession within the Sarajevo exclusion zone described above under Unprofor control, and to refrain from attacks launched from the current confrontation lines in the city . . . calls upon the parties to respect the cease-fire . . . decides that, ten days from 2400 GMT 10 February 1994, heavy weapons of any of the parties found within the Sarajevo exclusion zone, unless controlled by Unprofor, will, along with their direct and essential military support facilities, be subject to Nato air strikes which will be conducted in close coordination with the UN secretary-general.' (The greatest pressure came from France and the USA. The UK was lukewarm. Canada was one of the most reluctant and Greece actually dissociated itself from the statement. Prior to the meeting Manfred Wörner, Nato secretary-general, who was chairman despite being very ill, said: 'It is time to act. We have had enough words.' He died of cancer on 13 August 1994.)

The Bosnian prime minister and the Croatian foreign minister agree to ask the UN to arrange for international control of their frontier.

The UN agrees to set up a commission of inquiry into the Sarajevo market massacre.

The Geneva talks resume.

The USA is to become more actively involved with the Bosnian government in order to draw up a 'bottom line' negotiating position.

11 February 1994. The UN secretary-general delegates authority to his special representative in the former Yugoslavia both to initiate a first air strike against gun positions around Sarajevo and to order close air support to protect UN troops anywhere in Bosnia.

12 February 1994. The Geneva talks are called off for the time being.

14 February 1994. Disagreements emerge between Nato and the UN about what precisely is meant by 'control' of heavy weapons and the deadline for compliance. The precise chain of authority for issuing air strike orders is also not crystal-clear. (The Bosnian Serbs take advantage of the confusion to prevaricate and try to deepen differences between Nato and the UN. But differences also emerge among Bosnian Serb political and military leaders.)

A Bosnian Serb is arrested in Germany for alleged war crimes.

16 February 1994. The UN requests member governments to provide up to 3,000 extra troops for the Sarajevo operation (the response of the Western countries to the appeal for fresh troops was poor, most of those arriving being merely redeployed from other areas).

17 February 1994. Russia's special representative, Vitali Churkin, announces an agreement with the Bosnian Serbs to pull back their heavy weapons from around Sarajevo within thirty-six hours. Russia will also provide troops for the Sarajevo operation, 400 redeployed from Croatia and 400 fresh ones.

20–21 February 1994. The midnight deadline passes and it is agreed that 'virtually all' heavy weapons have been withdrawn or are under UN control; there are to be no air strikes 'at this stage'.

22 February 1994. Senior Foreign Ministry officials from the EU, the USA, Canada and Russia meet in Bonn.

23 February 1994. Yeltsin calls for a one-day summit involving Russia, the USA, Germany, France and the UK.

Military leaders of the Bosnian government and the Bosnian Croats, meeting in Zagreb, announce agreement on a cease-fire starting at noon on 25 February. Heavy weapons will be withdrawn by 7 March between six and twelve miles from the front lines or surrendered to UN control. UN troops will be positioned at key locations. (The Croatian foreign minister, Mate Granic, said that Croatia had withdrawn about 1,200 troops from the western Hercegovina region of Bosnia.)

25 February 1994. The cease-fire begins.

The Russian parliament approves the sending of an extra 300 troops.

27 February 1994. Lieutenant-General Rose says that a further 3,000–5,000 UN troops are needed to implement the Bosnian government–Bosnian Croat cease-fire agreement.

28 February 1994. Nato (US) fighters shoot down four (out of six) Bosnian Serb jet aircraft that were bombing targets in central Bosnia.

(This was not only the first enforcement of the 'no fly' resolution, but also the first ever combat role for Nato. More than 1,600 violations of the flight ban had been recorded, 1,397 between 9 October 1992 and 1 January 1994: *FT*, 1 March 1994, pp. 2, 22.)

(The UN was to have begun a new policy of simply giving notice of relief convoys passing through Bosnia rather than negotiating their way through. But the aid convoys were halted because of the Nato action. They resumed the following day, 1 March.)

1 March 1994. Preliminary agreement is announced in Washington (the USA was the broker) on the Bosnian government–Croat plan for a federation in Bosnia (see above).

The Bosnian Serbs and Russia announce in Moscow that Tuzla airport will be reopened, although for humanitarian aid only: 'Russian observers will take part in monitoring the non-military use of the airport.' (The UN had, in fact, already accepted a Russian offer of fifty observers, while the UN commander in Bosnia had already set a deadline of 7 March for the reopening of the airport; it was closed down in May 1992.)

The USA and the UK announce a joint planning mission of reconstruction experts for Sarajevo.

3 March 1994. The UN's special envoy to the former Yugoslavia, Yasushi Akashi, claims that an extra 10,650 troops are needed to implement the cease-fires, 4,600 around Sarajevo and 6,050 in central and southern Bosnia. (There are currently some 29,000 UN troops in the former Yugoslavia, 13,900 of them in Bosnia. France contributes some 6,000 and the UK 2,300.) (The response was far better than before. Within a few weeks some 7,000 fresh or redeployed troops were pledged, e.g. 900 from the UK and 800 from France.)

4 March 1994. The UN Security Council passes a resolution on Sarajevo commending complete freedom of movement for the civilian population, the free circulation of relief supplies and the restoration of 'normal life' in the city. In addition the secretary-general is asked to report on the feasibility of lifting the sieges of Mostar, Vitez and Maglaj.

6 March 1994. The Bosnian Serbs agree to allow two air corridors into Tuzla.

7 March 1994. UN troops take control of Tuzla airport.

9 March 1994. The UN Human Rights Commission in Geneva says that both the Serbs and the Croats have practised 'ethnic cleansing' in Bosnia, but 'the primary though not sole responsibility lies with the Serbian forces' (*The Independent*, 10 March 1994, p. 12).

10 March 1994. The Bosnian Serbs turn back an aid convoy attempting to get to Maglaj.

13 March 1994. UN military observers enter Maglaj for the first time in nine months.

14 March 1994. The UN Security Council calls for an end to the siege of Maglaj by the Bosnian Serbs.

16 March 1994. Lieutenant-General Bertrand de Lapresle (France) replaces General Cot.

17 March 1994. The Bosnian government and the Bosnian Serbs agree on a partial and highly regulated restoration (as of 23 March) of freedom of movement of civilians in and around Sarajevo.

18 March 1994. The formal signing takes place in Washington of the Bosnian government–Croat plan for Bosnia.

The British prime minister, John Major, visits Bosnia. He pledges £12 million in aid for Sarajevo.

20 March 1994. The first humanitarian road convoy since 22 October 1993 reaches Maglaj (under strong Unprofor protection, including aircraft). (The Bosnian Serbs had withdrawn from front-line positions the day before.)

In another sign of normality a soccer match takes place in the Olympic stadium (Sarajevo FC's B side beat Unprofor four goals to nil). (Trams had begun to run again recently in Sarajevo.)

21 March 1994. UN troops discover a large cache of Bosnian Serb heavy weapons just within the exclusion zone.

22 March 1994. The first UN (not humanitarian) flight to Tuzla airport takes place. The first talks for about two years begin between representatives of Croatia and the Serbs in Krajina.

23 March 1994. A small number of family reunions begin the easing of restricted civilian movement in and around Sarajevo.

The Bosnian Serbs hi-jack and loot an aid convoy headed for Maglaj.

The UN secretary-general recommends to the Security Council that Turkish troops should be used in Bosnia (to monitor the Bosnian government–Croat accord).

24 March 1994. Turkey announces that 2,700 troops are available for duty in Bosnia.

The 'parliament' of the 'Bosnian Serb parliament' votes not to join the new Bosnian government–Croat federation.

26 March 1994. The assembly of the Bosnian Serbs' self-proclaimed 'Herceg-Bosna' votes to accept the new federation.

27 March 1994. Izetbegovic is re-elected chairman of the Party of Democratic Action (the main Moslem party).

29 March 1994. The Bosnian Serbs begin a large-scale assault on Gorazde.

30 March 1994. The Bosnian parliament votes in favour of the new federation.

Croatia and the Serbs of Krajina agree to a cease-fire, to come into effect on 4 April. UN forces will be deployed in the buffer zone.

Seventeen Moslems and two Croats (all civilians) are murdered by Bosnian Serbs in Prijedor.

31 March 1994. The USA blocks a UN plan to mandate an additional 8,500 peacekeeping personnel for Bosnia (e.g. 1,027 from the UK), citing uncertainty about whether Congress would sanction the extra funding required of the USA (an additional thirty days would be needed to consider the UN resolution; the USA is supposed to contribute 31.7 per cent to the total peacekeeping costs). A compromise figure of 3,500 additional UN troops is agreed upon as part of the renewed six-month Unprofor mandate starting 1 April.

The Guardian (1 April 1994, p. 12) says that the current Unprofor deployment in the former Yugoslavia is 31,334, including 14,594 in Croatia, 14,433 in Bosnia and 1,048 in Macedonia (including 340 from the USA; on 31 March the USA announced that it would be sending up to 250 additional peacekeeping troops to Macedonia).

1 April 1994. Bosnian and Serb military commanders agree a tentative cease-fire in Bihac.

3 April 1994. Radovan Karadzic vows that 'the perpetrators of the crimes [in Prijedor] will be tried and severely punished before the eyes of the international public.'

The Bosnian Serbs give Red Cross officials a guarantee of safe passage for the thousands of Moslems and Croats who wish to leave the areas of conflict (apart from the atrocities in Prijedor, large-scale 'ethnic cleansing' by the Serbs has been going on in Banja Luka). (Note also that there has been heavy Serb shelling of Gorazde, whose population had swollen to 65,000 even before the 29 March offensive; before the war the town itself had a population of 3,500 and the entire enclave 37,000.)

4 April 1994. Karadzic refuses to allow the mass evacuation of Moslems and Croats from the Prijedor area unless there is a reciprocal movement of Serbs from elsewhere.

6 April 1994. Lieutenant-General Rose is prevented by the Bosnian Serbs from personally visiting Gorazde, but they ask him to arrange talks aimed at a 'global cessation of hostilities'.

7 April 1994. The Bosnian government announces a twenty-four-hour cease-fire. The Bosnian Serbs follow suit, but some fighting still goes on.

9 April 1994. The UN secretary-general orders UN forces to use 'all available means' to make the Bosnian Serbs withdraw from the territory recently occupied in the Gorazde enclave.

10 April 1994. The first ground attack takes place when two Nato (US) F-16 fighters bomb Bosnian Serb forces threatening to take Gorazde (which has been under sustained attack since the end of March). (The protection of UN personnel was stressed in the official explanations. Bombing was authorized under the UN's 'safe areas' resolution of 4 June 1993. The targets were tanks and a command post. Early reports talked of two tanks and the command post being destroyed. Note the argument that Bosnian Serb aggression against Gorazde had been encouraged by prior disagreements within the Clinton administration, with military/defence personnel essentially advising against action and the State Department arguing in favour.) (Although the UN Security Council authorized the dispatch of 7,600 peacekeeping forces to Bosnian 'safe areas' in June 1993, only 5,000 had arrived eight months later: *The Guardian*, 11 April 1994, p. 23. 'When the "safe areas" were voted into existence, the UN commander of the time requested some 900 peacekeepers for each of five such areas, and a much larger number for Sarajevo. He was turned down. Had that number of UN troops already been employed in Gorazde – there were just four observers in the town at the start of the latest fighting – the Serbs would probably not even have attempted to attack it': *The Economist*, 23 April 1994, p. 16.)

11 April 1994. Nato launches a second (US) air strike, which destroys a tank and seriously damages two personnel carriers.

President Yeltsin of Russia complains bitterly about the lack of 'prior consultation' and Zhirinovsky says that Russia should bomb Nato bases in Italy (where the fighters are stationed).

12 April 1994. The Bosnian Serb commander, General Ratko Mladic, says that his force will shoot down any Nato plane which threatens them. The Bosnian Serbs begin to harass UN personnel (e.g. some UN observers are put under house arrest) and to hinder aid convoys.

13 April 1994. Owen and Stoltenberg resume their negotiating role.

14 April 1994. The Bosnian Serbs continue to retaliate, e.g. by the detention of some peacekeeping troops, the banning of US journalists, attempting to regain control of some heavy weapons around Sarajevo and shelling Tuzla airport.

15 April 1994. In defiance of the UN, the Bosnian Serbs launch an all-out assault on Gorazde and capture all the strategic points in the enclave. Two UN (British) 'observers' (helping to guide the two previous air strikes in reality) are shot at by the Serbs (deliberately, according to the UN) and one later dies after being brought out by helicopter during a brief negotiated cease-fire (note that there were very few UN personnel in Gorazde, despite its being designated a 'safe area'). A UN (French) reconnaissance plane is hit by Serb anti-aircraft fire, but returns safely.

16 April 1994. A UN (British) jet is brought down over Gorazde by a Serb missile after a number of abortive bombing runs. (Note that Nato planes were only allowed to attack *specified* targets, which greatly hindered their effectiveness.)

17 April 1994. The UN is in disarray as the Bosnian Serbs effectively take control of Gorazde while a cease-fire (plus the withdrawal of Serb heavy weapons 3 km from the town) was being announced by Karadzic and Yasushi Akashi. The Russian special envoy, Vitali Churkin, declares that 'I have heard more broken promises in the last twenty-four hours than in my entire life'. A UN Security Council resolution condemns 'the escalating military activities of the Serbian forces around Gorazde.'

18 April 1994. Lieutenant-General Rose: 'The town is at their mercy and we are on the edge of a major humanitarian catastrophe. This is clearly a very sad week for the world when the UN peacekeeping operations have been so blatantly used to cover the prosecution of war by the Bosnian Serb authorities.'

Vitali Churkin: 'The time has come for Russia to stop all discussions with the Bosnian Serbs. The time for talking is past. They should be made to understand that Russia is a great power, not a banana republic . . . a group of Bosnian Serb extremists have fallen ill with the madness of war.' Russia should not allow them 'to use the policy of great Russia to cover their activities and drag other Serbs into their madness.' In response to a rumour that Nato may use air strikes, Churkin suggests that Russia should 'support them energetically'.

Warren Christopher, on the Bosnian Serbs: 'A tangle of lies and misleading statements that have seldom been equalled.'

19 April 1994. President Yeltsin of Russia says that 'the conflict in Bosnia-Hercegovina is on the brink of dangerous escalation.' He calls on the Bosnian Serbs 'to stop attacking Gorazde and leave the town' and to allow in UN troops. Yeltsin also calls for 'a summit between Russia, the United States and the European Union with the participation of the United Nations'.

The Russian foreign minister, Andrei Kozyrev, declares that 'in the most resolute manner I would not recommend to the Serbian side to continue to test the patience of the world community'.

The UN secretary-general calls on Nato to sanction, if so requested, the use of air strikes to defend all six 'safe areas' themselves (as opposed to merely Unprofor personnel).

In Sarajevo Bosnian Serbs take back eighteen anti-aircraft guns (although they are quickly returned).

Karadzic agrees to another cease-fire around Gorazde (which again means nothing).

20 April 1994. Nato says that the secretary-general's request has been 'considered in a positive light' and that Nato military planners will 'urgently' start drawing up plans in co-ordination with Unprofor.

President Clinton recommends the following: (1) the threat of the use of air strikes to defend the other five 'safe areas' along the lines of Sarajevo (he believes that the Bosnian Serbs must be made to pay a 'higher price' for their aggression); (2) the tightening of sanctions on Serbia; (3) a major diplomatic effort with Russia.

Yeltsin: 'The use of military force, especially air strikes, without agreement in the UN Security Council is unacceptable.'

Kozyrev: 'It would be a mistake to apply any decision on air strikes, at least without working out a co-ordinated policy.'

21 April 1994. Warren Christopher: 'We have a strategic interest in preventing the war from spreading.'

The attacking Bosnian Serbs issue an ultimatum to the defenders of Gorazde: abandon the remaining pockets of resistance on the left bank of the river Drina and move to the left bank or the town will be destroyed.

22 April 1994. Nato Secretary-General Manfred Wörner: 'The murderous and barbaric attacks on defenceless civilians in Gorazde are an outrage and a defiance of the United Nations. Still today the shelling has continued and it is clear that half-measures will not do.' Nato gives the Bosnian Serbs an ultimatum:

1. An immediate cease-fire.
2. The Bosnian Serbs to withdraw to a distance of at least 3 km from the centre of Gorazde by midnight (GMT) on 23 April (1.00 a.m. local time, 24 April). (Heavy weapons were to be withdrawn to a distance of at least 20 km from the centre of Gorazde by 1.00 a.m. GMT on 27 April; 2.00 a.m. local time.)
3. Access to Gorazde for UN forces, humanitarian relief convoys and medical workers.

If any of these demands are not met, Nato 'is authorized to conduct air strikes against Bosnian Serb heavy weapons and other military targets within a 20 km radius of the centre of Gorazde' (the UN secretary-general need approve only the first strike). (Similar arrangements are made later for the other 'safe areas' of Bihac, Srebrenica, Tuzla and Zepa.)

Yasushi Akashi announces an agreed cease-fire (as of noon local time, 23 April) after talks in Belgrade with the Bosnian Serb leaders (including General Ratko Mladic, who has personally led the assault on Gorazde).

23 April 1994. The assault continues, but Yasushi Akashi refuses to authorize air strikes before the midnight 23 April deadline.

Russia approves the use of air strikes around Gorazde if the Bosnian Serbs do not stop their offensive. Kozyrev says that 'the Bosnian Serbs' military command has criminally defied the elementary norms of humane behaviour, the demands of the United Nations and also of Russia. The only alternative to air strikes is compliance by the Bosnian Serbs with their commitments'.

UN (Ukrainian) troops reach Gorazde (they were joined the next day by other UN troops, although the French government ordered its troops not to go; positions were taken up on both banks of the river Drina).

24 April 1994. The Bosnian Serbs comply sufficiently with the ultimatum to avoid air strikes. But, among other things, the Serbs burn houses and destroy public installations as they withdraw.

The first humanitarian convoy arrives. The evacuation of the wounded begins. (A later estimate put the number of dead in Gorazde during the assault at up to 250 and the number of wounded at around 600. The original estimates were 715 and 1,970 respectively. On 10 June 1994 Tadeusz Mazowiecki, the UN's special investigator, reported that the Bosnian Serbs had committed war crimes in Gorazde. He estimated that nearly 2,000 people had been wounded and 700 killed: *IHT*, 11 June 1994, p. 4.)

25 April 1994. It is announced in London that a 'contact group' of leading officials from the USA, Russia, the EU (the UK, France and Germany) and the UN has been established (the first meeting to be held the following day). The focus of attention is the attainment of an overall cease-fire in Bosnia for four months and agreement on a map for settling the conflict. (Two days later Vitali Churkin was replaced as Russia's representative in the group by Alexei Nikiforov.)

There are disagreements within Russia. For example, Defence Minister Pavel Grachev is against the threat of air strikes, since they 'could lead to the conflict becoming unmanageable and growing, and not only in Bosnia'.

26 April 1994. The withdrawal of Serbian heavy weapons seems to be more or less accomplished within the deadline.

27 April 1994. The UN Security Council agrees to send 6,500 troops to Bosnia (the USA withdraws its opposition to funding).

Lieutenant-General Rose is (unofficially) recorded as saying in a private conversation that Gorazde 'had not been destroyed to the level which I had expected . . . they [the defenders] think we should be fighting their war for them . . . I think they basically turned and ran and left us to pick up the bits.' (He later tried to explain away his comments as being private and taken out of context while discussing military theory in answer to a question; he criticized the publication of his comments as being 'tittle-tattle'.)

29 April 1994. UN (UK) troops patrolling the borders of the Gorazde demilitarized zone come under attack from the Bosnian Serbs. (It is believed that three Serbs were killed and five seriously wounded when fire was returned.)

30 April 1994. The Bosnian Serbs shell a UN observation post near Tuzla. UN (Danish) troops use Leopard tanks in retaliation, killing an estimated nine Serbs and critically wounding up to five others.

1 May 1994. There is an incident involving vessels policing the embargo and those from the Yugoslav navy.

2 May 1994. The USA formally complains to the UN secretary-general about Yasushi Akashi's earlier criticism of the absence of US troops on the ground in Bosnia (he said that, after the withdrawal of troops from Somalia, the USA had become 'afraid, timid and tentative').

4 May 1994. Yasushi Akashi agrees that the Bosnian Serbs should be allowed to move a UN-escorted column of seven tanks through the Sarajevo exclusion zone (from the Serb headquarters at Pale to positions south of Mount Igman). In return the Serbs promise to allow an impeded UN convoy into Gorazde and to admit UN observers into the Serb-held area of Brcko (the first arrived on 8 May). (Five tanks were allowed through before much criticism caused the deal to be terminated. One of the two remaining tanks went 'missing' on 7 May.)

10 May 1994. The UN says that the Bosnian government has deployed men and weapons on Mount Igman in violation of the Sarajevo agreement.

11 May 1994. Shelling by Bosnian government forces kills three Serb civilians in Brcko. The Bosnian Serbs shell Tuzla in retaliation. (Bosnian government forces were to launch a number of offensives in central and north-east Bosnia.)

12 May 1994. The US Senate narrowly passes two resolutions, both by fifty votes to forty-nine. One requires the president to lift unilaterally the arms embargo against the Bosnian government and the other requires the president to try to persuade others in the UN and Nato to lift the embargo.

13 May 1994. The foreign ministers of the USA, Russia and five EU countries (the UK, France, Germany, Greece and Belgium) agree to try to persuade the warring factions to accept a four-month cease-fire during which to resume negotiations. The foreign ministers suggest that 51 per cent of the territory of Bosnia should go to the Bosnian government and Croats (despite the fact that on 11 May the Bosnian government and Croats agreed among themselves on 58 per cent). (The Bosnian government favoured a shorter truce of perhaps six weeks at most in order to minimize the chances of the consolidation of Serb gains. The Bosnian Serbs favoured an indefinite cease-fire.)

The State Duma in Russia resolves by 270 votes to one to recommend lifting the arms embargo on Serbia unilaterally if any other country lifts the embargo on the Bosnian government.

17 May 1994. France threatens to withdraw some 2,500 (of its 6,750) troops in the former Yugoslavia by the end of 1994. (Around 900 were already planned to be withdrawn from the Krajina, but troops would be withdrawn from Bihac if the peace negotiations were not successful. France plans to concentrate its forces around Sarajevo. One source puts the total number of French troops killed at about twenty and the number wounded at around 300: *IHT*, 18 May 1994, p. 4. The sixth British soldier was killed on 25 June.)

18 May 1994. The Bosnian Serbs release eleven French (civilian) aid workers they have been holding since 8 April.

22 May 1994. A cease-fire is due to begin around Gorazde. The Bosnian Serbs promise the UN to withdraw their remaining troops (disguised, for example, as policemen) from within the 3 km exclusion zone. (The pledge was not kept and the Bosnian government refused to sign the agreement.)

29 May 1994. The Bosnian Serbs allow UN troops to patrol freely within the heavy weapons exclusion zone around Gorazde.

2 June 1994. The Geneva talks fail to resume because Bosnian Serb troops are still within the Gorazde exclusion zone.

6 June 1994. The Geneva talks resume after the withdrawal of Bosnian Serb troops has been confirmed.

8 June 1994. A Bosnia-wide cease-fire is agreed. The warring parties agree, 'as a first step', to refrain from 'any offensive military operations or other provocative actions' for one month (starting at noon, local time, on 10 June). An exchange of prisoners is also part of the agreement.

9 June 1994. The US House of Representatives, by a vote of 244 to 178, adopts a resolution which requires the president to 'terminate the US arms embargo on the government of Bosnia and Hercegovina upon receipt from that government of a request for assistance in exercising its right of self-defence'. The house also authorizes up to $200 million in arms and training services to the Bosnian government. (President Clinton is not in favour of the unilateral lifting of the arms embargo.)

10 June 1994. The cease-fire begins. (It held generally at first, but not everywhere. The most notable exception was fighting in the Bihac area between Bosnian government forces and the supporters of Fikret Abdic, who did not take part in the cease-fire agreement. But the number of violations of the cease-fire increased, Bosnian government forces being the worst offenders. One of their main goals was the Mount Ozren area in north central Bosnia, where Serb-held land is finger-like in shape. Here ground was initially gained at the expense of the Serbs, with Bosnian government forces intent on fully securing the road between Zenica and Tuzla. But the Serbs successfully counter-attacked. The main potential flashpoint, however, remained the narrow strip of Serb-held land around Brcko in the Posavina corridor connecting the main Serb-held areas.)

14 June 1994. President Tudjman of Croatia visits Sarajevo to open the Croatian embassy there.

19 June 1994. A benefit concert is given in Sarajevo by international opera stars.

22 June 1994. The first contingent of Turkish troops arrive in the Croatian port of Split, *en route* for duty in Bosnia.

30 June 1994. The Serbs in Krajina take around twenty heavy weapons (including tanks) out of UN-monitored storage and move them over the border to the Bihac area.

1 July 1994. The US Senate, by the narrowest of margins, fails to support the resolution lifting the arms embargo on the Bosnian government passed by the House of Representatives on 9 June. The vote was fifty-fifty, with Vice-President Al Gore casting the decisive vote.

6 July 1994. The 'contact group' presents its plan, including the map, to the factions (see above, the various plans for Bosnia-Hercegovina).

7 July 1994. The Bosnian government says it will recommend the plan to parliament, while Karadzic says that the map provides a basis for further negotiations.

10 July 1994. The 'political G8' (which includes Russia) issue a communiqué which says that member countries 'strongly believe that the parties to the Bosnian conflict should accept the plan . . . If the opportunity is not seized, there is a grave risk of renewal of war on a larger scale . . . we shall ensure that the measures made known to the parties in the event of either acceptance or refusal are implemented.' The foreign ministers of France and the UK are sent on a two-day mission to talk to all sides (12–13 July 1994).

12 July 1994. There is agreement to extend the cease-fire (which expired at noon local time on 10 July).

14 July 1994. Bosnian government forces in the Bihac area make a brief incursion into Serb-held Krajina to counter cross-border artillery fire.

15 July 1994. Turkish President Suleyman Demirel visits his troops in Zenica, but cancels the planned visit to Sarajevo because the Serbs refuse to guarantee the safety of his flight.

16 July 1994. The Bosnian Croats accept the plan.

17 July 1994. Lieutenant-General Rose says that the UN peacekeeping force may have to be withdrawn by the end of the summer to make way for a Nato combat force if the Bosnian Serbs reject the plan.

18 July 1994. A joint session of the Bosnian parliament and the parliament of the new federation accepts the plan.

The Bosnian Serbs' self-proclaimed parliament begins its discussion of the plan.

19 July 1994. The Bosnian Serbs end their two-day meeting, but refuse to disclose their decision until their meeting with the 'contact group' in Geneva the following day.

21 July 1994. It is publicly revealed that the Bosnian Serbs do not accept the plan unconditionally: (1) 'further work is required on the proposed map'; (2) six points need further discussion, including 'constitutional arrangements', their share of Sarajevo, access to the sea and the lifting of sanctions.

Bosnian Serb forces are blamed for shooting at aircraft using Sarajevo airport for the second day running.

President Izetbegovic says that 'our unconditional yes ceased to be valid'.

Two (French) UN soldiers defect to the Bosnian Serbs, seemingly to protest against Moslem immigration into France.

22 July 1994. Bosnian Prime Minister Haris Silajdzic says that 'our Yes is still on the table', but the 'contact group' needs to 'stay true to its commitments'.

24 July 1994. Yasushi Akashi gives Croatian refugees blockading checkpoints on the demarcation line with the Krajina a week to end their action (which has been going on for three weeks and which has prevented supplies from reaching UN forces; the blockade was lifted in time).

25 July 1994. UN Secretary-General Boutros Boutros-Ghali says he will recommend the withdrawal of UN peacekeeping troops from the Balkans regardless of whether the plan is signed or not (because in the case of the former only troops from the 'contact group' countries can enforce the plan, while the latter makes UN troops vulnerable to attack).

For the second day running UN personnel protest at Bosnian Serb firing of heavy weapons into the Gorazde exclusion zone.

26 July 1994. Karadzic says that from the following day civilian traffic in and out of Sarajevo will be halted (i.e. only UN traffic will be allowed). He alleges violations such as using the route to smuggle arms to the Bosnian government.

27 July 1994. The Bosnian Serbs attack a UN convoy using the route near Sarajevo. There were a number of casualties and one soldier died (the seventh in total from the UK). (The Bosnian Serbs also attacked French UN soldiers who attempted to rescue the convoy.)

28 July 1994. The Bosnian Serb assembly ('parliament') insists on the need for further negotiations (the 'parliament' pointedly addressed its comments to Milosevic and Russia).

29 July 1994. Russian Foreign Minister Kozyrev says that Russia feels betrayed by the Bosnian Serbs.

30 July 1994. The 'contact group' decides, as initial measures, to recommend to the UN Security Council (1) a tightening of sanctions on the Federal Republic of Yugoslavia (and the Bosnian and Croatian Serbs by definition) and (2) 'strict enforcement' of the exclusion zones in Bosnia.

31 July 1994. Milosevic says that 'the proposal of the international community must be accepted. Who has the right to reject peace on behalf of the Serb people? No one has the right . . . It is not entirely just as far as the Serb side is concerned . . . but without doubt a compromise is necessary.'

1 August 1994. The Bosnian Serbs seek to reopen negotiations with the 'contact group'. Once agreement has been reached on changes to the map and on guaranteeing the sovereignty of the (self-proclaimed) 'Bosnian Serb Republic', 'the Serbs will be ready to accept the plan'.

2 August 1994. The Serbian government sends a letter to the leaders of the Bosnian Serbs: 'If at the moment when peace is being offered you usurp the right to decide about the fate of the Federal Republic of Serbia, you, as leaders, eliminate all possibility of further relations with us . . . If it is not enough that the Republic of Srpska exists and that peace is offered on that basis, then you are on the way to committing a crime against your own people by rejecting that . . . If you fail to accept peace, you will commit the greatest ever treason against Serb national interests.'

Kozyrev says that 'We cannot be a toy in the hands of the party of war. Therefore, I am not going to hold any talks with Mr Karadzic. I expect him to say yes [to the plan]. His interests have been fully taken into account. This is all we could do for him.'

3 August 1994. The Bosnian Serb Assembly decides to hold a referendum (27–28 August) on whether to accept the plan.

4 August 1994. The Federal Republic of Yugoslavia says that it is to bar entry to all Bosnian Serb leaders and close its borders with the Serb-held areas of Bosnia except for the movement of food, medicine and clothing.

Milosevic accuses the Bosnian Serb leaders of 'insane political ambitions and greed'. 'The Bosnian Serb leadership is acting in the interests of its own political aims and in the name of war profiteers.' (According to one report, Milosevic has moved to set up his own Socialist Party organization in Serb-held Bosnia in recent weeks: *The Times*, 5 August 1994, p. 12.)

An estimated 1,000 rebel Moslem soldiers surrender to Bosnian government forces in the town of Pecigrad (Bihac).

5 August 1994. The Bosnian Serbs raid a UN-monitored site in the Sarajevo zone and retrieve a tank, two armoured personnel carriers and an anti-aircraft gun. Nato jets respond with strikes (a tank buster is confirmed as destroyed). (The heavy weapons were quickly returned.) (Note that these events came on top of increasing violations of the cease-fire in Sarajevo, e.g. sniping and exchanges of fire in general. The UN has been taking a more aggressive stance on sniping.)

6 August 1994. Karadzic says that 'now we are totally, totally alone; only God is with us'. He orders full-scale mobilization of the work force (e.g. a ten-hour working day and the suspension of holidays). (The trams have stopped running in Sarajevo until 22 August.)

7 August 1994. Lieutenant-General Rose calls for the demilitarization of Sarajevo.

9 August 1994. Bosnian government forces make major advances in the Bihac area and many civilians and rebel soldiers flee across the border into Krajina.

US Secretary of State Warren Christopher says that sanctions against the Federal Republic of Yugoslavia could be eased if the sanctions it has imposed on the Bosnian Serbs prove to be effective.

10 August 1994. Lieutenant-General Rose threatens both Bosnian Serb and Bosnian government forces with air strikes if artillery exchanges continue within the Sarajevo heavy weapons exclusion zone.

The UN makes no attempt to extend the 'truce'.

11 August 1994. President Clinton comments on the possibility of lifting the arms embargo on the Bosnian government: 'If by 15 October the Bosnian Serbs have not accepted the contact group's proposal of 6 July 1994, it would be my intention within two weeks to introduce formally and to support a resolution at the UN Security Council to terminate the arms embargo.'

12 August 1994. The UN command in Bosnia says that lifting the arms embargo would make it difficult to retain peacekeeping troops in Bosnia.

14 August 1994. France says that it will withdraw its peacekeeping troops from Bosnia if the arms embargo is lifted.

An agreement is signed (effective the following day) to halt sniping in Sarajevo (the effectiveness of the agreement faded as time went on).

15 August 1994. Fikret Abdic announces a unilateral cease-fire in Bihac.

17 August 1994. The Bosnian Serbs say that as of the following day they will prevent UN aid convoys crossing their territory unless they are given fuel. The UN refuses to comply, calling it blackmail.

It is announced that the Pope will visit Sarajevo on 8 September and Zagreb on 10–11 September.

18 August 1994. The Bosnian Serb leaders call for a 'Greater Serbia'.

20 August 1994. The Croatian Serbs say that reunification should be postponed until after the war.

The UN attempts to mediate, but Fikret Abdic refuses to declare the 'autonomous province of western Bosnia' null and void.

21 August 1994. The Bihac enclave effectively falls when Abdic's castle stronghold of Velika Kladusha falls to Bosnian government forces. Thousands of civilians and troops flee across the border into the Krajina. The Bosnian government offers an amnesty to all but 'war criminals'. The government of Croatia refuses to allow the refugees to cross into territory it controls.

27–28 August 1994. The Bosnian Serbs hold their referendum: 'Are you in favour of the map for the territorial division of the former Bosnia-Hercegovina proposed by the International Contact Group?' There was an overwhelming 'no' vote. (Serbia refused to allow voting on its territory.)

29 August 1994. Russian Foreign Minister Kozyrev says that Milosevic should be rewarded by the lifting of certain sanctions.

6 September 1994. It is announced that the Pope's visit to Sarajevo, planned for 8 September, has been called off for security reasons. (The Orthodox Church opposed a visit to Belgrade.)

8 September 1994. The Serbs launch a two-pronged attack on Bihac, one by Croatian Serbs from the Krajina. An anti-aircraft missile is fired at two UN (British) jets patrolling the area.

9 September 1994. It is reported that Milosevic has agreed to accept international (civilian) observers to monitor Serbia's sanctions on the Bosnian Serbs.

10–11 September 1994. The Pope visits Zagreb.

EU foreign ministers agree (1) to recommend a relaxation of sanctions on Serbia if (135) monitors are allowed and (2) that the lifting of the arms embargo on the Bosnian government would have 'incalculable consequences'; it should be undertaken only as a 'last resort'.

On 11 September the EU's administrative headquarters in Mostar are hit by an anti-tank shell coming from the Croat district (the following day a Bailey bridge over the Neretva, built by the British army, was opened).

President Izetgegovic says that 'If you confront us with the choice between UN peacekeepers and weapons, we choose weapons. They at least guarantee our people's survival' (quoted in *The Times*, 12 September 1994, p. 1).

14 September 1994. The Federal Republic of Yugoslavia formally welcomes the use of international observers to monitor sanctions imposed on the Bosnian Serbs (parts of the Serbian press describe the observers as 'a group of humanitarian civilians' coming to help improve the provision of aid to Bosnia).

Presidents Tudjman and Izetbegovic meet in Zagreb to discuss the problems experienced in implementing the new Bosnian federation.

15 September 1994. Serbian action cuts off water, gas and electricity supplies to Sarajevo (not restored until 29 September).

16 September 1994. Nato decides to extend air operations to cover attacks on UN peacekeepers from Serb-held territory in Croatia.

18 September 1994. Serious fighting breaks out in Sarajevo and Lieutenant-General Rose warns both sides.

19 September 1994. Lieutenant-General Rose blames Bosnian government forces for starting the fighting and threatens air strikes. He wins an assurance that such action will stop (it seems as though Bosnian government forces attacked a Serb-held supply road).

22 September 1994. Nato jets destroy a tank after three Bosnian Serb attacks on UN forces (the empty and demobilized tank was not actually involved in any of the incidents).

23 September 1994. The UN Security Council votes to suspend certain sanctions on the Federal Republic of Yugoslavia for a trial period of 100 days, specifically to allow (1) direct passenger flights to Belgrade (and the restoration of ferry services between Italy and Montenegro) and (2) cultural and sporting exchanges. The suspension is dependent on a favourable response from the international observers.

The Security Council also tightens up economic sanctions on the Bosnian Serbs and bars their leaders from international travel.

25 September 1994. The Bosnian Serbs promise to allow the restoration of gas supplies to Sarajevo.

26 September 1994. The Bosnian government announces that it would be willing to suspend the lifting of the arms embargo for six months.

29 September 1994. Nato defence ministers recommend a tougher use of air strikes in Bosnia ('proportionate, robust and effective'). (On 5 October Nato recommended the possibility of multiple air strikes without warning.)

30 September 1994. The UN Security Council authorizes a further six months of peacekeeping by UN troops in the former Yugoslavia.

1 October 1994. The Bosnian Serbs promise to lift the ban on UN aid convoys going through their territory (imposed after the destruction of the tank on 22 September).

2 October 1994. The promise is not kept.

3 October 1994. A number of convoys are allowed to proceed.

5 October 1994. Following a positive response from the international observers, the limited lifting of sanctions on the Federal Republic of Yugoslavia comes into effect.

The Bosnian Serbs promise to allow Sarajevo airport (which has been closed for about two weeks) to reopen.

6 October 1994. A large exchange of prisoners takes place in Sarajevo.

UN troops find the bodies of sixteen Bosnian Serb soldiers and four female nurses (south of Sarajevo's demilitarized zone in the Mount Igman area). They were killed in a commando raid by Bosnian government forces. (Yasushi Akashi later withdrew his accusation that many of the bodies were mutilated.)

7 October 1994. UN troops drive some of the Bosnian government forces out of the zone.

UN flights into Sarajevo airport resume briefly after being halted by the Bosnian Serbs on 22 September.

9 October 1994. UN flights into Sarajevo resume in earnest.

14 October 1994. The international court for war crimes under Richard Goldstone names the first person to be charged. The charges against Dusan Tadic (a Bosnian Serb arrested earlier in the year in Germany) include murder, torture and rape during 'ethnic cleansing' in the Prijedor region of north-west Bosnia (Germany consented to his extradition on 31 March 1995 and he was actually extradited on 24 April 1995. On 26 April 1995 he pleaded not guilty to the charges of 'genocide, through the policy of ethnic cleansing, and crimes against humanity, such as assault, murder, rape and persecution based on religious grounds').

17 October 1994. The Bosnian Serbs hi-jack an aid convoy and steal medical supplies.

18 October 1994. The Bosnian Serbs attack an aid convoy near Gorazde, killing a driver.

20 October 1994. An alleged Serbian war criminal, Dusko Cvjetkovic, goes on trial in Austria (the first in a Western country). The trial is postponed until 5 December 1994.

21 October 1994. The Bosnian Serbs claim to have crushed an illegal network within the army and police (presumably under the instructions of Milosevic) plotting to undermine the state. Arrests take place of 'an illegal group who committed several crimes with the goal of crippling the functioning of state institutions'.

22 October 1994. The UN persuades the Bosnian government to withdraw its remaining 500 or so troops from the demilitarized zone, while the Bosnian Serbs agree to end their two-week blockade of fuel supplies (including those to UN forces). The Bosnian government also demands that the road through Mount Igman should be made safe from Bosnian Serb attack (it is the only access road under Bosnian government control).

24 October 1994. There is an exchange of fire between UN forces and Bosnian government forces in the demilitarized zone.

All eight parties in the Bosnian parliament in Sarajevo issue a statement (published in the press the following day) demanding the immediate dismissal of Lieutenant-General Rose (who is due to be replaced in January 1995). It is alleged that he 'does everything to water down the determination of the free world to punish crime and fascism . . . we are asking for an impartial, objective commander, one who will implement UN resolutions on the ground, a man who will be an official of the UN and not a general who protects the interests of his government.'

26 October 1994. Bosnian government forces begin a highly successful offensive in the Bihac area.

28 October 1994. The Bosnian Serbs threaten to shell Bihac and Sarajevo in retaliation for the Bihac offensive and commando raids around the capital.

Nato and the UN agree new guidelines for air strikes. There will be multiple targets in some way connected with the offensive (probably three or four targets) and warnings will generally not be given (a warning will be given in order to avoid civilian casualties).

The USA tables a Security Council resolution calling for an automatic six-month timetable for lifting the UN arms embargo on the Bosnian government.

29 October 1994. Bosnian government forces launch an attack from the demilitarized zone on Bosnian Serb positions. The UN, whose forces are fired on by the Bosnian government forces while attempting to intervene, threatens to use air strikes.

30 October 1994. President Izetbegovic promises to cease the attack and withdraw his troops.

The Pope makes Archbishop Vinko Puljic of Sarajevo a cardinal, the first ever in Bosnia.

31 October 1994. The Serbs from Krajina declare that they will help the Bosnian Serbs militarily.

1 November 1994. There are reports that Bosnian Croats have begun to help Bosnian government forces in the Bihac area and around Kupres in central Bosnia.

3 November 1994. Kupres falls to Bosnian government and Bosnian Croat forces, the first relatively important town lost by the Bosnian Serbs.

4 November 1994. The Bosnian Serb leaders declare a 'general mobilization' and announce that they will ask the Bosnian Serb 'parliament' to impose martial law. Karadzic says that 'We are going to declare a state of war in our assembly and to call a general mobilization and fight to the final victory.'

The UN denounces the firing of surface-to-air missiles into Bihac.

The UN General Assembly votes to lift the arms embargo on the Bosnian government after six months.

5 November 1994. The Bosnian Serbs counter-attack in the Bihac area and have some success.

The UN (successfully) warns both sides when fighting flares up in the Sarajevo area (seemingly started by Bosnian government troops).

7 November 1994. The international court for war crimes issues an arrest warrant for Dragan Nikolic, a Bosnian Serb still in the Serb-held area. He is charged with murder, torture and mutilation while commander of a detention camp.

8 November 1994. At the court's inaugural meeting Germany is asked to hand over Dusan Tadic.

9 November 1994. The Croatian Serbs launch air strikes against Bihac.

11 November 1994. The USA will cease to enforce the arms embargo on the Bosnian government as of midnight 12 November (except for weapons of mass destruction and missiles).

The Bosnian Serb 'parliament' empowers Karadzic to declare martial law in any area deemed appropriate.

The Bosnian Serbs have substantial success in their counter-offensive in the Bihac area (helped by Croatian Serb artillery fire from across the border; it is uncertain whether Croatian Serb personnel are involved).

13 November 1994. The UN Security Council condemns the escalation of fighting in the Bihac area and demands that the Croatian Serbs stay out of the conflict.

14 November 1994. The UN estimates that the Bosnian Serbs have regained about 80 per cent of the territory lost around the Bihac area. (Fikret Abdic has also sent people to fight on the side of the Bosnian Serbs.)

17 November 1994. The Bosnian Serbs hit the presidency building in Sarajevo with missiles and grenades.

18 November 1994. The Croatian Serbs launch an air attack against the Bihac area using napalm and cluster bombs.

19 November 1994. The UN Security Council and Nato both agree to make the Croatian Serb area (the Krajina) open to retaliatory air strikes. (The Croatian government gave its permission, for a week at first.)

21 November 1994. Thirty-nine Nato aircraft bomb the Udbina airfield in the Krajina. The airfield itself, missile sites and anti-aircraft defences were attacked, but (deliberately) not aircraft.

22 November 1994. A Bosnian Moslem (Refic Saric) is sentenced in Copenhagen to eight years in jail for torturing prisoners in a Bosnian Croat detention camp; two of the prisoners died.

23 November 1994. Nato planes attack three missile sites around the Bihac area (one in the Krajina) after the previous day's attempt to bring down two Nato aircraft.

The Bosnian Serbs appear to be on the verge of taking Bihac, with the help of Abdic and Croatian Serb forces.

Yasushi Akashi announces a peace package agreed to by Milosevic and the Bosnian Croat president, Milan Martic.

24 November 1994. The Bosnian Serbs enter the UN-designated 'safe area' of Bihac.

Nato fails to agree on a response, except to propose an extension of the no-fly zone to the Krajina and to refer the matter to the UN. The USA proposed a three-point plan: (1) to define clearly the 'safe area' and to extend it by 7 km; (2) to threaten the Bosnian Serbs with unlimited air strikes unless they withdraw their forces and weapons; (3) the area to be demilitarized and supervised by a lightly armed international police force (the Bosnian government forces would be given safe passage out of the area).

25 November 1994. Peace talks fail.

UN aircraft seek targets around Bihac, but fail to find them in the dark.

The USA sends three vessels and around 2,000 marines to the Adriatic in case UN or Nato forces need rescuing.

27 November 1994. The UN and Nato do nothing while the Bosnian Serbs continue to take over the 'safe area' of Bihac and detain more Unprofor forces as hostages. (On 29 November General Mladic demanded Nato flight plans in return for the hostages.)

US Secretary of State William Perry says that the Bosnian Serbs 'have demonstrated military superiority on the ground' and that Nato air strikes will not influence the situation in Bihac. 'Stopping the spreading of the war is the major national interest that the USA has today.'

Senator Robert Dole (Republican majority leader-elect in the US Senate) delivers a blistering attack and called for a lifting of the arms embargo on the Bosnian government. 'We have the United Nations vetoing targets, driven by the British and the French – primarily the British . . . The biggest stumbling block is the British. They are the ones who want to do absolutely nothing.' As for Lieutenant-General Rose and Yasushi Akashi, 'What they have done from the start is to help the Serb aggressors.' 'The UN protection forces are supposed to be there to protect civilians. They are not doing it. It may be time to get the UN protection forces out of there, redeploy them somewhere. They are not doing their job and they are in harm's way.' 'This is a classic failure where Nato has been tied in knots and almost become irrelevant. I think we have a complete breakdown of Nato.'

29 November 1994. Senator Dole again recommends that the arms embargo should be lifted: 'There has been no pressure on the Serbs and until there is some leverage it's going to be very difficult to stop the fighting.'

30 November 1994. Boutros Boutros-Ghali visits Sarajevo. He is jeered by a crowd of citizens and Radovan Karadzic refuses to meet him in Sarajevo (Karadzic wanted him to go to Pale).

Lady Thatcher returns to the attack. 'Every nation has the right to self-defence . . . they must have arms or you leave the innocent to suffer at the hands of ruthless Serb aggressors . . . What is going on in some of those safe havens is aggression, murder, almost amounting to genocide.' Nato has been robbed of its credibility. 'They have not stood up to the Serb aggressor; that is not a matter of opinion, that is a matter of fact.'

2 December 1994. There is great confusion about whether the UN requested Nato to stop (or at least scale down) air patrols over Bosnia to aid the peace negotiations.

The 'contact group' comes up with an amended plan (see above, on the various plans for Bosnia-Hercegovina).

Russia vetoes a Security Council resolution to block fuel supplies getting from the Federal Republic of Yugoslavia to the Croatian and Bosnian Serbs.

3 December 1994. Regular Nato air patrols resume. The Bosnian Serbs are warned that their missile sites will be attacked if they lock their radar on to Nato planes (there is speculation that new anti-aircraft systems from Russia have been employed, supplied via the Federal Republic of Yugoslavia).

4 December 1994. The foreign ministers of France and the UK visit Serbia and Milosevic backs the revised plan.

6 December 1994. The CSCE meeting in Budapest (5–6 December) ends in disarray. Russia vetoes any statement condemning Bosnian Serb aggression in Bosnia, especially a call for an end to the attack on Bihac by the Bosnian and Croatian Serbs. The Bosnian government is unwilling to support a statement simply calling for a cease-fire without naming the Serbs as aggressors. (The CSCE became the OSCE, Organization for Security and Co-operation in Europe.)

7 December 1994. The UN announces that up to 400 of the 1,200 Unprofor troops in Bihac are to be withdrawn 'temporarily'.

8 December 1994. The UN demands the immediate withdrawal from Bosnia of both the Croatian Serbs (fighting in the Bihac area) and Croatian army soldiers (fighting alongside Bosnian Croats west of Kupres). (On 30 November Croat or Bosnian Croat forces fired into the Krajina.)

10 December 1994. The EU issues a statement endorsing the 'contact group's' plan, condemning the Bosnian and Croatian Serb attack on Bihac, recommending an increase in the number of observers monitoring the embargo imposed by the Federal Republic of Yugoslavia on the Bosnian Serbs and ruling out the withdrawal of Unprofor troops supplied by EU countries for the moment at least (there are currently 23,600 Unprofor troops in total).

The Bosnian Serbs say that Unprofor forces will not be allowed to use armoured vehicles to escort aid convoys through territory controlled by the Serbs.

12 December 1994. The forces attacking Bihac deliberately fire at Unprofor forces, wounding several (one died later).

15 December 1994. Karadzic suggests that former US president Jimmy Carter should act as mediator.

The Organization of Islamic Conference (representing fifty-two countries) issues a statement after its meeting in Casablanca: 'we resolve to reconsider present economic relations between our countries and those which support the Serbian position'. There is no unilateral lifting of the arms embargo on the Bosnian government, but the statement says that the embargo 'cannot, legally or morally, be applied to the Republic of Bosnia-Hercegovina'.

17 December 1994. Velika Kladusa falls.

18 December 1994. Jimmy Carter starts his personal mission.

19 December 1994. Jimmy Carter says that the Bosnian Serbs have agreed to a four-month cease-fire, to stop hindering aid operations and to negotiate 'on the basis of' the 'contact group's' plan. (The Bosnian Serbs were aiming for a permanent cease-fire in order to freeze their gains, while the Bosnian government had in mind a three-month cease-fire at most.)

20 December 1994. Jimmy Carter announces that the Bosnian Serbs and the Bosnian government have agreed to a four-month cease-fire starting at noon on 23 December. They will try to negotiate a 'total cessation of hostilities' by 1 January 1995.

23 December 1994. The UN announces that the Bosnian government and the Bosnian Serbs have agreed to a cease-fire, starting at noon on 24 December, with negotiations until 1 January aimed at bringing about a four-month 'cessation of hostilities'. (There was no agreement on the questions of the exchange of prisoners and information on missing persons or the contact group's plan.)

25 December 1994. The Bosnian government threatens to call off the cease-fire if attacks on Bihac continue (the Bosnian government claims that Bosnian Serbs are helping the Croatian Serbs and Abdic forces, neither of which have signed the agreement).

28 December 1994. Lieutenant-General Rose says that Abdic has agreed to a cease-fire.

29 December 1994. The Bosnian Serb 'parliament' resolves 'to enter into negotiations on the basis of the agreement with Carter'.

Fighting in Bihac continues.

31 December 1994. The Bosnian government and the Bosnian Serbs agree to a four-month cessation of hostilities, to come into effect the following day. The agreement includes the following: the withdrawal of forces from front lines; the interposing of UN peacekeeping troops, who will monitor the cessation of hostilities and the removal of heavy weapons; the reopening of UN-secured civilian routes ('blue routes') into Sarajevo and the enclaves; complete freedom of movement for aid convoys; the removal of Bosnian government forces from the demilitarized zone on Mount Igman; the restoration of utility services; an exchange of prisoners; the removal of 'all foreign troops'.

1 January 1995. The cessation of hostilities comes into effect.

2 January 1995. The Bosnian Croats agree to the cessation of hostilities.

3 January 1995. Fighting continues in the Bihac area.

6 January 1995. The UN requests 6,000 additional peacekeeping troops.

The international monitoring team reports that Serbia has kept its promises on sanctions against the Bosnian Serbs to the best of its ability.

14 January 1995. The Bosnian Serbs do not keep their promise to open the 'blue routes' into Sarajevo and also bar relief columns for Unprofor troops from entering the eastern enclaves.

Bosnian government forces retake some land around Bihac. There is some shelling of Bihac.

16 January 1995. Some Bosnian government troops remain in the demilitarized zone on Mount Igman.

19 January 1995. The USA announces that it is to have direct talks with the Bosnian Serbs (they began the same day).

The cease-fire continues to unravel slowly. There is fierce fighting in the Bihac area and clashes are reported on several other fronts.

Lieutenant-General Rose fails to lift the nine-day-old blockade of Unprofor troops in their base at Tuzla airport by Bosnian government forces (objecting to the deployment of a Serb liaison officer, who is allegedly a war criminal).

In the first war crimes trial to be held in the Krajina a Croatian Serb, Dusan Boljevic, is sentenced to twenty years for killing seven unarmed prisoners.

20 January 1994. The Bosnian government and the Bosnian Serbs begin to exchange prisoners.

23 January 1995. At the end of his (ultimately controversial) official term as Unprofor commander in Bosnia, Lieutenant-General Rose is replaced by Lieutenant-General Rupert Smith (also from the UK; he arrived on 26 January).

It is announced that the 'blue routes' into Sarajevo will reopen on 1 February 1995.

27 January 1995. 'Contact group' representatives go home because of the lack of success with the Bosnian Serbs.

30 January 1995. There is heavy fighting in the Bihac area.

3 February 1995. The UN reports that more than fifteen helicopters from Serbia were seen flying to Bosnia, presumably on a resupply mission for the Bosnian Serbs. (In a four-day period the UN counted at least sixty-two helicopter sorties from Serbia to Bosnian Serb territory. There were also disputed reports of planes supplying Bosnian government forces: *IHT*, 22 February 1995, p. 5. There was ill feeling between the UN and Nato and some suspected the USA of surreptitiously, directly or indirectly, supplying arms to the Bosnian government.)

6 February 1995. Civilian traffic begins to use roads across Sarajevo airport.

13 February 1995. The international court for war crimes issues arrest warrants for twenty-one Serbs who ran prison camps, charged with war crimes and crimes against humanity. The only one in custody is Dusan Tadic (under arrest in Germany; note that, although the accused cannot be tried *in absentia*, evidence can be presented and a record of the crimes established). Zeljko Meakic, the commander of the Omarska camp in north-west Bosnia, is charged with genocide.

A spokesman for the UN High Commissioner for Refugees says that in Bihac some face starvation: 'The word starvation is now appropriate' (heavy fighting has continued in the Bihac area, with Bosnian Serbs, Croatian Serbs and Abdic 'rebels' fighting Bosnian government forces).

15 February 1995. An aid convoy reaches Bihac.

19 February 1995. Milosevic and Russian Foreign Minister Andrei Kozyrev issue a joint statement urging the lifting of sanctions on the Federal Republic of Yugoslavia: 'The lifting of sanctions is the first essential step towards a definitive solution to the Yugoslav crisis.'

20 February 1995. The Bosnian and Croatian Serbs form a joint 'supreme defence council' and agree to aid each other if attacked.

24 February 1995. There are reports that Bosnian government forces have started an offensive near Travnik.

25 February 1995. There are reports that the Bosnian Serbs have renewed 'ethnic cleansing' around Banja Luka.

27 February 1995. President Suleyman Demirel of Turkey is unable to fly into Sarajevo for fear of the plane being shot at by the Bosnian Serbs.

4 March 1995. The Bosnian Serbs allow a relief convoy for UN troops to reach Srebrenica.

6 March 1995. Croatia, the Bosnian government and the Bosnian Croat militia agree to form a military alliance, including the setting up of joint military headquarters (the Bosnian government later denied that joint headquarters were part of the deal, which only meant 'co-ordinated action').

9 March 1995. UN relief officials cut off aid to the Croatian Serbs and the Abdic forces for hindering aid supplies to Bihac.

Some results are revealed of a CIA report completed earlier in the year and based on techniques including aerial photography. Some 90 per cent of 'ethnic cleansing' in Bosnia had been undertaken by the Bosnian Serbs, 'the only party involved in a systematic attempt to eliminate all traces of other ethnic groups from their territory'. 'The systematic nature of the Serbian actions strongly suggests' that the Bosnian Serb leaders and 'perhaps Belgrade exercised a carefully veiled role in the purposeful destruction and dispersal of the non-Serb populations'. But while there was no 'conclusive evidence' of direct involvement by the Serb leaders, there was proof that Karadzic and others were aware of the existence of concentration camps controlled by the Bosnian Serbs.

A UN Human Rights Commission resolution condemns the Serbs for 'the systematic policy of ethnic cleansing and genocidal acts' in Bosnia and Croatia. The resolution also criticizes Serbia for discrimination against ethnic Albanians and Hungarians.

12 March 1995. The Bosnian Serbs cut off the 'blue routes' into Sarajevo when two Bosnian Serb girls are shot dead by snipers.

14 March 1995. Nine Unprofor (French) troops are killed and four seriously injured in a road accident on Mount Igman near Sarajevo.

15 March 1995. The UN reports widespread hunger and malnutrition in Bihac.

16 March 1995. A UN foot patrol is attacked by the Bosnian Serbs in Gorazde (the second attack in less than a week).

20 March 1995. Bosnian government forces launch a major offensive to capture Bosnian Serb positions on peaks around Tuzla and Travnik (the targets including communications towers). There is also an offensive around Gradacac. The Bosnian Serbs respond with heavy artillery barrages (there was heavy loss of life when a shell hit a Bosnian government barracks in Tuzla). (Sarajevo has been subjected to increasing sniping and shelling.)

The Bosnian Serbs take some heavy weapons from a UN-protected depot in Sarajevo.

25 March 1995. Radovan Karadzic calls for direct peace talks with the Bosnian government. (It was generally thought that this was due to some success achieved by Bosnian government forces in the offensives.)

The Bosnian Serbs shell Mostar and Gorazde.

26 March 1995. Karadzic orders general mobilization.

27 March 1995. Lieutenant-General Smith's spokesman says that attacks which come from outside a 'safe area' and which deliberately target civilians will meet a resolute response, including the use of air strikes. Bosnian government forces will not be protected if an attack comes from within a 'safe area'.

31 March 1995. Three resolutions are adopted by the Security Council as the current mandate of UN troops in the former Yugoslavia expires:

1. The creation of three separate but interlocking UN commands for Croatia, Bosnia and Macedonia.

2. The changing of the force names to UN Confidence Restoration Operation (Uncro) in Croatia, UN Protection Force for Bosnia and UN Preventative Deployment Force for Macedonia.

3. Extend the mandates for eight months to 30 November 1995.

The resolution on Croatia says that UN troops are to assist in 'controlling, by monitoring and reporting, the crossing of military personnel, equipment, supplies and weapons' over Croatia's international borders with Bosnia and the Federal Republic of Yugoslavia.

2 April 1995. Bihac is shelled.

5 April 1995. The third anniversary of the siege of Sarajevo (the killing of a civilian by a sniper while she was demonstrating against the raising of barricades by Bosnian Serbs is taken as the start of the war).

8 April 1995. Bosnian government forces claim to have taken Mount Vlasic, overlooking Travnik. (The Serbs then respond by, for example, shelling Sarajevo and Gorazde.)

10 April 1995. Unprofor issues a warning to the Bosnian Serbs about shelling Sarajevo.

12 April 1995. 'Contact group' envoys cancel their planned visit to Sarajevo when the Bosnian Serbs refuse to guarantee the safety of their plane.

14 April 1995. A French UN soldier is killed by a sniper in Sarajevo.

The Russian State Duma votes to lift sanctions on the Federal Republic of Yugoslavia.

15 April 1995. Another French soldier is killed by a sniper in Sarajevo.

There are reports that the USA may be tacitly accepting the delivery of arms by Iran to the Bosnian government (*IHT*, 15 April 1995, p. 1).

21 April 1995. Russia refuses to support a Security Council resolution to monitor air traffic as well as the land border with the Federal Republic of Yugoslavia. But only a seventy-five-day extension of the sanctions concessions is allowed (as opposed to the previous 100 days).

22 April 1995. Karadzic closes Sarajevo airport to all political delegations.

Three French soldiers are killed in an accidential explosion in Sarajevo.

24 April 1995. The international court for war crimes names Radovan Karadzic, General Ratko Mladic (the Bosnian Serb army commander) and Mico Stanisic (the former Bosnian Serb secret police chief) as suspected war criminals.

29 April 1995. Planes from the Krajina attack the Bihac enclave.

1 May 1995. The 'cease-fire' ends and is not extended. The Croats launch an attack in the Krajina (see Croatia).

7 May 1995. Eleven people are killed when Sarajevo is shelled (near the entrance to the tunnel which forms the city's link with the outside world). Prime Minister Haris Silajdzic says that 'People all over Europe and the world are celebrating the victory over fascism. Fascism is not dead.'

'Only resolute and, if necessary, continued Nato air strikes against Serbian artillery positions can end the siege and save the city' (Warren Zimmerman, *IHT*, 15 May 1995, p. 8).

8 May 1995. It is revealed that Yasushi Akashi (and General Bernard Janvier, overall commander of UN troops in the former Yugoslavia) turned down a request from Lieutenant-General Rupert Smith for air strikes on the Bosnian Serbs.

12 May 1995. Boutros Boutros-Ghali orders a 'fundamental review' of the role of UN peacekeeping troops.

16 May 1995. There are large-scale artillery exchanges in Sarajevo, the culmination of a gradual tightening of the siege of the city by the Bosnian Serbs.

Another French soldier, shot by a sniper in Sarajevo on 11 May, dies of his injuries.

24 May 1995. Lieutenant-General Smith threatens air strikes against any transgressor if the following deadlines are not met: (1) all heavy weapons to cease firing in the (20 km) Sarajevo exclusion zone by noon local time on 25 May and (2) all such weapons to be either outside the exclusion zone or in UN-controlled collection sites by noon on 26 May.

25 May 1995. Nato jets attack a Bosnian Serb ammunition dump near Pale when four guns taken from a UN collection site are not returned. The Bosnian Serbs respond by shelling Sarajevo and four other 'safe areas'. Seventy-one civilians are killed in Tuzla.

26 May 1995. Nato jets launch another attack on the ammunition dump.

The Bosnian Serbs retaliate by holding UN peacekeepers as hostages and using (unarmed) UN military observers as 'human shields' at likely targets of Nato air strikes.

27 May 1995. Two (French) UN soldiers and four Bosnian Serbs are killed in a heavy exchange of fire over control of an observation post on a bridge in Sarajevo.

28 May 1995. The UK announces that reinforcements will be sent after thirty-three British troops are taken hostage in Gorazde (1,200 more heavily armed troops immediately and 5,500 on stand-by). (France ordered an aircraft carrier to the Adriatic.)

The Bosnian foreign minister, Irfan Ljubijankic, is killed when his helicopter, en route from Bihac to Zagreb, is shot down over territory controlled by the Croatian Serbs.

29 May 1995. Andrei Kozyrev, Russia's foreign minister, says that 'We cannot allow barbaric treatment of the peacekeepers to be tolerated any longer.'

EU foreign ministers recommend the regrouping and more powerful arming of peacekeeping troops.

31 May 1995. UN Secretary-General Boutros Boutros-Ghali outlines the alternatives available to Unprofor. He recommends that a revised mandate should include 'only those tasks which a peacekeeping operation can realistically be expected to carry out' and regrouping existing forces to 'more defensible areas'.

President Clinton unexpectedly announces that 'I will carefully review any request for an operation involving the temporary use of our ground forces. If necessary, and after consultation with Congress, I believe we should be prepared to assist Nato if it decides to meet a request from the United Nations troops for help in withdrawal or in a reconfiguration and a strengthening of its forces.' (But on 3 June, Clinton specified that the only other contingency he had in mind was 'the remote, indeed highly unlikely event that Britain, France and other countries . . . become stranded and cannot get out of a particular place in Bosnia'. On 7 June US Defence Secretary William Perry stated that 'We should be prepared to assist Nato in an emergency extraction of units, whose positions had become untenable, to points of safety in Bosnia.' Previously the USA had offered ground troops only for a withdrawal or to help police a final peace settlement.)

Lord Owen announces that he is to resign as EU mediator (EU representative at the International Conference on the Former Yugoslavia; on 9 June 1995 he was replaced by Carl Bildt, the former prime minister of Sweden).

2 June 1995. An appeal from Milosevic results in the release of 121 UN hostages (about a third of the total). But the Bosnian Serbs take a further sixteen UN personnel hostage and shoot down a Nato (US) jet on routine patrol.

(Milosevic's envoy to the Bosnian Serbs is Jovica Stanisic, deputy prime minister and Serbian secret police chief.)

3 June 1995. Fifteen Western countries decide to set up a 'rapid reaction force' comprising up to 10,000 British, French and (to a much smaller extent) Dutch troops.

6 June 1995. Another 108 hostages are released, leaving around 150.

7 June 1995. Three more hostages are released.

8 June 1995. Under fire from the Bosnian Serbs US marines rescue the pilot of the jet shot down on 2 June.

9 June 1995. The US House of Representatives votes 318 to ninety-nine to lift the arms embargo at a time to be determined by the Bosnian government.

13 June 1995. Karadzic claims that, as a result of further releases, only fourteen hostages remain (a figure of twenty-six was generally reported in the Western media in the following days).

There are reports that Bosnian government forces are massing north-west of Sarajevo (in the Visoko area).

15 June 1995. Bosnian government forces launch attacks against the Bosnian Serbs on a number of fronts. Referring to Sarajevo, President Izetbegovic says that 'The world was doing nothing to prevent an obvious catastrophe. In this situation our army was ordered to undertake measures to prevent any further strangulation of the city.'

The Bosnian Serb assembly ('parliament') votes in favour of unification with the Croatian Serbs.

16 June 1995. The UN Security Council authorizes the deployment of up to 12,500 additional peacekeepers (including the 'rapid reaction force'), but the US Congress refuses to pay its share of the financing (President Clinton transfers some funds from the existing defence budget).

18 June 1995. The last twenty-six hostages are released.

Unprofor forces abandon the weapon collection points around Sarajevo, thus effectively ending the heavy weapons exclusion zone.

30 June 1995. The German Bundestag approves the use of German transport and fighter planes and the sending of a field hospital to support the 'rapid reaction force' and any future Nato withdrawal. The vote was 386 for, 258 against and eleven abstentions.

2 July 1995. The Bosnian Serbs shell UN headquarters in Sarajevo, seemingly deliberately.

6 July 1995. The Bosnian Serbs begin an assault on Srebrenica (they blame Bosnian government forces for launching raids out of the enclave).

8 July 1995. The Bosnian Serbs start overrunning UN observation posts in Srebrenica and take (Dutch) UN troops prisoner (later released) .

9 July 1995. The Bosnian Serbs are warned by the UN that Nato may be asked for 'close air support'.

10 July 1995. The Bosnian Serbs issue an ultimatum to UN troops to leave Srebrenica.

11 July 1995. The Bosnian Serbs capture Srebrenica despite two Nato air strikes on a tank column. (Srebrenica was the first 'safe area' to be declared and the first to fall.)

12 July 1995. The Bosnian Serbs begin transporting civilians out of Srebrenica and separating out males over the age of sixteen for them to be 'screened for war crimes'.

The UN Security Council unanimously passes a resolution demanding the immediate withdrawal of Bosnian forces from Srebrenica and full respect to be shown by both sides for Srebrenica's 'safe area' status.

13 July 1995. There are reports of widespread atrocities associated with the 'ethnic cleansing' of Srebrenica. (Tadeusz Mazowiecki later said he was convinced that these had taken place. In his final report, published on 23 August, he talked of 'significant direct and circumstantial evidence' of summary executions of individuals and small groups of people. 'On the question of mass executions, the evidence so far obtained leads to the chilling conclusion that these may have occurred.' On 10 August the USA claimed to have photographic evidence of mass graves containing the bodies of 2,000–2,700 men and boys).

14 July 1995. The Bosnian Serbs launch a major attack on the 'safe area' of Zepa.

19 July 1995. The Bosnian Serbs claim to have captured Zepa, but fighting continues.

21 July 1995. A conference of sixteen countries in London fails to issue an agreed communiqué, but the British foreign minister, Malcolm Rifkind, reads out the following statement: 'The current Bosnian Serb offensive and the siege of Sarajevo defy international law and opinion. The meeting therefore warned that in order to deter any attacks on Gorazde any such action will be met by a substantial and decisive response. There was strong support to include the use of air power, but great concerns were also expressed.'

Russia rejected any military action. UN commanders of the ground would retain a veto over air strikes, but Yasushi Akashi would not. (The exact chain of authority over air strikes was the subject of confusion and controversy. But on 26 July Boutros Boutros-Ghali announced that he was delegating authority to General Bernard Janvier, who was authorized to delegate authority to Lieutenant-General Rupert Smith.)

The USA, France and Britain later announced that they had warned General Mladic that air strikes could also be used in defence of other 'safe areas'.

The Organization of Islamic Conference meets to discuss the Bosnian crisis. The OIC's 'Islamic contact group' (Egypt, Iran, Malaysia, Morocco, Pakistan, Saudi Arabia, Senegal and Turkey) declares the UN arms embargo on the Bosnian government to be 'invalid'.

23 July 1995. Two French soldiers are killed in attacks by the Bosnian Serbs (France later denied rumours that it had carried out a bombing raid on Pale in retaliation).

Units of the 'rapid reaction force' (estimated at some 1,700 personnel) reinforce Unprofor in Sarajevo. Armed with long-range artillery and heavy mortars and deployed on Mount Igman, the new troops aim to protect UN convoys using the road over Mount Igman.

25 July 1995. Zepa falls.

The international court for war crimes issues arrest warrants for Radovan Karadzic and General Ratko Mladic: 'Beginning in July 1992 and continuing through July 1995, Bosnian Serb military forces, under the direction and control of Radovan Karadzic and Ratko Mladic, unlawfully fired on civilian gatherings that were of no military significance in order to kill, terrorize and demoralize the Bosnian Muslim and Bosnian Croat civilian population. Radovan Karadzic and Matko Mladic are charged with genocide and crimes against humanity . . . arising from atrocities perpetrated against the civilian population throughout Bosnia-Hercegovina, for the sniping campaign against civilians in Sarajevo, and for the taking of UN peacekeepers as hostages and their use as human shields.' The Croatian Serb leader Milan Martic 'is charged with war crimes in connection with the firing of cluster bombs into the central part of Zagreb on 2 May and 3 May 1995.' In total twenty-four Bosnian Serbs and Croatian Serbs are indicted, including commanders of detention camps.

26 July 1995. The US Senate votes sixty-nine to twenty-nine in favour of unilaterally lifting the arms embargo on the Bosnian government after the withdrawal of UN peacekeepers or ninety days after a formal request by the Bosnian government for their withdrawal (in addition, President Clinton would be able to call for successive thirty-day delays if the 'safety, security and successful completion' of the withdrawal were deemed to be in jeopardy).

Nato supports the idea of 'a degree of pre-emptive action' in the event of Bosnian Serb forces concentrating 'with the intent' of attacking Gorazde.

27 July 1995. Tadeusz Mazowiecki resigns. Recent events 'and above all the fact that the United Nations has allowed Srebrenica and Zepa to fall . . . oblige me to state that I do not see any possibility of continuing the mandate of Special Rapporteur entrusted to me by the Commission on Human Rights'. Mazowiecki also noted the 'effect of long-lasting policy' of the international community. 'I believe we have a certain hypocrisy as far as Bosnia is concerned, because we are claiming to defend it but in fact we are abandoning it.' Mazowiecki referred to evidence of 'barbarous' acts and terror on an enormous scale, 'the horrendous tragedy which has beset the population of those "safe havens" guaranteed by international agreements'.

Bosnian Croats, backed by units of the Croatian army, launch a major offensive to try to relieve the pressure of a three-pronged attack (beginning on 19 July) on Bihac by Bosnian Serbs, Croatian Serbs and forces loyal to Fikret Abdic. (Presidents Tudjman and Izetbegovic met on 22 July. Croatia would provide emergency military aid to help defend Bihac and a defence pact between Croatia and Bosnia was also agreed.)

28 July 1995. Karadzic declares martial law and full mobilization as the combined Croat forces make early gains in their Bosnian offensive (capturing the strategic Serb-held towns of Grahovo and Glamoc).

30 July 1995. After talks with the UN the Croatian Serbs agree to withdraw their troops from Bihac (it seems that few were actually withdrawn).

1 August 1995. Nato announces that pre-emptive air strikes could be used to deter attacks on all four remaining 'safe areas'.

The US House of Representatives votes 298 to 128 to lift the arms embargo on the Bosnian government (as with the Senate, a majority exceeding two-thirds; on 11 August President Clinton used his veto, which can be overridden only by another two-thirds majority in Congress).

3 August 1995. Prime Minister Haris Silajdzic offers to resign (the offer was withdrawn on 10 August). One interpretation of this friction is that Silajdzic is more strongly committed to a united secular culture than Izetbegovic. Other interpretations include (1) Silajdzic's resentment when Izetbegovic succeeded in temporarily amending the constitution to ensure that, in the event of the president's death during the war, he would be succeeded by a Moslem, and (2) personal rivalry between Silajdzic and Foreign Minister Muhamed Sacirbey.

5 August 1995. Bosnian government forces break out of Bihac and link up with Croatian government forces after their successful attack on the Krajina (see the section on Croatia below for details; Bosnian Foreign Minister

Muhamed Sacirbey expressed disquiet at the number of defeated Croatian Serb fighters moving into Bosnia).

Karadzic assumes personal command of the Bosnian Serb army, appointing General Mladic as co-ordinator of military operations between the Bosnian and Croatian Serbs. But Mladic refuses to relinquish control (he was backed by eighteen senior generals and then the general staff of the Bosnian Serb army, while the Bosnian Serb 'parliament' backed Karadzic; on 11 August Karadzic backed down, saying that he had 'decided to stop all announced changes in the army').

7 August 1995. Bosnian government forces drive Abdic forces from Velika Kladusa (in the Bihac enclave).

8 August 1995. Karadzic attacks Milosevic for betraying the Croatian Serbs: 'You have turned your back on the Serb cause. You have started yielding to outside pressure to an extent that borders on treason.'

12 August 1995. Bosnian government forces launch an attack on Donji Vakuf in central Bosnia.

There are reports that ethnic Croats and Moslems in Serbia and Bosnia have been evicted from their homes by Croatian Serb refugees.

Serbia announces that Croatian Serbs of fighting age will have to return to the Croatia–Bosnia front (but there is uncertainty about implementation, e.g. attempts to stop refugee families crossing the border were soon halted). Some of the refugees are being directed to Vojvodina and Kosovo.

14 August 1995. It is generally considered that the Bosnian Serbs have entered the final stage of 'ethnic cleansing' in the Banja Luka area.

16 August 1995. It is reported that Croatian government forces are massing for an attack on Serb-held Trebinje in Bosnia in order to push Serb artillery out of range of Dubrovnik.

18 August 1995. Croat forces claim to have captured Serb-held Drvar in western Bosnia.

The UN announces that the UN peacekeeping troops in Gorazde are to be withdrawn within weeks (around ninety from Ukraine and 180 from the UK; they are not expected to be replaced, but a small number of UN military observers will be stationed in Gorazde).

19 August 1995. Three US diplomats (including Robert Frasure, special envoy to the former Yugoslavia) and a French soldier are killed in an accident on the Mount Igman road.

20 August 1995. Four (British) members of the 'rapid reaction force' are killed in a helicopter accident off the coast of Croatia.

28 August 1995. Thirty-seven civilians are killed in a mortar attack on Sarajevo.

30 August 1995. Operation Deliberate Force begins. Nato planes launch a series of massive air strikes against Bosnian Serb targets around Sarajevo in particular but also around Tuzla, Gorazde, Zepa and Mostar. The 'rapid reaction force' also shells targets around Sarajevo, with the announced aim of clearing the exclusion zone of heavy weapons. Anti-aircraft batteries are the first targets to be attacked by Nato planes, with later targets including heavy weapons, ammunition dumps and command posts. (The intention is not to destroy substantially the heavy weapon capability of the Bosnian Serbs. Hence the subsequent attention to supply routes, e.g. bridges became targets.) One Nato (French) Mirage jet is shot down.

Boris Yeltsin talks of a 'cruel bombardment'.

Serbia announces that Milosevic will lead a joint negotiating team with the Bosnian Serbs (with Milosevic having the casting vote).

31 August 1995. Air strikes continue, albeit on a reduced scale.

There are reports that the Bosnian Serbs have begun to pull some heavy weapons out of the exclusion zone around Sarajevo.

1 September 1995. Nato suspends the air strikes for twenty-four hours.

The USA announces that the foreign ministers of Bosnia, Croatia and the Federal Republic of Yugoslavia are to meet in Geneva. (Note that the USA began to take the leading role in negotiations in August, the US team being led by Richard Holbrooke.)

3 September 1995. After unsuccessful talks the Bosnian Serbs are given an ultimatum (deadline 2300 local time on 4 September) to withdraw their heavy weapons from the exclusion zone around Sarajevo, to cease their attacks on the 'safe areas' and to ensure complete freedom of movement for UN personnel and those of the aid agencies.

UN troops open a road through Sarajevo airport without Bosnian Serb permission.

5 September 1995. Nato resumes air strikes and the Bosnian Serbs shell Sarajevo.

6 September 1995. The air strikes continue.

7 September 1995. There are more air strikes. Boris Yeltsin says that if they continue 'we will have to consider thoroughly our strategy, including our relations with the North Atlantic Alliance'.

Members of the 'contact group' and of the Organization of Islamic Conference meet and agree that the air strikes should continue.

8 September 1995. While air strikes continue the foreign ministers of Bosnia, Croatia and Serbia agree on the 'basic principles' of a political settlement. US Special Envoy Richard Holbrooke describes the agreement as 'an important milestone in the search for peace'. The main principles are as follows:

1. Bosnia-Hercegovina will continue its legal existence with its present borders and continuing international recognition.

2. Bosnia-Hercegovina will consist of two entities, the Federation of Bosnia and Hercegovina and the Republika Srpska. Each entity will continue to exist under its present constitution, although amended to accommodate the agreed basic principles. Both entities will have the right to

establish parallel special relationships with neighbouring countries, consistent with the sovereignty and territorial integrity of Bosnia-Hercegovina.

3. It is proposed that the Federation of Bosnia and Hercegovina will be assigned 51 per cent of the territory and the Republika Srpska will be assigned 49 per cent. But this territorial proposal is open for adjustment by mutual agreement.

4. The two entities will enter into reciprocal commitments (1) to hold complete elections under international auspices, (2) to adopt and adhere to normal international and human rights standards and obligations, including the obligation to allow freedom of movement and enable displaced persons to repossess their homes or to receive just compensation and (3) to engage in binding arbitration to resolve disputes between them. There is agreement in principle to establish a Commission for Displaced Persons and a Human Rights Commission; decisions will be binding on the entities.

5. The establishment of joint public corporations (e.g. transport) and of a Commission to Preserve National Monuments.

10 September 1995. US cruise missiles are used to attack anti-aircraft installations around Banja Luka.

EU foreign ministers endorse the idea of an aid programme along Marshall Plan lines for a post-war Bosnia.

12 September 1995. Air strikes continue. (General Mladic is considered to be the most reluctant of the Serb leaders to remove heavy weapons from the exclusion zone around Sarajevo. He claims that Bosnian Serb civilians would be vulnerable to attack.)

The Russian government declares that 'The survival of the present generation of Bosnian Serbs, which is threatened by genocide, is called into question'.

13 September 1995. The Bosnian Serbs suffer reverses in central Bosnia. Combined Bosnian government and Croat forces claim to have captured Donji Vakuf, while Croat forces claim to have taken Jajce.

A rocket-propelled grenade is fired at the US embassy in Moscow.

THE HUMAN TOLL IN THE FORMER YUGOSLAVIA

This section does not take account of the consequences of Croatia's military successes against the Croatian Serbs in August 1995 or contemporary events in Bosnia.

Refugees

Within the former Yugoslavia as a whole there were 3.5 million refugees and others needing humanitarian asssistance by the end of June 1993 and 595,000 had fled to other parts of Europe by December 1992: for example,

Germany (300,000), Switzerland (80,000), Austria (73,000), Sweden (62,000) and Hungary (40,000) (*The Times*, 21 July 1993, p. 10).

Of the 3,478,000 refugees or displaced persons, Bosnia accommodated 2,280,000, Croatia (including the Krajina) 613,000, Serbia and Montenegro 520,000, Slovenia 33,000 and Macedonia 32,000 (*The Independent*, 28 October 1993, p. 11).

The Guardian (24 May 1994, p. 11) compiled the following figures as of May 1994 (based on host government estimates; the real figures are thought to be higher):

1. The number of refugees or asylum seekers from the former Yugoslavia in European countries (excluding the former Yugoslavia itself): total, around 750,000 (at least half of whom are from Bosnia, overwhelmingly Moslems), including Germany (402,901), Sweden (58,824), Austria (55,000), the Netherlands (42,225), Turkey (32,817), Switzerland (32,149), Hungary (28,000), Denmark (21,517), France (15,918), Norway (12,761) and Italy (12,073).

2. The number of displaced people within the former Yugoslavia: Bosnia-Hercegovina, 2,776,000; Croatia, 518,000; Serbia, 405,000; Montenegro, 48,000; Slovenia, 33,000; Macedonia, 32,000.

(The numbers of men under arms and of tanks as of August 1994 were as follows: Bosnian army, 110,000 and 40; Bosnian Croats, 50,000 and 75; Croatia, 100,000 and 170; Bosnian Serbs, 80,000 and 330; Krajina Serbs, 50,000 and 240; the Federal Republic of Yugoslavia, 125,000 and 600: *The Economist*, 6 August 1994, p. 27.)

Rape

An EU report of late 1992 estimated that up to 20,000 Bosnian (mainly Moslem) women and girls had been raped by the Serbs (mass rape became a means of 'ethnic cleansing', not the result, the prospect of rape and other forms of terrorism driving people from their homes).

On 20 October 1993 a UN war crimes commission found evidence that the Serbs have used rape as a weapon of terror in the war in Bosnia (the largest number of victims were Moslems and the largest number of perpetrators were Serbs). But the number of provable cases may be substantially less than 20,000. Reports have been collected on about 3,000 cases and about 800 victims were identifiable by name (*IHT*, 21 October 1993, p. 2).

UN Protection Force losses

There are now only unofficial estimates, because the UN no longer issues figures of casualties. Up to sixty-five UN troops have lost their lives (*IHT*, 6 December 1993, p. 2). On 14 March 1995 nine UN troops died and four were seriously injured in a road accident. Up to then 140 had been killed in

Bosnia and 1,207 injured (*The Times*, 15 March 1995, p. 11). Since early 1992 158 UN peacekeepers have died in the former Yugoslavia, including fifty-seven in combat-related incidents (*IHT*, 15 April 1995, p. 2). Since 1992 159 peacekeepers have died in the former Yugoslavia, nearly a quarter of them French (*The Guardian*, 17 April 1995, p. 18). On 15 April 1995 the thirty-third French soldier died in the former Yugoslavia (*IHT*, 19 April 1995, p. 1). Three more French soldiers died in Sarajevo in an accidental explosion on 22 April 1995 and another was shot dead by a sniper the following month. 'In the whole peacekeeping operation 162 United Nations soldiers have been killed and 1,420 disabled or injured. France has sustained the largest number of casualties: thirty-seven dead' (Boutros Boutros-Ghali, *IHT*, 18 May 1995, p. 5).

As of 31 May 1994 there were 34,940 UN troops, observers and civilian police in the whole of the former Yugoslavia (*The Economist*, 25 June 1994, p. 19).

The countries contributing over a thousand troops in Bosnia (excluding those at headquarters) as of December 1994 were as follows: France, 3,611; the UK, 3,284; Pakistan, 3,017; the Netherlands, 1,615; Malaysia, 1,543; Turkey, 1,460; Spain, 1,269; Bangladesh, 1,230; Sweden, 1,045 (Russia's contribution was 505) (*The Economist*, 17 December 1994, p. 40).

The number of casualties in Bosnia-Hercegovina

The Bosnian government's Institute of Public Health issued revised estimates on 19 November 1993: 141,398 killed, missing or dead through malnutrition and cold; 157,827 wounded. These figures covered only certain areas and the overall death toll was thought to be over 200,000 (*IHT*, 20 November 1993, p. 2).

As of the end of November 1993 the casualty list was 141,502 dead (of which Sarajevo accounted for 9,575) and 158,164 wounded (55,711 in Sarajevo) (*The Guardian*, 27 December 1993, p. 19).

The Bosnian war has uprooted about 2 million people and killed an estimated 200,000 (*IHT*, 4 April 1994, p. 7).

More than 200,000 have been killed, tens of thousands raped or tortured in camps and a million and a half driven into exile (Kemal Kurspahic, *IHT*, 29 August 1994, p. 8). (Kemal Kurspahic was the editor-in-chief of Sarajevo's newspaper, *Oslobodenje*.)

An estimated 200,000 are dead and 2 million are homeless and displaced (Ian Traynor, *The Guardian*, 22 December 1994, p. 6).

The UN High Commissioner for Refugees estimates that out of the 837,000 non-Serbs (mainly Moslems) who lived in the now Serb-held areas of Bosnia before April 1992, only 80,000 remain; almost 10,000 have been driven out since mid-July 1994 (*The Independent*, 21 September 1994, p. 13).

'The UN High Commissioner for Refugees estimates that the Serbs have expelled, killed or imprisoned 90 per cent of the 1.7 million non-Serbs who once lived in Serbian-held areas of Bosnia . . . [since the summer of 1994] . . . the Serbs have stepped up their campaign of ethnic cleansing around Banja Luka in north-west Bosnia, Bijelina in the north-east and Rogatica north of the Gorazde enclave. About 800 Muslims a month are being forcibly expelled from their homes.' As the Clinton administration notes, 'the term "ethnic cleansing" was developed precisely to describe the Bosnian Serbs' explicit method . . . In contrast, the Bosnian government supports a multi-ethnic state, and where there have been violations by its local commanders it has renounced them' (leader by *The New York Times* in *IHT*, 5 January 1995, p. 6).

'Seventy per cent of our country is occupied. More than 200,000 civilians have been killed, including 17,000 children. More than 400,000 people have been wounded. More than 2 million have been expelled from their homes. All this, and our prewar population was only 4.3 million' (Haris Silajdzic, the prime minister of the Republic of Bosnia-Hercegovina, *IHT*, 23 February 1995, p. 8).

More than 10,000 residents of Sarajevo have been killed and 50,000 wounded (*IHT*, 6 April 1995, p. 7).

Around forty journalists have been killed (Roger Cohen, *IHT*, 14 March 1995, p. 22).

The number of casualties in Croatia

One-third of Croatia is controlled by Serbs (note that other sources put the proportion at 25 per cent, 27 per cent and 30 per cent) and the war toll in Croatia to date is 7,642 killed, 23,062 wounded and 13,153 missing. Over 40 per cent of Croatia's budget goes on defence (John Pomfret, *IHT*, 12 November 1993, p. 2).

The war in Croatia has to date resulted in at least 10,000 dead (Robert Block, *The Independent*, 15 September 1993, p. 1).

The war in Croatia left 10,000 dead or missing and created more than a million refugees (*Business Central Europe*, March 1995, p. 15).

(Note that the casualty figure for the ten-day war in Slovenia in 1991 was thirty-seven soldiers from the Yugoslav army and twelve Slovenes killed: Zimmerman 1995: 13.)

THE ECONOMIC TOLL

There has been massive destruction in the war zones (especially in Bosnia) and massive dislocation in most places.

There is very little information on Bosnia. In 1991 unemployment was 17 per cent and inflation was 117.4 per cent (*Business Europa*, April–May 1995,

p. 60). Industrial output fell by 16.2 per cent in 1991 and by 25 per cent in 1992 (United Nations Economic Commission for Europe 1994: 52, and 1995: 70).

The details are given in the sections below devoted to the individual countries.

Historical and religious treasures have also been vandalized or destroyed, e.g. the Serbs' early bombardment of Dubrovnik in Croatia, the loss of many priceless books when Sarajevo's National Library was destroyed and continuing wholesale destruction of mosques in Bosnia (the last two come under the category of what may be called 'cultural cleansing'). The Serbs started the shelling, but on 9 November 1993 it was the Croats who finally destroyed the famous Mostar bridge (*Stari Most* or 'Old Bridge'). It had been built over the river Neretva in 1557–66 by Suleiman the Magnificent.

THE PERSONALITIES INVOLVED IN THE DISINTEGRATION OF YUGOSLAVIA

This section is mainly devoted to a brilliant and convincing analysis of the role of key personalities in the disintegration of the former Yugoslavia by the former (and last) US ambassador to the country, Warren Zimmerman. Firstly the disintegration itself: 'The break-up of Yugoslavia is a classic example of nationalism from the top down – a manipulated nationalism in a region where peace has historically prevailed more than war and in which a quarter of the population were in mixed marriages. The manipulators condoned and even provoked local ethnic violence in order to engender animosities that could then be magnified by the press, leading to further violence . . . Milosevic's Serbia was at the heart of the complex of issues that destroyed Yugoslavia . . . [The Serbs'] tragic defect is an obsession with their own history; their hearts are in the past, not the future. In the Balkans, intellectuals tend to be standard-bearers of nationalism; in Serbia this is carried to fetishistic lengths. A lugubrious, paranoid and Serbo-centric view of the past enables the Serbs to blame everyone but themselves for whatever goes wrong' (Zimmerman 1995: 2–3). The chief manipulators were:

1. *Slobodan Milosevic.* Zimmerman arrived in Belgrade on 9 March 1989 (and remained ambassador until 1992). 'Milosevic, an ambitious and ruthless Communist Party official, had clawed his way to power several years before' (p. 3). 'Milosevic is an opportunist, not an ideologue, a man driven by power rather than nationalism. He has made a Faustian pact with nationalism as a way to gain and hold power. He is a man of extraordinary coldness. I never saw him moved by an individual case of human suffering; for him, people are groups (Serbs, Muslims) or simply abstractions . . . This chilling personality trait made it possible for Milosevic to condone, encourage and even organize the unspeakable atrocities committed by Serbian citizens in the Bosnian war. It also accounts for his habitual mendacity . . .

For Milosevic, truth has only a relative value. If it serves his objectives, it is employed; if not, it can be discarded . . . Milosevic cast himself as the apostle of [Yugoslav] unity. Not interested in unity *per se*, he wanted a unity that Serbia could dominate' (p. 5).

'Neither Milosevic nor Tudjman made any effort to conceal their designs on Bosnia from me. As a place where Serbs, Croats and Muslims had coexisted more or less peacefully for centuries, Bosnia was an affront to these two ethnic supremacists' (p. 15). (On 13 April 1995 it was revealed that a former member of the Serbian secret police had earlier produced purportedly genuine documents in which the Serbian security services had issued instructions to the Bosnian Serbs in 1992 about 'ethnic cleansing' and the running of the concentration camps.)

2. *Radovan Karadzic.* Of Karadzic Zimmerman says that: 'In the great tradition of nationalists who do not come from their nation (Hitler, Napoleon, Stalin), Karadzic is from Montenegro, not Bosnia . . . his outstanding characteristics were his stubbornness and deep-seated hostility to Muslims, Croats and any other non-Serb ethnic group in his neighbourhood . . . His disdain for the truth was absolute . . . His *apartheid* philosophy was as extreme as anything in South Africa. He was the architect of massacres in the Muslim villages, ethnic cleansing and artillery attacks on civilian populations. In his fanaticism, ruthlessness and contempt for human values, he invites comparison with a monster from another generation, Heinrich Himmler' (pp. 17–18). ('Back in May 1992 he described to me his intention of dividing the city [Sarajevo] into ethnic ghettoes, with walls and checkpoints, so that Serbs would not be contaminated by cohabitation with Muslims and Croats . . . Since its fifteenth-century occupation by the Ottoman Turks the city has been a haven for diverse ethnic groups and a symbol of racial tolerance. It has stood for precisely the values that the Serbian policy of *apartheid* is intended to stamp out . . . Only resolute and, if necessary, continued air strikes against Serbian artillery positions can save the city': *IHT*, 15 May 1995, p. 8.) 'There is no doubt that the two [Milosevic and Karadzic] were partners in crime' (p. 18).

3. *Franjo Tudjman.* The Croatian leader does not escape lightly either: 'Unlike Milosevic, who is driven by power, Tudjman is obsessed by nationalism . . . He presided over serious violations of the rights of the Serbs, who made up 12 per cent of the population of Croatia. They were dismissed from work, required to take loyalty oaths and subjected to attacks on their homes and property . . . Tudjman's saving grace, which distinguishes him from Milosevic, is that he really wants to be a Western statesman . . . Croatian nationalism is defined by Tudjman – intolerant, anti-Serb and authoritarian. These attributes – together with an aura of wartime fascism, which Tudjman has done nothing to dispel – help explain why many Serbs in Croatia reject Croatian rule and why the core hostility in the former Yugoslavia is still between Serbs and Croats' (pp. 7–8).

Croatia

POLITICS

20 April 1994. Defectors from the ruling Croatian Democratic Union form the Croatian Independent Democrats. The leading members of the new (liberal) party are Josip Manolic (then speaker of the upper house) and Stipe Mesic (then speaker of the lower house). (The new party has so far taken only seven defectors and not the twenty predicted: *EEN*, 1994, vol. 8, no. 14, p. 5.)

2 December 1994. Croatia signs an economic agreement with the Croatian Serbs, restoring road and rail links, use of the oil pipeline and water and gas supplies.

(An oil pipeline and a motorway have been reopened, but the Croatian Serbs are refusing to implement the accord's second stage, on telecoms and railway links, unless UN troops remain: *The Economist*, 4 March 1995, p. 14.)

12 January 1995. Croatia announces that the UN mandate will not be renewed on 31 March 1995 and the 15,000 or so Unprofor troops in the Serb-occupied areas of Croatia will be expected to leave by the end of June 1995. (Croatia points to the danger, for example, of a permanent division of the country and points out that refugees have not been allowed to return as agreed.)

30 January 1995. The representatives of the USA, Russia, the EU and the UN (known as the Zagreb Four, or Z-4) present their proposals. In return for recognizing Croatia's sovereignty and international borders (and full guarantees of human rights) the Croatian Serbs would be granted a high degree of autonomy in two of the four (UN-protected) areas they now occupy. These are the two where they had a majority before the fighting started, namely the area around Knin and the area of Glina. The Croatian Serbs would, for example, have their own president, parliament, flag, education system, police force and currency (albeit issued by the central bank of Croatia).

31 January 1995. The Croatian Serbs refuse even to consider the proposals unless guarantees are given that UN forces will remain. Milosevic refuses to see the Z-4 representatives.

12 March 1995. After talks with the USA, Tudjman announces that he is willing to allow UN troops to remain for another six months subject to certain conditions: (1) the numbers are reduced from around 12,000 to 5,000; (2) the troops also control Krajina's borders with Bosnia and the Federal Republic of Yugoslavia (Croatia stresses control rather than just monitoring); (3) they control the passage of aid to Bosnia; (4) they facilitate the implementation of the agreements with the Croatian Serbs (notably regarding the cease-fire and the economic accord) and encourage the re-integration of Croatia.

31 March 1995. Three resolutions are adopted by the Security Council as the current mandate for UN troops in the former Yugoslavia expires:

1. The creation of three separate but interlocking UN commands for Croatia, Bosnia and Macedonia.
2. The changing of the force names to UN Confidence Restoration Operation (Uncro) in Croatia, UN Protection Force for Bosnia and UN Preventative Deployment Force for Macedonia.
3. Extend the mandates for eight months.

The resolution on Croatia says that UN troops are to assist in 'controlling, by monitoring and reporting, the crossing of military personnel, equipment, supplies and weapons' over Croatia's international borders with Bosnia and the Federal Republic of Yugoslavia.

11 April 1995. The Russian commander of UN troops in Sector East (Krajina) is dismissed for profiteering and collaborating with the Croatian Serbs.

13 April 1995. The Serbs shell a suburb of Dubrovnik and the city's airport (since the cease-fire only occasional shelling had taken place).

21 April 1995. The UN secretary-general, Boutros Boutros-Ghali, recommends that the Security Council should fix the number of Uncro forces at 8,750 (approved) and set up stop-and-search checkpoints on the borders with Bosnia and the Federal Republic of Yugoslavia. 'In cases where military personnel, equipment, supplies and weapons are detected, [UN troops] will give notice that the crossing of such personnel and items would be in violation of Security Council resolutions and would be reported to the UN Security Council.'

1 May 1995. Croat forces launch a three-pronged attack on the Serb-held (isolated and most vulnerable) area in Sector West Krajina (western Slavonia; one of the four sectors of Krajina). The Croats seize a (twenty-mile) section of the motorway (closed by the Croatian Serbs after a series of incidents) and Croat planes attempt to destroy a bridge over the river Sava (a major supply route linking areas controlled by the Croatian and Bosnian Serbs). The Croatian Serbs shell Croat towns (such as Karlovac and Sisak) and capture UN civilian and military personnel.

2 May 1995. Croatia declares the two-day offensive a success when Okucani (the main town) is taken. The Croatian Serbs respond by undertaking a rocket attack on Zagreb (killing five) and continuing to shell other places.

The area of Croatia occupied by the Croatian Serbs was variously estimated at between 27 per cent and 33 per cent. According to John Pomfret, the two-day offensive reduced the proportion from 27 per cent to 24 per cent (*IHT*, 16 May 1995, p. 7).

3 May 1995. Zagreb is once again subject to a rocket attack and one person is killed (nearly 200 people were injured over the two days).

The UN gets the two sides to agree to a 'cessation of hostilities' and Croatian Serb civilians and military personnel (with side-arms only) are allowed to leave the enclave under UN protection.

4 May 1995. There is some fighting around Pakrac before Croatian Serbs surrender.

5 May 1995. The UN Security Council calls for a return to the situation as of 1 May.

Croatia sends some Croatian Serbs to detention camps in a search for war criminals.

7 May 1995. There is considerable controversy about whether Croat forces deliberately killed Croatian Serb civilians as they fled along with Croatian Serb military personnel.

President Tudjman lays down new terms for the UN presence. It would be confined to monitoring Croatian Serb rocket bases and the airport at Ubdina, and UN forces would be deployed along the internationally recognized borders of Croatia (*The Times*, 8 May 1995, p. 9).

20 May 1995. The Croatian Serb assembly votes in favour of unification with the Bosnian Serbs, but the process will be 'co-ordinated with the Federal Republic of Yugoslavia'.

27 July 1995. Bosnian Croats, backed by units of the Croatian army, launch a major offensive to try to relieve the pressure of a three-pronged attack (beginning on 19 July) on Bihac (Bosnia) by Bosnian Serbs, Croatian Serbs and forces loyal to Fikret Abdic. (Presidents Tudjman and Izetbegovic met on 22 July. Croatia would provide emergency military aid to help defend Bihac and a defence pact between Croatia and Bosnia was also agreed.)

28 July 1995. The combined Croat forces make early gains, capturing the strategic Serb-held Bosnian towns of Grahovo and Glamoc.

3 August 1995. Talks begin between the Croatian government and the Croatian Serbs (preceded by skirmishes between their military forces). The Bosnian Serbs shell the outskirts of Dubrovnik.

4 August 1995. Croatia launches a full-scale military assault on Sectors North and South Krajina (but not Sector East Krajina, known as eastern Slavonia).

5 August 1995. Croatian government forces make spectacular gains, even capturing Knin (considered by the Croatian Serbs to be their capital). (Note that during the offensive Nato aircraft knocked out Croatian Serb anti-aircraft positions.)

6 August 1995. Further gains are made, e.g. Petrinje and the Ubdina air base.

(The Croatian government claimed that 80 per cent of goals had been achieved by 6 August. Despite assurances given by the Croatian government there took place a massive exodus of Croatian Serb refugees; some later estimates put the figure at up to 200,000. The flood was encouraged by civilian attacks on fleeing refugees as well as looting and destruction of Serb property; later on there were claims that mass graves had been found. Croatian government forces were accused of deliberately targeting UN observation posts, killing three UN troops. An October EU report talked of a systematic campaign of killings, arson and looting by the Croatian army.)

7 August 1995. Croatia declares the military operation to be at an end, but some fighting continues (a cease-fire was agreed, but collapsed). An official figure of 118 Croatian government troops killed in the operation is given.

8 August 1995. The UN negotiates a cease-fire, with the UN collecting heavy weapons from the Croatian Serb forces in return for the safe passage of some 40,000 refugees in the northern part of the war zone.

9 August 1995. The UN reports that the last major pocket of Croatian Serb resistance has yielded when the town of Dvor falls.

Tudjman announces that he will accept Yeltsin's invitation to talks with Milosevic only if President Izetbegovic of Bosnia is also invited.

There are reports of a number of atrocities committed by Croatian and Bosnian government forces.

Radovan Karadzic and Milan Martic attack Milosevic.

10 August 1995. Yeltsin meets Milosevic in Moscow. The Russian president invites Milosevic, Tudjman and Izetbegovic to talks as a prelude to a summit of 'leading states'.

Yasushi Akashi says that most UN troops will be withdrawn from peacekeeping duties in Croatia.

12 August 1995. Croatian government forces attack Croatian Serb positions in the hills overlooking Dubrovnik, whose outskirts come under renewed attack.

16 August 1995. It is reported that Croatian government forces are massing for an attack on Serb-held Trebinje in Bosnia in order to push Serb artillery out of range of Dubrovnik.

25 August 1995. Serbia and Croatia sign a cease-fire over eastern Slavonia, but skirmishes are reported.

29 August 1995. The UN Security Council agrees to the secretary-general's request to reduce the number of UN peacekeeping troops in Croatia from around 12,000 to no more than 2,500. Two battalions are to remain in eastern Slavonia.

THE ECONOMY

Financial policy

Over 40 per cent of the budget goes on defence (John Pomfret, *IHT*, 12 November 1993, p. 2). (12.5 per cent of GDP in 1995: *Economist*, 11 November 1995.)

In mid-October 1993 parliament voted to rename the national currency the kuna ('marten': first used in the eleventh century, but it also circulated

1941–45, i.e. in the Ustasha period); it was reintroduced on 30 May 1994, replacing the Croatian dinar (which was introduced as a temporary currency in December 1991). An anti-inflation package was introduced in early October 1993, including a cap on pay increases for public-sector employees. There was also a devaluation of the dinar (*Business Central Europe*, November 1993, p. 15). A new personal and profit tax was introduced on 1 January 1994 and VAT was to follow on 1 July 1994. A managed floating exchange rate regime was established at the end of 1993; the currency is convertible for current transactions, with capital transactions still subject to restrictions (Deutsche Bank, *Focus: Eastern Europe*, 1994, no. 108, p. 3). The currency is in principle floating, but the national bank intervenes. There is now a high degree of current account convertibility, but some capital controls are still in force (EBRD 1994: 21, 109).

A wage freeze is in place for the state sector, supported until November 1994 by a 'social agreement' with unions. There are no wage restrictions on private enterprises (EBRD 1994: 21).

Monthly inflation fell from 40 per cent in October 1993 to zero by December 1993. It has stayed there ever since (*Business Central Europe*, October 1994, p. 19).

Inflation was brought down from +1,149 per cent in 1993 to –2.5 per cent in 1994. The (internally convertible) kuna has slightly appreciated against the Deutschmark (*Business Central Europe*, March 1995, p. 14).

'Croatia's third stabilization attempt, begun in October 1993, has been more consistently carried through and more successful' (Kraft 1995: 479). Inflation fell from 38.7 per cent a month in October 1993 to 1.4 per cent in November and was actually negative for the following six months. The main ingredients of the stabilization plan have been tight monetary and fiscal policy and a strict incomes policy (p. 480).

In the last quarter of 1994 the consumer price index was nearly 3 per cent below its level in the same period of 1993 (United Nations Economic Commission for Europe 1995: 96).

Prices

All direct price controls have now been removed. Some indirect controls remain, largely through government influence on major enterprises, particularly in the energy sector (EBRD 1994: 21).

Privatization

Applications for autonomous privatizations could be submitted by the enterprises themselves up to the end of 1992, but the war interrupted the process. Some 3,600 enterprises were listed for privatization and 2,500 submitted their proposals (only eighty-eight procedures were concluded; most were smaller units and sixty-five were purchased outright by the employees of the enterprises concerned) (Franz-Lothar Altmann, *The World Today*, June 1993, p. 114).

The rapid sale of shares was opted for. While enterprises initiated privatization, the final approval of any scheme was reserved for the government's Fund for Privatization. The deadline for the privatization of all socially owned enterprises was the end of June 1992; all shares not sold by that date (around 50 per cent of the value of all socially owned enterprises) were transferred to three state funds without compensation (United Nations Economic Commission for Europe 1993: 224).

The privatization law (which was passed in April 1991 and came into force in June that year) allows workers to buy shares of up to DM 20,000 in book value at a 20 per cent discount to the nominal value plus 1 per cent for every year they have worked. One-third of the remaining shares in each enterprise were transferred to two pension funds and the balance went to the Croatian Privatization Fund. These have subsequently sold off some of their shares to foreign companies (these made equity investments of $16 million in 1992 and $56 million in 1993). By the end of January 1994 1,907 enterprises had been privatized (Gavin Gray, *FT*, 31 March 1994, p. 32).

The Deutsche Bank (*Focus: Eastern Europe*, 14 June 1994, no. 108, pp. 5–6) reported that privatization was still making slow progress. The large majority of privatizations up to then had been management or worker buy-outs. Some 200 publicly owned enterprises which had not lodged their proposals for privatization passed completely into the hands of the Privatization Fund. Shares not sold when enterprises were converted were taken up by the Privatization Fund (two-thirds) and the Pension Fund (one-third). Ten per cent of capital was set aside as provision for restitution claims. Almost all the capital of small enterprises had passed into private hands. Enterprise employees and pensioners receive a discount of up to 50 per cent and have access to an interest-free loan for five years. The medium-sized enterprises were roughly half privately owned and large enterprises were almost entirely owned by the state (some, such as the state oil concern, are not to be privatized). Altogether, more than 50 per cent of the converted enterprises' capital was then still held by the state.

Writing in late 1994, Bartlett (forthcoming) reported that no large social-sector enterprises had been privatized.

There have been 2,877 applications for autonomous privatization, of which well over half (by number; less by value) have so far been privatized. The acceleration of privatization is now a government priority. Small privatization is now largely complete. There is no law on restitution. Workers' councils for enterprises have been replaced by management boards (EBRD 1994: 20). Some restructuring was undertaken in late 1994, including the closure of several large plants. A new Privatization Ministry was created in January 1995 with the task of accelerating privatization (EBRD 1995: 54).

The *FT* (16 February 1994, p. 3) reports a scheme to sell some forty companies in a debt-for-equity swap; citizens would be able to draw on foreign currency savings blocked since the disintegration of Yugoslavia.

According to official estimates, roughly 20 per cent of the economy is in private hands (*Business Central Europe*, September 1993, p. 22).

In mid-1994 the private sector accounted for roughly 40 per cent of GDP (EBRD 1994: 10).

The private sector has seen dynamic growth, especially in services such as retailing (*Business Central Europe*, March 1995, p. 15).

Foreign trade

The foreign trade system is liberal. There are no quantitative restrictions on imports. Most imports and exports are tariff-free. An import tax of 10 per cent was introduced as part of the government's macroeconomic stabilization programme in autumn 1993 (EBRD 1994: 21, 109).

Foreign aid

Croatia has reached agreement with the Paris Club of official creditors on rescheduling its foreign debt. The $1 billion debt would be repaid over fourteen years, with repayments starting in 1996. Another $100 million, borrowed after 1992, was to be repaid immediately (*Business Central Europe*, April 1995, p. 51).

Foreign investment

Direct foreign investment amounted to $46 million in the period 1990–93 (EBRD 1994: 123).

Economic performance

There has been real progress in the battle against inflation (after a massively high rate in 1993) and GDP grew in 1994 (see Table 26.1). But unemployment remains very high (see Table 26.2).

By mid-1993 output was about half the 1990 level (Kraft 1995: 479).

During 1991–92 around 30 per cent of fixed assets were damaged or destroyed. The level of industrial production in 1993 was 45 per cent of the maximum achieved in 1987 (Radosevic 1994: 490).

War damage has been estimated at $20 billion (James Hansen, *IHT*, 2 July 1994, p. 11).

Table 26.1 Croatia: selected economic indicators

Economic indicator	*1990*	*1991*	*1992*	*1993*	*1994*
Rate of growth of GDP (%)	−8.6	−14.4	−9.0	−3.2	0.8
Rate of growth of industrial output (%)	−11.3	−28.5	−14.6	−5.9	−3.0
Rate of growth of agricultural output (%)	−3.2	−7.2	−13.5	4.9	
Inflation rate (%)	610.0	123.0	665.5	1,515	97.5
Net foreign debt ($ billion)	2.5	2.5	2.4	1.9	1.3
Budget surplus or deficit (% GDP)		−5.0	−4.0	−1.0	1.7
Current account ($ billion)		−0.589	0.823	0.104	0.103
Net inflow of direct foreign investment ($ million)			−16	40	48

Sources: Various issues of United Nations Economic Commission for Europe, *Economic Survey of Europe*; Deutsche Bank, *Focus: Eastern Europe*; *Economics of Transition* and *Business Central Europe*; EBRD (1994: 154; 1995: 31); Bartlett (forthcoming)

Table 26.2 Croatia: unemployment

Date		*Unemployment rate (%)*
1990	December	11.4
1991	December	18.9
1992	January	
	February	
	March	18.8
	April	
	May	
	June	18.5
	July	
	August	
	September	18.5
	October	
	November	
	December	18.5
1993	January	18.5
	February	17.8
	March	17.9
	April	17.7
	May	
	June	17.2
	July	17.2
	August	
	September	17.3
	October	17.4
	November	17.4
	December	17.4
1994	January	17.6
	February	
	March	17.6
	April	
	May	

Table 26.2 Continued

Date	*Unemployment rate (%)*
June	17.0
July	
August	
September	
October	
November	
December	18.3

Sources: Various issues of United Nations Economic Commission for Europe, *Economic Survey of Europe*; Deutsche Bank, *Focus: Eastern Europe*; *Economics of Transition* and *Business Central Europe*; EBRD (1994: 154; 1995: 31); Bartlett (forthcoming)

The Former Yugoslav Republic of Macedonia

POLITICS

Demographic background

In the 1991 census, boycotted by most Albanians, the official figures showed that the population was split 65 per cent ethnic Macedonian and 21.7 per cent ethnic Albanian.

Likewise, the 21 June–10 July 1994 census was boycotted by most Albanians and to some extent by the Turk and Serb minorities. (All members of ethnic minorities had to complete two forms, one in Macedonian and one in the mother tongue, while all participants had to produce citizenship papers and residence permits.)

Ethnic Albanians claim that they constitute up to 40 per cent of the population. (The largest Albanian party, the Party of Democratic Prosperity, has split. At the congress held on 13 February 1994 the radical wing broke away: *EEN*, 2 March 1994, vol. 8, no. 5, p. 6.)

The final results of the 1994 census were not released until December. The total population was given as 1,936,877, of which Macedonians accounted for 1,288,330 (66.5 per cent) and Albanians 442,914 (22.9 per cent) (in 1953 the respective proportions were 65.59 per cent and 12.45 per cent). But in fact the number of Albanians is closer to 800,000 (40 per cent plus of the population) (*EEN*, 1995, vol. 9, no. 10, p. 2).

According to the 1994 census, the 2 million population was split 67 per cent Macedonian, 23 per cent ethnic Albanian, 4 per cent Turk,

2.3 per cent Gypsy and 2 per cent Serb (*Business Europa*, April–May 1995, p. 8).

Political developments

15 October 1993. Greece breaks off talks on the new name of Macedonia after the Greek general election.

10 November 1993. Two ethnic Albanian deputy ministers (of defence and health) are accused (along with a number of others) of plotting armed rebellion. Specifically they are charged with encouraging western Macedonia to secede. (Relations with Albania itself had earlier been adversely affected by incidents involving loss of life on the border.)

9 February 1994. The USA recognizes 'The Former Yugoslav Republic of Macedonia'.

16 February 1994. The Greek prime minister, Andreas Papandreou, says that 'the Greek government has decided to suspend the activities of its consulate in Skopje and on the suspension of goods to and from Skopje through the port of Salonika, except those that are absolutely necessary for humanitarian reasons, such as food and medicines' (the Foreign Ministry said later that the embargo would apply to all customs points in Greece). Salonika normally handles 70 per cent of Macedonia's imports and exports (*IHT*, 28 March 1994, p. 6); around 80 per cent of foreign trade, according to *The Independent* (29 March 1994, p. 8).

In late January there had been hints of a more conciliatory approach by the Greek government. These concerned possible concessions by Macedonia over: (1) the constitution, which states that 'The Republic cares for the status and rights of those persons belonging to the Macedonian people in neighbouring countries'; (2) the flag, specifically the use of the Star of Vergina (a sunburst symbol found on a gold casket in the tomb, unearthed in 1977, of Philip II of Macedon and also associated with his son Alexander the Great).

31 March 1994. More than a million Greeks demonstrate in Salonika in support of government policy.

6 April 1994. The EU gives Greece until 13 April to lift its blockade or face a referral to the European Court of Justice for violation of EU trade laws. Greece did not respond.

29 June 1994. The European Court of Justice refuses the EU's request for an emergency interim injunction (which can be granted only on the grounds of 'grave and irreparable harm' to the EU).

2 July 1994. All twenty-three ethnic Albanian MPs walk out of parliament when ten ethnic Albanians are sent to prison for allegedly forming paramilitary units in order to overthrow the government.

The Macedonian presidential and parliamentary elections of 16 October 1994

The parties competed for the 120 seats in parliament. There were long delays before the results were published, allegedly due to 'technical' factors (such as inadequate electoral rolls; the official electoral commission admitted that 10 per cent of voters were not on constituency registers, but they were still able to vote). Alleging serious irregularities, the Democratic Party and VMRO (see below) boycotted the second round (which took place on 30 October, when the turnout was only 35 per cent). International observers were far from being entirely happy, but thought the election results should stand. The presidential election was, as forecast, won by the incumbent, Kiro Gligorov, with 52.44 per cent of the registered vote (there was a high percentage of spoiled votes). The challenger, Ljubisha Georgievski (VMRO), received only 14.5 per cent of the vote.

Pro-Gligorov forces won about 82 per cent of the seats in parliament, with the under-represented opposition threatening civil resistance campaigns. The radical wing of the main Albanian party, the Party for Democratic Prosperity, polled well, gaining the majority of the seats taken by the Albanians. There was concern that Menduh Thaci (see below) was deprived of a parliamentary seat in Skopje on the third ballot by just ten votes after winning comfortably on the first two ballots (Pettifer 1995: 56).

The parties and their platforms

Alliance for Macedonia. The governing alliance, led by the Social Democratic Party (which is the party of Prime Minister Branko Crvenkovski) but also including the Liberal Party and the Socialist Party. In the first round the alliance gained 32.1 per cent of the vote and twelve seats.

Democratic Party. Founded a little over a year ago (in 1993), the party is led by Petar Gosev. The party campaigned on a platform of (1) nationalism (it refused to accept the principle of collective rights for the Albanian minority; it was against federalism and the granting of autonomy to ethnic Albanians) and (2) the free market (reduced taxes and faster privatization via vouchers). The slogan 'With clean hands' signified an anti-corruption stance. In the first round it won only 11.2 per cent of the vote.

Internal Macedonian Revolutionary Organization (VMRO). Hard-line nationalist party. In the first round it won 14.4 per cent of the vote and fewer than ten seats. It favours privatization (Pettifer 1995: 57).

Party for Democratic Prosperity. The ethnic Albanian party. As a result of the split in February 1994, some hard-liners ran as independents in the election (e.g. Menduh Thaci). In the first round it won two seats.

Political developments after the October 1994 general election

6 December 1994. There are reports that Greece has relaxed its embargo, e.g. allowing through fuel for humanitarian purposes.

16 February 1995. Ethnic Albanians open a university (in Tetovo) in defiance of government orders.

An Albanian protester has been shot dead, the founder of the university is in prison and Albanian MPs are boycotting parliament (Iso Rusi, *IHT*, 7 March 1995, p. 8).

'He was released four months later on bail . . . both communities have been careful not to let the situation get out of hand' (Kerin Hope and Anthony Robinson, *FT*, Survey, 7 July 1995, p. 36).

4 September 1995. Simultaneous announcements in Washington, Athens and Skopje reveal that the Greek and Macedonian foreign ministers are to meet to take the first steps towards 'the creation of a basis for friendly relations between the two countries'. Only the name of the former Yugoslav republic has yet to be agreed. But other disputes have been resolved. The star of Vergina is to be removed from the Macedonian flag, while sections of the Macedonian constitution considered by Greece to be threatening will be amended. In return Greece will lift its economic embargo (lifted on 15 October) and diplomatic relations will be established. (The USA will also establish diplomatic relations with the former Yugoslav republic.)

13 September 1995. The agreement is signed, effective after a month.

THE ECONOMY

Financial policy

The January 1994 reform programme, worked out with the IMF and the World Bank, was designed to bring inflation down from its current annual rate of 350 per cent to 70 per cent by the end of the year, reduce the budget deficit from 13.5 per cent of GDP to 6.6 per cent, start large-scale privatization and introduce a bank restructuring scheme (*Business Central Europe*, February 1994, p. 18; Deutsche Bank, *Focus: Eastern Europe*, 1994, no. 103, p. 5).

Liberalization of the price system is advanced, although a 'notification requirement' remains for milk, municipal rents, water, central heating and vehicle insurance (EBRD 1994: 25). There have been further moves towards cost recovery in the prices of electricity and oil derivatives (EBRD 1995: 56).

The Yugoslav dinar was withdrawn in April 1992 and replaced by coupons. The aim was to introduce a new currency, the denar, by the end of 1992 (actually achieved in May 1993). The denar has been floating since the beginning of 1994. There is near full current account convertibility except for citizens wishing to holiday abroad. Controls remain on the capital account. There are quotas on only 4 per cent of imports (mostly agricultural products). Export quotas were removed in January 1994 and over 90 per cent of exports are free of licensing requirements (EBRD 1994: 25, 109).

In April 1992 a public-sector pay freeze was announced and price controls were imposed on basic goods (Kerin Hope, *FT*, 4 August 1992, p. 2). A rigorous incomes policy has been in force since the end of 1993 (EBRD 1994: 25).

Pettifer (1995: 56) believes that economic viability has not been achieved. After admission to the IMF in December 1992 and to the World Bank in December 1993 substantial aid was mobilized. When an agreement on economic reconstruction was signed in February 1994 a stand-by loan of $80 million was arranged. Inflation has been reduced and the denar stabilized, but at considerable cost in terms of lost output and high unemployment. GDP in 1994 was only about 65 per cent of its 1992 level and unemployment stands at between 20 per cent and 30 per cent of the total work force.

The first stabilization package was introduced in April 1992 and the second in the autumn of that year. But a third one was needed. Introduced in December 1993, and this time sponsored by the IMF, inflation was brought down to quite low levels by March 1994 (Kraft 1995: 485). There has been heavy reliance on wage and price controls, e.g. in April 1993 wages were frozen for six months at 125 per cent of their March level (p. 487).

The exchange rate of the denar has been relatively stable for the past year (*Business Europa*, April–May 1995, p. 11).

Privatization

The aim is to take 1,450 companies out of the public sector (Mark Milner, *The Guardian*, 19 March 1994, p. 39).

The privatization law, passed in June 1993, was to come into force in spring 1994. In each case it is planned to sell at least 51 per cent of the capital of an enterprise at market prices to a dominant (domestic or foreign) investor; the main shareholder in larger enterprises will have five years during which to raise the stake to 51 per cent (Deutsche Bank, *Focus: Eastern Europe*, 1994, no. 103, p. 6).

The main approach is direct sales. Small and medium-sized enterprises can be bought (1) by anyone outright or in instalments over five years or (2) through an employee buy-out of at least 51 per cent of capital. By mid-1994 the (overwhelmingly private) small business sector accounted for 10 per cent of industrial output and 17 per cent of employment (Bartlett forthcoming).

The Law on the Transformation of Enterprises with Social Capital was passed in June 1993 (Koevski and Canning 1995: 3). The law refers only to those enterprises with social and mixed capital. At the end of 1993 a total of 1,931 enterprises with social capital (pure or mixed) were identified. Of these 1,009 had only social capital, while the remaining 922 had mixed capital, consisting mostly of 'internal' share capital (in those enterprises which began privatization under the federal laws; a significant number of enterprises underwent partial self-privatization under the federal programme during 1990–91, the principal participants being enterprise employees who received 'internal' shares; the extent of privatization then was greater in Macedonia than in all the other ex-Yugoslav republics combined: pp. 5, 33), social capital, state capital and, in a few cases, capital invested by an individual. A total of 414 enterprises (such as public utilities) were excluded from the first stage of the programme, as were the roughly 900 co-operatives. Thus the total number of enterprises with social capital earmarked for privatization was 1,517. They represent over 50 per cent of total corporate assets, with 115 classified as large, 325 as medium-sized and 1,077 as small (pp. 9–11). The process is to take place on a commercial basis, i.e. privatization by sale (p. 9). 'The new privatization strategy of the Macedonian government is a multi-track, "commercial" one, aiming to establish a durable pattern of responsible ownership, with active core shareholders (e.g. banks) providing corporate control' (p. 1). 'The new, multi-track privatization scheme emphasizes the creation of a durable pattern of responsible ownership, with dominant "inside" control groups. Full control rights can be obtained by initial purchase of only 10 per cent in the case of large enterprises and 20 per cent of capital equity in the case of medium-sized enterprises, with the obligation to buy 51 per cent of the entire capital within the subsequent five years . . . foreign investors are given equal treatment' (p. 33). A range of options are available:

1. Small (up to fifty employees) and medium-sized (fifty to 250 employees) enterprises are free to choose their privatization method(s).

Small enterprises may be sold whole or in part by public auction, competitive tender or by direct agreement with an interested buyer. Employees have the opportunity to buy the enterprise outright by paying an amount equivalent to 51 per cent of the value of its enterprise and undertaking to pay the remainder in instalments over five years.

Medium-sized enterprises may choose from a variety of methods, including public auction or tender, direct acquisition and a management buy-out.

2. Large enterprises (over 250 employees) are able to select an appropriate method in consultation with the Privatization Agency. Broadly the same range of options available to medium-sized enterprises is applicable here (pp. 11–12).

Although the primary strategy is privatization by sale, preferential rights are available to a number of groups. Discounts are available to present and former employees, citizens are able to use the hard currency deposits frozen in 1990, and former owners (or their heirs) whose property was confiscated under communism are to be compensated. In addition, 15 per cent of enterprise equity is to be transferred to the Pension Fund (p. 13).

The initiative for commencing privatization rests with the enterprise (i.e. the workers' council or the board of directors), but enterprises failing to meet the prescribed deadlines will be privatized by the agency. In the case of enterprises with no share capital the deadlines for presenting their privatization plans were December 1994 for small and medium-sized enterprises and December 1995 for large ones. In the case of enterprises which began their privatization under the former Yugoslav federal laws the deadline was June 1995 (pp. 16–17). A pilot privatization has been initiated, involving twenty-one enterprises (eight large, eight medium-sized and eight small). At the end of 1994 privatization was under way in three cases and a further ten were expected to be approved in early 1995 (p. 17). Overall, as of November 1994, the agency had approved enterprise privatization plans in a total of fifty-four cases, while final approval had been granted by the government commission on the proposed privatization transactions to go ahead in thirteen cases, seven of which had participated in the federal process. These companies have now been fully privatized (p. 18). Overall, progress so far has been slow but may be expected to gather momentum from the beginning of 1995 (p. 33).

The Privatization Agency revealed that it had an agreement with the World Bank to privatize 940 enterprises by the end of 1995, while the agency itself was looking for two-thirds of the economy to be in private hands by April 1996 (*Business Europa*, April–May 1995, p. 8). It was also revealed that privatization had been completed in 145 small and medium-sized enterprises (of which only six were actually management buy-outs); of these 145 enterprises 110 were small ones which became completely employee-owned (p. 9). The first public share offering was scheduled for spring 1995 (p. 15). Bids were received in March 1995 for stakes in three processing plants (p. 46).

In mid-1994 the private sector accounted for roughly 35 per cent of GDP (EBRD 1994: 10). Private activity, including that in the informal sector, probably accounts for 25–40 per cent of GDP. About 400 larger enterprises are expected to apply for privatization by the end of 1995. The others will then have restructuring or privatization imposed upon them. Twenty-five large enterprises have been selected for immediate privatization and a further forty are under consideration. Over 90 per cent of small enterprises are already privately owned. A draft law on restitution is in preparation. The 1989 bankruptcy law is still in force (p. 24).

Writing in March 1995, Pettifer (1995: 57) mentioned the 'almost total lack of progress' in the area of privatization.

In 1994 eighty-four large enterprises were privatized and another 200 were identified for privatization in the first half of 1995. A draft law on restitution was in preparation (EBRD 1995: 56).

So far some 250 enterprises have been privatized. The privatization agency planned to sell 790 out of 1,200 on its list by December 1995. Another group of twenty-five large loss-making enterprises were to be restructured in 1995 with the aim of privatizing the viable and liquidating the remainder (Kerin Hope, *FT*, Survey, 7 July 1995, p. 34).

The privatization agency announced that 130 enterprises had been privatized by July 1995. A further 467 were to be processed by the end of the summer (*Business Central Europe*, September 1995, p. 19).

Foreign investment

'Beyond 1990 it appears that, due to regional instability and doubts with regard to the nature and internal stability of the fledgling Macedonian state, foreign investment effectively ceased . . . current legislation does not permit land ownership by foreigners' (Koevski and Canning 1995: 14).

Economic performance

GDP growth was negative through 1994 and unemployment is very high. But inflation peaked in 1992 and there have been signs of progress in that regard (see Table 26.3). There have been somewhat varying interpretations of economic circumstances.

Unemployment has been pushed up from around 25 per cent to an estimated 30 per cent of the labour force and at times during 1994 to as much as 40 per cent (Koevski and Canning 1995: 2).

Helena Smith (*The Guardian*, 25 September 1993, p. 12) paints an encouraging economic picture, e.g. credits from and new export markets in the West, an upsurge of private activity and a stable currency. (There were also so many violations of the UN sanctions against the Federal Republic of Yugoslavia that Macedonia was told by the UN on 6 September 1993 to

Table 26.3 The Former Yugoslav Republic of Macedonia: selected economic indicators

Economic indicator	*1990*	*1991*	*1992*	*1993*	*1994*
Rate of growth of GDP (%)	−9.9	−12.1	−14.0	−14.1	−7.2
Rate of growth of industrial output (%)	−10.6	−17.2	−17.3	−15.9	−9.4
Rate of growth of agricultural output (%)	−10.2	17.6	0.4	−20.0	8.5
Inflation rate (%)	708.0	215.0	1,690.7	247.6	118.9
Net foreign debt ($ billion)	0.5	0.4	0.6	0.8	0.8
Budget surplus or deficit (% GDP)		−3.6	−7.2	−11.1	−2.6
Current account ($ billion)	−0.400	−0.262	−0.019	−0.088	−0.170
Unemployment rate (end of year, %)	22.9	24.5	26.8	30.3	33.2

Sources: Various issues of United Nations Economic Commission for Europe, *Economic Survey of Europe*; Deutsche Bank, *Focus: Eastern Europe*; *Economics of Transition*; EBRD (1994: 157; 1995: 34); *Business Europa*, 1994, no. 103, p. 4; Bartlett (forthcoming)

tighten up.) In a later article (*The Guardian*, 17 December 1993, p. 10) she describes Macedonia as having, with Slovenia, the highest standard of living in the whole of the former Yugoslavia.

Kerin Hope (*FT*, 25 January 1994, p. 3), however, perceives a more negative situation: GDP has fallen by more than 30 per cent since 1991; *per capita* income has dropped by half to less than $700; industrial production is collapsing (steel and nickel producers are close to shutting down because of difficulties in exporting and the textile industry is operating at 30 per cent of capacity); and agricultural output fell by more than 20 per cent in 1993. More than 40 per cent of the work force are unemployed or on forced leave from factories that have shut down (*FT*, 14 October 1994, p. 2).

Leonard Doyle (*The Independent*, 17 December 1993, p. 10) talks of economic free fall. *The Economist* of 3 April 1993 (p. 48) estimated that income per person was then less than half what it was in 1989.

Deutsche Bank (*Focus: Eastern Europe*, 1994, no. 103, p. 6) thinks that Macedonia has borne up relatively well despite the burdens. One reason is that UN sanctions on Serbia/Montenegro have in some cases been ignored.

'Its economy in ruins as a result of United Nations sanctions against Yugoslavia and trade barriers imposed by Greece, Macedonia is also torn by ethnic division' (Iso Rusi, *IHT*, 7 March 1995, p. 8).

'The output decline has bottomed out. However, about one-third of the labour force is unemployed or on involuntary leave' (IMF, *World Economic Outlook*, June 1995, p. 55).

The Federal Republic of Yugoslavia: (1) Montenegro

STATISTICAL, HISTORICAL AND POLITICAL BACKGROUND

Area, 5 per cent of the former Yugoslavia. Population (1989), 0.7 million (3 per cent of the Yugoslav total); 69 per cent Montenegrins, 13 per cent Moslems and 6 per cent Albanians. Contributed 2 per cent of Yugoslav GNP. Index of *per capita* income, 73 (Yugoslav average = 100). The 1991 census gave a population of 616,327, of which Montenegrins accounted for 61.8 per cent, Slav Moslems 14.6 per cent, Serbs 9.3 per cent and Albanians 6.6 per cent (*EEN*, 1995, vol. 9, no. 10, p. 4). The capital was known as Titograd before the name was changed to Podgorica. On 29 December 1993 the Montenegrin parliament reinstated Cetinje as the capital, although Podgorica was to remain the seat of government.

Independent in 1799, Montenegro was first a prince-bishopric (1799–1851), then a principality (1851–1910) and finally a kingdom (1910–18), under intermittent Russian patronage. Montenegro is poor and mountainous (its name means 'black mountain'). The December 1990 election produced a win for the Communist Party, which became known as the Democratic Party of Socialists in June 1991. The president is Momir Bulatovic. Montenegro supported Serbia as the threat of disintegration grew. A referendum held on 1 March 1992 attracted a turnout of 66 per cent, and 96 per cent voted to remain part of Yugoslavia. On 27 April 1992 Serbia and Montenegro declared a new Federal Republic of Yugoslavia, with 44 per cent of the area and 39 per cent of the population of the old one. (Montenegro accounts for only about 5 per cent of the population, GNP and assets of the Federal Republic of Yugoslavia: *The Economist*, 23 July 1994, p. 42.) The 31 May 1992 general election is discussed below in the section on Serbia. There were also elections on 20 December 1992 (see below). Bulatovic won 43 per cent of the votes in the first round of the Montenegrin presidential election, with Branko Kostic (who favours close ties with Serbia) winning 24 per cent. In the second round, held on 10 January 1993, Bulatovic was re-elected with 63.3 per cent of the votes (the latter secured 36.7 per cent). The distribution of seats in the eighty-five-seat Montenegrin assembly was as follows: the Democratic Party of Socialists, forty-six; the People's Party, fourteen; the Liberal Alliance, thirteen; the Serbian Radical Party, eight; the Social Democratic Party of Reformists, four.

Bulatovic is increasingly distancing himself from Milosevic and an attempt to declare Montenegrin independence cannot be ruled out (an 'attempt' because Serbia may well resist such a move with force of arms). For example, the then federal prime minister Milan Panic survived a vote of no confidence on 4 September 1992 with the help of Montenegrin MPs. Even more dramatically on 2 November 1992 Panic survived by the narrowest of margins another vote of no confidence only when (having lost decisively in the lower house) Montenegrin representatives in the upper house (where they have an equal share of seats) supported him. Montenegrin parliamentarians tried to save Yugoslav president Cosic when he was dismissed on 1 June 1993 (see below). Montenegro favoured allowing UN monitors along the Serbia–Bosnia border to enforce the sanctions which were supposed to be (but never were) imposed on the Bosnian Serbs after 8 May 1993 (and Montenegro would have welcomed a mission from the CSCE). President Bulatovic visited Albania on 20 September 1993. On 31 October 1993 the Autocephalous Montenegrin Orthodox Church was re-established despite resistance from the Serbian Orthodox Church (the two were merged in 1920). The new patriarch is Antonije Abramovic, who lived in Canada for over forty years.

THE ECONOMY

There is very little information on the economy as a separate entity. One report says that: 'Since the introduction of UN sanctions, local industry has either closed or cut production to 20 per cent or less of capacity. The huge KAT aluminium plant in the Zeta valley, which once produced nearly half the republic's foreign exchange earnings, works at 20 per cent capacity . . . its large, modern commercial fleet (once responsible for 25 per cent of foreign exchange earnings) is stranded or impounded around the world. The tourist industry, aside from its Yugoslav clients, is virtually dead. Unemployment is high but hard to quantify (well over 15 per cent)' (*EEN*, 15 March 1995, vol. 9, no. 6, p. 3).

Montenegro objected to a new company law drawn up by the Serbian Socialist Party, which argued that the proposed law would prevent the new bourgeoisie from grabbing state assets. The Montenegrin government, in contrast, believed that the law as drafted would slow down privatization and effectively reintroduce 'self-management' (*EEN*, 28 April 1995, vol. 9, no. 9, p. 5). Montenegro hoped to complete the privatization of all 'socially owned' enterprises by the end of 1995 (*EEN*, 24 August 1995, vol. 9, no. 17, p. 2).

The Federal Republic of Yugoslavia: (2) Serbia

POLITICS

The political background

Milosevic was born in Serbia but is of Montenegrin descent. He has built up (from around 40,000) a powerful police force, where his power lies. One estimate puts it as big as 110,000, compared with about 125,000 personnel in the army (James Whittington, *FT*, 7 October 1994, p. 3).

Ibrahim Rugova, who was elected president of Kosovo by the Albanian majority there (over 90 per cent), has expressed the opinion that Kosovo should be a UN protectorate. The president of Albania, Sali Berisha, also thought that Kosovo should be under UN control and declared a neutral zone. On 17 July 1995 sixty-nine ethnic Albanian former policemen were sentenced to prison terms ranging from one to eight years for allegedly forming an illegal police force (bringing the total convicted to eighty-five).

Relations with Montenegro have become increasingly strained. President Momir Bulatovic has increasingly distanced himself from Milosevic. For example, Montenegrin politicians tried to save Yugoslav president Cosic when he was dismissed on 1 June 1993. Montenegro favoured allowing UN monitors along the Serbia–Bosnia border to enforce the promised sanctions on the Bosnian Serbs (supposed to start on 8 May 1993, but never implemented). (Montenegro accounts for only about 5 per cent of the population, GNP and assets of the Federal Republic of Yugoslavia: *The Economist*, 23 July 1994, p. 42.)

The cost of the war

Around 20 per cent of Serbian GNP goes to the Bosnian and Croatian Serbs (Milos Vasic, *IHT*, 25 August 1993, p. 4).

The figure of 20 per cent is an official one. Some independent estimates put the proportion at closer to 40 per cent of GNP (Laura Silber, *FT*, 22 July 1993, p. 3).

Local economists and Western diplomats estimate that from 5 per cent to 20 per cent of Yugoslav GDP is spent on military and financial support for the Bosnian Serb forces (*IHT*, 5 August 1994, p. 1).

Around 75 per cent of the federal Yugoslav budget goes on defence (*The Times*, 22 October 1993, p. 21).

Political developments

19 December 1993. The Serbian general election takes place (with some reruns on 26 December owing to irregularities). All parties played the nationalist tune and played on the collective paranoia of almost the whole world seeming to be against Serbia. Draskovic openly advocated a Greater Serbia and even criticized Milosevic for supporting the Owen–Stoltenberg proposals. The Socialist Party won 123 seats, just three short of an absolute majority in the 250-member Serbian National Assembly. The Democratic Movement of Serbia (DEPOS) won forty-five seats and the Serbian Radical Party (led by Vojislav Seselj) thirty-nine. The Serbian Unity Party (founded on 3 November 1993 and led by the neo-fascist warlord and Milosevic supporter Zeljko Raznjatovic, known as 'Arkan' and accused of war crimes: see 3 November 1993 entry in the section on Bosnia) did surprisingly poorly (winning only one seat). (Six of the forty-five DEPOS MPs went over to Milosevic soon after the election: *The Economist*, 23 July 1994, p. 42.)

29 September 1994. Vojislav Seselj is arrested on charges of 'physical assault' (spitting, it seems) at the speaker of parliament, Radoman Bozovic. Seselj is sentenced to thirty days in jail (he already has an eight-month suspended sentence for an earlier incident in parliament). On 28 October he was jailed for three months.

23 December 1994. The district court of Belgrade cancels the private company licence (registered in September 1991) of *Borba*, the leading independent newspaper.

27 December 1994. The Yugoslav federal government pronounces itself owner of *Borba* and names the federal minister of information as acting director and editor-in-chief. (The staff resisted and began publishing their own edition of the newspaper on 25 December. The new paper is called *Nasa Borba.*)

4 June 1995. Vojislav Seselj is sentenced to twenty days in jail (generally thought to be connected with the fact that he has campaigned against Milosevic's policy on Bosnia and Croatia).

THE ECONOMY

The economic system

'In so far as he [Milosevic] has any economic ideas, he is wary of reform and suspicious of free-market capitalism' (*The Economist*, 23 July 1994, p. 42).

Despite the generally heavy fall in output, Serbia's ability to feed itself has always been a positive factor. But there have been problems. Hyperinflation and controls on the prices paid to farmers have led to reluctance to make deliveries to the state (*EEN*, 20 July 1993, vol. 7, no. 15, p. 1). The government has moved steadily towards a barter economy, e.g. buying farm products with cooking oil taken from state reserves (Michael Montgomery, *The Daily Telegraph*, 26 November 1993, p. 17).

On 18 August 1993 it was announced that the Federal Republic of Yugoslavia would put the prices of staple products under direct government control, enforce deliveries and declare war on speculators. There have been reports that Serbia has prevented supplies of basic products such as sugar, flour and oil from reaching Montenegro because of severe shortages. In early September the Yugoslav government introduced rationing of some foodstuffs and other basic products (*The Times*, 7 September 1993). The government promised that from 1 September 1993 each family would receive a special package of essential goods at a reduced price, but this promise was then postponed to 15 September (*EEN*, 7 September 1993, vol. 7, no. 18, p. 3). The promised supplies of cheap staples such as milk, sugar and flour have not materialized (Yigal Chazan, *The Guardian*, 30 September 1993, p. 10). The government promised to supply pensioners with food parcels in January 1994 (*The Times*, 28 December 1993, p. 8).

Privatization

New privatization legislation was passed in August 1991. It envisaged a state-dominated system favouring workers and managers and extensive state involvement (Bicanic forthcoming).

In the past few years industry has been gaining ground, but there are no plans to pursue the vigorous privatization of big state enterprises (*The Economist*, 23 July 1994, p. 43).

The Serbian parliament has passed a law calling for the reappraisal of all privatized enterprises. In short, what little privatization has been achieved, less than 10 per cent of state enterprises, will be largely reversed (Laura Silber, *FT*, 29 December 1994, p. 2).

The ruling Socialist Party of Serbia opposes privatization, while Montenegro favours it. Differences over this issue resulted in the federal law of 'transformation' (privatization) being withdrawn from the federal parliament (*EEN*, 24 August 1995, vol. 9, no. 17, p. 2).

Economic performance

Serbia has had to grapple with hyperinflation of world record proportions:

1. By the end of 1992 the annualized inflation rate was 20,000 per cent (United Nations, *World Economic Survey 1993*, p. 44).
2. The annual rate of inflation had reached 32,701,709 per cent by August 1993 (Bicanic forthcoming), 64,422,464 per cent by September 1993 (United Nations Economic Commission for Europe 1994: 75) and 320 million per cent by December 1993 (*The Economist*, 23 July 1994, p. 43).
3. Inflation ran to 1 million per cent in December 1993 alone (Laura Silber, *FT*, 29 March 1995, p. 2; 15 June 1995, p. 2).
4. Table 26.5 (see p. 628) shows monthly inflation rates for 1993. By way of comparison the peak monthly inflation rate in Germany during the Weimar Republic was 45,213 per cent in October 1923. Hyperinflation is generally considered to begin when the monthly inflation rate is 50 per cent.

On 30 September 1993 six zeroes were struck off the currency and on 29 December nine zeroes were struck off dinar notes. (Note that the Serbian-held areas of Bosnia and Croatia print their own currencies, which can be legally exchanged at par with the Yugoslav dinar. This has aggravated inflation: Marcus Tanner, *The Independent*, 2 December 1993, p. 14.)

A new 'super-dinar' was introduced on 24 January 1994 as part of an anti-inflation package (John Kifner, *IHT*, 26 January 1994, p. 11; Laura Silber, *FT*, 25 January 1994, p. 3). The new dinar was to be backed by gold and hard currency reserves and convertible into Deutschmarks at par (the Deutschmark came to dominate transactions during the hyperinflation; new dinars could be exchanged at banks for Deutschmarks, but transfers of more than DM 100 required written notice and a waiting period). The government hoped that hard currency savings would be traded in for new dinars at banks. The old currency would be used for an interim period (initially exchangeable at a rate of 13 million old dinars to one new one). There was to be a new guaranteed minimum wage of twenty new dinars a month, income in excess of this being taxed at a rate of 35 per cent. A steep rise in taxes, especially in the private sector, was another element of the stabilization package. There was also a steep rise in water, electricity and telephone charges.

The United Nations Economic Commission for Europe (1994: 76) commented that the monthly inflation rate in the Federal Republic of Yugoslavia reached 180,000 per cent in December 1993: 'it is uncertain whether the programme also includes the necessary cuts in budgetary expenditure which would be required to eliminate the underlying sources of inflationary pressures'.

The early consequences of the introduction of the 'super-dinar' were encouraging. Tim Judah (*The Times*, 30 April 1994, p. 13) described the results after three months as 'impressive': the monthly rate of inflation had been brought down to zero; the uncontrolled printing of dinars had been brought to a halt; the new dinar had held its value; the authorities had been zealous in collecting taxes; production in March 1994 had increased by 22 per cent compared with the same period of 1993 (although the economy was operating at about a third of its pre-war level); empty shops had been replenished; real incomes had doubled; 'Dragoslav Avramovic, architect of the plan, is being hailed as a Serbian folk hero.' (Avramovic is governor of the Yugoslav National Bank and at some time in the past worked for the World Bank.)

The government used gold coins to pay farmers for the 1993 harvest. The farmers were the first to get gold coins if they wanted them instead of paper money or goods, but any citizen may buy the coins (*Business Central Europe*, October 1994, p. 22).

Economic performance since the introduction of the 'super-dinar' in January 1994

The Economist (7 May 1994, pp. 49–50) notes that by the end of 1993 industry was running at barely one-third capacity. But in February 1994 (according to the Serbian government) industrial production was up 12 per cent on the same period of 1993 and in March it was up 22 per cent. The use of the new currency has been fostered by a ban on interest on foreign currency accounts but not on dinar accounts. (Avramovic also says that subsidies to the Bosnian and Croatian Serbs have been reduced.) But the problems may soon reappear. 'It is hard to see how a second collapse can be avoided, perhaps in the autumn, as foreign reserves run out and inflationary pressures return' (*The Economist*, 23 July 1994, p. 43).

Laura Silber (*FT*, 3 June 1994, p. 3) saw signs of tentative improvement. Industrial output grew over the previous four months; it rose, according to official figures, by 3 per cent in April 1994 compared with March, though this followed a 24 per cent increase over February. There are harsh penalties for black-market hard currency dealing, from three months to three years in prison. While the printing presses have stopped, so far the enormous demands on the budget have not been eliminated (Laura Silber, *FT*, 9 May 1994, p. 4).

The results, says James Whittington, eight months after the 'super-dinar' was introduced, have confounded critics and exceeded all expectations:

1. Inflation was brought down to −0.8 per cent in March 1994. In September the rate stood at 0.2 per cent.
2. The industrial production index in August 1994 was up 70 per cent over January.
3. Average monthly wages rose from DM 30 in January 1994 to DM 200 in September.
4. Shops have been surprisingly full.

But there are signs of trouble: (1) the reappearance of the currency black market signals a weakening of the dinar; (2) shop prices are showing inflationary pressures; and (3) by mid-1994 the money supply began to increase more quickly than the growth of foreign exchange reserves (James Whittington, *FT*, 6 October 1994, p. 3).

After nine months' respite from hyperinflationary economic collapse, Serbia appears to be on the brink of a second slump. The dinar is slipping, meat and cooking oil are again beginning to disappear from supermarkets, and prices are rising (*EEN*, 5 October 1994, vol. 8, no. 20, p. 8).

The black-market rate for the dinar has slipped to about 1.7 to the Deutschmark and prices are still rising (*The Independent*, 20 December 1994, p. 9).

The dinar has gone from 2.1 to 2.7 to the Deutschmark on the black market, while price controls were due to end on 1 April 1995 (Emma Daly, *The Independent*, 27 March 1995, p. 10).

Just previously the dinar had slumped to 4.5 to the Deutschmark on the black market, but has now strengthened to 2.6 (Laura Silber, *FT*, 29 March 1995, p. 2).

On 27 March 1995 dealers were selling the Deutschmark for varying rates around the country, from 2.7 to five dinars (*Transition*, 1995, vol. 6, no. 3, p. 18). 'An exchange rate-based stabilization programme put a sudden end to extreme hyperinflation in early 1994, but growing fiscal and quasi-fiscal imbalances spurred renewed high open inflation in late 1994' (IMF, *World Economic Outlook*, June 1995, p. 55). Monetary policy was relaxed after July 1994 to counter the continued fall in production (United Nations Economic Commission for Europe 1995: 96). On 26 November 1995 the dinar was officially devalued to 3.3 dinars to the Deutschmark.

Further economic statistics

The picture for GDP was very grim until 1994. Agriculture has fared much better than industry and Serbia has always been able to feed itself (see Tables 26.4 and 26.5).

Table 26.4 The Federal Republic of Yugoslavia: selected economic indicators

Economic indicator	*1990*	*1991*	*1992*	*1993*	*1994*
Rate of growth of GDP (%)	−8.4	−11.2	−26.2	−27.7	6.5
Rate of growth of industrial output (%)	−11.7	−17.6	−22.4	−37.4	1.2
Rate of growth of agricultural output (%)	−7.0	9.7	−17.8	−3.3	4.0
Budget surplus or deficit (% GDP)				−28.0	
Current account ($ billion)		−0.035	−1.284		
Inflation rate (annual, %)	580.0	120.0	8,990.9	2.2E+14[1]	

1 United Nations Economic Commission for Europe (1995: 97)
Sources: Various issues of United Nations Economic Commission for Europe, *Economic Survey of Europe*; United Nations, *World Economic Survey*; *Business Central Europe*, *The Financial Times*, *The Times*, *The Independent* and *The Guardian*

Table 26.5 The Federal Republic of Yugoslavia: inflation and unemployment

Rate (%)	*1991*	*1992*	*1993*	*1994*
Inflation (monthly)				
January				
February			212.0	
March				−0.8
April				
May				
June			366.7	
July			430.0	
August			1,882	
September			1,890	−0.2
October			1,900	
November			20,190	
December			180,000	
Unemployment				
December	21.5	22.8	24.0	23.9

Sources: Various issues of United Nations Economic Commission for Europe, *Economic Survey of Europe*; United Nations, *World Economic Survey*; *Business Central Europe*, *The Financial Times*, *The Times*, *The Independent* and *The Guardian*

The Belgrade Institute of Statistics reckons that 75 per cent of the population now lives at a minimum subsistence level (*EEN*, 30 March 1993, vol. 7, no. 7, p. 7).

In Serbia there are 550,000 working citizens, 750,000 unemployed and 1.4 million on temporary lay-off (Roger Boyes, *The Times*, 9 January 1993, p. 11).

More than 1 million workers (about 40 per cent of the Serbian work force) have been laid off by closures but still receive 80 per cent of their former salary (Kerin Hope, *FT*, 1 June 1993, p. 3). Some 750,000 workers (25 per cent of the work force) are registered as unemployed and 1.2 million more are on paid leave. GDP is now only a third of the 1990 level, while dramatic falls in industrial output mean that agriculture now accounts, officially, for more than 50 per cent of GDP. But the black economy may be the equivalent of 33 per cent of GDP (*FT*, 14 February 1994, p. 2).

People on 'forced leave' (due to factors such as sanctions) receive 80 per cent of their former salary (*EEN*, 1993, vol. 7, no. 5, p. 2).

Real incomes in Serbia are a tenth of what they were three years ago and about 60 per cent of the labour force is out of work (*The Economist*, 14 August 1993, p. 69). Today 60 per cent of workers in industry, services and administration are unemployed. Industry is working at 20–30 per cent of its pre-war capacity. GNP has fallen by half since 1989, while 40 per cent of all economic activity is believed to take place on the black market. Only agricultural output and oil output have remained constant. Before the war Serbia produced up to a quarter of the oil it needed (*The Economist*, 12 February 1994, p. 36). Unofficially, the Federal Republic of Yugoslavia conducted foreign trade worth $1 billion in 1993, i.e. 20 per cent of the pre-war level. This was achieved despite sanctions and an economy functioning at only one-third of its previous capacity (*The Economist*, 2 July 1994, p. 34).

Workers who earned the equivalent of DM 540 a month in 1990 were earning only DM 50 in June 1993. The UN High Commissioner for Refugees estimates that around 3 million of the 10 million people in the Federal Republic of Yugoslavia are at or below the poverty line (Tony Barber, *The Independent*, 3 September 1993, p. 10; 22 October 1993, p. 13).

Real wages in the Federal Republic of Yugoslavia fell by 5 per cent in 1991 and by 50 per cent in 1992 (United Nations Economic Commission for Europe 1993: 226).

In real terms the average monthly salary in Serbia is only a tenth of that of five years ago (Laura Silber, *FT*, 18 December 1993). GNP per head has fallen to $350 from $3,060 in 1989. Some 60–70 per cent of the Serbian population live below the poverty line. More than half Serbia's factories have temporarily closed (*FT*, 22 July 1993, p. 3). Almost half the 2.4 million non-agricultural labour force are without a job, while the average monthly wage in 1993 fell to DM 10 from DM 550 in 1990 (*FT*, 26 January 1994, p. 3). Industrial production has fallen to a third of its level in 1990 and factories are operating at below half capacity. *Per capita* GNP has fallen from $2,148 to less than $1,000. Unemployment is running as high as 50 per cent, including those on 'forced holiday' (*FT*, 2 June 1994, p. 3).

According to some estimates, the black economy makes up about a third of GNP. Taxes on corporate profits have already been abandoned in an attempt to encourage the black market into the registered private sector (James Whittington, *FT*, 6 October 1994, p. 3).

There has been a heavy 'brain drain' from Serbia. One source cites an unofficial estimate of over 100,000 people, mostly educated and/or young (Kerin Hope, *FT*, 2 March 1994, p. 2).

Slovenia

Political developments

The election of 6 December 1992 led to a coalition government. The Liberal Democratic Party won twenty-two seats in the ninety-member Chamber of Representatives. Its partners included the Christian Democrats (fifteen seats; led by Lojze Peterle, who is foreign minister), the Associated List of Social Democrats (fourteen seats) of four left-wing parties (deemed necessary to facilitate the passing of painful measures) and the Social Democratic Party (four seats).

15 January 1993. Slovenia becomes a member of the IMF (followed by membership of the World Bank in February and the conclusion of a trade and economic co-operation agreement with the EU in April).

12 May 1993. Slovenia becomes a member of the Council of Europe.

12 March 1994. A new ruling four-party alliance (Liberal Democracy of Slovenia) is formed under the leadership of Prime Minister Janez Drnovsek; the alliance comprises the Liberal Democratic Party, the Christian Democratic Party, the Socialist Party and the Green–Ecological Party (*EEN*, 1994, vol. 8, no. 7, p. 8; 1995, vol. 9, no. 14, p. 5).

28 March 1994. Defence Minister Janez Jansa (head of the Social Democratic Party) is dismissed following allegations of illegal intelligence operations. (The Social Democratic Party then left the coalition government.) (The interior minister resigned in mid-June: *EEN*, 22 June 1994, vol. 8, no. 13, p. 2.)

18 September 1994. Foreign Minister Lojze Peterle resigns (effective 1 October). (A new coalition government comprising the Liberal Democratic Party and the Asssociated List was formed. The Christian Democrats stayed in the coalition government. In return for losing the Foreign Affairs Ministry they were given the Ministry of Economic Relations and Development. The new foreign minister was Zoran Thaler of the Liberal Democratic Party.)

December 1994. Local elections see gains made by the right-wing Slovene People's Party, led by Marjan Podobnik (*FT*, Survey, 6 April 1995, p. 36).

6 March 1995. Italy lifts its veto on Slovenia having an association agreement with the EU (negotiations on associate status began on 15 March; Slovenia and the EU initialled a trade and political co-operation agreement on 15 June 1995). The dispute was about the property rights of Italians who fled from the Istrian peninsula after the Second World War.

Italy demanded that the property rights of Italian citizens who left the territory of Slovenia after 1945 should be restored. This contradicts the stipulations of the 1975 Osimo Treaty and of the Rome Agreement of 1983, which provides for fair indemnity for such property. The Slovene government has undertaken to submit to parliament legislation harmonizing its laws with those on property rights in force in the EU member states. Under present Slovene law foreign physical persons can inherit property (including land) and can acquire and own buildings (but not land), while foreign-owned legal persons are allowed to acquire all kinds of business-related property (Anton Bebler, *The World Today*, May 1995, vol. 51, no. 5, p. 98). In 1975 Italy and Yugoslavia signed a treaty which agreed compensation for property losses and all other outstanding issues (*FT*, Survey, 6 April 1995, p. 35). The promise to the EU does not mean that Italians will be allowed to claim back their property or to take part in auctions of real estate.

9 June 1995. A tentative debt agreement is reached with Western commercial banks, with the signing possibly taking place in September. Slovenia will be responsible for 18 per cent of the former Yugoslavia's total debt of $4.65 billion owed to the banks, Slovenia's share being swapped into bonds maturing in 2006. Slovenia has already secured debt rescheduling with the Paris Club of creditor governments (*FT*, 12 June 1995, p. 2).

THE ECONOMY

Financial policy

The aim was a budget deficit of 1.8 per cent in 1993 (Anthony Robinson, *FT Survey*, 30 March 1993, p. 36). Tight monetary and fiscal policies have been supplemented by wage controls in the battle against inflation.

The central bank is independent of the government (Harold Jackson and John Glover, *The Guardian*, 23 January 1993, p. 37).

The 27 January 1993 banking law provided for some of the bad debts of commercial banks to be swapped for government bonds (Anthony Robinson, *FT Survey*, 30 March 1993, p. 36).

In May 1994 an excess wage tax was imposed on all companies (*Business Central Europe*, July–August 1994, p. 24).

'Both monetary and fiscal policy have supported stabilization and wage pressure has been kept to a manageable level' (Kraft 1995: 474). The Bank of Slovenia Law, passed immediately after the declaration of Slovene political independence, established the independence of the central bank. The bank was not allowed to extend loans to the government for more than 5 per cent of the budget (p. 475). Incomes policy has also played a role in the stabilization effort, e.g. a wage freeze was introduced in February 1993 (pp. 478–9).

Prices

Price liberalization is almost complete (EBRD 1994: 37).

Privatization

The privatization bill went through a number of controversial drafts. Anthony Robinson (*FT*, Survey, 30 March 1993, p. 36) reports that the enabling law was approved in November 1992, but detailed regulatory legislation was still needed. Each enterprise is responsible for drawing up its own privatization proposal. The aim was to privatize 400 enterprises in 1993 and nearly 1,600 in 1994.

The privatization law (the Law on the Ownership Transformation of Enterprises) was passed on 11 November 1992 and included practically all possible methods of privatization (Zizmond 1993: 902–3). Privatization decrees were issued in March 1993. By March 1994 enterprises involved in the programme (about 55 per cent by value of all Slovenian enterprises) were to decide their privatization method and carry it out; otherwise it would be done for them. Harold Jackson and John Glover (*The Guardian*, 23 January 1993, p. 37) report that the book value of each enterprise would be allocated as follows: 10 per cent to a restitution fund (to compensate for seized property); 10 per cent to a staff pension fund; 20 per cent to employees; 20 per cent to a new central development fund, which, in turn, would distribute it in the form of vouchers to the population; 40 per cent to be sold on the open market (Zizmond refers to a 'labour buy-out' of 20 per cent and employees having priority in the sale of a further 20 per cent: 1993: 902). Socially owned enterprises can, however, also be privatized by being sold completely, in part or by fresh capital investment exceeding 30 per cent of the enterprise's value. If a foreign buyer's share exceeds Ecu 10 million the sale must be approved by the privatization agency (Zizmond 1993: 902).

Deutsche Bank (*Focus: Eastern Europe*, 17 December 1993, no. 95, pp. 3–4) reports that the November 1992 legislation was amended in June 1993. Some 2,700 enterprises are to be privatized, but so far only about eighty have submitted applications to the privatization agency. Privatization applications have to be submitted to the agency by the end of 1994. Failure to do so means that management and ownership fall to the development fund. Since privatization is just getting under way, the private sector currently accounts for roughly 15 per cent of GDP and 20 per cent of employment. The basic approach is as follows: 10 per cent of share capital is transferred to a restitution fund and 10 per cent to a pension fund; 20 per cent of the share capital is to go to a development fund (at a later date these shares will be sold to investment funds, which in turn will sell units to the population in exchange for vouchers, allocated according to age); 20 per cent of the share capital will be sold to the employees of the enterprise in exchange for vouchers; the remaining 40 per cent can be purchased by employees (at a 50 per cent discount off the purchase price, with payment spread over four years) or sold at auction or by tender. Enterprises are free to choose the privatization method. In the case of a proposal (which must be approved) to sell the entire share capital to a foreign investor, the revenue raised will be allocated to the funds.

Up to now privatization has made little headway. Of the 1,500–1,800 socially owned enterprises (originally put at 2,600 and inflated partly by double registrations) only about 700 have applied to the agency for privatization. Of the roughly 350 approved cases only something like seventy to 100 have actually initiated the process to date. Fewer than ten enterprises have completed privatization. The bulk of privatization is on the basis of a management and employee buy-out. One of the first enterprises to pass into private hands under the ownership scheme is the Lek pharmaceutical and chemical company (Deutsche Bank, *Focus: Eastern Europe*, 8 November 1994, no. 119, p. 3). By some estimates the underground economy accounts for around 7 per cent of GDP (p. 4).

It was generally expected that all but the largest enterprises would end up being controlled by their managers and employees, but the success of the first public offering of shares in February 1994 may make a difference. Only a handful of enterprises have been privatized so far (*Business Central Europe*, May 1994, p. 21). The first share-for-voucher auction, involving fifty of the 2,000 enterprises in the mass privatization programme, was planned for December 1994 (*Business Central Europe*, October 1994, p. 15). Sixty of the 1,350 enterprises in the programme were to take part in the first auction on 7 December 1994. A second auction was expected in early February 1995, followed by further auctions every two months (*Business Central Europe*, December 1994–January 1995, p. 53). Investment funds took part in the first real share auction on 8 March 1995. Over 65 per cent of enterprises were scheduled for privatization by the end of 1995 (*Business Central Europe*, April 1995, p. 20).

Only forty-nine out of the top 300 Slovenian companies are privately owned (*Transition*, July–August 1994, vol. 5, no. 6, p. 20).

Patrick Blum (*FT*, Survey, 12 April 1994, p. 32) adds the following:

1. Restructuring has had to precede privatization because of the sudden loss of markets in the former Yugoslavia.

2. Mira Puc, managing director of the Agency for Restructuring and Privatization, says that 'Conditions are different in each country. The political conditions here would make it impossible to do it [privatization] all through the state, as in Germany, because all managers here believe they already own the companies.'

3. The development fund has already sold about thirty companies.

4. There are no limits on the size of the stake an investment fund can have in any one company. Individual funds, however, can have no more than 10 per cent of their portfolio in a single company.

By mid-1994 small enterprises and craft firms employed 150,000 people out of a total work force of 700,000 (Bartlett forthcoming).

In mid-1994 the private sector accounted for roughly 30 per cent of GDP (EBRD 1994: 10). Large privatization has been slow, but is likely to become comprehensive by about the end of 1995. The programme involves about

2,700 enterprises and by mid-1994 215 had submitted privatization plans. Almost all small trade and service activity is operated by the private sector. Under the 1993 law land and buildings can be returned to the former owners (EBRD 1994: 36, 65). By the end of 1994 over 92 per cent of the enterprises that had been earmarked for privatization under the mass privatization programme had submitted plans to the agency. About 40 per cent of them had completed the first phase of privatization and were awaiting registration by the courts (EBRD 1995: 64).

Gavin Gray (*FT*, Survey, 6 April 1995, p. 36) provides the following information:

1. By the end of 1994 more than 1,300 of the socially owned enterprises had drawn up plans for privatization. (Some 1,350 enterprises: *IHT*, Survey, 6 April 1995, p. 11.)
2. Mira Puc believed that most of them would be in private hands by early 1996.
3. Only steel, postal services and a few other strategic industries would be owned by the state.
4. The role of the privatization agency is to check that the submitted plans conform with the law.
5. It seemed that most small and medium-sized enterprises would end up 40 per cent owned by investment funds, with the remaining shares controlled by workers and managers.
6. Larger enterprises were likely to be privatized by a combination of worker buy-outs, public share issues and transfers to investment funds.
7. The law is flexible. Some enterprises would be 100 per cent privatized straight away, but very few enterprises would be sold to foreign investors.
8. Private investment funds would own 20 per cent of the shares of most enterprises.

Anthony Robinson (*FT*, Survey, 6 April 1995, p. 35) argues that: 'The attempt to privatize the economy ran into resistance. This led to the adoption in most cases of privatization through a form of management or worker buy-out. In effect, privatization Slovene-style means that workers and managers generally retain ownership through the issue of free or discounted shares in their enterprise . . . Most "socially owned" enterprises are expected to be privatized by the end of this year, using variants of the free or discounted share-offer formula. But in the meantime enterprise managers have been unable to resist demands for higher wages and have been unwilling to invest.'

Foreign trade

Imports and exports are now generally free from quantitative restrictions. There is a floating exchange rate regime. Convertibility is full for current account purposes and the remaining restrictions on the capital account are to be phased out (EBRD 1994: 37, 109). By the end of 1994 98 per cent of imports were free from restrictions. The government is committed to further liberalization and to the elimination of all non-tariff barriers (EBRD 1995: 64).

On 1 September 1995 the tolar became externally convertible in accordance with Article 8 of the IMF (*Business Central Europe*, October 1995, p. 17).

Exports of goods and services account for 62 per cent of GDP (*Business Central Europe*, May 1994, p. 20).

Serbia had imposed a boycott on all Slovenian goods, but later substituted a 25 per cent tariff (*Business Europa*, January–February 1993, pp. 19–20).

A co-operation agreement was signed with the EU in 1993, giving tariff-free access to the EU for about 90 per cent of Slovenian industrial products. The EU now accounts for more than half of Slovenia's foreign trade, with Germany taking 29.5 per cent of exports in 1993 (Patrick Blum, *FT*, Survey, 12 April 1994, p. 32).

In 1994 the EU accounted for more than 60 per cent of commodity trade, with Germany alone responsible for more than 30 percentage points (*FT*, Survey, 6 April 1995, p. 35).

In 1994 more than 70 per cent of exports went to the EU, which supplied a near-equal amount of imports (*IHT*, Survey, 6 April 1995, p. 11).

On 23 February 1995 Slovenia signed a free-trade pact with the four remaining EFTA countries (Iceland, Liechtenstein, Norway and Switzerland). The pact would come into force on 1 July 1995 as far as the four were concerned, but Slovenia was to have a seven-year transition period.

Foreign investment

The constitution does not allow the sale of land to foreigners (*FT*, Survey, 6 April 1995, p. 35). (See Bebler above, p. 631.)

All sectors are open to foreign investors operating through joint ventures. But wholly owned foreign companies are restricted in certain fields, such as military equipment, transport and communications (*IHT*, Survey, 6 April 1995, p. 12).

A new company take-over law was introduced in July 1995, designed to place foreign and domestic investors on an equal footing. Share purchases that add up to a greater than 25 per cent interest in a company were to be subject to investigation (*Business Europa*, July–August 1995, p. 46).

Around 40 per cent of foreign capital is German, 25 per cent Austrian and 15 per cent Italian (Harold Jackson and John Glover, *The Guardian*, 23 January 1993, p. 37).

More than $1 billion of foreign capital has been invested since 1990 (Patrick Blum, *FT*, Survey, 12 April 1994, p. 32). There are still restrictions in sensitive sectors such as defence, aviation, telecommunications and the media (p. 33).

The total value of foreign investment is over $1 billion (*Transition*, July–August 1994, vol. 5, no. 6, p. 20).

Direct foreign investment amounted to $275 million in the period 1990–93 (EBRD 1994: 123).

Economic performance

Slovenia is the one really bright spot in the former Yugoslavia, although problems remain. GDP growth turned positive in 1993. The annual rate of inflation peaked in 1990, but it had still not reached single figures by 1994 (see Table 26.6). The unemployment rate was also still in double figures at the end of 1994 (see Table 26.7).

Table 26.6 Slovenia: selected economic indicators

Economic indicator	*1990*	*1991*	*1992*	*1993*	*1994*
Rate of growth of GDP (%)	−4.7	−8.1	−5.4	1.3	5.5
Rate of growth of industrial output (%)	−10.3	−12.4	−13.2	−2.8	6.4
Rate of growth of agricultural output (%)	1.6	−3.3	−6.0	−3.5	1.6
Inflation rate (%)	549.7	117.7	201.0	32.3	19.8
Net foreign debt ($ billion)	1.9	1.8	1.0	1.1	0.7
Budget surplus or deficit (% GDP)	−0.3	2.6	0.2	0.5	−1.0
Current account ($ billion)	0.526	0.190	0.926	0.150	0.485
Net inflow of direct foreign investment ($ million)	−2	41	113	112	88

Sources: Various issues of United Nations Economic Commission for Europe, *Economic Survey of Europe*; Deutsche Bank, *Focus: Eastern Europe*; *Economics of Transition* and *Business Central Europe*; EBRD (1994: 169; 1995: 46); Zizmond (1993: 887–905)

Table 26.7 Slovenia: unemployment

Date		*Unemployment rate (%)*
1990	December	4.7
1991	December	10.1
1992	January	
	February	
	March	
	April	
	May	
	June	
	July	
	August	
	September	

Table 26.7 Continued

Date		*Unemployment rate (%)*
	October	
	November	
	December	13.4
1993	January	13.5
	February	13.5
	March	13.5
	April	14.1
	May	14.0
	June	14.4
	July	14.9
	August	15.0
	September	15.1
	October	15.4
	November	15.3
	December	15.5
1994	January	15.2
	February	
	March	14.8
	April	14.5
	May	14.2
	June	14.1
	July	14.4
	August	14.4
	September	14.5
	October	14.5
	November	14.3
	December	14.3

Sources: Various issues of United Nations Economic Commission for Europe, *Economic Survey of Europe*; Deutsche Bank, *Focus: Eastern Europe*; *Economics of Transition* and *Business Central Europe*; EBRD (1994: 169; 1995: 46); Zizmond (1993: 887–905)

The unemployment rate is around 14.8 per cent, with about 122,000 workers out of a job (*IHT*, Survey, 6 April 1995, p. 13). According to ILO calculations, unemployment peaked at 9.1 per cent in 1993 and has only slightly eased since. But 'the unemployment figures should be taken with a pinch of salt. Many of the allegedly unemployed are working in Slovenia's thriving "shadow economy", now estimated to be worth 30 per cent of the official one' (p. 11).

Part IV

CHINA, CUBA, MONGOLIA, NORTH KOREA AND VIETNAM

27

CHINA

BACKGROUND

After relinquishing the titles of political office, Deng Xiaoping's only remaining formal title was 'Most Honorary President of the China Bridge Association'.

Yang Shang Kun and his half-brother Yang Baibing were thought to be building up a power base in the army and this explains the decline in their influence after October 1992 (note, however, that Yang Shang Kun is generally seen as a reformer).

There are 54 million members of the Communist Party. About 1.7 million new members have been added in each of the last two years (Lena Sun, *IHT*, 11 October 1994, p. 7).

Work on the controversial Three Gorges Dam started on 14 December 1994.

Demographic aspects

The population was 1.17 billion at the end of 1992, 1.185 billion at the end of 1993 and 1.2 billion in mid-February 1995. The population growth rate was 1.298 per cent in 1991 and 1.16 per cent in 1992 (EIU, *Country Report*, 1993, First Quarter, p. 2).

The birth rate (per thousand) was 23.33 in 1987, 21.00 in 1990 and 18.24 in 1992 (*IHT*, 28 April 1993, p. 4).

The crude death rate (per thousand) was ten in 1965 and seven in 1989 (Nolan 1992: 49).

Population growth in 1993 was 1.1 per cent (*FT*, 15 February 1995, p. 6).

The infant mortality rate was thirty per thousand in 1989 (Nolan 1992: 49).

Life expectancy at birth (in years) was sixty-seven in 1981 and seventy in 1989 (Nolan 1992: 49). *The Economist* (Survey, 30 October 1993, p. 12) cites figures of forty-three in 1965 and sixty-nine in 1991.

The literacy rate in 1990 was 82 per cent (*China Briefing*, February 1994, p. 6). The adult literacy rate was 73 per cent in 1991 (*The Economist*, Survey, 30 October 1993, p. 12).

Officially China is made up of fifty-six nationalities, with the Han comprising some 91 per cent of the population. The fifty-five official 'minority' nationalities are mostly scattered along China's borders, like the Mongolians and Uygurs in the north and the Zhuang, Yi and Bai in southern China. In the eight years to 1990 the Han population grew by 10 per cent and the minorities as a whole grew by 35 per cent. There is actually a wide variety of culturally and ethnically diverse groups within the majority Han population, groups which have recently begun to rediscover and reassert their different cultures, languages and histories (factors include more rapid economic development in certain regions). Han peoples differ in many ways, e.g. they speak eight mutually unintelligible tongues (Dru Gladney, *IHT*, 22 February 1995, p. 8).

On 27 October 1994 the Maternal and Infant Health Care Law was approved by the National People's Congress, aimed at 'improving the quality of the population'. 'Those suffering from mental and contagious diseases will have to defer their marriage when the diseases are serious and likely to affect others.' Foetuses found to be carrying hereditary diseases and to be seriously abnormal should be aborted. Women whose pregnancies are a serious threat to their own health would be advised to have an abortion.

The new law took effect on 1 June 1995. People diagnosed as having some genetic diseases ('carriers of genetic disorders') are not permitted to marry unless they agree to be sterilized or to adopt long-term contraceptive measures. The law also implies that parents who have had an abnormal child may be forced to terminate future pregnancies (*The Times*, 5 June 1995, pp. 11, 19).

The new law stipulates compulsory antenatal tests. Although the final decision on abortion lies with healthy mothers, there is concern that 'advice' can turn into forceful persuasion (*The Guardian*, 6 June 1995, p. 10).

The dissident movement

The leading dissident is Wei Jingshen, who first came to prominence in the pro-democracy or 'Democracy Wall' movement of 1978–79. He was arrested on 31 March 1979 and sentenced to fifteen years in prison for 'counter-revolutionary activity'. On his release on 14 September 1993 (part of the bid to host the next Olympic Games) he had about six months left to serve of his sentence. He was rearrested on 1 April 1994 (for meeting a US diplomat in February). He was supposed to have been paroled on 4 October 1994, but no one has seen him since April 1994 (officially he is under 'administrative detention' or 'residential surveillance').

Another well known dissident is Xu Wenli, who was released in May 1993 after serving twelve years of a fifteen-year prison sentence (police harassment continued). Wang Juntao was released on 23 April 1994 and allowed to go the USA for medical treatment; he was sentenced to thirteen years in prison in 1991 for his role in Tiananmen.

The regime continually stresses the need for 'social stability' and is especially fearful of the dissident movement linking up with discontented workers and peasants at a time of post-Deng anticipation. China has a huge labour camp network (*laogai*: 'reform through labour'). Former camp inmate Harry Wu estimates 10 million prisoners, while the Chinese government admits to less than 1.5 million (*The Guardian*, 19 May 1994, p. 27). Harry Wu (then Wu Hongda) was arrested in 1957 for criticizing the 1956 Soviet invasion of Hungary and was a labour camp inmate for nineteen years (from 1960 to 1979). He later became famous for undercover reports of life in the camps and for his allegation that China, apart from exporting goods made by prisoners, runs a highly profitable trade in the organs of executed prisoners. After emigrating to the USA in 1985 he became a naturalized American. Harry Wu was detained on 19 June 1995 when crossing into China from Kazakhstan. He was later arrested and charged with spying. On 24 August 1995 he was expelled from China immediately after receiving a fifteen-year jail sentence. There are at least 3,000 political prisoners (*IHT*, 20 May 1994, p. 3). There are 1,700 people in jail for their political or religious beliefs (*IHT*, 4 May 1995, p. 7).

Even tougher regulations against those who threaten the 'social order' were issued on 12 May 1994. Eighteen new rules banned certain activities by unregistered social or religious groups, persons under official surveillance or persons deprived of their political rights.

On 13 July 1994 new laws dealing with internal dissent and espionage were published. Foreign institutions, organizations and foreigners in China were considered hostile if they financed, colluded with or engaged in subversive activities endangering state security. Subversive activities were defined as the organization of terrorist activities, the fabrication or distortion of facts or the spreading of views that endanger state security, and the use of religion to incite ethnic strife.

On 1 October 1994 three dissidents were sentenced to three-year terms of 're-education through labour'. They were Yang Zhou (released in July 1995 on health grounds), Bao Ge and Yang Qinheng. On 18 October Li Guotao received the same sentence.

On 6 November 1994 four dissidents (sentenced after Tiananmen) and four Tibetan dissidents were released from prison.

Nine dissidents were sentenced to prison terms ranging from three to twenty years on 16 December 1994.

On 22 December 1994 Dai Xuechong was jailed for three years, allegedly for tax evasion but in reality for being a member of the Association of

Human Rights based in Shanghai (he was the fourth member to be sentenced in the previous three months).

A compensation law came into effect on 1 January 1995. Citizens who have been the victims of torture and other physical or mental violence are able to sue government officials.

On 5 January 1995 it was disclosed in the West that China had been operating a black list since May 1994. On the list were forty-nine dissidents living abroad, who were to be either banned from entering China or arrested on arrival at the border.

A Justice Ministry official has said that China does not classify its 2,679 'counter-revolutionaries' as political prisoners (*FEER*, 9 February 1995, p. 13).

A number of petitions were presented to the National People's Congress (which began on 5 March 1995), calling for greater democracy, an independent judiciary and an end to corruption. The petitions were not accepted.

On 8 March 1995 China survived by just one vote a UN Human Rights Commission's resolution (it was defeated by twenty-one to twenty, with twelve abstentions). Since Tiananmen (1989) attempts have been made by Western countries to pass a resolution condemning China's record on human rights, but until 1995 China had successfully ensured that a vote was not even held (this time Russia supported the holding of the vote, but then voted against the resolution). The draft resolution 'expressed concern at continuing reports of violations of human rights and fundamental freedoms in China . . . severe restrictions on the right of citizens to freedom of assembly, association, expression and religion, as well as to due legal process and a fair trial'. The resolution cited reports of torture and other accusations of violations, but it also praised China for improving the economic situation of many of its people and changing its legal system.

Forty-five eminent scientists and intellectuals issued a signed petition on 16 May 1995 pleading for the release of those imprisoned after Tiananmen and in general for those incarcerated for their beliefs.

In the run-up to the 4 June anniversary of Tiananmen further petitions were submitted and more dissidents were detained (e.g. Wang Xizhe on 20 May 1995 and Wang Dan the following day).

An Amnesty International report said that political and religious repression in Tibet increased in 1993 and 1994 (*IHT*, 30 May 1995, p. 4).

POLITICAL DEVELOPMENTS, CONGRESSES AND CENTRAL COMMITTEE SESSIONS

The Eighth National People's Congress, 15–31 March 1993

There were a number of significant personnel changes. Jiang Zemin, now described as the 'core' of the (collective) leadership, added the title president (he was already party secretary and chairman of the party's Central Military Commission; this was a sign of the abandonment of the earlier policy of separating party and state). (He replaced Yang Shangkun as president; Yang's half-brother Yang Baibing, the former chief political commissar of the People's Liberation Army, had been demoted at the Fourteenth Party Congress in October 1992.) Prime Minister Li Peng was re-elected for a second five-year term of office, while Zhu Rongji was promoted to (sole) senior vice-premier. Rong Yiren, the chairman of CITIC, became vice-president (the new chairman of CITIC is Wei Mingyi). The phrase 'socialist market economy' was formally enshrined in the new constitution.

In his speech on the opening day of the congress Li Peng reaffirmed that 'our great socialist motherland will stand as firm as a rock in the east for ever'. But the Dengist line on economic policy was strongly proclaimed. He did warn that 'the amount of bank credit and currency put into circulation has risen too fast and there is a constant threat of inflation' and he called for a 'basic balance between supply and demand'. But Li Peng formally raised the target for the average annual rate of growth of national income for the remaining three years of the five-year plan to 8–9 per cent (originally it was only 6 per cent). The 1993 target was set at 8 per cent, but the prime minister acknowledged that 'unforeseen circumstances' could cause it to be exceeded. He also mentioned regional variations: 'where conditions permit, a higher rate can and should be achieved'. Should the growth targets be met, the goal of quadrupling the 1980 value of national income could be achieved within five years. Particular attention should be paid over the next five years to infrastructure, services and agriculture.

The prime minister said that 'reforming the administration and structure of the government is essential to the establishment of a socialist market economy and accelerating economic development'. Specifically, he announced that the number of civil servants serving the central government was to be reduced by 25 per cent over the next three years, with the number of ministries and other bodies directly under the State Council falling from eighty-six to fifty-nine. (Note that this was a reflection of the growing decentralization of the economy. Mass unemployment was not envisaged, e.g. some people would be transferred to commercial organizations and some functions were to be transferred to the State Economic and Trade Commission.) Li Peng mentioned the growing importance of labour contracts and added that workers should no longer be seen as 'belonging permanently to one sector or another of the economy'. 'Small' state enterprises could be sold or leased 'by public bidding'. He called for the decontrol of grain prices and the conversion of state agricultural subsidies into a 'relief fund for natural disasters'. In other markets, too, the state should opt for a 'price regulation fund' or 'commodity reserves' as opposed to direct state intervention.

Finance Minister Liu Zhongli spoke on 16 March. He warned of 'great financial difficulties'. Another budget deficit was forecast, albeit slightly lower than 1992. Although the losses of state enterprises fell by 4.2 per cent in 1992, Liu warned that the government would 'resolutely stop subsidizing those enterprises that have no prospect of making a profit'. Spending on defence would again increase (by 12.4 per cent in 1993), the fourth annual increase in a row.

Political developments since the March 1993 congress

27–29 April 1993. Representatives of so-called 'semi-official' organizations from China and Taiwan meet in Singapore. This is the first high-level direct contact since 1949. Mostly technical matters are discussed, but regular future talks are to take place.

14 June 1993. Li Peng appears in public for the first time since 26 April after a mystery illness (heart trouble was later suggested). This led to speculation about his political future.

25 August 1993. On the final day of a six-day session of the party's Central Commission for Discipline Inspection a new code of conduct bars party and government officials from the following: engaging in business on their own account or helping relatives and friends to profit from their activities; trading in securities; accepting gifts (of money or securities) or credit cards; using public funds to acquire membership of clubs or to take part in expensive recreational activities; engaging in paid media activities. (A survey of companies in Hong Kong that do business in China suggested that about 5 per cent of their operating costs were taken up in bribes: *EIU Country Report*, 1993, Third Quarter, p. 13.) Over the space of three days, namely 23–25 October 1993, three anti-corruption edicts were issued: (1) various government and party departments were ordered to close down or sell off, because of conflicts of interest, any businesses they operated; (2) an end to fees being charged for what should be public services (e.g crime investigation by the police); (3) government-financed trips abroad must have a clear official purpose that cannot include sightseeing (*IHT*, 26 October 1993, p. 7).

7 September 1993. China and India sign a provisional border pact, including a reduction of troops: 'Pending a boundary settlement [to be decided through 'friendly negotiation'], India and China have agreed to respect and observe the line of actual control.' (The border has been a contentious issue, especially after the October 1962 war which India lost.)

23 September 1993. Beijing fails in its bid to stage the Olympic Games in the year 2000, after a heated debate in international political circles and in the international media on China's human rights record. In the final round of voting Sydney (Australia) wins by forty-five votes to forty-three.

5 October 1993. China conducts an underground nuclear test.

31 October 1993. 'High-level' military contacts with the USA resume (the first since Tiananmen). (This was another sign of warmer relations in general between the two countries, e.g. visits of US officials to discuss agriculture, trade and human rights. Relations reached a low point by mid-September and the Clinton administration determined to improve matters.) Note that in October China cracked down on satellite television dishes and other forms of telecommunications such as portable telephones (these needed to be registered). But there seems to have been significant flouting of the regulations.

11 November 1993. China and Russia sign a defence co-operation pact and agree to hold regular military exchanges.

15 November 1993. Chancellor Kohl of Germany begins a visit to China.

19 November 1993. President Clinton meets President Jiang Zemin in Seattle during the Asia-Pacific Economic Co-operation (Apec) forum. They clash over the issue of human rights. (Two days earlier China had been informed that a supercomputer would be removed from the sanctions list and that other exceptions were being considered.)

26 December 1993. The 100th anniversary of the birth of Mao Tse-Tung (who died in September 1976).

The third plenary session of the fourteenth Central Committee, 11–14 November 1993

Prior to the session Deng Xiaoping had reportedly called for economic reform and development to be 'as fast as possible'; 'development at a slow pace is not socialism'. His ideas in general were endorsed in the communiqué issued on 14 November 1993 (the document was entitled 'Decision on issues concerning the establishment of a socialist market economic structure'). The aim was to 'speed up the process of establishing a socialist market economic system and bring about sustained, swift and sound development of the national economy . . . economic construction should be taken as the central task . . . a programme of action to restructure the economy in the 1990s'. The socialist market economy (defined as 'making the market the fundamental factor in the disposition of resources under state macro-control') was to be completed by the end of the century. In the meantime the establishment of 'a sound microeconomic control system would continue' and 'greater efforts should be made in comprehensive improvement of social order. Political stability and unity should be consolidated and developed.' The main points were as follows:

1. Public ownership was to remain the 'mainstay' of the economy. But there was a call for a 'modern enterprise system which suits the requirements of a market economy'. There should be a separation of 'government administration from enterprise management' as part of the transformation of state enterprises. The enterprise should be more responsible for its own

profits and losses. The Communist Party would be removed from the boardroom, company directors being responsible for appointing management (*IHT*, 6 January 1994, p. 13). A start was to be made on a 'step by step' conversion of some state enterprises into corporations (the first corporation law was due to be considered by the National People's Congress in early 1994). The aim was to turn as many as possible into limited liability companies (and in some cases joint stock companies), which would stand on their own feet (responsible for their own profits and losses, i.e. no automatic subsidies). In a document issued on 16 November it was stated that persistently loss-making state enterprises should apply for bankruptcy (the failing enterprises would be 'eliminated in the market competition'). Small state enterprises could be leased or sold. But these changes 'should be adopted in a gradual manner after experiments. It must not be done for show or rashly on a mass scale.' (On 20 June 1995 an experimental plan was announced whereby profitable state enterprises that merge with unprofitable ones will assume the total debt, which must be repaid over five years. But interest will not be charged for two years on loans used for circulating funds or for three years on fixed asset loans. Eighteen enterprises were already targeted, but all eligible state enterprises would be able to participate: *IHT*, 21 June 1995, p. 17.)

Official figures showed that in the first quarter of 1994 49.6 per cent of state enterprises were making a loss, up from 34.2 per cent a year earlier (*IHT*, 18 April 1994, p. 14). This figure went down to 46.3 per cent in the first six months of 1994 (*IHT*, 19 July 1994, p. 13) and to 44.5 per cent in the first nine months of 1994 (*IHT*, 19 October 1994, p. 4). Zhu Rongyi is cited as saying that in 1994 40 per cent of state enterprises were in the red, compared with 60 per cent in 1993 (*IHT*, 8 February 1995, p. 17). Official statistics showed that nearly a third of state enterprises were making a loss by the end of 1994, largely because they were employing 20 million more workers than were needed (*IHT*, 1 March 1995, p. 15). There are other estimates: (1) according to the World Bank, at least a third of the state enterprises lose money; budgetary subsidies to them amount to about 3 per cent of GDP or one and a half times the size of the fiscal deficit (Ernest Stern, *IHT*, 20 May 1994, p. 6); (2) about two-thirds of the estimated 76,000 state enterprises are either losing money or are on the verge of bankruptcy (*IHT*, 31 December 1994, p. 11); (3) two-thirds of the 100,000 state enterprises lose money or merely break even (*The Economist*, 25 February 1995, p. 94); (4) in 1994 45 per cent of medium-sized and large state enterprises made a loss (Tony Walker, *FT*, 12 January 1995, p. 15); about one-third of the 100,000 state enterprises at the township level or above are in the red (this includes the 14,000 medium-sized and large enterprises) (Tony Walker, *FT*, 6 March 1995, p. 5).

The need for a new social security system stems from such factors as rising unemployment. Such concern led to the following announcement by the Ministry of Labour on 29 April 1994: enterprises would need government permission to lay workers off; enterprises would have to pay for workers' job searches; state aid should go to unprofitable enterprises with potential, while those that go bankrupt would have to set aside funds from their remaining assets to aid laid-off workers; the central government would send emergency funds to areas where the unemployment rate ran out of control (*IHT*, 30 April 1994, p. 94). It is also worth mentioning at this point that, whereas urban workers have typically been allocated housing by enterprises or municipalities at highly subsidized rents, farmers have typically provided their own housing on land owned and allocated by the community. There have been many local experiments since 1982 involving the sale of public housing, but the first serious proposals for urban housing reform were published by the central government in February 1988. The proposed rent increases, coupled with wage compensation, and house purchases were supposed to begin in 1990. But there has, in fact, been no serious attempt to introduce the reforms on a large scale; substantial reforms have been confined to very few cities, e.g. Shanghai (Pudney and Wang 1994: 4–5).

Patrick Tyler (*IHT*, 25 November 1993, pp. 1, 21), *FEER* (9 December 1993, p. 75) and *IHT* (6 January 1994, p. 13) reported a pilot scheme to operate in 1994 (later postponed to 1995). Around 100 large state enterprises were to become corporations (limited liability companies owned jointly by the state and by shareholders), shedding social welfare activities but assuming responsibility for the failure or success of the business. (A payroll tax would pay for welfare services such as pensions, health care and unemployment benefit, while private insurance schemes could act as a supplement: *The Economist*, 20 November 1993, p. 85.) If successful, the reform would spread to all 11,000 medium-sized and large enterprises within three to five years. Some enterprises could become multinational corporations. According to Carl Goldstein (*FEER*, 23 December 1993, p. 46), the new plan permits major stakes (in some cases even majority stakes) in state enterprises to be sold to private or foreign investors (although the state has to retain control in, for example, arms manufacture and other basic industries). On 7 January 1994 it was announced that the enterprises in the pilot scheme would be granted autonomy in wage determination (provided that wage increases did not exceed 'a rate representing economic efficiency') and the authority to dismiss workers in the name of efficiency (note that on the same day a regionally varying minimum wage scheme for urban areas was announced; it requires provinces and municipalities to pay at least the average wage in the region) (*IHT*, 8 January 1994, p. 13). On 3 November 1994 it was announced that the enterprises had been selected.

To date very little progress has been made with the enterprise reform programme because of the social implications, e.g. unemployment.

(Reformers call for intensified efforts to restructure the governance of state enterprises by distributing shares among multiple owners – provincial and local governments, other state enterprises, banks, newly established asset management companies and individuals – in the expectation that arm's-length relations between owners and managers will enhance performance: Jefferson and Rawski 1994: 65. By the end of 1992 only 120 state enterprises had been authorized to sell their shares to the public, although a much larger number were making less formal arrangements for shared ownership between state enterprises: Perkins 1994: 40.)

2. A new taxation system, to be phased in from the start of January 1994. The details were announced on 1 December 1993:

1. A unified system for sharing tax revenues raised in the localities between the central government and the thirty provinces and municipalities, increasing the proportion received by the central government to 60 per cent.

In the late 1980s a new system was introduced whereby each province negotiated a three-to-four-year tax-sharing contract with the central government, but enforcement was difficult. The central government's present share is just under 40 per cent (DIW, *Economic Bulletin*, 1994, vol. 31, no. 9, p. 22). (Note that the fall in central tax revenues has helped undermine fiscal policy as a policy instrument.)

The ratio of budgetary revenue to GNP went down from 31.6 per cent in 1978 to 14.1 per cent in 1993 (Tsang Shu-ki and Cheng Yuk-shing, *Asian Survey*, 1994, vol. XXXIV, no. 9, p. 774). The central government's revenue share in the total budget fell from around 60 per cent to about 40 per cent during the reform period. Up to 1993 central–local revenue arrangements were dominated by the fiscal contract system. There were two sorts: (1) a fixed or adjusted quota arrangement applied to provinces such as Guangdong and Fujian, under which the local government remitted to or received from the central government a fixed amount of revenue or subsidy which could be adjusted upwards and (2) a proportional sharing scheme in which the two levels of government shared revenue according to a pre-agreed ratio. By the mid-1980s most local authorities had adopted the proportional sharing scheme. But a few of them, including Shanghai, shifted to the fixed or adjusted quota arrangement in the late 1980s. In 1994 the government launched a tax assignment system under which taxes were divided into three categories, namely central, local and shared. The goal was to move from the central–local tax revenue ratio of about 40 : 60 in 1993 to one of 60 : 40, although no specific date was fixed (pp. 776–8).

The first time that the central government collected taxes direct was in 1994; previously it had had to rely on the provinces to collect taxes. The level of compliance in forwarding revenue to the central government varied greatly. The central bank estimated that on average provinces turned over about half the tax receipts. It has been estimated that the central government's share of total tax revenue rose from about 40 per cent to 65 per cent in 1994 (Steven Mufson, *IHT*, 7 March 1995, p. 4).

In 1994 the central government's actual tax share was 65 per cent (Lincoln Kaye, *FEER*, 16 March 1995, p. 15).

The official budget deficit is probably half the real figure (*The Economist*, 7 March 1995, p. 4). Consolidated budget deficits have averaged 4–5 per cent of GDP in recent years, financed primarily from the central bank's printing presses (*The Economist*, Survey, 18 March 1995, p. 10).

2. A uniform 33 per cent corporate tax on all enterprises (medium-sized and large state enterprises currently pay 55 per cent, while the standard rate on foreign-invested enterprises is 24 per cent: *IHT*, 6 December 1993, p. 13). The preferential tax treatment of foreign-invested enterprises would be preserved by such devices as tax rebates. Tax refunds would be available for a period of five years or until an enterprise's contract expired, whichever came first (although such refunds would not be available to foreign-invested enterprises set up after 1 January 1994). China has no plans to abolish preferential income tax rates for foreign investors in the special economic and development zones (*IHT*, 13 January 1994, p. 15).

'The unification of the income tax rates at 33 per cent may be regarded as a move to achieve breakthrough as the management contract system implemented since 1987 has been abolished as well' (Tsang Shu-ki and Cheng Yuk-shing, *Asian Survey*, 1994, vol. XXXIV, no. 9, p. 787). 'Management contracts that obliged state enterprises to pay lump-sum income taxes have been cancelled, as have income adjustment taxes. The preferential rate of 15 per cent for foreign-invested enterprises in the SEZs has not been changed' (p. 783).

3. A simplified and extended VAT (from July 1994 onwards). The rate is 17 per cent for most products and 13 per cent for staple commodities. There will be additional excise taxes on goods such as cigarettes, alcohol, petrol, cars and jewellery. The central government will receive 75 per cent of VAT revenue.

4. A uniform personal income tax system for Chinese and foreign citizens alike (the nine tax rates range from 5 per cent to 45 per cent). But foreigners' personal earnings would be protected by changes in deductions (*IHT*, 6 December 1993, p. 13).

5. A sales tax of 3 per cent to 5 per cent on the turnover of enterprises in the service sector (such as those in entertainment, food, insurance, finance and transport).

6. Special taxes on the extractive industries.

7. Other taxes include those on property, stock exchange dealings and inheritance.

(The overall tax burden on enterprises operating in China is supposed to remain unchanged, despite the introduction of new taxes: *IHT*, 27 December 1993, p. 7.)

3. Strengthening the powers of the central bank along Western lines in order to exercise more effective monetary control. The crude macroeconomic controls have been blamed for 'stop–go' cycles ('boom–bust') instead of finer tuning of the economy. Particular concern has been expressed about the rapid growth of non-bank financial intermediaries since the mid-1980s (such as those set up by banks), which have undermined monetary control.

The reform details were announced on 3 December 1993. The People's Bank of China was to become more like a Western central bank (responsible to the government). It would not engage in commercial or even policy-related lending. The existing four 'specialized banks' (Industrial and Commercial Bank, Agriculture Bank, People's Construction Bank and Bank of China) were to become commercial banks, while 'policy loans' would become the prerogative of three new 'policy banks' (Long-term Development and Credit Bank, Export–Import Bank and Agricultural Development Bank).

4. The income distribution system should be based on work and individual responsibility.

5. The 'open door' policy would be enhanced. It was later revealed that a new unified managed floating exchange rate regime would be aimed for in 1994 (with restricted current account convertibility) and full convertibility by about the turn of the century. The new regime was actually introduced on 1 January 1994, somewhat earlier than expected. All import subsidies would be withdrawn in 1994, tariffs were to be reduced over the next few years and all but a few commodities would be freed from licences and quotas over the next four years (*IHT*, 13 December 1993, p. 9). (For actual developments, see below in the section on foreign trade.)

The company law

The first company law came into effect on 1 July 1994, the result of work which began in 1983. Limited liability companies and joint stock companies were covered, regardless of ownership. Companies registered before 1 July 1994 were to be given time to comply. Arbitrary government intervention in company operations was to be reduced and stress laid on the independent economic and legal status of companies. Note that the law relating to foreign-invested companies was to take precedence (*China Briefing*, October 1994, pp. 1–4).

The Ninth National People's Congress, 10–22 March 1994

Prime Minister Li Peng delivered the opening speech to the 2,978 delegates. 'In a turbulent and volatile international environment, and amid a worldwide recession, our great socialist motherland stood firm as a rock in the

East, enjoying economic growth, political stability, unity among the ethnic groups and social progress.' But there were still 'some major contradictions and problems in the midst of progress', e.g. inflation, excessive growth in fixed investment, loss-making state enterprises, crime and corruption ('the fight against inflation is a matter of life and death for our nation'). 'Economic development is the centre of all our work . . . Social stability, in turn, is an indispensable prerequisite for economic development and smooth progress in reform . . . Government at all levels should try to raise farmers' incomes . . . It will be an outstanding achievement if we can keep the GDP growing at 8 or 9 per cent for a few more years.' The target rate of growth of industrial output was to be 10.7 per cent and for inflation 10 per cent. Anti-inflation policies were to include the following:

1. Holding the mayors of big cities 'responsible' for a 'market basket' system to guarantee the stability of the prices of key goods.

2. Financing the entire budget deficit by new (high interest) bonds rather than relying heavily on bank borrowings (note that the budget would henceforth be calculated more in line with standard international practice, e.g. an end to the peculiar Chinese practice of counting borrowed funds as revenue).

Defence spending was to increase by 22.4 per cent. The CIA puts the annual defence budget at $16 to $17 billion, more than twice the publicly stated amount; using the World Bank's purchasing power parity method of calculation, the figure comes out at around $21 billion, but this is still only about half the amount spent by Japan and a fraction of the spending of the major nuclear powers (Gary Klintworth, *IHT*, 21 May 1994, p. 6). The International Institute for Strategic Studies estimated the 1994 defence budget in the range $28.5 billion to $45 billion (*FEER*, 4 August 1994, p. 16). Independent estimates of China's annual military expenditure vary from $10 billion to $50 billion. Official figures reveal a 200 per cent increase since 1988. China has a 2.9 million-strong army (Nayan Chanda, *FEER*, 13 April 1995, pp. 24–5). Michael Richardson (*IHT*, Survey, 24 April 1995, p. 18) cites one US estimate of $20 billion to $30 billion a year.

3. Enterprise and banking reforms would continue. Enterprises in 'dire straits' would receive some assistance but in the end 'must rely on their own efforts to extricate themselves from their predicament'.

4. New capital spending would be restricted to construction projects already under way, with special emphasis on infrastructure.

On 23 March President Jiang Zemin repeated the main theme of the congress, stressing the need to 'protect reforms while preserving stability'.

US Secretary of State Warren Christopher visited China on 11–14 March 1994. Before, during and after his visit China harassed and arrested leading dissidents. Since a major topic was the link between trade and human rights, this greatly soured the atmosphere. A similar thing happened during the 7–10 April 1994 visit of French Prime Minister Edouard Balladur.

Political developments since the March 1994 congress

18–28 April 1994. Li Peng visits Uzbekistan, Turkmenistan, Kyrgyzstan, Kazakhstan and Mongolia.

26 May 1994. President Clinton announces that 'most favoured nation' status for China's exports would be renewed (see foreign trade below).

10 June 1994. China undertakes its fortieth nuclear bomb test since 16 October 1964 (including one on 5 October 1993, two in 1992 and two in 1990).

5–9 July 1994. Li Peng visits Germany. Many economic agreements are signed, but human rights demonstrations upset the Chinese prime minister.

13 July 1994. New laws dealing with internal dissent and espionage are published. Foreign institutions, organizations and foreigners in China are considered hostile if they finance, collude with or engage in subversive activities endangering state security. Subversive activities are defined as the organization of terrorist activities, the fabrication or distortion of facts or the spreading of views that endanger state security, and the use of religion to incite ethnic strife.

7 August 1994. Negotiators from China and Taiwan reach agreement on a number of issues, such as fishing disputes and the possible repatriation of aircraft hi-jackers and illegal immigrants. (The approval of both governments is needed.)

22 August 1994. Deng's ninetieth birthday.

29 August 1994. During the visit of a US trade mission led by the commerce secretary (Ron Brown) the two countries agree on a framework to expand commercial ties and sign a number of contracts. (Ron Brown said that 'private representations' would be made about human rights. China pledged to discuss the topic at the UN in September.)

28 September 1994. At the end of a four-day meeting of the Central Committee a document entitled 'The resolution on strengthening grass-roots party organizations' is published: 'it is necessary to safeguard central authority and forcefully implement the party's line, principles and policies'. The mayor of Shanghai, Huang Ju, is promoted to full membership of the politburo. He is a protégé of President Jiang Zemin, who is described as 'core leader'.

7 October 1994. China conducts an underground nuclear test. (This was China's forty-first nuclear test since 1964, compared with forty-four by Britain, 210 by France and more than 1,000 by the USA: Patrick Tyler, *IHT*, 8 October 1994, p. 8.)

16–19 October 1994. US Defence Secretary William Perry visits China (the first by a defence secretary since 1989). A Joint Defence Conversion Commission is agreed to. The USA will help in the conversion from military to civilian production, e.g. to free air traffic control from the (90 per cent) dominance of the military and to produce 'environmentally safe' vehicles.

The Tenth National People's Congress, 5–18 March 1995

Qiao Shi, who became chairman of the National People's Congress (NPC) in October 1992, has attracted considerable attention, given the imminent demise of Deng Xiaoping. He was made a member of the politburo in 1985 and of the Standing Committee of the politburo in 1987. Qiao Shi abstained in the vote to declare martial law in 1989 (Lincoln Kaye, *FEER*, 11 May 1995, p. 15), but he is thought to be broadly a supporter of Deng's policies.

5 March 1995. In Prime Minister Li Peng's opening address to the 2,811 delegates familiar concerns came up:

1. Inflation needs to be reduced. The aim was to keep overall output growth in 1995 down to 8–9 per cent (the target for industrial growth was 13 per cent) and inflation down to 15 per cent. The government should tighten 'control and supervision over prices, especially those for daily necessities'. There would be no major price adjustments in 1995.

2. Loss-making enterprises should be merged or declared bankrupt: 'Enterprises which have been operating at a loss for a long time without an end in sight and have failed to repay debts should be allowed to declare bankruptcy.' Those enterprises which produce outdated goods should be allowed to 'change hands'.

3. State enterprises should separate productive activities from social ones, with the latter gradually transferred to the state.

4. The aim of all the measures should be 'to invigorate the state sector as a whole so as to give fuller scope to its dominant role'.

5. Agricultural performance should be improved through measures such as increased investment and action to control the loss of land to agriculture. Provincial governors were to be responsible for grain output (their 'rice bag') and municipal leaders were to be responsible for non-staple food output (their 'vegetable basket'). This has been termed the 'leadership responsibility system' for agricultural output (*China Briefing*, July 1995, p. 8).

6. Not only should crime and corruption be combated but 'we should oppose money-worship, ultra-individualism and decadent life styles, advocate healthy and civilized life styles and create a society with high ethical standards'. 'It is necessary to adhere over a long period of time to the principle of plain living and hard struggle, and of building up the country with industry and thrift.'

6 March 1995. The defence budget was increased by 21 per cent (the sixth nominal increase in a row).

17 March 1995. Two members of the politburo, who had the backing of President Jiang Zemin, met resistance from the NPC when it came to voting (by secret ballot) for their elevation to deputy prime minister (thus making six vice-premiers in total). Jiang Chunyun (party secretary of Shandong Province) received only 63 per cent support for his agriculture portfolio (1,746 for, 605 against, 391 abstained and ten did not vote). The party secretary of Shanghai, Wu Bangguo (responsibility for the reform of state enterprises), did better, with 86 per cent support (2,366 for, 210 against, 161 abstained and fifteen did not vote).

18 March 1995. The Central Bank Law had only 66 per cent support (1,781 for, 509 against, 360 abstained and twenty-eight did not vote). The law increased the central bank's independence, but some delegates wanted a stronger supervisory role for the NPC. The final draft placed the central bank under the direct supervision of the State Council (cabinet), but also obliged the bank to submit work reports to the Standing Committee of the NPC.

Details of the People's Bank of China Law are to be found in *China Briefing* (July 1995, pp. 1–2). The central bank was to implement monetary policy under the leadership of the State Council, without interference from government departments, local government, civil bodies or individuals. Monetary stability was to be the prime policy goal. The use of indirect monetary control measures was endorsed, but their use was not expected to be immediate.

The Education Law had 74 per cent support.

Political developments since the March 1995 congress

22 March 1995. A US warship visits a Chinese port for the first time since 1989 (and only the third time ever; the first visit was in 1986 and the second in May 1989).

9 April 1995. One of Beijing's two vice-mayors (and the chairman of the municipal planning commission), Wang Baosen, commits suicide (apparently) after being accused of corruption. (On 4 July it was announced that he had committed 'serious economic crimes'.)

10 April 1995. Chen Yun dies, aged ninety.

12 April 1995. Li Peng says that 'The core of political leadership has already been transferred from Deng Xiaoping, the second generation leader, to President Jiang Zemin, who represents the third generation of Chinese leadership' (*IHT*, 13 April 1995, p. 1).

27 April 1995. Chen Xitong is forced to resign as party chief (secretary of the Central Committee) of the capital, Beijing (although he remains a member of the national politburo).

An old comrade of Deng Xiaoping, Chen Xitong was placed under house arrest and his son was arrested (on 4 July it was announced that Chen Xitong was to be investigated for corruption). This was generally seen not only as part of the anti-corruption drive (reaching high places for a change), but also as part of the process of establishing Jiang Zemin (from Shanghai) as the 'core' of the leadership. In February Zhou Guanwu had suddenly retired as chairman of the Shougang Company (the country's largest steel producer and a company having Deng Xiaoping's personal support) after his son, Zhou Beifang, had been arrested on charges of 'serious economic crimes' in connection with the Hong Kong operations of Shougang's real estate and investment company (headed by Deng Xiaoping's son Deng Zhifang). On 4 May 1995 it was announced that two executives of Shougang subsidiaries had been given suspended death sentences for accepting bribes.

3–7 May 1995. The prime minister of Japan visits China.

10 May 1995. The start of a week-long visit by the prime minister of South Korea.

11 May 1995. The Nuclear Non-proliferation Treaty is extended indefinitely.

15 May 1995. China conducts an underground nuclear test (its forty-second).

22 May 1995. Japan announces that, as a protest against the test, it will reduce its grant aid to China (a largely symbolic move, since grants constitute only a small part of the total aid programme).

China vehemently protests about the USA's decision to allow the president of Taiwan a visa for a private visit. (No president of Taiwan has been allowed a visa to enter the USA since 1979 when Beijing was recognized as the sole government of China. Thereafter the USA had only 'cultural, commercial and other unofficial relations with the people of Taiwan'. Beijing had taken Taiwan's seat in the United Nations in 1971.)

29 May 1995. State enterprise officials are banned from setting up private businesses, using their influence to help relatives or diverting enterprise assets for themselves. This move followed one the previous week ordering state and party officials to declare their incomes and a string of earlier edicts banning government workers from accepting meals, gifts and other favours from the public (*IHT*, 30 May 1995, p. 4).

30 June 1995. Zhu Rongyi steps down as governor of the central bank and is replaced by Dai Xianglong.

1 August 1995. US Secretary of State Warren Christopher meets Foreign Minister Qian Qichen in Brunei.

17 August 1995. China conducts an underground nuclear test (its forty-third). (Japan announced that it would cut off most grant aid.)

22 August 1995. Deng's ninety-first birthday.

4–15 September 1995. The Fourth World Conference on Women takes place in Beijing. The Non-governmental Organizations Forum started on 30 August and finished on 8 September. It took place in Huairou, some 50 km from Beijing. (The holding of the world conference in China was controversial and there were protests about restrictions imposed by China on participation and about harassment and excessive surveillance by security officials.)

ECONOMIC REFORMS

An overview

Perkins (1994: 23–5) makes the following points:

1. When the economic reform process began with the party plenum of December 1978, there was nothing like Eastern Europe's desire to be like Western Europe. China faced no economic crisis that required immediate and fundamental change, only dissatisfaction with the pace of existing growth (a dissatisfaction fuelled in part by increasing awareness of the far superior economic performance of China's neighbours).

2. There was no economic reform blueprint. But *per capita* grain output in 1978 was the same as it had been in the mid-1950s and Mao's bias against foreign technology and products had severely impeded modernization. Thus the sequence of economic reforms emerged which placed agriculture and foreign trade first and industry only later.

3. China began its reform period in a more advantageous position than Eastern European countries and members of the CIS after 1989. China had already substantially reorientated itself to trade with the West, it was not heavily indebted and did not have to begin with a macroeconomic stabilization programme.

Rawski thinks that 'there was no clear strategy and no planned sequence of reform measures. Policy-makers responded to a succession of problems and opportunities with *ad hoc* improvisation' (1994: 272). 'China's leaders initiated industrial reform in the hope of eliciting better performance, but with no specific vision of a desirable post-reform industrial system. Not surprisingly, China's reforms have followed an evolutionary path marked by frequent shifts of direction and *ad hoc* responses to unanticipated outcomes. Bottom-up initiative, experimentation, learning and adaptation stand at the core of the reform process in Chinese industry' (Jefferson and Rawski 1994: 65.)

Woo (1994: 279) argues that 'gradualism in China is the result of the political deadlock between the Stalinists and the reformers'. 'Gradual reform in China was not the optimal reform for China' (p. 306).

Thomas Bickford (*FEER*, 1994, vol. XXXIV, no. 5, p. 473) discusses the extensive business activities of the People's Liberation Army: 'While it is doubtful that the military establishment likes depending on the market to generate extra income, that dependence gives the military a stake in continuing the economic reform.'

Planning, the market and the reform process

Cyril Lin talks of 'the overwhelming importance of the market mechanism in China today: only 12 per cent of total industrial output was subject to planning in 1992, and [the figure] is expected to fall to 7 per cent this year'. Only 25 per cent of investment is centrally planned and 83 per cent of sales are through the market (reported by Alexander Nicholl, *FT*, 24 May 1993, p. 17).

Robert Thompson (*FT*, Survey, 18 November 1993, p. viii) reported a fall in the proportion of planned industrial output from 12 per cent to 6.5 per cent. In addition there was 'guidance' in the form of estimates for about 25 per cent of production (compared with 34 per cent a year earlier).

According to Prybyla (1994: 657–8), in 1979 the share of central plan allocation in gross industrial output value was 90 per cent. Today it is 20 per cent, although not all the remaining portion is allocated by real markets in response to free prices – probably about half. By 1990 55 per cent of industrial capital goods were being sold at free or floating (between state-set limits) prices, compared with zero in 1978.

By 1993 central plans controlled only 7 per cent of industrial output value (Jefferson and Rawski 1994: 63). The share of industrial products sold through markets surpassed 50 per cent in the late 1980s and now exceeds 80 per cent. Mandatory plans now control less than 10 per cent of industrial output (Rawski 1994: 272).

Nicholas Kristof (*IHT*, 7 September 1993, p. 1) describes the Chinese economic and political system as 'market Leninism'.

Apart from the relatively high degree of regional decentralization of decision-making in the pre-reform economy (and hence a tradition of local initiative), 'the economy was segmented into semi-autarkic cells each with its own complement of industries, and the nationwide division of labour was weak. Such segmentation, although it implied massive inefficiencies, also gave the economy resilience to disruptions and flexibility. It facilitated the *laissez-faire* approach of letting particular regions experiment with reforms without a disruption to the rest of the economy' (Hussain and Stern 1994: 10–11).

(See the sessions of the NPC and the Central Committee discussed above.)

Financial policy

The spring of 1993 saw a tightening of credit policy to try to contain inflationary pressures (there was an investment boom, especially in construction). For example, interest rates were raised on 15 May 1993. On 11 June 1993 Deng was reported as saying that 'Emphasizing speed does not mean encouraging unreasonably high speed. We must still be down-to-earth and demand efficient, co-ordinated and stable development.' In March 1993 the government resumed the practice of the compulsory sale of its bonds to state employees (EIU, *Country Report*, 1993, Second Quarter, p. 21). The government had great difficulty in selling its bonds and the compulsory sale of them to enterprises and workers was one way round the problem (regions would not be allowed to issue new bonds until completion of the troubled bond sale; this was planned to be by 15 July but an announcement of completion was not made until 7 August 1993).

On 2 July 1993 it was confirmed that the governor of the People's Bank of China, Li Guixian, was to be dismissed because of the failure to contain inflationary pressures. Senior vice-premier Zhu Rongji was to assume his position. On 5 July 1993 Zhu said that 'China must rectify financial order and strengthen financial discipline', having just issued a sixteen-point austerity plan (the World Bank's advice was sought). The aim of the plan was to dampen growth to about 10 per cent a year and reduce inflationary pressures by measures such as the following: increasing interest rates (the People's Bank would have to strengthen its role as a central bank and improve its macroeconomic functions); cutting administrative outlays by state organizations by 20 per cent (purchases would be restricted too, with motor vehicle imports more or less ceasing in the second half of 1993); recovering bank loans used for 'speculative' purposes (e.g. speculation in property and shares) (including loans to affiliated non-bank financial institutions; these institutions are owned by banks and are used to evade credit ceilings); a reduction in investment in capital construction (although funds for agriculture, including those for state purchases of farm products, and major state construction projects such as transport must be guaranteed); the suspension of new price reform measures (except for those already implemented) for the rest of 1993; forced bond sales; inspection teams would visit all regions to ensure the implementation of the measures.

On 25 July tighter land use regulations were announced. On 17 August it was announced that 'only profit-making enterprises will be allowed to increase wages and bonuses . . . state-owned enterprises which make no effort to pay off their debts will gradually lose their government subsidies'. On 22 August the 1993 bond issue authorization total for enterprises was reduced; no bond applications for new projects would be approved at all for the rest of the year. On 6 September 1993 measures were announced to control investment in fixed assets by regions and departments. Priority should be given to sectors such as agriculture, transport, telecommunications, power and the production of raw materials at the expense of projects such as hotels and offices. In addition a price freeze had been ordered on goods and services subsidized by the state for the rest of 1993, while local governments were ordered to prevent the prices of vegetables and non-staple foods sold on free markets from soaring (*IHT*, 7 September 1993, p. 11) (see below). (There has also been a clamp-down on corruption, e.g. the execution of eight young accountants, including a woman, on 27 September 1993 for embezzlement. The month before a Bank of China official had been executed and further executions followed. On 5 July 1994 two senior officials from state commercial enterprises were executed.)

There were visible signs of a relaxation of credit constraints in August–October 1993. This seems to have been the result of pressure from state enterprises adversely affected by the squeeze.

In a New Year interview Prime Minister Li Peng said that there would be an attempt to slow down economic growth from 13 per cent in 1993 to 9 per cent in 1994 (*IHT*, 4 January 1994, p. 1).

On 30 January 1994 further restraints on investment in non-priority sectors for the remainder of the year were announced.

In May 1994 Zhu Rongji appealed for an easing of the credit restrictions on state enterprises, although good enterprises should be differentiated from the bad; 'long-term loss-makers that have no hope of turning a profit' should be allowed to go bankrupt, at first on a trial basis and then 'more broadly' (*IHT*, 24 May 1994, p. 9).

On 20 August 1994 Zhu Rongji spoke of the need for strict controls on credit in the second half of 1994 (investment had increased rapidly in July).

On 28 August 1994 Li Peng made inflation the top priority, but the month saw a selective relaxation of financial constraints on ailing state enterprises.

On 17 September 1994 the inflation target for the year was raised from 9 per cent to 15 per cent and interest rates on long-term savings were increased.

On 1 December 1994 the priorities were said to be (1) inflation and (2) the management of state enterprises and the maintenance of social order.

It was announced that approval would not be given during 1995 for any new large or medium-sized fixed-asset investment project (*IHT*, 6 January 1995, p. 9). The State Council issued an order stating that 'Local governments may not run a budget deficit and have no right to issue bonds overseas.' Provinces are not among the thirteen authorized borrowing 'windows', i.e. institutions such as banks permitted to borrow abroad (Tony Walker, *FT*, 17 February 1995, p. 4).

On 24 January 1994 the central bank began Western-style open market operations, trading the first batch of 1994 Treasury bonds on the Shanghai securities exchange; the move came after decades of limiting money supply by imposing bank lending quotas (*IHT*, 24 January 1994, p. 11). The central government completed its bond sales for the whole of 1994 within the first six months of the year (*IHT*, 2 July 1994, p. 13).

(See the sessions of the NPC and the Central Committee discussed above.)

Prices

Nolan (1993: 76) cites figures showing the proportion of (1) retail trade, (2) agricultural products sold by farmers, and (3) 'ex-factory means of production for industrial use' sold at different types of prices in 1978 and 1990 respectively:

1. State-controlled, 97.0 per cent and 29.7 per cent; state-guided, 0.0 per cent and 17.2 per cent; market-regulated, 3.0 per cent and 53.1 per cent.

2. State-controlled, 94.4 per cent and 25.2 per cent; state-guided, 0.0 per cent and 22.6 per cent; market-regulated, 5.6 per cent and 52.2 per cent.

3. State-controlled, 100.0 per cent and 44.4 per cent; state-guided, 0.0 per cent and 18.8 per cent; market-regulated, 0.0 per cent and 36.8 per cent.

In March 1993 the trade minister announced that 80 per cent of prices were already free and that there was a commitment to continue the process of freeing the remaining 15 per cent of agricultural prices, 10 per cent of industrial prices and 30 per cent of raw materials prices (EIU, *Country Report*, 1993, Second Quarter, p. 32). One official estimate is that 80 per cent of prices are now set by the market, but the remaining 20 per cent cover vital products, e.g. significant proportions of energy, raw materials and some food costs (and even some 'market prices' in reality require approval of the local price bureaus). On 3 August 1993 city governments were ordered to 'pay great attention' to maintaining stable prices for cooking oil, grain and vegetables, using 'economic and legal means' supplemented, if necessary, by administrative methods (EIU, *Country Report*, 1993, Third Quarter, p. 19).

The Economist (20 November 1993, p. 85) talked of 90 per cent of prices then set by supply and demand. Tony Walker (*FT*, 17 March 1994, p. 4) said that the 90 per cent referred to the deregulation of the prices of consumer items and basic commodities in the market.

By mid-1993 80 per cent of production goods and 90 per cent of consumer goods had been freed of controls (DIW, *Economic Bulletin*, 1994, vol. 31, no. 9, p. 22).

By early 1994 the prices of more than 90 per cent of capital goods and 95 per cent of consumer goods were fully liberalized (*FEER*, 20 October 1994, p. 30).

By 1990 75 per cent of farm and sideline products were being sold at free or floating (between state-set limits) prices (zero in 1978), and 55 per cent of industrial capital goods (zero in 1978) (Prybyla 1994: 657–8).

Price controls on heating oil were removed in midwinter 1992 (*The Economist*, 20 March 1993, p. 80).

On 10 May 1993 Beijing ended grain and cooking oil rationing (Shanghai, Tianjin, Guangdong and Sichuan had done so the previous year). Monthly subsidies were paid to workers to help offset the price increases (*FEER*, 20 May 1993, p. 71).

About 60 per cent of coal production is sold at regulated prices, but there are plans to liberalize prices. In 1993 fully half of China's projected oil output would be sold at market prices (Carl Goldstein, *FEER*, 1 April 1993, pp. 66–7). (Coal accounts for 76 per cent of energy consumption, oil 17 per cent and hydro/natural gas 7 per cent: Carl Goldstein, *FEER*, 12 November 1992, p. 53.) January 1993 saw deregulation of the price of coal for power generation and of washed coal. An official forecast said that 83 per cent of the national output of coal will 'enter the market directly this year', i.e. be sold at a market price in 1993 (EIU, *Country Report*, 1993, no. 1, p. 17). *IHT* (24 December 1993, p. 15) reports a plan to decontrol coal prices in early 1994.

On 20 December 1993 Zhu Rongji announced that grain prices would be lowered by means such as releasing stocks and lowering prices in state stores. The following day price controls were reimposed on twenty-seven basic commodities by the Beijing municipal authorities (e.g. rice, cooking oil and eggs).

On 28 December 1993 Zhu Rongji said that prices for grain and edible oils had to be immediately lowered to a 'reasonable level' (*IHT*, 29 December 1993, p. 9).

On 8 March 1994 the State Council ordered nationwide price controls and warned of 'severely punishing' offenders. The measures ranged from maintaining reserves of staple foods and funds for intervening in grain markets to 'temporary' price ceilings on vital goods. Prices of chemical fertilizers, plastic crop coverings, pesticides and diesel oil were among those subject to limits (*IHT*, 9 March 1994, p. 11).

A State Council order published on 13 March 1994 gave price departments the right, with the approval of local governments, to impose temporary ceilings on prices and undertake 'appropriate interference' in the market for widely used consumer goods. The twenty items included wheat flour, edible vegetable oil, pork, milk, eggs, sugar, soy sauce, detergent, domestic coal and natural gas, rent, water, public transport and fees for schools and hospitals (*IHT*, 14 March 1994, p. 9). Traders and producers who wished to raise prices had to obtain permission from the local authorities, while provincial governments had to report rises to the State Planning Commission (*FEER*, 24 March 1994, p. 59). The State Council ordered city and provincial leaders to investigate prices (*IHT*, 26 March 1994, p. 13).

On 25 May 1994 it was announced that the prices of ten staple commodities (such as salt, coal, petrol and housing rents) would be set by the state, while the prices of twenty-four others (including rice, edible oil, sugar and pork) would be monitored (*IHT*, 26 May 1994, p. 15).

Some local authorities have reintroduced rationing for food products like grain and edible oil (*IHT*, 13 June 1994, p. 9).

Some cities in six provinces have reintroduced food-ration coupons. These allow the purchase of rice and edible oil at 25 per cent below market prices (*IHT*, 20 January 1995, p. 15).

Since late 1994 grain ration coupons have been revised in twenty-nine big cities to ensure supplies for the poor at a price below market levels (*IHT*, 28 April 1995, p. 17).

(Price controls as part of the 1993 austerity programme are also discussed above.)

Financial markets

The 'renminbi' means 'people's currency' and the 'yuan' means 'dollar'. 'H' shares are traded on the Hong Kong stock exchange (the first company involved was the Tsingtao Brewery in July 1993), while 'N' shares are traded on Wall Street (USA).

Dipchand (1994: 45–58) discusses the development of the interbank (money) market, in which financial institutions with surplus funds provide short-term loans to banks that need them. A regional experiment started in 1983 and significant expansion came in 1986. The State Council gave its official sanction in January that year. The central bank is in overall control: 'the terms and maximum interest rates for interbank lending and borrowing are fixed and adjusted by the People's Bank of China in line with the supply and demand for funds' (p. 52).

On 4 January 1993 an end was announced to the short moratorium on the development of new stock markets (EIU, *Country Report*, 1993, no. 1, p. 29).

The official inquiry into the Shenzhen riots found evidence of massive fraud and corruption (*The Economist*, 20 February 1993, p. 101).

The first national regulations were published on 4 April 1993 (the Securities Regulatory Commission took over the supervisory functions of the central bank). For example, if demand for new issues exceeds supply a fair means of allocation must be employed (such as ballots). National regulations governing the issue and trading of shares took effect on 4 May 1993. In the case of a new company coming to the market, for example, at least 25 per cent of shares must be sold to the public and no more than 10 per cent of that 25 per cent may be issued to its own employees (Shufang Qiu, *The CEA (UK) Newsletter*, 1993, vol. 5, no. 2, p. 16).

In June 1993 the Shanghai stock exchange invited a number of foreign firms to pay for seats and Shenzhen followed (*FEER*, 26 August 1993, p. 52).

Teresa Poole (*The Independent*, 25 November 1993, p. 16) reports on the activities of illegal stock exchanges. In theory most of the shares issued by state enterprises should not be traded at all by the public. Staff are supposed to retain them for three years before selling them outside the enterprise. But these and illegally issued shares continue to be traded.

China Briefing (September 1993, pp. 2–3) provides a history of commodity exchanges. Rural reforms allowed for some limited local trading in the mid-1980s, but it was not until October 1990 that the first large-scale, national wholesale market (for grain) was established in Zhengzhou in Henan province. Approximately twenty exchanges are now operating (e.g. for metals, coal, timber, petroleum and rubber) and another thirty may soon open.

Treasury bond futures trading was introduced on the Shanghai Securities Exchange on 28 December 1992 (*China Briefing*, April 1995, p. 1).

The first Western-style futures market was opened on 9 March 1993, namely the Nanjing petroleum exchange (*IHT*, 10 March 1993, p. 14). The network rapidly widened and various concerns led to the announcement of strict state controls on futures trading on 15 June 1994.

In late February 1995 there was a major bond trading scandal in the Shanghai stock market. It led to a tightening of regulations (*IHT*, 1 March 1995, p. 15, 2 March 1995, p. 15, 7 March 1995, p. 15, and 9 March 1995, p. 15; *China Briefing*, April 1995, p. 2). Bond-futures trading was suspended in Shanghai on 17 May 1995.

Banks

In the mid-1980s four 'specialized' banks were established (in effect government departments and accounting for about 85 per cent of bank assets; e.g. the Industrial and Commercial Bank of China) and also so-called 'comprehensive' ones (which now number about eight, e.g the Shanghai Bank of Communications). It is officially admitted that as many as 30 per cent of the loans of specialized banks are made for 'policy' reasons, i.e. to support weak state enterprises. The Shanghai Bank of Communications claims it has no policy loans. But deposit and loan rates are fixed (well below market rates) by the central bank, acting on government instructions (*The Economist*, 27 March 1993, p. 116). (Henny Sender says that only 30 per cent of loans are made on the basis of commercial criteria, while 70 per cent are 'policy-based': *FEER*, 14 January 1993, p. 41.)

Four foreign banks continued to operate in China throughout the communist period (there are now more than 100 foreign banks). For most of the time the four banks were restricted to foreign trade and foreign exchange dealings, but in 1985 they were permitted to take deposits and lend in foreign currency (*Banking World*, February 1994, p. 38).

The Banker (March 1993, p. 18) noted that the commercial activities of foreign banks were limited to foreign currency lending, trade settlements, leasing, advisory services and financial derivatives (such things as swaps, futures and options). Consideration was to be given to local currency dealings.

In late December 1993 it was announced that in 1994 Shanghai would allow five foreign banks to engage in local currency deals connected with their existing activities (such as trade financing and corporate loans, i.e. not retail banking, since they are not permitted to establish a branch network) (*IHT*, 28 December 1993, p. 13).

The first foreign bank was allowed to open a branch (as opposed to a representative office) in Beijing on 18 July 1995.

The State Development Bank (Long-term Development and Credit Bank) was set up in April 1994 to fund state priority infrastructure projects in fields such as energy and transport and communications (thus relieving commercial banks of 'policy' loans). Two other 'policy' loan banks were to be set up. The Export–Import Bank of China began operating on 1 July 1994, to stimulate, in particular, exports of machinery, electronics and complete sets of plant and equipment. The third was the Agriculture Development Bank, established in November 1994. These were all part of the programme to restructure the banking system and make the People's Bank more like a conventional central bank (*FEER*, 9 September 1993, p. 67; Tony Walker, *FT*, 31 August 1993, p. 4). (See above.)

Approval has been given for the first private bank, with shareholders from domestic private companies (no foreign shareholders are allowed in this case) (*FT*, 2 September 1994, p. 4).

On 24 October 1994 it was announced that the first international bank was to be set up. This was the Beijing-based China International Capital Corporation, dealing with international banking and advisory services. The shareholders were the Construction Bank of China (42.5 per cent), the Morgan Stanley Group of the USA (35 per cent) and three others. The new bank would make direct investments in China with its own capital and assist foreign investors in making investments in Chinese enterprises. The bank claimed that it would be the first joint-venture operation allowed to do business using local currency (*FEER*, 3 November 1994, p. 55).

The National People's Congress passed the Commercial Banking Law on 11 May 1995 (effective 1 July 1995). Commercial banks are given unprecedented autonomy, but the State Council has the power to order the banks to make doubtful loans provided the government compensates them (*IHT*, 12 May 1995, p. 19).

(See the sessions of the NPC and the Central Committee discussed above for more recent developments.)

Manpower

The urban work force at the end of 1990 was 147.3 million (*EIU Country Profile*, 1992, p. 25). The figure was later put at 150 million (*FEER*, 16 June 1994, p. 32).

China's 100,000 state enterprises employ 100 million workers (Henny Sender, *FEER*, 27 October 1994, p. 72). (Estimates of the total number of state enterprises of all sizes range between 150,000 and 200,000: Tony Walker, *FT*, 12 May 1994, p. 4.)

The urban unemployment rate in the summer of 1992 was 2.8 per cent, but this excludes the 50 million to 80 million migrant workers in cities as well as young people waiting for their first jobs (EIU, *Country Report*, 1993, First Quarter, p. 21). The official figure for urban unemployment was 2.5 per cent in March 1993 and 2.3 per cent in July 1993. But this, in effect, covers only that part of the work force in the state's employ in cities. At the end of June 1993 there were a further 3.6 million people who were 'waiting for employment', i.e. they had just finished education and were not yet classified as unemployed (EIU, *Country Report*, 1993, Second Quarter, p. 28; 1993, Third Quarter, p. 28).

The official figure for urban unemployment at the end of 1994 was 2.8 per cent.

Around 1.4 million people or 1 per cent of the urban work force, had been laid off since the end of 1991 (*IHT*, 15 June 1992, p. 12), but a quarter had been given new jobs and many others had been trained or reassigned (*IHT*, 19 February 1993, p. 15). In December 1992 the coal industry announced that it was to shed 400,000 jobs by 1995; it had already lost 100,000 (187,000 have been laid off, but 86,900 of these have moved into service industries or processing jobs: *IHT*, 4 October 1993, p. 13). Wuhan Iron & Steel announced it was to cut its 120,000 work force by 80,000 (although these would be found jobs by the enterprise; 50,000 had already been shifted to newly formed 'sister' enterprises and the intention was to reassign the remainder: *IHT*, 23 March 1993, p. 17).

In the first half of 1992 fifteen state enterprises went bankrupt (*IHT*, 6 August 1992, p. 13).

On 6 April 1994 for the first time ever a state-owned company filed for bankruptcy (*The Economist*, 9 April 1994, p. 74).

According to one account, five state enterprises went bankrupt in 1993 (Patrick Tyler, *IHT*, 6 May 1994, p. 1). There are 109 million workers in state-owned industry and 11,000 large state enterprises (p. 7). (There are 13,000 large and medium state enterprises: *IHT*, 8 July 1993, p. 15.) Of the several hundred thousand state and other enterprises, no more than 1,500 have applied for bankruptcy since China passed its first bankruptcy law in 1988 (Patrick Tyler, *IHT*, 17 December 1994, p. 13). Only around 2,000 (out of 72,000) state-owned industrial enterprises have been allowed to default (*FT*, 30 December 1994, p. 3).

The vice minister of the State Trade and Economic Commission said that 20 per cent of workers in state enterprises were not needed. About 1,500 enterprises had gone bankrupt, but fewer than half were state-owned (*IHT*, 29 October 1994, p. 15). Official statistics showed that by the end of 1994 state enterprises were employing 20 million more workers than they needed. In the countryside some 160 million workers were surplus (*IHT*, 1 March 1995, p. 15).

So far only about 1,000 enterprises have gone bankrupt, fewer than half of them state-owned and almost all of them small (Lincoln Kaye, *FEER*, 23 February 1995, p. 54).

China has invited the World Bank to help develop a policy framework to reform its unprofitable state enterprises (*IHT*, 7 April 1993, p. 15). On 17 August 1993 it was reported that the China National Petroleum Corporation planned to cut its work force of 1.5 million by one-third; it had already moved 150,000 workers to jobs in service industries (*IHT*, 18 August 1993, p. 15).

An unemployment insurance scheme started in Beijing in July 1994. Both enterprises and employees have to contribute to the insurance funds. If an enterprise is bankrupted, streamlined or abolished by the state, or if its employees are dismissed, the workers receive three to twenty-four months of unemployment benefit and a percentage of medical benefits (*IHT*, 5 July 1994, p. 13).

Teresa Poole (*The Independent*, 19 October 1993, p. 16) reported the first National Talented Personnel Fair (held in Beijing), aimed at highly educated people looking for jobs ('swimming' in the talent market). Nearly 1,000 talent exchange centres have been established throughout China.

By the end of 1992 21 per cent of state enterprise employees had labour contracts (Edward Balls, *FT Survey*, 18 November 1993, p. x). By the end of June 1994 27.6 per cent of state enterprises had adopted labour contracts (Simon Holberton, *FT*, Survey, 7 November 1994, p. v). The proportion of employees in state enterprises on contracts rose from 3.7 per cent in 1985 to 18.9 per cent in 1992 (Zhu 1995: 42).

There have been increasing complaints about labour conditions and growing labour unrest (due, for example, to disregard of health and safety regulations, e.g. loss of life in fires in foreign-invested enterprises in the Shenzhen Special Economic Zone). On 20 March 1993 it was reported that there would be an inspection of labour conditions in state and foreign-invested enterprises during the period 1 April–30 June 1994. According to a Chinese trade union official, less than 10 per cent of the 47,000 foreign-funded enterprises (employing 6 million workers) have unions (*IHT*, 11 May 1994, p. 9). Some 30 per cent of foreign-invested enterprises have established unions (Zhu 1995: 46).

In June 1994 it was decreed that every foreign-invested enterprise had to establish state-controlled trade unions by the end of the year. But an October amendment stated that only companies in the flourishing coastal areas had to meet this deadline (*FT*, 28 October 1994, p. 7).

A labour law aimed at protecting workers' rights was published on 6 July 1994, to become effective on 1 January 1995 (Tony Walker, *FT*, 7 July 1994, p. 6). The provisions included the following: (1) an eight-hour day and a maximum forty-four-hour week; (2) a minimum wage; (3) workers are guaranteed one day off a week; (4) women are not required to work beyond their seventh month of pregnancy and are entitled to a ninety days' maternity leave; women are also relieved from working in hardship locations such as mines; (5) there are penalties for the mistreatment of workers.

The new labour law provides a legal framework for the protection of workers' rights. The law includes the following: (1) compulsory written contracts between employers and employees; (2) a maximum of forty-four working hours per week and one hour overtime per day; (3) stipulated overtime payments; (4) a minimum wage; (5) other issues such as working, safety and hygiene conditions (Zhu 1995: 36).

The new labour law was to give state enterprises some leeway in setting wages. The government would set a minimum wage, a process to decide wage levels and special criteria for the payment of overtime and other special forms of remuneration. Enterprises would be allowed to provide bonuses and cost-of-living subsidies as a safeguard against inflation (*IHT*, 12 September 1994, p. 9). The new law would make it easier for enterprises to hire and fire workers (Simon Holberton, *FT*, Survey, 7 November 1994, p. v). Dismissed workers who have held jobs for a year are entitled to receive a month's salary, with compensation rising with length of service to a maximum of a year's pay (*IHT*, 4 January 1995, p. 13).

As of 1 May 1995 government workers were to be on a five-day rather than a five-and-a-half-day working week (*The Daily Telegraph*, 27 March 1995, p. 17). As of 1 May 1995 a five-day working week was introduced, i.e. down from a forty-four-hour to a forty-hour working week; it was officially claimed that this would help create 1 million jobs (*IHT*, 28 March 1995, p. 17). China introduced a forty-hour five-day week in state industries on 1 May 1995. In 1994 the working week had been cut from six days to five and a half days because of traffic congestion and energy shortages (*The Economist*, 1 April 1995, p. 6). As of 1 May 1995 the official working week was reduced from forty-four to forty hours. It was officially claimed that the move would create an estimated 1 million jobs, mostly in the service sector. It was also claimed that the previous year's reduction from forty-eight to forty-four hours had helped industry to raise productivity by 30 per cent (*FEER*, 6 April 1995, p. 85).

Results of reforms in the state sector of industry

Groves *et al.* (1994) argue that the gradual and partial reforms in state industry have significantly improved productivity. The reforms include the ability to retain some fraction of profits and to sell some output and buy some inputs in free markets (although other factors have also enhanced productivity, e.g. competition from non-state firms: p. 185). The 1988 study by Chen *et al.* is cited to show that total factor productivity grew at an average annual rate of only 0.4 per cent between 1957 and 1978, while between 1978 and 1985 industrial productivity grew at an average annual rate of 4.8 per cent. For the sample of firms in the empirical study by Groves *et al.*, total factor productivity grew at an average annual rate of 4.5 per cent over the period 1980–89 (p. 185). The authors conclude that the industrial reforms have 'met with significant success. While enterprises remain subject to many of the problems associated with state ownership in Eastern Europe and elsewhere, increases in enterprise autonomy have induced measurable changes in behaviour at the enterprise level. With autonomy in output decisions and with higher marginal profit retention rates, enterprises increased their use of bonus payments and hired more fixed-term contract workers. This strengthening of workers' incentives was correlated with higher productivity. The improved productivity raised the workers' incomes (but not the managers' incomes), and resulted in more investment by the enterprises, but did not lower subsidies or increase profits' (p. 208).

Jefferson and Xu (1994) evaluate the progress of socialist industrial enterprises towards satisfying one of the principal efficiency conditions of a competitive market economy, namely the equalization of marginal revenue factor products across enterprises (p. 597). They conclude that 'during China's reform decade of the 1980s, returns to labour, capital and materials became more and more equal among large and medium-sized enterprises within various industrial branches. While such a pattern of convergence can potentially arise from numerous sources, the consistency of the pattern suggests that, even among large and medium-sized enterprises within the core of China's system of state planning, greater market exposure and stronger profit-seeking behaviour associated with the reform programme are having the desired effect of motivating gains in efficient production. Despite the existence of market rigidities and the presence of bargaining, patronage, soft budget constraints, and other phenomena that shielded state-owned enterprises from external pressure, during the 1980s profit-seeking behaviour and market forces appear to have exerted regular and increasing pressure on Chinese industrial managers to economize on factor inputs' (p. 612). China's urban industrial sector is a model of gradual and partial reform, e.g. the enterprise contract responsibility system and dual pricing. 'In this light, prior findings that TFP [total factor productivity] has accelerated in state industry to levels of approximately 2–3 per cent per annum as compared with virtual stagnation during the pre-reform period, and the finding in this article concerning gains in efficient production within the core of Chinese state industry provides strong evidence that China's programme of gradual and partial reform has yielded substantial improvement in the economic performance of that country's industrial economy' (p. 613).

Jefferson and Rawski (1994) point to some encouraging results of the reforms in state industry: (1) data reveal a substantial and growing link between profit and retained earnings (p. 52); (2) reforms in general have meant expansion of both markets and competition (p. 52); (3) 'there is little room to doubt that profit has become the dominant objective of managers in state industries' (p. 53); (4) 'Apparently, many of China's state-owned enterprises are gaining ground in the international market place' (p. 56); (5) market forces create a tendency to equalize financial returns to factors employed in different lines of business and several studies identify measurable improvements of this sort (p. 57); (6) a variety of evidence indicates that reform has substanitially accelerated innovation in state enterprises; (7) total factor productivity in the state sector increased at an average annual rate of 1.8 per cent in 1980–84, 3.0 per cent in 1984–88 and 2.5 per cent in 1988–92, while the respective figures for labour productivity were 3.8 per cent, 6.2 per cent and 4.7 per cent (p. 56).

But Woo *et al.* (1994: 412) say that 'our results contradict those of the revisionist papers that have come to dominate the discussion since 1988. We found that TFP [total factor productivity] growth in SOEs [state-owned enterprises] has been zero at best in the 1984–88 period . . . [we] . . . raise the possibility that the high TFP growth in some studies might have been due to a mixture of underdeflation of gross output and overdeflation of intermediate inputs.'

A group of 202 workers have bought their factory from the state and become its sole owners. This is the first such case (*IHT*, 14 June 1994, p. 13).

There have been reports of substantial illegality in the use of state assets. Methods include (1) underestimating state assets contributed to joint ventures and underreporting profits to state-owned parent companies, (2) government organizations go into business for themselves using public property and funds without reporting their activities to the ministries that supervise them and (3) declaring false bankruptcies and selling assets at deep discounts to related parties. 'If it were legal, the widespread, under-the-table asset shuffle might be considered the world's largest privatization programme' (Kevin Murphy, *IHT*, 26 April 1995, p. 11).

(See the sessions of the NPC and the Central Committee discussed above for more recent developments.)

The defence industry

In 1979 only 8 per cent of the defence industry's output was civilian, but a figure of two-thirds was predicted in 1993 (Jonathan Mirsky, *The Times*, 12 July 1993, p. 9).

Around 70 per cent of the defence industry's output is for civilian consumption (Tai Ming Chung, *FEER*, 14 October 1993, p. 70).

In 1992 civilian output accounted for 70 per cent (John Gittings, *The Guardian*, 13 November 1993, p. 29).

An overwhelming number of Chinese sources from 1991 to 1993 put the civilian percentage of the defence industry's output from 66 per cent to over 70 per cent (Dennis Blasco, *FEER*, 3 March 1994, p. 37).

A Chinese estimate puts the average share of civilian production in the defence industries at about 76 per cent (Simon Holberton and Tony Walker, *FT*, 28 November 1994, p. 19).

'China's army now gets half of its budget from its vast empire of corporations' (Thomas Friedman, *IHT*, 16 January 1995, p. 6).

The non-state, non-agricultural sector

Hussain and Stern (1994: 10) point out that the rural industrialization drive in the 1960s resulted in a sizeable rural industry mostly established through local initiative. Many rural localities thus already had a group of people with the relevant experience and benefited from a large and relatively flexible labour market.

Naughton (1994: 266–70) describes the growth of township and village enterprises (TVEs). Most 'collectives' are a form of publicly owned enterprise. Most TVE industrial output is produced by firms that are controlled by local township and village governments. The label 'collective' was attached because they were established by agricultural collectives. When these were dissolved in the early 1980s most TVEs became subordinate to the township and village governments that replaced the former communes and agricultural collectives. This creates a misleading impression that TVEs are in some sense owned by local communities as a whole. In most cases that have been studied township and village officials in their official capacity possess all the key components of property rights. TVEs are responses to the early creation of product markets and the lagged creation of factor and asset markets. By the mid-1980s markets and market prices existed for nearly all commodities. But markets for labour and land really emerged only in the 1990s and financial institutions are still in the midst of a gradual adaptation to market forces. TVEs provided a way to convert assets into income streams without solving the difficult problems of privatization (mass privatization being ruled out on ideological grounds). (See Weitzman in the section in Chapter 1 devoted to China as a model.)

Chang and Wang (1994) see the township–village enterprise as the product of an environment in which an authoritarian government with monopolistic political power plays a dominant role in economic life. In such an environment a cost–benefit analysis explains why the right of control is given to the township–village government (TVG) (p. 450) ('managerial nominees of the TVG are rarely, if ever, disapproved by the workers': p. 438). The TVE is nominally owned by local citizens but controlled by the TVG. 'It assigns nominal ownership to the township–village citizens as a commitment that most benefits produced by the TVE will be retained locally . . . it specifies explicit sharing rules that at the same time provide the TVG officials with incentives to improve the performance of the TVE and prevent these officials from abusing their powers and giving excessive benefits to themselves' (p. 448). The centre requires the largest share, about 60 per cent of (post-tax) profit, to be retained by the enterprise for production expansion. In many cases a relatively small portion is used as bonuses for workers, while a larger portion is paid as fees to the TVG. These fees are used (1) to support communal social programmes and infrastructure projects, such as education, roads and irrigation systems ('another important policy is that the TVG should spend sizeable amounts of fees from TVEs' profits for rural programmes and infrastructure': p. 441) and (2) for the operation of the TVG, including benefits enjoyed by officials (pp. 439–40). 'It seems fair to say that the residual benefits of the TVE are shared between the TVG and the citizens, with the citizens the main beneficiaries' (p. 441). This ownership structure can be viewed as the solution to the central government's problem of improving citizens' welfare subject to the constraint that the current political system must be preserved and that local agents must be provided with incentives (p. 434). The right of control is given to the TVG because ordinary citizens cannot provide security and access to resources that are critical for the success of the TVE (p. 434). These resources include access to bank loans (p. 444). Central government control of the TVG would have disadvantages: (1) 'The centre, without giving the control right to the TVG, cannot ensure the support and co-operation of the TVG so that a TVE located within its jurisdiction can perform well' (p. 445) and (2) 'Another likely problem associated with direct control by the centre is the soft budget constraint' (p. 446). In 1993 TVEs produced about 40 per cent of total industrial production (p. 435).

The United Nations (*World Economic Survey 1993*, pp. 185–201) provides the following information. The non-state sector consists of (1) collectives owned by local governments and/or workers; (2) 'individual' enterprises (employing fewer than eight persons) and 'private' enterprises (employing eight or more persons); (3) foreign-owned enterprises, including wholly foreign-owned enterprises and joint ventures. The share of the non-state sector in total industrial output increased from 24 per cent in 1980 (24 per cent, 0 per cent and 0.5 per cent respectively) to 47 per cent in 1991 (36 per cent, 5.7 per cent and 5.7 per cent respectively). The policies announced in 1984 on the development of the rural sector reaffirmed the importance of rural collective enterprises and officially sanctioned private household enterprises, involving the use of hired workers (up to eight non-family workers). In reality these limits were often exceeded and a 1987 amendment to the constitution removed the limit. Local governments sometimes sell off small state enterprises.

A decade ago state enterprises accounted for 78 per cent of industrial output, collectives for 21 per cent and the private sector for the remaining 1 per cent. Today the respective figures are 53 per cent, 36 per cent and 11 per cent (Elizabeth Perry, *Asian Survey*, January 1993, vol. XXXIII, no. 1). Naughton (1994: 267) puts the respective 1978 figures at 78 per cent, 22 per cent and negligible. Jefferson and Rawski (1994: 48) and Rawski (1994: 272) put the respective figures as follows: 76 per cent, 23.6 per cent and 0.5 per cent in 1978, and 48.4 per cent, 38.2 per cent and 13.3 per cent in 1992.

State enterprises account for just under half of industrial output and 68 per cent of the industrial labour force (Kevin Murphy, *IHT*, Survey, 30 May 1994, p. 12).

In 1994 state enterprises accounted for 43 per cent of industrial output (compared with 78 per cent in 1978) and employed about 70 per cent of industrial workers. In 1993, according to the World Bank, state enterprises undertook 70 per cent of industrial investment, compared with 61 per cent in 1989 (*The Economist*, 10 June 1995, p. 69).

According to World Bank figures, there are 104,700 state enterprises (among 9.9 million industrial enterprises, most of them tiny). State enterprises account for 43 per cent of the gross value of industrial output (Tony Walker, *FT*, 18 May 1995, p. 8). Their share in total fixed investment is 61 per cent. Collectives account for 38 per cent of industrial output (p. 23). (In 1994 the figure for collectives was 39 per cent: *IHT*, 19 June 1995, p. 2.)

In 1994 overall industrial output grew by 18 per cent, the state sector by only 5.5 per cent and the remainder by 28 per cent (*IHT*, 1 March 1995, p. 15).

According to the Ministry of Agriculture, rural enterprises account for nearly half of total industrial output and employ about 120 million people (Emily Thornton, *FEER*, 9 March 1995, p. 56).

State enterprises still consume more than 60 per cent of all fixed-asset investment, although their share of gross industrial output has fallen from two-thirds in 1985 to little more than 40 per cent now. Almost all their investment is financed by bank credit (*The Economist*, Survey, 18 March 1994, p. 9). Township and village enterprises have raised their share of industrial output from 10 per cent to 40 per cent in fifteen years and now employ 120 million (p. 23).

Wang Zhonghui (1993: 16) discusses rural enterprises, including those run collectively by villages or townships as well as those owned by individuals. Total industrial output value increased by an average annual rate of 28.6 per cent in the period 1981 to 1989. In 1989 93.67 million people were employed in rural enterprises, representing 23 per cent of the rural labour force. Despite general state encouragement since 1978 there is still considerable discrimination against rural enterprises compared with state enterprises, especially in the supply of raw materials and credit in times of economic stringency (p. 25).

Edward Balls (*FT Survey*, 18 November 1993, pp. vii, x) states that less than half of the non-agricultural work force now work in state enterprises. Township and village enterprises account for 40 per cent (their share of exports has risen from less than 5 per cent in 1985 to over 20 per cent; 25 per cent of exports in 1992: Alexander Nicholl, *FT Survey* p. xiii).

Qian and Xu (1993: 135–70) stress the importance of regional devolution in encouraging the growth of the non-state sector, this providing the flexibility and opportunity for carrying out experiments.

Foreign trade

The reforms did not allow many domestic industrial enterprises to deal directly with foreign markets until well into the 1980s. Instead, the foreign trade corporations were decentralized to the provinces and regions and allowed to compete for business (Perkins 1994: 33). The formidable marketing talents of Hong Kong and Taiwan have been grafted on to the manufacturing capacity of the mainland. For example, in 1979 22.6 per cent of exports went to Hong Kong and 21 per cent of those were re-exported. By 1987 the respective figures were 31.1 per cent and 62 per cent (p. 34).

The World Bank has said that 'whereas in 1978 . . . foreign trade was monopolized by twelve Foreign Trade Corporations, today over 3,600 FTCs compete increasingly fiercely for export business' (*FT*, Survey, 7 November 1994, p. v).

On 28 May 1993 the USA renewed China's 'most favoured nation' status (for the year starting 3 June), but further renewal would be conditional on 'overall, significant progress' in human rights. On 25 August 1993 the USA banned the export of certain high-technology items (such as satellites and the means of launching them) to China for two years because of alleged Chinese exports of advanced missile technology to Pakistan in violation of the Missile Technology Control Regime (the ban was lifted on 4 October 1994). China came no way near to meeting the conditions laid down by the USA regarding human rights. Despite this, on 26 May 1994 President Clinton announced not only the renewal of MFN status but also his preference for severing the linkage (he was swayed by the economic argument, the importance of China in international affairs – such as the North Korean problem – and the idea that the 'open door' policy was the best way to further human rights in the long run). The only penalty that President Clinton imposed was a ban on the import of Chinese guns and ammunition.

On 31 December 1994 the USA threatened China with punitive tariffs (up to 100 per cent) on Chinese exports valued at $2.8 billion. The twenty-three categories of products included electronic goods, footwear and toys. This was in retaliation for alleged continuing massive copyright piracy of intellectual property, e.g. videos, films and compact discs (the USA has expressed great concern about twenty-nine factories producing pirated compact discs). The deadline for implementation was moved from 31 December 1994 to 4 February 1995 to allow further negotiations. On the latter date the USA announced that, in the absence of any agreement by 26 February, it would impose 100 per cent tariffs on $1.08 billion worth of Chinese imports (including silk blouses, answering machines, cellular phones, bicycles and sportswear). 'China's failure to enforce the intellectual property rights of US companies and its persistent denial of market access for intellectual property-based products and industries' were the reasons given. China announced that it would retaliate with tariffs on US imports (such as cigarettes, alcohol, cosmetics, videos, films and cassette tapes) and a freeze on negotiations with US car manufacturers interested in investing in China. It was then announced that further talks were to be held on 13

February 1995. (Note that China had improved its intellectual property laws in January 1992, but they were poorly enforced.)

A deal was announced on 26 February 1995, the negotiations going hours beyond the formal deadline. China agreed on tighter enforcement of its laws protecting intellectual property, including the creation of a task force (with extensive powers) and the announcement of a six-month 'special enforcement period' starting on 1 March 1995. In addition, China would improve access to US imports and exercise greater control over exports of pirated items. (To show goodwill China had, during the negotiations, closed down seven factories, two of them among the twenty-nine listed by the USA.)

On 12 March 1995 China and the USA signed an agreement that eased access for US products in exchange for increased US support for China's entry into the WTO (specifically China would honour the 1992 bilateral memorandum of understanding obliging China to ease access to imports from the USA). (In the negotiations about entry to the WTO China has demanded concessions on the grounds of being a developing country). (In 1994 China had a trade surplus with the USA of $29.5 billion, second only to Japan's surplus with the USA: *IHT*, 13 March 1995, p. 11. China says $7.4 billion only; the US figure includes re-exports from Hong Kong.)

The USA renewed MFN status for a further year, starting 3 June 1995.

(See the section below on the geographical distribution of trade for further details of trade relations with the USA.)

China and Gatt (WTO)

China did not succeed in gaining founder membership of Gatt's successor, the World Trade Organization (WTO), when it was established on 1 January 1995 (although 'founder' membership may be retroactively awarded). The so-called Uruguay Round of Gatt negotiations, which finished in December 1993, liberalized trade in manufacturing more sweepingly than trade in primary products. Thus China would be one of the world's biggest gainers on entry to the WTO. This is because China's export growth has centred on manufacturing, especially textiles. The World Bank estimates that China's exports to the USA, the EU and Japan would increase by 40 per cent under a post-Uruguay Gatt (*The Economist*, 14 May 1994, p. 83).

Trade restrictions

The World Bank estimates that fully 50 per cent of imports remain subject to some form of non-tariff barrier, such as quotas or licensing requirements (Carl Goldstein, *FEER*, 28 April 1994, p. 69).

According to Reginald Dale (*IHT*, 8 April 1994, p. 11), more than half of imports are still subject to controls, as are 15 per cent of exports and over 50 per cent of exchange earnings.

China has pledged to phase out import quotas by 1997; China currently restricts imports of about fifty items, most of them capital goods and electronics (*FEER*, 14 April 1994, p. 69).

The World Bank complains about strict controls over exporters' use of their foreign currency, high import tariffs, complicated non-tariff controls, currency rationing and import cartels (*The Economist*, 30 April 1994, p. 97).

On 1 January 1994 China abolished quotas and import licences on 283 products (including coffee and civil aircraft) and reduced tariffs on 234 products (including fertilizers, lead and zinc). But at the same time a list was published of electronic and machinery products that would continue to be protected through means such as quotas. Inport controls would be strengthened in the case of eighteen products on the quota list, including cars, motor cycles, video recorders and computers. Also published was a list of 171 products (including machinery used for textile production, communications and shipbuilding) that would be protected by insisting that purchases should be made using 'international procedures' such as quotas and tariffs.

January 1994 was the first major deadline under the terms of the 11 October 1992 accord with the USA, which included China agreeing to remove three-quarters of its non-tariff trade barriers within two years (*IHT*, 3 January 1994, p. 7).

On 30 March 1994 it was announced that 'within the next three years China will gradually cancel licences for most of the existing fifty-three categories that still require an import licence' (Tony Walker, *FT*, 31 March 1994, p. 4).

According to *IHT* (31 March 1994, p. 9), China said it would remove all quota and licensing barriers on imports by 1997.

On 26 May 1994 China announced a reduction in import licences and quotas applying to 195 items. There would also be further gradual reductions in the future; licences and quotas still apply to over 700 products (*FT*, 27 May 1994, p. 7).

China's share of world trade

China's share in world exports (average annual) was 1 per cent in 1978–82, 1.4 per cent in 1982–86, 1.8 per cent in 1986–90 and 2.1 per cent in 1990–92. Over this period of time China's rank among world exporters advanced from thirty-second to thirteenth (IMF, *World Economic Outlook*, May 1993, p. 53).

China's share of world exports was 0.6 per cent in 1977 (Alexander Nicholl, *FT*, 28 April 1994, p. 8). It rose to 0.9 per cent in 1980 and 1.73 per cent in 1989 (Nolan 1992: 34).

In 1992 China accounted for 2.3 per cent of world trade in goods (*FEER*, 28 April 1994, p. 66).

China was the world's eleventh largest trader in 1992 (*FT*, 20 April 1993, p. 4). According to Gatt, China has moved up to number eleven on the list of the world's largest exporters (DIW, *Economic Bulletin*, 1993, vol. 30, no. 6, p. 6).

A decade ago China ranked twentieth as a world trader, with exports amounting to 4 per cent of GDP and less than 1 per cent of world trade. Projected exports for 1993 would represent 20 per cent of GDP and more than 2.5 per cent of world trade. China is expected to be among the top ten world traders in 1993 (Tony Walker, *FT*, 16 February 1993, p. 6). (By way of contrast the UK accounts for 5.3 per cent of world trade: *FT*, 19 March 1993, p. 14.)

In 1993 China ranked eleventh and accounted for 3 per cent of world trade (Michael Richardson, *IHT*, 12 May 1994, p. 5). (By way of comparison, in the 1930s China's share of world trade was 2.3 per cent: Junhao Hong, *Asian Survey*, 1994, vol. XXXIV, no. 4, p. 34.)

China is the world's eleventh biggest exporter, accounting for 2.5 per cent of world trade, compared with the USA's 12.5 per cent (*The Economist*, Survey, 1 October 1994, p. 10). In 1993 China became a net importer of oil for the first time since the early 1970s (p. 34). 'Following two decades as an oil exporter, China became a net importer at the end of 1993' (Paul McDonald, *The World Today*, July 1995, p. 145).

China's share of world merchandise trade rose from 0.6 per cent in 1977 to 2.5 per cent in 1993 (the world's eleventh largest exporter) (Martin Wolf and Tony Walker, *FT*, 5 November 1994, p. 15).

China achieved a trade surplus of $5.3 billion in 1994, compared with a deficit of $12.2 billion the previous year (*IHT*, 16 January 1995, p. 11).

The importance of trade

Merchandise trade as a percentage of GNP (measured using the official exchange rate) increased from 12.8 per cent in 1980 to 38 per cent in 1992 (Edward Balls, *FT*, Survey, 18 November 1993, p. vii).

The ratio of exports plus imports to GDP had risen from 7 per cent in the 1960s to 21 per cent by the 1980s and 33 per cent in the 1990s (Gelb *et al.* 1993: 429).

In 1992 the ratio of trade to GDP (measured at market prices) was 32.7 per cent, but the ratio of trade to GNP (measured at purchasing-power parity) was only 9.5 per cent (Martin Wolf, *FT*, 21 November 1994, p. 24).

The commodity structure and geographical distribution of trade

The share of manufactured items in exports rose from 50 per cent in 1980 to 80 per cent in 1992. (The figure was 49 per cent in 1979 and 70 per cent in 1989: Nolan 1992, p. 34; DIW, *Economic Bulletin*, 1992, vol. 29, no. 7, p. 12, reports that the share of manufactures in total exports had risen to over 80 per cent in 1991.) Textiles and footwear accounted for one-third of exports in 1992, but machinery, electronic and transport equipment are the fastest growing (the share of machinery and transport equipment in total exports was 16 per cent in 1992, compared with 6 per cent in 1988).

The United Nations (*World Economic Survey 1993*, p. 67) provides the following information. During the period 1978–91 GNP growth averaged 8.6 per cent per annum, while the total value of trade increased by more than 15 per cent per year. Export value increased at over 16 per cent, with the result that the ratio of exports to GNP rose from 4.7 per cent in 1978 to about 19 per cent in 1991 (in 1993 the ratio of exports to GDP was about 17 per cent: *World Economic and Social Survey*, 1994, p. 57). Among the world's exporters China rose from twenty-seventh place in 1980 to eleventh place in 1992. In 1980 exports were divided more or less equally between primary commodities and manufactured products. By 1991 the share of manufactures in total exports had risen to over 77 per cent. In 1981 about 42 per cent of exports went to Japan, the USA and Europe; in 1991 the figure was 63.5 per cent.

Manufactured items accounted for 49.8 per cent of total exports in 1980 and 78.5 per cent in 1993 (Tony Walker, *FT*, 12 October 1994, p. 8).

About 15 per cent of capital goods/raw materials and 8 per cent of consumer goods are imported (*FEER*, 20 October 1994, p. 30).

Before 1993 grain imports exceeded grain exports, but in the past two years China has become a net grain exporter (*IHT*, 12 January 1995, p. 15).

Oil exports first became significant in the mid-1970s. They increased dramatically during the 1980s, reaching a peak of 36 million tonnes in 1985 (29 per cent of production). China began to import a small quantity of oil in the mid-1980s (*China Briefing*, August 1994, pp. 6–8).

China became a net oil importer in 1994. China has only 2.4 per cent of proven global oil reserves and 1 per cent of gas reserves (Michael Richardson, *IHT*, 3 June 1995, p. 9).

About 30 per cent of China's exports go to the USA (Lena Sun, *IHT*, 13 May 1993, p. 7). Around half China's exports to the USA are produced in the private sector (Nancy Dunne, *FT*, 20 May 1993, p. 5). On 6 January 1994 the USA announced that the 1994 quota for imports of textiles and clothing from China was to be cut by 25–35 per cent because of the lack of agreement on controlling Chinese goods being imported via other countries (and thus avoiding the quota). On 17 January 1994, however, an agreement was announced by both countries concerning these transshipments: China promised to slow the growth of exports and accepted a penalty clause in the event of proven quota violations. In 1994 more than 30 per cent of exports went to the USA, compared with only 10 per cent in 1985 (*The Economist*, 4 March 1995, p. 104).

China–Taiwan trade amounted to $7.4 billion in 1992 (*IHT*, 29 April 1993, p. 4). In 1994 it amounted to $16.51 billion (*FT*, 3 March 1995, p. 5). (Note that on 5 January 1995 the government of Taiwan proposed one of its ports as an 'offshore' facility for direct trade with China. On 4 May 1995 the Taiwan cabinet approved the 'transshipment centre plan', under which shipping links between Taiwan and China would be permitted for the first time since 1949: *IHT*, 5 May 1995, p. 19.)

Russia accounts for only 4 per cent of China's trade (*IHT*, 29 January 1994, p. 4).

(See the relevant section on the third plenary session above.)

Swap markets

A forward foreign exchange market has been operating in Shanghai since 1 June 1992 (*China Briefing*, September 1993, p. 4).

On 16 April 1993, for the first time, the regulations governing the swap centres were disclosed: 'if market rates fluctuate too sharply the People's Bank of China will adopt economic, administrative and legal measures to stabilize the price'. In a further development, however, the yuan was allowed to float freely in swap markets on 1 June 1993, i.e. price ceilings were removed. One aim of the move was to try to eliminate the black market.

There were three exchange rates in China:

1. The official rate. This was used by tourists, for some of the imports of state enterprises and for the conversion of some foreign investment (EIU, *Country Report*, 1993, Fourth Quarter, p. 21). (Prior to the reform foreign investors' capital contributions and some operating expenses in foreign exchange were officially required to be valued or converted at the official rate: *China Briefing*, February 1994, p. 2.) Foreigners working or travelling in China had to buy Foreign Exchange Certificates (FECs; introduced in 1979) at the official rate, while state enterprises had been forced to use the swap markets to an increasing extent. According to the *FT* (30 December 1993, p. 11), foreign investors had to register capital in new ventures at the official rate and repatriate profits at the swap rate.

2. Rates determined in the swap markets (first established in 1985). The swap markets were used by approved enterprises and financial institutions. It was unclear exactly how important the approximately 100 swap markets were. A common figure was around 80 per cent of current account transactions (e.g. *FT*, 30 December 1993, p. 11). According to Chinese officials, over 80 per cent of foreign exchange transactions were conducted at swap rates (*China Briefing*, February 1994, p. 3). Some 80 per cent of foreign exchange transactions in 1993 were thought to have been conducted in the swap markets or unofficially at the benchmark rates established by them (*The Economist*, 8 January 1994, p. 71). As of late 1993 80 per cent of

currency dealings were conducted in swap markets or on the black market (Lincoln Kaye, *FEER*, 13 January 1994, p. 80). But the EIU (*Country Report*, Fourth Quarter, 1993, p. 21) warned that estimates of the volume of business conducted at swap or black-market rates rather than the official rate varied from about 40 per cent to 80 per cent of total transactions.

3. The black market rate.

On 1 January 1994 the official and swap rates were unified, with the yuan (renminbi) subjected to a managed float: 'This unitary and controlled floating exchange rate system based on market demand and supply will replace the current dual-track system.' The FECs were to be phased out and no new ones issued (old ones would continue to be redeemed at the old official rate in the meantime so as not to penalize the holders). Initially the central bank would set the exchange rate for a particular day on the basis of the previous day's average dollar price on the swap markets. The swap markets would subsequently be replaced by a national interbank foreign exchange market (a National Foreign Exchange Centre would be established). (FECs were banned from circulation at the beginning of 1995 and withdrawn from all trading on 30 June 1995: *IHT*, 19 July 1995, p. 16.)

The original intention was to abolish swap markets on 1 April 1994 and replace them with an interbank currency market (centred on Shanghai), with banks engaged in currency transactions with Chinese and foreign-invested enterprises. Chinese banks were to use the interbank market to trade foreign currencies for domestic clients. Access to this market for foreign banks would be limited to the proceeds of export sales by their Chinese customers. But on 27 March it was announced that foreign-invested enterprises would not be allowed to buy hard currency at state-designated banks. Instead, swap markets would be kept open for them, such enterprises thus having to rely on finding individual trading partners with opposite currency needs. It appears that the swap markets would be obliged to use rates based on the mid-rate of the previous day's trading on the interbank market. (*IHT*, 28 March 1994, p. 9; 1 April 1994, p. 15.) Originally the idea was to use the rate prevailing at the close of trading on the previous day, but the rates actually applying in the swap markets track the weighted average of the interbank market (Tony Walker, *FT*, 5 April 1994, p. 4).

The yuan is internally convertible in a restricted sense. Complex rules were issued on access to foreign exchange, which would, for example, be especially difficult for ordinary Chinese citizens. Foreign currency would be bought and sold at banks, and enterprises would have to show import licences and all relevant payment documents in order to purchase foreign currencies. The government said it would enforce a ban on the circulation of foreign currency within China. *China Briefing* (February 1994, p. 2) provides further details: foreign exchange earnings by domestic Chinese entities must all be sold to authorized banks; abolition of the foreign exchange retention system for Chinese exporters; abolition of planned allocation of foreign exchange use for Chinese entities. (In March 1993 China, for the first time, legally allowed individuals to take renminbi out of the country: Perkins 1994: 33.) The aim is to achieve current account convertibility by the year 2000 (*IHT*, 19 December 1994, p. 9).

Shanghai (which already had the largest swap market) was destined to regain its status as China's financial centre. Until 1992, when Deng expressed regret that it had not been made a Special Economic Zone, Shanghai had been neglected (an important factor was the city's history of extreme left politics).

Foreign debt

Platte (1994) analyses China's foreign debt, which amounted to $52.5 billion in 1990 and $60.6 billion in 1991 (p. 485). China has not traditionally been an importer of capital. China undertook limited borrowing to expand its industrial base during the First Five Year Plan (1953–57), but then foreign loans were ended. There was no government borrowing until the 'open door' policy began at the end of 1978 (p. 481). Following the large increase in foreign debt in 1985, the authorities decided to subject all external borrowing to centralized reporting and control. But if a foreign bank lender does not ask for a guarantee of the Bank of China or another major guarantor, authorization requirements are difficult to enforce. Moreover, in 1987 the central government began to encourage local-level units to negotiate loans direct with foreign countries, which resulted in a dramatic surge in borrowing from commercial sources. The multitude of borrowing units, many of them with direct access to international finance markets, make it difficult, if not impossible, to control and limit total debt accumulation (p. 484). Total foreign debt is a small amount relative to China's economic size and population (p. 486). Throughout the period 1979–91 China enjoyed a credit rating well above the global average (p. 487). Most of China's borrowing has added to its productive capacity rather than financed consumption (p. 488). China's debt–service ratio of 10.3 per cent in 1990 was in the lowest quarter of all developing country debtors reporting under the World Bank's Debtor Reporting System (p. 490). The bulk of foreign debt is owed to private creditors, mostly to commercial banks (p. 492). China's record in servicing its debt has been good (p. 493).

Foreign debt amounted to $52.6 billion in 1990, $60.6 billion in 1991 and $69.3 billion in 1992. The debt–service ratio was 10.3 per cent, 11.2 per cent and 11.8 per cent respectively (DIW, *Economic Bulletin*, 1993, vol. 30, no. 6, pp. 2, 4).

The foreign debt was $83.5 billion at the end of 1993 and the debt–service ratio was 9.7 per cent (*FT*, 25 July 1994, p. 2).

The ratio of debt service to exports is about 12 per cent. The State Council has issued an order stating that 'Local governments may not run a budget deficit and have no right to issue bonds overseas.' Provinces are not among the thirteen authorized borrowing 'windows', i.e. institutions such as banks permitted to borrow abroad (Tony Walker, *FT*, 17 February 1995, p. 4). The IMF and the World Bank put the debt–service ratio at about 12 per cent. The foreign debt rose from $83.5 billion at the end of 1994 to $100 billion in 1994 (Tony Walker, *FT*, 27 March 1995, p. 1).

Note that there has been increasing concern about debt repayment by Chinese state enterprises, including money owed to Western companies operating in international currency and commodity markets. Zhu Rongyi told the Davos economic forum in Switzerland that default claims 'are purely commercial disputes and have nothing to do with the government' (*FEER*, 9 February 1995, p. 45).

Foreign investment

General comments on foreign investment

Perkins (1994: 34–5) notes the following:

1. Investment designed to supply the Chinese domestic market can perhaps be explained by the lure of over a billion customers.

2. The rapid growth of export-orientated foreign investment, in the face of insecure property rights, is easier to understand if one recognizes how much of this foreign investment comes from Hong Kong and other overseas Chinese and goes into Guangdong province (adjacent to Hong Kong). In 1990 55 per cent of all realized foreign investment came from Hong Kong/Macao and 46 per cent of all investment whose regional destination could be identified went to Guangdong. Fujian (opposite Taiwan) came next with 9 per cent. Most Hong Kong investments were small-scale and the pay-back periods were short, while overseas Chinese could exploit *guangxi*.

The structure of inward investment has changed. According to Wall (1993: 246), foreign investment has moved away from the Special Economic Zones to a broader geographical spread, there has been a move away from a concentration on real estate development (including hotels and other tourist facilities) towards industry (investment in industry accounted for 84 per cent of the total in 1990) and there has been a move away from joint-venture investment towards wholly owned enterprises (from almost none in 1979 to more than a quarter of the total in 1990 and rising fast). (Note the problem of measuring the value of 'foreign' investment, due to such factors as mainland Chinese capital returning via Hong Kong in order to take advantage of tax concessions. This is referred to as 'round-tripping'. According to an estimate cited in *The Economist*, it accounts for 'a good quarter' of total direct foreign investment: 26 August 1995, p. 60.)

The growth in direct foreign investment did not really begin to accelerate until after the mid-1980s, when a variety of measures were adopted to improve the investment climate. In the period 1979 to 1993 China absorbed a cumulative total of nearly $60 billion in actual realized direct foreign investment, accounting for 44.2 per cent of total foreign capital inflows of $135.79 billion (the remainder comprising principally loans) (Chen *et al.* 1995: 693). The location of Shenzhen next to Hong Kong, Zhuhai adjacent to Macao, and Xiamen and Shantou opposite Taiwan suggests that they were chosen to facilitate the eventual reunification of China (p. 692). There has been a substantial transfer of low and intermediate technology, but high technology has not been forthcoming on a large scale, since Hong Kong, the most important single source of direct foreign investment, is not known as a major source of such technology (p. 702). Successful foreign-invested enterprises have had significant 'demonstration and synergy effects' on their domestic counterparts. The opening of the economy to foreign trade and capital 'not only forced the domestic manufacturers to compete globally, but it also progressively made the plant managers and government officials develop and adopt the rules and the laws of a market economy' (p. 699).

The amount of foreign investment

The amount of direct foreign investment actually utilized was $1.80 billion in 1979–83, $1.26 billion in 1984, $1.87 billion in 1986, $3.19 billion in 1988, $3.49 billion in 1990 and $11.16 billion in 1992. As a proportion of total domestic productive investment its share increased from about 3 per cent in 1985 to almost 7 per cent in 1991 (United Nations, *World Economic Survey 1993*, p. 194).

The official figure for 1993 was $27 billion (Alexander Nicholl, *FT*, 20 January 1994, p. 4).

Foreign investors accounted for 10.6 per cent of total investment in 1992 (Henny Sender, *FEER*, 2 September 1993, p. 38).

According to official estimates, foreign capital now accounts for around 10 per cent of investment in fixed assets and foreign-invested firms accounted for 8.5 per cent of industrial output (EIU, *Country Report*, 1993, Third Quarter, p. 35).

By mid-1993 around 135,000 enterprises had overseas participation, with projected investment of nearly $170 billion and actual investment of some $44 billion. In 1992 a fifth of direct foreign investment was in inland provinces, while enterprises with foreign participation produced about 6 per cent of total industrial output (Frances Williams, *FT*, 15 September 1993, p. 4).

Tony Walker (*FT*, 16 February 1993, p. 6; 14 June 1993, p. 2) and Sheryll WuDunn (*IHT*, 16 February 1993, p. 12) report the following. Official figures for 1992 show that the contracted value of newly approved direct foreign investment was $57.51 billion (i.e. the amount pledged during the lifetime of the contracts), a 380 per cent increase on the year before. (Note that other sources give a 1992 figure of $68.5 billion of signed agreements, e.g. *FT*, Survey, 18 November 1993, p. vi.) Foreigners actually invested only $11.16 billion, up 160 per cent (Hong Kong accounted for two-thirds). The $11.16 billion in 1992 was greater than the $8 billion or so invested by foreigners during the previous thirteen years. In 1992 China received about a quarter of funds invested in developing countries as a whole. Between 1978 and 1991 China signed contracts to the value of $48 billion, of which half was actually invested. Of the actual (i.e. utilized) direct investment of about $37 billion from 1979 to the end of 1992, the five leading contributors were as follows: Hong Kong and Macao, $21.2 billion; Japan (recently becoming more involved), $3.9 billion; the USA, $3.2 billion; Taiwan, $1.9 billion; Germany, $0.47 billion. Since 1979 $52 billion has actually been invested out of a total contracted investment of nearly $200 billion; foreign-invested enterprises employ 5 million people (Tony Walker, *FT*, 8 November 1993, p. 5; *FT*, Survey, 18 November 1993, p. i).

In 1993 official figures revealed that $110.9 billion of direct foreign capital was contracted and $25.76 billion actually utilized (*IHT*, 1 March 1994, p. 19; *IHT*, Survey, 11 April 1994, p. 12.) (The latter figure was the world's second largest, the USA attracting $32 billion: *IHT*, 24 October 1994, p. 9.) The nearly $26 billion accounted for 13 per cent of total fixed investment in China (compared with an average of 2.5 per cent in the 1980s (Tony Walker, *FT*, 5 December 1994, p. 4).

In 1994 $82.6 billion was pledged and $33.5 billion actually utilized (Tony Walker, *FT*, 18 April 1995, p. 7). In 1994 'contracted' foreign investment fell to $81.4 billion from $122.7 billion in 1993, while 'disbursed' investment rose 22.9 per cent to $33.8 billion (*The Economist*, 26 August 1995, p. 60).

Other aspects of foreign investment

By the end of 1992 there were 84,000 foreign-funded enterprises in China (these generated nearly a quarter of foreign trade: p. 9), compared with 47,000 at the end of 1991 (*EIU Country Report*, 1993 no. 1, p. 29).

All enterprises with outside investment, including joint ventures and wholly foreign-owned firms, accounted for 25 per cent of total imports and exports in 1992; their share in total exports in 1992 was 20 per cent compared with 1.1 per cent in 1985 (United Nations, *World Economic Survey 1993*, pp. 67, 197).

In 1993 foreign-funded enterprises accounted for 37.1 per cent of trade (*IHT*, 13 April 1994, p. 17).

In the previous two years the recipients of direct foreign investment (foreign-owned companies and joint ventures) accounted for less than

5 per cent of output (*The Economist*, 30 April 1994, p. 97). In 1993 foreign-funded firms accounted for 27.5 per cent of exports (*The Economist*, Survey, 18 March 1995, p. 19).

Foreign-funded enterprises account for more than a third of total exports (Jon Liden, *IHT*, Survey, 24 April 1995, p. 15).

China itself invests overseas. In 1992 the investment amounted to $1.94 billion (Tony Walker, *FT*, 16 February 1993, p. 6).

The IMF estimates that in 1992 the net flow of direct investment into China was around $5.6 billion, after deducting $1.4 billion in Chinese investment overseas (Sheryll WuDunn, *IHT*, 16 February 1993, p. 12).

Chinese investment in Hong Kong now exceeds Hong Kong's investment in China (*The Economist*, 26 June 1993, p. 71).

Wall (1993: 246) cites one estimate that in 1992 China's foreign holdings amounted to over $5 billion.

Henny Sender (*FEER*, 2 September 1993, p. 40) quotes one estimate that all told $13 billion to $28 billion left the country in 1991 and even more in 1992 (capital flight amounted to some $15 billion to $20 billion in 1990 and to some $30 billion to $40 billion in 1993: FEER, *Asia 1994 Yearbook*, 1994, p. 119). Friedrich Wu (*FEER*, 20 January 1994, p. 17) reports the official estimates that by the end of 1992 China had 4,117 enterprises operating in 120 countries and territories. Its cumulative, worldwide direct investment amounted to slightly more than $4 billion during the period 1979–92. But Wu says that these figures almost certainly grossly underestimate China's real capital outflows, most of which are illicit and without official approval. An official Chinese source has said that the number of Chinese-funded enterprises overseas hit 380 in 1993, involving Chinese investment of $120 million. To date China has funded a total of 4,497 enterprises in foreign countries, with Chinese investment of $5.16 billion (*IHT*, Survey, 30 May 1994, p. 8). By the end of June 1995, according to official figures, China had set up 4,739 businesses overseas. This represented a total Chinese investment of $5.33 billion (*IHT*, 29 July 1995, p. 11).

There are also foreign loans to China; in 1992 the contractual value of loans amounted to $10.7 billion and the utilized value to $7.35 billion (*China Briefing*, March 1993, no. 44, p. 1).

Relaxation of the regulations governing foreign investment

On 21 June 1992 it was announced that for the first time a foreign (actually a Hong Kong) company had taken a majority (51 per cent) share in a state-owned enterprise (a textile company) (*IHT*, 13 July 1992, p. 13).

In late 1992 China issued its first licence to a foreign insurance company, though it was restricted to Shanghai (*IHT*, 16 February 1995, p. 13). On 12 July 1995 it was announced that foreign companies would also be allowed to sell insurance in Guangzhou (*IHT*, 13 July 1995, p. 17).

There are six cities where foreign ventures can engage in retailing: Beijing, Tianjin, Shanghai, Guangzhou, Dalian and Qingdao (*IHT*, 11 April 1994, p. 12). In 1995 China plans to allow one or two foreign retailers to operate supermarket chains in joint ventures. The Chinese partner's stake would exceed 50 per cent (*IHT*, 2 January 1995, p. 7). According to the original policy in 1992, only 'one or two' Sino-foreign joint ventures are permitted in the twelve locations (the five SEZs, Shanghai, Beijing, Tianjin, Guangzhou, Dalian and Qingdao). It was recently announced that only one Sino-foreign joint venture would be permitted to operate a national chain of stores. In August 1994 it was confirmed that a further six cities would be open to joint ventures in retailing (Harbin, Wuhan, Nanjing, Xian, Shenyang and Chongqing) (*China Briefing*, December 1994, no. 49, pp. 7–8).

On 6 August 1993 it was announced that joint ventures would be allowed in road and dock management.

On 25 January 1993 China announced that foreigners would be allowed to invest solely or jointly in the construction of motorways, bridges and tunnels and to invest solely in the construction of private docks and waterways for cargo shipping (*FT*, 26 January 1993, p. 4).

China recently announced that it would allow 100 per cent foreign ownership of power utilities (Tony Walker, *FT*, 30 March 1993, p. 32).

In April 1994 it was announced that no more joint ventures for cars would be approved for up to three years. After that new car-assembly plants would be approved only if they bought at least 40 per cent of their components inside China and raised the proportion to 60 per cent within three years (*The Economist*, 16 April 1994, p. 103). China's vehicle sector policy was issued in February 1994 and published in full in July. No new manufacturing joint ventures were to be approved until 1996. Preference would be given to foreign-invested companies operating in China whose operations included an element of component manufacture (*China Briefing*, October 1994, p. 5).

On 10 May 1993 it was announced that foreign companies were to be prohibited from participating in the management of or from holding shares in telecommunications services (as opposed to manufacturing plants) (*IHT*, 11 May 1993, p. 11).

On 5 December 1993 it was announced that joint-venture airlines would be allowed in 1994. Foreigners would also be permitted to invest in commercial airports and run all operations except air traffic control. Similar investment would be allowed in other parts of the transport system and infrastructure (*IHT*, 6 December 1993, p. 5). The details were announced on 27 May 1994 (*IHT*, 28 May 1994, p. 15; *FT*, 28 May 1994, p. 4): (1) there would be a small number of initial experiments; (2) foreign investors would be restricted to a maximum stake of 35 per cent in airlines and of 49 per cent in airports; (3) foreigners would be allowed a maximum 25 per cent of voting rights; (4) the positions of chairman and general manager would go to (mainland) Chinese.

On 26 June 1994 it was announced that foreign ownership would be allowed in the shipping industry, but generally only on a minority basis (Tony Walker, *FT*, 27 June 1994, p. 4).

On 13 May 1993 an agreement was signed between the Singapore authorities and China to develop an industrial township in Suzhou, near Shanghai. The Singapore Labour Foundation (a quasi-state body) and the Suzhou municipal government were to put together a consortium of companies to develop the new town (Kieron Cooke, *FT*, 14 May 1993, p. 4).

On 29 June 1993 the Tsingtao brewery became the first Chinese company to sell shares in Hong Kong.

On 20 July 1994 it was announced that China Unicom would be allowed to compete with the Ministry of Post and Telecommunications in the provision of telephones. But direct foreign investment was still ruled out.

On 12 October 1994 preliminary agreement was reached on a deal to involve foreign companies in telecommunications. But two days later it was made clear that foreigners could not take part in the equity or the management of phone services, being eligible only to build networks, to advise on their operation and to reap returns on the investment (*IHT*, 15 October 1994, p. 15).

China has opened up ten gold mines to foreign investment. Investors must sell all output to the state at 10 per cent below market prices (*FEER*, 1 December 1994, p. 81). (On 4 September 1994 China published its first official figure for gold production, namely 90 tonnes in 1993.)

Special economic zones

Wall (1993: 243–60) provides the following information. The Shekou Industrial Zone established in 1979 actually provided the initial impetus for SEZs, but was then subsumed in the Shenzhen SEZ. Quite soon after the establishment of the four SEZs the whole of Guangdong and Fujian provinces was opened up. The concept of labour contracts had to be introduced into the SEZs. Contracts were originally between the enterprises and the local labour bureau, but over time there has been greater flexibility in the form of direct recruitment and dismissal and freedom for workers to move between firms at the end of contracts (or even, by agreement, during contracts). The labour bureau now plays more of a supervisory or monitoring role. It acts as arbitrator and facilitator as regards recruitment as well as the conduit for welfare fund payments collected from enterprises in lieu of the direct provision of welfare benefits which they would otherwise be required to supply. There have also been experiments, starting with Shenzhen, involving university graduates finding their own jobs. But wages are still set at the centre for national enterprises, while foreign-funded enterprises have their rates controlled, albeit loosely, by local labour bureaus. Land leases are granted for variable periods, depending on the life of the project. Initially they were for short periods (typically ten years), but periods of seventy-five years are now common and some leases are even open-ended. (Wall notes that domestic Chinese state and collective enterprises are the principal investors in the SEZs, either in wholly owned enterprises or in joint ventures with foreign companies, mainly overseas Chinese companies but also overseas companies owned by mainland Chinese enterprises: pp. 249–50. Zhang Jun also points out that 'most investments and industries, including joint ventures with foreigners, that have taken place in the special zones are in fact based on investment from other parts of the same country. Up to 1990, the bulk of the investment and the overwhelming number of enterprises in SEZs came from China itself.' Zhang Jun draws attention to the efficiency losses associated with those activities merely relocated to take advantage of the special benefits available in the zones. 'The main argument . . . is that SEZs tend to produce to a large extent a "protection effect" on zone firms . . . state firms relocating into zones are actually protected instead of being forced to compete': *The CEA (UK) Newsletter*, 1993, vol. 5, no. 4, pp. 15–17.)

In the late 1970s Shenzhen was a small town of 30,000 people; it is now a metropolitan area of some 3 million (*IHT*, Survey, 11 April 1994, p. 14). *FEER* (16 June 1994, p. 35) talks of Shenzhen's population growing from 100,000 in 1979 to 2.5 million by the end of 1993.

No new SEZs as such have been approved. But there has been a proliferation of 'economic development zones' broadly defined, with various other titles as well (such as 'economic and technological development zones', 'high technology zones' and 'free trade zones').

On 7 February 1993 it was announced that the government would curb the spread of economic development zones to help dampen the construction boom. No new development zones were to be approved below the level of the provincial authority (*IHT*, 18 May 1993, p. 16). One hundred and seventeen development zones had been approved by the end of 1991, but estimates by various Chinese bodies of the current number vary from 1,700 to 9,000 (*IHT*, 8 February 1993, p. 7).

It was announced in December 1992 that there existed 8,700 economic development zones, of which only 213 had received central or provincial government approval (EIU, *Country Report*, 1993, Second Quarter, p. 18).

According to the government, around 3,000 economic development zones are in the planning stage or have actually been established; but the government has approved only about 300 development areas (Tony Walker, *FT*, 26 July 1993, p. 1).

It was announced that foreign-funded enterprises would have to re-register in order to nullify those tax concessions granted by local authorities in violation of national policy (*IHT*, 2 August 1993, p. 7).

On 12 August 1993 it was revealed that more than 1,000 unauthorized economic development zones had recently been closed down in the coastal regions and 200 were being inspected; only thirty zones had been approved by the State Council (note that returning land to agricultural use is one reason for this measure).

On 18 August 1993 a policy of promoting zones in inland regions was announced.

Also on 18 August 1993 the port of Tianjin opened a zone for investors from South Korea, the first such area in China. The zone is within the Tianjin economic and technology zone and is being developed by the state-owned Korea Land Development Corporation, which has a fifty-year contract for the use of the land (*IHT*, 19 August 1993, p. 13). (Nicholas Kristof, *IHT*, 7 April 1993, p. 15, reports that South Korean investment is orientated so much towards Shandong province, opposite South Korea, that it is possible that a sort of special zone or province is beginning to take shape; note the geographical positions of Shenzhen and Xiamen.)

China Briefing (September 1993, p. 7) reports a change in the type of Hong Kong investment in Guangdong province. In the 1980s the main investment forms were processing and assembly, simple manufacturing and some services (mainly catering and hotels), but in the 1990s new forms have begun to supplement these (such as higher technology and higher value-added activities). Guangdong (population 63 million) now has the most market-orientated economy in China and its growth rate has outstripped that of China as a whole (the average annual rate of growth of GDP was 12.6 per cent in 1980–92, compared with 8.9 per cent for China as a whole; the respective figures for industrial output were 19.4 per cent and 12.8 per cent; by 1992 Guangdong had quadrupled its 1980 economic output) (p. 5).

(Note that China was the World Bank's largest borrower during the fiscal year ending July 1994, with loans of $3 billion. The World Bank's accumulated lending to China since 1981 was $19.4 billion: *Transition*, 1994, vol. 5, no. 6, p. 24.)

Agriculture

The term 'Household Responsibility System' (HRS) derives from households having a responsibility to meet sales quotas and so on.

Background

At the start of the reform period in 1978 the rural sector involved 82 per cent of the total population, 74 per cent of the work force and 37.5 per cent of GNP (Jun Tian, *The CEA (UK) Newsletter*, 1993, vol. 5, no. 4, p. 13).

In 1991 73.6 per cent of the population was rural, compared with 82.1 per cent in 1978 and 89.4 per cent in 1949. In 1992 72 per cent of the population was rural and agriculture accounted for 73 per cent of employment in the period 1990–92 (industry 14 per cent and services 13 per cent). There are 450 working-age farmers (*The Economist*, Survey, 8 April 1995, p. 4; 14 October 1995, p. 99).

Fifteen years ago 80 per cent of the population lived off the land. Today 65 per cent does (Lena H. Sun, *IHT*, 11 October 1994, p. 7).

Today 72 per cent of the population is rural, but only 40 per cent actually farm (Ian Johnson, *The Guardian*, 3 November 1994, p. 13).

Cultivable land per rural household is a mere 0.4 ha and falling (Hussain and Stern 1994: 15). The land is relatively equally distributed.

Over the past forty years farmland *per capita* has fallen from 0.018 ha to 0.0086 ha (*IHT*, 12 January 1995, p. 15).

By the latter half of the 1980s around 60 per cent of agricultural commodities were bought and sold on competitive markets, compared with only 8 per cent in 1978. 'Decollectivization happened more or less spontaneously. What began as experiments to help the poorest areas in certain provinces spread quickly to other regions' (Perkins 1994: 26).

Land ownership

Ling and Zhongyi (1993) describe the confusion over the question of land ownership. 'The allocative function of the villages was initially brought about by the change in collective ownership. Owing to the institutional changes . . . some property which was formerly owned by production teams (e.g. farmland) or production brigades (e.g. non-agricultural enterprises) was transferred to community ownership. Though the constitution declared that there is still collective ownership of farmland, confusion has arisen from the fact that the agricultural production collectives no longer exist . . . With the emergence of communal property rights, village communities have assumed responsibility for community-based resource management. First, given that a land market is prohibited, the committees are in charge of the distribution and redistribution of farmland among family farms within each village for specified periods' (pp. 444–5). 'Given that the ownership of land has not yet been defined and that farmland cannot officially be bought and sold, land transfers have occurred mainly through redistribution within a village community, involving agreement between the village committee and the farmers of a given village' (p. 455). 'Though the state has always regulated land tenure and land use, it does not own the land. The state cannot directly dispose of village farmland because it is in collective ownership . . . most cases of land dispute in relation to the land tenure and land use systems are settled by village committees . . . However, community ownership of land is incomplete, since communities do not have the right to sell or to lease land. While every member of a village community does have a share of the property rights to the land of his/her community, this share is not embodied in any concrete form such as a title-deed stock, so that there is neither a market for transferring the usufruct right nor a real tenant-farming system' (p. 447).

'The "decollectivization" of farmland was not followed by the establishment of private property rights in land. The Chinese Communist Party did not wish to allow the emergence of a landlord class, and, therefore, land could not be bought and sold. Rather, the village community remained the owner of farmland, controlling the terms on which it was operated by peasant households . . . A striking feature of the "land reform" of the early 1980s is that land was contracted to households mostly on an equal *per capita* basis within each village' (Nolan 1993: 74).

Productivity

Gaynor and Putterman (1993: 357–9) examine the productivity effects of the manner of distributing collective land to households under the HRS. Land was distributed by a formula putting weight on both household size and household labour force. Virtually all the land distributed was divided among the households belonging to a given production team either on the basis of equal division by population (usually adjusted for age and sex differences), on the basis of equal division by labour forces, or by some combination of the two methods. Because neither land sub-letting nor agricultural labour markets emerged as significant phenomena in most of rural China, especially in the early years following the adoption of the HRS, the labour forces of recipient households could be expected to have been the main determinant of the amount of labour actually applied to each parcel. The authors conclude that 'agricultural output is concave in the proportion of land distributed according to work force as opposed to household size. Output increases initially as the work force-based share of land distributed is increased, but then reaches a maximum and declines . . . Assuming the continued use of administrative rules . . . the analysis suggests that productivity concerns require that land distribution give weight to both household work forces and household populations . . . The data from Dahe township [the former commune in Hebei province which provided the empirical data for 1985 on sixty-one production teams] suggest that this was in fact done; most teams chose distribution rules that appear to have been reasonably close to what would have maximized productivity' (p. 381). Further research is needed to determine the generality of this conclusion (some commentators have expressed concern that the division of land on an equal *per capita* basis would lead to more uneven use and lower average productivity than would distribution according to household labour force: p. 359).

Wen (1993: 1–41) estimates changes in total factor productivity over the period 1952–89 (defined as the ratio of output to the weighted sum of inputs). Wen suggests that there are three ways to increase production, namely an increase in inputs, institutional innovation and technological progress. Three sub-periods are distinguished:

1. *The pre-commune period, 1952–57.* This includes the mutual aid teams and elementary co-operatives, which farmers could leave if they so wished. Total factor productivity was not lowered (p. 2). (Farmers lost the ownership of land and capital during the short-lived advanced co-operative movement of 1957.)

2. *The commune period, 1958–78.* During this period land productivity was raised, but labour productivity fell (p. 2). 'Output growth came mainly from increased inputs. The rigidity of the system prohibited institutional innovation and the technological progress embodied in the modern inputs was overshadowed by the rampant inefficiency of the commune system' (pp. 34–5).

3. *The Household Responsibility System, 1979–89.* The HRS showed a clear advantage over the commune system in increasing total factor productivity. The productivity of both land and labour was raised. 'The rapid growth of output and the concomitant fall in inputs from 1982 to 1985 provide a classic example of an efficiency improvement induced by a dominantly institutional innovation' (p. 2). Since 1985, however, 'the increase in output once more required an increase in inputs' (p. 35). The growth rates of both the land productivity index of crop output and the total factor productivity index have slowed since 1985 (p. 36). The slower growth of crop production suggests the possibility that the long-run advantage of the current form of the HRS may lie in its ability to increase non-crop production rapidly (p. 2). Since 1986 the slow growth of crop production has triggered a debate in China (pp. 35–6). Almost all those taking part in the debate agree that (1) under the HRS the rural infrastructure, especially land, has been underinvested in and (2) the slow-down in the growth of both land productivity and crop production suggests that the gains from institutional innovations which started in the late 1970s have been largely exhausted. But there has been disagreement about the solution. Some suggest the need to increase the scale of farm operations through government intervention (there have been experiments since 1987 where plots have been taken away from farmers even before the expiry of contracts and reassigned to a smaller number of pre-selected farm households). Others believe that the fall in land investment is due in part to the omission of the responsibility to maintain the rural infrastructure by the government as well as by the farmers' insecurity with respect to land use rights. The government has a responsibility to maintain and expand the rural infrastructure, especially land-related investment such as roads, large-scale irrigation projects and flood control schemes. The idea of improving property

rights in land to enhance the potential of the HRS stems from this second school of thought.

Bramall (1993) disputes the conventional argument that the impressive agricultural performance after 1978 was largely due to the abolition of collective farms. Instead 'the source of the miracle [lies] in a favourable conjuncture of a shift in the intersectoral terms of trade towards agriculture and increased production of modern farm inputs, especially chemical fertilizers' (p. 271). The net value of farm output per head grew by an average annual rate of 4.4 per cent between 1978 and 1990, compared with an average annual decline of 0.1 per cent in the thirteen years before 1978 (p. 272).

Rural income increased at an average annual rate of 12.8 per cent 1978–85 (the figure for rural *per capita* income in real terms was 7.5 per cent) and in the period 1978–91 consumption among the agricultural population increased by 126 per cent in real terms. But the growth was markedly more rapid in the first half of the period. In 1984 farmers were formally allowed to engage solely in non-agricultural production and leases became transferable (United Nations, *World Economic Survey 1993*, pp. 187, 197).

The Labour Ministry estimates that 130 million of the total 333 million agricultural labour force is now surplus to requirements (Edward Balls, *FT*, Survey, 18 November 1993, p. x).

Lin's argument (see Jeffries 1993: 140) that the main cause of the 1959–61 agricultural disaster was the retraction of the right to withdraw from a collective in autumn 1958 has been subjected to considerable criticism on both theoretical and empirical grounds (see, for example, *Journal of Comparative Economics*, 1993, vol. 17, no. 2, pp. 471–559).

Current problems

There are a number of current problems:

1. Concern has been expressed about the loss of grain-producing land to commercial development and other forms of agriculture. Between 1990 and 1994 China lost about 1.5 million ha of farmland, or about 1 per cent of the total acreage sown to wheat and other grain crops annually. *Per capita* farmland had fallen by 1994 to below one mu, a mu being around one-fifteenth of a hectare and the level regarded by China as the minimum needed to guarantee self-sufficiency in grain production. The loss of about 500,000 ha of farmland in 1994 (about 63 per cent of the total loss) was attributed to farmers switching from grain to cash crops. Commercial development accounted for another 20 per cent, while natural disasters also took their toll (Tony Walker, *FT*, 2 March 1995, p. 33).

The Economist (Survey, 18 March 1995, p. 24) cites one estimate that China has already lost about a third of its cropland over the past forty years to soil erosion, desertification, energy projects and, at an accelerating pace, to industrial and housing development.

According to official figures, 10.6 million acres of arable land have been lost since 1978 (Patrick Tyler, *IHT*, 11 April 1995, p. 4).

2. Investment in agriculture has fallen from 6 per cent of all national investment in 1981 to 1 per cent in 1993, although it appears to have picked up again in 1994 (*The Economist*, Survey, 18 March 1995, p. 23).

3. There have been reports of growing peasant discontent over declining profitability and increasing local taxation. Many have left the land. There were riots in Fujia village in Sichuan province in late May to early June 1993 over the fees and charges used to finance local projects. There were more than 200 incidents of rural unrest in 1993 (Tony Walker, *FT*, 2 February 1994, p. 19).

In December 1991 the government issued a regulation limiting the total amount of fees and taxes on peasants to 5 per cent of the previous year's income (Sheryl WuDunn, *IHT*, 20 May 1993, p. 2). On 21 June 1993 the State Council issued a decree (effective 10 July) ordering local authorities to cancel thirty-seven levies.

In 1993, according to Chinese press reports, at least 830 incidents of rural rebellion involving more than 500 people each were recorded, including twenty-one cases involving crowds of more than 5,000 (*The Economist*, Survey, 18 March 1995, p. 23).

4. In 1992 the average urban wage was 1,800 yuan plus perks, while the rural figure was 780 yuan (Teresa Poole, *The Independent*, 13 May 1993, p. 11).

Average urban income in 1992 was 2,000 yuan and average rural income 770 yuan (*The Economist*, 19 June 1993, p. 69). Since the mid-1980s rural real incomes 'have done little better than remain stagnant.' There is already a 'floating population' (people not formally classified as urban residents) of more than 90 million rural workers who have left the land in search of higher earnings. (The official figure is around 20 million, but Western estimates vary from 70 to 150 million.)

In 1992 the average income of a farmer was less than half that of an urban resident. When subsidies to city dwellers and taxes on farmers are taken into account the figure becomes a quarter. In 1978 the rural–urban income ratio was 1 : 2.5; it fell to 1 : 1.7 in 1985 and then widened again to 1 : 2.3 in 1992 (Sheryl WuDunn, *IHT*, 20 May 1993, p. 2). (The real difference may be 1 : 4 once rural *ad hoc* levies and urban state subsidies are taken into account: Lincoln Kaye, *FEER*, 2 September 1993, p. 40.) On 16 June 1993 Deng expressed concern that 'the peasants' burden has already surpassed the limits of their endurance'.

In 1993 the average yearly urban income was 2,337 yuan, compared with 921 yuan in rural areas; there was a report in a Chinese newspaper of a serious breakdown of law and order in parts of the countryside (*IHT*, 4 May 1994, pp. 1, 6).

In 1994 *per capita* real income for urban residents was 3,150 yuan and for rural residents 1,200 yuan (*FEER*, 9 February 1995, p. 58).

In 1994 official figures showed that the *per capita* income of city dwellers was 3,179 yuan, compared with 1,220 yuan for rural residents (*IHT*, 1 March 1995, p. 15).

The deeply unpopular IOUs ('white slips') continued to be used through 1992 (partly because local authorities used funds provided by the central government for other purposes, such as property speculation). In January 1993 the government ordered all grain purchase departments to redeem all IOUs (by the Chinese New Year), but it is not certain that it happened (EIU, *Country Report*, 1993, no. 1, p. 23). The sixteen-point austerity programme of 4 July 1993 contained a ban on the issue of IOUs as well as an assurance of sufficient loans for agriculture (*FEER*, 15 July 1993, p. 69). (Farmers have also been antagonized by the difficulties experienced in cashing money orders sent by relatives working in the towns; 'green IOUs' have often been given instead of cash.)

(The problems of agriculture have featured prominently in sessions of the NPC and the Central Committee. See above.)

ECONOMIC PERFORMANCE

Output

See Table 27.1. China's record as regards GDP growth rates in the first half of the 1990s was world-class. But agricultural growth was relatively slow and the sluggish state sector held back the overall rate of growth of industry. The reason why the government expressed concern at above-target GDP growth rates was concern at above-target inflation rates.

World ranking in terms of GDP

The IMF has pushed China up from tenth to third place in the international ranking of total GDP, behind the USA and Japan (*World Economic Out-*

Table 27.1 China: selected economic indicators

Economic indicator	*1990*	*1991*	*1992*	*1993*	*1994*
Rate of growth of GDP (%)	5.2	8.2	13.1	13.4	11.8
Rate of growth of industrial output (%)	7.8	12.9	20.8	23.6	18.0
Oil output (million tonnes)		140.0		143.7	
Rate of growth of agricultural output (%)	7.6	3.0	3.7	4.0	3.5
Grain output (million tonnes)	435.0	435.3	442.6	456.4	444.5
Inflation (retail, %)	2.1	2.9	5.4	13.0	21.7

Sources: Various issues of United Nations, *World Economic and Social Survey*; United Nations, *Economic and Social Survey of Asia and the Pacific*; IMF, *World Economic Outlook*; *China Briefing*, *Economist Intelligence Unit*, *The Economist*, *The Financial Times* and *The International Herald Tribune*

look, 1993, pp. 116–19; see also reports in the following: *The Economist*, 15 May 1993, p. 95; *FT*, 24 May 1993, p. 17; *IHT*, 20 May 1993, p. 2, 25 May 1993, p. 20, and 5 June 1993, p. 8; *The Times*, 21 May 1993, p. 12). This is the result of using purchasing-power parity (PPP) rather than the official (actual or market) exchange rate between currencies.

Purchasing-power parity is the rate of exchange between currencies that gives equal purchasing power over commodities. PPP is computed by selecting a comparable bundle of both internationally traded and non-traded goods and services and estimating the purchasing-power equivalent of each item in one country as compared with others. This, for example, helps compensate for the relatively low price of services in foreign currency terms in developing countries. Peter Norman (*FT*, 30 December 1994, p. 3) talks of adjustment for the purchasing power of currencies in home markets. He cites the World Bank's definition, namely the number of units of a country's currency required to buy the same amount of goods and services in the domestic market that $1 would buy in the USA.

The figures for 1992 using the official exchange rate and PPP are as follows:

1. GDP: $440 billion and almost $2,000 billion. The PPP figure gives China a 6.1 per cent share of world GDP (1.9 per cent previously), compared with the following: the USA, 22.47 per cent (26.07 per cent); Japan, 7.63 per cent (14.61 per cent); Asia, 17.67 per cent (7.29 per cent); the developing countries, 34.38 per cent (17.71 per cent); Eastern Europe and the former Soviet Union, 11.16 per cent (9.06 per cent); the industrialized economies, 54.44 per cent (73.21 per cent).

2. GDP *per capita*: $370 and $1,680 (compared with $22,130 in the USA, $19,390 in Japan, $16,340 in the UK, $6,930 in Russia and $1,150 in India).

The UN International Comparison Programme has calculated the following figures for 1992, using PPP: (1) GDP, $2,700 billion; (2) GDP *per capita*, $1,950.

Further studies

The annual report of the Bank for International Settlements (reported by Peter Marsh, *FT*, 15 June 1993, p. 6) estimates that between 1960 and 1990 China increased its share of world income from 7.3 per cent to 11.5 per cent. During the 1980s the income of the average person increased at an average annual rate of 6.9 per cent.

The World Bank has estimated that China's 1992 GNP at the market exchange rate was only $506 billion, smaller than Spain's and eighth largest in the world. The PPP estimate was $2,220 billion. The respective figures for national income *per capita* were $470 and $1,910. Other estimates of (PPP) national income per head vary between $1,000 and $3,000 (Martin Wolf, *FT*, 7 November 1994, p. 24). (But the World Bank cautions that 'For

China no reliable PPP-survey price data exist and the $1,910 figure is subject to wide margins of error which probably impart an upward bias': Tony Walker, *FT*, 3 April 1995, p. 6.) According to successive World Development Reports, GDP per head (market exchange rate) rose from $260 in 1979 to $370 in 1991 (*FT*, Survey, 7 November 1994, p. iv). The World Bank has calculated that in 1993 the market exchange rate figure for GNP *per capita* was $490 and the PPP figure was $2,120 (Peter Norman, *FT*, 30 December 1994, p. 3).

China's GDP per head (market exchange rate) was $85 in 1965 and $370 in 1991. GDP per head (PPP) in 1990 was $1,990 (*The Economist*, Survey, 30 October 1993, pp. 6, 12). China's GDP per head (PPP) is $2,100, compared with Taiwan's $14,000, Hong Kong's $20,100 and the USA's $23,200 (*The Economist*, 6 August 1994, p. 57). The World Bank found that GDP per head in 1990 was $370 on an exchange rate basis and $1,950 on a PPP basis. Other PPP estimates put the figure at up to $2,600. But the use of other measures as a check on PPP estimates has made some of the higher PPP calculations look improbable; a figure of around $2,000 for 1994 might be guessed at (*The Economist*, Survey, 18 March 1995, p. 9).

In 1993, according to the IMF, world GDP (PPP) was divided up as follows: the developed countries, 55.7 per cent; developing countries, 33.4 per cent; Eastern Europe and the former Soviet Union, 10.9 per cent. The World Bank put China's GDP (PPP) in 1993 at around $2,500 billion (*The Economist*, 14 January 1995, p. 114).

Poverty

According to a 1993 World Bank study, the number of people living in absolute poverty fell from 220 million in 1980 to 100 million in 1990 (Nicholas Kristof, *IHT*, 8 September 1993, p. 6).

The percentage of the population living in poverty fell from 33 per cent in 1970 to 9 per cent in 1990, with 95 per cent of the 100 million to be found in the countryside (more often in northern and western provinces) (Edward Balls, *FT Survey*, 18 November 1993, pp. iii, x).

One-tenth of the population still live in 'absolute poverty' (Lewis Preston, then president of the World Bank, *IHT*, 7 April 1993, p. 15).

The World Bank has calculated that 9 per cent of the population live in poverty. The figure was brought down from 33 per cent in 1978 to 11 per cent in 1984 (*The Economist*, 4 March 1995, p. 78).

Ernest Stern, the managing director of the World Bank, says that 'since 1985 progress in reducing poverty has been slow. A very large minority of Chinese (the World Bank estimates as many as 100 million) has essentially missed out on the growing prosperity. Carefully targeted programmes need to be launched to help them' (*IHT*, 20 May 1994, p. 6).

Inflation

See Table 27.1. The 'cost-of-living index for staff and workers' represents the retail prices of consumption goods and services in urban areas only. The 'general retail price index' covers consumption goods (but not services) sold in rural as well as urban areas (Imai 1994: 128). 'Although China has experienced a significant rise in inflationary pressure since the initiation of economic reforms in 1979, the repressed inflation rate dropped considerably over this period because the prices of consumption goods became less rigid through price decontrol. Available information suggests that China's consumption goods market by and large regained equilibrium by 1990' (p. 152).

The 'cost-of-living index' includes services. The 'retail price index' is heavily weighted towards food and clothing (Tony Walker, *FT*, 17 March 1994, p. 4). (In 1993 the former was 14.7 per cent and the latter 13 per cent.)

The inflation rate for thirty-five major cities captures price rises in the deregulated service sector (*FEER*, 21 April 1994, p. 76).

Hussain and Stern (1993: 80–1) ask how China has managed to avoid high or hyper-inflation rates when tax revenue has lagged and large subsidies have been needed to support the many loss-making enterprises (at the expense of infrastructure: p. 62). They suggest five main reasons: (1) the exceptionally high propensity to save of households and their willingness to hold most of their savings in bank deposits (an important factor in explaining this thrift is saving up for the increasingly available consumer goods in the absence of a well developed consumer credit system) (the savings rate has been around 30 per cent of GNP for much of the 1980s and early 1990s: United Nations, *World Economic Survey 1993*, p. 186); (2) the small size of the state sector relative to East European economies, which mitigates the problem of subsidizing loss-makers; (3) the very high rates of growth of output coupled with increased absorption due to the monetarization of the rural economy; (4) the government retains a considerable degree of control over the economy, especially over wages, the banking system and the sanctioning of investment, control which can be tightened when necessary; (5) workers are prepared to take a long-run view and restrain wages to promote investment in their enterprise.

McKinnon (1994: 438) believes that major price inflation was avoided by a huge, voluntary build-up of household financial assets, mainly claims on the state banking system.

The rate of inflation in 1992 was 6.4 per cent; 70 per cent of this was due to price deregulation, according to government officials (*IHT*, 19 February 1993, p. 15).

28

CUBA

THE POLITICAL BACKGROUND

Exiles and refugees

The 1966 Cuban Adjustment Act meant that Cubans who arrived in the USA were effectively granted immediate political asylum (those who were rescued making the perilous sea journey to Florida were in reality treated the same; Cubans became eligible for permanent residence after one year). The situation changed on 19 August 1994 (see below). Phil Davison (*The Independent*, 14 September 1993, p. 12; 23 June 1994, p. 16) points out that it is the tight limit on the number of US visas that is the problem rather than the number of Cuban exit visas. Under a 1984 agreement with Cuba the USA could grant up to 20,000 visas a year, but in 1993 only 2,700 were actually awarded. Until 1991 Cuba would not let anyone under the age of fifty-five apply for a US visa. But now anyone over twenty can apply, except university graduates, who are expected to repay the costs of their education by working for at least five years. (Under the embargo only Americans travelling on government business, journalists, academic researchers and Cuban-American exiles with relatives in Cuba are allowed to visit Cuba. Groups may apply for special licences to deliver humanitarian aid to Cuba. The travel ban was first imposed in 1963, briefly lifted by President Carter and reinstated by President Reagan. Groups opposed to the ban have made defiant visits: David Adams, *The Times*, 11 October 1993, p. 10.)

Human rights activists in Cuba say that there are over 1,000 political prisoners, but the government has never confirmed this figure (Pascal Fletcher, *FT*, 8 May 1995, p. 4).

22–24 April 1994. A three-day conference was held in Havana at which representatives of the Cuban government met (for the first time since 1978) 'moderate' Cuban exiles from the USA and twenty-eight other countries. A number of concessions resulted, such as (1) the lifting of the five-year waiting period for return visits (though this would apply only to those who left Cuba legally); (2) a small number of children of exiles would be allowed to study at Cuban universities (though fees would have to be paid); (3) the creation of a special section of the Foreign Ministry to deal with the affairs of exiles.

29 May 1994. Up to 124 Cuban asylum-seekers occupy the Belgian embassy in Havana.

13 June 1994. Twenty-one asylum-seekers drive a lorry through the fence of the German embassy.

15 June 1994. Nine asylum-seekers force their way into the Chilean embassy.

The government's reaction to all the occupations involved carrot and stick: (1) those leaving would not be prosecuted for the occupation itself, although charges were not to be ruled out for crimes such as the theft of the lorry; (2) the occupiers would never gain official permission to leave the country. The occupiers gradually began to return home.

5 August 1994. Serious anti-government riots (involving over 1,000 demonstrators, it is estimated) break out in the port area of Havana following a spate of ferry hi-jackings by Cubans wishing to flee the country. Thirty-five people are injured in the worst outbreak of civil disorder since 1959 (two policemen were killed during an attempted ferry hi-jacking the previous day). Castro threatens the USA with a repeat of the Mariel boatlift of 1980 (the 125,000 Cubans sent from the port of Mariel to the USA over a five-month period included criminals and mental patients).

18 August 1994. The governor of Florida declares a state of emergency to deal with the growing seaborne influx of Cuban refugees (6,872 since the beginning of 1994, compared with 3,656 for the whole of 1993: *IHT*, 19 August 1994, p. 1).

19 August 1994. President Clinton announces that 'illegal refugees from Cuba will not be allowed to enter the United States'. Those picked up at sea would be taken to the US Guantanamo naval base on Cuba, while those making it to the USA would be taken to detention centres ('pending a determination of how they should be processed'). Cubans would be treated the same as other illegal immigrants. US citizens trying to help refugees flee Cuba would be prosecuted. (The Guantanamo base is leased, although Cuba refuses to accept the payments. The Platt amendment of 1902 was revoked in 1934, thus ending the right of the USA to intervene. The lease was reaffirmed, albeit for ninety-nine years instead of in perpetuity.)

20 August 1994. The USA announces further measures against Cuba, including an end to cash transfers, curtailed charter flights, restrictions on visits by relatives, increased radio and television broadcasts and a quest for resolutions in the UN condemning human rights violations. Gift parcels would be limited to food, medicine and other humanitarian items.

23 August 1994. The USA makes it clear that all Cubans picked up at sea ('rafters') are not entitled to consideration for refugee status unless they apply through the US diplomatic office in Havana (the USA has a Special Interests section in the Swiss embassy), i.e. they need to be repatriated first. (The immediate reaction was a surge in the number of those attempting to make the journey.)

24 August 1994. The USA is to ease the official quota (now a maximum of 27,845 annually) by, for example, broadening the categories eligible for consideration.

28 August 1994. Castro orders his personnel to stop children under sixteen, the elderly and pregnant women from being taken on unsafe rafts and boats.

The USA and Cuba agree to talk about the flight of illegal refugees (starting on 1 September).

6 September 1994. The first Cuban refugees in Guantanamo are sent for up to six months to camps in Panama (one of the few countries the USA persuaded to accept them).

8 September 1994. Roberto Robaina, the foreign minister of Cuba, announces that he has held talks with the leaders of three (moderate) exiled dissident groups.

9 September 1994. The USA and Cuba reach agreement: (1) the USA agrees to grant visas to 6,000 Cubans on the waiting list plus at least 20,000 each year; (2) Cuba will 'take effective measures in every way it possibly can to prevent unsafe departures, using mainly persuasive methods' and promises not to maltreat any refugees who return.

Some 35,000 Cubans have fled since the start of 1994 (*IHT*, 12 September 1994, p. 1). Since 1 August 1994 there have been 30,291 known refugees (*The Times*, 12 September 1994, p. 13).

2 May 1995. The USA announces that some 15,000 of the 21,253 Cubans held in Guantanamo will be allowed to enter the USA (the grounds for rejection include ill health and a criminal record). The 15,000 will be part of the agreed annual quota, but spread over three years. Those Cubans attempting to reach the USA illegally in the future will be returned to Cuba if intercepted at sea (unless the USA is satisfied that their lives are in jeopardy; those reaching shore will be given the opportunity to apply for asylum, but will be treated like all other illegal immigrants). The Cuban government promised not to take reprisals against those returned.

9 May 1995. The USA returns the first 'rafters' (thirteen of them) to Cuba.[1]

Political developments

24 February 1993. Direct and secret elections to the 589-member National Assembly take place (previously directly elected municipal councillors chose provincial representatives who in turn chose National Assembly deputies). Only around 70 per cent of delegates are formally Communist Party members, but there was only a single list and all candidates it seems were approved by the local branches of the Communist Party (formally the party was not supposed to be involved in the nominating process). The turnout was 99.6 per cent, but, although all the candidates were elected (including Castro himself), even the party admitted that 7.2 per cent either voted against or cast blank or spoiled ballot papers (14.3 per cent in Havana) (unofficial estimates put the average figure as high as 20 per cent). Also directly elected for the first time were 1,190 delegates to provincial assemblies. (Voters were able to choose between two and eight candidates; municipal or town elections had taken place by the usual secret and direct ballot on 20 December 1992.) (Note that on 11 July 1992 the National Assembly had increased the powers of the president, e.g. granting him the right to declare a state of emergency.)

25 February 1993. Castro says that he hopes it will not be necessary for him to be re-elected in 1998. He says he may step down in five years if the economic crisis is overcome, especially if the US embargo is lifted.

15 March 1993. The National Assembly re-elects Castro as president of the Council of State for the next five years.

23 May 1993. Cuba and Russia sign a memorandum on trade, joint ventures and production sharing, e.g. collaboration to reopen an oil refinery and oil terminal.

15 June 1993. A further reduction in the size of the army is announced (a reduction had also been announced in April). The government claims that Russia has not delivered arms since 1990 and only some spares in 1991.

The last of the Russian combat troops leave, numbering around 300 (the 3,000-strong motorized infantry brigade was introduced in 1962). (There were 40,000 Soviet troops in Cuba at the peak: Gary Prevost, *The World Today*, August–September 1993, p. 143.)

22 June 1993. It is announced that, owing to factors such as the economic situation, there will be no mass rally on 26 July to celebrate Castro's attack on the Moncada army barracks in Santiago on 26 July 1953 (although the attack itself was unsuccessful, it is regarded as the real starting point of the revolution; it was subsequently chosen as the date on which to celebrate the revolution).

22 November 1993. President Jiang Zemin of China pays a visit.

24 December 1993. The newspaper *Granma* reports that the Central Committee has approved a series of austerity measures, including cuts in subsidies to state enterprises and the gradual introduction of new taxes on income and property (David Adams, *The Times*, 27 December 1993, p. 9; Frances Kerry, *The Times*, 30 December 1993, p. 9).

29 December 1993. Castro says that although Cuba has been forced to make some compromises owing to the economic crisis, he will never renounce socialism: 'I have some convictions that I shall never renounce. What I feel is loathing for capitalism, not prejudice . . . the more I know about capitalism, the more I love socialism.'

1 May 1994. There was no May Day celebration. It was a normal working day and the National Assembly met in special session on 1–2 May (see below).

26 October 1994. The UN General Assembly votes to end the USA's economic embargo on Cuba. The votes were 101 'for' and two 'against' (the USA and Israel), with forty-eight abstentions. (In 1993 the vote was eighty-eight for, with fifty-seven abstentions.)

30 October 1994. The Pope announces that a Cuban is to become a cardinal.

25 November 1994. A direct-dial telephone service with the USA resumes after a break of around thirty years.

24 January 1995. There is a government reshuffle in which reform-minded individuals are promoted, e.g. Osvaldo Martinez as economy and planning minister and Francisco Soberon Valdes as president of the central bank.

13–15 March 1995. After attending the United Nations Social Development ('poverty') summit in Copenhagen, Castro visits France in a private capacity as the guest of Unesco. He is received by President François Mitterrand, who earlier described the US embargo on Cuba as 'stupid' (Mitterrand's wife Danielle is actively sympathetic to Castro's Cuba, e.g. she is patron of a charity that gives medicial supplies to hospitals in Cuba). Castro decided to stay an extra day. During the visit Castro tentatively agreed to a fact-finding mission on political prisoners in Cuba (*IHT*, 16 March 1995, p. 5). (Six political prisoners were released on 23 May and a seventh was admitted to hospital.)

25 March 1995. Cuba signs the 1967 treaty banning nuclear weapons in Latin America.

9 April 1995. Cuba and Chile restore full diplomatic relations (broken off after the military coup in Chile in 1973).

12 May 1995. Economy Minister Osvaldo Martinez retires on health grounds. He is replaced by Finance Minister Jose Luis Rodriguez (who also becomes a vice-president). His deputy, Manual Millares, takes over as finance minister.

31 July 1995. The EU donates Ecu 15 million towards Cuba's health service (*IHT*, 1 August 1995, p. 5).

ECONOMIC REFORM

Views from the West

Zimbalist (1993b: 152) summarized the situation as of early to mid-1993: 'A number of economic reforms initiated before 1989 are being continued, others are being accelerated and some new programmes are being put in place. The current emphasis on foreign investment and tourism, structural reforms in the operation of foreign trade and the impossibility of central planning in the presence of pervasive supply uncertainties have combined to transform the nature of Cuba's economy. Yet the needed and more concerted introduction of a broader market mechanism has not been forthcoming.' 'Although central planning was long ago abandoned, the value of trade on the black market easily surpasses official retail trade . . . Most of Cuba's production capacity goes unused because of shortages of raw materials and spare parts . . . With few exceptions, new productive investment has virtually ceased over the past three years' (p. 162). 'The structural and psychological momentum toward a mixed economy is strong' (p. 163). Western consultants are teaching Western management techniques (p. 163).

Pastor and Zimbalist (1995: 705) argue that: 'Cuba has attempted to adjust to external crisis via tighter rationing to curtail demand and traditional planning and sectoral strategies to expand the supply of tradables . . . prior sectoral-based efforts to adjust to the trade shocks of the 1980s have been extremely limited in their success and offer no road out of the crisis . . . Cuba has recently begun timid steps toward a more market-oriented approach . . . Given that the recent spate of half-hearted measures . . . has likely worsened distributional inequities, distorted incentives and failed to improve the macro economy, we suggest an alternative centred on the massive privatization of state assets to Cuban nationals residing within Cuba . . . which can be designed to absorb the monetary overhang, widely distribute assets and protect the social safety net.'

Perez-Lopez (1995a: 14) argues that: 'Cuba's economic strategy of opening the economy to foreign investment, coupled with its piecemeal adoption of economic liberalization measures, may prolong the Castro regime's life, but it will not turn the economy around. Comprehensive political and economic reforms that can turn Cuba into a market economy are essential if Cuba's economy is to grow and prosper.' 'Only bold economic and political reforms that create a market economy can provide a framework for sustainable economic growth' (Perez-Lopez 1995b: 149). But 'the Cuban leadership has adamantly rejected comprehensive political and economic reforms' (p. 135).

Events within Cuba

Cuban citizens who obtained foreign currencies (e.g. as tips or remittances from abroad) were required to exchange them at the official (inflated) exchange rate of the peso. In June 1993 ten categories of Cuban citizens were allowed to exchange foreign currencies at a preferential rate and to open bank accounts denominated in foreign currencies (Perez-Lopez 1995b: 140–1). In his 26 July 1993 speech Castro formally announced that legislation would be introduced to allow ordinary Cuban citizens (legally) to possess and use dollars and other foreign currencies in retail trade (he had hinted of the change at the end of June). This had also been made more explicit in mid-July by Vice-President Carlos Lage, who is in charge of economic policy. A chain of special shops would be set up to accept hard currency. The aim of the reform was to stimulate dollar remittances from the USA, but foreign currencies may not be used to pay wages or to stimulate domestic output directly (Jorge Dominguez, *FT*, 26 January 1994, p. 21). A decree issued on 13 August 1993 legalized the possession and use of foreign currencies by Cuban citizens, including the right to open bank accounts denominated in foreign currencies (Perez-Lopez 1995b: 141). It is estimated that about 15 per cent of Cuba's population has access to dollars, either through working in the tourist industry or joint ventures, or from money received from abroad (Douglas Farah, *The Guardian*, 9 February 1994, p. 12). (The so-called 'dollar' or 'diplomatic shops' were still theoretically barred to Cubans, but some citizens of Cuba have managed to use them in the past and the prospective change in the law encouraged quite open purchases. Dollars have, of course, been used on the black market. Prices in the 'dollar' shops were increased by 50 per cent on 10 August because of the surge in demand.)[2]

Until 20 August 1994 Cuban exiles in the USA were allowed to transfer $1,200 a year (per family) to each household in Cuba in which they have relatives; $400 million to $500 million probably enters Cuba each year in this way. US law allows the spending of up to $100 a day by those permitted to visit Cuba (Phil Gunson, *The Guardian*, 17 March 1994, p. 14). The dollars are converted into pesos at a special rate determined by the Cuban government, currently 25 pesos to the dollar instead of the official one peso (*The Economist*, 24 July 1993, p. 52). About one-fifth of Cubans receive such monies from Miami (*The Economist*, 9 October 1993, p. 80). There are some 1.1 million Cuban-Americans, of whom about 700,000 live in south Florida (*The Economist*, 16 July 1994, p. 46). Remittances from abroad amounted to $300 million in 1992 (Michael Reid, *The Guardian*, 21 July 1993, p. 9). Cubans abroad send home about $400 million a year in cash and goods (Stephen Fidler, *FT*, 29 April 1994, p. 18). *IHT* (22 August 1994, p. 1) put the sum transferred at $500 million to $600 million a year. The cash value of past remittances is estimated to have been between $250 million and $400 million annually (Pastor and Zimbalist 1995: 709).

Other reforms have also been in the air. Prior to the hard currency reform, in a 23 July 1993 speech, Castro declared that 'We have serious problems and we have to solve them to survive. There are two different sets of things: the things we have to do to perfect socialism and the things we have to do for the revolution to survive' (reported by Douglas Farah, *IHT*, 26 July 1993, p. 1). Carlos Lage said that future possible changes included expansion of the private sector (such as small retail shops) and the reopening of the free farmers' markets. A decree actually followed on 8 September 1993. More than 100 occupations in the trades, crafts and services sectors were opened up to legal *individual* private enterprises (self-employed people, i.e. non-relatives cannot be employed), such as those of taxi drivers, mechanics, plumbers, carpenters, painters, hairdressers, shoemakers, cooks, domestics, craftsmen, farm produce salesmen and computer programmers (those still not on the list include enterprise directors and university graduates, especially doctors and teachers). (Douglas Farah puts the number of occupations at about 140: *IHT*, 17 February 1994, p. 3; *The Guardian*, 9 February 1994, p. 12.) 'Direct sales to the population of goods and services produced by these people will be permitted' and prices can be negotiated between buyer and seller. But there would be state licensing and monitoring, a monthly flat-rate fee would be charged (because of the difficulties of administering a progressive tax system) and state authorities would decide whether a state employee could resign and go into business. An ambiguity in the September 1993 law has allowed flourishing though formally illegal 'home restaurants' (*paladares* or 'palates'): the law legalized the sale of 'light foods (drinks, sandwiches, candies, *etcetera*'). The 'etcetera' has now been removed, but 'light foods' are still allowed (Douglas Farah, *IHT*, 17 February 1994, p. 3). Phil Davison (*The Independent*, 29 June 1994, p. 12) reported that in the previous few weeks almost all the private restaurants ('tastebuds') had been closed down. As soon as self-employment was authorized private eateries sprang up all over the country. But the government moved in quickly to eliminate them, arguing that they were not consistent with the provisions of the law (Perez-Lopez 1995a: 12–13). The government ordered the shutting down of private restaurants in December 1993. Where there are abuses or clearly excessive profits in self-employment activities prices may be regulated by the state. In October 1993 eighteen new categories were added to the list of occupations deemed suitable for self-employment (Perez-Lopez 1995b: 142).

On 13 June 1995 nineteen new activities were added to the list of trades and services that can be legally practised by self-employed individuals. The *paladares* were legalized, albeit on condition of the payment of hefty licensing fees, the observance of strict regulations (such as those related to hygiene) and a ban on the employment of people outside the family. 'The government had until now been turning a blind eye to the dozens of private restaurants, known as *paladares* after a word borrowed from a popular Brazilian television soap opera [a food processing company], which had sprung up in homes and back yards in Havana and other cities . . . Street vendors of food products and individuals who prepare food for sale directly to homes were required to pay a lower fee than the home restaurants' (Pascal Fletcher, *FT*, 15 June 1995, p. 4).

On 1 July 1995 new rules were issued allowing certain kinds of public employees (teachers, doctors and engineers) to earn extra income privately in 140 categories of work (though they are still unable to practise their professions privately) (*IHT*, 3 July 1995, p. 3).

Entrepreneurs get round the ban on hiring any other person by forming 'co-operatives' which charge workers a fee for using the owner's capital equipment (Pastor and Zimbalist 1995: 717).

In his 26 July 1993 speech Castro said that 'we are ready to do everything necessary to save the country, the revolution and the triumphs of socialism; that is to say, we will be neither dogmatic nor mad'. Cubans could not expect 'miracles'. There were no 'magic formulas', but encouragement would be given to tourism (including a relaxation of the restrictions on overseas Cubans visiting their relatives) and foreign investment.

On 4 August 1993 new ministers are appointed for agriculture, sugar, communications and finance.

David Adams (*The Times*, 6 November 1993, p. 14) reports the sending of students abroad to study capitalist business techniques. In addition the economics course at the University of Havana had recently been adapted to include classes on capitalism.

Stephen Fidler (*FT*, 29 April 1994, p. 18) argues that 'so far, the reforms have done little more than legitimize already rampant black market activity . . . the National Assembly may agree to the closure of some state enterprises – 69 per cent of which lost money last year, according to the government, and many of which have ceased production.'

On 26 October 1994 it was announced that consumer goods produced by individual craftsmen or by state enterprises in excess of state targets could be sold direct to the public at market prices through authorized outlets. Tax would be levied.

In December 1994 the government announced plans to allow non-agricultural retail sales at deregulated prices, after state quotas have been met, and with important restrictions. Perhaps the most significant aspect is the ability of state enterprises to sell unused raw materials (Pastor and Zimbalist 1995: 709).

The special session of the National Assembly, 1–2 May 1994

A number of issues were discussed:

1. Details of a law against black-market activity were published on 5 May 1994. The authorities would be allowed to seize goods and income from people who 'increase their means without legitimate cause, disproportionately with their legal income'. Illicit means were listed as 'robbery, speculation, diversion of resources belonging to state bodies, participation in shady business, activities in the black market and other forms of enrichment that harm the vital interests of society'. The state would have powers to confiscate as a cautionary measure after an initial investigation. The confiscation could be annulled if the accused could prove that the goods had been obtained legitimately. (According to Gillian Walker, most Cubans eat on the black market at least once a week. Official figures estimate that more

than 30 per cent of all food and goods are bought that way. There was a crackdown on illegal traders in April: *The Guardian*, 9 May 1994, p. 12. A law against 'improper enrichment' went into effect in May 1994. The law granted the government sweeping powers to confiscate the cash, goods and other assets of individuals found guilty of profiteering and it provided for retrospective application of sanctions: Perez-Lopez 1995a: 13.)

2. The possible introduction of a convertible peso alongside the old one. (In December 1994 the convertible peso was introduced to replace gradually the dollar and other foreign currencies. Valued at par with the dollar, the convertible peso would eventually be used in tourism and at the 'dollar outlets' authorized in mid-1993. Bonus payments made to workers in certain key industries that generate hard currency, such as tourism, tobacco and oil extraction, were to be paid in convertible pesos rather than in foreign currencies: Perez-Lopez 1995a: 14.)

3. Austerity measures were outlined: (1) income tax to apply to a far greater number of people; (2) increases in the prices of goods and services, such as transport, water, the post, telephoning, food, medicines, alcohol, cigarettes, petrol and sporting and cultural events.

Cuba was to impose taxes on property and income at the start of 1995. Taxes were to be levied first on the self-employed and on Cubans with earnings from foreign sources. The legislation, passed by the National Assembly, included provision for taxes on salaried workers when the economy improved. The legislation also imposed taxes on a range of property and on some services. The rates were to be announced within three months. The government announced a 50 per cent cut in the armed forces' budget (Canute James, *FT*, 9 August 1994, p. 6).

In August 1994 the National Assembly approved a new tax code, to be implemented gradually from the beginning of 1995. The new tax system would be expanded to tax enterprise income, including that of joint ventures with foreign investors, as well as enterprise assets. Also included were taxes on personal income, though the application of this provision has been deferred. Subsidies to the public and to enterprises have been slashed (Perez-Lopez 1995a: 13).

On 23 May 1994 the government announced that sharp increases in the prices of certain goods and services would come into force on 1 June, e.g. cigarettes 566 per cent), cigars, alcohol (rum 300 per cent and beer 100 per cent), petrol (270 per cent), electricity (122 per cent), postal and telephone services and non-urban transport. On 8 July 1994 Cuba announced the introduction of modest (but ideologically painful) charges for state-provided services, e.g. school meals, sports events, museums and art galleries. A vitamin supplement also attracted a charge. Living allowances for students in higher education were to be replaced by a loan system, although good students were to be excused paying back part or even the whole of the loan (Noll Scott, *The Guardian*, 9 July 1994, p. 14).

The monetary overhang is probably approaching 100 per cent of domestic output, aggravated by a state deficit of the order of 30 per cent of estimated GDP (Pastor and Zimbalist 1995: 708). The budget deficit was slashed in 1994 (Perez-Lopez 1995a: 12; p. 13 cites an actual figure of 7.3 per cent of GDP). In 1993 it was 33 per cent (*FT*, 26 September 1995, p. iii).

Manpower

David Adams (*The Times*, 27 December 1993, p. 9) maintains that many employees have been sent home on 40 per cent of their salaries. If they have not found a job within three months, they are told to take agricultural jobs or lose their benefits.

According to *The Economist* (4 December 1993, p. 98), laid-off workers are paid 40–60 per cent of their salaries, but only for three months. They are then told to find a job in the countryside.

New regulations covering the treatment of unemployed workers came into effect in September 1994. Workers made redundant should be assigned to other available jobs or to strategic social or economic tasks. If no job can be found immediately, workers have the right to receive one month's full pay and 60 per cent thereafter (a trade union official stated that the salary guarantee could extend 'for long periods') (Pascal Fischer, *FT*, 9 May 1995, p. 4).

Those made redundant receive 60 per cent of pay for several months depending on how long they have worked (Douglas Farah, *IHT*, 24 May 1995, p. 1).

The government has begun streamlining state enterprises, eliminating some and merging others (Pushpinder Khaneka, *The Independent*, 3 May 1994, p. 14). Nearly 70 per cent of state enterprises lose money (Canute James, *FT*, 4 May 1994, p. 6).

Foreign trade

Zimbalist (1993b: 162–3) argues that 'Cuba's economy, especially its foreign sector, has been transformed over the past three years. Some 500 enterprises are self-financing in their foreign trade and are unencumbered by most central rules and regulations. Dozens of trading companies, some domestic and some foreign, have sprung up.' From 1987 to 1989 imports as a share of GDP averaged more than 35 per cent (p. 152). Imports from the former Comecon countries fell by more than 90 per cent between 1989 and 1992 (p. 152). By 1992 the value of total trade turnover between Cuba and the former Soviet bloc countries had fallen to only 7 per cent (approximately) of the 1989 level (p. 152). Oil imports from the Soviet Union decreased from 13.3 million tonnes in 1989 to 1.8 million tonnes in 1992 (and 1.8 million tonnes in 1993: *The Times*, 3 September 1994, p. 12). Overall the value of imports fell from $8.1 billion in 1989 to less than $3 billion in 1992 (p. 154). (Of the 13 million tonnes of oil formerly imported, 11.5 million tonnes were consumed and the rest exported to Western markets: Canute James, *FT*, 15 December 1993, p. 28.)

Jose Rodriguez (*Cuba Business*, 7 September 1993, vol. 7, no. 7, pp. 4–5) provides the following information. In 1989 83.1 per cent of Cuba's trade was with the socialist countries (65–70 per cent with the Soviet Union alone), 9.9 per cent with developed capitalist countries and 7.0 per cent with developing countries. In 1990 Cuban imports from Eastern Europe fell by 26 per cent; trade as a whole with Eastern Europe fell to very low levels in 1991 and in 1992 practically vanished. In 1990 imports from the Soviet Union fell by 11 per cent (they were 29 per cent below commitments); trade as a whole declined by 11.5 per cent. In late December 1993 Cuba and Russia signed a trade and economic co-operation agreement. Russia would exchange oil for unrefined sugar. The official Russian estimate is that Cuba's debt to Russia amounts to more than $20 billion (*CDSP*, 1993, vol. XLV, no. 52, pp. 18–19). Russia agreed to supply 2,500,000 tonnes of oil in exchange for 1,050,000 tonnes of sugar. But on 1 November 1994 Russia announced that oil deliveries (after 1.5 million tonnes had been sent) were being suspended because Cuba had delivered only 500,000 tonnes of sugar. The Russian and Ukrainian sugar beet harvests have been so poor that both countries have resumed oil deliveries in an attempt to revive the 'sugar for oil' barter trade (*Transition*, 3 March 1995, vol. 6, no. 3, p. 13).

On 4 June 1993 Cuba announced the suspension of sugar exports for forty-five days. This followed an earlier estimate of the worst sugar harvest since 1959, of only 4.2 million tonnes (although an assurance was then given that the oil-for-sugar agreement with Russia would be honoured). In 1992 sugar accounted for around 65 per cent of hard currency export earnings (Simon Tisdall, *The Guardian*, 9 August 1993, p. 16). In 1993 sugar accounted for around 40 per cent of export earnings (Pascal Fletcher, *FT*, 27 September 1994, p. 5). Exports of sugar and sugar products averaged 77 per cent of total exports over the period 1984–89 (Pastor and Zimbalist 1995: 706).

In his 26 July 1993 speech Castro forecast that imports in 1993 would be only $1.7 billion, compared with $2.2 billion in 1992 and $8.1 billion in 1991 (Damian Fraser, *FT*, 28 July 1993, p. 4). According to an official estimate, exports fell from $8.1 billion in 1989 to $1.7 billion in 1993 (Stephen Fidler, *FT*, 3 June 1994, p. 7). Before 1990 the former Soviet Union and Eastern Europe accounted for $7 billion a year in Cuban imports, 85 per cent of the total. In 1992 Cuba bought fewer than $1 billion worth of goods from them, less than half its imports (Juanita Darling, *The Guardian*, 12 August 1993, p. 11).

On 25 July 1993 the US administration announced its decision to permit US telephone companies to share their future revenues with Cuba (although earlier revenues, accumulated since the embargo was imposed and amounting to $80 million, were to remain in an escrow account in New York). The move was in response to the re-routing of calls to Cuba via Canada.

The US Treasury Department estimates that in 1991 foreign subsidiaries of US companies conducted more than $700 million of trade with Cuba. The volume of trade has fallen significantly since then because of the Cuban Democracy Act of October 1992, which widened the ban on unlicensed trading with Cuba to foreign subsidiaries (Dean Baquet, *IHT*, 28 December 1993, p. 13).

In 1993 crude oil and oil products made up 44 per cent of Cuba's imports (in value terms), compared with 32 per cent in 1989. This sharp increase in the share of oil in (shrinking) imports meant that purchases of consumer goods, raw materials and machinery had to be cut back (Perez-Lopez 1995a: 11).

Foreign aid

Zimbalist (1993a: 50) is very critical of the CIA estimate that in 1983 Soviet aid to Cuba amounted to $4.1 billion and that, of that total, $2.8 billion (or 68.3 per cent) originated in sugar subsidies.

On 24 April 1993 a 'flotilla of mercy' set sail from Key West (Florida) for Cuba carrying privately donated humanitarian aid in the form of food and medicines (to be distributed by Church organizations). Both the US and Cuban governments approved.

On 8 July 1993 Russia agreed to provide Cuba with a $350 million credit. It was to be used to continue the construction of projects begun with Soviet assistance. These projects, mainly connected with Cuba's export potential, include nickel, sugar and oil refining. A separate line in the agreement earmarked $30 million for mothballing the nuclear power plant (work on which had been suspended on 5 September 1992). The intention was to continue with the construction of the plant some time in the future with capital investments from third countries (*CDSP*, 1993, vol. XLV, no. 27, p. 23). Within the past few weeks Russia has agreed to provide credits to complete the nuclear power station (Phil Gunson, *IHT*, 2 November 1994, p. 12).

In June 1994 Canada resumed its humanitarian and economic development aid after a sixteen-year interval; projects would be funded via private companies and non-governmental organizations (Phil Davison, *The Independent*, 27 June 1994, p. 23).

Foreign investment

Foreign investment over the past two years has surpassed $500 million. More than 100 joint ventures are now in operation and they are allowed to contract independently with local producers (Zimbalist 1993b: 163).

Jorge Dominguez is quoted as saying that total direct foreign investment probably amounts to less than $1 billion (Rosie Hayes and Stephen Fidler, *FT*, 3 December 1993, p. 6).

There are 120 joint ventures in Cuba (Douglas Farah, *The Guardian*, 9 February 1994, p. 12).

Official figures show that as of November 1994 there were 165 joint ventures with partners from thirty-five countries, mostly in tourism. By the end of 1994 these joint ventures had attracted $1.5 billion in foreign capital (the figure probably includes pledged as well as realized investment) (Perez-Lopez 1995a: 12).

The Cuban government reported that as of June 1994 there were 140 joint ventures, but hard data on investment levels are scarce (Pastor and Zimbalist 1995: 708). There are now more than 150 joint ventures, comprising over $1.5 billion in value (p. 714).

Official figures indicate that more than $1.5 billion has been invested in over 200 joint ventures (John Carvel, *The Guardian*, 26 May 1995, p. 15).

Cuban officials give an accumulated total of $2.1 billion for foreign investment, but it is not clear whether these are funds actually disbursed rather than simply committed (Pascal Fletcher, *FT*, 18 July 1995, p. 4).

The Cuban central bank plans to allow foreign banks to set up branches in partnership with the Cuban government (Damian Fraser, *FT*, 17 July 1993, p. 3).

In the summer of 1993 the first Western mining company signed an exploration agreement with the Cuban mining agency Geominera (Bernard Simon, *FT*, 17 November 1993, p. 44).

The decision to open up mineral resources to foreign exploration and investment has led to a scramble by Western mining companies. Minerals include nickel, cobalt, gold, silver, copper and zinc. A letter of intent with an Australian company envisages giving it a 65 per cent stake, thus exceeding the 49 per cent usually conceded to foreign investors. A new mining code was approved by the National Assembly on 21 December 1994, establishing the state's right of ownership over subsoil, mines and mineral resources, and regulating the granting of concessions (Pascal Fletcher, *FT*, 5 January 1995, p. 25).

In mid-June 1994 Grupo Domos of Mexico announced that it would take a 49 per cent share in Cuba's telephone monopoly Emtel-Cuba, with the aim of modernizing telecommunications. The deal included an element of debt–equity swap.

On 30 October 1994 it was announced that more sectors would be opened up to foreign investment, including sugar, real estate and services.

A new foreign investment law was approved by the National Assembly on 5 September 1995. Among the clauses were the following: (1) all sectors would be open to foreign investment except defence, health and education (although all investment proposals would continue to be examined on a case-by-case basis and foreign investors would still have to hire workers from state employment agencies, except in unspecified 'exceptional cases'); (2) Cuban exiles would be eligible to invest; (3) free-trade and export manufacturing zones would be set up enjoying concessions in areas such as customs, tax and manpower; (4) 100 per cent foreign-owned companies would be allowed (Pascal Fletcher, *FT*, 27 July 1995, p. 4; 5 September 1995, p. 7; Stephen Fidler and Pascal Fletcher, *FT*, 7 September 1995, p. 4). The law offers guarantees similar to those in other countries for transfers of capital and compensation for expropriation. It allows investors to own housing, offices and other buildings, although it does not address the question of land ownership. The Cuban government says that 212 foreign-Cuban associations have already invested more than $2 billion in tourism, mining, transportation and other sectors, some under majority ownership (Mireya Navarro, *IHT*, 8 September 1995, p. 11). The new law allows foreigners to take out long leases on the land their enterprises stand on. Apart from 'exceptional cases' foreigners will continue to hire through a state employment agency, paying the agency in dollars. The agency will continue to pass the pay on in pesos, but the practice of 'a second, under-the-table dollar wage paid direct' will no doubt survive (*The Economist*, 9 September 1995, p. 63).[3]

Agriculture

Some details of the role of sugar in the economy are given by Pollitt and Hagelberg (1994). Cuba's share of world output fell from 12 per cent in the late 1950s to under 8 per cent in the late 1980s, but Cuba remained the world's largest sugar exporter. In 1989 sugar accounted for roughly three-quarters of all merchandise exports, while sugar cane growing and processing contributed 10 per cent of global social product (p. 547). In 1959 nearly 60 per cent of sugar exports went to the USA at a quota premium 80 per cent over the world market price (p. 564).

According to Castro (interviewed by Jas Gowronski in *The Guardian*, 21 December 1993, p. 11), some private farmers own as much as 110 acres.

Zimbalist (1993a: 48) reports the following. In 1977 the National Association of Small Farmers (representing the private sector) endorsed the gradual transformation of the private sector into production co-operatives formed by individual farmers voluntarily pooling their land and equipment and electing their own management. Each co-operative is run collectively as an autonomous enterprise within the constraints set by the economic plan; it receives low-interest credit and preferential access to materials. By 1987 there were 68,000 co-operative members on some 1,400 co-operative farms, accounting for roughly 63 per cent of private land holdings. In 1980 23 per cent of the labour force was employed in agriculture (p. 53).

Reliable data on the distribution of farmland were not available until the 1987 census. In that year 74.3 per cent of agricultural land was owned by the state. The remaining 25.7 per cent was split as follows: production co-operatives, 11.4 percentage points; peasants belonging to Credit and Service Co-operatives, 10.9 percentage points; non-organized individuals, 3.4 percentage points (Deere *et al.* 1995: 214).

In (mid) September 1993 agricultural workers on state farms were allowed to form private co-operatives, subject to three limitations: (1) only the state has title to the land; (2) no one can work by himself or herself, i.e. workers must join a co-operative; (3) all commercial output must still be sold to the Ministry of Agriculture (Jorge Dominguez, *FT*, 26 January 1994, p. 21).

According to Douglas Farah (*IHT*, 7 February 1994, p. 6), most state farms have been turned over to semi-autonomous co-operatives. They are self-financed and workers are given financial rewards for exceeding work quotas. The co-operatives can also dismiss inefficient workers and lay off surplus labour.

Co-operative members have their own bank accounts and elect their own management (Perez-Lopez 1995a: 13). The party decreed the break-up of state farms and the creation of 'basic units of co-operative production'. The latter were to operate as production co-operatives within each state farm, with wage workers becoming co-operative members whose earnings would be connected with the profitability of their units. Some land could be set aside to meet own consumption needs (Perez-Lopez 1995b: 139). The reforms 'have been instituted expeditiously' (p. 144).

Deere *et al.* (1994) analyse in depth the decentralizing reforms affecting state farms since 1990:

1. The Technical, Organization and Payment System according to Final Production Results was first developed in 1990 and gradually extended. Within the planned system work teams were made directly accountable for all aspects of production in a given area and were paid by results (p. 202).

2. Between January 1992 and September 1993 state enterprises were divided into 'large farms', which, in turn, were subdivided into smaller units (p. 3).

3. During 1992 state farms began allowing workers (usually groups but also individuals) to cultivate parcels of unused state farm land for their own provisioning (pp. 11–12). (An aspect of the 'special period in a time of peace' has been increased emphasis on 'self-provisioning' of foodstuffs within state farms: p. 208.)

4. In September 1993 the Council of Ministers announced approval of the formation of production co-operatives ('basic units of co-operative production') on state farms. Collectives of workers are leased (rent-free) state farmland in permanent usufruct and given autonomy over management. The state enterprise continues to plan the 'primary line of production' for

each (financially independent) co-operative. The co-operative's production, outside of what it produces for 'self-provisioning', can be sold only to the state (procurement contracts are signed with the state marketing agency). The worker collectives elect their own management. There is flexibility in terms of the size of unit. Taxes will be paid to the state (p. 206). Transformation was achieved quickly in sugar cane production (by December 1993–January 1994). But generally 'our expectation is that the conversion of state enterprises to truly co-operative structures will be quite slow and uneven' (p. 207).

Deere *et al.* (1994: 231) conclude that: 'The relatively high incomes that many CPA [agricultural production co-operative] members earn are indicative of the higher profitability and, hence, productivity of Cuba's production co-operatives as compared to the state farms. Given the drastic shortfall in inputs resulting from the abrupt drop in imports from the former socialist trading bloc after 1989, the Cuban leadership had no alternative but to attempt to emulate, on the state farms, the incentive system governing the private production co-operatives.'

On 17 September 1994 it was announced that as of 1 October all producers (licensed and subject to tax) of agricultural produce (except sugar producers) would be able to sell on the open market at freely determined prices. Farmers would still be required to meet state delivery quotas before such sales. According to Pascal Fletcher (*FT*, 19 September 1994, p. 7), senior Cuban officials said that over seventy markets were already operating experimentally.

The government said that state farms would, in 1995, receive only 40 per cent of their subsidies and would be expected to be self-financing in 1996 (Pastor and Zimbalist 1995: 717).

Economic performance

The collapse of communism, especially the demise of the Soviet Union, left Cuba in dire straits, although some sectors have fared better than others and the government claimed that the economy as a whole grew by 0.7 per cent in 1994 (see Table 28.1).

Rationing is now pervasive. The state even offers a service whereby people can be hired to stand in a queue to pick up a family's weekly rations (Gary Prevost, *The World Today*, August–September 1993, p. 142). *The Economist* (24 April 1993, p. 74) cites a Cuban study: of 415 items defined as essential for domestic production, 226 were not available in 1992 and the availability of the others varied between 5 per cent and 26 per cent of the 1980s levels.

A report published in November 1992 by the Cuban-American National Foundation (right-wing Cuban exiles in the USA) said that Cuba's GNP had fallen to 37 per cent of the average level of 1986–89; the report,

Table 28.1 Cuba: selected economic indicators

Economic indicator	*1989*	*1990*	*1991*	*1992*	*1993*	*1994*
Rate of growth of GDP (%)	0.1	−3.1	−25.0	−14.0	−20.0	0.7
Sugar output (million tonnes)	7.3	8.1	7.7	7.0	4.2	3.3
Oil output (tonnes)			550,000	882,000	1,106,000	1,280,000
Nickel and cobalt output (tonnes)	46,591				30,200	26,772
Hard currency debt ($ billion)	6.2	7.0	8.4	10.0	10.8	9.1

Sources: Pastor and Zimbalist (1995: 708); Zimbalist (1993b: 152, 164); Pollitt and Hagelberg (1994: 565–6); Perez-Lopex (1995a: 11–14); various issues of *The Economist* and *The Financial Times*

allegedly based on a Cuban government report, forecast complete economic collapse by July 1993 (*IHT*, 1 April 1993, p. 2).

Between 1989 and 1992 national income fell by about 45 per cent (Zimbalist 1993b: 154). Since 1989 the economy is reckoned to have shrunk by about half (Damian Fraser, *FT*, 23 July 1993, p. 3). According to Cuban government figures, GDP has fallen by 75 per cent since 1989 and industry is operating at only 25 per cent of its capacity (Tom Rhodes and David Adams, *The Times*, 3 September 1994, p. 12). The period 1989–93 saw an estimated 50.2 per cent shrinkage in GDP (Pastor and Zimbalist 1995: 707). Figures provided by the Ministry of the Economy and Planning and the National Statistics Office show GDP growth of +0.7 per cent in 1989, −2.9 per cent in 1990, −10.7 per cent in 1991, −11.6 per cent in 1992, −14.9 per cent in 1993 and +0.7 per cent in 1994 (in 1994 the percentage change on 1989 was −34.3 per cent) (Pascal Fletcher, *FT*, 18 July 1995, p. 4). In a speech delivered on 26 July 1995 Castro claimed that the economy had grown by 2 per cent in the first half of 1995 (Pascal Fletcher, *FT*, 28 July 1995, p. 3).

'In the early 1990s, half of Cuba's formal economy disappeared, according to the Cuban government's own statistics. Export earnings fell by about 60 per cent between 1989 and 1992, while imports fell by about 70 per cent in the same period' (Jorge Dominguez, *FT*, 26 January 1994, p. 21).

In 1993 the US State Department published a report entitled *Transition in Cuba: New Challenges for US Policy*, under the direction of Lisandro Perez. Jorge Dominguez forecast 'a prolonged, slow decline' as Cuba awaited 'a catastrophe' (cited by Hugh Davies, *The Daily Telegraph*, 1 December 1993, p. 10). 'The most optimistic conclusions set the date for an appreciably more liberal, more democratic and more prosperous Cuba no sooner than the beginning of the millennium' (cited by Howard French, *IHT*, 22 November 1993, p. 3).

Douglas Farah (*IHT*, 7 February 1994, p. 1) painted a more optimistic picture: 'a series of once unthinkable high-risk reforms, coupled with favourable world prices for key commodities, are improving Cuba's devastated economy . . . world oil prices have dropped sharply and the price of sugar . . . has climbed . . . Although no one is predicting a rapid revival, and the economy . . . is still far from healthy, Cuban leaders . . . say that the economic free-fall has ended.'

The president of the Economic Commission of Cuba's National Assembly estimated that the economy had shrunk by 30–35 per cent since the collapse of the Soviet Union. He forecast modest growth in 1995 (Stephen Fidler, *FT*, 3 June 1994, p. 7).

Perez-Lopez points out that official information on the Cuban economy is virtually non-existent. The latest published statistical yearbook dates back to 1989, but in October 1994 a local weekly magazine published selected official statistics for the period 1988–93 (Perez-Lopez 1995a: 11). GDP in 1993 was only a little more than half that produced in 1989, merchandise exports and imports were 69 per cent and 75 per cent lower respectively, and the budget deficit almost tripled (amounting to nearly 50 per cent of GDP in 1993) (p. 11). Carlos Lage (vice-president of the Council of State) claimed in late January 1995 that the economy grew by 0.7 per cent in 1994, but 'considering the poor sugar harvest and the lacklustre performance of other sectors, it can be assumed that the Cuban economy in 1994 experienced negative growth' (p. 12). In 1993–94 up to 80 per cent of Cuba's factories stood idle, owing to lack of fuel, raw materials, machinery and spare parts (p. 11). Nevertheless, 1993–94 saw modest improvement in some key sectors of the economy, such as tourism, agriculture and oil production (p. 11). In 1993 oil production exceeded the 1 million tonne mark for the first time, although domestically produced oil still accounts for less than 20 per cent of total oil consumption (p. 11). The free-fall of the economy that began in the early 1990s seems to have been arrested by the fourth quarter of 1993, but the 'modest improvements in the economy in late 1993 and early 1994 . . . probably reflect mostly favourable changes in world prices for sugar and crude oil . . . and some small increases in revenue from tourism' (Perez-Lopez 1995b: 146–7).

Between the end of 1991 and the end of April 1993 nearly 26,000 cases had been reported (43,412 by the end of May and around 50,000 by the end of August) of a mystery illness affecting the nervous system (blurred eyesight, with 70 per cent loss of eyesight in the worst cases, weight loss and muscle problems; no deaths were recorded and only 1,300 cases have shown any signs of retaining any permanent disability). Various causes were suggested (including a virus and food poisoning exacerbated by vitamin deficiency due to poor diet), but even international specialists were baffled. By September it was reported that the disease (identified as 'neuropathy') was under control (*IHT*, 11 September 1993, p. 2). Edward Luce (*The Guardian*, 30 September 1993, p. 13) and *IHT* (30 September 1993, p. 2) report the World Health Organization's praise of the Cuban medical system for bringing the outbreak of the eye disease (optic neuritis) to a rapid end through such means as education and a massive vitamin distribution programme (in addition the disease was confined to the twenty-five to sixty-five age bracket because of the provision of free milk and other essential nutrients to the young and old): 'After careful research we have come to the conclusion that the disease was probably caused by the effects of some sort of household toxin combined with poor nutrition levels. It was clear, however, that no virus or other microbe had been responsible.'

NOTES

1. On 6 October 1995 President Clinton announced an easing of travel restrictions for Cuban Americans and for Americans engaged in educational, religious and human rights work. US news organizations would be permitted to establish bureaux in Cuba and vice versa.
2. In mid-October 1995 eight official exchange kiosks began operating, allowing citizens to buy and sell foreign currencies on the open market. The kiosks offer about the same exchange rate as the black marketeers (Larry Rohter, *IHT*, 10 November 1995, p. 7).
3. Three free-trade zones are proposed. Under the foreign investment law taxes on corporate profits will be 30 per cent, although this may be waived 'in cases of national interest'. Companies will continue to pay an 11 per cent payroll tax and a social security contribution of 14 per cent on top of employee salaries. Many foreign companies make top-up salary payments in hard currency, ostensibly to cover expenses. Hirings will continue to be made through a Cuban state intermediary, although the intermediary may be the Cuban partner in the project (Stephen Fidler, *FT*, Survey, 26 September 1995, p. ii). While the government has opened up the sugar industry to foreign financing and is known to be seeking foreign capital and technology to help refine raw sugar, it is not offering ownership shares in mills or cane plantations (Pascal Fletcher, *FT*, Survey, 26 September 1995, p. vi).

29

MONGOLIA

BACKGROUND

Mongolia is half the size of India, but sparsely populated (Milne *et al.* 1991: 2). It has a homogeneous population, with around 95 per cent Mongol-speaking. It is rich in mineral resources.

The urban population increased from 44 per cent of the total in 1969 to 58 per cent in 1990 (Milne *et al.* 1991: 2). The urban population is 60 per cent, and 25 per cent of the total population lives in the capital (Asian Development Bank 1992: xiii, 121–2).

The population was 2.18 million in 1992 (EIU, *Country Report*, 1993, First Quarter, p. 5).

The literacy rate is 97 per cent. The death rate fell from 22 per thousand in 1940 to 8.4 per thousand in 1989 (Denizer and Gelb 1992: 5).

There are various estimates of *per capita* income: $658 in 1988 (official Mongolian estimate); $552 in 1989 (IMF); less than $240 (Asian Development Bank in a mid-1991 survey); $440 in 1991 (Michael Kaser, *Economics of Transition*, 1994, vol. 2, no. 2, pp. 266–7). *Per capita* real NMP (at 1986 prices) declined to perhaps less than $200 in 1991 (Asian Development Bank 1992: 91). In 1989 GDP *per capita* was $522 (Milne *et al.* 1991: 2).

Agriculture's contribution to employment has decreased over time: 61 per cent in 1960; 47 per cent in 1970; 40 per cent in 1980; 29 per cent in 1990; 26.2 per cent in 1991 (industry, 21.1 per cent) (Asian Development Bank 1992: xiii, 28, 121–2).

POLITICAL DEVELOPMENTS

In the general election of June 1992 the National and Social Democrats received only five seats between them (they now have six) in the seventy-six-seat Great Hural, despite having won some 40 per cent of the vote. The ruling Mongolian People's Revolutionary Party's 'inclination [is] to monopolize the political scene' (Alan Sanders, *The World Today*, June 1994, vol. 50, no. 6, p. 105).

The MPRP won 93 per cent of the parliamentary seats with only 56 per cent of the popular vote (Ginsburg 1995: 467). 'Mongolia's reform path has been remarkably peaceful when compared with its former patron to the north or the ethnically diverse nations of Central Asia' (p. 471). Ginsburg attributes the MPRP's success to a number of factors:

1. 'Among the population, the close identification of the MPRP with the successful anti-Chinese nationalist movement of the 1920s is critical for understanding its survival today' (pp. 460–1).

2. The importance of personal contacts combined with the party's extensive network in the countryside (p. 470).

3. Pragmatism as regards policy. 'Throughout the transition the MPRP has not launched a serious challenge to an economic reform agenda largely dictated by international donors and the political opposition . . . it has also served as a kind of umbrella for a wide spectrum of political views' (pp. 470–1).

A new opposition party was formed on 25–26 October 1992 under the leadership of Davaadorjiyn Ganbold. The Mongolian National Democratic Party was the result of a merger between the Mongolian Democratic Party (the leading party in the Democratic Coalition), the National Progress Party, the Mongolian Renewal Party and the Mongolian United Party. The Social Democratic Party remained a separate party. (Note that five smaller parties which did not do well in the 1992 general election formed the 'Third Force' alliance. The Coalition of Four Associations has also been formed.)

In January 1993 a new treaty was signed with Russia, which excluded the mutual military assistance clause of the previous (1966) treaty (Tsedendambyn Batbayar, *Asian Survey*, 1994, vol. XXXIV, no. 1, p. 44).

6 June 1993. The presidential election (92.7 per cent turnout) was won by the incumbent Punsalmaagiyn Ochirbat although as the candidate of the opposition National Democratic Party and the Social Democratic Party. (The MPRP did not adopt him as their candidate because of the president's increasingly independent stance, e.g. in July 1992 Ochirbat called for a coalition government and more recently the Constitutional Court upheld his view that the fixing of tax rates was the prerogative of the Great Hural and not of the government: Alan Sanders, *The World Today*, May 1993, p. 84.) Ochirbat attracted 57.8 per cent of the vote, while the MPRP candidate, Lodongiyn Tudev (editor of the party newspaper), attracted only 38.7 per cent.

18 June 1993. Ochirbat is sworn in as the first democratically elected president of Mongolia. He expresses a strong commitment to democracy and a market-orientated economy, his priorities being the strengthening of public order, social protection for the most vulnerable groups affected by the transition and the speeding up of privatization and other elements of the reform package (Tsendendambyn Batbayar, *Asian Survey*, 1994, vol. XXXIV, no. 1, p. 43).

April 1994. A hunger strike in Ulan Bator lasting twelve days is organized by the Mongolian Democratic Union. At its peak forty-one strikers demanded the resignation of the Jasrai government and the dissolution of parliament on the grounds of bribery, corruption and general incompetence. Sheldon Severinghaus (*Asian Survey*, 1995, vol. XXXV, no. 1, pp. 70–1) believes the root of the strike is to be found in the 1992 parliamentary election, in which opposition forces, despite winning around 40 per cent of the vote, were essentially denied any meaningful outlet in parliament because of the small number of seats they won. But the strike ended peacefully through negotiation and compromise. President Ochirbat and the heads of the three political parties represented in parliament agreed that: (1) the electoral law would be revised so that the results of the next general election (1996) would more accurately reflect the will of the people; (2) the drafting of a law to create independent media free of government control and interference; (3) measures would be taken to combat corruption (note that a banking scandal surfaced in September 1994: p. 73). Severinghaus argues that the power of the Mongolian People's Revolutionary Party is being modestly checked by three factors: (1) the elected president through his veto power, his right to initiate legislation and his role as ombudsman; (2) the Constitutional Court; and (3) the immature but committed and growing group of non-governmental organizations.

THE ECONOMY

The transition to the market

The State Planning Commission was abolished in September 1990 and a two-tier banking system was approved in August 1990 (Milne *et al.* 1991: 10, 30).

By October 1992 the Mongolbank had raised its interest rate to 160–214 per cent (i.e. positive in real terms); the central bank exercises direct regulatory authority, such as the establishment of minimum interest rates on time deposits and quantitative ceilings on access to its overdraft facility (Tsedendambyn Batbayar, *Asian Survey*, 1994, vol. XXXIV, no. 1, p. 43).

Despite progress on the privatization front, Mongolia had not created a market economy by 1993. The economy was becoming increasingly dollarized as people lost confidence in the tugrik (Pomfret 1993: 5). Interest rates were raised after September 1992 (p. 6). During the second half of 1992 economic reform appeared to be in danger of running out of steam, but it was about to gather speed again (p. 7). Monetary policy will be helped by tax reforms introduced in January 1993, which are moving the government's revenue base away from a turnover tax and towards profit and sales taxes (p. 9). In 1993 further budget cuts were decided upon (p. 7).

Denizer and Gelb (1992: 13–15) pointed to a slowing of the economic reform programme and an increase in administrative controls in the period July 1991–February 1992 (due to factors such as the drying up of Soviet aid and the collapse of foreign trade) and a pick-up in the pace of reforms after February 1992.

The EIU (*Country Report*, 1993, no. 1, p. 30) detects a lukewarm attitude towards economic reform, due largely to a wish to avoid the associated political costs. The government's priorities are food production, exports and the infrastructure.

Boone (1994: 330–2) detects a lack of consensus about the speed and direction of reform, e.g. the central government is divided into several factions. This results in varying speeds of and inconsistency in the reform process.

A bankruptcy law was passed in 1992 (Denizer and Gelb 1992: 7). EIU (*Country Report*, 1993, Fourth Quarter, p. 37) reported that a sheepskin tannery had ceased production in July 1993, the first state enterprise to go bankrupt.

Prices

In 1987 the government freed the prices of customer services from state control. Until 16 January 1991 only the retail prices of customer services and some luxury goods (such as furniture, fine leather and coats) covering some 20 per cent of total sales were liberalized. In the aftermath of the 16 January 1991 decree retail prices covering 50 per cent of food sales and 70 per cent of sales of other items, comprising more than 60 per cent of total sales, were liberalized. Some thirty-five groups of articles were still subject to fixed retail prices (e.g. coal, meat, flour, bread, milk and eggs), although these were increased by about 100 per cent on average. All wholesale prices were freed except for thirty items, such as petroleum products, power generation, steel, copper, wheat, livestock, water, electricity and heat (these thirty items comprised about 40 per cent of gross social product). There followed further gradual price liberalization. In October 1991 the number of commodities with fixed prices was reduced to seventeen. Beginning in March 1992 the prices of most commodities were freed, with the exception of items like fuel and rice (Asian Development Bank 1992: 81, 85).

By the end of 1991 the prices of goods remaining subject to government intervention were estimated to account for only 20 per cent of all prices, covering meat, milk, flour, eggs, children's clothing, coal and public utilities such as electricity and water (Milne *et al.* 1991: 30).

Denizer and Gelb (1992: 9) reported the introduction of consumer rationing in January 1991. Half the rationed items, including sugar, rice and flour, involved imports. Meat rations covered about one-third of previous consumption levels.

Tsedendambyn Batbayar (*Asian Survey*, 1993, vol. XXXIII, no. 1, pp. 63–4) reported that by March 1992 the prices of 90 per cent of all commodities and services had been freed. In late September 1992 the government freed the prices of flour, bread, meat, domestic electricity, public transport and livestock feed, thus completing price liberalization.

But the EIU (*Country Report*, 1993, no. 1, p. 35) argues that reports indicating the lifting of price controls on all items except heating, water and sewerage are somewhat misleading. A range of basic foodstuffs, including rationed goods, are still subject to controls of some sort, although the government did allow price rises on 1 October 1992 and 1 January 1993 (e.g. domestic electricity and bus and air fares).

The government's approach to price reform has been conservative. 'They equate administered increases in prices to price liberalization' (Pomfret 1993: 6). The government was reluctant to abandon rationing, but by spring 1993 only flour and meat remained on the ration list. Utility prices, rents and bus services continued to be subject to controls, leaving their prices well below costs (p. 6).

Oil and gas prices were raised by almost 30 per cent in October 1994, the first time in sixteen months (Sheldon Severinghaus, *Asian Survey*, 1995, vol. XXXV, no. 1, p. 73).

Privatization

The privatization programme announced in 1991 (effective 1 July) aimed to privatize 344 large enterprises and 1,601 small enterprises by the end of 1992. Each citizen was entitled to three red vouchers (tradable on secondary markets) and one blue one (non-tradable). Red vouchers, with a face value of 1,000 tugriks, were for the privatization of small enterprises and agricultural assets (except land and livestock). The total book value of small assets was 9.4 billion tugriks. Blue vouchers, with a face value of 7,000 tugriks, were for the privatization of the 344 large enterprises with a book value of 10.8 billion tugriks. Small assets were to be privatized at auctions, but workers employed in the small enterprises had the first right to acquire them at a value determined by the Privatization Commission. By the beginning of February 1992 around 80 per cent of all small enterprises were in private hands. Large enterprises were also to be privatized by voucher auction after having their plans approved by the Privatization Commission. Ten per cent of their shares would be granted to employees. Investment funds would not be able to control more than 20 per cent of the shares of a given enterprise. Foreigners would be able to buy shares only when secondary trading began (Denizer and Gelb 1992: 9–13).

Approximately 85 per cent of the assets of small shops and enterprises were sold to insiders (i.e. their employees) (Boone 1994: 350). The auctions for large enterprises began in early 1992 (p. 350). All small retail shops and enterprises have been sold for vouchers and by March 1993 250 large enterprises (i.e. 60 per cent) had been converted to joint stock companies and sold for vouchers. Around 83 per cent of livestock is now privately owned. The aim was to complete the privatization programme by the end of 1993. A survey of the first 105 privatized enterprises found that 43 per cent of shares were held by employees and relatives of employees (p. 351).

The 1991 companies Act laid down that state and co-operative enterprises were to convert to joint stock companies in that year. On average around 65 per cent of the assets of large enterprises were eventually to be privatized. The industrial sector comprises mainly state enterprises and several large joint ventures with former Comecon countries. The private sector is only now developing and, although large in number (with some 4,200 enterprises), it is quite small in terms of employment (about 8.6 per cent). The emerging private sector is concentrated in retail trade and in small manufacturing and handicraft activities (Asian Development Bank 1992: 60, 83, 111).

In July 1992 the prime minister said that 60 per cent of total livestock, 40 per cent of state enterprises and almost 100 per cent of retail trade and services had been privatized. (The centralized distribution and state procurement systems for agricultural products had been dismantled.) In the first half of 1992 the private sector produced 4.8 per cent of total industrial output (Tsedendambyn Batbayar, *Asian Survey*, 1993, vol. XXXIII, no. 1, p. 63).

Prime Minister Puntsagiyn Jasray has claimed that as of July 1993 privatization was 90 per cent complete in trade and services and 80 per cent in livestock farming. Individual herdsmen owned 27 per cent (and townspeople 19 per cent) of Mongolia's 18 million head of privately owned livestock (54 per cent of so-called 'privately owned' livestock belonged to companies and co-operatives, which are the old herding co-operatives) (FEER, *Asia 1994 Yearbook*, 1994, p. 173).

Large privatization under the law of May 1991 was proceeding at a slower pace than planned. Around 70 per cent of livestock was in private hands by January 1993, with the remainder the property of co-operatives or joint stock companies. A new law on land would allow citizens to buy or lease agricultural plots. Housing would be sold in three ways, namely to existing tenants under a voucher system, for cash or by extended payment (EIU, *Country Report*, 1993, First Quarter, p. 34). The EIU (*Country Report*, 1993, Second Quarter, p. 39) reports the announcement in April 1993 that 73.5 per cent of state properties earmarked for transfer were in private hands (over 4,000 small enterprises and 600 large ones) and the hoped-for completion date of the process was August 1993. The private sector now accounts for around 60 per cent of industrial output (EIU, *Country Report*, 1993, Third Quarter, p. 40).

The initial intention was to complete the privatization of large enterprises by September 1992 (a schedule that was not met). The State Privatization

Commission estimated that 92 per cent of state enterprises (65 per cent by value) would be privatized (although there are lower estimates). By May 1993 267 enterprises had been privatized, employing 74,925 people. By the spring of 1993 over half the assets of large enterprises had been covered by the share sales. Almost all trade, food and other service enterprises had been privatized by the summer of 1993. Over 70 per cent of livestock has been transferred to private ownership. New developments in 1993 were the decisions to privatize 170 incomplete construction projects and to begin the privatization of housing accommodation. In 1992 the private sector accounted for about half national income (Pomfret 1993: 5).

Kaser (*Economics of Transition*, 1994, vol. 2, no. 2, pp. 266–7) cites Murrell's estimates that by the end of 1993 nearly 80 per cent of state enterprises had been sold off and that 67 per cent of all privatized enterprises ended up wholly owned by 'insiders' (managers, employees, pensioners and their families – children born by 31 May 1991 qualified). The share of foreign ownership in the total reached only 8 per cent.

Korsun and Murrell ascribe the rapidity of the privatization process to the fact that: 'The overwhelming proportion of privatization has simply resulted in the transfer of ownership to those already inside the organizations being privatized . . . Paradoxically, the privatization process might have achieved one of the primary objectives of its designers, speed, precisely because it did not achieve another of its goals, the creation of outside ownership' (Korsun and Murrell 1995: 486).

Employees were given preferential rights to obtain shares in both small and large enterprises (pp. 477–8). From mid-1991 to mid-1992 both agricultural privatization and small privatization in the trade and service sectors were virtually completed. When worker buy-outs in small enterprises began in Ulan Bator there were significant discounts for workers. An attempt was made to moderate the discounts, but 'Ultimately valuation procedures were redesigned to yield valuations equal to estimates of a heavily discounted auction price' (p. 485). The beginning of large privatization was delayed until early 1992, but by mid-1993 it was nearly three-quarters complete (p. 478). Throughout 1994 the pace of large privatization slowed. But 'this was not only a reflection of the government's preferences; the major task was over, since virtually all of the industrial, service and trade sectors were now private. The large enterprises remaining under state control were in the utility, mining and transportation sectors' (p. 484). Employees and their families have invested their vouchers predominantly in their own enterprises. Mutual funds garnered only 2 per cent of shares (p. 484).

Lee (1993: 630–1) argues that: 'In addition to the absence of price liberalization, the monetary and labour market institutions appropriate to a market economy had not yet been developed. The privatized commercial banks were controlled by state enterprises which pre-empted credit disbursements, hence crowding-out borrowing by the private sector . . . Administered wage scales from the central planning system still applied in state enterprises . . . There was little evidence of enterprise restructuring and related steps to improve economic efficiency . . . the industrial structure which had developed under central planning was highly concentrated . . . It is not surprising, therefore, that the change in ownership was not accompanied by changes in the management and control of privatized enterprises.'

Much-delayed trading on the stock exchange was due to begin by spring 1995. 'Since privatization scarcely altered management practices, most of the country's enterprises still lose money' (Teresa Poole, *The Independent*, 12 January 1995, p. 13).[1]

Foreign trade

Mandatory state orders for exports were eliminated in 1992 (Denizer and Gelb 1992: 7).

Foreign exchange earnings on a substantial part of exports still had to be surrendered to the state at the official exchange rate (Lee 1993: 630).

Most export licences were abolished in January 1993, but a clause in the decree permits the imposition of quantitative export restrictions through border controls (Boone 1994: 349).

On 28 May 1993 the tugrik was allowed to float on the new Interbank Currency Exchange (EIU, *Country Report*, 1993, Third Quarter, p. 41).

At first the government maintained a dual exchange rate system. Enterprises were required to turn over a percentage of their foreign currency earnings to the state at the official exchange rate (the percentage varied according to the activity, with a maximum of 90 per cent). The surrender requirements were supported by strict regulation of exports. Administrators appear to have used the threat of withholding licences to ensure that exporters fulfilled state orders at domestic prices. There was a large devaluation of the tugrik at the start of 1993; in May the exchange rate was unified and the tugrik was allowed to float (Pomfret 1993: 6–7).

Russia is still the most important trading partner, accounting for 56 per cent of Mongolia's exports (the Soviet Union, 78.3 per cent in 1990) and 52 per cent of imports (the Soviet Union, 77.5 per cent in 1990). China now accounts for 18 per cent of Mongolia's imports (compared with 2.4 per cent in 1990) but the figure for exports is much lower (EIU, *Country Report*, 1993, no. 1, pp. 5, 36–7). China has become Mongolia's second largest trading partner; in the first half of 1993 China accounted for 25.7 per cent of exports and 20.7 per cent of imports (Tsendendambyn Batbayar, *Asian Survey*, 1994, vol. XXXIV, no. 1, p. 45). In 1992 China accounted for 14.5 per cent of trade, compared with only 1.3 per cent in 1990 (Boone 1994: 349).

By 1991 imports had fallen to one-third of their 1989 level (Lee 1993: 625). In the period 1989–91 exports fell by 56 per cent and imports by 75 per cent (Denizer and Gelb 1992: 13). In the past two years the volume of trade between Russia and Mongolia has been cut in half, while fuel consumption in Mongolia is only 40 per cent of the 1989 level (*CDSP*, 17 February 1993, vol. XLV, no. 3, p. 17).

In 1992 trade between Mongolia and Russia fell by 57 per cent; China accounted for 12 per cent of trade and Japan 9 per cent (FEER, *Asia 1994 Yearbook*, 1994, p. 175).

Exports and imports fell by more than half between 1990 and 1993 (*The Economist*, 26 November 1994, p. 89).

Foreign aid

By the late 1980s Soviet aid was equivalent to 25–30 per cent of GDP (Lee 1993: 624).

Large-scale financial assistance was provided by the Soviet Union and the other Comecon countries from the mid-1950s; in the period 1985–90 grants and loans averaged 30 per cent of GDP a year (Denizer and Gelb 1992: 3, 13). But Soviet financial assistance to cover the budget deficit halved in 1988–90, a loss equivalent to 15 per cent of Mongolia's GDP (p. 6). At the beginning of 1991 Soviet financial assistance totally dried up (p. 13).

According to Boone (1994: 330), the Soviet Union cut financial assistance to Mongolia by an amount equal to 46 per cent of Mongolian GDP, from 53 per cent of GDP in 1989 to 7 per cent of GDP in 1991.

In 1989–90 Soviet aid amounting to a third of GDP was abruptly withdrawn (Teresa Poole, *The Independent*, 12 January 1995, p. 13).

The international donors held a further round of consultations on 14–15 October 1992 on the $320 billion aid package pledged in May 1992. Concern had been expressed at Mongolia's lack of success in meeting the conditions laid down and in August 1992 the IMF (Mongolia became a member on 14 February 1991) withheld some of its aid (EIU, *Country Report*, 1993, First Quarter, p. 36).

The June 1992 agreement with Russia allowed for the postponement of Mongolia's 1991–95 debt repayments until the year 2000 on an interest-free basis (Tsedendambyn Batbayar, *Asian Survey*, 1993, vol. XXXIII, no. 1, p. 64).

In 1992 aid totalled $220 million (Lynne O'Donnell, *FT*, 8 July 1993, p. 36).

The Mongolia Assistance Group Conference met in Tokyo on 13–14 September 1993, and aid pledges of $150 million to $170 million were made (compared with $155 million in 1991 and $320 million in 1992) (EIU, *Country Report*, 1993, Fourth Quarter, p. 40).

According to FEER (*Asia 1994 Yearbook*, 1994, p. 174), the donors agreed $150 million and Japan had earlier issued a separate loan of $20 million. Total international pledges for 1993 stood at $356.7 million in financial aid and $414.9 million in project aid and technical assistance. Disbursement of part of a $35 million stand-by credit from the IMF was halted in August 1992 because of the failure to limit the budget deficit. But a satisfied IMF granted an 'enhanced structural facility' worth $30 million in April 1993 and that opened the way to World Bank and Asian Development Bank loans which had also been withheld.

At the meeting in Tokyo held on 8–9 November 1994 donor countries pledged $210 million for the next twelve months (*The Economist*, 26 November 1994, p. 92).

Foreign investment

The March 1990 Foreign Investment Law contained provisions, subject to negotiations, for a maximum ceiling of 40 per cent on income tax and a three-year tax holiday. But the results were disappointing, only about two or three dozen small joint ventures with firms from China, Hong Kong and Japan (focusing on the restaurant and tourist industries) being established (Asian Development Bank 1992: 75).

A new law was passed in May 1993. There are no tax or any other concessions in the mining of precious metals, but most minerals and oil and gas carry a five-year tax holiday followed by a further five years at half the normal tax rate (Lynne O'Donnell, *FT*, 8 July 1993, p. 36).

The Law on Foreign Investment came into force on 1 July 1993. Investors in power, transport and telecommunications are offered a ten-year tax-free period and an additional five years at half the normal tax rate. Investors in mining and metallurgy (excluding precious metals) need pay no tax for five years. Any joint venture exporting more than half its output will enjoy a three-year exemption and a further three years of tax at 50 per cent of the normal rate. Imported equipment is exempt from customs duty and sales tax for five years. Land may be leased to foreign companies for a period of sixty years with a forty-year extension (EIU, *Country Report*, 1993, Third Quarter, p. 45).

A new set of laws was to take effect in April 1995 allowing private citizens to own land and foreigners to lease it (*Transition*, January–February 1995, p. 22). A new mining law was passed in January 1995, permitting full foreign ownership of mining ventures, including those involving precious metals. No longer are gold producers forced to sell to the Mongolian central bank at prices below the prevailing international price (Kenneth Gooding, *FT*, 16 June 1995, p. 31).

The only flourishing joint ventures are small service-sector ventures (Pomfret 1993: 4).

By mid-1993 more than 100 joint ventures had been registered, with partners coming from twenty countries (Tsedendambyn Batbayar, *Asian Survey*, 1994, vol. XXXIV, no. 1, p. 44).

Agriculture

In 1989 the limit on private ownership of livestock was increased by twenty-five per household (Asian Development Bank 1992: 82). Restrictions on the private ownership of herds were eliminated altogether in 1990 (Denizer and Gelb 1992: 7).

As mentioned above, Batbayar reports the gradual dismantling of the centralized distribution and state procurement systems for agricultural products by July 1992 (*Asian Survey*, 1993, vol. XXXIII, no. 1, p. 63). Prior to this the government had reduced the number and output coverage of targeted goods, especially meat, so that production in excess of state orders could be sold freely at higher prices (Asian Development Bank 1992: 84). In January 1991 farm-gate prices for products such as skins, wool and butter were raised. State orders were reduced to cover only 50 per cent of meat output, 80 per cent of wool and 10 per cent of hides. Farm-gate prices on goods to meet state orders remained subject to control, although production in excess of these orders could be sold at freely negotiated prices (Milne *et al.* 1991: 13). The procurement price for grain in September 1992 was 4.2 tugriks per kilo (compared with a free-market producer price of 25–30 tugriks) and for mutton 36 tugriks per kilo (compared with 80–100 tugriks). Even the privatized food-processing enterprises (such as abattoirs and bakeries) and retail shops were still expected to sell part of their output at controlled prices in order to implement the rationing system (Lee 1993: 628).

According to Boone (1994: 349), state procurement of meat and other products fell sharply in 1991 and 1992. In 1993 obligatory state orders were abolished and the Ministry of Agriculture began paying market prices for agricultural products. Each co-operative and state farm was permitted to choose its own method of privatization. Early reports suggest that co-operatives are breaking up into smaller family groups similar to the structure of the 1950s. The state farms have been maintained as large holding companies, with 51 per cent share ownership by the government. Around 83 per cent of livestock is now privately owned (p. 351).

Private ownership of (small areas of) urban land had been allowed in the 1990 constitutional amendment. Partial private ownership of agricultural land is provided for in the new constitution of 1992, although the Land Law has yet to be passed (Asian Development Bank 1992: 84, 181).

A new set of laws was to take effect in April 1995 allowing private citizens to own land and foreigners to lease it (*Transition*, April 1995, p. 22).

Land privatization remains the most controversial element of the programme, despite the fact that most land is pasture and barred from privatization by the constitution. Therefore the most ambitious reformers envisage privatizing only land in urban areas (0.3 per cent of the land mass) in the first phase and arable land (an additional 2–3 per cent of the land mass) in the second phase. After many attempts a land law was passed in late 1994, but it explicitly defers consideration of the mechanism for effective ownership transfer to later legislation. The current law explicitly prohibits foreign ownership (Korsun and Murrell 1995: 485). Co-operatives were given control over their own privatization (p. 477). In some cases members voted to break the co-operatives up into smaller units or to become completely independent (p. 482). The private share of livestock increased from 32 per cent in 1990 to 80 per cent by 1993 (p. 481).

According to EIU (*Country Report*, 1993, Fourth Quarter, p. 38), all arable farming is now in the private sector.

A third of camels have been butchered since privatization began, with animals distributed indiscriminately to those who know nothing about livestock as well as to those who are skilled herders (*FT*, 16 February 1995, p. 21).

Economic performance

Mongolia had a rough time after the collapse of communism, especially with the demise of the Soviet Union (see Table 29.1). But inflation fell to 70 per cent by the end of 1994 and preliminary figures suggest that the economy actually grew in 1994 (Teresa Poole, *The Independent*, 12 January 1995, p. 13). Inflation was reduced from an annual high of 320 per cent in 1992 to an expected 70 per cent in 1994. GDP was expected to show growth of 2.5 per cent in 1994 after four consecutive years of negative growth, while a trade surplus of $85.9 million was registered for the first eight months of 1994 (Sheldon Severinghaus, *Asian Survey*, 1995, vol. XXXV, no. 1, p. 72).

In November 1994 the UN's Food and Agriculture Organization said that Mongolia needed exceptional food assistance (food rationing, in operation since 1991, was ended in August 1993). The cumulative loss in national income in the period 1989–93 was 20 per cent and real consumption per person fell by a third. According to official figures, a quarter of the population now lives below the poverty line (*The Economist*, 26 November 1994, pp. 89, 92).

There are a number of estimates of unemployment:

1. By early 1992 urban unemployment was 20 per cent (Denizer and Gelb 1992: 28).

2. In January 1993 the unemployment rate was 10 per cent (EIU, *Country Report*, 1993, Second Quarter, p. 40).

3. The unemployment rate was 6 per cent at the end of 1990 and 11 per cent in mid-1991 (Asian Development Bank 1992: 7).

Table 29.1 Mongolia: selected economic indicators

Economic indicator	*1990*	*1991*	*1992*	*1993*	*1994*
Rate of growth of GDP (%)	−2.0	−9.9	−7.6	−1.3	2.5
Rate of growth of industrial output (%)	−1.9	−13.2	−13.1	−5.5	
Rate of growth of agricultural output (%)	−0.8	−5.1	−3.9	−7.0	
Inflation rate (%)	−0.5	20.2	202.6	268.4	87.6
Foreign debt ($ billion)	0.125	0.236	0.342	0.386	
Foreign debt (transferable roubles, billion)	10.4	10.6			
Budget surplus or deficit (% GDP)	−14.0	−10.5	−9.9		−5.0
Current account ($ billion)	−0.644	0.076	−0.120		

Sources: United Nations, *Economic Survey of Asia and the Pacific*; IMF, *World Economic Outlook*, May 1993, pp. 59, 146; FEER, *Asia Yearbook 1994*, pp. 174–5; Economist Intelligence Unit (various reports); Asian Development Bank (1992: xiv, 75, 226); Lee (1993: 626); Sheldon Severinghaus (*Asian Survey*, 1995, vol. XXXV, no. 1, p. 72); *Transition* (January–February 1995, p. 22)

4. In January 1992 the unemployment rate was 6.1 per cent (Lee 1993: 628).

5. Unemployment is now 8.5 per cent (*The Economist*, 26 November 1994, p. 89).

6. Unemployment has almost doubled since 1991 (Sheldon Severinghaus, *Asian Survey*, 1995, vol. XXXV, no. 1, p. 72).

Aid agencies estimate that 25 per cent of Mongolians live below the poverty line (Peter Hannam, *FEER*, 9 December 1993, p. 67).

One in four of the population lives below the poverty line (Alan Sanders, *The World Today*, June 1994, vol. 50, no. 6, p. 104).

According to a study sponsored by the United Nations Development Programme, about 25 per cent of the population live below the poverty line (Sheldon Severinghaus, *Asian Survey*, 1995, vol. XXXV, no. 1, p. 72).

NOTE

1. The stock exchange began public trading on 28 August 1995 (*Transition*, 1995, vol. 6, nos 9–10, p. 21).

30

NORTH KOREA

THE POLITICAL BACKGROUND

Demographic aspects

In 1980 only 15 per cent of the population (compared with 41 per cent in South Korea) were allowed to reside in urban areas. Those permitted to pursue higher education or to live in the cities are the elite of society (Sungwoo Kim, *Asian Survey*, 1993, vol. XXXIII, no. 9, p. 864).

Ten million or so Koreans are separated from their relatives as a result of the Korean War (*The Economist*, 25 June 1994, p. 69).

Farmers account for barely a quarter of the civilian work force, compared with 44.4 per cent in 1960 (EIU, *Country Profile*, 1993–94, p. 59).

Military aspects

The armed forces number 1,132,000 in North Korea and 633,000 in South Korea (*The Economist*, 3 April 1993, p. 74). In 1992 the armed forces numbered 1.1 million in North Korea and 633,000 in South Korea (plus 36,500 from the USA) (*The Economist*, 28 May 1994, p. 24). The North Korean armed forces number 1,111,000 with a civilian militia of perhaps 5 million (EIU, *Country Profile*, 1993–94, p. 50).

The North Korean armed forces number 1,127,000, compared with South Korea's 633,000 (plus 35,500 from the USA) (*The Times*, 17 June 1994, p. 12).

The armed forces of North Korea number about a million, while those of South Korea number 750,000 (plus 37,000 from the USA) (*IHT*, 27 January 1995, p. 6).

The North Korean armed forces are the fifth largest in the world after China, Russia, the USA and India (*The Independent*, 17 March 1993, p. 17).

There are various estimates of the proportion of national income spent on defence: a third (*The Economist*, 3 April 1993, p. 74); as much as 30 per cent (5 per cent in South Korea) (John Burton, *FT*, 18 March 1993, p. 4); 30 per cent (Kevin Rafferty, *The Guardian*, 18 June 1994, p. 14); 24 per cent in

1991 (the official figure was 12 per cent) (Sungwoo Kim, *Asian Survey*, 1993, vol. XXXIII, no. 9, p. 877); more than 20 per cent (Andrew Mack, *IHT*, 3 June 1994, p. 6). In 1993 North Korea's military spending was 8.9 per cent of GDP, compared with 3.8 per cent for South Korea (*The Economist*, Survey of South Korea, 3 June 1995, p. 9).

Defence spending as a proportion of the budget was planned to be 12.6 per cent in 1993 compared with 11.4 per cent in 1992 (EIU, *Country Report*, 1993, Second Quarter, p. 36).

Political developments

12 March 1993. North Korea withdraws from the Nuclear Non-proliferation Treaty (NNPT). Formally the withdrawal is not effective until three months have elapsed, i.e. until 12 June. Treaty signatories with nuclear power plants are required come to an agreement (instantly ended if a country so desires) to permit inspectors from the International Atomic Energy Agency (IAEA; set up in 1957) to ensure that nuclear fuel is not diverted to military purposes.

North Korea may have begun its nuclear programme in the mid-1960s after the 1962 Cuban missile crisis (President Nixon's visit to China in 1972 was also influential). According to *The Economist* (9 April 1994, pp. 75–6), both Koreas began to try to build a bomb in the early 1970s. Pressure from the USA deterred South Korea, while China stopped all nuclear co-operation with North Korea in 1987. North Korea did not join the NNPT until 1985. The safeguard agreements, authorizing inspections by the IAEA, were, however, signed only in 1992 (see main text). A number of inspections followed, but North Korea refused special inspections by the IAEA to check two nuclear waste sites (at Yongbyon, sixty-two miles north of Pyongyang); the agency suspected that plutonium (derived from spent fuel rods) was being produced in quantities far greater than those admitted to by North Korea (perhaps sufficient to allow North Korea to produce nuclear weapons; whether such weapons have actually been produced is the source of considerable disagreement).

15 March 1993. North Korea says that war could break out 'at any time' and the country is put on a 'semi-war' footing (done in the name of Kim Jong Il, seemingly as a way of boosting his standing with the armed forces). Foreigners are forbidden to enter the country and restrictions are increased on those already there.

The new South Korean government of Kim Young Sam puts prospective future investment in North Korea on hold.

18 March 1993. The IAEA gives North Korea until 31 March to allow inspections.

23 March 1993. China opposes sanctions and even taking North Korea to the UN Security Council. (The 1961 China–North Korea treaty of friendship and mutual assistance obliges the other to offer immediate military and other assistance if one country is attacked. There is no obligation to assist if either country is the aggressor in a war.)

24 March 1993. The end is announced of the 'semi-war' footing.

1 April 1993. The IAEA refers the case to the UN Security Council.

9 April 1993. Kim Jong Il becomes chairman of the National Defence Committee (he was made supreme commander of the army on 25 December 1991).

11 May 1993. A UN Security Council resolution urges North Korea to open the two sites to inspection and reconsider its decision to withdraw from the NNPT. The UN would consider further action if necessary.

4 June 1993. North Korea orders all foreigners (except accredited diplomats) to leave the country by 15 June. The issuing of visas is to be suspended until the end of July.

11 June 1993. After talks with the USA, North Korea decides to 'suspend' its withdrawal from the NNPT.

19 July 1993. North Korea announces that consultations are to resume with the IAEA over inspections.

3 August 1993. Officials from the IAEA resume inspections in North Korea (but it turns out that they are not allowed to visit the two disputed sites).

24 August 1993. A North Korean army defector reports an attempted coup by Moscow-educated military leaders in 1992; ten generals were executed (in late 1992) when the coup failed (*FEER*, 9 September 1993, p. 16; Kevin Rafferty. *The Guardian*, 25 August 1993, p. 11).

Mid-September 1993. Kim Il Sung, in remarks to a visiting legislative delegation from China, praises China's 'tremendous success' in reform and opening up to the outside world (John Merrill, *Asian Survey*, 1994, vol. XXXIV, no. 1, p. 14).

9 December 1993. A communiqué issued by the Central Committee publicly acknowledges North Korea's economic difficulties: 'the internal and external situation remains grim and complex.' Reference is made to 'the grave situation and grim trials during the Third Seven Year Plan period [1987–93]', when industrial output grew at an average annual rate of growth of 5.6 per cent compared with a target of 10 per cent (electric power, steel and synthetic fibres in particular experienced difficulties). North Korea has had to 'divert a large proportion of the economy to national defence'. A period of economic adjustment lasting up to three years is needed, when priority will be given to agriculture, light industry and exports.

Personnel changes are also announced. Kim Il Sung's younger brother, Kim Yong Ju (aged seventy-one), is rehabilitated by being appointed to the politburo (he disappeared from view in 1975, having been deputy prime minister until then and a possible successor to Kim Il Sung). (The day before Kim Dal Hyon, the chairman of the State Planning Commission, had been dismissed.) Kim Yong Ju was made one of the four vice-presidents on 12 December (the other is Kim Pyong Sik).

24–26 December 1993. UN Secretary-General Boutros Boutros-Ghali visits North Korea.

1 January 1994. In his New Year's address Kim Il Sung called for an overhaul of the economy and suggested that North Korea would have to change dramatically in order to develop foreign markets (*IHT*, 3 January 1994, p. 5). The 1994–96 period was to be one of adjustment to implement 'agriculture-first, light industry-first and foreign trade-first policies' (cited by Samuel Kim, *Asian Survey*, 1995, vol. XXXV, no. 1, p. 25).

15 February 1994. North Korea accepts IAEA inspection of the seven *declared* nuclear facilities (i.e. not including 'special inspection' of the two suspected nuclear waste dumps).

Late February 1994. There are rumours that ten military officers have been executed for plotting against the North Korean regime.

1–15 March 1994. IAEA personnel are not allowed to carry out full inspections even of the seven declared facilities.

21 March 1994. President Clinton announces that patriot anti-missile batteries are to be sent to South Korea.

24 March 1994. The IAEA reports to the UN Security Council.

31 March 1994. A weakly phrased UN Security Council resolution (with no threat of sanctions) gains China's approval. The resolution is critical of the North Koreans for 'not allowing IAEA inspectors . . . to conduct indispensable inspection activities at their seven declared nuclear sites'. North Korea is urged to allow IAEA personnel to complete their inspections within six weeks of the date of their recent return. The council would 'consider further Security Council action if necessary'.

14 May 1994. North Korea announces that it has started withdrawing spent fuel rods from a nuclear reactor (no IAEA inspectors are present).

17 May 1994. IAEA inspectors arrive (they resumed their inspection the following day).

20 May 1994. The IAEA announces that although North Korea was in breach of the NNPT, no spent nuclear fuel has been diverted since 14 May (note that North Korea allowed observation only of the withdrawal and not of the testing).

22 May 1994. North Korea agrees to receive an IAEA mission when the USA decides to resume high-level talks with North Korea.

27 May 1994. The IAEA declares the mission a failure, since it is not possible to examine the fuel rods (the inspectors flew home two days later).

30 May 1994. The UN Security Council urges North Korea to allow examination of the fuel rods.

8 June 1994. North Korea offers to allow inspections if the USA agrees to a third round of talks. (Note that by then the withdrawal of fuel rods had probably been completed.)

10 June 1994. The IAEA withdraws technical aid. In retaliation, North Korea says that it is no longer able to guarantee continuity of nuclear safeguards and will ask the two remaining IAEA inspectors to leave. (North Korea has repeatedly said that economic sanctions would constitute an 'act of war'.)

13 June 1994. North Korea says it will withdraw from the IAEA and will no longer allow inspectors into the country.

16 June 1994. Former US president Jimmy Carter visits North Korea and says that 'President Kim Il Sung has committed himself to maintain the inspectors on site at the disputed nuclear reactor and also guarantees that surveillance equipment would stay in good operating order so long as good-faith efforts are being made jointly by the USA and North Korea to resolve the entire nuclear problem.' (A short while before Selig Harrison reported that North Korea would be willing to freeze work on a new nuclear reactor and its fuel reprocessing plant in return for Western assistance in constructing light-water reactors for peaceful purposes; this sort of reactor produces less plutonium than the graphite-moderated type.)

17 June 1994. Ex-president Jimmy Carter says that the USA has 'stopped the sanctions activity in the United Nations' (the Clinton administration is upset by this presumption).

18 June 1994. During Carter's (four-day) visit Kim Il Sung offers to meet President Kim Young Sam of South Korea (who immediately accepted).

21 June 1994. North Korea grants a two-week extension to the visas of the two IAEA inspectors (the visas were due to run out at the end of June).

22 June 1994. The USA and North Korea agree that a third round of bilateral talks should begin (later fixed for 8 July; the first two were in June and July 1993). The USA is to suspend moves to impose sanctions. North Korea is to freeze its nuclear programme and allow inspectors.

28 June 1994. North Korea and South Korea begin talks about the proposed meeting of the two presidents (the first between presidents since the split). The negotiators agree that the venue should be Pyongyang on 25–27 July 1994.

8 July 1994. Kim Il Sung dies of a heart attack at the age of eighty-two (he was born on 15 April 1912).

The planned succession of Kim Jong Il (born 16 February 1942) represents the first 'dynastic' succession in socialist history. Kim Il Sung was prime minister 1948–72, president (1972–94) and general secretary of the Korean Workers' Party (formed in August 1946 when the Korean Communist Party united with the New Democratic Party; the party currently has 3 million members: *FEER*, 21 July 1994, p. 15). He was born Kim Song Ju and he adopted the name Kim Il Sung after a famous guerrilla who fought the Japanese ('Il Sung' means 'One Star').

9 July 1994. The talks with the USA (which began the day before) are suspended when the death of Kim Il Sung is officially announced.

11 July 1994. North Korea announces the postponement of the 25–27 July summit.

13 July 1994. Radio Pyongyang announces that 'Our Dear Leader and Comrade Kim Jong Il, the sole successor to our Great Leader, now holds the revered positions at the top of the party, the government and the revolutionary forces.'

16 July 1994. The funeral is delayed (from 17 July to 19 July).

19 July 1994. The funeral takes place (organized by Kim Jong Il). Radio Pyongyang refers to Kim Jong Il as 'the great leader of our party and our people who is national defence committee chairman and concurrently the supreme comander of the armed forces'.

20 July 1994. Senior military and government people pledge their support for Kim Jong Il at a memorial ceremony in Pyongyang.

21 July 1994. The USA and North Korea agree in principle to resume talks (the date is later fixed for 5 August).

(Note that after an initial respite in the usual 'war of words' following the announcement of the death of Kim Il Sung, relations between North Korea and South Korea were aggravated in a number of ways, e.g. South Korea sent no condolences, published documentary proof that Kim Il Sung had started the Korean War and arrested students who wanted to mourn publicly and/or take up North Korea's invitation to attend the funeral.)

27 July 1994. South Korea reveals a defector who claims to be the son-in-law of the prime minister of North Korea (Kang Song San). The defector says he was told that North Korea already has five nuclear bombs and intends to produce another five before openly declaring the country to be a nuclear power. (Kang Song San regained the premiership in 1993, after having been prime minister from 1984–86. He is considered to be broadly in favour of economic reform.)

28 July 1994. It is announced that Russians are to embalm Kim Il Sung's body.

5 August 1994. Talks with the USA resume.

12 August 1994. The USA and North Korea reach preliminary agreement. In return for a freeze in North Korea's nuclear programme, the USA is to move towards diplomatic relations, reduce barriers to trade and investment, and help arrange for the construction of light-water reactors (South Korea offers to provide the reactors 'if and when the North guarantees the transparency of its nuclear activities', while Japan is likely to help with the finance). Alternative energy supplies are to be provided until the new reactors come on stream. The details are to be discussed in talks to begin on 23 September.

17 August 1994. The USA and South Korea agree that the two undeclared North Korean sites must be inspected before the new reactors are provided.

22 August 1994. North Korea reiterates its refusal to allow special inspections of the two sites, but offers to help clear up 'nuclear suspicion'.

28 August 1994. North Korea rejects the idea of reactors from South Korea.

2 September 1994. China withdraws its delegate from the Military Armistice Commission. (The commission oversees the armistice proclaiming the end of the Korean War; the three original delegates were from China, North Korea and the UN command dominated by the USA. North Korea has boycotted the commission since 1991, when a South Korean officer was appointed by the UN, and withdrew its delegate in April 1994.)

10–13 September 1994. In talks with the USA (in Pyongyang and Berlin), North Korea agrees to allow two extra inspections (two minor sites previously off-limits to IAEA inspectors).

23 September 1994. Talks with the USA resume. (During the talks North Korea complains about a US naval exercise off the Korean peninsula.)

16 October 1994. Kim Jong Il makes his first public appearance at the end of the 100-day mourning period.

21 October 1994. The USA and North Korea formally sign an agreement on the latter's nuclear programme (the chief negotiators were Robert Gallucci for the USA and Kang Sok Ju for North Korea). There are to be three stages that give each side leverage against the other reneging:

1. At the end of the first stage (about five years), with construction of the first light-water reactor well under way but before key nuclear components have been supplied, North Korea will allow special inspections of the two nuclear waste sites.

2. As construction proceeds on the two light-water reactors North Korea will gradually ship its 8,000 spent fuel rods abroad for reprocessing (this will take about three years, so something like eight years will have elapsed before the last rods leave the country).

The source of the new reactors soon became a bone of contention. The USA argued that there was a clear understanding that South Korea would supply them, though based on US technology, since it would be bearing by far the largest share of the cost. But North Korea subsequently demanded that the new reactors should come from elsewhere (Russia was mentioned early on). Japan was to contribute the second largest share of the estimated $4 billion or so cost. In March 1995 a US-led consortium, the Korean Peninsula Energy Development Organization (Kedo), was set up to deal with the problem. Further tortuous negotiations between the USA and North Korea led to an announcement on 13 June 1995 that provisional agreement had been reached. The source of the reactors (still South Korea in reality) was disguised by the following statement: 'The reactor model, selected by Kedo, will be the advanced version of US-origin design and technology currently in production.' The programme was to be co-ordinated by a US company and North Korea's claim for an extra $1 billion for related facilities (such as power transmission lines) was to be the subject of further negotiations with Kedo.

3. As the second replacement reactor nears completion (after several more years) North Korea will dismantle all its facilities, including its old graphite reactors and the reprocessing plant. North Korea currently has a small reactor and two larger ones under construction. Interim alternative energy supplies in the form of oil will be provided. North Korea will also resume its dialogue with South Korea on the denuclearization of the peninsula.

(Note that in February 1995 the USA claimed that some of the fuel oil it had supplied had been diverted by North Korea to factory use rather than being used for 'heating and electricity production'. On 18 May 1995 the USA announced that the second shipment of oil, due in July, would not be undertaken unless arrangements were made to prevent any such diversion.)

The USA will begin to ease restrictions on trade and investment, and at some time diplomatic liaison offices will be opened in Pyongyang and Washington. The USA promised never to use nuclear weapons against North Korea. The 1994 'Team Spirit' military exercise between the USA and South Korea was cancelled.

31 October–4 November 1994. Prime Minister Li Peng of China visits South Korea. A number of economic deals are signed, e.g. a joint venture to build a civilian aircraft.

1 November 1994. North Korea announces that work has stopped on the construction of the two nuclear reactors and that the existing reactor has been shut down.

7 November 1994. President Kim Young Sam of South Korea says that South Korea intends gradually to ease restrictions on economic links with North Korea. These were later said to include: (1) direct trade and investment (although an individual investment project would initially be limited to $5 million); (2) permission for businessmen to visit North Korea for discussions, to undertake pilot projects and feasibility studies and to set up representative offices; (3) the management of North Korean enterprises; and (4) the sending of materials and equipment used for reprocessing in North Korea.

10 November 1994. There is a cool response from North Korea: 'co-operation and confrontation are incompatible'.

17 December 1994. A US helicopter strays into North Korean air space and is shot down. One of the two pilots is killed. North Korea says it was on a spying mission, but the USA blames navigational error.

22 December 1994. The pilot's body is returned.

North Korea announces that it is planning to allow commercial airliners from other countries to fly over its territory and land at its airports.

24 December 1994. The USA sends a formal letter of regret for the incident.

30 December 1994. The surviving pilot is returned (the USA expresses 'sincere regret' for the incident).

9 January 1995. It is announced that, as of mid-January, North Korea will lift restrictions on trade and financial transactions with the USA, remove the ban on port calls by US commercial vessels and open telecommunication services between the two countries. (Later in the month the USA announced a partial relaxation of its embargo, allowing telecommunication transactions, some banking and credit card activities and purchases of magnesite, a mineral used in steelmaking. In mid-February 1995 the first US investment mission went to North Korea: *IHT*, 13 February 1995, p. 9.)

16 February 1995. Kim Jong Il's (fifty-third) birthday is designated 'the greatest holiday of the nation'.

25 February 1995. Defence Minister Marshal O Jin U dies at the age of seventy-seven. He was generally considered to be the second-ranking official in the country.

16 March 1995. Four new members of the Central Military Commission are appointed.

28–29 April 1995. North Korea hosts an International Sports and Cultural Festival for Peace.

3 May 1995. North Korea announces that its lone north–south border crossing has been closed to cease-fire monitors and journalists: 'personnel and journalists of the US Army side and officials of the Neutral Nations Supervisory Commission are totally prohibited from coming over to the section on our side'.

To replace the armistice that ended the 1950–53 Korean War, North Korea wants direct peace negotiations with the USA that would exclude South Korea. On 28 February 1995 North Korea forcibly evicted the Polish delegation to the Neutral Nations Supervisory Commission, which monitors violations of the cease-fire. North Korea had earlier forced out the Czech delegation (refusing to accept it as a substitute for the Czechoslovak one), leaving no outside monitors on the northern side of the border. North Korea argues that Poland and the Czech Republic are no longer its allies (*IHT*, 4 May 1995, p. 4).

8 September 1995. Russia forwards a new draft treaty to replace the 1961 accord. The clause calling for Russia's automatic intervention in the event of war involving North Korea is not in the new draft (*IHT*, 9 September 1995, p. 5).

THE ECONOMY

Coal provides 70 per cent of energy consumption (EIU, *Country Report*, 1993, Second Quarter, p. 38) and 50 per cent of electricity (Sungwoo Kim, *Asian Survey*, vol. XXXIII, no. 9, p. 866).

National income

There are various estimates of *per capita* income in North Korea: $1,038 in 1991 ($6,498 in South Korea) (EIU, *Country Report*, 1992, no. 3, pp. 5, 35;

1993, First Quarter, pp. 5, 35); $1,064 in 1991 (*Asian Survey*, 1993, vol. XXXIII, no. p. 347); $904 in 1993 (Kevin Rafferty, *The Guardian*, 18 June 1994, p. 14). In 1993 GDP per head was $859 in North Korea and $8,479 in South Korea (*The Economist*, Survey on South Korea, 3 June 1995, p. 9).

There are various estimates of total national income in North Korea: $22.9 billion in 1991 ($280.8 billion in South Korea) (EIU, *Country Report*, 1992, no. 3, pp. 5, 35; 1993, First Quarter, pp. 5, 35); $23 billion in 1992 ($297 billion in South Korea) (*The Economist*, 28 May 1994, p. 24); $20.3 billion in 1993 (*The Times*, 11 June 1994, p. 14); $20.5 billion (John Burton, *FT*, 14 July 1994, p. 6).

Economic planning

A major theme of the Third Seven Year Plan (1987–93) was a revitalization of the economy through automation, computers and robots. An especially important target was electricity. Significant technical assistance was hoped for from the GDR, whose scientific and technological achievements North Korea had always sought to emulate (Sungwoo Kim, *Asian Survey*, 1993, vol. XXXIII, no. 9, pp. 865–6). As a partial remedy for the shortage of consumer goods, the regime introduced the 'Third of August People's Consumer Goods Programme'. This involves the use of local industrial wastes and by-products to produce consumer goods for local consumption. Its success is shown by the fact that more than 10 per cent of the country's total consumer needs are now supplied this way (p. 869).

Foreign trade

General aspects

In 1992 Kim Jong Il introduced the 'new economic regime'. It allowed provincial governments greater autonomy to conduct foreign trade and gave state enterprises greater freedom to set their own production priorities for export-orientated goods. This relatively unknown policy is said to have boosted border trade with China (two-way trade with China, ranked number one, amounted to $700 million in 1993) (Shim Jae Hoon, *FEER*, 4 August 1994, p. 50).

Trade accounts for 13 per cent of North Korea's GNP of $20.5 billion (John Burton, *FT*, 14 July 1994, p. 6).

North Korea depends on imported oil for 10 per cent of its energy needs (*IHT*, 22 November 1993, p. 6).

Oil imports fell from 2.54 million tonnes in 1990 to 1.35 million tonnes in 1992 (*FEER*, 29 April 1993, p. 9).

The main destinations of exports in 1991 were the Soviet Union (40.1 per cent), Japan (20.2 per cent), South Korea (11.7 per cent), other Asian countries (6.4 per cent), Western Europe (6.4 per cent) and China (6.1 per cent). The main origins of imports in 1991 were the Soviet Union (37.2 per cent), China (22.7 per cent), Japan (9.7 per cent), Hong Kong (5.4 per cent), other Asian countries (4.3 per cent) and Western Europe (2.8 per cent) (EIU, *Country Report*, 1993, Second Quarter, p. 5).

There have been a number of estimates of the value of North Korea–South Korea trade in 1992: $210 million, $198.8 million of northern exports and only $11.4 million of imports (EIU, *Country Report*, 1993, no. 1, p. 38); $213 million, compared with $192 million in 1991 (*IHT*, 10 April 1993, p. 8); $174 million, with South Korea accounting for 6 per cent of North Korea's trade (David Sanger, *IHT*, 16 March 1993, p. 7). South Korea's trade with North Korea amounted to $180 million in 1993 (John Burton, *FT*, 4 June 1994, p. 3). In 1993 North Korea's exports to South Korea amounted to $178 million (mostly gold, zinc, cement and copper), while its imports from the latter came to only $8 million. South Korea ranked fourth in trade terms behind China, Japan and Russia; North Korea's total trade was $2.6 billion in 1993 (Shim Jae Hoon, *FEER*, 4 August 1994, p. 50). North–South trade amounted to about $200 million in 1994 (Bridges 1995: 106); $194 million (John Burton, *FT*, 4 July 1995, p. 4).

In 1993 Japan was the second largest trading partner, with an estimated volume of $480 million (John Burton, *FT*, 22 March 1994, p. 6).

North Korea's trade with the Soviet Union fell from $2.57 billion in 1990 to $470 million in 1991. The figures for oil imports from the Soviet Union were 440,000 tonnes and 40,000 tonnes respectively (Sungwoo Kim, *Asian Survey*, 1993, vol. XXXIII, no. 9, p. 867). Total foreign trade fell from $3.09 billion in 1990 to $2.72 billion in 1991, i.e. by 16 per cent (FEER, *Asia 1994 Yearbook*, 1994, p. 149).

China had announced that all trade with North Korea was to be on a cash basis from the start of 1993, but China continued to supply some oil and grain on 'friendship terms' (EIU, *Country Report*, 1993, no. 1, p. 37). At least two-thirds of trade with China is in the form of barter; in 1993 China provided 72 per cent of food imports and 75 per cent of oil imports (Ed Paisley, *FEER*, 10 February 1994, p. 23). About 65 per cent of oil comes by pipeline from China on concessionary terms; about 40 per cent of grain is imported, a good portion from China (*IHT*, 13 June 1994, p. 2). North Korea imports anything from 25 per cent to 75 per cent of its oil from China, according to widely differing estimates (Lena Sun, *IHT*, 17 June 1994, p. 4).

North Korea has established a trade-company office in Taiwan (John Merrill, *Asian Survey*, January 1993, vol. XXXIII, no. 1, p. 52).

David Watts (*The Times*, 18 March 1993, p. 12) reports on trade between the USA and North Korea. US exports to North Korea had been all but forbidden under the Trading with the Enemy Act, owing to the lingering technical state of hostility since the end of the Korean War in 1953 and the fact that North Korea is on the list of countries allegedly supporting international terrorism. In 1989, however, the Bush administration quietly changed the regulations to allow commercial shipments of humanitarian items such as food and medical equipment. President Bush hoped to influence North Korea's attitude towards international terrorism and nuclear weapons. (See the entries for 21 October 1994 and 9 January 1995.)

Trade between South Korea and China and Russia

In 1992 two-way trade between China and South Korea amounted to $8 billion, up 39 per cent on the 1991 figure and more than double the 1990 level (*IHT*, 7 April 1993, p. 15). In the first half of 1994 China–South Korea trade amounted to $4.96 billion (a 59.5 per cent increase on the same period of 1993), while China–North Korea trade fell by 21.9 per cent to $336 million (*IHT*, 1 November 1994, p. 6).

South Korea's seventh largest trading partner in 1993, China advanced to third position in 1994. Two-way trade increased rapidly from $4.4 billion in 1991 to $9.08 billion in 1993 and possibly over $12 billion in 1994 (Chong-Sik Lee and Hyuk-Sang Sohn, *Asian Survey*, 1995, vol. XXXV, no. 1, p. 35).

Russian–South Korean trade turnover increased from $859 million in 1992 to $1.58 billion in 1993 (Tsuneo Akaha, *Asian Survey*, 1995, vol. XXXV, no. 1, p. 107). In June 1994 Yeltsin said that Russia would let the 1961 Treaty of Friendship, Co-operation and Mutual Assistance with North Korea expire at the end of 1996 (p. 108). (Moscow had already reinterpreted the treaty to stress that assistance would be given only if North Korea were to be attacked and not if North Korea committed an act of aggression.)

Foreign aid

Charles Smith (*FEER*, 9 September 1993, p. 23) cites one estimate that the Chosen Soren (General Association of Koreans in Japan) either collects or helps to channel $600 million to $700 million to North Korea every year, the flow of funds including cash carried by hand (by those travelling to the country) and bank remittances. There are 100,000 or so pro-North Koreans living in Japan. According to David Sanger (*IHT*, 2 November 1993, pp. 1, 8; 15 January 1994, p. 1), 800,000 Koreans live in Japan and around 150,000 are sympathetic to North Korea; the sum transferred annually is in the range $600 million to $1 billion. In a later article (*IHT*, 23 March 1994, p. 5), David Sanger refers to 300,000 professing loyalty and sending between $600 million and $1.6 billion a year (later still he cites $600 million to $1.8 billion: *IHT*, 9 June 1994, p. 1; so does *The Economist*: 11 June 1994, p. 72). Another source cites an annual figure of $570 million (*IHT*, 16 December 1993, p. 10). According to the *FT* (21 April 1994, p. 4), there are 700,000 ethnic Koreans in Japan; of these about a third are believed to owe allegiance to North Korea (*IHT*, 17 June 1994, p. 4). The Japanese Foreign Ministry said it had inconclusive evidence that Korean residents in Japan were supplying North Korea with as much as $1.81 billion a year in financial support (*IHT*, 29 December 1993, p. 6). Ed Paisley (*FEER*, 10 February 1994, p. 23) cites $1.8 billion for 1993. John Burton (*FT*, 22 March 1994, p. 6) cites estimates in the range $600 million to $1.8 billion a year provided by the estimated 260,000 pro-North Korean Japanese. *The Economist* (26 March 1994, p. 87; 28 May 1994, p. 24) talks of $600 million to $1.8 billion provided by 250,000 or so sympathizers.

Note that it is not certain how voluntary the flow of funds is, e.g. family members still living in North Korea may be under threat. An editorial in *FEER* (16 June 1994, p. 5) said that the Korean population in Japan 'is more or less blackmailed into remitting millions in funds'.

Foreign debt

In 1991 total debt amounted to $9.3 billion, of which $3.5 billion was owed to industrialized countries (Sungwoo Kim, *Asian Survey*, 1993, vol. XXXIII, no. 9, p. 87).

Foreign banks are owed $1.6 billion (John Burton, *FT*, 14 July 1994, p. 6).

The sum borrowed from Western banks is $1.2 billion (*The Economist*, 12 November 1994, p. 107).

The principal owed to international banks amounted to $747 million, but this has doubled because of interest (*FT*, Survey, 23 June 1994, p. iv).

Foreign investment

Only about $150 million in direct foreign investment flowed in over the period 1984–92 (Ed Paisley, *FEER*, 10 February 1994, p. 23).

Approved foreign investment amounts to about $140 million (John Burton, *FT*, 4 July 1995, p. 4).

Some further information is available on the October 1992 foreign investment law. Workers can be fired, although both hirings and firings have to be done through the competent labour department rather than by contracting directly with individual workers (EIU, *Country Report*, 1992, no. 4, p. 38). The (what in effect are) special economic zones are exempt from income tax for the first three years of profit; they are entitled to a further two years of reduced tax and the rate thereafter is 14 per cent (said to be a reduction on the rate prevailing elsewhere) (p. 38). The corporate profit tax rate is 25 per cent outside the zones (Sungwoo Kim, *Asian Survey*, 1993, vol. XXXIII, no. 9, p. 870). The government has approved legislation allowing foreign bank operations and foreigners to lease land and visit free-trade zones without visas (John Burton, *FT*, 14 December 1993, p. 6).

Since 1991 the South Korean conglomerate Lucky Goldstar (and a few other South Korean companies) have sent materials (plus design specifications) to North Korea for processing into final products such as toys and garments. The products have either been reimported or exported to China (*The Economist*, 16 July 1994, p. 20; 22 October 1994, p. 88). Lucky Goldstar has been asked to take over North Korea's largest steelworks (*The Economist*, 22 October 1994, p. 88).

John Merrill (*Asian Survey*, January 1993, vol. XXXIII, no. 1, p. 48) reports the following. Around 170 joint ventures have been established, e.g. garments, musical instruments and diamond-cutting. North Korea has pushed ahead with plans to develop a free-trade zone in the Rajin–Sonbong area and make Chongjin a free-trade port. North Korea seems determined to go ahead rather than wait for agreement on the Tumen River Development Programme (costing $30 billion over a decade). North Korea wants South Korea to participate (the South Korean government has made progress on the nuclear issue a precondition for allowing any investment in North Korea: Aidan Foster-Carter, *The Independent*, 28 June 1994, p. 18). In a later article (*Asian Survey*, 1994, vol. XXXIV, p. 16), John Merrill mentions new laws having been passed in 1993 on the leasing of land by foreigners. He also cites an estimate that by 1993 Korean residents in Japan had invested over $100 million in 120 projects in North Korea.

The *FEER* (27 May 1993, p. 71) reports that China, Russia and North Korea have agreed in principle to lease out land for a twenty-year $30 billion port and industrial project along the Tumen river. UN officials said that the land, which straddles all three countries, would be managed by an independent international corporation.

The Rajin–Sonbong free economic and trade zone is North Korea's contribution to the Tumen River development area. A meeting held in May 1993 decided to push the project forward. A private-sector corporation, the Tumen River Area Development Corporation, was scheduled to be registered. Headed by an American, the corporation is to oversee developments in the North Korean, Chinese and Russian zones (Mark Clifford, *FEER*, 30 September 1993, p. 72).

Special investment areas have been created, including a site at Nampo (near Pyongyang) and another near the border with China. Progress on the Tumen project has been slow. Most of the Japanese–Korean joint ventures have been failures, according to Paul Abrahams (*FT*, 23 June 1994, p. iv).

North Korea claims that foreign companies have already pledged $200 million to the Rajin–Sonbong zone, of which $40 million has been committed (John Burton, *FT*, 29 April 1995, p. 3). 'So far next to nobody has invested there' (*The Economist*, Survey on South Korea, 3 June 1995, p. 9). So far not much has been achieved in the way of attracting foreign investors to the zone (Bridges 1995: 105).[1]

On 30 May China, Russia and North Korea agreed to the establishment of the Tumen River Area Development Co-ordination Committee, whose task would be to boost trade and investment. South Korea and Mongolia joined the three in agreeing to a consultative commission with broad responsibility for developing trade, infrastructure, finance and banking (Tony Walker, *FT*, 31 May 1995, p. 5).

On 28 February 1995 it was announced that North Korea and a Hong Kong investment company were to set up a joint venture development bank to help finance the state's development projects (*IHT*, 1 March 1995, p. 15; *FT*, 1 March 1995, p. 7).

On 17 May 1995, for the first time, South Korea approved two joint ventures between North and South Korean firms, producing textiles and other light industrial goods (the approval of North Korea was still needed). 'North Korea has adopted joint venture laws to attract foreign investment and has designated a free-trade zone, but no actual investment has been made so far' (*IHT*, 18 May 1995, p. 13).

Agriculture

About 37 per cent of the work force is still employed on the land, compared with 15 per cent in South Korea (Philip Bowring, *IHT*, 11 July 1994, p. 6).

'North Korea's economic problems have also led to the emergence of primitive capitalism in the form of black markets. The government allows those with small garden plots to sell vegetables at the informal markets to help relieve growing food shortages' (John Burton, *FT*, 16 May 1995, p. 18).

The cost of reunification

A South Korean Ministry of Finance report published in January 1993 put the cost of reunification (if it took place in the year 2000) for the first decade at $980 billion (EIU, *Country Report*, 1993, no. 1, p. 28). To put this in some perspective, South Korea's GNP in 1991 was $280.8 billion (EIU, *Country Report*, 1992, no. 3, p. 35).

According to David O'Rear (*IHT*, 31 May 1993, p. 6), the authorities in South Korea estimate that reunification would cost more than $46 billion a year for four years and $9 billion in each of the subsequent six years.

The ten-year cost of reunification has been variously estimated at $200 billion to $300 billion, an annual sum equivalent to more than 3 per cent of South Korea's GNP (Andrew Mack, *Asian Survey*, 1993, vol. XXXIII, no. 4, p. 357). This estimated $200 billion to $300 billion cost over ten years is also mentioned by John Burton (*FT*, 11 July 1994, p. 17), but he cites $250 billion to $400 billion over ten years in a later article (*FT*, 24 October 1994, p. 22). (An estimated 7 million South Koreans, one-sixth of the population of South Korea, are either refugees from North Korea or their descendants: John Burton, *FT*, Weekend, 31 December 1994, p. ii.)

Kang Suk Rhee (*Asian Survey*, 1993, vol. XXXIII, no. 4, pp. 372–4) reports the two estimates produced by the Korean Development Institute (affiliated to the South Korean government):

1. Abrupt, German-style reunification would require an investment of $816.7 billion (at 1990 prices) over the ten-year period 2001–10 in order to bring North Korea's productivity up to 60 per cent of that of South Korea's. It is also calculated that South Korea might pay between $46.05 billion and $47.88 billion every year for the first four years, an amount equivalent to South Korea's present budget and 8.2 per cent of its GDP.

2. A gradual process of reunification would bring the respective figures down to $773.9 billion and $17.43 to $18.95 billion.

Kang Suk Rhee also quotes an Economist Intelligence Unit estimate of the cost to the South Korean government and private sector of $61 billion a year for ten years (p. 374).

Bringing North Korea up to South Korea's living standard will cost an estimated $500 billion to $800 billion over ten years (Philip Bowring, *IHT*, 29 April 1994, p. 6). North Korea's economy is roughly where it was in 1970, when it was first surpassed by South Korea. Estimates of the capital needed over ten years to bring the former up to the latter's levels range from $600 million to $1,000 million (Philip Bowring, *IHT*, 11 July 1994, p. 6).

A study by Korea University puts the cost of bringing North Korea's economy up to the standard of South Korea at $1,200 billion, i.e. four times the latter's GNP (*The Economist*, Survey of South Korea, 3 June 1995, p. 10). Another estimate is cited. If reunification came in the year 2000 and Chinese-style economic reforms were undertaken before then, South Korea would have to invest around $90 billion in North Korea in the following decade (mainly on infrastructure). But if no reforms are undertaken and North Korea collapses in 2000, the sum would increase to $230 billion (*The Economist*, 16 July 1994, p. 20).

The cost of reunification would be more than $1,000 billion, spread over ten years (Steven Brull, *IHT*, 11 July 1994, p. 9, and 10 November 1994, p. 16).[2]

Economic performance

What actually happened to the North Korean economy in the first half of the 1990s is not known with any certainty. But things looked pretty bleak and it seems that growth was consistently negative (see Table 30.1).

According to David O'Rear (*IHT*, 31 May 1993, p. 6), two cuts in food rations in 1992 reportedly caused riots. There have been further reports of food riots and even worse incidents in the countryside, especially in the spring of 1993 (e.g. T. R. Reid, *IHT*, 19 August 1993, p. 1). But there is

Table 30.1 North Korea: selected economic indicators

Economic indicator	*1990*	*1991*	*1992*	*1993*	*1994*
Rate of growth of GDP (%)	−3.7	−5.2	−7.6	−4.3	−1.7
Rate of growth of agricultural output (%)			−2.7	−9.0	
Rate of growth of manufacturing output (%)			−17.8		
Rate of growth of mining output (%)			−6.1		

Sources: Various issues of the *FEER*, the Economist Intelligence Unit, *The Economist*, *The Financial Times*, *The Times* and *The Guardian*

uncertainty about the seriousness of these events. There may only be certain cases of food shortages and perhaps isolated raids on grain depots and food supply lorries.

Food shortages have reportedly been widespread in the countryside, while factories operate at about one-third capacity (*FT*, 26 March 1994, p. 9). Energy shortages have forced factories to work at half their capacity or less. Food shortages have been caused by four years of poor harvests; there is an estimated 40 per cent shortfall in grain supplies needed to feed the population (John Burton, *FT*, 14 July 1994, p. 6).

Flora Lewis (*IHT*, 14 April 1994, p. 4) cites one estimate that industry is operating at 50 per cent capacity.

Industry is now estimated to be working at between one-third and one-half capacity (*The Economist*, 28 May 1994, p. 24).

In 1993 a 'two meals a day' campaign was reportedly conducted in most of the country and malnourishment was said to affect even the military. Some Russian economists estimated that factories were operating at about half capacity, no worse and in some cases probably slightly better than in 1992 (John Merrill, *Asian Survey*, 1994, vol. XXXIV, no. 1, p. 15).

Foreign visitors report factories running at only two-thirds capacity. North Korea appears to be suffering from food shortages in some areas and small-scale food riots have been reported intermittently since 1992. Defectors report that an active black market even in basic necessities is developing (Bridges 1995: 105).

North Korea asked for emergency loans of rice from Japan on 26 May 1995 and from Unesco on 31 May 1995. After five days of direct talks with North Korea in Beijing, South Korea announced (on 21 June 1995) that it would supply 150,000 tonnes of rice free of charge and with no labelling to indicate its source. (A quarrel over the first South Korean ship being made to fly the North Korean flag while in port was patched up when North Korea formally apologized. On 9 August 1995 North Korea seized a South Korean ship and accused the crew of spying. This incident was defused when South Korea expressed 'regret' that a crew member had taken personal photographs while in port.) Japan made its contribution dependent on such an agreement. Half its 300,000 tonnes would be provided free of charge and the other half provided under a thirty-year loan with a ten-year grace period.

In 1991 South Korean civic organizations collected 5,000 tonnes of rice for North Korea, although the latter never officially acknowledged the shipment. This was a reversal of the situation in 1984 when North Korea sent 7,000 tonnes of rice to South Korea to aid flood victims (Shim Jae Hoon, *FEER*, 29 June 1995, p. 23).

On 29 August 1995 North Korea asked the UN for emergency relief aid after severe flooding. North Korea 'also made an unprecedented appeal to private US organizations and to European governments for emergency relief' (*IHT*, 4 September 1995, p. 4). (A UN team was allowed to visit North Korea. At the end of the visit the team issued an urgent appeal for aid.) On 7 September 1995 North Korea asked Japan for humanitarian aid. On 3 October 1995 Japan agreed to provide 200,000 tonnes of emergency rice supplies. This was to be paid for over a thirty-year period at 2 per cent a year for the first ten years, rising to 3 per cent. On 23 November 1995 the UN announced that its shipment 'represents the first UN food aid ever sent to the country'.

NOTES

1. The Rajin-Sonbong free-trade zone was founded in 1991. North Korea says that investment commitments total only $200 million to date, of which $20 million has actually been spent. There is full freedom from import duties and firms enjoy a tax holiday for three years after a venture starts to make money (Peter Montagnon, *FT*, 27 September 1995, p. 8).
2. Estimates of the cost of reunification range from less than $100 million, predicated on a gradual process, to more than $1 trillion assuming a collapse of North Korea and an attempt to equalize living standards (Steven Brull, *IHT*, 26 September 1995, p. 17).

31

VIETNAM

POLITICS

Political and economic background

Vietnam means 'land to the south' (of China). Over the past fifty years the forest cover has declined from 44 per cent to less than 24 per cent (Murray Hiebert, *FEER*, 3 February 1994, p. 21). On a *per capita* basis Vietnam is not at all well endowed with natural resources, e.g. with over 900 people per square kilometre of agricultural land Vietnam is far more densely populated than Thailand or China, whose population densities are less than 300 (Dollar 1994: 358).

In 1993 some 50,000 people joined the Communist Party, which now has a membership of almost 3 million (Iain Simpson, *FT*, 25 January 1994, p. 4).

In late 1988 Vietnam formally introduced a comprehensive fertility policy encouraging parents to have no more than two children ('one or two children') to try to reduce a population growth rate of over 2 per cent a year (Goodkind 1995: 85). North Vietnam's two-or-three-child norm was promoted in 1963 but not enforced (p. 89). Members of ethnic minorities, who constitute about 13 per cent of Vietnam's population today, are formally allowed to have up to three children (p. 90). Vietnam's policy is less draconian than China's (p. 107), but the means of implementation include fines, job penalties and social persuasion (p. 105).

The government of Vietnam gives a *per capita* income figure of $220 (William Keeling, *FT*, Survey, 30 November 1993, p. 32). A figure of $250 is cited later (*FT*, Survey, 8 December 1994, p. 37).

A World Bank report refers to a *per capita* income of less than $200 and to 51 per cent of the population living in absolute poverty (Peter Montagnon, *FT*, 24 February 1995, p. 4).

The Asian Development Bank put GDP per head in 1990 at about $200, as against $1,400 for Thailand. Allowing for differences in purchasing power, the UN Development Programme put the respective figures at $1,000 and $3,570 (*The Economist*, 20 March 1993, p. 26).

On a PPP (purchasing-power parity) basis GDP per head in 1990 was $1,100 (*The Economist*, Survey, 30 October 1993, p. 6).

On 3 April 1995 the government released, for the first time, figures on the Vietnam War. In the period 1954–75 the communist forces (North Vietnamese and Viet Cong soldiers) suffered over 1.1 million dead, 600,000 wounded and 300,000 listed as missing. Previous Western estimates had put the communist death toll at 666,000. Government statistics also showed that nearly 2 million Vietnamese civilians were killed and another 2 million injured. In addition the government said that about 50,000 children were born deformed because of the use of Agent Orange by US forces. According to the USA, 58,153 Americans were killed in Vietnam and 300,000 were wounded from 1965 to 1975. The number of South Vietnam soldiers killed was 223,748 and the number wounded was 500,000. More than 5,200 South Koreans, Australians (424), New Zealanders and Thai soldiers also died. The number of American soldiers listed as missing in Indochina is put at 2,211, including 1,651 in Vietnam (*IHT*, 5 April 1995, p. 4; *The Daily Telegraph*, 4 April 1995, p. 13).

Vietnam's armed forces number 572,000 (*FEER*, 13 April 1995, p. 26).

The 'boat people'

A background article on the 'boat people' by Frederick Balfour is to be found in *FEER* (4 March 1993, pp. 28–30). Vietnam agreed to voluntary repatriation in 1989. The UNHCR and the Hong Kong immigration authorities had earlier taken action. Beginning in June 1988, arrivals were screened to distinguish economic migrants from political refugees. In 1989 other countries did the same. The UNHCR set 27 September 1991 as the cut-off date for direct assistance to asylum-seekers (local authorities in Vietnam receive aid to help those returning). In 1992 only twelve boat people arrived in Hong Kong and fewer than fifty were picked up in other countries. At the time of writing only Hong Kong carried out forced repatriation.

There are still 25,903 Vietnamese in Hong Kong (Simon Holberton, *FT*, 2 December 1994, p. 4).

More than 50,000 Vietnamese still remain in South East Asian camps (*FEER*, 3 November 1994, p. 18).

The UNHCR has to repatriate the remaining Vietnamese (estimated at 50,000) still in camps in South East Asian countries. In January 1995 Malaysia, Vietnam and the UNHCR signed an agreement on the repatriation of the remaining 5,000 Vietnamese in Malaysia, while a similar agreement has been signed for the repatriation of 6,000 from Indonesia. China will not permit Hong Kong to remain a place of asylum after 1997 (*IHT*, 22 February 1995, p. 4).

A two-day international meeting was held on 22–23 February 1995 to discuss the UN's 1989 Comprehensive Plan of action to persuade all

40,000 refugees who do not qualify for political asylum in third countries to return home by the end of 1995. It was agreed that all Vietnamese in Asian camps would be repatriated (by force of necessary) by the end of 1995, except in Hong Kong (holding 22,000) where the last would be repatriated 'shortly afterwards' (probably in 1996) (*IHT*, 24 February 1995, p. 4).

The UNHCR said that only 5.5 per cent of the 839,000 people who left Vietnam after 1975 were still in the Asian 'first asylum' countries. Some 70,000 Vietnamese had returned home, with a small allowance, where they have benefited from programmes financed principally by the EU. The UNHCR's monitoring teams have never recovered any convincing cases of official harassment or of discrimination against any of those returning (*IHT*, 16 March 1995, p. 4).

On 16 March 1995, at a meeting in Geneva, the UNHCR said that it was time to wind up the 1989 programme. The target date for the completion of repatriation was confirmed as the end of 1995 (with Hong Kong being allowed a couple more months). Of the 42,000 remaining in South East Asian camps, over 22,000 were in Hong Kong. Since 1975 over 839,000 Vietnamese have sought asylum, of whom 753,000 have been resettled. The UNHCR said that there was 'no substantive evidence of any ill-treatment' of the 70,000 who have already returned to Vietnam (Frances Williams, *FT*, 17 March 1995, p. 6).

There was a riot in Hong Kong on 19–20 May 1995 when security forces moved 'economic migrants' from one detention centre to another. One factor adding to the unrest was a bill being discussed in the US Congress to increase the number of Vietnamese allowed into the USA. There followed a riot in a camp in Malaysia.

(Note that on 11 January 1995 Vietnam and Germany agreed to repatriate around 40,000 Vietnamese by the year 2000 in return for export credits and development aid. Some 60,000 Vietnamese are unaffected, because of their acceptance as political refugees or immigrants. There are some 95,000 Vietnamese living in Germany, of whom only 55,000 are legal residents. Of the remainder, 10,000 tried to enter Germany illegally after reunification, another 10,000 are guest workers from the former GDR and 20,000 are asylum-seekers whose requests for refugee status have been rejected: *FEER*, 9 February 1995, p. 28. The agreement was formally signed on 21 July 1995.)

The 2 million Vietnamese living abroad send their relatives in Vietnam $600 million to $700 million each year (*Vietnam Report*, 1995, issue 3, p. 3).

Political developments

2 July 1993. President Clinton announces that the USA is no longer opposed to Vietnam's reinstatement in the IMF and the World Bank. On 29 September fifteen 'Friends of Vietnam' (including France, Japan, Australia,

Belgium, Canada, Germany and Sweden) announced a financial package to clear the $140 million owed to the IMF. This comprised a bridging loan of $85 million (to be repaid on 6 October by means of an IMF stand-by loan of that amount) and $55 million in grants from donor countries. Vietnam's arrears needed to be cleared before new loans were granted. On 4 October 1993 an IMF loan of $223 million was agreed. (The IMF's first loan was in January 1977; Vietnam defaulted in the early 1980s. The World Bank's first loan was in April 1978; the project was suspended in 1980: *FEER*, 15 July 1993, p. 10.)

17 July 1993. Agreement in principle is announced for three US diplomats to be posted in Hanoi (the first since 1955), formally to handle consular matters (Vietnam formally agreed on 5 August).

5 August 1993. The USA announces that a congressional delegation will visit Vietnam on 12–15 August to study investment and trade prospects.

14 September 1993. President Clinton only partially lifts the US embargo by allowing US companies to bid for participation in projects funded by international organizations such as the World Bank and the Asian Development Bank. (The unilateral US embargo does not seem to be very effective as regards trade in goods.)

10 November 1993. President Le Duc Anh begins a visit to China, the first by a head of state since Ho Chi Minh in 1959.

20–25 January 1994. A special national conference of the Communist Party takes place, the first of its kind to be held between congresses (held every five years, the next one being due in 1996). The economic reform programme was generally given the green light (the building of a 'socialist-orientated market mechanism under state management'), but action was urged on social and economic problems such as unemployment, poverty, corruption, smuggling, drug addiction and prostitution. The need to retain political stability was stressed. The politburo was increased by four to seventeen (the new members including Foreign Minister Nguyen Manh Cam and the director of the party's economic commission, Nguyen Ha Phan). The Central Committee was increased by twenty to 161 members (including Deputy Foreign Minister Le Mai).

27 January 1994. The US Senate, in a non-binding vote, urges the president to lift the economic embargo.

3 February 1994. President Clinton announces that the economic embargo on Vietnam is to be lifted.

23 February 1994. A former energy minister is sentenced to three years for corruption and fraud (eight others were also sentenced).

26 May 1994. It is announced that Vietnam and the USA are to establish diplomatic missions in both countries.

16 June 1994. Vietnam and Russia sign a new friendship treaty.

20 June 1994. The National Assembly approves a law permitting strikes for better wages and working conditions (after negotiations have been exhausted and provided that equipment is not damaged and there is no 'public disorder').

5 July 1994. An Australian delegation calls off a planned visit during which the issue of human rights would have figured strongly. (Vietnam refused to grant a visa to one member of the delegation.)

24 July 1994. Foreign ministers of Asean say they are ready to accept Vietnam as a member, but set no date. (The Association of South East Asian Nations, established in 1967, consists of Brunei, Indonesia, Malaysia, the Philippines, Singapore and Thailand.)

26 August 1994. The first visit by a prime minister of Japan.

20–22 November 1994. President Jiang Zemin of China visits Vietnam. The two countries agree to form a group of experts to consider the dispute over the Spratly Islands. (Brunei, China, Malaysia, the Philippines, Taiwan and Vietnam dispute ownership of the islands, with China, Taiwan and Vietnam each claiming all of them. As a result of a clash in 1974 China seized the Paracel Islands from South Vietnamese forces. In the 1988 Spratly incident the Chinese navy inflicted significant damage on Vietnamese naval vessels and seized a number of reefs. There have since been disputes over oil exploration. In January 1995 the Philippines accused China of building a base on one of the reefs.)

28 January 1995. The USA and Vietnam sign an agreement (1) to open liaison offices, thus allowing diplomatic links (although not full diplomatic relations) and (2) dealing with the question of diplomatic properties seized in 1975.

3 February 1995. Vietnam claims that at a meeting on 26 January 1995 Asean decided to admit Vietnam as its seventh member.

12 April 1995. General Secretary Do Muoi begins a visit to South Korea.

30 April 1995. The twentieth anniversary of victory in the Vietnam War is celebrated in low key (partly for diplomatic reasons, but Vietnam generally stresses the reunification of the country rather than victory as such).

14 June 1995. US Secretary of State Warren Christopher recommends that the USA establishes full diplomatic relations with Vietnam.

11 July 1995. President Clinton announces that the USA is to establish full diplomatic relations with Vietnam (formally established on 5 August).

17 July 1995. The EU and Vietnam sign an economic co-operation accord.

28 July 1995. Vietnam becomes the seventh member of Asean.

Vietnam agreed to join the Asean free-trade plan at the beginning of January 1996, although it would have until 2006 (instead of the usual 2003) to reduce tariffs on most manufactured goods to a maximum 5 per cent (*IHT*, 31 July 1995, p. 9; *FEER*, 10 August 1995, p. 15).

2 September 1995. The fiftieth anniversary of the declaration of independence.

THE ECONOMY

Financial policy

'Vietnam launched an ambitious reform programme that, within a short time, completely reoriented its economic system. At the heart of the renovation (*doi moi*) introduced in 1989 were agricultural reforms and price liberalization . . . the removal of price controls in Vietnam was complete in the agricultural sector and nearly as comprehensive in industry and services . . . the regime for foreign trade and investment was liberalized. Restrictions on imports and exports of important products, such as rice, were relaxed. The exchange rate was unified and sharply devalued . . . interest rates were raised to very high levels . . . the government also tried to curb credit financing of the budget' (Dollar 1994: 361). 'The fiscal deficit was reduced sharply from 11.4 per cent of GDP in 1989 to 2.5 per cent in 1991. The deficit increased modestly to 3.8 per cent of GDP in 1992' (p. 366). 'Vietnam's macroeconomic performance in the 1989–92 period compares very favourably with the experiences of other transition economies' (p. 373).

On 23 July 1993 the first interbank money market started trading in dong. The main aim is to provide financial institutions with short-term credit from banks with surplus dong (Murray Hiebert, *FEER*, 5 August 1993, p. 57).

The dong is not convertible on international exchanges. The dollar is rapidly becoming an accepted means of payment for goods and services in Vietnam as well as the only way foreign investors can take profits out (*IHT*, 11 June 1994, p. 17). On 9 August 1994 it was announced that restrictions were to be placed on the use of the US dollar and companies would be required to deposit foreign currency in bank accounts (as of 1 October). Businesses that charge for their services in dollars would be required to accept dong, with only duty-free shops and at the airports and others authorized by the central bank taking foreign currency (*IHT*, 10 August 1994, p. 13; *FEER*, 18 August 1994, p. 55).

In early August the government decreed that as of 1 October 1994 all domestic transactions had to be conducted in dong. The decree failed to distinguish between foreign and domestic enterprises when requiring them to convert all foreign currency not being used for import and export purposes into dong. But the best guess is that a clarifying circular will be issued to differentiate between accounts held by foreigners and those held by Vietnamese. Under the foreign investment law foreigners are granted the right to hold foreign exchange accounts (Michael Vatikliotis, *FEER*, 6 October 1994, p. 54).

Since 1 October 1994 hotels, airlines, taxis and shops have not been allowed to advertise prices in dollars and have only been able to accept payment in dong. Vietnamese organizations now have to channel their hard currency earnings through banks, rather than holding cash. Foreign investors, especially in the hotels sector, were thought likely to be keen to seek exemptions so that they could convert their dong earnings into dollars. It was understood that the State Bank had set a deadline (the end of October) by which applications had to be made (*FT*, 12 October 1994, p. 7).

It subsequently turned out that the August decree appeared to affect only domestic transactions and that it was being enforced only gradually (Victor Mallet, *FT*, Survey, 8 December 1994, p. 38).

In February 1995 the central bank announced that efforts would be made to gain stricter control over foreign exchange transactions, e.g. joint ventures would only be able to open an account at one bank. Some foreign-invested companies, primarily those involved in import substitution, are allowed to buy foreign currency with dong if they obtain permits from the central bank and the investment approval agency (Adam Schwarz, *FEER*, 27 April 1995, p. 68).

The State Bank ordered privately operated foreign exchange outlets to close from 30 June 1995, because they did not transfer sufficient amounts of foreign currency to the State Bank (*FEER*, 6 July 1995, p. 71).

Prices

From early 1989 prices were substantially decontrolled; by the end of that year only the prices of electricity, oil and goods transport were still centrally controlled (Andreff 1993: 522). Some prices, including petroleum, are still determined by the government. Tariffs on utilities, public services and transport are still set administratively (Dinh 1993: 542).

The state sector

'The failure to develop a heavy industrial base may now turn out to be something of an advantage . . . Vietnam has few of the large, inefficient industrial plants that plague other socialist economies' (Dollar 1994: 359). 'Vietnam . . . relies on a few hundred large firms, all state-owned, to provide most government revenue' (p. 367).

Between 2,500 and 3,000 state enterprises have been dissolved in the past two years. Of the remaining 9,000–9,500 state enterprises, 46 per cent at the provincial level and 20 per cent at the national level face serious problems (*FEER*, 25 March 1993, p. 71). A Vietnamese minister claims that the government has shut down 2,000 state enterprises and may close another 800 (*FEER*, 3 June 1993, p. 71).

According to official statistics, the number of state enterprises has been reduced by mergers and liquidations in the last eighteen months from 12,000 to 7,000 (Victor Mallet, *FT*, Survey, 24 September 1993, p. xx).

Murray Hiebert (*FEER*, 3 February 1994, p. 45) reports that the state sector employs only 8 per cent of the work force. Restructuring has reduced the number of state enterprises from about 12,000 in mid-1992 to around 7,000. Most of those that disappeared were small, loss-making enterprises belonging to provincial governments. Just over half were integrated into larger, more efficient enterprises, while the rest were either leased to private businessmen or sold to pay off their debts. The National Assembly approved a bankruptcy law in December 1993. Direct subsidies to state enterprises have been abolished, but indirect support remains in the form of low-interest loans. Since 1990 some 2,000 state enterprises have been closed and 3,000 have been merged, reducing state enterprise employment to 1.7 million people (Nayan Chanda, *FEER*, 23 February 1995, pp. 49–50).

According to Philip Bowring (*IHT*, 30 November 1993, p. 6), state enterprises now account for less than a quarter of GDP. Kevin Murphy (*IHT*, 9 June 1994, p. 9) adds that in 1989 the state sector accounted for only 23.7 per cent of GDP and 7.7 per cent of the work force. Moreover, state employees have never enjoyed a system of extensive welfare benefits like China's 'iron rice bowl'. The number of state enterprises has shrunk from about 12,300 in 1989 to around 6,000, with as many as 2,000 businesses liquidated and the rest merged with healthier companies.

The government says that Vietnam has some 7,000 state-owned enterprises, down from 12,000 in 1990. Most of the enterprises that the government has merged or closed down had fewer than 500 employees. Total employment in state enterprises fell from 2.7 million in 1988 to 1.7 million in 1993. The remaining state enterprises have been given greater freedom to hire and fire and to market their goods. They must seek their own financing, because the government has slashed their subsidies. Furthermore, a new bankruptcy law passed in 1994 should make it easier for banks to seize the assets of insolvent state enterprises and shut them down. Officially 76 per cent of state enterprises make a profit and 15 per cent break even. The National Assembly was to consider a new law on state enterprises in April 1995 (Adam Schwarz, *FEER*, 2 March 1995, p. 56). State enterprises dominate the industrial sector. To improve international competitiveness, the government is trying to assemble several dozen conglomerates, known as general corporations, in areas such as steel, coal, power, rice, coffee and textiles (Adam Schwarz, *FEER*, 26 October 1995, p. 57).

The number of state enterprises in 1991 was 12,084, of which 1,695 were managed by ministries and 10,389 were managed by local authorities. The state sector contributed 33.4 per cent on average to GDP in the period 1986–90. The state enterprise sector employed 12 per cent of total social labour. About 40 per cent of state enterprises were breaking even, 30 per cent were operating at a loss and only 30 per cent were profitable (Tai and Hare 1995: 1–2). The number of existing state enterprises is about 7,000 at present (p. 4). Only about 6 per cent of the labour force is employed by state enterprises in industry (p. 11).

William Brannigin (*IHT*, 18 October 1993, p. 7) reports that the army (whose regular forces totalled 1.2 million in the 1980s, complemented by 3.5 million reservists, and whose number is now down to 600,000 regulars) has set up more than 300 commercial enterprises (employing 66,400 full-time workers, mostly soldiers).

Thomas Friedman (*IHT*, 16 January 1995, p. 6) expresses some concern at the fact that: 'Every Vietnamese ministry has been ordered to start businesses to support itself . . . I fear this short cut to capitalism will haunt the Vietnamese. When ministries become the biggest entrepreneurs, it means that there is no civil service upholding the public interest. That is why bridges collapse in Seoul and why twelve-year-old girls are trapped in factory fires in China. It was Asian capitalist talent, harnessed by a professional civil service, that made Japan rich and stable.'

On 1 July 1994 a state-owned cement producer became the first Vietnamese enterprise to issue a corporate bond (*IHT*, 1 July 1994, p. 17).

The state telecommunications monopoly is to be ended, with the military being allowed to set up a rival telephone company (*FT*, 6 July 1995, p. 5).

The non-state sector

The non-state sector comprises private and co-operative (collective) enterprises (for details see Jeffries 1993: 222).

In 1993 the non-state sector accounted for approximately 75 per cent of GDP (*Foreign Affairs*, Survey, vol. 73, no. 3, p. 6).

In 1993 small family businesses produced 23 per cent of total industrial output and probably employ over 30 per cent of the active labour force today (*Small Enterprise Development*, 1994, vol. 5, no. 3, p. 59).

The private sector's share of GDP has risen to 45 per cent. There are still only a few substantial Vietnamese private companies (Victor Mallet, *FT*, Survey, 8 December 1994, p. 37).

The 'equitization' programme

An experimental 'equitization' plan to privatize some state enterprises has been stalled for a year (*FEER*, 3 June 1993, p. 71). Murray Hiebert (*FEER*, 1 July 1993, p. 64) reports that Vietnam has so far failed to begin the privatization process. Six of the seven enterprises listed in June 1992 for partial privatization have either withdrawn because of resistance from managers and workers or were struck off the list because of valuation difficulties. During the previous year eleven new enterprises had been added to the list, but only two had received approval to begin selling shares.

It has been reported that the first partially privatized enterprise, the Legamex garment producer, has sold some shares (*FEER*, 12 August 1993,

p. 79). (In April 1994 the director and deputy director of Legamex were dismissed for alleged corruption. The sale of shares to the public was subsequently suspended: *The Economist*, 4 June 1994, p. 79.) The second state enterprise (Hiep An Footwear) began offering shares in mid-October 1993 (*FEER*, 25 November 1993, p. 61).

A detailed update is provided by Murray Hiebert (*FEER*, 3 February 1994, p. 45). In October 1993 a small shipping enterprise (General Forwarding & Agency Company) became the first state enterprise to be 'equitized'. The Transport Ministry retained 18 per cent of the shares, while 42 per cent were sold to employees of the enterprise and 40 per cent were sold to ministry staff. The only other to complete the process is Refrigeration Electrical Engineering Company, in December 1993 (the authorities in Ho Chi Minh City retained 30 per cent of the shares, while the employees of the enterprise bought 50 per cent of the shares and 20 per cent of the shares were sold to the public. Legamex has sold about 8 per cent of the enterprise, while Hiep An Footwear has also sold some shares. The Finance Ministry has approved sale plans by seven other enterprises and is considering eight more. *IHT* (11 June 1994, p. 17) reported that ten state enterprises had applied to privatize, e.g. Vietnam Airlines was awaiting government approval to sell a 30 per cent equity stake to a foreign partner.

The privatization of state enterprises has stalled. Of the more than 6,000 state enterprises that survive only three (in transport, shoes and refrigeration) have so far successfully prepared for privatization (Victor Mallet, *FT*, Survey, 8 December 1994, pp. 37–8).

Since 1992 the government has run a pilot 'equitization programme' in which it has sought to issue shares for twenty-one small state enterprises. The government typically keeps about 30 per cent of the shares and sells the rest to employees and outside buyers. To date only three of the enterprises have been sold off. About ten have dropped out of the programme, mostly because employees see 'equitization' as the first step towards losing their jobs. Employees have bought most of the shares and their purchases have been financed by government loans and the enterprises' own welfare funds. But 'privatization of a quieter sort continues unchecked: state-owned firms are selling off assets to joint ventures controlled by foreigners. Just under a thousand foreign-investment projects have been approved since 1988' (Adam Schwarz, *FEER*, 2 March 1995, p. 58.)

Tai and Hare (1995) tackle the question of why the 'equitization' process has stalled. State enterprise equitization entails the transformation of state enterprises into equity companies (limited liability companies which are allowed to issue shares). This measure was introduced by a 10 May 1990 resolution of the Council of Ministers. A 'movement for the equitization of state-owned enterprises' began in the latter half of 1992. As an experiment seven state enterprises were put forward. In early 1993 four of them withdrew from the programme without official explanation. The government took action in March and May 1993 to encourage the process. Eighteen others joined the experiment, raising the total number to twenty-one. But at the end of 1993 only two had converted themselves into equity companies, most of the rest being quietly withdrawn (p. 4). The General Maritime Transport Company is a small enterprise (fifty employees) in which the managers and workers have bought 33.1 per cent of the shares for cash, others (mostly officers and staff employees of the Ministry of Transport) purchased 48.9 per cent and the state retained 18 per cent. The Electric Equipment Enterprise had 174 workers. The managers and employees bought 50 per cent of the shares, others purchased 20 per cent and the state retained 30 per cent (p. 5). Legamex is a large and relatively modern state enterprise in the footwear and garment sector employing around 7,000 people. The first issue involved cash from the workers, the management and outside borrowers (including foreign companies and organizations). But after three months only a quarter of the shares had been sold and the experiment had to be suspended because of allegations of malpractices such as insider dealing (p. 5). Factors hindering the process of 'equitization' include (1) the problems of land use (all land belongs to the state, so land use rights must be bought or rented) and (2) disputes about asset ownership (many state enterprises have had to mobilize capital from different sources, including loans from the informal market and stakes from managers and workers; this capital is referred to as 'own capital' and directors think that it should be taken into account in the enterprise evaluation process). Although the private sector is now being encouraged, the official orientation that 'the state enterprise must be dominant' is giving rise to serious uncertainty in the minds of many individual investors (p. 9).

The food processing enterprise Long An Export (employing 1,200 people) announced that shares were to be sold on 19 June 1995. The state was to retain 30 per cent of the capital, 40 per cent would be offered to employees and the remainder was to go to domestic enterprises. Foreigners would not be allowed to invest in the enterprise. There are 6,240 state enterprises in Vietnam, but only five have become stock-issuing enterprises since 1992 (*IHT*, 16 June 1995, p. 15).

Foreign companies are not yet allowed to buy shares in the roughly twenty state enterprises currently being privatized. But under new banking rules joint stock commercial banks and finance companies are to be allowed to raise up to 30 per cent of capital from foreign shareholders. A single foreign shareholder will be limited to 10 per cent of a company's total capital (*FEER*, 23 December 1993, p. 55).

A decree has been issued allowing foreign residents and companies to buy bonds and shares issued by state enterprises (*Transition*, September 1994, vol. 5, no. 7, p. 18).

The government has recently announced a series of 'intermediate' measures, including the selling or leasing of state-owned premises or machinery to workers and managers (Kevin Murphy, *IHT*, 3 July 1993, p. 13).

In late January 1993 an experimental stock trading centre was authorized to deal in government bonds and shares in state-owned enterprises (*FEER*, 18 February 1993, p. 9). The Ho Chi Minh City stock exchange was expected to open in 1994 (initially dealing only in government bonds) and one was also planned for Hanoi later on (*IHT*, 7 December 1993, p. 13).

Vietnam plans to grant state enterprises the right to issue stock and bonds. A law due to take effect on 1 October 1994 would enable state enterprises to sell securities to Vietnamese individuals and companies, as well as to foreign joint ventures (*FEER*, 6 October 1994, p. 89).

Members of the Communist Party are formally not allowed to hire non-family labour, but examples are to be found in real life (Murray Hiebert, *FEER*, 30 September 1993, p. 64).

Foreign trade

Vietnam is now a highly open economy; in 1992 the share of trade in output was 55 per cent (Irvin 1995: 732).

Vietnam is the third largest rice exporter after Thailand and the USA (*The Economist*, 20 March 1993, p. 26).

Rice exports total 1.9 million tonnes (Murray Hiebert, *FEER*, 27 May 1993, p. 59). In 1992 unprocessed farm products accounted for 40 per cent of exports and crude oil for 32 per cent (5.4 million tonnes) (Murray Hiebert, *FEER*, 28 January 1993, p. 43).

The oil industry now accounts for two-thirds of exports (Victor Mallet, *FT*, Survey, 24 September 1993, p. xx). Oil is the largest earner of foreign currency (Victor Mallet, *FT*, Survey, 8 December 1994, p. 39).

Japan accounts for 35 per cent of exports, the EU for 17.1 per cent and Hong Kong for 6 per cent. The respective figures for imports are 14.8 per cent, 12.6 per cent and 30.8 per cent (*FT*, Survey, 30 November 1993, p. 33).

According to Dorothy Avery (*Asian Survey*, 1993, vol. XXXIII, no. 1, p. 71), in 1992 Vietnam achieved a balance of trade surplus for the first time since independence. But there were trade deficits of $200 million in 1993 and $900 million in 1994 (*Transition*, January–February 1995, p. 20). The trade deficit in 1994 was later put at $1.4 billion (*FT*, 30 March 1995, p. 8).

Foreign aid

Soviet economic aid was estimated to average $1.1 billion annually between 1981 and 1985, while aid from other Comecon countries averaged $500 million a year (Andreff 1993: 517).

President Mitterrand of France visited Vietnam on 9–10 February 1993, the first visit by a Western head of state since 1975. He pledged a doubling of aid. French aid amounted to $1 million in 1988 and $35 million in 1992; $65 million was the target for 1993 (*The Economist*, 13 February 1993, p. 63).

Prime Minister Vo Van Kiet visited Japan the following month, while diplomatic relations were opened with South Korea at ambassadorial level on 22 December 1992.

Later developments

7 September 1993. A $30.9 million soft loan from the World Bank for the development of the rubber industry.

26 October 1993. A $76.5 million soft loan from the Asian Development Bank for irrigation purposes.

1 November 1993. Two soft loans amounting to $228.5 million from the World Bank, $70 million for primary education and $158.5 million to upgrade the main north–south highway.

9–10 November 1993. During a donors' conference in Paris sponsored by the World Bank and the UN Development Programme (the USA did not formally attend, but did send an observer) Vietnam was promised $1.86 billion. Around 53 per cent of the aid (which was mainly in the form of soft loans) was to come from governments (Japan promised the largest amount, $557.4 million), while the remaining 47 per cent was to come from the IMF, the World Bank and the Asian Development Bank. Vietnam said that most of the aid was to be spent on education, health, child nutrition and infrastructure. Only around $400 million of the pledged aid was actually disbursed in 1994. According to *Transition* (January–February 1995, p. 20), only $400 million of the $3.82 billion pledged since 1991 has reached Vietnam. (The lack of infrastructure and the necessary legal and financial institutions are real hindrances to development in general and foreign investment in particular.)

15–16 November 1993. The conference pledges $2 billion for 1995, 80 per cent in the form of soft loans and 20 per cent in the form of grants. Japan's commitments in 1995 amount to $650 million, while the World Bank and the Asian Development Bank have promised $450 million and $340 million respectively.

Foreign debt

Apart from its debt to multilateral lenders, Vietnam owes about $4 billion to other governments (plus 11 billion roubles to former Comecon countries) and about $500 million to commercial banks (Kevin Murphy, *IHT*, 10 December 1993, p. 17).

Some $10 billion of Vietnam's debt is still outstanding from the Soviet era

(*Moscow News*, 17–23 June 1994, p. 1).

The total external debt, including the rouble component, was $15.4 billion in 1992 (*FT*, Survey, 30 November 1993, p. 33). The total external debt was $14.6 billion in 1990, $15.3 billion in 1991, $15.4 billion in 1992 and $17.7 billion in 1993 (*FT*, Survey, 24 September 1993, p. xx, and 8 December 1994, p. 40).

In 1991 the foreign debt amounted to $8.63 billion, of which the convertible area accounted for $3.94 billion (Dinh 1993: 535, 537).

At the end of 1992 the hard currency debt was over $3 billion. In addition Vietnam had borrowed 10 billion transferable roubles from the Soviet Union (Dollar 1994: 359, 372).

The Russians say Moscow granted Vietnam 15 billion roubles in military aid. The remaining 10 billion roubles, primarily project funding and traded goods, was lent (Nayan Chanda, *FEER*, 16 March 1995, p. 21). Russia has said that Vietnam is the only Soviet debtor that has made payments, albeit on a very modest scale. A Western diplomat said that for several years Vietnam had been paying Russia $100 million a year, mostly in goods like rice and clothing. Vietnam does not wish Russia's rent for the use of Cam Ranh Bay to be taken out of the debt owed to Russia (under the terms of the 1978 friendship treaty Moscow is entitled to use the facilities there until 2003) (p. 22).

In 1989 Vietnam's outstanding debt to the former Soviet Union was $11 billion, 'which at the current rouble exchange rate is almost negligible' (Irvin 1995: 734).

Foreign investment

Foreign investment commitments since 1988 have totalled $4.6 billion, with Taiwan in first place and Hong Kong a close second (Dorothy Avery, *Asian Survey*, January 1993, vol. XXXIII, no. 1, pp. 71–2).

Since 1986 foreign companies, led by those from Taiwan and Hong Kong, have invested $5.2 billion (Charles Wallace, *IHT*, 15 May 1993, p. 13).

By early April 1993 Vietnam had granted 626 licences valued at $5.3 billion (Murray Hiebert, *FEER*, 27 May 1993, p. 59).

By May 1993 foreign companies had been granted licences for $6.05 billion worth of projects (i.e. registered investment capital) (Victor Mallet, *FT*, 16 September 1993, p. 26).

The 671 investment licences issued so far are valued at $6.3 billion, but only $1.6 billion has actually been disbursed (Murray Hiebert, *FEER*, 23 September 1993, p. 92). William Keeling (*FT*, Survey, 30 November 1993, pp. 32–3) reports the following. As of June 1993 695 projects had been approved, involving $6.214 billion in approved investment and $1.4 billion in implemented investment. By the time the survey had been published the respective figures were 780 (only seven of these concerned private Vietnamese enterprises, of which three were later revoked), \$6.8 billion and \$2 billion. Ten foreign banks have been licensed to open branches, two joint ventures between foreign and state-owned banks have been established and more than twenty 'shareholding' banks have been created (most of these are majority-owned by state institutions, but all have mixed ownership including private enterprises, co-operatives and individuals).

Approved foreign investment amounted to \$2.86 billion in 1992. Since 1987 the total sum approved has amounted to \$7.5 billion (Taiwan accounting for \$1.5 billion), although only about \$2 billion has actually been spent (oil exploration accounting for much of this) (Victor Mallet, *FT*, 13 January 1994, p. 4). The State Committee on Co-operation and Investment has licensed 863 foreign investment projects with a total approved capital of nearly \$7.46 billion over the six years from 1987 to 1993. In 1992 alone 260 projects were licensed with total approved capital of \$2.8 billion. Initially most foreign investment went into oil exploration and hotel construction, but in 1992 investment in industrial production, including cement and steel, rose to 45 per cent of the total registered capital (*IHT*, 24 January 1994, p. 9). In 1994 foreign companies pledged \$3.7 billion to projects, taking the total pledged since 1988 to \$10.9 billion (*IHT*, 3 January 1994, p. 11).

Approved investment in 1993 amounted to \$2.86 billion (*The Economist*, 4 June 1994, p. 79). Actual investment in 1993 amounted to something over \$700 million (Murray Hiebert, *FEER*, 3 February 1994, p. 44). Between 1988 and the end of May 1994 the total value of licences amounted to \$8.9 billion, but actual investment reached only \$2.1 billion by the end of 1993 (Murray Hiebert, *FEER*, 23 June 1994, p. 53). By September 1994 contracted investment amounted to \$10 billion (*FT*, 20 October 1994, p. 6). Since the beginning of 1988 948 foreign-invested projects have been approved, with a combined value of just over \$10 billion. But less than one-third of the \$10 billion has been implemented and almost 10 per cent of approved projects have been cancelled (Adam Schwarz, *FEER*, 29 December 1994, p. 96). Of the \$17 billion in investment contracts only about \$5 billion has actually been invested (*FEER*, 26 October 1995, p. 7). 'Problems facing foreign investors range from lengthy bureaucratic delays in getting licenses, to higher than expected costs for labour, power and telecommunications services… Adding to the licensing morass are confusing policies on land-use rights, the shortage of local financing options, the absence of an effective dispute settlement mechanism, corruption' (p. 57; Adam Schwarz).

Joint venture companies with foreigners do not have the right to get mortgages on land (*The Economist*, 22 October 1994, p. 91).

In late March 1993 the Ministry of Finance said that foreigners would be allowed to buy shares in Vietnamese enterprises on an experimental basis (*FEER*, 15 April 1993, p. 67).

On 26 April 1993 the Vietnam America Trade and Investment Company opened for business in Hanoi. What is significant about this consultancy firm is that it was the first US company to operate officially in Vietnam since 1975.

A late 1993 State Bank edict permitted the establishment of joint stock domestic banks with foreign partners. Joint stock banks are able to sell up to 30 per cent of their capital to foreign investors, although a single foreign shareholder is limited to 10 per cent (*FEER*, 23 December 1993, p. 55; 6 October 1994, p. 54).

In January 1994 foreign insurance companies were allowed to set up branches or joint ventures with local enterprises (*FEER*, 3 February 1994, p. 57).

In February 1995 the central bank announced that efforts would be made to gain stricter control over foreign exchange transactions, e.g. joint ventures would only be able to open an account at one bank. Some foreign-invested companies, primarily those involved in import substitution, are allowed to buy foreign currency with dong if they obtain permits from the central bank and the investment approval agency (Adam Schwarz, *FEER*, 27 April 1995, p. 68).

Vietnam has started granting licences for 'concentrated industrial zones' to complement the six export processing zones already approved. The former will be permitted to sell some output on the domestic market, while the latter are obliged to export all production (Victor Mallet, *FT*, Survey, 8 December 1994, p. 39). The approved export processing zones are in Ho Chi Minh City (two), Hanoi, Haiphong, Danang and Can Tho in the Mekong Delta (*FT*, 14 February 1995, p. 5).

The six approved export processing zones are manufacturing areas where imports and exports are tax-free (*IHT*, 3 January 1995, p. 11).

Industrial zones have been approved in the northern port of Haiphong and near Ho Chi Minh City (*FEER*, 19 January 1995, p. 55).

Amended rules specify that new foreign joint ventures in garments and shoes must export at least 80 per cent of production, with the figure rising to 90 per cent for wholly owned foreign businesses. New hotels in Ho Chi Minh City that involve foreign investors must have at least 150 rooms and $8 million in investment capital; the respective figures for Hanoi are 100 rooms and $5 million (*FEER*, 29 December 1994, p. 99).

A decree took effect on 1 January 1995 that speeded up approval of foreign investments: (1) the State Committee on Co-operation and Investment would have a maximum of forty-five days to consider applications; (2) unless ministries or provinces came up with written objections to a project proposal sent to them by the committee within twenty days, the project would be automatically approved (*IHT*, 2 January 1995, p. 7).

In December 1994 the prime minister approved a project (commonly termed 'Saigon South') to build a new city of more than 500,000 south of Ho Chi Minh City. The new city is to become an international business and financial centre. The majority partner (with a 70 per cent stake) in the project is a Taiwanese company. The Ho Chi Minh City People's Committee (the local authority) has a 30 per cent stake (Kieran Cooke and Laura Tyson, *FT*, 3 January 1995, p. 4; *FT*, 14 February 1995, p. 5).

Some significant events in the oil and gas sectors were as follows (note that Vietnam's total oil output in 1993 was 6.3 million tonnes):

1. In April 1993 a twenty-three-year production-sharing agreement was signed with a consortium led by Australia's Broken Hill Proprietory Company to explore the Dai Hung (Big Bear) oilfield off the south-east coast. In October 1993 commercial quantities of oil were found. The oil started flowing on 15 October 1994.

2. In August 1993 BP announced a big gas find.

3. On 20 June 1994 the Mitsubishi Oil Company announced a significant offshore oil find.

4. On 15 September 1994 BP announced a big gas find.

Adam Schwarz (*FEER*, 16 March 1995, p. 54) stated that 'a few recent oil and gas finds have renewed interest in the country's mostly untapped offshore fields'. But 'none of the discoveries announced last year have yet proved to be commercially viable' (p. 55).

5. On 18 July 1995 BP/Statoil announced a significant offshore gas discovery.

Recent oil and gas discoveries in the South China Sea have sharply increased foreign companies' interest. Oil companies have said that six new finds, the most recent in April 1995, have led to a major upgrading of Vietnam's oil prospects and added gas to the list of potential exports (Michael Richardson, *IHT*, 25 May 1995, p. 17).

Agriculture

State-sector farms now account for only about 4 per cent of the agricultural sector (Victor Mallet, *FT*, Survey, 8 December 1994, p. 39).

Under the production contract system the user may not on his own turn agricultural land to non-agricultural purposes and he cannot let it lie fallow or reduce the fertility of the soil. If necessary the state can take land back after paying some appropriate compensation to the user (Andreff 1993: 527).

A new law was passed by the National Assembly on 14 July 1993 and was planned to come into force on 15 October 1993 (*IHT*, 16 July 1993, p. 17; *FT*, 6 August 1993, p. 5). Land still belongs to the state, but farmers are allowed to buy, sell, transfer, mortgage, rent and inherit the right to use land: 'Land belongs to the people . . . [which] . . . the state allots to land users to till on a long-term basis.' Farmers are entitled to use farmland for up to twenty years for annual crops such as rice and fifty years for perennial crops such as fruits. Each household is allotted a maximum of 3 ha (7.4

acres). Land rentals to subtenants are permitted for up to three years, with exceptions in special cases. The tax on farmers was also reduced. Until then farmers had to reserve 10 per cent of their harvest for the state, but henceforth the rate was to be reduced to 5 per cent. In addition the levy was to be based on local output criteria and the state of the soil and not just on the size of the harvest. According to FEER (*Asia 1994 Yearbook*, 1994, p. 224), peasants would no longer be taxed on production but on the quality of land and its proximity to markets.

Murray Hiebert (*FEER*, 30 September 1993, p. 64) talks of a formal limit of 3 ha per person. But some private land holdings are, in reality, much larger than this and one Vietnamese source suggests that the restriction is on 'farming fields' rather than total land.

In 1994 the length of leases was extended to ninety-nine years (Irvin 1995: 730).

A decree was issued on 1 January 1995 which reaffirmed the state's ownership and control over land (strictly speaking land belongs to the people and is administered by the state). The decree converted land use rights to leases for which rents must be paid to the government. For some types of land use a tax has been charged, but in most cases fees have been nominal and collection has been poorly enforced (Adam Schwarz, *FEER*, 27 April 1995, p. 68).

Economic performance

Vietnam is still a very poor country, but growth rates in the first half of the 1990s were impressive and substantial progress was made on the inflation front (see Table 31.1).

The UN calculates that 51 per cent of the population live below the most basic poverty line, although that figure is down from 70 per cent a decade

Table 31.1 Vietnam: selected economic indicators

Economic indicator	*1990*	*1991*	*1992*	*1993*	*1994*
Rate of growth of GDP (%)	4.9	6.0	8.6	8.1	8.8
Rate of growth of industrial output (%)	2.5	9.9	12.6	10.5	12.9
Rate of growth of agricultural output (%)	1.5	2.2	6.3	3.0	3.9
Food production (paddy equivalent, million tonnes)	21.49	21.7	23.9	24.5	24.3
Inflation rate (%)	67.0	68.1	17.5	5.2	14.4
Budget surplus or deficit (% GDP)	−8.0	−2.5	−3.8	−6.2	−3.5
Current account ($ billion)	−0.121	−0.278	−0.008	−0.869	

Sources: Various issues of the *FEER*, *The Financial Times*, *The International Herald Tribune* and *The Economist*; Dollar (1994: 362, 368); *Transition* (January–February 1995, p. 20); Irvin (1995: 730–8)

ago (Victor Mallet, *FT*, Survey, 8 December 1994, p. 37). Most are in rural areas (p. 39).

The World Bank has calculated that 51 per cent of the population live in poverty, compared with only 9 per cent in China. Rural poverty in Vietnam runs at 57 per cent, compared with just 27 per cent in the towns (*The Economist*, 4 March 1995, p. 78).

Murray Hiebert provides a number of figures for unemployment: (1) 22 per cent of the urban work force have no job and 28 per cent of the rural work force are underemployed (*FEER*, 28 January 1993, p. 43); (2) there are 3.5 million urban jobless and 5 million lack jobs in the countryside (*FEER*, 4 February 1993, p. 27); (3) urban unemployment is about 20 per cent (*FEER*, 27 May 1993, p. 60); (4) official statistics put the unemployment rate at 6 per cent of the work force of 34 million (in urban areas the rate is 9–12 per cent), but the Asian Development Bank puts the unemployment rate at 20 per cent, more than three times the government's figure; loss-making state enterprises have laid off roughly 800,000 workers in the past three years (*FEER*, 2 September 1993, p. 16).

More than 70 per cent of the population live in the countryside. About 20 per cent of peasants are unemployed and an additional 20 per cent are underemployed (Clare Hollingworth, *IHT*, 4 April 1995, p. 8).

Nearly 800,000 workers, about one-third of the 1988 total, have been laid off from state enterprises (Dollar 1994: 369).

A United Nations study by the International Labour Office was published in May 1995 (*IHT*, 12 May 1995, p. 19). The report estimated that over 2 million workers are unemployed and a million new entrants have to be absorbed each year into the work force of 40 million. An annual growth rate of around 10 per cent is needed simply to absorb the new entrants. Although agriculture absorbs over 70 per cent of the work force it accounts for only about one-third of GDP. Since the first labour code came into effect in January 1995 stoppages have become common, particularly at foreign-run enterprises in the south of the country. The report found that:

1. Since 1988 about 1.5 million workers have lost their jobs in state industries and the government bureaucracy, a number equivalent to one-fifth of the urban work force.
2. Since 1988 over 1 million soldiers have been demobilized, 200,000 workers have returned home from former Soviet bloc countries and 65,000 refugees and asylum-seekers have been repatriated from camps in Hong Kong and South East Asia.
3. Official unemployment has risen to 6 per cent nationally from 'almost negligible levels' in the late 1980s. The unemployment rate reaches 25 per cent or more in cities and towns.
4. In the last decade wages have generally lagged behind the rate of inflation and in the state sector have fallen by one-third in real terms.

POSTSCRIPT

THE PRIVATE SECTOR OF THE ECONOMY

The EBRD's estimates of the private sector's share of GDP in mid-1995 are as follows (EBRD, *Transition Report*, 1995, p. 11): Russia, 55 per cent; Armenia, 45 per cent; Azerbaijan, 25 per cent; Belarus, 15 per cent; Estonia, 65 per cent; Georgia, 30 per cent; Kazakhstan, 25 per cent; Kyrgyzstan, 40 per cent; Latvia, 60 per cent; Lithuania, 55 per cent; Moldova, 30 per cent; Tajikistan, 15 per cent; Turkmenistan, 15 per cent; Ukraine, 35 per cent; Uzbekistan, 30 per cent; Albania, 60 per cent; Bulgaria, 45 per cent; Czech Republic, 70 per cent; Slovakia, 60 per cent; Hungary, 60 per cent; Poland, 60 per cent; Romania, 40 per cent; Croatia, 45 per cent; Former Yugoslav Republic of Macedonia, 40 per cent; Slovenia, 45 per cent. The tables have been amended to take account of the data contained in the 1995 report, but it has not been possible to make alternations to the text itself. A very large postscript would be needed to accommodate all the rich material to be found in this excellent report.

RUSSIA

The loans-for-shares scheme. The 31 August 1995 decree laid down the procedure for loans using state-owned shares as collateral, with the lender acting as the state's trustee for the shares. Interest was to be paid and the loan was to be repaid in three years at the original value 'adjusted' for the intervening change in the rouble value of the Ecu. If the lender and the state property committee agree, the former could at any time sell the shares and keep the 'adjusted' value of the loan plus 30 per cent of the excess of the sale price over that value. For each block of shares there would be a competition and the block would be awarded to the one offering the largest loan. For strategic decisions the voting rights of shares could be exercised only with the agreement of the state property committee (*RET*, Monthly Update, 19 September 1995, p. 11). It was necessary to enter into discussions with banks on the loans-for-shares scheme because of the extremely low level of privatization proceeds in 1995 (*RET*, Monthly update, 19 October 1995, p. 12). The range of possible lenders was opened to include banks, other financial institutions, and domestic and foreign companies. The highest bidder at the auction will receive the shares. If the loan is not repaid (with interest) by the end of 1995 the creditor has the right to sell the shares within three years. The first list, of twenty-nine enterprises, was published on 25 September 1995 (Deutsche Bank, *Focus: Eastern Europe*, 1995, no. 139, pp. 1–3). On 2 November 1995 the president signed a decree deferring the earliest date when investors could be given permission to sell the acquired shares from 1 January 1995 to 1 September 1995 (*RET*, Monthly Update, 14 November 1995, p. 10). 'In practice, there may be little competition, and lenders will probably have understandings with the management of the companies involved. The result may well be a series of de facto management buy-outs, mostly at below-market prices' (*The Economist*, 18 November 1995, p. 100).

ALBANIA

An auction of six enterprises was held in December 1994, but only one was bid for. By 11 September 1995, when twenty enterprises were offered for sale as the start of large privatization, some 900,000 people had received part of their voucher entitlement. People over fifty-five years of age receive twice as many vouchers as the under-thirty-five-year-olds. The first phase of mass privatization was set to end in June 1996. Strategic industries such as telecommunications were to be handled separately (Jane Martinson, *FT*, Survey, 2 October 1995, p. iv). In August 1995 the government removed the bar on non-nationals owning land (p. iv). The average farm consists of 1.5 ha split into 3.3 separate parcels of differing quality. A law passed in August 1995 allowed the buying and selling of farmland for the first time. In order to encourage land consolidation a farmer who wishes to sell must offer it to his family and neighbours before putting it on the open market. The government estimates that 96 per cent of agricultural land has been distributed, but only half has been legally entitled (p. iii).

A voucher-based mass privatization programme was approved in early 1995, with voucher distribution starting in June. The scheme involved about 1,100 enterprises, including utilities and subsidiaries in the mining and petroleum sectors but excluding enterprises under the defence ministry. Actual completed privatization of large enterprises has been insignificant. In July 1995 a law was passed which allowed foreign individuals or companies to buy land if they combine the purchase with a three times as large investment in the usage of land. Another law allowed the sale and purchase of agricultural land and also transformed the titles to usage of the land into property titles (EBRD, *Transition Report*, 1995, p. 33).

SLOVAKIA

Under the new legislation voucher holders were to receive five-year bands. These may be held until maturity or used for purposes such as the purchase of shares in privatized companies in which the holders are employed or the purchase of shares from assets in the national property fund portfolio. Most of the assets to be privatized in the new programme were to be by means of direct sales, including management and employee buy-outs. The law relating to state interests identified over twenty enterprises which were not to be privatized (mainly in gas and electricity generation, telecommunications, armaments and agriculture). It also listed a further forty enterprises (some of which had already been partially privatized) which were defined as 'strategically important' (mainly in mining, chemicals, construction, engineering and the agricultural sectors). The state was to retain ownership in these and enjoy special voting rights (EBRD, *Transition Report*, 1995, p. 57).

THE FORMER YUGOSLAVIA

The success of the Bosnian government and Croat/Bosnian Croat offensives in north-west and central Bosnia in mid-September 1995 rapidly reduced the area held by the Bosnian Serbs from around 70 per cent to some 50 per cent (i.e. almost in line with their proposed share of 49 per cent). The siege of Sarajevo began to be lifted in return for a suspension of Nato air strikes. On 26 September 1995 the foreign ministers of Bosnia, Croatia and Serbia agreed on the constitutional principles for Bosnia. For example, there were to be free and democratic elections for parliament and the presidency, with two-thirds of both elected from the territory of the Federation and one-third from the territory of the Republika Srpska. Foreign policy was to be centrally determined. On 5 October a cease-fire was agreed. It formally came into effect on 11 October (slightly late), but it took more than a week for the fighting to die down in north-west Bosnia, with the Bosnian Serbs losing more ground (some estimates put their share at 48 per cent). There was deep international concern about continuing atrocities and 'ethnic cleansing' by the Bosnian Serbs. Croatia also came in for strong condemnation for its activities in the Krajina. Talks about a Bosnian peace settlement began in the USA on 1 November 1995, attended by Presidents Izetbegovic, Tudjman and Milosevic.

On 10 November an agreement was signed which strengthened the Federation of Bosnia and Hercegovina. A peace agreement was initialled by Presidents Izetbegovic, Tudjman and Milosevic on 21 November 1995. Additional points of agreement included the following: a reunited Sarajevo under federal authority; an 'effective' central government responsible for foreign policy, foreign trade, monetary policy, citizenship and immigration (the presidency to rotate, one of the three members to be a Bosnian Serb); individuals charged with war crimes to be excluded from political and military life; a land corridor to link Sarajevo and Gorazde; the problem of Brcko and the Posavina corridor to be submitted to international arbitration (the Bosnian Serbs were awarded land in western Bosnia which they lost in the summer of 1995); Nato to provide a 60,000 strong implementation force, including 20,000 US troops (on 8 November 1995 the USA and Russia announced that a Russian combat brigade would participate as part of a US division, though under US rather than Nato control); on 22 November the UN Security Council announced a lifting of the arms embargo on the countries of the former Yugoslavia and the suspension of economic sanctions on the Federal Republic of Yugoslavia.

On 12 November 1995 Croatia and the Croatian Serbs signed an agreement relating to eastern Slavonia drafted by Tudjman and Milosevic during the talks in the USA. Eastern Slavonia was to return to Croatian control after a transitional period of UN administration of at least one year and no more than two years. In the general election in Croatia, held on 29 October 1995, Tudjman's Croatian Democratic union was victorious, stressing the recent military victories. But the party was disappointed not to win the two-thirds majority in parliament necessary to change the constitution in favour of a stronger presidency. Opposition parties played on economic and social problems such as unemployment and on corruption in political life.

CHINA

The new banking law does not have an immediate impact on the operations of foreign and Sino-foreign joint venture banks (which will continue to be governed by separate, existing legislation for an indefinite period). As regards Chinese commercial banks, both deposit and lending rates have to be set within a certain range set by the central bank. Commercial banks have to provide loans 'under the guidance of state industrial policies'. Wholly state-owned commercial banks have to provide loans for designated projects approved by the State Council, with compensation forthcoming for any ensuing losses. Commercial banks are not allowed to invest in non-banking financial institutions (*China Briefing*, October 1995, pp. 2–4).

VIETNAM

To date only enterprises have actually sold shares in the 'equitization' programme (Adam Schwarz, *FEER*, 26 October 1995, p. 53).

BIBLIOGRAPHY

PERIODICALS AND REPORTS

Abecor *Country Reports* are distributed in Britain by Barclays Bank on behalf of an association of European banks. The *Vietnam Courier* was published in Hanoi until it ceased publication in 1992. Periodicals and reports mentioned in the text are abbreviated as follows:

CDSP *Current Digest of the Soviet Press* (since 5 February 1992 *Post-Soviet*)
DIW Deutsches Institut für Wirtschaftsforschung (Berlin)
EEN *Eastern Europe Newsletter*
EIU Economist Intelligence Unit
FEER *Far Eastern Economic Review*
FT *Financial Times*
IHT *International Herald Tribune*
RET *Russian Economic Trends*

Note the following changes of title: *Soviet Economy* to *Post-Soviet Studies*; *Soviet Studies* to *Europe–Asia Studies*.

BOOKS AND JOURNALS

Acks, Z. and FitzRoy, F. (1993) *A Constitution for Privatized Eastern Enterprise*, University of St Andrews: Discussion Paper 9302.
Adam, J. (1993) 'Transformation to a market economy in the former Czechoslovakia', *Europe–Asia Studies*, vol. 45, no. 4.
Afanasyev, Y. (1994) 'Russian reform is dead', *Foreign Affairs*, vol. 73, no. 2.
Aghion, P. and Blanchard, O. (1994) *On the Speed of Transition in Central Europe*, Nuffield College Oxford: Discussion Paper no. 87.
Akerlof, G., Rose, A., Yellen, J. and Hessenius, H. (1991) 'East Germany in from the cold; the economic aftermath of currency union', *Brookings Papers on Economic Activity*, no. 1.
Ali, R. and Lifschultz, L. (1994) 'Why Bosnia?', *Third World Quarterly*, vol. 15, no. 3.
Andreff, W. (1993) 'The double transition from underdevelopment and from socialism in Vietnam', *Journal of Contemporary Asia*, vol. 23, no. 4.
Ash, T. (1993) 'Agriculture in the former centrally-planned economies in transition', *Economics of Transition*, vol. 1, no. 4.
Ash, T. and Hare, P. (1994) 'Privatization in the Russian Federation: changing enterprise behaviour in the transition period', *Cambridge Journal of Economics*, vol. 18, no. 6.

Asian Development Bank (1992) *Mongolia: a Centrally Planned Economy in Transition*, Hong Kong: Oxford University Press.

Åslund, A. (1994a) 'Lessons of the first four years of systemic change in Eastern Europe', *Journal of Comparative Economics*, vol. 19, no. 1.

—— (1994b) 'Russia's success story', *Foreign Affairs*, vol. 73, no. 5.

—— (1995) 'Ukraine's turnaround', *Foreign Policy*, no. 100.

—— (forthcoming) 'Introduction: the Balkan transformation in perspective' in Jeffries and Teodorescu (forthcoming).

Åslund, A. and Layard, R. (eds) (1993) *Changing the Economic System in Russia*, London: Pinter.

Åslund, A. and Sjöberg, Ö. (1991) *Privatization and Transition to Market Economy in Albania*, Stockholm Institute of Soviet and East European Economics: Working Paper no. 27.

Balcerowicz, L. (1993) 'Transition to market economy: Central and East European countries in comparative perspective', *British Review of Economic Issues*, vol. 15, no. 37.

—— (1994) 'Common fallacies in the debate on the transition to a market economy', *Economic Policy*, no. 19 (Supplement).

Bartholdy, K. (1993) 'Statistical review', *Economics of Transition*, vol. 1, no. 1.

Bartholdy, K. and Szegvari, I. (1993) 'Statistical review', *Economics of Transition*, vol. 1, no. 2.

Bartlett, W. (forthcoming) 'From reform to crisis: economic impacts of secession, war and sanctions in the former Yugoslavia' in Jeffries and Teodorescu (forthcoming).

Begg, D. (1991) 'Economic reform in Czechoslovakia: should we believe in Santa Klaus?', *Economic Policy*, no. 13 (October).

—— (1993) *Economics: Update*, no. 3 (winter/spring).

Begg, D. and Portes, R. (1993a) 'Enterprise debt and economic transformation', *Economics of Transition*, vol. 1, no. 1.

—— (1993b) 'East Germany since reunification: wage subsidies remain a better way', *Economics of Transition*, vol. 1, no. 4.

Bennett, A. (1993) 'The operation of the Estonian currency board' *IMF Staff Papers*, vol. 40, no. 2.

Berkowitz, D., Berliner, J., Gregory, P., Linz, S. and Millar, R. (1993) 'An evaluation of the CIA's analysis of Soviet economic performance', *Comparative Economic Studies*, vol. XXXV, no. 2.

Bicanic, I. (forthcoming) 'The economic divergence of Yugoslavia's successor states' in Jeffries and Teodorescu (forthcoming).

Bim, A., Jones, D. and Weisskopf, T. (1993) 'Hybrid forms of enterprise organization in the former USSR and the Russian Federation', *Comparative Economic Studies*, vol. XXXV, no. 1.

Blanchard, O. (1994) 'Transition in Poland', *Economic Journal*, vol. 104, no. 426.

Blanchard, O., Dornbusch, R., Krugman, P., Layard, R. and Summers, L. (1991) *Reform in Eastern Europe*, Cambridge, Mass.: MIT Press.

Blanchard, O. and Layard, R. (1990) *Economic Change in Poland*, London: Centre for Research into Communist Economies (New Series 1, July).

Blaszczyk, B. and Dabrowski, M. (1993) *The Privatization Process in Poland 1989–1992*, London: Centre for Research into Communist Economies.

Blejer, M. *et al.* (1992) *Albania: from Isolation toward Reform*, IMF: Occasional Paper no. 98.

Bogetic, Z. (1993) 'The role of employee ownership in privatization of state enterprises in Eastern and Central Europe', *Europe–Asia Studies*, vol. 45, no. 3.

Bogetic, Z. and Fox, L. (1993) 'Incomes policy during stabilization: a review and lessons from Bulgaria and Romania', *Comparative Economic Studies*, vol. XXXV, no. 1.

Bojcun, M. (1995) 'The Ukrainian general elections in March–April 1994', *Europe–Asia Studies*, vol. 47, no. 2.

Bolton, P. (1995) 'Privatization and the separation of ownership and control: lessons from Chinese enterprise reform', *Economics of Transition*, vol. 3, no. 1.

Bolton, P. and Roland, G. (1992) 'Privatization policies in Central and Eastern Europe', *Economic Policy*, no. 15.

Boone, P. (1994) 'Grassroots macroeconomic reform in Mongolia', *Journal of Comparative Economics*, vol. 18, no. 3.

Boote, A. and Somogyi, J. (1991) *Economic Reform in Hungary since 1968*, IMF Occasional Paper no. 83, Washington, D.C.: IMF.

Borensztein, E. and Kumar, M. (1991) 'Proposals for privatization in Eastern Europe', *IMF Staff Papers*, vol. 38, no. 2.

Borensztein, E., Demekas, D. and Ostry, J. (1993) 'An empirical analysis of the output decline in three Eastern European countries', *IMF Staff Papers*, vol. 40, no. 1.

Boycko, M. (1991) 'Price decontrol: the microeconomic case for the "big bang" approach', *Oxford Review of Economic Policy*, vol. 7, no. 4.

Boycko, M., Shleifer, A. and Vishny, R. (1994) 'Voucher privatization', *Journal of Financial Economics*, vol. 35, no. 2.

Brada, J. (1993) 'The transformation from communism to capitalism: how far? how fast?', *Post-Soviet Affairs*, vol. 9, no. 2.

Brada, J. and King, A. (1992) 'Is there a J-curve for the economic transition from socialism to capitalism?', *Economics of Planning*, vol. 25, no. 1.

—— (1993) 'Is private farming more efficient than socialized agriculture?', *Economica*, vol. 60, no. 237.

Bramall, C. (1993) 'The role of decollectivization in China's agricultural miracle, 1978–90', *The Journal of Peasant Studies*, vol. 20, no. 2.

Bridges, B. (1995) 'North Korea after Kim Il Sung', *The World Today*, vol. 51, no. 6.

Brom, K. and Orenstein, M. (1994) 'The privatized sector in the Czech Republic: government and bank control in a transitional economy', *Europe–Asia Studies*, vol. 46, no. 6.

Brooks, K. (1992) 'Stabilization, sectoral adjustment and enterprise reform in the agricultural sector of Russia', *American Journal of Agricultural Economics*, vol. 74, no. 5.

Brooks, K., Guash, L., Braverman, A. and Csaki, C. (1991) 'Agriculture and the transition to the market', *Journal of Economic Perspectives*, vol. 5, no. 4.

Brooks, K. and Meurs, M. (1994) 'Romanian land reform, 1991–93', *Comparative Economic Studies*, vol. XXXVI, no. 2.

Bruno, M. (1993a) 'Stabilization and the macroeconomics of transition – how different is Eastern Europe?', *Economics of Transition*, vol. 1, no. 1.

—— (1993b) *Crisis, Stabilization and Economic Reform: Therapy by Consensus*, Oxford: Clarendon Press.

Brus, W. (1993) 'Marketization and democratization: the Sino-Soviet divergence', *Cambridge Journal of Economics*, vol. 17, no. 4.

Bryson, P. (1984) *The Consumer under Socialist Planning: the East German Case*, New York: Praeger.

Bryson, P. and Melzer, M. (1991) *The End of the East German Economy: from Honecker to Reunification*, London: Macmillan.

Brzezinski, Z. (1967) *The Soviet Bloc*, Cambridge, M.A.: Harvard University Press.

—— (1994) 'The premature partnership', *Foreign Affairs*, vol. 73, no. 2.

Buck, T., Filatotchev, I. and Wright, M. (1994) 'Employee buy-outs and the transformation of Russian industry', *Comparative Economic Studies*, vol. XXXVI, no. 2.

Buechtemann, C. and Schupp, J. (1992) 'Repercussions of reunification: patterns and trends in the socio-economic transformation of East Germany', *Industrial Relations Journal*, vol. 23, no. 2.

Burda, M. (1993) 'Unemployment, labour markets and structural change in Eastern Europe', *Economic Policy*, no. 16.

Cable, V. and Ferdinand, P. 'China as an economic giant', *International Affairs*, vol. 70, no. 2.

Calvo, G. and Coricelli, F. (1993) 'Output collapse in Eastern Europe', *IMF Staff Papers*, vol. 40, no. 1.

Calvo, G. and Frenkel, J. (1991a) 'From centrally planned to market economy', *IMF Staff Papers*, vol. 38, no. 2.

—— (1991b) 'Credit markets, credibility, and economic transformation', *Journal of Economic Perspectives*, vol. 5, no. 4.

Capek, A. and Sazama, G. (1993) 'Czech and Slovak economic relations', *Europe–Asia Studies*, vol. 45, no. 2.

Carlin, W. and Mayer, C. (1992) 'Restructuring enterprises in Eastern Europe', *Economic Policy*, no. 15.

Cepl, V. (1991) 'A note on the restitution of property in post-communist Czechoslovakia', *Journal of Communist Studies*, vol. 7, no. 3.

Chai, J. (1992) 'Consumption and living standards in China', *China Quarterly*, no. 131.

Chang, C. and Wang, Y. (1994) 'The nature of the township–village enterprise', *Journal of Comparative Economics*, vol. 19, no. 3.

Charemza, W. (1992) 'Market failure and stagflation: some aspects of privatization in Poland', *Economics of Planning*, vol. 25, no. 1.

Chen, C., Chang, L. and Zhang, Y. (1995) 'The role of foreign direct investment in China's post-1978 economic development', *World Development*, vol. 23, no. 4.

Chen, K., Hongchang, W., Yuxin, Z., Jefferson, G. and Rawski, T. (1988) 'Productivity changes in Chinese industry', *Journal of Comparative Economics*, vol. XII.

Chen, K., Jefferson, G. and Singh, I. (1992) 'Lessons from China's economic reform', *Journal of Comparative Economics*, vol. 16, no. 2.

Chubais, A. and Vishnevskaya, M. (1993) 'Main issues of privatization in Russia' in Åslund and Layard (1993).

Clague, C. (1992) 'Introduction: the journey to a market economy' in Clague and Rausser (1992).

Clague, C. and Rausser, G. (eds) (1992) *The Emergence of Market Economies in Eastern Europe*, Oxford: Blackwell.

Cnossen, S. (1992) 'Key questions in considering a value-added tax for Central and Eastern European countries', *IMF Staff Papers*, vol. 39, no. 2.

Cochrane, N. (1988) 'The private sector in East European agriculture', *Problems of Communism*, March–April.

—— (1990a) 'Reforming agricultural prices in Eastern Europe', *Problems of Communism*, January–February.

—— (1990b) 'Reforming socialist agriculture: Bulgarian and Hungarian experience and implications for the USSR' in Wädekin (1990b).

—— (1993) 'Central European agrarian reforms in a historical perspective', *American Journal of Agricultural Economics*, vol. 75, no. 3.

Collier, I. and Siebert, H. (1991) 'The economic integration of post-Wall Germany', *American Economic Review*, Papers and Proceedings, May.

Corbett, J. and Mayer, C. (1991) 'Financial reform in Eastern Europe: progress with the wrong model', *Oxford Review of Economic Policy*, vol. 7, no. 4.

Davidova, S. (1991) 'Bulgarian farm structure: from paralysis to reform', *Food Policy*, vol. 16, no. 3.

Deere, C., Gonzales, E., Perez, N. and Rodriguez, G. (1995) 'Household incomes in Cuban agriculture: a comparison of the state, co-operative and peasant sectors', *Development and Change*, vol. 26, no. 2.

Deere, C., and Meurs, M. (1992) 'Markets, markets everywhere? Understanding the Cuban anomaly', *World Development*, vol. 20, no. 6.

Deere, C., Perez, N. and Gonzales, E. (1994) 'The view from below: Cuban agriculture in the "special period in peacetime"', *Journal of Peasant Studies*, vol. 21, no. 2.

Demekas, D. and Khan, M. (1991) *The Romanian Reform Programme*, IMF: Occasional Paper no. 89.

Demougin, D. and Sinn, H.-W. (1994) 'Privatization, risk-taking and the communist firm', *Journal of Public Economics*, vol. 55, no. 2.

Denizer, C. and Gelb, A. (1992) *Mongolia: Privatization and System Transformation in an Isolated Economy*, World Bank: Working Paper WPS 1063.

Dinh, Q. (1993) 'Vietnam's policy reforms and its future', *Journal of Contemporary Asia*, vol. 23, no. 4.

Dipchand, C. (1994) 'The interbank market in China', *Development Policy Review*, vol. 12, no. 1.

Dobozi, I. and Pohl, G. (1995) 'Real output decline in transition economies: forget GDP, try power consumption data', *Transition*, vol. 6, nos 1–2.

Dollar, D. (1990) 'Economic reform and allocative efficiency in China's state-owned industry', *Economic Development and Cultural Change*, vol. 39, no. 1.

—— (1994) 'Macroeconomic management and the transition to the market in Vietnam', *Journal of Comparative Economics*, vol. 18, no. 3.

Eastwood, R. and Durski, A. (1993) *Financial Reform in Poland: Some Parallels with Chilean Experience 1973–83*, University of Sussex: Discussion Paper no. 3/93.

Eberstadt, N. (1994a) 'Demographic shocks after communism: Eastern Germany, 1989–93', *Population and Development Review*, vol. 20, no. 1.

—— (1994b) 'Demographic shocks in Eastern Germany, 1989–93', *Europe–Asia Studies*, vol. 46, no. 3.

EBRD (1994) *Transition Report*, London: European Bank for Reconstruction and Development.

—— (1995) *Transition Report Update* (April), London: European Bank for Reconstruction and Development.

Economist Surveys:

—— (1985) 'Comecon', 20 April.

—— (1988) 'The Soviet Economy', 9 April.

—— (1989) 'Eastern Europe', 12 August.

—— (1989) 'Russia's anti-drink campaign', 23 December.

—— (1990) '*Perestroika*', 28 April.

—— (1990) 'The new Germany', 30 June.

—— (1990) 'The Soviet Union', 20 October.

—— (1991) 'Business in Eastern Europe', 21 September.

—— (1992) 'Germany', 23 May.

—— (1992) 'China', 28 November.

—— (1992) 'Russia', 5 December.

—— (1993) 'Eastern Europe', 13 March.

—— (1993) 'Asia', 30 October.

—— (1994) 'Poland', 16 April.
—— (1994) 'Ukraine', 7 May.
—— (1994) 'Germany', 21 May.
—— (1995) 'China', 18 March.
—— (1995) 'Russia's emerging market', 8 April.
—— (1995) 'Vietnam', 8 July.
Eichengreen, B. (1993) 'A payments mechanism for the former Soviet Union: is the EPU a relevant precedent?', *Economic Policy*, no. 17.
Eichengreen, B. and Uzan, M. (1992) 'The Marshall Plan: economic effects and implications for Eastern Europe and the former USSR', *Economic Policy*, no. 14.
Elliott, J. (1992) 'The future of socialism: Vietnam, the way ahead?', *Third World Quarterly*, vol. 13, no. 1.
Ellman, M. (1986) 'Economic reform in China', *International Affairs*, vol. 62, no. 3.
—— (1989a) *Socialist Planning*, 2nd edn, London: Cambridge University Press.
—— (1989b) *The USSR in the 1990s*, London: EIU.
—— (1993) 'General aspects of transition' in Ellman *et al.* (1993).
—— (1994) 'The increase of death and disease under "katastroika"', *Cambridge Journal of Economics*, vol. 18, no. 4.
Ellman, M., Gaidar, E. and Kolodko, G. (editor Admiraal, P.) (1993) *Economic Transition in Eastern Europe*, Oxford: Blackwell.
Estrin, S. and Richet, X. (1993) 'Industrial restructuring and microeconomic adjustment in Poland: a cross-sectional approach', *Comparative Economic Studies*, vol. XXXV, no. 4.
Estrin, S. and Xavier, R. (1993) 'Industrial restructuring and microeconomic adjustment in Poland: a cross-sectional approach', *Comparative Economic Studies*, vol. XXXV, no. 4.
Faber, M. (1990) 'Mongolia: moves towards *perestroika*', *Development Policy Review*, vol. 8, no. 4.
Fan, Q. and Schaffer, M. (1994) 'Government financial transfers and enterprise adjustments in Russia, with comparisons to Central and Eastern Europe', *Economics of Transition*, vol. 2, no. 2.
Feder, G., Lau, L., Lin, J. and Luo, X. (1992) 'The determinants of farm investment and residential construction in post-reform China', *Economic Development and Cultural Change*, vol. 41, no. 1.
Filatotchev, I., Buck, T. and Wright, M. (1992) 'Privatization and buy-outs in the USSR', *Soviet Studies*, vol. 44, no. 2.
Financial Times (various surveys):
Albania: 21 July 1994; 2 October 1995.
Armenia: 7 June 1995.
Azerbaijan: 7 March 1994.
Baltic Basin States: 16 December 1992.
Bulgaria: 7 December 1984; 27 October 1988; 17 May 1991; 5 May 1993; 13 October 1994.
China: 9 December 1985; 20 August 1986; 5 September 1986; 22 September 1986; 29 September 1986; 30 September 1986; 18 December 1986; 18 December 1987; 12 December 1989; 24 April 1991; 16 June 1992; 2 June 1993; 18 November 1993; 7 November 1994; 20 November 1995.
Counter-trade: 11 February 1986; East–West Trade: 13 December 1988; 6 June 1989; 8 December 1989.
Cuba: 17 February 1989; 26 September 1995.
Czechoslovakia: 23 October 1985; 8 November 1991.
Czech Republic: 11 January 1993; 24 March 1993; 19 December 1994; 2 June 1995.

Eastern Europe: 4 February 1991.
Estonia: 19 April 1994.
GDR: 3 October 1989.
Germany: 29 October 1990; 10 April 1991; 28 October 1991; 26 October 1992; 25 October 1993; 4 May 1994 (Restructuring of Eastern Germany); 21 November 1994; 23 October 1995.
Hungary: 11 September 1987; 17 September 1990; 30 October 1991; 29 October 1992; 17 November 1993; 11 November 1994; 21 November 1995.
IMF: World Economy and Finance: 24 September 1993.
Korea: 23 June 1994.
Latvia: 18 November 1994.
Macedonia: 7 July 1995.
Poland: 25 May 1989; 20 November 1990; 2 May 1991; 28 April 1992; 17 June 1993; 18 March 1994; 28 March 1995; 29 September 1995.
Privatization in Eastern Europe: 3 July 1992.
Romania: 3 May 1994; 25 May 1995.
Russia: 13 May 1992; 27 May 1993; 27 June 1994; 10 April 1995.
Slovakia: 2 November 1993; 16 December 1994.
Slovenia: 30 March 1992; 30 March 1993; 12 April 1994; 6 April 1995.
Soviet Union: 12 March 1990.
Ukraine: 27 January 1993.
Vietnam: 14 November 1991; 30 November 1993; 8 December 1994; 13 November 1995.
Yugoslavia: 18 June 1984; 21 December 1984; 21 June 1985; 17 December 1985; 17 June 1986; 16 December 1986; 22 December 1987; 22 June 1988; 6 December 1988; 29 June 1989; 5 December 1989; 6 July 1990; 17 December 1990; 27 June 1991.

Fischer, S. (1992a) 'Stabilization and economic reform in Russia', *Brookings Papers on Economic Activity*, no. 1.

—— (1992b) 'Privatization in East European transformation' in Clague and Rausser (1992).

Fischer, S. and Frenkel, J. (1992) 'Macroeconomic issues of Soviet reform', *American Economic Review*, Papers and Proceedings, May.

Fischer, S. and Gelb, A. (1991) 'The process of socialist economic transformation', *Journal of Economic Perspectives*, vol. 5, no. 4.

Flemming, J. and Matthews, R. (1994) 'Economic reform in Russia', *National Institute Economic Review*, no. 149.

Fry, M., and Nuti, D. (1992) 'Monetary and exchange-rate policies during Eastern Europe's transition: some lessons from further east', *Oxford Review of Economic Policy*, vol. 8, no. 1.

Frydman, R. and Rapaczyncki, A. (1993) 'Insiders and the state: overview of responses to agency problems in East European privatization', *Economics of Transition*, vol. 1, no. 1.

Frydman, R., Rapaczynski, A., Earle, J. *et al.* (1993) *The Privatization Process in Central Europe*, London: Central European University Press.

Gaynor, M. and Putterman, L. (1993) 'Productivity consequences of alternative land division methods in China's decollectivization', *Journal of Development Economics*, vol. 42, no. 2.

Gelb, A., Jefferson, G. and Singh, I. (1993) 'Can communist economies transform incrementally? The experience of China', *Economics of Transition*, vol. 1, no. 4.

Gills, B. (1992) 'North Korea and the crisis of socialism: the historical ironies of national division', *Third World Quarterly*, vol. 13, no. 1.

Ginsburg, T. (1995) 'Political reform in Mongolia: between Russia and China', *Asian Survey*, 1995, vol. XXXV, no. 5.

Goodkind, D. (1995) 'Vietnam's one-or-two-child policy in action', *Population and Development Review*, vol. 21, no. 1.

Gregory, P. and Stuart, R. (1990) *Soviet Economic Structure and Performance*, 4th edn, New York: Harper & Row (2nd edn 1981 and 3rd edn 1986).

—— (1994) *Soviet and Post-Soviet Economic Structure and Performance*, 5th edn, New York: Harper Collins.

Groves, T., Hong, Y., McMillan, J. and Naughton, B. (1994) 'Autonomy and incentives in Chinese state enterprises', *Quarterly Journal of Economics*, vol. CIX, no. 1.

The Guardian (various surveys):

China: China 13 October 1986; regional China – Jiangsu and Guangdong 16 October 1987; Shanghai: 19 November 1987.

Hungary: 31 October 1985; 20 October 1986; 5 May 1988; 8 February 1991.

Soviet Union: 6 November 1987; 24 June 1988; 13 December 1988; 5 April 1989.

Yugoslavia: 27 October 1986.

Slovenia, 16 May 1988.

Gungwu, W. (1993) 'Greater China and the Chinese overseas', *China Quarterly*, no. 136.

Gwiazda, A. (1994) 'National minorities in Poland and the Baltic States', *International Relations*, vol. XII, no. 1.

Handelman, S. (1994) 'The Russian mafiya', *Foreign Affairs*, vol. 73, no. 2.

Hansson, A. (1993) 'The trouble with the rouble: monetary reform in the former Soviet Union' in Åslund and Layard (1993).

Hare, P. (1990a) 'Creating market economies: Eastern Europe in the 1990s', *The Economic Review*, vol. 7, no. 5.

—— (1990b) 'From central planning to market economy: some microeconomic issues', *Economic Journal*, vol. 100, no. 401.

—— (1991) 'Eastern Europe: the transition to a market economy', *The Royal Bank of Scotland Review*, no. 169 (March).

—— (1992) 'Hungary' in Jeffries (1992b).

—— (1993) 'Competitiveness and restructuring: issues for Eastern Europe', *British Review of Economic Issues*, vol. 15, no. 37.

Hare, P. and Revesz, T. (1992) 'Hungary's transition to the market: the case against a "big-bang"', *Economic Policy*, no. 14.

Havel, V. (1994) 'A call for sacrifice: the co-responsibility of the West', *Foreign Affairs*, vol. 73, no. 2.

Havrylyshyn, O., Miller, M. and Perraudin, W. (1994) 'Deficits, inflation and the political economy of Ukraine', *Economic Policy*, no. 19.

Heady, C., Rajah, N. and Smith, S. (1994) 'Tax reform and economic transition in the Czech Republic', *Fiscal Studies*, vol. 15, no. 1.

Hexter, D. (1993) 'The bad debt problem in Eastern Europe', *Economics of Transition*, vol. 1, no. 1.

Holzman, F. (1976) *International Trade under Communism*, New York: Basic Books.

—— (1987) *The Economics of Soviet Bloc Trade and Finance*, Boulder and London: Westview Press.

—— (1991) 'Moving towards rouble convertibility', *Comparative Economic Studies*, vol. XXXIII, no. 3.

Holzman, R. (1992) 'Tax reform in countries in transition', *Public Finance*, Supplement to vol. 47.

Hough, J. (1994) 'The Russian general election of 1993: public attitudes toward economic reform and democratization', *Post-Soviet Affairs*, vol. 10, no. 1.

Hrncir, M. (1993) *Economic Recovery and Foreign Exchange Regime: the Case of the Czech Republic*, University of Cambridge: Discussion Paper on Economic Transition DPET 9301.

Hughes, G. and Hare, P. (1991) 'Competitiveness and industrial restructuring in Czechoslovakia, Hungary and Poland' in *European Economy.*

—— (1992) 'Industrial policy and restructuring in Eastern Europe', *Oxford Review of Economic Policy*, vol. 8, no. 1.

—— (1994) 'The international competitiveness of industries in Bulgaria, Czechoslovakia, Hungary and Poland', *Oxford Economic Papers*, vol. 46, no. 2.

Hughes, M. (1993) 'Eastern pain and Western promise: the reaction of Western governments to the economic plight of the "New Eastern Europe"', *International Relations*, vol. XI, no. 6.

Hughes Hallet, A. and Ma, Y. (1993) 'East Germany, West Germany, and their Mezzogiorno problem: a parable for European economic integration', *Economic Journal*, vol. 103, no. 417.

—— (1994) 'Real adjustment in a union of incompletely converged economies: an example from East and West Germany', *European Economic Review*, vol. 38, no. 9.

Hume, I. and Pinto, B. (1993) 'Prejudice and fact in Poland's industrial transformation', *Finance and Development*, vol. 30, no. 2.

Husain, A. and Sahay, R. (1992) 'Does sequencing of privatization matter in reforming planned economies', *IMF Staff Papers*, vol. 39, no. 4.

Huskey, E. (1995) 'The rise of contested politics in Central Asia: elections in Kyrgyzstan, 1989–90', *Europe–Asia Studies*, vol. 47, no. 5.

Hussain, A. (1992) *The Chinese Economic Reforms in Retrospect and Prospect*, LSE: CP no. 24.

Hussain, A. and Stern, N. (1991) 'Effective demand, enterprise reforms and public finance in China', *Economic Policy*, no. 12.

—— (1993) 'The role of the state, ownership and taxation in transitional economies', *Economics of Transition*, vol. 1, no. 1.

—— (1994) *Economic Transition on the Other Side of the Wall: China*, LSE: Discussion Paper CP no. 29.

Ickes, B. and Ryterman, R. (1993) 'Road block to economic reform: inter-enterprise debt and the transition to markets', *Post-Soviet Affairs*, vol. 9, no. 3.

Ickes, B. and Slemrod, J. (1992) 'Tax implementation issues in the transition from a planned economy', *Public Finance*, Supplement to vol. 47.

Imai, H. (1994) 'Inflationary pressure in China's consumption goods market: estimation and analysis', *The Developing Economies*, vol. XXXII, no. 2.

Information Mongolia (1990) Compiled and edited by the Mongolian Academy of Sciences, Oxford: Pergamon Press.

Inotai, A. (1994) 'Transforming the East: Western illusions and strategies', *The Hungarian Quarterly*, vol. 35, no. 133.

International Herald Tribune (various surveys):

China: 15 September 1986; 9 July 1986; 11 April 1994; 30 May 1994; 13 March 1995; 24 April 1995.

Czech Republic: 25 June 1994; 26 June 1995; 22 November 1995.

East–West Trade: 6 June 1989.

Germany: 10 April 1991; 16 December 1992; 23 April 1993; 15 December 1993; 1 March 1994; 7 December 1994 (Germany: the New States); 15 December 1994; 3 April 1995.

Hungary: 12 June 1985; 4 March 1991; 7 October 1993; 19 April 1994; 5 December 1994.

Latvia: 4 November 1994; 9 June 1995.

Poland: 6 May 1994; 24 June 1995.

Russia: 8 December 1993; 2 December 1994.

Slovenia: 6 April 1995.

Soviet Union: 7–8 November 1985; 7 November 1988.

Irvin, G. (1995) 'Vietnam: assessing the achievements of doi moi', *Journal of Development Economics*, vol. 31, no. 5.

Jackman, R. (1994) 'Economic policy and employment in the transition economies of Central and Eastern Europe: what have we learned?', *International Labour Review*, vol. 133, no. 3.

Jefferson, G. and Rawski, T. (1994) 'Enterprise reform in Chinese industry', *Journal of Economic Perspectives*, vol. 8, no. 2.

Jefferson, G. and Xu, W. (1991) 'The impact of reform on socialist enterprises in transition: structure, conduct, and performance in Chinese industry', *Journal of Comparative Economics*, vol. 15, no. 1.

—— (1994) 'Assessing gains in efficient production among China's industrial enterprises', *Economic Development and Cultural Change*, vol. 42, no. 3.

Jeffries, I. (ed.) (1981) *The Industrial Enterprise in Eastern Europe*, New York: Praeger.

—— (1990) *A Guide to the Socialist Economies*, London: Routledge.

—— (1992a) 'The impact of reunification on the East German economy' in Osmond (1992).

—— (ed.) (1992b) *Industrial Reform in Socialist Countries: from Restructuring to Revolution*, Aldershot: Edward Elgar.

—— (1993) *Socialist Economies and the Transition to the Market*, London: Routledge.

Jeffries, I., Melzer, M. (eds), and Breuning, E. (advisory ed.) (1987) *The East German Economy*, London: Croom Helm.

Jeffries, I. and Teodorescu, A. (eds) (forthcoming) *The Problems of Economic and Political Transformation in the Balkans*, London: Pinter.

Jenkins, G. (1992) 'Privatization and pension reform in transition economies', *Public Finance*, Supplement to vol. 47.

Joskow, P., Schmalensee, R. and Tsukanova, N. (1994) 'Competition policy in Russia during and after privatization', *Brookings Papers on Economic Activity (Microeconomics)*.

Jürgens, U., Klinzing, L. and Turner, L. (1993) 'The transformation of industrial relations in Eastern Germany', *Industrial and Labour Relations Review*, vol. 46, no. 2.

Karatnycky, A. (1992) 'The Ukrainian factor', *Foreign Affairs*, vol. 71, no. 3.

Kaser, M. (1990) 'The technology of decontrol: some macroeconomic issues', *Economic Journal*, vol. 100, no. 401.

—— (1992) 'Mongolia' in Jeffries (1992b).

—— (1995) *Privatization in the CIS*, London: Royal Institute of International Affairs.

Kaser, M. and Allsopp, C. (1992) 'The assessment: macroeconomic transition in Eastern Europe, 1989–91', *Oxford Review of Economic Policy*, vol. 8, no. 1.

Kaser, M. and Mehrotra, S. (1992) *The Central Asian Economies after Independence*, London: Royal Institute of International Affairs.

Kay, C. (1988) 'Cuban economic reforms and collectivisation', *Third World Quarterly*, vol. 10, no. 3.

Kazlauskiene, N. (1992) 'Transition of agriculture in the Baltics', *American Journal of Agricultural Economics*, vol. 74, no. 5.

Kenen, P. (1991) 'Transitional arrangements for trade and payments among the CMEA countries', *IMF Staff Papers*, vol. 38, no. 2.

Kipp, J. (1994) 'The Zhirinovsky threat', *Foreign Affairs*, vol. 73, no. 3.

Kiss, Y. (1992) 'Privatization in Hungary: two years later', *Soviet Studies*, vol. 44, no. 6.

—— (1993) 'Lost illusions? Defence industry conversion in Czechoslovakia, 1989–92', *Europe–Asia Studies*, vol. 45, no. 6.

Klaus, V. (1992a) 'Policy dilemmas of Eastern European reforms: notes of an insider' in A. Prindle (ed.) *Banking and Finance in Eastern Europe*, London: Woodhead-Faulkner.

—— (1992b) 'Transition: an insider's view', *Problems of Communism*, January–April.

Koevski, G. and Canning, A. (1995) *Privatization in the Former Yugoslav Republic of Macedonia*, Heriot-Watt University: Discussion Paper no. 95/10.

Kolodko, G. (1993a) 'Recession and growth during transition to a market economy' in Ellman *et al.* (1993).

—— (1993b) 'From recession to growth in post-communist economies: expectations versus reality', *Communist and Post-Communist Studies*, vol. 26, no. 2.

—— (1993c) 'Perverse effect of fiscal adjustment in transition economies', *Economics of Transition*, vol. 1, no. 3.

Korsun, G. and Murrell, P. (1995) 'Politics and economics of Mongolia's privatization programme', *Asian Survey*, vol. XXXV, no. 5.

Koslowski, R. (1992) 'Market institutions, East European reform, and economic theory', *Journal of Economic Issues*, vol. XXVI, no. 3.

Kozminski, A. (1992) 'Transition from planned to market economy: Hungary and Poland compared', *Studies in Comparative Communism*, vol. XXV, no. 4.

Kraft, E. (1995) 'Stabilizing inflation in Slovenia, Croatia and Macedonia: how independence has affected macroeconomic policy outcomes', *Europe–Asia Studies*, vol. 47, no. 3.

Kramer, H. (1993) 'The European Community's response to the "new Eastern Europe"', *Journal of Common Market Studies*, vol. 31, no. 2.

Laban, R. and Wolf, H. (1993) 'Large-scale privatization in transition economies', *American Economic Review*, vol. 83, no. 5.

Lambeth, B. (1995) 'Russia's wounded military', *Foreign Affairs*, vol. 74, no. 2.

Landesmann, M. (1993) *Industrial Policy and the Transition in East-Central Europe*, University of Cambridge: Discussion Paper on Economic Transition DPET 9204.

Le Duc Thuy, Luong Xuan Quy and To Xuan Dan (1991) 'The market mechanism in the new economic management system in Vietnam' in Ronnas and Sjöberg (1991a).

Le Trang (1990) 'Renewal of industrial management policy and organisation' in Ronnas and Sjöberg (1990).

Lee, E. (1993) 'Initiating transition in a low-income dualistic economy: the case of Mongolia', *International Labour Review*, vol. 132, nos 5–6.

Lee, K. (1990) 'The Chinese model of the socialist enterprise: an assessment of its organization and performance', *Journal of Comparative Economics*, vol. 14, no. 3.

—— (1993) 'Property rights and the agency problem in China's enterprise reform', *Cambridge Journal of Economics*, vol. 17, no. 2.

Levine, R. and Scott, D. (1993) 'Old debt and new beginnings: a policy choice in transitional socialist economies', *World Development*, vol. 21, no. 3.

Lewis, B. (1961) *The Emergence of Modern Turkey*, London: Oxford University Press.

Lin, J. (1988) 'The household responsibility system in China's agricultural reform; a theoretical and empirical study', *Economic Development and Cultural Change*, vol. 36, no. 3 (Supplement).

—— (1990) 'Collectivization and China's agricultural crisis in 1959–61', *Journal of Political Economy*, vol. 98, no. 6.

—— (1992) 'Rural reforms and agricultural growth in China', *American Economic Review*, vol. 82, no. 1.

Ling, Z. and Zhongyi, J. (1993) 'From brigade to village community: the land tenure system and rural development in China', *Cambridge Journal of Economics*, vol. 17, no. 4.

Lipton, D. and Sachs, J. (1990a) 'Creating a market in Eastern Europe: the case of Poland', *Brookings Papers on Economic Activity*, no. 1.

—— (1990b) 'Privatization in Eastern Europe: the case of Poland', *Brookings Papers on Economic Activity*, no. 2.

—— (1992) 'Prospects for Russia's economic reforms', *Brookings Papers on Economic Activity*, no. 2.

Lorinc, H. (1992) 'Foreign debt, debt management and implications for Hungary's development', *Soviet Studies*, vol. 44, no. 6.

Lueschen, L. (1994) 'Collective farms in transition in the former German Democratic Republic', *Comparative Economic Studies*, vol. XXXVI, no. 2.

Maciaszek-Roberts, B. (1993a) 'Transition in Eastern Europe: does the sequence of privatization matter?', *Journal of International Development*, vol. 5, no. 2.

—— (1993b) 'The sequence of privatization: the case of Poland', *British Review of Economic Issues*, vol. 15, no. 37.

McFaul, M. (1995) 'Eurasia letter: Russian politics after Chechnya', *Foreign Policy*, no. 99.

McKinnon, R. (1992a) 'Taxation, money, and credit in a liberalizing socialist economy', *Economics of Planning*, vol. 25, no. 1.

—— (1992b) 'Taxation, money and credit in a liberalizing socialist economy' in Clague and Rausser (eds).

—— (1994) 'Financial growth and macroeconomic stability in China, 1978–92: implications for Russia and other transitional economies', *Journal of Comparative Economics*, vol. 18, no. 3.

Mencinger, J. (1993) 'How to create a currency? The experience of Slovenia', *Weltwirtschaftliches Archiv*, vol. 129, no. 2.

Messerlin, P. (1993) 'The EC and Central Europe: the missed rendez-vous of 1992?', *Economics of Transition*, vol. 1, no. 1.

Metcalf, G. and Ambrus-Lakatos, L. (1992) 'The optimal rate of privatization in a dynamic economy', *Public Finance*, Supplement to vol. 47.

Michalopoulos, C. and Tarr, D. (1993) 'Energizing trade of the states of the former Soviet Union', *Finance and Development*, March.

Milne, E. *et al.* (1991) *The Mongolian People's Republic: toward a Market Economy*, IMF: Occasional Paper no. 79.

Mizsei, K. (1992) 'Privatization in Eastern Europe: a comparative study of Poland and Hungary', *Soviet Studies*, vol. 44, no. 2.

Mladek, J. and Hashi, I. (1993) 'Voucher privatization, investment funds and corporate governance in Czechoslovakia', *British Review of Economic Issues*, vol. 15, no. 37.

Mullineux, A. (1992a) *Banks, Privatization and Restructuring in Poland*, University of Birmingham: Discussion Paper IFGWP-92-02.

—— (1992b) *Privatization in the UK and Germany: Lessons for Central and Eastern Europe*, University of Birmingham: Discussion Paper IFGWP-92-01.

Mullineux, A. and Belka, M. (1993) *Hardening Micro Budget Constraints: Bank Behaviour and Corporate Governance in Poland*, University of Birmingham: Discussion Paper IFGWP-93-08.

Murrell, P. (1990) *The Nature of Socialist Economies: Lessons from Eastern European Foreign Trade*, Princeton, NJ: Princeton University Press.
—— (1992a) 'Evolutionary and radical approaches to economic reform', *Economics of Planning*, vol. 25, no. 1.
—— (1992b) 'Evolution in economics and in the economic reform of the centrally planned economies' in Clague and Rausser (1992).
—— (1993) 'What is shock therapy? What did it do in Poland and Russia?', *Post-Soviet Affairs*, vol. 9, no. 2.
Naughton, B. (1994) 'Chinese institutional innovation and privatization from below', *American Economic Review*, vol. 84, no. 2.
Nelson, G. (1993) 'Agricultural policy reform in Eastern Europe', *American Journal of Agricultural Economics*, vol. 75, no. 3.
Neuber, A. (1993) 'Towards a political economy of transition in Eastern Europe', *Journal of International Development*, vol. 5, no. 5.
Nguyen Tuong Lai and Nguyen Thanh Bang (1991) 'A new development policy for human resources within the socio-economic strategy of Vietnam up to the year 2000' in Ronnas and Sjöberg (1991b).
Nguyen Van Huy (1990) 'Renewal of economic policies and economic management organisation in Vietnam' in Ronnas and Sjöberg (1990).
Nikonov, A. (1992) 'Agricultural transition in Russia and the other former states of the USSR', *American Journal of Agricultural Economics*, vol. 74, no. 5.
Nolan, P. (1992) *Transforming Stalinist Systems: China's Reforms in the Light of Russian and East European Experience*, University of Cambridge: Discussion Paper on Economic Transition DPET 9203.
—— (1993) 'China's post-Mao political economy: a puzzle', *Contributions to Political Economy*, no. 12.
Noren, J. (1993) 'The FSU economies: first year of transition', *Post-Soviet Geography*, vol. XXXIV, no. 7.
Nourzhanov, K. and Saikal, A. (1994) 'The new Kazakhstan: has something gone wrong?', *The World Today*, vol. 50, no. 12.
Nove, A. (1961) *The Soviet Economy*, London: Allen & Unwin.
—— (1981) 'The Soviet industrial enterprise' in Jeffries (1981).
—— (1986) *The Soviet Economic System*, 3rd edn, London: Allen & Unwin.
—— (1987) 'Soviet agriculture: light at the end of the tunnel?', *Detente*, nos 9–10.
—— (1994) 'A gap in transition models? A comment on Gomulka', *Europe–Asia Studies*, vol. 46, no. 5.
OECD (1992) *Bulgaria: an Economic Assessment*, Geneva: OECD.
Orlowski, L. (1993) 'Indirect transfers in trade among former Soviet Union republics: sources, patterns and policy responses in the post-Soviet period', *Europe–Asia Studies*, vol. 45, no. 6.
Osmond, J. (ed.) (1992) *German Reunification: a Reference Guide and Commentary*, London: Longman.
Pallot, J. (1993) 'Update on the Russian Federation land reform', *Post-Soviet Geography*, vol. XXXIV, no. 3.
Pashko, G. (1991) 'The Albanian economy at the beginning of the 1990s' in Sjöberg and Wyzan (1991).
—— (1993) 'Obstacles to economic reform in Albania', *Europe–Asia Studies*, vol. 45, no. 5.
—— (forthcoming) 'Problems of the transition in Albania, 1990–94' in Jeffries and Teodorescu (forthcoming).
Pastor, M. and Zimbalist, A. (1995) 'Waiting for change: adjustment and reform in Cuba', *World Development*, vol. 23, no. 5.

Perez-Lopez, J. (1986) 'Cuba's economy in the 1980s', *Problems of Communism*, vol. XXXV, no. 5.

—— (1989) 'Sugar and structural change in the Cuban economy', *World Development*, vol. 17, no. 10.

—— (1990) 'Rectification at three: impact on the Cuban economy', *Studies in Comparative International Development*, vol. 25, no. 3.

—— (1991) 'Bringing the Cuban economy into focus: conceptual and empirical challenges', *Latin American Research Review*, vol. 26, no. 3.

—— (1992) 'The Cuban economy: rectification in a changing world', *Cambridge Journal of Economics*, vol. 16, no. 1.

—— (1994) 'Completing China's move to the market', *Journal of Economic Perspectives*, vol. 8, no. 2.

—— (1995a) 'Castro tries survival strategy', *Transition*, vol. 6, no. 3.

—— (1995b) 'Cuba's socialist economy toward the mid-1990s', *Journal of Communist Studies and Transition Politics*, vol. 11, no. 2.

Perkins, D. (1988) 'Reforming China's economic system', *Journal of Economic Literature*, vol. XXVI, no. 2.

Pettifer, J. (1995) 'Macedonia: still the apple of discord', *The World Today*, vol. 51, no. 3.

Pinto, B., Belka, M. and Krajewski, S. (1993) 'Transforming state enterprises in Poland: evidence of adjustment by manufacturing firms', *Brookings Papers on Economic Activity*, no. 1.

Platte, E. (1994) 'China's foreign debt', *Pacific Affairs*, vol. 66, no. 4.

Pollitt, B. and Hagelberg, G. (1994) 'The Cuban sugar economy in the Soviet era and after', *Cambridge Journal of Economics*, vol. 18, no. 6.

Pomfret, R. (1993) 'Mongolia's economic reforms: background, contents and prospects', *Economic Bulletin for Asia and the Pacific*, vol. XLIV, no. 1.

Portes, R. (1994) 'Transformation traps', *Economic Journal*, vol. 104, no. 426.

Poznanski, K. (1992) 'Privatization of the Polish economy: problems of transition', *Soviet Studies*, vol. 44, no. 4.

Priewe, J. (1993) 'Privatization of the industrial sector: the function and activity of the Treuhandanstalt', *Cambridge Journal of Economics*, vol. 17, no. 3.

Prybyla, J. (1994) Review in *Economic Development and Cultural Change*, vol. 42, no. 3.

Pryor, F. (1991) 'Third World decollectivization: Guyana, Nicaragua and Vietnam', *Problems of Communism*, vol. XL, no. 3 (May–June).

—— (1992) *The Red and the Green: the Rise and the Fall of Collectivized Agriculture in Marxist Regimes*, Princeton, NJ: Princeton University Press.

—— (1993) 'Problems of decollectivization with special attention to East Germany' in Somogyi (1993).

Purcell, S. (1990) 'Cuba's cloudy future', *Foreign Affairs*, vol. 69, no. 3.

—— (1992) 'Collapsing Cuba', *Foreign Affairs*, vol. 71, no. 1.

Pudney, S. and Wang, L. (1994) *Housing and Housing Reform in Urban China: Efficiency, Distribution and the Implications for Social Security*, LSE: EF no. 8.

Qian, Y. (1994) 'A theory of shortage in socialist economies based on the soft budget constraint', *American Economic Review*, vol. 84, no. 1.

Qian, Y. and Xu, C. (1993) 'Why China's economic reforms differ: the M-form hierarchy and entry/expansion of the non-state sector', *Economics of Transition*, vol. 1, no. 2.

Radosevic, S. (1994) 'The generic problems of competitiveness at company level in the former socialist economies: the case of Croatia', *Europe–Asia Studies*, vol. 46, no. 3.

Rausser, G. (1992) 'Lessons for emerging market economies in Eastern Europe' in Clague and Rausser (eds) (1992).

Rausser, G. and Johnson, S. (1993) 'State–market–civil institutions: the case of Eastern Europe and the Soviet republics', *World Development*, vol. 21, no. 4.

Rawski, T. (1994) 'Chinese industrial reform: accomplishments, prospects and implications', *American Economic Review*, vol. 84, no. 2.

Rich, V. (1995) 'An East Slavic Union?', *The World Today*, vol. 51, no. 3.

Riedel, J. (1993) 'Vietnam: on the trail of the Tigers', *World Economy*, vol. 16, no. 4.

Riskin, C. (1987) *The Political Economy of Chinese Development since 1949*, London: Oxford University Press.

Roesler, J. (1994) 'Privatization in Eastern Germany: experience with the Treuhand', *Europe–Asia Studies*, vol. 46, no. 3.

Roland, G. (1994a) 'The role of political constraints in transition economies', *Economics of Transition*, vol. 2, no. 1.

—— (1994b) 'On the speed and sequencing of privatization and restructuring', *Economic Journal*, vol. 104, no. 426.

Roland, G. and Verdier, T. (1994) 'Privatization in Eastern Europe: irreversibility and critical mass effects', *Journal of Public Economics*, vol. 54, no. 2.

Rollo, J. and Smith, A. (1992) *The Political Economy of Central Europe Trade with the European Community: Why so Sensitive?*, London: Royal Institute of International Affairs.

—— (1993) 'The political economy of Eastern European trade with the European Community', *Economic Policy*, no. 16.

Ronnas, P. (1991a) 'The economic legacy of Ceausescu' in Sjöberg and Wyzan (1991).

—— (forthcoming) 'Romania: transition to underdevelopment' in Jeffries and Teodorescu (forthcoming).

Ronnas, P. and Sjöberg, Ö. (eds) (1990) *Doi Moi: Economic Reforms and Development Policies in Vietnam*, Stockholm: Swedish International Development Authority.

—— (1991a) 'Economic reform in Vietnam: dismantling the centrally planned economy', *Journal of Communist Studies*, vol. 7, no. 1.

—— (1991b) (eds) *Socio-economic Development in Vietnam: the Agenda for the 1990s*, Stockholm: Swedish International Development Authority.

Rosati, D. (1992) 'The CMEA demise, trade restructuring, and trade destruction in Central and Eastern Europe', *Oxford Review of Economic Policy*, vol. 8, no. 1.

—— (1994) 'Output declines during the transition from plan to market: a consideration', *Economics of Transition*, vol. 2, no. 4.

Rosenberg, J. (1992) 'Cuba's free-market experiment: los mercados libres campesinos, 1980–86', *Latin American Research Review*, vol. 27, no. 3.

Rothschild, K. (1993) 'Notes on the German reunification drama', *Cambridge Journal of Economics*, vol. 17, no. 3.

Rybczynski, T. (1991) 'The sequencing of reform', *Oxford Review of Economic Policy*, vol. 7, no. 4.

Sachs, J. (1992) 'The economic transformation of Eastern Europe: the case of Poland', *Economics of Planning*, vol. 25, no. 1.

—— (1994) *Poland's Jump to the Market Economy*, Cambridge, Mass.: MIT Press.

—— (1995) 'Consolidating capitalism', *Foreign Policy*, no. 98.

Sachs, J. and Lipton, D. (1990) 'Poland's economic reform', *Foreign Affairs*, vol. 69, no. 3.

Sachs, J. and Woo, W. (1994) 'Structural factors in the economic reforms of China, Eastern Europe and the former Soviet Union', *Economic Policy*, no. 18.

Sagers, M. (1993) 'The energy industries of the former USSR: a mid-year survey', *Post-Soviet Geography*, vol. XXXIV, no. 6.

Sakwa, R. (1995) 'The Russian elections of 1993', *Europe–Asia Studies*, vol. 47, no. 2.

Sanders, A. (1987) *Mongolia: Politics, Economics and Society*, London: Pinter.

Sandström, P. and Sjöberg, Ö. (1991) 'Albanian economic performance: stagnation in the 1980s', *Soviet Studies*, vol. 43, no. 5.

Schimmerling, H. (1991) 'Agricultural development in Czechoslovakia: prospects after the 1989 revolution', *Food Policy*, vol. 16, no. 3.

Schmiedling, H. (1993) 'From plan to market: on the nature of the transformation crisis', *Weltwirtschaftliches Archiv*, vol. 129, no. 2.

Schnytzer, A. (1982) *Stalinist Economic Strategy in Practice: the Case of Albania*, London: Oxford University Press.

—— (1992) 'Albania: the purge of Stalinist economic ideology' in Jeffries (1992b).

Schwartz, G. (1991) 'Privatization: possible lessons from the Hungarian case', *World Development*, vol. 19, no. 12.

Schwartz, G. and Lopes, P. (1993) 'Privatization: expectations, trade-offs and results', *Finance and Development*, vol. 30, no. 2.

Scott, N. (1992) 'The implications of the transition for foreign trade and investment', *Oxford Review of Economic Policy*, vol. 8, no. 1.

Shaw, D. (1992) 'Further progress with land reform', *Post-Soviet Geography*, vol. XXXIII, no. 8.

Shlapentokh, V. (1993) 'Privatization debates in Russia: 1989–1992', *Comparative Economic Studies*, vol. XXXV, no. 2.

Siebert, H. (1991a) *German Unification: the Economics of Transition*, Kiel Institute of World Economics Working Paper no. 468.

—— (1991b) 'German unification: the economics of transition', *Economic Policy*, no. 13 (October).

Silberman, J., Weiss, C. and Dutz, M. (1994) 'Jump-starting ex-communist economies: a leaf from the Marshall Plan', *Foreign Affairs*, vol. 75, no. 1.

Simoneti, M. (1993) 'A comparative review of privatization strategies in four former socialist countries', *Europe–Asia Studies*, vol. 45, no. 1.

Sinn, H.-W. (1992) 'Privatization in East Germany', *Public Finance*, Supplement to vol. 47.

Siszov, A. (1993) 'Land reform developments in Russia', *Economics of Transition*, vol. 1, no. 4.

Sjöberg, Ö. (1989) *The Agrarian Sector in Albania during the 1980s: a Changing Regional Focus*, Economic Research Institute of the Stockholm School of Economics: Research Report no. 4.

—— (1990) *The Albanian Economy in the 1980s: the Nature of a Low-performing System*, Economic Research Institute of the Stockholm School of Economics: Working Paper no. 10.

—— (1991a) 'The Albanian economy in the 1980s: coping with a centralised system' in Sjöberg and Wyzan (1991).

—— (1991b) *Rural Change and Development in Albania*, Boulder: Westview Press.

—— (forthcoming) 'The regional effects of economic transformation in Albania: towards an assessment' in Jeffries and Teodorescu (forthcoming).

Sjöberg, Ö. and Wyzan, M. (eds) (1991) *Economic Change in the Balkan States: Albania, Bulgaria, Romania and Yugoslavia*, London: Pinter.

Smith, A. (1993) *Russia and the World Economy: Problems of Integration*, London: Routledge.

Snower, D. (1992) *Revenue-sharing Subsidies as Employment Policy: Reducing the Cost of Stimulating East German Employment*, Birkbeck College (University of London): Discussion Paper 15/92.
Somogyi, L. (ed.) (1993) *The Political Economy of the Transition Process in Eastern Europe*, Aldershot: Edward Elgar.
Soros, G. (1995) 'Toward open societies', *Foreign Policy*, no. 98.
Steinherr, A. and Ottolenghi, D. (1993) 'Yugoslavia: was it a winner's curse?', *Economics of Transition*, vol. 1, no. 2.
Summers, L. (1992) 'The next decade in Central and Eastern Europe' in Clague and Rausser (eds) (1992).
Summers, M. (1992) 'Privatization by coupon in Czechoslovakia', *Economic Affairs*, vol. 12, no. 3.
Sundakov, A., Ossowski, R. and Lane, T. (1994) 'Shortages under free prices: the case of Ukraine in 1992', *IMF Staff Papers*, vol. 41, no. 3.
Sutela, P. (1994) 'Insider privatization in Russia: speculations on systemic change', *Europe–Asia Studies*, vol. 46, no. 3.
Sword, K. (ed.) (1991) *The Times Guide to Eastern Europe*, 2nd edn, London: Times Books.
Tai, N. and Hare, P. (1995) *State Enterprise Ownership Transformation in Vietnam*, Heriot-Watt University: Discussion Paper no. 95/2.
Tarr, D. (1994) 'The terms-of-trade effects of moving to world prices on the countries of the former Soviet Union', *Journal of Comparative Economics*, vol. 18, no. 1.
Tesche, J. (1994) 'Fiscal decentralization in the Russian Federation', *Comparative Economic Studies*, vol. XXXVI, no. 3.
The Times (1986) Survey on China, 10 October.
—— (1995) Survey on the Czech Republic, 2 May.
—— (1995) Survey on the Russian Federation, 31 May.
—— (1995) Survey on Hungary, 21 June.
—— (1995) Survey on Albania, 26 June.
—— (1995) Survey on the Czech Republic, 10 July.
—— (1995) Survey on Poland, 10 August.
The Times Guide to Eastern Europe (1990) ed. by Keith Sword, London: Times Books.
Thompson, S. (1993) 'Agrarian reform in Eastern Europe following World War I: motives and outcomes', *American Journal of Agricultural Economics*, vol. 75, no. 3.
United Nations (1993) *World Economic Survey 1993*, New York: United Nations.
United Nations Economic Commission for Europe (1992) *Economic Survey of Europe in 1991–92*, New York: United Nations.
—— (1993) *Economic Survey of Europe in 1992–93*, New York: United Nations.
—— (1994) *Economic Survey of Europe in 1993–94*, New York: United Nations.
—— (1995) *Economic Survey of Europe in 1994–95*, New York: United Nations.
Van Atta, D. (1993) 'The current state of agrarian reform in Uzbekistan', *Post-Soviet Geography*, vol. XXXIV, no. 9.
Van Brabant, J. (1994) 'Agrarian reform in post-Soviet Russia', *Post-Soviet Affairs*, vol. 10, no. 2.
—— (1993) 'Lessons from the wholesale transformations in the East', *Comparative Economic Studies*, vol. XXXV, no. 4.
—— (1994) 'Trade, integration and transformation in Eastern Europe', *Journal of International Affairs*, vol. 48, no. 1.
Van Wijnbergen, S. (1993) 'Enterprise reform in Eastern Europe', *Economics of Transition*, vol. 1, no. 1.

Vincentz, V. (1991) *Privatization in Eastern Germany: Principles and Practice*, Munich Eastern Europe Institute Working Paper, no. 146.

Wädekin, K.-E. (ed.) (1990a) *Communist Agriculture: Farming in the Far East and Cuba*, London: Routledge.

—— (1990b) *Communist Agriculture: Farming in the Soviet Union and Eastern Europe*, London: Routledge.

—— (1990c) 'Private agriculture in socialist countries: implications for the USSR' in Gray (1990).

Wall, D. (1991) 'Special economic zones and industrialisation in China', Discussion Paper no. 01/91, International Economics Research Centre at the University of Sussex.

—— (1993) 'China's economic reform and opening-up process: the Special Economic Zones', *Development Policy Review*, vol. 11, no. 3.

Wang Xiao-qing (1993) *'Groping for Stones to Cross the River': Chinese Price Reform against the 'Big Bang'*, University of Cambridge: Discussion Paper DPET 9305.

Wang Zhonghui (1993) 'China's policies towards collective rural enterprises', *Small Enterprise Development*, vol. 4, no. 1.

Wanniski, J. (1992) 'The future of Russian capitalism', *Foreign Affairs*, vol. 71, no. 2.

Weber, S. (1994) 'Origins of the European Bank for Reconstruction and Development', *International Organization*, vol. 48, no. 1.

Wegren, S. (1992a) 'Private farming and agrarian reform in Russia', *Problems of Communism*, May–June.

—— (1992b) 'Agricultural reform in the nonchernozem zone; the case of Kostroma oblast', *Post-Soviet Geography*, vol. XXIII, no. 10.

—— (1994) 'Rural reform and political culture', *Europe–Asia Studies*, vol. 46, no. 2.

Weitzman, M. (1993) 'Economic transition: can theory help?', *European Economic Review*, vol. 37, nos 2/3.

Weitzman, M. and Xu, C. (1993) *Chinese Township–Village Enterprises as Vaguely Defined Co-operatives*, LSE: CP no. 26.

—— (1994) 'Chinese township–village enterprises as vaguely defined co-operatives', *Journal of Comparative Economics*, vol. 18, no. 2.

Wen, G. (1993) 'Total factor productivity in China's farming sector, 1952–89', *Economic Development and Cultural Change*, vol. 42, no. 1.

Williamson, J. (1993) 'Why did output fall in Eastern Europe?' in Somogyi (1993).

Woo, W. (1994) 'The art of reforming centrally planned economies: comparing China, Poland and Russia', *Journal of Comparative Economics*, vol. 18, no. 3.

Woo, W., Hai, W., Jin, Y. and Fan, G. (1994) 'How successful has Chinese enterprise reform been? Pitfalls in opposite biases and focus', *Journal of Comparative Economics*, vol. 18, no. 3.

Wyzan, M. (1989) 'The small enterprise and agricultural initiative in Bulgaria: a comment on Robert J. McIntyre', *Soviet Studies*, vol. XLI, no. 4.

—— (1990a) 'Bulgarian agriculture: sweeping reform, mediocre performance' in Wädekin (1990b).

—— (1990b) 'The Bulgarian experience with centrally planned agriculture: lessons for Soviet reformers' in Gray (1990).

—— (1990c) *The Bulgarian Economy in the Immediate Post-Zhivkov Era: a Western Perspective*, Stockholm Institute of Soviet and East European Economics: Working Paper no. 7.

—— (1991) 'The Bulgarian economy in the immediate post-Zhivkov era' in Sjöberg and Wyzan (1991).

Wyzan, M. (1992) 'Bulgaria: shock therapy followed by steep recession', *Radio Free*

Europe/Radio Liberty Research Report, vol. 1, no. 45.

—— (forthcoming) 'Economic change in Bulgaria since the fall of communism' in Jeffries and Teodorescu (forthcoming).

Zhu, Y. (1995) 'Major changes under way in China's industrial relations', *International Labour Review*, vol. 134, no. 1.

Zimbalist, A. (1987) 'Cuba's socialist economy toward the 1990s', *World Development*, vol. 15, no. 1.

—— (ed.) (1988a) *Cuban Political Economy*, Boulder and London: Westview Press.

—— (1988b) 'Cuba's statistical and price systems: interpretation and reliability', *Latin American Perspectives*, vol. 15, no. 2.

—— (1988c) 'Cuba's external economy: reflections on export dependence, Soviet aid and foreign debt', *Comparative Economic Studies*, vol. XXX, no. 2.

—— (1989) 'Incentives and planning in Cuba', *Latin American Research Review*, vol. XXIV, no. 1.

—— (1992a) 'Industrial reform and the Cuban economy' in Jeffries (1992b).

—— (1992b) 'Teetering on the brink: Cuba's current economic and political crisis', *Journal of Latin American Studies*, vol. 24, no. 2.

—— (1993a) 'Cuba in the age of *perestroika*', *Latin American Perspectives*, vol. 20, no. 1.

—— (1993b) 'Dateline Cuba: hanging on in Havana', *Foreign Policy*, no. 92.

Zimbalist, A. and Eckstein, S. (1987) 'Patterns of Cuban development: the first twenty-five years', *World Development*, vol. 15, no. 1.

Zimbalist, A., Sherman, H. and Brown, S. (1989) *Comparing Economic Systems: a Political–Economic Approach*, 2nd edn, New York: Harcourt Brace Jovanovich.

Zimmerman, W. (1995) 'The last ambassador: a memoir of the collapse of Yugoslavia', *Foreign Affairs*, vol. 74, no. 2.

Zizmond, E. (1993) 'Slovenia – one year of independence', *Europe–Asia Studies*, vol. 45, no. 5.

Zukowski, R. (1993) 'Stabilization and recession in a transitional economy: the case of Poland', *World Development*, vol. 21, no. 7.

GLOSSARY

agrarno-promishlen komplex (APK) Agro-industrial complex in socialist Bulgaria. Normally a horizontal integration of co-operative farms, state farms and their servicing centres.

Basic Organization of Associated Labour (BOAL) A legal and economic unit in Yugoslavia. The smallest unit producing a marketed or marketable product.

'big bang' The rapid, comprehensive transformation of a centrally planned economy into a market economy. Sometimes the term is used interchangeably with 'shock' therapy, but it may be more useful to think of 'shock' treatment as a series of austerity measures dealing with severe macroeconomic disequilibrium (see below).

bilateral trade The balancing of trade between two countries over a period of time. Characterizes trade between command economies.

cartel A trade association that restricts competition among its members.

centrala 'Central' in socialist Romania, usually the result of country-wide, horizontal integration of one large enterprise with smaller ones.

Charter 77 A Czechoslovak civil and human rights group founded in 1977. It led to the setting up of Civic Forum in November 1989.

Chuch'e The North Korean policy of 'self-reliance'.

Civic Forum See *Charter 77*.

civil society Widespread activities by individuals who voluntarily associate together in various forms outside the control of the state. Life outside the state. The self-organization of individuals in society.

Comecon (CMEA) Council of Mutual Economic Assistance. Set up in 1949, there were eventually ten full members: the Soviet Union, Bulgaria, Czechoslovakia, Hungary, Poland, Romania, the GDR, Mongolia, Cuba and Vietnam. Wound up in 1991.

Cominform The Communist Information Bureau was set up in September 1947 to promote international communism and Soviet control over the movement. It was dissolved in 1956. Its predecessor was the Comintern (1919–43).

commercialization See *corporatization.*

Commonwealth of Independent States (CIS) The successor to the Soviet Union, set up towards the end of 1991.

Commune ('people's commune') Key institution during the Chinese Great Leap Forward.

Comprehensive (Complex) Programme A 1971 Comecon programme for the further extension and improvement of co-operation and development of socialist integration to the year 2000.

control figures Initial, tentative output targets passed down by the State Planning Commission.

convertibility R. Holzman (1991: 6) defines 'resident' or 'internal' convertibility to mean that a country's citizens and enterprises are free to purchase foreign currency for use in either current account (to purchase goods and services) or capital account (e.g. to invest abroad) transactions. Internal convertibility has been adopted by some of the countries studied in this book. But there are sometimes restrictions even on the purchase of foreign currency for current account transactions, and controls relating to capital account transactions are the rule. (Note that the domestic currency is not bought and sold on international foreign exchange markets and not used to make international payments.) An internally convertible currency enables individuals and enterprises to buy foreign exchange and, therefore, imports. This exposes resident enterprises to foreign competition.

'full' convertibility Implies the unconstrained freedom of any enterprise or person to buy or sell a nation's currency for foreign currencies at the existing exchange rate.

corporatization (commercialization) Frydman *et al.* (1993: 35, 140) define corporatization as the process by which state enterprises are converted into commercial companies with structures familiar in the West (such as joint stock or limited liability companies; the shares of the former, which may also enjoy limited liability, are publicly traded, whereas the shares of the latter are not publicly traded). Prior to privatization the state or appropriate municipality remains the owner. According to Clague (1992: 15), state enterprises 'are put in the charge of boards of directors and allowed to act independently'.

Council of Europe Promotes democracy and human rights: 'the principles of the rule of law and of the enjoyment by all persons within [the member states'] jurisdiction of human rights and fundamental freedoms.'

counter-plans Designed as an inducement to managers of socialist enterprises to adopt more demanding targets than those set out in the five-year plan.

CSCE Conference on Security and Co-operation in Europe. The Paris CSCE conference was held on 19–21 November 1993 and signified the formal end of the Cold War. On 6 December 1994 the CSCE became known as the Organization for Security and Co-operation in Europe (OSCE).

Cultural Revolution Officially covered the period 1966–76 in China, but the more extreme elements were ended by 1969.

danwei The workplace in China. Not only a production unit, but historically represents an important provider of housing and the chief provider of welfare services.

destatization (destatification) (razgosudarstvleniye) A broader concept than privatization. In the initial stages joint stock companies may be formed, whose shares could be held by state holding companies. It can involve, for example, leasing, employee ownership and co-operative ownership.

doi moi 'Renovation' or 'new way' (Vietnam).

Durzhavenski Stopanski Obedineniya (DSO) State Economic Organization. The basic production unit in socialist Bulgaria, comprising horizontally integrated enterprises.

EBRD European Bank for Reconstruction and Development. An organization set up in 1990 mainly to promote the private sector in Eastern Europe.

EC The European Community. Called the European Union since the Maastricht Treaty came into force on 1 November 1993.

Economic Community Gorbachev's failed attempt at setting up a mechanism in the Soviet Union to co-ordinate economic policy among sovereign republics.

economic levers Prices, taxes, interest rates and so on, used to steer the economy indirectly.

Ecu The EC's monetary unit, whose value is determined by a weighted basket of twelve currencies.

edinonachalie The principle of one-man responsibility and control, applying to the management of the Soviet enterprise by the director.

emerging (or new) democracies (emerging market economies or transitional economies) The post-communist regimes.

ethnic cleansing Ethnically mixed areas are 'cleansed' by forcibly driving out other ethnic groups.

European Economic Area (EEA) A free trade zone formed on 1 January 1994 by the twelve EC countries and five of the European Free Trade Area (EFTA) countries (Austria, Finland, Iceland, Norway and Sweden).

European Union See *EC*.

extensive growth Growth of the economy achieved mainly through increasing inputs.

foreign direct investment 'The transfer by a firm of resources – including capital, technology and personnel – into a foreign business venture with the objective of acquiring control of the venture. In the transition economies, equity stakes have often been acquired by foreigners through in-kind contributions. As a result, the volume of FDI is hard to assess on the basis of financial flows alone. Even for balance of payments data, comparability across countries is often limited, given definitional problems such as different thresholds for the equity stake that distinguishes direct investment from portfolio placement and failure to record reinvested earnings . . . The IMF recommends measuring FDI as cross-border equity participations whose original capital share surpasses a 10 per cent benchmark, reinvested earnings and long-term loans by parent companies' (EBRD 1994: 122). 'An investment is considered to constitute FDI when a lasting relationship is established between a legal person or entity resident in one country (the foreign investor) and an entity resident in another country (the foreign-investment enterprise), in which the foreign investor obtains a controlling interest. This type of investment can be contrasted with (foreign) portfolio investment, in which the investor is not interested in exerting significant influence over management decisions' (Barbara Peitsch, *The OECD Observer*, April–May 1995, no. 193, p. 33).

G7 Group of Seven leading 'Western' industrial democracies (Canada, France, Germany, Italy, Japan, the UK and the USA). (On 10 July 1994 Russia formally joined the political talks only and the term 'political G8' was informally coined.)

G24 Group of Twenty-four 'Western' countries.

Gatt General Agreement on Tariffs and Trade.

GDP and GNP (see *Net Material Product*) Gross Domestic Product (GDP) is a measure of the goods and services produced annually within the geographical area of a country, while Gross National Product (GNP) is a measure of the national income accruing to residents of a country. The difference between the two is net (inflows minus outflows) of income from factor services, e.g. wages and salaries earned by residents working abroad and profits earned by foreign companies.

GEMU German economic and monetary union.

glasnost Openness. Freedom of speech.

glavki Chief administrations. Bodies linking ministries and enterprises in the traditional Soviet economic system.

GLF Great Leap Forward in China 1958–60.

goods inconvertibility If one command economy has a trade surplus with another, the surplus cannot automatically be converted into a claim on particular goods in the latter country, because of the lack of direct and free exchange between ultimate purchaser and supplier. The claim can be met only by negotiations and provisions in central plans.

Gosbank The Soviet State Bank.

Gosplan The Soviet State Planning Commission.

Gospriomka The Soviet State Quality Commission.

Gossnab The Soviet State Committee for Material-Technical Supply.

goszakazy State orders in the Soviet Union.

Grand Bargain Large-scale Western aid in return for a programme to adopt political democracy, a market economy and macroeconomic stabilization measures.

guangxi An informal system of personal connections in China.

guidance planning In China, the use of suggested rather than mandatory plan targets; the state encourages compliance by means of economic levers.

hard goods Those commodities particularly sought after in Comecon, because the internal price system undervalued them and they could be sold and purchased on the world market for hard (convertible) currencies (e.g. foodstuffs, fuels and raw materials).

Helsinki Final Act (Helsinki Accords) The Helsinki Conference lasted from 3 July 1973 to 1 August 1975, when the Helsinki Final Act was signed by thirty-five countries. All the European nations were represented (with the exception of Albania) plus Canada and the USA. The Final Act was a sort of substitute for the general peace conference which never took place after the Second World War. There were three so-called 'baskets': security in Europe (confirmation of existing boundaries in particular); co-operation in economics, science and technology and the environment; and human rights (although this 'basket' was widely ignored by the Soviet and East European regimes, it proved crucial in the long term by giving legitimacy and power to the dissident movements). There were follow-up conferences.

higher-level co-operative In Vietnamese agriculture this differs from the 'lower-level co-operative' in that labour is the sole source of remuneration.

higher-type agricultural co-operative A transitional institution in socialist Albania towards a full state farm, differing from the traditional co-operative in ways such as the fact that it received state budgetary grants instead of repayable long-term loans.

Household Responsibility System (HRS) The household is now the basic production unit in Chinese agriculture. After meeting sales quotas, tax obligations and payments for collective services, the household is able to make its own output and input decisions.

Hural Mongolian parliament, with the Great and Little Hurals (or councils).

IMF International Monetary Fund. Set up in 1944 to provide short-term finance for countries with temporary balance of payments problems. But today provides credit and technical advice in return for the implementation of anti-inflationary and pro-market policies. The designated repayment period for 'stand-by' credits is up to five years and for 'extended facility' credits up to ten years. The IMF's new 'systemic transformation facility' is available for countries committed to economic transformation. At least the first tranche of credit is issued on easier terms than normal.

initial (primary) stage of socialism The stage in China that started in the 1950s and which could last beyond the mid-twenty-first century. A process of gradually moving towards a modern industrial economy.

intensive growth Output increases largely accounted for by increases in the efficiency of input use, especially by means of an improvement in the application of modern science and technology.

Intensivierung Intensification in the GDR. Approximately equivalent to 'intensive growth'.

internal convertibility See *convertibility.*

'iron rice bowl' Literally, everyone eats from the same pot, regardless of work effort. Chinese workers are assured of a job and a wage.

Junta Central de Planification (Juceplan) Cuban Central Planning Board.

khozraschyot Economic accounting. On this basis the Soviet industrial enterprise is a financially separate and accountable unit for the purpose of efficiently implementing the *tekhpromfinplan.*

'know-how' fund Aid in the form of technical advice for setting up a market economy, e.g. the UK fund.

kolkhoz The Soviet collective farm.

Kombinat The GDR combine. A horizontal and vertical amalgamation of enterprises under the unified control of a director-general.

link A small Soviet agricultural group that is given responsibility for a piece of land or livestock, allocated inputs and set broad output targets. The group is paid according to results, but is not set work assignments.

London Club Western creditor banks.

lower-level co-operative (production collective) A farm in Vietnam where individual income depends on both labour and contributed land and means of production.

macroeconomic disequilibrium See *'big bang', 'shock' therapy* and *macroeconomic stabilization.*

macroeconomic stabilization Anti-inflationary measures involving tight fiscal, monetary and incomes policies, e.g. expenditure cuts, high interest rates, price liberalization (including the reduction of subsidies on basic products) and wage inflation taxes. A cure for macroeconomic disequilibrium.

market socialism A market economy in which social ownership predominates.

marketization Progress away from command planning and towards the introduction of a market economy.

Marshall Plan The US programme to aid the post-Second World War recovery of Europe. Launched in April 1948.

material balances The basic planning technique used in command economies, involving the drawing up of the major sources of supply and demand for a particular commodity with the aim of attaining a rough balance.

materials allocation The administrative distribution of raw materials, intermediate goods and capital goods.

MOFERT The Chinese Ministry of Foreign Economic Relations and Trade.

monetary overhang Unplanned accumulation of cash and savings accounts ('forced savings') because of the lack of desired goods and services. Ellman (1989a: 244) defines the term as the excess of purchasing power over the total supply of goods and services at effective prices.

monobank The 'one bank' arrangement in the traditional Soviet economic system, with no separation of the central bank from independent commercial banks.

'moral economy' stage During the Cuban development of 1966–70 emphasis was placed on moral incentives and collective interests rather than on individual material incentives.

naryad Soviet allocation certificate for non-labour inputs.

National Salvation Front Took over the reins of government after the fall of the Ceausescu regime in Romania.

NEP The New Economic Policy in the Soviet Union (1921–28), characterized by considerable concessions to private enterprise and the restoration in large part of the market mechanism.

Net Material Product (NMP) The Soviet 'material product system' differs from the 'system of national accounts' recommended by the United Nations and used in the West in that it excludes so-called 'non-productive' services. These include (with some variation) defence, general administration, education, finance and credit, and transport and communications serving households. 'NMP produced' minus exports plus imports, measured in domestic prices, and minus losses due to abandoned construction and accidental damage, gives 'NMP utilized'. As a very rough approximation, the Soviet definition gives a figure about 20 per cent less than its Western counterpart.

Neues Ökonomisches System (NES) The GDR's New Economic System 1963–70 was a period that saw the greatest use of indirect steering of the economy by means of mainly monetary instruments.

New Economic Mechanism (NEM) Introduced in Hungary on 1 January 1968. The term was also used in Bulgaria throughout the 1970s, but any resemblance to the Hungarian system was in name only.

new economic zones Resettlement plan in Vietnam to move mainly northern people to zones in central and south Vietnam.

nomenklatura A system whereby the Communist Party makes all the important appointments, including those in the economy.

normative net output Required as opposed to actual wage costs, social insurance and profit. A sort of 'shadow price' that can be used to determine the entire NNO for the enterprise by multiplying it by the actual output.

Noul Mecanism Economico-Financiar Socialist Romania's New Economic and Financial Mechanism, introduced at the start on 1979.

Nov Sistem na Rukovodstvo Socialist Bulgaria's New System of Management.

NPK Socialist Bulgaria's 'scientific–productive complex', incorporating scientific institutes.

obedineniye The Soviet association, a mainly horizontal amalgamation of enterprises.

OECD Organization for Economic Co-operation and Development. The OECD replaced the OEEC (Organization for European Economic Co-operation), founded in 1948, in 1961. In March 1990 the OECD created the Centre for Co-operation with European Economies in Transition.

'open door' policy Introduced in China in 1978 to open the economy to foreign trade, capital, technology and know-how.

Ordnungspolitik Government policy which merely provides a framework for the operation of market forces, i.e. creating the right environment for the private sector to flourish in the form of a basic infrastructure, a sound currency and a competitive environment.

OSCE See *CSCE*.

PAK Socialist Bulgaria's 'industro-agrarian complex', a vertical merger of farms with industrial enterprises processing and selling agricultural products.

Paris Club Western creditor governments.

perestroika The Soviet term for the restructuring of the whole of economic and social life. All-round economic and social reforms associated with Mikhail Gorbachev.

Phare Poland, Hungary, Aid for Reconstruction of the Economy. Essentially a technical assistance programme for Hungary and Poland of July 1989. Other countries were subsequently included (the Federal Republic of Yugoslavia was subsequently expelled). The EC co-ordinates G24 aid.

Plan tekniko-industrial-financiar Socialist Albania's technical–industrial–financial plan for the industrial enterprise.

Planungsordnung The GDR's Order of Planning.

polny khozraschyot 'Full economic accounting'. All expenditure incurred by the Soviet enterprise, including investment, had to be covered from revenue earned or credit borrowed.

predpriyatiye The Soviet enterprise.

Preisausgleich 'Price equalization'. The mechanism by which exports and imports in a command economy are involved in a sort of price equalization with world and domestic prices respectively.

prestavba Socialist Czechoslovakia's term for *perestroika*.

Prinzip der Einzelleitung Principle of individual management in the GDR. The equivalent of *edinonachalie*.

privatization Usually refers to the transformation of state into private ownership. 'Major' or 'large' privatization applies to large enterprises, while 'minor' or 'small' applies to small enterprises such as shops and restaurants. The private sector also includes privately established enterprises. When calculating the share of the private sector in GDP, the EBRD measures 'the whole value added of privately controlled enterprises even if they buy inputs, including the services of leased equipment, from the state and sell their output to it and even if the state, or state-owned organs, are (non-controlling) minority shareholders' (EBRD 1994: 10).

prodrazvyorstka Compulsory requisitioning of agricultural products during the Soviet War Communism period, 1918–21.

property rights Van Brabant (in Ronnas and Sjöberg 1991: 220): 'A property right is a socially recognized and legally enforceable right to select users of scarce goods. The crucial element is Roman law, i.e. the right of use, enjoyment of the fruits, and disposal of the object of ownership (*ius utendi, fruendi et abutendi*).'

raspilenie sredstv 'Scattering' (excessive spread) of investment resources in command economies. Construction projects whose completion times are excessive relative both to the plan and to those taken in market economies.

ratchet effect ('base-year approach'; 'planning from the achieved level') This period's achievement by the socialist enterprise is the starting point for next period's plan.

rectification campaign The period 1966–70 in Cuba, when emphasis was placed on moral incentives and collective (group) interests rather than on individual material incentives.

regulated market economy Gorbachev's proposal for a mixed (in terms of ownership) market economy regulated by the state.

resident convertibility See *convertibility*.

restitution Physical (natural) restitution refers to the return of property to former owners or their heirs. Financial compensation or coupons exchangeable for shares in enterprises to be privatized may be available if this is not possible or desired.

samofinansirovanie Soviet 'self-financing'. Both operating costs and capital expenditure had to be covered out of revenue earned by the enterprise; investment was normally to be financed out of retained profit or from credits that had to be repaid.

samookupaemost This concept entails at least a minimum rate of return on Soviet investment, whatever the source of finance.

samoupravleniye Soviet 'self-management'. The work force takes a more active part in enterprise plan formulation and in the election of management.

second economy The non-regulated sector, including both legal and illegal activity.

Sejm Polish parliament.

self-management Self-management of the 'socially owned' Yugoslav industrial enterprise by the workers via an elected workers' council.

'sequencing' or 'sequential' ('staged') programming The transition from a centrally planned to a market economy, involving various sequences or orders of reforms.
shinechiel Mongolian *perestroika*; renewal.
'shock' therapy (treatment) Severe austerity measures involving strict fiscal, monetary and incomes policies to combat a high degree of macroeconomic disequilibrium in the form of open and/or repressed inflation. See *'big bang'*.
shturmovshchina The Soviet term for 'storming'. A mad rush by enterprises to fulfil the plan towards the end of the planning period.
Sistema de Direccion de la Economia The Cuban System of Economic Management and Planning.
social market economy A market economy with the government intervening in forms such as the provision of a comprehensive social security safety net.
'socialism or death' Fidel Castro's response to and rejection of the Eastern European path to democracy and the market after 1989.
soft budget constraint State financial support in the form of subsidies, price increases or tax reductions to cover any losses incurred by enterprises.
soft goods The reverse of *hard goods* (see above). Includes examples such as low quality, obsolete machinery and equipment.
Solidarity Polish trade union and political organization.
sovkhoz The Soviet state farm. Literally, 'Soviet economic unit'.
Special Economic Zones (SEZs) An important feature of China's 'open door' policy. Direct foreign investment is attracted by special concessions such as low tariff and tax rates.
stabilization fund Here refers to Western aid in the form of a hard currency fund to support the convertibility of a formerly inconvertible currency.
state orders See *goszakazy.*
stavka Basic wage rate set for a particular branch of Soviet industry.
storming See *shturmovshchina.*
structural (commodity) bilateralism The balancing of trade in *'hard'* and *'soft'* goods (*q.v.*) separately.
subsidy-based bureaucratic centralism model The Vietnamese term for the traditional Soviet-type economic system with a soft budget constraint.
supply-side recession An economic recession (low level of economic activity) due not to lack of demand but to the disruption of supply links (lack of inputs) as the old command system disintegrates and a new market system has not yet been set up.
'systematization' ('systemization') (sistematizare) Ceausescu's programme to destroy many Romanian villages and create 'agro-industrial centres' instead.
'systemic transformation facility' See *IMF.*
taut planning Implies pressure to squeeze maximum output from given resources.
technical aid 'Technical aid is needed to help in the creation of the institutional structures of a market economy and in training the people to operate it effectively' (United Nations Economic Commission for Europe 1993: 17).
tekhpromfinplan The technical–industrial–financial plan to be fulfilled by the enterprise in the traditional Soviet economic system.
Tiananmen The bloody suppression by the army of Chinese students demonstrating in favour of democracy in Tiananmen Square (Beijing) on 4 June 1989.
togrog (tugrik, meaning 'disc') The Mongolian currency unit. Equals 100 mongo.
tolkachi Soviet 'pushers', unofficial supply agents.
transferable rouble A unit of account used in transacting intra-Comecon trade.
Treuhandanstalt (THA) A trust body dealing with privatization, restructuring, liquidation and credit guarantees in East Germany. The THA was disbanded at the end of 1994.

trudoden The Soviet agricultural 'work day'. Not literally a calendar day, but each particular piece of work is valued at so many 'work days'.

turnover tax Essentially the difference between the wholesale and retail price. Typically the tax is price-determined, that is, the residual resulting from attempts to equate supply and demand.

Union of Sovereign States (USS) See *Union Treaty.*

Union Treaty Gorbachev's failed attempt to form a *Union of Sovereign States* to succeed the Soviet Union.

Unprofor The United Nations Protection Force in the former Yugoslavia.

uskorenie The Soviet term for 'acceleration' of growth achieved by means such as increasing investment.

valovaya produktsiya The Soviet term for gross output. Measures the value of finished output plus net change in the value of goods in the process of production.

valuta Foreign currency.

'velvet revolution' The relatively peaceful process of change to political democracy and the market in Czechoslovakia after November 1989.

Vervollkommnung 'Perfecting' of planning, management and economic accounting in the GDR.

vstrechnye plany Soviet term for counter-plans. See *counter-plans.*

vyrobni hospodarska jednotka (VHJ) Socialist Czechoslovakia's industrial association.

War Communism The period 1918–21 in the Soviet Union, characterized by extreme nationalization and an attempt at a form of moneyless administration.

wielkie organizacje gospodarcze Polish 'large economic organizations'.

zastoi The Soviet term for 'stagnation'. Refers to the stagnation of the Brezhnev era.

zayavka The Soviet indent (request) for non-labour inputs.

'zero option' Castro's programme of severe austerity measures for coping with post-1989 disrupted Comecon trade links and rapidly diminishing Soviet aid.

zjednoczenie 'Association' of enterprises in socialist Poland.

zrzeszenie 'Amalgamation' of enterprises in socialist Poland.

zveno The Soviet term for *link*. See *link.*

INDEX